The Handbook of Sexuality in Close Relationships

The Handbook of Sexuality in Close Relationships

Edited by

John H. Harvey
University of Iowa

Amy Wenzel
University of North Dakota

Susan Sprecher
Illinois State University

LEA
LAWRENCE ERLBAUM ASSOCIATES, PUBLISHERS
2004 Mahwah, New Jersey   London

Senior Editor:	Debra Riegert
Cover Design:	Sean Trane Sciarrone
Textbook Production Manager:	Paul Smolenski
Full-Service Compositor:	TechBooks
Text and Cover Printer:	Hamilton Printing Company

This book was typeset in 10/12 pt. Palatino, Italic, Bold, and Bold Italic.
The heads were typeset in Palatino and Americana, Bold, Italics, and Bold
Italics.

Lawrence Erlbaum Associates, Inc., Publishers
10 Industrial Avenue
Mahwah, New Jersey 07430
www.erlbaum.com

Library of Congress Cataloging-in-Publication Data

The handbook of sexuality in close relationships / edited
   by John H. Harvey, Amy Wenzel, Susan Sprecher.
      p.   cm.
   Includes bibliographical references.
   ISBN 0-8058-4548-8 (casebound : alk. paper)
   1. Sex.   2. Sex customs.   3. Couples.   I. Harvey, John H.,
   1943–   II. Wenzel, Amy.   III. Sprecher, Susan, 1955–
   HQ21.H3233   2004
   306.7—dc22   2003026962

Books published by Lawrence Erlbaum Associates are printed on
acid-free paper, and their bindings are chosen for strength and durability.

Printed in the United States of America
10 9 8 7 6 5 4 3 2 1

This book is dedicated to pioneers in the study of close relationships and sexuality, respectively, including: Harold Kelley, Elaine Hatfield, Ellen Berscheid, and Alfred Kinsey, on whose shoulders we have stood in doing our own work in these fields.

CONTENTS

PREFACE

This project emerged from conversations the first two editors had in trying to access the status of the literature at the intersection of sexuality and close relationships. Our conversations led us to believe that this intersection had been relatively neglected and that a major edited volume would contribute to stimulating the interface of sexuality and close relationships. Fortunately, our mutual expertise in this area was enhanced greatly when we were joined by the third editor, who had worked at this intersection for years and who had a vast knowledge of issues and researchers.

We also then had the fortune of gaining the interest of a large number of diverse scholars doing valuable work on sexuality and relationships and in attaining the support of Debra Riegert, Senior Editor at Lawrence Erlbaum Associates, Publishers. This effort is truly a collective enterprise of many people, especially including our wonderful chapter authors and commentators.

The editors wish to thank the reviewers of this project and Debra Riegert of LEA for their valuable help in developing this volume. We also thank the reviewers of the proposal for this volume for their helpful suggestions about authors and material to include. We appreciate the efforts of those involved in the production process—Paul Smolenski, Textbook Production Manager at LEA and Susan Detwiler of TechBooks.

Although sexuality is central to romantic close relationships, oddly there has been relatively little work linking the ideas from the extensive subfields of work on close relationships and work on sexuality. Researchers in communication studies, sociology, family studies, psychology, and psychiatry, among other disciplines, have made major advances in both of these broad subfields. Our goal was to integrate this research and scholarship into one edited volume. It has been several years since an edited book had been done to link these two areas (Sprecher & McKinney, 1991). Chapters included in this handbook reflect well the intersection of the definitions of sexuality that embraces sexual behaviors, arousal, as well as attitudes, desires, affect, attraction, and communication, and of close relationships that involve strong, frequent, diverse interdependence between two people, who mutually view themselves as seriously involved. The chapters represented in this volume focus on sexual behaviors, physiological responses, and attitudes within the context of close relationships.

This volume was designed to bring together researchers from the diversity of fields working on close relationship topics to explore past contributions and new directions in sexuality. The handbook emphasizes theoretical integration and stimulation, methodological rigor, and critical analysis of what we know about sexuality in close relationships.

We challenged authors to focus on sexuality and its many manifestations as it affects and is affected by ongoing close relationships. We believe that this challenge was met well by our authors and that existing data from both fields were seen in a new light.

As described in chapter 1, the spectrum of phenomena that represent the interface of sexuality in close relationships indeed is vast. It extends from the beginnings of a relationship to middle parts of relationships, to how well relationships are maintained, and to the many forces that signal the conflict and dissolution of close relationships. The "dark side" of the intersection of sexuality and close relationships (e.g., abuse) is another dimension represented in this volume. The book contains major theoretical and methodological analyses and several chapters that involve significant work on therapy and applications. Over 50 authors came together in the writing of 25 chapters to make this volume comprehensive in dealing with sexuality in close relationships.

It is our hope that in the 21st century, sexuality in close relationships will become a major subtopic both in the study of sexuality and the study of close relationships. Such a development will require systematic efforts aimed at linking the two topics at scholarly meetings and in major journals representing these fields. This handbook is one of the first steps to make this subfield a reality.

—John H. Harvey
—Amy Wenzel
—Susan Sprecher

I

Introduction

Why a Handbook on Sexuality in Close Relationships is Warranted

John H. Harvey
University of Iowa

Amy Wenzel
University of North Dakota

Susan Sprecher
Illinois State University

Although sexuality is an integral part of close, romantic relationships, research linking these two constructs has been less systematic and less developed than some other areas of inquiry pertaining to close relationships. To some degree, this lack of development speaks to the difficulty of defining either close relationships or sexuality, to the absence of a reference to close relationships in definitions of sexuality, and to the absence of references to sexuality in definitions of close relationships. In an early, significant collection of writings about sexuality within various types of close relationships, McKinney and Sprecher (1991) defined sexuality as referring to "sexual behaviors, arousal, and responses, as well as to sexual attitudes, desires, and communication" (p. 2). Similarly, a close relationship has been defined as a relationship involving "strong, frequent, and diverse interdependence [between two people] that lasts over a considerable period of time" (p. 38, Kelley et al., 1983). Added to this latter definition might be the stipulation that the two people mutually consider themselves as involved in a close relationship (Harvey & Weber, 2002).

Although research that links sexuality and close relationships has not been fully systematic or developed, it exists and can be found in a variety of sources. To date, researchers in communication, sociology, family studies, psychology, and psychiatry, among other disciplines, have made significant advances in both of these broad fields. Our goal was to integrate this research and scholarship into one edited volume. It has been several years since an edited book had been done to link these two areas (see Sprecher & McKinney, 1993).

In the main, the chapters included in this handbook reflect well the intersection of the two definitions previously presented. The sexuality definition focuses on behavior, physiological response, and attitudes. The close relationship definition focuses on patterns of behavior over time and the interpretive act of seeing oneself in an involved, personal relationship. The reviews represented in this volume focus on sexual behaviors, physiological responses, and attitudes within the context of close relationships.

This handbook was designed to bring together major scholars from the diversity of fields working on close relationship topics to explore past contributions and new directions in sexuality. The volume emphasizes theoretical integration and stimulation, methodological rigor, and critical analysis of what we know about sexuality in close relationships. It is hoped that it will serve as a forum for enhancement of dialogue about the centrality of sexual issues in close relationships. As will be attested by the contributions to this volume, there are major programs of work and exciting theoretical and methodological developments that can be brought together and that can readily define the intersection of sexuality in close relationships. That is what the present volume has attempted to do. In the editing process, we have repeatedly challenged authors to hone in on sexuality and its many manifestations in ongoing relationships and as it affects and is affected by ongoing close relationships. Indeed, we noticed that many leading sexuality researchers consider close relationship variables in their work and that many leading close relationships researchers consider sexuality variables in their work. We challenged them to make the intersection between the two the focus of their chapters. In the process, existing data from both fields were seen in a new light.

Do these developments warrant a handbook? We believe so. A handbook should report a significant collection of scholarly work that helps define a field or subfield. It should be relatively comprehensive of developments to date in a field. It should integrate the major theoretical approaches from the field to interpret existing data. It should stimulate further theory and research. It should raise questions about facets of the phenomena in question that have not been answered by work to date. Indeed, it is our hope that in the 21st century, sexuality in close relationships will become a major subfield both in the study of sexuality and the study of close relationships. If that development is to occur, there will need to be systematic efforts aimed at linking the two topics at scholarly meetings and in major journals representing these fields. We view this handbook as the first step to make this subfield a reality.

As will be seen in the chapters in this handbook, we believe that the spectrum of phenomena that represent the interface of sexuality in close relationships is vast. It stretches in time from the beginnings of a relationship (attraction phenomena; see chapters by Regan and Metts) to middles and how well relationships are maintained (see chapter by Christopher & Kisler) to endings, and the diverse forces that signal the conflict and dissolution of close relationships (see Sprecher & Cate). From examination of the chapters in this volume, it may be deduced that this spectrum relates to topics such as attitudes, mores, love, personality, the family, jealousy, and aggression. It relates to same-sex and heterosexual phenomena. It relates to special issues, such as sexuality during the transition to parenthood and sexuality in the context of one partner struggling with a sexual dysfunction. It relates to, but is not restricted to, sexual intercourse.

Once we decided that there was a need for an edited *Handbook on Sexuality in Close Relationships*, we began identifying topics and inviting authors. Fifty authors became involved in the writing of 23 chapters along with three additional scholars writing the commentaries. It was a pleasure to work with all of these hard-working authors and with each other in producing this handbook. We believe that this handbook will be of interest to scholars, students, and other professionals in multiple disciplines.

The book is divided into six parts. The chapters in Part I represent major conceptual, theoretical (DeLamater & Hyde) and methodological statements (Wiederman) about the issues in studying sexuality in close relationships. They reflect a landscape of theoretical directions, problems in investigative techniques, general attitudes and practices (Willetts, Sprecher, & Beck) and individual differences (Simpson, Wilson, & Winterheld) as they relate to the study of sexuality in relationships. These chapters provide a critical analysis of theoretical approaches that have been applied to the study of sexuality in close relationships to date and highlight methodological advances as well as areas on which future research can improve.

Part II contains chapters on how sexuality is involved in the formation, development, and maintenance of close relationships. It begins with coverage of the initial attraction and dating period (Regan) and first sexual intercourse (Metts). It proceeds through love and sex (Hendrick & Hendrick), attachment and sex (Feeney & Noller), exchange and sex (Byers & Wang), and concludes with sexual satisfaction and expression as predictors of relationship satisfaction and stability (Sprecher & Cate). After reading these chapters, the reader will have an understanding of the psychological, behavioral, emotional, and social determinants that contribute to the manner in which sexuality is experienced at various stages of close relationships.

The chapters in Part III reflect the dark side of close relationships as they interface with sexuality. They include coverage of unrequited sexual lust (Cupach & Spitzberg), sexual aggression (Christopher & Kisler), and sexuality jealousy (Guerrero, Spitzberg, & Yoshimura). These chapters demonstrate that the dark side of sexuality in close relationships can emerge at different stages of relationship development and is not limited to circumscribed settings or age ranges.

The chapters in Part IV concern sexuality in special types of close relationships and contexts of relating. They include coverage of sexuality in lesbian and gay couples (Peplau, Fingerhut, & Beals), marital sexuality (Christopher & Kisler), families and sexuality (Fisher), sexuality during pregnancy and the postpartum period (Haugen, Schmutzer, & Wenzel), sexuality in midlife and later life couples (Burgess), and sexuality in relationships reflecting strong gender drifts—"his versus her" relationships (Vohs, Catanese, & Baumeister). Although all of these chapters show that sexuality is an important facet of all types of relationships, they also demonstrate the important point that the specific nature of sexual experience in relationships depends in part on external forces that compete for energy and attention. These chapters also highlight the point that programs of research are just now beginning to be developed to focus on sexuality in these types of close relationships, and they call for more systematic inquiry in the future.

We were also committed to having applications in this handbook. Part V contains chapters that relate specifically to applications and clinical aspects of sexuality and close relationships. They pertain to sexual dysfunction (Aubin & Heiman), contraceptive use and safe sex issues (Noar, Zimmerman, & Atwood), the effects of psychopathology on sexual functioning (Wenzel, Jackson & Brendle), and sex therapy and couples therapy (McCarthy, Bodnar, & Handal). Material included in these chapters has important implications for both health professionals and policymakers.

We were pleased to obtain two commentaries on the chapters within this volume. We asked a past president of the interdisciplinary scientific organization on sexuality (Society for Scientific Study of Sexuality) and a past president of the interdisciplinary scientific organization on close relationships (currently International Association for Relationship Research) to write commentaries. In the first commentary, Pepper Schwartz discusses some of the themes of the book and places them in a real-world context and challenges future researchers to new topics. In the second commentary, Daniel Perlman and his coauthor, Susan Campbell, critically evaluate the rigor of theories that have been applied to the study of sexuality and close relationships and outline the historical and political forces with which sexuality researchers have contended over the years. Together, these commentaries provide compelling insights into where we have been, where we are now, and where it will be important to go with the study of sexuality in close relationships.

In the end, we recognize that the present volume represents a very small step in contributing to our understanding of a huge topic that has occupied the minds of human beings since humans began to bond. It is our hope that this handbook will stimulate other workers to view the intersection of sexuality and close relationships as a fertile nexus for future inquiries.

REFERENCES

Harvey, J. H., & Weber, A. L. (2002). *Odyssey of the heart: Close relationships in the 21st Century* (2nd. ed.). Mahwah, NJ: Lawrence Erlbaum Associates.

Kelley, H. H., Berscheid, E., Christensen, A., Harvey, J., Huston, T., Levinger, G., McClintock, E., Peplau, A., & Peterson, D. (1983). *Close relationships*. San Francisco: Freeman.

McKinney, K., & Sprecher, S. (1991). Introduction. In K. McKinney & S. Sprecher (Eds.), *Sexuality in close relationships* (pp. 1–8). Hillsdale, NJ: Lawrence Erlbaum Associates.

Sprecher, S., & McKinney, K. (1993). *Sexuality*. Newbury Park, CA: Sage.

1

Conceptual and Theoretical Issues in Studying Sexuality in Close Relationships

John DeLamater
Janet Shibley Hyde
University of Wisconsin–Madison

The study of sexuality in close relationships involves key conceptual issues that must be clearly identified and addressed. These include:

- The definition of sexuality.
- The need to construct dyadic, interactional models rather than individual-level models.
- The impact of gender and the issue of whether distinct models are needed for males and females.
- The necessity of integrating race/ethnicity into theoretical models and research.
- The importance of taking a developmental approach to both individuals and relationships.
- The need for multiple levels of analysis of the phenomena of sexuality in relationships.

A complete theory of sexuality in close relationships would integrate individual, dyadic, biological, and sociocultural processes. Cutting edge approaches to studying affect must also be integrated, and the heterosexism of most theories must be corrected. We address all of these issues, and then review and evaluate the major contemporary theories relevant to the study of sexuality in close relationships: evolutionary theory, social exchange theory, script theory, symbolic interaction theory, and role theory.

CONCEPTUAL ISSUES

The Definition of Sexuality

Our understanding of the role and importance of sexuality in relationships is hampered by a narrow conception of sexuality. Much of the research has narrowly focused on sexual behavior, on the incidence and frequency of kissing, genital touching, and oral, anal, and vaginal intercourse. Some researchers, especially those who study adolescents, focus more narrowly on penile–vaginal intercourse (Savin-Williams & Diamond, in press). This has been especially characteristic of quantitative studies, as a legacy of behaviorism. This perspective dominates research and treatment on sexual disorders, where the emphasis is on sexual performance and bodily functioning, and the use of masturbation, medicines, and devices to treat a wide array of difficulties.

One limitation of this conceptualization is that it recognizes only a small number of behaviors as "sexual." This leads to the view that only a few behaviors count, that is, constitute "real sex" (a view held by many young adults; Sanders & Reinisch, 1999). In daily life and relationships, by contrast, a wide range of behaviors may contribute to the experience of physical/sexual intimacy by a person, including prolonged eye contact, holding hands, hugging, dancing, and massage, in addition to behaviors that involve the sex organs. One author expressed the need for a broader focus by calling for an emphasis on *outercourse* instead of intercourse (Chalker, 1995), on physical intimacy instead of penetration.

Another limitation of this narrow conceptualization is that it focuses on genital and physiological aspects of sexual behavior; it ignores the nonbehavioral aspects of sexuality, and, by implication, of sexual relationships. We need to expand our focus in several ways. In the 1980s, the cognitive revolution in the behavioral sciences led to calls to incorporate cognition into models of sexuality. In the 1990s, there were calls to incorporate emotion in the study of relationships; DeLamater (1991) outlined the connections between emotion and sexuality. Tiefer, in response to the contemporary medicalization of female sexual functioning, called our attention to the role of psychological factors such as sexual inhibition or aversion due to past experience, and to sociocultural factors such as access to information about sexuality, conflicting social norms, and the impact of family and work obligations (Tiefer, 2001). Thus, what is needed is a broad, *biopsychosocial* conception of sexuality (DeLamater & Sill, 2003).

Several sources call for a more expansive conceptualization of sexuality. In his *Call to Action to Promote Sexual Health and Responsible Sexual Behavior*, former Surgeon General David Satcher wrote, "sexuality encompasses more than sexual behavior. . . . the many aspects of sexuality include not only the physical, but the mental and spiritual as well, and . . . sexuality is a core component of personality. Sexuality is a fundamental part of human life" (Office of the Surgeon General, 2001, ii). Robinson, Bockting, Rosser, Miner, & Coleman (2002) presented the *sexual health model*. "Sexual health involves an ability to be intimate with a partner, to communicate explicitly about sexual needs and desires, to be sexually functional, to act intentionally and responsibly, and to set appropriate sexual boundaries" (p. 45). Robinson and colleagues identified several dimensions of sexuality, including intimacy, communication, sexual behavior, and self-regulation. Other dimensions they discussed include sexual self-esteem, a community aspect, and issues of consent.

Thus, an expanded definition of sexuality would recognize that sexual behavior is only one aspect, that other aspects include cognition (knowledge, thoughts, identity), emotion, and sociocultural factors. Such a definition would directly implicate relationship processes in the study of sexuality.

Models for Dyadic, Interactional Phenomena

The behavioral focus of much of the research on sexuality is closely tied to another limitation. Much of the literature focuses primarily on the individual. Numerous studies link sexual behavior to attitudes, motives, prior experience, age, gender, and race, all characteristics of the individual. Much of the research on adolescent sexuality links it to parent–child relationships, media and peer influences, biological drive, and puberty;

only rarely does research consider romantic relationships (Brown, Feiring, & Furman, 1999). Yet most forms of sexual expression involve two (or more) people. Thus, what behaviors or interaction sequences occur reflect an interactional sequence involving those present, and perhaps mental representations of others (parents, peers, other lovers) as well. Most sexual expression is interpersonal; relying on individualistic explanatory models limits our understanding.

The influence of partner(s) is clear in incidents of sexual assault; in such cases, knowing the characteristics of the individual victim may be of little value in predicting the victim's sexual behavior. But such influence is involved in a broad range of sexual interactions. Research documents the occurrence of "unwanted" sexual activity, in which an unwilling person engages in sexual activity as a result of influence by the partner. Such experiences occur in male–female (O'Sullivan & Allgeier, 1998), male–male (Kalichman et al., 2001), and female–female interactions/relationships (Struckman-Johnson & Struckman-Johnson, 2002). In other circumstances, there may be unwanted abstinence or celibacy; the fact that sexual behavior does not occur may reflect a partner's refusal to participate (Donnelly, Burgess, Anderson, Davis, & Dillard, 2001), or lack of a partner.

The importance of the couple as the unit around which societies organize sexual norms or scripts is the point of a recent paper by Gagnon and colleagues (2001). Analyses of data from the National Health and Social Life Survey in the United States ($N = 3,432$) and the Analysis of Sexual Behavior in France ($N = 4,580$) support the conclusion that one of the principal influences on sexual activity is whether the individual is in a long-term, couple relationship. Living as a couple (compared to living alone) and the type of coupled relationship are major correlates of type and frequency of sexual activity. "The role of *living in a couple* [is] a primary regulator of the sexual behavior of individuals in western societies" (Gagnon, Giami, Michaels, & de Colomby, 2001, p. 24).

In some cases, adherence to an individualistic model reflects commitment to a discipline or theoretical perspective that emphasizes individual characteristics in explaining behavior. Such a view is congenial with the American cultural emphasis on the importance of the individual. The predominance of theories and research methods that focus on the individual create a barrier to taking the couple into account. There are few conceptual frameworks or methods of gathering data that are designed to be employed with the couple. One attempt to conceptualize interaction in a dyad is the *interdependence* framework (Kelley et al., 1983). This model analyzes interaction as a sequence of actions by two persons; it can be used in the study of a variety of aspects of close relationships. It is an application of exchange theory, which will be discussed in more detail in the following. Another model with the potential to illuminate couple interaction is *script theory* (Gagnon & Simon, 1973). Scripts are explicitly conceptualized as occurring at three levels: intrapsychic, interactional, and social/cultural. This conceptualization will also be discussed in the following.

Another barrier to the study of couples is methodological. Most of the methodologies sexuality researchers traditionally rely on involve measuring the behavior and psychological responses of the individual. Some experiments involve careful attention to the temporal order of behavior; such research typically studies a very short sequence of activity. Some observational studies have captured interaction over time. Limits on the observer can be overcome by audiotaping and videotaping. Conversational analysis provides one useful approach to such data. Some research on marriage is leading the way in developing multimethod strategies, involving real time recording of interaction and physiological processes, and postinteraction interviews to assess the meaning of interactional events to the participant (e.g., Gottman, Conn, Carrere, & Swanson, 1998). Audio and video recording has not been used in the study of sexuality in close relationships. Ethical considerations preclude the use of these methods to study sexual behavior, but these methods could be used for research on communication and negotiations about sexual activity.

The Impact of Gender and Gender Roles: "His and Hers" Sex?

In an influential 1972 book, sociologist Jesse Bernard made the case that marriage is really "his and hers" marriage—that is, that marriage is experienced differently by husbands and wives. She presented data indicating that, in terms of mental health and physical health, men benefit from marriage and women are hurt by it, compared with their single counterparts. More recent data indicate that these trends have changed somewhat, and that marriage now benefits both men and women, although it still benefits men more than women (Kiecolt-Glaser & Newton, 2001; Ross et al., 1990; Waite & Gallagher, 2000). The picture is more complex than simple comparisons based on marital status though, because marital quality is more important than marital status in predicting mental and physical health (Barnett & Hyde, 2001; Steil, 2001).

The argument about his and hers marriage raises the question of whether there may be his and hers sex in marriage and other close relationships. That is, do women and men in heterosexual relationships experience the sexual relationship differently? Are there gender differences in sexuality in close relationships? By what processes do gender roles shape any gender differences? We know that marital satisfaction is linked to sexual frequency and satisfaction (Christopher & Sprecher, 2000), but does this linkage differ for men and women?

Most research on these questions has used quantitative methods; these are and will continue to be important. However, some questions—for example, do women and men in heterosexual relationships experience the sexual relationship differently—can best be answered with qualitative research. Although these methods are represented in other areas of sexuality research (e.g., adolescent girls' sexuality; Tolman & Szalacha, 1999; Tolman, 2002), there have been few qualitative studies of gender and sexuality in close relationships. One exception is Lawson's (1988) use of in-depth interviews with persons who had been involved in extramarital sex.

Most research on gender differences in sexuality has been based on samples of college students, most of whom are unmarried and many of whom are not in a long-term relationship (Oliver & Hyde, 1993, 1995). These studies may yield considerably greater gender differences than exist at other times in the life span and in the context of marriage or a long-term relationship.

Experts have suggested that, in late adolescent and early adult years, men are very body-centered in their sexuality, focusing on physical pleasures, whereas women are very person-centered, focusing on the relationship (Kaplan & Sager, 1971). Over time, men add a person-centered focus and women develop their capacity for body-centered sexuality.

Meta-analytic results from a study by Oliver and Hyde indicate large gender differences in masturbation, with males having the higher incidence, and attitudes toward casual sex, with males being more approving (Oliver & Hyde, 1993). The studies included in this meta-analysis used self-report methods and covered a wide range of ages, with an overrepresentation of college samples.

DeLamater (1987a) reviewed the literature on these and other gender differences and suggested that male and female sexual scenarios or scripts do differ, at least among adolescents and young adults. Data from research conducted in the 1960s through 1980s suggested that males view sexual activity as an end in itself, a means of gratification, whereas females view it as a means to an end, in the context of romantic relationships. Yet gender similarities are present as well; for example, there are no gender differences in subjective sexual satisfaction (Oliver & Hyde, 1993).

The forces of gender roles and the gender differentiation they create may be considerably stronger for unmarried college students than for married or cohabiting adults. One essential feature of gender roles is the double standard, which in its traditional form was more disapproving of premarital sex for women than men, and in its modern form is more disapproving of casual premarital sex for women than men (Sprecher, McKinney, & Orbuch, 1987; Sprecher & Hatfield, 1996). The modern double standard is completely approving of women's sexual expression within marriage and in long-term relationships, thus removing—at least in the context of marriage—one obstacle to women's sexuality and opening the possibility for gender similarities in these contexts. Nonetheless, other aspects of gender roles—such as the man's role as sexual initiator and the woman's as passive or willing recipient—may remain potent in many long-term relationships, potentially creating gender differences in the experience of sexuality.

In sum, research on sexuality in close relationships has attended to gender and gender roles, yet gender must continue to be a major focus of analysis in future research, remaining open to the possibility of both gender differences and gender similarities.

Integrating Race

In contrast to the attention given to gender, research on sexuality in close relationships has seldom focused on race or ethnicity. Many of the important samples have been White or predominantly White. Yet the evidence that does exist suggests that there may be important variations among ethnic groups in sexual patterns.

Data from the National Health and Social Life Survey (NHSLS; Laumann, Gagnon, Michael, & Michaels, 1994) indicate that 38% of Black women, but only 26% of White women, always have an orgasm during sex with their primary partner (Laumann and colleagues' race analyses aggregate across relationship statuses making it impossible, for example, to know if this differential exists between married Black and married White women). Among Hispanic men, 34% have engaged in anal intercourse at some time in their life, compared with 15% for Asian-American men (Laumann et al., 1994). Seventy-nine percent of White women, compared with 49% of Black women, have received oral sex at least once in their life (Laumann et al., 1994).

Examination of race/ethnicity should not be limited to analyses of race differences. For example, although statistics noted earlier indicated a race difference in orgasm consistency for Black compared with White women, race similarities hold for men: 75% of Black men and 75% of White men always have an orgasm during sex with their primary partner (Laumann et al., 1994, p. 117). The mean age of first intercourse is 16.3 for Mexican-American males and 16.3 for White males (Day, 1992). Recognition of ethnic group similarities should balance considerations of difference.

Studies of ethnicity provide sex researchers with an unique opportunity to understand the impact of culture on sexuality. If analyses stop with findings of race differences or similarities, they provide no insight into the cultural processes that create these patterns. (For guidelines on research with people of color, see McDonald, 2000; Myers, Abdullah, & Leary, 2000; Santos de Barona & Barona, 2000; Sue & Sue, 2000). As an example, among American ethnic groups, Asian-American women have a notably higher percentage of conceptions terminated by abortions, compared with Black, White, and Hispanic women (Laumann et al., 1994). The likely explanation is that the last three ethnic groups are part of cultures strongly influenced by the Judeo-Christian tradition which, in many cases, has been vocally opposed to abortion. In contrast, Asian cultures have not been so influenced by that religious tradition, and abortion is routine in countries such as Japan and China. The meaning and acceptability of abortion for a woman, then, depends heavily on the cultural heritage of her ethnic group.

Developmental Issues and the Life Course Approach

Much of the literature on sexuality and on relationships is cross-sectional in nature. Thus, we have a substantial literature on adolescent sexuality (for a recent review, see Savin-Williams & Diamond, in press), the sexual expression of college students, marital sexual behavior and satisfaction (Christopher & Sprecher, 2000; Sprecher & Cate, chapter 10, this volume), and extramarital sexual activity. Each of these literatures exists in relative isolation. Studies of marital sexuality rarely consider the premarital experience of respondents. Studies of teenagers, both gay and straight, often ignore the fact that their sexual activity reflects childhood experience and perceptions of their future lifestyle and relationships. An exception is Thompson's research (1995), involving individual interviews with 400 teenage females about the role of sexuality in their lives. Two of the eight types of female adolescents Thompson identified regulate their sexual activity based in part on their beliefs about the future. Young women who view the future as full of infinite possibilities are motivated to avoid unprotected intercourse; those who view their future as limited to motherhood may be ready to have a baby while still in high school.

We need a developmental or life-course model of sexuality. DeLamater and Friedrich (2002) provided an overview of the development of sexuality over the life course. Each stage of development—childhood, adolescence, adulthood, and later life—is associated with biological development and changes, distinctive social influences, and developmental and coping tasks. In childhood, for example, infants typically develop an attachment relationship with caregiver(s); this relationship may serve as the prototype for the person's emotional attachments in later life (Hazen & Shaver, 1987). Children grow physically, developing characteristics that determine their physical attractiveness. They explore and learn about bodies, influencing the nature of later sexual motivation. Children develop a gender identity, and in late childhood or early adolescence may consider issues of sexual orientation. The distinctive social influences are parents or other caregivers, and peers.

In adolescence, puberty occurs, directly influencing sexual interest via hormones and the development of adult physical characteristics, which in turn may lead others to express sexual interest in the young person. Social influences interact with these pubertal changes, either facilitating or inhibiting sexual interaction (Udry, 1988). Reactions to these changes will be influenced by childhood sexual experiences. Many young people engage in oral, anal, or vaginal intercourse by age 19 (Centers for Disease Control and Prevention, 2000), and some will experience outcomes such as pregnancy, abortion, childbirth, or sexually transmitted infection (STI). These may in turn have a lifelong impact on the person's sexual expression and relationships. In part, these consequences occur because many adults view these activities as problems and treat the young person accordingly.

In adulthood, the process of achieving sexual maturity, broadly defined, continues. Biological changes are mute, unless injury or illness intervene. The major developmental task involves attempts to integrate one's gender identity, sexual orientation, and sexual expression with partners. A second task is making informed decisions about reproduction and the prevention of STIs, as emphasized by the sexual health model (Robinson et al,. 2002), discussed earlier. Adults in U.S. society have several lifestyles to choose from, including celibacy, singlehood, cohabitation, and marriage. Choices will be influenced not only by characteristic level of sexual desire, gender identity, and sexual orientation, but also by ethnic/racial group identification and membership, and economic circumstances. This is an excellent example of the necessity of an expanded conception of sexuality in order to understand sexual expression.

In later life biology again becomes significant. Physical signs of aging, such as gray hair or weight gain, may affect body image and self-schema, leading to changes in behavior in relationships and in sexuality. This is another topic that has not been the subject of research. In women, the decline in estrogen at menopause may reduce lubrication and make penile–vaginal intercourse uncomfortable. Men may experience a lengthening of the time required to attain an erection and reduced firmness of erections. Both women and men may notice a decline in sexual desire (see Burgess, chapter 18, this volume). Knowledgeable persons will be aware of ways to counter or adapt to these changes, but for others, these changes may result in reduced frequency of sexual activity (voluntary or involuntary), sexual dissatisfaction, and sexual disorders. Obvious social influences are the partner, if available, and family (parents, siblings, children). An important factor is negative attitudes toward sexual expression among the elderly. According to the cultural stereotype, it is inappropriate for two elderly people to engage in intercourse, and especially inappropriate for an 80-year-old to masturbate. A survey of 1,384 men and women over the age of 45 included measures of attitudes toward sex, illness, use of medications, demographic variables, and sexual desire and sexual behavior. Regression analyses indicate that the person's attitudes toward sexual activity for older persons are more closely related to sexual desire than medical/biological factors such as number of chronic illnesses and medications taken regularly (DeLamater & Sill, 2003).

Some scholars reject developmental models of sexuality. Diamond, Savin-Williams, and Dube (1999) criticize such models, arguing that they specify normative progressions and fail to allow for atypical progressions or atypical types of relationships (i.e., the experiences of gay, lesbian, and bisexual youth). They argue that such models are responsible for the uneven emphasis in past work, discussed previously—an emphasis on heterosexual dating and marriage. However, such emphases are not inherent in developmental models. One can create models that include "turning points" at which the person may continue in one of several directions. Similarly, one can point to patterns without giving them normative status. The emphases noted in past work reflect social norms and the fact that conformity to these norms makes some patterns much more common than others.

We need not only a model of sexual development of the individual but also a model of the development of relationships over time. More effort has been made to develop such models. One such perspective is provided by social penetration theory (Altman & Taylor, 1973). This theory emphasizes the development of intimacy over time through self-disclosure by each individual. The theory also includes propositions about changes over time in the nature of self-disclosure within a relationship. But it assumes that every relationship follows the same pattern. It seems plausible that the developmental process changes as the individual gains experience in relationships. For example, the definition of an "intimate" disclosure may be very different for an adolescent of 14 and a divorced person in his 50s. In another example, Diamond et al. (1999) suggested that relationships differ in their motivations, characteristics, and functions. They differentiate four types of intimate peer relationships: sexual, romantic, dating relationships, and passionate friendships. Whereas sexual relationships involve sexual intimacy, the other three may not. Romantic relationships and passionate friendships involve emotion, whereas dating and sexual relationships may not. One can speculate that dating relationships and passionate friendships are more common at some life stages (adolescence), and that the functions of dating relationships are different in adulthood than in adolescence.

Developmental patterns may also characterize the succession of relationships over time spans of years or decades. A common pattern in marital relationships (and other sexual relationships) is a declining frequency of sexual activity over time (Christopher & Sprecher, 2000; Willetts, Sprecher, & Beck, chapter 3, this volume). This suggests that persons who leave a marriage/sexual relationship and enter a new one will experience an initial increase in the frequency of activity. An analysis of the NHSLS data focused on sexual activity following termination of a cohabiting relationship or divorce; the results indicated that newly single people enter relationships fairly quickly, with the number of relationships influenced by parental status, gender, and class (Wade & DeLamater, 2002). Sexual intimacy may occur more quickly in the new relationship, and the repertoire of behaviors may be broader in the new relationship compared with the old. Decline may still occur, but it may occur earlier or later in succeeding relationships.

THEORETICAL ISSUES

Integrating Biological Processes

Like other social scientists, sex researchers have often been so busy fighting the nativist–empiricist wars that they have had little time to conceptualize theoretical models in which biological processes and learning processes are integrated. In the meantime, biological research and sociocultural research have both made impressive advances, and much can be gained by weaving the two strands together.

A major new trend in biological research is to focus on neural plasticity (Davidson, Jackson, & Kalin, 2000). In contrast to older models in which biology was believed to be fixed and to influence or control behavior, the newer models investigate the reverse process, how behavior and experience affect biology—for example, by adding or pruning neural connections. This trend in neuroscience facilitates efforts to integrate biological and cultural approaches, because in this context, experience and culture are seen as major factors leading to the proliferation or pruning of neural connections.

An example is the work of Marler and her colleagues on the social behavior of two species of mice (*Peromyscus*), the monogamous California mouse and the polygamous white-footed mouse native to Wisconsin. Monogamous California males engage in care of their young and are more aggressive toward intruders than their white-footed male counterparts are (Bester-Meredith, Young, & Marler, 1999).

Bester-Meredith and Marler (2001) conducted a cross-fostering experiment with these two species. Half of the California mouse pups were raised by California parents, and half were raised by white-footed parents. White-footed pups were similarly fostered. Behaviorally, male California mice raised by white-footed parents were significantly less aggressive than California mice raised by California parents. Arginine vasopression (AVP) is a neurotransmitter. Research, over several species, shows that AVP is associated with both aggressive behavior and parental behavior. Under normal rearing conditions, California mice, the more aggressive species, show more AVP-releasing neurons in the bed nucleus of the stria terminalis than white-footed mice do (Bester-Meredith et al., 1999). California mice raised by white-footed parents had significantly fewer AVP-releasing neurons in that same region than California mice raised by California parents. Essentially, then, early rearing conditions—social relationships—influenced the biology, the neurons of the California mice.

This phenomenon—that social experience modifies biology—has been replicated with other species and with other social interactions influencing biology (e.g., dominance in golden hamsters, Delville, Melloni, & Ferris, 1998; for a review of data with humans, see Cacioppo, Berntson, Sheridan, & McClintock, 2000).

What are the implications for research on sexuality in close relationships? We need theoretical models that integrate biological and sociocultural influence. For example, researchers must make more progress toward understanding the brain centers and circuitry that are involved in various aspects of sexuality, including sexual desire, sexual arousal, and choice of sexual partner. At the same time, researchers must investigate the impact of experience on these centers, considering both positive and negative effects. For example, what neural effects does child sexual abuse have? And what impact will those neural effects have on the individual's ability to form romantic attachments as an adult and to function well sexually? The most recent research indicates that the hippocampus is shrunken in size in adults with Post-Traumatic Stress Disorder (PTSD) and adults who experienced childhood sexual abuse (Bremner et al., 1997; Sapolsky, 2000; Teicher, Andersen, Polcari, Anderson, & Navalta, 2002; Villareal et al., 2002)

Neural plasticity is not limited to childhood or to destructive effects. Researchers should begin to explore questions such as: Does a long-term, supportive romantic relationship in adulthood have detectable neural effects? Does an active, happy sex life have neural effects?

Integrating Affect

The Cognitive Revolution, beginning in the 1980s, has dominated conceptual models in psychology and, to a lesser extent, sociology. Exchange theory and script theory, both reviewed later in this chapter, are examples of cognitive models. Lost in the Cognitive Revolution was emotion, yet surely emotion is as important as cognition in understanding sexuality in close relationships (DeLamater, 1991). It is crucial that new theoretical models integrate cognition and affect.

A number of promising new lines of research are beginning to draw emotion into sex research. Janssen, Vorst, Finn, and Bancroft (2002) have developed a measure of the emotional tendency toward sexual inhibition or sexual excitation and find that the measure predicts sexual response in men (see also Beauregard, Levesque, & Bourgouin, 2001). Both lust and romantic attraction can be conceptualized as emotions or as part of an emotion-motivation system (Fisher, Aron, Mashek, Li, & Brown, 2002). Byrne's theory of erotophobia–erotophilia, an individual differences variable, is based implicitly on the emotion of anxiety as it relates to sexuality (Byrne, 1977, 1983). Erotophobes feel anxious and guilty about sex, whereas erotophiles feel comfortable with it. Erotophobes have strong negative emotional responses to sexually explicit films, whereas erotophiles respond with sexual arousal to such films.

Of course, for some time anxiety has been integrated into theoretical models of sexual dysfunctions such as erectile dysfunction (Masters & Johnson, 1970). Exposure to emotion-inducing films stimulates contraction of the pelvic floor muscles in women when the film is threatening but not when it is neutral or erotic (van der Velde & Everaerd, 2001). And one hypothesis is that Selective Serotonin Reuptake Inhibitors (SSRIs; a category of antidepressants) induce sexual dysfunctions because SSRIs blunt or dampen emotions (Opbroek et al., 2002). There is every reason to incorporate affect in theorizing about sexuality.

This research on affect and sexuality has typically focused on the individual. The important next step will be to examine the role that affect plays in sexual relationships. Love is a key relational emotion. Love has been theorized in isolation (e.g., Sternberg, 1986); we need to theorize its role specifically in the sexual relationship. Jealousy, too, plays a key role in close relationships (see Guerrero, Spitzberg, & Yoshimura, chapter 13, this volume). Shame and guilt are powerful emotions that some children are socialized to associate with sexuality. They can be expected to exert a strong effect on sexuality in close relationships, and perhaps even in legitimized relationships such as marriage.

Emotional experience and expression are strongly gendered and this gender differentiation may be a powerful force in heterosexual relationships. Women are expected to experience most emotions more than men, including embarrassment, fear, guilt, happiness, love, and shame (Plant, Hyde, Keltner, & Devine, 2000)—all emotions that potentially link to sexuality. At the same time, men are restricted by norms demanding nonexpression of these same emotions, potentially crippling them from the experience of intimacy in romantic relationships (Zilbergeld, 1999). Anger is one of the few "masculine" emotions (Plant et al., 2000), and it seems likely that it is linked to sexual coercion in relationships, such as marital rape.

In short, sexuality in close relationships is bubbling over with emotion, and theoretical models must incorporate this crucial aspect. Models that combine cognition and affect hold much promise for the future.

Same-Gender Relationships

One problem with many of the theories of sexuality in close relationships is that they are heterocentric—that is, they are framed from a heterosexual point of view and focus on heterosexual relationships (Rose, 2000). Sexual Strategies Theory (Buss & Schmitt, 1993), discussed later in this chapter, is a prime example. This heterocentric pattern raises the question of whether the major existing theories can adequately account for same-gender intimate relationships. It also poses a challenge to theorists of the future to frame models that will account equally well for heterosexual and homosexual relationships.

Certainly we have theories of sexual orientation (e.g., Bell, Weinberg, & Hammersmith, 1981; Bem, 1996). But these theories conceive sexual orientation as an individual differences variable rather than as a relationship variable. One exception is the work of Peplau and colleagues (Peplau, Cochran, Rook, & Padesky, 1978; Peplau & Garnets, 2000) who studied women's lesbian and heterosexual relationships extensively. They found that women's approach to intimate relationships seems more determined by their gender than by their sexual orientation. That is, both lesbian and heterosexual women are relational or partner-centered in their approach to sexual relationships (Peplau & Garnets, 2000). (For a more extended discussion, see Peplau, Fingerhut, & Beals, chapter 14, this volume.)

Contemporary Theories: Review and Evaluation

Evolutionary Theory. Sociobiologists (Symons, 1979, 1987; Wilson, 1975) and evolutionary psychologists (e.g., Buss & Schmitt, 1993) have contributed a great deal of theorizing about sexuality.

Sociobiology examines how evolution has shaped social behaviors, including sexual behavior (Wilson, 1975). Evolution operates through natural selection, which is based on the differential fitness of individuals. Fitness refers to the individual's relative contribution of genes to the next generation, and clearly sexual behaviors are closely linked to fitness.

Originally proposed by Darwin, sexual selection is a mechanism that acts in parallel to natural selection and produces gender differences. Sexual selection creates different selection pressures on males and females. It involves two processes: (1) intrasexual selection, in which members of one gender (usually males) compete among themselves for sexual access to members of the other gender; and (2) intersexual selection, in which members of one gender (usually females) have preferences for mating with certain members of the other gender and not others. These principles of natural selection and sexual selection have been used by sociobiologists to explain numerous phenomena, including patterns of courtship, infidelity, and rape (Fisher, 1992; Thornhill & Palmer, 2000).

Evolutionary psychology is an updated and elaborated version of sociobiology, proposed by (Buss, 1994; Buss & Schmitt, 1993; see also Tooby & Cosmides, 1992). Buss' writings on the topic of sexuality are so voluminous that they cannot all be discussed in detail here, in view of space limitations and fairness to other theories. We therefore focus on Sexual Strategies Theory (SST), the centerpiece of his theoretical work.

According to SST, men and women have, over many centuries, faced different adaptive problems in regard to mating (Buss & Schmitt, 1993). They have also faced different problems in short-term mating (casual sex) compared with long-term mating (sex in a committed relationship). According to SST, because it is to men's evolutionary advantage to inseminate many females, men put more of their energy into short-term mating. Women, having the greater parental investment, are more interested in ensuring that their offspring survive and therefore put more of their energy into long-term mating strategies that will ensure the long-term commitment of a man who will provide resources for them and their children. Men's evolutionary problems centered around identifying fertile females and removing the uncertainty of paternity. Women, in contrast, had to identify men willing to make a long-term commitment, who were also willing and able to provide resources. Thus, men have evolved psychological mechanisms that lead them to prefer as sexual partners women who are in their 20s—even if the man is in his 60s—because women are at their peak fertility in their 20s. In addition, men are notoriously jealous about their mates' sexual infidelity because of the problem of paternity certainty, according to evolutionary theories. Women evolved psychological mechanisms that lead them to prefer long-term mates who possess resources such as wealth, or qualities such as ambition or a law degree that should indicate a good capacity to provide resources in the future. Buss (1989) provided data supporting his theory from numerous small studies and from his 37 cultures study, in which he collected data on mate preferences in 37 distinct cultures around the world and found results generally consistent with his predictions. In brief, the data indicated that men place a higher premium on physical attractiveness in a short-term than in a long-term partner, presumably because physical attractiveness is a quick indicator of fertility (Buss & Schmitt, 1993). Women, too, prefer a mate who is physically attractive, but they also rate as important qualities such as "has a promising career," and they rate this feature as more important in a long-term mate than a short-term mate (for similar results, see Buss, 1989; Buss, Larsen, & Westen, 1996; but see Miller, Putcha-Bhagavatula, & Pedersen, 2002; Pedersen, Miller, Putcha-Bhagavatula, & Yang, 2002).

Many criticisms have been leveled at these evolutionary theories. Some have argued that sociobiologists and evolutionary psychologists ignore the importance of culture and learning in human sexual behavior (Eagly & Wood, 1999). Buss does explicitly acknowledge the importance of environment, calling his theory a contextual-evolutionary theory (Buss & Schmitt, 1993). However, this acknowledgment remains at the level of lip service, because measurement of environmental context is not incorporated into his research designs. Sociobiology has been criticized for resting on an outmoded version of evolutionary theory that modern biologists consider naive (Gould, 1987). For example, sociobiology has focused mainly on the individual's struggle for survival; whereas modern biologists focus on more complex issues such as the survival of the species or group and the evolution of a successful adaptation between a species and its environment.

Most of the data supporting evolutionary theories have come from evolutionary theorists, with few independent attempts to test predictions of the theory. One exception is the work of Freese and Meland (2002). They examined the much-publicized claim of the evolutionary psychologists regarding heterosexual men's mate preferences—that over the years both Miss America contest winners and *Playboy* centerfold models consistently have a waist-to-hip ratio (WHR) of .70—that is, that their waist measurement is 70% of their hip measurement (Buss, 1999; Singh, 1993). Freese and Meland checked the archives to make sure that they had accurate data on the measurements of these revered women, covering 1921 to 1986 for Miss Americas and 1966 to 2001 for *Playboy* centerfold models. Contrary to the claims of the evolutionary theorists, the WHRs varied considerably. For Miss Americas they ranged from 0.61 to 0.78, and for *Playboy* centerfolds from 0.52 to 0.79. Moreover, there was a significant

negative correlation between WHR and year, indicating that the WHR of these beau-
ties has declined over time, i.e., waists are now smaller relative to hips than they were
decades ago. These findings directly contradict the claims of evolutionary theorists
that a certain WHR was fixed as attractive (purportedly useful as an indicator of
fertility) to men thousands of years ago.

Eagly and Wood (1999) have provided one of the most elegant empirical critiques
of evolutionary psychology, while also proposing an alternative theoretical account
for the pattern of data—social-structural theory. Reanalyzing Buss's 37 cultures data
and adding to them United Nations data on gender equality in the nations in which
Buss collected data, they showed high correlations between nations' gender inequality and the magnitude of the difference between women and men in that society on
measures of mate preferences. Again, if mate preferences were determined by evolution thousands of years ago, they should not vary across cultures and they should
not correlate with a society's gender equality. Eagly and Wood proposed, instead,
that gender inequality in a culture produces a strongly gendered division of labor, in
which women are more responsible for home and family and men specialize in paid
employment in male-dominated occupations. Under conditions of marked gender
inequality, women are, of course, most interested in men's earning power.

Finally, it is important to note that sociobiologists and evolutionary psychologists
fail to specify the biological mechanisms from evolution to behavior. Their basic arguments are that evolution occurred over millions of years, resulting in a certain
pattern of gender differences in sexual and relationship behaviors in the 21st century.
But evolution can act only through genes, and genes influence behavior because they
direct the synthesis of certain proteins and not others, leading to differing levels of
biochemicals such as neurotransmitters or hormones. This is the era of the Human
Genome Project, in which specific genes that create specific medical conditions and
behaviors are being identified. Sociobiologists and evolutionary psychologists have
failed to incorporate this work and fail to specify which genes and biochemicals are
responsible for the patterns of gender differences that they claim have evolved.

Social Exchange Theory.   Social exchange theory (Homans, 1974; Kelley & Thibaut,
1978) uses the concept of reinforcement, as developed in psychology, to explain a
number of aspects of relationships. The theory assumes that individuals have freedom
of choice and often must choose among alternative actions. Each choice or action
provides rewards and entails costs. There are many kinds of material and socially
mediated rewards—money, goods, services, prestige or status, approval by others,
and the like. Similarly, there are many types of costs—physical and mental effort,
time, money, and anxiety or embarrassment. The theory posits that individuals are
hedonistic—they try to maximize rewards and minimize costs. Consequently, they
choose actions that produce good profits (profits = rewards − costs) and avoid actions
that produce poor profits.

This theory views relationships primarily as exchanges of goods and services
among persons. People participate in relationships only if they find that these provide profitable outcomes. These principles are used to explain entering, staying in,
and leaving relationships. Each individual uses two standards in evaluating the profits she or he receives. In general, the person expects to receive profits at least equal to
the average he or she has attained in past relationships; this is referred to as the *comparison level*. Generally, an individual will be attracted to a potential relationship that
offers profits above the comparison level. An individual judges the attractiveness of
an ongoing relationship by comparing the profits it provides against those available in
other, alternative relationships. If a person is participating in a social relationship and
receiving certain outcomes, then the level of outcomes available in the best alternative
relationship is termed that person's *comparison level for alternatives* (Thibaut & Kelley,

1959). If an alternative relationship offers greater profit than the one the person is in, the theory predicts that the individual will leave the present one for the alternative.

Social exchange theory could be used to generate predictions about how an individual would choose among potential sexual partners, but to our knowledge such choices have never been studied. Drigotas and Rusbult (1992) included sexual gratification as one of the six individual needs that may be met in a relationship, and assessed the relative importance to the individual of each of the six needs. Persons to whom sexual gratification is of great importance may, in fact, include it in their assessment of the profits associated with present and potential partners. Such assessments of potential partners may be influenced by cultural stereotypes of the sexual drive and preferences of persons belonging to specific racial or ethnic groups.

There is a good deal of empirical support for other propositions derived from the theory. Studies of heterosexual couples in long-term dating relationships show that rewards and costs can explain whether persons stay in or exit from such relationships (Rusbult, 1983; Rusbult, Johnson, & Morrow, 1986). Results of these studies indicate that individuals are more likely to stay when the partner is physically and personally attractive, when the relationship does not entail undue hassle (e.g., high monetary costs, broken promises, arguments), and when romantic involvements with attractive outsiders are not readily available. In other words, they are more likely to stay when the rewards are high, the costs are low, and the comparison level for alternatives is low.

Exchange theory also predicts the conditions under which people try to change or restructure their relationships. Central to this is the concept of *equity* (Adams, 1963; Walster (Hatfield), Walster, & Berscheid, 1978). A state of equity exists in a relationship when the individual feels that the rewards received are proportional to the costs. Applied to relationships, the theory predicts that couples will be satisfied when they perceive that each is receiving rewards that are proportionate to their costs. This is the basis for the interpersonal model of sexual satisfaction, developed by Byers and her colleagues (Lawrance & Byers, 1995; Byers & Wang, chapter 9, this volume). According to this theory, sexual satisfaction is high when rewards are high, costs are low, and rewards exceed costs; the couple's sexual satisfaction is high when the profits received by each are equal.

If, for some reason, a participant feels the allocation of rewards and costs in a relationship is inequitable, then the relationship is potentially unstable. People find inequity difficult to tolerate—they may feel cheated or exploited and become angry. Social exchange theory predicts that people will try to modify an inequitable relationship. Most likely, they will attempt to reallocate costs and rewards so that equity is established. One study tested the prediction that persons who felt their marriage was inequitable would be more likely to engage in extramarital sex; the results showed that such men and women began engaging in extramarital sex earlier in their marriages and reported more extramarital partners than those who felt equitably treated (Hatfield, 1978).

Social exchange theory has been fruitfully applied to the study of romantic and of sexual relationships. As noted, it enjoys considerable empirical support in some areas. However, it also has shortcomings (Sprecher, 1998). First, it is difficult to measure the key concepts of rewards, costs, and equity. Often researchers rely on single item or global measures that tap the commonsense understandings of respondents. One problem is the absence of a metric for comparing rewards or costs; what is the value of a physically attractive partner compared to the value of one who earns $100,000 per year? Second, exchange theory makes predictions about the effects of rewards and costs on outcomes, but does not consider the possibility of the reverse, that outcomes influence rewards and costs. For example, an outcome experienced frequently may become less rewarding; or the experience of a sexual dysfunction may make sexual interactions more costly than rewarding psychologically. Finally, there are aspects of close relationships and of sexual relationships to which exchange theory cannot readily be applied, such as physiological and emotional aspects.

Script Theory.   A potentially powerful theory for understanding both relationships and sexual interactions is script theory. This theory begins with the assumption that much of social life and interaction is governed by social norms. These norms are organized around situations and types of relationships that are recognized in the society or group. The result is a script, much like the script for a play. A *script* specifies the definition of the situation (a date, job interview, or sexual encounter); the social identities of the actors involved (eligible man and woman, job seeker and interviewer); and the range and sequence of permissible behaviors.

Script theory has been applied to the initiation and development of relationships. There are scripted ways to initiate a conversation, for example, talking about the weather. This opening line often includes an *identification display*, a signal that we believe the other person is a potential partner in a specific kind of relationship. The person who is approached, in turn, decides whether she is interested in that type of relationship. If she is, she engages in an *access display*, a signal that further interaction is permissible. It can be argued that this initial exchange heavily influences the subsequent interaction by defining the situation for the participants.

Once initiated, scripts specify the permissible next steps. American society, or at least the subculture of college students, is characterized by a specific script for first dates (Rose & Frieze, 1993). When asked to describe actions which a woman (man) would typically do both men and women identified a *core action sequence*: dress, (be) nervous, pick up (date), leave (meeting place), confirm plans, get to know, evaluate, talk, laugh, joke, eat, attempt to make out and accept or reject, take (date) home, kiss, go home. In general, both men and women ascribed a proactive role to the male and a reactive role to the female.

Can scripts contribute to the understanding of ongoing relationships? Some analysts would argue that as a relationship develops, the couple moves from interacting based on a widely shared cultural script to an individualized, primary relationship. It can be argued, however, that scripts continue to govern even intimate relationships. Every couple develops patterned ways of interacting, and these patterns often repeat themselves for many years. If the concept of script allows for adapting scripts to particular circumstances, and scripts can be shared by as few as two people, these patterns can be seen as scripted. Furthermore, even though unique in some aspects, the interaction is probably like the interactions of other couples in many ways.

The concept of script was first applied to sexual interactions by Gagnon and Simon (1973). They argued that sexual behavior is not spontaneous; it is the result of elaborate prior learning that teaches us how to behave sexually. The script tells us the who, what, where, when, and why of sexual behavior. The who specifies what types of persons we may have sex with, etc. One study of the scripts in U.S. society for heterosexual interactions gave participants 25 sentences, each describing an event in a heterosexual interaction (Jemail & Geer, 1977). People were asked to arrange the sentences in a sequence that was most sexually arousing and then to do it again in the order events were most likely to occur. There was a high degree of agreement about what the sequence should be. There was also high agreement between males and females. The standard sequence was kissing, hand stimulation of the breasts, hand stimulation of genitals, mouth stimulation of genitals, penile–vaginal intercourse, and orgasm. Note that this is not only the sequence in a single encounter, but also the sequence as a couple becomes sexually intimate over time.

How do we learn these scripts? One source is the mass media. Both men and women learn about relationships and how to handle them from popular magazines.

A study of magazines oriented toward women (*Cosmopolitan, Glamour,* and *Self*) and men (*Playboy, Penthouse,* and *GQ*) found that they portray relationships in similar terms (Duran & Prusank, 1997). The dominant focus in both types was sexual relationships. In women's magazines (January 1990 to December 1991), the themes were: women are less skilled and more anxious about sex and sex is enjoyed most in caring relationships. In men's magazines during the same period, themes were: men are under attack in sexual relationships and men have natural virility and strong sexual appetites. Also, articles in women's magazines portray men as incompetent about relationships. There is also evidence that young people's attitudes and perhaps scripts are influenced by television (Ward & Rivadeneyra, 1999).

Obviously, script theory is primarily concerned with behavioral sequences. It is well suited to the study of sexual and romantic interactions. DeLamater (1987b) integrated script theory with a sociological emphasis on social institutions and values. According to his model, an individual's scripts depend on the groups to which the person belongs and is socialized into; family and friendship groups in turn are connected to social institutions such as education, religion, and the stratification system of the society. Such an integration produces a multilevel, interdisciplinary model. It calls attention to the way in which social class, religion, race/ethnicity, and gender influence the scripts that individuals learn. Gagnon and Simon (1973) discussed the operation of scripts at the intrapsychic level, that is, within the individual, referring to the motivational elements of sexual activity; motivation arises from the attribution of meaning to internal biological processes. This aspect of the theory has not been developed and researched to the same extent as the interactional level. A strict version of the theory would argue that the individual's thoughts and feelings are all the result of social learning, leaving little room for biological and emotional influences per se on sexual behavior.

Script theory has great potential as a theory of sexual interactions. With a focus on the meaning of behaviors, it is complementary to exchange theory, with its emphasis on the outcomes of interaction. Script theory has generated research into some types of sexual interaction, for example, sadomasochistic activity (Weinberg, 1994) and sex worker–client interactions(Weinberg, Shaver, & Williams, 1999). But on the whole it has not generated as much research as one might expect. This may reflect its processual focus and the lack of developed methodologies for studying couples.

Symbolic Interaction Theory.   The basic premise of symbolic interaction theory is that human nature and social order are products of symbolic communication among people (Mead, 1934; Stryker, 1980). In this perspective, a person's behavior is constructed through give-and-take during interaction with others. Behavior is not merely the result of evolutionary adaptation, profit maximization, or conformity to norms embedded in scripts. Rather, a person's behavior emerges continually through communication with others. People can communicate successfully with one another only to the extent that they ascribe *similar meanings* to objects. An object's meaning for a person depends not so much on the properties of the object itself but on what the person might do with the object. An object takes on meaning only in relation to a person's plans.

Symbolic interaction theory views humans as proactive and goal seeking. People formulate plans of action to achieve their goals. Many plans, of course, can be brought to realization only through cooperation with other people. To establish cooperation with others, meanings of things must be shared and consensual. If the meaning of something is unclear or contested, an agreement must be developed through give-and-take before cooperative action is possible. For example, if a man invites a woman up to his apartment, exactly what meaning does this proposed visit have? The two people will have to achieve some agreement about the purpose of the visit before successful joint action is possible. The man and woman might achieve this through explicit negotiation or perhaps through tacit, nonverbal communication. This emphasis on establishing shared meanings has led to numerous studies of sexual subcultures such as nudists, gays, polyamorists, and shoe fetishists (Weinberg, Williams, & Calhan, 1995), focusing on shared meanings and on how new members are socialized into the subculture.

Symbolic interactionism portrays social interaction as having a tentative, developing quality. To fit their actions together and achieve consensus, people interacting with one another must continually negotiate new meanings or reaffirm old meanings. Each person formulates plans for action, tries them out, and then adjusts them in light of responses by others. Thus, social interaction always has some degree of unpredictability and indeterminacy. Even though romantic and sexual interactions are scripted, it is unlikely that those present will always behave as expected, especially, for example, in initial sexual interactions.

Symbolic interaction theory emphasizes that a person can act not only toward others but also toward the *self*. That is, an individual can engage in self-perception, self-evaluation, and self-control, just as he or she might perceive, evaluate, and control others. One important component of self is identity, the person's understanding as to who he or she is. For interaction among persons to proceed smoothly, there must be some consensus with respect to the identity of each. A number of qualitative studies have identified the interactional and personal processes involved in the development of types of sexual identity.

The self occupies a central place in symbolic interaction theory because social order is hypothesized to rest in part on self control (Charon, 1998). The individual strives to maintain self-respect in her own eyes, but because she is continually engaging in role taking, she sees herself from the standpoint of the others with whom she interacts. To maintain self-respect, she thus must meet the standards of others, at least to some degree. Of course, the individual will care more about the opinions and standards of some persons than about those of others. The persons whose opinions she cares most about are called *significant others*. Typically, these are people who control important rewards or who occupy central positions in groups to which the individual belongs. Because their positive opinions are highly valued, significant others have relatively more influence over the individual's behavior. Self-control based on concern for the opinions of others is a major source of conformity to norms governing sexual expression.

In sum, the symbolic interactionist perspective has several strong points. It recognizes the importance of the self in social interaction. It stresses the central role of symbolic communication and language. It addresses the processes involved in achieving consensus and cooperation. Critics of symbolic interactionism have pointed to various shortcomings (Longmore, 1998). One criticism is that this perspective overemphasizes rational, self-conscious thought and de-emphasizes unconscious or emotional states. A second criticism concerns the model of the individual implicit in symbolic interaction theory. The individual is depicted as a specific personality type—an "other-directed" person who is concerned primarily with maintaining self-respect by meeting others' standards. A third criticism of symbolic interactionism is that it places too much emphasis on consensus and cooperation and therefore neglects or downplays the importance of conflict. The perspective does recognize, however, that interacting people may fail to reach consensus, despite their efforts to achieve it. The symbolic interactionist perspective is at its best when analyzing fluid, developing encounters with significant others; it is less useful when analyzing self-interested behavior or principled action.

Role Theory.   Role theory (Biddle, 1979, 1986; Turner, 1990) holds that a substantial proportion of observable, day-to-day social behavior is simply persons carrying out their roles, much as actors carry out their roles on the stage or ballplayers perform theirs on the field.

The following propositions are central to the role theory perspective (Michener, DeLamater, & Myers, 2004):

1. People spend much of their lives participating as members of groups and organizations.

2. Within these groups, people occupy distinct positions (husband, sex worker, police officer).

3. Each of these positions entails a *role*, which is a set of functions performed by the person for the group. A person's role is defined by expectations (held by other group members) that specify how he or she should perform.

4. Groups often formalize these expectations as norms, rules specifying how a person should behave, what rewards will result for performance, and what punishments will result for nonperformance.

5. Individuals usually carry out their roles and perform in accordance with prevailing norms. In other words, people are primarily conformists; they try to meet the expectations held by others.

6. Group members check each individual's performance to determine whether it conforms to the norms. If an individual meets the role expectations held by others, then he or she will receive rewards in some form (acceptance, approval, money, and so on). If he or she fails to perform as expected, however, then group members may embarrass, punish, or even expel that individual from the group. The anticipation that others will apply sanctions ensures performance as expected.

Thus, to understand a person's behavior, we need to know the person's position and the expectations associated with it. Many types of interaction involving sexuality can be viewed as persons enacting roles, such as sex worker and client, sadist and masochist, and persons attending a swingers' party. Research in sexuality has documented the extent to which various activities are governed by role expectations and maintained by group sanctions (e.g., Frank, 2002). According to role theory, a person's role is embedded in a group or organization. Thus, an interaction cannot necessarily be changed by the immediate participants; the norms and sanctioning ability of the larger social unit may limit the participant's freedom. For example, parental control is an important influence on adolescent sexual behavior (Miller, 2002). In this regard, role theory differs from symbolic interactionism.

In order to change a person's behavior, it is necessary to change or redefine his or her role. This might be done by changing the role expectations held by others with respect to that person or by shifting that person into an entirely different role (Allen & Van de Vliert, 1982). Again, this calls our attention to the processes by which people are socialized, in this case into specific roles.

Role theory maintains that a person's role determines not only behavior but also beliefs, attitudes, and self-image. In other words, individuals bring their attitudes and self-perceptions into congruence with the expectations that define their roles. These processes are clearly shown in various qualitative studies. For example, as college athletes become the focus of media attention, their attitudes toward sports and academics undergo change, and they come to perceive themselves as stars (Adler & Adler, 1989).

Despite its usefulness, role theory has difficulty explaining certain kinds of social behavior. Foremost among these is *deviant behavior*, which is any behavior that violates or contravenes the norms defining a given role. Most forms of deviant behavior, whether simply a refusal to perform as expected or something more serious like commission of a crime, disrupt interpersonal relations. Deviant behavior poses a challenge to role theory because it contradicts the assumption that people are essentially conformist—deviant behavior violates the demands of roles. Of course, a certain amount of deviant behavior can be explained by the fact that people are sometimes ignorant of the norms. Deviance may also result whenever people face conflicting and/or incompatible expectations from several other people. This is the situation of many adolescents with regard to sexuality, caught between conflicting expectations of parents, close friends, and romantic or sexual partners; similarly, a participant in extrarelationship sexuality is caught between social standards, expectations of partner, and those of the lover. People in such situations may behave impulsively and may suffer considerable anxiety and guilt. Also, role theory does not and cannot explain how role expectations came to be what they are in the first place. Symbolic interactionism, on the other hand, can readily explain the development of role expectations through social interaction.

Comparison of Theories.   Earlier in this chapter, we identified several conceptual issues in research and in theorizing about sexuality and close relationships. We have reviewed five relevant theoretical perspectives. In this section, we briefly compare these theories in regard to the conceptual issues.

Table 1.1 lists five of the conceptual issues, and provides a thumbnail assessment of the five theories on each criterion. We argued that conceptualizations should be based on a *broad definition of sexuality*, one that includes cognition and affect in addition to genital sexual behavior. We believe that none of the theories meet this criterion. All five focus on one aspect to the exclusion of the others. Evolutionary psychology focuses on mating, that is, heterosexual intercourse. Social exchange theory focuses broadly on behavior, and role theory more narrowly on sexual behavior; neither considers nonbehavioral aspects. Script theory is focused on behavioral sequences. Symbolic interaction theory is concerned primarily with sexual identity, which is cognitive and affective, and downplays behavior.

With regard to the second criterion, four of the five do focus on the *dyad*. The central concepts vary, including interdependence (of outcomes), verbal and nonverbal communication, and interaction in role. Evolutionary psychology is the exception, with its focus on the individual.

None of the five include a *developmental model of sexuality*. On the other hand, two of the five conceptualize the *development of relationships*. Social exchange theory recognizes the development of utilities across interactions and relationships. Script theory considers the development over time of personal scripts.

Finally, we argued for theories that incorporate *multiple levels of analysis*. Only script theory explicitly identifies more than one level, considering intrapsychic, interactional, and cultural levels. Three of the theories focus exclusively on social interaction, which is perhaps the essential core of sexual activity; all three ignore biology. Evolutionary psychology focuses on the individual and ignores culture.

Sexual script theory emerges as more comprehensive than the others. It incorporates both a focus on the dyad and a developmental model of relationships. Evolutionary psychology, while the most visible perspective in the past decade, is the least comprehensive. Its visibility reflects the amount of published research based on the theory, and mass media attention. Given its limited focus on the individual, it has been able to generate research by relying on surveys of college students responding to hypothetical scenarios. More convincing evidence requires longitudinal surveys of adults in a cross section of ongoing relationships, such as the work of Rusbult and colleagues.

The major weaknesses in contemporary theories are two: reliance on limited, behavioral definitions of sexuality; and the failure to incorporate models of the development of sexuality over the life course.

TABLE 1.1

Comparison of Theoretical Perspectives

Conceptual Criterion	Theories				
	Evolutionary Psychology	*Social Exchange*	*Sexual Scripts*	*Symbolic Interaction*	*Role Theory*
1. Broad definition? Focus:	No Mating	No Behavior	No Behavioral sequence	No Sexual identity	No Sexual behavior
2. Focus on dyad?	No	Yes; Interdependence	Yes	Yes; Communication	Yes; Interaction in role
3. Developmental model of sexuality?	No	No	No	No	No
4. Developmental model of relationship?	No	Yes; Development of utilities	Yes; Development of personal script	No	No
5. Multiple levels of analysis? Primary level: Ignores:	Individual Culture	Interactional Biology	Several Biology	Interactional Biology	Interactional Biology

SEXUAL DISORDERS AND THERAPY: A POSITIVE EXAMPLE?

In many ways, research on sexual disorders and the application of that research in sex therapy have overcome some of the key conceptual issues we have raised, and we would be remiss not to acknowledge these accomplishments. For example, we argued that too much sex research has focused on the individual rather than on the dyad. In contrast, Masters and Johnson insisted, from the outset, that the couple and their relationship should be the focus of sex therapy (Masters & Johnson, 1970), and that view continues to shape the practice of sex therapy today. We noted that too much research has focused on sexuality as defined only by sexual behavior, ignoring other aspects such as cognition and affect. Masters and Johnson's (1966, 1970) research and therapy, developed during the era of behavior analysis and behavior therapy, are vulnerable to that criticism. However, other theorists developed models of sexual function and dysfunction that acknowledge cognition (Walen & Roth, 1987) and affect, specifically sexual desire (Kaplan, 1974, 1979). Cognitive-behavioral therapy for sexual disorders is common today (McCarthy, 1989; Wincze & Carey, 1991). Researchers who investigate sexual disorders should be poised to develop biopsychosocial models, although the advent of Viagra and the rush to medicalize sexual disorders represents a trend to focus on the biology to the neglect of the psychosocial. See chapter 20 in this volume for a fuller discussion of issues related to sexual disorders.

CONCLUSION

A broad understanding of an individual's or couple's sexual expression necessitates a conceptualization that incorporates multiple levels of analysis. In discussing the need for a life course approach, we noted three levels of analysis: biological (sexual anatomy, hormones, maturation), psychological (gender identity, sexual self-perceptions), and social (partner, family, peers). We need a biopsychosocial model in order to incorporate these potential influences on sexual expression. Furthermore, DeLamater (1987b) suggested that the individual and couple's behavior are influenced by sexual scripts and social norms that reflect group and subcultural memberships, which in turn are embedded in social institutions with characteristic structures and value orientations. Such a model enables us to incorporate the influence of social processes at two levels beyond the level of the couple.

Clearly, in any particular research project we will focus on a segment of this multiple-level process. But we need to be aware of and call attention to points of linkage with other levels, in order to facilitate integration of what are too-often isolated bodies of literature. This is also, inevitably, a call for a multidisciplinary approach to the study of sexual relationships. Fortunately, both the study of relationships and of sexuality have become increasingly multidisciplinary in the last three decades. The challenge is to integrate the two.

We have identified several other conceptual issues in contemporary research and scholarly writing on sexuality in close relationships. Our intent is not to discourage those interested in this area, but to encourage them to broaden their vision, to expand beyond narrowly focused theoretical models and research and work toward multilevel, biopsychosocial theories that illuminate the diverse phenomena involved in interpersonal sexuality. Our review indicates that, in common with other subdisciplines in the social sciences, we need to incorporate race and ethnicity, affect, and same-gender relationships into our vision. Our review of theories indicates that we have several rich theoretical traditions that we can draw on. In some cases, extant theory could help us understand phenomena as yet unstudied, for example applying exchange theory to choices among potential sexual partners. In other cases, bodies of literature already exist, and the need is for integration. The study of sexuality has advanced tremendously since the publication of the first Kinsey volume 55 years ago. The study of close relationships has advanced greatly since the now-famous First International Conference on Personal Relationships held in Madison, Wisconsin, in 1982. The time is ripe for a union of these specialties that will foster major advances in knowledge.

REFERENCES

Adams, J. S. (1963). Toward an understanding of inequity. *Journal of Abnormal and Social Psychology, 67*, 422–436.

Adler, P. A., & Adler, P. (1989). The gloried self: The aggrandizement and the construction of self. *Social Psychology Quarterly, 52*, 299–310.

Allen, V. L., & Van de Vliert, E. (1982). A role theoretical perspective on transitional processes. In V. L. Allen and E. Van de Vliert (Eds.), *Role transitions: Explorations and explanations.* New York: Plenum, 3–18.

Altman, I., & Taylor, D. A. (1973). *Social penetration: The development of interpersonal relationships.* New York: Holt, Rinehart, & Winston.

Barnett, R. C., & Hyde, J. S. (2001). Women, men, work, and family: An expansionist theory. *American Psychologist, 56*, 781–796.

Beauregard, M., Levesque, J., & Bourgouin, P. (2001). Neural correlates of conscious self-regulation of emotion [article No. RC 165]. *Journal of Neuroscience, 21*.

Bell, A. P., Weinberg, M. S., & Hammersmith, S. K. (1981). *Sexual preference.* New York: Simon & Schuster.

Bem, D. J. (1996). Exotic becomes erotic: A developmental theory of sexual orientation. *Psychological Review, 103*, 320–335.

Bernard, J. (1972). *The future of marriage.* New York: Bantam.

Bester-Meredith, J. K., & Marler, C. A. (2001). Vasopressin and aggression in cross-fostered California mice (*Peromyscus californicus*) and white-footed mice (*Peromyscus leucopus*). *Hormones and Behavior, 40*, 51–64.

Bester-Meredith, J. K., Young, L. J., & Marler, C. A. (1999). Species differences in paternal behavior and aggression in *Peromyscus* and their associations with vasopressin immunoreactivity and receptors. *Hormones and Behavior, 36*, 25–38.

Biddle, B. J. (1979). *Role theory: Expectations, identities, and behaviors.* New York: Academic Press.

Biddle, B. J. (1986). Recent developments in role theory. In A. Inkeles, J. Coleman, and N. Smelser (Eds.), *Annual Review of Sociology*, Vol. 12 (pp. 67–92). Palo Alto, CA: Annual Reviews.

Bremner, J., Randall, P., Vermetten, E., Staib, L., Bronen, R., Mazure, C., Capelli, S., McCarthy, G., Innis, R., & Charney, D. (1997). Magnetic resonance imaging-based measurement of hippocampal volume in posttraumatic stress disorder related to childhood physical and sexual abuse: A preliminary report. *Biological Psychiatry, 41*, 23–32.

Brown, B. B., Feiring, C., & Furman, W. (1999). Missing the Love Boat: Why researchers have shied away from adolescent romance. In W. Furman, B. B. Brown, & C. Feiring (Eds.), *The development of romantic relationships in adolescence* (pp. 1–16). Cambridge, England: Cambridge University Press.

Buss, D. M. (1989). Sex differences in human mate preferences: Evolutionary hypotheses tested in 37 cultures. *Behavioral and Brain Science, 12*, 1–49.

Buss, D. M. (1994). *The evolution of desire: Strategies of human mating.* New York: Basic Books.

Buss, D. M. (1999). *Evolutionary psychology: The new science of the mind.* Needham Heights, MA: Allyn & Bacon.

Buss, D., Larsen, R., & Westen, D. (1996). Sex differences in jealousy: Not gone, not forgotten, and not explained by alternative hypotheses. *Psychological Science, 7*, 373–375.

Buss, D. M., & Schmitt, D. P. (1993). Sexual strategies theory: An evolutionary perspective on human mating. *Psychological Review, 100*, 204–232.

Byrne, D. (1977). Social psychology and the study of sexual behavior. *Personality and Social Psychology Bulletin, 3*, 3–30.

Byrne, D. (1983). Sex without contraception. In D. Byrne & W. Fisher (Eds.), *Adolescents, sex, and contraception* (pp. —). Hillsdale, NJ: Lawrence Erlbaum Associates.

Cacioppo, J. T., Berntson, G. G., Sheridan, J. F., & McClintock, M. K. (2000). Multilevel integrative analyses of human behavior: Social neuroscience and the complementing nature of social and biological approaches. *Psychological Bulletin, 126*, 829–843.

Centers for Disease Control and Prevention. (2000). Youth risk behavior surveillance—United States, 1999. *Morbidity and Mortality Weekly Report, 50*, 262–265.

Chalker, R. (1995). Sexual pleasure unscripted. *Ms, 6*, 49–52.

Charon, J. M. (1998). *Symbolic interactionism: An introduction, an interpretation, an integration.* Upper Saddle River, NJ: Prentice-Hall.

Christopher, F. S., & Sprecher, S. (2000). Sexuality in marriage, dating, and other relationships: A decade review. *Journal of Marriage and the Family, 62*, 999–1017.

Davidson, R. J., Jackson, D., & Kalin, N. (2000). Emotion, plasticity, context, and regulation: Perspectives from affective neuroscience. *Psychological Bulletin, 126,* 890–909.

Day, R. D. (1992). The transition to first intercourse among racially and culturally diverse youth. *Journal of Marriage and the Family, 54,* 749–762.

DeLamater, J. (1987a). Gender differences in sexual scenarios. In K. Kelley (Ed.), *Females, males, and sexuality: Theories and research* (pp. 127–139). Albany, NY: SUNY Press.

DeLamater, J. (1987b). A sociological perspective. In J. H. Geer & W. T. O'Donohue (Eds.), *Theories of human sexuality* (pp. 237–256). New York: Plenum.

DeLamater, J. (1991). Emotions and sexuality. In K. McKinney & S. Sprecher (Eds.), *Sexuality in close relationships* (pp. 49–70). Hillsdale, NJ: Lawrence Erlbaum Associates.

DeLamater, J., & Friedrich, W. N. (2002). Human sexual development. *Journal of Sex Research, 39,* 10–14.

DeLamater, J., & Sill, M. (2003). Sexual desire in later life (Working Paper No. 2003–05). Madison, WI: Center for Demography and Ecology.

Delville, Y., Melloni, R. H., & Ferris, C. F. (1998). Behavioral and neurobiological consequences of social subjugation during puberty in Golden hamsters. *Journal of Neuroscience, 18,* 2667–2672.

Diamond, L. M., Savin-Williams, R. C., & Dube, E. M. (1999). Sex, dating, passionate friendships and romance. In W. Furman, B. B. Brown, & C. Feiring (Eds.), *The development of romantic relationships in adolescence* (pp. 175–210). Cambridge, England: Cambridge University Press.

Donnelly, D., Burgess, E., Anderson, S., Davis, R., & Dillard, J. (2001). Involuntary celibacy: A life course analysis. *Journal of Sex Research, 38,* 159–169.

Drigotas, S. M., & Rusbult, C. E. (1992). Should I stay or should I go? A dependence model of breakups. *Journal of Personality and Social Psychology, 62,* 62–87.

Duran, R. L., & Prusank, D. T. (1997). Relational themes in men's and women's popular nonfiction magazine articles. *Journal of Social and Personal Relationships, 14,* 165–189.

Eagly, A. H., & Wood, W. (1999). The origins of sex differences in human behavior: Evolved dispositions versus social roles. *American Psychologist, 54,* 408–423.

Fisher, H. (1992). *Anatomy of love: The mysteries of mating, marriage, and why we stray.* New York: Ballantine.

Fisher, H. E., Aron, A., Mashek, D., Li, H., & Brown, L. L. (2002). Defining the brain systems of lust, romantic attraction, and attachment. *Archives of Sexual Behavior, 31,* 413–419.

Frank, K. (2002). *G-Strings and Sympathy: Strip Club Regulars and Male Desire.* Durham, NC: Duke University Press.

Freese, J., & Meland, S. (2002). Seven tenths incorrect: Heterogeneity and change in the waist-to-hip ratios of *Playboy* centerfold models and Miss America Pageant winners. *Journal of Sex Research, 39,* 133–138.

Gagnon, J., Giami, A., Michaels, S., & de Colomby, R. (2001). A comparative study of the couple in the social organization of sexuality in France and the United States. *Journal of Sex Research, 38,* 24–34.

Gagnon, J., & Simon, W. (1973). *Sexual conduct.* Chicago: Aldine-Atherton.

Gottman, J., Conn, J., Carrere, S., & Swanson, C. (1998). Predicting marital happiness and stability from newlywed interactions. *Journal of Marriage and the Family, 60,* 5–22.

Gould, S. J. (1987). *An urchin in the storm.* New York: Norton.

Hatfield, E. (1978). Equity and extramarital sexuality. *Archives of Sexual Behavior, 7,* 127–141.

Hazen, C., & Shaver, P. (1987). Love conceptualized as an attachment process. *Journal of Personality and Social Psychology, 52,* 511–524.

Homans, G. C. (1974). *Social behavior: Its elementary forms.* New York: Harcourt Brace Jovanovich.

Janssen, E., Vorst, H., Finn, P., & Bancroft, J. (2002). The Sexual Inhibition (SIS) and Sexual Excitation (SES) Scales: II. Predicting psychophysiological response patterns. *Journal of Sex Research, 39,* 127–132.

Jemail, J. A., & Geer, J. (1977). Sexual scripts. In R. Gemme & C. C. Wheeler (Eds.), *Progress in sexology* (pp. —). New York: Plenum.

Kalichman, S. C., Benotsch, E., Rompa, D., Gorg-Felton, C., Austin, J., Luke, W. (2001). Unwanted sexual experiences and sexual risks in gay and bisexual men: Associations among revictimization, substance use, and psychiatric symptoms. *Journal of Sex Research, 38,* 1–9.

Kaplan, H. S. (1974). *The new sex therapy.* New York: Brunner/Mazel.

Kaplan, H. S. (1979). *Disorders of sexual desire.* New York: Simon & Schuster.

Kaplan, H. S., & Sager, C. (1971, June). Sexual patterns at different ages. *Medical Aspects of Human Sexuality,* 10–23.

Kelley, H. H., Berscheid, E., Christensen, A., Harvey, J. H., Huston, T. L., Levinger, G. (1983). *Close relationships.* New York: W. H. Freeman.

Kelley, H. H., & Thibaut, J. W. (1978). *Interpersonal relations: A theory of interdependence.* New York: Wiley.

Kiecolt-Glaser, J. K., & Newton, T. L. (2001). Marriage and health: His and hers. *Psychological Bulletin, 127,* 472–503.

Laumann, E. O., Gagnon, J. H., Michael, R. T., & Michaels, S. (1994). *The social organization of sexuality.* Chicago: University of Chicago Press.

Lawrance, K., & Byers, E. S. (1995). Sexual satisfaction in long-term heterosexual relationships: The interpersonal exchange model of sexual satisfaction. *Personal Relationships, 2,* 267–285.

Lawson, A. (1988). *Adultery: An analysis of love and betrayal.* New York: Basic Books.

Longmore, M. A. (1998). Symbolic interactionism and the study of sexuality. *Journal of Sex Research, 35,* 44–57.

Masters, W. H., & Johnson, V. E. (1970). *Human sexual inadequacy.* Boston: Little, Brown.

Masters, W. H., & Johnson, V. (1966). *Human sexual response.* Boston: Little, Brown.

McCarthy, V. W. (1989). Cognitive-behavioral strategies and techniques in the treatment of early ejaculation. In S. R. Leiblum & R. C. Rosen (Eds.), *Principles and practice of sex therapy* (2nd ed., pp. —). New York: Guilford.

McDonald, J. D. (2000). A model for conducting research with American Indian participants. In Council of National Psychological Associations for the Advancement of Ethnic Minority Interests, *Guidelines for research in ethnic minority communities* (pp. 12–15). Washington, DC: American Psychological Association.

Mead, G. H. (1934). *Mind, self, and society.* Chicago: University of Chicago Press.

Michener, H. A., DeLamater, J. D., & Myers, D. J. (2004). *Social psychology,* Belmont, CA: Wadsworth.

Miller, B. C. (2002). Family influences on adolescent sexual and contraceptive behavior. *Journal of Sex Research, 39,* 22–26.

Miller, L. C., Putcha-Bhagavatula, & Pedersen, W. C. (2002). Men's and women's mating preferences: Distinct evolutionary mechanisms? *Current Directions in Psychological Science, 11,* 88–93.

Myers, L. J., Abdullah, S., & Leary, G. (2000). Conducting research with persons of African descent. In Council of National Psychological Associations for the Advancement of Ethnic Minority Interests, *Guidelines for research in ethnic minority communities* (pp. 5–8). Washington, DC: American Psychological Association.

Office of the Surgeon General. (2001). *The Surgeon General's call to action to promote sexual health and responsible sexual behavior.* Rockville, MD: U.S. Public Health Service.

Oliver, M. B., & Hyde, J. S. (1993). Gender differences in sexuality: A meta-analysis. *Psychological Bulletin, 114,* 29–51.

Oliver, M. B., & Hyde, J. S. (1995). Gender differences in attitudes toward homosexuality: A reply to Whitley and Kite. *Psychological Bulletin, 117,* 155–158.

Opbroek, A., Delgado, P. L., Laukes, C., Mcgahuey, C., Katsanis, J., Moreno, F., & Manber, R. (2002). Emotional blunting associated with SSRI-induced sexual dysfunction: Do SSRIs inhibit emotional responses? *International Journal of Neuropsychopharmacology, 5,* 147–151.

O'Sullivan, L. F., & Allgeier, E. R. (1998). Feigning sexual desire: Consenting to unwanted sexual activity in heterosexual dating relationships. *Journal of Sex Research, 35,* 234–243.

Pedersen, W. C., Miller, L. C., Putcha-Bhagavatula, A. D., & Yang, Y. (2002). Evolved sex differences in the number of partners desired. *Psychological Science, 13,* 157–161.

Peplau, L. A., Cochran, S., Rook, K., & Padesky, C. (1978). Loving women: Attachment and autonomy in lesbian relationships. *Journal of Social Issues, 34*(3), 7–27.

Peplau, L. A., & Garnets, L. D. (2000). A new paradigm for understanding women's sexuality and sexual orientation. *Journal of Social Issues, 56,* 329–350.

Plant, E. A., Hyde, J. S., Keltner, D., & Devine, P. G. (2000). The gender stereotyping of emotions. *Psychology of Women Quarterly, 24,* 81–92.

Robinson, B. E., Bockting, W. O., Rosser, B., Miner, M., & Coleman, E. (2002). The sexual health model: Application of a sexological approach to HIV prevention. *Health Education Research, 17,* 43–57.

Rose, S. (2000). Heterosexism and the study of women's romantic and friend relationships. *Journal of Social Issues, 56,* 315–328.

Rose, S., & Frieze, I. H. (1993). Young singles' contemporary dating scripts. *Sex Roles, 28,* 499–509.

Ross, C. E., Mirowsky, J., & Goldsteen, K. (1990). The impact of the family on health: Decade in review. *Journal of Marriage and the Family, 52,* 1059–1078.

Rusbult, C. E. (1983). A longitudinal test of the investment model: The development (and deterioration) of satisfaction and commitment in heterosexual involvements. *Journal of Personality and Social Psychology, 45,* 101–117.

Rusbult, C. E., Johnson, D. J., & Morrow, D. G. (1986). Predicting satisfaction and commitment in adult romantic involvements: An assessment of the generalizability of the investment model. *Social Psychology Quarterly, 49,* 81–89.

Sanders, S. A., & Reinisch, J. M. (1999). Would you say you "had sex" if. . . ? *Journal of the American Medical Association, 281,* 275–277.

Santos de Barona, M., & Barona, A. (2000). A model for conducting research with Hispanics. In Council of National Psychological Associations for the Advancement of Ethnic Minority Interests, *Guidelines for research in ethnic minority communities* (pp. 9–11). Washington, DC: American Psychological Association.

Sapolsky, R. M. (2000). Glucocorticoids and hippocampal atrophy in neuropsychiatric disorders. *Archives of General Psychiatry, 57,* 925–935.

Savin-Williams, R. C., & Diamond, L. (in press). Sex. In R. M. Lerner, & L. Steinberg (Eds.), *The Handbook of Adolescent Psychology.* San Francisco, CA: Jossey-Bass.

Singh, D. (1993). Adaptive significance of female physical attractiveness: Role of waist-to-hip ratio. *Journal of Personality and Social Psychology, 65,* 293–307.

Sprecher, S. (1998). Social exchange theories and sexuality. *Journal of Sex Research, 35,* 32–43.

Sprecher, S., & Hatfield, E. (1996). Premarital sexual standards among U.S. college students: Comparison with Russian and Japanese students. *Archives of Sexual Behavior, 25,* 261–288.

Sprecher, S., McKinney, K., & Orbuch, T. L. (1987). Has the double standard disappeared? An experimental test. *Social Psychology Quarterly, 50,* 24–31.

Steil, J. (2001). Marriage: Still "his" and "hers"? In J. Worell (Ed.), *Encyclopedia of gender* (pp. 677–686). San Diego: Academic Press.

Sternberg, R. J. (1986). A triangular theory of love. *Psychological Review, 93,* 119–135.

Struckman-Johnson, C., & Struckman-Johnson, D. (2002). Sexual coercion reported by women in three midwestern prisons. *Journal of Sex Research, 39,* 217–227.

Stryker, S. (1980). *Symbolic interactionism: A social structural version.* Menlo Park, CA: Benjamin/Cummings.

Sue, S., & Sue, D. W. (2000). Conducting psychological research with the Asian American/Pacific Islander population. In Council of National Psychological Associations for the Advancement of Ethnic Minority Interests, *Guidelines for research in ethnic minority communities* (pp. 2–4). Washington, DC: American Psychological Association.

Symons, D. (1979). *The evolution of human sexuality.* New York: Oxford University Press.

Symons, D. (1987). An evolutionary approach: Can Darwin's view of life shed light on human sexuality? In J. H. Geer & W. T. O'Donohue (Eds.), *Theories of human sexuality* (pp. 91–126). New York: Plenum.

Teicher, M., Andersen, S., Polcari, A., Anderson, C., & Navalta, C. (2002). Developmental neurobiology of childhood stress and trauma. *Psychiatric Clinics of North America, 25,* 397.

Thibaut, J. W., & Kelley, H. H. (1959). *The social psychology of groups.* New York: Wiley.

Thompson, S. (1995). *Going all the way: Teenage girl's tales of sex, romance and pregnancy.* New York: Hill and Wang.

Thornhill, R., & Palmer, C. T. (2000). *A natural history of rape: Biological bases of sexual coercion.* Cambridge, MA: MIT Press.

Tiefer, L. (2001). A new view of women's sexual problems: Why new? Why now? *Journal of Sex Research, 38,* 89–96.

Tolman, D. L. (2002). *Dilemmas of desire: Teenage girls talk about sexuality.* Cambridge, MA: Harvard University Press.

Tolman, D. L., & Szalacha, L. A. (1999). Dimensions of desire: Bridging qualitative and quantitative methods in a study of female adolescent sexuality. *Psychology of Women Quarterly, 23,* 7–40.

Tooby, J., & Cosmides, L. (1992). The psychological foundations of culture. In J. Barkow, L. Cosmides, & J. Tooby (Eds.), *The adapted mind: Evolutionary psychology and the generation of culture* (pp. 19–136). New York: Oxford University Press.

Turner, R. H. (1990). Role change. In W. R. Scott & J. Blake (Eds.), *Annual Review of Sociology* (Vol. 16, pp. 87–110). Palo Alto, CA: Annual Reviews.

Udry, J. R. (1988). Biological predispositions and social control in adolescent sexual behavior. *American Sociological Review, 53,* 709–722.

Van der Velde, J., & Everaerd, W. (2001). The relationship between involuntary pelvic floor muscle activity, muscle awareness, and experienced threat in women with and without vaginismus. *Behaviour Research and Therapy, 39,* 395–408.

Villareal, G., Hamilton, D., Petropoulos, H., Driscoll, I., Rowland, L., Griego, J., Kodituwakku, P., Hart, B., Escalona, R., & Brooks, W. (2002). Reduced hippocampal volume and total white matter volume in posttraumatic stress disorder. *Biological Psychiatry, 52,* 119–125.

Wade, L., & DeLamater, J. D. (2002). Relationship dissolution as a life stage transition: Effects on sexual attitudes and sexual behaviors. *Journal of Marriage and the Family, 64,* 898–914.

Waite, L. J., & Gallagher, M. (2000). *The case for marriage: Why married people are happier, healthier, and better off financially.* New York: Doubleday.

Walen, S. R., & Roth, D. (1987). A cognitive approach. In J. H. Geer & W. T. O'Donohue (Eds.), *Theories of human sexuality* (pp. 335–362). New York: Plenum.

Walster (Hatfield), E., Walster, G. W., & Berscheid, E. (1978). *Equity: Theory and research.* Boston, MA: Allyn & Bacon.

Ward, L. M., & Rivadeneyra, R. (1999). Contributions of entertainment television to adolescent's sexual attitudes and expectations: The role of viewing amount versus viewer involvement. *Journal of Sex Research, 36,* 237–249.

Weinberg, M. S., Shaver, F. M., & Williams, C. J. (1999). Gendered sex work in the San Francisco tenderloin. *Archives of Sexual Behavior, 28,* 503–521.

Weinberg, M., Williams, C., & Calhan, C. (1995). "If the shoe fits . . . ": Exploring male homosexual shoe fetishism. *Journal of Sex Research, 32,* 17–27.

Weinberg, T. S. (1994). Research in sadomasochism: A review of sociological and social psychological literature. *Annual Review of Sex Research, 5,* 57–279.

Wilson, E. O. (1975). *Sociobiology: The new synthesis.* Cambridge, MA: Harvard University Press.

Wincze, J. P., & Carey, M. P. (1991). *Sexual dysfunction: A guide for assessment and treatment.* New York: Guilford.

Zilbergeld, B. (1999). The new male sexuality. (Rev. ed.). New York: Bantam.

2

Methodological Issues in Studying Sexuality in Close Relationships

Michael W. Wiederman
Columbia College

The study of sexuality within close relationships involves scholars from various disciplines, each with their own research methodological traditions and preferred approaches. Rarely do scholars receive formal training in the particular methodological issues inherent in studying sexuality, especially when examined within the context of interpersonal relationships. In this chapter the primary methodological issues in sexuality research within close relationships are addressed under three broad categories: sampling, measurement of variables, and research design and data analysis. Many of the issues discussed are relevant for behavioral research in general, but there are several issues inherent in studying sexuality within close relationships that warrant special attention because of the sensitive nature of sexuality data and particular methodological issues that arise when studying couples rather than individuals.

Research on close relationships and sexuality is characterized by its cross-disciplinary nature (McKinney & Sprecher, 1991; Wiederman & Whitley, 2002). Rather than being a field unto itself, particular scholars within family studies, psychology, sociology, anthropology, communication studies, public health, and a host of medical and other fields study certain facets of human sexual experience within the context of close relationships. Although the cross-disciplinary nature of couple research on sexuality is advantageous with regard to the possible topics studied and the approaches taken, the result is that there is no set of agreed-on research methods (Reiss, 1999). Also, methodological advances in one traditional discipline may not be known to researchers studying couples' sexuality from the perspective of a different traditional discipline.

Despite the differences among researchers, there are some generalizations that can be made about social scientific research on sexuality within close relationships. The vast majority of research on human sexuality has been focused on the individual as the unit of study, even when the issue of interest entails a close relationship. Also, the primary sources of data have been self-report in nature (either surveys or interviews).

Why? Most likely because of convenience or necessity. Human sexuality is a sensitive topic, which certainly influences the research methods employed to study it. Masters and Johnson (1966, 1970) were pioneers for their physiological and observational research on individuals and couples engaged in sexual activity; more recently, such research is relatively rare. For many topics involving sexuality within close relationships, experimental or observational studies are liable to be unethical, or they would at least result in very unrepresentative samples due to the self-selection inherent in the unusual nature of participation in such types of research (Janssen, 2002).

When studying sexuality as experienced within close relationships, often about the best researchers can do is to ask respondents to report on their experiences, and then correlate such self-reports with other variables. With this crude generalization as a backdrop, the focus of this chapter is on the primary methodological issues inherent in studying sexuality within close relationships. Despite the apparent importance of a relationship context for understanding most people's experience of their sexuality, research on sexuality specifically within couples has been relatively rare (Orbuch & Harvey, 1991). Such research shares the methodological concerns inherent in sexuality research generally, and also entails some special methodological considerations. In this chapter, the review of specific methodological issues is organized according to three categories: sampling, measurement of variables, and research design and data analysis.

SAMPLING

Researchers recognize the importance of studying samples that are representative of the population of interest. Otherwise, how can one generalize from the sample to the population? The primary barriers to representativeness are *coverage error*, where substantial portions of the population of interest are not eligible to participate because the methods used to sample people exclude them, and *nonresponse error*, where people chosen for the sample refuse to participate to one degree or another (Dunne, 2002). Obtaining representative or unbiased samples may be especially problematic when research participation involves "unusual" demands (such as answering questions about sexuality), or the population of interest is small or difficult to access. If the population of interest is a potentially stigmatized group, such as gay or lesbian couples, researchers often must be creative in gaining access to a sample from that group. In these cases, frequently the goal is to obtain a large enough sample to warrant statistical analysis, rather than a representative sample per se. So, the issue of generalizability from such samples remains an important issue.

Research results are often presented in such a way as to imply that they accurately describe *people in general*, or at least all people in the population of interest. For example, researchers may write that, based on their results, "couples experience such-and-such," or "relationships that are this way also tend to exhibit these sexual characteristics." However, not everyone from the population of interest is given the opportunity to participate in research (coverage error) and not everyone who is given the opportunity actually agrees to do so (nonresponse error). Because people are free to decline an invitation to participate in research (ethical principles demand it), some people will choose that option, perhaps simply because they do not have the time or interest to participate. This is true about research in general, especially in an age when consumers are bombarded with mail and telephone solicitation (and use caller ID and voicemail to screen out such solicitation). Imagine how the issue may be most relevant when the research is on a sensitive topic such as sexuality within close relationships. So, perhaps it is not surprising that even in the most extensive and well-conducted national sexuality surveys, where great care is taken to select a nationally representative sample and great effort and expense goes into securing cooperation, only about 70 to 80% of those people initially selected to participate actually do so (Dunne, 2002; Seidman & Rieder, 1994; Turner, Danella, & Rogers, 1995).

Are there differences between those individuals who agree to participate in sexuality research and those who do not? With regard to general national surveys in the United States, certain demographic groups tend to be underrepresented: people at both extremes of the age continuum, males, the wealthy, those living in large cities, and people who work long hours (Visser, Krosnick, & Lavarakas, 2000). These characteristics seem to point to people who simply spend less time at home during which they might be contacted by researchers. However, nonparticipation may result from either explicit refusal or simply being unavailable to participate, and each of these groups of nonparticipants appear to be demographically distinct. Turner (1999) examined potential participants for a national sexual behavior survey who either refused participation twice or who were still not contacted for recruitment after 17 attempted telephone calls. More than 1,500 such individuals who had not participated in the initial survey were sent a follow-up questionnaire. Not surprisingly, a minority returned the survey (27% of the refusers and 40% of the difficult-to-contact). Interestingly, compared to participants in the initial sexual behavior survey, refusers were older, more religious, and more distrustful of researchers. In contrast, the difficult-to-reach sample displayed an overrepresentation of men, Blacks, and those with high numbers of sexual partners.

Depending on how sexuality studies are presented to potential participants, particular sampling biases may apply. When asked whether they would volunteer for sexuality research, agreeable responses are most likely from males, the relatively young, and people who are relatively more sexually experienced, more comfortable with sexual topics, and more liberal in their sexual attitudes (Wiederman, 1999). In addition to these differences, the more sensitive or revealing the information requested, or the more sexually explicit the requirements of participation, the more likely the sample may deviate from the general public (Plaud, Gaither, Hegstad, Rowan, & Devitt, 1999; Wiederman, 1999). For example, if asked to complete a brief, anonymous survey on one's attitudes about past sexual relationships, a small proportion of potential respondents will refuse. If the same sample of potential participants is asked to complete a face-to-face interview regarding their sexual experiences within relationships, a larger proportion of people will refuse. If the same group is asked to engage in some form of sexual behavior with his or her partner while psychophysiological responses are recorded using special instruments, an even greater proportion of people will refuse. The more sensitive or involved the research, the more concern there should be about the generalizability of the results.

The differences between participants and nonparticipants in sexuality research has been investigated almost exclusively among individuals. However, imagine the issues inherent in obtaining a representative sample of couples to participate in sexuality research. The key question is whether volunteer and nonvolunteer couples differ systematically. Not surprisingly, the available data suggest differences. For example, Karney et al. (1995) contacted more than 3,600 couples who had applied for a marriage license and asked whether they would be willing to participate in a longitudinal study of couples. Less than 20% agreed, a typical participation rate for such studies (Brehm, Miller, Perlman, & Campbell, 2002). However, compared to those couples who refused, volunteers were better educated, employed in higher-status jobs, and more likely to be living together at the time of applying for the marriage license. Of course there are myriad other ways volunteer couples may differ from nonvolunteers, but the public information available from marriage license applications is limited.

Consider the issue of motivation. An unwillingness or inability to participate by one partner nixes the couple from inclusion in the sample. So, couples with an imbalanced commitment to research participation are likely to be underrepresented. Perhaps least likely of all to participate are couples who have yet to engage in sexual intercourse. Participation in a study on sexuality within relationships may seem irrelevant to these couples, or presumptuous at that stage in their relationship. Who are the couples who are most motivated to participate jointly? Such couples are liable to be either sexually confident and/or sensation seeking relative to the larger population (and thereby comfortable with, and intrigued by, sexual topics) or those who are most in distress and hopeful that participation will benefit them personally or as a couple. This latter extreme is probably most likely to occur when the topic of investigation is sexual functioning. Some individuals or couples may hope that participation in the research is therapeutic, or at least calls attention to the problem he, she, or they are experiencing. So, a call for participants in research on sexual functioning in couples may result in overrepresentation of couples at the extremes of the function–dysfunction continuum. These speculations need to be investigated empirically.

Potential problems sampling couples apply especially when the couples of interest are nonheterosexual. Due to their minority status, simply identifying a large enough group of couples comprised of gay, lesbian, or bisexual members from which to sample often represents a formidable challenge (Dunne, 2002), regardless of their degree of representativeness. Because nonheterosexual individuals and couples are stigmatized, asking for research participation from members of that identified group equates to asking for "more" than would be the case when sampling heterosexual couples. Simply identifying oneself as a member of a stigmatized group may result in perceptions of vulnerability to negative outcomes. Accordingly, nonresponse error may be greater when sampling nonheterosexual individuals and couples compared to heterosexual research participants.

Does the representativeness of the sample really make that much difference? Like so many questions, the answer is "it depends." Logically, sampling bias most seriously hampers attempts to describe the incidence or prevalence of attitudes or experiences in a population (i.e., what is normative). However, what about statistical relationships between variables? Some people have argued that if a researcher's hypothesis is that two particular variables are related among people in general, then it really does not matter that one is testing the hypothesis with a biased sample because the relationship should still exist (Brecher & Brecher, 1986). It is possible, however, that the relationships exist for some groups of people and not others, or that the strength of the relationship between the variables varies across groups (Visser et al. 2000). If participants are chosen because of their status on one such variable, the resulting correlational analyses are liable to be hampered by restriction in range on that variable. Research with any one particular sample may result in an inaccurate portrayal of the relationships among variables.

In conclusion, the issue of generalizability is an important one, and one that ultimately needs to be addressed empirically. In other words, additional research focused on the same or similar topics but with different samples helps to reveal whether the results of any one study generalize well. Beyond the issues inherent in sampling, there are many considerations related to measurement of variables.

MEASUREMENT OF VARIABLES

As noted, researchers typically rely on self-reports from research participants when studying sexuality within close relationships. A small set of relevant variables can be assessed through observation (Moore, 2002) or psychophysiological measures (Janssen, 2002). However, many of the variables of interest to relationship researchers are hypothetical constructs or involve behavior that is private and cannot be observed, so self-reports constitute the majority of data in published research on sexuality within close relationships. A number of self-report scales have been created to measure variables of interest to researchers studying sexuality within close relationships. Unfortunately, these measures have been developed typically using simplistic psychometric analysis on data from convenience samples (Weinhardt, Forsyth, Carey, Jaworski, & Durant, 1998). Self-report measures of all types are vulnerable to a number of sources of error and bias (Baker & Brandon, 1990). In this chapter, these concerns are organized according to reliability of measurement, validity of measurement, and factors affecting self-reports of sexual attitudes and experiences specifically.

Reliability of Measurement

A measure is said to be reliable if it is *consistent,* or *stable,* or *dependable* in its measurement (Anastasi & Urbina, 1997; Kerlinger, 1986; Whitley, 1996). Theoretically, if one could administer a highly reliable measure multiple times simultaneously with the same research participant, one would obtain the same results each time. In this theoretical case, if the results varied across administrations of the instrument, the measure would be said to contain some degree of unreliability. Why might this occur? With imperfect measures and imperfect respondents, there will be some random factors that influence scores on the measure (e.g., inconsistent interpretation of some test items, carelessness or inattentiveness by the test taker). These factors are collectively referred to *as random error in measurement.* Scores on a highly reliable measure contain less random error than do scores on a less reliable measure.

In the hypothetical case in the preceding paragraph, reliability was assessed by administering the same measure multiple times simultaneously to the same respondent. Of course, in reality this cannot be accomplished, so researchers must rely on less direct ways of assessing reliability. There are several ways to assess reliability in measurement (Anastasi & Urbina, 1997), but the focus here is on three of the most commonly used methods: test–retest reliability, internal consistency of scales, and interrater reliability.

Test–Retest Reliability. In attempting to assess the reliability of self-reported behavior or attitudes, researchers may ask for the same information at two or more separate points in time (e.g., Carballo-Dieguez, Remien, Dolezal, & Wagner, 1999), and then compare each respondent's answers to assess the degree to which those answers are consistent (i.e., reliable) across time. Such consistency is typically calculated as a correlation coefficient or percentage agreement between the two scores taken from the two points of assessment. In some instances the information is asked for at two separate points in the same questionnaire or interview, whereas in other instances the information is asked for during separate assessment sessions, sometimes spaced up to months apart. Each approach entails advantages and disadvantages.

For example, suppose researchers wished to assess the reliability of responses to the question, "How many times have you and your spouse engaged in vaginal intercourse during the previous 4 weeks?" An investigator who asks the question during two separate interviews, each conducted 3 months apart, is not asking about the same reference period, so there is likely to be some discrepancy between the reports gathered during each session because the respondents may have had changes in their sexual experience. In the second interview the researcher could attempt to specify "in the 4 weeks prior to the previous interview," but it is unclear (and doubtful) whether respondents would be able to effectively draw boundaries in their memories around the span of time the researcher designates as of interest.

Sexuality researchers could circumvent this problem by assessing the number of acts of vaginal intercourse during the previous 4 weeks at two different points in the same interview. However, a high degree of consistency might simply indicate that the respondents were able to accurately recall their first response over the relatively short span of the interview.

Sexuality variables are often measured with single interview or questionnaire items, such as the one about frequency of sexual intercourse over the preceding 4 weeks. With regard to theoretical constructs, however, multiple-item scales are often used because such scales are generally more reliable than single-item measures (Gardner, Cummings, Dunham, & Pierce, 1998). Single-item measures are relatively more vulnerable to measurement error because such error is more concentrated, or liable to affect the final overall score, compared to multiple-item measures. For example, suppose two researchers measure sexual satisfaction within respondents' current relationship, and one uses a single item whereas the other uses a 10-item scale designed to measure the same construct. If a respondent is careless in responding to the single-item measure, or if it contains language that is ambiguous, the measurement error introduced will have a tremendous effect on the value ascribed to that respondent. In the case of the 10-item measure, the effect of careless responding to a few items, or ambiguous wording in some items, will be watered down when a single score is generated across the items (some of which are better items than the problematic ones). Therefore, the 10-item scale will demonstrate greater reliability relative to the single-item measure.

To assess test–retest reliability of scales one would administer them to the same individuals or couples at two points in time, and the correlation between the two sets of scores would indicate the test–retest reliability of the measure. Such an index of reliability is inappropriate, however, for tests measuring constructs that are, by their nature, unstable. For example, suppose researchers developed a self-report inventory of sexual arousal. Although sexual arousal may entail a component best conceptualized as a trait (i.e., some individuals tend to experience more frequent or intense sexual arousal than do others) and as a feature of the relationship (i.e., members of some couples tend to experience more frequent or intense sexual arousal than do others), certainly a large component of sexual arousal involves the individual's current state (i.e., situational variables are probably most prominent). Accordingly, we might expect a fair degree of variation in sexual arousal across situations, even though the same respondent and the same sexual partner are involved in all of the situations. The researcher's inventory might in fact be highly reliable, yet appear to be unreliable because the influence of situational variables such as stimuli present during testing, the respondents' levels of fatigue or stress, respondents' recent sexual activity, and other factors that vary between testing sessions results in low correlations between administrations.

Regardless of whether a self-report scale measures a state or a trait variable, generally the longer the span of time between the two administrations, the lower the test–retest correlation (Anastasi & Urbina, 1997; Kerlinger, 1986). Accordingly, Anastasi and Urbina advocated that "the interval between retests should rarely exceed six months" (p. 92). Because test–retest reliability requires repeated access to the same sample, as well as the ability to match responses from the repeated sessions, researchers typically rely on alternative measures of reliability.

Internal Consistency of Scales. The most common index of reliability for self-report scales appears to be the coefficient of internal consistency (typically Cronbach's alpha), which is derived from the mean correlation between scores on all possible halves of the measure (Kerlinger, 1986). In other words, one could split any multiple-item scale into two sets, with half the items in one set and the other half of the items in the other set, and calculate the correlation between scores on the two halves. As there are multiple ways the sets could be generated, the internal consistency coefficient is based on averaging the results obtained across all possible pairs of sets. Spearman

(1904) was among the first to use the internal consistency of a scale as a measure of the scale's reliability. He reasoned that if the items in a scale all measure the same latent construct, responses to those items should display substantial covariation. If responses to a set of scale items are not highly related to one another, then those items presumably are not measuring the same construct (and hence the scale has low internal consistency).

A common statement regarding scale reliability in published reports of sexuality research fits the following formula: "In a large sample [or in a previously published study], the X scale exhibited a high degree of reliability with an internal consistency coefficient of .86." Typically, such authors refer to their scale (or subscale) as reliable and as measuring a single construct, mostly based on the acceptably high internal consistency coefficient. However, both conclusions may be inaccurate.

First, the internal consistency coefficient tells us about the reliability of the data generated by the measure in that particular sample (Vacha-Haase, 1998). As Thompson and Snyder (1998) noted, "Put simply, *reliability is a characteristic of scores for the data in hand*, and not of a test per se" (p. 438, emphasis in the original). The internal consistency coefficient derived from a particular sample could be viewed as an estimate for the internal consistency coefficient one would find for the population from which the sample was drawn. Taking the mean internal consistency coefficient across several such samples would be an even better estimate. There will be sample-to-sample variations from this mean, sometimes very large ones. So, it is important that internal consistency coefficients be calculated each time a scale is used with a new sample. Only when researchers have access to numerous internal consistency coefficients for a particular scale, each of which was generated based on an independent sample from a larger population of interest (e.g., college students), might they be able to generalize from that set of coefficients to a conclusion about the scale's reliability in that population (Vacha-Haase, 1998).

The authors of many published reports of research on sexuality within close relationships (as well as other types of research) mistakenly imply that a relatively high internal consistency coefficient is evidence that the items are homogeneous and the scale or subscale is unidimensional. However, several writers have explained why a high internal consistency coefficient is a necessary but far from sufficient condition for unidimensionality in a scale (Boyle, 1991; Clark & Watson, 1995; Cortina, 1993; John & Benet-Martinez, 2000). The problem stems from confusion over the difference between item *homogeneity* and item *interrelatedness*. Homogeneous items are those that all measure the same construct. Interrelated items are those whose scores are correlated with one another; they may or may not measure the same construct. The internal consistency coefficient is *not* a measure of item homogeneity and is a poor measure of item interrelatedness because its value is a function of the number of scale items as well as the degree of interrelatedness among them. A relatively large set of items will have a high internal consistency coefficient as long as the correlations among the items are greater than 0 (Cortina, 1993). For example, a 30-item scale in which the average inter-item correlation is .12 will have an internal consistency coefficient of .81 (Green, Lissitz, & Mulaik, 1977), as will a 10-item scale in which the average inter-item correlation is .30 (John & Benet-Martinez, 2000).

Perhaps even more problematic is the fact that, regardless of the length of the scale, the internal consistency coefficient will be high as long as the *average* intercorrelation among items is larger than 0, even if such an average intercorrelation derives from subsets of items that are highly related to one another but totally unrelated to the items in the other subsets. In other words, if a scale is comprised of several subscales, each of which contains relatively homogeneous sets of items, the internal consistency coefficient for the entire scale will be high even when the subscales are unrelated to one another (John & Benet-Martinez, 2000). Cortina (1993) demonstrated this fact with a hypothetical 18-item scale comprised of three distinct 6-item subscales. The average inter-item correlations within each subscale was .70, yet the correlations among the subscale scores were all zero. The overlap among subscales was nil, yet the overall internal consistency coefficient for the entire 18-item scale was .84! Based on misuse of the internal consistency coefficient, the user of the scale might mistakenly conclude that the scale is unidimensional.

What should researchers do instead of relying on the internal consistency coefficient as an index of item homogeneity? If the goal is to demonstrate that a particular scale is unidimensional, researchers should perform factor analysis (see Comrey, 1988; Floyd & Widaman, 1995) and pay more attention to the inter-item correlations than to the overall internal consistency coefficient (Clark & Watson, 1995). The range and mean of inter-item correlations provide a straightforward measure of internal consistency that avoids the potential problems noted in the hypothetical case from Cortina (1993).

Is there reason to be concerned about whether purported unidimensional scales are indeed measuring only one construct? Misspecification of the number of factors composing a scale has grave implications for the validity of relationships found with measures of other constructs (Smith & McCarthy, 1995). For example, Wryobeck and Wiederman (1999) analyzed the factor structure of the 25-item Hurlbert Index of Sexual Narcissism (ISN) among a sample of male undergraduates. Hurlbert, Apt, Gasar, Wilson, and Murphy (1994) presented the scale as unidimensional, citing a high internal consistency coefficient, and advocated use of an overall score. Wryobeck and Wiederman found, however, that 16 of the items comprised four distinct subscales, and that the remaining 9 items did not load clearly or consistently on any factors. They went on to show that, depending on the sexuality construct under consideration, some subscales were significantly related whereas others were not. Simply using the overall scale score would obscure potentially important theoretical relationships between individual facets of the larger construct (sexual narcissism) and other sexuality measures (also see Carver, 1989).

Perhaps more surprising, Wryobeck and Wiederman (1999) found that the multiple correlation between various sexuality constructs and scores on the four subscales was as high, and sometimes higher, than the correlation between the sexuality constructs and the score on the 25-item ISN. How can this be when the full ISN contains all of the items comprising the four subscales? Part of the answer lies in the fact that sometimes a particular subscale score correlated negatively with the sexuality construct under consideration, whereas the remaining subscale scores correlated positively. In these cases, using the overall score resulted in a loss of predictive power. Also, the 9 ISN items that did not load on the four primary factors apparently were not related to the other sexuality constructs in consistent ways, resulting in the introduction of error variance when using the full 25-item ISN.

Inter-Rater Reliability. Inter-rater reliability is sometimes used in research on sexuality within close relationships to compare reports of the same phenomena (e.g., frequency of sexual intercourse) from two or more respondents. For example, with regard to partnered sexual activity, researchers sometimes attempt to assess reliability by comparing reports from each member of an ongoing couple (e.g., Carballo-Deguez et al., 1999; Ochs & Binik, 1999). Relevant questions might be to what degree do sexual partners agree in their self-reported frequency of sexual intercourse and to what extent do partners agree that each of several sexual behaviors did or did not occur? Depending on the nature of the data, a sexuality researcher might attempt to answer these questions by computing kappa (for nominally scaled data), weighted kappa (for ordinally scaled data), or the intraclass correlation coefficient (for dimensionally scaled data). Calculation and interpretation of these statistics are discussed in Ochs and Binik and in Siegel and Castellan (1988).

Inter-rater reliability of sexual experiences within couples is far from a gold standard. Unlike objective observers, members of a sexual dyad are liable to be influenced by their present feelings about their sexual relationship and/or partner (Grote & Frieze, 1998). Discrepancies in partners' reports of sexual activity are common. For example, Upchurch et al. (1991) compared the reports of men and women composing 71 couples who attended sexually transmitted disease clinics. When asked to report the number of experiences of vaginal intercourse during the previous 4 weeks, the men reported an average of 8.8 such experiences compared to an average of 11.5 reported by their female partners. Padian, Aral, Vranizan, and Bolan (1995) examined consistency of reports among more than 300 heterosexual couples. When asked whether they had ever experienced vaginal intercourse together (yes/no), 100% of couples displayed agreement. However, for a similar question about ever having engaged in anal intercourse together, more than 12% of couples were discordant (one member of the couple indicated having experienced anal sex with their current partner whereas the partner denied such experience). When there is such a discrepancy, which partner's report is more accurate? Even if there is no such discrepancy within a particular couple, unfortunately it is still possible that both members of the couple reported inaccurately (and there would be no way for the researcher to know).

Validity of Measurement

Behaviorally we can only measure that which can be observed. However, researchers are commonly interested in variables such as sexual satisfaction, sexual anxiety, and sexual conflict, that cannot be directly observed. To assess such hypothetical constructs, researchers typically create self-report scales intended to indirectly measure the construct of interest. Such measures may include items based on past or current behavior (e.g., assessment of sexual activity with one's partner) or attitudes toward a referent (e.g., sexual satisfaction with one's partner). The goal of the scale developer is to create a set of items that reflect the construct being measured. The theory underlying the scale development process is that the hypothetical construct influences people's responses to items such that higher scores on the scale represent higher (or lower) levels of the construct. To the extent that this relationship between item responses and the hypothetical construct actually exists, the researcher can infer that those responses are indicative of the respondents' underlying degree of sexual satisfaction, or sexual anxiety, or sexual conflict, for example. That is, the strength of the hypothetical construct is inferred from the strength of the respondents' answers to the items that compose the measure. Is this an accurate inference?

Measurement validity refers to the degree to which a measuring instrument accurately assesses what it is intended to measure (Foster & Cone, 1995; Whitley, 1996). As noted previously, random error in measurement results in decreased reliability. The oft-cited principle that reliability is a necessary but not sufficient condition for validity points to the importance of evaluating measurement reliability when assessing validity of an instrument. If a measure is unreliable, it contains a high degree of random error and so, by definition, it cannot be a good measure of a construct. However, a measure can be highly reliable, yet demonstrate a low degree of validity. This may occur because the source of low validity in measurement is *systematic error*. Responses to a measure may be a function of systematic factors other than what the measure is intended to assess. In essence, the measure may be assessing, perhaps even consistently (reliably), some construct or phenomenon other than that intended. For example, responses to the items may be influenced by the respondent's attempts to portray the self in a socially desirable light.

In general terms, researchers assess the validity of a measure by examining relationships between responses on the measure and other variables and considering the pattern that emerges (Foster & Cone, 1995; Whitley, 1996). A valid measure should demonstrate substantial and predictable relationships with some variables (convergent validity) and a lack of relationship, or very modest relationships, with others (discriminant validity). The variables used to demonstrate convergent validity might entail a behavioral or group membership criterion or scores on measures of other, related theoretical constructs. Discriminant validity would be demonstrated by a lack of relationship to theoretically unrelated variables. For example, scores on a measure of sexual satisfaction with one's partner should be inversely related to sexual conflict (indicating convergent validity) yet not related to scores on measures of particular personality variables such as conscientiousness (indicating discriminant validity).

Ideally, evidence for convergent validity should entail different methods of measurement (Brewer, 2000). For example, evidence for convergent validity of a self-report scale of sexual passion toward one's partner should include demonstration of predictable relationships with group membership (e.g., couples who have engaged in genital sexual activity vs. those who have not) and behavior (e.g., frequency of sexual activity with one's partner), as well as perhaps physiological response (e.g., autonomic nervous system arousal in response to imagining sexual activity with one's partner). If evidence for convergent validity comes only from other measures based on self-report, one is left wondering whether the resulting correlational relationships simply reflect shared method variance (i.e., it is possible that the correlations result from individuals tending to be consistent in the general ways they respond to self-report scales, regardless of the content of such scales). If only self-report measures are used to assess the validity of a measure, it is imperative to demonstrate discriminant validity using self-report instruments as well (Foster & Cone, 1995).

Another potential problem is when two or more self-report scales purportedly measure distinct concepts, yet the individual items composing each scale overlap conceptually or practically. The labels attached to scales designed to measure hypothetical constructs are derived from the judgment of the scholars developing the scales, so there is room for variation. For example, suppose one scale has been labeled a measure of "sexual self-disclosure" to one's partner, whereas another scale has been labeled a measure of "sexual trust" in one's partner. In reality, the items composing each scale might be very similar (despite the fact that the respective developers of each scale thought of the underlying hypothetical construct in different terms). A researcher administering both scales to a sample would find a strong, positive correlation between scores on each and go on to try to explain why people who indicate greater trust in their partners also report disclosing more to their partners. Such a relationship makes sense and would likely not engender any suspicion. However, perhaps some of the items composing each scale are very similar, thereby explaining the correlation, whereas the constructs the scales are meant to measure are not related (or at least to the extent thought).

Last, in establishing the validity of a measure, researchers should keep in mind that the demonstrated validity of a measure may apply only to the samples and uses that have been investigated. In other words, it is dubious to proclaim unconditional validity for a measure whose validity has not been assessed under a variety of conditions.

> Because of the conditional nature of validation, it should rarely be assumed that an assessment instrument has unconditional validity. Statements such as "... has been shown to be a reliable and valid assessment instrument" do not reflect the conditional nature of validity and are usually unwarranted (Haynes, Richard, & Kubany, 1995, p. 241).

The validity of a measure may also change over time as the construct it measures evolves with additional research and conceptual modification (Haynes et al., 1995). Accordingly, the validity of measures must be re-established over time.

In the end, evaluating the validity of a measure is a somewhat subjective process of weighing the evidence for both convergent and discriminant validity and entails evaluating multiple sources of evidence. Ideally, conclusions as to a measure's validity are drawn on the basis of numerous relationships demonstrated between the measure and other constructs (these being assessed using a variety of methods) involving data from several different, recent samples (Brewer, 2000).

Factors Influencing the Reliability and Validity of Self-Reports

Regardless of whether a researcher measures variables with individual questions or multiple-item scales, respondents' sexual experiences and attitudes are considered sensitive information, so researchers typically must rely on self-reports from research participants (Weinhardt et al., 1998). Such self-reports are vulnerable to a number of sources of error and bias that can adversely affect reliability and validity of measurement (Baker & Brandon, 1990; Krosnick, 1999; Tourangeau, Rips, & Rasinski, 2000). In this section the most prominent sources of error and bias in self-reports in the context of sexuality research are reviewed.

Suppose researchers presented the following question to respondents: "How often have you and your current partner engaged in vaginal intercourse during the previous 6 months?" Who would most likely be able to provide an accurate response? Probably those respondents who have not engaged in vaginal intercourse during at least the previous 6 months, or perhaps those respondents who have done so only a few times. Now consider a respondent who in actuality experienced vaginal intercourse 83 times during the previous 6 months. With experiences that occur more than a few times, it is unlikely that each instance will be distinct in memory (the few instances that are distinct are liable to be so because those instances were unusual—positively or negatively). Certainly it is unrealistic to expect that our hypothetical respondent could remember each instance of vaginal intercourse, even if highly motivated and given enough time to try.

How do respondents produce answers to questions about their sexual behavior when it is impossible to recall and count every actual instance of the behavior? In the end, most respondents estimate their experience, and respondents do so in different ways depending on the frequency and regularity of the behavior about which they are being asked (Brown, 1995, 1997; Conrad, Brown, & Cashman, 1998; Croyle & Loftus, 1993). For example, when asked for the number of sex partners one has had in one's lifetime, respondents who have had several partners are liable to give a round, "ballpark" estimate (Brown & Sinclair, 1999; Wiederman, 1997). Indeed, respondents with more than about 10 partners typically provide numbers that are multiples of 5 (e.g., 15, 25, 30, 100; Tourangeau et al., 2000).

Considering responses to frequency questions such as the vaginal intercourse question just posed, it appears that people who have had numerous such experiences go through a cognitive process to arrive at an estimate (Brown, 1995, 1997; Conrad et al., 1998; Jaccard & Wan, 1995). The thinking of our hypothetical respondent might go something like this, "Well, my partner and I typically have sex about three times a week, and 4 weeks in each month results in 24 weeks over the past 6 months. Three times 24 is 72, so I guess we had sex about 72 times." Notice that this cognitive process is liable to occur in the course of just a few seconds, and that the respondent does not even attempt to remember each instance because to do so is impossible. How accurate the resulting estimate is depends on how regularly the respondent engages in the behavior as well as the accuracy of his or her recall (or estimation) of that typical frequency (Downey, Ryan, Roffman, & Kulich, 1995; Sudman, Bradburn, & Schwartz, 1996). Minor exceptions (e.g., that week the respondent was on vacation or was ill or was fighting with the partner) are typically not factored in when arriving at global estimates. Whether the respondent is proficient in the mathematics involved in the calculation is yet another matter.

It is probably the case that individuals have a more difficult time recalling particular behaviors (e.g., condom usage, sexual disagreements) over longer rather than shorter periods of time (Thompson, Skowronski, Larsen, & Betz, 1996). So, all else being equal, researchers should have more faith in responses to the question "Did you and your partner both experience orgasm during your most recent experience of vaginal intercourse?" than in responses to the question "How often did both you and your partner experience orgasm while engaging in vaginal intercourse during the previous 12 months?" In responding to this latter question, couples who recently have been emotionally closer and experiencing orgasms more consistently might tend to overestimate orgasm frequency during the past year compared to couples who perhaps used to experience orgasms consistently but less so over the past few months. In actuality both couples might have had the same overall rates of orgasm over the past year, but their more recent experiences bias their estimates for the year-long time span.

Some questions sexuality researchers pose to respondents contain an element requiring location of an event or behavior in time. For example, "When in your relationship did you first begin engaging in oral sex?" Unfortunately, it does not appear that human memory contains a component having to do with remembered time per se. That is, people use different methods for trying to locate a remembered event in time, and these methods may be prone to distortion, particularly as the event become more distant in time (Friedman, 1993). In the end, researchers should be cautious of the absolute accuracy of answers respondents provide about events that occurred several years ago or when the individuals were very young, regardless of the nature of the events (Henry, Moffitt, Caspi, Langley, & Silva, 1994; Thompson et al., 1996).

In addition to asking questions that rely on respondents' memories, sometimes sexuality researchers ask respondents to answer *why* questions. These questions may not actually contain the word *why*, but yet they ask for some degree of introspection as to motives or decision making nonetheless. For example, "What factors led to your decision to have sexual intercourse the first time with your partner?" Similar questions may explicitly ask *why* the respondent did something: "Why did you fall in love with your partner? Why did you breakup with your most recent partner?" Such questions not only demand recall but also a great degree of insight into one's own motives and the factors that led to particular emotions and decisions. However, people apparently do not have good insight into these mental processes (Brehmer & Brehmer, 1988; Nisbett & Ross, 1980; Nisbett & Wilson, 1977), and this is especially likely to be true with complex feelings and decisions. Survey questions regarding motives are based on an assumption that all such motives are conscious. However, researchers have made the distinction between *implicit* motives, which are outside of conscious awareness, and *self-attributed* motives, which are conscious or are based on the individual's beliefs about what his or her motives should be (McClelland, Koestner, & Weinberger, 1989).

When asked questions about their motives or decisions, people do readily provide responses. "He was the kindest person I had ever met." "We were no longer communicating and just grew apart." These are typical, self-attributed motives people might provide in response to the questions about falling in love and breaking up in the previous paragraph, yet it is doubtful that they capture all of the complexity (and implicit motives) that went into the experience of falling in love or the potentially difficult decision to end a meaningful relationship. People apparently provide such answers based on stereotypes or beliefs they hold regarding the causes of relationship events (Baldwin, 1992; 1995; Knee, 1998), which may or may not accurately reflect what occurred within the respondent's life.

Many times researchers are interested in how things may have changed over time within people's close sexual relationships. Such research questions beg for longitudinal studies, but these are costly and difficult in many ways. Accordingly, it is tempting to ask respondents to tell the researcher how their respective relationship has changed over time (Stone, Catania, & Binson, 1999; Visser et al., 2000). The problem? Because people's beliefs about close relationships in general affect how each person perceives his or her actual relationship partner (Baldwin, 1992, 1995; Knee, 1998), any questions or measures that rely on respondents' memories or perceptions of how things used to be within the relationship are vulnerable to distortion. Over time, as couples develop a history together and construct stories to make sense out of that history, their recollection of earlier events, feelings, and perceptions within the relationship tend to be influenced by the stories themselves (LaRossa, 1995; McGregor & Holmes, 1999). Also, people tend to overestimate the degree to which earlier feelings toward their current relationship partners were similar to their present feelings (Grote & Frieze, 1998; McFarland & Ross, 1987). Research based on such measures may lead to results that are highly questionable if taken at face value. Indeed, one comparison between actual change and perceived change in number of sexual partners over a span of just 1 year demonstrated a statistically significant degree of disagreement between the data derived from the two methods (Stone et al., 1999).

An extension of the problem of asking people to report on changes in their attitudes, thoughts, or feelings is the case of trying to evaluate the effect of some event or intervention. If researchers ask people about their behavior, attitudes, or feelings subsequent to some notable event (e.g., disclosure of extramarital sex by one's spouse), respondents are liable to provide answers commensurate with their expectations for how their attitudes, feelings, or behavior should have changed. For example, when people believe they have participated in an intervention that should affect their behavior, they tend to report such improvements in their behavior, even if there has not been any such improvement (Dawes, 1988). One explanation of this phenomenon is that people often do not remember precisely what their attitudes, feelings, or behavior were prior to the event or intervention, so it is possible to recall that things were better (or worse) than they were because of the assumption that the intervening experience must have had some effect. These *expectancy* or *placebo effects* have been studied most in regard to drug trials and psychotherapy outcome (Critelli & Neumann, 1984; Horvath, 1988; Quitkin, 1999), yet the phenomena have important implications for sexuality researchers relying on self-reports. For example, when people participate in a sexual counseling program, they may report (and honestly believe) there has been at least some improvement in their sexual lives, regardless of whether the intervention was effective.

One possible improvement over asking respondents to remember certain experiences, or to compare the past to the present, is to have them report on the experiences very shortly after they occur. Such methods involve event sampling or diaries. With event sampling, research participants are cued (e.g., with a beeper) to pay attention to their immediate experience and complete a rating or reporting sheet about their experience at that point (Reis & Gable, 2000). With diaries, participants are asked to complete the rating or reporting sheet at prescribed times (e.g., immediately after target experiences, or each evening immediately before bedtime). In either case, there is still the risk that respondents will fail to comply, or put off completing the measure until later, or distort their responses; and there are specific issues to consider, such as the frequency of data collection and retrieval (Okami, 2002). The primary advantage over other self-report methods, however, is that presumably the length of time of recall is considerably shorter with event sampling and diaries, thereby lessening the chance of omission or distortion of data regarding particular experiences. However, researchers garner different data depending on whether respondents complete the diaries each day or are telephoned and interviewed each day (Morrison, Leigh, & Gillmore, 1999).

In addition to issues of memory and beliefs affecting responses to questions, it appears that respondents vary systematically in their tendency to provide certain responses regardless of the content of the items (Austin, Deary, Gibson, McGregor, & Dent, 1998; Greenleaf, 1992). For example, when presented with a response scale, some people tend to use the extreme ends of the scale, whereas others may tend to gravitate toward the middle of such scales (or least avoid using the end points). Similarly, some respondents may tend to agree with survey items (acquiescence response bias), seemingly regardless of the content of such items. In an attempt to address this form of potential response bias, some researchers advocate inclusion of reverse-scored items so that respondents will be prompted to consider both positively and negatively worded items. However, often it is difficult to construct positively and negatively worded items that are equivalent. For example, Snell and Papini (1989) constructed a self-report measure of sexual preoccupation and included both positively and negatively worded items. Examples of each include: "I think about sex more than anything else" and "I hardly ever fantasize about having sex." After reverse scoring the second item, would one expect comparable scores on each item? If they are both measuring the same phenomenon, the answer should be "yes." However, Wiederman and Allgeier (1993) found that the positively and negatively worded items each comprised their own factors in data collected from college student respondents. Understandably, respondents did not seem to equate an absence of sexual preoccupation as synonymous with an absence of sexual thoughts and fantasies.

Some research participants distort their responses, consciously or unconsciously, to present themselves in a positive light (Nicholas, Durrheim, & Tredoux, 1994; Siegel, Aten, & Roughman, 1998; Tourangeau et al., 2000). For example, if a respondent believes that the frequency of sexual activity within a relationship is an indication of the value or closeness of that relationship, she or he may tend to overestimate the frequency of sexual activity. Conversely, if a respondent believes that frequent sexual activity is shameful or cheapens the nonsexual qualities of the relationship, he or she may not remember or report as much sexual activity as actually occurred. Researchers refer to these types of distortion as *social desirability response bias*, and it has been a long-time bane of the researcher's existence when attempting to understand sexuality (Meston, Heiman, Trapnell, & Paulhus, 1998; Wiederman, 1997).

Almost without exception, the potential impact of social desirability response bias has been tested by examining correlations between scores on sexuality measures and the Marlowe-Crowne measure of socially desirable responding (Crowne & Marlowe, 1964). This instrument is purported to measure the respondent's general tendency toward unrealistically positive self-presentation. There has been debate as to what the Marlowe-Crowne scale actually measures, and space limitations here prevent going into the potential conceptual problems associated with the measure (see Paulhus, 1991). However, the assumption that a relatively low correlation between scores on a sexuality measure and scores on the Marlowe-Crowne measure indicates a lack of social desirability response bias in the first set of scores is dubious. This may explain the general lack of relationship between scores on the Marlowe-Crowne measure and reports of sexual behavior (e.g., Gibson, Hudes, & Donovan, 1999).

So far, the forms of measurement error covered here have focused on factors related to the respondent. There are, however, aspects of the research itself that may result in measurement error and hence compromise reliability and validity of the respondent's self-reports. Why? Because researchers must rely on words, either spoken or printed, to form the questions. The problem is that any time we use words there is the possibility for misunderstanding or multiple interpretations (Binson & Catania, 1998; Catania et al., 1996; Krosnick, 1999). Can the researcher be sure that the words used in an interview or questionnaire have the same meaning to all respondents as they do to the researcher? Researchers often take great care in choosing the wording for questions, sometimes pilot testing the items prior to conducting the study. However, it is easy for different meanings to arise (Huygens, Kajura, Seeley, & Burton, 1996; Visser et al., 2000). Consider these questions:

> *How many sex partners have you had during your lifetime?*
> *How often have you and your partner engaged in sex during the past month?*
> *How often do you experience sexual passion?*
> *Have you ever forced your partner to have sex? (Or, has your partner ever forced you to have sex against your will?)*

Respondents generate answers to these types of questions quite readily, especially if a scale is provided to indicate frequency. However, respondents may interpret the meaning of certain words in a variety of ways. In the first two questions, what does the term *sex* mean? Heterosexual respondents are liable to interpret *sex* to mean vaginal intercourse. To many such individuals, if there was not a penis moving around inside a vagina, there was no sex. However, others will interpret *sex* to include oral or manual stimulation of the genitals (Sanders & Reinisch, 1999). This ambiguity may occur even when researchers do what they can to avoid it. For example, Carballo-Dieguez et al. (1999) studied reports from both members of 75 male couples and found that different interpretations of what constitutes sex was a primary cause of inter-partner discrepancies in reporting, despite precise and clear definitions that were provided within the assessment.

What about lesbian women and definitions of sex (Rothblum, 1994)? Heterosexual definitions of sex rely on the involvement of a penis, and episodes of sex typically are marked by ejaculation from that penis. So, if a heterosexual couple is asked the second question ("How often have your and your partner engaged in sex during the past month?"), the response will likely be based on the number of times the man ejaculated after having been inside his partner's vagina, regardless of the number of orgasms the woman did or did not have. Lesbian respondents may arrive at an answer to the same question in a variety of ways, yet one may ask whether the question would even have meaning for most such respondents (Rothblum, 1994).

The last questions in the list (*Have you ever forced your partner to have sex? Or, has your partner ever forced you to have sex against your will?*) may elicit images of physical restraint and use of physical force to achieve penetration, and certainly most respondents would include such experiences in their definition of forced sex. Generally, these are the kinds of experiences that researchers are interested in when studying rape within close relationships. However, because many respondents may not have had such an experience, some may tend to take a more liberal definition of "forced" (Allgeier, 2002). For example, Ross and Allgeier (1996) had college men individually complete a questionnaire containing several commonly used questions having to do with forcing or coercing women into having sex. Afterward, each respondent was individually interviewed to find out how each had interpreted the meaning of the words used in some of the questions. Interestingly, there was a variety of ways the men interpreted what was meant by each question, and some of the interpretations of the questions had nothing to do with physical force. There is also variation in how research participants interpret response choices to sexuality questions; so two respondents giving the same answer may mean different things (e.g., see Cecil & Zimet, 1998; Wright, Gaskell, & O'Muircheartaigh, 1997).

When people respond to questions in a questionnaire or interview, they do not respond to each question in a vacuum (Krosnick, 1999; Tourangeau et al., 2000). As such, the questions surrounding a target question may influence responses to that particular item. For one, people's answers to the target question may be influenced by their responses to related questions within the questionnaire or interview, coupled with a desire to be consistent in one's behavior or viewpoints. There is even evidence that at least some people may go back and change responses to earlier items in a self-administered questionnaire to make them more consistent with later responses (Schwartz & Hippler, 1995).

Respondents also consider the questions surrounding a particular question when trying to determine what the researchers mean by the question (Krosnick, 1999; Schwartz, 1999; Sudman et al., 1996). So, if respondents are asked to rate their degree of satisfaction with their primary relationship, and that question was preceded by a series of questions about the sexual aspects of that relationship, respondents are liable to interpret the satisfaction question as referring to the nonsexual aspects of their relationships (because sex had already been assessed).

Context effects can also influence how people evaluate their attitudes or feelings (Council, 1993; Tourangeau et al., 2000). Because respondents typically provide the first appropriate answer that comes to mind (Ottati, 1997), previous questionnaire or interview items may influence responses to a current question because those previous items called to mind particular experiences, attitudes, or feelings. Consider the previous example pertaining to a question about overall satisfaction with a partner preceded by multiple questions about the sexual aspects of the relationship. The sexuality questions may "prime" the respondent to think about the sexual aspects of the relationship, and therefore these aspects may disproportionately affect the general satisfaction rating (Marsh & Yeung, 1999). Such an instance would inflate the apparent correlation between sexual satisfaction and satisfaction with life.

Apart from the questions asked, the scales used, and the context in which those items are embedded, researchers may affect respondents' answers by the conditions under which they ask participants to respond (Catania, 1999; Kaplan, 1989). Imagine asking respondents to answer questions about their first sexual experiences and asking respondents to answer such questions either when alone or in the presence of their relationship partner. Under what circumstances would respondents feel most comfortable and free to answer openly and honestly?

As a general rule, people are more comfortable and more willing to admit personal, potentially embarrassing information about their sexuality when they are completing an anonymous questionnaire compared to when they believe others have access to their answers (Sudman et al., 1996; Tourangeau et al., 2000). The important factor is whether the respondents *believe* that others might see or hear their answers, not necessarily whether others actually could. So, all else being equal, people are probably most likely to admit to masturbation or extramarital sex when completing an anonymous questionnaire compared to answering the same questions posed in a face-to-face interview. Accordingly, some research has shown that people are more likely to provide sensitive sexual information when interviewed by a computer program compared to a human interviewer (Gribble, Miller, Rogers, & Turner, 1999; Turner et al., 1998), or when asked in a mailed survey compared to a telephone interview (Acree, Ekstrand, Coates, & Stall. 1999). Compared to anonymity, or being asked questions only in the presence of a stranger, asking sensitive questions in the presence of family members or a group of peers might result in even lower rates of admitting particular sexual experiences (e.g., Johnson, 1970; but see Gibson et al., 1999; and Laumann et al., 1994, for important exceptions).

In summary, there are numerous issues sexuality researchers need to consider regarding measurement reliability and validity, and the factors that may influence peoples' responses to questions posed by the researchers. The process of constructing a meaningful and sound interview schedule or a questionnaire is a complex one (Krosnick, 1999; Tourangeau et al., 2000; Visser et al., 2000). Previous reviews of the numerous potential influences on self-reports have revolved around research on nonsexual topics, although such work has direct implications for research studying sexuality in close relationships. For those readers desiring more detail, Thompson et al. (1996) provide a fascinating review of research, including their own, on the factors affecting autobiographical memory. Schwartz and Sudman (1994) also provide an excellent collection of chapters, by authors from various disciplines, on the topic of autobiographical memory and the validity of retrospective reports. Finally, Sudman et al. (1996) and Tourangeau et al. (2000) each review the cognitive and other processes and influences involved in responses to survey questions and highlight many of the conclusions with examples from their own numerous studies.

RESEARCH DESIGN AND DATA ANALYSIS

After considering issues inherent in sampling and measurement of variables, sexuality researchers are faced with issues involved in research design and analysis of data. Sexuality researchers are frequently interested in causal questions: What causes or influences the phenomenon of interest? However, given the nature of sexuality within close relationships, experimental research designs are prohibited. Typically, such research is correlational, as researchers measure variables of interest and examine potential relationships among them. Examining relationships among variables involves inferential statistics, and the thorny issue of statistical significance comes into play.

Statistical Significance and Effect Size

The overriding goal of researchers appears to be generating results that attain statistical significance, despite the urging of various writers over the past several decades to focus on effect sizes instead. Using the traditional probability cut-off of .05, what does "statistical significance" mean? Simply put, *if there is absolutely no difference or relationship between the variables in question in the population, the odds that the researcher would have obtained the results she or he did purely by chance are less than 5%*. Not terribly exciting on the face of it. If one has a large enough sample, the odds of any obtained difference or relationship between variables being due to chance are slim. So, ironically, although people seem to be impressed by results based on large samples, they should be more impressed by statistically significant results in a relatively small sample, because the difference or relationship between variables must have been large for it to be statistically significant in a small sample.

It is unfortunate that the term "statistical significance" was chosen to describe the state of relationships between variables being unlikely if there is no such relationship in the population. In common parlance the word "significant" translates into "important" or "impressive." So, when we encounter reports of statistically significant findings, it is easy to assume the findings are important. However, what if the term "statistically unlikely" had been chosen instead? To encounter a claim that certain research results were "statistically unlikely" would beg the question: How large or substantial is the difference or relationship?

The issue of the absolute size of a statistical relationship or difference (the effect size) is typically the issue that is of most importance to nonresearchers. Sometimes small relationships or differences are important for scientific theory (Prentice & Miller, 1992), but for most people, the primary issue is whether the research findings are large enough to be of practical importance. Are they impressive? The only way to know is to have the results presented in a form that is intuitively understandable. Effect size indicators were developed for just such a purpose, and there are a variety of such statistics. Pearson's correlation coefficient r is one of them, but it lacks strongly intuitive meaning. The convention has been to square the value of r, resulting in a number that is believed to represent the proportion of variance in one variable that is "accounted for" or "determined" by the other variable. However, this interpretation of r^2 rests on certain assumptions that only rarely apply, making the estimate too conservative (Ozer, 1985). Although calculation of the numerous other effect size statistics is beyond the scope of this chapter, other writers have provided easy-to-use guides (see Rosenthal & Rosnow, 1991; Rosnow & Rosenthal, 1996, 1999).

One effect size indicator that is perhaps the most intuitive is the Common Language Effect Size Statistic (CL; McGraw & Wong, 1992), and fortunately it is easy to calculate. Imagine that you repeatedly sampled one member of each of the two groups being compared in a particular study. As you compared these individual pairings one at a time, in what proportion of instances would the member of one of the particular groups have the greater value on the variable of interest? If there was no difference between the two groups, the answer would be 50%. As you get a value that deviates further from 50%, there is a stronger relationship between group membership and the variable of interest.

To consider a concrete example, suppose the research question is whether people in second marriages report greater sexual satisfaction than do people in first marriages. If the researcher hypothetically paired individual respondents from the sample (one being in a first marriage and the other being in a second marriage), and in each such case examined who had the higher satisfaction score, in what proportion of the cases would the person in the second marriage demonstrate the higher degree of sexual satisfaction? If there was no difference between people in a first marriage versus a second marriage, the person in the first marriage would report the greater degree of satisfaction in 50% of the pairings and the person in the second marriage would indicate the greater satisfaction in the remaining 50% of the pairings. In this hypothetical instance, suppose that the CL revealed that people in their second marriage reported the greater degree of satisfaction in 64% of the hypothetical pairings, and people in their first marriages reported the greater satisfaction in the remaining 36% of cases. Now we have an intuitive measure of the degree to which people in their first versus second marriage differed within this particular sample. For continuous variables, correlation coefficients can be quickly translated into the CL using the table provided by Dunlap (1994).

Without effect size statistics, the conclusion that one group differed "significantly" from another can be too easy taken to mean that the members of the first group *typically* or invariably differ from members of the second group. This may indeed have been the case. However, a statistically significant difference between the groups may have resulted from a small subset of people in the first group who provide extreme scores. In this case, the *typical* member of each group may have given very similar responses to the questions researchers posed, yet the groups differ in the *average* response because of those relatively few respondents who gave very atypical reports (and hence inflated their group's average). Unfortunately, it is quite easy to fall into the trap of taking the mean score for a sample and describing the "average" respondent in that sample as exhibiting that score when in fact most respondents had a notably different score (Allgeier, 2002).

Another potential problem with interpreting the meaning of "statistically significant" findings is that it is easy to fall into the trap of assuming that the inverse of the probability (p) value is the likelihood that there is a difference or relationship in the population. So, if the obtained p value is less than .05, researchers may be tempted to assume that the likelihood that there is indeed a relationship or difference in the population is at least .95. However, this is not true. Again, the p value obtained from an inferential test pertains only to the likelihood of the obtained data given the null hypothesis (the assumption that there is absolutely no difference or relationship in the population of interest). Although it may seem obvious, it is also worth noting that the p value says nothing about the likelihood that the research (alternate) hypothesis is correct (although rejecting the null hypothesis may be taken as a bit of evidence supporting the research hypothesis—and typically other alternative hypotheses as well). Unfortunately, by the time some researchers write about the implications of their findings, this point seems to be lost.

Determining Causality

Researchers are typically interested in causal relationships, yet because true experiments are generally prohibited when studying sexuality within close relationships, alternatives are necessary. Quasi-experimental approaches allow for matching groups as closely as possible, or statistically controlling for relevant variables, thereby attempting to allow for causal inferences based on some manipulation applied to one group and not the control group. When might quasi-experimental designs apply to research on sexuality in close relationships? One such example involves tests of effects of some intervention (e.g., sex therapy or sexuality education) when it is prohibitive to randomly assign couples to conditions.

Another option for attempting to investigate issues of causality is to conduct longitudinal research. Such within-subjects designs typically have been neglected in research on intimate relationships (Gable & Reis, 1999), yet they allow for examination of environmental variables, both in terms of their possible main effects and possible role as moderators. Particularly when studying intimate relationships, employing a mixed between-subjects and within-subjects design allows for the important examination of dispositional (intrapersonal) variables as well as situational ones (including interpersonal variables), thereby allowing for examination of possible statistical interactions or moderator variables (Kashy & Snyder, 1995).

What might such a mixed between-subjects and within-subjects design look like? Suppose a researcher is interested in examining the determinants of sexual activity within couples. Overall, some couples engage in sexual activity more frequently than do other couples. To account for such differences, the researcher will need to consider between-subjects variables such as age of members of the couple, the duration of the relationship, their religious beliefs, and so forth. Still, within each couple, certain factors probably influence the frequency of sexual activity. So, the researcher will also need to consider within-subjects variables such as fluctuation in emotional intimacy, time together, familial duties, and so forth. Obviously such mixed between-subjects and within-subjects designs are complex, but so are the phenomena researchers are typically interested in when attempting to understand sexuality within close relationships. At best, employing only a between-subjects or a within-subjects design results in an incomplete picture of the sexual phenomenon under study.

Compared to between-subjects, cross-sectional designs, longitudinal research designs provide obvious advantages but also additional costs and complications. Greater time and other resources are needed to conduct longitudinal rather than cross-sectional research, and special issues such as participant attrition complicate data analysis and interpretation (Collins & Sayer, 2000; Everitt, 1998). Also, the very act of participating in research has been shown to affect couples' relationships (Hughes & Surra, 2000; Rubin & Mitchell, 1976; Veroff, Hatchett, & Douvan, 1992). Researchers had long known about reactivity, or the fact that simply measuring behavior or psychological phenomena may alter these variables of interest (Brewer, 2000), and this may be especially true with longitudinal research that requires multiple measurements made over time (Collins & Sayer).

Given the costs and potential problems with longitudinal research, why not conduct a cross-sectional study with people who are in relationships of various duration and infer change over time from how relationship duration correlates with the variables of interest? A primary concern with such inferences from cross-sectional designs is that any observed difference as a function of group membership may be the result of at least three causes: age, cohort, and time (Collins & Sayer, 2000). For example, if researchers collect data on frequency of sexual intercourse within couples from a sample of respondents in relationships of various duration and find a negative correlation between relationship duration and sexual frequency, the interpretation of such results is ambiguous. Relationship duration and cohort are confounded because people who have been in the relationships of longest duration tend to be older (and hence from an earlier birth cohort). Is the negative correlation between relationship duration and sexual experience due to respondents having come from different historical cohorts or being different ages? Is the relationship due to changes over time as couples habituate to one another? Or is there an interaction between cohort and time, such that length of relationship has differential effects depending on the cohort to which individuals belong?

When researchers perform correlational studies they recognize that correlation is not synonymous with causation. Some third variable or set of variables may be related to the two variables demonstrating the correlation, and it is therefore the third variable that explains the observed correlation (Brewer, 2000). However, it is difficult to not let causal thinking or language creep into the interpretation of results, particularly when the observed correlation "makes sense" in terms of a causal link between the two variables. Rosenthal (1994) referred to researchers' tendencies to imply causal relationships between their correlated variables as "causism." He noted that writers may not come out and say that their correlational results indicate a causal relationship, yet they may describe their findings using such words as *effect, impact, consequence*, or *the result of.* Such words distract the reader from the important point that the results are simply correlational, and that all we can say for sure is that the two variables demonstrate a statistical relationship (and perhaps a weak, yet statistically significant, one).

If researchers do not consider possible third variables that might explain the correlation between any two variables, there is the possibility that the findings will be misleading. For example, researchers reported that respondents with less than a high school education were about half as likely to report having had a sexually transmitted disease (STD) compared to respondents with at least a high school education (Tanfer, Cubbins, & Billy, 1995). If that is the only statement we encounter, it might be tempting to conclude that people with greater education are actually more likely to contract an STD. However, STD infections were self-reported, and educational level may be related to both awareness of STDs and the likelihood of having access to healthcare (so that an STD might be detected). It is very likely that the most educated respondents in the sample were most aware of STDs and their symptoms, and most likely to seek medical care that might result in detection of any STDs that are present. Accordingly, all we can conclude from this study is that more educated respondents were more likely to *report* having had an STD, with a strong emphasis on the word *report*. One possible interpretation is that respondents with the least education reported the fewest STDs not because of a reduced incidence of STDs among this group, but because of a greater tendency to distort their memory of having had STDs or a greater tendency to lie about having had STDs.

Before leaving the topic of misinterpreting results, it is worth noting what have been called "Type III" statistical errors—providing the right answer for the wrong question (Kimball, 1957). In particular, it is easy to fall into taking results that pertain to interindividual variation as implying an explanation for changes between populations or across historical periods (Schwartz & Carpenter, 1999). For example, suppose that there has been an increase in sexual satisfaction among women within a particular culture over a specific period of time. Of course it is impossible to go back in time to conduct longitudinal studies to examine possible explanations for such a cultural shift.

However, researchers may find that gender-role traditionalism is related to less sexual satisfaction within a current sample of women involved in ongoing relationships. It may be tempting to use these findings to speculate that the cultural shift in sexual satisfaction is due to women adhering less to traditional gender roles now than in the past. Unfortunately, however, the causes of within- and between-group variation in a particular phenomenon may be very different (Schwartz & Carpenter, 1999).

Complex and Messy Data

Understanding all of the influences on sexual phenomena is often messy business. The potential complexity in the way variables are related poses difficulties for researchers who must often focus on a relatively small set of variables, measured in a particular sample with measures that are too often imprecise. When researchers take on the challenge, they may be faced with data and statistical issues for which they were not prepared in their formal education.

When studying sexuality within close relationships, the investigator is often faced with the issue of interdependent observations. That is, the data gathered from one member of a couple is not independent from the data gathered from the other member, and this statistical dependence needs to be taken into account when performing statistical tests (Kashy & Kenny, 2000; Kashy & Snyder, 1995; Kenny, 1988). An initial issue is whether the members of the couples are distinguishable (Kashy & Kenny). For example, in heterosexual couples, each member is distinguishable according to sex. In this case, the researcher can compute a correlation between men's and women's scores (although there is still the issue of separating the dyad-level and individual-level components of such a correlation; see Gonzalez & Griffin, 1999).

What about same-sex couples? The members of these couples are indistinguishable (or exchangeable) in that a score from one particular member may serve as either an X variable or a Y variable when computing a correlation coefficient between members' scores across couples. Does it matter? Kashy and Kenny (2000) created a hypothetical example involving data from 10 couples. Each member of each couple provided a rating (on a 9-point scale) of how much the respondent liked the other member. Kashy and Kenny randomly assigned scores from each member of each couple to serve as the X or the Y variable. The resulting Pearson correlation coefficient was .53 ($p < .12$). However, by simply reversing the scores for the last five couples (so that the X variable within those couples is now the Y variable, and vice versa), the resulting correlation was .79 ($p < .01$). This example illustrates that different analytic techniques are needed for data from indistinguishable couples compared to distinguishable couples. Kashy and Kenny described the intraclass correlation as an appropriate alternative to the Pearson correlation in such cases (also see Griffin & Gonzalez, 1995).

In analyzing data from couples, it is also important to distinguish two types of "couple" variables: those that are inherently based on a quality of the relationship (e.g., length of relationship, whether the couple has children, or amount of time the couple spends together engaged in leisure activities), and those that are based on the degree of similarity between members (Kashy & Snyder, 1995; Kenny & Cook, 1999). Theoretically, there is only one score or value for each variable of the first type (but there is still the issue of handling discrepancies that can arise if each member of the couple reports on the variable). The second type of couple variables, the degree of similarity within the couples, is often represented by a difference score on the variable of interest. The type of difference score that should be calculated varies as a function of the type of statistical relationship the researcher expects between couple similarity and the variable of interest. For example, does the researcher expect that absolute degree of similarity within the couple is the important thing to consider, or is it important to examine the effect that occurs when particular members within each couple (e.g., wives) are the ones with the greater value on the variable of interest when there is a discrepancy? Griffin, Murray, and Gonzalez (1999) provide guidance as to calculation and use of difference score correlations when studying couples.

There are numerous other statistical issues that arise when dealing with data gathered from couples, or collected longitudinally, or both. Fortunately, writers have tackled many such issues in attempts to improve the appropriateness and accuracy of data analysis. For example, others have considered the analysis of actor, partner, and interaction effects (Campbell & Kashy, 2002; Kashy & Kenny, 2000; Kenny & Cook, 1999), statistical modeling of growth and change over time (Collins & Sayer, 2000; Warner, 1998), and handling data that do not conform to the statistical assumptions on which inferential tests are based (McClelland, 2000).

IN CLOSING

The multiple disciplines represented by researchers studying sexuality in close relationships stands as both a strength and a weakness. The diversity in training and experiences provides for the possibility that sexual and relationship phenomena will be studied from multiple theoretical perspectives and with a variety of research methods. However, researchers interested in studying sexuality in close relationships rarely receive formal training in conducting research on sexuality or relationships specifically. Arguably, most of the issues and considerations when studying sexuality within close relationships are the same as those when conducting other types of behavioral or psychological research. The objective of this chapter was to highlight some of the issues that may be specific to empirical investigation of human sexuality. However, there is a risk in doing so. By pointing to all of the potential problems when conducting such research, it is easy to come away with a defeatist attitude: "What's the point of trying when the result will likely be flawed?" However, the only alternative to flawed research is no research at all, and that does not seem like an acceptable alternative. The value of the collective enterprise of science lies in the fact that multiple researchers, each contributing their flawed pieces to the puzzle, will enable the scientific community to better understand the experience of sexuality within close relationships.

REFERENCES

Acree, M., Ekstrand, M., Coates, T. J., & Stall, R. (1999). Mode effects in surveys of gay men: A within-individual comparison of responses by mail and by telephone.*The Journal of Sex Research, 36*, 67–75.

Allgeier, E. R. (2002). Interpreting research results. In M. W. Wiederman & B. E. Whitley, Jr. (Eds.),*The handbook for conducting research on human sexuality* (pp. 371–392). Mahwah, NJ: Lawrence Erlbaum Associates.

Anastasi, A., & Urbina, S. (1997). *Psychological testing* (7th ed.). Upper Saddle River, NJ: Prentice-Hall.

Austin, E. J., Deary, I. J., Gibson, G. J., McGregor, M. J., & Dent, J. B. (1998). Individual response spread in self-report scales: Personality correlations and consequences. *Personality and Individual Differences, 24*, 421–438.

Baker, T. B., & Brandon, T. H. (1990). Validity of self-reports in basic research. *Behavioral Assessment, 12*, 33–51.

Baldwin, M. W. (1992). Relational schemas and the processing of social information. *Psychological Bulletin, 112*, 461–484.

Baldwin, M. W. (1995). Relational schemas and cognition in close relationships. *Journal of Social and Personal Relationships, 12*, 547–552.

Binson, D., & Catania, J. A. (1998). Respondents' understanding of the words used in sexual behavior questions. *Public Opinion Quarterly, 62*, 190–208.

Boyle, G. J. (1991). Does item homogeneity indicate internal consistency or item redundancy in psychometric scales? *Personality and Individual Differences, 3*, 291–294.

Brecher, E. M., & Brecher, J. (1986). Extracting valid sexological findings from severely flawed and biased population samples. *The Journal of Sex Research, 22*, 6–20.

Brehm, S. S., Miller, R. S., Perlman, D., & Campbell, S. M. (2002). *Intimate relationships* (3rd ed.). New York: McGraw-Hill.

Brehmer, A., & Brehmer, B. (1988). What have we learned about human judgment from thirty years of policy capturing? In B. Brehmer & C. R. B. Joyce (Eds.), *Human judgment: The SJT view* (pp. 75–114). New York: Elsevier.

Brewer, M. B. (2000). Research design and issues of validity. In H. T. Reis & C. M. Judd (Eds.), *Handbook of research methods in social and personality psychology* (pp. 3–16). New York: Cambridge University Press.

Brown, N. R. (1995). Estimation strategies and the judgment of event frequency. *Journal of Experimental Psychology: Learning, Memory, and Cognition, 21,* 1539–1553.

Brown, N. R. (1997). Context memory and the selection of frequency estimation strategies. *Journal of Experimental Psychology: Learning, Memory, and Cognition, 23,* 898–914.

Brown, N. R., & Sinclair, R. C. (1999). Estimating number of lifetime sexual partners: Men and women do it differently. *The Journal of Sex Research, 36,* 292–297.

Campbell, L., & Kashy, D. A. (2002). Estimating actor, partner, and interaction effects for dyadic data using PROC MIXED and HLM: A user-friendly guide. *Personal Relationships, 9,* 327–342.

Carballo-Dieguez, A., Remien, R. H., Dolezal, C., & Wagner, G. (1999). Reliability of sexual behavior self-reports in male couples of discordant HIV status. *The Journal of Sex Research, 36,* 152–158.

Carver, C. S. (1989). How should multifaceted personality constructs be tested? Issues illustrated by self-monitoring, attributional style, and hardiness. *Journal of Personality and Social Psychology, 56,* 577–585.

Catania, J. A. (1999). A framework for conceptualizing reporting bias and its antecedents in interviews assessing human sexuality. *The Journal of Sex Research, 36,* 25–38.

Catania, J. A., Binson, D., Canchola, J., Pollack, L. M., Hauck, W., & Coates, T. J. (1996). Effects of interviewer gender, interviewer choice, and item wording on responses to questions concerning sexual behavior. *Public Opinion Quarterly, 60,* 345–375.

Cecil, H., & Zimet, G. D. (1998). Meanings assigned by undergraduates to frequency statements of condom use. *Archives of Sexual Behavior, 27,* 493–505.

Clark, L. A., & Watson, D. (1995). Constructing validity: Basic issues in objective scale development. *Psychological Assessment, 3,* 309–319.

Collins, L. M., & Sayer, A. G. (2000). Modeling growth and change processes: Design, measurement, and analysis for research in social psychology. In H. T. Reis & C. M. Judd (Eds.), *Handbook of research methods in social and personality psychology* (pp. 478–495). New York: Cambridge University Press.

Comrey, A. L. (1988). Factor-analytic methods of scale development in personality and clinical psychology. *Journal of Consulting and Clinical Psychology, 56,* 754–761.

Conrad, F. G., Brown, N. R., & Cashman, E. R. (1998). Strategies for estimating behavioural frequency in survey interviews. *Memory, 6,* 339–366.

Cortina, J. M. (1993). What is coefficient alpha? An examination of theory and applications. *Journal of Applied Psychology, 78,* 98–104.

Council, J. R. (1993). Context effects in personality research. *Current Directions in Psychological Science, 2,* 31–34.

Critelli, J. W., & Neumann, K. F. (1984). The placebo: Conceptual analysis of a construct in transition. *American Psychologist, 39,* 32–39.

Crowne, D. P., & Marlowe, D. (1964). *The approval motive: Studies in evaluative dependence.* New York: Wiley.

Croyle, R. T., & Loftus, E. F. (1993). Recollections in the kingdom of AIDS. In D. G. Ostrow & R. C. Kessler (Eds.), *Methodological issues in AIDS behavioral research* (pp. 163–180). New York: Plenum.

Dawes, R. M. (1988). *Rational choice in an uncertain world.* New York: Harcourt Brace Jovanovich.

Downey, L., Ryan, R., Roffman, R., & Kulich, M. (1995). How could I forget? Inaccurate memories of sexually intimate moments. *The Journal of Sex Research, 32,* 177–191.

Dunlap, W. P. (1994). Generalizing the common language effect size indicator to bivariate normal correlations. *Psychological Bulletin, 116,* 509–511.

Dunne, M. P. (2002). Sampling considerations. In M. W. Wiederman & B. E. Whitley, Jr. (Eds.), *The handbook for conducting research on human sexuality* (pp. 85–112). Mahwah, NJ: Lawrence Erlbaum Associates.

Everitt, B. S. (1998). Analysis of longitudinal data. *British Journal of Psychiatry, 172,* 7–10.

Floyd, F. J., & Widaman, K. F. (1995). Factor analysis in the development and refinement of clinical assessment instruments. *Psychological Assessment, 7,* 286–299.

Foster, S. L., & Cone, J. D. (1995). Validity issues in clinical assessment. *Psychological Assessment, 7,* 248–260.

Friedman, W. J. (1993). Memory for the time of past events. *Psychological Bulletin, 113,* 44–66.

Gable, S. L., & Reis, H. T. (1999). Now and then, them and us, this and that: Studying relationships across time, partner, context, and person. *Personal Relationships, 6,* 415–432.

Gardner, D. G., Cummings, L. L., Dunham, R. B., & Pierce, J. L. (1998). Single-item versus multiple-item measurement scales: An empirical comparison. *Educational and Psychological Measurement, 58,* 898–915.

Gibson, D. R., Hudes, E. S., & Donovan, D. (1999). Estimating and correcting for response bias in self-reported HIV risk behavior. *The Journal of Sex Research, 36,* 96–101.

Gonzales, R., & Griffin, D. (1999). The correlational analysis of dyad-level data in the distinguishable case. *Personal Relationships, 6,* 449–469.

Green, S. B., Lissitz, R. W., & Mulaik, S. A. (1977). Limitations of coefficient alpha as an index of test unidimensionality. *Educational and Psychological Measurement, 37,* 827–838.

Greenleaf, E. A. (1992). Measuring extreme response style. *Public Opinion Quarterly, 56*, 328–351.

Gribble, J. N., Miller, H. G., Rogers, S. M., & Turner, C. F. (1999). Interview mode and measurement of sexual behaviors: Methodological issues. *The Journal of Sex Research, 36*, 16–24.

Griffin, D., & Gonzalez, R. (1995). Correlational analysis of dyad-level data in the exchangeable case. *Psychological Bulletin, 118*, 430–439.

Griffin, D., Murray, S., & Gonzalez, R. (1999). Difference score correlations in relationship research: A conceptual primer. *Personal Relationships, 6*, 505–518.

Grote, N. K., & Frieze, I. H. (1998). "Remembrance of things past:" Perceptions of marital love from its beginnings to the present.*Journal of Social and Personal Relationships, 15*, 91–109.

Haynes, S. N., Richard, D. C. S., & Kubany, E. S. (1995). Content validity in psychological assessment: A functional approach to concepts and methods. *Psychological Assessment, 7*, 238–247.

Henry, B., Moffitt, T. E., Caspi, A., Langley, J., & Silva, P. A. (1994). On the "remembrance of things past": A longitudinal evaluation of the retrospective method. *Psychological Assessment, 6*, 92–101.

Horvath, P. (1988). Placebos and common factors in two decades of psychotherapy research. *Psychological Bulletin, 104*, 214–225.

Hughes, D. K., & Surra, C. A. (2000). The reported influence of research participation on premarital relationships. *Journal of Marriage and the Family, 62*, 822–832.

Hurlbert, D. F., Apt, C., Gasar, S., Wilson, N. E., & Murphy, Y. (1994). Sexual narcissism: A validation study. *Journal of Sex & Marital Therapy, 20*, 24–34.

Huygens, P., Kajura, E., Seeley, J., & Burton, T. (1996). Rethinking methods for the study of sexual behaviour. *Social Science and Medicine, 42*, 221–231.

Jaccard, J., & Wan, C. K. (1995). A paradigm for studying the accuracy of self-reports of risk behavior relevant to AIDS: Empirical perspectives on stability, recall bias, and transitory influences. *Journal of Applied Social Psychology, 25*, 1831–1858.

Janssen, E. (2002). Psychophysiological measurement of sexual arousal. In M. W. Wiederman & B. E. Whitley, Jr. (Eds.), *The handbook for conducting research on human sexuality* (pp. 139–171). Mahwah, NJ: Lawrence Erlbaum Associates.

John, O. P., & Benet-Martinez, V. (2000). Measurement: Reliability, construct validation, and scale construction. In H. T. Reis & C. M. Judd (Eds.), *Handbook of research methods in social and personality psychology* (pp. 339–369). New York: Cambridge University Press.

Johnson, R. E. (1970). Some correlates of extramarital coitus. *Journal of Marriage and the Family, 32*, 449–456.

Kaplan, H. B. (1989). Methodological problems in the study of psychosocial influences on the AIDS process. *Social Science and Medicine, 29*, 277–292.

Karney, B. R., Davila, J., Cohan, C. L., Sullivan, K. T., Johnson, M. D., & Bradbury, T. N. (1995). An empirical investigation of sampling strategies in marital research. *Journal of Marriage and the Family, 57*, 909–920.

Kashy, D. A., & Kenny, D. A. (2000). The analysis of data from dyads and groups. In H. T. Reis & C. M. Judd (Eds.), *Handbook of research methods in social and personality psychology* (pp. 451–477). New York: Cambridge University Press.

Kashy, D. A., & Snyder, D. K. (1995). Measurement and data analytic issues in couples research. *Psychological Assessment, 7*, 338–348.

Kenny, D. A. (1988). The analysis of data from two-person relationships. In S. W. Duck (Ed.), *Handbook of personal relationships* (pp. 57–77). New York: Wiley & Sons.

Kenny, D. A., & Cook, W. (1999). Partner effects in relationship research: Conceptual issues, analytic difficulties, and illustrations. *Personal Relationships, 6*, 433–448.

Kerlinger, F. N. (1986). *Foundations of behavioral research* (3rd ed.). San Francisco, CA: Holt, Rinehart & Winston.

Kimball, A. W. (1957). Errors of the third kind in statistical consulting. *Journal of the American Statistical Association, 52*, 133–142.

Knee, C. R. (1998). Implicit theories of relationships: Assessment and prediction of romantic relationship initiation, coping, and longevity. *Journal of Personality and Social Psychology, 74*, 360–370.

Krosnick, J. A. (1999). Survey research. *Annual Review of Psychology, 50*, 537–567.

LaRossa, R. (1995). Stories and relationships. *Journal of Social and Personal Relationships, 12*, 553–558.

Laumann, E. O., Gagnon, J. H., Michael, R. T., & Michaels, S. (1994). *The social organization of sexuality: Sexual practices in the United States.* Chicago: University of Chicago Press.

Marsh, H. W., & Yeung, A. S. (1999). The lability of psychological ratings: The chameleon effect in global self-esteem. *Personality and Social Psychology Bulletin, 25*, 49–64.

Masters, W. H., & Johnson, V. E. (1966). *Human sexual response.* New York: Little, Brown.

Masters, W. H., & Johnson, V. E. (1970). *Human sexual inadequacy.* New York: Little, Brown.

McClelland, D. C., Koestner, R., & Weinberger, J. (1989). How do self-attributed and implicit motives differ? *Psychological Review, 96*, 690–702.

McClelland, G. H. (2000). Nasty data: Unruly, ill-mannered observations can ruin your analysis. In H. T. Reis & C. M. Judd (Eds.), *Handbook of research methods in social and personality psychology* (pp. 3–16). New York: Cambridge University Press.

McFarland, C., & Ross, M. (1987). The relation between current impressions and memories of self and dating partners. *Personality and Social Psychology Bulletin, 13*, 228–238.

McGraw, K. O., & Wong, S. P. (1992). A common language effect size statistic. *Psychological Bulletin, 111,* 361–365.

McGregor, I., & Holmes, J. G. (1999). How storytelling shapes memory and impressions of relationship events over time. *Journal of Personality and Social Psychology, 76,* 403–419.

McKinney, K. & Sprecher, S. (Eds.) (1991). *Sexuality in close relationships.* Hillsdale, NJ: Lawrence Erlbaum Associates.

Meston, C. M., Heiman, J. R., Trapnell, P. D., & Paulhus, D. L. (1998). Socially desirable responding and sexuality self-reports.*The Journal of Sex Research, 35,* 148–157.

Moore, M. M. (2002). Behavioral observation. In M. W. Wiederman & B. E. Whitley, Jr. (Eds.),*The handbook for conducting research on human sexuality* (pp. 113–137). Mahwah, NJ: Lawrence Erlbaum Associates.

Morrison, D. M., Leigh, B. C., & Gillmore, M. R. (1999). Daily data collection: A comparison of three methods. *The Journal of Sex Research, 36,* 76–81.

Nicholas, L. J., Durrheim, K., & Tredoux, C. G. (1994). Lying as a factor in research on sexuality. *Psychological Reports, 75,* 839–842.

Nisbett, R. E., & Ross, L. (1980). *Human inference: Strategies and shortcomings of social judgment.* Englewood Cliffs, NJ: Prentice-Hall.

Nisbett, R. E., & Wilson, T. D. (1977). Telling more than we can know: Verbal reports on mental processes. *Psychological Review, 84,* 231–259.

Ochs, E. P., & Binik, Y. M. (1999). The use of couple data to determine the reliability of self-reported sexual behavior. *The Journal of Sex Research, 36,* 374–384.

Okami, P. (2002). Dear diary: A useful but imperfect method. In M. W. Wiederman & B. E. Whitley, Jr. (Eds.),*The handbook for conducting research on human sexuality* (pp. 195–207). Mahwah, NJ: Lawrence Erlbaum Associates.

Orbuch, T. L., & Harvey, J. H. (1991). Methodological and conceptual issues in the study of sexuality in close relationships. In K. McKinney & S. Sprecher (Eds.), *Sexuality in close relationships* (pp. 9–24). Hillsdale, NJ: Lawrence Erlbaum Associates.

Ottati, V. C. (1997). When the survey question directs retrieval: Implications for assessing the cognitive and affective predictors of global evaluation. *European Journal of Social Psychology, 27,* 1–21.

Ozer, D. J. (1985). Correlation and the coefficient of determination.*Psychological Bulletin, 97,* 307–315.

Padian, N. S., Aral, S., Vranizan, K., & Bolan, G. (1995). Reliability of sexual histories in heterosexual couples. *Sexually Transmitted Diseases, 22,* 169–172.

Plaud, J. J., Gaither, G. A., Hegstad, H. J., Rowan, L., & Devitt, M. K. (1999). Volunteer bias in human psychophysiological sexual arousal research: To whom do our research results apply? *The Journal of Sex Research, 36,* 171–179.

Paulhus, D. L. (1991). Measurement and control of response bias. In J. P. Robinson, P. R. Shaver, & L. S. Wrightsman (Eds.), *Measures of personality and social psychological attitudes* (pp. 17–59). New York: Academic Press.

Prentice, D. A., & Miller, D. T. (1992). When small effects are impressive. *Psychological Bulletin, 112,* 160–164.

Quitkin, F. M. (1999). Placebos, drug effects, and study design: A clinician's guide. *American Journal of Psychiatry, 156,* 829–836.

Reis, H. T., & Gable, S. L. (2000). Event sampling and other methods for studying everyday experience. In H. T. Reis & C. M. Judd (Eds.), *Handbook of research methods in social and personality psychology* (pp. 190–222). New York: Cambridge University Press.

Reiss, I. L. (1999). Evaluating sexual science: Problems and prospects. *Annual Review of Sex Research, 10,* 236–271.

Rosenthal, R. (1994). Science and ethics in conducting, analyzing, and reporting psychological research. *Psychological Science, 5,* 127–134.

Rosenthal, R., & Rosnow, R. L. (1991). *Essentials of behavioral research: Methods and data analysis* (2nd ed.). New York: McGraw-Hill.

Rosnow, R. L., & Rosenthal, R. (1996). Computing contrasts, effects sizes, and counternulls on other people's published data: General procedures for research consumers. *Psychological Methods, 1,* 331–340.

Rosnow, R. L., & Rosenthal, R. (1999). *Beginning behavioral research: A conceptual primer* (3rd ed). Upper Saddle River, NJ: Prentice-Hall.

Ross, R., & Allgeier, E. R. (1996). Behind the pencil/paper measurement of sexual coercion: Interview-based clarification of men's interpretations of Sexual Experience Survey items. *Journal of Applied Social Psychology, 26,* 1587–1616.

Rothblum, E. D. (1994). Transforming lesbian sexuality. *Psychology of Women Quarterly, 18,* 627–641.

Rubin, Z., & Mitchell, C. (1976). Couples research as couples counseling. *American Psychologist, 31,* 17–25.

Sanders, S. A., & Reinisch, J. M. (1999). Would you say you "had sex" if . . . ? *JAMA: Journal of the American Medical Association, 281,* 275–277.

Schwartz, N. (1999). Self-reports: How the questions shape the answers. *American Psychologist, 54,* 93–105.

Schwartz, N., & Hippler, H. J. (1995). Subsequent questions may influence answers to preceding questions in mail surveys. *Public Opinion Quarterly, 59,* 93–97.

Schwartz, N., & Sudman, S. (Eds.). (1994). *Autobiographical memory and the validity of retrospective reports.* New York: Springer-Verlag.

Schwartz, S., & Carpenter, K. M. (1999). The right answer for the wrong question: Consequences of type III error for public health research. *American Journal of Public Health, 89,* 1175–1180.

Seidman, S. N., & Rieder, R. O. (1994). A review of sexual behavior in the United States. *American Journal of Psychiatry, 151,* 330–341.

Siegel, D. M., Aten, M. J., & Roughman, K. J. (1998). Self-reported honesty among middle and high school students responding to a sexual behavior questionnaire. *Journal of Adolescent Health, 23,* 20–28.

Siegel, S., & Castellan, N. J. (1988). *Nonparametric statistics for the behavioral sciences* (2nd ed.). New York: McGraw-Hill.

Smith, G. T., & McCarthy, D. M. (1995). Methodological considerations in the refinement of clinical assessment instruments. *Psychological Assessment, 7,* 300–308.

Snell, W. E., & Papini, D. R. (1989). The Sexuality Scale: An instrument to measure sexual-esteem, sexual-depression, and sexual-preoccupation. *The Journal of Sex Research, 26,* 256–263.

Spearman, C. (1904). The proof and measurement of association between two things. *American Journal of Psychology, 15,* 72–101.

Stone, V. E., Catania, J. A., & Binson, D. (1999). Measuring change in sexual behavior: Concordance between survey measures. *The Journal of Sex Research, 36,* 102–108.

Sudman, S., Bradburn, N. M., & Schwartz, N. (1996). *Thinking about answers: The application of cognitive processes to survey methodology.* San Francisco: Jossey-Bass.

Tanfer, K., Cubbins, L. A., & Billy, J. O. G. (1995). Gender, race, class, and self-reported transmitted disease incidence. *Family Planning Perspectives, 27,* 196–202.

Thompson, B., & Snyder, P. A. (1998). Statistical significance and reliability analyses in recent *Journal of Counseling & Development* research articles. *Journal of Counseling & Development, 76,* 436–441.

Thompson, C. P., Skowronski, J. J., Larsen, S. F., & Betz, A. L. (1996). *Autobiographical memory: Remembering what and remembering when.* Mahwah, NJ: Lawrence Erlbaum Associates.

Tourangeau, R., Rips, L. J., & Rasinski, K. (2000). *The psychology of survey response.* New York: Cambridge University Press.

Turner, H. A. (1999). Participation bias in AIDS-related telephone surveys: Results from the National AIDS Behavioral Survey (NABS) non-response study. *The Journal of Sex Research, 36,* 52–58.

Turner, C. F., Danella, R. D., & Rogers, S. M. (1995). Sexual behavior in the United States, 1930–1990: Trends and methodological problems. *Sexually Transmitted Diseases, 22,* 173–190.

Turner, C. F., Ku, L., Rogers, S. M., Lindberg, L. D., Pleck, J. H., & Sonenstein, F. L. (1998). Adolescent sexual behavior, drug use, and violence: Increased reporting with computer survey technology. *Science, 280,* 867–873.

Upchurch, D. M., Weisman, C. S., Shepherd, M., Brookmeyer, R., Fox, R., Clenetano, D. D., Colletta, L., & Hook, E. W. (1991). Interpartner reliability of reporting of recent sexual behaviors. *American Journal of Epidemiology, 134,* 1159–1165.

Vacha-Haase, T. (1998). Reliability generalization: Exploring variance in measurement error affecting score reliability across studies. *Educational and Psychological Measurement, 58,* 6–20.

Veroff, J., Hatchett, S., & Douvan, E. (1992). Consequences of participating in a longitudinal study of marriage. *Public Opinion Quarterly, 56,* 315–327.

Visser, P. S., Krosnick, J. A., & Lavarakas, P. J. (2000). Survey research. In H. T. Reis & C. M. Judd (Eds.), *Handbook of research methods in social and personality psychology* (pp. 223–252). New York: Cambridge University Press.

Warner, R. M. (1998). *Spectral analysis of time-series data.* New York: Guilford.

Weinhardt, L. S., Forsyth, A. D., Carey, M. P., Jaworski, B. C., & Durant, L. E. (1998). Reliability and validity of self-report measures of HIV-related sexual behavior: Progress since 1990 and recommendations for research and practice. *Archives of Sexual Behavior, 27,* 155–180.

Whitley, B. E. (1996). *Principles of research in behavioral science.* Mountain View, CA: Mayfield.

Wiederman, M. W. (1997). The truth must be in here somewhere: Examining the gender discrepancy in self-reported lifetime number of sex partners. *The Journal of Sex Research, 34,* 375–386.

Wiederman, M. W. (1999). Volunteer bias in sexuality research using college student participants. *The Journal of Sex Research, 36,* 59–66.

Wiederman, M. W., & Allgeier, E. R. (1993). The measurement of sexual-esteem: Investigation of Snell and Papini's (1989) Sexuality Scale. *Journal of Research in Personality, 27,* 88–102.

Wiederman, M. W., & Whitley, B. E., Jr. (Eds.) (2002). *The handbook for conducting research on human sexuality.* Mahwah, NJ: Lawrence Erlbaum Associates.

Wright, D. B., Gaskell, G. D., & O'Muircheartaigh, C. A. (1997). How response alternatives affect different kinds of behavioural frequency questions. *British Journal of Social Psychology, 36,* 443–456.

Wryobeck, J. M., & Wiederman, M. W. (1999). Sexual narcissism: Measurement and correlates among college men. *Journal of Sex & Marital Therapy, 25,* 321–331.

3

Overview of Sexual Practices and Attitudes Within Relational Contexts

Marion C. Willetts
Susan Sprecher
Frank D. Beck
Illinois State University

This chapter presents what is currently known about adolescents' and adults' attitudes and behaviors with regard to sexuality within a relational context. We summarize findings primarily from U.S. national data sets, such as the National Health and Social Life Survey and the General Social Survey. We also highlight relevant findings from smaller scale studies that are unique in some way (e.g., cohort, longitudinal data). The findings across studies suggest that most adults, regardless of age, race, social class, and gender, engage in sexual behavior within relational contexts and approve of sex in committed relationships. However, there is variation across various sociodemographic aggregates in terms of how acceptable and likely sex is in a partnership that is in the initial stage of development. In addition, there is variation in the number of relational (sexual) partners Americans have over a specific span of time (e.g., 5 years) and the particular sexual practices in which they engage. We discuss trends and variations in sexual attitudes and practices of Americans and focus on the following types of sexuality: (a) adolescent and young adulthood sexuality in relational contexts, (b) adult sexual behavior within primary partnerships, and (c) extramarital and extradyadic sex. Within each of these sections, we provide descriptive data on current patterns, discuss (where possible) longitudinal trends, highlight any differences based on sociodemographic aggregates, and (where available) compare U.S. trends to those in other countries. We conclude by offering suggestions for future research directions.

INTRODUCTION

Conservative commentators such as David Popenoe and Barbara Dafoe Whitehead argue that a breakdown in sexual morality is occurring (Popenoe, 1993; Popenoe & Whitehead, 1999). They express concern that a high divorce rate, combined with the enormous popularity of cohabitation, indicates that marriage has become a less stable social institution. There is also a concern that our society is currently experiencing an unmarried pregnancy crisis, as approximately 33% of all births are to unmarried women (Ventura & Bachrach, 2000). These commentators assert that these social problems are occurring because individuals are no longer interested in devoting themselves to family life, instead thinking only about their own self-fulfillment. The result, according to Popenoe, is that individuals act irresponsibly, particularly with regard to sexual behaviors.

Scholarly research in this area, however, indicates that most dyadic human sexual behavior does indeed occur within an emotionally bonded relational context. Although individuals vary in the extent to which they are emotionally committed to their partners (and even partners of the same couple may differ with regard to their emotional commitment to each other and to their union), most dyadic sexual behavior occurs among those who mutually agree that they are in some form of emotionally bonded relationship. This chapter presents descriptive information on both sexual attitudes and behaviors within a relational context. We focus mainly on heterosexual, emotionally bonded relationships in the U.S. (Although we briefly discuss sexuality in homosexual relationships, it is the focus of the chapter by Peplau, Fingerhut, & Beals in this volume). Throughout the chapter, we review the existing research on sexual attitudes and behaviors in relationships, both in the United States and in other countries where data are available. We also discuss differences among various sociodemographic aggregates, such as those based on race/ethnicity and social class. Where appropriate to our discussion, we also highlight longitudinal changes in attitudes and behaviors.

We begin by summarizing the best available national data sets, particularly the National Health and Social Life Survey (Laumann, Gagnon, Michael, & Michaels, 1994) and the General Social Survey (Davis, Smith, & Marsden, 2002). We also discuss smaller scale studies in the United States, as well as those conducted in other countries. Based on these data, the second section describes sexuality in nonmarital emotionally bonded relationships among adolescents and young adults.[1] In particular, we focus on attitudes toward such nonmarital sexuality, the conditions under which first sexual experiences occur, the average number of premarital sexual partners, and the types of sexual activities in which adolescents and young adults engage. In the third section, we review the literature on adult sexual behavior within a primary emotionally bonded relationship, focusing on the types of sexual partnerships formed, sexual frequency in primary dyads, sexual practices and preferences, and the number of sexual partners. We follow this discussion with a review of the available literature on extramarital and extradyadic sex, with a focus on attitudes toward this form of sexual experience, the incidence of sex with a secondary partner, and the characteristics of such relationships. We then conclude with recommendations for future research on sexuality within emotionally bonded relationships.

---

[1] For the purposes of this chapter, adolescence is defined as teenagers under the age of 18. Young adults primarily are those in their late teens to early 20s. Adults are those in their mid-20s and older.

SOURCES OF DATA ON CURRENT TRENDS IN RELATIONAL SEXUALITY

It is only in the last 15 years or so that representative national-level data on sexuality, and specifically sexuality in a relational context, have become available. The National Health and Social Life Survey (NHSLS; Laumann, et al., 1994), the General Social Survey (GSS; Davis et al., 2002), and other data sets have added to our knowledge, not only about sexuality overall in the United States, but also sexuality within close relationships.

National Health and Social Life Survey

Not since the Kinsey reports of the 1940s and 1950s (Kinsey, Pomeroy, & Martin, 1948; Kinsey, Pomeroy, Martin, & Gebhard, 1953) has anyone even claimed to have nationally representative data. In fact, given the manner in which Kinsey collected his data via volunteers and nonrandom sampling of organizations and their members, the NHSLS is the first ever, nationally representative data collection effort focused on human sexuality in the United States. Originally, the team sought a sample of 20,000 persons in order to make generalizations about subsets of the population (e.g., homosexuals); however, once government funding was blocked by a conservative political climate, the team had to rely on a smaller pool of private funds. As a result, data were collected from a smaller sample, although the final sample of 3,432 persons is still larger than most political polls (Laumann et al., 1994). The team was comprised of University of Chicago scholars and survey experts working in sociology and public policy, as well as experts from the well-respected National Opinion Research Center (NORC). The stratified cluster random sample they obtained is representative of the adult, noninstitutionalized U.S. population ages 18 through 59. Blacks and English-speaking Hispanics were oversampled (Laumann et al., 1994). Populations not included or sampled at a less than optimal level include homosexuals, persons age 60 and over, those in group quarters (e.g., prisons, college dorms, or military barracks), and households where Spanish is the only language spoken.

The NHSLS is the first such study of its kind. It is clear that the goal of the study was to move sexuality away from its historical home in the disciplines of biology and psychology. Much of the work in the area is individualistic in nature; however, sexuality is typically not an individualistic enterprise, as it happens in a relational context. By paying attention to social networks (dyads) and marital/cohabitation status, the NHSLS makes a strong case for research on sexuality as a social phenomena as well. For instance, the authors were able to relate sexual frequency, number of partners, sexual satisfaction, manner of sexual activity, same sex attraction and behavior with marital/cohabiting status. Contraceptive use was related to marital/cohabiting status as well. There are data on whether partners match on preferences for different sexual activities, as well as where a couple met or who introduced them. Data on many of these issues will be discussed later in this chapter, as well as in many other chapters in this handbook.

The team was extremely careful in their sampling strategy, training of interviewers, and pretesting of the questionnaire for language/vocabulary issues. It is clear from reading *The Social Organization of Sexuality* that Laumann and his colleagues (1994) are forthright in their descriptions of the data collection process—both its strengths and shortcomings. For instance, an issue of concern is that 21% of the interviews were conducted with another person present; often this was a child or stepchild of the respondent. The presence of a third party, particularly the primary partner, was found to be associated with a lower likelihood of the respondent reporting two or more sex partners in the past year and with some of the attitudinal items. However, the team checked to see if dollars spent to recruit the interviewee might have introduced some selectivity or response bias in the sample; the tests showed no such effects. Further, the NHSLS team extensively checked the quality of their data against other representative samples, finding that their respondents fit national patterns (Laumann et al., 1994). The data are now available through the Inter-University Consortium for Political and Social Research (www.icpsr.umich.edu).

The General Social Survey

Another national dataset employing a representative sample is the General Social Survey (GSS). It is administered annually to a representative sample of U.S. residents by NORC at the University of Chicago. The sample sizes range anywhere from 1,500 to approximately 3,000. The data are available online (http://www.icpsr.umich.edu/GSS/). Among the vast array of data collected by the GSS are attitudinal questions regarding respondents' opinions of premarital sex, extramarital sex, and sex among teens. Because these data have been collected since the early 1970s, it is possible to conduct trend analyses on the measures. Beginning in 1988, in response to the need for information related to the AIDS crisis, the GSS began to ask questions about the frequency of sexual acts, number of partners, and condom use. The GSS has also asked whether the married respondents had sex with individuals other than their spouse, such as friends, neighbors, coworkers, acquaintances, someone they just met, or whether they have paid for sex. Questions on the number of partners the respondent had in the last 12 months, last 5 years, and since they were 18 were also asked in 1988 and subsequently. GSS respondents have been asked about their general attitudes toward homosexuality since 1972, with more specific attitudinal questions beginning in 1988. Also in 1988, additional questions were added on the respondent's homosexual activity in the last year and previous 5 years.

Additional U.S. Data Sets

Representative data on sexuality among U.S. adults are also available from other sources. Although these data sets are not focused exclusively on sexuality, scholars have been able to glean from them information on sexuality in relational contexts. For example, Donnelly (1993), using data from the National Survey of Families and Households (NSFH; a panel study of a nationally representative sample of the noninstitutionalized population between the ages of 18 to 75, with data collected in 1987 to 1988 and 1992 to 1994, with a third wave currently underway), correlated sexual inactivity with level of marital happiness, shared activity within a relationship, arguments over sex, number of children, and violence in the relationship. Also, Forste and Tanfer (1996), using data from the National Survey of Women (NSW; a longitudinal study with data collected in 1983 and 1991 from a nationally representative sample), studied the effect of relationship type (non-cohabiting, cohabitation, or marriage), length of relationship, and homogamy on sexual exclusivity. Furthermore, the National Survey of Men (NSM) includes nationally representative data on sexual activity among 3,321 men in the contiguous 48 states and includes measures of marital status, cohabitation, and whether the men have a "regular partner" (Billy, Tanfer, Grady, & Klepinger, 1993).

The National Longitudinal Study of Adolescent Health (AddHealth) data on sexuality are quite extensive (http://www.cpc.unc.edu/addhealth/); questions on the survey include age at first intercourse, number of partners, frequency, and sexual orientation. Other questions focus on close relationships, cohabitation, interest in marriage, frequency of sex and condom usage with a partner, kinds of and timing of sexual acts with primary partners, and partner expectations for various sexual acts. Note, however, that these data are not exclusively focused on adolescent sexuality per se, but instead are focused on adolescent health, including sexual health. Finally, another large, though unrepresentative, national study (Blumstein & Schwartz, 1983) collected survey responses from over 12,000 persons and interviewed 300 couples. Because the data were collected from both partners in the relationship (including both married and cohabiting couples, and heterosexual and homosexual couples), the researchers were quite thorough and were able to situate sexuality within relational contexts. Included are data on negotiations in the bedroom, relationship satisfaction, sexual initiation, number of sex partners outside the primary relationship, and more.

International Studies

Internationally and in response to AIDS, two studies (one French and one British) have looked at sexuality in those respective countries (Spira, Bojas, & ACFS Group, 1994; Wellings, Field, Johnson, & Wadsworth, 1994). Spira et al. telephone interviewed over 20,000 people ages 18 to 69 in France. They included the standard sexuality items on age at first intercourse, sexual frequency, and condom use, as well as questions on the different strategies respondents employ in finding partners. The British work of Wellings et al. interviewed a nationally representative sample of 18,876 men and women ages 16 to 59 in England, Wales, and Scotland with a 65% response rate. Last, new representative data from China are just now being analyzed. They consist of responses from more than 2,900 men and women on questions covering extramarital sex, premarital sex, and masturbation (Laumann & Parish, 2001).

By far, these studies are not exhaustive of the work done on sexuality. Certainly, studies more qualitative in nature (e.g., Richardson, 1988) or those focused on more geographically accessible populations (e.g., Ford & Norris, 1997; Glass & Wright, 1992; Sprecher & Hatfield, 1996) exist. The focus of this chapter will be on the scholarship of sexuality that employs the nationally representative data discussed and describes sexuality within relational contexts.

ADOLESCENT AND YOUNG ADULTHOOD SEXUALITY WITHIN (NONMARITAL) RELATIONAL CONTEXTS

Nearly 85% of men and 80% of women in the United States have experienced premarital sexual intercourse in adolescence, adulthood, or both (Laumann et al., 1994). In this section, we review the literature on attitudes among both adults and adolescents regarding premarital heterosexual intercourse, particularly that occurring in a relational context (Carver, Joyner, & Udry, 2003; Laumann et al.). We then discuss first sexual experiences within relationships; most notably, the age at which individuals become sexually experienced via intercourse, what factors contribute to a first experience at an early age, and the relational context in which this experience occurs. Next, we discuss the average number of sexual partners prior to legal marriage and conclude with a discussion of the sexual techniques in which adolescents and young adults engage.

Attitudes Regarding Premarital Sex

U.S. adults are approving of premarital sex for adults in general. For example, in the 1998 GSS data, nearly 44% of adults stated that it is "not wrong at all" if "a man and woman have sex relations before marriage," without reference to whether that sex occurs within the context of an emotionally bonded relationship (Davis et al., 2002).

Another 21% stated that premarital sex is "wrong only sometimes." In contrast, 26% of adults stated that premarital sexual activity is "always wrong," with another 9% having stated that such activity is "almost always wrong."

Unfortunately, the GSS and other national data sets are limited in that they typically include measures concerning approval of premarital sex without specifying whether such activity occurs within a relational context. Smaller scale studies, however, have provided more information regarding the degree of approval of premarital sex in a variety of relational contexts. For example, Sprecher, McKinney, Walsh, and Anderson (1988), in a study conducted with a probability sample of college students at one midwestern university, found that respondents were most likely to approve of premarital sex for an engaged couple, compared to a pre-engaged couple, followed by those "seriously dating," "casually dating," and finally those on a "first date." These findings were confirmed by Sprecher (1989) and by Sprecher and Hatfield (1996) in studies also conducted with undergraduates. In addition, this research indicated that both men and women were more approving of sexual activity for men than for women, particularly in the very early stages of relationships. This pattern of results suggests that a sexual double standard in which men are permitted greater permissiveness than women continues to persist.

Furthermore, most measures of approval of premarital sexual activity typically do not distinguish between premarital sexual activity engaged in by adults versus by adolescents. One exception is the NHSLS data, which indicated that nearly 61% of adults surveyed stated that premarital sex among teenagers is always wrong (Michael, Gagnon, Laumann, & Kolata, 1994, p. 234). Another exception is the 1998 GSS data, which showed that nearly 72% of adults agreed that premarital sex among those about 14 to 16 years old is "always wrong" (only 3.5% of adults reported that such activity is "not wrong at all"; Davis et al., 2002). Again, however, neither data set measured attitudes toward premarital sex for adolescents specifically in the context of an emotionally bonded relationship.

Less is known about attitudes among adolescents regarding premarital sex (for either adolescents or for adults), and most studies that have been conducted with this age aggregate made use of convenience samples, thereby limiting the generalizability of the results (e.g., Wein's 1970 study was conducted on street youth in two major cities; de Gaston, Weed, & Jensen's 1996 study was conducted among junior high school students enrolled in sex education courses; Werner-Wilson conducted his 1998 study on high school students enrolled in health, parenting, or home economics classes in three southwestern cities). These studies resulted in mixed findings, likely as a result of reliance on disparate convenience samples. For example, Wein found that a majority of adolescents approve of premarital sex for adolescents. However, de Gaston and colleagues found that a majority of adolescents disapprove of premarital sex. Meanwhile, Werner-Wilson found that adolescents, on average, are "neutral" in their attitudes.

There are numerous predictors of permissive attitudes toward premarital sex, both in general and within an emotionally bonded relationship. These include gender—males express more permissive attitudes than females (de Gaston et al., 1996; Somers & Paulson, 2000; Thornton, 1990; Walsh, Ganza, & Finefield, 1983); religious participation—members of mainstream religious organizations hold the most conservative attitudes (Werner-Wilson, 1998); and age—older adolescents express more permissive attitudes than do younger adolescents, and adolescents in general express more permissive attitudes than do adults (Huerta-Franco, de Leon, & Malacara, 1996; Werner-Wilson, 1998). Furthermore, prior sexual experience is a correlate of attitudes, as teens that hold permissive attitudes regarding sexuality are also more likely than those with more conservative attitudes to engage in sexual intercourse (Bingham, Miller, & Adams, 1990; Miller & Olson, 1988; Udry & Billy, 1987).

First Sexual Intercourse

Large-scale studies conducted on initial sexual intercourse have generally examined two issues: the percent of teens who have engaged in sexual intercourse by a certain age and the average age at initiation of intercourse. Laumann and colleagues (1994) indicated that among those born between 1953 and 1972, 48% of men and 37% of women experienced first intercourse by the age of 16, a finding confirmed by smaller studies (e.g., Kivisto's 2001 study of midwestern high school students). Additionally, research points to an increasingly early age at initiation of coitus, though Furstenberg (1998) predicted it will hit a plateau, if it has not already. According to Laumann and colleagues (1994), the modal age at first intercourse among those born between 1933 and 1952 (between the ages of 40 to 59 at time of data collection) was approximately 17 years of age for men and about 18 years of age for women. However, among those born between 1953 and 1972 (between the ages of 20 to 39 at time of data collection), the modal age at first intercourse for men was 16, while for women, the mode was nearly 17. Black adolescents tended to be younger than their counterparts of other racial/ethnic groups at age of first coitus, followed by Hispanics and then Whites (Day, 1992; Gibson & Kempf, 1990; Hofferth, Kahn, & Baldwin, 1987; Laumann et al.; Sonenstein, Ku, Lindberg, Turner, & Pleck, 1998; Zelnik & Shah, 1983).

There is substantial international variation with regard to the incidence of premarital sex and the age at which initial sexual intercourse occurs. For example, Wulf and Singh (1991) found in Hispanic countries that the incidence rates of premarital sex ranged from 46% to 63%, with substantial variation within a particular country based on urbanity (higher rates are found in more urban areas; see Huerto-Franco et al., 1996, and Morris, Nunez, Monroy de Velasco, Bailey, Cardenas, & Watley, 1988). Also, although adolescent males in the United States were more likely to have acquired sexual experience than were females of the same age, adolescent females in some European countries were more sexually experienced than were males of the same age. For example, in Bologna, Italy, Zani (1991) found, using a sample of high school and vocational school students and nonstudents in the city, that 38% of adolescent females but only 6% of adolescent males had experienced sexual intercourse by the age of 15, the difference due in large part to younger females becoming sexually involved with older males. The same pattern is found in Sweden (Lewin, 1987).

According to Hyde and DeLamater's (2000) review of data from the Demographic and Health Surveys Program, some other countries tend to have a somewhat higher average age at initiation of sexual intercourse among women (data for men were not reviewed), such as Bolivia (median = 19.6 years), Brazil (median = 18.7 years), Nigeria (median = 18.1 years), and Nicaragua (median = 18.1 years), compared to a median of 17.4 years in the United States. There are countries, however, that have a lower average age at initiation of sexual intercourse, such as Mexico (median = 17.0 years), Zambia (median = 16.6 years), and Cameroon (median = 16.3 years).

Numerous factors are associated with the age at which adolescents first experience sexual intercourse. According to Leigh, Weddle, and Loewen (1988) and Thornton (1990), an early initiation into dating strongly influenced the age at which adolescents first engaged in sexual intercourse. Furthermore, AddHealth data show that over one third of adolescents had romantic relationship experience by the time they reached the age of 12, whereas more than 80% did by the age of 18, with older adolescents having reported relationships longer in duration. A relational context provides more opportunity for sexual activity (Carver et al., 2003). An appreciable increase in the percent of girls who had engaged in sexual intercourse occurred between the ages of 16 and 17; for boys; this sizable increase occurred between the ages of 18 and 19, coinciding with an increase in the proportion of adolescents with emotionally bonded relationship experience.

Adolescents also are influenced by their families. For example, Sorensen (1973) found that having parents or friends with sexually permissive attitudes was associated with a younger age at first intercourse, which suggests that social networks influence sexual behavior. Also, living with a single parent was associated with a younger age at first intercourse (Billy, Brewster, & Grady, 1994; Brooks-Gunn & Furstenberg, 1989; Flewelling & Bauman, 1990; Joyner & Laumann, 2001; Laumann et al., 1994; Murry, 1994). This may be a function of supervision by two parents versus one (Hogan & Kitagawa, 1985), role modeling—an adolescent may have witnessed her single mother's dating behavior and adopted the same behavior for herself (Fox, 1980), or parental control—a moderate level of parental control has been found to be associated with a later age at start of sexual intercourse, compared to either low or high levels of parental control (Hogan & Kitagawa; Murry, 1994; Newcomer & Udry, 1987). Furthermore, having a nonemployed or less well-educated mother (Laumann & Michael, 2001; Murry) and a lower family income (Billy et al., 1994; Murry) were associated with a younger age at first intercourse, indicating the influence of social class on sexual behavior. Also, having an older brother who had engaged in sexual intercourse, which may serve as a role model for initiation to sexual intercourse, was associated with a younger age at initiation of intercourse (Widmer, 1997).

Other factors that have been found to be associated with the age at which adolescents commence sexual activity include permissive sexual attitudes (Udry & Billy, 1987), early sexual development (Joyner & Laumann, 2001; Murry, 1994), and childhood sexual abuse (Butler & Burton, 1990; Huerta-Franco & Malacara, 1999). These factors lend further support to the contention that attitudes and behaviors are indeed related. Low academic ability and the use of cigarettes, alcohol, or illegal drugs also are associated with a younger age at start of sexual activity (Rosenbaum & Kandel, 1990), indicating that these behaviors may go together. Infrequent church attendance (Billy et al., 1994; Laumann et al., 1994; Marsiglio & Mott, 1986; Miller & Olson, 1988; Murry, 1994) and residing in an urban area (Murry) were also associated with a younger age at start of sexual activity.

The Context of Initial Premarital Sex

For both adolescents and young adults, initial premarital sexual activity is highly likely to occur within the context of an emotionally bonded relationship (de Gaston, Jensen, & Weed, 1995; DeLamater & MacCorquodale, 1979; Sprecher, Barbee, & Schwartz, 1995; Thornton, 1990), reflecting a pattern that has been found since the 1920s, although historically, unmarried couples would only engage in sexual activity after becoming engaged to be married (Burgess & Wallin, 1953; Mintz & Kellogg, 1988; Scanzoni, 1995). Since the 1960s, however, couples are likely to engage in sexual activity as long as there is some emotional commitment between the partners, although not necessarily an engagement (Sherwin & Corbett, 1985).

Christopher and Cate (1985), in their study of college students enrolled in psychology and human development courses at a northwestern university, identified three factors that are associated with the decision to engage in sexual intercourse among emotionally bonded couples (adolescents and young adults). First is the extent to which the partners like or love each other, including the commitment they feel toward each other and toward their relationship. For many girls and women, love of one's partner is the primary reason for engaging in sexual activity regardless of marital intentions, both in the United States and in other countries (Christopher, 1996; Huerta-Franco & Malacara, 1999; Laumann et al., 1994). Second is the extent to which the partners are sexually aroused and how receptive they are to each other's sexual advances. Men are more likely than women to report that they engaged in first intercourse out of sexual curiosity or physical pleasure (Laumann et al.). Third is what

Christopher and Cate referred to as "circumstances," which include the sexual activity level of the partners' respective friends. Other research has indicated that individuals have friends who have a similar level of sexual experience as themselves, although it is difficult to determine whether the friendship networks influence one's behavior or whether the members of the network change *after* an adolescent has engaged in sexual activity (Christopher & Roosa, 1991; Keith, McCreary, Collins, Smith, & Bernstein, 1991; Rodgers & Rowe, 1990). Circumstances also include whether the intercourse was planned ahead of time and the extent to which alcohol or drugs were used by the partners.

The use of contraception at first sexual intercourse is relatively low, with 34% of all men and 38% of all women in the Laumann et al. (1994) study having reported use. The proportion of those who used contraception at first intercourse was higher among younger adult cohorts, so that 50% of those in the youngest group (those born between 1963 and 1967) reported using contraception the first time they had sexual intercourse. Furthermore, those who engaged in first sexual intercourse within the context of an emotionally bonded relationship were more likely to use contraception. According to an analysis of the 1995 National Survey of Family Growth conducted by Manning, Longmore, and Giordano (2000), just over half (52%) of adolescents who had recently met their first sexual partner used no method of contraception, compared to 24% of those who were in an emotionally bonded relationship. Furthermore, among teenagers in Britain, researchers found that the duration of a relationship increased the likelihood that a couple would discuss contraception prior to first intercourse, which in turn increased the likelihood that a couple would use contraception at first intercourse (Stone & Ingham, 2002).

Several factors are associated with the likelihood that a teenager will use contraception at first intercourse. In an analysis of the 1995 National Survey of Family Growth, researchers found that adolescents with well-educated parents were more likely to use contraception than were those with less well-educated parents (Hogan, Sun, & Cornwell, 2000). Whites and those who attended religious services regularly were more likely to use contraception than were Blacks or Hispanics and those who did not attend religious services regularly. Furthermore, as adults, those with a higher level of educational attainment were more likely to use contraception at first intercourse, as were Jewish individuals and those with no religious affiliation (Laumann et al., 1994; for a further discussion of contraceptive use, refer to Noar, Zimmerman, & Atwood, chapter 21, this volume).

Number of Partners

A variety of studies employing various samples and conducted in a myriad of ways show that adolescent and young adult males have more sex partners than females at the same ages (Laumann et al., 1994; Miller, Sabo, Farrell, Barnes, & Melnick, 1999; Murphy, Rotheram-Borus, & Reid, 1998; Reinisch, Hill, Sanders, & Ziemba-Davis, 1995; Reinisch & Sanders, 1992).[2] Thornton (1990) is exemplary of this pattern. Using a sample of 18-year-old males and females in Detroit, he found that 43% of men but only 30% of women have had more than one partner. Furthermore, almost 17% of the men but only 6% of the women claimed to have had six or more partners. Specific research on the number of sexual partners of adolescents and young adults within a relational context is more scant.

---

[2] Some literature does question the difference in reporting bias of sexual activity by gender, noting that men are likely to exaggerate their numbers, whereas women deflate them (Laumann et al., 1994; Schwartz & Rutter, 1998).

The NHSLS has provided the most detailed information on number of sexual part-ners in relationships. Laumann and colleagues found that both men and women ages 18 to 29 have engaged in a pattern of having numerous partners in short intervals both before a union, cohabitation, or formal marriage is formed and after it dissolves. However, those young men and women whose first residential union was cohabi-tation rather than marriage had more sexual partners prior to the residential union, were less likely to have had no sexual partners prior to the union, and were much more likely to have had five or more sexual partners prior to the union. Those young cohabiting men and women whose relationships led to marriage were more likely to have had sex with only that one partner and have had fewer other partners during the union than those cohabiting men and women for whom the cohabiting partner did not become a spouse (Laumann et al., 1994).

Using data from a 1980 survey of 18-year-old males and females in Detroit, Thornton (1990) found that the number of partners for both men and women was significantly related to the ages at which they started dating, first became an exclusive couple, and engaged in first intercourse. For those who have ever had sex, the number of part-ners was unrelated to recent dating but was related to recently being in an exclusive relationship. Both men and women who had been in an exclusive relationship with the same person for awhile or who were planning to marry had fewer numbers of partners.

Another study of college students indicated that the mean number of sex part-ners in the past year for both men and women varied by the sexual exclusivity of the relationship—7.0 for men and 4.6 for women in nonexclusive relationships, and 2.3 for men and 1.8 for women in exclusive relationships (Reinisch & Sanders, 1992). In addition, Baumer and South (2001), using data from Wave 3 of the National Sur-vey of Children, found that sex in general, and the number of partners specifically (2.4 in the year prior to the interview) among 18 to 22 year olds, was affected by adolescent–parent relationships and peer relationships after holding constant race, socioeconomic status (SES), and neighborhood characteristics. Peer support for pre-marital sex was associated with a greater number of partners. Parents' awareness of their child's friends was associated with a lower number.

Types of Sexual Activities

In the previous discussion of first sexual experiences and number of sexual partners, the focus was on sexual intercourse. However, in their dating relationships, adoles-cents usually engage in deep kissing, breast fondling, and genital fondling for a period of time before they progress to sexual intercourse. This is evidenced in studies that have included a Guttman-type list of sexual behaviors that asked respondents to indi-cate in which behaviors they have engaged. For example, DeLamater and MacCorquo-dale (1979) conducted a large-scale survey on premarital sexuality with a probability sample of both university students and non-student young adults in Madison, Wis-consin, and asked the respondents whether they had ever in their lives and with their current partner engaged in several sexual behaviors, ranging from necking to female mouth contact with male genitals. Although almost all of the participants (more than 90%) had engaged in necking, French kissing, and breast fondling, only about two thirds of the respondents had engaged in the most intimate sexual behaviors: inter-course, male mouth contact with female genitals, and female mouth contact with male genitals, both ever and with their current partner.

Similarly, Carver et al. (2003) found a smaller incidence of sexual intercourse (41%) than of either behaviors involving touching each other under clothing (57%) or touch-ing each other's genitals (52%) among the AddHealth respondents, who ranged in age from 12 to 19. Furthermore, they found the differences in the incidences of noncoital behaviors versus sexual intercourse were greater for the younger respondents than for the older respondents. Halpern, Joyner, Udry, and Suchindran (2000) reported on data for 10 sexual activities (ranging from kissing to sexual intercourse) for a group of adolescents in North Carolina who were surveyed multiple times over a 2- to 3-year period. They reported that sexual intercourse was the least common activity, and that holding hands and kissing were the most common (85 to 97%). They also reported that the incidence of sexual activity increased over the period of study and hence as the adolescents became older.

Based on rates of sexual activities found among adolescents, including at different ages, some researchers have concluded that adolescents follow a regular progression through these sexual behaviors (moving from nongenital behaviors to genital and coital behaviors) in their overall sexual development, and that this progression can occur over several years and involve several partners (e.g., Christopher, 2001; DeLamater & MacCorquodale, 1979; Smith & Udry, 1985). A similar progression of sexual activities occurs within one specific relationship as well. For example, research conducted with smaller college samples indicates that people agree about the order in which sexual behaviors should occur (e.g., breast fondling occurs before genital fondling) in a relationship (Geer & Broussard, 1990). The implicit norms that develop about which particular behaviors are appropriate and the order in which they should occur are referred to as a sexual script (Gagnon, 1990).

Earlier, we presented evidence to indicate that during the past few decades the incidence of adolescent sexual intercourse has increased. Because most research studies, particularly those based on national samples, have focused only on sexual intercourse and not also on other types of sexual behaviors, we know less about how the incidences of noncoital sexual behaviors have changed over time. We speculate, however, that the incidence of these behaviors has probably not increased to nearly the same degree as has sexual intercourse. In earlier times, noncoital sexuality was the behavior to which most dating couples progressed but generally did not proceed beyond. A change, however, is that contemporary adolescents may engage in noncoital sexual behaviors with a greater number of partners than did adolescents from earlier generations.

Most experts, however, conclude that there has been a dramatic increase in the incidence of oral sex in adolescent sexual relationships. For example, this was concluded by Rubin (1990), who compared different generations represented in an in-depth interview study conducted with 375 people of different ages from around the United States and a survey study conducted with 600 others, mostly college students. In addition, by comparing data from the Kinsey studies (Kinsey et al., 1948, 1953), which indicated that 17% of respondents reported that they had premarital fellatio and 11% reported they had premarital cunnilingus, with the data collected in recent smaller scale studies of teenage sexuality, Newcomer and Udry (1985) concluded that the incidence of oral sex in teenage relationships has increased. For example, they found percentages closer to 50% for various adolescent samples obtained in the 1970s and early 1980s.

In some studies, particularly those of younger teens, a greater proportion of the sample has reported engaging in oral sex than in sexual intercourse (Newcomer & Udry, 1985), indicating that oral sex occurs before sexual intercourse for many adolescents. Oral sex may occur before sexual intercourse in part because oral sex does not carry the risk of pregnancy (Newcomer & Udry; Rubin, 1990). In addition, adolescents often define themselves as still a virgin while experimenting with oral sex without having yet engaged in sexual intercourse (Rubin). Among sexually experienced and/or older teens, sexual intercourse appears to be as common as oral sex and often more common (DeLamater & MacCorquodale, 1979; Weinberg, Lottes, & Gordon, 1997).

Although oral sex may be common among adolescents, it is not likely to occur during the sexual episode in which vaginal sexual intercourse is experienced for the first time. In the NHSLS data, only 16% of male respondents and 8% of female respondents said they had oral sex during the same sexual encounter in which they had first vaginal intercourse, leading the researchers to conclude that first intercourse is a goal-directed experience for most people (Laumann et al., 1994).

Evidence is mixed as to whether fellatio or cunnilingus is more likely to be experienced in adolescent heterosexual relationships. In Kinsey's data (as reported in Newcomer & Udry, 1985), fellatio was more common than cunnilingus in premarital relationships. In her description of teenage sexuality, Rubin (1990) also reported that fellatio was more common than cunnilingus. Newcomer and Udry found just the opposite, and still other studies have found no differences (e.g., DeLamater & Mac-Corquodale, 1979; Hass, 1979). It is probably safe to conclude that it is as common in adolescent relationships to give as to receive oral sex for both genders.

Anal sex, although probably also increasing over time (Story, 1985), is not common in adolescent relationships, according to the few studies that have asked about this sexual activity. Reinisch and colleagues (1995) conducted a study of sexual behavior with a probability sample of heterosexual undergraduates at a midwestern university and found that among those who were sexually experienced, only 17% had experienced anal intercourse. Slightly smaller percentages had anal intercourse according to another midwestern U.S. sample; the percentages ranged from 8% to 16%, depending on the year of data collection and whether active or passive (Story). In addition, in the NSHLS data, only 1% of the respondents reported having anal intercourse during the sexual encounter in which they experienced their first vaginal intercourse (Laumann et al., 1994).

Very little research exists on how sexual techniques practiced in adolescent sexual relationships vary by sociodemographic variables. Weinberg et al. (1997) found, based on a probability sample conducted at a midwestern university, almost no differences in sexual behavior based on social class. Christopher (2001) cited evidence, including that in Smith and Udry (1985), indicating that the progression of sexual activity discussed earlier, from kissing to touching breasts, touching genitals, and then oral sex and sexual intercourse, is found for White and Hispanic youth, but not for Blacks, who tend to progress from kissing to sexual intercourse but "fail to follow a discernible pattern" for the other noncoital behaviors (p. 49). Consistent with the National Study of Adolescent Health, Carver et al. (2003) reported that African-American adolescents report higher levels of sexual intercourse than Whites but lower levels of noncoital behaviors.

In sum, adolescents engage in a variety of sexual behaviors, but typically progress gradually through the sequence of sexual behaviors.

ADULT SEXUAL BEHAVIOR WITHIN PRIMARY PARTNERSHIPS

Whereas the previous section focused on formative sexual experiences, this section focuses on the sexual behavior that occurs in the context of adult sexually based primary partnerships. Once again, the focus is on a *description* of sexual behavior, based primarily on national, representative samples. We begin with a description of with *whom* and *how* sexually based primary partnerships are typically formed. Then, we discuss how often couples have sex, as well as the types of behaviors in which they engage. Finally, we present information on how many sexually based primary partnerships adults typically have over a lifetime.

Types of Sexual Partnerships Formed

People do not form sexual relationships with just anyone. Laumann et al. (1994) concluded, based on the National Health and Social Life Survey (NHSLS), that individuals form sexually based relationships with those who are similar to themselves on age, race/ethnicity, education, and religion. Of the social attributes examined in their study, the greatest degree of homophily (or homogamy) was found for race (occurring in 90% of the couples), and the lowest degree, although still occurring in more than 50% of the couples, was found for religion. They also found homophily on social characteristics to be common across several types of sexually based partnerships: marriage, cohabitation, long-term noncohabiting relationships, and short-term noncohabiting relationships. There are many reasons that people choose someone who is similar as a sexual partner. Laumann et al. (1994) noted that the similarity makes it easier to interact and thus increases the chances for sexual compatibility between the partners. They also noted that social networks and social institutions encourage people to form sexual relationships with those who are similar.

The influence of social networks on sexual partnerships formed is also evidenced in the NHSLS data on how the respondents met their partners. The researchers asked two specific questions: Where did they meet their partner? And, who (if anyone) introduced them? Among the sexual partnerships represented in this national sample, the three most common locations for meeting partners were school, work, and private parties. Introductions by third parties (most often mutual friends) were very common, occurring in approximately 60% of all sexual partnerships. Self-introductions were slightly more common in short-term, noncohabitation partnerships, although still slightly over 50% of such relationships began through an introduction by a third party. Other research, based on both national (although unrepresentative) samples (Simenauer & Carroll, 1982) and smaller community or college samples (Knox & Wilson, 1981; Parks & Eggert, 1991), also suggest that introductions by mutual friends are a very common way that sexually bonded primary partnerships begin.

The data on relationship formation from the NHSLS highlight the importance of social networks. As noted by Laumann et al. (1994), the vast majority of sexual partnerships originate within tightly circumscribed social settings, resulting in relatively few partnerships between people with sharply different social characteristics (p. 255). Mate selection research and attraction research in social psychology, often based on small convenience (college) samples, have identified a number of other predictors of sexual/romantic attraction in addition to homophily or similarity. These factors, which probably operate within the constraints of social network factors, include: the physical attractiveness of the partner, mystery, something very special or unique about the other, and arousal coming from extraneous sources (for a review of this literature, see Orbuch & Sprecher, 2003 and Simpson & Harris, 1994).

Frequency of Sexual Behavior

In most adult romantic partnerships, particularly those characterized by affection and some commitment, sexual activity occurs. Where there is more variation, however, is in *how often* couples engage in sex. Some couples have sex frequently, whereas for other couples, sex is a rare event and may even cease over time. Variation in sexual behavior is likely to be related to personal dispositions of the members of the couple, including sex drive. However, the major sources of variation in the frequency of sexual activity are the age of the partners and the duration of the relationship. Sexual frequency decreases with age and duration of the relationship, regardless of the type of relationship (e.g., cohabiting, marital, homosexual).

One source of information on sexual frequency is the National Survey of Families and Households (NSFH). Although not focusing per se on sexuality, this national data set included a question about sexual frequency. In analyses based on Wave 1 data (collected between 1987 and 1988), Call, Sprecher, and Schwartz (1995) reported that married respondents had an overall mean frequency of sex of 6.3 times per month. Married couples under the age of 24 had a mean frequency of 11.7, but the frequency declined with each subsequent age group (analyses based on the NSFH are also reported in Donnelly, 1993; Marsilgio & Donnelly, 1991; and Rao & DeMaris, 1995). Call et al. also reported that cohabitors had sex more frequently than did married respondents of similar ages. These results are consistent with earlier data collected in a national (but nonprobability) sample of over 12,000 individuals by Blumstein and Schwartz (1983), who reported that cohabitation is a sexier living arrangement than marriage. More specifically, Blumstein and Schwartz found that heterosexual cohabiting couples had more frequent sex than heterosexual married couples. They also reported more frequent sex among male homosexual couples than among heterosexual couples and the least frequent sex among lesbian couples.

Data from the National Health and Social Life Survey (NHSLS) support a frequency of marital sex similar to the rate reported in NSFH (Laumann et al., 1994; Michael, et al., 1994). The NHSLS mean frequency of sexual activity per month was 6.9 for married men and 6.5 for married women. Cohabitors in the sample had a higher frequency of sexual activity, whereas single individuals had the lowest frequency. Laumann and colleagues (1994) also reported a decrease in sexual frequency with age.

The General Social Survey (GSS) also includes data on sexual frequency. As reported in Smith (1998), married respondents in the recent GSS data engaged in sexual intercourse an average of 61 times per year, which is slightly over once a week. Similar to the results for NSFH and NHSLS, the frequency rates were highest among the young and those married less than 3 years, and declined with age and number of years married. Other studies conducted with both national samples and smaller, geographical-limited samples have also found comparable rates of overall sexual frequency, and lower rates associated with age and number of years married (e.g., Blumstein & Schwartz, 1983; Edwards & Booth, 1976; Greeley, 1991; James, 1983; Trussell & Westoff, 1980; Westoff, 1974).

Smith (1998) concluded, based on GSS data and other data collected in the United States, that sexual frequency increased for (married and unmarried) adults from the 1960s to the 1970s, declined in the 1980s, and then has not changed significantly since the 1980s. The increase in sexual frequency in the 1960s may have been due to the sexual revolution that affected not only premarital sex but also marital sex. In addition, the advent of the birth control pill made it possible for couples to enjoy spontaneous sex without having to worry about conception. On the other hand, the 1980s have been described as a somber sexual age, with the beginning of the AIDS epidemic and the maturity of the baby boom generation (Schwartz & Rutter, 1998), which may account for the slight dip in sexual frequency during that decade.

The decline in sexual frequency with age, found consistently across studies, seems to be due to psychological, social, and biological factors associated with the aging process (Call et al., 1995). Decreases due to habituation, or the reduction in novelty because of being with the same partner, are also likely to occur, but habituation may explain primarily the decrease that occurs early in marriage or a marriage-like relationship, which is the specific period of time that has the greatest decrease in sexual frequency. A habituation perspective can also explain the finding from NSFH that remarriage was associated with an increase in marital sex, controlling for other factors including age (Call et al.). Blumstein and Schwartz (1983), based on their data, suggest that both age and duration in a relationship contribute uniquely to the decrease in sexual frequency, and that the male's age contributes to the decrease more than the female's age, although some research has shown just the opposite (e.g., Udry, Deven, & Coleman, 1982; Udry & Morris, 1978).

Other factors in addition to age and duration of the relationship also are likely to be associated with sexual frequency. In particular, overall relationship satisfaction has been found to be associated with the frequency of sex, an issue discussed by Sprecher and Cate (see chapter 10, this volume). Variation in sexual frequency is not, however, strongly associated with social demographic characteristics other than age. More specifically, people of different races, religions, social classes, and ethnic groups generally tend to have sex at approximately the same frequency (e.g., Laumann et al., 1994; Smith, 1998). Nonetheless, a number of sociodemographic factors have been found to be modestly associated with a decreased sexual frequency, at least in some studies, including demanding jobs, being Catholic, and living in a rural area (Call et al., 1995; Edwards & Booth, 1976; Trussell & Westoff, 1980; Westoff, 1974).

It might be surprising to some that so much attention has been given to sexual frequency in marriage and other sexually bonded relationships. However, social scientific interest in this variable has arisen in part from its presumed association with marital quality and fertility (Christopher & Sprecher, 2000). Recent studies have advanced beyond earlier ones by using multivariate analyses to examine several predictors (relational and sociodemographic) of sexual frequency (e.g., Call et al., 1995). This research indicates that only a modest amount of variance in marital sexual frequency is explained, despite examining a large number of predictor variables including age and relationship satisfaction.

Sexual Practices and Preferences

The studies examining sexual frequency generally have focused on sexual intercourse, although occasionally respondents are simply asked how often they engage in sexual activity or sex (Laumann et al., 1994). A couple that engages in sexual intercourse is usually engaging in other sexual behaviors as well, and typically these behaviors occur in a particular order (e.g., breast and genital fondling occur before sexual intercourse). As we noted earlier, sociologists refer to a sexual script, which people learn in society about what types of sexual behaviors are appropriate to engage in and when during the relationship (e.g., Gagnon, 1990).

Some detail about specific sexual practices was obtained in the NSHLS (Laumann et al., 1994). However, the researchers focused primarily on genital sexual activities and did not also ask about hugging, kissing, and other behaviors. Ninety-five percent of the respondents reported having vaginal sex the last time they had sex, and 80% reported having vaginal sex every time they had sex in the past year. Although a majority of the respondents had engaged in oral sex in their lifetime, less than 30% reported having oral sex during the last time they had sex. Anal sex was reported to be experienced infrequently, ever (10%) and in the last sex event (1 to 2%). Some differences in specific sexual practices were found based on sociodemographic variables. In particular, oral sex and anal sex were more commonly experienced among the young adults (than among the older adults), among the more educated, and among Whites (as compared to Blacks and Hispanics).

Blumstein and Schwartz (1983), in their national (but nonrepresentative) sample, found that the percentage of couples that usually or always have oral sex when they have sex was 50% for gay couples, 39% for lesbian couples, and approximately 30% for heterosexual couples. Although most couples that engage in oral sex treat it as a foreplay behavior to sexual intercourse, occasionally it is the final sex act, according to Blumstein and Schwartz's (1983) data. They found that heterosexual couples that had more oral sex had less sexual intercourse, and gay couples were more likely than other types of couples to have oral sex while having sex.

According to national data sets, couples also include some variety in their sexual activity. Based on telephone surveys conducted with two national samples of married couples, Greeley (1991) found that one half of the couples had experimented with new ways of having sex at least some of the time. For example, the percentage who reported that they engaged in the following behaviors a lot or sometimes were: take showers or baths together (39%), go to a hotel or motel to spend time alone with each other (34%), abandon all your sexual inhibitions (32%), make love outdoors (22%), buy erotic underclothes (21%), watch X-rated videos (21%), and swim nude together (19%).

In some studies, respondents also have been asked what behaviors they would *like* to do sexually. For example, the respondents in the NSHLS were asked what sexual practices they found appealing. The list included vaginal intercourse, oral sex, anal sex, and a variety of other behaviors. Vaginal intercourse was found to be the most appealing behavior, and second in preference was watching the partner undress. Oral sex was also found to be appealing by a large number of respondents, but many also found this behavior to be unappealing. Respondents preferred to receive oral sex to giving it. Most of the other behaviors included in the list were found to be appealing to only a small minority of respondents. These included behaviors such as group sex, watching others do sexual things, and forcing someone to do something sexual (this behavior was most unappealing of all). With the exception of vaginal intercourse, younger respondents found the behaviors to be more appealing (or less unappealing) than older respondents. In addition, men rated most of the behaviors more appealing (or less unappealing) than did women. In research conducted with smaller samples on preferences for various types of sexual behavior, Hatfield, Sprecher, Pillemer, Greenberger, and Wexler (1989) also found that men desired more types of sexual behaviors than did women. For example, men to a greater degree than women wanted their partner to be more rough, experimental, willing to initiate sex, play the dominant role in sex, and to be wild and sexy.

Number of Recent and Lifetime Sexual Partners

Another question typically asked in large-scale, national studies on sexuality is the number of sexual partners, either ever or in a specific period of time (e.g., a year). Although not all sexual partners are also relational partners, most of them are likely to be defined as such (i.e., someone for whom affection and interdependence are experienced). For example, Smith (1998) reported, based on GSS data, that most sexual partners were described to be a married or cohabiting partner. Only 3 to 4% of sexual partners were prostitutes or one-night stands and another 4 to 5% were acquaintances (e.g., neighbors, coworkers) but not a regular partner. Thus, we can estimate, conservatively, that approximately 80% of lifetime sexual partners reported by individuals are also relational partners. However, there may be complete overlap between relational partners and sexual partners for those people who have only a few sexual partners in their lifetime, whereas for those people having 100 or more sexual partners, only a few may be relational partners.

A majority of participants in national surveys have stated that they had one sexual partner in the past year. For example, among both the NHSLS and the GSS respondents, 68% and 69%, respectively of men and 76% (for both samples) of women stated they had one sexual partner in the last year. The next most common response (11–14%) was no or zero partners. Only a small proportion of the participants had five or more sexual partners in the past year, and they were primarily male, young, and not married or cohabiting (Laumann et al., 1994).

When asked about lifetime sexual partners since the age of 18, the respondents in the GSS reported an overall mean of 7 partners (Smith, 1998). The mean was 12.4 for men and 4.0 for women. Although older cohorts generally had more partners than younger cohorts due to the accumulation of partners over a lifetime, Smith reported that the oldest cohorts in the GSS study (60 and older) had a lower number of lifetime partners than did the middle cohorts (ages 40–59), probably because the older respondents married relatively early and had not experienced the sexual revolution. For the NHSLS sample, Laumann et al. (1994) reported a *median* number of three partners for the entire sample, with six for men and two for women. They reported that the number of partners in adulthood has increased over time because of three major social trends: first intercourse beginning at an earlier age, people entering marriage at a later age, and an increased divorce rate, which allows for a period of postmarital sexual activity for many individuals and hence an increase in number of lifetime partners.

As noted, both the GSS and the NHSLS reported a greater number of sexual partners for men than for women. Similar differences between men and women in number of sexual partners have been found in national data collected in other countries, including Britain, France, New Zealand, and Norway (as reported in Wiederman, 1997b). The discrepancy between the genders in number of partners is found for both premarital activity and postmarital activity (Schwartz & Rutter, 1998). A number of authors have discussed this gender discrepancy (Brown & Sinclair, 1999; Laumann et al., 1994; Schwartz & Rutter, 1998; Wiederman, 1997b). The major explanations provided for it are:

1. Men may have more male sexual partners than women have female sexual partners.
2. Men may be having sex with a group of women who are out of the sampling frame for the study, including younger females (under the age of 18) or women from out of the country.
3. There may be a small group of hyper-sexual women and prostitutes who have sex with many men.
4. Men and women may define sexual activity and sexual partners in different ways. For example, men may include any type of sexual partner, whereas women may have a more restrictive definition of a partner, and report only those to whom some affection is experienced.
5. Men may exaggerate their reports of lifetime partners and/or women may minimize their reports.

Although all of the above factors may contribute to the gender differences found, experts suggest that the major explanation may be the last one (e.g., Laumann et al., 1994; Schwartz & Rutter, 1998). Wiederman (1997b) argued that older women may be especially likely to minimize the number of sexual partners because of the norms, common to their generation, that women do not have multiple sex partners. Based on the GSS data, Wiederman presented strong evidence that the gender discrepancy increases with age.

Although large gender differences are found in number of sexual partners reported, most other sociodemographic variables (e.g., social class) are unrelated to number of sexual partners (e.g., Laumann et al., 1994). One exception found in the NHSLS was for education, which was positively associated with the number of sexual partners. Laumann et al., speculated that it was because those with more education were more likely to postpone marriage and hence accumulate more sexual partners prior to marriage. Those with more education may also be more likely to have liberal sexual attitudes and have more opportunities to meet sexual partners.

According to the NHSLS, the accumulation of additional sexual partners occurs primarily prior to marriage and during a postdivorce period for those who have a marriage dissolve.

EXTRAMARITAL AND OTHER FORMS OF EXTRADYADIC SEX

As discussed, most adults have several consecutive primary relationships that include sexual activity throughout adolescence and the adult life course. In addition, some individuals engage in sexual activity in secondary relationships while maintaining their primary unions. In this section, we discuss attitudes among adults regarding sexual activity outside of legal marriage (extramarital sex) or outside of a primary relationship that does not include marriage (extradyadic sex). We also describe the incidence of this sexual activity, as well as characteristics of these secondary relationships.

Attitudes Regarding Extramarital Sex

Researchers have explored two types of attitudinal standards. First, many researchers have examined what typically are referred to as "normative standards," which refer to how acceptable or appropriate extramarital/extradyadic sex is for adults in general, or for a specific category of adults, based on demographic variables or some other defining characteristics (e.g., Reiss & Lee, 1988; Sponaugle, 1989; Sprecher & McKinney, 1993). One of the most common measures assessing normative standards is a single item from the General Social Survey (Davis et al., 2002), also employed in numerous other studies, such as the National Health and Social Life Survey (Laumann et al., 1994). Respondents are asked whether extramarital sex in general is "always wrong, almost always wrong, wrong only sometimes, or not wrong at all." Another well-established measure of normative standards is the Extramarital Sexual Permissiveness Scale, in which a series of vignettes is provided and the respondent reacts to each by assessing the extent to which each provides a justification for engaging in sex with a secondary partner (Reiss & Lee, 1988). Other measures include an attitudinal scale regarding the acceptability of sex with a secondary partner in four situations constructed from a typology of a happy versus an unhappy marriage and affection versus lack of affection for an extramarital partner (Saunders & Edwards, 1984), a scale assessing intentions to engage in extramarital sexual activity (Buunk, 1998) or presenting respondents with a series of behaviors (such as emotional involvement with others and/or engaging in behaviors such as kissing) to determine the extent to which each was an act of infidelity (Roscoe, Cavanaugh, & Kennedy, 1988).

"Personal" (Sprecher & McKinney, 1993) or "self-focused" (Sponaugle, 1989) standards, on the other hand, are measures assessing the extent to which respondents believe that sex with a secondary partner is acceptable or permissible for oneself. According to Sponaugle, there are two types of personal standards—one assessing personal behavior and one assessing personal desires or intentions. An example of the former is the Projective Involvement scale developed by Neubeck and Schletzer (1962), which assesses respondents' reactions to a scenario in which they have an opportunity to engage in flirtatious behavior (such as going out to dinner with a neighbor of the opposite sex, spending an evening together in the living room, and dancing together). An example of a personal desire or intent measure asks respondents a series of questions as to whether they desire or intend to engage in sexual activity outside of marriage (Sponaugle).

Regardless of whether normative or personal standards are studied, however, the overwhelming majority of U.S. adults express strong opposition to sexual activity outside of a primary relationship (most of this research, however, has assessed attitudes toward extramarital sex, rather than extradyadic sex; Bringle & Buunk, 1991; Greeley, 1991; Sprecher & McKinney, 1993). Indeed, with regard to normative standards, the percent of U.S. adults having stated that extramarital sex is "always wrong" (80%) was higher than the percent of adults who responded to the same question in 23 other countries studied by Widmer, Treas, and Newcomb (1998), with the exceptions of Northern Ireland (81%) and the Philippines (88%). These data were collected using standardized questionnaires administered to nationally representative samples from the International Social Survey Program. The U.S. figure is supported by Laumann et al. (1994), who found that 77% of the NHSLS sample stated that extramarital sexual activity is "always wrong," while their secondary analysis of 1991 GSS data showed that 74% of respondents stated that extramarital sexual activity is "always wrong." Another 20.5% of the NHSLS and 16.3% of the GSS sample stated that extramarital sex is "almost always wrong," resulting in nearly all respondents in the NHSLS and over 90% of respondents in the GSS having disapproved of extramarital sex.

Whereas most research has been conducted on normative standards, a few studies have examined personal standards (e.g., Buckstel, Roeder, Kilmann, Laughlin, & Sotile, 1978; Weis & Slosnerick, 1981). These studies have found that even among more liberal college students, most are opposed to extramarital sexual activity.

Despite this widespread disapproval of extramarital sex, however, certain characteristics are predictive of a more tolerant attitude toward sexual behavior outside of one's primary relationship. First, both Sponaugle (1989) and Thompson (1983) reported, in their reviews of the literature, that acceptance of premarital sex was the strongest predictor of acceptance of extramarital sex. In addition to attitudes, Buunk and van Driel (1989), in their review of the literature, found that gender (men were more tolerant of sex outside of one's primary relationship than women), age (younger individuals were more likely to approve), education (those with higher levels of educational attainment were more accepting), social class (upper-middle class individuals were more likely to approve), religiosity (those with a weaker religious affinity were more tolerant), region (those living in urban areas were more accepting), and political orientation (those more liberal politically were more likely to approve) all significantly affected attitudes regarding sex outside of one's primary relationship.

In addition, Saunders and Edwards (1984), who drew a sample from a "judicious selection of occupations" (p. 829) in one standard metropolitan statistical area, found that when women perceived an opportunity to engage in extramarital sex (what the authors refer to as the "diffuse intimacy conception"), they were more likely to approve of it. Saunders and Edwards also found that low levels of marital satisfaction were associated with greater acceptance of extramarital sex.

Furthermore, Glass and Wright (1992), in their nonrepresentative sample from the Baltimore area, found that men and women differed in their approval of the justifications employed to engage in extramarital sex, with men being more likely than women to be accepting of sexual reasons for engaging in extramarital sex, whereas women were no more likely than men to approve of any form of justifications for involvement. However, in comparing only those men and women who currently were involved in an extramarital relationship or who had been involved in the past, women were more likely than men to approve of such relationships when the reason for such involvement was to receive love and affection or falling in love.

As discussed earlier, attitudes and behaviors do not necessarily correlate. That is, although many U.S. adults disapprove of extramarital sex, some engage in it anyway. In the next section, we discuss the available research on behavioral engagement in extramarital and extradyadic sex.

Incidence of Extramarital and Extradyadic Sex

Statistics abound on the percentage of married men and women who have had sexual experience outside of their primary relationships. These statistics vary widely, as a result of some studies relying on nonscientific sampling and data collection measures, the resulting statistics of which reflect very high levels of extramarital sex. For example, Yablonsky (1979), in a national but nonrepresentative sample of 771 married men in the United States, reported that over half engaged in extramarital sex at some point. Earlier studies also based on nonrepresentative samples, such as those of Kinsey and colleagues (1948, 1953), indicated that approximately half of married men and one fourth of married women engaged in extramarital sex.

Research based on rigorous sampling and data collection procedures, however, shows that a much smaller percentage of married men and women have had experience with extramarital sex. According to the NHSLS, approximately one fourth of men and 15% of women have engaged in extramarital sexual activity (Laumann et al., 1994). Laumann and colleagues also found in their analysis of 1991 GSS data that nearly 22% of men and just over 13% of women between the ages of 18 to 59 have engaged in extramarital sex. Wiederman (1997a), using 1994 GSS data, reported a similar incidence, with 22.7% of men and 11.6% of women at some point having had sex with someone other than one's spouse. These percentages are comparable to those found by Blumstein and Schwartz (1983) in a national but nonrepresentative study. They found that approximately one fourth of husbands and one fifth of wives engaged in extramarital sex. Finally, Forste and Tanfer (1996), in analyzing data from the 1991 National Survey of Women, found that only a small percentage of married women (4%) have engaged in sex with someone other than their primary partner.

In one of the few studies conducted on extradyadic sex among cohabitors, Blumstein and Schwartz (1983), in a national but nonrepresentative sample, found that a third of male and a third of female cohabitors had engaged in sex with someone other than their primary partner. Laumann and colleagues (1994) also reported that cohabitors exhibited a higher rate of sexual activity outside of their primary relationship than did marrieds. Forste and Tanfer (1996) found that 20% of cohabiting women had engaged in extradyadic sex. They also found that "dating" relationships were similar to cohabitations, in that 18% of women in nonresidential relationships had engaged in extradyadic sex.

As was the case with attitudes, certain characteristics were predictive of an increased likelihood to engage in sex outside of one's primary relationship. For example, men were more likely to have engaged in extramarital/extradyadic sex than were women, though there was no gender difference among young respondents (Blumstein & Schwartz, 1983; Wiederman, 1997a). Also, representative data from the 1990/91 National AIDS Behavioral Survey found that African-Americans reported the highest incidence of extramarital sex in the past year (6.1%), followed by 4% for Hispanics and 2.5% for Whites (Choi, Catania, & Dolcini, 1994; also see Smith, 1998 and Wiederman, 1997a). Forste and Tanfer (1996) found that married African-American women and married Hispanic women were more likely than married White women to have engaged in extramarital sexual relationships, whereas Hispanic women in noncohabitation unions were more likely than White women in similar unions to have engaged in extradyadic sex (there were no racial/ethnic differences among cohabiting women).

Although confounded with duration of the primary union, age may be an important factor in the lifetime incidence of extramarital sex. Smith (1998), using GSS data, found that a recent experience of extramarital sex was more common among younger adults. More specifically, he found that nearly 7% of those between the ages of 18 and 29 had experienced an extramarital sexual relationship in the last year, compared to 3% among those in their 30s, 4% of those in their 40s, another 3% in their 50s, and only approximately 1% among those in their 60s or older. When looking at lifetime incidence, however, the proportion that reported having had at least one extramarital sexual relationship increased with age, in that 12.6% between the ages of 18 and 29 reported such a relationship, compared to 14.5% in their 30s and 20.7% in their 40s, after which the proportion began to decrease. Although older respondents who had been married for longer periods of time were at greater risk for having had an extramarital sexual relationship, these numbers suggest that extramarital sex is becoming more common for younger individuals. Wiederman (1997a), using cross-sectional GSS data, found cohort effects in that the incidence of extramarital sex for men increased with each age group except the oldest (70 years and older), when the incidence decreased. For women, there was a curvilinear relationship, likely related to the sexual revolution of the 1960s/1970s: the percent of women having reported that they had ever engaged in extramarital sex increased from women in their 20s through women in their 40s, and then began to decrease with women in their 50s. And, Forste and Tanfer (1996) found that women in nonmarital and noncohabitational relationships (i.e., dating relationships) were more likely to engage in extradyadic sex as they became older. That is, older respondents (those over the age of 25) were more likely than those under the age of 25 to have engaged in extradyadic sex.

Other factors associated with a higher incidence of extramarital/extradyadic sex include infrequent attendance at religious services (Buunk, 1980a; Choi et al., 1994; Smith, 1998); women's affiliation with a religion other than Catholicism or mainstream Protestantism, or no religious affiliation (Forste & Tanfer, 1996); and residing in urban areas (Choi et al.; no comparison was made to only rural areas). However, some studies found no significant relationship between community size and the incidence of extramarital sex (e.g., Wiederman, 1997a). Still others found a significant relationship only for extramarital sex occurring within the last twelve months (Smith, 1988).

In addition, the effect of educational attainment on the incidence of extramarital/extradyadic sex was mixed in the literature. Specifically, some studies reported that extramarital sex was more likely to occur in the preceding 12 months among the less educated, although the lifetime incidence with regard to educational attainment was unclear (Smith, 1998). Others found that African-Americans with low levels of educational attainment, but not their White counterparts, were more likely to engage in extramarital sex than were those with moderate levels of education (Choi et al., 1994). Still others, however, found that both cohabiting and noncohabiting women with low levels of educational attainment were *less* likely to engage in extradyadic sex than were their well-educated counterparts. And, some studies found the same relationship among married individuals (Buunk, 1980a).

Forste and Tanfer (1996), in analyzing data from the National Survey of Women, found that educational heterogamy also was a factor, in that women with higher levels of educational attainment than their partners were more likely to engage in extramarital/extradyadic sex compared to women in homogamous relationships. Women with lower levels of educational attainment relative to their partners were less likely to engage in extramarital/extradyadic sex, compared to women in homogamous relationships (Forste & Tanfer, 1996).

In the same study, relationship experience also was associated with the incidence of sex with a secondary partner, with women who cohabited prior to marriage being more likely to have engaged in extramarital sex than were women without this prior cohabiting experience (Forste & Tanfer, 1996). Furthermore, Spanier and Margolis (1983), in their sample of divorced or separated individuals in Pennsylvania, found a higher incidence of extramarital sex among those who had been separated and/or divorced than other researchers found among the general population (also see Laumann et al., 1994; Smith, 1998; and Wiederman, 1997a).

Premarital sexual activity may also be important. Forste and Tanfer (1996) found that women with several sex partners prior to their current primary relationship were much more likely to have engaged in extramarital/extradyadic sex, compared to women who had few sex partners prior to the current union. However, Spanier and Margolis (1983) found, among their sample of separated or divorced individuals, that premarital sexual experience as measured by the number of partners had no relationship to the incidence of extramarital sex. Indeed, they found that only the length of marriage increased the likelihood of engaging in extramarital sex.

Finally, some researchers have examined whether primary relationship satisfaction (sexual and emotional) has an impact on the likelihood of engaging in extramarital/extradyadic sexual activity. Earlier studies (conducted prior to the 1990s) indicated that extramarital sex was more common among those less satisfied with their marriages, particularly for women (see Christopher & Sprecher, 2000, for reviews). Later studies confirmed the finding that lower levels of marital satisfaction were related to the likelihood of extramarital sex (Bringle & Buunk, 1991; Smith, 1998).

As we have established, despite widespread disapproval of extramarital and extradyadic sex, a substantial number of U.S. adults engage in these behaviors. What characterizes these secondary unions? What are the benefits and costs of such relationships?

Characteristics of Extramarital and Extradyadic Relationships

Lampe (1987), in his discussion of Morton Hunt's (1969) research into extramarital relationships, reported that secondary sexual relationships are typically short term, with only one fourth lasting at least 2 years. More recent qualitative studies, however, such as that done by Atwater (who recruited interviewees nationally by placing an ad in *Ms.* Magazine; 1982) and Richardson (who "announced my research interest to nearly everyone I met" to recruit interviewees; 1985, p. x), indicated that many individuals who have engaged in extramarital sexual activity did so in the context of ongoing, long-term relationships with someone other than their primary partner. Despite the duration, however, these secondary unions rarely were transformed into a subsequent marriage (Richardson, 1985).

Consistent with attitudes regarding the acceptability of sex with a secondary partner, men and women do not engage in these unions for the same reasons. Blumstein and Schwartz (1983) found that men tend to look for sexual variety, whereas women look for more of an emotional connection (see also Atwater, 1982, and Glass & Wright, 1985). These findings support evolutionary theories (see Guerrero, Spitzberg, & Yoshimura, this volume) to explain men's and women's differing behaviors. Other reasons explaining why men and women have engaged in extramarital/extradyadic sex, as reviewed by Schwartz & Rutter (1998), include boredom with the primary partner, retaliation against a partner's secondary relationship or other behaviors, and an inability to resist the attention being given by someone else.

There are different forms of extramarital/extradyadic relationships. As discussed by Lampe (1987), these forms vary along an emotional continuum (ranging from a strong emotional commitment to sex as a game with little or no emotional feeling) and a physical continuum (ranging from simply fantasizing about sex with someone else, minor sexual activity such as kissing, to actual intercourse). Unfortunately, due to a lack of research in this area relying on nationally representative samples, it is unknown what percent of individuals have engaged in extramarital/extradyadic sex within an emotionally bonded relationship.

Because secondary sexual relationships typically are conducted in secret, the partners face unique challenges, such as finding a place to get together without anyone else knowing and finding a mutually convenient time to be together, which complicate the relationship (Hunt, 1969). The lack of support from one's social network also may result in additional costs to maintaining the secondary union, increasing the likelihood of dissolution (Laumann et al., 1994; Sprecher, Felmlee, Orbuch, & Willetts, 2002). These challenges give the married partner (if only one partner is married) in the secondary relationship more power, as he/she dictates the conditions under which the couple will spend time together, while the nonmarried partner arranges his/her schedule to suit the married partner's needs.

Despite attempts at secretly maintaining the extradyadic relationship, however, researchers note that "the vast majority of people learn about it sooner or later if their partner has had sex outside the relationship," with cohabitors being less secretive than married individuals (Blumstein & Schwartz, 1983, p. 268). The reactions of the faithful spouse or partner take several different forms, with the majority reacting with anger, jealousy, depression, and sometimes violence (Bringle & Buunk, 1991; Lampe, 1987).

Sometimes, couples construct a new sexual arrangement upon learning of one partner's infidelity that includes open marriage, where one or both partners are permitted secondary relationships. In those instances where open marriage is permitted for both partners/spouses, rules are set to which both partners must conform to make the arrangement successful. These norms often include continuing to define the marriage to be the most important relationship, that the secondary relationships be brief and involve little emotion, and that the partners either keep each other informed of their other unions or agree not to flaunt them to each other (Buunk, 1980b). Unfortunately, there is little current information about open marriages or relationships, after a flurry of research interest in the 1970s. Blumstein and Schwartz (1983) provide the best information. They report that despite rules that allowed for secondary relationships while maintaining the primary relationship, many couples, cohabitors in particular, had such negative experiences with an open relationship that they subsequently more strongly adhered to monogamy.

Regardless of the reactions of the faithful partner, secondary sexual relationships are infrequently the *main* cause of the termination of the primary relationship. Indeed, according to Richardson (1985), most married men engaging in extramarital relationships never divorce their wives. Research indicates that cohabiting relationships are more likely to end, particularly if the male partner engaged in extradyadic sex early in the cohabiting union (Blumstein & Schwartz, 1983). When primary relationships do end, however, men are much more likely than women to hold their wives' extramarital relationships, as opposed to their own, as responsible for the demise of their marriages, whereas women were more likely to attribute dissolution to other problems in the relationship, which likely caused both the start of a secondary relationship(s) and the subsequent termination of the primary relationship (Buunk, 1987).

CONCLUSIONS AND IMPLICATIONS FOR FUTURE RESEARCH

We have presented the current state of knowledge on sexual attitudes and practices especially within relational contexts. We described available data, with a focus on national studies. We discussed sexuality among adolescents and young adults, followed by a discussion of adult sexual behavior in primary relationships. We then presented information on extramarital and extradyadic sex. Finally, we conclude with suggestions for future research.

There are numerous directions that future research should undertake. First, more representative samples are needed to study the issues we address in this chapter. As noted throughout, much research in this area makes use of convenience samples, leading in some cases (e.g., approval among adolescents of premarital sex) to inconsistent results and thereby limiting the generalizability of the results. Ideally, large national studies based on probability sampling methods and focused on sexuality should be conducted. These data collection efforts would include obtaining responses from adolescents as well as adults. Most research protocols are aimed at persons 18 years or older because of human subjects provisions. It is important, however, to uncover patterns of sexuality among adolescents when they are adolescents; under this scenario, recall error should be less. In addition, these efforts could clarify many of the results presented here (such as why men report a higher number of lifetime sexual partners than do women). New data that more fully explore extramarital and extradyadic sex (including the proportion of these sexual events that occur within the context of an emotionally bonded relationship) would also add greatly to our understanding of these forms of sexuality. Furthermore, such research knowledge would allow for greater development of public policy regarding adolescent sexuality and disease prevention among all Americans. Obviously, funding issues represent a significant challenge to collecting nationally representative data. Despite this problem, however, we could still move beyond small convenience samples in one geographical location (based primarily on students) by initiating greater cooperation among researchers to combine resources. Researchers in different U.S. locations, and even those in other countries, could collaborate to enhance the quality of the data.

Second, we need large-scale studies that focus more on sexuality specifically within a relational context. We need more information on the proportion of lifetime sexual partners that are also involved in an emotionally bonded relationship, characteristics of relationships, including the sexual negotiation process in the dyad itself, the frequency at which couples engage in a variety of sexual behaviors, as well as psychosocial characteristics of primary and secondary partners. Additionally, data collected from members of a respondent's social network (e.g., family members and friends) would be enormously useful in determining how others contribute to and detract from sexuality in a relational context. More specifically, how do these network members influence the development of sexuality in relationships? How is sexuality in relationships mediated through network members in the maintenance of the primary relationship? These questions have not been adequately addressed in prior research.

Similarly, we need more longitudinal research in order to examine the sequence of sexual events within a relational context, and how this sequence changes over time. Longitudinal research would more accurately explore how sexuality is related to the development of relationships, how it is negotiated in those relationships, and the role it plays in the dissolution of unions. We also recommend longitudinal analysis of sexuality in various union types. Multiple waves employing a variety of methods would best allow us to research the progression of sexual behaviors.

Fourth, more precise measures should be developed and employed in these large-scale studies. For example, some measures currently in use to explore sexuality in a relational context do not differentiate among types of individuals or types of attitudes or behaviors (e.g., adolescent vs. young adult; attitudes toward extramarital sex vs. extradyadic sex; coitus vs. other sexual behaviors). Large-scale studies are needed that include these more precise measures, in order for us to better understand attitudes and behaviors regarding sexuality in a relational context.

Fifth, there should be greater intellectual exchange and cooperation between those who design and administer large-scale studies and those who focus more on the theoretical rationales explaining sexual attitudes and behaviors. As our chapter illustrates, the research that has been conducted on attitudes and behaviors regarding sexuality in a relational context is largely descriptive. Examining such attitudes and behaviors within some of the existing theoretical frameworks currently employed in sexuality research (e.g., social exchange, network theories) would be fruitful.

Overall, although much descriptive information is currently available regarding attitudes and behaviors toward sexuality in a relational context, further research, particularly that relying on nationally representative data, is needed to better clarify some of these results. Furthermore, the application of various theoretical perspectives to interpret these results is needed. Although this chapter described much in the way of attitudes and behaviors, less is known specifically as to *why* adolescents and adults think and act in the ways that they do. The partnership of method and theory would enhance our understanding of sexuality in relational contexts and would be instrumental in the development of public health policy.

REFERENCES

Atwater, L. (1982). *The extramarital connection: Sex, intimacy, and identity.* New York: Irvington.

Baumer, E. P., & South, S. J. (2001). Community effects on youth sexual activity. *Journal of Marriage and Family, 63,* 540–554.

Billy, J. O. G., Brewster, K. L., & Grady, W. R. (1994). Contextual effects on the sexual behavior of adolescent women. *Journal of Marriage and the Family, 56,* 387–404.

Billy, J. O. G., Tanfer, K., Grady, W. R., & Klepinger, D. H. (1993). The sexual behavior of men in the United States. *Family Planning Perspectives, 25,* 52–60.

Bingham, C. R., Miller, B. C., & Adams, G. R. (1990). Correlates of age at first sexual intercourse in a national sample of young women. *Journal of Adolescent Research, 5,* 18–33.

Blumstein, P., & Schwartz, P. (1983). *American couples: Money, work, sex.* New York: Morrow.

Bringle, R. G., & Buunk, B. (1991). Extradyadic relationships and sexual jealousy. In K. McKinney & S. Sprecher (Eds.), *Sexuality in close relationships* (pp. 135–153). Hillsdale, NJ: Lawrence Erlbaum Associates.

Brooks-Gunn, J., & Furstenberg, F. F. (1989). Adolescent sexual behavior. *American Psychologist, 44,* 249–257.

Brown, N. R., & Sinclair, R. C. (1999). Estimating number of lifetime sexual partners: Men and women do it differently. *The Journal of Sex Research, 36,* 292–297.

Buckstel, L. H., Roeder, G. D., Kilmann, P. R., Laughlin, J., & Sotile, W. M. (1978). Projected extramarital sexual involvement in unmarried college students. *Journal of Marriage and the Family, 40,* 337–340.

Burgess, E. W., & Wallin, P. (1953). *Engagement and marriage.* Philadelphia: Lippincott.

Butler, J. R., & Burton, L. M. (1990). Rethinking teenage childbearing: Is sexual abuse a missing link? *Family Relations, 39,* 73–80.

Buunk, B. (1980a). Extramarital sex in the Netherlands: Motivation in social and marital context. *Alternative Lifestyles, 3,* 11–39.

Buunk, B. (1980b). Sexually open marriages: Ground rules for countering potential threats to marriage. *Alternative Lifestyles, 3,* 312–328.

Buunk, B. (1987). Conditions that promote break-ups as a consequence of extradyadic involvements. *Journal of Social and Clinical Psychology, 5,* 237–250.

Buunk, B. (1998). Extramarital behavioral intentions scale. In C. M. Davis, W. L. Yarber, R. Bauserman, G. Schreer, & S. L. Davis (Eds.), *Handbook of sexuality-related measures* (pp. 224–225). Thousand Oaks, CA: Sage.

Buunk, B. & van Driel, B. (1989). *Variant lifestyles and relationships.* Newbury Park, CA: Sage.

Call, V., Sprecher, S., & Schwartz, P. (1995). The incidence and frequency of marital sex in a national sample. *Journal of Marriage and the Family, 57,* 639–650.

Carver, K., Joyner, K., & Udry, J. R. (2003). National estimates of adolescent romantic relationships: In P. Florsheim (Ed.), *Adolescent romantic relations and sexual behavior* (pp. 23–56). Mahwah, NJ: Lawrence Erlbaum Associates.

Choi, K. H., Catania, J. A., & Dolcini, M. M. (1994). Extramarital sex and HIV risk behavior among U.S. adults: Results from the National AIDS Behavioral Survey. *American Journal of Public Health, 84,* 2003–2007.

Christopher, F. S. (1996). Adolescent sexuality: Trying to explain the magic and the mystery. In N. Vanzetti & S. Duck (Eds.), *A lifetime of relationships* (213–240). Pacific Grove, CA: Brooks/Cole.

Christopher, F. S. (2001). *To dance the dance: A symbolic interactional exploration of premarital sexuality.* Mahwah, NJ: Lawrence Erlbaum Associates.

Christopher, F. S., & Cate, R. M. (1985). Anticipated influences on sexual decision making for first intercourse. *Family Relations, 34,* 265–270.

Christopher, F. S., & Roosa, M. W. (1991). Factors affecting sexual decision in the premarital relationships of adolescents and young adults. In K. McKinney & S. Sprecher (Eds.), *Sexuality in close relationships* (pp. 111–133). Hillsdale, NJ: Lawrence Erlbaum Associates.

Christopher, F. S., & Sprecher, S. (2000). Sexuality in marriage, dating, and other relationships: A decade review. *Journal of Marriage and the Family, 62,* 999–1017.

Davis, J. A., Smith, T. W., & Marsden, P. V. (2002). *The General Social Survey: 1972–2000 cumulative codebook.* Chicago: National Opinion Research Center, University of Chicago. Retrieved September 2, 2002 from http://www.icpsr.umich.edu/GSS/

Day, R. D. (1992). The transition to first intercourse among racially and culturally diverse youth. *Journal of Marriage and the Family, 54,* 749–762.

de Gaston, J. F., Jensen, L., & Weed, S. (1995). A closer look at adolescent sexual activity. *Journal of Youth and Adolescence, 24,* 465–479.

de Gaston, J. F., Weed, S., & Jensen, L. (1996). Understanding gender differences in adolescent sexuality. *Adolescence, 31,* 217–231.

DeLamater, J., & MacCorquodale, P. (1979). *Premarital sexuality: Attitudes, relationships, behavior.* Madison, WI: The University of Wisconsin Press.

Donnelly, D. A. (1993). Sexually inactive marriages. *The Journal of Sex Research, 30,* 171–179.

Edwards, J. N., & Booth, A. (1976). Sexual behavior in and out of marriage: An assessment of correlates. *Journal of Marriage and the Family, 38*, 73–81.

Flewelling, R. L., & Bauman, K. E. (1990). Family structure as a predictor of initial substance use and sexual intercourse in early adolescence. *Journal of Marriage and the Family, 52*, 171–181.

Ford, K., & Norris, A. (1997). Sexual networks of African-American and Hispanic youth. *Sexually Transmitted Diseases, 24*, 327–333.

Forste, R., & Tanfer, K. (1996). Sexual exclusivity among dating, cohabiting, and married women. *Journal of Marriage and the Family, 58*, 33–47.

Fox, G. L. (1980). The mother–adolescent daughter relationship as a sexual socialization structure: A research review. *Family Relations, 29*, 21–28.

Furstenberg, F. F., Jr. (1998). When will teenage childbearing become a problem? The implications of Western experience for developing countries. *Studies in Family Planning, 29*, 246–253.

Gagnon, J. H. (1990). The implicit and explicit use of the scripting perspective in sex research. *Annual Review of Sex Research, 1*, 1–43.

Geer, J. H., & Broussard, D. B. (1990). Scaling heterosexual behavior and arousal: Consistency and sex differences. *Journal of Personality and Social Psychology, 58*, 664–671.

Gibson, J. W., & Kempf, J. (1990). Attitudinal predictors of sexual activity in Hispanic adolescent females. *Journal of Adolescent Research, 5*, 414–430.

Glass, S. P., & Wright, T. L. (1985). Sex differences in type of extramarital involvement and marital dissatisfaction. *Sex Roles, 12*, 1101–1120.

Glass, S. P., & Wright, T. L. (1992). Justifications for extramarital relationships: The association between attitudes, behaviors, and gender. *The Journal of Sex Research, 29*, 361–387.

Greeley, A. M. (1991). *Faithful attraction: Discovering intimacy, love, and fidelity in American marriage.* New York: Doherty.

Halpern, C. T., Joyner, K., Udry, J. R., & Suchindran, C. (2000). Smart teens don't have sex (or kiss much either). *Journal of Adolescent Health, 26*, 213–225.

Hass, W. (1979). *Teenager sexuality.* New York: Macmillan.

Hatfield, E., Sprecher, S., Pillemer, J. T., Greenberger, D., & Wexler, P. (1989). Gender differences in what is desired in the sexual relationship. *Journal of Psychology & Human Sexuality, 1*, 39–52.

Hofferth, S. L., Kahn, J. R., & Baldwin, W. (1987). Premarital sexual activity among U.S. teenage women over the past three decades. *Family Planning Perspectives, 19*, 46–53.

Hogan, D. P., & Kitagawa, E. M. (1985). The impact of social status, family structure, and neighborhood on fertility of black adolescents. *American Journal of Sociology, 90*, 825–855.

Hogan, D. P., Sun, R., & Cornwell, G. T. (2000). Sexual and fertility behaviors of American females aged 15–19 years: 1985, 1990, and 1995. *American Journal of Public Health, 90*, 1421–1425.

Huerta-Franco, R., de Leon, J. D., & Malacara, J. M. (1996). Knowledge and attitudes toward sexuality in adolescents and their association with the family and other factors. *Adolescence, 31*, 179–191.

Huerta-Franco, R., & Malacara, J. M. (1999). Factors associated with the sexual experiences of underprivileged Mexican adolescents. *Adolescence, 34*, 389–401.

Hunt, M. (1969). *The affair: A portrait of extra-marital love in contemporary America.* New York: Signet.

Hyde, J. S., & DeLamater, J. (2000). *Understanding human sexuality,* (7th ed). New York: McGraw-Hill.

James, W. H. (1983). Decline in coital rates with spouses' ages and duration of marriage. *Journal of Biosocial Science, 15*, 83–87.

Joyner, K., & Laumann, E. O. (2001). Teenage sex and the sexual revolution. In E. O. Laumann & R. T. Michael (Eds.), *Sex, love, and health in America: Private choices and public policies* (pp. 41–71). Chicago: The University of Chicago Press.

Keith, J. B., McCreary, C., Collins, K., Smith, C. P., & Bernstein, I. (1991). Sexual activity and contraceptive use among low-income urban black adolescent females. *Adolescence, 26*, 769–785.

Kinsey, A. C., Pomeroy, W. B., & Martin, C. E. (1948). *Sexual behavior in the human male.* Philadelphia: Saunders.

Kinsey, A. C., Pomeroy, W. B., Martin, C. E., & Gebhard, P. H. (1953). *Sexual behavior in the human female.* Philadelphia: Saunders.

Kivisto, P. (2001). Teenagers, pregnancy, and childbearing in a risk society: How do high-risk teens differ from their age peers? *Journal of Family Issues, 22*, 1044–1065.

Knox, D., & Wilson, K. (1981). Dating behaviors of university students. *Family Relations, 30*, 255–258.

Lampe, P. E. (1987). Adultery and the behavioral sciences. In P. E. Lampe (Ed.), *Adultery in the United States: Close encounters of the sixth (or seventh) kind* (pp. 165–198). Buffalo, NY: Prometheus Books.

Laumann, E. O., Gagnon, J. H., Michael, R. T., & Michaels, S. (1994). *The social organization of sexuality: Sexual practices in the United States.* Chicago: The University of Chicago Press.

Laumann, E. O., & Michael, R. T. (2001). Introduction: Setting the scene. In E. O. Laumann & R. T. Michael (Eds.), *Sex, love, and health in America: Private choices and public policies* (pp. 1–39). Chicago: The University of Chicago Press.

Laumann, E. O., & Parish, W. (2001, October). An overview of the national survey of sexual practices in China. Paper presented at the Annual Meetings of the Society for the Scientific Study of Sexuality. San Diego, CA.

Leigh, G. K., Weddle, K. D., & Loewen, I. R. (1988). Analysis of the timing of transition to sexual intercourse for black adolescent females. *Journal of Adolescent Research, 3*, 333–344.

Lewin, B. (1987, September). *Adolescent sexuality: Changing behaviour and lasting trust in the family.* Paper presented at CFR/CYR International Seminar on Young People and their Parents, Munich, Germany.

Manning, W. D., Longmore, M. A., & Giordano, P. C. (2000). The relationship context of contraceptive use at first intercourse. *Family Planning Perspectives, 32*, 104–110.

Marsiglio, W., & Donnelly, D. (1991). Sexual intercourse in later life: A national study of married persons. *Journal of Gerontology, 46*, 338–344.

Marsiglio, W., & Mott, F. L. (1986). The impact of sex education on the sexual activity, contraceptive use, and premarital pregnancy among American teenagers. *Family Planning Perspectives, 18*, 151–162.

Michael, R. T., Gagnon, J. H., Laumann, E. O., & Kolata, G. (1994). *Sex in America.* Boston: Little, Brown.

Miller, B. C., & Olson, T. D. (1988). Sexual attitudes and behavior of high school students in relation to background and contextual factors. *The Journal of Sex Research, 24*, 194–200.

Miller, K. E., Sabo, D. F., Farrell, M. P., Barnes, G. M., & Melnick, M. J. (1999). Sports, sexual behavior, contraceptive use, and pregnancy among female and male high school students: Testing cultural resource theory. *Sociology of Sport Journal, 16*, 366–387.

Mintz, S., & Kellogg, S. (1988). *Domestic revolutions: A social history of American family life.* New York: The Free Press.

Morris, L., Nunez, L., Monroy de Velasco, A., Bailey, P., Cardenas, C., & Watley, A. (1988). Sexual experience and contraceptive use among young adults in Mexico City. *International Family Planning Perspectives, 14*, 147–152.

Murphy, D. A., Rotheram-Borus, M. J., & Reid, H. M. (1998). Adolescent gender differences in HIV-related sexual risk acts, social cognitive factors and behavioral skills. *Journal of Adolescence, 21*, 197–208.

Murry, V. M. (1994). Black adolescent females: A comparison of early versus late coital initiators. *Family Relations, 43*, 342–348.

National Longitudinal Study of Adolescent Health. Carolina Population Center. University of North Carolina. Retrieved August 21, 2002 from http://www.cpc.unc.edu/addhealth/

Neubeck, G., & Schletzer, V. (1962). A study of extramarital relationships. In G. Neubeck (Ed.), *Extramarital relations* (pp. 146–152). Englewood Cliffs, NJ: Prentice-Hall.

Newcomer, S. F., & Udry, J. R. (1985). Oral sex in an adolescent population. *Archives of Sexual Behavior, 14*, 41–46.

Newcomer, J. F., & Udry, J. R. (1987). Parental marital status effects on adolescent sexual behavior. *Journal of Marriage and the Family, 49*, 235–240.

Orbuch, T., & Sprecher, S. (2003). Attraction and interpersonal relationships. In J. DeLamater. (Ed.), *Handbook of social psychology* (pp. 339–362). New York: Kluwer-Plenum.

Parks, M. R., & Eggert, L. L. (1991). The role of social context in the dynamics of personal relationships. In W. Jones & D. Perlman (Eds.), *Advances in personal relationships* (Vol. 2, pp. 1–34). London: Jessica Kingsley.

Popenoe, D. (1993). American family decline, 1960–1980: A review and appraisal. *Journal of Marriage and the Family, 55*, 527–555.

Popenoe, D., & Whitehead, B. D. (1999). *Should we live together? What young adults need to know about cohabitation before marriage.* New Brunswick, NJ: The National Marriage Project.

Rao, K. V., & DeMaris, A. (1995). Coital frequency among married and cohabiting couples in the U.S. *Journal of Biosocial Science, 27*, 135–150.

Reinisch, J. M., Hill, C. A., Sanders, S. A., & Ziemba-Davis, M. (1995). High-risk sexual behavior at a midwestern university: A confirmatory survey. *Family Planning Perspectives, 27*, 79–82.

Reinisch, J. M., & Sanders, S. A. (1992). High-risk sexual behavior among heterosexual undergraduates at a midwestern university. *Family Planning Perspectives, 24*, 116–122.

Reiss, I. L., & Lee, G. R. (1988). *Family systems in America* (4th ed.). New York: Holt, Rinehart & Winston.

Richardson, L. (1985). *The new other woman: Contemporary single women in affairs with married men.* New York: The Free Press.

Richardson, L. (1988). Secrecy and status: The social construction of forbidden relationships. *American Sociological Review, 53*, 209–219.

Rodgers, J. L., & Rowe, D. C. (1990). Adolescent sexual activity and mildly deviant behavior. *Journal of Family Issues, 11*, 274–293.

Roscoe, B., Cavanaugh, L. E., & Kennedy, D. R. (1988). Dating infidelity: Behaviors, reasons and consequences. *Adolescence, 13*, 35–43.

Rosenbaum, E., & Kandel, D. B. (1990). Early onset of adolescent sexual behavior and drug involvement. *Journal of Marriage and the Family, 52*, 783–798.

Rubin, L. B. (1990). *Erotic wars: What happened to the sexual revolution?* New York: Farrar, Straus, & Giroux.

Saunders, J. M., & Edwards, J. N. (1984). Extramarital sexuality: A predictive model of permissive attitudes. *Journal of Marriage and the Family, 46*, 825–835.

Scanzoni, J. (1995). *Contemporary families and relationships: Reinventing responsibility.* New York: McGraw-Hill.

Schwartz, P., & V. Rutter. 1998. *The gender of sexuality.* Thousand Oaks, CA: Pine Forge Press.

Sherwin, R., & Corbett, S. (1985). Campus sexual norms and dating relationships: A trend analysis. *The Journal of Sex Research, 21*, 258–274.

Simenauer, J., & Carroll, D. (1982). *Singles: The new Americans*. New York: Simon & Schuster.

Simpson, J. A., & Harris, B. A. (1994). Interpersonal attraction. In A. L. Weber & J. H. Harvey (Eds.), *Perspectives on close relationships* (pp. 46–66). Boston: Allyn & Bacon.

Smith, E. A., & Udry, J. R. (1985). Coital and non-coital sexual behaviors of white and black adolescents. *American Journal of Public Health, 75*, 1200–1230.

Smith, T. W. (1998). American sexual behavior: Trends, socio-demographic differences, and risk behavior. *GSS Topical Report No. 25*. Chicago: National Opinion Research Center, University of Chicago.

Somers, C. L., & Paulson, S. E. (2000). Students' perceptions of parent-adolescent closeness and communication about sexuality: Relations with sexual knowledge, attitudes, and behaviors. *Journal of Adolescence, 23*, 629–644.

Sonenstein, F. L., Ku, L., Lindberg, L. D., Turner, C. F., & Pleck, J. H. (1998). Changes in sexual behavior and condom use among teenaged males: 1988–1995. *American Journal of Public Health, 88*, 956–959.

Sorensen, R. C. (1973). *Adolescent sexuality in contemporary America*. New York: World.

Spanier, G. B., & Margolis, R. L. (1983). Marital separation and extramarital sexual behavior. *The Journal of Sex Research, 19*, 23–48.

Spira, A., Bajos, N., & the ACFS Group. (1994). *Analyse des Comportements Sexuel en France*. Brookfield, VT: Avebury.

Sponaugle, G. C. (1989). Attitudes toward extramarital relations. In K. McKinney & S. Sprecher (Eds.), *Human sexuality: The societal and interpersonal context* (pp. 187–209). Norwood, NJ: Ablex.

Sprecher, S. (1989). Premarital sexual standards for different categories of individuals. *The Journal of Sex Research, 26*, 232–248.

Sprecher, S., Barbee, A., & Schwartz, P. (1995). Was it good for you, too?: Gender differences in first sexual intercourse experiences. *The Journal of Sex Research, 32*, 3–15.

Sprecher, S., Felmlee, D., Orbuch, T. L., & Willetts, M. C. (2002). Social networks and change in personal relationships. In A. Vangelisti, H. Reis, & M. A. Fitzpatrick (Eds.), *Stability and change in relationship behavior* (pp. 257–284). New York: Cambridge University Press.

Sprecher, S., & Hatfield, E. (1996). Premarital sexual standards among U.S. college students: Comparison with Russian and Japanese students. *Archives of Sexual Behavior, 25*, 261–288.

Sprecher, S., & McKinney, K. (1993). *Sexuality*. Newbury Park, CA: Sage.

Sprecher, S., McKinney, K., Walsh, R., & Anderson, C. (1988). A revision of the Reiss Premarital Sexual Permissiveness Scale. *Journal of Marriage and the Family, 50*, 821–828.

Stone, N., & Ingham, R. (2002). Factors affecting British teenagers' contraceptive use at first intercourse: The importance of partner communication. *Perspectives on Sexual and Reproductive Health, 34*, 191–197.

Story, M. D. (1985). A comparison of university student experience with various sexual outlets in 1974 and 1984. *Journal of Sex Education and Therapy, 11*, 35–41.

Thompson, A. P. (1983). Extramarital sex: A review of the research literature. *The Journal of Sex Research, 19*, 1–22.

Thornton, A. (1990). The courtship process and adolescent sexuality. *Journal of Family Issues, 11*, 239–273.

Trussell, J., & Westoff, C. F. (1980). Contraceptive practice and trends in coital frequency. *Family Planning Perspectives, 12*, 246–249.

Udry, J. R., & Billy, J. O. G. (1987). Initiation of coitus in early adolescence. *American Sociological Review, 52*, 841–855.

Udry, J. R., Deven, F. R., & Coleman, S. J. (1982). A cross-national comparison of the relative influence of male and female age on the frequency of marital intercourse. *Journal of Biosocial Science, 14*, 1–6.

Udry, J. R., & Morris, N. M. (1978). Relative contribution of male and female age to the frequency of marital intercourse. *Social Biology, 25*, 128–134.

Ventura, S. J., & Bachrach, C. A. (2000). Nonmarital childbearing in the United States, 1940–99. *National Vital Statistics Report, 48*, 16.

Walsh, R. H., Ganza, W., & Finefield, T. (1983, April). *A fifteen-year study about sexual permissiveness*. Paper presented at the Midwest Sociological Society Annual Meetings, Kansas City, MO.

Wein, B. (1970). *The runaway generation*. New York: McKay.

Weis, D. L., & Slosnerick, M. (1981). Attitudes toward sexual and nonsexual extramarital involvements among a sample of college students. *Journal of Marriage and the Family, 43*, 349–358.

Weinberg, M. S., Lottes, I. L., & Gordon, L. E. (1997). Social class background, sexual attitudes, and sexual behavior in a heterosexual undergraduate sample. *Archives of Sexual Behavior, 26*, 625–642.

Wellings, K., Field, J., Johnson, A., & Wadsworth, J. (1994). *Sexual behavior in Britain: The National Survey of Sexual Attitudes and Lifestyles*. New York: Penguin.

Werner-Wilson, R. J. (1998). Gender differences in adolescent sexual attitudes: The influence of individual and family factors. *Adolescence, 33*, 519–531.

Westoff, C. F. (1974). Coital frequency and contraception. *Family Planning Perspectives, 6*, 136–141.

Widmer, E. D. (1997). Influence of older siblings on initiation of sexual intercourse. *Journal of Marriage and the Family, 59*, 928–938.

Widmer, E. D., Treas, J., & Newcomb, R. (1998). Attitudes toward nonmarital sex in 24 countries. *The Journal of Sex Research, 35*, 349–358.

Wiederman, M. W. (1997a). Extramarital sex: Prevalence and correlates in a national survey. *The Journal of Sex Research, 34*, 167–174.

Wiederman, M. W. (1997b). The truth must be in here somewhere: Examining the gender discrepancy in self-reported lifetime number of sex partners. *The Journal of Sex Research, 34*, 375–386.

Wulf, D., & Singh, S. (1991). Sexual activity, union and childbearing among adolescent women in the Americas. *International Family Planning Perspectives, 17*, 137–144.

Yablonsky, L. (1979). *The extra-sex factor: Why over half of America's married men play around.* New York: Times Books.

Zani, B. (1991). Male and female patterns in the discovery of sexuality during adolescence. *Journal of Adolescence, 14*, 163–178.

Zelnik, M., & Shah, F. K. (1983). First intercourse among young Americans. *Family Planning Perspectives, 15*, 64–72.

4

Sociosexuality and Romantic Relationships

Jeffry A. Simpson
Carol L. Wilson
Heike A. Winterheld
Texas A&M University

In this chapter, we review and critique extant theory and research on sociosexuality and romantic relationships. We begin by recounting the origins of sociosexuality, focusing first on earliest descriptive research and then on the development of the sociosexuality construct and inventory (Gangestad & Simpson, 1990; Simpson & Gangestad, 1991). Following this, we review three sets of theoretical models—life-history models, Sexual Strategies Theory, and a model of strategic pluralism—that might explain the large amount of within-sex variation that exists on most sociosexual attitudes and behaviors. We then review and attempt to integrate nearly all of the published and several unpublished empirical investigations of sociosexuality. This empirical review is divided into two major sections: (1) patterns of relations between sociosexuality and other individual difference measures (e.g., personality traits, attachment styles, gender roles), and (2) patterns of relations between sociosexuality and mating proclivities (e.g., mating motives, romantic partner preferences, relationship initiation styles, patterns of romantic interaction, early family history, and cross-cultural differences). We conclude by discussing several important future directions and implications of sociosexuality. These include the possible biological/evolutionary origins of sociosexuality, the different motives that might generate restricted versus unrestricted sociosexual orientations, the cues that may signal or convey restricted versus unrestricted orientations in each gender, and the effects that restricted versus unrestricted sociosexual orientations might have on the functioning and well-being of established romantic relationships.

INTRODUCTION

In the 1940s, Alfred Kinsey and his colleagues embarked on the most extensive and ambitious study of human sexuality ever conducted. Kinsey's primary objective was to document population norms—means, standard deviations, and ranges—for different kinds of sexual attitudes, preferences, and behaviors. One of the most striking features of his data was the tremendous variability in many of what he termed *sociosexual* attitudes and behaviors (see Kinsey, Pomeroy, & Martin, 1948; Kinsey, Pomeroy, Martin, & Gebhard, 1953). The past 20 years of research has confirmed that individuals vary considerably on several core facets of sociosexuality, including the desire for many versus few sex partners, past sexual behavior (e.g., number of lifetime sex partners), anticipated sexual behavior (e.g., number of sex partners expected in the future), willingness to engage in concurrent sexual relationships (e.g., extramarital affairs), the frequency of sexual fantasies about people other than one's current or primary partner, and attitudes about engaging in "casual" sex, i.e., sex without much emotional closeness or commitment. (For relevant reviews, see Buss and Schmitt, 1993; Gangestad and Simpson, 2000; Laumann, Gagnon, Michael, and Michaels, 1994).

Given that many of these sociosexual attitudes, preferences, and behaviors are correlated, Gangestad and Simpson (1990) argued that they might tap a unique individual difference dimension reflecting *sociosexual orientation*. Individuals at one end of this continuous dimension—those who have a more restricted sociosexual orientation—may expect greater love, commitment, and emotional closeness and, thus, may require more time in relationships before having sexual intercourse with romantic partners. Restricted individuals, it turns out, do claim that they must feel emotionally close to romantic partners before having sex with them, report having fewer different mates in the past, and rarely if ever have sex with someone on only one occasion (Simpson & Gangestad, 1991). Unrestricted individuals anchor the other end of the continuous sociosexuality dimension. They require less time in a relationship before having sex and are more comfortable engaging in sex without love, closeness, or commitment. Such persons, in fact, report that they could and sometimes do enjoy casual sex with different partners, have had multiple partners, and have engaged in "one-night stands" (Simpson & Gangestad, 1991).

Some of the variance underlying sociosexual attitudes and behaviors is, of course, linked to gender differences. Relative to women, men tend to have more permissive attitudes about casual sex, fantasize more often about having sex with different partners, and engage in more unrestricted sociosexual behaviors (see Buss & Schmitt, 1993; Eysenck, 1976; Griffit & Hatfield, 1985; Hendrick, Hendrick, Slapion-Foote, & Foote, 1985). On virtually every indicator of sociosexuality, however, the variability in responses that exists *within* each gender greatly exceeds that which exists *between* men and women (Hendrick et al., 1985; Kinsey et al., 1948; Kinsey et al., 1953; Simpson & Gangestad, 1991). Gangestad and Simpson's (2000) re-analyses of data reported by Buss and Schmitt (1993), for example, reveal that gender differences account for only about 16% of the variance in seeking short-term mates, 9% of the variance in the number of sex partners desired within a specific period of time, and 20% of the variance in the probability of consenting to sex after knowing an attractive, opposite-sex person a short period of time. Similarly, a recent meta-analysis found that gender differences in interest in casual sex explain only 25% of the variance in this dimension (Oliver & Hyde, 1996). In fact, approximately 30% of U.S. men have *less* favorable attitudes about casual sex relative to the median attitudes of U.S. women (Gangestad & Simpson, 2000).

These data indicate that socialization differences associated with gender explain only a fraction of the total variance underlying sociosexuality, at least in European and North American samples. What else accounts for this variability? What theoretical models are capable of explaining the large amount of within-sex variation observed for most sociosexual attitudes and behaviors? How do measures of sociosexuality correlate with other constructs that tap personality traits and mating strategies? These are some of the questions that we address in this chapter.

The chapter is divided into four sections. In the first section, we briefly review the history and origins of the sociosexuality construct. In doing so, we discuss the way in which within-sex variation in sociosexual attitudes and behaviors was conceptualized prior to the development of the sociosexuality construct, and we note some limitations of earlier views. We then describe the Sociosexual Orientation Inventory (SOI: Simpson & Gangestad, 1991; Simpson, 1998) and the original sociosexuality construct (Gangestad & Simpson, 1990), both of which were developed to offer a better and more comprehensive theoretical account of the within-sex variation underlying sociosexual attitudes and behaviors.

In the second section, we review recent theories of human mating that offer slightly different interpretations for why individuals vary so much in sociosexual orientation, and why many men tend to be more unrestricted than most women. Specifically, we describe and summarize three contemporary models of human mating that elucidate how and why both short-term *and* long-term mating strategies could have evolved within each gender.

In section three, we review virtually all published (and several unpublished) studies that have investigated sociosexuality using the SOI. As a rule, these studies have examined how people with restricted and unrestricted sociosexual orientations differ in terms of: (a) *personality dimensions* (e.g., the Big Five, attachment styles, masculinity vs. femininity), and (b) *mating strategies/tactics* (e.g., motives for entering sexual relationships, specific mate preferences, the display of short-term vs. long-term mating strategies). In the final section, we highlight some important directions for future research. We conclude by outlining some of the possible implications that restricted and unrestricted sociosexual orientations might have for understanding the maintenance, stability, and emotional well-being of long-term romantic relationships, particularly marriages.

HISTORY AND ORIGINS OF SOCIOSEXUALITY

Early Descriptive Research

Several early, independent lines of research investigated the within-sex variation evident in sociosexual attitudes and behaviors. Most of the earliest work focused on how global attitudes about different sex-related topics (e.g., homosexuality, pornography, prostitution, abortion, sexual permissiveness) were related to an individual's level of erotophobia (Byrne & Sheffield, 1965; Fisher, 1984; Gerrard, 1980; Gerrard & Gibbons, 1982), sex guilt (Mosher, 1979; O'Grady, Janda, & Gillen, 1979), and social/sexual anxiety (Leary & Dobbins, 1983). As a group, these studies revealed that people who espouse more conservative views on these issues are more erotophobic (i.e., fearful of sex) and report higher levels of sex guilt and social/sexual anxiety.

Early research also documented that certain personality traits and individual difference measures systematically covary with several sociosexual attitudes and behaviors. For example, individuals who are more extraverted (Eysenck, 1974; 1976), more disinhibited (Zuckerman, Bone, Neary, Mangelsdorff, & Brustman, 1972; Zuckerman, Tushup, & Finner, 1976), and who score higher in self-monitoring (Snyder, Simpson, & Gangestad, 1986) and psychoticism (Eysenck, 1976) all hold more permissive attitudes toward uncommitted sex and are more likely to engage in unrestricted forms of sexual behavior relative to individuals who score lower on these traits. Compared to less permissive persons, individuals who are more sexually permissive also tend to be less religious (Byrne, 1983; Reiss, 1967; Zuckerman et al., 1976), less politically and socially conservative (Curran, Neff, & Lippold, 1973; D'Augelli & Cross, 1975; Eysenck, 1976; Griffit, 1973), and better educated (Alston & Tucker, 1973; Hunt, 1974).

Unfortunately, the vast majority of early research on sociosexual attitudes and behaviors was atheoretical. One notable exception was work that endorsed a "sex-drive" view (e.g., Eysenck, 1976; Kelley, 1978; Libby, Gray, & White, 1978; Reiss, 1982). Proponents of this view claimed that individual differences in sociosexuality might be attributable to variation in general interest in sex, with more unrestricted persons simply having stronger "sex-drives" than their restricted counterparts. This perspective suffered from two major shortcomings. First, it did not conceptualize sociosexual attitudes and behaviors in the context of ongoing relationships (where sex and sexuality frequently have their strongest impact on people). Second, early "sex-drive" models predicted that two markers of general interest in sex—willingness to engage in sex without emotional ties, and the frequency of sex in a committed relationship—should be highly correlated given that each variable should, in theory, be a manifestation of greater general interest in sex (cf. Kelley, 1978). As we shall see, this assumption proved to be incorrect.

The Sociosexuality Inventory and Construct

Realizing the need for a validated measure and theoretical construct capable of explaining the variation underlying sociosexuality, Gangestad and Simpson (1990) launched a program of research on the topic. Informed by earlier work on personality and sexuality (Eysenck, 1976; Snyder et al., 1986), Simpson and Gangestad (1991) developed and validated a short self-report measure—the Sociosexual Orientation Inventory (SOI)—that was designed to assess restricted versus unrestricted sociosexual orientations in heterosexual persons (see also Simpson, 1998). The SOI measures five components of sociosexuality: (1) the number of different sex partners (where "sex" connotes sexual intercourse) in the past year; (2) the number of "one-night" stands; (3) the number of sex partners anticipated in the next 5 years; (4) the frequency of sexual fantasies involving persons other than the current (or most recent) romantic partner; and (5) attitudes toward engaging in casual, uncommitted sex. These five components are weighted and then summed to form a single sociosexual orientation score (see Simpson & Gangestad, 1991, for information on weighting and scoring). Higher scores reflect a more "unrestricted" sociosexual orientation, and lower scores reflect a more "restricted" orientation. Although the terms unrestricted and restricted are used for convenience to describe high versus low scorers, the SOI is a continuously distributed scale. One implication of this is that many people score closer to the middle of the scale and, therefore, exhibit a mixture of restricted and unrestricted characteristics. Simpson and Gangestad confirmed that individual differences in several aspects of sexuality—satisfaction with sex, sex-related guilt, and sex-related anxiety—were *not* highly correlated with individual differences in sociosexuality. They also argued that unrestricted sociosexuality differs from sexual promiscuity in that unrestricted people, although more willing to engage in sex without love and commitment, still prefer being involved in stable, serially monogamous relationships (unlike promiscuous people).

When validating the SOI, Simpson and Gangestad (1991) also found that, contrary to a "sex-drive" perspective, the frequency of sexual intercourse was *not* significantly correlated with willingness to engage in uncommitted sex with different partners (see also Hendrick et al., 1985; Snyder et al., 1986). In other words, individual differences in the preferred frequency of sex were distinct from individual differences in preference for sexual variety (e.g., wanting sex with multiple vs. only one partner). Though counter to a "sex-drive" perspective, these results make sense when viewed from an evolutionary standpoint. The amount of time, level of commitment, and strength of emotional bonds that an individual requires before having sex with someone for the first time should have been shaped by different selection pressures in our evolutionary past than those that shaped the desire for frequent sex in committed relationships (see Mellen, 1981; Symons, 1979). During our ancestral past, uncommitted sex and frequent sex should typically have been associated with different levels of relationship investment. Uncommitted sex should have covaried with a lack of willingness to invest in long-term mateships (Buss & Schmitt, 1993; Symons, 1979). Frequent sex in close, established relationships, in contrast, should have been systematically linked with—and may have fueled—greater investment in the relationship (Mellen, 1981).

Various models have been developed to explain variation in social and mating behavior, not only within and between the sexes but also across societies. Most models have focused on how different social role requirements (e.g., Eagly & Wood, 1999) or gender-role socialization processes (e.g., Lytton & Romney, 1991) could have generated behavioral differences in women and men. These models have identified important proximal causes of social and sexual behavior (i.e., conditions in the immediate environment that instigate, sustain, or terminate certain behavioral tendencies), but they have not fully addressed more distal causes of behavior (e.g., the evolutionary forces that gave rise to the adaptive value of certain mating propensities in the first place). As a result, these models do not fully explain *why* individuals preferentially engage in certain mating strategies and tactics in certain social and developmental contexts. By considering how natural selection should have shaped mating motivations and behaviors in humans, evolutionary approaches can supplement other approaches by providing distal reasons for why different mating orientations exist, when they should be expressed, and why they might change across development. Both proximal and distal explanations are required in order to understand human mating completely.

To gain a deeper theoretical understanding of *why* so much within-sex variation exists in sociosexuality, Gangestad and Simpson (1990) turned to basic evolutionary principles of mating. They did so because, throughout evolutionary history, sex and mating were directly tied to reproduction, which in turn was intimately linked to reproductive success and differential fitness. Indeed, if selection pressures shaped *any* form of human social behavior, sex and mating behaviors would have been prime theoretical candidates.

Trivers' (1972) parental investment theory has served as the foundation on which many contemporary theories of human mating are based. According to this theory, the *initial* amount of investment that each gender must devote to offspring should affect what males and females desire and value in mates. Parental investment theory primarily explains why the gender that initially invests more in offspring (usually women in humans, due to pregnancy, childbirth, and lactation) tends to be more discriminating and more restricted in mating behavior, and why the gender that initially invests less (usually men) is often less discriminating and more unrestricted (see Trivers, 1985). Nevertheless, the theory also posits that, for species in which biparental care is critical to infant survival (i.e., humans), "mixed" mating strategies also could have evolved within each gender. Until recently, this additional feature of the theory has been neglected or overlooked by many scholars.

For species whose offspring require substantial care, Trivers (1972) proposed that mating decisions should be governed by three mate criteria: (1) parental investment (individuals should, on average, be attracted to mates who can and will invest in their offspring); (2) fitness/viability (individuals should, on average, be attracted to mates who show signs of being healthy and in good physical condition); and (3) certainty of parenthood (individuals should, on average, be attracted to mates whose offspring are certain to be their own). Because women bear children, certainty of maternity is never in doubt. Certainty of paternity, however, is not guaranteed because women can bear the children of other men. Given this disparity, certainty of parenthood should not be a mating concern for women. The other two criteria, however, should have a direct bearing on women's reproductive fitness and, therefore, ought to be weighed heavily in their mating decisions.

Cognizant of these basic principles, Gangestad and Simpson (1990) proposed that women in evolutionary history who adopted a restricted sociosexual orientation might have done so to extract more parental investment from their mates, thereby increasing their offspring's chances of survival and, ultimately, their own reproductive fitness. Women who pursued an unrestricted orientation, by comparison, might have done so to attract mates who had better physical health or fitness, which might have elevated their reproductive fitness by passing on the "good genes" of these desirable mates to their own offspring. In a detailed set of analyses, Gangestad and Simpson (1990) demonstrated that (a) genetic (heritable) variance underlies the SOI (see also Martin & Bailey, 1999), (b) the SOI shares variance with two higher-order personality dimensions known to contain genetic variance (extraversion and lack of constraint), and (c) the genetic variance that underlies sociosexuality could have been maintained by frequency-dependent selection processes.[1]

The original sociosexuality construct had two principle limitations. First, frequency-dependent mating strategies, though possible, may have been less likely to evolve than strategies that were responsive to events in individuals' past or current environments (e.g., ecologically contingent strategies; Gangestad & Simpson, 2000). Second, the original sociosexuality construct did not adequately explain why men vary so much in their sociosexual orientations.

RECENT THEORETICAL MODELS EXPLAINING VARIATION IN SOCIOSEXUALITY

Recent theoretical models have redressed these drawbacks. Most models of human mating draw a clear distinction between two general types of mating strategies[2]: short-term strategies (enacted by individuals who have unrestricted sociosexual orientations), and long-term strategies (enacted by those who have restricted sociosexual orientations). Three major theoretical models are particularly germane to understanding variation in long-term (restricted) versus short-term (unrestricted) mating strategies in both genders.

Life-History Models

According to life-history theory (see Stearns, 1992), humans should have evolved to use alternate, ecologically contingent behavioral strategies and tactics to solve the major, recurrent problems associated with survival, growth, and reproduction during evolutionary history. Depending on the environments in which individuals are raised,

---

[1] According to this form of selection, the "value" of enacting a restricted orientation depends on how common it is in the local environment relative to an unrestricted orientation. The rarer a given orientation or strategy, the more valuable it tends to be.

[2] Mating strategies are defined as integrated sets of adaptations that organize and guide an individual's reproductive effort. They influence how individuals select mates, how much mating effort they expend, how much parental effort they expend, and so on. Mating strategies are *not* necessarily formulated consciously or even accessible to awareness. They usually are defined as genetically based programs (i.e., decision rules) that individuals use to allocate their somatic (e.g., growth and development of the body) and reproductive (e.g., mating and parenting) effort to specific alternative phenotypes (i.e., mating tactics) in adaptive ways. Tactics, in turn, are the specific actions and behaviors that individuals engage in when pursuing a given strategy. A mating strategy often entails multiple tactics.

"optimal" solutions to problems at earlier stages of development (e.g., enhancing one's chances of survival, given a specific history of caregiving from parents) should affect later stages of development (e.g., one's pattern or style of mating and parenting in adulthood). Life-history models propose that, across development, individuals should invest different amounts of time, energy, and resources at different rates of expenditure into somatic effort (e.g., growth and development of the body) versus reproductive effort (e.g., mating effort and parenting effort), contingent on local environmental conditions.

Inspired by life-history theory, Belsky, Steinberg, and Draper (1991) developed a life-span model of human social development. They conjecture that, in our evolutionary past, early social experiences provided children with diagnostic information about the kinds of social and physical environments they would most likely encounter during their lifetimes. This information may have helped individuals adopt appropriate mating strategies—strategies that could have increased their reproductive fitness—in future environments. Hinde (1986), for instance, proposed that if harsh environments induced maternal rejection when competition for limited resources was intense, offspring who were aggressive and noncooperative may have had higher reproductive fitness as adults than offspring who lacked these opportunistic attributes. Conversely, offspring raised in less hostile environments that contained abundant resources might have increased their reproductive fitness by developing cooperative, communal long-term relationships with others in adulthood.

The Belsky et al. (1991) model contains 5 stages. It proposes that (1) early contextual factors in the family of origin (e.g., the amount of stress, spousal harmony, financial resources) impact (2) early childrearing experiences (e.g., the level of sensitive, supportive, and responsive caregiving). Across time, these experiences affect (3) psychological and behavioral development (e.g., patterns of attachment, internal working models), which influences (4) somatic development (how quickly sexual maturation is reached) and, ultimately, (5) the adoption of alternate reproductive strategies in adulthood. Two developmental trajectories are believed to culminate in two different mating strategies. One strategy involves adopting a short-term, opportunistic orientation to mating and parenting in which sexual intercourse with multiple partners occurs earlier in life, pair bonds are shorter and less stable, and parental investment is lower. According to the model, this "unrestricted" strategy is geared toward increasing the *quantity* of offspring. The second strategy involves adopting a long-term, investing orientation in which sex occurs later in life with fewer partners, pair bonds are longer and more stable, and parental investment is higher. This "restricted" strategy ostensibly increases the *quality* of offspring. Research has supported several segments of this model (see, for example, Barber, 1998b; Simpson, 1999).

According to the Belsky et al. (1991) model, therefore, much of the variation in sociosexuality within each gender can be understood as responses to certain types of early social experiences (i.e., being reared in stable/abundant vs. unstable/harsh environments) that shunt individuals down different developmental pathways.[3] One limitation of the model is that it does not explain why men are more inclined to engage in unrestricted, short-term mating, and why women are more likely to engage in restricted, long-term mating.

---

[3] Chisholm (1993, 1996) has proposed a similar model based on local mortality rates. According to this model, local mortality may serve as a proximal environmental cue that shunts people down different developmental pathways. Higher local mortality rates should lead people to adopt short-term mating strategies (i.e., early, rapid reproduction and investment in more offspring), whereas lower local mortality rates should be associated with long-term mating strategies (i.e., delayed reproduction and investment in fewer offspring).

Sexual Strategies Theory

Buss and Schmitt (1993) developed Sexual Strategies Theory (SST) to offer a more complete evolutionary account of why different sexual strategies exist both between and within men and women. According to SST, human mating is "strategic" in that people seek out mates to solve specific adaptive problems that our ancestors recurrently faced. Mate preferences and mating strategies, therefore, are believed to have been molded by specific selection pressures in evolutionary history. SST contends that mating strategies should be context-dependent, resulting in both short-term and long-term strategies in each gender. To the extent that women and men confronted different adaptive problems in evolutionary history, different principles should govern when and how often the sexes adopt different mating strategies.

Many of SST's core assumptions are grounded in Trivers' (1972) parental investment theory. As discussed, Trivers conjectured that one principle force driving sexual selection should have been the minimal amount of initial parental investment that women and men were obliged to devote to their offspring. Because women tend to be the more "investing" gender in humans (due to fertilization, internal gestation, placentation, and lactation) and they are able to have a relatively small number of offspring in their lives, women should be more selective and discriminating than men when choosing mates. Conversely, because men do not necessarily have to provide high initial parental investment and can conceivably have larger numbers of offspring, men should be less discriminating and more inclined to compete for mates than women. Accordingly, SST explains how and why ancestral men could have benefited from adopting short-term (i.e., unrestricted) mating strategies, and how and why ancestral women could have benefited from enacting long-term (i.e., restricted) strategies. The theory also identifies a few of the circumstances in which both genders might have benefited from adopting or shifting to alternate ("mixed") mating strategies.

According to SST, the potential costs of long-term mating should have been greater for men than for women in many situations. Men should have adopted long-term mating strategies when doing so allowed them to gain greater control over a woman's lifetime reproductive potential, when more resources or better social alliances could have been forged through cooperation with a mate's extended family, when women with higher mate value could be attracted (especially if such women demanded greater commitment and investment), when the costs of unsuccessfully pursuing short-term mates were very high, or when greater cooperation from one's current mate needed to be secured (see Buss & Schmitt, 1993).

Even though the potential costs of short-term mating should have been steeper for women than men, SST suggests that there could have been situations in which short-term mating yielded greater fitness advantages for women. Short-term mating strategies might have expedited the extraction of resources from men, allowed women to gauge a man's prospects as a long-term mate more accurately, or helped women judge their own mate value better (e.g., by determining how many desirable men they could attract). Short-term strategies might also have been used by women to assess a potential mate's true intentions or actual personal characteristics, including his mate value. In certain contexts, short-term mating may also have offered women greater protection, especially those not involved in long-term relationships. At base, however, SST contends that women in evolutionary history should have used short-term strategies to identify and screen men who might be good long-term mates. In other words, SST claims that women's short-term mating was primarily rooted in long-term motivations and goals.

Through its focus on gender differences, SST explains why, from an evolutionary perspective, many women engage in more long-term (restricted) mating strategies, and why many men display more short-term (unrestricted) strategies. However, SST does not specify the contextual variables that should motivate men and women to adopt alternate mating strategies, and it says little about how an individual's personal attributes and immediate environment might elicit different mating strategies. More important, SST does not explain why considerably *more* variation in sociosexuality and related mating strategies/tactics exists within men and women than between them. If short-term strategies are so well-suited to enhancing the reproductive fitness of men given how they reproduce, and if long-term strategies are better-suited to enhancing the reproductive fitness of women given how they reproduce, why do a sizable percentage of women pursue short-term (unrestricted) mating strategies? And why do a notable percentage of men pursue long-term (restricted) ones?

Strategic Pluralism

The Strategic Pluralism Model (SPM; Gangestad & Simpson, 2000) was developed to address some of the shortcomings of SST. SPM blends principles from "good-provider" and "good-genes" models of sexual selection to account for the variation in mating strategies observed both within *and* between the sexes. Building from the original sociosexuality construct (Gangestad & Simpson, 1990), SPM posits that women evolved to evaluate men on two basic dimensions: the degree to which a potential mate is likely to be a good provider/investor in offspring, and the degree to which a potential mate shows evidence of good genetic quality. Assuming that it would have been difficult for most individuals to attract and retain mates who scored high on both dimensions (given that such "stellar" mates should have been desired and may have been constantly pursued by other attractive people), SPM contends that most women in evolutionary history probably had to make "trade-offs" between the two dimensions when choosing mates. The way in which trade-offs were made should have depended on the attributes a woman possessed (e.g., her health, physical attractiveness, access to resources) along with the demands of the local environment (e.g., whether it was harsh with scarce resources or benign with plentiful resources). The model also posits that men who possessed higher genetic viability (indexed by variables such as physical symmetry) should have been able to reproduce without investing as much time, energy, and resources in their mates as did less viable men. In other words, men who had higher viability should have been more successful at pursuing a short-term (unrestricted) mating strategy, which both Trivers (1972) and Buss and Schmitt (1993) claim should have been the "default" mating strategy of men. Men who possessed less viability, on the other hand, should have offered their mates greater investment (devoting more time, energy, and exclusive commitment to a single mate). Such men, therefore, should have pursued a long-term (restricted) mating strategy.

SPM also predicts that local environmental conditions should have influenced when short-term or long-term mating strategies were enacted by women and men. In ancestral environments where biparental care was critical to infant survival, good parenting qualities in men should have been valued more by women. Conversely, when pathogens and disease were prevalent, the health and fitness of men should have become more important in mate selection decisions. If women were repeatedly exposed to both types of environments across evolutionary time, they could have evolved to make adaptive trade-off decisions when weighing a mate's investment qualities against his genetic viability, calibrating their decisions to the "demands" of the local environment.

Additional factors should also have influenced the value of male parenting effort. One factor might have been whether or not women had access to resources. Women who had sufficient resources, for instance, should have placed less emphasis on male investment and more on male genetic viability. These same factors should have affected the mating strategies that most men adopted. In environments where biparental care was necessary for infant survival, a larger proportion of men should have devoted more time and effort to parental investment, reducing the variance in men's reproductive success (see Gangestad & Simpson, 2000). When pathogens or disease had particularly pernicious effects on infant mortality, a larger proportion of men should have allotted more time and effort to short-term mating, eventually increasing the variance in men's reproductive success.

In sum, the Strategic Pluralism Model describes how an individual's personal attributes and local environment could have influenced the adoption of different mating strategies in our evolutionary past. Some of the psychological, motivational, and emotional remnants of these evolutionary forces—lust, empathy, compassion, love— remain with us today. SPM also explains why more variation in sociosexuality and associated mating strategies exists within women and men than between them. Despite the fact that most women should have wanted greater investment from men than most men wanted to provide, some women should have "shifted" their mating strategies in facultative, cost-effective ways, depending on their personal and environmental circumstances. Men, in turn, should have tailored their mating strategies to what most women wanted, what they (men) had to offer, and local environmental conditions. Although short-term strategies might have been the "optimal" way for men to increase their reproductive fitness, few males in evolutionary history may have been able to pursue short-term mating successfully, regardless of environmental conditions (see Gangestad & Simpson, 2000). As a consequence, many men—especially those with lower viability—may have shifted to the use of long-term mating strategies.

RECENT EMPIRICAL INVESTIGATIONS OF SOCIOSEXUALITY

There has not been a comprehensive review of the sociosexuality literature since the publication of the Sociosexual Orientation Inventory (SOI; Simpson & Gangestad, 1991). How do individual differences in sociosexual orientation correlate with other theoretically relevant constructs? In this section, we review relevant findings from all published and several unpublished studies that have used the SOI or measures very similar to it. The review focuses primarily on within-sex correlates of sociosexuality for purposes of clarifying what the SOI is and is not related to within each gender. Relevant gender differences, however, are also discussed. The review is structured around how sociosexuality covaries with individual difference measures (personality traits, attachment styles, and masculinity/femininity) as well as measures reflecting different mating strategies (e.g., the motives, preferences, and behaviors associated with short-term and long-term mating).[4]

Sociosexuality and Individual Difference Measures

Sociosexuality and Personality Traits. Several researchers have explored how sociosexuality correlates with dispositional components of personality, including facets of the Big Five personality model. Gangestad and Simpson (1990), for example, documented that the SOI is related to two higher-order personality dimensions, which they labeled *Extraversion* (tapped by measures of social potency, extraversion, and self-monitoring) and *Lack of Constraint* (tapped by measures of disinhibition, lack of harm avoidance, and poor ego control). Individuals with unrestricted sociosexual

---

[4] In the review of empirical investigations that follows, most of the significant correlations between sociosexuality and other measures were low or medium in terms of effect size (i.e., rs ranged between .15 and .40).

orientations tend to be more extraverted, more aggressive, more disinhibited, and more likely to lack control than restricted individuals, who typically score higher on social closeness and well-being.

Using the NEO-Personality Inventory (Costa & McCrae, 1992) and a modified version of the SOI, Wright and Reise (1997) found that unrestricted sociosexuality was most strongly associated with higher extraversion and lower neuroticism in Asian college students, and with lower agreeableness in Caucasian students. More unrestricted women scored higher in extraversion (particularly Asian women) and lower in agreeableness (particularly Caucasian women). Both Asian and Caucasian unrestricted men reported being less agreeable than their restricted counterparts. Caucasian individuals who were more restricted also scored higher in ego development, which signifies better impulse control, greater maturity, and enhanced socialization. Among Asian individuals, however, sociosexuality did not correlate with differential ego development. As a group, unrestricted individuals also reported being more erotophilic, which was the single strongest predictor of sociosexual orientation.

In a follow-up study, Wright (1999) confirmed that higher levels of extraversion and lower agreeableness predict greater unrestrictedness in women. Having a more unrestricted orientation was also associated with greater anger/hostility, more impulsiveness, more excitement-seeking, and less deliberation in women. This cluster of temperamental traits suggests that unrestricted women may be more emotionally labile, adventurous, and pleasure-seeking than their restricted counterparts. By comparison, more restricted women reported being less open to new ideas and values, more depressed, more self-conscious, and more compliant. This suite of characteristics suggests that restricted women prefer more conventional attitudes and behaviors, and are less willing to accept or tolerate deviations from established rules.

In a dissertation, Probst (1999) found a negative relation between sociosexuality and agreeableness in both sexes, confirming that more unrestricted individuals tend to be more difficult to interact with and less trustworthy. Unlike earlier studies, however, sociosexuality was not significantly correlated with extraversion (although restricted individuals did score higher in conscientiousness and lower in openness relative to unrestricted persons). Openness proved to be a particularly good predictor of unrestricted sociosexuality within women in this sample.

Using the California Q-Sort (CAQ; Block, 1978) and a modified version of the SOI, Reise and Wright (1996) found that several other trait-like measures are associated with more unrestricted sociosexuality in men. These include lack of warmth/capacity for close relationships, undependability/irresponsibility, lack of productivity, not feeling guilty about personal matters, being distrustful of other people, claiming to be physically attractive, and not being ethically consistent. The measures that predicted greater unrestricted sociosexuality in women were enjoying sensuous experiences, having unconventional thoughts, constantly comparing oneself to others, viewing oneself as physically attractive, regarding oneself as interesting/attention-grabbing, not being concerned with philosophical matters, adopting different and varied roles, not being conservative, not being moralistic, and not being ethically consistent. The CAQ prototypes of narcissism and psychopathy both predicted greater unrestricted sociosexuality in men. This evidence suggests that emotional immaturity, egocentrism, and lack of self-insight are all tied to an interest in casual sex, and these traits/characteristics could hinder the development of close, long-term relationships.

Schmitt and Buss (2000) examined how sociosexuality was related to four individual difference facets of sexuality: the number of current (ongoing) romantic relationships, the duration of each relationship, the sexual fervor (i.e., erotophilia) of each relationship, and the emotional engagement (i.e., emotional investment) that characterized each relationship. Sociosexuality was negatively correlated with "relationship exclusivity" (indexed by the number and duration of an individual's current romantic relationships). Greater relationship exclusivity (i.e., being more restricted), in turn, was associated with lower extraversion and higher agreeableness in men, and with higher agreeableness and higher conscientiousness in women. Moreover, women and men who scored higher in erotophilia (a correlate of unrestricted sociosexuality) described themselves as more extraverted and less agreeable than did individuals who scored lower, and erotophilic women also described themselves as less conscientious. Finally, both men and women who scored higher in emotional relationship investment (reflective of a restricted sociosexual orientation) claimed that they were slightly more extraverted (an unexpected finding) and highly agreeable.

Sociosexuality and Attachment.   A second major area of research has focused on sociosexuality and attachment (see also Feeney and Noller, chapter 8, this volume). Attachment orientations can be conceptualized as different strategies for regulating negative emotions, particularly in stressful situations (Simpson & Rholes, 1994). At least three primary attachment orientations have been identified in infant–caregiver and adult romantic relationships. Securely attached individuals tend to be comfortable depending on and trusting their attachment figures (e.g., romantic partners), and they turn to them for comfort and support when upset. Avoidantly attached individuals either fear being rejected by their attachment figures (fearful-avoidants) or discount the importance of closeness and intimacy in relationships (dismissive-avoidants). Consequently, avoidant people habitually distance themselves from their romantic partners physically, psychologically, and emotionally, especially when they are distressed. Anxiously attached individuals persistently worry about being abandoned by their romantic partners. As a result, they tend to be clingy, possessive, and hypervigilant to cues that their partners might leave them.

Given this backdrop, Brennan and Shaver (1995) examined relations between sociosexuality and attachment orientations. They documented that avoiding sustained intimacy and emotional dependence in relationships is associated with the tendency to engage in casual, short-term relationships. In particular, unrestricted individuals were more likely to have avoidant attachment orientations. Unrestricted persons were also more inclined to feel greater ambivalence toward their partners (i.e., lacking clear, unconflicted feelings about them), greater frustration with their partners (i.e., pent-up anger due to feelings of being under-appreciated or unloved), and stronger needs to maintain self-reliance (i.e., not asking their partners for help). Unrestricted individuals also scored lower on attachment security, proximity-seeking, and trust/confidence in both their partners and relationships.

Corroborating these results, Simon (1997) found that secure attachment is associated with harboring more negative attitudes about casual sex (i.e., with having a more restricted sociosexual orientation). By contrast, people with dismissive-avoidant and fearful-avoidant attachment orientations held more positive attitudes about casual sex (i.e., they had a more unrestricted orientation). No significant effects were found between attachment orientations and sexual behaviors (as opposed to sexual attitudes). In other words, sexual behaviors did *not* correlate with individuals' attachment orientations in this sample, even though attitudes toward casual sex clearly did.[5]

Examining love schemas, Stephan and Bachman (1999) reported that individuals classified as clingy (corresponding to anxious attachment), skittish (corresponding to avoidance), and fickle (corresponding to discomfort with both independence and closeness) scored intermediately on the SOI and did not differ from people with either

---

[5] Barber (1998a) found that attachment security was linked with greater restricted sociosexuality in women, but with unrestricted sociosexuality in men. This unexpected result for men is difficult to interpret and is at odds with most other studies.

"secure" or "casual/uninterested" love schemas (the former being more restricted than the latter). Relative to fickle or casual/uninterested people, however, those with secure love schemas reported wanting more emotional sex, which is indicative of having a more restricted sociosexual orientation.[6]

Sociosexuality, Masculinity/Femininity, and Gender Roles.   A third area of work has examined how sociosexuality relates to masculinity/femininity and gender roles. Mikach and Bailey (1999) hypothesized that unrestricted women might be more masculine than restricted women, perhaps due to differential masculinization of the brain in response to prenatal androgens. They tested this idea in a community sample of heterosexual women, half of whom reported a large number of lifetime sexual partners (25–200) and half of whom reported a smaller number (10 or less). Women who had more lifetime partners claimed to have greater interest in casual sex and scored higher on three dimensions of masculinity: recalling having been more masculine during childhood, considering themselves more masculine as adults, and being rated (by interviewers) as more physically and behaviorally masculine. Despite these significant associations, the mean SOI scores of the two groups were not significantly different.[7]

Extending this line of work, Walker, Tokar, and Fischer (2000) examined whether different masculinity factors correlate with sociosexuality (SOI) scores in undergraduate men. As a group, more unrestricted men held less liberal gender role attitudes than did more restricted men. This is consistent with the notion that a preference for nonintimate sexuality (i.e., having an interest in unrestricted, short-term sex) might reinforce men's adherence to more traditional, less egalitarian gender role beliefs, especially those that are more closely linked with masculinity in our society.

In a recent study conducted in Scotland and Northern Ireland, Cunningham and Russell (2002) found a positive connection between sociosexuality and scores on the Bem Sex Role Inventory (BSRI; Bem, 1974), with unrestricted women and men both scoring higher in masculinity. Unrestricted individuals also rated a potential romantic partner's commitment and status as less important and their physical attractiveness as more important than did restricted people. Sex-typing (indexed by BSRI scores), however, was a stronger predictor of these partner preferences than sociosexuality was.

Investigating sexual orientation and sociosexuality, Bailey, Gaulin, Agyei, and Gladue (1994) found that although lesbian and heterosexual women did not differ in their sociosexuality (SOI) scores, gay men were, on average, more unrestricted than heterosexual men. When SOI scores were broken down into the behavioral and attitudinal components, however, gay men scored higher than heterosexual men on only the behavioral component. No component differences emerged for women. These findings suggest that gay men may have more short-term sex partners than heterosexual men due to differences in opportunity rather than inherent psychological differences between the two groups.

---

[6] Two unpublished studies have reported null results concerning the relation between attachment orientations and sociosexuality. Januszewski (1997) administered the Adult Attachment Interview (AAI; Main & Goldwyn, 1994) to African-Americans and European-Americans. No significant relation between AAI attachment and SOI scores emerged in the total sample. Within each ethnic group, however, more dismissive (avoidant) people had more unrestricted sociosexual attitudes than did secure/autonomous people. In an African-American sample, Wensley (2000) found no relation between various romantic attachment measures and sociosexual orientation, contrary to both previous findings in general and Januszewski's findings for African-Americans in particular.

[7] In a recent study where trained raters evaluated the attractiveness of photographed women, Campbell, Cronk, Milroy, and Simpson (2003) found that women who reported being more unrestricted were rated by males as less attractive, less feminine, and poorer long-term mates compared to women who reported being more restricted.

Finally, Seal and Agostinelli (1994) investigated sociosexuality and high-risk decision making, particularly with regard to sex. They discovered that more unrestricted people tended to be more impulsive when making decisions, took more risks, and were more responsive to immediate situational demands and cues. Unrestricted individuals also reported having had more different sex partners in the past 3 years with whom condoms were *not* used, suggesting that they might be at greater risk than restricted individuals for contracting AIDS or other sexually-transmitted diseases.

In summary, mounting evidence indicates that unrestricted individuals tend to be more extraverted, less agreeable, more erotophilic, more disinhibited, more impulsive, more likely to take risks, and more insecurely (avoidantly) attached. Restricted individuals, on the other hand, tend to be more introverted, more agreeable, more erotophobic, more socially constrained, less impulsive, less likely to take risks, and more securely attached. Possible links between sociosexuality and masculinity, though provocative, remain inconclusive.

The constellation of personal characteristics possessed by unrestricted individuals—heightened sociability, disinhibition, risk-taking, and avoidance of emotional intimacy—are likely to help these individuals pursue short-term mating strategies more effectively and successfully. Similarly, the cluster of characteristics possessed by restricted individuals—greater introversion, self-control, impulse control, and attraction to emotional intimacy and commitment—should facilitate the efficient and successful enactment of long-term mating strategies. What still remains unclear is whether sociosexuality should be considered a stable, trait-like dimension, or whether it should be viewed as a more labile individual difference that fluctuates across the life span and changes in response to varying environmental contexts. This general issue is addressed in the next section.

Sociosexuality and Mating Tendencies

Gangestad and Simpson's (2000) Strategic Pluralism Model (SPM) describes how different environmental conditions, and the cues that signal them, should affect trade-offs between parental investment and genetic viability, thereby shaping individual differences in sociosexuality. Differences in sociosexual orientation, therefore, should reflect the enactment of different mating strategies and tactics within each gender. In the past decade, several studies have investigated the way in which individual differences in sociosexuality correlate with mating strategies and related behaviors, ranging from the motives that people have for entering and maintaining romantic relationships, to the criteria they use when selecting partners for short-term versus long-term sexual relationships, to the enactment of short-term and long-term mating strategies and the verbal and nonverbal cues that may signal them.

Sociosexuality and Mating Motives. Previous research (Simpson & Gangestad, 1991; 1992) suggests that restricted individuals harbor different relationship motives than their unrestricted counterparts. Jones (1998), for instance, found that restricted individuals (relative to unrestricted ones) indicate that greater intrinsic motivation (e.g., to seek mutual satisfaction in relationships) explains why they tend to get involved in and maintain romantic relationships. Restricted individuals also experience greater commitment in their relationships than do unrestricted individuals, and the association between restricted sociosexuality and greater commitment is mediated through heightened intrinsic motivation. Jones also found that sociosexuality is not correlated with various extrinsic motivations (e.g., seeking relationships/partners in order to obtain rewarding outcomes).

Greiling and Buss (2000) compared restricted and unrestricted women's cost–benefit evaluations of short-term mating, particularly extra-pair mating. Restricted and unrestricted women differed substantially in the nature and magnitude of perceived benefits. Relative to restricted women, unrestricted women perceived greater sexual benefits (e.g., having a partner willing to experiment sexually, obtaining greater arousal, being appreciated sexually, experiencing the novelty of a new partner), resource benefits (e.g., receiving expensive clothing, jewelry, gifts), and improvement of their attraction and seduction skills as positive outcomes of short-term, extra-pair mating. For men, sociosexuality was not systematically associated with any particular short-term benefits.

Extending this line of work, Bleske-Rechek and Buss (2001) investigated how sociosexuality impacts individuals' preferences for opposite-sex friends and their motivations for initiating and ending opposite-sex friendships. Unrestricted women and men rated sexual attraction and the desire for possible sex as more important reasons for launching opposite-sex friendships, and a lack or loss of these attributes as more important reasons for dissolving them.

Townsend (1995) has investigated the emotional-motivational mechanisms that mediate sexual attraction in each sex. He proposes that these mechanisms differ for men and women, and that the primary motivation behind selecting mates for most women is gaining high-quality paternal investment, regardless of their sociosexual history. Even when women do not want to become emotionally attached to romantic partners, they often report that sexual intercourse makes them feel emotionally vulnerable and leads them to contemplate their partners' level of investment. In contrast, the more sex partners men have, the more they desire sexual relations without emotional involvement, the less they are concerned about their partners' investment, and the less emotionally vulnerable they feel. An unrestricted sexual history, therefore, may make it easier for men to separate sex from emotional attachment. For women, however, sex may elicit stronger emotional bonding, the desire for more investment, and greater emotional vulnerability.

Pursuing a related program of work, Townsend and Wasserman (1997) found that women's sociosexuality did not predict their ratings of the sexual attractiveness of male targets. Unrestricted men, however, rated female targets as generally more sexually attractive than did restricted men. Townsend and Wasserman (1998) also documented that unrestricted men report stronger sexual desire when viewing attractive models, whereas restricted men show more interest in the social traits presumably possessed by attractive models. Unrestricted and restricted women, by comparison, do not differ in their sexual desire for attractive male models based solely on their physical features. However, unrestricted women do report being more willing to have sex with attractive models, are more interested in their popularity, and are less interested in their willingness to commit compared to restricted women. In addition, information about the models' ambitions and income affected women's willingness to date, have sex with, and potentially marry them, even when women's scores on sociosexuality (the SOI) were statistically controlled. Townsend (1999) concludes that, similar to restricted women, unrestricted women have cognitive mechanisms geared to assess the quality of parental investment (cf. Buss & Schmitt, 1993). Unrestricted women, however, may overestimate their chances of extracting investments from potential mates, and may underestimate the strength of their emotional attachments, especially to physically attractive mates.[8]

---

[8] Townsend (1993; 1995) also found that women with multiple partners wanted to marry at the same age as did women with fewer partners, but more unrestricted women were less likely to believe they would marry someone they would meet in college. In contrast, men's SOI scores and number of past sex partners was positively correlated with the desire to delay marriage, and unrestricted men were more likely to believe they might marry someone from college. Townsend suggests that, particularly in women, unrestricted sociosexuality may represent a mating "stage" rather than a stable mating strategy that remains constant across the lifespan.

Compared to men, women also feel more distress, degradation, and exploitation when their sexual partner's level of investment is seen as inadequate, regardless of their past sociosexual history. Townsend (1995) postulates that it is not engaging in sexual behavior with little or no commitment per se that generates these negative feelings; it is the lack of control over the partner's level of investment that does. These conclusions fit with Simpson's (1987) findings that unrestricted women report greater emotional distress following romantic breakups than restricted women do. If unrestricted women believe that they have made greater sexual or emotional investments at earlier points in their romantic relationships than is true of most restricted women, the heightened postdissolution distress of unrestricted women could stem from greater perceived disparities between the investments they made relative to what their former partners made or what they actually received from them.

In coded interviews, Townsend (1995) documented the various techniques that unrestricted women use to mitigate negative emotional reactions to low-investing men. These techniques include dating other men, keeping a reliable mate "in reserve," suppressing their emotions, and avoiding low-investing partners altogether. They also "test" their partners for evidence of investment by looking for signs that their partners become jealous, are dominant, or are willing to be affectionate in relevant situations. Even the most unrestricted women claim that they withhold sex if their partners' investment drops below a minimally acceptable threshold.[9]

Sociosexuality and Mate Preferences.   Given the divergent motives and goals they possess for romantic/sexual relationships, restricted and unrestricted individuals should be attracted to different types of romantic partners. Wiederman and Dubois (1998) examined short-term mating preferences in men and women, focusing on the importance they placed on six partner attributes: physical attractiveness, financial resources, generosity, sexual experience/interest, current relationship status (single vs. involved), and desired commitment. Men rated short-term mates as more desirable than women did. Men also placed more emphasis on physical attractiveness in short-term mates, whereas women weighted financial resources, generosity, sexual experience/interest, and current relationship status more heavily. Unrestricted men and women viewed short-term mates with greater sexual experience/interest as more desirable, and unrestricted women rated short-term mates who were *not* involved in an exclusive relationship as most desirable.[10]

Sprecher, Regan, McKinney, Maxwell, and Wazienski (1997) also found that sociosexuality is related to preferences for sexual experience among women. Unrestricted women rated moderate and extensive levels of experience in male partners as more desirable than did restricted women. Restricted women, on the other hand, rated partners' sexual inexperience as more desirable than did unrestricted women. Among men, sociosexuality was unrelated to preferences for sexual experience in a partner. Sprecher and her colleagues conjecture that this might be due to the fact that men were much more unrestricted than women in their sample. Moreover, previous research (e.g., Sprecher & Regan, 1996) suggests that men who have little or no sexual

---

[9] Studying a community sample (18–54 years in age), Bleske-Rechek and Buss (2001) did not find a gender difference in SOI scores, which contradicts past research on younger samples (e.g., college students). They conjecture that gender differences in sociosexuality might decrease with age as women's use of short-term mating increases. Furthermore, women may become more skilled at controlling their emotional involvement and gaining greater investment from their romantic partners as they grow older (Townsend, 1995). If they do not receive sufficient investment, however, they should terminate current relationships and search for new ones, leading older women to acquire a larger number of mates.

[10] When using a different method (policy-capturing), fewer sex differences emerged and more within-sex variation was found.

experience often want to gain more, but cannot because of a scarcity of willing mates. As a result, the preferences of restricted men may mimic those of unrestricted men.

A considerable amount of research has investigated links between sociosexuality and the importance of physical attractiveness and status in potential mates. Besides the Cunningham and Russell (2002) study previously discussed, Townsend (1993) has found that unrestricted men and women, relative to restricted ones, emphasize their spouses' physical attractiveness more and are more willing to support them financially. Although actual socioeconomic resources did not correlate with women's SOI scores in this study, unrestricted men reported higher anticipated (future) incomes. Townsend speculates that unrestricted men might use their future economic resource potential as a tactic to attract short-term mates.

In a series of studies, Simpson and Gangestad (1992) tested whether restricted and unrestricted individuals desire and actually acquire romantic partners who have different attributes. As predicted, unrestricted individuals rated a potential mate's physical attractiveness and sex appeal as more important than restricted individuals did. Restricted individuals, in contrast, placed more weight on characteristics indicative of good personal and parenting qualities (e.g., kind/affectionate, responsible, loyal/faithful) than did unrestricted individuals. A similar pattern was found when individuals evaluated potential romantic partners who were described in vignettes as being either physically attractive/socially visible/high in status (but deficient in personal and parenting qualities) or as possessing stellar personal/parenting qualities such as responsibility and faithfulness (but were less attractive). Unrestricted individuals rated the more attractive/poor parent mate as more desirable, whereas restricted individuals preferred the less attractive/better parent mate. These findings are consistent with those of Fletcher, Simpson, Thomas, and Giles (1999), who showed that unrestricted individuals rated their ideal standards for partner warmth/trustworthiness and relationship intimacy/loyalty as less important than did restricted individuals. Simpson and Gangestad (1992) also examined the attributes of the dating partners of individuals with different sociosexual orientations. Unrestricted individuals had dating partners (described by both themselves *and* their partners) who were more socially visible and more physically/sexually attractive. Conversely, restricted individuals were involved with partners who were more committed to the relationship and were more affectionate, responsible, and faithful/loyal.

Similar mate preference patterns were documented by Herold and Milhausen (1999), who studied differences in women's perceptions of "nice guys" versus "bad boys." Women who said that sex was less important to them, had fewer past sexual partners, and were less accepting of men with more sexual experience preferred inexperienced nice guys over more experienced and attractive bad boys. The bad boys were preferred by sexually experienced women who typically sought short-term relationships and viewed nice guys as unexciting or boring.

Sociosexuality and Relationship Initiation. How do proverbial bad boys and nice guys present themselves when competing for potential mates? In a simulated "dating game" study, Simpson, Gangestad, Christensen, and Leck (1999) found that unrestricted men were more likely to display direct competition tactics associated with short-term mating (e.g., showing off, bragging about past accomplishments, derogating their "competitor") when they were interviewed for a possible date. Restricted men, in contrast, presented themselves as nice guys, emphasizing their positive personal qualities (e.g., their kindness, agreeableness, and easy-going nature). These qualities, needless to say, should be of higher value in long-term, committed relationships. No parallel effects were found for women, and sociosexuality did not predict tactics that might convey an interest in establishing a long-term relationship in either gender. Simpson et al. conjecture that long-term tactics (e.g., expressing a keen interest in really getting to know and understand a potential mate) could be easily faked and, therefore, might be considered as unreliable indicators of true interest in developing long-term, committed relationships.

To clarify the manner in which individuals convey their interest in short-term versus long-term relationships nonverbally, Simpson, Gangestad, and Biek (1993) conducted a study in which college students believed they were being interviewed for a date by an attractive opposite-sex person (actually a trained experimental accomplice). Unrestricted men were more likely to smile, display flirtatious glances and head cants, and laugh, and were rated by observers as generally behaving in a more socially engaging, dominant, and pretentious manner nonverbally. Unrestricted women were more likely to lean forward (i.e., show interest in the potential date) and cant their heads during the interview. Interestingly, sociosexuality (SOI) scores did not correlate with individuals' self-reported interest in dating the attractive interviewer, despite the clearer nonverbal signs of sexual interest expressed by unrestricted people. Thus, unrestricted individuals are more inclined than their restricted counterparts to communicate "contact readiness" via specific nonverbal cues.

Extending this work, Gangestad, Simpson, and DiGeronimo (1994) examined whether restricted and unrestricted individuals are differentially attracted to certain nonverbal behaviors in relationship initiation settings. As expected, unrestricted individuals were more attracted to potential dating partners who cast more flirtatious glances, displayed intermittent gaze aversions, and canted their heads. Restricted individuals were more drawn to persons who expressed more loyalty/faithfulness and kindness/understanding, and who came across as being more restricted. In addition, unrestricted women were strongly attracted to physically attractive and sexually provocative men who appeared more unrestricted. Gangestad et al. speculate that the more frequent display of flirtatious glances and head cants by unrestricted men and the greater attraction to such cues on the part of unrestricted women may facilitate the development of sexual intimacy without closeness and commitment. This might be particularly true in couples where both partners are unrestricted.

Other research has revealed that men may perceive sociosexuality more accurately in women than women do in men. Gangestad, Simpson, DiGeronimo, and Biek (1992) found that men who were given visual but not auditory information about female targets were more accurate perceivers of targets' (i.e., women's) actual SOI scores than were women who rated the sociosexuality of male targets. These effects held even after controlling for the observer-rated physical attractiveness of female and male targets. This gender difference could be fueled by the greater importance for men of accurately detecting female sociosexuality (perhaps to gauge paternity concerns). Gangestad et al. also found that people tend to perceive targets' actual levels of sociosexuality more accurately than their other traits (i.e., social potency, social closeness, stress reaction). The superior assessment of sociosexuality appears to be attributable to enhanced cue utilization (i.e., using valid cues more effectively) rather than to deficient cue availability (i.e., the lack of valid cues to use).

Sociosexuality and Relationship Interactions. Using a diary methodology, Hebl and Kashy (1995) explored relations between sociosexuality, everyday social behavior, and perceptions of romantic partners. Unrestricted women reported having a larger number of daily social interactions with men than did restricted women. Unrestricted individuals also rated interactions with their best friends (nonromantic partners) as lower in quality (defined by pleasantness, satisfaction, and feelings of acceptance) than did restricted individuals. In addition, unrestricted people perceived somewhat more negativity in their daily interactions with their romantic partners, reported lower sexual interest in their partners, and rated them as less physically attractive (all largely unanticipated results).

Two studies have examined the conditions under which unrestricted individuals are more willing to betray their current romantic partners. Seal, Agostinelli, and Hannett (1994) found that unrestricted individuals involved in exclusive dating relationships report being more willing to entertain and pursue other romantic involvements than is true of restricted individuals. Unrestricted individuals are also more willing to engage in physically intimate behaviors with hypothetical opposite-sex strangers than are restricted individuals. Extradyadic sexual involvement is much less probable in the eyes of restricted individuals, especially if they report being highly committed to their partners or having dated them for long periods of time. Unrestricted individuals, on the other hand, indicate that their extradyadic behaviors would be less affected by either commitment or relationship length. However, both restricted and unrestricted individuals perceived a hypothetical stranger's involvement in another established relationship as a barrier to extradyadic involvement.

Recent research by Feldman and Cauffman (1999) has shown that unrestricted individuals are also more likely to view betrayal or "cheating" as acceptable under certain conditions (e.g., when involved in a bad relationship, when magnetically attracted to someone else, when able to escape detection, when a relationship needs to be "tested," to vindicate a partner's own infidelity). Supporting earlier work, they also found that unrestricted individuals report engaging in more cheating and actual betrayals than do restricted individuals.

To ascertain how restricted and unrestricted individuals perceive and communicate about sex in their ongoing relationships, Seal (1997) assessed interpartner concordances (rates of agreement) for various self-reported sexual behaviors in couples who were exclusively dating, exploring differences between couples who were more versus less concordant. Higher concordance was observed among couples in which the male was younger and more restricted than his partner. Seal speculates that, because these men had more limited sexual experiences, all sexual encounters should be more salient and, therefore, recalled more accurately. Sexual experiences should be less salient and more poorly recalled by older (i.e., more unrestricted) men. Considering that unrestricted men also tend to have a more impulsive decision-making style (Seal & Agostinelli, 1994), impulsivity might further bias their recounting of past sexual behaviors.

Sociosexuality and Early Family Environments.   In recent years, there has been growing interest in understanding how individual differences in sociosexuality fit within life-history models of human development. Barber (1998b) has investigated connections between sociosexuality, parental investment, and the grade point averages (GPAs) of college students. Exposure to marital instability during childhood (one marker of low parental investment) predicts higher levels of unrestricted sociosexuality and poorer academic performance in adulthood, particularly among women. The single component of marital instability that predicted sociosexuality and college GPA the best appears to be the number of stepsiblings in the family of origin. The impact of earlier marital instability on college GPA was direct for both genders. For women, however, there was also an indirect effect mediated through sociosexuality. Women whose parents had more unstable marriages were more unrestricted as young adults, which in turn predicted their poorer academic performance in college.

Investigating divorce, Barber (1998a) also found that the adult male children of divorced parents tend to be more unrestricted than the adult male children of parents who did not divorce. No similar pattern, however, has been found for daughters. Other research (e.g., Mikach & Bailey, 1999), however, has failed to find that early childhood stress and parental discord forecast unrestricted sociosexuality in adulthood.

Sociosexuality Across Cultures.   Schmitt, Alcalay, Allik et al. (2003) translated the SOI into 25 languages and administered it to people in more than 50 countries. They found that the SOI is reliable and valid across cultures and then tested theories that make predictions about the prevalence of restricted versus unrestricted sociosexuality in different cultures, regions, and climates. The findings revealed that sex ratios (i.e., the proportion of women to men in a given region) and environments that pose greater challenges to reproduction are related in theoretically consistent ways to mean (national average) SOI scores in both women and men. Specifically, the SOI correlates positively with men's self-reported physical attractiveness in nearly all cultures, and gender differences in sociosexuality (with women being on average more restricted than men) are evident in all cultures. Moreover, gender differences in sociosexuality tend to be larger in environments that pose more daunting barriers to reproduction (e.g., in harsh or pathogen-prevalent environments), and smaller in cultures that have greater political and economic gender equality.

In summary, restricted people report possessing stronger intrinsic motives for entering romantic relationships and, once formed, they are more committed to maintaining them. They prefer mates who, like themselves, value intimacy and commitment, and who are affectionate, trustworthy, and faithful. In their quest to attract such mates, restricted men accentuate their personal qualities, especially those that may be viewed as valuable by others in long-term relationships. These characteristics are all cardinal features of long-term mating tactics.

Unrestricted individuals, in contrast, become involved in fleeting, short-term relationships that contain less commitment and more guarded emotional intimacy. They prefer physically attractive and high status mates, and they weight sexual attraction and the potential for sex more heavily when choosing opposite-sex friends. Unrestricted individuals are also more likely to cheat (or say that they might be more willing to cheat) on their partners. Unrestricted women perceive sexual rewards, resource acquisition, and the refinement of their seduction skills as positive consequences of short-term mating. When trying to attract mates, unrestricted men resort to direct, competitive tactics such as showing off, bragging about their past accomplishments, or belittling other men. They also display nonverbal behaviors that convey "contact readiness" (e.g., smiles, flirtatious glances, head cants), which may pave the way for the rapid development of sexual intimacy without accompanying closeness and commitment. All of these characteristics are quintessential short-term mating tactics. Some evidence, however, suggests that unrestricted women at times may use short-term mating to evaluate, attract, and possibly retain long-term mates, which does not appear to be true of unrestricted men.

CAVEATS AND FUTURE DIRECTIONS

Several caveats must be considered when one interprets what has been presented in this chapter. First, the review of the sociosexuality research literature characterizes the personality, individual difference, mating, and relationship correlates of restricted and unrestricted orientations as being fairly clear and distinct. Most people, however, score between the restricted and unrestricted extremes of the sociosexuality continuum, meaning that they often exhibit attributes that are combinations of the two prototypic orientations. Second, neither sociosexual orientation is inherently "better than" or "more optimal than" the other one. Restricted and unrestricted individuals both possess some desirable as well as some undesirable traits and attributes. When viewed from the standpoint of reproductive fitness, the degree to which one orientation might be "more optimal" than the other should be dependent on the nature of the local environments in which individuals are raised (see Gangestad & Simpson, 2000).

Third, it is difficult to tell which of the theoretical models that explain within-sex variation in sociosexuality—life-history models, Sexual Strategies Theory, or the Strategic Pluralism Model—provides the best fit to the data on sociosexuality reviewed. Most of the existing data was either not collected to test between these alternate models, or it was collected before they were developed (this is particularly true of strategic pluralism). Future research should identify and test the critical points at which each model makes unique, different, or conflicting predictions.

The last decade of research on sociosexuality has raised several intriguing questions, many of which suggest promising paths for future work. In this final section, we highlight what we consider to be a few of the more promising and important directions for future work.

Biological and Evolutionary Origins of Sociosexuality

Several critical questions remain about the possible biological or evolutionary underpinnings of individual differences in sociosexuality. Recent research by Mikach and Bailey (1999), for example, implies that three models could explain the strong links between unrestricted sociosexuality and masculine gender/role identity. It is possible that (1) unrestricted sociosexuality and masculine gender/role identity might both be indicators of greater prenatal masculinization of the brain, (2) a history of unrestricted sociosexuality might cause greater masculinization of gender/role identity during social development, or (3) greater masculine gender/role identity might lead people to become more unrestricted over time. These models should be tested.

In addition, the role that testosterone may assume in promoting unrestricted behavior needs to be explored in much greater depth. Noting that testosterone, social dominance, and unrestricted sexual behavior are more highly correlated in men than in women, Townsend (1999) has speculated that testosterone might play a pivotal role in the development and maintenance of these gender differences and, perhaps, in the behavioral subsystems that support them (e.g., extraversion).

Future research should also clarify the extent to which individual differences in sociosexuality are heritable, are shaped by exposure to early environmental variables (e.g., parenting practices, family conflict, father absence), and/or are affected by environmental cues in adulthood that motivate people to shift their sociosexual orientations in "adaptive" ways. A recent study of Australian twins suggests that some of the variance underlying sociosexuality is heritable and some of it has environmental origins (Martin & Bailey, 1999). Elucidating the specific environmental factors that lead people to adopt restricted versus unrestricted orientations should be a major mission of future research. It is conceivable that certain experiences early in life (e.g., prolonged parent absence, the presence of stepfathers, high local mortality rates) shunt individuals down different reproductive pathways, yet mating behavior remains malleable in response to certain ecologically contingent cues (e.g., pathogen prevalence, the need for biparental care and heavy investment) if or when they are encountered at later points in development.

Motivations Underlying Sociosexuality

Another agenda of future research should be to pinpoint the different psychological motives that account for why individuals adopt unrestricted or restricted sociosexual orientations. What motives might underlie unrestricted sociosexuality? Some individuals may adopt an unrestricted orientation because they enjoy casual, novel sex with different partners. Others may be unrestricted because they do not want to—or cannot—develop closeness, intimacy, and strong emotional ties with romantic partners. Others might be unrestricted because they fear what could happen if they developed too much closeness and emotional intimacy or because their partners are unrestricted. And others (primarily women, according to Buss and Schmitt, 1993) may use unrestricted mating to attract and retain desirable long-term mates.

What motives might fuel restricted sociosexuality? Some individuals may adopt a restricted orientation because they enjoy the reassuring predictability of being involved with a single partner. As Jones (1998) has shown, other persons may be restricted because they value and enjoy the deep emotional bonds that can be forged with long-term partners. Still others might be restricted because they are involved with partners who are also restricted. And some (particularly certain men, according to Gangestad and Simpson, 2000) may be restricted because it is their best means of attracting and retaining desirable mates. These are just some of the possible motives that might underlie unrestricted and restricted sociosexual orientations.

Cues Signaling Sociosexuality

Another promising avenue for future inquiry is how individuals signal or communicate who they are and what they want from prospective romantic relationships. Several investigators (e.g., Cunningham & Russell, 2002; Gangestad et al., 1992) have insinuated that individuals might be biologically predisposed to "read" behavioral cues that honestly convey a potential mate's sociosexuality. Future work should clarify whether perceivers are differentially attracted to specific verbal and nonverbal signals (or unique combinations of signals) that convey an interest in short-term *and* long-term relationships in initiation settings. We currently know that unrestricted people are attracted to nonverbal gestures thought to communicate "contact readiness." However, we know little about the specific cues that restricted people find preferentially attractive. Future research should identify the verbal and nonverbal cues that honestly communicate the desire to form close, loyal, and committed long-term relationships and the cues that regulate interactions in highly committed, long-term relationships.

Sociosexuality and Long-Term Relationships

One of the most glaring gaps in research on sociosexuality is the impact that sociosexual orientations have on long-term relationships, especially marriages. The paucity of research on this topic may stem from the fact that the behavioral component of the SOI (e.g., number of sex partners in the past year, number of partners foreseen in the next 5 years) is not relevant to most people who are involved in long-term, committed relationships. However, the attitudinal component of the SOI (e.g., global attitudes toward sex without love or commitment) *is* germane to married people and should be assessed in such samples. Past research indicates that restricted people tend to choose mates based on attributes that may foster greater relationship stability and commitment (e.g., their faithfulness, personal compatibility, capacity for affection), whereas unrestricted people select partners according to attributes that may not promote stability and commitment (e.g., their physical appearance, social status, personal charisma).

Future work should determine whether these same criteria also influence the amount of satisfaction with, and the reasons for dissolving, long-term relationships. Are unrestricted individuals more likely to base their judgments of relationship satisfaction on the attractiveness, status, and charisma of their mates? Given their willingness to contemplate extradyadic involvements, are unrestricted persons more likely to have marriages that contain greater real or imagined jealousy and perhaps physical violence? Are they more inclined to terminate their marriages, especially if their spouses decline in attractiveness, charisma, and status or if extradyadic jealousies intensify? Or are unrestricted individuals more likely to end their marriages when relationship problems arise simply because they believe that good alternative partners can always be found?

On the flip side, are restricted persons more likely to base their evaluations of relationship satisfaction on the loyalty, compatibility, and affectionate qualities of their mates? Are they more motivated to leave their marriages when their spouses are no longer able or willing to provide these attributes? Might they be more sensitive to potential infidelity, given the premium they place on faithfulness and monogamy, and could these concerns make restricted people even more prone to jealousy and relationship violence than unrestricted individuals?

We also know very little about what happens when individuals with a history of being unrestricted settle into long-term, monogamous relationships (e.g., marriage). Do they have a more difficult time making this transition than their restricted counterparts? How do restricted and unrestricted individuals sustain high levels of commitment? Do restricted individuals focus more on the investments they have already made or the satisfaction they have derived from their partners/relationships in the past? Do unrestricted individuals sustain commitment by discounting, downplaying, or ignoring potential alternative partners (see Miller, 1997)? Indeed, is the process of sustaining commitment even the same for unrestricted and restricted persons, and does gender moderate any differences?

Surprisingly little is also known about how partner "mismatches" in sociosexuality (i.e., cases in which one partner is highly restricted and the other is highly unrestricted) impact relationship functioning and outcomes. How do mismatched couples "negotiate" their discrepant pasts, develop ways to meet each other's unique needs, and forge emotionally strong and stable marriages? Are mismatched couples more likely to divorce or need marital counseling than matched ones? All of these questions merit further study.

In conclusion, some of the most intimate and meaningful events that occur in relationships center on sex and sexuality. The nature and quality of these experiences depend not only on each individual, but also on his/her partner and the unique relationship they share. Important theoretical and empirical advances in our understanding of sociosexuality have occurred during the last decade. The field has moved from merely describing aspects of sociosexual attitudes and behaviors to achieving a provisional understanding of *how and why* both genders vary so much in their sexual and mating orientations. These theoretical advances have provided good roadmaps for research, suggesting several new and promising directions that future investigators should follow enroute to enriching and extending our understanding of how individual differences in sociosexuality affect what transpires in romantic relationships.

REFERENCES

Alston, J. P., & Tucker, F. (1973). The myth of sexual permissiveness. *Journal of Sex Research, 9*, 34–40.

Bailey, J. M., Gaulin, S., Agyei, Y. A., & Gladue, B. A. (1994). Effect of gender and sexual orientation on evolutionarily relevant aspects of human mating psychology. *Journal of Personality and Social Psychology, 66*, 1081–1093.

Barber, N. (1998a). Sex differences in disposition towards kin, security of adult attachment, and sociosexuality as a function of parental divorce. *Evolution and Human Behavior, 19*, 125–132.

Barber, N. (1998b). The role of reproductive strategies in academic attainment. *Sex Roles, 38*, 313–323.

Bem, S. L. (1974). The measurement of psychological androgyny. *Journal of Consulting and Clinical Psychology, 42*, 410–415.

Belsky, J., Steinberg, L., & Draper, P. (1991). Childhood experience, interpersonal development, and reproductive strategy: An evolutionary theory of socialization. *Child Development, 62*, 647–670.

Bleske-Rechek, A. L., & Buss, D. M. (2001). Opposite-sex friendship: Sex differences and similarities in initiation, selection, and dissolution. *Personality and Social Psychology Bulletin, 27*, 1310–1323.

Block, J. (1978). *The Q-sort method in personality assessment and psychiatric research*. Palo Alto, CA: Consulting Psychologists Press.

Brennan, K. A., & Shaver, P. R. (1995). Dimensions of adult attachment, affect regulation, and romantic relationship functioning. *Personality and Social Psychology Bulletin, 21*, 267–283.

Buss, D. M., & Schmitt, D. P. (1993). Sexual Strategies Theory: A contextual evolutionary analysis of human mating. *Psychological Review, 100*, 204–232.

Byrne, D. (1983). The antecedents, correlates, and consequents of erotophobia–erotophilia. In C. M. Davis (Ed.), *Challenges in sexual science* (pp. 53–75). Philadelphia: Society for the Scientific Study of Sex.

Byrne, D., & Sheffield, J. (1965). Response to sexually arousing stimuli as a function of repressing and sensitizing defenses. *Journal of Abnormal Psychology, 70*, 114–118.

Campbell, L., Cronk, L., Milroy, A., & Simpson, J. A. (2003). Sociosexuality and physical appearance. Unpublished data, Rutgers University, New Brunswick, NJ.

Chisholm, J. S. (1993). Death, hope, and sex: Life-history theory and the development of reproductive strategies. *Current Anthropology, 34*, 1–24.

Chisholm, J. S. (1996). The evolutionary ecology of attachment organization. *Human Nature, 7*, 1–38.

Costa, P. T., Jr., & McCrae, R. R. (1992). *The revised NEO personality inventory (NEO-PI-R) and NEO five-factor inventory (NEO-FFI) professional manual*. Odessa, FL: Psychological Assessment Resources.

Cunningham, S. J., & Russell, P. A. (2002). *Individual differences and sexual strategies: The influence of sex-type and sexual restrictiveness*. Unpublished manuscript, University of Aberdeen, England.

Curran, J. P., Neff, S., & Lippold, S. (1973). Correlates of sexual experience among university students. *Journal of Sex Research, 9*, 124–131.

D'Augelli, J. F., & Cross, H. J. (1975). Relationship of sex guilt and moral reasoning to premarital sex in college women and couples. *Journal of Consulting and Clinical Psychology, 43*, 40–47.

Eagly, A. H., & Wood, W. (1999). The origins of sex differences in human behavior: Evolved dispositions versus social roles. *American Psychologist, 54*, 408–423.

Eysenck, H. J. (1974). Personality, premarital sexual permissiveness, and assortative mating. *Journal of Sex Research, 10*, 47–51.

Eysenck, H. J. (1976). *Sex and personality*. London: Open Books.

Feldman, S. S., & Cauffman, E. (1999). Your cheatin' heart: Attitudes, behaviors, and correlates of sexual betrayal in late adolescents. *Journal of Research on Adolescence, 9*, 227–252.

Fisher, W. A. (1984). Predicting contraceptive behavior among university men: The roles of emotions and behavioral intentions. *Journal of Applied Social Psychology, 14*, 104–123.

Fletcher, G. J. O., Simpson, J. A., Thomas, G., & Giles, L. (1999). Ideals in intimate relationships. *Journal of Personality and Social Psychology, 76*, 72–89.

Gangestad, S. W., & Simpson, J. A. (1990). Toward an evolutionary history of female sociosexual variation. *Journal of Personality, 58*, 69–96.

Gangestad, S. W., & Simpson, J. A. (2000). The evolution of human mating: Trade-offs and strategic pluralism. *Behavioral and Brain Sciences, 23*, 573–587.

Gangestad, S. W., Simpson, J. A., & DiGeronimo, K. (1994). *"Good looking, but not my type": Heterosexual attraction as a function of nonverbal displays and perceiver sociosexuality*. Unpublished manuscript, University of New Mexico, Albuquerque.

Gangestad, S. W., Simpson, J. A., DiGeronimo, K., & Biek, M. (1992). Differential accuracy in person perception across traits: Examination of a functional hypothesis. *Journal of Personality and Social Psychology, 62*, 688–698.

Gerrard, M. (1980). Sex guilt and attitudes toward sex in sexually active and inactive female college students. *Journal of Personality Assessment, 44*, 258–261.

Gerrard, M., & Gibbons, F. X. (1982). Sexual experience, sex guilt, and sexual moral reasoning. *Journal of Personality, 50*, 345–359.

Greiling, H., & Buss, D. M. (2000). Women's sexual strategies: The hidden dimension of extra-pair mating. *Personality and Individual Differences, 28*, 929–963.

Griffit, W. (1973). Response to erotica and the projection of response to erotica in the opposite sex. *Journal of Experimental Research in Personality, 6*, 330–338.

Griffit, W., & Hatfield, E. (1985). *Human sexual behavior*. Glenview, IL: Scott, Foresman.

Hebl, M. R., & Kashy, D. A. (1995). Sociosexuality and everyday social interaction. *Personal Relationships, 2*, 371–383.

Hendrick, S., Hendrick, C., Slapion-Foote, M. J., & Foote, F. H. (1985). Gender differences in sexual attitudes. *Journal of Personality and Social Psychology, 48*, 1630–1642.

Herold, E. S., & Milhausen, R. R. (1999). Dating preferences of university women: An analysis of the nice guy stereotype. *Journal of Sex and Marital Therapy, 25*, 333–343.

Hinde, R. A. (1986). Some implications of evolutionary theory and comparative data for the study of human prosocial and aggressive behavior. In D. Olweus, J. Block, & M. Radke-Yarrow (Eds.), *Development of antisocial and prosocial behavior* (pp. 13–32). Orlando, FL: Academic Press.

Hunt, M. (1974). *Sexual behavior in the 1970s*. Chicago: Playboy Press.

Januszewski, B. A. (1997). Associations between attachment representations and patterns of sexuality. *Dissertation Abstracts International, 58*, 2681B.

Jones, M. (1998). Sociosexuality and motivations for romantic involvement. *Journal of Research in Personality,* *32,* 173–182.

Kelley, J. (1978). Sexual permissiveness: Evidence for a theory. *Journal of Marriage and the Family, 40,* 455–468.

Kinsey, A., Pomeroy, W., & Martin, C. (1948). *Sexual behavior in the human male.* Philadelphia: Saunders.

Kinsey, A., Pomeroy, W., Martin, C., & Gebhard, P. (1953). *Sexual behavior in the human female.* Philadelphia: Saunders.

Laumann, E. O., Gagnon, J. H., Michael, R. T., & Michaels, S. (1994). *The social organization of sexuality: Sexual practices in the United States.* Chicago: University of Chicago Press.

Leary, M. R., & Dobbins, S. E. (1983). Social anxiety, sexual behavior, and contraceptive use. *Journal of Personality and Social Psychology, 45,* 1347–1354.

Libby, R. W., Gray, L., & White, M. (1978). A test and reformulation of reference group and role correlates of premarital sexual permissiveness theory. *Journal of Marriage and the Family, 40,* 79–92.

Lytton, H., & Romney, D. M. (1991). Parents' differential socialization of boys and girls: A meta-analysis. *Psychological Bulletin, 109,* 267–296.

Main, M., & Goldwyn, R. (1994). *Adult attachment scoring and classification systems.* Unpublished scoring manual, University College, London.

Martin, N. G., & Bailey, J. M. (1999, June). *Origins of sociosexuality: A twin study.* Paper presented at the annual meeting of the Human Behavior and Evolution Society, Salt Lake City, UT.

Mellen, S. L. W. (1981). *The evolution of love.* Oxford, England: Freeman.

Mikach, S. M., & Bailey, J. M. (1999). What distinguishes women with unusually high numbers of sex partners? *Evolution and Human Behavior, 20,* 141–150.

Miller, R. S. (1997). Inattentive and contented: Relationship commitment and attention to alternatives. *Journal of Personality and Social Psychology, 73,* 758–766.

Mosher, D. L. (1979). Sex guilt and sex myths in college men and women. *Journal of Sex Research, 15,* 224–234.

O'Grady, K. E., Janda, L. H., & Gillen, H. B. (1979). A multi-dimensional scaling analysis of sex guilt. *Multivariate Behavioral Research, 14,* 415–434.

Oliver, M. B., & Hyde, J. S. (1996). Gender differences in sexuality: A meta-analysis. *Psychological Bulletin, 114,* 29–51.

Probst, S. S. (1999). Long- and short-term mating strategies and the five-factor model of personality. *Dissertation Abstracts International, 60,* 0560B.

Reise, S. P., & Wright, T. M. (1996). Personality traits, cluster B personality disorders, and sociosexuality. *Journal of Research in Personality, 30,* 128–136.

Reiss, I. L. (1967). *The social context of premarital sexual permissiveness.* New York: Holt, Rinehart & Winston.

Reiss, I. L. (1982). Trouble in paradise: The current status of sexual science. *Journal of Sex Research, 18,* 97–113.

Schmitt, D. P., Alcalay, L., Alik, J. et al. (2003). *Universal sex differences in the desire for sexual variety: Tests from 52 nations, 6 continents, and 13 islands. Journal of Personality and Social Psychology, 85,* 85–104.

Schmitt, D. P., & Buss, D. M. (2000). Sexual dimensions of person description: Beyond or subsumed by the Big Five? *Journal of Research in Personality, 34,* 141–177.

Seal, D. W. (1997). Interpartner concordance of self-reported sexual behavior among college dating couples. *The Journal of Sex Research, 34,* 39–55.

Seal, D. W., & Agostinelli, G. (1994). Individual differences associated with high-risk sexual behavior: Implications for intervention programs. *AIDS Care, 6,* 393–397.

Seal, D. W., Agostinelli, G., & Hannett, C. A. (1994). Extradyadic romantic involvement: Moderating effects of sociosexuality and gender. *Sex Roles, 31,* 1–22.

Simon, E. P. (1997). Adult attachment style and sociosexuality. *Dissertation Abstracts International, 57,* 5966B.

Simpson, J. A. (1987). The dissolution of romantic relationships: Factors involved in relationship stability and emotional distress. *Journal of Personality and Social Psychology, 53,* 683–692.

Simpson, J. A. (1998). Sociosexual orientation inventory. In C. M. Davis, W. L. Yarber, R. Bauserman, G. Schreer, & S. L. Davis (Eds.), *Handbook of sexuality-related measures* (pp. 565–566). Thousand Oaks, CA: Sage.

Simpson, J. A. (1999). Attachment theory in modern evolutionary perspective. In J. Cassidy & P. R. Shaver (Eds.), *Handbook of attachment theory and research* (pp. 123–150). New York: Guilford.

Simpson, J. A., & Gangestad, S. W. (1991). Individual differences in sociosexuality: Evidence for convergent and discriminant validity. *Journal of Personality and Social Psychology, 60,* 870–883.

Simpson, J. A., & Gangestad, S. W. (1992). Sociosexuality and romantic partner choice. *Journal of Personality, 60,* 31–51.

Simpson, J. A., Gangestad, S. W., & Biek, M. (1993). Personality and nonverbal social behavior: An ethological perspective of relationship initiation. *Journal of Experimental Social Psychology, 29,* 434–461.

Simpson, J. A., Gangestad, S. W., Christensen, P. N., & Leck, K. (1999). Fluctuating asymmetry, sociosexuality, and intrasexual competitive tactics. *Journal of Personality and Social Psychology, 76,* 159–172.

Simpson, J. A., & Rholes, W. S. (1994). Stress and secure base relationships in adulthood. In K. Bartholomew & D. Perlman (Eds.), *Attachment processes in adulthood: Advances in personal relationships* (Vol. 5, pp. 181–204). London: Jessica Kingsley.

Snyder, M., Simpson, J. A., & Gangestad, S. (1986). Personality and sexual relations. *Journal of Personality and Social Psychology, 51,* 181–190.

Sprecher, S., & Regan, P. C. (1996). College virgins: How men and women perceive their sexual status. *The Journal of Sex Research, 33*, 3–15.

Sprecher, S., Regan, P. C., McKinney, K., Maxwell, K., & Wazienski, R. (1997). Preferred level of sexual experience in a date or mate: The merger of two methodologies. *The Journal of Sex Research, 34*, 327–337.

Stearns, S. (1992). *The evolution of life histories.* New York: Oxford University Press.

Stephan, C. W., & Bachman, G. F. (1999). What's sex got to do with it?: Attachment, love schemas, and sexuality. *Personal Relationships, 6*, 111–123.

Symons, D. (1979). *The evolution of human sexuality.* New York: Oxford University Press.

Townsend, J. M. (1993). Sexuality and partner selection: Sex differences among college students. *Ethology and Sociobiology, 14*, 305–330.

Townsend, J. M. (1995). Sex without emotional involvement: An evolutionary interpretation of sex differences. *Archives of Sexual Behavior, 24*, 173–206.

Townsend, J. M. (1999). Extraversion, sexual experience, and sexual emotions. *Behavioral and Brain Sciences, 22*, 537.

Townsend, J. M., & Wasserman, T. (1997). The perception of sexual attractiveness: Sex differences in variability. *Archives of Sexual Behavior, 26*, 243–268.

Townsend, J. M., & Wasserman, T. (1998). Sexual attractiveness: Sex differences in assessment and criteria. *Evolution and Human Behavior, 19*, 171–191.

Trivers, R. (1972). Parental investment and sexual selection. In B. Campbell (Eds.), *Sexual selection and the descent of man, 1871–1971* (pp. 136–179). Chicago: Aldine-Atherton.

Trivers, R. (1985). *Social evolution.* Menlo Park, CA: Benjamin/Cummings.

Walker, D. F., Tokar, D. M., & Fischer, A. R. (2000). What are eight popular masculinity-related instruments measuring? Underlying dimensions and their relations to sociosexuality. *Psychology of Men and Masculinity, 1*, 98–108.

Wensley, L. A. (2000). Measurement of adult attachment. *Dissertation Abstracts International, 60*, 4936B.

Wiederman, M. W., & Dubois, S. L. (1998). Evolution and sex differences in preferences for short-term mates: Results from a policy capturing study. *Evolution and Human Behavior, 19*, 153–170.

Wright, T. M. (1999). Female sexual behavior: Analysis of Big Five trait facets and domains in the prediction of sociosexuality. *Dissertation Abstracts International, 59*, 5611B.

Wright, T. M., & Reise, S. P. (1997). Personality and unrestricted sexual behavior: Correlations of sociosexuality in Caucasian and Asian college students. *Journal of Research in Personality, 31*, 166–192.

Zuckerman, M., Bone, R. N., Neary, R., Mangelsdorff, D., & Brustman, B. (1972). What is the sensation seeker? Personality trait and experience correlates of the Sensation Seeking Scales. *Journal of Consulting and Clinical Psychology, 39*, 308–321.

Zuckerman, M., Tushup, R., & Finner, S. (1976). Sexual attitudes and experience: Attitude and personality correlates and changes produced by a course in sexuality. *Journal of Consulting and Clinical Psychology, 44*, 7–19.

II

Role of Sexuality in the Formation, Development, and Maintenance of Close Relationships

5

Sex and the Attraction Process: Lessons from Science (and Shakespeare) on Lust, Love, Chastity, and Fidelity

Pamela C. Regan
California State University, Los Angeles

This chapter explores the ways in which an individual's sexual responses and his or her sexual attributes or characteristics are implicated in the attraction process and in the initial stages of romantic relationships. The first section focuses on the association between one particular sexual response—sexual desire or lust—and the state of passionate love. Theoretical discourse from a number of disciplines suggests that sexual desire is a distinguishing feature of the passionate love experience and may promote romantic attraction and relationship development. Empirical research substantiates this hypothesis. People believe that sexual desire is part and parcel of the state of being in love, assume that couples who desire each other sexually also are passionately in love, and report a similar association when reflecting on their own dating relationships. In addition to experiencing desire (and other sexual responses) for their partners, individuals possess various sexual attributes or characteristics whose behavioral expression within a beginning relationship may have significant consequences for the partners and the relationship itself. The second section of this chapter focuses on four of these attributes—sex appeal, sexual passion, sexual chastity, and sexual fidelity. A consideration of social context and evolutionary theories, as well as a growing body of empirical work, suggests that men and women are most attracted to romantic partners who possess high levels of sex appeal (which primarily consists of an attractive physical appearance), who demonstrate sexual passion, who possess lower rather than higher levels of prior sexual experience, and who are sexually loyal or faithful (i.e., who confine their sexual responses to the primary relationship). The chapter ends with suggestions for additional research that might serve to advance knowledge in this area.

INTRODUCTION

People experience and express a variety of sexual responses within their romantic relationships. These responses may include *sexual desire* (a motivational state that can be understood broadly as an interest in sexual objects or activities, or as a wish, need, or drive to seek out sexual objects or to engage in sexual activities; Regan & Berscheid, 1999), *physiological/genital sexual arousal* (a state of reflex activation that involves the sex organs and nervous system; Masters, Johnson, & Kolodny, 1982, 1994), *subjective sexual arousal* (the subjective awareness of physiological/genital arousal; Green & Mosher, 1985), *sexual activity* (overt behavioral responses; e.g., kissing, "petting," intercourse), and *sexual feelings* that are associated with these responses (e.g., satisfaction, intimacy, fulfillment). Although sexual desire, arousal, and activity can and often do co-occur, they are considered separate and distinct phenomena that have different interpersonal consequences and that become more or less important at different stages of relationship development (see Regan & Berscheid, 1999). One of these responses—sexual desire or lust—appears to play an especially important role in the attraction process and in the beginning stages of romantic relationships, particularly as people begin to experience that state known variously as passionate, erotic, or romantic love. The first part of this chapter considers theory and research that explores the association between an individual's feelings of sexual desire for another and romantic attraction (see Hendrick & Hendrick, chapter 7, this volume, which presents a more general overview of the relation between sexuality and love).

In addition to the sexual responses that they experience for a partner and express within a relationship, people also possess a variety of sexual attributes that may have interpersonal consequences. Some of these attributes are dispositional in nature. For example, considerable empirical attention has been paid to such intra-individual traits as erotophobia–erotophilia (i.e., the disposition to respond to sexual cues with positive or negative affect and evaluation; Fisher, Byrne, White, & Kelley, 1988) and sociosexual orientation (i.e., the dispositional tendency to require [or not require] emotional intimacy and commitment prior to sexual involvement; Gangestad & Simpson, 1990; Simpson & Gangestad, 1991; also see Simpson, Wilson, & Winterheld, this volume). Other sexual attributes are not dispositional per se but rather consist of a constellation of personal characteristics and attitudinal and behavioral tendencies. The second section of this chapter focuses on four of these attributes—sex appeal, sexual passion, sexual chastity or level of prior sexual experience, and sexual fidelity or exclusivity. Social context and evolutionary theories, and a growing body of empirical research, suggest that these attributes are significant predictors of romantic attraction.

SEXUAL DESIRE AND PASSIONATE LOVE

The idea that sexual desire or lust causes feelings of passionate love, focuses the lovers' attention exclusively on each other, and promotes the initiation and development of romantic relationships is not a new one. For centuries, poets, playwrights, and other artists have vociferously touted the notion that sexual attraction is the force that propels individuals to fall in love with one another. Shakespeare, for example, clearly was aware of the havoc that sexual desire could wreak on human lives; his dramatic tragedies are filled with examples of the negative consequences of unbridled lust, ranging from kidnapping, rape, and murder to war, the pillage of cities, and the decimation of entire armies (see *Hamlet, Troilus and Cressida*, and *Titus Andronicus*, for examples). However, he also viewed desire as an essential element of passionate love and as a powerful force that prompted individuals to seek out and enter romantic relationships. It is desire that causes Romeo and Juliet to defy their families and secretly wed, a desire that is very evident in the eager anticipation with which Juliet awaits their first night together and the sexual consummation of their union:

> Spread thy close curtain, love-performing night!
> That runaway's eyes may wink, and Romeo
> Leap to these arms, untalk'd of and unseen!
> Lovers can see to do their amorous rites
> By their own beauties; or, if love be blind,
> It best agrees with night. Come, civil night,
> Thou sober-suited matron, all in black,
> And learn me how to lose a winning match,
> Play'd for a pair of stainless maidenhoods.
> Come, night! Come Romeo!
> O! I have bought the mansion of a love,
> But not possess'd it, and, though I am sold,
> Not yet enjoy'd. So tedious is this day
> As is the night before some festival
> To an impatient child that hath new robes
> And may not wear them.
>   (*Romeo and Juliet*, Act III, Scene II)

Closely allied with this Shakespearian theme is the notion that satiated or consummated desire is antithetical to passionate love. Throughout much of the play *Troilus and Cressida*, Cressida resists Troilus' advances and remains "stubborn-chaste against all suit," because she believes that he will cease to love her once his desire is quenched:

> Women are angels, wooing:
> Things won are done; joy's soul lies in the doing:
> That she belov'd knows naught that knows not this:
> Men prize the thing ungain'd more than it is:
> That she was never met, that ever knew
> Love got so sweet as when desire did sue.
>   (*Troilus and Cressida*, Act I, Scene II)

(Ironically, it is the sexual attraction that Cressida herself develops for another man that destroys her relationship with Troilus).

Although Shakespeare's goal was to entertain rather than to advance the state of knowledge about lust, love, and related phenomena, theory and research from a number of disciplines suggest that his assumptions were fundamentally correct.

Theoretical Discourse

Early theorists from disciplines as diverse as sexual pathology and medicine (e.g., H. Ellis, 1897–1928/1901–1928; 1933/1963; Krafft-Ebing, 1886/1945), psychiatry and psychoanalysis (e.g., A. Ellis, 1954; Freud, 1908/1963, 1912/1963; Reik, 1944, 1945), existential philosophy (e.g., Fromm, 1956), psychology (e.g., James, 1890/1950), and religious theology (e.g., Lewis, 1960) posited that sexual desire (in particular, *unsated* sexual desire) is strongly implicated in, and may be a necessary feature of, the experience of passionate love and the initiation of romantic relationships. For example, Capellanus (1184/1960), a 12th century French courtier and scholar, posited that all heterosexual love relationships began with the occurrence of sexual desire ("he begins to lust after her in his heart," p. 29) which, in turn, prompts relationship initiation ("he begins to plan how he may find favor with her, and he begins to seek a place and a time opportune for talking," p. 29). Love depends, at least partly, on the continued presence of lust; once desire is sated via "the final act of Venus," Capellanus opined that love "quickly fails" (p. 122).

Similarly, German physician Krafft-Ebing (1886/1945) argued that sexual desire differentiated passionate or *sensual love* from other varieties of love. He wrote, for example, "Since love implies the presence of sexual desire it can only exist between persons of different sex capable of sexual intercourse. When these conditions are wanting or destroyed it is replaced by friendship" (p. 13). His contemporary William James (1890/1950) also argued that sexual appetite formed the basis for the love that occurred between men and women (see, for example, pp. 437–439). Although antiquated (e.g., both Krafft-Ebing and James refused or failed to acknowledge that passionate love and sexual desire can and do occur between same-sex partners), the assertion that sexual desire is an essential feature of passionate love has been made by many other theorists throughout the past century.

Psychotherapist Albert Ellis (1954) also believed that sexual desire was the force that propelled individuals into the state of "being in love" with one another. Following a thorough examination of earlier discourse, literature, and popular mass media, as well as his own psychoanalytic observations, he concluded in his classic work *The American Sexual Tragedy* that (thwarted) sexual desire was the single most powerful cause of passionate love:

> Romantic love, again, is largely based on the sexual teasing and blocking of modern courtship. Its very intensity, to a large part, grows out of the generous promises combined with the niggardly actualities of sex fulfillment which exist during the courtship stages. (p. 113)

Ellis believed that the heady, emotionally volatile state of being in love could survive only as long as sexual desire was permitted no outlet. Once the urgent pangs of lust were sated via intercourse, Ellis hypothesized that passionate love would perish—"sexual and marital consummation indubitably, in the vast majority of instances, maims, bloodies, and finally kills romanticism until it is deader than—well, yesterday's romance" (p. 116).

This theme is echoed by religious theologian C. S. Lewis (1960/1988) in *The Four Loves*. Like other love types, erotic love or the "state which we call 'being in love'" (p. 91) was posited to contain a "carnal or animally sexual element" (p. 92) that essentially is an individualized sexual desire directed toward the beloved (as opposed to a more general appetite for sex). It is the transitory nature of this carnal element, coupled with lovers' (unrealistic) beliefs in its permanence, that Lewis felt gave erotic love its unique blend of "strength, sweetness, terror and high port" (p. 115).

Contemporary theorists have similarly targeted sexual desire as an important component of the passionate love experience (see Hendrick & Hendrick, 1992, 2000, and Sternberg & Barnes, 1988, for a review of theoretical statements about passionate love). For example, Lee (1973, 1988) concluded that passionate (or what he termed erotic) love always begins with a strong sexual attraction—the erotic lover is "eager to get to know the beloved quickly, intensely—and undressed" (1988, p. 50). Similarly, Tennov (1979, 1998) suggested that sexual desire is a particularly important hallmark of "limerence" or the state of being in love. She wrote:

> I am inclined toward the generalization that sexual attraction is an essential component of limerence. This sexual feeling may be combined with shyness, impotence or some form of sexual dysfunction or disinclination, or with some social unsuitability. But LO, in order to become LO, must stand in relation to the limerent as one for whom the limerent is a potential sex partner. Sexual attraction is not "enough," to be sure. Selection standards

for limerence are, according to informants, not identical to those by which "mere" sexual partners are evaluated, and sex is seldom the main focus of limerence. Either the potential for sexual mating is felt to be there, however, or the state described is not limerence. (1979, pp. 24–25)

In addition, Hatfield and Berscheid, two of the first social psychologists to begin a dialogue on the nature of passionate love, have continued to argue that sexuality (in particular, thwarted or unsated sexual desire) is intricately linked with the experience of being in love (see, for example, Berscheid, 1988; Berscheid & Walster [Hatfield], 1974; Hatfield & Rapson, 1993; Regan & Berscheid, 1999; Walster [Hatfield] & Berscheid, 1971).

Empirical Evidence

Considered together, the aforementioned theoretical statements suggest that sexual desire is a powerful correlate (and even antecedent) of passionate love; an individual who experiences sexual desire for another person, in association with other events or feelings, may characterize his or her state as one of "being in love," and consequently may seek to initiate or intensify a romantic relationship. Some (albeit mostly indirect) evidence for these theoretical suppositions exists. Certainly people *believe* that sexual desire is an essential component of passionate love. When Ridge and Berscheid (1989) asked a sample of undergraduates whether they thought that there was a difference between the experience of being in love with and that of loving another person, almost all (87%) emphatically claimed that there indeed was a difference between the two experiences. When asked to specify the nature of that difference, sexual desire was listed as a key distinguishing feature (i.e., participants were much more likely to cite sexual desire as descriptive of the "in love" than of the "loving" experience).

Similar results were reported by Regan, Kocan, and Whitlock (1998), who conducted a prototype analysis of the concept of passionate love. Participants in this study listed in a free response format all of the features that they considered to be characteristic or prototypical of the state of "being in love." Out of 119 spontaneously generated features, *sexual desire* received the second highest frequency rating (65.8%). In other words, when thinking of passionate love, two thirds of the participants automatically thought of sexual desire. In addition, this feature was viewed as more important to the passionate love concept than behavioral sexual events, including *caresses* (cited by only 1.7% of participants), *kissing* (cited by 10%), and *sexual activity* (cited by 25%).

Two person-perception experiments provide support for these prototype study results. In the first experiment, Regan (1998) provided a sample of 60 undergraduate men and women with two self-report questionnaires ostensibly completed by "Rob" and "Nancy," a student couple enrolled at the same university. The members of this couple reported experiencing no sexual desire for each other or a high amount of sexual desire for each other and were currently engaging in sexual intercourse with each other or were not sexually active. Participants then estimated the likelihood that the partners experienced passionate love as well as a variety of other relationship phenomena. The results revealed that both men and women believed that dating partners who desire each other sexually are more likely to be in love with one another than dating partners who do not desire each other sexually, regardless of their current level of sexual activity.

A second experiment, a conceptual replication of the first, confirmed these results. Here, men and women received information about the members of a heterosexual, dating "student couple" who ostensibly reported that they were currently passionately in love with each other, that they loved each other, or that they liked each other.

Participants then estimated the likelihood that the members of the couple experience sexual desire for each other and the amount of desire that they feel for each other. Analyses revealed that participants perceived partners who were characterized as being passionately in love as more likely to experience sexual desire than partners who loved each other or who liked each other. Similarly, partners who were passionately in love were believed to experience a greater amount of sexual desire for each other than partners who loved each other or who liked each other. Interestingly, sexual desire was believed to be no more likely in a "loving" relationship than in a "liking" relationship, and greater amounts of sexual desire were not believed to occur in loving relationships than liking relationships. Again, it seems that sexual desire is viewed as an important feature of passionate love relationships—and not of relationships characterized by feelings of love and/or liking.

Research conducted with individuals involved in ongoing romantic relationships, although scarce, also supports the association between sexual desire and passionate love. For example, during the process of scale validation, Hatfield and Sprecher (1986) administered their Passionate Love Scale (PLS) and a battery of other measures to students involved in romantic (e.g., dating, cohabiting) relationships. These researchers found that PLS scores for both men and women were significantly positively correlated with several measures of current desire for sexual and/or physical interaction with the partner (including self-reported desire to be held by the partner, to kiss the partner, and to engage in sex with the partner). In other words, individuals who are very passionately in love also tend to experience higher levels of sexual desire for their partners than do individuals who are less passionately in love.

Research conducted by Berscheid and Meyers (1996) also provides evidence for the association between lust and passionate love. Using what they termed a "social categorical method," these researchers asked a large sample of undergraduate men and women to list the initials of all the people they currently loved, the initials of all those with whom they were currently in love, and the initials of all those toward whom they currently felt sexual attraction or desire. For each respondent, the researchers calculated the probability that persons named in the "sexually desire" category also were named in the "in love" and "love" categories. These sets of probabilities then were averaged across respondents, and the results indicated that 85% of the persons listed in the "in love" category also were listed in the "sexually desire" category, whereas only 2% of those listed in the "love" category (and not cross-listed in the "in love" category) were listed in the "sexually desire" category. Thus, the objects of respondents' feelings of passionate love (but not their feelings of love) also tended to be the objects of their lust.

More recently, Regan (2000) asked a sample of men and women currently involved in dating relationships to indicate the amount of sexual desire, passionate love (further defined as the state of being "in love with" the partner), liking, and love they currently experienced in their relationships (assessed via single-item measures). She found that sexual desire and passionate love were positively correlated; the more participants desired their dating partners sexually, the more they reported being in love with those partners. Similar associations were not found between sexual desire and liking, or between sexual desire and loving.

This set of empirical findings suggests that sexual desire or lust is indeed an important component of the state of being in love with another person. What is yet to be—and what must be—empirically determined is whether the experience of sexual attraction for another individual produces or significantly contributes to the sense that one is falling in love with that person, and whether sexual attraction promotes actual romantic relationship initiation and/or propels partners in an already existing relationship into a further stage of development (e.g., from casual dating to serious dating, from uncommitted to committed and "in love").

SEXUAL ATTRIBUTES AND ROMANTIC ATTRACTION

The theory and research reviewed in the first section of this chapter suggest that people use their feelings of lust to gauge the magnitude of their passionate love for, and emotional involvement with, the partner. Thus, an individual's sexual responses to an actual or potential partner appear to have important interpersonal consequences. In addition to these sexual responses, both the individual and the partner possess various sexual characteristics and attributes that undoubtedly also influence the attraction process. This section examines theory and research on the relationship between romantic attraction and four characteristics that are associated with sexuality—sex appeal, sexual passion, sexual chastity, and sexual fidelity.

Theoretical Discourse

At least two broad theoretical frameworks can be utilized to predict the factors that will determine an individual's sex appeal and the impact that this and other sexual variables will have on attraction and partner preference.

Social Context Frameworks. Social context frameworks focus on proximal mechanisms—forces located in the contemporary social, cultural, and historical milieu—that are implicated in the dynamics of sexuality and human mating. For example, *social exchange or equity models* (e.g., Blau, 1964; Murstein, 1970, 1976; Walster, Walster, & Berscheid, 1978) assume that people are sensitive to the rewards they gain and the costs they incur in social interaction. Furthermore, these theories propose that people will actively attempt to maximize their profits (rewards minus costs) in social interaction and will seek out those persons with whom social interaction is expected to be most profitable while avoiding those from whom less profit is anticipated. Applied to romantic attraction and human mating, these principles imply that most men and women will be attracted to, and attempt to pair with, individuals who possess high amounts of socially desirable characteristics. Insofar as physical attractiveness is an attribute that generally produces a great deal of social profit for its bearer (see, for example, Dion, Berscheid, & Walster, 1972), this theoretical perspective predicts that physical appearance attributes will be an important determinant of sex appeal and will influence romantic preferences (for additional discussion of the social exchange perspective applied to sexuality, see Byers & Wang, chapter 9, this volume).

Other social forces also act to shape romantic attraction and mating behavior, including *social and cultural scripts* (e.g., Reiss, 1967, 1981, 1986; Simon & Gagnon, 1986) and *social learning processes* (e.g., Hogben & Byrne, 1998; Mischel, 1966). Sociocultural scripts define and organize social experience, are developed through social interaction via observational or social learning, and are used to guide and assess behavior in social situations (Gagnon & Simon, 1973; Simon, 1974). This framework posits that beliefs, expectations, and behavior in the realm of sex, love, and mating are affected by the sociocultural scripts experienced, and by the patterns of punishment and reinforcement received, by people during their lifetimes. Applied to romantic attraction, social context theories suggest that men and women will be attracted to and prefer as mates individuals who are sexually or reproductively mature, physically attractive, and sexually receptive and responsive. In contemporary Western cultures, it is not considered socially acceptable to desire (and initiate sexual/romantic relationships with) preadolescent, unattractive, and/or unwilling or uninterested partners, and men and women who possess these desires are indirectly or directly discouraged from acting in service of them. Similarly, as social mores regarding premarital sexuality have become increasingly relaxed over the past several decades (Sherwin & Corbett, 1985) and as increasing numbers of adolescents and young adults are engaging in premarital intercourse (see Christopher, 2001), this perspective suggests that sexual chastity will become an increasingly unimportant or undesirable sexual attribute, and that sexual passion or responsiveness will become an increasingly important characteristic for an individual to possess.

Evolutionary Frameworks.   A second category of theoretical approaches focuses on distal rather than contemporary mechanisms that are implicated in attraction and mating dynamics. *Evolutionary models* are grounded in the theoretical principles of evolutionary psychology, which posit that "the mind is a set of information-processing machines that were designed by natural selection to solve adaptive problems faced by our hunter-gatherer ancestors" (Cosmides & Tooby, 1997, p. 1). Specifically, evolutionary psychologists focus on the design of the human mind (the neural circuitry humans possess that processes information), and they conceptualize the mind as comprised of many, specialized processing systems (e.g., we possess neural circuitry specialized for mate selection, which is different from the circuitry we possess for language acquisition or food choice). Evolutionary psychologists also acknowledge that the human mind—our specialized neural circuitry—was designed by the processes of natural and sexual selection originally articulated by Darwin (1859, 1871) and was designed to solve adaptive problems (i.e., recurrent problems in human evolutionary history that had implications for reproduction and survival). Finally, evolutionary psychology—and, therefore, all models of attraction and mating based on evolutionary principles—is oriented toward the human species' very distant past. Insofar as natural selection takes time, the human mind was designed to solve problems that existed thousands of years ago that affected the daily existence of our hunter–gatherer forebears.

With these principles in mind, evolutionary models of human mating consider the ways in which sexual attraction and mating dynamics are influenced by psychological heuristics or mechanisms that were selected because they overcame obstacles to reproduction and enabled our ancestors to make "appropriate" mating decisions. From an evolutionary perspective, an appropriate mating decision is one that results in a high(er) probability of gene replication and the production of viable offspring (i.e., offspring who survive to reach reproductive maturity), whereas an inappropriate mating decision is one that produces a low(er) chance of reproductive success for the individual. Thus, an appropriate decision is simply an adaptive one (i.e., one that enhances reproductive success) rather than one that is morally or ethically or socially acceptable, and an appropriate partner is one who possesses attributes that enhance, and/or who lacks attributes that hinder, reproductive success (for additional discussion of this point, see Regan, 2002; the reader also is referred to discussions of evolutionary theory and sexuality provided by DeLamater & Hyde, chapter 1, and Hendrick & Hendrick, chapter 7, this volume).

A consideration of evolutionary principles suggests that for both sexes reproductive success in the ancestral environment would have been dependent on selecting a physically fit partner; that is, a sexually mature, healthy individual who was capable of reproduction, who would pass on "good" genetic material to any resulting offspring, and who would be physically able to contribute to the reproductive relationship, the partner, and the offspring. Insofar as physical appearance may function as an external indicant of underlying genetic fitness, reproductive status, and health, this framework suggests that appearance attributes may constitute an important determinant of sex appeal. Reproductive success also would have been affected by a mate's relational fitness or ability and motivation to become exclusively attached to the primary partner, to have intercourse and reproduce with that partner, to confine his or her sexual and/or reproductive activities to the primary relationship, and to avoid the temptations posed by other potential partners. Thus, we might expect contemporary humans to prefer partners with limited (as opposed to extensive) prior sexual experience who possess relatively high levels of sexual passion and who demonstrate sexually fidelity or exclusivity.

Empirical Work

The empirical interpersonal attraction and mate preference literatures are enormous and generally substantiate many of the predictions generated by the aforementioned theoretical frameworks.

Sex Appeal.   In accordance with predictions generated from both social context and evolutionary theories, research suggests that physical appearance is an important component of sex appeal. For example, Regan and Berscheid (1995) asked a group of men and women to list all the characteristics a man and a woman could possess that would cause them to be sexually desirable to others. According to their participants, sex appeal in both men and women was assumed to primarily be a function of appearance. Although a number of attributes were mentioned, almost all of the participants (90%) specified an attractive physical appearance as an essential determinant of female sex appeal. Examples of participants' responses included:

> I think men want women to be willing, attractive, and interesting . . . Physically, I think a desirable woman would be soft, yet athletic, not fat, but not overly thin, with lots of curves and a nice face. [male respondent]

> Her appearance. Nothing else is needed . . . The easiest way to get a man interested in a woman is for his friends to say how good the girl looks. I truly feel that besides the body—no other characteristics are needed. [male respondent]

> Definitely an attitude that portrays that she wants "it." Flirtation seems to help men become more interested. A confident characteristic that would suggest that she is good at "it." Overall attractiveness (skinny, tall, nice smile). [female respondent]

> Could be very thin with long, thin legs, long hair, white teeth. Could be voluptuous—I guess what I'm getting down to is physical attraction. [female respondent]

Male sex appeal was presumed to be caused by a very similar constellation of features. Again, appearance was the most frequently mentioned characteristic (cited by 76%):

> I think a well-built, strong man would cause desire as opposed to a sloppy, overweight guy or a really skinny guy. I think women desire a guy who is open, honest, and is interested in pleasing them, instead of the opposite. . . . Physical qualities would probably include muscles, and cleanliness or being well-groomed. [male respondent]

> Women like men to be funny and caring. A major thing for women is that they want a man to be sensitive to their needs as women. Physical attractiveness is important to women, although they don't tend to show this as much as men do. I wish I knew more about this question myself—believe me! [male respondent]

> A great fit body, and nice clothes. This doesn't mean that's all I'm looking for, but to be sexually attracted—yes. [female respondent]

> Based on physical characteristics I would say the way a person looks such as his face, eyes, lips, and a well-toned body. A man must be caring, kind, and gentle. He must be able to show his feelings and let you know he cares about you. [female respondent]

It is apparent from these responses that although men and women believed that a number of attributes determine sex appeal, physical attractiveness was considered the most important.

In addition to overall physical appearance, specific morphological features may be important elements of an individual's sexual attractiveness. One of these morphological features is body fat distribution, which is quantified by computing a ratio of the circumference of the waist to the circumference of the hips. Before puberty, both sexes exhibit a similar waist-to-hip ratio; however, after puberty, women deposit more fat in the gluteofemoral region (buttocks and thighs); whereas men deposit more fat in the central and upper body regions (shoulders, abdomen, and nape of the neck). Typically, the waist-to-hip ratio ranges from .67 to .80 in healthy, premenopausal women (an hourglass shape), and from .80 to .90 in healthy men (a straighter shape). Research reveals that men and women of different ages, races, and cultural backgrounds assign higher attractiveness ratings to individuals with a sex-typical waist-to-hip ratio (e.g., Furnham, Tan, & McManus, 1997; Henss, 1995; Singh, 1993, 1994, 1995; Singh & Luis, 1995).

General body size also may be an important determinant of sex appeal. Both men and women perceive thinner or average weight people of both sexes to be more physically attractive than extremely thin or very overweight individuals (e.g., Clayson & Klassen, 1989; Davis-Pyles, Conger, & Conger, 1990; Furnham & Radley, 1989; Lamb, Jackson, Cassiday, & Priest, 1993; Singh, 1993; Wiggins, Wiggins, & Conger, 1968). In addition, a study conducted by Regan (1996) suggests that obese individuals are not perceived to be as sexually appealing as average weight individuals. In this study, men and women received information about a man or woman who was characterized either as obese or average weight; they then made various inferences about the target individual's sexual characteristics. Participants viewed both the obese man and woman as less sexually attractive and desirable than their average weight counterparts.

In addition to body features, there are certain facial characteristics that seem to be universally preferred. For example, men and women in a variety of cultures rate "average" faces with symmetrical features as particularly desirable (e.g., Grammer & Thornhill, 1994; Jones & Hill, 1993; Langlois & Roggman, 1990). There are also specific configurations of facial features that most adults find appealing (although the superficial features, including skin tone and pigment, eye color, and lip size, that are considered attractive vary widely). A series of studies conducted by Cunningham and his colleagues (e.g., Cunningham, 1986; Cunningham, Barbee, & Pike, 1990) provides evidence that the most attractive male and female faces possess a combination of three types of attribute: neonate or babyish features (e.g., relatively large, wide-set eyes, a smallish nose), sexually mature features (prominent cheekbones and thinner cheeks, and, in men, a strong chin), and expressive features (including a wide smile and high eyebrows).

Although researchers have devoted little attention to the concept of sexual *un*desirability, data collected by Regan and her colleagues (e.g., Regan & Chapman, 2001; Regan, Whitlock, & Salgado, 2000) as part of an ongoing exploration of sexual desire substantiates the association between physical attractiveness and sex appeal. These researchers asked 900 heterosexual men and women to list or describe in a free response format all the characteristics that would render an opposite-sex individual sexually undesirable or repellant. Although participants considered a variety of characteristics to be sexually unappealing, the most commonly cited attribute category concerned physical appearance (over 80% mentioned appearance variables, ranging from general overall unattractiveness to specific facial or morphological features).

As before, then, Shakespeare was right. Romeo and Juliet truly were "bewitched by the charm of looks," and desire does appear to lie "not truly in [our] hearts, but in [our] eyes."

Sexual Passion.   Another sexual characteristic that has implications for attraction is sexual passion. Insofar as lust is believed by most people to be associated with passionate love and other important interpersonal phenomena, we might expect men and women to prefer a partner who is capable of both experiencing and expressing feelings of sexual passion. Few researchers have directly examined preferences for this particular partner attribute. However, there is some evidence in support of this hypothesis. For example, Sprecher and Regan (2002) asked a large sample of men and women to indicate how much "sexual passion" they preferred in three types of potential mate: a casual sex partner, a dating partner, and a marriage partner. Participants also were asked to report how important it was that they obtain a partner with that particular level of sexual passion. No differences were found between men and women or between types of potential mate in the amount desired of, or the importance placed on, this particular sexual attribute. Participants preferred equally high levels (close to 8 on a 9-point scale) of sexual passion from all three types of potential mate, and they placed equal importance on obtaining these desired high levels.

Employing a percentile ranking procedure, Regan, Levin, Sprecher, Christopher, and Cate (2000) also examined preferences for sexual passion. Participants in this study used percentiles to indicate where they would like their potential partners to rank on a particular characteristic relative to other same-sex individuals (e.g., a score of 50% indicated a preference for a partner who was average with respect to the characteristic). The results revealed that both men and women desired a romantic partner who ranked well above average on the attribute "sexually passionate/high sex drive." Specifically, men preferred that their potential mate possess more sexual passion and a higher sex drive than 80% of other women, and women preferred that their potential mate score higher on this attribute than 73% of other men.

Buss and Schmitt (1993, pp. 212–213) obtained similar results when they examined men's preferences for the partner attributes "low sex drive" and "prudish" (these attributes were not defined for participants but presumably reflect low levels of sexual passion). Their participants considered both a low sex drive and prudishness to be extremely undesirable in potential partners for short-term and long-term mating relationships.

More recently, Regan and Joshi (2003) asked a sample of adolescent boys and girls (average age = 15 years) to rate how important three attributes reflective of sexual passion—"sexually passionate," "high sex drive," and "sexually responsive"—were in a short-term, casual sex partner and a long-term, romantic partner. The ratings for these attributes were summed to create a composite preference score for each participant. The results revealed that both boys and girls believed that sexual passion was a highly desirable partner attribute (this composite variable received the highest importance rating in the casual sex partner condition and the third highest importance rating in the romantic partner condition). The results from partner preference studies, then, demonstrate that people prefer partners who demonstrate sexual passion and who possess a relatively high need for and interest in sex.

Although not much is known about the correlates and consequences of the attribute of sexual passion as it is expressed by partners in the early stages of ongoing romantic relationships, clinical surveys of couples in established (e.g., marital) relationships suggest that a marked loss or absence of sexual passion is interpreted by both partners as a sign of interpersonal dysfunction and as a problem that requires therapeutic intervention (e.g., Kaplan, 1979; Leiblum & Rosen, 1988; Talmadge & Talmadge, 1986; Trudel, 1991). In addition, results from person perception experiments indicate that men and women view an individual who does not sexually desire his or her dating partner (i.e., who possesses low levels of sexual passion for the partner) as feeling unhappy and dissatisfied with the quality of the romantic relationship and as being very likely to terminate that relationship (Regan, 1998, Experiment 3).

Considered together, these results support predictions generated from both social contextual and evolutionary theories.

Sexual Experience.   A person's level of sexual experience also may be an important predictor of attraction. Certainly Shakespeare extolled the virtue of virginity (particularly for women)—in *Romeo and Juliet*, the title characters proudly offer each other their "stainless maidenhoods" on their wedding night, and in *Much Ado About Nothing* Claudio refuses to wed Hero until she convinces him that "surely as I live, I am a maid" (a virgin).

Research does suggest that very high levels of premarital sexual experience are considered undesirable. For example, when Regan and Berscheid (1997) asked a group of men and women to rank order a list of characteristics, including several related to sexuality, in terms of their desirability in a potential romantic partner, their participants selected "being sexually available or 'easy'" as the least desirable attribute. Similar results were reported by Buss and Schmitt (1993, see Tables 2 and 3), who asked two samples of men to rate the sexual attributes "promiscuous," "sleeps around a lot," and "sexually experienced" in terms of their desirability in a potential long-term (romantic) partner. Participants viewed all three characteristics as undesirable. Although descriptive information (e.g., means, standard deviations) was not provided, the researchers reported that a sample of women also judged these characteristics to be highly undesirable in romantic partners (see p. 217).

Similar results are provided by person perception experiments. In one such study, Bettor, Hendrick, and Hendrick (1995) asked a group of college students to read a brief vignette about two target persons who were depicted as being involved in either a casual or a serious romantic relationship. In the casual relationship vignette, "Bob" and "Cathy" (the two targets) had met recently at a grocery store and exchanged phone numbers and within a week had gone on their first date (during which they had sex). In the serious relationship condition, the targets were described as meeting a year ago in a grocery store and dating steadily ever since, now feeling that they were in love, and having sex for the first time very recently. After reading the two vignettes, participants were asked to estimate the likelihood that Bob would consider marrying "a girl like Cathy" and that Cathy would consider marrying "a guy like Bob." The results revealed that participants thought that Bob would be much more likely to marry Cathy, and Cathy would be more likely to marry Bob, when the relationship was depicted as serious rather than casual. In other words, targets described as having engaged in sexual intercourse on a first date with someone they had just met were not considered as "marriageable" as those who were depicted as having waited to have sex until they were in a loving, committed relationship. Similar results were reported by O'Sullivan (1995). Participants in her study rated target persons described as having few past sexual partners as more desirable as dating partners and spouses than targets with numerous previous sex partners. In addition, targets presented as engaging in intercourse within a committed relationship were preferred more for both dating and marriage than targets described as engaging in sex in an uncommitted, casual relationship.

Similar findings are provided by researchers who examined the influence of a target person's sexual *attitudes*—rather than his or her sexual behavior—on romantic attraction. In one experiment, for example, Oliver and Sedikides (1992) asked men and women to rate the marriage desirability of an opposite-sex individual who ostensibly had completed the Sexual Permissiveness Scale (created by Hendrick & Hendrick, 1987) and who was extremely permissive (e.g., viewed casual, uncommitted sex as acceptable) or extremely nonpermissive (e.g., believed that sexual activity should be confined to marriage). Both men and women judged the highly sexually permissive target less favorably than the nonpermissive target in terms of marriage desirability.

In sum, the bulk of the evidence from self-report preference surveys and person perception experiments suggests that most adults view a high level of premarital sexual experience as a fairly undesirable partner attribute. However, this does not mean that people desire a partner who possesses absolutely no sexual experience whatsoever. Jacoby and Williams (1985) provided men and women with information about an opposite-sex target person who had high (sexual intercourse), moderate (some petting), or low (none) levels of lifetime sexual experience. The moderately experienced individual was preferred more than the other two as both a dating and marriage partner. Similar findings were reported by Sprecher, McKinney, and Orbuch (1991), who asked men and women to judge the dating desirability of either a male or a female target who was characterized as engaging in low, moderate, or high levels of sexual activity in his or her current relationship. Overall, the targets with moderate and high levels of sexual activity received higher dating desirability ratings than did the targets with no current sexual activity.

In addition, data from self-report mate preference studies conducted over the past several decades suggest that chastity or complete sexual inexperience has become increasingly unimportant to both men and women. For example, in one of the earliest mate preference studies (Hill, 1945), men and women received a list of 18 attributes that they ranked in terms of importance in a romantic partner. Chastity, defined as "no previous sexual experience," was ranked 10th in importance by participants, followed by 8 other attributes. A replication study conducted approximately 2 decades later by Hudson and Henze (1969) revealed that chastity had fallen to 15th in importance as a partner attribute (indeed, these researchers noted that chastity "declined [in importance] to a greater degree than did any other characteristic," p. 773). Ten years after that study, another replication conducted by Hoyt and Hudson (1981) revealed that chastity had continued to decline in importance—women ranked chastity second to last (17th), and men ranked it last (18th), in importance. Participants in yet another, and more recent, replication by Sprecher, Regan, McKinney, Maxwell, and Wazienski (1997) continued to place little value on chastity (women ranked it 17th in importance, and men ranked it 15th, in a marriage partner). Thus, although high levels of sexual experience are not considered extremely desirable in a potential mate, neither is complete sexual inexperience—at least among adults living in modern-day Western societies. Chastity may have been prized during previous eras; however, men and women today apparently want someone with just the "right" amount of sexual experience (neither too much nor too little), a finding that is more readily explained by a consideration of social context theories than of evolutionary perspectives.

Sexual Fidelity.   A fourth sexual attribute that plays a role in attraction is sexual exclusivity or fidelity. In the dramatic world created by Shakespeare, a high premium is placed on fidelity (even the merest hint of infidelity produces dire consequences ranging from relationship dissolution and social censure [*Troilus and Cressida, Much Ado About Nothing*] to violent death [*Othello, Hamlet*]). Our own world is no different; social scientific research consistently demonstrates that sexual fidelity between partners is one of the most fundamental beliefs that people hold about the nature of committed romantic relationships (Davis & Smith, 1991; Feldman, Cauffman, Jensen, & Arnett, 2000; Glenn & Weaver, 1979; Wiederman & Allgeier, 1996). Although infidelity does occur (e.g., Michael, Gagnon, Laumann, & Kolata, 1994; Wiederman, 1997), the general presumption in all human societies is that once an individual is romantically committed to another, he or she will confine sexual activities to that relationship (e.g., Fisher, 1992; Frayser, 1989).

Few researchers have directly investigated the association between sexual fidelity as a partner attribute or behavior and attraction in the initial or beginning stages of romantic relationships. However, the fact that men and women who imagine their dating partner having intercourse with another person subsequently report experiencing high levels of distress or emotional upset (for a review of this literature, see Harris, 2000; also see Guerrero, Spitzberg, & Yoshimura, chapter 13, this volume) certainly suggests that sexual fidelity is a desirable partner characteristic or behavioral tendency.

More direct evidence is provided by research on undesirable partner attributes, called "social allergens" by Cunningham and his colleagues (e.g., Cunningham, Barbee, & Druen, 1996; Rowatt et al., 1997). These researchers found that men and women are highly repulsed by romantic partners whose behavior suggests an inability or an unwillingness to be sexually exclusive (e.g., who look longingly at others; who brag about their sexual prowess; who talk often about previous romantic/sexual partners). Similar results were found by Buss and Dedden (1990), who asked a sample of undergraduates to list all the "things people do to make others of their same sex *undesirable* to members of the opposite sex" (p. 401, emphasis in original). A second sample of participants then rated these tactics in terms of their effectiveness in accomplishing the specified goal (i.e., making someone undesirable to members of the opposite sex). The results revealed that questioning the individual's sexual fidelity (e.g., accusing him/her of "cheating" on partners or of being unable to "stay loyal" to partners) was considered one of the most effective methods for rendering a man or woman romantically undesirable.

Two studies of desirable and undesirable partner attributes conducted by Buss and Schmitt (1993, p. 217, Table 3) also suggest that fidelity is an important sexual attribute to possess and demonstrate to one's partner. In the first study, men rated the desirability of the characteristics "faithful" and "sexually loyal"; in the second study, another sample of men evaluated the attribute "unfaithful." The results revealed that both fidelity and sexual loyalty were considered highly desirable in a potential romantic partner, whereas infidelity was seen as the single most undesirable characteristic in a potential mate. As before, the researchers did not provide descriptive statistical information but noted that they collected similar data from women and found nearly identical results.

This pattern of findings supports the predictions generated by the social context and evolutionary theories reviewed earlier.

CONCLUSIONS AND SUGGESTIONS

There are a number of conclusions and suggestions to offer to scholars interested in lust, love, and related phenomena. My first conclusion is that sexual desire is an important human experience and one that merits scientific attention. Largely because of its association with passionate love, this aspect of human sexual response takes on great significance in initial encounters between potential partners and during very early relationship stages (e.g., a person who experiences sexual desire for another individual may assume that he or she is becoming romantically interested in, or even falling in love with, that other; this conclusion, in turn, may prompt the initiation or intensification of a romantic relationship). This conclusion—that we should study sexual desire—may seem commonsensical to many readers; however, sexual desire has been recognized only very recently as a separate and distinct aspect of human sexuality (in fact, Masters and Johnson included desire in the human sexual response cycle for the very first time in the mid-1990s; see Masters et al., 1994). Consequently, we know less about sexual desire than we do about other sexual phenomena, and there is a great need to delineate more clearly the factors that are implicated in the experience of sexual desire, explore the interpersonal context of lust (particularly the meanings that people give to sexual desire in their ongoing romantic relationships), and construct reliable and valid measures of desire. Because sexual desire is a motivational (as opposed to a physiological or behavioral) construct, this latter task may prove particularly challenging; nonetheless, it is a necessary undertaking if we wish to empirically examine the antecedents, correlates, and interpersonal consequences of this sexual response (and we can take heart from the fact that a number of reliable measures of love—a concept that, like desire, was for many years not considered amenable to scientific investigation—have been constructed and utilized; see, for example, scales crafted by Hatfield and Sprecher [1986] and Hendrick and Hendrick [1990]).

My second conclusion, to which I alluded briefly in the previous paragraph, is that much more attention needs to be paid to the dynamics of lust and its role in ongoing romantic relationships. Over 10 years ago, a number of theorists and researchers contributed chapters to an edited book entitled *Sexuality in Close Relationships* (McKinney & Sprecher, 1991). In addition to discussing their topics, several authors outlined questions and avenues of investigation they believed would be fruitful—and necessary—for future research to explore. For example, Orbuch and Harvey (1991) called for longitudinal research that would provide more comprehensive information on how sexual events causally influence (and are influenced by) nonsexual events in ongoing relationships, for the adoption of a dyadic approach to relational sexuality and the collection of data from both members of couples, and for more direct investigations of the interpersonal meanings that couples place on the occurrence (or the cessation) of sexual activities within their relationship. Much of what these authors said a decade ago remains relevant today, particularly with respect to sexual desire, and can serve as a springboard for future research on this topic. For example, does sexual attraction experienced for a dating partner predict subsequent feelings of passionate love? Does sexual attraction between dating partners contribute to relationship commitment and intensification? Does frequent sexual activity between dating partners result in a satiation or diminution of desire and, if so, does this diminution of desire result in lowered levels of passionate love? Does the absence or loss of sexual desire for a romantic partner produce interpersonal distress and/or relationship termination? What is the impact of mismatched levels of sexual desire in the beginning stages of romantic relationships? These and other questions warrant sustained investigation.

A similar issue arises with respect to the various sexual attributes considered in this chapter. Most of the empirical research that has been conducted on such characteristics as chastity, sex appeal, sexual fidelity, and sexual passion or sex drive has focused on preferences for these attributes (usually with respect to hypothetical mates) rather than on the personal and interpersonal consequences they may have for individuals involved in ongoing romantic relationships. We know, for example, that people prefer that their potential dates and marital partners possess sex appeal (i.e., physical attractiveness) and a high sex drive, have lower rather than higher levels of prior sexual experience, and demonstrate sexual fidelity. What we do not know is how much weight people give to these attributes when initiating actual relationships, or how important these attributes continue to be over the course of a romantic relationship. Does a change in sex appeal produce a change in romantic attraction within an already existing relationship? Does infidelity in beginning relationships have the same kind of deleterious impact that it seems to have in established relationships? It is difficult to capture the experiences of partners who are in the very initial stages of a romantic relationship (e.g., these associations are fragile, frequently unstable, and often lack a clear beginning, and partners may not even recognize or identify their association as a "relationship" until they have passed beyond the stages of empirical interest). Nonetheless, this type of research clearly is needed if we are to gain an understanding of the importance (or unimportance) of sexual attributes in determining romantic attraction.

My third conclusion is that it would be helpful if those of us who use social context and evolutionary theories to generate our hypotheses about sex, love, and mating would make a greater effort to systematically examine the theories themselves (in particular, the mechanisms that they propose create and sustain human behavior). For example, evolutionary theories suggest that physical attractiveness is an important component of sex appeal because physical appearance was an adaptively significant attribute in ancestral times (i.e., attractiveness advertised a person's underlying health and fitness, and those early humans who selected mates based on that attribute enjoyed greater reproductive success than those who did not). We cannot travel back in time, but we can at least investigate whether, for example, attractiveness actually correlates with physical, genetic, or reproductive health in contemporary societies. Some researchers are, in fact, exploring this issue, and their work provides valuable information on the utility of the evolutionary framework (e.g., Singh [1993, 1995] has extensively documented the correlation between waist-to-hip ratio and health and reproductive status; Kalick, Zebrowitz, Langlois, and Johnson [1998] have examined the relationship between facial attractiveness and health status). Similarly, social context theories posit that socialization processes and the rewards and punishments meted out by social objects (e.g., parents, peers) shape our sexual preferences and behaviors. It is just as impossible to travel back to our participants' early childhoods and examine their interactions with parents and peers as it is to journey back into the origins of our species. However, we can search the developmental, sociological, and social psychological literatures for evidence about the norms that exist with respect to sexuality in children and adolescents. I am not proposing that each scientist devote his or her professional life to theory testing. Rather, I am suggesting that we (and I include myself in this) use existing theories as more than window dressing for our hypotheses and data, and that we also familiarize ourselves with literature from our own and from other disciplines that speaks to the utility and validity of these theories.

My fourth and final conclusion is that Shakespeare really knew what he was talking about (and he said it beautifully). Lust is powerfully and intimately connected with the experience of being in love, physical appearance is a potent component of sex appeal, and fidelity, chastity, and passion are important sexual attributes to possess and seek in a romantic partner. It is essential that contemporary scholars keep sight of the past, and remain in touch with earlier discourse—some scientific, some not so scientific—on their particular topics. Many of the ideas and concepts put forth by those who have gone before us have stood the test of time and are amenable to empirical investigation. I close by simply noting that, while I do not underestimate the value of theory construction and hypothesis testing, or the necessity of following the tenets of the scientific method, a lot can be gained from spending a little time with a good book.

REFERENCES

Berscheid, E. (1988). Some comments on love's anatomy: Or, whatever happened to old-fashioned lust? In R. J. Sternberg & M. L. Barnes (Eds.), *The psychology of love* (pp. 359–374). New Haven, CT: Yale University Press.

Berscheid, E., & Meyers, S. A. (1996). A social categorical approach to a question about love. *Personal Relationships, 3*, 19–43.

Berscheid, E., & Walster, E. (1974). A little bit about love. In T. L. Huston (Ed.), *Foundations of interpersonal attraction* (pp. 355–381). New York: Academic Press.

Bettor, L., Hendrick, S. S., & Hendrick, C. (1995). Gender and sexual standards in dating relationships. *Personal Relationships, 2*, 359–369.

Blau, P. M. (1964). *Exchange and power in social life.* New York: Wiley.

Buss, D. M., & Dedden, L. A. (1990). Derogation of competitors. *Journal of Social and Personal Relationships, 7*, 395–422.

Buss, D. M., & Schmitt, D. P. (1993). Sexual strategies theory: An evolutionary perspective on human mating. *Psychological Review, 100*, 204–232.

Capellanus, A. (1960). *The art of courtly love.* (J. J. Parry, Trans.). New York: Columbia University Press. (Original work written approximately 1184)

Christopher, F. S. (2001). *To dance the dance: A symbolic interactional exploration of premarital sexuality*. Mahwah, NJ: Lawrence Erlbaum Associates.

Clayson, D. E., & Klassen, M. L. (1989). Perception of attractiveness by obesity and hair color. *Perceptual and Motor Skills, 68*, 199–202.

Cosmides, L., & Tooby, J. (1997). *Evolutionary psychology: A primer*. Retrieved September 26, 2003 from http://www.psych.ucsb.edu/research/cep/primer.html

Cunningham, M. R. (1986). Measuring the physical in physical attractiveness: Quasi-experiments on the sociobiology of female facial beauty. *Journal of Personality and Social Psychology, 50*, 925–935.

Cunningham, M. R., Barbee, A. P., & Druen, P. B. (1996). Social allergens and the reactions that they produce: Escalation of annoyance and disgust in love and work. In R. M. Kowalski (Ed.), *Aversive interpersonal behaviors* (pp. 189–214). New York: Plenum.

Cunningham, M. R., Barbee, A. P., & Pike, C. L. (1990). What do women want? Facialmetric assessment of multiple motives in the perception of male facial physical attractiveness. *Journal of Personality and Social Psychology, 59*, 61–72.

Darwin, C. (1859). *On the origin of the species by means of natural selection, or, preservation of favoured races in the struggle for life*. London: J. Murray.

Darwin, C. (1871). *The descent of man, and selection in relation to sex*. London: J. Murray.

Davis, J. A., & Smith, T. (1991). *General social surveys, 1972–1991*. Storrs, CT: University of Connecticut, Roper Center for Public Opinion Research.

Davis-Pyles, B., Conger, J. C., & Conger, A. J. (1990). The impact of deviant weight on social competence ratings. *Behavioral Assessment, 12*, 443–455.

Dion, K., Berscheid, E., & Walster, E. (1972). What is beautiful is good. *Journal of Personality and Social Psychology, 24*, 285–290.

Ellis, A. (1954). *The American sexual tragedy*. New York: Twayne.

Ellis, H. (1901–1928). *Studies in the psychology of sex* (Vols. 1–7). Philadelphia, PA: F. A. Davis. (Original work published 1897–1928)

Ellis, H. (1963). *Psychology of sex*. New York: New American Library of World Literature. (Original work published 1933)

Feldman, S. S., Cauffman, E., Jensen, L. A., & Arnett, J. J. (2000). The (un)acceptability of betrayal: A study of college students' evaluations of sexual betrayal by a romantic partner and betrayal of a friend's confidence. *Journal of Youth and Adolescence, 29*, 499–523.

Fisher, H. (1992). *Anatomy of love: A natural history of mating, marriage, and why we stray*. New York: Fawcett Columbine.

Fisher, W. A., Byrne, D., White, L. A., & Kelley, K. (1988). Erotophobia-erotophilia as a dimension of personality. *The Journal of Sex Research, 25*, 123–151.

Frayser, S. G. (1989). Sexual and reproductive relationships: Cross-cultural evidence and biosocial implications. *Medical Anthropology, 11*, 385–407.

Freud, S. (1963). "Civilized" sexual morality and modern nervousness. In P. Rieff (Ed.), *Sexuality and the psychology of love* (pp. 20–40). New York: Collier Books. (Original work published 1908)

Freud, S. (1963). The most prevalent form of degradation in erotic life. In P. Rieff (Ed.), *Sexuality and the psychology of love* (pp. 58–70). New York: Collier Books. (Original work published 1912)

Fromm, E. (1956). *The art of loving*. New York: Harper & Row.

Furnham, A. F., & Radley, S. (1989). Sex differences in the perception of male and female body shapes. *Personality and Individual Differences, 10*, 653–662.

Furnham, A., Tan, T., & McManus, C. (1997). Waist-to-hip ratio and preferences for body shape: A replication and extension. *Personality and Individual Differences, 22*, 539–549.

Gagnon, J. H., & Simon, W. (1973). *Sexual conduct: The social sources of human sexuality*. Chicago: Aldine-Atherton.

Gangestad, S. W., & Simpson, J. A. (1990). Toward an evolutionary history of female sociosexual variation. *Journal of Personality, 58*, 69–96.

Glenn, N. D., & Weaver, N. (1979). Attitudes toward premarital, extramarital, and homosexual relations in the U.S. in the 1970s. *The Journal of Sex Research, 15*, 108–119.

Grammer, K., & Thornhill, R. (1994). Human (*homo sapiens*) facial attractiveness and sexual selection: The role of symmetry and averageness. *Journal of Comparative Psychology, 108*, 233–242.

Green, S. E., & Mosher, D. L. (1985). A causal model of sexual arousal to erotic fantasies. *The Journal of Sex Research, 21*, 1–23.

Harris, C. R. (2000). Psychophysiological responses to imagined jealousy: The specific innate modular view of jealousy reconsidered. *Journal of Personality and Social Psychology, 78*, 1082–1091.

Hatfield, E., & Rapson, R. L. (1993). *Love, sex, and intimacy: Their psychology, biology, and history*. New York: HarperCollins.

Hatfield, E., & Sprecher, S. (1986). Measuring passionate love in intimate relationships. *Journal of Adolescence, 9*, 383–410.

Hendrick, C., & Hendrick, S. S. (1990). A relationship-specific version of the Love Attitudes Scale. *Journal of Social Behavior and Personality, 5*, 239–254.

Hendrick, S. S., & Hendrick, C. (1987). Multidimensionality of sexual attitudes. *The Journal of Sex Research, 23*, 502–526.

Hendrick, S. S., & Hendrick, C. (1992). *Liking, loving, & relating* (2nd ed.). Pacific Grove, CA: Brooks/Cole.

Hendrick, S. S., & Hendrick, C. (2000). Romantic love. In C. Hendrick & S. S. Hendrick (Eds.), *Close relationships: A sourcebook* (pp. 202–215). Thousand Oaks, CA: Sage.

Henss, R. (1995). Waist-to-hip ratio and attractiveness: Replication and extension. *Personality and Individual Differences, 19,* 479–488.

Hill, R. (1945). Campus values in mate-selection. *Journal of Home Economics, 37,* 554–558.

Hogben, M., & Byrne, D. (1998). Using social learning theory to explain individual differences in human sexuality. *The Journal of Sex Research, 35,* 58–71.

Hoyt, L. L., & Hudson, J. W. (1981). Personal characteristics important in mate preference among college students. *Social Behavior and Personality, 9,* 93–96.

Hudson, J. W., & Henze, L. F. (1969). Campus values in mate selection: A replication. *Journal of Marriage and the Family, 31,* 772–775.

Jacoby, A. P., & Williams, J. D. (1985). Effects of premarital sexual standards and behavior on dating and marriage desirability. *Journal of Marriage and the Family, 47,* 1059–1065.

James, W. (1950). *The principles of psychology* (Vol. 2). New York: Dover. (Original work published 1890)

Jones, D., & Hill, K. (1993). Criteria of facial attractiveness in five populations. *Human Nature, 4,* 271–296.

Kalick, S. M., Zebrowitz, L. A., Langlois, J. H., & Johnson, R. M. (1998). Does human facial attractiveness honestly advertise health? Longitudinal data on an evolutionary question. *Psychological Science, 9,* 8–13.

Kaplan, H. S. (1979). *Disorders of sexual desire and other new concepts and techniques in sex therapy.* New York: Simon & Schuster.

Krafft-Ebing, R. von. (1945). *Psychopathia sexualis* (12th ed.). New York: Pioneer. (Original work published 1886)

Lamb, S. C., Jackson, L. A., Cassiday, P. B., & Priest, D. J. (1993). Body figure preferences of men and women: A comparison of two generations. *Sex Roles, 28,* 345–358.

Langlois, J. H., & Roggman, L. A. (1990). Attractive faces are only average. *Psychological Science, 1,* 115–121.

Lee, J. A. (1973). *Colours of love: An exploration of the ways of loving.* Toronto, Canada: New Press.

Lee, J. A. (1988). Love-styles. In R. J. Sternberg & M. L. Barnes (Eds.), *The psychology of love* (pp. 38–67). New Haven, CT: Yale University Press.

Leiblum, S. R., & Rosen, R. C. (Eds.). (1988). *Sexual desire disorders.* New York: Guilford.

Lewis, C. S. (1988). *The four loves.* New York: Harcourt Brace. (Original work published 1960)

Masters, W. H., Johnson, V. E., & Kolodny, R. C. (1982). *Human sexuality.* Boston: Little, Brown.

Masters, W. H., Johnson, V. E., & Kolodny, R. C. (1994). *Heterosexuality.* New York: HarperCollins.

McKinney, K., & Sprecher, S. (Eds.) (1991). *Sexuality in close relationships.* Hillsdale, NJ: Lawrence Erlbaum Associates.

Michael, R. T., Gagnon, J. H., Laumann, E. O., & Kolata, G. (1994). *Sex in America: A definitive survey.* Boston: Little, Brown.

Mischel, W. (1966). A social-learning view of sex differences in behavior. In E. E. Maccoby (Ed.), *The development of sex differences* (pp. 56–81). Stanford, CA: Stanford University Press.

Murstein, B. I. (1970). Stimulus-value-role: A theory of marital choice. *Journal of Marriage and the Family, 32,* 465–481.

Murstein, B. I. (1976). *Who will marry whom? Theories and research in marital choice.* New York: Springer.

Oliver, M. B., & Sedikides, C. (1992). Effects of sexual permissiveness on desirability of partner as a function of low and high commitment to relationship. *Social Psychology Quarterly, 55,* 321–333.

Orbuch, T. L., & Harvey, J. H. (1991). Methodological and conceptual issues in the study of sexuality in close relationships. In K. McKinney & S. Sprecher (Eds.), *Sexuality in close relationships* (pp. 9–24). Hillsdale, NJ: Lawrence Erlbaum Associates.

O'Sullivan, L. F. (1995). Less is more: The effects of sexual experience on judgments of men's and women's personality characteristics and relationship desirability. *Sex Roles, 33,* 159–181.

Regan, P. C. (1996). Sexual outcasts: The perceived impact of body weight on sexuality. *Journal of Applied Social Psychology, 26,* 1803–1815.

Regan, P. C. (1998). Of lust and love: Beliefs about the role of sexual desire in romantic relationships. *Personal Relationships, 5,* 139–157.

Regan, P. C. (2000). The role of sexual desire and sexual activity in dating relationships. *Social Behavior and Personality, 28,* 51–60.

Regan, P. C. (2002). Functional features: An evolutionary perspective on inappropriate relationships. In R. Goodwin & D. Cramer (Eds.), *Inappropriate relationships: The unconventional, the disapproved, and the forbidden* (pp. 25–42). Mahwah, NJ: Lawrence Erlbaum Associates.

Regan, P. C., & Berscheid, E. (1995). Gender differences in beliefs about the causes of male and female sexual desire. *Personal Relationships, 2,* 345–358.

Regan, P. C., & Berscheid, E. (1997). Gender differences in characteristics desired in a potential sexual and marriage partner. *Journal of Psychology and Human Sexuality, 9,* 25–37.

Regan, P. C., & Berscheid, E. (1999). *Lust: What we know about human sexual desire.* Thousand Oaks, CA: Sage.

Regan, P. C., & Chapman, W. (2001, July). *Sexual turn-offs: Beliefs about repellant partner characteristics.* Paper presented at the joint conference of the International Network on Personal Relationships and the International Society for the Study of Personal Relationships, Prescott, AZ.

Regan, P. C., & Joshi, A. (2003). Ideal partner preferences among adolescents. *Social Behavior and Personality, 31*, 13–20.

Regan, P. C., Kocan, E. R., & Whitlock, T. (1998). Ain't love grand! A prototype analysis of romantic love. *Journal of Social and Personal Relationships, 15*, 411–420.

Regan, P. C., Levin, L., Sprecher, S., Christopher, F. S., & Cate, R. (2000). Partner preferences: What characteristics do men and women desire in their short-term sexual and long-term romantic partners? *Journal of Psychology & Human Sexuality, 12*, 1–21.

Regan, P. C., Whitlock, T., & Salgado, S. (2000, April). *Sexual turn-offs: Beliefs about repellant partner characteristics.* Paper presented at the annual conference of the Western Psychological Association, Portland, OR.

Reik, T. (1944). *A psychologist looks at love.* New York: Farrar & Rinehart.

Reik, T. (1945). *Psychology of sex relations.* New York: Grove Press.

Reiss, I. L. (1967). *The social context of premarital sexual permissiveness.* New York: Holt, Rinehart, & Winston.

Reiss, I. L. (1981). Some observations on ideology and sexuality in America. *Journal of Marriage and the Family, 43*, 271–283.

Reiss, I. L. (1986). *Journey into sexuality: An exploratory voyage.* Englewood Cliffs, NJ: Prentice-Hall.

Ridge, R. D., & Berscheid, E. (1989, May). *On loving and being in love: A necessary distinction.* Paper presented at the annual convention of the Midwestern Psychological Association, Chicago, IL.

Rowatt, T. J., Cunningham, M. R., Rowatt, W. C., Miles, S. S., Ault-Gauthier, L. K., Georgianna, J., & Shamblin, S. (1997, July). *Men and women are from Earth: Life-span strategy dynamics in mate choices.* Paper presented at the meeting of the International Network on Personal Relationships, Oxford, OH.

Shakespeare, W. (1943). *Romeo and Juliet.* In *The tragedies of Shakespeare* (Vol. I, pp. 277–364). New York: The Modern Library. (Original work published 1599)

Shakespeare, W. (1943). *Troilus and Cressida.* In *The tragedies of Shakespeare* (Vol. I, pp. 1–96). New York: The Modern Library. (Original work published 1609)

Sherwin, R., & Corbett, S. (1985). Campus sexual norms and dating relationships: A trend analysis. *The Journal of Sex Research, 21*, 258–274.

Simon, W. (1974). The social, the erotic, and the sensual: The complexities of sexual scripts. In J. K. Cole & R. Deinstbier (Eds.), *The Nebraska symposium on motivation, 1973* (pp. 61–82). Lincoln: University of Nebraska Press.

Simon, W., & Gagnon, J. H. (1986). Sexual scripts: Permanence and change. *Archives of Sexual Behavior, 15*, 97–120.

Simpson, J. A., & Gangestad, S. W. (1991). Individual differences in sociosexuality: Evidence for convergent and discriminant validity. *Journal of Personality and Social Psychology, 60*, 870–883.

Singh, D. (1993). Adaptive significance of female physical attractiveness: Role of waist-to-hip ratio. *Journal of Personality and Social Psychology, 65*, 293–307.

Singh, D. (1994). Body fat distribution and perception of desirable female body shape by young Black men and women. *International Journal of Eating Disorders, 16*, 289–294.

Singh, D. (1995). Female judgment of male attractiveness and desirability for relationships: Role of waist-to-hip ratio and financial status. *Journal of Personality and Social Psychology, 69*, 1089–1101.

Singh, D., & Luis, S. (1995). Ethnic and gender consensus for the effect of waist-to-hip ratio on judgment of women's attractiveness. *Human Nature, 6*, 51–65.

Sprecher, S., McKinney, K., & Orbuch, T. L. (1991). The effect of current sexual behavior on friendship, dating, and marriage desirability. *The Journal of Sex Research, 28*, 387–408.

Sprecher, S., & Regan, P. C. (2002). Liking some things (in some people) more than others: Partner preferences in romantic relationships and friendships. *Journal of Social and Personal Relationships, 19*, 463–481.

Sprecher, S., Regan, P. C., McKinney, K., Maxwell, K., & Wazienski, R. (1997). Preferred level of sexual experience in a date or mate: The merger of two methodologies. *The Journal of Sex Research, 34*, 327–337.

Sternberg, R. J., & Barnes, M. L. (Eds.) (1988). *The psychology of love.* New Haven, CT: Yale University Press.

Talmadge, L. D., & Talmadge, W. C. (1986). Relational sexuality: An understanding of low sexual desire. *Journal of Sex & Marital Therapy, 12*, 3–21.

Tennov, D. (1979). *Love and limerence.* New York: Stein and Day.

Tennov, D. (1998). Love madness. In V. C. de Munck (Ed.), *Romantic love and sexual behavior: Perspectives from the social sciences* (pp. 77–88). Westport, CT: Praeger.

Trudel, G. (1991). Review of psychological factors in low sexual desire. *Sexual and Marital Therapy, 6*, 261–272.

Walster, E., & Berscheid, E. (1971). Adrenaline makes the heart grow fonder. *Psychology Today, 5*, 47–62.

Walster, E., Walster, G. W., & Berscheid, E. (1978). *Equity: Theory and research.* Boston: Allyn & Bacon.

Wiederman, M. W. (1997). Extramarital sex: Prevalence and correlates in a national survey. *The Journal of Sex Research, 34*, 167–174.

Wiederman, M. W., & Allgeier, E. R. (1996). Expectations and attributions regarding extramarital sex among young married individuals. *Journal of Psychology and Human Sexuality, 8*, 21–35.

Wiggins, J. S., Wiggins, N., & Conger, J. C. (1968). Correlates of heterosexual somatic preference. *Journal of Personality and Social Psychology, 10*, 82–90.

6

First Sexual Involvement in
Romantic Relationships: An
Empirical Investigation of
Communicative Framing,
Romantic Beliefs, and
Attachment Orientation in the
Passion Turning Point

Sandra Metts
Illinois State University

This chapter examines the immediate and long-term consequences of first sexual involvement in dating couples. Drawing on the "passion turning point" construct articulated by Baxter and Bullis (1986), research is reviewed that suggests the events or elements within the passion turning point (first kiss, first sex, "I love you," and the whirlwind phenomenon) are not only conceptually related, but also temporally related. More specifically, an argument is advanced that when expressions of love occur prior to first sexual involvement in dating relationships, the event is more likely to have positive consequences for the relationship both immediately and over time for relationships that continue to develop. In addition, research is reviewed to suggest that attachment orientations may contribute to how variations in the sequencing of the passion turning point are interpreted both immediately after first sex and over time. A survey study of college students who have experienced first sex in a current or recent past relationship is presented as a preliminary test of the arguments derived for related literature.

The author would like to thank Allison Rattenborg for her assistance with this project.

INTRODUCTION

The notion that relationships move through stages of increased intimacy and interdependence or, alternatively, through stages of decreased intimacy and separateness has been a prevailing view in the interpersonal area for some time (e.g., Altman & Taylor, 1973; Knapp, 1984). In recent years, scholars began to examine the affective and behavioral events, transitions, or "turning points" that people use as interpretative signals of change in the commitment, intensity, definition, or stage of development in their romantic relationships (e.g., Baxter & Bullis, 1986; Bullis, Clark, & Sline, 1993; Huston, Surra, Fitzgerald, & Cate, 1981; Lloyd & Cate, 1985; Surra, 1987). It is not surprising that sexual involvement emerges as a particularly salient indicator of increasing commitment in many dating relationships, although certainly not all. The question that still intrigues relationship scholars is what aspects of the first sexual involvement experience in dating relationships predict positive emotional and relational outcomes, or alternatively, dissatisfaction and relationship instability or termination.

This chapter focuses on this question by exploring both the contextual aspects of the first sexual involvement and the dispositional or personality traits of the individuals involved. Relationship events are contextual in that they are constituted within and given meaning through the conversations of partners (Baxter & Montgomery, 1996; Duck, 1995), but events and the messages that accompany them are also processed through the interpretive screens of individual dispositions and previous experiences. This dynamic is echoed in the distinction between the proximal context and distal context in Bradbury and Fincham's (1989) Contextual Model of Marital Interaction. As these authors demonstrate, messages sent during interactions in the proximal context and their interpretation are influenced by and subsequently influence the relatively enduring traits and dispositions that partners bring to the interaction from the distal context.

Accordingly, the first section of this chapter reviews research on the contextual or situational factors relevant to the "passion turning point" (Baxter & Bullis, 1986). An argument is developed that the sequencing of events entailed by the passion turning point, specifically expressions of love prior to sexual involvement, is consistent with cultural expectations or sexual scripts. As a result, events consistent with this sequence are more likely than events not consistent with this sequence to be followed by positive relational and emotional outcomes, both immediately after first sex and over time for relationships that continue to develop. The second section reviews research on two dispositional or personality variables that are influential in relationship development, and presumably, therefore, influential in responses to first sexual involvement in dating relationships. These factors are romantic beliefs and attachment orientation. For example, a person who is generally secure in his or her attachment orientation may not need to hear the statement, "I love you," to feel positive about sexual involvement or may readily accept the statement as a sincere measure of relationship commitment if it is spoken. A person who is generally fearful or anxious in his or her attachment orientation, on the other hand, may need to hear expressions of affection but, ironically, may question the legitimacy of the message and feel ambivalence about sexual involvement even when the message is direct and explicit.

Of course, these speculations invite empirical investigation to determine their validity. Thus, the third section of this chapter presents an empirical investigation of the extent to which individual dispositions in attachment and romantic beliefs also contribute to the personal and relational outcomes of the passion turning point both immediately following the event and over time. The chapter closes with a summary of the findings and offers directions for future research on the nature of and consequences following first sexual involvement in romantic relationships.

CONTEXTUAL FACTORS: THE PASSION TURNING POINT

Building on the early work of Bolton (1961), Baxter and Bullis (1986) initiated their systematic investigations of transition relevant junctures or "turning points" in relationship development. According to Baxter and Bullis (1986), a turning point is "any event or occurrence that is associated with change in a relationship" (p. 470). Based on interviews with 80 romantic partners, they derived 13 broad categories of turning points from the 579 events generated during the interviews. In order of frequency, these included: (1) get-to-know time (first meeting, activity time, first date); (2) quality time (meet the family, getting away time); (3) physical separation; (4) external competition (new rival, competing demands, old rival); (5) reunion; (6) passion (first kiss, first sex, "I love you," whirlwind phenomenon); (7) disengagement; (8) positive psychic change; (9) exclusivity; (10) negative psychic change; (11) making up; (12) serious commitment (living together, marital plans); and (13) sacrifice (crisis help, favors, gifts). As indicated by the ordering in this list, the passion turning point was recalled with moderate frequency; the 48 instances reported constituted about 6% of all turning points recalled. Among the more specific events that were collapsed within the passion turning point rubric, first sex was the most frequently reported (23), followed by first kiss (10), statements of "I love you" (9), and whirlwind phenomenon (i.e., experiencing "love at first sight" [6]). In addition, the passion turning point, along with exclusivity, making up, disengagement, and serious commitment, was likely to involve meta-communication or talk about the relationship, and to mark a positive increase in commitment as indicated by respondents on the Retrospective Interview Technique graph (Huston et al., 1981).

In a subsequent study of perceptions of dialectical contradictions associated with these categories of turning points, Baxter and Erbert (2000) interviewed 50 heterosexual dating couples. Not only did Baxter and Erbert identify three more turning points (network interaction, conflict, and relationship talk), but they also found a complicated association between the passion turning point and three primary relational dialectics: Openness–Closedness, Autonomy–Connection, and Predictability–Novelty. Respondents characterized the passion turning point as evoking the strongest tension in the Openness–Closedness dialectic. Thus, when respondents experienced the passion turning point, they felt a tension between the competing desires to fully reveal their feelings (openness) while at the same time wanting to protect themselves and avoid being vulnerable (closedness). In addition, however, respondents described how their passion turning point created tension related to the dialectics of Autonomy–Connection and Predictability–Novelty as well. They described feeling tension between the desires to maintain some degree of independence (autonomy) but also be intimately connected to their partner (connection), and to have consistency and clear expectations in the relationship (predictability) without succumbing to boredom and losing the excitement of the unexpected (novelty). According to Baxter and Erbert, the simultaneous interplay of these three dialectics was evident when respondents described the verbal ("I love you") and nonverbal (first sex) expressions of passion. Specifically, respondents indicated emerging tensions in these dialectics as they "grappled with the uncertain implications of such an expression for relational development" (p. 561). Using these same interviews in a follow-up study of how couples communicatively remember turning points in their reminiscing, storytelling, relational idioms, and celebrations, Baxter and Pittman (2001) found that the passion turning point was among those most frequently "remembered" or "commemorated" by couples in their communication rituals.

In sum, as indicated in the studies reviewed, the passion turning point is highly salient to dating couples. Further, although it might evoke some degree of dialectical strain as couples adjust to the open expression of emotional involvement that it represents and to the uncertainty of its relational implications, it is generally considered a positive force in the trajectory of the relationship. Three points about this line of research, however, merit additional comment.

First, when intact couples are interviewed about the turning points in their relationships, events that resulted in termination will not likely surface. The "breaking up" turning point and its correlate, the "making up" turning point, will emerge, but these two events are necessarily embedded within an overall progression toward relationship development. Although this is of little consequence when the researcher's goal is to understand turning points in relationships that continue toward advanced levels of commitment, it can be problematic when the goal is to understand the nature of turning points whose consequences are negative and ultimately derail developing relationships. Thus, a sample containing both continuing and terminated relationships would yield a fuller understanding of the passion turning point and its relational consequences.

Second, the four elements or specific events that constitute the passion turning point—first kiss, first sex, "I love you," and the whirlwind phenomenon—are not treated as separate units in the turning points analyses. Given the research goals of Baxter and her colleagues (i.e., to identify the events that function as relational turning points, to explain their characteristics, and to determine their association with other processes such as dialectical contradictions), collapsing more specific events into fewer supracategories for purposes of analysis is certainly reasonable. However, closer examination of the four elements collapsed within the passion turning point suggests that they might be temporally related, rather than simply conceptually linked. More specifically, they may represent different moves or scenes in a sort of "miniscript" for first sexual involvement in a relationship (Simon & Gagnon, 1986; see Metts & Cupach, 1989, for a review). If so, sequences that reflect cultural expectations about sexual episodes in romantic relationships might function as a more positive force in relationship development than those that do not. For example, a traditional sequence might unfold with the first kiss, expressions of love and commitment, and then "first sex." If first sex occurs before expressions of love, or occurs in the absence of expressions of love, this turning point might seem to partners less indicative of relationship advancement and more indicative of "casual sex," possibly evoking a sense of personal vulnerability and risk. By contrast, if it should be the case that the explicit expression of "I love you" occurs before even the first kiss in a dating relationship, one or both partners might perceive this to be a reversal of the more traditional sequence of affection intensifying into emotional commitment. Of course the interpretation of any particular sequence and its impact on the direction of relationship development might be attenuated by the presence of the whirlwind phenomenon, or as Baxter and Bullis (1986) say, "the proverbial love-at-first-sight phenomenon." For individuals who believe they are experiencing love at first sight, the temporal ordering of moves within the passion turning point may not be particularly salient because the rapture of sudden and intense infatuation frames any sequence as the "right" one.

A third observation related to turning point research, and one that is relevant to the previous, is that the component "first sex" may itself include several levels of sexual intimacy, depending on what respondents had in mind when they reported on their turning point experiences. For example, Sanders and Reinisch (1999) asked 599 college students to respond to the question, "Would you say you 'had sex' with someone (yes, no) if the most intimate behavior you engaged in was..." followed by 11 behaviors (e.g., "a person had oral contact with your breasts or nipples," "you touch, fondle, or manually stimulated a person's genitals," "you had oral contact with a person's genitals," "penile–vaginal intercourse [penis in vagina]"). Although there was almost uniform consensus that deep kissing was not having "had sex" and that penile–vaginal intercourse was having "had sex," there was considerable variability in the other types of behavior. For example, 81% considered penile–anal intercourse as having "had sex," whereas only 40% indicated they would consider oral–genital contact as having had sex.

In a scenario study of whether a hypothetical male, "Jim," and a hypothetical female, "Susie," were perceived to have had sex when certain behaviors were performed, Bogart, Cecil, Wagstaff, Pinkerton, and Abramson (2000) found that although 97% of the college sample believed that vaginal intercourse was "having sex" and 93% believed that anal intercourse was "having sex," only 44% believed that oral–genital intercourse was "having sex." Moreover, judgments as to what counted as sex varied depending on who received stimulation and who reached orgasm. Thus, when we seek to find patterns of relationship change associated with the passion turning point, the type of event that constitutes "first sex" may influence whether change occurs and if so, whether it is positive or negative. Furthermore, in terms of temporal sequencing within the passion turning point, expressions of love and commitment may be more likely to accompany certain types of behaviors (i.e., those more generally perceived as "having sex") than other types of behaviors (i.e., those not typically perceived as "having sex").

These three observations about the current state of research on the passion turning point are not intended to suggest that the passion turning point lacks conceptual integrity. Rather, they are intended to suggest that focusing on the temporal sequences among elements may provide additional insight into how this turning point influences relationship movement toward greater (or less) commitment and satisfaction. Indeed, this more narrow focus is reflected in the typology characterizing four pathways to sexual involvement in dating couples offered by Christopher and Cate (1985b): rapid-involvement couples, gradual-involvement couples, delayed-involvement couples, and low-involvement couples. Each type of couple is characterized by the extent of sexual activity (from kissing to mutual orgasm) and how quickly it occurs during the dating period. Unfortunately, we do not know whether the occurrence of sex in these couple types precedes or follows expressions of affection nor whether any particular sequence is more likely to contribute to positive relational consequences in the immediate context or over time if the relationship remains intact. In the next section, this issue is explored more fully by reviewing the research on two elements of the passion turning point: emotional expression and sexual behavior.

Love, Commitment, and Sex in Developing Relationships

Before answering the question of whether the temporal sequencing of expressions of love as a framing device prior to sexual involvement leads to different short- and long-term consequences, the definitional web that connects the concepts of love and sex must be untangled. As noted previously, Baxter and Bullis (1986) assume that "I love you" and sexual behavior are both expressions of affection, which of course, in some cases, they are. Indeed, the now classic assessment of intimacy, the PAIR inventory (Schafer & Olson, 1981), characterizes sexual intimacy as representing both expressions of affection and sexual acts. However, as Sprecher and McKinney (1993) illustrate in their review of the research, sex in romantic relationships can function not only an act of affection and love, but also an act of self-disclosure, intimacy, interdependence, maintenance, and exchange (see Sprecher & Cate, chapter 10, this volume, for further discussion of this issue). In addition, according to the findings of Browning, Kessler, Hatfield, and Choo (1999) and those who study sexual coercion (e.g., Koss & Cleveland, 1997; Koss, Gidycz, & Wisneiwski, 1987; Lottes & Weinberg, 1997), sex is sometimes also a way to assert dominance or control in a relationship.

More recently, in a multistage study to determine how young adults (college students) conceptualize the association between love and sex in their own current or past romantic relationships, Hendrick and Hendrick (2002) found four emergent views (subscales): "Love is Most Important (love is the primary entity); Sex Demonstrates Love (sex is important but in some ways subsumed by love); Love Comes Before Sex (love comes first); and Sex is Declining (sex is no longer as much a part of the relationship)" (p. 374). Although these factors suggest different conceptions of love in romantic relationships and were statistically distinct in how they related to other constructs such as types of love (e.g., eros, ludic, storge), sex attitudes, relationship constructs (e.g., commitment), and romantic beliefs (e.g., Love Finds a Way, One and Only), the first three do seem to suggest that love frames the meaning of sex rather than the reverse.

Thus, the key issue here is not whether relational emotions such as love and commitment are necessarily expressed as sexual action or whether sexual action is necessarily an expression of relational emotion. Rather the key issue is whether couples in developing relationships that have expressed love and commitment prior to the occurrence of first sexual involvement are more likely to interpret the event as relationally significant and positive than those that have not. Based on the prominent role of love as both a precursor and a superordinate construct in Hendrick and Hendrick's (2002) subscales, this assumption seems reasonable.

The assumption is also supported by the several studies identifying the prevailing theme of emotional investment and affection as reasons or motivations to have sex in a dating relationship. When asked what they perceive to be reasons or motivations to have sex, individuals report emotional investment or being in love as an important precondition with men and women differing somewhat in perceptions of its importance. For example, Hill (2002) provided college students with scenarios of hypothetical dating relationships that varied in terms of emotional investment and relationship stage. As predicted, ratings of likelihood of sexual involvement (kissing, intimate touching, and vaginal/oral intercourse) were greatest for both men and women in those scenarios with the highest level of emotional involvement and designation as serious dating (rather than casual). In low investment scenarios, however, men indicated no distinctions between levels of relationship development, whereas women associated sexual involvement with the more serious relational stage. These findings are consistent with self-report patterns in actual sexual history. Cohen and Shotland (1996) found that 70% of both men and women in their sample of 242 college students reported sexual experience only in conditions where both emotional closeness and physical attraction were present. By contrast, only 5% of the women but 34% of the men reported having sex in relationships where neither emotional closeness nor physical attraction was present.

A number of studies approached this issue by asking young adults what conditions or factors might encourage them to have sex for the first time in a dating relationship. Christopher and Cate (1985a) factor analyzed 43 items derived from existing literature on premarital sex and augmented by items derived from respondents' open-ended responses to the question of why they might engage in sexual intercourse with an "ideal partner." Three factors emerged: general physical arousal (e.g., both participant's and partner's arousal prior to intercourse), relationship factors (e.g., liking and love between participant and partner and the possibility of eventual marriage), and circumstances (e.g., alcohol and drugs, friends engaging in intercourse). As described by Christopher and Cate, the relationship factor "is composed of items that deal with the affective qualities of the relationship, the commitment level at the time of first sexual intercourse" (p. 267). Of interest here is the fact that the relationship factor accounted for almost 24% of the variance. In another study by the same authors, a similar factor (Positive Affect/Communication) accounted for 41% of the variance in decisions to have intercourse (Christopher & Cate, 1984).

The influence factors that emerged in the Christopher and Cate (1985a) study were also associated with expectations for the type of relationship in which sexual intercourse would first occur and in slightly different ways for women and men. Those participants who reported high scores on the relationship factor also reported that they would be more likely to have sex in a serious dating or engaged relationship than to have sex in a causal stage of dating. Also, women reported that the relationship factor was more important as a motivation to have sex compared to men, a finding that is consistent with Christopher and Cate (1984). This finding is also consistent with Leigh (1989) who found that women rated expressing emotional closeness as a more important reason to have sex compared to men, whereas men rated pleasure and pleasing partner as a more important reason compared to women. Likewise, Carroll, Volk, and Hyde (1985) found that women's primary motives for having sex were emotional expression, love, and commitment, whereas men's primary reasons were pleasure and physical release.

In a comparison of African-American and White adolescents, Eyre and Millstein (1999) noted several differences in reported reasons for having sex. For example, African-American males and females both reported that "nice body" was a necessary factor for engaging in sex, whereas White males and females did not, and males in both groups reported sexual arousal as an important criterion. However, of importance here is the fact that all four subsamples included "you love the person" and "time is right" as important criteria for having sex in a dating relationship.

In a more direct test of the importance of affectionate communication as a precursor to sexual intercourse and its effect on intact premarital relationships, Cate, Long, Angera, and Draper (1993) used items similar to those of Christopher and Cate (1984; 1985a) to measure relationship quality as recalled at the time of first intercourse (i.e., how much you loved your partner; how important the degree of commitment was between you and your partner at the time of first intercourse; how much you discussed the meaning of sexual intercourse). Regression results indicated that for both men and women, the degree to which the preexisting quality of the relationship was a factor in deciding to have sex was the primary predictor of positive relational effects.

In a particularly comprehensive examination of the moderating effects of gender differences in precursors to sexual involvement, Taris and Semin (1997) collected data at two points in time (1 year apart) from 253 English adolescents (15–18 years old). Factor analysis of items measuring attitudes toward love and sex based on Time 1 data revealed that the construct of "love motive" was constituted of three dimensions: relational commitment (e.g., "I would have to be in a committed long-term relationship with the person before having sex with them"), emotional commitment or love (e.g., "I would have to be in love with them," and "I would have to know that they really loved me"), and sexual permissiveness (e.g., "It does not really matter whether men and women have sex before marriage"). Results indicated that males and females were about equally likely to have had sex at both time points (Time 1: 38% of males and 35% of females; Time 2: 62% of males and 64% of females). However, females were more likely than males to report having a "steady relationship" at Time 2 and to be having sex with only their steady partner. Females were also more likely than males to stress the importance of emotional and relational commitment as motives for engaging in a sexual relationship, particularly when sexual behaviors move from kissing and holding hands to more physically intimate acts such as petting and sexual intercourse.

In sum, although it is certainly possible that sexual involvement can and does occur with no prior expressions of affection and commitment, research findings support the assumption that the passion turning point will be qualitatively different for a couple when sexual involvement follows after (or is perceived to be the manifestation of) explicit statements of love and commitment. To the extent that having dated for a period of time and having feelings of being in love, or at least emotionally attached, are linked to the "typical" sexual script for many dating adolescents and young adults, deviations from that expectation may be somewhat more problematic than circumstances consistent with the script. We might expect, for example, that some degree of personal regret and relationship doubt might emerge when no love is expressed and the sexual behavior is primarily physical and/or circumstantial, whereas positive feelings and some degree of relationship escalation might follow when expressions of love and commitment frame the event as relationally motivated.

Further, these immediate consequences of regret or positive relationship change may ripple through the relationship over time as well. For example, if this turning point is uncomfortable for one or both partners (associated with regret) it might contribute to lessened commitment and satisfaction or even to the eventual termination of the relationship. If the turning point is perceived positively, it may contribute to further relationship development and to high commitment and satisfaction in the future. In addition, given the strong evidence that emotional investment as a motivation for having sex is especially salient to women, deviations from the expected script of love before sex are likely to be more problematic for women in dating relationships compared to men, both in the short term and over time. A full appreciation of this pattern, however, requires consideration of two personality factors: the belief in love at first sight and attachment orientation.

DISPOSITIONAL FACTORS

Romantic Beliefs: Love at First Sight

In the initial formulation of the passion turning point, Baxter and Bullis (1986) noted that when asked to describe turning points in their relationship some respondents described the overwhelming feeling that they were swept away or had fallen in love almost immediately after meeting a partner. Baxter and Bullis labeled this experience "the whirlwind phenomenon" and included it within the supracategory of the passion turning point. Thus, Baxter and Bullis do not characterize this element of the passion turning as a dispositional factor. However, related research suggests that people do differ in the extent to which they believe such experiences are possible and/or likely to happen to them. Thus, previous research on individual differences in romantic beliefs, especially the belief in "love at first sight," is useful in elaborating the element referred to by Baxter and Bullis as the whirlwind phenomenon.

Using a sample of college dating couples, Sprecher and Metts (1989) created and validated the Romantic Beliefs Scale as a measure of dispositional tendencies to endorse four domains of the romantic love ideology: Love Finds a Way (e.g., love can overcome all obstacles), One and Only (e.g., there is only one true love), Idealization (e.g., the relationship and partner will be perfect), and Love at First Sight (e.g., falling in love soon after meeting). Although Love Finds a Way, One and Only, and Idealization were associated with several measures of relationship quality (e.g., liking and love for partner), Love at First Sight was not. Indeed, its only significant associations were with the Eros love style and number of dates prior to falling in love. In a second study using the same measure of Romantic Beliefs, Sprecher and Metts (1999) found that total romanticism score as well as the three specific beliefs of Love Finds a Way, One and Only, and Idealization were associated with love, satisfaction, and commitment. However, Love at First Sight was associated only with satisfaction and commitment, and only for men.

These findings may seem to argue against the notion that Love at First Sight would be a factor in the consequences of the passion turning point; however, as Sprecher and Metts (1999) suggest, "this belief may influence behaviors and relational affect only at the very early stages of relationship development, and may not influence relational dynamics once the relationship has been established" (p. 847). Thus, belief in love at first sight may be very important in the immediate consequences of the first sex experience, but contribute relatively little to later satisfaction and commitment, especially when compared to the other romantic beliefs. On the other hand, as Vangelisti (2002) concludes from a review of empirical work on relationship beliefs and standards, "When individuals' relational standards or beliefs are met or upheld, they are relatively satisfied with their relationships; when their standards or beliefs are not fulfilled, they are likely to become dissatisfied or distressed" (p. 652). To the extent that a person believed that he or she had fallen love at a first meeting, or on a first or second date, only to realize later that this was not the case, he or she might be prone to greater disappointment compared to someone who experienced the slow evolution of feelings of love, particularly as the inevitable challenges of maintaining the relationship intensify over time. Thus, the effect would not show up in the immediate context of first sexual involvement, but might well emerge in later levels of satisfaction and commitment.

Returning to the argument being developed here, if the passion turning point is indeed a microscript for first sexual involvement, what role might we expect for the belief that love at first sight is possible? The answer to this question depends in part on the type of outcome that is examined, that is, the immediate consequence or the long-term relational outcome. A person who believes that he or she can fall in love very quickly may interpret sexual involvement as a positive turning point indicating relationship confirmation, even if love and commitment have not yet been explicitly expressed. However, if the relationship does not live up to initial "whirlwind" love expectations over time (a sort of regression toward the mean), early sexual involvement prior to or in the absence of explicit expressions of love and commitment may be associated with lower satisfaction and commitment.

Before exploring these speculations, however, another dispositional variable is reviewed briefly. Although attachment styles or attachment orientation is not included in the passion turning point, the predisposition to feel comfortable with relationship commitment and interdependence or to feel uneasy and anxious has emerged in numerous studies as a strong contribution to relationship characteristics and processes. It is difficult to imagine that a rigorous examination of elements within the passion turning point and their effects of immediate and long-term consequences could be complete without including attachment as a control variable. The following overview provides the justification for this assumption.

Attachment Styles/Orientations

Hazan and Shaver (1987, 1990) piloted important research that tied attachment patterns first observed between infants and caregivers (Bowlby, 1969) to attachment patterns in adult romantic relationships. Drawing from a model of three attachment styles in children described by Ainsworth, Blehar, Waters, & Wall (1978), Hazan and Shaver (1987) found comparable patterns in descriptions of romantic love among adults. More specifically, "secure lovers described their most important love experience as especially happy, friendly, and trusting." Avoidant lovers "were characterized by fear of intimacy, emotional highs and lows, and jealousy" and anxious-ambivalent lovers "experienced love as involving obsession, desire for reciprocation and union, emotional highs and lows, and extreme sexual attraction and jealousy" (p. 515). Subsequently, Bartholomew (1990) proposed a four-category system of attachment based on quadrants derived from two dimensions: Model of Others (positive or negative) and Model of Self (positive or negative). The four attachment styles embedded within the model are secure, dismissing, preoccupied, and fearful. More recently, Brennan,

Clark, and Shaver (1998) proposed that although these four attachment styles are reasonable labels, the dimensions that underlie them are actually anxiety and avoidance (high and low). Further, they argue that attachment "style" might be better represented as attachment "orientation," characterized by relatively greater/less anxiety and avoidance, although they do allow that categorization of respondents sometimes fits the needs of a research agenda (see also Fraley & Waller, 1998).

Of relevance here are the several studies suggesting a link between attachment style and sexual practices (for more detail see Feeney & Noller, chapter 8, this volume). Feeney, Noller, and Patty (1993) used both questionnaires and diary records to measure attachment style, relationship history, attitudes toward sex, and interaction patterns among unmarried individuals. Not surprising, persons with a secure attachment style (i.e., comfortable with relational interdependence and commitment) were more likely than insecure (i.e., avoidant and anxious–ambivalent) persons to have sex within an established relationship and to report high relationship quality. Persons with an avoidant attachment style (i.e., uncomfortable with relational intimacy and commitment) held the least negative attitudes toward casual sex compared to persons with secure or anxious–ambivalent attachment styles. Last, persons with an anxious–ambivalent attachment style (i.e., longing for relational union but never feeling they get as close as they want to) engaged in fewer interactions with strangers as recorded in their diaries compared to secure respondents. Further, anxious–ambivalent males and avoidant females were the least likely of all groups to have engaged in sexual intercourse over the 6-week period constituting the diary study.

Hazan, Zeifman, and Middleton (1994) conducted a comprehensive study that made a strong link between attachment and sexuality. Results indicated that secure attachment partners were more committed to their primary relationship and more likely to engage in mutually initiated sex than people with other attachment styles. Avoidants reported more "one-night stands" in their sexual history compared to other attachment groups. They also reported a preference for "sex without love," and a preference for sexual behaviors such as oral and anal sex compared to less explicitly sexual behaviors such as kissing and cuddling. Brennan and Shaver (1995) also made connections between avoidant attachment style and sexuality. Using the Sociosexual Orientation Inventory (Simpson & Gangestad, 1991), they found that the avoidant attachment style was associated with an unrestricted (uncommitted, casual, and short-term) sexual orientation, possibly as a way "to get physically close to partners without incurring the psychological vulnerability of prolonged intimacy and dependency" (p. 268).

Taken together, these studies suggest that, at the very least, the secure attachment style and the avoidant attachment style exhibit characteristic patterns of sexual behavior in relationships and perhaps influence how partners respond to expressions of love and commitment prior to sexual involvement. For example, "I love you" prior to sexual involvement may evoke positive feelings and increased commitment from a person who has a secure attachment style, but may evoke discomfort and reduced commitment from a person who is fearful or avoidant. Although this assumption is only speculative, it suggests that any examination of the personal and relational effects of the passion turning point would be enhanced with the inclusion of attachment orientations in the analysis. The following section describes a study that was conducted to assess the possible contribution of attachment orientation.

UNPACKING THE PASSION TURNING POINT: A STUDY OF RELATIONAL CONSEQUENCES

As noted previously, the goal of this chapter is to bring the lens of investigation more clearly into focus on the passion turning point by examining both the contextual factor (i.e., the sequencing of expressions of love and commitment prior to sexual involvement) and dispositional factors (i.e., attachment orientation and romantic beliefs, especially "love at first sight") that might explain variation in outcomes. Integration of the literature reviewed to this point suggests two hypotheses and two research questions.

The first hypothesis is concerned with predictors of the immediate consequences of first sexual involvement, both relational consequences (i.e., relationship confirmation and escalation) and personal consequences (i.e., regret). The logic that guides this hypothesis is that occurrence of explicit statements of love and commitment prior to sexual involvement communicatively frames the event as an "act of love" rather than an "act of lust." Although a partner's love and commitment might be inferred from acts of kindness and general dating routines, explicit verbal expression is far more salient and far less ambiguous. Thus, when sexual involvement follows after these expressions, and thereby instantiates the traditional cultural script, we would expect the relationship to escalate and would expect the individuals to feel less regret. However, as noted in the research reviewed previously, one's orientation toward attachment influences sexual behavior and how it is situated within relational goals. Thus, more formally stated, the first hypothesis predicts:

> H1: Expressions of love and commitment prior to first sexual involvement will be a positive predictor of relationship escalation and a negative predictor of regret following the sexual experience, even after controlling for background variables (i.e., age, time dating prior to sex, and number of previous sexual partners) as well as attachment orientation.

The second hypothesis is concerned with aspects of the passion turning point that might predict relationship quality over time for relationships that continue to develop after the first sexual involvement. The logic guiding the second hypothesis is that the immediate consequences of first sexual involvement in terms of relationship escalation or personal regret probably have a greater effect on relationship satisfaction and commitment over time than does the initial sequencing of explicit expressions of love and commitment. Although the effects of the temporal sequencing of explicit expressions of love and commitment may contribute some variance to current satisfaction and commitment, its effect is probably subsumed over time by the relational and emotional consequences it fostered in the first place. We can't know the direction of influence, but it is likely that any relational or personal effects that linger from first sexual involvement are likely to influence or be influenced by current levels of satisfaction and commitment in the relationship. Once again, however, attachment orientations may account for differences in current satisfaction and commitment suggesting that the most rigorous test of the lingering effects of the passion turning point should include attachment orientation as a control variable. Thus, the second hypothesis predicts:

> H2: The degree of relationship escalation and regret that followed immediately after the first sexual experience and to a lesser degree, expressions of love and commitment prior to first sexual involvement, will be significant predictors of relational satisfaction and commitment in those relationships that continue to develop over time, even after controlling for background variables (i.e., age, time dating prior to sex, number of previous sexual partners, and length of relationship) and attachment orientation.

Two research questions are also derived from the previous review of research. First, because love at first sight or the whirlwind phenomenon is an element within the passion turning point, it merits attention. However, as noted previously, it is treated as an "emotion of the moment" rather than a relatively enduring disposition. Thus, no directly pertinent research is available to guide a prediction. However, based on the analogous construct of romantic beliefs, a research question is offered to examine its contribution to immediate and long-term consequences.

> RQ1: To what extent does the romantic belief, Love at First Sight, contribute to the immediate and long-term consequences of first sexual involvement beyond the contributions made by expressions of love and commitment and attachment orientation?

Second, the literature reviewed also suggests that men and women view emotional involvement and sexual involvement somewhat differently and thus may respond in different ways to the sequencing of expressions of love and commitment prior to sexual involvement and possibly experience its consequences differently over time. Thus, a second research question is also posed.

RQ2: Do patterns of influence associated with expressions of love and commitment differ for immediate and long-term consequences depending on the biological sex of the individual describing the experience?

Sample and Measures

In order to test the hypotheses and answer the research questions, a survey was distributed to a large population of undergraduate students at Illinois State University recruited from lower division general education courses and introductory communication courses. Recruitment from a younger student population was intentional because the goal was to assess respondents who might not have yet formed long-term relationships and whose first sexual experience in a new relationship would still be salient. A cover letter described the project as a study of turning points in romantic relationships. Students were told that they would be asked to call to mind their current or most recent past romantic relationship and to provide information on two events that are typically considered turning points in the development of a relationship: the first fight and the first occurrence of sexual involvement. The survey began with questions focused on the first fight and then moved to questions focused on the first sexual involvement. The two sections were identical in format but only responses to the first sexual involvement section were used for analysis.

After eliminating 38 respondents who left the sexual involvement section blank (see instructions in the following) and 8 respondents who reported their current status as married, the sample used for analysis consisted of 286 respondents (96 males and 190 females). The average age was 19.6 years, ranging from 18 to 31. The predominant ethnic group was White (89%), followed by African-American (5.6%), Asian (1.4%), Hispanic (1.4%) and other ethnic groups (2.6%). The majority of the respondents reported on relationships that were still intact ($n = 163$, 57%). Most of these continuing relationships were characterized by the respondent as "seriously dating" ($n = 123$), with a smaller number of "casual dating" partners ($n = 33$), or engaged ($n = 8$). Other respondents reported on relationships that were terminated or no longer "romantic" in nature, i.e., just friends, not dating ($n = 123$, 43%). The average length of the continuing relationships was slightly over 16 months, ranging from less than a month to just over 2 years (2 years and 3 months).

The questionnaire contained several sections, some with open-ended questions and some with scales to assess the variables of interest. Each section is described in the following.

Descriptions of First Sexual Involvement.   Respondents were asked to think back to the first significant sexual involvement they had in their current relationship. If not currently dating anyone or in a relationship that had not had sexual involvement, respondents were asked to recall the first sexual involvement in a recent past relationship. Respondents were instructed to skip this section if they had not had sex in a current or past relationship or were not comfortable reporting on their sexual experience. They were instructed to move to the third section of the questionnaire (the Romantic Beliefs Scale).

Those respondents who chose to complete the "First Sex" section were asked to describe their first sexual involvement in a current or recent past relationship (e.g.,

Describe the event. Where did it happen? What were the circumstances surrounding it? What was the extent of sexual involvement?). Follow-up questions also asked how long the relationship had existed prior to sexual involvement, who had initiated the sexual involvement (partner, self, or both), and how many sexual relationships the respondent had previously.

Descriptions of the sexual event were coded for type of sexual behavior described: (1) kissing only (e.g., we just kissed for a long time, passionately, and then stopped); (2) petting (e.g., "we played around, touching and being close, but did not take all of our clothes off"); (3) oral sex for one or both partners ("We went down on each other but stopped there"); and (4) sexual intercourse ("We made love," "We went all the way"). No respondent explicitly described anal intercourse as the first type of sexual involvement. Two research assistants coded the descriptions for type of sex following a brief training session. Each coded the same 50 surveys and compared codings. Intercoder agreement was high (agreement across the four categories ranged from .89 to .93). One research assistant then coded the remaining surveys.

Contextual Factors. A set of 18 items generated by the author and a research assistant followed the open-ended question asking for a description of first sexual involvement. These 18 items were derived from the turning points literature and were designed to assess three contextual aspects of the passion turning point: (1) extent of pre-sexual communication framing through expressions of love and commitment, (2) immediate positive relationship consequences, and (3) immediate negative relational consequences. Respondents were asked to rate each item on a 5-point Likert scale from 1 = Strongly Disagree to 5 = Strongly Agree. Factor analysis of these items confirmed the coherence and reliability of the intended dimensions. The first factor (*alpha* = .89) contained six items and was labeled *explicit expression of love and commitment* to represent communication that explicitly stated strong affection and relationship commitment prior to sexual involvement (e.g., "I told my partner 'I love you' prior to the event," "My partner had told me he or she loved me," "My partner had expressed his or her commitment to me prior to the event," and "My partner expressed his or her commitment to the relationship prior to the event"). The second factor (*alpha* = .84) contained five items and was labeled *regret* to represent feelings that the event was unfortunate and should not have occurred (e.g., "I regret having the experience," "We both apologized after the event," "What happened caused problems in our relationship," and "After the event, I told my partner that it was a mistake"). The third factor (*alpha* = .81) contained four items and was labeled *relationship escalation/confirmation* to indicate that a significant positive turning point had occurred and partners felt an increase in satisfaction, commitment, and understanding in the relationship (e.g., "The event was a significant turning point in our relationship," "The event led to greater understanding in our relationship," "The event led to more satisfaction in our relationship").

Romantic Beliefs. The 15-item Romantic Beliefs Scale (Sprecher & Metts, 1989) was used to measure romanticism generally and love at first sight specifically. Factor analysis indicated the same four dimensions as those that emerged in previous research (Sprecher & Metts, 1989; 1999): Love at First Sight (*alpha* = .79), One and Only (*alpha* = .84), Love Finds a Way (*alpha* = .82), and Idealization (*alpha* = .81).

Attachment Style. Twenty-five items from Brennen et al.'s (1998) 36-item Measure of Adult Romantic Attachment scale were used to measure attachment orientations (1 = Disagree Strongly; 7 = Agree Strongly). Brennen et al. provide detailed instructions for converting the anxiety and avoidance scores into categories of attachment styles; however, Fraley and Waller (1998) present a strong case for treating attachment orientations as continuous variables. For this reason, the Brennen et al. scale was factor analyzed. Four dimensions emerged and were fully consistent with the theoretical underpinnings of the original scale: secure (e.g., "I am very comfortable being close to romantic partners"), fearful (e.g., "I worry a lot about my relationships"), anxious/preoccupied ("I need a lot of reassurance that I am loved by my partner"), and avoidant/dismissive ("I prefer not to be too close to romantic partners"). All dimensions yielded strong reliability: secure, *alpha* = .81; fearful, *alpha* = .86; anxious/preoccupied, *alpha* = .82; avoidant/dismissive, *alpha* = .88.

The questionnaire closed with demographic questions asking about age and sex of respondent and his or her partner, ethnic background, current status of the relationship (i.e., terminated, friends but not dating, casual dating, serious dating, engaged, married), and how long the relationship had lasted. Finally, respondents who were still in their relationship were asked to rate their own levels of *satisfaction* and *commitment* (1 = extremely low; 7 = extremely high) as well as what they perceived to be their partner's level of *satisfaction and commitment* (1 = extremely low; 7 = extremely high). The length of the questionnaire and the desire to allow respondents sufficient time to describe their first fight and first sex encouraged single-item measures of current satisfaction and commitment for intact relationships rather than longer scales.

Results

The first hypothesis predicted that passion turning points in which explicit expressions of love and commitment provide communicative framing for sexual involvement result in more positive and less negative relational consequences after controlling for the influence of background variables and attachment orientation. To test this assumption and simultaneously answer the research questions, four hierarchical regression analyses were performed. Two regressions were conducted using relationship escalation as the outcome variable, one for men and one for women. Two other regressions were performed using regret as the outcome variable, again one for men and one for women. In all cases, variables were entered in four blocks. The first block included control variables (i.e., respondent's age, number of previous sexual partners, and time dating prior to sexual involvement). The second block included the four attachment orientations (avoidant/dismissive, anxious, secure, and fearful). The third block contained only the expression of love and commitment. The final block contained the four romantic beliefs (Love at First Sight, One and Only, Love Finds a Way, and Idealization) although Love at First Sight was the primary belief of interest.

As Table 6.1 indicates, expression of love and commitment prior to sexual involvement predicted relationship escalation/confirmation for both men and women, although it contributed relatively more variance beyond the control variables for women (12%) than for men (4%). This contribution emerged even after the significant contributions of avoidance attachment orientation for men and anxious and secure attachment orientations for women. Romantic beliefs failed to contribute significant variance to relationship escalation/confirmation.

As Table 6.2 indicates, expression of love and commitment prior to sexual involvement was a negative predictor of regret for both men and women to about the same degree, 4% additional variance for men and 3% additional variance for women. Interestingly, neither attachment orientation nor romantic beliefs contributed to regret for either men or women, but the number of previous sexual partners for men was a strong (positive) predictor of regret. The tendency for men to feel more regret following

TABLE 6.1

Predictors of Relational Escalation/Confirmation for Males ($N = 96$) and Females ($N = 190$)

Blocks	Males			Females		
	R^2chg	$Fchg$	Beta	R^2chg	$Fchg$	Beta
Control variables	.03	.97		.02	1.53	
Age			−.07			−.12
Time prior to sex			−.17			−.11
Previous sex partners			−.07			−.04
Attachment	.12	3.18*		.10	5.21**	
Avoid			−.30*			.04
Anxious			.09			−.17*
Secure			.04			.27**
Fearful			−.17			−.01
Expression love/commit.	.04	3.70*	.22*	.12	28.21**	.43**
Romantic beliefs	.02	.61		.02	.95	
Love at first sight			−.15			−.06
One and only			−.06			.03
Love finds a way			.01			.03
Idealization			.12			.11

$^*p < .05; ^{**}p < .01$

TABLE 6.2

Predictors of Regret for Males ($N = 96$) and Females ($N = 163$)

Blocks	Males			Females		
	R^2chg	$Fchg$	Beta	R^2chg	$Fchg$	Beta
Control variables	.12	4.03**		.01	.84	
Age			.01			.02
Time prior to sex			−.10			.08
Previous sex partners			.30**			.06
Attachment	.06	1.53		.06	3.01*	
Avoid			.06			.03
Anxious			.18			.08
Secure			−.13			−.14
Fearful			.01			.11
Expression love/commit.	.04	4.45*	−.23**	.03	5.15*	−.31**
Romantic beliefs	.02	.44		.02	.99	
Love at first sight			.14			.11
One and only			−.05			.03
Love finds a way			−.03			.07
Idealization			.01			−.03

$^*p < .05; ^{**}p < .01$

first sexual involvement in a dating relationship as the number of their previous sexual partners increases is not easy to explain. It could be the case that some of the men in this sample were not reporting on a significant dating relationship, but on yet "another sexual fling" in a casual or short-term relationship that they subsequently regretted. However, variance due to length of the relationship being reported on was controlled in the regression model. Moreover, length of the relationship did not differ significantly between men and women—even in the terminated relationship group. So this explanation is not compelling. Additional reflection, however, suggests two other possible explanations. First, despite the common cultural depiction of men as sexual seekers who do not necessarily link sexual behavior and emotional investment, the lack of novelty or "specialness" for sex in a new relationship when there have been many previous sexual partners may induce some sense of regret that "this time" could not be the "first time." Alternatively, a second explanation could be that men who have a relatively greater number of previous sexual partners have been unwilling or unable to sustain long-term committed relationships. Thus, first sex in a new relationship evokes regret or fear that "this relationship" will also dissolve or will involve undesired commitments as had been experienced in the past.

The second hypothesis proposed that the immediate effects of first sexual involvement, and to a lesser degree, the expressions of love and commitment prior to sexual involvement, would contribute to current levels of relational satisfaction and commitment for couples who remained together after first sexual involvement. Once again, separate regressions were performed for each of the criterion variables (satisfaction and commitment) and separately for men and women controlling for background variables, attachment orientation, and adding the immediate consequences of relationship escalation/confirmation and regret. Only those relationships that remained intact ($n = 163$) were examined.

As Table 6.3 indicates, current satisfaction appears to be a function of secure attachment orientation for both men and women (positive predictor), as well as an anxious attachment orientation only for women (negative predictor). Expression of love and commitment prior to first sexual involvement does not seem to contribute to current satisfaction; however, the regret associated with first sex for men negatively contributes to current satisfaction and the relationship escalation/confirmation associated with first sex positively contributes to current satisfaction for women. Given the contribution of expression of love and commitment to regret and relational escalation at the time of first sexual involvement, it is likely that its contribution to later satisfaction is simply subsumed by the lingering regret that men felt and the lingering sense of relationship confirmation that women felt after the first sexual experience. Romantic beliefs did not contribute significantly to satisfaction beyond these other variables.

The profile for current commitment is more complex. As Table 6.4 indicates, regret for men and relationship escalation/confirmation for women contribute to commitment in much the same way they contribute to satisfaction. Likewise secure attachment orientation contributes to commitment for both men and women as it did for current satisfaction. However, the anxious attachment dimension emerges as a negative predictor for both men and women and the avoidant dimension only for women. Apparently, attachment orientation is a more salient feature of one's felt commitment than one's level of satisfaction.

Finally, time dating prior to first sexual involvement is a negative predictor of commitment for men and belief in love at first sight is a positive predictor of commitment for women. This finding for women underscores the culturally expected integration for women among love, sex, and relationships. Believing that love at first sight is possible justifies premarital sex, but sexual involvement also encourages commitment. The finding for men may seem counterintuitive at first. Why would rapid sexual

TABLE 6.3
Predictors of Satisfaction for Males ($N = 46$) and Females ($N = 117$) in Continuing Relationships

Blocks	Males			Females		
	R^2chg	$Fchg$	Beta	R^2chg	$Fchg$	Beta
Control variables	.07	1.02		.02	.79	
Age			−.15			−.06
Time prior to sex			−.13			−.14
Previous sex partners			−.24			−.01
Length of relationship			.14			.11
Attachment	.38	6.44**		.23	8.24**	
Avoid			.09			−.17
Anxious			−.11			−.31**
Secure			.51**			.19
Fearful			−.18			.10
Passion point elements	.13	3.49*		.09	5.05**	
Expression love/commit.			.03			.01
Rel. escalation/confirm.			−.11			.36
Regret			.07			.07
			−.38*			
Romantic beliefs	.06	1.05		.04	1.34	
Love at first sight			.20			.17
One and only			−.01			−.01
Love finds a way			.09			−.06
Idealization			.06			.10

$^*p < .05; ^{**}p < .01$

TABLE 6.4
Predictors of Commitment for Males ($N = 46$) and Females ($N = 117$) in Continuing Relationships

Blocks	Males			Females		
	R^2chg	$Fchg$	Beta	R^2chg	$Fchg$	Beta
Control Variables	.21	3.68*		.03	1.33	
Age			−.09			.11
Time prior to sex			−.46**			−.17
Previous sex partners			−.14			−.02
Length of relationship			−.12			.08
Attachment	.29	5.54**		.28	11.12**	
Avoid			−.08			−.31**
Anxious			−.38**			−.22*
Secure			.50**			.19*
Fearful			.09			−.06
Passion point elements	.10	2.79*		.04	1.78	
Expression love/commit.			.12			−.13
Rel. escalation/confirm.			.04			.22*
Regret			−.34*			−.01
Romantic beliefs	.04	.96		.06	1.05	
Love at first sight			.05			.23**
One and only			−.06			−.02
Love finds a way			.18			.08
Idealization			.09			.01

$^*p < .05; ^{**}p < .01$

involvement predict greater commitment for men? Although not immediately apparent, these different predictors for men and women may actually be tapping similar processes. That is, engaging in sex early in a relationship may contribute positively to later commitment for men in much the same way that believing in love at first sight contributes to later commitment for women in that early sexual involvement for men may be the behavioral manifestation of an intuitive, but seldom articulated belief that love at first sight is possible. Modest support for this position is evident in a post hoc correlation analysis between endorsement of the belief in love at first sight and time prior to sexual involvement. For men who reported on intact relationships, these two variables are related in the expected direction ($r = -.24$; $p < .02$). However, there was no correlation for men who reported on relationships that had terminated after first sexual involvement. Thus, men may interpret and/or respond to rapid sexual involvement in two ways. When it is recalled from the vantage point of an enduring and committed relationship, rapid sexual involvement may be interpreted as the logical manifestation of passionate love (i.e., love at first sight or the whirlwind phenomenon). When recalled from the vantage point of a terminated or short-lived relationship, it may be interpreted as a manifestation of sexual desire and/or sexual opportunity that did not lead to commitment.

SUMMARY AND DISCUSSION

This chapter began with a general question of whether the elements or events subsumed within the passion turning point (Baxter & Bullis, 1986) can be viewed as sequentially related as well as conceptually related. Based on the literature reviewed and assuming that the cultural level sexual script holds, an expected pattern would be for expressions of emotional investment to precede sexual involvement, thereby framing it as a relational event rather than a physical release or moment of pleasure. Experiences consistent with this sequence were expected to evoke positive feelings and to escalate the relationship toward greater commitment and confirmation. Violations of this sequence were expected to evoke feelings of regret. Moreover, the effects of emotional expression prior to sexual involvement were expected to be more salient for women than for men. A second concern was the possible long-term effects of emotional and sexual sequencing during the first sexual experience on subsequent relational satisfaction and commitment for intact relationships. These two primary concerns are addressed before giving attention to the contributions of attachment orientations.

The results of the study suggest the following profiles for the passion turning point. First, for both men and women, the explicit expression of love and commitment prior to sexual involvement in a dating relationship appears to provide communicative framing for the personal and relational meaning of sexual actions immediately following the event. When emotional expression is present, sexual experience is perceived to be a positive turning point in the relationship, increasing understanding, commitment, trust, and sense of security. When emotional expression does not precede sexual involvement, the experience is perceived to be a negative turning point, evoking regret, uncertainty, discomfort, and prompting apologies. Although regret was low in this sample (Mmales $= 1.45$; Mfemales $= 1.34$) and relationship escalation/confirmation was relatively high (Mmales $= 3.89$; Mfemales $= 4.06$), they did not differ significantly between men and women, even in the sample representing intact relationships. Thus, this appears to be a profile characterizing both men and women.

It should also be noted, however, that consistent with sex role expectations and previous research, post hoc comparisons indicate that women reported significantly higher levels of explicit expressions of love and commitment prior to sexual involvement ($M = 3.66$) than did men ($M = 3.09$) ($t = 3.89$, $p = .000$). In addition, this type of communicative framing explained relatively more variance in the perceptions of positive relationship change for women (12%) than for men (4%). Thus, although the pattern holds for both men and women, women seem even more responsive to expressions of emotional investment compared to men.

Second, for later relationship quality, communicative framing (i.e., expressions of love and commitment) prior to first sexual involvement does not contribute directly to satisfaction or commitment over time. However, communicative framing may be an indirect influence through the lingering effects of regret and relationship escalation. Specifically, regret is a significant (negative) predictor of both satisfaction and commitment for men, whereas positive relationship change is a significant (positive) predictor of both satisfaction and commitment for women. An explanation for this pattern is speculative at this point, but it may be attributable to an underlying sex role expectation for the role of first sex in a developing relationship. For men, the absence of regret following first sexual involvement may be a sufficient indicator that the relationship would endure, and they base their current satisfaction and commitment on this "default" case. For women, however, a stronger indicator is necessary. Women may embed their current levels of satisfaction and commitment within recollections that are consistent with the sex role expectation for women to have sex in emotionally invested relationships. Thus, it is not the *absence* of regret that predicts future satisfaction and commitment after first sexual involvement, but rather the *presence* of increased relationship escalation. Interestingly, whatever dynamic is operating for men and women, it is not manifested in different levels of satisfaction or commitment; the means for men and women reporting on intact relationships were virtually identical (satisfaction: Mmales = 5.63; Mfemales = 5.50; commitment: Mmales = 5.78; Mfemales = 5.81). Clearly, the differential contributions of regret (for men) and relationship escalation (for women) to current relationship quality after first sexual involvement merits additional investigation.

One variable adapted from the passion turning point literature that offers little new additional insight in this study is the romantic belief in love at first sight. The decision to measure this construct as a dispositional variable, rather than asking respondents directly whether they experienced love at first sight prior to *this particular sexual experience,* may have been misguided. Nevertheless, what the current investigation offers is the conclusion that for women, belief in love at first sight is a predictor of commitment to their partner over time after the first sexual involvement. This is consistent with the contribution to commitment made by positive relationship change after first sex. No doubt these two constructs work together to reinforce a woman's decision to stay in her relationship.

Finally, the profiles for the passion turning point and its consequences must be situated within the strong contributions made also by adult attachment orientations. In some ways, the findings for the contextual variables of communicative framing, positive relationship change, and regret assume even greater significance considering that attachment orientations were entered before them in all regression models, and yet they still emerged as significant features of the passion turning point profile. However, the contributions of the attachment orientations cannot be ignored.

First, and perhaps most interesting is the fact that the only outcome to which attachment orientation does not contribute significant variance is regret. Apparently, regret is the one outcome variable following first sexual involvement that is most fully responsive to the communicative framing provided by expressions of love and commitment. This supports the reasoning presented previously that violations of the sequence associated with the cultural script for sexual involvement evokes uneasiness and even regret that the event occurred.

Second, for positive relational change represented here as relational escalation/confirmation, three attachment orientations emerged as significant. The tendency to avoid relationship commitment among men and the tendency to be anxious or ambivalent toward relationship commitment among women lessens the likelihood that positive relationship change will follow the first sexual experience in a dating relationship. Having a secure attachment orientation for women, however, tends to increase the likelihood that positive relationship change will follow the first sexual experience in a dating relationship. These patterns are consistent with previous research. Hazan et al. (1994), for example, found that the avoidant attachment style was associated with a preference for "sex without love" and Brennan and Shaver (1995) found the avoidant style was associated with uncommitted, casual, and short-term sexual relations. In addition, the findings reported here fall in line with the perspective that sex-role expectations may interact with attachment orientations (Davis, 1999). Sex-role expectations that casual sex is more "costly" for women compared to men may intensify the role of anxious attachment orientations in predicting less relationship escalation after sexual involvement for women but not for men. Conversely, women who are generally secure in their views of relationships may be less concerned with possible negative evaluations (from self or other) when they engage in premarital, and potentially casual, sex compared to women who are more anxious and therefore are more likely to experience relationship escalation after sexual involvement. If so, this would explain why secure attachment orientation does not contribute to relationship escalation for men following first sexual involvement; it is less salient than the more individual disposition to simply avoid relationship commitment after sex.

Some support for this line of reasoning is evident in the correlations for men and women. When controlling for explicit expressions of love and commitment, the correlation between avoidant attachment orientation for men and relationship escalation/confirmation remains high ($r = -.35$, $p = .001$). The same holds true for women who feel secure attachment orientation ($r = .24$, $p = .001$). However, for women who are anxious in their orientation toward relationships, the presence of explicit expressions of love and commitment mediates the association between attachment orientation and relationship escalation yielding a nonsignificant association ($r = -.11$, $p = .09$). Apparently, the presence of communicative framing of first sexual involvement is particularly important for women who are not secure in their view of relationships, at least in assessing the consequences immediately following the event.

Third, patterns of attachment orientations as predictors of relationship quality over time for couples who stay together after first sexual involvement seem to reflect the profiles established in previous research on dating and married couples (e.g., Davis, 1999; Kirkpatrick, 1998; Koski & Shaver, 1997). As we would expect, secure attachment orientation predicts increased relationship satisfaction and commitment for both men and women over time following the first sexual experience in a dating relationship. Anxious and avoidant attachment orientations predict lower commitment for both men and women over time. In addition, being anxious or ambivalent predicts lower satisfaction for women over time. These patterns are generally consistent with previous research on the associations between attachment styles and relationship quality. They no doubt index the more complicated role of attachment orientations in relationship processes once individuals begin negotiating the demands of relationship maintenance. Indeed, the interconnectedness among, for example, the tendency to be anxious about relationships for dating women, their partners' communication, and their satisfaction in the relationship may be similar to that found for husbands and their wives' communication in other studies (Feeney, 1994). The association among attachment orientations, partner communication, and relationship quality in dating couples who have experienced first sexual involvement merits additional investigation.

Several other directions for future research are also suggested by these findings and their implications. These are presented in the following discussion.

FUTURE DIRECTIONS

The motivation for this chapter and goal of the preliminary study was to explore the structure, process, and outcomes of the passion turning point in romantic, premarital relationships. For this reason, only variables directly suggested by the passion turning point literature and the obvious dispositional variable of attachment style were included. However, reflection on the findings that emerged suggests limitations inherent in this study and several directions for future research.

First, any questionnaire that asks respondents to recall critical events in their relationship invites some degree of recall bias. In the current investigation, respondents were asked to recall the extent to which certain messages preceded first sexual involvement. It is possible that respondents who experienced positive relational development after the event recalled expressions of love and commitment that were not explicitly spoken. It is also possible that respondents who experienced negative relational outcomes and/or regret retrospectively discounted (underreported) expressions of love and commitment, believing them to have been spoken insincerely or prematurely. Although several background variables, including age, previous sexual partners, time prior to sexual involvement, and length of continuing relationships were included as control variables in the analyses, these variables may not fully account for recall biases. Thus, although it may be a more challenging design, future research should employ diaries that track developing relationships over time, beginning at a point early in the relationship prior to first sexual involvement.

Second, the fact that belief in love at first sight was predictive only of commitment and only for females was unexpected. Its lack of contribution to the outcome variables is no doubt due in part to its inclusion last in the regression models. In addition, however, the disconnect between Baxter and Bullis' (1986) original presentation of the phenomenon as being overwhelmed by love early in a particular relationship and its operationalization here as a more enduring personality trait may also explain the lack of findings. Future research should attempt to refine the operational definition of the "whirlwind phenomenon."

Third, the dispositional variable of love styles should be considered for inclusion in future investigations of the passion turning point. The associations between love styles and attitudes toward love and sex as evidenced in the research of Hendrick and Hendrick (2002) noted previously suggests several possibilities relevant to the immediate consequences of first sexual involvement. For example, a ludic lover (game-playing approach to relationships) or an eros lover (attracted to physical traits of the love object) may be less inclined to escalate a relationship following first sexual involvement and less inclined to feel regret. A storge lover (anchoring romantic relationships in friendship) may wait longer to engage in sex and may also be more likely to escalate the relationship following first sexual involvement. Interestingly, a manic lover (insecure and possessive in romantic relationships) might well respond to first sex in much the same way that anxious women do—seeking and depending on explicit expressions of love and commitment before escalating the relationship. In terms of relationship quality over time for those couples who stay together after first sexual involvement, research on other aspects of love styles also indicates that love styles contribute to relationship satisfaction and stability as well (e.g., Meeks, Hendrick, & Hendrick, 1998).

Fourth, as the terminology used in the previous paragraph indicates, the implicit stance taken in making speculations and interpreting the findings from the study presented is that "an individual" escalates or does not escalate the relationship following first sexual involvement. Clearly the progression of a relationship following any turning point, sexual or otherwise, is a function of both individuals involved. Certain aspects of an individual's personality or relationship competence may lead him or her to less adequately accomplish relationship development, but much of the success also depends on the needs, goals, and dispositions of the other person. Moreover, certain types of individuals may seek out, however unconsciously, certain other types of individuals. For example, Hahn and Blass (1997) found that respondents exhibited a preference for stimulus persons who were similar to them in love style. Thus, a ludic lover may be drawn to another ludic lover or perhaps a manic lover, and a storge lover may be attracted to another storge lover. Certain attachment orientations may also be drawn to or attract people with particular love styles; for example, a person who has an anxious attachment orientation may be drawn to or attract a ludic lover. Some combinations of attraction are no doubt more likely to lead to relationship escalation after first sexual involvement than are other combinations. This possibility can be assessed only by obtaining responses from both members of a couple and indicates an essential next step in this line of research.

Finally, future investigations of the passion turning point would be enriched by including a far more diverse sample than was used in this investigation. Younger college students were intentionally selected to tap the most traditional prototype of first sex in dating relationships. However, generalizing these findings to the broader population must be done with caution until other samples are used. For example, individuals who are dating at an older age, often in middle age following a divorce, may exhibit very different patterns of response to first sexual involvement in a new relationship compared to never-married, 18 to 20-year-old college students. Likewise, to the extent that sexual scripts derive largely from sex-role expectations for men and women in relation to each other, same-sex couples may exhibit different patterns of response to first sexual involvement in their relationships compared to heterosexual couples. Investigations of more diverse samples are necessary to confirm the conclusions offered here about both the sequencing of explicit expressions of love and commitment and their influence on immediate relationship change and quality over time.

CONCLUSION

This chapter has explored in detail the elements within the passion turning point and their contribution to immediate and long-term consequences. Consistent with the literature that was reviewed, as explicit expressions of love and commitment preceding sexual involvement increase, the likelihood of relationship escalation increases, but the likelihood of regret decreases. This suggests validity to the argument that elements within the passion turning point can be temporally organized as well as conceptually integrated. Indeed, not only does expression of love and commitment enhance relationship development after first sex and minimize regret, but it also distinguishes those relationships that terminate after first sex ($M = 3.30$) from those relationships that remain intact ($M = 3.60$) ($t = 2.03$, $p < .04$). Although expressions of love and commitment are not salient in later relationship satisfaction and commitment, the lingering effects of regret (even though the relationship remains intact) contribute to decreased commitment over time for men and the lingering effects of relationship escalation contribute to increased commitment for women over time. Thus, the underlying premise of the contextual model of interaction (Bradbury & Fincham, 1989) is evident here: Initial positive and negative consequences of first sexual involvement apparently take their place in the distal context influencing the messages sent and attributions made in future interactions.

Furthermore, attachment orientations appear to be unrelated to feelings of regret following first sexual involvement, but appear to be salient predictors of whether relationships continue to develop and the degree to which individuals remain satisfied and committed to those relationships. Again, distal factors seem to influence at least one of the immediate outcomes of first sexual experiences and to contribute to subsequent interactions.

Although these findings are preliminary and stimulate more questions than they answer, they do underscore the important role of both interactional and dispositional factors in framing the meaning of first sexual involvement. It is hoped that the arguments advanced here and the patterns that emerged in the findings provide direction for continued research in the passion turning point as a complex and sequenced event that has both immediate and long-term effects for relationship development.

REFERENCES

Ainsworth, M. D. S., Blehar, M. C., Waters, E., & Wall, S. (1978). *Patterns of attachment*. Hillsdale, NJ: Lawrence Erlbaum Associates.

Altman, I., & Taylor, D. A. (1973). *Social penetration: The development of interpersonal relationships*. New York: Holt, Rinehart & Winston.

Bartholomew, K. (1990). Avoidance of intimacy: An attachment perspective. *Journal of Social and Personal Relationships, 7*, 147–178.

Baxter, L. A., & Bullis, C. (1986). Turning points in developing romantic relationship. *Human Communication Research, 12*, 469–493.

Baxter, L. A., & Erbert, L. A. (2000). Perceptions of dialectical contradictions in turning points of development in heterosexual romantic relationships. *Journal of Social and Personal Relationships, 16*, 547–569.

Baxter, L. A., & Montgomery, B. M. (1996). *Relational dialectics: A dialogic approach to communication in personal relationships*. New York: Guilford.

Baxter, L. A., & Pittman, G. (2001). Communicatively remembering turning points of relational development in heterosexual romantic relationships. *Communication Reports, 14*, 1–17.

Bogart, L. M., Cecil, H., Wagstaff, D. A., Pinkerton, S. D., Abramson, P. R. (2000). Is it "sex"?: College students' interpretations of sexual behavior terminology. *The Journal of Sex Research, 37*, 108–116.

Bolton, C. D. (1961). Mate selection as the development of a relationship. *Marriage and Family Living, 23*, 234–240.

Bowlby, J. (1969). *Attachment and loss: Vol. 1. Attachment*. New York: Basic Books.

Bradbury, T. N., & Fincham, F. D. (1989). Behavior and satisfaction in marriage: Prospective mediating processes. In C. Hendrick (Ed.), *Close relationships* (pp. 119–143). Newbury Park, CA: Sage.

Brennan, K. A., Clark, C. L., & Shaver P. R. (1998). Self-report measurement of adult attachment: An integrative overview. In J. A. Simpson & W. S. Rholes (Eds.), *Attachment theory and close relationships* (pp. 46–76). New York: Guilford.

Brennan, K. A., & Shaver, P. R. (1995). Dimensions of adult attachment, affect regulation, and romantic relationship functioning. *Personality and Social Psychology Bulletin, 21*, 267–283.

Browning, J. R., Kessler, D., Hatfield, E., & Choo, P. (1999). Power, gender, and sexual behavior. *The Journal of Sex Research, 36*, 342–347.

Bullis, C., Clark, C., & Sline, R. (1993). From passion to commitment: Turning points in romantic relationships. In P. Kalbfleisch (Ed.), *Interpersonal communication: Evolving interpersonal relationships* (pp. 213–236). Hillsdale, NJ: Lawrence Erlbaum Associates.

Carroll, J. L., Volk, K. D., & Hyde, J. S. (1985). Differences between males and females in motives for engaging in sexual intercourse. *Archives of Sexual Behavior, 14*, 131–139.

Cate, R. M., Long, E., Angera, J. J., & Draper, K. K. (1993). Sexual intercourse and relationship development. *Family Relations, 42*, 158–164.

Christopher, F. S., & Cate, R. M. (1984). Factors involved in premarital sexual decision-making. *Journal of Sex Research, 20*, 363–376.

Christopher, F. S., & Cate, R. M. (1985a). Anticipated influences on sexual decision-making for first intercourse. *Family Relations, 34*, 265–270.

Christopher, F. S., & Cate, R. M. (1985b). Premarital sexual pathways and relationship development. *Journal of Social and Personal Relationships, 2*, 271–288.

Cohen, L. L., & Shotland, F. L. (1996). Timing of first sexual intercourse in a relationship: Expectations, experiences, and perceptions of others. *Journal of Sex Research, 33*, 291–299.

Davis, K. E. (1999). What attachment styles and love styles add to the understanding of relationship commitment and stability. In J. M. Adams & W. H. Jones (Eds.), *Handbook of interpersonal commitment and relationship* (pp. 221–237). New York: Kluwer Academic/Plenum.

Duck, S. (1995). Talking relationships into being. *Journal of Social and Personal Relationships, 12,* 535–540.

Eyre, S. L., & Millstein, S. G. (1999). What leads to sex? Adolescent preferred partners and reasons for sex. *The Journal of Research on Adolescence, 9,* 277–307.

Feeney, J. A. (1994). Attachment style, communication patterns, and satisfaction across the life cycle of marriage. *Personal Relationships, 1,* 333–348.

Feeney, J. A., Noller, P., & Patty, J. (1993). Adolescents' interactions with the opposite sex: Influence of attachment style and gender. *Journal of Adolescence, 13,* 169–186.

Fraley, R. C., & Waller, N. G. (1998). Adult attachment patterns: A test of the typological model. In J A. Simpson & W. S. Rholes (Eds.), *Attachment theory and close relationships* (pp. 77–114). New York: Guilford.

Hahn, J., & Blass, T. (1997). Dating partner preferences: A function of similarity of love styles. *Journal of Social Behavior and Personality, 12,* 257–272.

Hazan, C., & Shaver, P. (1987). Romantic love conceptualized as an attachment process. *Journal of Personality and Social Psychology, 52,* 511–524.

Hazan, C., & Shaver, P. (1990). Love and work: An attachment-theoretical perspective. *Journal of Personality and Social Psychology, 59,* 270–280.

Hazan, C., Zeifman, D., & Middleton, K. (1994, July). *Adult romantic attachment, affection, and sex.* Paper presented at the 7th International Conference on Personal Relationships, Gronigen, The Netherlands.

Hendrick. S. S., & Hendrick, C. (2002). Linking romantic love with sex: Development of the perceptions of love and sex scale. *Journal of Social and Personal Relationships, 19,* 361–378.

Hill, C. A. (2002). Gender, relationship stage, and sexual behavior: The importance of partner emotional investment within specific situations. *Journal of Sex Research, 39,* 228–240.

Huston, T. L., Surra, C., Fitzgerald, N. M., & Cate, R. (1981). From courtship to marriage: Mate selection as an interpersonal process. In S. Duck & R. Gilmour (Eds.), *Personal relationships 2: Developing personal relationships* (pp. 53–88). New York: Academic Press.

Kirkpatrick, L. A. (1998). Evolution, pair-bonding, and reproductive strategies: A reconceptualization of adult attachment. In J. A. Simpson & W. S. Rholes (Eds.), *Attachment theory and close relationships* (pp. 353–393). New York: Guilford.

Knapp, M. L. (1984). *Interpersonal communication and human relationships.* Boston: Allyn & Bacon.

Koski, L. R., & Shaver, P. R. (1997). Attachment and relationship satisfaction across the life span. In R. J. Sternberg & M. Hojjat (Eds.), *Satisfaction in close relationships* (pp. 26–55). New York: Guilford.

Koss, M. P., & Cleveland, H. H. (1997). Stepping on toes: Social roots of date rape lead to intractability and politicization. In M. D. Schwartz (Ed.), *Researching sexual violence against women: Methodological and personal perspectives* (pp. 4–21). Thousand Oaks, CA: Sage.

Koss, M. P., Gidycz, C. A., & Wisniewski, N. (1987). The scope of rape: Incidence and prevalence of sexual aggression and victimization in a national sample of higher education students. *Journal of Consulting and Clinical Psychology, 55,* 162–170.

Leigh, B. C. (1989). Reasons for having and avoiding sex: Gender, sexual orientation, and relationship to sexual behavior. *Journal of Sex Research, 26,* 199–209.

Lottes, I. L., & Weinberg, M. S. (1997). Sexual coercion among university students: A comparison of the United States and Sweden. *Journal of Sex Research, 34,* 67–76.

Lloyd, S. A., & Cate, R. M. (1985). The developmental course of conflict in dissolution of premarital relationships. *Journal of Social and Personal Relationships, 2,* 179–194.

Meeks, B. S., Hendrick, S. S., & Hendrick, C. (1998). Communication, love, and relationship. *Journal of Social and Personal Relationships, 15,* 755–773.

Metts, S., & Cupach, W. R. (1989). The role of communication in human sexuality. In K. McKinney & S. Sprecher (Eds.), *Human sexuality: The societal and interpersonal context* (pp. 139–161). Norwood, NJ: Ablex.

Sanders, S. A., & Reinisch, J. M. (1999). Would you say you "had sex" if . . . ? *JAMA, 281,* 275–277.

Schaefer, M. T., & Olson, D. H. (1981). Assessing intimacy: The PAIR Inventory. *Journal of Marital and Family Therapy, 7,* 47–60.

Simon, W., & Gagnon, J. H. (1986). Sexual scripts: Permanence and change. *Archives of Sexual Behavior, 15,* 97–120.

Simpson, J. A., & Gangestad, S. W. (1991). Individual differences in sociosexuality: Evidence for convergent and discriminant validity. *Journal of Personality and Social Psychology, 60,* 870–883.

Sprecher, S., & McKinney, K. (1993). *Sexuality.* Newbury Park, CA: Sage.

Sprecher, S.. & Metts, S. (1989). Development of the "Romanic Beliefs Scale" and examination of the effects of gender and gender-role orientation. *Journal of Social and Personal Relationships, 6,* 387–411.

Sprecher, S., & Metts, S. (1999). Romantic beliefs: Their influence on relationships and patterns of change over time. *Journal of Social and Personal Relationships, 16,* 834–851.

Surra, C. A. (1987). Reasons for changes in commitment: Variations by courtship type. *Journal of Social and Personal Relationships, 4,* 17–33.

Taris, T. W., & Semin, G. R. (1997). Gender as a moderator of the effects of the love motive and relational context on sexual experience. *Archives of Sexual Behavior, 26,* 159–177.

Vangelisti, A. L. (2002). Interpersonal processes in romantic relationships. In M. L. Knapp & J. A. Daly (Eds.), *Handbook of interpersonal communication* (3rd ed., pp. 643–679). Newbury Park, CA: Sage.

7

Sex and Romantic Love: Connects and Disconnects

Clyde Hendrick
Susan S. Hendrick
Texas Tech University

Sex and romantic love are complexly related. The various links between love and sex are broadly surveyed, including the views of undergraduates, philosophers, psychologists, evolutionary biologists, and close relationships scholars, among others. Aron and Aron (1991) devised a dimensional approach for relating love and sex, with sex dominant at one end of the dimension, love at the other end, and both equally important at the midpoint. This approach is used in a general way to organize the chapter. The "love is really sex" endpoint of the dimension captures a broad range of naturalistic/biological perspectives. We discuss the evolution of sex, speculate on an appropriate "unit of selection," and consider the evolution of love, particularly passionate love, along with mating strategies. We also analyze the relation of adult attachment to love and sex. The "sex is really love" end of the dimension as well as the middle area includes a wide array of psychological and sociological approaches. We survey such topics as passionate versus companionate love, the double standard, and orientations toward sexuality. Several recent studies (e.g., Sprecher & Regan, 1998) have found interesting associations between sexual desire and passionate love. We also describe our own work on love and sexual attitudes, taking the position that people hold belief systems about love and sex and how (not whether) the two are related. Gender differences and similarities are attended to as well in this research description. We conclude that the intersection of sex and love perhaps captures the real essence of humanity: The union of our biological nature with our personhood as enacted through the gift of love.

INTRODUCTION

Our research program on close relationships has always included the study of belief systems about romantic love and sexuality, as well as the relationship satisfaction that emerges (or fails to emerge) from love and sex. From the outset, we noticed that love and sex, as areas of scholarly research, were basically unconnected. Different groups of scholars, even different professional societies, were relatively concerned with love or sex, but not both. Such a separation is understandable through the foibles of the history of academic discipline formation. But it makes no sense for the actual study of two of life's most vital forces. The evidence of our senses, every day, suggests a strong connection between romantic love and sexual behavior (e.g., Berscheid, 1988).

Much of our own research has been devoted to bridging the gap between these two domains. Our first attempt at synthesis occurred many years ago in a chapter entitled "Love and Sex Attitudes: A Close Relationship" (S. Hendrick & Hendrick, 1987a). We have pursued the synthesis of love and sex since then in numerous papers and conference addresses (e.g., S. Hendrick & Hendrick, 1997).

More recently, advocacy for studying love and sex together has increased. For example, Regan (1998) noted that many researchers on love evolved out of an older interpersonal attraction paradigm, an approach that viewed love more or less as sexless. Regan protested against this approach: "My own research provides evidence that romantic love is a qualitatively different experience from such other varieties of interpersonal attraction as loving and liking, and that sexual desire in particular is one of its essential components" (pp. 102–103). In a seminal chapter, Aron and Aron (1991) sketched the various possible connections between love and sex as they had appeared in the historical literature. This chapter is loosely organized around the continuum that Aron and Aron proposed. In the initial section, we describe their model in some detail and make a few modest conceptual emendations.

After presentation of Aron and Aron's model, we provide four major sections that grapple with the relation between love and sex. We start with a broad sampling of philosophers, including a few observations from our "student philosophers." We divide the many social science approaches to love and sex into two broad categories that we have labeled "naturalistic/biological" and "psychological/sociological" approaches. These two categories roughly approximate the two halves of the conceptual continuum that Aron and Aron (1991) proposed.

Following these discussions, we present a section summarizing our own work. Our approach construes love and sex as "attitudes" or "belief systems," and this cognitive approach has been fertile in outcomes.

ARE SEX AND ROMANTIC LOVE RELATED, AND IF SO, HOW?

Most people today, at least in the Western world, tend to associate romantic love with sexuality and marriage. In fact, the perceived bond among the three concepts has grown over the previous century. For example, Simpson, Campbell, and Berscheid (1986) found that over a 30-year period, romantic love was increasingly perceived as the only legitimate basis for marriage, and for staying in a marriage. Falling out of love became a sufficient basis for divorce.

People often assume that the way things are now is the way things have always been. Thus, today, falling in love (i.e., romantic love) is a sufficient basis for having sex and getting married—or first getting married and then having sex, depending on one's belief system. However, today's local customs are not necessarily universal experiences. Lindholm (1995) provided compelling evidence that, for most of the world for most of human history, marriage has not been associated closely with romantic love. The purpose of marriage was to produce children, a task accomplished by sexuality that seldom included romantic love. The latter was found outside of marriage; sometimes it included sexuality, but in many cases such romantic love remained chaste. So, historically, there have been varying combinations of love, sex, and marriage.

The complexity of the relationship between love and sex increases when one attempts to construe romantic love and sexual expression as universal human experiences. Sexuality is a clear case (we wouldn't be here otherwise), but the universal reality of romantic love has been debated. Jankowiak and Fischer (1992), in a cross-cultural study of 166 cultures, provided clear evidence that romantic love is a "near" empirical universal, a conclusion also drawn by Hatfield and Rapson (1987). However, proof of the universality of romantic love says little about how love is related to sexual expression. In fact, there may be cultural inconsistency between conceptions of sex and love, leading to wide variation in perceptions of how love and sex are related. Jankowiak (1995a) argued:

> Every culture highlights either sexuality or love, but has a very difficult time in blending the two together. Every culture, including the intellectuals of that culture, prefer to speak in idioms that stress the benefits of either love or sex—rarely both. This is especially true of the intellectual history of the Western world, which has repeatedly demonstrated a continuous and pronounced ambivalence toward sexuality and love. (p. 6)

Jankowiak further concluded that:

> The inability to satisfactorily blend and integrate the two emotions accounts for the push/pull tension between love as desire and love as enduring affection. It may also account for some of the misunderstanding and turmoil often found in male–female relationships. (p. 7)

Many other examples may be found in Jankowiak's (1995b) edited volume.

This background makes apparent the arduous task that Aron and Aron (1991) set for themselves; namely, an attempt to systematize the historical relations between love and sexuality (limited to "the Western cultural context," p. 25). Their approach was to locate both love and sex on a single dimension of relative importance, with sex at one end of the dimension, love at the other end, and equality of importance of love and sex at the midpoint of the dimension. Five location points on the dimension were identified and elaborated.

Prior to consideration of these levels, however, we need to consider carefully the Arons' definitions of love and sex. "*Love is the constellation of behaviors, cognitions, and emotions associated with a desire to enter or maintain a close relationship with a specific other person*" (Aron & Aron, 1991, p. 26 [italics in original]). This definition stresses motivation (desire), but it is a broad definition. In fact, it could include friendship as well as romantic love. The breadth was intended by the Arons to maintain neutrality with regard to whether love is learned, based on social scripts, genetically programmed, etc.

The Arons defined sex more complexly, but also more narrowly: "*Sexuality is the constellation of sensations, emotions, and cognitions that an individual associates with physiological sexual arousal and that generally gives rise to sexual desire and/or sexual behavior*" (p. 27 [italics in original]). This definition is also motivational in nature (sexual desire) and is intended to be neutral with respect to whether sexuality is mostly biological or mostly socially constructed.

These definitions of sex and love affect the way various theories are classified. Different definitions (e.g., broader or narrower) might have yielded different classifications. The Arons' five positions on the dimension are sketched briefly:

Position A: Approaches to sexuality that ignore love, or see it as an outcome of sexuality. Obviously this position gives little or no importance to love. Sex is everything. The Arons view this approach as most congruent with various evolutionary approaches.

Position B: Approaches that emphasize sexuality, but view love as a minor part of sexuality. The Arons view attachment theory in this category, as well as research that emphasizes hormones, neurotransmitters, and other physiological processes (e.g., Liebowitz, 1983).

Position C: Approaches that consider love and sex as separate and probably equal (in importance). The authors discuss six widely varying theories under this category. As Aron and Aron (1991, p. 41) noted, there are three possibilities: (1) Love and sex are interrelated and exhibit mutual causality, (2) love and sex are independent, essentially uncorrelated, or (3) any relation between love and sex is spurious, being caused by some third factor such as general physiological arousal or desire for self-expansion (Aron & Aron, 1986). The fact that the midpoint of a dimension allows for several interpretations is troublesome, suggesting other intersecting dimensions may exist. However, we can not pursue that possibility here.

Position D: Approaches that emphasize love and consider sexuality a minor part of love. Examples of this position include passionate versus companionate love (e.g., Walster & Walster, 1978), Sternberg's (1986) triangular theory of love, and Lee's (1973) love styles. With regard to scales, Aron and Aron (1991, p. 33) considered the type of love measured by the Passionate Love Scale (Hatfield & Sprecher, 1986) as falling into this category. Because of the definitional emphasis that Hatfield placed on emotional and physiological arousal, we believe that her approach to passionate love belongs at least in the previous category (Position C).

Position E: Approaches to love that ignore sexuality or construe sex as a result of love. A variety of approaches are reviewed, ranging from social science contributions to Platonic notions of Eros and the Christian concept of agape. In these varied approaches, love is the driving force that makes the world go round. Sexuality is a pale and weak phenomenon compared to the power of love.

Aron and Aron (1991) did an excellent job in this first pass at sorting out joint conceptions of love and sex. They note correctly that "our own culture seems to link sexuality and love rather closely" (p. 38), and "love is primary and sex must wait for it" (p. 38). Thus, the modal folk psychology approach in our culture is Positions E and D (love causes sex), whereas much of the relevant scientific culture focuses on Positions A and B (sex causes love).

The span of possible linkages between love and sex implies the ambivalence that Jankowiak (1995a) noted; namely, that every culture has difficulty in perfectly blending "love as desire and love as enduring affection" (p. 7). This pan-cultural difficulty perhaps stems from our recognition that we are both *animals* and *persons*. Sexuality is what all higher animals do to procreate. Human sexuality is uniformly (though not universally) performed in privacy, perhaps for the same reason we wear clothes, apparently to hide our physical, animal nature. In contrast, love is an emotional transaction between *persons*. No one can say exactly what a "person" is, but to be a person is certainly to be more than an animal. Perhaps to be a person is to be slightly "less than an angel!" So humans are trapped between a carnal biological nature and personhood. It is small surprise, then, that we may have difficulty in integrating sexuality with love.

PHILOSOPHICAL VIEWS ON SEX AND LOVE

We provide only a brief sampling here; the literature is so voluminous that a full summary would require its own book.

Undergraduates as Philosophers

Reading undergraduates' views on the relationship between sex and romantic love can be a fascinating experience. We have sometimes collected comments at the end of a questionnaire as responses to the question "If you have any additional thoughts or ideas about the way love and sex are linked together in a close, romantic relationship, please write your comments below." The answers range from a detailed comparison of love and sex to amusing commentary. The first response below clearly distinguishes love from sex.

> Love and lust are often interpreted as the same thing, but they are very different. Lust stems from a need to fill a void in a person's life. The void can be traced to many things in the person's background. Love is a mutual trust on a whole other level than something physical. A lust between two people can be very satisfying for a short period of time, but only love transcends time.

This importance of love over sex is also shown in the next vignette.

> Love is something not easily attained. Sex is. Therefore I feel that love is a much more precious and genuine emotion which actually enhances sex.

Some students accounted for love and sex in terms of some third variable, as noted by Aron and Aron (1991). For example: "In a close relationship, love and sex are linked together by trust."

The last vignette, in its amusing style, recognizes that love and sex can be linked, but do not have to be: "Sex, when in love, can be the best thing in this world. Sex for the hell of it is still good though."

The differences in opinion among the undergraduates are just as wide as some people who get paid to speculate about the relation between love and sex—some professional philosophers.

Philosophers Look at Love and Sex

Philosophers have been as varied as social scientists and undergraduates in their views on love. For example, Solomon (1981) stated "Romantic love ... is essentially sexual, secular, personal and always tentative, tenuous, never certain" (p. xxvi). Solomon viewed love as a complex emotion, and sex serves as a medium of expression of this emotion. To two people deeply in love, sex is a sanctified ritual, an expression of their love, and a merging of flowing, creative desire. Sex becomes a vehicle for the merging of two separate identities into a single identity.

Vannoy (1980) proposed that sex without love is equal or superior to sex with love. The basic argument was that sex per se is good. It is a natural act that should be an end value in itself. Sex can be used for instrumental purposes (e.g., dominance), and thus, violates Kant's edict that people should always be treated as ends, and never as means to other ends. To engage in sex for any other reason than sex itself is to use sex as a means for some other end. And that includes love. To engage in sex for the sake of love is to make sex an instrument of love, and therefore morally wrong.

Vannoy makes a strong and interesting case for sex for its own sake. Strenuous disagreements were to be expected. Solomon (1988) said that Vannoy was wrong. Sex, with love, expresses something that is delightful; namely, love. Sex without love can express less desirable impulses, such as conquest, overcoming insecurity, proving ones masculinity/femininity, etc. Solomon declared "sex in love is the ecstasy of the moment made possible by the promise of unending ecstasy to come" (p. 140).

Sex always occurs within a context. Very few of our behaviors serve as pure and simple ends in and of themselves. Sex may mean multiple things simultaneously: pure physical pleasure, expression of love, reduction of boredom, etc. (S. Hendrick & Hendrick, 1992b). Further, as we interact with others, we tend to treat them as persons, rather than just as roles or useful objects (S. Hendrick & Hendrick, 1992a). Because sex is a strong form of interaction, it is very difficult over time to keep sex separate from other aspects of the person. Personal involvement with the sexual partner is almost inevitable. Thus, Vannoy (1980) may be analytically correct in his abstract analysis of love and sex, but utterly false about what happens in the concrete reality of the ongoing human world.

Brown (1987) treated love as an emotion, but one different from all others. According to Brown, humans are unable to live without love. He also noted that sexual desire can't be independent of other human needs (also contradicting Vannoy). Although sex and love are not equivalent, sexual activity tends to develop into sexual love, unless prevented by social institutions. The mutual contextualization of love and sex is nicely illustrated by Brown (1987):

> For once we begin to care for a person and express our attraction to the person rather than express our appreciation of the person's body and physical performance, we are no longer merely playing a sexual game. We are initiating a personal relationship whose outcome is uncertain. (p. 53)

As a last example, Wilson (1980) argued that there is no intrinsic connection between love and sex. Sexuality can be disconnected from romantic love. But personal involvement in sex is almost inevitable because people bring themselves and their emotions into their sexual encounters. Thus, love and sex tend to become interconnected, an argument similar to our own position (S. Hendrick & Hendrick, 1992a, 1992b).

This small sampling of philosophers' views indicates a broad range of positions. If a large sample were collected, they might well distribute across the entire length of Aron and Aron's (1991) dimension.

We now turn our attention to scientific discussions and research on the relation between romantic love and sexuality. We first consider naturalistic/biological approaches, followed by discussion of psychological/sociological approaches. The former tend to map onto Aron and Aron's (1991) Positions A and B, and the latter map onto Positions C, D, and E.

NATURALISTIC/BIOLOGICAL APPROACHES TO SEX AND LOVE

We can only sample from the vast literature that falls within the naturalistic/biological domain. We consider two general approaches: (a) evolutionary processes involved in love and sex, and (b) the role of attachment processes. These approaches roughly match Aron and Aron's (1991) Positions A and B, respectively. At the outset, we note that there is scarcely more agreement on the relation between love and sex in naturalistic/biological approaches than among philosophers.

EVOLUTION, LOVE, AND SEX

There are several issues to be considered. The most basic issue is whether sexuality is an evolved adaptation. Most biological scholars believe that it is. Less certain is whether romantic love is also an evolved adaptation. Assuming for the moment that love is an adaptation, the large question remains as to how (or whether) romantic love and sexuality are evolutionarily linked together, and if so, how tightly linked? Finally, assuming evolution is important in these matters, we need to consider mating strategies, and especially whether there are evolved gender differences in mating strategies.

Evolution of Sex

Explaining why sex evolved is not an easy matter, at least not for evolutionary biologists. Sex needs to be considered in terms of three concepts: recombination of genetic material, reproduction of offspring, and gender (Stearns, 1987). Recombination is crucial because it leads to genetic diversity. But recombination is not automatically a part of reproduction. "The production of offspring can occur sexually or asexually, with or without recombination" (Stearns, 1987, p. 16). The gender of an organism ". . . is the principal consequence of a history of sexual selection" (Stearns, p. 17). Across all species, recombination, reproduction, and gender are relatively independent of each other. However, sexual species, in most cases, have vastly superior genetic recombination than do asexual species.

What is the adaptive significance of sex? Although Darwin argued for sexual selection at the individual level, later theorizing postulated a positive adaptive effect for sex at the species level. That is, the adaptive benefit of sex accrued to the species at large, not to specific individuals. Group selection was challenged in the 1970s by a series of writings that proposed an adaptive value for sex at the individual level (Ghiselin, 1988). A number of individual advantages of sex were proposed by distinguished biologists (e.g., Ghiselin, 1974; Maynard Smith, 1978; Williams, 1975). Among these advantages were repair of defective DNA through sexual recombination, gene diversification, faster evolutionary response to changing environments, and success in the "coevolutionary arms race" with predators, parasites, and diseases.

However, for each advantage, a disadvantage can be imagined. Genetic immortality is only possible through asexual reproduction. This fact was one reason that adaptation for the species as a whole was long held to be the primary function of sex. Sexual reproduction is costly to the individual (e.g., Lewis, 1987). Such costs have even led to proposals that the gene itself is the unit selected, not the individual organism (e.g., Dawkins, 1989). However, it is unlikely that gene replication per se is of key importance in the adaptive significance of sex. An asexual creature that reproduces by dividing into pairs (without any genetic recombination) would, in 25 generations, reproduce 33,554,432 exact genetic replicas of itself. In contrast, a sexual creature bears the "cost" of loss of half of its remaining genetic material in each succeeding generation. Thus, children are related one-half, grandchildren one-fourth, and so on. After 25 generations, less than three parts in 10 million of the sexual creature's original genetic material remain in the direct descendent line (C. Hendrick, 2002).

Thus, survival of copies of the genome cannot be the reason most species engage in sexual reproduction. What, then, is the adaptive significance of sex? The truth is that no one yet knows for sure. "No one has yet given a convincing, single-generation, microevolutionary and experimental demonstration of the advantages of sex, which must nevertheless exist" (Stearns, 1987, pp. 26–27). But Stearns also asserted that "we now know that explanations for the maintenance of sex that are based strictly on selection of individuals do work in principle and are increasingly well-supported by experimental evidence" (p. 27).

Thus, we are left with the conclusion that sex is an evolved adaptation, although why it is superior to asexual reproduction (for complex animals) is still not fully understood. Most of us are undoubtedly quite happy, however, to accept nature's verdict of sexual reproduction.

What Is the Unit of Selection?

Recent evolutionary theorizing was stimulated by Hamilton's (1964) concept of inclusive fitness and theory of kin selection (Simpson, 1999). By postulating selection at the level of the gene, Hamilton was able to account for several puzzles. For example, not every individual tries to maximize its own reproduction; sometimes the individual sacrifices its own chance in order to assist the reproduction of close kin. One classic example is an adult child who stays at home and cares for aging parents until they die. This altruistic behavior allows the siblings to pursue their vocations and to reproduce. However, the altruist is too old to reproduce by the time their responsibilities for the parents have ended. Comparable examples have been observed across many species.

We have no wish to challenge the general theory of kin selection! Based on the facts pointed out for sexually reproducing creatures, however, the gene is not, per se, a promising unit for selection's work. Even with the added component of kin's genes, in several generations only a miniscule fraction of hereditary relatedness would remain.

What, then, is the unit of selection? We believe that it is everyday human behavior, including attributes such as similarity, familiarity, communicative intimacy, and the physical bonding of attachment. There is a massive literature that shows that similarity (Byrne, 1971) and familiarity (Zajonc, 1968) both stimulate liking. We aid and sacrifice for those we like and love (Clark & Mills, 1993). If humans evolved as small-group animals, all of these processes, and more, would have operated. Most groups were extended family kin groups. Thus, genetic relatedness would be closely correlated with degree of similarity, familiarity, and communication within the group. Said differently, these attributes were confounded with degree of genetic relatedness. To us, it makes more sense to view these behavioral attributes as the basic units of evolutionary selection. We would dub this approach the *social* theory of kin selection.

Attributes as complex as similarity recognition, communication, and the emotional adaptation of familiarity are undoubtedly complexly polygenic. There may be multiple genetic patterns through which each attribute can be manifested. Thus, genetic relatedness may be most important as a general pattern device that controls complex behaviors (e.g., mother–infant bonding at birth based on repeated contact). Such polygenic patterns are associated with many behavioral complexes within the kin group. Because these polygenic patterns can have different configurations that lead to the same complex behavior pattern, the behavior pattern, therefore, becomes relatively independent of any specific gene. Therefore, the behavior pattern (e.g., love of infants) can be maintained even though specific genes change widely over generations. Thus, a 25th generation descendant may still love an infant just as intensely as the line founder did 25 generations earlier. But in 25 generations, the specific genetic relatedness is nil. Therefore, stable or slowly changing polygenic patterns can be linked with stable patterns of familial behavior, generation after generation, long after one's own specific configuration of genes has passed into oblivion.

This polygenic social behavior theory of kin selection can account for certain anomalous observations. For example, based on the traditional view of the gene as a discrete unit, Kirkpatrick (1998, p. 356) correctly observed that spouses should not be expected to provide much costly caregiving to each other because they are not genetically related. Yet, many people would sacrifice their lives for a spouse before they would do so for a genetic relative. Also, infant adoption may lead to parent–child bonds just as intense as for biological parent–child bonding. This focus on sociality is completely consistent with scientific perspectives on the human brain as a "social brain" that has fostered "our success as a species . . . [due to] our gregarious nature" (Taylor, 2002. p. 37).

Complex, polygenic patterns are associated with complex behavior patterns. Evolution selected to bond with, protect, perhaps love, and reproduce with a mate. It is a very powerful pattern. Likewise, the complex patterns of attraction to and bonding with an infant are more general than any specific gene. These vast polygenic patterns free us from behavioral slavery to our own *specific* gene configuration.

This social approach to kin selection may deserve serious consideration. Belsky (1999) stated: "genetic replication is the goal of [all] life, and thus the ultimate target of natural selection" (p. 141). We agree; the only question is the conceptual unit of selection. Because discrete gene patterns are eventually dispersed, we have argued that polygenic patterns for complex behaviors are the most useful conceptual units of selection.

Evolution of Love

Is love an evolved adaptation? There are many biological arguments to believe that it is. However, there are equally many good arguments to believe that love is mostly a cultural invention. But what is love? As we noted, Aron and Aron (1991) defined love broadly, such that it could include parental love, friendship, etc. Most people distinguish romantic love from other types of love. We are interested in both general love and romantic love, but with primary emphasis on the latter.

It could be that love (e.g., parental love) in general is an evolved adaptation, but that romantic love is a cultural overlay or perhaps both parental and romantic love are evolved adaptations. Or perhaps both are cultural products stemming from some third (unknown) evolved mechanism. We mostly emphasize evolutionary possibilities, though some cultural counterarguments are noted. We focus on five specific arguments.

1. *Emotion.* There is general consensus that a core set of emotions are part of our physiological equipment, although some social constructionists dispute the matter. Darwin (1873) believed that emotional expression is part of the evolutionary heritage. Mallon and Stich (2000), in a detailed conceptual analysis, argued that proponents for the social constructionist approach to emotions were actually quite similar in their arguments to accounts for emotion based on evolutionary theory.

So, is love an emotion? We have argued that it is (C. Hendrick & Hendrick, 2003). Shaver, Morgan, and Wu (1996) also argued convincingly that love is a basic emotion, fundamental to many other complex, nuanced emotional states. Such a view makes love a central human experience (thus likely an evolved adaptation). This conception of love as a core emotion is consistent with Baumeister and Leary (1995) in their argument that humans have a fundamental need to belong, as a need for attachment and connection with others as part of our evolutionary heritage.

2. *Communication.* Humans are group animals in incessant communication. Communication keeps us in contact as part of a "gregarious bonding herd" (S. Hendrick & Hendrick, 1992b). What drives this incessant communication? Buck and Ginsburg (1991) provide an interesting answer. Love serves as a bonding glue of sociality that keeps us organized as a group species. Without the emotional/behavioral/interactional force called love, most of the centripetal force that bonds us together would be absent. Thus, communication may be an evolved adaptation in the service of love.

3. *Species generality.* It is difficult to prove that other species experience love. Daily interaction with pets suggests that they do love—unconditionally! Something like maternal love is also clearly evident across species in protection of the young. Beyond such anthropomorphism, however, there is good research evidence. For example, Harlow (1974) started a research tradition in studying the development of love in rhesus monkeys. Harlow described an infant monkey's need to cling to its mother as "organic affection." Infants deprived of such contact comfort did not mature normally. In particular, infant monkeys deprived of motherly love could not form later peer or mating relations in adulthood. This research has been replicated many times and generalized to other monkey and ape species (Suomi, 1999). To a considerable extent, "monkey love" is now studied as part of the research tradition on attachment.

4. *Evolution of romantic love?* In an interesting volume, Mellen (1981) speculated on how love might have evolved. Because females bear children, they require assistance

when the infant is born. Males foraged for food, especially meat. Protection by the male would have given at least a slight survival edge to the infant. As S. Hendrick and Hendrick (1992b) noted, with respect to love:

> One mechanism to ensure such protection was the development of a type of emotional bondedness between breeding pairs of males and females. In Mellen's terms this was the beginning of love. Love for a female and, presumably, her offspring served to ensure care and protection by the male, increasing offspring survival. Thus love would have had an evolutionary advantage among early humans. (p. 9)

In a slightly different approach, Buss (1988) argued that love should be construed as a natural category of acts that is an outcome of evolution. If love is related to evolution, it must be manifest in behavior. Such "love acts" should be most clearly observed in rituals of courtship and mating behavior. Love acts include a range of behaviors, from resource displays, to sexual intimacy, to parental investment in offspring. In this approach, romantic love becomes virtually the entire complex of mating behavior.

5. *Universality of romantic love.* For romantic love to be an evolved adaptation, it should be experienced everywhere among human groups. We noted earlier the research by Jankowiak and Fischer (1992) that found romantic love to be "near" universal across human cultures. Hatfield also provided strong arguments and data for the universality of passionate love (Hatfield, 1988; Hatfield & Rapson, 1987, 1996; Hatfield & Sprecher, 1986). Research shows that passionate love has occurred in all eras and across all ethnic groups. Males and females equally experience passionate love, and pre-pubertal children may fall in love. If romantic love is indeed a universal part of human experience, it may be an evolved adaptation.

Passionate Love: Two Sides of the Same Coin?

Passionate/romantic love has been discussed as if love and sex were conceptually independent. Perhaps sex and romantic love co-evolved as adaptations so that they are functionally the same thing. The theorizing of Buss (1988) and Mellen (1981) suggests such a conclusion. In a famous quote, Berscheid (1988) imagined herself before a firing squad, to be executed if she did not give the correct definition of romantic love. She said that she would whisper "it's about 90 percent sexual desire as yet not sated" (p. 373). In an equally memorable quote on the same page, Berscheid (1988) concluded:

> I am certain that to continue to discuss romantic love without also prominently mentioning the role sexual arousal and desire plays in it is very much like our printing a recipe for tiger soup that leaves out the main ingredient. (p. 373)

As noted previously, Regan (1998) saw sexual desire as an important part of romantic love, a conclusion reinforced in a volume by Regan and Berscheid (1999).

So, from one point of view, sexual attraction and desire virtually equate with romantic love. However, romantic (i.e., passionate) love was defined by Hatfield (1988) as "a state of intense longing for union with another" (p. 193). That longing might include sexual union, but it need not. For example, a child with a passionate crush may not even know what "sexual union" is. Hatfield's definition of passionate love closely approximates Tennov's (1979) concept of limerence. Sexual attraction is not the main component of limerent longing, and may be absent altogether. The intensity of limerence (as is true for Hatfield's passionate love) is for reciprocity from the beloved; sex may be a sign of such reciprocity.

Fisher (2000) viewed lust (sex) and attraction (passionate love) as two of three independent, but highly interrelated emotion systems in service of mating, reproduction, and parenting (also see Fisher, 1992, 1998). Attachment is the third system, reviewed in the next major section. Fisher (2000) made a strong case that the three emotion systems of lust, love, and attachment are separate neural systems, each with its own set of neurotransmitters. The three systems evolved separately, but became interconnected over time. But the connections are not causally tight. Thus, cultural invention, in interaction with genetic endowment, leads to endless variety. Sometimes romantic love *is* 90% lust, but sometimes it may be 90% desperate yearning for union, with no sexual desire at all.

Perhaps the best conclusion at this time is that romantic love and lust are both co-evolved systems, but they are systems that are endlessly rearranged into new configurations by culture. This interplay of genes and culture shows up clearly in mating strategies.

Mating Strategies and Gender

There is a voluminous literature in evolutionary psychology on gender differences in mating strategies (i.e., methods of attracting a mate). Space precludes extensive review. As one example, in a textbook on evolutionary psychology, Buss (1999) devotes three chapters (nearly 100 pages) to the long-term and short-term mating strategies of men and women. Other extended discussions may be found in Buss (1994, 1995, 1996), Buss and Kenrick (1998), Kenrick (1987), and Kenrick and Trost (1989).

Anatomical differences in males and females suggest different mating strategies. The differential parental investment model proposed by Trivers (1972) implies an empirical sequence of such gender differences: (a) women must invest more effort than men in producing and raising children, (b) reproductive success for women requires protection and economic security for their young (thus economics are relatively more important for women), (c) men invest relatively little in a reproductive act, focusing primarily on female beauty and health as signs of reproductive potential, and (d) men are inclined to have more sexual partners than women have. Buss and Barnes (1986) provided some initial evidence for such gender differences, and many relevant studies are reviewed in detail in Buss (1999) and Kenrick and Trost (1989).

In addition, males are never as certain of paternity as females are of maternity. One implication is that male jealousy tends to focus more on guarding sexual access, whereas females may be more concerned with emotional unfaithfulness (a signal of potential loss of economic support). Such gender differences in certainty about parental status suggest that males should be more sexually territorial than females. In fact, Symons (1979) claimed that sex is always a service that females perform for males, regardless of the female's own sexual satisfaction. Given that sex for pay is overwhelmingly a female occupation, there may be an element of truth in this observation.

Many more examples of differences in mating strategies could be given. However, for every evolutionary claim, cultural theorists can provide reasoned rebuttals. For example, Eagly and Wood (1999) attributed many of the observed gender differences to societal differences in power. By and large, men have the power. If gender roles were reversed, very different mating strategies might be observed.

So the argument goes. Clearly it is not evolution *or* culture, but rather evolution *and* culture. The problem is that we do not understand at present how culture and evolution interact and in what degree of complexity. A tradition is developing that explores linkages between evolution and culture. An excellent summary of work on evolutionary approaches to culture is provided by Janicki and Krebs (1998). This tradition poses questions such as how biological and cultural evolution are related, how evolved psychological mechanisms (such as learning) create and transmit culture, and the like. As one example, Dawkins (1989) viewed biological and cultural processes as *independent* evolutionary systems. As noted previously, Dawkins identified the gene as the basic unit of biological selection. He coined the term "meme," in analogy, as the basic unit of cultural evolution. Memes include ideas, fashions, songs, etc.; in general, any specific symbol unit that can be transferred from one mind to another.

The notion of memes has generated a substantial literature. One strand is the possible coevolution of genes and culture. Another branch is the use of evolution as a model for the growth of scientific knowledge. There are many other fertile ideas in process, but we cannot pursue them here. For a broader perspective of evolutionary psychology, see de Waal (2002).

ATTACHMENT, LOVE, AND SEX

Attachment theory and research is currently a sprawling field of endeavor. We must therefore be very selective in our discussion. We focus primarily on the relation of attachment to romantic love and sex. Attachment theory was originally a conceptual creation of Bowlby (1969), based in part on evolutionary thinking, but also on systems theory, ethology, and depth psychology. The placement of attachment theory on Position B of Aron and Aron's (1991) dimension seems correct.

Originally, attachment was construed narrowly as "a biobehavioral safety-regulating system in which the parent is the child's primary protector and haven of safety" (Goldberg, Grusec, & Jenkins, 1999, p. 476). Goldberg et al. complained that the history of the concept was one of steady broadening, until, at the extreme, "attachment" meant parent–child relationships. They argued for a return to a more narrow definition of attachment.

The change in meaning of the term in developmental and family psychology is nothing compared to what researchers on *adult* attachment have done. The initial study by Hazan and Shaver (1987) has had a profound impact on later research. As an analog to attachment research on infants using the Strange Situation (Ainsworth, Blehar, Waters, & Wall, 1978), Hazan and Shaver composed three vignettes representing secure, avoidant, and anxious/ambivalent types, and asked adults to classify themselves as one of the three attachment types in terms of their romantic relationship. In conceptual articles, Shaver and Hazan (1988), and Shaver, Hazan, and Bradshaw (1988) argued for strong similarities between infant attachment and romantic love. Ultimately, Shaver et al. construed romantic love as the integration of *attachment*, *caregiving*, and *sexuality*, in parallel to three behavioral systems proposed by Bowlby (1969).

The simple classification of three attachment love styles did not long endure. For example, Bartholomew and Horowitz (1991) proposed four attachment categories. Research on reliability and stability of attachment type and on measures of attachment proliferated (e.g., Scharfe & Bartholomew, 1994). This vast mass of literature on adult attachment as romantic love was ably summarized by Feeney (1999) and Feeney, Noller, and Roberts (2000).

Two issues deserve brief consideration: issues of measurement and new theoretical directions. We consider measurement issues first. There has been a tremendous proliferation of scales. Brennan, Clark, and Shaver (1998) found 60 attachment scales and factored them. These 60 scales reduced to 12 factors, and second-order analysis recovered two dimensions: avoidance (high or low) and anxiety (high or low). The matter was further complicated by scaling research by Fraley and Waller (1998) who used taxometric procedures developed by Meehl (e.g., 1995) to determine if attachment styles best fit a typological model (e.g., Hazan & Shaver, 1987) or a dimensional, continuous model. Their analyses strongly suggested a dimensional approach. The results were so strong as to lead Brennan, Clark, and Shaver (1998) to conclude "it is difficult to justify categorical measures except on grounds of convenience" (p. 68). There is an irony here because Shaver's original categorical approach stimulated scores of typological studies! Thus, how infant attachment may (or may not) be related to romantic love remains an unsolved research issue (e.g., Harvey & Weber, 2002).

The era of construing romantic love as attachment may be changing. The most valiant attempt in this direction is probably Hazan's theory of adult romantic pair bonds as attachment processes (e.g., Hazan & Zeifman, 1999). Kirkpatrick (1998) reconstrued this tradition in arguing that the attachment system (as a system) is not centrally involved in adult romantic relationships. Basically, Kirkpatrick pointed out the wide variety of ways in which adult bonding differs from infant attachment. He also reconstrued emotions, especially love, as *commitment devices*. Commitment means selecting a mate, bonding, reproducing and caring for the young. Kirkpatrick (1998) suggested that "romantic relationships might involve neither the caregiving system nor the attachment system per se, but rather are organized around a single component shared by those systems: the emotional bond of love" (p. 361). Hazan and Zeifman (1999, p. 345) denied Kirkpatrick's reconstrual by arguing for a broad definition of attachment. As noted, many of the disputes in this area revolve around the meaning of attachment (e.g., a narrow or broad construal of "protection").

In infancy, the sexual system is not very relevant. However, the infant's attachment system and the parent's caregiving system are highly relevant to the infant's survival and future reproduction. Kirkpatrick's main point is that love is a bonding glue that links infant attachment to adult caregiving. This kernel of infant love remains in adult relations, but the relations among the three systems (attachment, caregiving, and sex) cannot remain as they were in infancy. In fact, Berman and Sperling (1994) suggested that in adulthood, attachment and caregiving collapse into a single system.

If this is true, then attachment/caregiving, sexuality, and love become the "big three" interlocking variables. These are the same three variables that Fisher (e.g., 1998) identified as attachment, lust, and attraction, respectively. Further, these three were posited as evolved independent systems that became loosely linked over time.

We find this approach compelling. Attachment is *not* romantic love, and romantic love is *not* sex. Yet they are all highly interrelated in the formation of reproducing pair bonds that successfully raise offspring to the point of the offspring's own reproduction. It appears that all three systems are required for complex, sexually reproducing creatures, and thus, perhaps, for most if not all mammals. (For an extended discussion of attachment, see Feeney and Noller, chapter 8, this volume.)

We have puzzled at length over naturalistic/biological approaches to love and sex. Evolution and attachment are very important. But their theoretical languages are still not adequate to capture all the nuances of love and sex. To attempt to do so more completely, we next consider several psychological/sociological approaches to love and sex.

PSYCHOLOGICAL/SOCIOLOGICAL APPROACHES TO SEX AND LOVE

Initial Approaches to Love and Sex

Sociologists and psychologists have been interested for the most part in either sexuality or love, rather than in the connection between them. Yet much of the work on love or sex at least implicitly addresses such connections. The following section will highlight some of the major approaches to sex and love, with special attention to how love approaches implicitly address sex and how sex approaches implicitly address love.

Passionate love, for example, was discussed at some length earlier in this chapter as falling somewhere around the midpoint of the Arons' (1991) continuum. But predating Hatfield's (1988) focus solely on passionate love was Walster and Walster's (1978) discussion of two different kinds of love: passionate and companionate. Whereas passionate love involves intense emotionality, physiological arousal, and a need for almost constant interaction with the loved one, companionate love is "the affection we feel for those with whom our lives are deeply intertwined" (Walster & Walster, p. 9). Although this perspective on romantic love is not focused on sex directly, the excitement of sexual interaction is an obvious aspect of passionate love and appears to be much less relevant to companionate love. In fact the whole nature of passionate and companionate love is premised on the roaring sexual flame of passionate love settling down to the only mildly warm embers of companionship.

Almost parallel with some of the early work on love was Reiss's (1960, 1967) articulation of sexual "standards" as one way to frame people's beliefs and values about sexuality. Reiss defined four broad sexual standards referring specifically to premarital sexuality. The first standard, *abstinence*, views premarital sexual intercourse as wrong for both women and men. The second standard, the *double standard*, essentially gives less sexual freedom to women than to men. The third standard, *permissiveness with affection*, expresses "the notion that premarital sex is appropriate for both men and women in stable, affectionate relationships" (Sprecher & McKinney, 1993, p. 4). The fourth standard, *permissiveness without affection*, viewes consensual adult premarital sex as appropriate for both men and women, without regard for emotional involvement or commitment. Although Reiss's standards are explicitly about sex, the third standard is at least implicitly about love, because the acceptability of premarital sex is made contingent on the context of an affectional, presumably loving relationship.

Viewing sex even more broadly than in terms of standards, DeLamater (1989) proposed three general orientations toward sexuality. These refer to global frameworks for human sexual interaction rather than to specific standards for premarital sexuality. The *procreational* orientation proposes that reproduction, or perpetuation of the species, is the essential purpose of sexual intercourse. Sex may well occur within the context of a stable, caring relationship and may well be pleasurable for both persons; however, neither the relationship nor the pleasure is the central purpose of the sexual experience. Although this orientation would seem on the face of it to be an evolution-based, naturalistic approach to sex, it appears rather to be based on a conservative political/religious perspective (similar to Reiss's standard of abstinence) that places sex (and perhaps love) in the service of procreation. The *relational* orientation, reminiscent of Reiss's permissiveness with affection standard, and also referred to as "person-centered sex" (Sprecher & McKinney, 1993) views sex as "a way of expressing love and affection and a way to help increase the emotional intimacy of a relationship" (Sprecher & McKinney, p. 3). Thus, although sex within this relational context may be highly pleasurable and may result in the birth of children, the central purpose here is relational. Finally, the *recreational* orientation views sex as pleasurable activity for consenting adults, nothing more and nothing less. This orientation is very similar to Reiss's permissiveness without affection, and has also been called "body-centered sex" (Sprecher & McKinney). Sex may enhance an ongoing relationship or may even result in children, but the central theme here is sex as pleasure. Thus, a particular example of two people sexually involved with one another could appear very similar within each of these global frameworks/orientations, but the central theme for the couple would vary. Although love is not addressed centrally in these orientations, it is clearly an important aspect of the relational orientation, though it appears to be absent in the recreational one, and its role is unclear in the procreational perspective. The orientations could fall on points A, B, or C of the Arons' continuum (1991).

Later Approaches to Love and Sex

More recently, Laumann and his colleagues (Laumann, Gagnon, Michael, & Michaels, 1994) developed designated "groups" based on the specific sexual attitudes, values, and behaviors reported by a large, representative sample of persons in the United States. The groups were labeled *Traditional, Relational*, and *Recreational*, conforming in a general sense to DeLamater's (1989) orientations. Yet within these broad groups, there were a number of subgroups, sometimes reporting an interesting mixture of social and religious attitudes and values. For example, the Traditional designation (similar to Procreational) includes groups labeled Conservative and Pro-Choice. The Relational designation includes groups labeled Religious, Conventional, and Contemporary Religious. The Recreational designation contains a Libertarian group (liberal on all values) and a Pro-Life group (combining "liberal positions on extramarital sex and pornography with relatively conservative positions on homosexuality and abortion" (Laumann et al., p. 516). And these groups differed somewhat on the basis of age, race, and especially gender (with women more relational and men more recreational; Michael, Gagnon, Laumann, & Kolata, 2000). Clearly, orientations to sex, and by implication to sex and love, are very complex, and people may hold what appear to be discrepant attitudes and values regarding the two.

One of Laumann et al.'s (1994) findings that is particularly interesting is that in assessing people's satisfaction with their sexual lives, those reporting the greatest physical pleasure and emotional satisfaction are those in monogamous relationships. As the authors concluded, "having one sex partner is more rewarding in terms of physical pleasure and emotional satisfaction than having more than one partner, and it is particularly rewarding if that single partner is a marriage partner, next most if that partner is a cohabitational partner, and so forth" (p. 364). These persons also reported the greatest overall happiness. What might be so special about having sex within a monogamous, committed relationship? "Love" seems like the obvious answer.

Just as much of the research on sexual standards, orientations, and value designations have contained implicit references to love, so also have the various perspectives on love, such as passionate and companionate love, discussed earlier, contained implicit references to sex. Sternberg's (1986, 1987) triangular theory of love proposed that love has three primary components that can be combined in multiple ways to form eight different types of love. The eight types are variously high or low in some or all of the primary components, and of the eight types, four are high in passion, which could at the very least be considered a sexualized component of love. These four types of love include Infatuated love (high passion, low intimacy and commitment); Fatuous love (high passion and commitment, low intimacy); Romantic love (high passion and intimacy, low commitment); and Consummate love (high on all three primary components).

One relationship researcher who has been very concerned with the intersection of sex and love is Regan (e.g., Regan & Berscheid, 1999), whose overall perspective is that sexual desire is an integral aspect of both romantic love and sexual expression, and as such might be one of the strongest links between the two. Passionate love and sexual desire are indeed linked, as Sprecher and Regan (1998) found when assessing the relationships between companionate and passionate love and a variety of relationship constructs. They found that "for both men and women, the experience of sexual excitement was more strongly correlated with passionate love scores than with companionate love scores, whereas feelings of sexual intimacy were more strongly related to companionate love scores than to passionate love scores" (Regan & Berscheid, 1999, p. 127). It appears that different aspects of love may be associated variously with different aspects of sexuality, but an essentially important finding is that the two *are* associated.

The several sociological and psychological approaches to love and sexuality just discussed are placed variously on the Aron and Aron (1991) continuum, with the love approaches more nearly approximating the "sex is really love" pole, and the sexuality approaches more nearly approximating the "love is really sex" pole. Regan's (1998) perspective is more centered on the continuum, however, in that she attempts to tie romantic/passionate love and sexual desire together, thus explicitly linking sex and love as interrelated and mutually causal.

A social-psychological approach to love and sex that has rather consistently attempted to link the two phenomena in intimate, romantic relationships is presented in some detail in the following section.

BELIEF SYSTEMS ABOUT SEX AND LOVE

Love Attitudes and Sexual Attitudes

The question of whether sex and romantic love may be linked, or how they may have come to be linked, has earned commentary from philosophers, evolutionary biologists, social scientists, and others. Yet at some juncture, scholars accept the reality of the connection—at least for most humans—and go on about the business of assessing "how" love and sex intersect. That intersection has been of interest to us for nearly 2 decades.

As noted earlier, we began with the premise that love and sex are complex emotional and behavioral phenomena that are exceedingly difficult to measure in their entirety. Thus, we focused on the two from an attitudinal perspective, setting out to measure love attitudes and sexual attitudes as coherent belief systems comprised of cognitive structures, affect, and behavioral tendencies.

When we began working in the area of romantic love, our first goal was to develop an attitude scale that would represent the six major love styles proposed by Lee (1973) and included in a scale previously developed by Lasswell and Lasswell (1976). The initial 54-item version of the Love Attitudes Scale (C. Hendrick, Hendrick, Foote, & Slapion-Foote, 1984) was subsequently refined to a 42-item, psychometrically solid, scale that had seven items representative of each of the six love styles (C. Hendrick & Hendrick, 1986). These include Eros (passionate, intimate love); Ludus (game-playing, uncommitted love); Storge (love based in friendship); Pragma (practical, calculating love); Mania (possessive, dependent love), and Agape (altruistic, partner-supportive love).

Although sexuality was not central to Lee's approach, each love style incorporates sexual elements somewhat differently (S. Hendrick & Hendrick, 1992a). Eros has "a strong physical component . . . and seeks early sexual relations with the partner" (p. 100). Ludus "enjoys sex and variety in sexual activity, but tends to consider sex (merely) good fun" (p. 100). The Storge lover "tends to be shy about intense contact and sexual behavior, assuming that after full commitment any sexual difficulties will be worked out" (p. 100). The manic lover is so obsessed with the partner that intimacy, including sexual intimacy, may be elusive. In contrast, Pragma "believes that sexual compatibility is important, but that any problems can be worked out mutually" (p. 101). Finally, Agape is so focused on selflessness and concern for the partner that sex is likely very much in the background. Love is spiritual rather than biological. These love styles as measured by the Love Attitudes Scale have provided the basis for an extensive research program. The Love Attitudes Scale has several forms, including a partner-specific form (C. Hendrick & Hendrick, 1990) and a short form (C. Hendrick, Hendrick, & Dicke, 1998).

At the same time the love scale was being developed, we searched the existing literature for measures of sexual attitudes that offered the multidimensional perspective to sex that Lee's work offered to love. Although we found solid, established measures that captured a single aspect of sexual attitudes (e.g., Reiss, 1967), no measures offered the breadth that we were looking for. We found it necessary to develop our own measure, the Sexual Attitudes Scale (S. Hendrick, Hendrick, Slapion-Foote, & Foote, 1985). An earlier version was reduced in subsequent studies (S. Hendrick & Hendrick, 1987c) to 43 items, represented by four factors. The factors include: Permissiveness (casual, uncommitted sex; 21 items); Sexual Practices (tolerant, responsible sex; 7 items); Communion (sex as a peak experience; 9 items); and Instrumentality (biological, self-focused sex; 6 items). The measure was psychometrically strong and related in predictable ways to other measures of sexual attitudes as well as to selected individual and relationship characteristics. For example, Permissiveness was correlated strongly and positively with a measure of sensation seeking (S. Hendrick & Hendrick, 1987c), and is related negatively to relationship satisfaction (S. Hendrick & Hendrick, 1995).

Although refinement of the Sexual Attitudes Scales, and the Love Attitudes Scale as well, continued for some time, the two measures were employed together from their inception. For example, the Love Attitudes Scale was one of the measures used to establish construct validity of the Sexual Attitudes Scale (S. Hendrick & Hendrick, 1987c).

It was deemed important to explore fully the relationships between the Sexual Attitudes Scale and the Love Attitudes Scale (and presumably the belief systems/attitude constellations that they measured). Early relevant work was detailed most fully in S. Hendrick and Hendrick (1987a) as a research program "concerned with attitudes toward love, attitudes toward sex, and the relations between the two" (p. 142).

Across several studies, we correlated the six love attitude subscales and four sexual attitude subscales, finding that although correlation patterns differed slightly, some fairly consistent central relationships appeared. Correlations between game-playing love (Ludus) and casual sex (Permissiveness) were consistently strong, which was not surprising. A game-playing lover who seeks to avoid commitment is likely to endorse a casual, less-than-serious approach to sex. Ludus was also related consistently to Instrumentality, indicating a relationship between game-playing love and self-focused, somewhat utilitarian sex. The other romantic love–sex relationships with substantial consistency were between passionate love (Eros) and both idealized sex (Communion) and tolerant, responsible sex (Sexual Practices). Eros and Communion both express an intense and in some ways idealized notion of love and sex, respectively. Finally, altruistic love (Agape) was modestly but consistently negatively correlated with casual sex and fairly consistently and positively related to idealistic sex (Communion). Logically, altruistic love should be congruent with idealized sexuality, but discrepant with a casual orientation to sex.

There were other significant correlations among the scales (e.g., friendship love [Storge] and practical love [Pragma] negatively related to Permissiveness; possessive, dependent love [Mania] positively related to Sexual Practices), but these relationships were not completely consistent across studies.

To conclude our initial exploratory analyses of the Sexual Attitudes Scale and Love Attitudes Scale, we factored the 10 subscales, with the best solution extracting three factors. Permissiveness, Instrumentality, and Ludus loaded positively on the first factor, with Agape loading negatively. This factor seemed to represent a "game-playing, mechanistic love/sex relationship" (S. Hendrick & Hendrick, 1987c, p. 516). The second factor contained positive loadings by Eros, Mania, Agape, Sexual Practices, and Communion (three love and two sex attitudes scales). This factor appeared to represent an emotional and somewhat idealistic, yet responsible, orientation to sex and love. Storge and Pragma loaded solidly on Factor Three, which also had a modest positive loading by Mania and a modest negative loading by Permissiveness. "The content of this factor could perhaps be characterized as 'stable' in the sense that Storge and Pragma are both solid, steady love styles. To the extent that Permissiveness represents more free-ranging sexuality, it would logically relate negatively to the other two. Mania's secondary loading on this factor may reflect the Manic tendency to fixate solidly on one's partner" (p. 516).

More recently, we have refactored the love and sex scales, using a shorter, 24-item version of the Love Attitudes Scale (C. Hendrick et al., 1998) and a shorter, 25-item version of the Sexual Attitudes Scale (S. Hendrick, 2002). This analysis resulted in three factors, which differed slightly from the earlier analysis. The game-playing factor looked very similar (positive loadings by game-playing love and casual and self-focused sex), but the other two factors showed slightly different configurations. In this analysis, idealistic and responsible sexuality were combined with passionate and friendship-based love, while the third factor seemed to be a general love factor (e.g., loadings by Eros, Pragma, Mania, and Agape). Nevertheless, sex and love still showed substantial linkages.

Based on the correlations and the factor analyses contained in the early work, we concluded that there was a considerable relationship between the love scales and the sex scales, and we believed that the relationship was conceptual as well as psychometric. We proposed that "Love and sex are inextricably linked, with love as the basis for much of our sexual interaction, and sex as the medium of expression for much of our loving" (S. Hendrick & Hendrick, 1987a, p. 159).

After establishing these connections between the sex and love scales early in the development of the research program, we employed the scales in tandem in the studies that followed. Highlights of those studies are noted briefly.

Although we envision sex and love as attitude constellations, we explored their relationships with more dispositional constructs such as self-disclosure and sensation seeking in one study (S. Hendrick & Hendrick, 1987b). Indeed, self-disclosure to a lover was related positively to passionate and altruistic love and idealized sexuality, as well as more modestly related to manic love. It was related negatively to game-playing love. An aspect of sensation seeking, Disinhibition, was related strongly to game-playing love and permissive sexuality, and moderately to self-focused sex. Other dimensions of disclosure and sensation seeking were also related to love and sex attitudes, variously for women and men.

Sexual attitudes and love attitudes are also related to specific behavior patterns such as eating disorders (Raciti & Hendrick, 1992) and contraceptive behavior (Adler & Hendrick, 1991). In the former study, specific eating disorder characteristics are most consistently positively related to possessive love and instrumental sexual attitudes, and most consistently negatively related to passionate love. In the latter study, passionate love and an absence of game-playing love predict more consistent contraceptive behavior for women, whereas passionate love and idealistic sex attitudes predict more consistent contraceptive behavior for men.

We also explored how sexual attitudes and romantic love attitudes might differ for people who are currently in love versus those not in love (C. Hendrick & Hendrick, 1988). Respondents who are in love report themselves to be more passionate and giving and less game-playing in their love attitudes as well as less casual and self-focused in their sexual attitudes. Factor analyses of the love and sex attitude scales conducted separately for those in love versus those not in love indicated slightly different factor structures for the two groups. The three-factor structure found previously was replicated for the "not in love" group, but for the "in love" group, only the first two factors were intact. The third factor split into two factors, one of which contained passionate, possessive, and altruistic love (with a modest loading by practical love). This "romantic love" factor thus appeared only for the in love group and indicated that people who are in love do view the world somewhat differently from people who are not in love.

One study with a cross-cultural perspective assessed love and sex attitudes, as well as marital satisfaction and other variables, in a sample of Mexican-American (divided into Hispanic-oriented and bicultural) and European-American married couples (Contreras, Hendrick, & Hendrick, 1996). Both love attitudes and sexual attitudes show some cultural differences (ethnic differences on three love scales and two sex scales), but these are modest. For example, both Mexican-American groups endorse more game-playing love attitudes than do the European-American group, which in turn is more endorsing of tolerant, responsible sexuality than are either of the Mexican-American groups. The Hispanic-oriented group has more practical love attitudes than do the other two groups, whereas the European-American and bicultural groups have more idealistic sexual attitudes than do the Hispanic-oriented group. So although there are some universal themes common to all the groups, there appear to be cultural differences as well.

Similarity is the case also in a comparison of homosexual and heterosexual men from two locations on both love attitudes and sexual attitudes (Adler, Hendrick, & Hendrick, 1986). Gay men and heterosexual men differ significantly only on the love attitude of Agape, with gay men from one location significantly less endorsing of Agape than gay men from the other location or heterosexual men from either location. For sexual attitudes, the only difference is for Permissiveness, with heterosexual men less endorsing than gay men.

Gender

Our research program was not initiated with the expectation that gender issues would be an important ongoing component of the research. Early in the process, however, it was apparent that women and men differed on a number of love attitudes (C. Hendrick et al., 1984) and sexual attitudes (S. Hendrick et al., 1985), particularly at the item level. For example, women appear to be more friendship-oriented and practical as well as less game-playing in their love styles than do men. Men are more inclined toward casual sexuality than are women. Once the sex and love scales were in final form, gender differences tended to appear consistently on the total subscale scores, as they had on individual items. In addition to exploring gender differences, we also surveyed gender role categories (Bailey, Hendrick, & Hendrick, 1987), based on the Bem Sex Role Inventory (Bem, 1974). We found gender differences consistent with previous work as well as an impressive number of differences based on gender role (significant effects for three of the sex scales and five of the love scales). As an example, "masculine" participants are more strongly endorsing of game-playing love, whereas "feminine" participants are least endorsing. We concluded that "gender role as well as biological sex were related to basic attitudes toward love and sexuality" (Bailey et al., p. 647).

Although potential gender differences were explored consistently across various studies, we did not assume that such differences were invariant. Indeed, cohorts change, and even within cohorts, samples may differ. How questions are asked, as well as what questions are asked, can influence findings, including those based on gender. For example, the Love Attitudes Scale: Short Form (24 items) was developed as an alternative to the longer, 42-item version (C. Hendrick et al., 1998). Across three studies, gender comparisons were performed for both the long and short forms of the Love Attitudes Scale, and although some gender differences were consistent across forms, other differences appeared with the short form. Men, more than women, endorse altruistic love and to some extent possessive, dependent love. These findings are basically new and appear to result from the specific items that had been retained in the shorter version of the scale.

Over the years we have found that useful comparisons between women and men in sex and love attitudes must attend to both mean differences and patterns of correlations. Using a sample of nearly 1,100 respondents (S. Hendrick & Hendrick, 1995), we found gender differences consistent with previous work. Men are more endorsing of casual and self-focused sex and game-playing love, whereas women are more endorsing of friendship, practical, and possessive love. Yet when correlation patterns for romantic love and sex attitudes and several other relationship quality and relationship history variables are examined, out of 60 pairs of correlations (i.e., correlations for men vs. correlations for women), only 11 of these pairs are significantly different. "Only 5 of the 11 pairs involved correlations greater than .30 for at least one gender; of these, 4 of the 5 pairs involved sexual permissiveness" (p. 61). We conclude that although scholars cannot ignore gender differences, it is also important not to overemphasize them. "What *can* [italics in original] be concluded based on the current research is that any discussion of gender and sexuality in intimate relationships must embrace both gender differences and gender similarities" (S. Hendrick & Hendrick, p. 65).

Considerable research had shown that love attitudes and sexual attitudes intersect psychometrically. In addition, both attitude constellations are related to a variety of dispositional (e.g., sensation seeking) and behavioral (e.g., contraception) variables as well as to relationship status (in love versus not in love) and gender. Yet ultimately we wanted to investigate further some of the underlying linkages between romantic love and sex.

Linking Sex With Romantic Love

Although scholars may have differing ideas about whether or how sex and love may be linked, we decided to approach the issue from a folk psychology perspective (see also Weis, Slosnerick, Cate, & Sollie, 1986, for a linkage of love, sex, and marriage). We simply asked research participants (advanced undergraduates, some of whom were nontraditional students) to "Please tell us how love and sex (meaning any type of physical affection) are related in your relationship" (S. Hendrick & Hendrick, 2002). Participants' free-form responses varied from a few sentences to a couple of pages, with two excerpts provided below.

> We are extremely sexually active. It is one way we both enjoy showing each other how much we love each other. We both often tell each other sex is not everything, but that we both do enjoy it and it is definitely a good part of our relationship. We have many other ways of showing our love for each other also.

> Both my partner and I believe that physical affection makes our relationship stronger. Whether it is hugging, kissing, holding hands, making love, or just lying next to each other. I believe sex is not necessary to have love but it can make love stronger in a relationship. In my relationship, our love is made stronger with sex. It brings us closer.

These responses were analyzed qualitatively, with the result that 27 "themes" were extracted and put into rating item format. These items, along with several relationship measures, were employed in three studies. After extensive analyses, a 17-item, four-factor scale was retained. Although this measure clearly did not contain all the themes offered by the research participants, it nevertheless provided a window into how people view the linkages between sex and love. The first subscale, Love is Most Important, reflects the idea that indeed, the emotion of love is more important than anything else. This is consistent with the Arons' (1991) observations of our culture, noted earlier. The second subscale, Sex Demonstrates Love, seems to argue that although sex is very important in a romantic relationship, it is a means of showing the deeper sentiment of love. (This seems very consistent with the sexual standard of "relational sexuality," discussed earlier.) The third subscale, Love Comes Before Sex, is centered on chronology, positing that love comes before and "drives" sex, not the reverse. Finally, subscale four, Sex is Declining, focuses on diminishing sex in a relationship and was an extremely strong negative predictor of relationship satisfaction.

Overall, we were pleased with the results of that research endeavor. We found it very significant that when asked about how love and sex might be linked, none of the research participants replied "they're not." People do appear to link sexuality and romantic love in their relationships, even as scholars may debate the issue.

CONCLUSIONS

Philosophers, evolutionary theorists, sociologists, psychologists, and other relationship scholars all have varying perspectives on sex and love and their meaning within the human condition. Consistent with the Arons' (1991) model of a continuum, discussed at length earlier in this chapter, some believe that sex is more important than love, others that love is more important than sex, and still others that the two are equally important but separate or equally important and overlapping.

In related research, many scientists have rediscovered the view of mind and body as interwoven entities in the service of the positive organismic growth of each person. The Positive Psychology perspective (e.g., Snyder & Lopez, 2002) promotes actively the notion of maximally positive human functioning, and one essential ingredient of such functioning is positive intimate relationships.

A romantic relationship is one significant form of an intimate relationship, and it is in a romantic relationship that the nexus of sex and love is found. As we have commented previously, we view sex and love not as subsumable one by another but rather as equally important in partnered intimate relationships. Consistent with position C on the Arons' (1991) continuum, sex and love are viewed as interrelated and exhibiting mutual causality. It is essential to define sex broadly, because sexual intimacy includes a variety of forms of physical affection rather than relying solely on sexual intercourse. Part of the "need to belong" (Baumeister & Leary, 1995) is a need for contact, for touching, and sexual touching in the context of an intimate relationship is a very meaningful form of touch. Perhaps that is why sex and love are important across cultures, across age groups, and across levels of physical ability/disability.

Finally, the intersection of sex and love is a very special "place." Although humans may be at our most admirable when we are the most spiritual, we in fact may be most "real" at this interface between love and sex. For it is here that our essentially biological nature meets our personhood, and it thus may be here where we are most fully human.

REFERENCES

Adler, N. L., & Hendrick, S. S. (1991). Relationships between contraceptive behavior and love attitudes, sex attitudes, and self-esteem. *Journal of Counseling and Development, 70*, 302–308.

Adler, N. L., Hendrick, S. S., & Hendrick, C. (1986). Male sexual preference and attitudes toward love and sexuality. *Journal of Sex Education & Therapy, 12*(2), 27–30.

Ainsworth, M. D. S., Blehar, M. E., Waters, E., & Wall, S. (1978). *Patterns of attachment: A psychological study of the strange situation.* Hillsdale, NJ: Lawrence Erlbaum Associates.

Aron, A., & Aron, E. N. (1986). *Love and the expansion of self: Understanding attraction and satisfaction.* Washington, DC: Hemisphere.

Aron, A., & Aron, E. N. (1991). Love and sexuality. In K. McKinney & S. Sprecher (Eds.), *Sexuality in close relationships* (pp. 25–48). Hillsdale, NJ: Lawrence Erlbaum Associates.

Bailey, W. E., Hendrick, C., & Hendrick, S. S. (1987). Relation of sex and gender role to love, sexual attitudes, and self-esteem. *Sex Roles, 16*, 637–648.

Bartholomew, K., & Horowitz, L. M. (1991). Attachment styles among young adults: A test of a four-category model. *Journal of Personality and Social Psychology, 61,* 226–244.

Baumeister, R. F., & Leary, M. R. (1995). The need to belong: Desire for interpersonal attachments as a fundamental human motivation. *Psychological Bulletin, 117,* 497–529.

Belsky, J. (1999). Modern evolutionary theory and patterns of attachment. In J. Cassidy & P. R. Shaver (Eds.), *Handbook of attachment: Theory, research, and clinical applications* (pp. 141–161). New York: Guilford.

Bem, S. L. (1974). The measurement of psychological androgyny. *Journal of Consulting and Clinical Psychology, 42,* 155–162.

Berman, W. H., & Sperling, M. B. (1994). The structure and function of adult attachment. In M. B. Sperling & W. H. Berman (Eds.), *Attachment in adults: Clinical and developmental perspectives* (pp. 3–28). New York: Guilford.

Berscheid, E. (1988). Some comments on love's anatomy: Or whatever happened to old-fashioned lust? In R. J. Sternberg & M. L. Barnes (Eds.), *The psychology of love* (pp. 359–374). New Haven, CT: Yale University Press.

Bowlby, J. (1969). *Attachment and loss: Vol. 1. Attachment.* New York: Basic Books.

Brennan, K. A., Clark, C. L., & Shaver, P. R. (1998). Self-report measurement of adult attachment: An integrative overview. In J. A. Simpson & W. S. Rholes (Eds.), *Attachment theory and close relationships* (pp. 46–76). New York: Guilford.

Brown, R. (1987). *Analyzing love.* New York: Cambridge University Press.

Buck, R., & Ginsburg, B. (1991). Spontaneous communication and altruism: The communicative gene hypothesis. In M. S. Clark (Ed.), *Prosocial behavior* (pp. 149–175). Newbury Park, CA: Sage.

Buss, D. M. (1988). Love acts: The evolutionary biology of love. In R. J. Sternberg & M. L. Barnes (Eds.), *The psychology of love* (pp. 100–117). New Haven, CT: Yale University Press.

Buss, D. M. (1994). *The evolution of desire.* New York: Basic Books.

Buss, D. M. (1995). Evolutionary psychology: A new paradigm for psychological science. *Psychological Inquiry, 6,* 1–30.

Buss, D. M. (1996). The evolutionary psychology of human social strategies. In E. T. Higgins & A. W. Kruglanski (Eds.), *Social psychology: Handbook of basic principles* (pp. 3–38). New York: Guilford.

Buss, D. M. (1999). *Evolutionary psychology: The new science of the mind.* Boston: Allyn & Bacon.

Buss, D. M., & Barnes, M. (1986). Preferences in human mate selection. *Journal of Personality and Social Psychology, 50,* 559–570.

Buss, D. M., & Kenrick, D. T. (1998). Evolutionary social psychology. In D. T. Gilbert, S. T. Fiske, & G. Lindzey (Eds.), *The handbook of social psychology: Vol. 2.* (4th ed., pp. 982–1026). Boston: McGraw-Hill.

Byrne, D. (1971). *The attraction paradigm.* New York: Academic Press.

Clark, M. S., & Mills, J. (1993). The difference between communal and exchange relationships: What it is and is not. *Personality and Social Psychology Bulletin, 19,* 684–691.

Contreras, R., Hendrick, S. S., & Hendrick, C. (1996). Perspectives on marital love and satisfaction in Mexican American and Anglo couples. *Journal of Counseling and Development, 74,* 408–415.

Darwin, C. (1873). *The expression of emotions in man and animals.* New York: Appleton.

Dawkins, R. (1989). *The selfish gene* (New ed.). New York: Oxford University Press.

DeLamater, J. (1989). The social control of human sexuality. In K. McKinney & S. Sprecher (Eds.), *Human sexuality: The societal and interpersonal context* (pp. 30–62). Norwood, NJ: Ablex.

de Waal, F. B. M. (2002). Evolutionary psychology: The wheat and the chaff. *Current Directions in Psychological Science, 11,* 187–191.

Eagly, A. H., & Wood, W. (1999). The origins of sex differences in human behavior. *American Psychologist, 54,* 408–423.

Feeney, J. A. (1999). Adult romantic attachment and couple relationships. In J. Cassidy & P. R. Shaver (Eds.), *Handbook of attachment: Theory, research, and clinical practice* (pp. 355–377). New York: Guilford.

Feeney, J. A., Noller, P., & Roberts, N. (2000). Attachment and close relationships. In C. Hendrick & S. S. Hendrick (Eds.), *Close relationships: A sourcebook.* Thousand Oaks, CA: Sage.

Fisher, H. E. (1992). *Anatomy of love: The natural history of monogamy, adultery, and divorce.* New York: Norton.

Fisher, H. E. (1998). Lust, attraction, and attachment in mammalian reproduction. *Human Nature, 9,* 23–52.

Fisher, H. E. (2000). Lust, attraction, attachment: Biology and evolution of three primary emotion systems for mating, reproduction, and parenting. *Journal of Sex Education and Therapy, 25,* 96–104.

Fraley, R. C., & Waller, N. G. (1998). Adult attachment patterns: A test of the typological model. In J. A. Simpson & W. S. Rholes (Eds.), *Attachment theory and close relationships* (pp. 77–114). New York: Guilford.

Ghiselin, M. T. (1974). *The economy of nature and the evolution of sex.* Berkeley, CA: University of California Press.

Ghiselin, M. T. (1988). The evolution of sex: A history of competing points of view. In R. E. Michod & B. R. Levin (Eds.), *The evolution of sex: An examination of current ideas* (pp. 7–23). Sunderland, MA: Sinauer Associates.

Goldberg, S., Grusec, J. E., & Jenkins, J. M. (1999). Confidence in protection: Arguments for a narrow definition of attachment. *Journal of Family Psychology, 13,* 475–483.

Hamilton, W. D. (1964). The genetical evolution of social behavior. *Journal of Theoretical Biology, 7,* 1–52.

Harlow, H. F. (1974). *Learning to love.* New York: Jason Aronson.

Harvey, J. H., & Weber, A. L. (2002). *Odyssey of the heart: Close relationships in the 21st century* (2nd ed.). Mahwah, NJ: Lawrence Erlbaum Associates.

Hatfield, E. (1988). Passionate and companionate love. In R. J. Sternberg & M. L. Barnes (Eds.), *The psychology of love* (pp. 191–217). New Haven, CT: Yale University Press.

Hatfield, E., & Rapson, R. L. (1987). Passionate love: New directions in research. In W. H. Jones & D. Perlman (Eds.), *Advances in personal relationships: Vol. 1* (pp. 109–139). Greenwich, CT: JAI Press.

Hatfield, E., & Rapson, R. L. (1996). *Love and sex: Cross-cultural perspectives.* Boston: Allyn & Bacon.

Hatfield, E., & Sprecher, S. (1986). Measuring passionate love in intimate relationships. *Journal of Adolescence, 9*, 383–410.

Hazan, C., & Shaver, P. R. (1987). Romantic love conceptualized as an attachment process. *Journal of Personality and Social Psychology, 52*, 511–524.

Hazan, C., & Zeifman, D. (1999). Pair bonds as attachments: Evaluating the evidence. In J. Cassidy & P. R. Shaver (Eds.), *Handbook of attachment: Theory, research, and clinical applications* (pp. 336–354). New York: Guilford.

Hendrick, C. (2002). A new age of prevention? *Journal of Social and Personal Relationships, 19*, 621–627.

Hendrick, C., & Hendrick, S. S. (1986). A theory and method of love. *Journal of Personality and Social Psychology, 50*, 392–402.

Hendrick, C., & Hendrick, S. S. (1988). Lovers wear rose colored glasses. *Journal of Social and Personal Relationships, 5*, 161–183.

Hendrick, C., & Hendrick, S. S. (1990). A relationship specific version of the Love Attitudes Scale. *Journal of Social Behavior and Personality, 5*, 239–254.

Hendrick, C. & Hendrick, S. S. (2003). Romantic love: Measuring Cupid's arrow. In S. J. Lopez & C. R. Snyder (Eds.), *Positive psychological assessment: A handbook of models and measures* (pp. 235–249). Washington, DC: American Psychological Association.

Hendrick, C., Hendrick, S. S., & Dicke, A. (1998). The Love Attitudes Scale: Short Form. *Journal of Social and Personal Relationships, 15*, 147–159.

Hendrick, C., Hendrick, S. S., Foote, F. H., & Slapion-Foote, M. J. (1984). Do men and women love differently? *Journal of Social and Personal Relationships, 1*, 177–195.

Hendrick, S. S. (2002, July). Intricate linkages between sex and love. In J. H. Harvey (Chair), *New directions in understanding sexuality in close relationships.* Paper presented at the International Conference on Personal Relationships, Halifax, Nova Scotia.

Hendrick, S. S., & Hendrick, C. (1987a). Love and sex attitudes: A close relationship. In W. H. Jones & D. Perlman (Eds.), *Advances in personal relationships: Vol. 1* (pp. 141–169). Greenwich, CT: JAI Press.

Hendrick, S. S., & Hendrick, C. (1987b). Love and sexual attitudes, self-disclosure, and sensation seeking. *Journal of Social and Personal Relationships, 4*, 281–297.

Hendrick, S. S., & Hendrick, C. (1987c). Multidimensionality of sexual attitudes. *The Journal of Sex Research, 23*, 502–526.

Hendrick, S. S., & Hendrick, C. (1992a). *Liking, loving & relating* (2nd ed.). Pacific Grove, CA: Brooks/Cole.

Hendrick, S. S., & Hendrick, C. (1992b). *Romantic love.* Newbury Park, CA: Sage.

Hendrick, S. S., & Hendrick, C. (1995). Gender differences and similarities in sex and love. *Personal Relationships, 2*, 55–65.

Hendrick, S. S., & Hendrick, C. (1997, June). *Love and sex in romantic relationships.* Invited address to the 1997 conference of the International Network on Personal Relationships, Miami University, Oxford, OH.

Hendrick, S. S., & Hendrick, C. (2002). Linking romantic love with sex: Development of the Perceptions of Love and Sex Scale. *Journal of Social and Personal Relationships, 19*, 361–378.

Hendrick, S. S., Hendrick, C., Slapion-Foote, M. J., & Foote, F. H. (1985). Gender differences in sexual attitudes. *Journal of Personality and Social Psychology, 48*, 1630–1642.

Janicki, M. G., & Krebs, D. L. (1998). Evolutionary approaches to culture. In C. Crawford & D. L. Krebs (Eds.), *Handbook of evolutionary psychology: Ideas, issues, and applications* (pp. 163–207). Mahwah, NJ: Lawrence Erlbaum Associates.

Jankowiak, W. (1995a). Introduction. In W. Jankowiak (Ed.). *Romantic passion: A universal experience?* (pp. 1–19). New York: Columbia University Press.

Jankowiak, W. (Ed.). (1995b). *Romantic passion: A universal experience?* New York: Columbia University Press.

Jankowiak, W. R., & Fischer, E. F. (1992). A cross-cultural perspective on romantic love. *Ethnology, 31*, 149–155.

Kenrick, D. T. (1987). Gender, genes, and the social environment: A biosocial interactionist perspective. In P. Shaver & C. Hendrick (Eds.), *Sex and gender* (pp. 14–43). Newbury Park, CA: Sage.

Kenrick, D. T., & Trost, M. R. (1989). A reproductive exchange model of heterosexual relationships: Putting proximate economics in ultimate perspective. In C. Hendrick (Ed.), *Close relationships* (pp. 92–118). Newbury Park, CA: Sage.

Kirkpatrick, L. A. (1998). Evolution, pair-bonding, and reproductive strategies: A reconceptualization of adult attachment. In J. A. Simpson & W. S. Rholes (Eds.), *Attachment theory and close relationships* (pp. 353–393). New York: Guilford.

Lasswell, T. E., & Lasswell, M. E. (1976). I love you but I'm not in love with you. *Journal of Marriage and Family Counseling, 38*, 211–224.

Laumann, E. O., Gagnon, J. H., Michael, R. T., & Michaels, S. (1994). *The social organization of sexuality: Sexual practices in the United States*. Chicago: University of Chicago Press.

Lee, J. A. (1973). *The colors of love: An exploration of the ways of loving*. Don Mills, Ontario: New Press.

Lewis, W. M., Jr. (1987). The cost of sex. In S. C. Stearns (Ed.), *The evolution of sex and its consequences* (pp. 33–57). Boston: Birkhauser Verlag.

Liebowitz, M. R. (1983). *The chemistry of love*. Boston: Little, Brown.

Lindholm, C. (1995). Love as an experience of transcendence. In W. Jankowiak (Ed.), *Romantic passion: A universal experience?* (pp. 57–71). New York: Columbia University Press.

Mallon, R., & Stich, S. P. (2000). The odd couple: The compatibility of social construction and evolutionary psychology. *Philosophy of Science, 67*, 133–154.

Maynard Smith, J. (1978). *The evolution of sex*. New York: Cambridge University Press.

Meehl, P. E. (1995). Bootstrap taxometrics: Solving the classification problem in psychopathology. *American Psychologist, 50*, 266–275.

Mellen, S. L. W. (1981). *The evolution of love*. San Francisco: Freeman.

Michael, R. T., Gagnon, J. H., Laumann, E. O., & Kolata, G. (2000). Sex and society. In A. J. Cherlin (Ed.), *Public and private families: A reader* (2nd ed., pp. 159–169). Blacklick, OH: McGraw-Hill.

Raciti, M., & Hendrick, S. S. (1992). Relationships between eating disorder characteristics and love and sex attitudes. *Sex Roles, 27*, 553–564.

Regan, P. C. (1998). Romantic love and sexual desire. In V. C. de Munck (Ed.), *Romantic love and sexual behavior: Perspectives from the social sciences* (pp. 91–112). Westport, CT: Praeger.

Regan, P. C., & Berscheid, E. (1999). *Lust: What we know about human sexual desire*. Thousand Oaks, CA: Sage.

Reiss, I. L. (1960). *Premarital sexual standards in America*. New York: Free Press.

Reiss, I. L. (1967). *The social context of premarital sexual permissiveness*. New York: Holt, Rinehart & Winston.

Scharfe, E., & Bartholomew, K. (1994). Reliability and stability of adult attachment patterns. *Personal Relationships, 1*, 23–43.

Shaver, P. R., & Hazan, C. (1988). A biased overview of the study of love. *Journal of Social and Personal Relationships, 5*, 473–501.

Shaver, P., Hazan, C., & Bradshaw, D. (1988). Love as attachment: The integration of three behavioral systems. In R. J. Sternberg & M. L. Barnes (Eds.), *The psychology of love* (pp. 68–99). New Haven, CT: Yale University Press.

Shaver, P. R., Morgan, H. J., & Wu, S. (1996). Is love a "basic" emotion? *Personal Relationships, 3*, 81–96.

Simpson, J. A. (1999). Attachment theory in modern evolutionary perspective. In J. Cassidy & P. R. Shaver (Eds.), *Handbook of attachment: Theory, research, and clinical applications* (pp. 115–140). New York: Guilford.

Simpson, J. A., Campbell, B., & Berscheid, E. (1986). The association between romantic love and marriage: Kephart (1967) twice revisited. *Personality and Social Psychology Bulletin, 12*, 363–372.

Snyder, C. R., & Lopez, S. J. (Eds.) (2002). *The handbook of positive psychology*. Oxford, England: Oxford University Press.

Solomon, R. C. (1981). *Love: Emotion, myth and metaphor*. New York: Anchor Press.

Solomon, R. C. (1988). *About love: Reinventing romance for our times*. New York: Simon & Schuster.

Sprecher, S., & McKinney, K. (1993). *Sexuality*. Newbury Park, CA: Sage.

Sprecher, S., & Regan, P. C. (1998). Passionate and companionate love in courting and young married couples. *Sociological Inquiry, 68*, 163–185.

Stearns, S. C. (1987). Why sex evolved and the differences it makes. In S. C. Stearns (Ed.), *The evolution of sex and its consequences* (pp. 15–31). Boston: Birkhauser Verlag.

Sternberg, R. J. (1986). A triangular theory of love. *Psychological Review, 93*, 119–135.

Sternberg, R. J. (1987). Liking versus loving: A comparative evaluation of theories. *Psychological Bulletin, 102*, 331–345.

Suomi, S. J. (1999). Attachment in rhesus monkeys. In J. Cassidy & P. R. Shaver (Eds.), *Handbook of attachment: Theory, research, and clinical applications* (pp. 181–197). New York: Guilford.

Symons, D. (1979). *Evolution of human sexuality*. New York: Oxford.

Taylor, S. E. (2002). *The tending instinct*. New York: Henry Holt.

Tennov, D. (1979). *Love and limerence: The experience of being in love*. New York: Stein & Day.

Trivers, R. L. (1972). Parental investment and sexual selection. In B. Campbell (Ed.), *Sexual selection and the descent of man, 1871–1971* (pp. 136–179). Chicago: Aldine.

Vannoy, R. (1980). *Sex without love: A philosophical exploration*. Buffalo, NY: Prometheus Books.

Walster, E., & Walster, G. W. (1978). *A new look at love*. Reading, MA: Addison-Wesley.

Weis, D. L., Slosnerick, M., Cate, R., & Sollie, D. L. (1986). A survey instrument for assessing the cognitive association of sex, love, and marriage. *The Journal of Sex Research, 22*, 206–220.

Williams, G. C. (1975). *Sex and evolution*. Princeton, NJ: Princeton University Press.

Wilson, J. (1980). *Love, sex, and feminism: A philosophical essay*. New York: Praeger.

Zajonc, R. B. (1968). Attitudinal effects of mere exposure. *Journal of Personality and Social Psychology Monographs, 9* (2, Pt. 2).

8

Attachment and Sexuality in Close Relationships

Judith A. Feeney
Patricia Noller
University of Queensland

In recent decades, researchers studying human sexuality have paid increasing attention to its relational context. Attachment theory, which addresses the processes by which bonds of affection are developed and maintained, has particular relevance to this topic. In this chapter, we describe studies that link individual differences in adults' "felt security" to diverse aspects of sexuality, including sexual communication, sexual self-efficacy, attitudes to casual sex, beliefs about condoms, and safer sex practices. These studies have employed a range of samples, research designs, and data collection methods and suggest that the link between attachment and sexuality is relatively robust. Further, the findings support the proposition that attachment-related differences in sexuality reflect the interaction goals of the different attachment styles, particularly with regard to intimacy and autonomy. We argue that the attachment perspective extends recent efforts to provide theory-based explanations of sexuality and offers the advantage of integrating early and later relationship experiences.

Early studies of human sexuality focused primarily on documenting the frequencies of various kinds of sexual behaviors (e.g., Kinsey, Pomeroy, & Martin, 1948). In contrast, the last 2 decades have seen a growing interest in the *relational* context of sexuality, linking sexual expression to such relationship phenomena as attraction, love, intimacy, and commitment. Although some of this work has been atheoretical, recent studies and reviews have advocated the use of a number of theoretical perspectives, including social exchange theory, social learning theory, systems theory, and evolutionary theories (see Christopher & Sprecher, 2000; DeLamater & Hyde, chapter 1, this volume). In this chapter, we argue that attachment theory has particular relevance to the study of sexuality: This theory addresses the normative processes involved in developing and maintaining bonds of affection, together with the origins and consequences of individual differences in felt security (attachment style). As Feeney and Raphael (1992) noted, differences in attachment style are likely to have far-reaching implications for the meaning that partners place on their sexual relationship and for sexual attitudes and behaviors.

ATTACHMENT AND SEXUALITY: THEORETICAL CONSIDERATIONS

Since the early 1970s, attachment principles have provided a major theoretical perspective on children's social and emotional development (e.g., Ainsworth, Blehar, Waters, & Wall, 1978; Bowlby, 1979). More recently, Hazan and Shaver (1987) proposed that romantic love could be understood as an attachment process. According to this perspective, adults' romantic relationships (particularly those between committed partners) meet basic needs for comfort, closeness, and security. Further, differences in adult attachment security, based in part on early attachment experiences, are reflected in emotions, cognitions, and behaviors that influence relationship outcomes. Hazan and Shaver's (1987) empirical studies provide preliminary support for these propositions: A simple self-report measure in which respondents categorized themselves as secure, avoidant, or anxious–ambivalent was related in predictable ways to reports of early attachment relationships, working models of attachment, and romantic love experiences.

Shortly after, Shaver, Hazan and Bradshaw (1988) presented a conceptual paper outlining the major differences between attachments in childhood and in adulthood; most notably, adult attachments involve reciprocal caregiving, together with sexual attraction and mating. Based on this analysis and on Bowlby's (1969) discussion of behavioral systems, the authors proposed that romantic love involves the integration of three behavioral systems: attachment, caregiving, and sexual mating. They further proposed that the link between sexual mating and attachment can be explained in evolutionary terms: Attachment between adult lovers is not necessary for reproduction itself to occur, but is likely to offer a survival advantage by promoting parental health, stability, and investment in offspring.

Although all three systems of behavior are innate and have important biological functions, the attachment system is seen as preeminent. Attachment appears very early in the course of individual development; moreover, attachment experiences lead to the formation of mental models of self and others, which influence later relationships by shaping responses to interaction partners (Shaver et al., 1988). Thus, individual differences in attachment orientation should be reliably related to sexual attitudes and behaviors, as well as to patterns of caregiving. More specifically, childhood experiences of warm and responsive caregiving should promote secure attachment, together with the capacity to give and receive care and to strive for mutual intimacy and sexual pleasure. Conversely, all three behavioral systems are vulnerable to distortions caused by negative socialization experiences (Shaver & Hazan, 1988; Shaver et al., 1988).

These arguments fit with the work of Belsky and colleagues (Belsky, Steinberg, & Draper, 1991) on the pathways involved in interpersonal development. Belsky et al. described two divergent paths, related to early family experiences. One path involves a relatively stress-free child-rearing environment, leading to secure attachment to parents and the later formation of stable pair bonds; the other path involves a stressful child-rearing environment, insecure attachment to parents, precocious sexuality in adolescence, and the formation of unstable pair bonds. Belsky et al. reviewed studies supporting the various associations proposed in this model. However, as we will see shortly, a simple dichotomy of secure and insecure attachment obscures important differences between different forms of insecurity and their links with sexuality.

In this regard, it is important to note the rapid advances that have been made in the conceptualization and measurement of individual differences in adult attachment orientation. As mentioned earlier, Hazan and Shaver (1987) assessed attachment style using a simple measure that required participants to endorse either a secure, avoidant, or anxious–ambivalent (preoccupied) prototype. A few years later, Bartholomew (1990;

Bartholomew & Horowitz, 1991) presented theoretical and empirical evidence of four adult attachment styles, defined by positive and negative working models of self and others. This typology differs from that of Hazan and Shaver (1987) in describing two forms of avoidance: Dismissing avoidants (positive model of self, negative model of other), emphasize achievement and self-reliance at the expense of intimacy; whereas fearful avoidants (negative model of self, negative model of other) desire intimacy but feel very vulnerable to loss and rejection.

Although both these typologies have reasonable predictive power, there is growing consensus that individual differences in attachment are best conceptualized in terms of continuous dimensions, rather than discrete types (Fraley & Waller, 1998). Empirical studies (e.g., Brennan, Clark, & Shaver, 1998; Feeney, 1994) point to two major dimensions underlying adult attachment style: anxiety (or anxiety over relationships) and avoidance (or discomfort with closeness). These dimensions are clearly related to the major styles: Secure and preoccupied groups (which have positive models of others) report less avoidance than fearful and dismissing groups, and secure and dismissing groups (which have positive models of self) report less anxiety than preoccupied and fearful groups. Despite reliable links between different measures of adult attachment, the diversity of measures has hampered integration of findings linking attachment with sexuality and other aspects of relationship functioning.

Before discussing studies of attachment and sexuality, we wish to note that the aim of attachment research is not simply to document attachment-related differences in various aspects of sexuality. Rather, attachment theorists argue that these differences should be related in meaningful ways to individuals' *interaction goals* (Feeney & Noller, 1996). This emphasis is evident in the broader literature linking romantic attachment style with relational attitudes and behavior (for a review of this literature, see Feeney, 1999). In terms of the three-group typology, for example, secure individuals adopt strategies that support their goals of establishing intimacy, while seeking a balance between closeness and autonomy. Specifically, these individuals hold relatively positive expectations of their partners, while accepting their faults and limitations; they are comfortable with both support-seeking and support-providing and engage in mutual negotiation in response to couple conflict. In contrast, avoidant individuals seek to limit intimacy, pursue impersonal achievements, and satisfy their needs for autonomy and independence. These goals are achieved by limiting self-disclosure and emotional expression, especially in situations involving stress and conflict. Finally, anxious–ambivalent individuals seek to establish extreme levels of intimacy, and to gain approval and validation from others. Consistent with these goals, they experience intense attractions and "love at first sight," become hypervigilant to signs of rejection, and are prone to jealousy and coercive responses to conflict.

EMPIRICAL STUDIES OF ROMANTIC ATTACHMENT AND SEXUALITY

The following discussion of studies of romantic attachment and sexuality focuses on research conducted in our own laboratory. Throughout, however, we integrate our findings with those of other researchers. We present four studies from our laboratory in the order in which they were conducted. In this way, we trace the development of research questions covering a range of issues, samples, measures, and methods.

Attachment, Sexual Permissiveness, and Sexual Restraint

Our first study on this topic (Feeney, Noller, & Patty, 1993) was based on a sample of 193 young adults (ages 17 to 20 years), and combined questionnaire and diary methods. The aims of the study were to clarify attachment-related differences in sexual attitudes and in patterns of interaction with the opposite sex and to see whether these differences were influenced by gender roles.

Questionnaire-Based Findings.   Questionnaire measures in this study included the three-group measure of attachment style, items tapping attitudes to casual sex, and aspects of relationship history. The most consistent finding was the link between avoidant attachment and a more permissive approach to sexuality: Avoidant individuals were more accepting of casual sex and sex without love than were secure and anxious–ambivalent individuals, and were more accepting of sex without commitment than were secure individuals. However, among those in steady dating relationships, secure respondents were *more* likely than insecure respondents to report having been sexually active with the current partner.

As suggested earlier, the link between avoidance and a more permissive approach to sex can be understood in terms of avoidant individuals' interaction goals: namely, to maintain distance and a sense of independence and autonomy. In fact, this is one of the most robust findings concerning attachment-related differences in sexuality. Simpson and Gangestad (1991) proposed that early attachment experiences (involving distant or rejecting caregivers) may push avoidant individuals to adopt an "unrestricted" sexual orientation; that is, to feel more comfortable in short-term sexual relationships that involve limited closeness and commitment (see also Simpson, Wilson, & Winterheld, chapter 4, this volume). Consistent with this argument, Brennan and Shaver (1995) and Gentzler and Kerns (2001) found that avoidant attachment is related to measures of unrestricted sexuality, both attitudinal (acceptance of sex without love or commitment) and behavioral (e.g., number of sexual partners). Similar results emerged from Stephan and Bachman's (1999) study, based on Hatfield and Rapson's (1996) model of love types: secure, clingy (cf. preoccupied), skittish (uncomfortable with closeness, comfortable with independence), fickle (uncomfortable with closeness *and* independence), casual (interested only in problem-free relationships), and uninterested (detached from all kinds of relationships). Note that the last four groups all tend to avoid intimacy, although they do not correspond neatly to previous attachment types. Using this typology, Stephan and Bachman (1999) found consistent differences between secure individuals and those from the fickle and casual groups: The latter groups were less sexually restrictive, more interested in emotionless sex and more likely to report engaging in relationship-destructive behaviors such as infidelity and deception.

Diary-Based Findings.   Although questionnaires provide useful information about sexual attitudes and behaviors, structured diary records enable participants to document sexual (and other social) interactions soon after they occur. Thus, they are likely to give a more complete and accurate picture of the events in question. In the study by Feeney et al. (1993), diary records were completed by a subset of participants ($N = 85$), sampled to ensure adequate coverage of the three attachment styles. Respondents were asked to record all interactions with members of the opposite sex that lasted 10 minutes or longer, over a 6-week period. They were also asked to classify each interaction according to the type of partner (friend, acquaintance, stranger) and the highest level of intimacy involved (from chatting and handholding, through to petting and sexual intercourse).

Overall, avoidant females and anxious–ambivalent males were the *least* likely to report engaging in intercourse during the 6-week period, even when relationship status was controlled. However, interactions involving sexual intercourse were reported by a small number of individuals who were *not* in steady relationships, and who did not regard the sexual partner as a "friend"; these individuals were mainly avoidant in attachment style. In addition, a minority of insecure respondents reported that a relatively high proportion of their interactions with the opposite sex involved sexual intercourse, suggesting an overemphasis on sexual activity as a form of relating.

These data have two major implications, both attesting to the complex link between attachment and sexuality. First, the diary data suggest that gender and attachment style may *jointly* influence sexual behavior. This result fits with the findings of some other researchers. For example, Gangestad and Thornhill (1997) found that, for women only, anxious–ambivalent attachment was associated with a greater number of sexual partners outside of the primary relationship. Gender differences also emerged in Hazan, Zeifman and Middleton's (1994) comprehensive study of the links between attachment style and the frequency and enjoyment of various sexual behaviors. In this study, secure men and women reported little involvement in one-night stands and extra-relationship sex, but there were marked gender differences in the correlates of insecure attachment, especially anxious–ambivalence. Anxious–ambivalent females were likely to have engaged in voyeurism, exhibitionism, and bondage, whereas anxious–ambivalent males were much more sexually reticent. There has been little attempt to explain these findings. Shaver (1994) suggested possible effects of *partners'* attachment style, but issues concerning attachment-related goals and gender-role expectations may also be relevant. For example, the sexual reticence of anxious–ambivalent males may reflect a tension between their strong needs for intimacy, affection, and reassurance, and societal pressures to be independent and achievement-oriented. Given that anxious–ambivalent individuals crave approval but suffer from self-doubts (Feeney & Noller, 1996), performance anxiety may also be an issue for anxious–ambivalent males.

The second implication of our results concerns the importance of studying a range of dependent variables. Recall that avoidant individuals showed relatively accepting attitudes toward casual sex, but that avoidant females reported low levels of actual sexual activity. Thus, it is important to study both sexual attitudes and sexual behaviors. A full understanding of the link between attachment and sexual expression also requires assessment of a range of behaviors. For example, our data indicate that young adults who are insecure report less intimate sexual involvement with steady partners, but sometimes adopt an indiscriminate approach to sex (engaging in sex with acquaintances or strangers, or allowing social encounters to be dominated by sexual activity).

Attachment and Relationship Functioning in Gay Males and Lesbians

Our second study (Ridge & Feeney, 1998) focused on attachment and sexuality in samples of gay males ($N = 77$) and lesbians ($N = 100$), but also included a comparison sample of heterosexuals ($N = 150$). In this study, we assessed attachment in terms of the four-group typology (secure, preoccupied, dismissing and fearful; see Bartholomew, 1990, Bartholomew & Horowitz, 1991); this typology, which distinguishes between dismissing and fearful avoidance, has gained increasing acceptance over the last decade. The aim of this study was to explore similarities and differences in attachment processes within homosexual and heterosexual samples, and to assess the predictive validity of attachment style for the relationship functioning of gay males and lesbians.

All samples in the study consisted primarily of university students, with the focal samples recruited through gay and lesbian organizations at the various institutions. The study addressed four issues concerning attachment and sexuality among gay males and lesbians: the relative frequencies of the different attachment styles; the links among attachment style, attachment history and working models of attachment; the associations between attachment style and aspects of intimate relating (love experiences and sexual attitudes); and the implications of attachment style for the experience of "coming out."

Relative Frequencies of Attachment Styles.   First, with regard to the relative frequencies of attachment styles, it is important to note that some clinicians (e.g., Colgan, 1987) have discussed the prevalence of problems of "over-attachment" and "over-separation" in gay males. These patterns, which are thought to be linked to the experience of stigmatization, appear similar to preoccupied and avoidant attachment, respectively. However, using both categorical and continuous measures to assess the four attachment styles, we found that the distributions of responses were similar among the homosexual and heterosexual groups.

This finding suggests that insecurity is no more prevalent in gay populations, although it is possible that individuals who are recruited through gay and lesbian organizations are less "closeted" and more secure in their attitudes to close relationships than is the larger population. Data from Kurdek's (1997) study of neuroticism, attachment and relationship commitment suggest a similar conclusion. This study included samples of gay, lesbian, and heterosexual (married) couples. Although Kurdek did not specifically test for group differences in the attachment measures (positivity of models of self and other), mean scores on these variables were no lower for gay males and lesbians than for heterosexual spouses.

Attachment Style, Attachment History and Working Models of Attachment.   As expected, Ridge and Feeney (1998) found that gay individuals' attachment style showed similar links with items tapping working models of attachment as reported in heterosexual samples. For example, secure and dismissing respondents expressed less dependence, mistrust, and self-doubt than did preoccupied and fearful respondents. Attachment style was unrelated, however, to reports of attachment history (early relationships with parents). This result contrasts with a substantial body of findings from heterosexual samples, linking security to warm and responsive parenting (Rothbard & Shaver, 1994). Thus, it seems that, for gay individuals, attachment security may be influenced more strongly by peer relationships than by early parenting.

This suggestion is consistent with other data showing the particular importance of the peer community and peer relations (both friendship and intimate) to gay individuals (e.g., Kurdek, 1988). Further, in their study of identity formation among gay men, Elizur and Mintzer (2001) found that secure attachment was predicted by self-acceptance and support from friends, but not by support from family. This finding does not mean that family support is unimportant to gay males' sense of identity; in this study, support from family did predict disclosure of sexual orientation (Elizur & Mintzer). These results support a multidimensional view of identity formation in gay males, involving interrelated processes of self-definition, self-acceptance, and disclosure. They also support the idea that friends are key sources of support for gay males, particularly when parents are unaware of, or reacting negatively to, their offspring's sexual orientation.

Attachment Style and Intimate Relating.   In Ridge and Feeney's (1998) study, gay individuals' attachment style showed meaningful links with aspects of intimate relating. For example, relationship satisfaction was related positively to secure attachment, and intensity of love experiences was related positively to preoccupied attachment and negatively to dismissing attachment. Dismissing attachment was also linked to permissive and instrumental attitudes to sex; in other words, dismissing respondents were relatively accepting of casual sex and multiple partners, and tended to equate sex with physical pleasure rather than with intimacy and communication.

These findings suggest that attachment security generally plays a similar role in relationship processes in same-sex *and* opposite-sex couples. An emerging literature on attachment and gay relationships supports this conclusion. For example, Greenfield and Thelen (1997) showed that, for both gay males and lesbians, avoidance was associated with greater fear of intimacy; this result parallels findings from heterosexual samples (Feeney & Noller, 1990). Similarly, data reported by Mohr (1999) suggest that, for both gay males and lesbians, security is linked to greater relationship satisfaction and to less communication apprehension and aversive interaction. Finally, in Kurdek's (1997) study, attachment security (model of self and other) mediated the link between depression and low relationship commitment, for both gay and heterosexual couples. In other words, the lower commitment reported by depressed individuals can be explained by their negative models of self and others, which serve to weaken relationship commitment. Specifically, those with negative models perceive their relationships as involving fewer rewards and more costs and as falling well short of their ideal. These findings highlight the destructive role of negative evaluations of self and others.

Attachment Style and Coming Out. The last issue addressed by Ridge and Feeney (1998) concerned the implications of attachment style for the experience of coming out. As expected, attachment style was linked to both the timing and the reported effects of coming out. Dismissing and fearful individuals reported having come out substantially later than others (on average, about 4 years later). In addition, although almost all respondents reported a deterioration in their relationships with their parents when their sexual orientation was first disclosed, preoccupied and dismissing females reported particularly severe difficulties in their relationships with their mothers at that time (see Fig. 8.1). Further, for dismissing females, these difficulties were reported as ongoing. Importantly, these attachment-related differences in the quality of maternal relationships remained significant when time since disclosure was statistically controlled. It seems that dismissing females may react to their mother's initial negativity defensively, by distancing themselves from her and downplaying the importance of the relationship; this approach is likely to result in issues remaining unresolved. An alternative explanation is that the poor quality of these relationships is driven largely by the mother's behavior: Quality of maternal relationships before coming out was unrelated to attachment style, but mothers of dismissing daughters may be particularly cold and rejecting in response to disclosure.

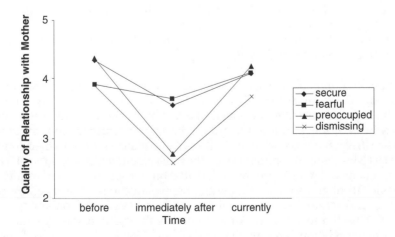

FIG. 8.1. Lesbians' reports of the quality of relationship with mothers, before "coming out," immediately after, and currently.

These results pertaining to coming out support the relevance of attachment the-ory for relational issues unique to homosexual groups, as well as for general issues concerning intimacy and satisfaction. Links between gay men's attachment style and disclosure of sexual orientation are also reported by Elizur and Mintzer (2001). In this study, secure attachment was positively related to all three variables assessing sexual identity formation: self-definition, self-acceptance, and disclosure of sexual orienta-tion. Disclosure was also predicted by support from family, with the effect of general family support mediated by the more specific form of family acceptance of same-sex orientation. In other words, gay men who rated their family relationships as gen-erally supportive also perceived family members as more accepting of their sexual orientation, and this perception predicted greater verbal and behavioral disclosure to friends and family. Together, these studies suggest that there may be reciprocal relations among secure attachment, disclosure of sexual orientation, and the quality of family relationships. Longitudinal studies are needed to examine these relations more fully.

Attachment, Communication, Attitudes and Behaviors: Predicting Sexual Risk Taking

Issues concerning sexual risk taking have featured prominently in research literature over the last couple of decades, prompted largely by the HIV/AIDS epidemic. Our third study of attachment and sexuality focused on these issues, and was a short-term longitudinal study of young adults ($N = 470$) in the early stages of sexual experience. (At the start of the study, only 56% of the sample reported having had sexual expe-rience.) This is an important time to study sexual attitudes and behavior, given that early experiences are likely to be quite formative.

This study involved a two-stage process of data collection: Individual difference variables (such as attachment security and general communication variables) were assessed at Time 1, and safer sex behaviors were assessed at Time 2 (8 weeks later). This procedure has the important advantages of minimizing the effect of common-method variance and facilitating recall of sexual behaviors by fixing the start of the recall period to the initial assessment session. In addition, this study used a multiple-item measure of attachment that yielded scores on the dimensions of discomfort with closeness (referred to as discomfort) and relationship anxiety (referred to as anxiety). These multiple-item scales are likely to provide more sensitive measurement of individual differences in attachment than are forced-choice items or global ratings (Feeney & Noller, 1996). (As noted earlier, secure and preoccupied groups report less discomfort than fearful and dismissing groups, and secure and dismissing groups report less anxiety than preoccupied and fearful groups.)

Attachment, Communication and Safer Sex.   The first report of this study (Feeney, Kelly, Gallois, Peterson, & Terry, 1999) was based on an initial sample of 195 partici-pants. This report focused on the effects of attachment and communication variables (difficulty in assertion, attitudes toward discussing AIDS prevention) on actual safer sex practice (frequency of condom use with current or most recent partner; condom use over the last 8 weeks; and condom use on the most recent sexual encounter). We tested a mediational model, which proposed that attachment security would influence safer sex behavior through its association with positive attitudes toward communication. This type of mediational model is featured in several studies of romantic attachment (see Fig. 8.2), with researchers seeking to identify the mechanisms by which security promotes better relationship functioning (Feeney, 1994; Keelan, Dion, & Dion, 1998).

The mediational model was tested using regression techniques, with the primary criterion for mediation being a reduction in prediction by the attachment dimensions

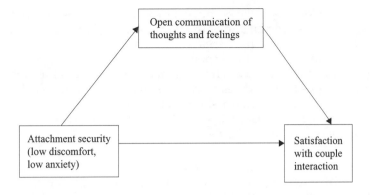

FIG. 8.2. Mediational model linking attachment security and relationship functioning.

when communication measures were added to the equation (Feeney et al., 1999). The analyses revealed a robust link between anxiety and unsafe sex: Highly anxious individuals reported less condom use with the current or most recent partner, less condom use over the last 8 weeks, and less condom use on the most recent encounter. The role of communication variables in predicting condom use was more complex. Negative attitudes toward discussing AIDS prevention predicted less frequent condom use *with the current or most recent partner*, and these attitudes mediated the effect of anxiety. However, the other two measures of condom use did not yield support for the mediational model. Negative attitudes toward discussing AIDS prevention predicted less condom use over the last 8 weeks, but this effect was independent of the effect of anxiety. Further, the communication variables failed to predict condom use on the most recent encounter (and thus could not play a mediating role).

In short, condom use was consistently related to low anxiety, but less consistently related to attitudes toward communication. Attitudes toward communication seem to provide better prediction of *general* measures of safer sex than measures specific to a given encounter, partly because behavior in any single encounter may be affected by a number of situational factors. Further, anxiety and attitudes toward communication provided *independent* prediction of condom use over the 8-week period. Therefore, the robust link between anxiety and less condom use may reflect several mechanisms, including reluctance to risk alienating partners by talking about AIDS-related issues and difficulties in negotiating sexual encounters when arousal is high or when partners pressure for unprotected sex.

The broader literature on adult attachment (e.g., Feeney, Noller, & Callan, 1994; Hazan & Shaver, 1987) shows that individuals high in relationship anxiety report such tendencies as yearning for intimacy, strong feelings of attraction, belief in love at first sight, doubts about self-worth, and poor communication skills. Together with our results linking anxiety to unsafe sex and to reluctance to discuss AIDS prevention, these findings suggest that anxious individuals may use sexuality in an attempt to forge intimacy. In other words, as noted earlier, attachment-related differences in sexual behavior reflect the interaction goals of the different attachment styles. Similarly, in their study of young adults, Bogaert and Sadava (2002) found that, for women, anxious attachment was related to erotophilia, or highly positive affect with regard to a variety of sexual experiences. Women's anxious attachment was also related to composite measures assessing promiscuity (early first intercourse, number of lifetime partners), infidelity (by self and partner), and recent sexual experience (condom use, number of partners in the last year). This last result, which suggests greater condom use among anxious women, appears to run counter to our own findings (Feeney et al.,

1999). However, follow-up analyses showed that this result was due to the nature of the composite variable; women's anxious attachment was linked to more sexual partners, but not to more condom use (Bogaert & Sadava, 2002).

Of importance, in the study by Feeney et al. (1999), only the anxiety dimension of attachment predicted condom use. The fact that discomfort was unrelated to condom use suggests that positive attitudes toward intimacy do not necessarily encourage safer practices, and caution against simplistic generalizations about the benefits of a secure attachment style. This issue is further highlighted when we consider later analyses from this study, discussed next.

Attachment, Sexual Self-Efficacy and Sexual Risk: Linking Attitudes and Behaviors. A later report of this study (Feeney, Peterson, Gallois, & Terry, 2000) was based on the full sample of 470 participants and involved a detailed assessment of the links between attachment dimensions and sexual attitudes and behavior. This report focused on six sets of variables related to sexuality: openness of communication; sexual self-efficacy and locus of control; beliefs about condoms; perceived risk of contracting HIV/AIDS; actual sexual behaviors (past and current); and, for those not currently sexually active, reasons for *not* having sex. The results for each of these sets of variables are outlined next, and Table 8.1 summarizes key findings for the more complex sets (sexual self-efficacy and locus of control, beliefs about condoms, and sexual behaviors).

Both discomfort and anxiety were related to women's reports of less open communication about sex with their sexual partners. In other words, insecure women (those high in discomfort or high in anxiety) reported that their romantic relationships involved less open exchange of information and advice about contraception, safer sex, and general sexual matters. In addition, for sexually active women, discomfort was related to reports of less open communication with mothers and fathers. These findings support the broader literature on romantic attachment, linking attachment security

TABLE 8.1

Correlations Between Attachment Dimensions and Sexual Attitudes and Behaviors for Sexually Active Respondents (Selected Results Only)

	Relationship Anxiety		Discomfort with Closeness	
	Men	Women	Men	Women
Sexual locus of control				
Internal	−.06	−.28 (**)	−.45 (***)	−.06
External	.33 (***)	.28 (**)	.60 (***)	.36 (***)
Self-efficacy (negotiation)	−.33 (**)	−.23 (*)	−.07	−.05
Belief items: Condoms....				
Are boring	.19	.26 (**)	−.09	−.20 (*)
Protect against HIV	.14	−.11	.39 (**)	.05
Reduce intimacy	.29 (*)	.26 (**)	−.25 (*)	−.01
Destroy spontaneity	.39 (**)	.30 (***)	−.16	−.11
Recent sexual behavior				
Discussing HIV/AIDS	−.11	−.26 (**)	.34 (**)	.05
Frequency of condom use	−.56 (***)	−.15	.07	.12
Condom use every time	.02	−.24 (**)	.28 (*)	.11
Injecting drugs before sex	.49 (***)	−.05	.38 (**)	.04
Other drug use before sex	.49 (***)	−.28 (**)	.39 (**)	−.06

$*p < .05, **p < .01, ***p < .001.$

with self-disclosure and with more open discussion of contentious issues (Feeney et al., 1994; Keelan et al., 1998).

For both sexes, discomfort and anxiety were related to more external, and less internal, locus of control. That is, insecure individuals saw themselves as less responsible for, and less in control of, the course of their sexual interactions; they tended to see sexual outcomes as being influenced by other people, or by chance. Anxiety was also related to less perceived self-efficacy in negotiating sexual encounters; that is, anxious individuals reported less ability to discuss sexual issues and to resist pressure from others to engage in unwanted or unprotected sex. In short, insecurity was linked to lack of confidence in relation to sexual outcomes. A recent study by Shafer (2001) provides indirect support for this finding. In this study, a single-factor measure of trait sexuality (defined by such terms as "sensuous" and "sexy") was related both to secure attachment and to measures tapping confidence in engaging in sexual activity (e.g., sexual self-esteem and sexual assertiveness).

In Feeney et al.'s (2000) study, the items tapping beliefs about condoms showed relatively complex links with attachment. Anxious individuals thought that condoms were boring and saw them as destroying spontaneity, interrupting foreplay, reducing pleasure, and reducing intimacy; however, some of these associations were specific to women or to respondents who reported being sexually active. Discomfort with closeness showed a different pattern of effects: Sexually active men who were high in discomfort saw condoms as protecting against AIDS and other STDs and *rejected* the notion that condoms reduce intimacy. Divergent effects of the two attachment dimensions were also evident for perceived risk of contracting HIV/AIDS: Anxiety was related to men's perceptions that they were at low risk compared to others, whereas discomfort was related to their perceptions of high risk (both in absolute terms and compared to others).

Measures of sexual behavior included past involvement in risky behaviors (unprotected sex and nonexclusive relationships), and current involvement in safer-sex discussions, condom use, and drug use shortly before sex. Links between attachment dimensions and past sexual behavior were restricted to women. Anxious women reported more high-risk behaviors, including nonexclusivity, together with less willingness to change their risky practices. In contrast, women high in discomfort reported *less* involvement in unprotected sex (both vaginal and anal). Links between attachment and current sexual behavior were again relatively complex. Anxious individuals reported less discussion of contraception and HIV/AIDS, less condom use (assessed using slightly different measures from those in the earlier report), and more use of alcohol, injectable drugs, and other drugs before sex. However, most of these links were gender-specific. For men, discomfort also predicted more drug use before sex (marijuana, injectable drugs, and other drugs). On the other hand, and consistent with perceptions of risk and beliefs about condoms, men's discomfort predicted *greater* discussion of issues about HIV/AIDS and the use of condoms for every sexual encounter.

Finally, attachment dimensions were linked with reported reasons for *not* having sex. For men, discomfort was strongly related to citing worry about AIDS and worry about other STDs (consistent with the finding that discomfort predicted more discussion of HIV/AIDS and more consistent condom use). For women, discomfort was related to citing worry about AIDS, whereas anxiety was related to citing practical constraints such as lack of opportunity or lack of privacy.

In summary, this study linked anxiety to difficulty in negotiating and controlling sexual encounters, and to unsafe practices. As noted earlier, these findings probably reflect anxious individuals' strong desires for affection and reciprocation, together with their low sense of self-worth. Interestingly, anxiety was also linked with perceptions of low risk of contracting HIV and with less willingness to change risky practices. This pattern of interrelated cognitions and behaviors suggests that anxious individuals may be quite resistant to safer-sex messages. Discomfort, like anxiety, predicted drug use before sex—behavior that invites less reasoned decision making, and thus, unsafe sex. However, discomfort predicted more discussion of HIV/AIDS and more consistent condom use. This finding suggests, rather ironically, that young people who are comfortable with intimacy tend to see intimacy as incompatible with safe-sex talks and with protected sex. This potential "downside" of comfort with closeness may become more problematic as relationships develop and partners become increasingly motivated to achieve and demonstrate mutual trust. Overall, this study suggests that attachment is relevant to the broad range of sexual expression, from motivations to engage (or not to engage) in sex, to perceptions of control and self-efficacy, sexual communication, and sexual practices. At the same time, it highlights the complexity of these issues, with many findings being specific to one gender or one dimension of attachment.

The findings from this study (Feeney et al., 2000) are consistent with data derived from a large, representative sample of adolescents in the United States (Tracy, Shaver, Cooper, & Albino, 2003). This study relied on a simple measure of the three major attachment styles (secure, avoidant, and anxious–ambivalent), but used both interviewer-administered and self-administered questions to assess sexual attitudes and behaviors (self-administered questions are particularly appropriate for highly sensitive topics). Like our own work, this study linked secure attachment to higher sexual self-efficacy and perceived sexual competence and to less intoxication and other substance use prior to sexual encounters. In addition, secure adolescents were less likely to report being victims or perpetrators of sexual aggression. The researchers also studied attachment-related differences in reported reasons for having sex (a question which complements our own work on reasons for *not* having sex). Both secure and anxious–ambivalent adolescents reported having sex in order to express love for the partner, but anxious–ambivalent adolescents also reported fear of losing the partner as a reason for having sex. In contrast, avoidant adolescents reported engaging in sex in order to lose their virginity and rated their sexual encounters as of little importance. Again, these findings support the argument that attachment-related differences in sexual expression reflect differences in interaction goals, particularly in relation to needs for intimacy and autonomy.

Attachment and Sexual Expression in Married Couples

Our most recent study of attachment and sexuality was a study of the transition to parenthood (Feeney, Hohaus, Noller, & Alexander, 2001). There are important reasons for focusing on attachment during this period of transition. According to attachment theory, attachment styles arise from early experiences with caregivers and involve rules and strategies for dealing with attachment-related distress. Thus, attachment-style differences may be most pronounced in stressful circumstances, and security is seen as a "core resource" that helps people cope with difficult events (Mikulincer & Florian, 1998). Many studies of adult attachment and responses to stress have focused on relationship conflict as the stressor. However, first-time parenthood is a major event that should make attachment issues *particularly* salient, given that partners' attachment bond must change to incorporate a new and highly dependent family member.

Participants in this longitudinal study were 107 married couples who were expecting their first child (we refer to these as "transition couples"), and 100 married couples who had no children and were not planning to embark on parenthood in the near future ("comparison couples"). The couples completed three assessment sessions: These sessions occurred in the second trimester of pregnancy and when the babies were about 6 weeks and 6 months of age (for comparison couples, sessions occurred at similar times). Attachment security was again defined by the dimensions of anxiety and discomfort.

Unlike the studies described to this point, our study of marriage and parenthood clearly focused on highly committed relationships. In this study, we were interested in how partners felt about their sexual relationship, rather than how often they engaged in specific behaviors. To measure these feelings, we began with items drawn from several previous measures, tapping sexual desire, satisfaction, and communication. Factor analysis of the item set revealed two major dimensions. The first factor assessed sexual desire; that is, levels of sexual drive, and amount of sexual interest and involvement with the partner. Sample items include, "I look forward to having sex with my partner" and "Just thinking about having sex with my partner excites me." The second factor assessed sexual communication; that is, partners' ability to communicate about their sexual needs and preferences and the level of satisfaction with these aspects of communication. Sample items from this factor include, "I tell my partner when I am especially sexually satisfied" and "My partner shows me by the way s/he touches me if s/he is satisfied."

Group and Gender Effects. In reporting the results of this study, we have chosen to focus on the first and second assessments (from midway through pregnancy to 6 weeks postbirth, for the transition couples). At the beginning of the study, transition and comparison couples reported similar levels of sexual desire. However, transition couples were somewhat less satisfied with their sexual communication than were comparison couples. This small difference may indicate that transition couples were already starting to focus on discussing other important issues in their lives, such as their plans for the baby. Alternatively, or in addition, it may reflect the arrival of new sexual concerns and challenges, related to the physical and emotional changes that accompany pregnancy. Gender differences were evident in both groups, with women reporting somewhat less sexual desire than men, but greater satisfaction with their sexual communication. These group and gender differences were also evident at the second assessment, with no significant change in scores occurring in that time period.

Predictive Effects of Attachment. When we first reported this study (Feeney et al., 2001), we focused on the predictive power of the individual's own attachment security; that is, on the link between respondents' initial attachment dimensions and their later (Time 2) levels of sexual desire and communication. These results are shown in the top half of Table 8.2. Initial scores on anxiety were related negatively to later sexual desire and sexual communication for both groups of husbands (but not for either group of wives). In addition, initial scores on discomfort were related negatively to sexual communication for both groups of husbands and for comparison wives. We will discuss these results in more detail shortly.

Before doing so, it is important to note another advantage of studying couples, rather than individuals. Specifically, we are able to assess "partner effects," or how the attachment characteristics of an individual may influence the *partner's* perceptions of the sexual relationship. We conducted additional analyses to explore this issue (see Table 8.2, bottom half). Husbands' initial anxiety and discomfort predicted comparison wives' low scores on sexual desire and sexual communication. Husbands' discomfort also predicted transition wives' low scores on sexual communication. Interestingly, these partner effects remained significant when the respondent's own attachment scores were partialed out. In other words, these effects cannot be dismissed as due to confoundings between partners' attachment characteristics (commonly known as "partner matching").

Overall, when we consider the entries in Table 8.2, the correlations between attachment and sexuality may not seem particularly high. However, given the 5-month

TABLE 8.2

Correlations Between Own and Partner's Attachment Dimensions and Measures of Sexual Desire and Satisfaction With Sexual Communication

	Relationship Anxiety				Discomfort With Closeness			
	Husbands		Wives		Husbands		Wives	
	Trans	Comp	Trans	Comp	Trans	Comp	Trans	Comp
Own reports								
Desire	−.23*	−.24*	−.13	−.15	−.18	−.08	−.01	−.15
Satis. comm.	−.39**	−.39**	−.12	−.14	−.29**	−.24*	−.12	−.28*
Partner's reports								
Desire	−.03	−.30**	−.08	.11	.09	−.29**	.01	−.04
Satis. comm.	−.17	−.26*	−.19	−.09	−.24*	−.22*	.04	−.15

Note. Trans = transition group; Comp = comparison group; satis. comm. = satisfaction with sexual communication.
* $p < .05$, ** $p < .01$.

time-lag between assessments and the complex variables that affect sexual responding (particularly among new parents), the effects of earlier attachment are quite convincing. In short, predictive effects were obtained mainly for *husbands'* attachment, which predicted sexuality scores for self (in both groups) and partner (mainly in the comparison group). At this stage, it is not clear why the effects should be stronger for husbands' attachment. It is possible that gender roles are again relevant. In long-term relationships, for example, sexual expression may be more strongly linked to men's security, whereas some aspects of communication may be more strongly linked to women's security. However, this suggestion clearly requires further testing.

It is worth noting that discomfort was negatively linked mainly to satisfaction with sexual communication, whereas anxiety affected *both* aspects of sexuality. It is not surprising that discomfort with intimacy affects sexual communication, given the highly intimate nature of this topic and the sense of vulnerability that may surround disclosures of such personal thoughts and feelings. The pervasive effects of relationship anxiety also make sense, given the nature of this attachment dimension. By definition, relationship anxiety involves deep-seated concerns about the partner's love and commitment and about the viability of the relationship. It is understandable that these concerns impact negatively on the individual's own sexual desire and perceptions of sexual communication. These findings remind us that, particularly in ongoing relationships, sexual expression is firmly embedded in the broader relational context.

Similarly, the negative effects of *partners'* insecurities are understandable given the interdependence that characterizes marital bonds. Insecurity often manifests itself in negative attributions for partner's behavior and negative communication patterns such as coercion and withdrawal, particularly in response to stress (Feeney & Noller, 1996). Over time, these processes are likely to affect both partners' attitudes toward their relationship. It is interesting to note that partner effects of husbands' attachment were mainly confined to comparison couples. This finding may seem surprising given that attachment-related differences are thought to be more marked when partners face challenging events, such as new parenthood. However, differences in sexual expression following childbirth may be an exception to this rule. Indeed, new mothers' sexual desire and perceptions of sexual communication may be influenced less by partner's security than by the myriad of variables related to pregnancy, delivery, and the demands of infant care.

To our knowledge, no other study has explored the predictive relations between attachment and one's own and one's partner's perceptions of sexuality in marriage. However, several findings from other studies (most of which we have already discussed) suggest that security promotes healthy long-term sexual relationships. First, questionnaire studies have linked attachment security to comfort with touch in close relationships: Compared with other attachment groups, secure respondents report less touch aversion and more positive attitudes toward the use of touch to show affection and to express sexuality (Brennan, Wu & Love, 1998). Second, questionnaire and diary data link secure attachment with greater frequency of mutually initiated sex, greater enjoyment of physical contact (both sexual and nonsexual), and willingness to experiment sexually within the primary relationship (Hazan et al., 1994). Third, a measure of trait sexuality relates both to secure attachment and to indices of confidence and interest in sexual activity, including sexual motivation and sexual assertiveness (Shafer, 2001). Finally, a recent study (Bogaert & Sadava, 2002) links secure attachment to self-perceptions of physical attractiveness. Together, these diverse findings suggest that secure individuals' positive models of self and others foster a sense of confidence in the self as a sexual being, together with an appreciation of the intimate nature of sexual interactions. In other words, positive models of self and others are played out in attitudes and behaviors that promote active and satisfying sexual relationships.

STUDYING ATTACHMENT AND SEXUALITY: LIMITATIONS AND FUTURE DIRECTIONS

When evaluating existing studies linking attachment and sexuality, the limitations of the research must be kept in mind. As with most studies of sexuality, data have been gathered by self-reports, using either questionnaires, interviews, or structured diaries. As other researchers have noted (e.g., Catania, Gibson, Chitwood, & Coates, 1990), questions can be raised about the validity of self-reports of sexual behavior. Barriers to valid reporting include those typically associated with self-report methods (e.g., difficulty in recalling events fully and accurately), together with those that may be particularly problematic in this research area (e.g., embarrassment, desire for privacy, desire to embellish one's experience).

In addition, the direction of causal relations is not always clear. As noted earlier, attachment theorists propose that working models of attachment develop relatively early in life and influence the expression of sexuality. Moreover, theory and research into social cognitive processes suggest that new relationship experiences tend to be assimilated to fit existing working models; thus, these models should be relatively stable (Collins & Read, 1994). However, powerful relationship events may disconfirm existing models, producing change in self-reported attachment. In a 4-year prospective study, for example, Kirkpatrick and Hazan (1994) found that relationship dissolution was associated with change from secure to insecure attachment. Therefore, with cross-sectional studies of attachment and sexuality, it is possible that causation is in the reverse direction; that is, from sexual behavior to attachment style. Such reverse causation is most plausible in the case of very powerful experiences, such as sexual coercion. Of course, longitudinal studies play an important role in establishing causal relations. In particular, using earlier attachment scores to predict later measures of sexuality minimizes potential confounds such as mood. However, even with these designs, social desirability response bias could conceivably inflate associations between security and positive sexual attitudes and behaviors.

With regard to sampling, it should be acknowledged that several studies of attachment and sexuality have used samples of undergraduate students, with respondents therefore being quite restricted in terms of age and education. However, a substantial minority of studies have extended this base by investigating broader samples of adults or couples who are in marital, gay, or lesbian relationships. The move toward less restrictive samples is an important development. For example, cross-sectional data from broad samples suggest that levels of relationship anxiety may decrease with age (e.g., Feeney, 1994). Although long-term longitudinal studies are needed to confirm this suggestion, it is worth noting that some of the tendencies associated with relationship anxiety (such as avoidance of topics that might alienate partners) may be less marked in older samples.

The studies reported in this chapter point to some robust findings, such as the association between anxious–ambivalence (relationship anxiety) and less consistent condom use, and between avoidance (discomfort with closeness) and a more permissive approach to sex. Given current concerns related to HIV / AIDS and other sexually transmitted diseases, it may be tempting to read moral messages into these findings. However, it is crucial to bear in mind that significant associations between attachment and sexual variables are usually small to moderate in size. Thus, the expression of sexuality is likely to vary considerably across individuals and relationships, even when attachment characteristics are taken into account. For this reason, it is important to exercise caution in making generalizations about the implications of particular attachment styles.

It is also worth noting that attachment has been linked to other theoretical constructs in the area of romantic love. For example, there is evidence of links between the major attachment styles and the components of Sternberg's (1986) triangular model of love: intimacy, commitment, and passion. Specifically, all three components are related positively to secure attachment and negatively to avoidant and anxious–ambivalent attachment, although the associations are modest in size (Levy & Davis, 1988). Links between the three attachment styles and the love styles discussed by Lee (1973) are more informative, involving differential links with the two forms of insecurity (Feeney & Noller, 1990; Levy & Davis, 1988). The most robust links are between secure attachment and eros (romantic, passionate love), avoidant attachment and ludus (game-playing, uncommitted love), and anxious–ambivalent attachment and mania (possessive, dependent love). Given previous data linking love styles and sexual attitudes (Hendrick & Hendrick, 1988), meaningful patterns are emerging that support the convergent validity of findings and integrate the different theoretical approaches. For example, research points to interrelations among avoidance, ludus, and sexual permissiveness, and among secure attachment, eros, and sexual attitudes emphasizing intimacy and communication.

Given the firm theoretical base linking attachment and sexuality, we expect that this topic will continue to be of interest to researchers. As already noted, multiple-item attachment scales are likely to provide sensitive measurement of adults' attachment concerns, and this development should enhance future research. In terms of research directions, perhaps the greatest need is for studies that focus on the dyad, rather than the individual. The broader literature on adult attachment has clearly moved in this direction, with fruitful results. There is now abundant evidence that perceptions of relationships are influenced not only by the attachment characteristics of the reporter, but also by those of the partner (see Feeney, 1999). Further, there are reports of *interactive* effects of partners' attachment characteristics (e.g., Feeney, 1994; Roberts & Noller, 1998). These latter effects clearly highlight the dyadic nature of attachment bonds, indicating, for example, that an individual's discomfort with closeness may be played out differently, depending on the characteristics of the partner. Specific developmental stages also warrant further research. On the one hand, there is a need for further study of the early stages of sexual experience, given their formative nature. On the other hand, current rates of separation and divorce suggest a need to study the sexual attitudes and behaviors of older adults, following the breakup of long-term relationships.

SUMMARY AND CONCLUSIONS

In summary, the studies we have described in this chapter link avoidance with greater endorsement of casual sex, more involvement with nonintimate partners, more concern about STDs, and greater belief in the benefits of condoms. Avoidance is also related to delays and difficulties in gay persons' disclosure of their sexual orientation. By contrast, anxiety is linked to low self-efficacy for sexual negotiation, fears that requests for sexual discussions will alienate partners, negative beliefs about condoms, less exclusivity, less condom use, and less willingness to change risky practices. Finally, secure attachment is linked to sexual confidence, open sexual communication, mutual initiation of sex, sexual enjoyment, and fidelity. All these links are consistent with the interaction goals of the different attachment styles, particularly with regard to intimacy and autonomy.

Overall, the studies we have reviewed also suggest that the association between attachment and sexuality is quite robust. This association has now been tested using concurrent and predictive designs, heterosexual and homosexual samples, categorical and continuous measures of attachment, and questionnaire, interview, and diary-based assessments of sexuality. The attachment perspective clearly fits with recent attempts to study sexuality in its relational context, and offers the additional advantage of integrating early and later relationship experiences. We think that Shaver (1994) provided quite an understated comment on the richness of attachment theory when he noted that this perspective allows researchers to see sex as more than simple mechanics.

REFERENCES

Ainsworth, M. D. S., Blehar, M. C., Waters, E., & Wall, S. (1978). *Patterns of attachment: A study of the strange situation.* Hillsdale, NJ: Lawrence Erlbaum Associates.

Bartholomew, K. (1990). Avoidance of intimacy: An attachment perspective. *Journal of Social and Personal Relationships, 7,* 147–178.

Bartholomew, K., & Horowitz, L. M. (1991). Attachment styles among young adults: A test of a four-category model. *Journal of Personality and Social Psychology, 61,* 226–244.

Belsky, J., Steinberg, L., & Draper, P. (1991). Childhood experience, interpersonal development, and reproductive strategy: An evolutionary theory of socialization. *Child Development, 62,* 647–670.

Bogaert, A. F., & Sadava, S. (2002). Adult attachment and sexual behavior. *Personal Relationships, 9,* 191–204.

Bowlby, J. (1969). *Attachment and loss: Vol. 1. Attachment.* New York: Basic Books.

Bowlby, J. (1979). *The making and breaking of affectional bonds.* London: Tavistock.

Brennan, K. A., Clark, C. L., & Shaver, P. R. (1998). Self-report measurement of adult attachment: An integrative overview. In J. A. Simpson & W. S. Rholes (Eds.), *Attachment theory and close relationships* (pp. 46–76). New York: Guilford.

Brennan, K. A., & Shaver, P. R. (1995). Dimensions of adult attachment, affect regulation, and romantic relationship functioning. *Personality and Social Psychology Bulletin, 21,* 267–283.

Brennan, K. A., Wu, S., & Love, J. (1998). Adult romantic attachment and individual differences in attitudes toward physical contact in the context of adult romantic relationships. In J. A. Simpson & W. S. Rholes (Eds.), *Attachment theory and close relationships* (pp. 394–428). New York: Guilford.

Catania, J. A., Gibson, D. R., Chitwood, D. D., & Coates, T. J. (1990). Methodological problems in AIDS behavioral research: Influences on measurement error and participation bias in studies of sexual behavior. *Psychological Bulletin, 108,* 339–362.

Christopher, F. S., & Sprecher, S. (2000). Sexuality in marriage, dating, and other relationships: A decade review. *Journal of Marriage and the Family, 62,* 999–1017.

Colgan, P. (1987). Treatment of identity and intimacy issues in gay males. *Journal of Homosexuality, 14,* 101–123.

Collins, N. L., & Read, S. J. (1994). Cognitive representations of attachment: The structure and function of working models. In K. Bartholomew & D. Perlman (Eds.), *Advances in personal relationships: Vol. 5: Attachment processes in adulthood* (pp. 53–90). London: Jessica Kingsley.

Elizur, Y., & Mintzer, A. (2001). A framework for the formation of gay male identity: Processes associated with adult attachment style and support from family and friends. *Archives of Sexual Behavior, 30,* 143–167.

Feeney, J. A. (1994). Attachment style, communication patterns and satisfaction across the life cycle of marriage. *Personal Relationships, 1,* 333–348.

Feeney, J. A. (1999). Adult romantic attachment and couple relationships. In J. Cassidy & P. R. Shaver (Eds.). *The handbook of attachment: Theory, research, and clinical applications* (pp. 355–377). New York: Guilford.

Feeney, J. A., Hohaus, L., Noller, P., & Alexander, R. (2001). *Becoming parents: Exploring the bonds between mothers, fathers, and their infants.* Cambridge, England: Cambridge University Press.

Feeney, J. A., Kelly, L., Gallois, C., Peterson, C., & Terry, D. J. (1999). Attachment style, assertive communication, and safer-sex behavior. *Journal of Applied Social Psychology, 29,* 1964–1983.

Feeney, J. A., & Noller, P. (1990). Attachment style as a predictor of adult romantic relationships. *Journal of Personality and Social Psychology, 58,* 281–291.

Feeney, J. A., & Noller, P. (1996). *Adult attachment.* Thousand Oaks, CA: Sage.

Feeney, J. A., Noller, P., & Callan, V. J. (1994). Attachment style, communication and satisfaction in the early years of marriage. In K. Bartholomew & D. Perlman (Eds.), *Advances in personal relationships: Vol. 5: Attachment processes in adulthood* (pp. 269–308). London: Jessica Kingsley.

Feeney, J. A., Noller, P., & Patty, J. (1993). Adolescents' interactions with the opposite sex: Influence of attachment style and gender. *Journal of Adolescence, 16,* 169–186.

Feeney, J. A., Peterson, C., Gallois, C., & Terry, D. J. (2000). Attachment style as a predictor of sexual attitudes and behavior in late adolescence. *Psychology and Health, 14,* 1105–1122.

Feeney, J. A., & Raphael, B. (1992). Adult attachments and sexuality: Implications for understanding risk behaviours for HIV infection. *Australian and New Zealand Journal of Psychiatry, 26,* 399–407.

Fraley, R. C., & Waller, N. G. (1998). Adult attachment patterns: A test of the typological model. In J. A. Simpson & W. S. Rholes (Eds.), *Attachment theory and close relationships* (pp. 77–114). New York: Guilford.

Gangestad, S. W., & Thornhill, R. (1997). The evolutionary psychology of extrapair sex: The role of fluctuating asymmetry. *Evolution and Human Behavior, 18,* 69–88.

Gentzler, A. L., & Kerns, K. A. (2001). *Insecure attachment and sexual experiences: Explaining associations between the two.* Manuscript submitted for publication.

Greenfield, S., & Thelen, M. (1997). Validation of the Fear of Intimacy Scale with a lesbian and gay male population. *Journal of Social and Personal Relationships, 14,* 707–716.

Hatfield, E., & Rapson, R. L. (1996). *Love and sex: A cross-cultural perspective.* New York: Allyn & Bacon.

Hazan, C., & Shaver, P. R. (1987). Romantic love conceptualized as an attachment process. *Journal of Personality and Social Psychology, 52,* 511–524.

Hazan, C., Zeifman, D., & Middleton, K. (1994, July). *Adult romantic attachment, affection, and sex.* Paper presented at the 7th International Conference on Personal Relationships, Groningen, The Netherlands.

Hendrick, C., & Hendrick, S. S. (1988). Lovers wear rose colored glasses. *Journal of Social and Personal Relationships, 5,* 161–183.

Keelan, J. P. R., Dion, K. K., & Dion, K. L. (1998). Attachment style and relationship satisfaction: Test of a self-disclosure explanation. *Canadian Journal of Behavioural Science, 30,* 24–35.

Kinsey, A. C., Pomeroy, W. B., & Martin, C. E. (1948). *Sexual behavior in the human male.* Philadelphia: Saunders.

Kirkpatrick, L. E., & Hazan, C. (1994). Attachment styles and close relationships: A four-year prospective study. *Personal Relationships, 1,* 123–142.

Kurdek, L. A. (1988). Perceived social support in gays and lesbians in cohabitation relationships. *Journal of Personality and Social Psychology, 54,* 504–509.

Kurdek, L. A. (1997). The link between facets of neuroticism and dimensions of relationship commitment: Evidence from gay, lesbian, and heterosexual couples. *Journal of Family Psychology, 11,* 503–514.

Lee, J. A. (1973). *The colors of love: An exploration of the ways of loving.* Ontario, Canada: New Press.

Levy, M. B., & Davis, K. E. (1988). Lovestyles and attachment styles compared: Their relations to each other and to various relationship characteristics. *Journal of Social and Personal Relationships, 5,* 439–471.

Mikulincer, M., & Florian, V. (1998). The relationship between adult attachment styles and emotional and cognitive reactions to stressful events. In J. A. Simpson & W. S. Rholes (Eds.), *Attachment theory and close relationships* (pp. 143–165). New York: Guilford.

Mohr, J. J. (1999). Same-sex romantic attachment. In J. Cassidy & P. R. Shaver (Eds.), *Handbook of attachment: Theory, research, and clinical applications* (pp. 378–394). New York: Guiford.

Ridge, S. R., & Feeney, J. A. (1998). Relationship history and relationship attitudes in gay males and lesbians: Attachment style and gender differences. *Australian and New Zealand Journal of Psychiatry, 32,* 848–859.

Roberts, N., & Noller, P. (1998). The associations between adult attachment and couple violence: The role of communication patterns and relationship satisfaction. In J. A. Simpson & W. S. Rholes (Eds.), *Attachment theory and close relationships* (pp. 317–350). New York: Guilford.

Rothbard, J. C., & Shaver, P. R. (1994). Continuity of attachment across the life span. In M. B. Sperling & W. H. Berman (Eds.), *Attachment in adults: Theory, assessment, and treatment* (pp. 31–71). New York: Guilford.

Shafer, A. B. (2001). The Big Five and sexuality trait terms as predictors of relationships and sex. *Journal of Research in Personality, 35,* 313–338.

Shaver, P. R. (1994, August). *Attachment, caregiving, and sex in adult romantic relationships.* Paper presented at the Conference of the American Psychological Association, Los Angeles, CA.

Shaver, P. R., & Hazan, C. (1988). A biased overview of the study of love. *Journal of Social and Personal Relationships, 5,* 473–501.

Shaver, P. R., Hazan, C., & Bradshaw, D. (1988). Love as attachment: The integration of three behavioral systems. In R. J. Sternberg & M. Barnes (Eds.), *The psychology of love* (pp. 68–99). New Haven, CT: Yale University Press.

Simpson, J. A., & Gangestad, S. W. (1991). Individual differences in sociosexuality: Evidence for convergent and discriminant validity. *Journal of Personality and Social Psychology, 60,* 870–883.

Stephan, C. W., & Bachman, G. F. (1999). What's sex got to do with it? Attachment, love schemas, and sexuality. *Personal Relationships, 6,* 111–123.

Sternberg, R. J. (1986). A triangular theory of love. *Psychological Review, 93,* 119–135.

Tracy, J. L., Shaver, P. R., Cooper, M. L., & Albino, A. W. (2003). Attachment styles and adolescent sexuality. In P. Florsheim (Ed.), *Adolescent romance and sexual behavior: Theory, research, and practical implications* (pp. 137–159). Mahwah, NJ: Lawrence Erlbaum Associates.

9

Understanding Sexuality in Close Relationships From the Social Exchange Perspective

E. Sandra Byers
Adrienne Wang
University of New Brunswick

The social exchange framework has been important to our understanding of inter-personal interactions within close relationships but has only occasionally been used to explain *sexuality* within close relationships. However, the social exchange perspective can be useful in understanding sexuality in close relationships because it takes the interpersonal context into account. In this chapter, we review existing research and theory supporting the utility of the social exchange perspective for understanding sexuality in close relationships. We start by defining the four components that comprise the social exchange framework. To do this we incorporate the components contained in a number of different social exchange models each of which emphasizes some but not all of these components. These four components are: the balance of rewards and costs, equity/equality, comparison level, and comparison level for alternatives. We then examine theoretical and empirical evidence to support the importance of each of these components to four important aspects of sexuality in close relationships: sexual partner selection, sexual frequency, sexual satisfaction, and extradyadic sexual activity. We conclude by suggesting a number of potentially fruitful directions for future research. In particular, future research needs to: (a) be based on the complete social exchange framework; (b) examine the relative contributions of sexual exchanges compared to nonsexual exchanges to sexual relationships; (c) examine developmental changes over the course of the relationship in the exchange components and in the relationships of the exchange components to the sexual relationship, (d) include neglected populations such as gays and lesbians, ethnocultural minority groups, and distressed couples; and, (e) examine neglected topics such as sexual coercion/unwanted sexual activity and sexual communication.

INTRODUCTION

The social exchange framework has been important to our understanding of a number of aspects of interpersonal interactions within close relationships including relationship development, relationship satisfaction, and relationship stability (Cate, Lloyd, & Long, 1988; Huston & Burgess, 1979; Laursen & Jensen-Campbell, 1999; Rusbult, 1983; Rusbult, Johnson, & Morrow, 1986). However, the social exchange perspective has only occasionally been used to explain *sexuality* within close relationships (Lawrance, 1994; Sprecher, 1998). Until fairly recently, research on sexuality within close relationships has focussed on the individual and largely ignored the interpersonal context in which it occurs (Christopher & Sprecher, 2000). Thus, although there is an extensive literature to explain and explore, for example, sexual responses, sexual problems and concerns, sexual attitudes, and contraceptive use from individual characteristics, the interpersonal aspects of sexuality largely have been neglected (McKinney & Sprecher, 1991). Of course, sexual behaviour does not occur in all close relationships, nor is a close relationship necessary for sexual activity. However, in Western culture at least, most people believe that sexual activity should take place mainly within a close, intimate relationship; and most sexual activity does take place in this context (Christopher & Sprecher, 2000; Cramer, 1998; Laumann, Gagnon, Michael, & Michaels, 1994; McKinney & Sprecher, 1991).

The social exchange perspective takes the interpersonal context into account and thus, provides a theoretical framework from which sexuality in close relationships can be understood. This chapter examines how well this framework explains four important aspects of sexuality in close relationships: partner selection, sexual frequency, sexual satisfaction, and extradyadic sexual activity. Because there has been little or no research applying a social exchange framework to sexuality in same-sex relationships (see Steinman, 1990 for an exception), we have limited our discussion to heterosexual relationships.

SOCIAL EXCHANGE THEORIES

There have been a number of variations of social exchange theory within social psychology since it was first proposed by Thibaut and Kelley (1959) including: reinforcement theory (Homans, 1961), equity theory (Walster [now Hatfield] Berscheid, & Walster, 1973), interdependence theory (Cramer, 1998) and its variation the investment model (Rusbult, 1983), and the interpersonal exchange model of sexual satisfaction (Lawrance & Byers, 1995). All of these models assume that interpersonal behavior consists of a series of exchanges and examine interpersonal relationships with reference to what the partners put in to and get out of the relationship (Kelley et al., 1983; Nye, 1982; Thibaut & Kelley, 1959). The basic premise of the social exchange framework and of each of these theories, then, is that each individual in a dyad engages in a diverse set of interpersonal interactions or exchanges in order to influence his or her partner and attain the most favorable outcomes—that is, to maximize rewards and minimize costs. Thus, the social exchange approach is particularly suitable for understanding sexuality within close relationships because most sexual activities occur within the context of an intimate relationship within which partners interact and influence each other on many levels, sexual and nonsexual (Kirkendall & Libby, 1966; Sprecher 1998).

There are four concepts that are central to the social exchange framework as it may apply to sexuality within close relationships: the balance of rewards and costs, equity/equality, comparison level, and comparison level for alternatives. However, each of the existing social exchange models emphasizes different components within the social exchange framework. Reinforcement theory emphasizes the individual's outcomes (rewards and costs) and fails to take the interpersonal context (i.e., equity/equity) or expectations (i.e., comparison level) into account. Equity theory includes both outcomes and the equity of inputs and outcomes but omits the subjective evaluation of these outcomes (i.e., comparison level). In contrast, interdependence theory incorporates outcomes and the process by which individuals subjectively evaluate the value of rewards and costs in their relationship but omits equity/equality. The interpersonal exchange model of sexual satisfaction incorporates rewards, costs, equality, and expectations or comparison level, but excludes a consideration of the availability of attractive alternative relationships. Thus, each of these theories is incomplete; sexuality within close relationships can be best understood by considering all four of the social exchange theory components.

SOCIAL EXCHANGE COMPONENTS

As noted, there are four components that are central to a social exchange framework: the balance of rewards and costs, equity/equality, comparison level, and comparison level for alternatives. As these terms have specific meaning within social exchange theory, we start by defining each of these components.

Rewards and Costs

Rewards are exchanges that are positive, gratifying, or pleasurable to the individual, whereas costs are exchanges that inflict pain, embarrassment or anxiety, or demand mental or physical efforts and include missed opportunities in the relationship (Kelley & Thibaut, 1978; Thibaut & Kelley, 1959). In interpersonal relationships, rewards and costs can include material goods and services. However, they can also include the experience of love and affection, sharing of interests, quality of communication, accrued status, sexual pleasure, and so on (Foa & Foa, 1980; Swenson, 1973). Basically, social exchange theories propose that, in a close relationship, partners strive for the most profitable outcomes—that is, they engage in interpersonal exchanges that will maximize rewards and minimize costs (Sprecher, 1998; Thibaut & Kelley, 1959). A more favorable balance of rewards to costs results in greater satisfaction (Cate, Lloyd, Henton, & Larson 1982; Cate et al., 1988; Rusbult, 1983; Rusbult et al., 1986).

Both sexual and nonsexual rewards and costs may influence sexuality in close relationships. For example, Regan and Sprecher (1995) found that, in close relationships, both men and women value some sexual exchanges, such as being passionate, as highly or more highly than nonsexual exchanges. Lawrance and Byers (1992) had undergraduates list the sexual rewards they had experienced in their relationship and found that a wide range of exchanges are experienced as sexual rewards and costs. They used this information to develop the Rewards/Costs Checklist, a list of 46 sexual exchanges that can be either rewards or costs in a sexual relationship (Lawrance & Byers, 1995; 1998). The Rewards/Costs Checklist includes a wide range of items including items related to affection, communication, intimacy, sexual response, the performance sexual script (i.e., the nature of lovemaking), sexual exclusivity, and spontaneity. Each item can be identified as a sexual reward, a sexual cost, both a reward and a cost, or neither a reward nor a cost.

Specific sexual exchanges are not inherently sexual rewards or sexual costs in and of themselves. Rather, people differ in which sexual exchanges they experience as rewarding and/or costly. For example, in a study of couples in long-term relationships, Lawrance and Byers (1995) asked participants to indicate whether each of the 46 items on the Rewards/Costs Checklist was generally a reward in their sexual relationship, generally a cost, both a reward and a cost, or neither a reward nor a cost. They found that on average men and women identified 28 items as sexual rewards and 11 items as sexual costs. Each of the 46 items was identified as a sexual reward by at least 21% of the men and 16% of the women. Some items were identified as sexual rewards by more than 90% of participants. Similarly, each of the 46 items was identified as a sexual cost by some participants; some items by 40 to 50% of respondents. Thus, although there is a wide range of exchanges that are experienced as generally being sexual rewards and sexual costs, some exchanges are particularly likely to be experienced as rewarding or as costly. Whether a particular individual experiences a specific exchange as a sexual reward or a sexual cost may reflect the nature of the couple's performance sexual script (i.e., what lovemaking consists of). Alternately, it may reflect the match between the performance script and the individual's ideal sexual script. Thus, for example, oral sex might be endorsed as a reward if it occurs in the sexual relationship and the individual enjoys it. However, it might be experienced as a cost if it occurs in the relationship and the individual does not enjoy it, or if it occurs more or less often than the individual desires. Byers and her colleagues have demonstrated that all of the 46 items on the Rewards/Costs Checklist also are experienced as both rewards and costs in heterosexual dating relationships and in long-term relationships in other cultures (i.e., China; Byers, Demmons, & Lawrance, 1998; Renaud, Byers, & Pan, 1996).

Equity and Equality

Equity and equality are also important exchange concepts. Equity models propose that a couple's interactions are not driven exclusively by each individual's motivation to maximize their own rewards and minimize their own costs. They are also driven by both partners' desires to maintain equity or equality in the relationship. Equity refers to the individual's perception of how his or her own inputs (that is, own positive or negative contributions to the relationship) and outcomes (that is, the rewards and costs he or she experiences in the relationship) compare with the partner's inputs and outcomes. A relationship is equitable when the perceived inputs and outcomes are the same for both partners (Sprecher, 1998; Sprecher & Schwartz, 1994; Walster et al., 1973). However, whether a relationship or a specific aspect of a relationship (e.g., sexual communication) is judged to be equitable or inequitable depends on the individual's perceptions; perceptions, in turn, are influenced by how much the individual values various inputs and outcomes in the relationship exchange. Further, the value a person places on a particular contribution may be different if he or she makes it than if the contribution is made by the partner (Regan & Sprecher, 1995). Of course, partners may exchange one type of reward for another if they place different values on various exchanges (Hatfield, Utne, & Traupmann, 1979). Nonetheless, partners may reach different conclusions about the equity of their relationship. For example, Sprecher (2001) found that although there is a significant positive association between partners' ratings of sexual equity in their relationship, the magnitude of this association is small, accounting for only 5% of the variance in the equity ratings.

Equality is another distributive justice norm that plays an important role in intimate relationships (Deutsch, 1975). However, unlike equity, equality focuses only on the balance between partners' relative outcomes. A relationship is deemed equal insofar as both partners are receiving the same level of outcomes, regardless of the level of their contributions (inputs) to the relationship (Sprecher, 1998; Sprecher & Schwartz, 1994).

Implicit in the principles of equity and equality is the assumption that individuals are motivated to reciprocate the rewards and costs received in the relationships so as to achieve equity or equality with the partner (Gouldner, 1960; Sprecher, 1998). In turn, greater equity and equality are associated with greater relationship satisfaction (Cate et al., 1982, 1988; Davidson, 1984; Hatfield, Greenberger, Traupmann, &

Lambert, 1982; Michaels, Edwards, & Acock, 1984; Morton & Douglas, 1981; Walster, Walster, & Berscheid, 1978). In contrast, inequity and inequality are associated with distress and dissatisfaction. Although this is true for both the partner who is overbenefited (gains more than their partner) and for the partner who is underbenefited (gains less than their partner), the underbenefited partner tends to experience more distress than does the overbenefited partner. For example, Sprecher (2001) found that underbenefited men experience greater depression, anger, and frustration; underbenefited women experience greater frustration, resentment, and depression. However, only guilt is associated with perceiving oneself to be overbenefited. Most individuals will attempt to reduce their distress by restoring equity/equality in one of two ways: by changing their own behavior or bringing about a change in their partner's behavior; or by changing their perceptions of their own and their partner's relative inputs and outcomes, possibly by altering their expectations or comparison level, such that they no longer perceive inequity or inequality within the relationship.

Researchers have found a high degree of overlap between the concepts of equity and equality in close relationships. It appears that the precise rules governing the exchanges (i.e., equity or equality) are relatively unimportant as long as partners perceive their exchanges to be balanced (Cate et al., 1982; Michaels et al., 1984; Morton & Douglas, 1981). Therefore, *equity* and *equality* will be treated as a single exchange component in this chapter. What is more important is whether researchers have assessed global equity/equality or equity/equality in the sexual relationship specifically. Sprecher (2001) found, in a sample of dating couples, that sexual equity is unrelated to any of four measures of global equity. Thus, global equity/equality and sexual equity/equality may play different roles with respect to various aspects of sexuality in close relationships.

Comparison Level and Comparison Level for Alternatives

According to social exchange theories, the values of rewards and costs are subjective, and people make cognitive comparisons in assessing the value of the rewards and costs they receive in their relationship (Kelley & Thibaut, 1978; Sabatelli, 1984; Thibaut & Kelley, 1959). There are two points of reference or sets of expectations that individuals use to evaluate their rewards and costs: comparison level and comparison level for alternatives (Cramer, 1998). Comparison level (CL) refers to the expected outcomes from the exchanges within the current relationship; that is, the level of rewards and costs that the individuals believe that they should receive from the relationship. In contrast, comparison level for alternatives (CL_{alt}) refers to the expected outcomes from alternative relationships, including the best currently available alternative to the present relationship (Kelley & Thibaut, 1978). A relationship remains satisfying and stable as long as the balance of rewards and costs compares favorably to expectations regarding the level of rewards and costs that the individual believes she or he should receive from the relationship, and the level of rewards and costs she or he expects to get in an alternative relationship (Berg & McQuinn, 1986; Felmlee, Sprecher, & Bassin, 1990; Michaels et al., 1984; Rusbult, 1983). Thus, satisfaction is based not only on the individual's absolute level of rewards and costs, but also on the level of rewards and costs experienced relative to her or his CL and CL_{alt}. The same balance of rewards and costs may have different values for different individuals, because each individual's past experiences and understanding of others in similar situations is unique. These, in turn, affect their expectations (Sabatelli, 1984).

CL_{alt} is particularly important for explaining relationship stability (Rusbult, 1983; Thibaut & Kelley, 1959). Thus, even when the present outcome is less favorable than expected, an individual is only likely to disrupt or leave the present relationship if what is available in the best alternative relationship, or indeed from not being in a relationship, exceeds the outcome in the current relationship. Conversely, partners will feel more committed to the current relationship and will be more likely to stay in it if the outcomes they receive are better than what they expect to receive from the best alternative. In other words, CL_{alt} affects feelings of commitment within the relationship as well as relationship satisfaction (Floyd & Wasner, 1994; Kelley & Thibaut, 1978; Sprecher, 1998). Further, partners' relationship satisfaction may influence their evaluations of the attractiveness of alternative relationships (Johnson & Rusbult, 1989).

PARTNER SELECTION

A sexual relationship does not typically occur spontaneously on the first encounter between two strangers. Most people are choosey about whom they become sexually involved with, going through a process of partner selection that is influenced by a number of factors. A social exchange framework may help to explain this process (Sprecher, 1998).

Rewards and Costs

People tend to be attracted to and seek out individuals with whom the interaction is most rewarding (Huston & Burgess, 1979; Lott & Lott, 1974). According to Byrne's law of attraction, our attraction to another person is proportional to the rewards we get from the person relative to the total number of rewards and costs (Byrne, 1997; Byrne & Nelson, 1965; Byrne & Rhamey, 1965). That is, consistent with social exchange theory, the balance of rewards to costs is seen as the basis for attraction. Further, there are various types of rewards that may lead to and influence attraction: direct rewards and rewards by association. Direct rewards are the benefits an individual obtains from being with a particular partner. These benefits can be tangible rewards, such as money and status, or intangible rewards, such as love, attention, or the partner's characteristics (e.g., trustworthiness, intelligence, good looks). According to the law of attraction, people prefer partners who are similar to them in age, ethnic background, education, and attitudes because interacting with them tends to be more rewarding and less punishing than is interacting with someone who is quite dissimilar (Byrne, 1961; Byrne & Blaylock, 1963; Byrne, Clore, & Worchel, 1966; Byrne, Ervin, & Lamberth, 1970; Byrne, Griffitt, & Stefaniak, 1967; Newcomb, 1956). Rewarding interactions, in turn, result in positive affect. In contrast, interacting with someone who is dissimilar results in negative affect. Thus, people are attracted to partners who are more similar to them because "at its simplest level ... people like feeling good and dislike feeling bad" (Byrne, 1997, p. 425). Further, people are more likely to stay in rewarding relationships (Sprecher, 1998).

There are two possible explanations for why people find particular characteristics rewarding. Social constructionists argue that the social norms that children learn through socialization determine the characteristics that people find attractive (Schwartz & Rutter, 1998). That is, information children receive from society in general, from their subcultural, and from their families shapes their perceptions of which characteristics are attractive in a partner and which are not. Thus, it may be that people prefer physically attractive partners because they are aware of the value placed on physical attractiveness in Western cultures. As a result, they hold this value themselves and also believe that people will have a higher opinion of them if they are with a more attractive partner (Hyde, DeLamater, & Byers, 2004). Thus, the rewards and costs and resultant positive affect associated with having a more physically attractive partner may come from both internal and external sources. The halo effect associated with physical attractiveness may also contribute to attraction (Dion, Berscheid, & Walster,

1972). That is, especially on first encounter, people who are more physically attractive are perceived to possess other positive and rewarding qualities such as being more sexually warm and responsive, sociable, and intelligent. Thus, the degree to which an interaction is viewed as rewarding or costly appears to depend on how physically attractive one perceives one's partner to be. Finally, people may prefer partners with high social status and earning potential both for the tangible rewards (the materials things that go along with money and status) and well as for the intangible rewards (status by association).

Evolutionary theory also provides an explanation for why people prefer physically attractive partners and partners with higher social status—that is, find having a physically attractive or high status partner more rewarding than having a less attractive, lower status partner (Allgeier & Wiederman, 1994; Buss, 1994; Buss & Schmitt, 1993; also see Simpson, Wilson, & Winterheld, chapter 4, this volume, for a more complete discussion of evolutionary theory). In fact, evolutionary theory identifies physical attractiveness and resources as the key aspects of attraction. According to sexual strategies theory, men and women who selected mates based on certain preferences were more successful at producing offspring and passing on their genes. Attractiveness is an indication of good health and fertility. Thus, there may be a genetic basis to a preference for attractive partners because we have evolved from ancestors who preferred attractive partners and thus had greater reproductive success. However, the most successful reproductive strategies for men and women are not the same, and thus, men's and women's priorities in selecting a mate should differ. According to evolutionary theory, men who were particularly concerned with finding a mate who is healthy and fertile (and thus able to produce healthy offspring to carry on their genes) would have had the most evolutionary success. However, because women have relatively few pregnancies, their best strategy would have been to choose a mate who was able to provide them with material and emotional resources and who would invest these resources in any offspring, thus ensuring their survival.

From a social exchange perspective, the key issue is that we are more likely to select partners who provide more rewards and fewer costs. It is not as important to determine whether it is individuals' learning history, their environment, and/or their genetic heritage that makes them find particular characteristics rewarding or costly. In fact, it is likely that both evolved mechanisms and environmental influences affect the characteristics that we find rewarding (Buss & Schmitt, 1993; Schwartz & Rutter, 2000).

Consistent with social exchange theory, there have been a large number of studies that have supported the view that people tend to prefer partners who are more physically attractive, have high socioeconomic status, and are more similar to them (Berscheid & Walster, 1974; Byrne, 1997; Curran & Lippold, 1975; Dion, 1981; Feingold, 1990; Hatfield & Sprecher, 1986; Sprecher, Sullivan, & Hatfield, 1994). However, various rewards and costs may be more important at different relationship stages or depending on whether the individual is looking for a short-term or a long-term partner. Thus, initially and in short-term sexual relationships, physical attractiveness may be the most salient reward; at later stages and in long-term relationships physical attractiveness becomes relatively less important and value similarity, compatibility, role fit, and intrinsic attributes such as honesty and trustworthiness become more salient rewards (Huston & Burgess, 1979; Kenrick, Groth, Trost, & Sadalla, 1993; Kenrick, Sadalla, Groth, & Trost, 1990; Murstein 1972; Nevid, 1984; Regan & Berscheid, 1997; Shanteau & Nagy, 1979; Sprecher & Regan, 2002). Further, consistent with evolutionary theory, the most salient rewards and costs for men in the initial and developing stages of relationships may differ from the most salient rewards and costs for women. For example, research suggests that women's physical attractiveness may be more important to men, whereas wealth and socioeconomic status may be more salient to women (Sprecher et al., 1994; Taylor & Glenn, 1976; Udry & Eckland, 1984). Similarly, although the quality of communication is important to attraction for both men and women, it is more important for women than for men (Sprecher & Duck, 1994). Nonetheless, there is greater variability within genders than there is between men and women. These individual differences may be influenced by sociosexual orientation (Simpson & Gangestad, 1991; Simpson, Wilson, & Winterheld, chapter 4, this volume). Thus, for example, for some women physical attractiveness is more important than status; for some men status and resources are more important than physical attractiveness.

In addition to the rewards directly provided by a partner or potential partner, rewards can be obtained by being with someone under pleasant circumstances (i.e., rewards by association). That is, people tend to be attracted to those whom they meet in happy occasions, despite the fact that those people are not necessarily responsible for the pleasant situation (Brehm, 1995). They are also more attracted to people they meet when they are physically aroused even when the arousal is due to exercise or anxiety rather than to the partner (termed misattribution of arousal) (Dutton & Aron, 1974; White, Fishbein, & Rutstein, 1981). That is, individuals' perceptions of others affect their attraction to them. However, perceptions are affected not only by the characteristics of the potential partner but also by the perceiver's internal state, mood, surroundings, circumstances, etc.

Researchers have rarely examined costs associated with attraction directly; they have largely assumed that the absence of the qualities found to be rewards are experienced as costs—that is, low physical attractiveness, low social status, low intelligence, value dissimilarity, incompatibility, or poor role fit are experienced as costs. In addition, for some people, the partner's prior sexual experience may be experienced as a cost. In general, extensive sexual experience tends to be seen as a cost by both men and women, whereas moderate sexual experience is not (Jacoby & Williams, 1985; O'Sullivan, 1995; Sprecher, McKinney, & Orbuch, 1991). Although it is likely that people experience their partner's use of verbal or physically coercive methods to influence them to engage in sexual activity as costs, sexual coercion and its effect on partner selection has rarely (if ever) been investigated from an exchange perspective.

Sexual coercion in dating relationships is not uncommon (Christopher & Kisler, chapter 12, this volume; Craig, 1990; Hogben, Byrne, & Hamburger, 1996; McConaghy & Zamir, 1995; Shapiro & Schwarz, 1997). For example, Koss, Dinero, and Seibel (1988) found that more than half of the sexual assaults experienced by the university women in their sample were committed by a steady partner. Other researchers have also found that sexual assault committed by a dating partner is more common than is sexual assault committed by a stranger (Byers & O'Sullivan, 1998; Finkelhor & Yllo, 1985; O'Sullivan, Byers, & Finkelman, 1998; Russell, 1984). Although women experience sexual coercion more often than men do, women sometimes are sexually coercive with their male partners. For example, O'Sullivan et al. (1998) found that 19% of the male and 43% of the female university students they surveyed reported that they had experienced unwilling sexual activity in the previous year; 20% of the men and 9% of the women reported that they had used sexual coercion. Further, studies in both Canada and in the United States have found that 8% of women report having been sexually assaulted by a current or former spouse (Russell, 1982, 1984; Statistics Canada, 1993). In addition, both men and women report engaging in unwanted sex because their partners threatened to end the relationships or find new partners, made them feel guilty or inadequate, or questioned their sexuality (Muehlenhard & Cook, 1988). Experience of unwilling sex with a partner, whether through physical force or verbal coercion, has been shown to be associated with a number of negative psychological outcomes such as emotional upset, depression, anxiety, fear, feelings of betrayal and humiliation, decreased trust, self-blame, anger, and decreased sexual satisfaction (Byers & O'Sullivan, 1998; Koss et al., 1988; Muehlenhard, Goggins, Jones, & Satterfield, 1991; O'Sullivan et al., 1998; Resick, 1993). These outcomes are costs in and of themselves but also suggest that sexual coercion is experienced as a cost. However, sexual coercion does not necessarily lead directly to the breakup of the relationship. For example, Byers and Eastman (1979) found that of the women who reported a sexually coercive experience, 29% had been sexually coerced by the same partner on a previous occasion. Thus, it appears that people weigh the cost associated with unwanted sex against the rewards they experience in the relationship.

Equity/Equality

If equity/equality affects partner selection, then people should choose partners who have qualities that result in a balance between their own attractiveness (i.e., inputs) and their partners' attractiveness (i.e., outcomes). In fact, equity theorists proposed the "matching hypothesis" that argues that: individuals expect partners to be similar in socially desirable characteristics (e.g., physical attractiveness, social status, intelligence) to themselves; and, couples who are matched in their social desirability are likely to have a more satisfying and enduring relationships than are couples who are mismatched (Walster, Aronson, Abrahams, & Rottmann, 1966).

Studies testing the matching hypothesis by setting opposite sex pairs up on artificial dates have found only limited support for the matching hypothesis (Sprecher, 1998). For example, Walster et al. (1966) examined dating choices among students matched on physical attractiveness attending a large college dance organized by the investigators. Contrary to their predictions, they found that, regardless of the participants' own attractiveness, the main determinant of their liking for their date, desire to date them again, or actually asking for another date is the desirability of the partner. Thus, they found support for the role of rewards in partner selection, but not for equity. In contrast, studies conducted with existing couples have found evidence for matching on physical attractiveness and other desirable characteristics (Aron, 1988; Huston & Burgess, 1979; Murstein, 1972; Price & Vandenberg, 1979). This may be because in real life, people fear social rejection, an important cost in partner selection (Berscheid, Dion, Walster, & Walster, 1971; Murstein & Christy, 1976). Thus, although people prefer the most socially desirable person, they choose a person to whom they are matched in order to maximize rewards and minimize the possibility of rejection (Aron, 1988; Kalick & Hamilton, 1986; Murstein, 1972). In contrast, an individual who has little or no fear of rejection would tend to choose a much more difficult goal (e.g., a much more attractive partner). For example, Bernstein, Stephenson, Snyder, and Wicklund (1983) found that when the possibility of rejection is salient, males are less willing to approach an attractive female. In contrast, Huston (1973) demonstrated that individuals are likely to prefer a more attractive partner when the probability of acceptance is assured.

CL and CL$_{alt}$

There are many different potential rewards and costs in intimate relationships. Thus, couples can be matched in ways that may not be immediately obvious to an outside observer. Further, as the old expression goes, beauty is in the eye of the beholder. Thus, an individual's perception of potential rewards and costs in a relationship and of equity/equality in the relationship is likely more important than their actual physical attractiveness or similarity (Curran & Lippold, 1975; Walster et al., 1966). In turn, individuals compare their perceptions to the overall level of rewards and costs they feel that they should receive in a relationship—that is, to their comparison level (Sprecher, 1998). Individuals will be more likely to continue in the relationship if their perception of the balance of rewards and costs compares favorably to their expectations.

Researchers have not examined CL and partner selection in a comprehensive fashion. However, some findings can be best understood with reference to comparison level. For example Sprecher et al. (1991) found that extensive sexual experience, but not moderate sexual experience, is perceived to be less desirable in a mate. In other words, high sexual experience in a partner is a cost. This suggests that individuals have *expectations* of a suitable partner based on their own experiences and their perceptions of socially desirable characteristics and use these expectations to evaluate whether a particular individual is the partner that they deserve. The partner's prior sexual experiences would be one component of these expectations. Thus, individuals might conceal their own extensive sexual history, fearing that such knowledge on the part of the partner would lead to rejection. Alternatively, they would be less likely to stay in a relationship with a highly sexually experienced partner if they perceived extensive sexual experience as an important relationship cost. The point at which moderate sexual experience (not seen as undesirable) becomes extensive sexual experience (seen as undesirable) would also be made with respect to the individual's comparison level. Further, the level at which low levels of certain desirable characteristics becomes a cost (rather than just the absence of a reward) is also likely made with reference to comparison level, which in turn is affected by the individual's self-evaluation. For example, if a moderately physically attractive individual experiences high physical attractiveness or similarity as a reward, does he or she also experience average physical attractiveness and moderate similarity as rewards (albeit weaker ones)? As costs? As neither rewards nor costs? What about the person who is low on physical attractiveness? Several researchers have found that individuals who rate their own qualities more positively tend to have higher expectations of these qualities in an ideal partner suggesting that self-evaluation affects comparison level (Kenrick et al., 1993; Kenrick et al., 1990; Murray, Holmes, & Griffin, 1996; Sprecher & Regan, 2002).

CL_{alt} may play a part in sexual partner selection (Kerckhoff & Davis, 1962). For example, when there are no other attractive alternative partners available, an individual might choose a partner who offers fewer rewards or more costs than the individual feels that he/she deserves. Consistent with this hypothesis, Sprecher and Regan (2002) found that men who perceived that there were more available dating partners have higher standards for a potential partner on desirable traits than do men who perceived that there are fewer potential partners available. Partner availability did not affect women's standards for potential partners. Finally, people are more likely to stay in a relationship if the relationship compares favorably to available alternatives.

FREQUENCY OF SEXUAL ACTIVITY

Scant attention has been given to conceptualizing sexual frequency within intimate relationships from a social exchange perspective. In fact, most researchers have ignored the dyadic processes that determine whether sexual activity occurs. Yet, the occurrence of consensual sexual activity is the result of a process in which one partner first considers initiating sex and then transforms the desire into verbal or nonverbal actions, and the other partner responds to the sexual initiation positively (Byers & Heinlein, 1989). Given the interpersonal nature of sexual interactions, it is likely that both the initiation of sexual activity and responses to sexual initiations (as well as the resultant frequency of sexual activity) can be understood within the social exchange framework.

Rewards and Costs

Sexual initiations, responses to initiations, and the frequency of sex can be sexual rewards and costs in and of themselves. Lawrance and Byers (1995) assessed the rewards and costs of 94 men and 150 women in long-term relationships using the Rewards/Costs Checklist. They found that a little more than half of the men and women identified the frequency of sexual activity as being a reward in their sexual relationship; just under half of the men and women identified the frequency of sexual activity as being a cost in their sexual relationship. Several other items on the Rewards/Costs Checklist are also related to frequency of sexual activity including *who initiates sexual activity, how your partner responds to your sexual advances, the amount of spontaneity in your sex life,* and *having sex when you are not in the mood.* Between 28% and 64% of men and between 19% and 86% of women identified these items as sexual rewards; between 34% and 47% of men and between 17% and 65% of women identified these items as sexual costs.

Gender may influence the extent to which the frequency of sexual activity and sexual initiations are experienced as rewards or costs. Men initiate sex more frequently then women do (Blumstein & Schwartz, 1983; Byers & Heinlein, 1989; O'Sullivan & Byers, 1992). Further, Lawrance, Taylor, and Byers (1996) found that men are more instrumental and less expressive then are women in sexual situations. Sexual initiation is, of course, an instrumental behavior. These results are consistent with predictions based both on evolutionary theory (see Simpson, Wilson, & Winterheld, chapter 4, this volume). They are also consistent with the prescribed gender role scripts for sexual situations, termed the traditional sexual script. Further, there is evidence that the sexual script delineating expected behavior for men and women in sexual situations is evolving and now prescribes high instrumentality and high expressiveness for both women and men, although not yet equality (Schwartz, 1994). For example, Lawrance et al. (1996) also found that women think that ideally women should be more instrumental in sexual situations than they themselves are, and men think that men should be more expressive in sexual situations than they themselves are. Further, Lawrance and Byers (1995) found that men and women do not differ in the extent to which they endorsed the frequency of sexuality activity or who initiates sexual activity as generally a reward or a cost in their sexual relationship. In addition, Byers and her colleagues found that although women refuse sex more frequently then men do, this is because men initiate sex more frequently (Byers & Heinlein, 1989; O'Sullivan & Byers, 1992). There was no difference in how likely men and women are to respond positively or negatively to their partner's sexual initiation when the frequency of sexual initiations was controlled.

Sexual initiations, responses to a partner's initiation, and the frequency of sexual activity are also outcomes that may be affected by the overall levels of rewards and costs in the relationship. From a social exchange perspective, then, factors that positively or negatively influence this outcome, both sexual and nonsexual, can be viewed as rewards or costs. For example, low relationship satisfaction is associated with lower sexual frequency (Blumstein & Schwartz, 1983; Call, Sprecher & Schwartz, 1995; Laumann et al., 1994; Udry, Deven, & Coleman, 1982). A sexual difficulty or dysfunction on the part of one or both partners may be experienced as a sexual cost that affects sexual initiations and/or responses to initiations and thus sexual frequency (Byers & Heinlein, 1989; Frank, Anderson, & Rubinstein, 1978). Variables such as adherence to traditional gender roles and/or affective orientation toward sexuality (erotophobia–erotophilia) may affect whether parts of the sexual script related to sexual frequency (i.e., sexual initiations and/or responses to initiations), and indeed the nature and pleasurability of the sexual activities that couples engage in, are experienced as rewards or costs (Blumstein & Schwartz, 1983; Byers & Heinlein, 1989; Fisher, Byrne, White, & Kelley, 1988; O'Sullivan & Byers, 1992). Thus, these individual factors may also affect sexual frequency.

To determine the extent to which sexual rewards and costs—that is rewards and costs associated specifically with the sexual relationship—affect sexual frequency, we conducted additional analyses both on data from a study of individuals in dating relationships (Byers & Demmons, 1999; Byers et al., 1998) and on data from a study of individuals in long-term relationships (Lawrance & Byers, 1995). For the daters, the level of rewards ($r = .36$, $p < .001$) but not the level of costs ($r = .11$, $p > .10$.) is associated with reported sexual frequency over the previous 4 weeks. However, the individuals in long-term relationships with a higher sexual frequency report both a higher level of sexual rewards ($r = .69$, $p < .001$) and a lower level of sexual costs ($r = -.51$, $p < .001$). These results provide support for the role of rewards and costs in determining sexual frequency, particularly in long-term relationships. The frequently reported decrease in sexual frequency with marital duration, particularly early in the marriage, may be due to a decrease in how rewarding individuals find their sexual relationship due to habituation (Call et al., 1995). However, Liu (2003) found that although longer duration relationships are associated with decreased sexual quality (assessed in terms of pleasure and emotional satisfaction), this relationship is weak, accounting for only a small percentage of the variance in sexual quality. Thus, sex may become less frequent over the course of a relationship, but not necessarily less pleasurable (Schwartz & Rutter, 2000).

Not all individual and interpersonal factors that are associated with the frequency of sexual activity influence the sexual script in the same way. That is, some factors may have a greater impact on sexual initiations, whereas other factors may have a greater impact on responses to initiations. For example, Byers and Heinlein (1989) had 77 individuals in long-term heterosexual relationships keep a diary of the sexual initiations and responses to initiations (positive or negative) by themselves and their partner. They found that participants who are younger, are cohabiting rather than married, have been romantically involved for a shorter period of time, and are more relationally and sexually satisfied report more frequent sexual initiations. When the number of initiations was controlled, more frequent negative responses to initiations were associated with less sexual pleasure for the woman and the man and lower relational and sexual satisfaction. Thus, age, relationship status, and length of romantic involvement are associated with the number of sexual initiations but not with whether partners respond positively or negatively to sexual initiations. In contrast, the extent of the man's sexual pleasure and the woman's sexual pleasure are associated with sexual responses but not with sexual initiations. Sexual satisfaction and relationship satisfaction are associated with both initiations and responses. Therefore, it is important to consider sexual initiation and responses to initiations as well as sexual frequency not only as exchangeable resources but also as outcomes.

Equity/Equality

Insofar as sexual frequency, sexual initiations, and responses to sexual initiations are considered to be rewards and costs, inequity and/or inequality in perceived frequency or quality of initiations and positive responses to initiations may contribute to lower sexual satisfaction (Hatfield et al., 1979). In this view, partners' sexual initiations and responses to initiations are one type of resource to be exchanged for other types of resources (e.g., love, money, status) in the relationship. Therefore, in order to maintain equity in the relationship, an individual may reciprocate with love, attention, or other favors if her or his partner engages in unwanted sexual activity. However, it is unlikely that either partner will experience these types of nonsymmetrical exchanges as satisfactory for two primary reasons (Foa & Foa, 1974). According to Foa and Foa, people prefer exchanges with their intimate partner in which love (and by extension lovemaking) is exchanged for reciprocated love. In particular, the exchange of love for money or goods is unlikely to be satisfying. Second, lovemaking when freely given and enjoyable to both partners, enhances the amount of love and pleasure experienced by the partners. This is different than the exchange of some other resources, such as material possessions, in which giving decreases the amount available to the giver. In contrast, engaging in sexual activity with a partner who is disinterested is likely to be experienced negatively. The disinterested partner, in particular, is likely to find these experiences not just neutral but as unpleasant, particularly over time. This is particularly true for women (Lawrance & Byers, 1995). Perhaps as a result, perceived inequality in sexual interest (as manifested through initiations and responses to initiations) as well as disagreements regarding the frequency of lovemaking are a common source of conflict and distress in many relationships, regardless of perceived equality in other aspects of the relationship (Blumstein & Schwartz, 1983; Carlson, 1976; Frank et al., 1978). That is, partners' satisfaction with the relationship in general, and the sexual relationship in particular, is affected by the extent to which they perceive such exchanges as equitable or equal.

Insofar as sexual frequency is considered to be an outcome, inequity/inequality in both the sexual and nonsexual aspects of the relationship may affect sexual frequency. Thus, for example, sexual frequency is likely to be higher if partners perceive equity/equality in exchanges related to communication, emotional investment, material investment, sexual and emotional fidelity, and degree of arousal during sexual activity (Lawrance & Byers, 1995; Peplau, Rubin, & Hill, 1977; Regan & Sprecher, 1995; Walster, Walster, & Traupmann, 1978). Further, the same exchanges may be assigned different values by the two partners. That is, one partner may attribute more value to, for example, his/her own sexual initiation than the sexual initiation made by the partner. Regan and Sprecher (1995) found that women value their partner's initiation more than their own, whereas men value initiations by both themselves and their partner equally. Similarly, men and women report more pleasure for themselves and for their partner from sexual interactions that result from an initiation by the man than from an initiation by the woman (Blumstein & Schwartz, 1983; O'Sullivan & Byers, 1992). This may be because men and women were more comfortable with, and thus derive more pleasure from, male initiations, an expected part of the male gender role. Conversely, Lawrance and Byers (1995) found that women are more likely than men to experience their partner's responses to their sexual advances as a reward and having sex when they are not in the mood as a cost. In fact, most men and women indicate that they prefer the man to initiate sex more often than the woman does (Blumstein & Schwartz, 1983). Similarly, Lawrance et al. (1996) found that although gender roles in sexual situations are less stereotyped than are gender roles in nonsexual situations, men and women still believe that ideally men should be more instrumental than women should be. However, there is no difference in ratings of how expressive men and women should ideally be in sexual situations. This suggests that ideally men would initiate sexual activity more frequently than women (an instrumental response), but that men and women would be equally likely to respond positively to the partner's initiation (an expressive response). Thus, as a result of the different values they place on sexual initiations, positive or negative responses to initiations, and sexual frequency, individuals involved in an equal relationship may not necessarily perceive their relationship as equitable and may disagree about the fairness or equity of their contributions. In turn, perceptions of inequity may affect the frequency of sexual activity either directly or indirectly through reduced sexual satisfaction (Blumstein & Schwartz, 1983; Byers & Heinlein, 1989; Sprecher, 1998).

There has been little research evaluating the extent to which perceived inequity/inequality of rewards and costs affects sexual frequency as a relationship outcome. Yet, low sexual and relationship satisfaction has been shown to be associated with low sexual frequency suggesting that sexual frequency serves as both a reward and/or cost and as an outcome (Blumstein & Schwartz, 1983; Byers & Heinlein, 1989; Call et al., 1995; Laumann et al., 1994). However, additional analyses of our research involving individuals both in dating and in long-term relationships (Byers et al., 1998; Byers & Demmons, 1999; Lawrance & Byers, 1995) found only limited support for the impact of the perceived equality of sexual rewards and costs, specifically, on sexual frequency. Consistent with the social exchange framework, individuals in long-term relationships who report greater equality of sexual costs engage in somewhat more frequent sexual activity, $r's = .15$, $p < .05$. However, the relationship between equality of sexual rewards and sexual frequency is not significant. Similarly, the equality of rewards and costs is not associated with sexual frequency in dating couples.

CL and CL$_{alt}$

People may base their beliefs about the expected frequency of sexual activity, and indeed the expected frequency of sexual initiations and positive responses to initiations, on a number of factors. First, they may be influenced by what they believe is expected of them by their partners. For instance, Carlson (1976) found that 64% of husbands and 85% of wives report that they usually (or always) participate in sexual activities when their partner desires to and they do not. Second, perceptions of social norms may influence couples' sexual frequency. For example, people may engage in sexual activity more frequently than desired if they believe that their preferred frequency of sexual activity is lower than what is "normal" or expected for people of their age, gender, and situation (Christopher & Sprecher, 2000). Their perceptions of social norms may come from a number of sources including the media, their sexual frequency with previous partners, and/or their sexual frequency with the current partner earlier in the relationship. Thus, for example, in keeping with prescribed gender roles, men initiate sex more often than women do in both long-term and dating relationships (Byers & Heinlein, 1989; O'Sullivan & Byers, 1992). Finally, an individual's appraisal of how the overall levels of rewards and costs they receive in the relationship compare to their expected levels of rewards and costs may influence sexual frequency. In fact, reanalysis of the data from our studies with individuals in dating and long-term relationships found that individuals in long-term relationships engage in sexual activity more frequently if their sexual rewards are higher ($r = .58$, $p < .001$) and their sexual costs are lower ($r = -.28$, $p < .001$) than their expected levels of rewards and costs. We found similar results with respect to comparison level for rewards ($r = .38$, $p < .001$) and costs ($r = -.26$, $p < .01$) for individuals in dating relationships.

CL$_{alt}$ may impact both the frequency of sexual activity as well as satisfaction with the frequency of sexual interactions within the primary relationship. CL$_{alt}$ is based on the actual or potential sexual frequency that an available alternative relationship could offer. Of course, an individual's expectations of what an alternative relationship can offer may be unrealistic if her or his perceptions of social norms are inaccurate. They may also be unrealistic if the individual assumes that a high sexual frequency early on in an alternate relationship is likely to be maintained over the long term. There is considerable research to show that the frequency of sexual activity declines with relationship duration (Blumstein & Schwartz, 1983; Call et al., 1995; Greenblat, 1983; Laumann et al., 1994; Udry et al., 1982). An available alternative relationship that is, for instance, perceived as being more able to meet one's expectation regarding the desired sexual frequency may lead to greater dissatisfaction with the current relationship. In turn, relationship dissatisfaction can lead to a decrease in the frequency of sexual initiation or positive responses to initiations in the current relationship, and/or to seeking sex outside the relationship. Application of the social exchange framework to involvement in extradyadic relationships is discussed later in this chapter.

SEXUAL SATISFACTION

Sexual satisfaction is closely linked to sexual frequency, to a variety of other aspects of sexual relationships, as well as to overall relationship satisfaction. However, even though relationship variables offer a better prediction of sexual satisfaction than do individual characteristics, early research failed to consider the dyadic aspects of sexuality that contribute to sexual satisfaction. Instead researchers largely focused on individual attributes, such as personality (Lawrance & Byers, 1995). The social exchange framework is particularly helpful in understanding sexual satisfaction. In fact, in comparison to other areas of sexuality, sexual satisfaction has been more thoroughly considered from an exchange perspective, both by equity theorists (e.g., Hatfield et al., 1979), and in the Interpersonal Exchange Model of Sexual Satisfaction (IEMSS; Lawrance & Byers, 1992, 1995).

The IEMSS differs from earlier social exchange models in two primary ways. First, although it takes the nonsexual aspects of the relationship into account, it focuses specifically on how exchanges within the sexual relationship—that is, sexual exchanges—impact on sexual satisfaction. Second, it is more comprehensive than many of the other social exchange models in that it includes the balance of rewards and costs, comparison level for rewards and costs, and equality of rewards and costs. It does not, however, include comparison level for alternatives. According to the IEMSS, the most satisfying sexual relationship is one in which the level of sexual rewards exceeds the level of sexual costs, the perceived levels of sexual rewards and sexual costs compare favorably to what is expected, equality is perceived to exist between one's own and one's partner's levels of sexual rewards and costs, and relationship satisfaction is high (Lawrance & Byers, 1995). Further, sexual satisfaction is hypothesized to be influenced by the history of exchanges between partners, rather than resulting from the sexual rewards or costs at any one point in time. Therefore, temporarily unfavorable or unequal sexual rewards or costs will not necessarily decrease sexual satisfaction, whereas ongoing unfavorable or imbalanced levels of sexual rewards and costs will decrease sexual satisfaction. In a series of studies, Byers and her colleagues have demonstrated the validity and predictive utility (accounting for between 58% and 79% of the variance in sexual satisfaction) of the IEMSS for heterosexual Canadian individuals in dating and long-term relationships (Byers et al., 1998; Lawrance & Byers, 1995), and Chinese individuals in marital relationships (Renaud, Byers, & Pan, 1997). Further, they demonstrated that the model works equally well for men and women.

In the following sections, we review the contribution of each component of the social exchange perspective to sexual satisfaction in close relationships.

Rewards and Costs

Individuals who are more sexually satisfied experience a more favorable balance of rewards to costs as well as a higher number of sexual rewards and a lower number of sexual costs (Byers & Demmons, 1999; Lawrance & Byers, 1995; Renaud et al., 1997). Further, many of both the sexual and nonsexual factors that have been shown to be associated with sexual satisfaction are better conceptualized as rewards and/or costs (Lawrance & Byers, 1992, 1995). For example, high orgasmic consistency, sexual pleasure, frequent sexual activity, and sexual self-disclosure have been shown to be associated with greater sexual satisfaction but actually represent rewards associated with the sexual relationship (Byers & Demmons, 1999; Chesney, Blakeney, Cole, & Chan, 1981; Frank et al., 1978; Laumann et al., 1994; LoPiccolo & Steger, 1974; MacNeil & Byers, 1997; Perlman & Abramson, 1982; Pinney, Gerrard, & Denney, 1987). Low levels on these factors—that is, low orgasmic consistency, pleasure, or meaningful self-disclosure—may be experienced as costs. In addition, sexual difficulties/dysfunctions, concerns about sexual adequacy, and dissimilar levels of sexual desire between partners may be experienced as sexual costs and negatively affect sexual satisfaction (Byers & Grenier, 2003; Davidson & Darling, 1988; Grenier & Byers, 2001; MacNeil & Byers, 1997; Nathan & Joaning, 1985; Snyder & Berg, 1983).

Sexual self-disclosure may serve as a reward in two ways (Byers & Demmons, 1999; Cupach & Metts, 1991). First, sexual self-disclosure may be rewarding in and of itself by enhancing relationship closeness and intimacy. In fact, people who self-disclose more in general, and more about their sexual likes and dislikes in particular, appraise their communication more positively (Byers & Demmons, 1999). Further, 66% of men and 61% of women endorse the item *extent to which partners communicate about sex* on the Rewards/Costs Checklist as a sexual reward (Lawrance & Byers, 1995). Second, sharing their sexual likes and dislikes enables partners to negotiate mutually and maximally pleasurable sexual scripts that include more sexual rewards and fewer sexual costs. In turn, experiencing high sexual rewards and low sexual costs leads to greater sexual satisfaction (Byers & Demmons, 1999; Cupach & Comstock, 1990; Cupach & Metts, 1991; Gordon & Snyder, 1986; MacNeil & Byers, 1997; Metts & Cupach, 1989; Purnine & Carey, 1997). In contrast, a lack of sexual self-disclosure in the relationship makes it difficult for partners to be aware of and thus incorporate each other's sexual preferences. Thus, in the Lawrance and Byers (1995) study, 34% of the men and 42% of the women identify the *extent to which you communicate with your partner about sex* as a sexual cost.

Nonsexual aspects of the relationship may also influence sexual satisfaction (Byers et al., 1998; Sprecher & McKinney, 1993). For example, individuals who engage in more nonsexual self-disclosure report higher sexual satisfaction (Byers & Demmons, 1999; Chesney et al., 1981; Fowers & Olson, 1989; MacNeil & Byers, 1997; Schenk, Pfrang, & Rausche, 1983). In addition, perceptions of the quality of communication in general, including the quality of emotional self-disclosure and perceptions of the partner's empathy to one's feelings, can serve as rewards and are closely linked to perceptions of the quality of the relationship (Pinney et al., 1987; Tiefer, 1988). In turn, higher relationship satisfaction and/or adjustment are shown to be associated with higher sexual satisfaction in both dating and long-term relationships (Byers et al., 1998; Davies, Katz, & Jackson, 1999; Haavio-Mannila & Kontula, 1997; Henderson-King & Veroff, 1994; Lawrance & Byers, 1995; Young, Denny, Young, & Luquis, 2000). Further, changes in sexual satisfaction are associated with changes in relationship satisfaction (Sprecher, 2002). Thus, exchanges that influence relationship satisfaction, whether sexual or nonsexual, may also affect sexual satisfaction (Blumstein & Schwartz, 1983; Byers, 1999). For example, partners' experiences of feeling or not feeling loved, unresolved conflicts, and emotional closeness or distance negatively impact sexual satisfaction (Davidson & Darling, 1988; Schenk et al., 1983).

There may be some gender differences in the rewards and costs associated with sexual satisfaction. Feminist authors have argued that, compared with men's sexual satisfaction, women's sexual satisfaction may be less dependent on physical gratification and more dependent on the emotional and relational qualities of the sexual relationship (Loulan, 1984; McCormick, 1994; Poulin, 1992). Moreover, women may be more likely to include psychological aspects and the relational context into their expectations of sexual arousal and satisfaction (Pinney et al., 1987; Poulin, 1992; The Working Group, 2001). In keeping with this view, Lawrance and Byers (1995) found that although women and men did not differ in their levels of sexual rewards, sexual costs, or sexual satisfaction, they did differ in the frequency with which they report certain exchanges as sexual rewards or costs. Specifically, women are more likely than men to report rewards reflecting the emotional, relational qualities of the sexual partner such as *being with the same partner each time you have sex, how your partner responds to your sexual advances*, and *how your partner treats you when you have sex*. In contrast, women are more likely than men to report costs reflecting the physical, behavioral aspects of sexual interactions, such as *how easily you reach orgasm* and *engaging in sexual activities that you dislike but your partner enjoys*.

The relative contributions of sexual exchanges and nonsexual exchanges to sexual satisfaction may change over the course of the relationship (Byers, 1999). Byers and her colleagues found that both overall relationship satisfaction and sexual exchanges contribute independently to sexual satisfaction in both dating and long-term relationships (Byers et al., 1998; Lawrance & Byers, 1995). However, relationship satisfaction makes a larger contribution to the sexual satisfaction of individuals in dating relationships than it does to the sexual satisfaction of individuals in long-term relationships— accounting for 67% versus 49% of the variance (Byers, 1999). In contrast, after taking relationship satisfaction into account, sexual rewards and costs make a larger contribution to the sexual satisfaction of individuals in long-term relationships (31%) than individuals in dating relationships (8%). Thus, in new relationships sexual exchanges may contribute only a small amount to sexual satisfaction compared to partners' overall feelings about the relationship. That is, for the most part, if daters are satisfied with the relationship overall, they are satisfied with the sexual relationship. Sexual exchanges have a more major influence in long-term relationships in that sexual satisfaction is the result of high rewards and low costs in both the sexual and the nonsexual aspects of the relationship.

Finally, although most of the research has considered sexual satisfaction as an outcome, it is also possible that sexual satisfaction can serve as a reward or cost. As such, the level of sexual satisfaction may affect the nonsexual aspects of the relationship (e.g., relationship satisfaction, frequency of conflict) and/or other sexual aspects of the relationship (e.g., sexual frequency, orgasmic consistency).

Equity/Equality

Equity theorists argue that equity leads to relationship and sexual satisfaction (Hatfield et al., 1982; Hatfield et al., 1979). In contrast, inequity leads to distress. Distress, in turn, can affect sexual satisfaction directly or indirectly through its effect on relationship satisfaction. That is, if individuals feel that their own and their partner's gains from the relationship are relatively equal, sex is likely to be satisfying. Individuals in inequitable relationships, on the other hand, may not experience satisfying sexual encounters. Both the angry underbenefited partner and the guilty overbenefited partner are likely to have trouble responding to their partner sexually and enjoying receipt of sexual pleasures from them. In keeping with these predictions, Hatfield et al. (1982) found that respondents who felt equitably treated tend to experience higher sexual satisfaction than do inequitably treated respondents. Moreover, among the inequitably treated respondents, underbenefited individuals experience lower sexual satisfaction than do overbenefited individuals. In fact, overbenefited individuals have similar sexual satisfaction to individuals who feel equitably treated (Traupmann, Hatfield, & Wexler, 1983). Nonetheless, as this study was based on correlational data, it is also possible that high sexual satisfaction leads to the perception of equity in the relationship rather than vice versa, as proposed. Further, Hatfield and her colleagues did not assess specifically how equity in the sexual relationship affects sexual satisfaction, nor the extent to which equity contributes to sexual satisfaction over and above the contribution of the sexual rewards and costs experienced in the relationship.

Byers and her colleagues examined the contributions of equality (not equity) of sexual rewards and costs to sexual satisfaction (Byers et al., 1998; Lawrance & Byers, 1995). In keeping with social exchange theory, individuals who perceive that the sexual rewards and costs in their relationship are more equal report higher sexual satisfaction.

Further, even in their highly satisfied sample, the equality of sexual rewards and costs contribute to sexual satisfaction over and above the contribution of the actual levels of rewards and costs experienced by the individual. However, Schwartz (1994) argued that even though equality in long-term heterosexual relationships, including egalitarianism in the sexual part of the relationship, increases intimacy and sexual comfort, it may negatively affect sexual passion unless partners work to prevent the loss of eroticism by "reinventing sexual acts." According to Schwartz, this is because, traditionally, sexual passion comes from the tensions associated with the differences between partners. Nonetheless, the distance and differences inherent in inequitable relationships may not lead to a mutually satisfying sexual script even if they are associated with passion.

All of these studies measured *perceived* equality between partners rather than directly comparing the actual levels of rewards and costs experienced by both partners directly. Byers and MacNeil (2003) studied both members of couples in long-term relationships. They found that the men's reports of their sexual rewards and costs add uniquely to the prediction of women's sexual satisfaction over and above the women's reports of their own sexual rewards and costs. Similarly, women's reports of their own sexual rewards and costs add uniquely to the prediction of men's sexual satisfaction. These results provide further support for the dyadic nature of sexual satisfaction. Both partner's experiences in the sexual interaction contribute to each partner's individual sexual satisfaction.

CL and CL$_{alt}$

Prior to the development of the IEMSS, researchers largely overlooked the contribution of CL to sexual satisfaction. Yet, Michaels et al. (1984) illustrated that comparison level accounts for substantially more variance in relationship satisfaction than equity or equality does. Further, in a study conducted by Lawrance and Byers (1992), most respondents (75%) report that they compare their current level of sexual rewards to a "general notion of how rewarding a sexual relationship should be" when evaluating their level of rewards. The majority of the participants (79%) also use this general guideline to evaluate their level of costs in the sexual relationship. Byers and her colleagues have shown that both comparison level for sexual rewards and comparison level for sexual costs are associated with sexual satisfaction such that individuals who evaluate their sexual rewards and costs favorably in comparison to their expectations report higher sexual satisfaction (Byers & Demmons, 1999; Lawrance & Byers, 1995). Further, these studies demonstrated that CL contributes to sexual satisfaction over and above the contribution of the actual level of sexual rewards and costs experienced in the relationship for both individuals in dating and in long-term relationships. This is important because research suggests that levels of rewards are highest in the early stage of a relationship, then decrease as the relationship continues (Greenblat, 1983; Hatfield & Rapson, 1993). Thus, it appears that the discrepancy between sexual rewards and costs experienced and those expected may remain relatively stable because, even if the balance of rewards to costs decreases over time, comparison level also varies over time.

Comparison level for alternatives has mainly been discussed in terms of the stability of the relationship and therefore is not included in the IEMSS. However, Floyd and Wasner (1994) argued that partners' overall satisfaction with their primary relationship affects their evaluation of the desirability of available alternatives. In other words, the available alternatives are judged less favorable when individuals' satisfaction with the primary relationship is high. Consistent with this view, Johnson and Rusbult (1989) found that people who are satisfied and committed to their relationship tend to devalue alternative opportunities that threaten their present relationship.

Therefore, the CL_{alt} may affect sexual satisfaction directly by reducing the attractiveness of other available alternatives. Alternatively, CL_{alt} may impact sexual satisfaction indirectly through its effect on relationship satisfaction.

EXTRADYADIC SEXUAL ACTIVITY

Every close relationship, and especially those that include a sexual component, encompasses some degree of exclusivity (Bringle & Buunk, 1991; McKinney & Sprecher, 1991). However, extradyadic relationships are far from rare. For example, in their well-sampled probability study, Laumann et al. (1994) found that 25% of the married men and 15% of the married women report having engaged in extramarital sex at least once. Canadian survey results, albeit from less comprehensive surveys, put the estimates for married Canadian men and women somewhat lower (Hyde et al., 2004). Individuals in dating relationships also engage in extradyadic sexual behavior, although men are more likely to do so than are women. For example, in one study of college students, 65% of the men and 49% of the women had experienced extradyadic kissing and fondling; 49% of the men and 31% of the women had experienced extradyadic sexual intercourse (Wiederman & Hurd, 1999). Nonetheless, there is a general disapproval of extradyadic involvement—that is, sex outside of the committed relationship (Bibby & Posterski, 1995; Christopher & Sprecher, 2000; Laumann et al., 1994; Lieberman, 1988; Thornton & Young-DeMarco, 2001; Wiederman, 1997). Thus, 77% of Americans and 60% of Canadians agree that extramarital sex is "always wrong." That is, implicit in most intimate sexual relationships is the assumption of exclusivity. Nonconsensual extradyadic involvement violates this basic assumption (Bringle & Buunk, 1991; Glenn & Weaver, 1979; McKinney & Sprecher, 1991; Thompson, 1984). The social exchange framework may provide some insight into why a significant percentage of people nonetheless engage in extradyadic sexual activity (Hatfield, Traupmann, Sprecher, Utne, & Hay, 1985; Sprecher, 1986, 1998; Walster et al., 1973; Walster, Walster, & Berscheid, 1978).

Rewards and Costs

Lawrance and Byers (1995) found that being with the same partner during each sexual encounter is identified as a sexual reward by most individuals (93% of women and 76% of men). Similarly, Regan and Sprecher (1995) found that both women and men rate being sexually faithful as one of the most valuable contributions to a relationship, although women value their own faithfulness more than men value their own sexual faithfulness. In keeping with this finding, Lawrance and Byers also found that only 19% of men and 5% of women identify being with the same partner during each sexual encounter as a sexual cost. Thus, sexual faithfulness is likely to be a reward in most relationships. However, men are more likely than women are to experience being with only one partner as a cost and thus to see extradyadic involvement as a reward. From a social constructionist perspective, this is because the traditional gender script prescribes high sexual interest in general, and in sexual variety in particular, for men (Byers, 1996; Zilbergeld, 1999). However, men's greater interest and involvement in extradyadic sexual activity is also consistent with evolutionary theory (see Guerrero, Spitzberg, & Yoshimura, chatper 13, this volume). Parental investment theory argues that men's best strategy for ensuring their genetic success is to engage in sex with (and thus impregnate) as many different women as possible. Thus, men who find having multiple partners rewarding would have been more successful at passing on their genes. In contrast, the best reproductive strategy for women (who are able to have relatively few pregnancies during their lifetime) is to have a mate who provides resources to ensure the survival of any offspring. Thus, women who were successful at maintaining this type of relationship would have had more reproductive success than would women who had multiple partners who were not invested in them and their offspring. Thus, according to evolutionary theory, men's great interest in extradyadic sexual activity is a result of our genetic heritage. It should be noted, however, that although both the social constructionist and the evolutionary arguments explain why more men than women are interested in and engage in extradyadic sexual activity, they do not explain why most men experience being with the same partner every time they have sex as a reward and only a minority of men experience it as a cost.

Researchers have invested a considerable amount of effort into identifying factors associated with extradyadic involvement (Hansen, 2001). Individual differences in sociosexual attitudes, preferences, and behaviors may explain some of the differences in whether the novelty of a new partner is experienced as a reward and the familiarity of an intimate partner is experienced as a cost (see Simpson et al., chapter 4, this volume, for a review). For example, individual characteristics such as liberal attitudes, perceived need for sexual variety, and desire for autonomy and freedom have been shown to be associated with extradyadic behavior (Buunk, 1980; Knapp & Whitehurst, 1977; Maykovich, 1976). These individual factors may be thought of as costs associated with being in a committed sexual relationship and/or as rewards resulting from extradyadic involvement. These rewards and costs, then, contribute to the likelihood that an individual will engage in extradyadic sexual activity. Thus, for example, the individual with a high perceived need for sexual freedom or a more unrestricted sociosexual orientation is more likely to experience sexual exclusivity as a cost. For this individual, the experience of sexual freedom or of partner novelty associated with extradyadic sexual involvement may be experienced as a reward. Of course, if the sexual activity violates the partner's expectations regarding exclusiveness in the relationship, the partner is likely to experience such extradyadic involvement as a cost. Further, most partners interpret sexual infidelity as an act of betrayal and thus, experience anger and jealousy as a result of the perceived threat to the relationship (Metts, 1994; Roscoe, Cavanaugh, & Kennedy, 1988). These emotions—betrayal, anger, sexual jealousy—are also likely experienced as costs. Jealousy itself may serve an evolutionary function in that jealousy would tend to increase reproductive success by helping to maintain the pair bond and thus increasing parental investment in the offspring (Buss, 1988; also see Guerrero, Spitzberg, & Yoshimura, chapter 13, this volume, for a more complete discussion of jealousy).

Extradyadic involvement may also be an outcome of rewards and costs experienced in the nonsexual aspects of the relationship. For example, dissatisfaction with the primary relationship, indicative of high costs relative to rewards, is one of the most frequently reported reasons for extradyadic involvement (Bell, Turner, & Rosen, 1975; Hunt, 1974). These relationship-specific sexual and nonsexual rewards and costs such as revenge/anger/jealousy, emotional dissatisfaction, and sexual dissatisfaction, in turn can influence whether an individual engages in extradyadic sexual activity (Bell et al., 1975; Buunk, 1980; Greene, Lee, & Lustig, 1974; Roscoe et al., 1988). However, research results suggest that relationship dissatisfaction plays only a minor role in predicting who will engage in extradyadic sexual activity (Christopher & Sprecher, 2000).

Equity/Equality

Hatfield and her colleagues argued that inequity contributes to relationship dissatisfaction and, therefore, to the likelihood of engaging in extradyadic sexual behavior (Walster, 1978; Walster, Traupmann, & Walster, 1978; see also Schwartz, 1994). According to equity theory, both the overbenefited and the underbenefited partner in a relationship experience some degree of psychological distress as a result of the perceived imbalance in the relationship. That is, overbenefited partners tend to experience slight guilt and uneasiness due to the fact that they perceive themselves to gain more from the relationship than their partner does. However, underbenefited partners tend to experience significant distress, anger, sadness, and frustration, as well as lower relationship satisfaction (Hatfield et. al., 1985; Sprecher, 1986; Walster et al., 1973; Walster, Walster, & Berscheid, 1978). Thus, underbenefited partners are more motivated and more likely than are overbenefited partners to engage in extradyadic relationships as one way in which they can restore equity to their relationship and thereby relieve their psychological distress. Consistent with this view, Walster, Traupmann, and Walster (1978) found that married individuals who felt underbenefited have more extramarital relationships than do either overbenefited individuals or individuals who felt their relationship was equitable. Further, among individuals who engaged in extradyadic sex, people who felt underbenefited tended to have their extradyadic relationships earlier in the relationship than did people who felt that they were either overbenefited or in an equitable relationship. Similarly, Prins, Buunk, and VanYperen (1993) found that, compared to women in equitable relationships, Dutch women who felt overbenefited or underbenefited in their global relationship have more extradyadic involvement and desire more extradyadic involvement. Further, inequity influenced extradyadic involvement over and above the contribution of overall relationship distress and normative disapproval. However, extradyadic involvement is not related to the quality of the relationship for men.

According to equity theorists, there are three reasons why individuals get involved in extradyadic relationships (Prins et al., 1993; Sprecher, 1998). First, as previously noted, extradyadic involvement may be an attempt to restore equity in a relationship. Extradyadic involvement may also be an attempt to establish equity through an alternative relationship, termed the equity-with-the-world phenomenon. That is, the underbenefited partner may feel entitled to engage in extradyadic affairs and seek compensations in an alternative relationship (Austin, 1974, cited in Sprecher, 1998). Finally, individuals in an inequitable relationship may engage in extradyadic activities because they are planning to terminate the unfair relationship, termed "leaving the field."

Individuals who learn of the clandestine extradyadic sexual behavior of their partner typically experience jealousy and may do a number of different things in an attempt to re-establish equity (Rusbult, Zembrodt, & Gunn, 1982). Some of these responses have a positive effect on the relationship, whereas others have a negative effect. For example, arguing, accusing, leaving the relationship, withdrawing emotionally or sexually, exhibiting extreme jealousy, using violence, seeking revenge, and reciprocating the extradyadic sexual behavior are responses that are likely to be experienced as costs by one or both partners. Thus, these behaviors can be both a cause and an effect of the inequity. In contrast, some responses such as discussing problems in the relationship that led to the extradyadic involvement, addressing the inequity in the relationship, seeking therapy, and renewing or increasing commitment to the relationship can be constructive for the relationship. Nonetheless, extradyadic sexual involvement is often a factor leading to divorce, suggesting that attempts to reestablish equity were unsuccessful (Betzig, 1989; Parker & Drummond-Reeves, 1993). It is likely that individual and relationship characteristics affect the partner's response. For example, Feldman and Cauffman (1999) found that individuals with an unrestricted sociosexual orientation are more likely to see extradyadic involvement as an acceptable response to their partner's infidelity.

CL and CL$_{alt}$

Individuals' *expectations* of the relationship may also be a factor that influences the occurrence of extradyadic sexual behavior, regardless of whether the relationship is equitable or equal. That is, an individual may engage in an extradyadic relationship because the primary relationship falls short of his/her expectations. The unfavorable balance of rewards and costs compared to expectations may occur either in the sexual or in the nonsexual parts of the relationship. On the other hand, individuals may be less likely to become involved in an extradyadic affair if their balance of rewards and costs is more favorable than expected. This may help to explain why some individuals do not engage in extradyadic activity even though they feel that the relationship is inequitable or unequal.

The important comparison may not be to expectations within the relationship but rather to social expectations. Thus, the traditional sexual script may explain, in part, why men are more likely to engage in extradyadic sexual behavior than women are. According to the traditional sexual script, men are more interested in sex in general and sex with multiple partners than are women (Byers, 1996; Zilbergeld, 1999). These different expectations for women and men may be a result of socialization, our genetic heritage, or both. Whatever the source, men are more likely to believe that it is acceptable for them, or at least normative, to engage in extradyadic sexual behavior. In turn, having a reference group that supports nonmonogamy and places a lower value on fidelity has been shown to play a role in facilitating extradyadic sexual behavior (Bringle & Buunk, 1991; Christopher & Sprecher, 2000). Consistent with this view, Prins et al. (1993) found that the quality of the relationship predicted extradyadic involvement for men but not for women. According to the authors, these findings reflect the double standard in that women feel that they need a better reason to justify their extradyadic involvement than men do. However, they are also consistent with an evolutionary explanation.

The availability of alternative attractive relationships may also influence extradyadic behavior (Felmlee et al., 1990; Kelley & Thibaut, 1978; Thibaut & Kelley, 1959). According to Berscheid and Campbell (1981), available alternatives may be the main reason that people in equitable relationships engage in extradyadic sexual behavior. The unavailability of attractive alternatives, on the other hand, may be an important reason why people do not engage in extradyadic behaviour, even though they would find these experiences rewarding or perceive their relationship as inequitable. In addition, the extent of investment in the primary relationship may explain why some people stay in an unsatisfying (sexual) relationship when a better alternative is available (Rusbult, 1980, 1983). Rusbult argued that CL_{alt}, relationship satisfaction, and the degree of investment in the relationship all contribute to relationship commitment. Individuals who are committed to their relationship are more likely to derogate attractive alternatives than those who are not committed (Johnson & Rusbult, 1989; Simpson, Gangestad, & Lerma, 1990). Alternatively, commitment may enhance the costs of extradyadic involvement (guilt, fear of the consequences of the partner finding out), and thus decrease the likelihood of extradyadic involvement.

CL and CL_{alt} may also affect an individual's response to his or her partner's extradyadic involvement (White & Mullen, 1989). Thus, it is likely that people compare their own attractiveness to the attractiveness of the person the partner was involved with. Their emotional and behavioral responses are likely influenced both by this comparison as well as by their perception of how likely they would be to find a more desirable partner.

CONCLUSIONS AND DIRECTIONS FOR FUTURE RESEARCH

The social exchange framework was developed to explain relationships in general rather than sexuality in intimate relationships specifically. Nonetheless, social exchange theory has great potential for explaining a wide range of sexual behaviors and experiences. Past research from a social exchange perspective has tended to employ one of the social exchange models (e.g., reinforcement theory, equity theory, independence theory) that include some but not all of the social exchange components reviewed in this chapter. Even so, research conducted within each of these models has been successful at predicting various aspects of sexual behavior. For example, there is good evidence that equity affects extradyadic behavior; that the balance of rewards and costs, comparison level, and equality affect sexual satisfaction; etc. However, we have argued that to gain a full understanding of the complex ways in which dyadic partners influence each other and influence the sexual relationship, it is important to consider all four social exchange components—the balance of rewards and costs, equity/equality, comparison level, and comparison level for alternatives. Research based on a complete social exchange model is likely to provide a more powerful explanation of sexual behavior within intimate relationships than past research has because, taken together, the social exchange components take into account the impact of individual, dyadic, cognitive, and affective processes on sexual behavior. Thus, the balance of rewards and costs captures the unique contributions and experiences that each partner brings to the relationship. Partners' perceptions of equity/equality within the relationship captures the dyadic aspects of the relationship and the fact that the experiences of each partner influences the experiences and behavior of the other partner. Comparison level and comparison level for alternatives capture the contributions of cognitive appraisals, and resulting affect, to experiences of exchanges in the relationship.

There are a number of possible reasons why, despite its promise, there has been relatively little research examining intimate sexuality from the social exchange perspective. First, much of the research in the sexuality area has focused on the individual and has largely ignored the interpersonal context in which sexual activity occurs (Christopher & Sprecher, 2000; McKinney & Sprecher, 1991). This may be because, from both a methodological and a data analysis perspective, it is easier to conduct research with individuals than with couples. Second, research in many areas of sexuality has proceeded atheoretically. That is, there is relatively little research testing any theory explaining sexual behavior, not just little research from a social exchange perspective. Although there is a considerable body of research testing evolutionary predictions regarding some aspects of sexual behavior, this research tests distal causes of sexual behavior—that is, our genetic heritage. Social exchange theory, in contrast, tests proximal causes of sexual behavior and experiences. Regardless of the distal causes (genetics, socialization), social exchange theory has the potential to provide insight into the behavior and choices of individuals within relationships.

Finally, it may be that researchers are put off by a perception that social exchange theory is mechanistic and thus passionless—that is, that the social exchange perspective proposes that people operate on a quid pro quo (tit for tat) basis in which they consciously weigh their rewards, costs, and alternatives and make rational decisions about their behavior (O'Sullivan, personal communication, February 28, 2003). Certainly, research has generally shown that relationships based on a quid pro quo rather than a communal approach tend to be less satisfying rather than more satisfying. Further, people are not good at predicting outcomes and thus, probably do not select the best course of action by weighing the pros and cons of various courses of action (Goldstein & Hogarth, 1997; Tversky & Kahneman, 1974). However, the social exchange perspective does not preclude an affective component. For example, Lawrance and Byers (1995) argued that sexual satisfaction *is an affective response arising from one's subjective evaluation of the positive and negative dimensions associated with one's sexual relationship* (p. 268). Thus, they distinguish satisfaction from purely affective constructs such as happiness and from purely evaluative constructs such as success. Further, social exchange theory proposes that behavior is affected by the history of exchanges in the relationship and not by exchanges at one point in time (see Lawrance & Byers, 1995, for support for this proposition with respect to sexual satisfaction). Similarly, it is likely that the affective responses to exchanges in a close relationship as well as the resultant sexual behavior, such as those discussed in this chapter (partner selection, sexual frequency, extradyadic sexual behavior), are based on an affective response to subjective evaluation of overall rewards, costs, equity/equality, comparison level, and comparison level for alternatives over an extended period of time.

From the social exchange perspective, there are a number of promising directions that future research on sexuality in close relationships could take. Some of these are indentified in the following sections.

Testing the Complete Social Exchange Framework

Researchers need to examine various aspects of sexuality within close relationships using the complete social exchange framework. This would have a number of advantages over testing only parts of the model. First, it would allow researchers to determine the extent to which the complete social exchange framework accounts for each of these sexual behaviors. Second, it would allow researchers to evaluate both the unique impact and the relative importance of each social exchange component on each of these behaviors. For example, does the balance of rewards and costs predict sexual initiations and responses to initiations? Does equity/equality add to the prediction of initiations and responses over and above the contribution of the balance of rewards and costs? Does comparison level and/or comparison level for alternatives? Which component is most strongly linked to these behaviors and to sexual frequency? Similar questions could be asked about the other sexual behaviors reviewed in this chapter as well as about aspects of sexual behavior in close relationships that have not yet been examined from a social exchange perspective such as contraceptive use and sexual coercion/unwanted sexual activity.

Sexual Exchanges Versus Global Exchanges

Most of the research from the social exchange perspective has examined the contributions of exchanges in the overall relationship rather than of sexual exchanges specifically. Thus, with the exception of sexual satisfaction, the importance of sexual exchanges to various aspects of sexual functioning is not known (Sprecher, 1998). For example, equity theorists examined the impact of global equity but not sexual equity on extradyadic sexual activity. This is problematic because the balance of sexual rewards and costs may differ considerably from the balance of nonsexual rewards and costs. Similarly, there may be differences between comparison level and perceptions of equity with respect to the sexual and nonsexual aspects of the relationship. For example, Sprecher (2001) found that equity in the sexual relationship is unrelated to global equity. It is likely that both sexual and nonsexual exchanges play a role in sexual behavior in close relationships. Thus, it is important to examine the specific contribution of sexual exchanges over and above the contribution of global exchanges on various aspects of sexual functioning.

In addition, although social exchange theory proposes that it is the overall balance of rewards and costs that affects sexual behavior, it is likely that not all sexual rewards and costs have the same impact on sexuality in close relationships. Thus, it would be interesting to know which rewards and costs contribute the most to perceptions of the overall balance of sexual rewards and costs, or to the perceived equity/equality of sexual rewards and costs. For example, for some individuals, sex that occurs less frequently than desired may contribute to the perception of a high level of costs relative to rewards, even if lovemaking is highly satisfying when it does occur. For others, the frequency of sexual activity may have less impact on overall perceptions than the quality of lovemaking.

Examining Changes Over the Developmental Course of the Relationship

There has been little research from the social exchange framework that has taken a lifespan perspective on sexuality in close relationships. Yet, relationships are not static but rather are constantly evolving and subject to reevaluation as a result of new input from within and without. Researchers need to determine whether the social exchange perspective is equally applicable to couples at different relationship stages. Researchers also need to examine the developmental course of each of the exchange components, as well as changes in their impact on the sexual relationship over the life course of the relationship. They also need to go beyond investigating the early stages of relationships to determining, from an exchange perspective, how partners influence each other and share meaning (Duck, 1991). For example, how do the levels and types of sexual rewards and costs change over the course of a relationship? How does comparison level change? Sprecher (2001) found that perceptions of sexual equity remain only somewhat stable and that men and women tend to feel more sexually underbenefited over time. What factors account most for a move from perceptions of equity to perceptions of inequity—increased costs, decreased rewards, comparison level? How do these changes in perceived equity impact the sexual relationship? It is also important to determine the relative importance of the various social exchange components at different relationship stages. For example, Byers (1999) found that sexual exchanges have a larger impact on the sexual satisfaction of individuals in long-term relationships than they do on the sexual satisfaction of daters.

Extending Research to Include Neglected Populations

For the most part, the extent to which the social exchange perspective is applicable to persons from ethnocultural minority groups in North America, to other countries and cultures, to gay men and lesbians, to older adults, and to distressed couples is not known. Thus, for the most part, the applicability of the social exchange framework to close sexual relationships in these diverse populations has yet to be demonstrated (see Renaud et al., 1997, and Steinman, 1990, for exceptions). For example, it would be interesting to examine the utility of the social exchange model in predicting extra-dyadic sexual activity among gay couples because studies show that many gay couples value sexual exclusivity less than do heterosexual couples (Kurdek, 1991). Similarly, it would be useful to examine differences in the contribution of sexual equity/equality to sexuality in close relationships between cultures with more egalitarian gender roles and those with less egalitarian gender roles. In addition, most research from a social exchange perspective has been conducted with relatively satisfied couples. This leaves a number of questions unanswered. For example, how well does a social exchange framework fit for couples with a sexual dysfunction? Does relationship or sexual distress affect each of the social exchange components equally or some components more than others? Can the social exchange perspective help to explain why some couples who have a sexual dysfunction nonetheless report high sexual satisfaction while others do not (Frank et al., 1978; MacNeil & Byers, 1997)?

Extending Research to Neglected Topics

There are some aspects of sexuality in close relationships that have yet to be examined from a social exchange perspective such as unwanted sexual activity, sexual self-disclosure, and contraceptive use, to name three. For example, how does unwanted sexual activity affect perceptions of the overall balance of sexual rewards to sexual costs? To what extent do perceptions of coercive behavior as rewarding in and of itself, or of sexual behavior with an unwilling partner as rewarding rather than costly, contribute to use of sexual coercion? To what extent does comparison level affect use of sexual coercion? Research has shown that there are a number of beliefs associated with use of sexual coercion in close relationship including the belief that partners have a right to sex (Muehlenhard et al., 1991). How do these beliefs affect perceptions of rewards and costs or comparison level? How do beliefs that equate sex with love affect perceptions of equity/equality? Might there be a downside to expectations of equality if partners experience these expectations as meaning that they do not have the right to refuse their partner's sexual initiations (Braun, Gavey, & McPhillips, 2003)? That is, are there some inherent pressures and obligations in expectations for reciprocity that may be experienced as costs if this means that partners engage in unwanted sex?

Also it would be interesting to examine the dynamics of self-disclosure associated with sexual exchanges. For example, how does communication of sexual likes and dislikes affect the sexual exchange components such as perceptions of equality/equity? Conversely, how does the perceived balance of rewards and costs affect sexual self-disclosure? That is, do people self-disclose more in more favorable or less favorable sexual relationships? There is some evidence that sexual rewards and costs mediate the relationship between sexual self-disclosure and sexual satisfaction in dating relationships (Byers & Demmons, 1999). However the extent to which the exchange components moderate or mediate the relationship between sexual communication and other sexual behaviors and outcomes has not been investigated.

SUMMARY

We have argued that the social exchange perspective can provide insight into various aspects of sexuality in close relationships. All four of the components—balance of rewards to costs, equity/equality, comparison level, and comparison level for alternatives—appear to be useful in explaining the four important aspects of sexuality in close relationships examined in this chapter. Yet there remain a large number of unanswered questions that could be fruitful if examined from the social exchange perspective. Future research needs to provide a more systematic and comprehensive application of social exchange theory to the range of sexual behaviors that occur over the developmental course of close relationships and to do so with diverse populations.

REFERENCES

Allgeier, E. R., & Wiederman, M. (1994). How useful is evolutionary theory for understanding contemporary human sexual behavior? *Annual Review of Sex Research, 5*, 218–256.

Aron, A. (1988). The matching hypothesis reconsidered again: Comment on Kalick and Hamilton. *Journal of Personality and Social Psychology, 54*, 441–446.

Bell, R. R., Turner, S., & Rosen, L. (1975). A multivariate analysis of female extramarital coitus. *Journal of Marriage and the Family, 37*, 375–384.

Berg, J. H., & McQuinn, R. D. (1986). Attraction and exchange in continuing and noncontinuing dating relationships. *Journal of Personality and Social Psychology, 50*, 942–952.

Bernstein, W. M., Stephenson, B. O., Synder, M. L., & Wicklund, R. A. (1983). Causal ambiguity and heterosexual affiliation. *Journal of Experimental Social Psychology, 19*, 78–92.

Berscheid, E., & Campbell, B. (1981). The changing longevity of heterosexual close relationships: A commentary and forecast. In M. J. Lerner & S. C. Lerner (Eds.), *The justice motive in social behaviour* (pp. 209–234). New York: Plenum.

Berscheid, E., Dion, K., Walster, E., & Walster, G. W. (1971). Physical attractiveness and dating choice: A test of the matching hypothesis. *Journal of Experimental Social Psychology, 7*, 173–184.

Berscheid, E., & Walster, E. (1974). Physical attractiveness. In L. Berkowitz (Ed.), *Advances in experimental social psychology* (pp. 157–215). New York: Academic Press.

Betzig, L. (1989). Causes of conjugal dissolution: A cross-cultural study. *Current Anthropology, 30*, 654–676.

Bibby, R. W., & Posterski, Donald, D. (1995). *The Bibby Report: Social trends Canadian style.* Toronto: Stoddart.

Blumstein, P., & Schwartz, P. (1983). *American couples.* New York: Morrow.

Braun, V., Gavey, N., & McPhillips, K. (2003). The "fair deal"? Unpacking accounts of reciprocity in heterosex. *Sexualities, 6*, 237–261.

Brehm, S. S. (1995). *Intimate Relationships* (2nd ed.). New York: McGraw-Hill.

Bringle, R. G., & Buunk, B. P. (1991). Extradyadic relationships and sexual jealousy. In K. McKinney, & S. Sprecher (Eds.), *Sexuality in close relationships* (pp. 135–153). Hillsdale, NJ: Lawrence Erlbaum Associates.

Buss, D. M. (1988). From vigilence to violence: Tactics of mate retention in American undergraduates. *Ethology and Sociobiology, 9*, 291–317.

Buss, D. M. (1994). *The evolution of desire: Strategies of human mating.* New York: Basic Books.

Buss, D. M., & Schmitt, D. P. (1993). Sexual strategies theory: An evolutionary perspective on human mating. *Psychological Review, 100*, 204–232.

Buunk, B. (1980). Extramarital sex in the Netherlands. *Alternative Lifestyles, 3*, 11–39.

Byers, E. S. (1996). How well does the traditional sexual script explain sexual coercion?: Review of a program of research. *Journal of Psychology and Human Sexuality, 8*, 7–25.

Byers, E. S. (1999). The interpersonal exchange model of sexual satisfaction: Implications for sex therapy with couples. *Canadian Journal of Counselling, 33*, 95–110.

Byers, E. S., & Demmons, S. (1999). Sexual satisfaction and sexual self-disclosure within dating relationships. *The Journal of Sex Research, 36*, 180–189.

Byers, E. S., Demmons, S., & Lawrance, K. (1998). Sexual satisfaction within dating relationships: A test of the interpersonal exchange model of sexual satisfaction. *Journal of Social and Personal Relationships, 15*, 257–267.

Byers, E. S., & Eastman, A. M. (1979, June). *Characteristics of unreported sexual assaults.* Paper presented at the meeting of the Canadian Psychological Association, Quebec City.

Byers, E. S., & Grenier, G. (2003). Premature or rapid ejaculation: Heterosexual couples' perceptions of men's ejaculatory behavior. *Archives of Sexual Behavior, 32*, 261–270.

Byers, E. S., & Heinlein, L. (1989). Predicting initiations and refusals of sexual activities in married and cohabiting heterosexual couples. *The Journal of Sex Research, 26*, 210–231.

Byers, E. S., & MacNeil, S. (2003, April). *Dyadic prediction of sexual satisfaction in heterosexual couples.* Paper presented at the meeting of the Eastern Region of the Society for the Scientific Study of Sexuality, Baltimore.

Byers, E. S., & O'Sullivan, L. F. (1998). Similar but different: Men's and women's experiences of sexual coercion. In P. B. Anderson & C. Struckman-Johnson (Eds.), *Sexually aggressive women.* New York: Guilford.

Byrne, D. (1961). Interpersonal attraction and attitude similarity. *Journal of Abnormal and Social Psychology, 62*, 713–715.

Byrne, D. (1997). An overview (and underview) of research and theory within the attraction paradigm. *Journal of Social and Personal Relationships, 14*, 417–431.

Byrne, D., & Blaylock, B. (1963). Similarity and assumed similarity of attitudes among husbands and wives. *Journal of Abnormal and Social Psychology, 67*, 636–640.

Byrne, D., Clore, G. L., & Worchel, P. (1966). The effect of economic similarity–dissimilarity on interpersonal attraction. *Journal of Personality and Social Psychology, 4*, 220–224.

Byrne, D., Ervin, C. R., & Lamberth, J. (1970). Continuity between the experimental study of attraction and real-life computer dating. *Journal of Personality and Social Psychology, 16*, 157–165.

Byrne, D., Griffitt, W., & Stefaniack, D. (1967). Attraction and similarity of personality characteristics, *Journal of Personality and Social Psychology, 5*, 82–90.

Byrne, D., & Nelson, D. (1965). Attraction as a linear function of proportion of positive reinforcement: *Journal of Personality and Social Psychology, 1*, 659–663.

Byrne, D., & Rhamey, R. (1965). Magnitude of positive and negative reinforcements as a determinant of attraction. *Journal of Personality and Social Psychology, 2*, 884–889.

Call, V., Sprecher, S., & Schwartz, P. (1995). The incidence and frequency of marital sex in a national sample. *Journal of Marriage and the Family, 57*, 639–650.

Carlson, J. (1976). The sexual role. In F. I. Nye (Ed.), *Role structure and analysis of the family* (pp. 101–110). Beverly Hills, CA: Sage.

Cate, R. M., Lloyd, S. A., Henton, J. H., & Larson, J. H. (1982). Fairness and reward level as predictors of relationship satisfaction. *Social Psychology Quarterly, 45*, 177–181.

Cate, R. M., Lloyd, S. A., & Long, E. (1988). The role of rewards and fairness in developing premarital relationships. *Journal of Marriage and the Family, 50*, 443–452.

Chesney, A. P., Blakeney, P. E., Cole, C. M., & Chan, F. A. (1981). A comparison of couples who have sought sex therapy with couples who have not. *Journal of Sex and Marital Therapy, 7*, 131–140.

Christopher, F. S., & Sprecher, S. (2000). Sexuality in marriage, dating and other relationships: A decade review. *Journal of Marriage and the Family, 62*, 999–1017.

Craig, M. (1990). Coercive sexuality in dating relationships: A situational model. *Clinical Psychology Review, 10*, 395–423.

Cramer, D. (1998). *Close relationships: The study of love and friendship.* London: Arnold.

Cupach, W. R., & Comstock, J. (1990). Satisfaction with sexual communication in marriage: Links to sexual satisfaction and dyadic adjustment. *Journal of Social and Personal Relationships, 7*, 179–186.

Cupach, W. R., & Metts, S. (1991). Sexuality and communication in close relationships. In K. McKinney & S. Sprecher (Eds.). *Sexuality in close relationships* (pp. 93–110). Hillsdale, NJ: Lawrence Erlbaum Associates.

Curran, J., P., & Lippold, S. (1975). The effects of physical attraction and attitude similarity on attraction in dating dyads. *Journal of Personality, 43*, 528–539.

Davidson, B. (1984). A test of equity theory for marital adjustment. *Social Psychology Quarterly, 47*, 36–42.

Davidson, J., & Darling, C. (1988). The sexually-experienced woman: Multiple sex partners and sexual satisfaction. *Journal of Sex Research, 24*, 141–154.

Davies, S., Katz, J., & Jackson, J. L. (1999). Sexual desire discrepancies: Effects on sexual and relationship satisfaction in heterosexual dating couples. *Archives of Sexual Behavior, 28*, 553–567.

Deutsch, M. (1975). Equity, equality and need: What determines which value will be used on the basis of distributive justice? *Journal of Social Issues, 31*, 137–150.

Dion, K. K. (1981). Physical attractiveness, sex roles, and heterosexual attraction. In M. Cook (Ed.), *The bases of human sexual attraction* (pp. 3–22). New York: Academic Press.

Dion, K. K., Berscheid, E., & Walster, E. (1972). What is beautiful is good. *Journal of Personality and Social Psychology, 24*, 285–290.

Duck, S. (1991) Afterword: Couples and coupling. In K. McKinney & S. Sprecher (Eds.), *Sexuality in close relationships* (pp. 155–175). Hillsdale, NJ.: Lawrence Erlbaum Associates.

Dutton, D. G., & Aron, A. P. (1974). Some evidence for heightened sexual attraction under conditions of high anxiety. *Journal of Personality and Social Psychology, 30*, 470–517.

Feingold, A. (1990). Gender differences in effects of physical attractiveness on romantic attraction: A comparison across five research paradigm. *Journal of Personality and Social Psychology, 59*, 981–993.

Feldman, S. S., & Cauffman, E. (1999). You're cheatin' heart: Attitudes, behaviors, and correlates of sexual betrayal in late adolescents. *Journal of Research on Adolescence, 9*, 227–252.

Felmlee, D., Sprecher, S., & Bassin, E. (1990). The dissolution of intimate relationships: A hazard model. *Social Psychology Quarterly, 53*, 13–30.

Finkelhor, D., & Yllo, K. (1985). *License to rape.* New York: Holt, Rinehart & Winston.

Fisher, W. A., Byrne, D., White, L., & Kelley, K. (1988). Erotophobia–erotophilia as a dimension of personality. *The Journal of Sex Research, 25*, 123–151.

Floyd, F. J., & Wasner, G. H. (1994). Social exchange, equity, and commitment: Structural equation modeling of dating relationships. *Journal of Family Psychology, 8*, 55–73.

Foa, E. Z., & Foa, U. G. (1980). Resource theory: Interpersonal behavior as exchange. In K. Gergen, M. Greenberg, and R. Willis (Eds.), *Social exchange: Advances in theory and research.* New York: Plenum.

Foa, U. G., & Foa, E. B. (1974). *Social structures of the mind.* Springfield, IL: Thomas.

Fowers, B. J., & Olson, D. H. (1989). ENRICH Marital Inventory: A discriminant validity and cross-validation assessment. *Journal of Marital and Family Therapy, 15*, 65–79.

Frank, E., Anderson, C., & Rubinstein, D. (1978). Frequency of sexual dysfunction in "normal" couples. *The New England Journal of Medicine, 299* 111–115.

Glenn, N. D., & Weaver, N. (1979). Attitudes toward premarital, extramarital and homosexual relations in the U.S. in the 1970s. *Journal of Sex Research, 15*, 108–119.

Goldstein, W. M., & Hogarth, R. M. (1997). Judgment and decision research: Some historical context. In W. M. Goldstein & R. M. Hogarth (Eds.), *Research on judgment and decision-making: Currents, connections, and controversies* (pp. 183–210). Cambridge, England: Cambridge University Press.

Gordon, S., & Snyder, C. W. (1986). *Personal issues in human sexuality.* Newton, MA: Allyn & Bacon.

Gouldner, A. (1960). The norm of reciprocity: A preliminary statement. *American Sociological Review, 15*, 451–463.

Greenblat, C. S. (1983). The salience of sexuality in the early years of marriage. *Journal of Marriage and the Family, 45*, 289–299.

Greene, B. L., Lee, R. R., & Lustig, N. (1974). Conscious and unconscious factors in marital infidelity. *Medical Aspects of Human Sexuality, 8*, 87–91.

Grenier, G., & Byers, E. S. (2001). Operationalizing premature or rapid ejaculation. *The Journal of Sex Research, 38*, 369–378.

Haavio-Mannila, E., & Kontula, O. (1997). Correlates of increased sexual satisfaction. *Archives of Sexual Behavior, 26*, 399–419.

Hansen, G. L. (2001). Extradyadic relations during courtship. In R. F. Baumeister (Ed.), *Social psychology and human sexuality* (pp. 285–291). Philadelphia: Psychology Press.

Hatfield, E., Greenberger, D., Traupmann, J., & Lambert, P. (1982). Equity and sexual satisfaction in recently married couples. *Journal of Sex Research, 18*, 18–31.

Hatfield, E., & Rapson, R. L. (1993). *Love, sex and intimacy: Their psychology, biology and history.* New York: HarperCollins.

Hatfield, E., & Sprecher, S. (1986). *Mirror, mirror . . . : The importance of looks in everyday life.* Albany: State University of New York Press.

Hatfield, E., Traupmann, J., Sprecher, S., Utne, M., & Hay, J. (1985). Equity and intimate relations: Recent research. In W. Ickes (Ed.), *Compatible and incompatible relationships* (p. 91–117). New York: Springer.

Hatfield, E., Utne, M. K., & Traupmann, J. (1979). Equity theory and intimate relationships. In R. L. Burgess & T. L. Huston (Eds.), *Social exchange in developing relationships* (pp. 99–133). New York: Academic Press.

Henderson-King, D. H., & Veroff, J. (1994). Sexual satisfaction and marital well-being in the first years of marriage. *Journal of Social and Personal Relationships, 11*, 509–534.

Hogben, M., Byrne, D., & Hamburger, M. E. (1996). Coercive heterosexuality in dating relationships of college students: Implications of differential male–female experience. *Journal of Psychology and Human Sexuality, 8*, 69–78.

Homans, G. C. (1961). *Social behaviour: Its elementary forms*. New York: Harcourt, Brace, & World.

Hunt, M. (1974). *Sexual behaviour in the 1970s*. Illinois: Playboy Press.

Huston, T. L. (1973). Ambiguity of acceptance, social desirability, and dating choice. *Journal of Experimental Social Psychology, 9*, 32–42.

Huston, T. L., & Burgess, R. L. (1979). Social exchange in developing relationships: An overview. In R. L. Burgess & T. L. Huston (Eds.), *Social exchange in developing relationships* (pp. 3–28). New York: Academic Press.

Hyde, J. S., DeLamater, J. D., & Byers, E. S. (Eds.) (2004). *Understanding human sexuality: Canadian edition*. (2nd ed.) Toronto: McGraw-Hill Ryerson.

Jacoby, A. P., & Williams, J. D. (1985). Effects of premarital sexual standards and behavior on dating and marriage desirability. *Journal of Marriage and the Family, 47*, 1059–1065.

Johnson, D. J., & Rusbult, C. F. (1989). Resisting temptation: Devaluation of alternative partners as a means of maintaining commitment in close relationships. *Journal of Personality and Social Psychology, 57*, 967–980.

Kalick, S. M., & Hamilton, T. E. (1986). The matching hypothesis re-examined. *Journal of Personality and Social Psychology, 51*, 673–682.

Kelley, H. H., & Thibaut, J. W. (1978). *Interpersonal relations: A theory of interdependence*. New York: Wiley.

Kelley, H. H., Berscheid, E., Christensen, A., Harvey, J. H., Huston, T. L., Levinger, G., McClintock, E., Peplau, L. A., Peterson, D. R. (1983). *Close relationships*. San Francisco: Freeman.

Kenrick, D. T., Groth, G. E., Trost, M. R., & Sadalla, E. K. (1993). Integrating evolutionary and social exchange perspectives on relationships: Effects of sex, self-appraisal, and involvement level on mate selection criteria. *Journal of Personality and Social Psychology, 64*, 951–969.

Kenrick, D. T., Sadalla, E. K., Groth, G. E., & Trost, M. R. (1990). Evolution, traits, and the stages of human courtship: Qualifying the parental investment model. *Journal of Personality, 58*, 97–116.

Kerckhoff, A. C., & Davis, K. E. (1962). Value consensus and need complementarity in mate selection. *American Sociological Review, 27*, 295–303.

Kirkendall, L., & Libby, R. W. (1966). Interpersonal relationships—crux of the sexual renaissance. *Journal of Social Issues, 22*, 45–59.

Knapp, J. J., & Whitehurst, R. N. (1977). Sexually open marriage and relationships: Issues and prospects. In R. W. Libby, & R. N. Whitehurst (Eds.), *Marriage and alternatives: Exploring intimate relationships* (pp. 147–160). Glenview, IL: Scott, Foresman.

Koss, M. P., Dinero, T. E., & Seibel, C. A. (1988). Stranger and acquaintance rape: Are there differences in victim's experiences? *Psychology of Women Quarterly, 12*, 1–24.

Kurdek, L. A. (1991). Sexuality in homosexual and heterosexual couples. In K. McKinney & S. Sprecher (Eds.), *Sexuality in close relationships* (pp. 177–191). Hillsdale, NJ.: Lawrence Erlbaum Associates.

Laumann, E. O., Gagnon, J. H., Michael, R. T., & Michaels, S. (1994). *The social organization of sexuality: Sexual practices in the United States*. Chicago: University of Chicago Press.

Laursen, B., & Jensen-Campbell, L. A. (1999). The nature and functions of social exchange in adolescent romantic relationships. In W. Furman, B. B. Brown, & C. Feiring (Eds.), *The development of romantic relationships in adolescence* (pp. 50–74). Cambridge, England: Cambridge University Press.

Lawrance, K. (1994). *Development and validation of the interpersonal exchange model of sexual satisfaction in long-term heterosexual sexual relationships*. Unpublished doctoral dissertation, University of New Brunswick, Fredericton, New Brunswick.

Lawrance, K., & Byers, E. S. (1992). Development of the interpersonal exchange model of sexual satisfaction in long-term relationships. *The Canadian Journal of Human Sexuality, 1*, 123–128.

Lawrance, K., & Byers, E. S. (1995). Sexual satisfaction in long-term heterosexual relationships: The interpersonal exchange model of sexual satisfaction. *Personal Relationships, 2*, 267–285.

Lawrance, K., & Byers, E. S. (1998). Interpersonal Exchange Model of Sexual Satisfaction Questionnaire. In C. M. Davis, W. L. Yarber, R. Baureman, G. Schreer, & S. L. Davis (Eds.), *Sexuality related measures: A compendium* (2nd ed., pp. 514–519). Thousand Oaks, CA: Sage.

Lawrance, K., Taylor, D., & Byers, E. S. (1996). Differences in men's and women's global, sexual, and ideal-sexual expressiveness and instrumentality. *Sex Roles, 34*, 337–357.

Lieberman, B. (1988). Extrapremarital intercourse: Attitudes toward a neglected sexual behaviour. *The Journal of Sex Research, 24*, 291–299.

Liu, C. (2003). Does quality of marital sex decline with duration? *Archives of Sexual Behavior, 32*, 55–60.

LoPiccolo, J., & Steger, J. C. (1974). The sexual interaction inventory: A new instrument for the assessment of sexual dysfunction. *Archives of Sexual Behaviour, 3*, 585–595.

Lott, A. J., & Lott, B. E. (1974). The role of reward in the formation of positive interpersonal attitudes. In T. L. Huston (Ed.), *Foundations of interpersonal attraction* (pp. 171–189). New York: Academic Press.

Loulan, J. (1984). *Lesbian sex*. San Francisco: Spinsters Ink.

MacNeil, S., & Byers, E. S. (1997). The relationships between sexual problems, communication, and sexual satisfaction. *Canadian Journal of Human Sexuality, 6,* 277–283.

Maykovich, M. K. (1976). Attitudes versus behavior in extramarital sexual relations. *Journal of Marriage and the Family, 33,* 183–187.

McConaghy, N., & Zamir, R. (1995). Heterosexual and homosexual coercion, sexual orientation and sexual roles in medical students. *Archives of Sexual Behavior, 24,* 489–502.

McCormick, N. (1994). *Sexual salvation: Affirming women's sexual rights and pleasures.* Westport CT: Praeger.

McKinney, K., & Sprecher, S. (1991). Introduction. In K. McKinney & S. Sprecher (Eds.), *Sexuality in close relationship* (pp. 1–8). Hillsdale, NJ: Lawrence Erlbaum Associates.

Metts, S. (1994). Relational transgressions. In W. R. Cupach & B. H. Spitzberg (Eds.), *The dark side of interpersonal communication* (pp. 217–239). Hillsdale, NJ: Lawrence Erlbaum Associates.

Metts, S., & Cupach, W. R. (1989). The role of communication in human sexuality. In K. McKinney and S. Sprecher (Eds.), *Human sexuality: The social and interpersonal context* (pp. 139–161). Norwood, NJ: Ablex.

Michaels, J. W., Edwards, J. N., & Acock, A. C. (1984). Satisfaction in intimate relationships as a function of inequality, inequity, and outcomes. *Social Psychology Quarterly, 47,* 347–367.

Morton, T. L., & Douglas, M. A. (1981). Growth of relationships. In W. Duck and R. Gilmour (Eds.), *Personal relationships 2: Developing personal relationships* (pp. 3–26). London: Academic Press.

Muehlenhard, C. L., & Cook, S. W. (1988). Men's reports of unwanted sexual activity. *Journal of Sex Research, 24,* 58–72.

Muehlenhard, C. L., Goggins, M. F., Jones, J. M., & Satterfield, A. T. (1991). Sexual violence and coercion in close relationships. In K. McKinney & S. Sprecher (Eds.), *Sexuality in close relationships* (pp. 155–175). Hillsdale, NJ: Lawrence Erlbaum Associates.

Murray, S. L., Holmes, J. G., & Griffin, D. W. (1996). The benefits of positive illusions: Idealizing and the construction of satisfaction in close relationships. *Journal of Personality and Social Psychology, 70,* 79–98.

Murstein, B. I. (1972). Physical attractiveness and marital choice. *Journal of Personality and Social Psychology, 22,* 8–12.

Murstein, B. I., & Christy, P. (1976). Physical attractiveness and marital adjustment in middle-aged couples. *Journal of Personality and Social Psychology, 34,* 537–542.

Nathan, E. P., & Joaning, H. H. (1985). Enhancing marital sexuality: An evaluation of a program for the sexual enrichment of normal couples. *Journal of Sex and Marital Therapy, 11,* 157–164.

Nevid, J. S. (1984). Sex differences in factors of romantic attraction. *Sex Roles, 11,* 401–411.

Newcomb, T. M. (1956). The prediction of interpersonal attraction. *American Psychologist, 11,* 575–586.

Nye, F. I. (1982). Family mini theories as special instances of choice and exchange theories. In F. I. Nye (Ed.), *Family relationships: Rewards and costs* (pp.171–183). Beverly Hills, CA: Sage.

O'Sullivan, L. F. (1995). Less is more: The effects of sexual experience in judgments of men's and women's personality characteristics and relationship desirability. *Sex Roles, 33,* 159–181.

O'Sullivan, L. F., & Byers, E. S. (1992). College students' incorporation of initiator and restrictor roles in sexual dating interactions. *Journal of Sex Research, 29,* 435–446.

O'Sullivan, L. F., Byers, E. S., & Finkelman, L. (1998). A comparison of male and female college students' experiences of sexual coercion. *Psychology of Women Quarterly, 22,* 177–195.

Parker, B. L., & Drummond-Reeves, S. J. (1993). The death of a dyad: Relational autopsy, analysis, and aftermath. *Journal of Divorce and Remarriage, 21,* 95–119.

Peplau, L. A., Rubin, Z., & Hill, C. T. (1977). Sexual intimacy in dating relationships. *Journal of Social Issues, 33,* 86–109.

Perlman, S., & Abramson, P. (1982). Sexual satisfaction among married and cohabiting individuals. *Journal of Sex and Marital Therapy, 9,* 171–181.

Pinney, E., Gerrard, M., & Denney, N. (1987). The Pinney Sexual Satisfaction Inventory. *The Journal of Sex Research, 23,* 233–251.

Poulin, C. (1992). Towards a multidimensional and multidirectional model of female sexual arousal. *The Canadian Journal of Human Sexuality, 1,* 129–132.

Price, R. A., & Vandenberg, S. G. (1979). Matching for physical attractiveness in married couples. *Personality and Social Psychology Bulletin, 5,* 398–400.

Prins, K. S., Buunk, B. P., VanYperen, N. W. (1993). Equity, normative disapproval and extramarital relationships. *Journal of Social and Personal Relationships, 10,* 39–53.

Purnine, D. M., & Carey, M. P. (1997). Interpersonal communication and sexual adjustment: The roles of understanding and agreement. *Journal of Consulting and Clinical Psychology, 65,* 1017–1025.

Regan, P. C., & Berscheid, E. (1997). Sex differences in characteristics desired in a potential sexual and marital partner. *Journal of Psychology and Human Sexuality, 9,* 25–37.

Regan, P. C., & Sprecher, S. (1995). Gender differences in the value of contributions to intimate relationships: Egalitarian relationships are not always perceived to be equitable. *Sex Roles, 33,* 221–238.

Renaud, C., Byers, E. S., & Pan, S. (1996). Factors related to sexual satisfaction in Mainland China. *The Canadian Journal of Human Sexuality, 5,* 243–252.

Renaud, C., Byers, E. S., & Pan, S. (1997). Sexual and relationship satisfaction in Mainland China. *The Journal of Sex Research, 34,* 399–410.

Resick, P. A. (1993). Psychological impact of rape. *Journal of Interpersonal Violence, 8,* 223–255.

Roscoe, B., Cavanaugh, L. E., & Kennedy, D. R. (1988). Dating infidelity: Behaviors, reasons and consequences. *Adolescence, 23,* 35–43.

Rusbult, C. E. (1980). Commitment and satisfaction in romantic associations: A test of the investment model. *Journal of Experimental Social Psychology, 16,* 172–186.

Rusbult, C. E. (1983). A longitudinal test of the investment model: The development (and deterioration) of satisfaction and commitment in heterosexual involvements. *Journal of Personality and Social Psychology, 45,* 101–117.

Rusbult, C. E., Johnson, D., & Morrow, G. (1986). Predicting satisfaction and commitment in adult romantic involvement: An assessment of the generalizability of the investment model. *Social Psychology Quarterly, 49,* 81–89.

Rusbult, C. E., Zembrodt, I. M., & Gunn, L. K. (1982). Exit, voice, loyalty, and neglect: Responses to dissatisfaction in romantic involvements. *Journal of Personality and Social Psychology, 43,* 1230–1242.

Russell, D. E. H. (1982). *Rape in marriage.* New York: Macmillan.

Russell, D. E. H. (1984). *Sexual exploitation Rape, child sexual abuse, and workplace harassment.* Beverly Hills, CA: Sage.

Sabatelli, R. M. (1984). The marital comparison level index: A measure for assessing outcomes relative to expectations. *Journal of Marriage and the Family, 46,* 651–662.

Schenk, J., Pfrang, H., & Rausche, A. (1983). Personality traits versus the quality of the marital relationship as the determinant of marital sexuality. *Archives of Sexual Behaviour, 12,* 31–42.

Schwartz, P. (1994). *Peer marriage: How love between equals really works.* New York: The Free Press.

Schwartz, P., & Rutter, V. (1998). *The gender of sexuality.* Walnut Creek, CA: AltaMira Press.

Shanteau, J., & Nagy, G. F. (1979). Probability of acceptance in dating choice. *Journal of Personality and Social Psychology, 37,* 522–533.

Shapiro, B. L., & Schwarz, J. C. (1997). Date rape: Its relationship to trauma soymptoms and sexual self-esteem. *Journal of Interpersonal Violence, 12,* 407–419.

Simpson, J. A., & Gangestad, S. W. (1991). Individual differences in sociosexuality: Evidence for convergent and discriminant validity. *Journal of Personal and Social Psychology, 60,* 870–883.

Simpson, J. A., Gangestad, S. W., & Lerma, M. (1990). Perception of physical attractiveness: Mechanisms involved in the maintenance of romantic relationships. *Journal of Personality and Social Psychology, 59,* 1192–1201.

Snyder, D. K., & Berg, P. (1983). Determinants of sexual dissatisfaction in sexually distressed couples. *Archives of Sexual Behaviour, 12,* 237–246.

Sprecher, S. (1986). The relationship between inequity and emotions in close relationships. *Social Psychology Quarterly, 49,* 309–321.

Sprecher, S. (1998). Social exchange theories and sexuality. *The Journal of Sex Research, 35,* 32–43.

Sprecher, S. (2001). A comparison of emotional consequences of and changes in equity over time using global and domain-specific measures of equity. *Journal of Social and Personal Relationships, 18,* 477–501.

Sprecher, S. (2002). Sexual satisfaction in premarital relationships: Associations with satisfaction, love, commitment, and stability. *The Journal of Sex Research, 39,* 190–196.

Sprecher, S., & Duck, S. (1994). Sweet talk: The importance of perceived communication for romantic and friendship attraction experienced during a get-acquainted date. *Personality and Social Psychology Bulletin, 4,* 391–400.

Sprecher, S., & McKinney, K. (1993). *Sexuality.* Newbury Park, CA: Sage.

Sprecher, S., McKinney, K., & Orbuch, T. L. (1991). The effect of current sexual behaviour in friendship, dating, and marriage desirability. *The Journal of Sex Research, 28,* 387–408.

Sprecher, S., & Regan, P. C. (2002). Liking some things (in some people) more than others: Partner preferences in romantic relationships and friendships. *Journal of Social and Personal Relationships, 19,* 463–481.

Sprecher, S., & Schwartz, P. (1994). Equity and balance in the exchange of contributions in close relationships. In M. J. Lerner, and G. Mikula (Eds.), *Entitlement and the affectional bond: Justice in close relationships* (pp. 11–41). New York: Plenum.

Sprecher, S., Sullivan, Q., & Hatfield, E. (1994). Mate selection preferences: Gender differences examined in a national sample. *Journal of Personality and Social Psychology, 66,* 1074–1080.

Statistics Canada (1993). The violence against women survey. *The Daily.* Catalogue #11-001E.

Steinman, R. (1990). Social exchanges between older and younger gay male partners. *Journal of Homosexuality, 20,* 179–206.

Swenson, C. (1973). *Introduction to interpersonal relations.* Glenview, IL: Scott, Foresman.

Taylor, P. A., & Glenn, N. D. (1976). The utility of education and attractiveness for females' status attainment through marriage. *American Sociological Review, 41,* 484–497.

Thibaut, J. W., & Kelley, H. H. (1959). *The social psychology of groups.* New York: Wiley.

Tiefer, L. (1988). A feminist critique of the sexual dysfunction nomenclature. *Women and Therapy, 7,* 5–21.

Thompson, A. P. (1984). Emotional and sexual components of extramarital relations. *Journal of Marriage and the Family, 46,* 35–42.

Thornton, A., & Young-DeMarco, L. (2001). Four decades of trends in attitudes toward family issues in the United States: The 1960s through the 1990s. *Journal of Marriage and the Family, 63,* 1009–1037.

Traupmann, J., Hatfield, E., & Wexler, P. (1983). Equity and sexual satisfaction in dating couples. *British Journal of Social Psychology, 22,* 33–40.

Tversky, A., & Kahneman, D. (1974). Judgment under uncertainty: Heuristics and biases. *Science, 185*, 1124–1131.

Udry, J. R. & Eckland, B. K. (1984). The benefits of being attractive: Different payoffs for men and women. *Psychological Reports, 54*, 47–56.

Udry, J. R., Deven, F. R., & Coleman, S. J. (1982). A cross-national comparison of the relative influence of male and female age on frequency of marital intercourse. *Journal of Biosocial Science, 14*, 1–6.

Walster, E. (1978). Equity and extramarital sexuality. *Archives of Sexual Behavior, 7*, 127–141.

Walster, E., Aronson, V., Abrahams, D., & Rottman, L. (1966). Importance of physical attractiveness in dating behaviour. *Journal of Personality and Social Psychology, 4*, 508–516.

Walster, E., Berscheid, E., & Walster, G. W. (1973). New directions in equity research. *Journal of Personality and Social Psychology, 25*, 151–176.

Walster, E., Traupmann, J., & Walster, G. W. (1978). Equity and extramarital sexuality. *Archives of Sexual Behaviour, 7*, 127–142.

Walster, E., Walster, G., & Berscheid, E. (1978). *Equity: Theory and research*. Boston: Allyn & Bacon.

Walster, E., Walster, G., & Traupmann, J. (1978). Equity and premarital sex. *Journal of Personality and Social Psychology, 36*, 82–92.

White, G. L., Fishbein, S., & Rutstein, J. (1981). Passionate love and the misattribution of arousal. *Journal of Personality and Social Psychology, 41*, 56–62.

White, G. L., & Mullen, P. E. (1989). *Jealousy: Theory, research and clinical strategies*. New York: Guilford.

Wiederman, M. W. (1997). Extramarital sex: Prevalence and correlates in a national survey. *The Journal of Sex Research, 34*, 167–174.

Wiederman, M. W. & Hurd, C. (1999). Extradyadic involvement during dating. *Journal of Social and Personal Relationships, 16*, 265–274.

Working Group for a New View of Women's Sexual Problems. (2001). Part I: A new view of women's sexual problems. In E. Kachak & L. Tiefer (Eds.), *A new view of women's sexual problems* (pp. 1–8). Binghamton, NY: Haworth.

Young, M., Denny, G., Young, T., & Luquis, R. (2000). Sexual satisfaction among married women. *American Journal of Health Studies, 16*, 73–84.

Zilbergeld, B. (1999). *The new male sexuality* (Rev. ed.). New York: Bantam.

10

Sexual Satisfaction and Sexual Expression as Predictors of Relationship Satisfaction and Stability

Susan Sprecher
Illinois State University
Rodney M. Cate
University of Arizona

Why do some intimate relationships endure and others do not? Of the stable relationships, why are some couples highly satisfied, whereas other couples become dissatisfied? Vast literatures have focused on theory and research on predictors of relationship stability and satisfaction. In this chapter, we examine how aspects of the sexual relationship are associated with overall relationship satisfaction and stability. We begin with a focus on the contribution of sexual satisfaction to overall relationship quality and stability. We then discuss how several types of sexual expression, including frequency of sexual activity, sexual communication, and sexual conflict are related to sexual satisfaction and thus also to relationship satisfaction and stability. Although most of the literature conceptualizes sexuality variables as distinct from relationship quality variables (e.g., satisfaction), sexuality is also a component of some relationship phenomena that are empirically and theoretically associated with sexual satisfaction and relationship quality. In this chapter, we also discuss sexuality as a dimension of the following relationship constructs: intimacy, love, exchange, and maintenance behaviors.

INTRODUCTION

Why do some intimate relationships endure whereas others dissolve? Relationship scholars have long been interested in answering this question as well as identifying the factors that lead to relationship satisfaction, assumed in many theoretical traditions to be one of the major predictors of relationship stability (e.g., Berscheid & Reis, 1998). Vast literatures have developed around both relationship satisfaction and relationship stability, and these literatures have identified a variety of predictors of both relationship outcome variables. The major goal of this chapter is to discuss that portion of these vast literatures that include predictor variables referring to sexuality.

Not surprising, the sexuality variable that has been examined most frequently for its association with relationship satisfaction and stability is *sexual satisfaction*. Thus, in our first section, we provide an overview to sexual satisfaction in a relationship context, focusing on definition/measurement issues, theories about sexual satisfaction, and a description of the degree to which couples report that they are sexually satisfied in their relationships. In the second section, we review the empirical literature documenting the associations of sexual satisfaction with relationship satisfaction and stability. In the third section, we review the literature showing how specific types of sexual expression, including frequency of sexual activity, sexual communication, and sexual conflict, are related to sexual satisfaction and thus also to relationship satisfaction and stability. In our fourth section, we discuss several higher-order constructs that include a dimension referring to sexuality and that have been linked to relationship satisfaction and stability. These include intimacy, love, maintenance acts, and exchange. In our final section, we offer several suggestions for additional research.

This chapter summarizes research conducted on various types of close, sexual relationships or what have been referred to as "sexually based primary partnerships" (Scanzoni, Polonko, Teachman, & Thompson, 1989). Research on married, cohabiting, and dating relationships is included, and for both heterosexual and homosexual partnerships.

OVERVIEW OF SEXUAL SATISFACTION

Definition and Measurement of Sexual Satisfaction

Sexual satisfaction is generally defined as the degree to which an individual is satisfied or happy with the sexual aspect of his or her relationship. For example, Lawrance and Byers (1998) defined sexual satisfaction as "an affective response arising from one's subjective evaluation of the positive and negative dimensions associated with one's sexual relationship" (p. 514).

Various multi-item scales have been developed to measure sexual satisfaction. One such scale is the Hudson Index of Sexual Satisfaction (Hudson, 1998; Hudson, Harrison, & Crosscup, 1981). The most recent version of this scale contains 25 items (with 7-point Likert responses) including such items as, "Our sex life is very exciting," "I think our sex is wonderful," "My partner does not satisfy me sexually," and "I feel that my sex life is lacking in quality." Another scale that also includes a variety of items is the Whitley Sexual Satisfaction Inventory (Whitley, 1998; Whitley & Paulsen, 1975). This scale asks participants to rate the level (on a 5-point response scale) of sexual satisfaction they would receive from various sexual activities with their partner (kissing, stroking, undressing, etc.). Several other scales also measure sexual satisfaction, including the Pinney Sexual Satisfaction Inventory (Pinney, Gerrard, & Denney, 1987), the Sexual Interaction Inventory (LoPiccolo & Steger, 1974), and the Derogatis Sexual Functioning Inventory (Derogatis & Melisaratos, 1979). Furthermore, some scales that were designed to measure marital or relationship satisfaction contain a subscale to measure sexual satisfaction (e.g., Snyder, 1979). The authors of these scales describe the scales as having adequate to excellent reliability and validity.

One problem, however, with some multi-item sexual satisfaction scales is that they include items that measure aspects of sexuality other than sexual satisfaction. For example, Lawrance and Byers (1995, 1998) note that some sexual satisfaction scales include items referring to the behaviors (e.g., sexual frequency) that are, in some studies, used as predictors of sexual satisfaction. Obviously, this confounding of measures precludes the analysis of how sexual behaviors predict sexual satisfaction, which is the goal of many studies. As part of a larger Interpersonal Exchange Model of Sexual Satisfaction (IEMSS), Lawrance and Byers (1995) developed the Global Measure of Sexual Satisfaction. This scale asks individuals to rate their sexual relationship on the following bipolar adjectives: good–bad, pleasant–unpleasant, positive–negative, satisfying–unsatisfying, and valuable–worthless. The scale seems to have good test–retest reliablity, high internal consistency, and is correlated with other measures of sexual satisfaction (Lawrance & Byers, 1998).

In many studies, however, particularly the large-scale, national studies, sexual satisfaction has been measured with only one or two global items. For example, Laumann, Gagnon, Michael, and Michaels (1994), in the National Health and Social Life Survey conducted with over 3,000 Americans, asked the participants two questions: "How physically pleasurable do you find your relationship with (Partner) to be?" and "How emotionally satisfying do you find your relationship with (Partner) to be?" In a telephone survey conducted by the Gallup organization (see Greeley, 1991), respondents (married couples throughout the United States), were asked: "How much satisfaction do you get out of your sexual relationship—a very great deal, a great deal, quite a bit, a fair amount, some, little, or none?" Blumstein and Schwartz (1983), in their study of over 12,000 adults who represented different relationship types, asked their participants how satisfied they were with the quality of their sex life. In a recent, smaller-scale study of sexual satisfaction in premarital relationships (Sprecher, 2002), sexual satisfaction was measured with two global items. One asked the respondents how sexually satisfying their relationship was and the other asked about the reward level of the sexual relationship. Just as it has been argued that relationship satisfaction might be best measured by one or more global items (see Fincham & Bradbury, 1987), sexual satisfaction might also be more usefully measured with global items than with multidimensional, detailed items.

Some researchers (e.g., Hunt, 1974), however, have rejected both multi-item scales and global items as being too subjective and as likely to be characterized by social desirability responses, and they recommend the use of the occurrence of an orgasm as an objective indicator of sexual satisfaction. For example, Laumann et al. (1994; Michael, Gagnon, Laumann, & Kolata, 1994) used a measure of the occurrence of orgasms as an alternative indicator of sexual quality, in addition to their questions on emotional satisfaction with sex and physical pleasure. However, for some women, orgasm is an infrequent occurrence, although a positive affective reaction of the sexual experience can still be experienced. Thus, we recommend that if the focus of the research study is on sexual satisfaction, a valid and reliable multi-item scale or one or more global items measuring respondents' *feelings or evaluations* about the quality of their sexual relationship be used to measure sexual satisfaction. Furthermore, the particular sexual satisfaction scales used should be related to the theory guiding the investigation. The next section discusses several theories about sexual satisfaction.

Theories About Sexual Satisfaction

A few theories address the association of sexual satisfaction with other properties of interpersonal relationships. These theories are of two types: biological/evolutionary and socially based theories.

Biological/Evolutionary Theories. Evolutionary theory (Buss, 1998) posits that sexuality in personal relationships is a result of an underlying motivation to maximize the transmission of one's genes to succeeding generations. According to the theory, males maximize the chance of passing on their genes by mating with as many women as possible, whereas females are more reproductively successful when they can attract men who can provide resources and protection that allow children to mature and reproduce. Consequently, over evolutionary time, both genders have developed various psychological mechanisms that serve to fulfill these reproductive needs.

From an evolutionary perspective, humans have evolved the capacity to develop quality relationships and sexual satisfaction in relationships in order to solve reproductive problems. For example, when people are sexually satisfied and/or generally satisfied with their relationships, they are more likely to have stable relationships that increase the odds of transmitting their genes to succeeding generations. Evolutionary scientists have focused most of their attention on people's sexual desires and evaluations, because overt sexual behavior is so sensitive to immediate contextual factors (e.g., the sexual partner; Buss, 1994). The most prominent evolutionary research centers on gender differences in the choice of mating partners. However, certain hypotheses can be derived about features of ongoing relationships and their association with sexual satisfaction. For example, in contrast to males, females should be more satisfied with sex and their relationships when their male partners generally act kindly and loving toward them (Buss, 1994). According to the theory, when women have mates who are kind and loving, men are more likely to maintain fidelity, which is indicative of the desire to continue supplying the resources that increase reproductive success. On the other hand, evolutionists predict that men who have female partners who maintain their sexual allure through maintaining and enhancing beauty are more sexually and generally satisfied with their partners than men whose partners do not enact such behaviors. Such behavior on the part of women signals the intention to maintain fidelity, which enhances reproductive success (Buss, 1994). Evolutionary theory assumes that underlying the immediate "proximate" cause (e.g., beauty enhancement influences sexual satisfaction) is an "ultimate" cause based in humans' evolutionary history (e.g., reproductive challenges lead to the development of strategies that maximize reproductive fitness).

Social-Based Theories.   In contrast to evolutionary theories, social-based theories place the major causal locus on factors that represent interaction between the individual and various contexts. Social-based theories highlight the influence of both macro and micro contexts on sexual/interpersonal relationships. The social-based approach to the theoretical study of sexuality in relationships is best represented by symbolic interaction theory (LaRossa & Reitzes, 1993), script theory (Gagnon, 1990), and exchange theories (Hatfield, Utne, & Traupmann, 1979).

Symbolic interaction (SI) theory (LaRossa & Reitzes, 1993) has been used to study sexuality for several decades. SI theory assumes that people are both active and reactive to the contexts in which they exist. From this perspective, the interactions of individuals with their partners (the interpersonal context) and other social contexts (various macro-level contexts) result in the social construction of relationships and the properties that characterize them. Rather than some ultimate cause (e.g., motivation to pass on one's genes) operating in relationships, SI assumes that relationship properties emerge from the interaction between partners. This leads to relationships that have some unique properties. The regularities that characterize most couple relationships emerge because partners bring some societally shared meanings about such relationships to their interactions (e.g., marital relationships should be loving in nature, quality relationships are sexually satisfying). Many of these shared meanings are those held about various social roles that people enact. Social roles and the expectations tied to them are particularly important in understanding relationships and their properties (e.g., sexual satisfaction). For example, sexual satisfaction could result when one spouse perceives that the partner adequately fulfills the spouse's conception of a "sexual partner." Similarly, according to SI, when both partners have similar conceptions of the "spouse" role, the likelihood of having a harmonious relationship is increased, thus contributing to sexual satisfaction. Conceptions of the "self" are equally important in SI. Not only do people assess the "role performance" of their partners, they also reflect on themselves as a sexual partner. When conceptions of self as sexual partners are positive, it follows that sexual satisfaction would be enhanced.

Script theory (Gagnon, 1990) and symbolic interactionism share several features. Script theory proposes that people in sexual relationships adhere to various sexual scripts, scripts that define the situation, the actors and their roles in the script, and the behaviors that accompany these scripts (Gagnon, 1990). Such sexual scripts are socially constructed at both the cultural and interpersonal levels. For example, cultures, in interaction with their inhabitants, construct scripts such as the proper age to become sexually involved, whether that involvement should come before or after marriage, and whether the sexual activity should result in conception of children, as well as the appropriate sequence in which those events should occur. At the interpersonal level, sexual partners can construct their own scripts that differ from the cultural ones, although cultural scripts are likely to influence greatly the social constructions at the interpersonal level. From a SI perspective, sexual satisfaction might result through at least two mechanisms. Individuals would be sexually satisfied when they perceive that (a) the other possesses a similar sexual script (i.e., shared meaning); and (b) the other is adequately enacting (i.e., role performance) the preferred script that they share.

Last, other theories propose that interpersonal behavior and evaluations are a result of rational choices on the part of partners. In particular, *social exchange theories* (Rusbult, 1983; Thibaut & Kelley, 1959) assume that people are hedonistic, but know that they must "give" in order to "get" in relationships. The currency of the exchange process is in the form of rewards (e.g., love, services, information, etc.) and costs/investments (e.g., time, effort, etc.). People strive to maximize their rewards and minimize their costs/investments. Individual partners are satisfied when the profits (rewards minus costs) exceed their expectations for the profits they should receive (comparison level). These expectations develop from previous relationships, societal norms, and the observation of other relationships. According to social exchange, satisfaction results when the overall profits in a relationship exceed the profits that people believe they deserve to receive. Thus, sexual satisfaction may be a result of general rewards, costs, and the comparison level, as well as rewards, costs, and comparison level specific to sexual interaction. Lawrence and Byers (1995) developed the Interpersonal Exchange Model of Sexual Satisfaction (IEMSS), an exchange model specific to sexual satisfaction. This model proposes that sexual satisfaction results from the rewards and costs in the sexual relationship, how the reward/cost balance compares to what the person is accustomed to receiving, and the perception that both partners are receiving equal levels of rewards/costs (Lawrence & Byers, 1995; also see Byers & Wang, chapter 9, this volume).

Other offshoots of exchange theory postulate that satisfaction is a result of factors other than present relationship profits compared to expectations for the profits deserved in the relationship. *Equity theory* (Hatfield et al., 1979; Sprecher, 1998) proposes that satisfaction in relationships results when partners perceive that the proportion of rewards to costs is equal for both partners. Partners could be receiving different levels of rewards but have equitable relationships because they are incurring different levels of costs/investments. In other words, people feel satisfied when they feel they are fairly treated. Thus, sexual satisfaction can result from feeling equitably treated in the relationship in general, or in the sexual aspect of the relationship (see Byers, & Wang, chapter 9, this volume).

How Sexually Satisfied Are Couples?

As previously indicated, the evolutionary perspective suggests that humans have developed the ability to have sexually satisfying relationships in order to solve reproductive issues. In addition, the exchange perspective reviewed suggests that individuals who remain in their relationship because they are rewarded and invest heavily in it should be satisfied with the overall relationship and with specific aspects of the relationship, including the sexual aspect. Thus, people who are involved in marriages or other committed relationships should report that they are generally sexually satisfied in their relationship. In fact, research indicates that most individuals involved in a committed relationship are sexually satisfied. For example, Laumann et al. (1994), with the NHSLS data, found that 88% of the married respondents report being either extremely or very physically pleased in their relationship. In addition, when asked to respond about specific feelings they experienced after having sex, a majority of the participants report positive feelings (i.e., felt "loved," "thrilled and excited") and only a small minority report any negative feelings (e.g, "anxious and worried"). In a national study of married couples, Greeley (1991) asked the respondents the question, "How much satisfaction do you get out of your sexual relationship—a very great deal, a great deal, quite a bit, a fair amount, some, little, or none?" One third of husbands and wives report "a very great deal" and another one third report "a great deal" (Greeley, 1991). Other studies of married couples also indicated high levels of sexual satisfaction (e.g., Edwards & Booth, 1994; Lawrance & Byers, 1995; Oggins, Leber, & Veroff, 1993). Sexual satisfaction is also common among those who are dating (e.g., Sprecher, 2002) and in both heterosexual and homosexual relationships (e.g., Blumstein & Schwartz, 1983; Kurdek, 1991). Some evidence suggests that sexual satisfaction may decrease slightly with age and/or time in the relationship (e.g., Greeley, 1991; Laumann et al., 1994), although the decline is not nearly as dramatic as the decline in sexual frequency, which is discussed elsewhere in this volume (see Willetts, Sprecher, & Beck, chapter 3).

Sexual Satisfaction in Different Relationship Types.   Many studies on relationships focus on only one type of relationship, for example, married couples (e.g., Edwards & Booth, 1994; Greeley, 1991). However, in some studies, several relationship types are represented in the sample, and therefore comparisons in sexual satisfaction can be made across relationship types. Laumann et al. (1994) made such relationship comparisons with the NHSLS data. They reported that married respondents report higher levels of emotional satisfaction and physical pleasure with sex than do cohabiting and single coupled (dating) adults. Furthermore, regardless of the relationship type, the respondents are most sexually satisfied with their primary sexual partner when they do not also have a secondary sexual partner.

In a follow-up study with the NHSLS data, Waite and Joyner (2001) conducted detailed analyses to compare sexual satisfaction across relationship types. They compared respondents from different relationship types on emotional satisfaction and pleasure with sex while controlling for demographic and background variables. In addition, they distinguished among single respondents based on their expectations for the future stability of the relationship. Their results indicated that there are no differences in emotional satisfaction and physical pleasure among men in different types of coupled relationships after controlling for demographic and background variables, except for a lower level of both emotional satisfaction and physical pleasure found among the single men who forecast that their relationship will not last. For women, physical pleasure is highest among the married and cohabiting respondents and also among the particular subset of singles who expect to be in their relationship forever, and, it is lowest among the singles who do not expect their relationship to last. In addition, married women experience more emotional satisfaction with sex, controlling for demographic and background characteristics, than do other women, with one exception. Single women who believe their relationship will last a lifetime experience emotional satisfaction to the same degree as married women. The research by Waite and Joyner (2001) suggests that the critical factor associated with higher levels of sexual satisfaction is not marital status but psychological commitment. In the next section, we discuss further how sexual satisfaction is associated with commitment and other aspects of the quality of the relationship.

THE ASSOCIATION BETWEEN SEXUAL SATISFACTION AND RELATIONSHIP OUTCOMES

Because modern culture gives emphasis to sexual expression in marriage and other committed relationships, sexual satisfaction is considered to be a barometer for the quality of a relationship. Next we discuss the evidence that demonstrates the associations of sexual satisfaction with relationship satisfaction and relationship stability.

Sexual Satisfaction and Relationship Satisfaction

Several studies show an association between sexual satisfaction and overall relationship satisfaction in marriage. More specifically, husbands and wives who say they are sexually satisfied in their marriage are also likely to report high levels of overall satisfaction with their relationship (e.g., Blumstein & Schwartz, 1983; Cupach & Comstock, 1990; Edwards & Booth, 1994; Henderson-King & Veroff, 1994). This positive association between sexual satisfaction and relationship satisfaction is also found in samples of dating couples (Byers, Demmons, & Lawrance, 1998; Davies, Katz, & Jackson, 1999; Sprecher, 2002). Sexual satisfaction and related subjective measures of sexuality (e.g., sexual intimacy) are also associated positively with other indicators of relationship quality, including love (Aron & Henkemeyer, 1995; Grote & Frieze, 1998; Sprecher & Regan, 1998; Yela, 2000; see Hendrick & Hendrick, chapter 7, this volume) and commitment or the likelihood that the relationship will last (Pinney et al., 1987; Sprecher, 2002; Sprecher, Metts, Burleson, Hatfield, & Thompson, 1995; Waite & Joyner, 2001). In addition, longitudinal evidence shows that a *change* in sexual satisfaction is associated with a *change* in relationship satisfaction (e.g., Edwards & Booth, 1994; Sprecher, 2002). Thus, there is strong evidence to indicate that sexual satisfaction is tightly linked to overall relationship satisfaction and to other indicators of relationship quality. Although it may not seem surprising that satisfaction in a specific area of the relationship (e.g., sex) is associated with overall relationship satisfaction, the association found between sexual satisfaction and love and commitment indicate that sexual satisfaction also has implications for how partners feel about each other and how committed they are to staying in the relationship. These results are consistent with social exchange framework (e.g., Rusbult, 1983; Sprecher, 1998) that suggests that positive social exchanges are associated with overall relationship quality.

However, two caveats are in order concerning the associations found between sexual satisfaction and relationship satisfaction. First, sexual satisfaction is only one specific type of satisfaction that contributes to relationship satisfaction. Satisfaction with other areas of the relationship (e.g., fairness in household work distribution, decisions about money) also contribute to overall relationship satisfaction (e.g., Glenn, 1990). Second, we cannot assume that an association found between sexual satisfaction and relationship satisfaction indicates that sexual satisfaction leads to relationship satisfaction. The causal linkage between sexual satisfaction and relationship satisfaction may go in either direction. Most studies that have demonstrated the association between sexual satisfaction and relationship satisfaction have been cross-sectional, and therefore causal direction cannot be determined in such studies. Although sexual satisfaction is likely to contribute to overall relationship satisfaction, it is equally plausible that relationship satisfaction leads to sexual satisfaction (e.g., Blumstein & Schwartz, 1983; Hendersen-King & Veroff, 1994). Attempts to determine causal direction with longitudinal data have been difficult in part because ceiling effects in sexual satisfaction and relationship satisfaction are reached early in the studies, resulting in little variance in change over time to be explained (Sprecher, 2002).

Sexual Satisfaction as a Predictor of Relationship Stability Versus Instability

If sexual satisfaction contributes to overall relationship quality, it is also likely to contribute, directly or indirectly, to relationship stability. A few longitudinal studies conducted over time with married couples have relevant data. Oggins et al. (1993), using data from the Early Years of Marriage project, reported that measures of sexual satisfaction at Year 1 predict (negatively) marital dissolution by the fourth year of marriage (also see Veroff, Douvan, & Hatchett, 1995). Furthermore, Edwards and Booth (1994) reported that a decline in sexual satisfaction between 1980 and 1983 is associated with the probability of divorce by 1988. White and Keith (1990), using a national sample of married individuals first interviewed in 1980 and again in 1983, reported that a measure of sexual problems (dissatisfaction) at Time 1 is associated positively with the likelihood of divorce by Time 2.

Prospective studies conducted with individuals in dating relationships have generally focused on sexuality variables other than sexual satisfaction. For example, in the Boston Dating Couples Study, Hill, Rubin, and Peplau (1976) found that whether or not the dating couple is sexually intimate at the time of the initial contact had no effect on the status of the relationship 2 years later. Furthermore, no difference was found in relationship stability between the couples who have sex early in their relationship and couples who have sex later (Peplau, Rubin, & Hill, 1977). However, in a 3-month longitudinal study of dating individuals, Simpson (1987) found that whether the couple has engaged in sexual intercourse has a significant and positive effect on relationship stability. Furthermore, Felmlee, Sprecher, and Bassin (1990) found that an index representing sexual intimacy is a positive predictor of the stability of premarital relationships, although it is not significant when included in a model with several other predictors (social network reactions, comparison level for alternatives).

In one recent study conducted with dating couples, Sprecher (2002) examined how sexual satisfaction is associated with the stability of the relationships over time. In this study, sexual satisfaction (measured at Time 1) is higher in couples who are still together 6 months later than in couples who broke up. In an analysis that included both sexual satisfaction and relationship satisfaction as predictors of relationship stability, sexual satisfaction (but not relationship satisfaction) is significant for men, whereas relationship satisfaction (but not sexual satisfaction) is significant for women.

Another way of examining the degree to which quality of sex (or lack of) is associated with the likelihood of breakups is to ask people who have experienced a recent breakup to indicate what factors led to the breakup of their relationship. In such studies, respondents are either provided with an investigator-generated list of reasons for the breakup and asked to rate the importance of each reason or asked to provide their own list of reasons in a free-response format. In such research, sexual incompatiblity and sexual problems are often rated as at least moderately important (e.g., Cleek & Pearson, 1985; Hill et al., 1976; Kurdek, 1991; Sprecher, 1994).

SEXUAL EXPRESSION AS A PREDICTOR OF SEXUAL SATISFACTION, RELATIONSHIP SATISFACTION, AND STABILITY

We have established that sexual satisfaction is associated with relationship satisfaction and stability. In this section, we step back and discuss the sexual behaviors and experiences that may contribute to sexual satisfaction and/or also, directly or indirectly, to relationship satisfaction and stability. We discuss the following sexual experiences and behaviors: (a) frequency of sexual behavior; (b) variety and type of sexual behavior; (c) orgasmic frequency and consistency; (d) sexual communication; and (e) sexual conflict. Although we present the literature on each of these topics separately, these behaviors coexist and are interrelated. For example, couples who have sex frequently are also likely to have variety in their sex. In addition, whereas these sexual behaviors may contribute to sexual satisfaction and overall relationship quality and stability, it is just as likely that sexual satisfaction and overall relationship quality affect the expression of sexuality.

Frequency of Sexual Activity

According to recent national studies (e.g., Call, Sprecher, & Schwartz, 1995; Laumman et al., 1994; Rao & DeMaris, 1995), married couples, especially early in their marriage, have sex on the average (i.e., the mean or median) about two times a week. However, there is variation in how often couples have sex, with this variation found to be linked to sexual satisfaction (and relationship quality).

Studies that have included measures of both sexual frequency and sexual satisfaction have found that they are positively associated (e.g., Hunt, 1974, Laumann et al., 1994; Trussell & Westoff, 1980). Thus, couples who have more frequent sex are generally also those who are most sexually satisfied; conversely, those who do not have frequent sex are less sexually satisfied. However, it should be noted that even though there appears to be an ubiquitous decline in sexual frequency with increasing age (or with time in the relationship), there is not a corresponding decline in sexual satisfaction (e.g., Edwards & Booth, 1994; Laumann et al., 1994). This may reflect the fact that the desired or expected level of sexual frequency, as well as its discrepancy from actual frequency, are factors that contribute to sexual satisfaction. Individuals may assume as they get older, sex will be less frequent and thus they do not become distressed when sexual frequency does decrease. Consistent with this, in an early study of marital relationships, Terman, Buttenweiser, Ferguson, Johnson, and Wilson (1938) found that small discrepancies between desired and actual frequency of sexual interaction are associated with marital satisfaction (and large discrepancies are associated with lower marital satisfaction).

The association between sexual frequency and sexual satisfaction is found even while controlling for relationship duration and other variables. For example, Blumstein and Schwartz (1983) found that for all couple types represented in their study (gay, lesbian, and heterosexual) sexual frequency is positively correlated with sexual quality, controlling for duration of the relationship, educational level, and other variables. Other research has examined the direct association of sexual frequency with relationship quality, and found a positive association. For example, Call et al. (1995) analyzed data from Wave 1 of the National Survey of Families and Households and examined several predictors of sexual frequency, including age and opportunity variables such as education, employment, and presence of children. Age is the strongest predictor of frequency of marital sex (its effect is negative), and marital satisfaction is the second strongest predictor (happy marriages are associated with a higher sexual frequency). Because Call et al. (1995) controlled for several other variables that are often associated with both marital satisfaction and sexual frequency (marital duration, presence of children), this research demonstrates that there is an unique relationship between sexual frequency and marital satisfaction that cannot be explained by other variables.

Variety and Type of Sexual Activity

Most of the research on the association between sexual frequency and sexual satisfaction, as discussed, has focused on the frequency of intercourse or coitus, at least for heterosexual respondents. However, most couples engage in other sexual behaviors in addition to sexual intercourse, either as foreplay behaviors or as other genital-focused behaviors that might lead to orgasm. For example, many couples engage in oral–genital sex (Blumstein & Schwartz, 1983; Laumann et al., 1994). A positive association is found between frequency of oral–genital sex and sexual satisfaction, for both heterosexual and homosexual couples (Blumstein & Schwartz, 1983). Blumstein and Schwartz (1983) also found that oral sex is more important to the sexual satisfaction of heterosexual men than to that of heterosexual women. It has also been found that couples who engage in some experimentation and variety in sex are more sexually satisfied (Greeley, 1991).

Orgasms

The apex of sexual pleasure is widely seen to reside in the sexual orgasm. The consistent failure to achieve orgasm, anorgasmia, in sexual interaction with a partner constitutes a major sexual dysfunction in both males and females (see American Psychiatric Association, 1994). The ability to experience orgasm is tied to physiological mechanisms, individual characteristics and behaviors, and interpersonal processes (Mah & Binik, 2001). Our focus here is on the connection of the frequency and consistency of orgasm to interpersonal/couple processes and other outcomes.

In the context of couple relationships, the occurrence and consistency of orgasm is positively related to the quality of the sexual relationship (Singh, Meyer, Zambarano, & Hurlbert, 1998; Young, Denny, Young, & Luquis, 2000; Young & Luquis, 1998) and the general quality of the relationship (Singh et al., 1998; Young et al., 2000; Young & Luquis, 1998). The bulk of research on orgasmic response has focused on females, because they exhibit much more variation than males in the likelihood of having an orgasm during sexual interaction. According to a study using the data collected in the National Health and Social Life Survey (Laumann, Paik, & Rosen, 1999), 22% to 28% of women have been unable to reach orgasm at least once in the preceding 12 months, while only 7% to 9% of men report this problem. Consequently, there is little variation to explain for the occurrence of male orgasm in relationships.

Orgasmic Frequency/Consistency and Sexual Satisfaction.   Several studies have shown the positive association between sexual satisfaction in relationships and orgasmic frequency/consistency (Birnbaum, Glaubman, & Mikulincer, 2001; Hyde, DeLamater, & Durik, 2001; Singh et al., 1998; Young et al., 2000). However, caution must be taken in interpreting some empirical findings connecting these two phenomena, as the occurrence of orgasm is sometimes used as a proxy for sexual satisfaction (see previous discussion concerning the definition and measurement of sexual satisfaction) or questions concerning orgasm may be included in multi-item measures of sexual satisfaction. Experiencing frequent orgasms does not ensure sexual satisfaction. For example, a man experiencing premature ejaculation with a partner may have orgasms consistently, yet be very sexually unsatisfied.

The mechanisms by which orgasm and sexual satisfaction are linked are not clear. We propose two possible causal links. First, from a social exchange perspective, people who experience orgasm consistently, as compared to those who do not, are likely to perceive high levels of sexual rewards, thus increasing sexual satisfaction. Symbolic interaction theorists might explain this same association through reference to "role performance." When partners consistently have orgasms during sexual interaction, they may view themselves and their partners as successfully fulfilling the role of "sexual partner," thus leading to greater sexual satisfaction.

Second, it is plausible that high sexual satisfaction may lead to the increased occurrence of orgasm. For example, sexually satisfied, as compared to sexually dissatisfied people, are more likely to engage in noncoital sexual activities such as oral–genital stimulation and extensive foreplay, thus increasing the likelihood of orgasm (Young & Luquis, 1998; Young et al., 2000).

Orgasmic Frequency/Consistency and General Relationship Quality.   Several studies (Birnbaum et al., 2001; Singh et al., 1998; Young & Luquis, 1998; Young et al., 2001) have shown that the occurrence of orgasm in sexual relationships is positively associated with various indicators of general relationship quality. Specifically, more frequent or consistent orgasms are associated with greater (a) love for the partner and feelings of being loved in return (Birnbaum et al., 2001); (b) sense of interdependence with the partner (Birnbaum et al., 2001; (c) general relationship satisfaction (Young & Luquis, 1998; Young et al., 2001); and (d) other positive nonsexual aspects (e.g., recreational companionship, shared activities; Young et al., 2001). The mechanisms by which orgasmic frequency/consistency are connected with relationship quality are largely unexplored. However, several potential explanations are evident.

First, it may be that relationship quality *leads* to greater likelihood of orgasm. Relationally satisfied partners may demonstrate their thoughtfulness and care for the partner through more active participation and uninhibitedness during sexual interaction, thus increasing the likelihood that orgasm will occur (Young & Luquis, 1998; Young et al., 2001). Second, orgasm may be more likely due to increased communication about sexual needs and desires by individuals in high-versus low-quality relationships (Byers & Demmons, 1999; Cupach & Comstock, 1990). Third, physiological explanations remain unexplored, but are potentially important. The recent research showing that marital quality is positively associated with immunocompetence and endocrine activity (Kiecolt-Glaser, McGuire, Robles, & Glaser, 2002) suggests that the examination of potential physiological pathways from relationship quality to orgasmic frequency is warranted. Some research findings, although mixed and sparse, suggest that oxytocin may play an enhancing role in producing orgasms in women (Anderson-Hunt & Dennerstein, 1994).

Last, the opposite causal direction between relationship quality and orgasmic frequency/consistency is also possible, but has not been examined. It is quite plausible that frequent and consistent orgasms lead to enhanced relationship quality. Unfortunately, longitudinal research that might clarify the causal direction between relationship quality and orgasmic frequency/consistency has not been conducted.

Sexual Communication

It is commonly accepted that communication about sexual issues is important in close relationships throughout their developmental course. The communication of sexual/relational interest to potential partners is an essential task in establishing relationships that may lead to sexual involvement and increasing long-term commitment. In accord with the purpose of this chapter, we are concerned with sexual communication and its association with various relationship outcomes in couples who have at least a modicum of commitment. Thus, we do not discuss sexual communication behaviors that operate in rather short-term pairings.

The study of sexual communication and its association with relationship factors is relatively sparse, despite its purported importance. Several factors contribute to this situation. First, much sexual communication occurs during sexual interaction, which makes it much less amenable to scientific study using observational methods (for an exception, see Masters & Johnson, 1966, 1979). Second, considerable sexual communication is transmitted through subtle nonverbal channels that may be relatively idiosyncratic to individual couples.

However, the extant research does show that sexual communication (at least as reported by the participants) is related to both sexual and nonsexual dimensions of relationships. The more couples talk about sex in general, the greater their satisfaction with both the sexual (Byers & Demmons, 1999; Chesney, Blakeney, Cole, & Chan, 1981) and nonsexual aspects of their relationships (Byers & Demmons, 1999; Yelsma, 1986). In addition, the *quality* of sexual communication is positively associated with both sexual and nonsexual relationship satisfaction (Banmen & Vogel, 1985; Cupach & Comstock, 1990) and the development of the relationship (Wheeless, Wheeless, & Baus, 1984). Other studies examined the specific mechanisms by which sexual communication is linked to both sexual and nonsexual relationship satisfaction. These studies explored the link of sexual and nonsexual satisfaction with how sexual desire is communicated and received (e.g., initiation and acceptance/refusal). In addition, other research examined how disclosure of sexual information is related to sexual and nonsexual satisfaction.

Sexual Initiation, Acceptance, and Refusal.   In a potential sexual episode, partners must first communicate to each other their interest or lack of interest in engaging in sexual interaction. Much of this communication is likely through nonverbal channels, but research has focused on the verbal expression of interest (or lack of interest) to a partner concerning a sexual interaction. As expected, men in heterosexual relationships initiate sexual interaction more often than do women (Brown & Auerback, 1981; Byers & Heinlein, 1989). Contrary to popular belief, women are as likely to accept their partners' initiations as men are to accept initiations from their partners, when the number of initiations is controlled (Byers & Heinlein, 1989). From the perspective of social exchange, sexual satisfaction should be higher when accepted initiations (e.g., rewards) are high and lower when refused initiations (e.g., costs) are high. The few studies done in this area support the exchange perspective. Increased refusals are related to lower sexual and relationship satisfaction, whereas increased levels of accepted initiations are positively related to sexual and relationship satisfaction (Byers & Heinlein, 1989). However, both directions of causality between these two constructs are plausible. Increased or decreased sexual or relationship satisfaction could lead to more initiations or refusals. Thus, we expect the tie between initiations and refusals/acceptances with relationship and sexual/relationship satisfaction is likely reciprocal. For example, women are more likely to actively refuse sexual initiations when they perceive that their partners will not react negatively (Morokoff et al., 1997).

Disclosure of Likes and Dislikes.   One function of sexual communication is for sexual partners to disclose their likes and dislikes concerning sexual interaction, thus increasing the possibility of pleasing sexual interaction. From the perspective of social exchange theory, when sexual disclosures are effective, partners are more likely to engage in sexual interaction that fulfills the likes (rewards) and avoids the dislikes (costs) of partners, thus leading to increased sexual and relationship satisfaction. The existing research is consistent with this perspective.

Early work by Masters and Johnson (1979) found that the subjective quality of sexual interaction is higher in homosexual couples than in heterosexual couples. These researchers attributed the higher subjective quality to the more extensive disclosure of likes and dislikes during sexual interaction for homosexual couples than for hetero-sexual couples. Results of more direct tests of the link between sexual self-disclosure and sexual satisfaction are consistent with those of Masters and Johnson (1979). More extensive sexual self-disclosure positively predicts sexual satisfaction in committed re-lationships (Byers & Demmons, 1999; MacNeil & Byers, 1997; Purnine & Carey, 1997). Similarly, sexual self-disclosure positively predicts relationship satisfaction in com-mitted relationships (Byers & Demmons, 1999) and relationship commitment (Herold & Way, 1988). As with communication of desire, a reciprocal relationship between sex-ual self-disclosure and sexual/relationship satisfaction is equally likely.

In summary, effective sexual communication is conducive to both sexual and re-lationship satisfaction. However, despite good communication, some level of conflict in sexual relationships is virtually inevitable. We turn to this aspect next.

Sexual Conflict and Partner Discrepancies

Conflict over sexual issues in relationships is a frequent source of tension or problems in committed relationships. A survey of therapists showed that over 50% of couples seeking therapy had problematic issues concerning sexuality (Geiss & O'Leary, 1981). Sexual conflict is also common in dating couples. One study revealed that 47% of daters had disagreements about sex at least once during a 4-month period (Byers & Lewis, 1988). In the preceding section we discussed areas that could potentially generate conflict over sex between partners, for example, how sexual desire is initiated, how sexual initiations are accepted or rejected, and the communication about their sexual likes and dislikes. There is a substantial literature concerning newly developing dating relationships and their conflict over engaging in various levels of sexual involvement (see Koss & Cleveland, 1997). Our concern here is sexual conflict in more established relationships, where the level of sexual involvement has likely been established. Only a few studies have directly investigated the association between conflict over sex and sexual/relationship quality. In addition, there is a small body of research on how sexual and relationship satisfaction is related to discrepancies between partners on various sexual dimensions (e.g., discrepancies in sexual desire). Although these latter studies do not look at conflict per se, the assumption is made that these discrepancies have the potential to cause conflict. First, we address the issue of sexual conflict and relationship/sexual satisfaction.

Sexual Conflict.   In light of the evidence that couples frequently have conflict over sexual issues (Geiss & O'Leary, 1981), it is somewhat surprising that relatively little empirical work has addressed the extent to which conflict over sexual issues impacts sexual and relationship satisfaction. However, some research on sexual conflict has been done with both premarital and marital relationships.

Studies of sexual conflict in ongoing relationships have addressed general conflict about sexual issues in the relationship and aggressive tactics used to force a partner to have intercourse. *General sexual conflict* refers to conflict not specific to a particular sex-ual issue. One study of premarital relationships examined the role of general sexual conflict (e.g., the extent to which the partners had conflict concerning 34 separate sex-ual issues) in relationship and sexual satisfaction (Long, Cate, Fehsenfeld, & Williams, 1996). Results showed that increased conflict over sexual issues is negatively related to both sexual and relationship satisfaction. More notably, sexual conflict predicted general relationship satisfaction over and above the contribution of general conflict in the relationship in a 4-month follow-up of the respondents. This suggests that sexual conflict plays an unique role in general satisfaction within premarital relationships.

General sexual conflict also has negative consequences for *marital* relationships. A study of married women who reported that they suffered from inhibited sexual desire found that sexual stress (e.g., conflict about frequency, inconsideration about sexual needs, lack of willingness to compromise about sexual activity) is negatively related to sexual compatibility (e.g., agreement on sexual values, level of interest in sex, etc.), but is not related to marital satisfaction (Hurlbert, Apt, Hurlbert, & Pierce, 2000). Next, we address the issue of how certain types of sexual conflict are associated with relationship factors.

Content specific sexual conflicts arise when partners have conflict over a specific sexual issue. Few studies have addressed the impact of specific sexual conflict on ongoing relationships. However, two studies have researched this issue, one examining premarital conflict and the other marital conflict.

Conventional wisdom suggests that sexual aggression in premarital relationships is more common in casual dating relationships than in more serious dating relationships. The rationale for that belief is that sexual interaction is the main focus of short-term pairings, whereas serious couples negotiate a mutually agreeable role for sexual interaction in their relationships. Consequently, the opportunity for sexual conflict is diminished. Research has not supported such a view. Women in serious dating relationships report *higher* levels of coercion and pressure to engage in sexual activity than those in casual relationships (Christopher, 1988). Christopher (1988) suggests that such coercive behavior may emanate from seriously dating individuals' beliefs that they have a "right" to sexual intimacy. One study has shown that exercise of that perceived right through sexual coercion is significantly related to general conflict in the relationship for both genders (Christopher, Madura, & Weaver, 1998). One other study with married individuals is consistent with this perspective (Buss, 1989). Women experience lower overall satisfaction and lower sexual satisfaction the more their husbands are sexually aggressive. Men are less satisfied overall and less sexually satisfied the more their wives are sexually withholding. These findings are consistent with a symbolic interaction perspective. For example, when women withhold sex and men are aggressive, men and women may view the partner as not fulfilling the role of "wife" or "husband" adequately, thus leading to dissatisfaction. On the other hand, an evolutionary interpretation might suggest that when women withhold sex (a strategy to increase reproductive fitness), it leads to emotional upset due to interference with men's reproductive strategies. For women, they are dissatisfied with aggressiveness by their husbands because it does not signal that husbands are committed to supporting their offspring. We next address discrepancies between partners on sexual dimensions that could induce conflict over sex.

Partner Discrepancies. Existing research has examined discrepancies between partners on sexual attitudes, sexual desire, and preferences for sexual behavior and the association of those discrepancies with relationship quality. The assumption is that when discrepancies exist between partners, there is either increased conflict or the potential for conflict, although it is not directly assessed in the studies we reviewed.

The association of sexual discrepancies with satisfaction differs somewhat between males and females. In a study using both dating and married individuals (Cupach & Metts, 1995), discrepancies (measured with difference scores between partners) in attitudes toward sexual responsibility (e.g., "using birth control is responsible," "men have equal responsibility for birth control") are negatively related to sexual and relationship satisfaction only for men (Cupach & Metts, 1995). These researchers speculated that women are more likely than men to be concerned with issues of sexual responsibility and have consequently adjusted to that situation. However, there is more consistency between the genders in relation to how similar their positivity toward sexual behavior is seen in their lives. The more similar the partners in the positivity of their attitudes toward sexuality in their lives, the more both men and women are sexually satisfied, although similarity in positivity is related to general relationship satisfaction only for men. It may be that the relative importance of sexuality to men (vs. women) may explain why discrepancies in positivity is more closely associated with men's relationship satisfaction.

Another study of married couples (Purnine & Carey, 1999) showed more congruence between males and females. This study examined similarity/difference in sexual behavior preferences (e.g., use of contraception, use of erotica, use of drugs/alcohol, foreplay, etc.). Both "objective" similarity (difference scores between partners' individual preferences) and people's individually based perceptions of similarity are generally positively related to sexual satisfaction for both partners, except that females' perceived similarity is not related to males' sexual satisfaction (Purine & Carey, 1999).

Some gender differences were also found in the association of sexual desire discrepancies with sexual and relationship satisfaction in dating couples (Davies, Katz, & Jackson, 1999). They found that the greater the "objective" discrepancy in sexual desire (difference between partners' individual desire levels), the lower the sexual and relationship satisfaction for women, whereas "objective" discrepancies are not related to sexual and relationship satisfaction for men. This gender difference could be due to the purported increased sensitivity of women versus men to relationship dynamics (Peplau & Gordan, 1985). The findings for men and women are more consistent when *perceived* discrepancies (i.e., the individual's perception of whether there is a discrepancy between partners) are examined. Each person's perception of a discrepancy in sexual desire is negatively related to their *own* sexual satisfaction and their *own* relationship satisfaction. Similarly, each person's perceived discrepancy in sexual desire is related to the *partner's* sexual satisfaction. In contrast, each person's perceived discrepancy is not related to the *partner's* relationship satisfaction. The lack of association between one partner's perceived discrepancy in desire and the other partner's relationship satisfaction cannot be readily explained. It is plausible that people may not always be aware that their partners perceive a discrepancy in desire. On the other hand, if lack of awareness of a partner's perception of a discrepancy accounts for the absence of a link to relationship satisfaction, one would also expect that there would also be no tie to sexual satisfaction. Consequently, we believe that the gender differences presented here must be viewed as tentative.

These findings are consistent with both social exchange and symbolic interaction theory. Theoretically, when people are not discrepant (i.e., are similar) on sexual dimensions, rewards are maximized and costs are minimized, thus promoting satisfaction in the sexual and general relationship. From an SI perspective, dissimilarities in sexual dimensions between partners is indicative of a lack of shared meaning between partners, thus producing dissatisfaction.

SEXUAL EXPRESSION AS A DIMENSION OF HIGHER-ORDER RELATIONSHIP CONSTRUCTS THAT ARE LINKED TO RELATIONSHIP SATISFACTION AND STABILITY

Thus far in this chapter, we have discussed how sexual satisfaction is associated with overall relationship quality and stability and how various types of sexual expression contribute to sexual satisfaction and therefore also to overall relationship quality. In the literature that we have reviewed, the sexuality variables have been conceptualized and operationalized as distinct from relationship quality variables (e.g., satisfaction). However, sexuality is also linked to relationship stability and satisfaction in its role as a *component* of relationship phenomena that are empirically and theoretically associated with sexual satisfaction and relationship quality. This issue is discussed in greater detail in Sprecher and McKinney (1993). In the following, we summarize briefly four relationship phenomena that include a sexuality dimension in their operationalization.

Intimacy

Intimacy has been defined as a feeling of closeness and sharing of emotions and physical experiences with another person (e.g., Schaefer & Olson, 1981). It has also been conceptualized as a type of interaction (Prager, 2000; Reis & Shaver, 1988). Several scales have been developed to measure intimacy, and most contain items that measure sexual intimacy or physical expression. For example, Schaefer and Olson (1981) measured five aspects of intimacy, and one of these is *sexual intimacy* (sharing affection and sexual activities). Example items are "Sexual expression is an essential part of our relationship" and "I am satisfied with our sex life." Other intimacy scales that include items that measure a sexual dimension are the Waring (1984) Intimacy scale (e.g., Waring, McElrath, Lefcoe, & Weisz, 1981) and the Psychosocial Intimacy Questionnaire (Tesch, 1985). Research has shown that intimacy is positively associated with relationship satisfaction and commitment (e.g., Sprecher et al., 1995).

Love

There are many different models or typologies of love (see Hendrick & Hendrick, 2000), and some specific types of love are defined to be more sexual than are others (see Hendrick & Hendrick, chapter 7, this volume). One sexual type of love is passionate love, which is often distinguished from the more low-keyed companionate love (e.g., Berscheid & Walster, 1969; Walster & Walster, 1978). Passionate love has several features, including that it is intensely emotional, that it can be inherently unstable, and that it contains a sexual component (Hatfield & Rapson, 1990; Sprecher & Regan, 1998). In the Passionate Love Scale developed by Hatfield and Sprecher (1986) to measure this intense type of love, several items refer to sexuality including "Sometimes my body trembles with excitement at the sight of ___," "I want ___ physically, emotionally, mentally," and "I sense my body responding when ___ touches me." Passionate love has been found to be associated with relationship satisfaction and other measures of relationship quality (Hendrick & Hendrick, 1989; Sprecher & Regan, 1998).

A type of love similar to passionate love is Eros, which is included as one of the love styles in the typology originally developed by Lee (1973), and studied empirically by Hendrick and Hendrick (2000). This type of love is measured by a subscale of the Love Attitudes Scale (Hendrick & Hendrick, 1986) and contains the items "Our lovemaking is very intense and satisfying," and "My love and I have the right physical 'chemistry' between us." Eros is found to be the love style most consistently predictive of relationship satisfaction and relationship stability (Hendrick, Hendrick, & Adler, 1988; Meeks, Hendrick, & Hendrick, 1998).

Exchange

In intimate relationships, partners exchange a variety of resources, including household tasks, money, services, and sexual favors. One partner's sexual factors can be exchanged for the other's sexual factors and/or exchanged for other types of rewards in the relationship (e.g., love, gifts, etc; e.g., Foa & Foa, 1974). Rewards, equity, and other exchange concepts have been measured through both global indicators and through detailed or domain-specific measures (Sprecher, 2001a). Many of the detailed measures include items referring to resources associated with sex. For example, a list of seven resources that has been used in several research studies consists of love, status, services, information, goods, money, and sex (Cate, Lloyd, Henton, & Larson,

1982; Michaels, Acock, & Edwards, 1986; Sprecher, 2001a). Sprecher (2001b) found that measures of equity, investments, and rewards based on these resources are associated with relationship satisfaction and commitment.

Maintenance Behaviors

Sexual behaviors are also an aspect of the larger-order construct, *relational maintenance*. As defined by Dindia (2000), relational maintenance is a "dynamic process" and refers to "all the cognitive, affective, and behavior dynamics involved in maintaining a relationship" (p. 288). Several researchers identified and measured *maintenance strategies*, common strategies that individuals engage in to help maintain their relationship. In some of this theoretical and empirical work, physical or sexual affection and engaging in sexual relations are identified as types of maintenance strategies (e.g., Bell, Daly, & Gonzalez, 1987; Dainton, 1991). Research indicates that there is a positive association between the perceived frequency of maintenance strategies (by both self and partner) and relationship satisfaction (for a review, see Dindia, 2000).

FUTURE RESEARCH DIRECTIONS AND CONCLUSIONS

This chapter documented evidence showing that couples who have more frequent and satisfying sex are more likely to be satisfied overall in the relationship and likely to remain together as compared to couples who have less frequent and less satisfying sex. However, experts on marriage (e.g., Edwards & Booth, 1994) observed that a small proportion of couples have good marriages but poor sexual relationships and another small group of couples have bad marriages but good sex. We encourage more research on these "outlier" couples, including in-depth interviewing, which may reveal how the discrepancy between the sexual aspect of the relationship and the other aspects of the relationship are managed.

We also encourage more research on the role of sexual experiences in contributing to relationship quality among older couples, including those who enter new romantic relationships later in life after widowhood or divorce. The proportion of the population over the age of 75 is increasing and therefore, it is important to know how sexuality is expressed in these couples and the effects of various types of sexual expression on satisfaction when one or both partners are limited physically. In addition, we encourage research on the influence of sexuality on relationship quality in other types of understudied relationships, including homosexual relationships and extramarital and other extradyadic relationships.

More research could be conducted using diverse and sophisticated methods to examine the association between sexuality and relationship quality and stability. For example, more research is needed with longitudinal designs in order to examine how sexual satisfaction changes over time in long-term relationships, and also on how the association between sexual satisfaction and relationship quality may change over time. Investigators of existing, ongoing longitudinal studies conducted with married couples are likely to continue to collect and analyze more waves of data with their samples and should be able to provide further insight into the role of sexuality in contributing to relationship quality and stability over time. These studies include The Early Years of Marriage Project based on a sample of Black and White married couples in the Detroit area (e.g., Oggins et al., 1993) and the Marital Instability Over the Lifecourse Project, which was based on a national sample of married individuals obtained through random digit dialing (e.g., Edwards & Booth, 1994). In addition, multiple-wave data collections can be combined with diary or frequent (daily) assessments of sexual activity and satisfaction in order to more accurately assess the fluctuations over time in sexuality variables. Such frequent assessments make it possible to examine the role of sexuality in the everyday life of couples. We need more research that examines the daily processes of couples (e.g., within couple analyses). For example, although we know that at the aggregate level, sexual satisfaction is associated with relationship satisfaction, will we find that these two variables co-vary within couples on a daily basis?

The 1990s were characterized by an increased availability of large-scale national studies on sexuality, with the most notable one being the National Health and Social Life Survey (e.g., Laumann et al., 1994). We call for continuing research to be conducted with large national data sets, including with both partners of the couple. Laumann and Parish (2001) have conducted a large-scale study in China similar to the NHSLS, and perhaps similar data collection efforts will be conducted in other countries as well in the next decade. Future research needs to validate the association between sexual satisfaction and relationship satisfaction in individuals of various ethnicities and cultural backgrounds.

We also believe that theoretical advances are necessary in order to advance research on the interplay of sexuality and close relationships. Our impression is that much research on sexuality and close relationships has no theoretical underpinnings. This situation reduces the likelihood that empirical findings will be integrated into a coherent whole that takes the field significantly forward. Theoretical work could utilize existing theories or focus on the development of new theories. In addition, other theoretical contributions could be made through the integration of existing research into theoretical or conceptual models. An excellent example of such work using symbolic interaction theory is the volume by Christopher (2001).

We also encourage that research be done on the specific practices that are suggested to enhance the sexual union. For example, recent attention has been given to Tantra sex (Mumford, 1993), which is an inclusion of the spirituality, creative use of sexual energy, and a focus on chakra or focal points throughout the body in order to heighten both the union with the other and the union with the Divine.

Regardless of how divine sex is in a close relationship, overall relationship quality is associated with whether couples have it, how often they have it, and how satisfied they are with it. The amount of time couples may engage in genital sexual activity may be very little compared to the time they spend doing other activities together (watching television, eating, sharing household tasks, etc.), but the quality of this time together can impact the rest of the relationship.

REFERENCES

American Psychiatric Association. (1994). *Diagnostic and statistical manual of mental Disorders* (4th ed.). Washington, DC: Author.

Anderson-Hunt, M., & Dennerstein, L. (1994). Increased female sexual response after oxytocin. *British Medical Journal, 309*, 929.

Aron, A., & Henkemeyer, L. (1995). Marital satisfaction and passionate love. *Journal of Social and Personal Relationships, 12*, 139–146.

Banmen, J., & Vogel, N. A. (1985). The relationship between marital quality and interpersonal sexual communication. *Family Therapy, 12*, 45–58.

Bell, R. A., Daly, J. A., & Gonzalez, C. (1987). Affinity-maintenance in marriage and its relationship to women's marital satisfaction. *Journal of Marriage and the Family, 49*, 445–454.

Berscheid, E., & Reis, H. T. (1998). Attraction and close relationships. In D. R. Gilbert, S. T. Fisk, & G. Lindzey (Eds.), *The handbook of social psychology* (Vol. 2, 4th ed., pp. 196–281). New York: McGraw-Hill.

Berscheid, E., & Walster, E. (1969). *Interpersonal attraction*. Reading: MA: Addison-Wesley.

Birnbaum, G., Glaubman, H., & Mikulincer, M. (2001). Women's experience of heterosexual intercourse—scale construction, factor structure, and relations to orgasmic disorder. *Journal of Sex Research, 38*, 191–204.

Blumstein, P., & Schwartz, P. (1983). *American couples*. New York: Morrow.

Brown, M., & Auerback, A. (1981). Communication patterns in initiation of marital sex. *Medical Aspects of Human Sexuality, 15,* 105–117.

Buss, D. M. (1989). Conflict between the sexes: Strategic interference and the evocation of anger and upset. *Journal of Personality and Social Psychology, 56,* 735–747.

Buss, D. M. (1994). *The evolution of desire: Strategies of human mating.* New York: Basic Books.

Buss, D. M. (1998). Sexual strategies theory: Historical origins and current status. *The Journal of Sex Research, 35,* 19–31.

Byers, E. S., & Demmons, S. (1999). Sexual satisfaction and sexual self-disclosure within dating relationships. *Journal of Sex Research, 36,* 180–189.

Byers, E. S., Demmons, S., & Lawrance, K. (1998). Sexual satisfaction within dating relationships: A test of the interpersonal exchange model of sexual satisfaction. *Journal of Social and Personal Relationships, 15,* 257–267.

Byers, E. S., & Heinlein, L. (1989). Predicting initiations and refusals of sexual activities in married and cohabiting heterosexual couples. *The Journal of Sex Research, 26,* 210–231.

Byers, E., S., & Lewis, K. (1988). Dating couples' disagreements over the desired level of sexual intimacy. *The Journal of Sex Research, 24,* 15–20.

Call, V., Sprecher, S., & Schwartz, P. (1995). The incidence and frequency of marital sex in a national sample. *Journal of Marriage and the Family, 57,* 639–652.

Cate, R. M., Lloyd, S. A., Henton, J. M., & Larson, J. H. (1982). Fairness and reward level as predictors of relationship satisfaction. *Social Psychology Quarterly, 45,* 177–181.

Chesney, A. P., Blakeney, P. E., Cole, C. M., & Chan, F. A. (1981). A comparison of couples who have sought sex therapy with couples who have not. *Journal of Sex and Marital Therapy, 7,* 131–140.

Christopher, F. S. (1988). An initial investigation into a continuum of premarital sexual pressure. *The Journal of Sex Research, 25,* 255–266.

Christopher, F. S. (2001). *To dance the dance: A symbolic interactional exploration of premarital sexuality.* Mahwah, NJ: Lawrence Erlbaum.

Christopher, F. S., Madura, M., & Weaver, L. (1998). Premarital sexual aggressors: A multivariate analysis of social, relational, and individual variables. *Journal of Marriage and the Family, 60,* 56–69.

Cleek, M. G., & Pearson, T. A. (1985). Perceived causes of divorce: An analysis of interrelationships. *Journal of Marriage and the Family, 47,* 179–183.

Cupach, W. R., & Comstock, J. (1990). Satisfaction with sexual communication in marriage: Links to sexual satisfaction and dyadic adjustment. *Journal of Social and Personal Relationships, 7,* 179–186.

Cupach, W. R., & Metts, S. (1995). The role of sexual attitude similarity in romantic heterosexual relationships. *Personal Relationships, 2,* 287–300.

Dainton, M. (1991, May). *Relational maintenance revisited: The addition of physical affection measures to a maintenance typology.* Paper presented to the International Communication Association, Chicago, IL.

Davies, S., Katz, J., & Jackson, J. L. (1999). Sexual desire discrepancies: Effects on sexual and relationship satisfaction in heterosexual dating couples. *Archives of Sexual Behavior, 28,* 553–567.

Derogatis, L. R., & Melisaratos, N. (1979). The DSFI: A multidimensional measure of sexual functioning. *Journal of Sexual and Marital Therapy, 5,* 244–281.

Dindia, K. (2000). Relational maintenance. In C. Hendrick & S. S. Hendrick (Eds.), *Close relationships: A sourcebook* (pp. 287–299).Thousand Oaks, CA: Sage.

Edwards, J. N., & Booth, A. (1994). Sexuality, marriage, and well-being: The middle years. In A. S. Rossi (Ed.), *Sexuality across the life course* (pp. 233–259). Chicago: The University of Chicago Press.

Felmlee, D., Sprecher, S., & Bassin, E. (1990). The dissolution of intimate relationships: A hazard model. *Social Psychology Quarterly, 53,* 13–30.

Fincham, F. D., & Bradbury, T. N. (1987). The assessment of marital quality: A reevaluation. *Journal of Marriage and the Family, 49,* 797–809.

Foa, U. G., & Foa, E. B. (1974). *Social structures of the mind.* Springfield, IL: Thomas.

Gagnon, J. H. (1990). The implicit and explicit use of the scripting perspective in sex research. *Annual Review of Sex Research, 1,* 1–43.

Geiss, S., & O'Leary, K. (1981). Therapist ratings of frequency and severity of marital problems: Implications for research. *Journal of Marital and Family Therapy, 7,* 515–520.

Glenn, N. D. (1990). Quantitative research on marital quality in the 1980s: A critical review. *Journal of Marriage and the Family, 52,* 818–831.

Greeley, A. M. (1991). *Faithful attraction: Discovering intimacy, love, and fidelity in American marriage.* New York: Doherty.

Grote, N. K., & Frieze, I. H. (1998). Remembrance of things past: Perceptions of marital love from its beginnings to the present. *Journal of Social and Personal Relationships, 15,* 91–109.

Hatfield, E., & Rapson, R. L. (1990). Passionate love in intimate relationships. In B. S. Moore & A. Isen (Eds.), *Affect and social behavior* (pp. 126–152). Cambridge, England: Cambridge University Press.

Hatfield, E., & Sprecher, S. (1986). Measuring passionate love in intimate relationships. *Journal of Adolescence, 9,* 383–410.

Hatfield, E., Utne, M. K., & Traupmann, J. (1979). Equity theory and intimate relationships. In R. L. Burgess & T. L. Huston (Eds.), *Social exchange in developing relationships* (pp. 99–133). New York: Academic Press.

Henderson-King, D. H., & Veroff, J. (1994). Sexual satisfaction and marital well-being in the first years of marriages. *Journal of Social and Personal Relationships, 11*, 509–534.

Hendrick, C., & Hendrick, S. (1986). A theory and method of love. *Journal of Personality and Social Psychology, 50*, 392–402.

Hendrick, C., & Hendrick, S. S. (1989). Research on love: Does it measure up? *Journal of Personality and Social Psychology, 56*, 784–794.

Hendrick, S. S., & Hendrick, C. (2000). Romantic love. In C. Hendrick & S. S. Hendrick (Eds.), *Close relationships: A sourcebook* (pp. 203–215). Thousand Oaks, CA: Sage.

Hendrick, S. S., Hendrick, C., & Adler, N. L. (1988). Romantic relationships: Love, satisfaction, and staying together. *Journal of Personality and Social Psychology, 54*, 980–988.

Herold, E., & Way, L. (1988). Sexual self-disclosure among university women. *The Journal of Sex Research, 24*, 1–14.

Hill, C. T., Rubin, Z., & Peplau, L. A. (1976). Breakups before marriage: The end of 103 affairs. *Journal of Social Issues, 32*, 147–168.

Hudson, W. W. (1998). Index of sexual satisfaction. In C. M. Davis, W. L. Yarber, R. Bauserman, G. Schreer, & S. L. Davis (Eds.), *Handbook of sexuality-related measures* (pp. 512–513). Thousand Oaks, CA: Sage.

Hudson, W. W., Harrison, D. F., & Crosscup, P. C. (1981). A short-form scale to measure sexual discord in dyadic relationships. *The Journal of Sex Research, 17*, 157–174.

Hunt, M. (1974). *Sexual behavior in the 1970s.* Chicago: Playboy Press.

Hurlbert, D. F., Apt, C., Hurlbert, M. K., & Pierce, A. P. (2000). Sexual compatibility and the sexual desire–motivation relation in females with hypoactive sexual desire disorder. *Behavior Modification, 24*, 325–347.

Hyde, J. S., DeLamater, J. D., & Durik, A. M. (2001). Sexuality and the dual-career couple, part II: Beyond the baby years. *Journal of Sex Research, 38*, 10–23.

Kiecolt-Glaser, J., McGuire, L., Robles, T., & Glaser, R. (2002). Emotions, morbidity, and mortality: New perspectives from psychoneuroimmunology. *Annual Review of Psychology 53*, 83–107.

Koss, M. P., & Cleveland, H. H. (1997). Stepping on toes: Social roots of date rape lead to intractability and politicization. In M. D. Schwartz (Ed.), *Researching sexual violence against women: Methodological and personal perspectives* (pp. 4–21). Thousand Oaks, CA: Sage.

Kurdek, L. A. (1991). Sexuality in homosexual and heterosexual couples. In K. McKinney & S. Sprecher (Eds.), *Sexuality in close relationships* (pp. 177–191). Hillsdale, NJ: Lawrence Erlbaum Associates.

LaRossa, R., & Reitzes, D. (1993). Symbolic interactionism and family studies. In P. G. Boss, W. J. Doherty, R. LaRossa, W. R. Schumm, & S. K. Steinmetz (Eds.), *Sourcebook of family theories and methods: A contextual approach* (pp. 135–166). New York: Plenum.

Laumann, E. O., Gagnon, J. H., Michael, R. T., & Michaels, S. (1994). *The social organization of sexuality: Sexual practices in the United States.* Chicago: University of Chicago Press.

Laumann, E. O., Paik, A., & Rosen, R. (1999). Sexual dysfunction in the United States: Prevalence and predictors. *Journal of the American Medical Association, 281*, 537–544.

Laumann, E. O., & Parish, W. (2001, November). *An overview of the national survey of sexual practices in China.* Paper presented at the Annual Meeting of the Society for the Scientific Study of Sexuality. San Diego, CA.

Lawrance, K., & Byers, E. S. (1995). Sexual satisfaction in long-term heterosexual relationships: The interpersonal exchange model of sexual satisfaction. *Personal Relationships, 2*, 267–285.

Lawrance, K., & Byers, E. S. (1998). Interpersonal exchange model of sexual satisfaction questionnaire. In C. M. Davis, W. L. Yarber, R. Bauserman, G. Schreer, & S. L. Davis (Eds.), *Handbook of sexuality-related measures* (pp. 514–519). Thousand Oaks, CA: Sage.

Lee, J. A. (1973). *The colors of love: An exploration of the ways of loving.* Don Mills, Ontario: New Press.

Long, E. C. J., Cate, R. M. Fehsenfeld, D. A., & Williams, K. M. (1996). A longitudinal assessment of a measure of premarital sexual conflict. *Family Relations, 45*, 302–308.

LoPiccolo, J., & Steger, J. D. (1974). The sexual interaction inventory: A new instrument for assessment of sexual dysfunction. *Archives of Sexual Behavior, 3*, 585.

MacNeil, S., & Byers, E. S. (1997). The relationships between sexual problems, sexual communication and sexual satisfaction. *The Canadian Journal of Human Sexuality, 6*, 277–283.

Mah, K., & Binik, Y. M. (2001). The nature of human orgasm: A critical review of major trends. *Clinical Psychology Review, 21*, 823–856.

Masters, W. H., & Johnson, V. (1966). *Human sexual response.* Boston: Little, Brown.

Masters, W. H., & Johnson, V. (1979). *Homosexuality in perspective.* Boston: Little, Brown.

Meeks, B. S., Hendrick, S. S., & Hendrick, C. (1998). Communication, love, and relationship satisfaction. *Journal of Social and Personal Relationships, 15*, 755–773.

Michael, R. T., Gagnon, J. H., Laumann, E. O., & Kolata, G. (1994). *Sex in America: A definitive survey.* Boston: Little, Brown.

Michaels, J. W., Acock, A. C., & Edwards, J. N. (1986). Social exchange and equity determinants of relational commitment. *Journal of Social and Personal Relationships, 3*, 161–175.

Morokoff, P. J., Quina, K., Harlow, L. L., Whitmire, L., Grimley, D. M., Gibson, D. R., & Burkholder, G. J. (1997). Sexual Assertiveness Scale (SAS) for women: Development and validation. *Journal of Personality and Social Psychology, 73*, 790–804.

Mumford, J. (1993). *Ectasy through Tantra.* St. Paul, MN: Llewellyn.

Oggins, J., Leber, D., & Veroff, J. (1993). Race and gender differences in black and white newlyweds' perceptions of sexual and marital relationships. *The Journal of Sex Research, 30*, 152–160.

Peplau, L. A., & Gordon, S. (1985). Women and men in love: Sex differences in close relationships. In V. O'Leary, R. Unger, & B. Wallston (Eds.). *Women, gender and social psychology* (pp. 257–291). Hillsdale, NJ: Lawrence Erlbaum Associates.

Peplau, L. A., Rubin, Z., & Hill, C. T. (1977). Sexual intimacy in dating relationships. *Journal of Social Issues, 33*, 86–109.

Pinney, E. M., Gerrard, M., & Denney, N. W. (1987). The Pinney Sexual Satisfaction Inventory. *The Journal of Sex Research, 23*, 233–251.

Prager, K. J. (2000). Intimacy in personal relationships. In C. Hendrick & S. S. Hendrick (Eds.), *Close relationships: A sourcebook* (pp. 229–242).Thousand Oaks, CA: Sage.

Purnine, D. M., & Carey, M. P. (1997). Interpersonal communication and sexual adjustment: The roles of understanding and agreement. *Journal of Clinical and Consulting Psychology, 65*, 1017–1025.

Purnine, D. M., & Carey, M. P. (1999). Dyadic coorientation: Rexamination of a method for studying interpersonal communication. *Archives of Sexual Behavior, 28*, 45–62.

Rao, K., V., & DeMaris, A. (1995). Coital frequency among married and cohabiting couples in the U.S. *Journal of Biosocial Science, 27*, 135–150.

Reis, H. T., & Shaver, P. (1988). Intimacy as interpersonal process. In S. W. Duck (Ed.), *Handbook of personal relationships: Theory, relationships, and interventions* (pp. 367–389). New York: Wiley.

Rusbult, C. E. (1983). A longitudinal test of the investment model: The development (and deterioration) of satisfaction and commitment in heterosexual involvements. *Journal of Personality and Social Psychology, 45*, 101–117.

Scanzoni, J., Polonko, K., Teachman, J., & Thompson, L. (1989). *The sexual bond: Rethinking families and close relationships.* Newbury Park, CA: Sage.

Schaefer, M. T., & Olson, D. H. (1981). Assessing intimacy: The PAIR inventory. *Journal of Marital and Family Therapy, 7*, 47–60.

Simpson, J. A. (1987). The dissolution of romantic relationships: Factors involved in relationship stability and emotional distress. *Journal of Personality and Social Psychology, 53*, 683–692.

Singh, D., Meyer, W., Zambarano, R., & Hurlbert, D. (1998). Frequency and timing of coital orgasm in women desirous of becoming pregnant. *Archives of Sexual Behavior, 27*, 15–29.

Snyder, D. K. (1979). Multidimensional assessment of marital satisfaction. *Journal of Marriage and the Family, 41*, 813–823.

Sprecher, S. (1994). Two sides to the breakup of dating relationships. *Personal Relationships, 1*, 199–222.

Sprecher, S. (1998). Social exchange theories and sexuality. *The Journal of Sex Research, 35*, 32–43.

Sprecher, S. (2001a). A comparison of emotional consequences of and changes in equity over time using global and domain-specific measures of equity. *Journal of Social and Personal Relationships, 18*, 477–501.

Sprecher, S. (2001b). Equity and social exchange in dating couples: Associations with satisfaction, commitment, and stability. *Journal of Marriage and Family, 63*, 599–613.

Sprecher, S. (2002). Sexual satisfaction in premarital relationships: Associations with satisfaction, love, commitment, and stability. *The Journal of Sex Research, 3*, 1–7.

Sprecher, S., & McKinney, K. (1993). *Sexuality.* Newbury Park, CA: Sage.

Sprecher, S., Metts, S., Burleson, B., Hatfield, E., & Thompson, A. (1995). Domains of expression interaction in intimate relationships: Associations with satisfaction and commitment. *Family Relations, 44*, 203–210.

Sprecher, S., & Regan, P. C. (1998). Passionate and companionate love in courting and young married couples. *Sociological Inquiry, 68*, 163–185.

Terman, L. M., Buttenweiser, P., Ferguson, L. W., Johnson, W. B., & Wilson, D. P. (1938). *Psychological factors in marital happiness.* New York: McGraw-Hill.

Tesch, S. A. (1985). The Psychosocial Intimacy Questionnaire: Validational studies and an investigation of sex roles. *Journal of Social and Personal Relationships, 2*, 471–488.

Thibaut, J. W., & Kelley, H. H. (1959). *The social psychology of groups.* New York: Wiley.

Trussell, J., & Westoff, C. F. (1980). Contraceptive practice and trends in coital frequency. *Family Planning Perspectives, 12*, 246–249.

Veroff, J., Douvan, E., & Hatchett, S. J. (1995). *Marital instability: A social and behavioral study of the early years.* Westport, CT: Praeger.

Waite, L. J., & Joyner, K. (2001). Emotional satisfaction and physical pleasure in sexual unions: Time horizon, sexual behavior, and sexual exclusivity. *Journal of Marriage and the Family, 63*, 247–264.

Walster, E., & Walster, G. W. (1978). *A new look at love.* Reading, MA: Addison-Wesley.

Waring, E. M. (1984). The measurement of marital intimacy. *Journal of Marital and Family Therapy, 10*, 185–192.

Waring, E. M., McElrath, D., Lefcoe, D., & Weisz, D. (1981). Dimensions of intimacy in marriage. *Psychiatry, 44*, 169–175.

Wheeless, L., Wheeless, V., & Baus, R. (1984). Sexual communication, communication satisfaction, and solidarity in the developmental stages of intimate relationships. *Western Journal of Speech Communication, 48*, 217–230.

White, L, & Keith, B. (1990). The effect of shift work on the quality and stability of marital relationships. *Journal of Marriage and the Family, 52*, 453–462.

Whitley, M. P. (1998). Sexual satisfaction inventory. In C. M. Davis, W. L. Yarber, R. Bauserman, G. Schreer, & S. L. Davis (Eds.), *Handbook of sexuality-related measures* (pp. 519–521). Thousand Oaks, CA: Sage.

Whitley, M. P., & Paulsen, S. B. (1975). Assertiveness and sexual satisfaction in employed professional women. *Journal of Marriage and the Family, 37,* 573–581.

Yela, C. (2000). Predictors of and factors related to loving and sexual satisfaction for men and women. *European Review of Applied Psychology, 50,* 235–243.

Yelsma, P. (1986). Marriage vs. cohabitation: Couples' communication practices and satisfaction. *Journal of Communication, 36,* 94–107.

Young, M., Denny, G., Young, T., & Luquis, R. (2000). Sexual satisfaction among married women. *American Journal of Health Studies, 16,* 73–84.

Young, M., & Luquis, R. (1998). Correlates of sexual satisfaction in marriage. *Canadian Journal of Human Sexuality, 7,* 115–127.

III

The Dark Side of Sex

11

Unrequited Lust

William R. Cupach
Illinois State University
Brian H. Spitzberg
San Diego State University

Although sexual attraction and desire can be potent forces that initiate and sustain personal relationships, they also can create discontent, distress, and relationship conflict. In this chapter we consider the phenomenon of *unrequited lust*. We draw on diverse literatures to explicate the manifestations and consequences of unrequited lust, as well as the coping mechanisms employed to manage it. The problematic nature of unrequited lust is illustrated in a variety of relational forms, including sexual tension in platonic friendships, sexual incompatibility in romantic relationships, sexual pursuit in cyberspace, sexual harassment in the workplace, and sexual coercion.

INTRODUCTION

Mutuality is a highly prized feature of most relationships. Few relationships we envision in everyday life succeed without a substantial dose of mutuality in perception and patterns of action. For example, *mutuality* of relationship commitment is positively associated with relational satisfaction, even after controlling for overall *level* of commitment (Drigotas, Rusbult, & Verette, 1999). When relational involvement is perceived to be unequal, the relationship tends to become unstable and the less involved partner is inclined to terminate the relationship (Drigotas & Rusbult, 1992; Hill, Rubin, & Peplau, 1976; Sprecher, Schmeeckle, & Felmlee, 2002). Perhaps the prototypical mismatch of relational intentions is reflected in the phenomenon of unrequited love, when one person's feelings of passionate love are rejected by the would-be lover (e.g., Aron, Aron, & Allen, 1998; Baumeister, Wotman, & Stillwell, 1993; Bratslavsky, Baumeister, & Sommer, 1998; Hill, Blakemore, & Drumm, 1997). In this chapter we explore a related concept that has received little attention—unrequited lust. We begin by defining lust. Then we examine the occurrence of unrequited lust in various relational forms, including platonic cross-sex friendships and romantic relationships. We also consider the special case of cyberlust. Next we review the role of lust in the contexts of sexual harassment and sexual coercion. Finally, we discuss how lust objects respond to unwanted sexual/romantic pursuit.

CONCEPTUALIZING UNREQUITED LUST

We adopt the ordinary language usage of lust as *sexual desire*, especially that which is overwhelming or obsessive (e.g., Morris, 1979). We use the terms lust and sexual desire interchangeably in this chapter. Because lust represents a particular type of want, it carries motivational force (Heider, 1958). As Regan and Berscheid (1999) explain, "desire is conceptualized as a psychological state that one *wants* to be doing or feeling or having something that one is *not* now doing, feeling, or having and whose fulfillment is associated with pleasure" (p. 15). For the purposes of this chapter, one who lusts possesses the wish to experience sexual union with another.

The experience of lust varies on both quantitative and qualitative dimensions (Hill & Preston, 1996; Regan & Berscheid, 1999). Lusting can be more or less intense with any given object of lust at any given time, and intensity can wax and wane over time. The experience of lust also varies in terms of frequency across lustful persons, lust objects, and over time. Qualitatively lust can vary in terms of the specificity of sexual activity and the specificity of the sex object. Desired sexual activity may be diffuse and general, such as the desire for some sort of sexual gratification in a vague sense. On the other hand, the desired sexual activity can be specific—anal intercourse or masturbation, for example. Regardless of the specificity of the objective (i.e., sexual activity), the object of lust also varies in specificity. The object of lust might exist in loosely formed and ill-defined erotic thoughts or fantasies, an idealized and more focused imaginary person, or a real person with whom the lustful individual is or is not acquainted. In this chapter we circumscribe our interest to those instances in which the lustful person's object is another real individual.

Although some authors collapse lust and other elements of sexuality under a more general rubric, lust is usefully distinguished from sexual arousal (e.g., erect penis, swollen clitoris) and sexual behavior (e.g., intercourse, oral copulation; Regan & Berscheid, 1999). The awareness of one's own physical stimulation does not necessarily entail desire for sexual union, although arousal can be either a precursor to or a consequence of lust. One can experience lustful desire without concomitant physical arousal. Similarly, sexual activity can occur with or without lust. The experience of lust may motivate sexual activity, or sexual activity may breed lust that leads to further sexual activity. However, sometimes the lust object does not desire sexual activity with the lustful person and sexual union is thwarted, which suggests the possibility of unrequited lust.

Lust is distinguished from, but associated with, the concept of love. Sprecher and Regan (1998) found that sexual excitement was associated more strongly with *passionate* love than with *companionate* love. Similarly, several investigations have demonstrated that sexual attraction is associated with "in love" relationships more than "love" relationships (Regan, 1998), "liking" relationships (Regan, 1998), or relationships characterized as "dating" or "friendship" (Pam, Plutchik, & Conte, 1975). Berscheid and Meyers (1996) found that being "in love" and feeling sexual desire co-occurred 85% of the time, whereas experiencing love (but not being "in love") and feeling sexual desire co-occurred only 2% of the time in their sample of college students. Regan, Kocan, and Whitlock (1998) performed a prototype analysis of the concept of romantic love and found that sexual desire was a central defining feature— even more so than sexual activities. Tennov (1979) studied the experience of intense, erotic, obsessive (and unreciprocated) love, for which she coined the neologism *limerance*. Tennov contends that sexual desire is an "essential component" of limerance. After reviewing the most recent empirical evidence, Regan and Berscheid (1999) conclude that sexual desire is a necessary, but not sufficient, condition for romantic love. They indicate that "sexual desire is the ingredient that puts the 'romantic' in romantic love. A person who does not sexually desire his or her partner may like, love, care for, or even altruistically be willing to die for that individual, but he or she is not likely to be romantically or passionately in love with that person" (pp. 133, 135). Thus, lust intensifies the experience of love, and thereby characterizes romantic, passionate, and limerant varieties of love.

Because lust is conceived as a motivational state, the lustful person formulates a relationship goal when the lust object is a specific person. Physical attraction frequently serves as the impetus for pursuit of a sexual and/or romantic relationship (e.g., Regan & Berscheid, 1995; Regan & Dreyer, 1999; Townsend & Levy, 1990) and even motivates the formation of some friendships (e.g., Bleske-Recheck & Buss, 2001). In order to realize the pleasure associated with lust fulfillment, the lustful person must interact with the lust object. At a minimum, sexual fulfillment requires the negotiation of a sexual relationship (however brief) with the sexual object. Even in a fleeting "hook up" (Paul & Hayes, 2002; Paul, McManus, & Hayes, 2000), the lustful person must coordinate sexual intentions and activity with the lust object. More commonly the lustful person must seek the lust object's affinity in order to create a relationship frame that validates mutual sexual activity. The lustful person pursues the goal of establishing a relationship with the lust object by enacting a positive self-presentation and by ingratiating the lust object (e.g., Bell & Daly, 1984). Rituals of flirtation (Givens, 1983) and courtship (Cate & Lloyd, 1992; Metts & Spitzberg, 1996) enable the development of psychological intimacy and relational interdependence. The lustful person pursues the relationship with the lust object to the extent that the relationship is perceived to be attainable and the perceived costs and risks of pursuing the relationship do not outweigh the anticipated pleasure associated with lust fulfillment. As the lustful person and lust object interact they typically develop attraction for each other that is not merely sexual. Feelings of liking or infatuation often co-occur with lust early on in relationship pursuit, and as the relationship develops, the co-occurrence of romantic love with lust is quite common (Berscheid & Meyers, 1996; Regan et al., 1998). These nonsexual feelings of positive sentiment toward a lust object undoubtedly reinforce the goal of developing and maintaining a romantic/sexual relationship. Indeed, lust and romantic love conflate and combine to energize pursuit of the relationship goal.

Relational partners' goals, meanings, and intentions are rarely isomorphic. For example, it is relatively uncommon for both relational partners to perceive that they are equally invested emotionally in their relationship (Sprecher et al., 2002). So it is with lust. Despite shared consensual activity and even mutual physical pleasure, it seems likely that levels of sexual desire are rarely identical for two sexual partners (or two individuals who seem attracted to one another in a more general sense). This is all the more likely given the vast literature revealing gender differences in motives for sex in general (i.e., males are more sexually motivated than females; e.g., McGuirl & Wiederman, 2000), acceptance and motives for casual sex (i.e., males are more accepting of casual sex than females; e.g., Clark, 1990; Oliver & Hyde, 1993; Regan & Berscheid, 1995; Regan & Dreyer, 1999; Symons & Ellis, 1989), sexual timetables (i.e., males expect sex earlier in romantic relationships than females; e.g., McCabe & Collins, 1984; Rosenthal & Smith, 1997), dating scripts (i.e., males envision more, and earlier, sexual experiences than females; e.g., Gilbert, Walker, McKinney & Snell, 1999; Laner & Ventrone, 1998; Metts & Spitzberg, 1996), sexual fantasies (i.e., males fantasize about sex more than females; e.g., Byers, Purdon, & Clark, 1998; Hicks & Leitenberg, 2001; Hsu et al., 1994; Leitenberg & Henning, 1995; Wilson, 1997), and sexual preoccupation (i.e., males think about sex more than females; e.g., Snell & Papini, 1989). "In general, then, the weight of evidence points strongly and unmistakably toward the conclusion that the male sex drive is stronger than the female" (Baumeister, Catanese & Vohs, 2001, p. 261). When the discrepancy in lust levels is substantial and when the disparity is apparent to relational partners, lust is unreciprocated. Unrequited lust represents an element of nonmutuality that can create a "relationship crisis" for partners (Morton,

Alexander, & Altman, 1976). To the extent that one partner possesses a strong sexual desire regarding the other partner and the other partner does not share that desire, the relationship incurs a disjunctive element that the partners must manage.

Which partner experiences unrequited lust in a relationship can change over the developmental and temporal course of the relationship. It is also possible for perceived unrequited lust to be mutual in nature. That is, two people may simultaneously misinterpret each other's level of sexual desire. This possibility is implied by research on pluralistic ignorance regarding making the first move in relationships (Vorauer & Ratner, 1996). This research shows that individuals are more likely to avoid making the first move in initiating relationships because of their fear of rejection, whereas they are more likely to view others' lack of initiative as based on lack of interest. Therefore, it is possible for people to lust after one another, yet never attempt relationship formation.

RELATIONAL FORMS OF UNREQUITED LUST

Unrequited lust occurs in various relational contexts. Here we consider the nature of unrequited lust in platonic friendships and romantic relationships. We also examine the unique circumstance of lust objects who are pursued in cyberspace.

Sexual Tension in Platonic Friendships

Lust in "platonic" relationships would seem to be an oxymoron. Nevertheless, "the attraction between friends is sometimes manifested as sexual desire or even sexual involvement" (Cupach & Metts, 1991, p. 94). Bratslavsky et al. (1998) contend "platonic friendships provide fertile soil for unrequited love" (p. 311). Given the connection between lust and romantic love (Berscheid & Meyers, 1996; Regan et al., 1998), friendships also create the opportunity for unrequited lust. The heterosexual composition of cross-sex friendships creates ambiguity regarding ways in which friends regard one another and define their relationship roles. In a landmark article, O'Meara (1989; also see Rawlins, 1982) delineated challenges that attend cross-sex friendship. Two of the four challenges identified by O'Meara are particularly relevant to our discussion. O'Meara argued that cross-sex friends struggle to discern the precise nature of their shared emotional bond. In addition, they must contend with managing the issue of sexuality in their relationship. Typically romance and sexuality are not the most important concerns in cross-sex friendships (e.g., Monsour, Harris, Kurzweil, & Beard, 1994; Monsour, Harvey, & Betty, 1997). Such concerns run contrary to the cultural definition of friendship. However, the unique nature of cross-sex friendships renders at least some cross-sex friendships vulnerable to issues of sex and romance.

The ambiguity of relational definition that cross-sex friends face is magnified by a number of factors. It is not uncommon for individuals to experience ambivalence regarding their sexual and relational intentions (e.g., O'Sullivan & Gaines, 1998). Friends experience greater relationship uncertainty compared to their romantic counterparts (Afifi & Burgoon, 1998), and this uncertainty is sustained to the extent that friends generally avoid overt discussion of their relationship (Baxter & Wilmot, 1985). Moreover, cross-sex friends often engage in behaviors that are ambiguous in their relational meaning and intent. For example, cross-sex friends often exhibit sexual teasing and flirting. Sometimes this merely represents a form of play, but other times it is designed to safely signal romantic or sexual attraction (Egland, Spitzberg, & Zormeier, 1996; Givens, 1983; Koeppel, Montagne-Miller, O'Hair, & Cody, 1993). The ambiguous meaning attached to flirtatious behavior permits the lustful person to deny sexual interest if challenged by a nonreciprocating partner.

Several studies have documented the experience of sexual attraction or tension on the part of at least one member among a significant minority of cross-sex friendships (Reeder, 2000; Sapadin, 1988; Werking, 1997). Kaplan and Keys (1997), for example, found that "57 percent of men and 32 percent of women reported at least moderate levels of current sexual attraction for their closest cross-sex friend" (p. 198). Perhaps this is not surprising given that sexual attraction motivates some individuals, especially young males, to initiate a cross-sex friendship (Bleske-Recheck & Buss, 2001; Rose, 1985). When sexual attraction is not mutual, the lustful friend sometimes terminates the friendship (Bleske-Recheck & Buss, 2001). Alternatively, sexual attraction may diminish over time and be displaced by "friendship" attraction. In Reeder's (2000) study of cross-sex friendships, 71% reported that their friendship attraction had increased over time, whereas 40% reported that subjective physical/sexual attraction had declined over time. Some cross-sex friendships, however, eventually evolve into romantic involvements (Swain, 1992). Still others incorporate sexual activity in their friendship (e.g., Bleske & Buss, 2000; Monsour, 1992), despite the fact that romance is not intended. Afifi and Faulker (2000) reported that about half of their sample of college students said they "'had sex' with an opposite-sex friend with whom they had no intentions of dating at the time of the sexual activity" (p. 217).

Afifi and Faulkner (2000) found sexual activity in cross-sex friendship is relationship-enhancing in some cases. In particular, friends who perceive that sexual activity enriches friendship closeness view sexual activity as positive. However, sexual activity is also associated with significant damage to the friendship for some participants. The onset of sexual activity usually represents a turning point in the developmental trajectory of a relationship (Baxter & Bullis, 1986), and sexuality is commonly tied to romance (Hendrick & Hendrick, 2002). A mismatch occurs when one friend enjoys the sexual activity within a friendship frame while the other friend perceives that the sexual activity means that the friendship is morphing into a romantic attachment. As Kaplan and Keys (1997) remark, "Managing sexuality in cross-sex friendships appears to be closely tied to managing an emotional bond" (p. 204). Consequently, some cross-sex friends strategically avoid sexual activity with each other in order to preserve the valued friendship (Messman, Canary, & Hause, 2000).

When heterosexual romantic relationships are dissolved, the former partners sometimes remain friends. In other words, romantic partners sometimes are able to redefine their once-romantic relationship into a friendship (Metts, Cupach, & Bejlovec, 1989). When one partner wants to deescalate intimacy more than the other (e.g., Hill et al., 1976; Sprecher, Felmlee, Metts, Fehr, & Vanni, 1998), it is likely that the rejected partner still harbors hope that the romantic and sexual aspects of the relationship can eventually be restored. Indeed, Kaplan and Keys (1997) found that prior romantic involvement and feelings of love are the most potent predictors of current sexual attraction in cross-sex friendships. Unfortunately, the unrequited sexual/romantic attraction strains the friendship. When lust is unrequited, it can be a source of overt conflict between friends (Samter & Cupach, 1998). Schneider and Kenny (2000) discovered that the friendships of individuals who previously were romantic partners exhibit lower quality than friendships that had no history of romantic involvement. Reeder (2000) found that being sexually (but not romantically) attracted to a friend is not deleterious to the friendship, and that the sexual attraction tends to wane over time. However, she also observed that "asymmetrical romantic attraction was the most detrimental condition for cross-sex friendships. The pressure of one person wanting to make the friendship romantic often caused these friendships to become strained and ultimately less close" (Reeder, 2000, p. 340). Ironically, being friends prior to developing a romantic relationship enhances the likelihood that ex-romantic partners can remain friends after the romantic breakup (Metts et al., 1989; Schneider & Kenny, 2000).

Finally, although most research has examined cross-sex friendships, the possibility exists that same-sex friendships can elicit analogous tensions among people who have same-sex preferences. For example, Nardi and Sherrod (1994) found gay and lesbian friendships to be similar to each other along a variety of dimensions, except conflict and likelihood of having previously been lovers. Specifically, gay men are more likely to report sex with their casual and close friends, but lesbians are much more likely to report having had sex with their best friend. The differences in handling conflict could not be tied to the sexual tensions of these relationships, but are at least suggestive that sexual tension could arise in same-sex platonic relationships.

Sexual Incompatibility in Romantic Relationships

Love and sex are seen as inextricably linked by romantic partners (Hendrick & Hendrick, 2002). Because romantic love typically entails lust (Berscheid & Meyers, 1996; Regan et al., 1998), romantic partners generally expect mutual sexual desire. In American culture, the pervasive sexual script suggests that shared intimacy or emotional closeness in a relationship legitimizes sexual activity (DeLamater, 1981; Sprecher, 1989). In particular, love that is passionate rather than companionate is strongly associated with lust (Hatfield & Rapson, 1987; Sprecher & Regan, 1998). The reciprocation of lust in a relationship enhances the likelihood of mutually satisfying sexual activity. The sexual element of the romantic relationship is associated with the more general climate of the relationship. Indeed, several studies have documented the substantial association between sexual satisfaction and relational satisfaction and adjustment in romantic relationships (Blumstein & Schwartz, 1983; Cupach & Comstock, 1990; Hudson, Harrison, & Crosscup, 1981; Perlman & Abramson, 1982; Snyder, 1979; also see Sprecher & Cate, chapter 10, this volume).

Even when partners perceive that they are fairly evenly matched in their lust levels at some point, several factors account for the potential erosion of mutuality on this dimension. First, although levels of sexual desire may be similar, each partner may possess conflicting sexual objectives. For example, one partner may have a strong preference for bondage that the other partner finds disgusting. Related to conflicting objectives, shared sexual activity may carry different meanings for relational partners (Cupach & Metts, 1991). Research indicates, for example, that men and women seek to fulfill different functions in a sexual relationship. Men tend to focus more on elements of arousal and tension release, whereas women tend to focus more on issues regarding love and intimacy (Brown & Auerback, 1981; Hatfield, Sprecher, Pillemer, Greenberger, & Wexler, 1988), although these differences apparently attenuate over the life span (Sprague & Quadagno, 1989).

Second, one's initial sexual desire may turn into a "fatal attraction" whereby the partner's erotic and sensual qualities eventually are perceived as a liability (Felmlee, 1995, 1998). The once-arousing lust object may come to be seen by the once-lustful partner as promiscuous or vane. Third, one partner's lust may decline more rapidly because of a higher need for sexual novelty and/or a nonmutual shift from passionate to companionate love. The decline in lust may be hastened by the appearance of a new lust object who is more sexually attractive compared to the object of waning lust and is perceived to be available. The lustful person displaces the object of waning lust with an object that stimulates more intense sexual desire. Fourth, over time one may find his or her partner to be less attractive because of changes in the partner's physical appearance, dissatisfaction with the partner's sexual skills, or dissatisfaction with the partner's personality or behavior. More generally, couples who experience relational conflict regarding other (nonsexual) issues can experience a decline in the quality of their sexual relationship (e.g., Blumstein & Schwartz, 1983). General dissatisfaction with the partner or the relationship can translate into a loss of sexual interest and sexual dissatisfaction, and the proportionate decline in lust may be asymmetrical.

When sexual desires are grossly mismatched between partners, the relationship itself is likely to suffer. Although nonmutuality of lust can be masked by either partner concealing his or her true level of sexual desire, nonmutuality creates a form of sexual incompatibility. Conflict about sexual issues and sexual dissatisfaction in romantic relationships can adversely affect other domains of the relationship, and ultimately lead to the demise of the relationship (Blumstein & Schwartz, 1983; Cleek & Pearson, 1985; Hill et al., 1976; Surra & Longstreth, 1990). The lustful partner is dissatisfied to the extent that his/her sexual desire remains unfulfilled, and he or she is predisposed to experience sexual jealousy and its attendant problems (see Guerrero, Spitzberg, & Yoshimura, chapter 13, this volume). Moreover, because the lustful person subscribes to the cultural script that the romantic relationship normally includes lust and concomitant sexual activity, expectations for the relationship are violated. In other words, if the lustful person perceives that lust is not mutual, it is seen as a form of interpersonal rejection and relational devaluation—i.e., the lustful person feels that his or her partner does not value the relationship as much as the lustful person would like (Leary, 2001). The feelings of rejection occur even when the lustful person knows that his/her partner accepts and likes (or even loves in a companionate sense) the lustful partner. Because lust mutuality is unlikely to be engineered by the lustful person, hurt feelings may motivate him or her to withdraw from the lust object or terminate the relationship altogether to avoid further rejection (e.g., Leary, Springer, Negel, Ansell, & Evans, 1998).

Although the lust object may be flattered that the lustful partner finds him or her attractive, the lust object is ultimately burdened by the constraint of the lustful partner's physical and emotional needs. Consequently, the lust object may decide to dissolve or scale back the relationship. The principle of least interest (Waller, 1938) suggests that the unreciprocating lust object has more power in the relationship and can more easily terminate the relationship because he or she is less emotionally involved and has less to lose (e.g., Hill et al., 1976; Sprecher et al., 2002). Regan's (1998) recent research supports this idea. She devised vignettes to manipulate characterizations of couples who possess various combinations of high or low levels of sexual desire. When couples are discrepant in their levels of sexual desire, the individual with low sexual desire is perceived as more likely to be unfaithful and more likely to terminate the relationship.

When a lust object terminates the relationship with a lustful partner, the rejected partner may attempt to reconcile the relationship. After all, the lustful person realizes that it is not uncommon for partners who breakup to get back together again (e.g., Davis, Ace, & Andra, 2000; Langhinrichsen-Rohling, Palarea, Cohen, & Rohling, 2000). The lustful person's sexual desire motivates attempts to reestablish the relationship that is necessary to achieve sexual fulfillment. The concomitant experience of continuing passionate love for the ex-partner magnifies the importance of regaining the ex-partner's affections and thereby escalates the lustful person's pursuit of a romantic relationship with the lust object. The more important it is to have a relationship with the lust object, the more persistent the lustful person will be in pursuing reconciliation (Cupach, Spitzberg, & Carson, 2000). Not infrequently, the unwanted pursuit of a rejecting partner by a rejected partner can be quite persistent and harassing (e.g., Clark & Labeff, 1986; Dunn, 1999, 2002; Jason, Reichler, Easton, Neal, & Wilson, 1984). When pursuit of a former partner becomes obsessive and threatening, it constitutes stalking (Cupach & Spitzberg, 1998; Emerson, Ferris, & Gardner, 1998; Spitzberg & Cupach, 2002).

Although the unwanted attention that a lust object receives can be annoying and frustrating, it also can be quite flattering, especially when the lustful person engages in romantic affinity-seeking behavior (Dunn, 2002). Overtures by the lustful person may make the lust object ambivalent about reconciliation, which reinforces the lust-ful person's hopes and efforts. The lust object also experiences guilt about rejecting the lustful person (Baumeister et al., 1993; Bratslavsky et al., 1998). These feelings, along with the desire to minimize hurt, often lead a rejecting partner to communicate rejection in an indirect and face-saving manner (e.g., Folkes, 1982; Metts, Cupach, & Imahori, 1992; Snow, Robinson, & McCall, 1991). As a consequence, the lustful person may take the ambiguous rejection as a sign of encouragement and intensify efforts to reconcile with the lust object.

The Special Case of Unrequited Cyberlust

Historically speaking, substantive technological changes in communication media have often produced revolutionary changes in culture, society, and interpersonal rela-tions (e.g., Inose & Pierce, 1984; Pool, 1981; Williams, 1991). From Gutenberg's printing press, to the telegraph, landline telephone, radio, television, satellite communications, and most recently the Internet and cellular telephone, each new revolution in media has facilitated significant structural and qualitative changes in how people relate to others. These changes sometimes are only recognized from a position of relative hindsight, as social evolution sometimes occurs very gradually. However, the Internet displays all the hallmarks, in even its brief contemporary history, of a true revolution in communication and human relations (e.g., Cerulo, 1997; Kedzie, 1997; Ronfeldt, 1992).

Research on the social effects of the Internet is in its infancy, and as a result there is minimal empirical evidence regarding its potential impact on unrequited lust (Good-son, McCormick & Evans, 2000; Ogilvie, 2001). However, there are several reasons why Internet use is likely to facilitate unrequited lust (Miceli, Santana, & Fisher, 2001). Be-fore these reasons are examined, a brief detour is needed to define the construct being examined. A close analogue of unrequited cyberlust—cyberstalking—will also be de-fined, which will illustrate the difficulties of defining a construct that is associated with a rapidly evolving technological landscape.

The term "cyberspace" was introduced into the social lexicon by Gibson (1984) in the fictional novel *Neuromancer*: "Cyberspace. A consensual hallucination...A graphic representation of data abstracted from the banks of every computer in the human system" (p. 51). The term was a prefix adaptation from *cybernetics* (Wiener, 1950), which is the scientific study of communication and signal control in machine and living systems. This term was derived from the Greek *kubernetes*, which refers to a steersman, which suggests the steering, or distribution and selection, of informa-tion. So the prefix *cyber* does not seem strictly to refer to any particular technology or medium. Consequently, in order to delimit the construct, *cyberlust* is defined here as *the computer mediated expression of sexual desire*. *Unrequited cyberlust*, therefore, is defined as *unreciprocated sexual desire expressed via computer mediated means*. Thus, un-requited cyberlust could include cellular telephone, pager, fax, PDA, and personal computer media, and any future technological innovations that rely on computer (or digital processing) networks for their transmission. As technological convergence increases across these media, the particular features of any specific technology (i.e., phone, PDA, and even television) become less important than the Internet-enabled interactional functions permitted by the entire class of technologies.

One of the earliest signs that cyberlust could migrate to, and implicitly across, communication media was the phenomenon of obscene and harassing phone calls. Research is scant on this phenomenon, in part because victims are often unsure they have been victims (e.g., a "hang-up" call may or may not be a harassing or targeted call), and even when they are certain, they may know nothing about the identity of the perpetrator or the meaning of the call. Nevertheless, some research indicates that obscene and hang-up calls are relatively common experiences, and some evidence suggests that sizable percentages of such calls are specifically targeted at the receiver (Katz, 1994; Murray, 1967; Savitz, 1986; Sczesny & Stahlberg, 2000; Sheffield, 1989; Smith & Morra, 1994; Warner, 1988). "Nastygrams" and inappropriate messages once relegated to paper and bulletin boards have likewise migrated to e-mail (Markus, 1994).

Whereas the telephone provided a new outlet or channel for transmitting lustful messages, the Internet, combined with the information processing power and accessibility of its enabling computers, radically expanded both the stimuli and opportunities for lustful interaction. The Internet is particularly facilitative of lustful communications in a variety of ways. First, it has engendered a vast expansion of access to pornography, and more extreme, deviant, and previously illicit sexual imagery and interaction than previous media permitted (McGrath & Casey, 2002). Such availability of sexual stimuli has been one of the factors associated with a new phenomenon of Internet addiction, and explicitly associated with Internet sex addiction and compulsivity (e.g., Griffiths, 2001). Most cybersex pursuits appear fairly incidental and inconsequential. Anderson (2001), for example, found college students surveyed spent only an average of less than 1 minute per day engaged in cybersex activities (9.8% of their sample met criteria for Internet dependence), even though among those who used the Internet, the average daily usage was 100 minutes per day (with only 6% of the sample spending more than 400 minutes per day). Cybersex was the least common use of the Internet for both the low- and high-user groups. In contrast, Pratarelli, Browne and Johnson (1999) found that 20% of their collegiate sample reported using the Internet for sexual arousal purposes. However, within such distributions of users are likely to be more compulsive cybersex users. Cooper, Delmonico and Burg (2000) found, in an Internet sample of over 9,000 MSNBC subscriber respondents (mean age 32–35, 14% female), almost 11% could be considered "to have some degree of difficulties with sexual behaviors (and may in fact be sexually compulsive)" (p. 11). Only 4.6% of the sample was considered explicitly "sexually compulsive," and only 1% met this criterion *and* spent more than 11 hours per week in "online sexual pursuits," therefore classifying them as cybersex compulsives. "The cybersex compulsives reported spending an estimated average of about 35 to 45 total hours per week online overall" (p. 13). Not surprisingly, 24% of cybersex addicts reported that online sexual pursuits jeopardized some area of their life (p. 17). Such compulsiveness and addiction may be reinforced by the medium because time on the Internet is generally time away from face-to-face (f-t-f) forms of interaction. The implications of diminished f-t-f forms of interaction may be significantly increased levels of loneliness and depression (Kraut et al., 1998), although other research has not replicated this finding (Wästlund, Norlander, & Archer, 2001). Certainly cybersex compulsives or addicts are likely to reflect higher proportions of diminished quality of life (Brenner, 1997), personality disorders (Black, Belsare, & Schlosser, 1999), loneliness (Pratarelli et al., 1999) depression and relational troubles (Griffiths, 1999, 2001; Schneider, 2000; Schwartz & Southern, 2000) than nonaddicted populations.

Second, the internet is increasingly becoming a normative space for meeting, courting, dating, and developing relationships with others (Merkle & Richardson, 2000; Nice & Katzev, 1998; Parks & Floyd, 1996). Such relationships initiated online often migrate from the cyberspace to the "real life" (RL) of f-t-f interaction (Parks & Floyd, 1996). Other research suggests that email and the internet are often used to supplement more traditional communication channels (Parks & Floyd, 1996; Parks & Roberts, 1998; Rumbough, 2001), although McKenna, Green and Gleason (2002) predict that the Internet serves a "gating" function in Internet-initiated relationships that it is unlikely to play in relationships that evolve initially through more personal media. Nevertheless, for the most part, such relationships are viewed as equivalent to f-t-f relationships along various dimensions of relational quality (Nice & Katzev, 1998; Parks & Floyd, 1996), even though the Internet may tend to exaggerate disclosure and compress normal relationship processes (Merkle & Richardson, 2000). As a space for relating and initiating relationships, the Internet opens a new arena in which lust can be expressed, and thereby unreciprocated as well.

Third, the Internet provides a variety of technological features that may reinforce the expression of lust. The Internet permits (a) a wider range of targeting of recipients through chatrooms and listserves and the like; (b) better investigative resources for locating personal information and potential objects of desire; (c) a partial illusion of relative anonymity, which may embolden the expression of lust; (d) relatively efficient, rapid escalation of intimacy (Merkle & Richardson, 2000); and (e) the linking of romantic and sexual pursuits (via pornography, computer dating services, etc.) and mundane communications in the same medium (i.e., the computer as a device specifically enables both audiovisual relating and sexual stimulation). In particular, computers and the Internet provide a 'Triple A Engine' of Access, Affordability, and Anonymity" to "turbocharge (i.e., accelerate and intensify) online sexual interactions" (Cooper, 2000, p. 2).

Finally, the Internet may be particularly facilitative of fantasy. The extensive proliferation of games and fantasy groups, combined with the relative anonymity and dissociation of geographic limitations, all give play to the pursuit of fantasy. This fantasy world may particularly appeal to lustful desires that might otherwise be normatively constrained through cultural standards and routines (McGrath & Casey, 2002).

Whether these features of computer-mediated communication facilitate unrequited lust has yet to be addressed extensively in any systematic empirical manner. If cyberstalking is taken as a reasonable prototype (or at least, analogue) of unrequited lust, then there is certainly tantalizing evidence for concern (Burgess & Baker, 2002). First, there are many specific cases of cyberpredators attempting or succeeding in exploiting both normal (e.g., see Cyber-predators, 2002) and vulnerable (e.g., Katz, 2001) populations. Second, what evidence exists suggests a substantial increase in the occurrence of, or at least awareness of, cyberstalking and predatorial use of computers. Cyber-predators (2002) notes that the FBI opened 113 cases of Internet child exploitation in 1996, and over 1,500 in 2001. Third, at least two studies of cyberstalking types of activities indicate cause for concern. In a nationally representative sample of over 1,500 youths ages 10 to 17, about 20% reported having received a sexual solicitation or approach through the Internet over the past year. Approximately 3% of regular Internet-using youths received an "aggressive sexual solicitation" in which the pursuer attempted some form of contact beyond the Internet (Finkelhor, Mitchell, & Wolak, 2000). Of those youths receiving aggressive sexual solicitations, 66% were girls. Although the age of the pursuer was unknown in 27% of cases, almost a fourth (24%) were believed to be adults (18 and older), and the remaining (48%) were perceived to be younger than 18. Only 24% of incidents were reported to parents, and even fewer (10%) were reported to an authority.

Spitzberg and Hoobler (2002) surveyed 235 college students using a measure of cyber-obsessional pursuit victimization. Relatively few respondents reported experiencing the more extreme forms of unwanted cyber pursuit. For example, fewer than 3% experienced someone attempting to disable their computer, altering or taking over their electronic identity (i.e., cyber-rape), directing others to the victim in threatening ways, meeting first online and then following, threatening, or stalking in RL. However, sizable proportions reported someone exposing the victim's private information (17%), sabotaging the victim's private reputation (12%), receiving unwanted pornographic or obscene images or messages (19%), and receiving excessively disclosive messages (26%), excessively needy or demanding messages (25%), or exaggerated messages of affection (31%). Clearly not all cyberstalking or cyberpredation is focused on lust, but just as clearly, much of it is. As such, the Internet has made it easier to express lust, and perhaps, more likely for such lust to be unrequited.

DARKER MANIFESTATIONS OF UNREQUITED LUST

So far we have been concerned primarily with unrequited lust when it is manifested in the context of negotiating a consensual relationship. Our brief discussion of cyberstalking, however, suggests that unrequited lust may be relevant to darker circumstances. In the following sections we consider the role of unrequited lust in two such contexts: sexual harassment and sexual coercion.

Sexual Harassment

Certain facets of sexual harassment may reflect unrequited lust. By definition, sexual harassment implies an unrequited (i.e., unwanted) element, so to the extent that such harassment has lustful motives, it is a form of unrequited lust. Sexual harassment has received extensive attention in the past 2 decades (see Charney & Russell, 1994; Eisaguirre, 1993; Fitzgerald, 1993; Gutek, 1985; Keyton, 1996; McKinney & Maroules, 1991; Rotundo, Nguyen, & Sacket, 2001). Conceptions of sexual harassment vary, but most definitions imply or require all of the following features: "the behavior is unwanted (as perceived by the victim) and/or repeated and/or deliberate, there is some harm or negative outcome for the victim, a wide range of behaviors is included, and the offender has more power than the victim" (McKinney & Maroules, 1991, p. 29). More recently, the term harassment has been extended to include peer relations in which a power discrepancy may not be inherent, ranging in contexts from the playground (e.g., McMaster, Connolly, Pepler, & Craig, 2002) to the organization (e.g., Pierce & Aguinis, 2001). Traditionally, sexual harassment is considered to take two basic forms: hostile environment and quid pro quo. *Hostile environment harassment* consists of a pattern of gender-directed behavior that creates an offensive, intimidating, or inimical working climate. Such hostility can be achieved both through behavior demeaning to a gender in general or through unwanted sexual attention paid to a particular person of gender (Fitzgerald, Gelfand, & Drasgow, 1995). *Quid pro quo harassment* is gender-directed behavior in which economic opportunity is made conditional on sexual activity or favor (Keyton, 1996; Welsh, 1999). Although both forms of harassment may be motivated by sexual desire, the latter seems more likely to be initially stimulated by lust. Other research suggests there is at least one additional and distinct component of sexual harassment: unwanted sexual attention (Gelfand, Fitzgerald, & Drasgow, 1995). Still another typology identifies five distinct types of harassment: pressure for dates/relationships, sexual comments, sexual posturing, sexual touching, and sexual assault (Gruber, 1990).

There are few sexually oriented behaviors that have been studied in as many large and small samples as sexual harassment. Estimates indicate somewhere between 15% and 90% of women, and perhaps 15% of men, experience sexual harassment during their lifetime (Charney & Russell, 1994; Welsh, 1999).[1] In a review of 18 studies, an average of 44% of women had been harassed (Gruber, 1990). Such wide variations in prevalence estimates suggest methodological sensitivity to type of sample, context, measurement, and perceiver. Most research approaches operationalize harassment in terms of its behavioral manifestations. One review (Rotundo et al., 2001) attempted a comprehensive coding scheme of sexually harassing behavior, which comprised

---

[1] Charney & Russell's (1994) review indicates only 1% to 7% of victims file formal complaints.

seven types of harassment: *derogatory attitudes—impersonal* ("behaviors that reflect derogatory attitudes about men or women in general"), *derogatory attitudes—personal* ("behaviors that are directed at the target that reflect derogatory attitudes about the target's gender"), *unwanted dating pressure* ("persistent requests for dates after the target has refused"), *sexual propositions* ("explicit requests for sexual encounters"), *physical sexual contact* ("behaviors in which the harasser makes physical sexual contact with the target"), *physical nonsexual contact* ("behaviors in which the harasser makes physical nonsexual contact with the target"), and *sexual coercion* ("requests for sexual encounters or forced sexual encounters that are made a condition of employment or promotion"). For the most part, the latter five categories are likely to overlap substantially with sexual desire.

Although harassment may intrinsically involve power and attempted influence, there is extensive evidence that sexual harassment also correlates to various factors consistent with a sexual motivation interpretation (Pierce & Aguinis, 2001; Studd, 1996; Williams, Giuffre, & Dellinger, 1999). This is hardly surprising, given that 15% to 33% of romantic or sexual relationships begin at work (Bureau of National Affairs, 1988; Dillard & Witteman, 1985; Laumann, Gagnon, Michael, & Michaels, 1994) and perhaps as many as 7% of workers' closest relationships with a coworker is sexually intimate (Lobel, Quinn, St. Clair, & Warfield, 1994). Pierce and Aguinis (2001) predict that different types of sexual harassment are more likely to occur as a result of different types of office romance. Specifically, they argue that dissolved companionate and passionate romances are more likely to result in hostile environment harassment, whereas romances in which one of the partners has job advancement motives (i.e., mutual user or utilitarian romances) are likely to result in quid pro quo harassment. However, organizational "flings" in which the primary motive is sexual excitement are predicted as unlikely to result in any sexual harassment on dissolution. Of course, such predictions are likely to be moderated by how unilateral or bilateral the dissolution was (Metts et al., 1989; Pierce & Aguinis, 2001), such that unilaterally dissolved romances are more likely to lead to sexual harassment than bilaterally dissolved romances.

In academic and organizational contexts, unwanted pursuit of romance, dates, and sex is commonly viewed as an element of sexual harassment. A very select sampling of studies illustrates some of the sexual nature of sexual harassment. For example, the U.S. Merit Systems Protection Board (1988) study of over 8,500 Federal employees found that more than 30% of females and more than 10% of males reported experiencing harassing "sexual remarks." Approximately 15% of females in 1987 experienced harassing pressure for dates, compared to 4% of males. A study of 916 family practice resident female physicians found 32% reported unwanted sexual advances (Vukovich, 1996). College populations also report victimization of sexually harassing behaviors. In one small study of college females, 24% reported being "followed for the purpose of sexual harassment;" and 61% reported receiving obscene phone calls (Herold, Mantle, & Zemitis, 1979, p. 70). Even child and adolescent populations experience sizable amounts of sexually harassing behaviors from their peers, such as unwanted sexual comments, physical contact, pressure for dates, sexual advances, and so forth (e.g., American Association of University Women, 1993; McMaster et al., 2002; Roscoe, Strouse & Goodwin, 1994). In sum, a substantial proportion of sexual harassment seems sexually motivated, regardless of its overlap with motives and means of power.

Sexual Coercion

Sexual interaction can be consensual or nonconsensual. When nonconsensual, the possibility of unrequited lust arises. The literature on nonconsensual sex tends to focus on sexual coercion and aggression (e.g., Belknap & Erez, 1995; Burkhart & Fromuth,

1991; Craig, 1990; Hall, 1990; Lloyd, 1991; Lundberg-Love & Geffner, 1989; Muehlen-hard, Harney, & Jones, 1992; Spitzberg, 1998; also see Christopher & Kisler, chapter 12, this volume). Spitzberg (1999) provided a statistical summary of 120 studies of sexual aggression. The analysis showed that approximately 13% of females have been raped, 18% have experienced attempted rape, 22% have been sexually assaulted, 24% have experienced unwanted sexual contact, and 25% have experienced sexual coercion. The rates for males, while lower, were nevertheless cause for concern. Approximately 3% of males have been raped, 5% to 6% have experienced attempted rape, 14% have been sexually assaulted, almost 8% experienced unwanted sexual contact, and 23% have been sexually coerced. Across all categories, males were far more likely to be the assaulter. Such sexual encounters represent instances in which sexual activity was pursued or achieved without reciprocal interest from the other party, and therefore, such encounters become relevant to an examination of unrequited lust.

If sexual consent is viewed on a continuum, from expressly preferred and consented to, to expressly dispreferred, sexual coercion reflects the range of dispreferred contexts. Such a continuum would envision a broader range of sexual consent and nonconsent than typically conceptualized in discussions of sexual interaction. Spitzberg (1998) identifies 10 types of sexual interaction along a consent continuum. The only purely consensual sex, in which the participants accurately express and perceive consent, is referred to as consensual sex. The other 9 types suggest the potential for lust to be unrequited. Rape, attempted rape, coerced sexual contact, acquiescence to sexual pressure, unwanted sex, refused sex, token resistance, and foregone opportunities for sex (due to mutual ignorance of the other's willingness) all suggest the possibility of sex occurring, or not occurring, because one person's lust is not shared or reciprocated. The darker shades of this continuum represent its coercive facet.

Coercion, defined broadly, extends to any sexual relations with another "taken with the intent of imposing harm on another person or forcing compliance" (Tedeschi & Felson, 1994, p. 348) or "compelled under duress or threat" to engage in sex against one's will (Sidman, 1989, p. 31). Such definitions, however, overlook domains of relevant coercive sexual interactions. Specifically, when sex is obtained through deception or intoxication, it can be viewed as nonconsensual if, given accurate or complete information or sobriety, a person would have withdrawn consent. In such cases, threat of harm may not be necessary to achieve sexual relations.

Several typologies of coercive tactics have been identified. Waldner-Haugrud and Magruder (1995), for example, examined eight types of sexual coercion: intoxication, relationship termination, blackmail, guilt, detainment, touching, use of lies, and false promises. Spitzberg (1998) reviewed dozens of studies and formulated a five-category typology of tactics: pressure and persistence (e.g., too aroused to stop, verbal pressure, bribery, continual arguments, etc.), deception (e.g., falsely profess love, mock force, lies, trickery, etc.), threat (e.g., threaten to terminate relationship, verbal threats or blackmail, physical intimidation, threat of bodily harm, weapon display, etc.), physical restraint (e.g., intoxication, physical restraint, twisting arm, holding down, etc.), and physical force/injury (e.g., physical harming, hitting, choking, beating, using weapon, etc.). These tactics suggest the intricate manner in which sex and power become entangled. Whereas various forms of coercion, especially rape, have often been viewed largely as being "the use of sex to achieve power" (Ellis, 1989; MacKinnon, 1989; Stock, 1991), other perspectives view most sexual coercion, especially among acquaintances, as "the use of power to obtain sex" (Ellis, 1989; Thornhill & Palmer, 2000; Thornhill & Thornhill, 1991). Ultimately, the distinction is likely to be more complicated (e.g., Muehlenhard, Danoff-Burg, & Powch, 1996; Spitzberg, 1998). Sexual coercion likely involves both power and sex motives (Drieschner & Lange, 1999; Malamuth, 1996; Wheeler, George, & Dahl, 2002). But where exerted power meets with resistance, the possibility of unrequited motives is apparent.

That sexual coercion is one of the darker extensions of unrequited lust is less complicated. Research abounds demonstrating the extensive negative psychological, social, and physical effects of sexual victimization (see Koss & Harvey, 1991; Spitzberg, 1998; Wiehe & Richards, 1995; Zweig, Barber & Eccles, 1997). Culture and society imbue an enormous amount of personal identity in, and normative structures around, sexuality. Therefore, when one's own sexuality is exploited or taken without consent, it is a deeply personal violation, and highly likely to be a traumatizing experience.

COPING WITH UNREQUITED LUST

The phenomena of unrequited lust are diverse, and it follows that the ways in which people respond or cope with unrequited lust are likely to be diverse as well. Here our interest is not in how the person experiencing unrequited lust will cope with his or her predicament, but in how the object of lust copes with what is often a pattern of unwanted sexual pursuit or attention. Research has explored responses to unwanted pursuit in a variety of arenas, including: unwanted sexual harassment and attention (e.g., Cochran, Frazier, & Olson, 1997; Dodd, Giuliano, Boutell, & Moran, 2002; Fritz, 1997; Quinn, Sanchez-Hucles, Coates, & Gillen, 1991), sexual refusal (e.g., Byers, 1988; Byers & Heinlein, 1989; Byers & Lewis, 1988; Emmers-Sommer, 2002; Motley & Reeder, 1995; O'Sullivan & Byers, 1993), and sexual coercion and rape resistance (e.g., Brady, Chrisler, Hosdale, Osowiecki, & Veal, 1991; Kanin, 1984; Koss, Dinero, Seibel, & Cox, 1988; Spitzberg, 1998). However, to date, few efforts have been made to integrate typologies of such responses into a comprehensive scheme, despite their potential common functions. Although these typologies reflect delimited scope due to their particular areas of application, responses to sexual harassment may have enough in common with responses to attempted rape to permit a comprehensive typology.

As an illustration, we extend our typology previously applied exclusively to stalking and obsessive relational pursuit (Spitzberg & Cupach, 2001; also see Spitzberg, 2002). We formulated a five-fold typology of coping responses: *moving inward* (i.e., engaging in activities to manage one's view of self, one's world view, or "escape" into oneself), *moving outward* (i.e., engaging assistance, input, feedback, and/or support of third-parties), *moving away* (i.e., attempts to avoid interaction with the pursuer), *moving toward/with* (i.e., engaging in activities to maintain an alternative preferred relationship with pursuer), and *moving against* (i.e., efforts to harm, punish, deter, intimidate, or otherwise impair the pursuer's efforts). In Table 11.1, we integrate literatures related to other forms of unwanted sexual and relational pursuit (e.g., Furby, Fischhoff, & Morgan, 1992; Tamres, Janicki, & Helgeson, 2002; Ullman, 2000) into this scheme. The five-fold typology reveals a reasonable fit to these diverse literatures, accommodating the efforts to cope with a full range of mild unwanted attention as well as more severe and threatening types of intrusion. In the few instances in which an obvious fit was not possible, it was typically because a strategy was overly vague (e.g., "problem solving;" Stith, Jester, & Bird, 1992) or overly mixed in function (e.g., "passive coping—ignored behavior or did nothing, avoided person, went along with behavior, made joke of behavior;" Stockdale, 1998). The first two responses are "extrarelational" in the sense that they do not involve the pursuer directly, whereas the latter three all reflect ways of interacting with the pursuer so as to eventually avoid or transform the relationship. Whereas these categories provide a reasonable a priori classification of strategies and tactics, we further speculate these response types may align themselves along two intersecting dimensions of *locus* (i.e., to whom the response is directed) and *function* (i.e., what is the intended valence of relational outcome).

Such an alignment produces a typology of five "mixed" clusters of coping responses to unwanted sexual pursuit. *Avoidance* reflects a relatively neutralizing function and

TABLE 11.1

Typology of Coping Responses to Unwanted Sexual Pursuit

MOVING OUTWARD (seeking constructive assistance from others)

Counsel—Formal: Counseling (Bjerregaard, 2000; Fisher, Cullen, & Turner, 1999; Levitt, Silver, & Franco, 1996); health professionals (Purcell, Pathé, & Mullen, 2001); lawyers (Pathé, Mullen, & Purcell, 2000); legal counsel (Kamphuis & Emmelkamp, 2001; Purcell et al., 2001); medical profession (Pathé et al., 2000); mental health care/professional, sought help (Blaauw, Winkel, Arensman, Sheridan, & Freeve, 2002); police (Pathé et al., 2000); police for assistance (Blackburn, 1999); social coping—seek medical attention, seek counseling from religious source, seek psychological counseling, discussed it with or got advice from someone unofficially, threatened to tell coworker (Malamut & Offermann, 2001); consulted family/friends (Purcell et al., 2001); defusion—social support (Gruber, 1989); sought help from friends/family (Pathé et al., 2000)

Social Support: Social support—talk to others with similar experiences, talk to someone about how you felt, seek advice (Cochran et al., 1997; Harnish, Aseltine, & Gore, 2000; Stith et al., 1992; Ullman, 2000)

Social Countersupport: Others told you that you could have done more to prevent the experience, others told you that you were irresponsible or not cautious enough, others told you that you were to blame or shameful (Ullman, 2000)

Disclosure: Talked to friends or relatives (Levitt et al., 1996); talked to someone—talked to family or friends, students or coworkers, counselor (Cochran et al., 1997); told doctor-social worker (Budd & Mattinson, 2000); told friend, relative, or neighbor (Budd & Mattinson, 2000); told partner or boy/girlfriend (Budd & Mattinson, 2000)

Tangible Aid/Information Support: Contacted local law enforcement (Miceli et al., 2001); others helped you get medical care, others provided information, others took you to police, others encouraged you to seek counseling (Ullman, 2000)

Third-party Egocentrism: Expressed so much anger at perpetrator that you had to calm person down, said she/he feels personally wronged by your experience, others so upset that she/he needed reassurance from you, others wanted to seek revenge against perpetrator (Ullman, 2000)

Third-party Protection: Arranged to have personal escort (Fremouw, Westrup, & Pennypacker, 1997); asked friends/family for protection (Nicastro, Cousins, & Spitzberg, 2000); became involved with new people (Levitt et al., 1996); contingency plan for family members (Guy, Brown, & Poelstra, 1992); contacted harasser's Internet service provider (Miceli et al., 2001); discussed safety issues with loved ones (Guy et al., 1992); family/friends talked to stalker (Brewster, 2000); security guard (Guy et al., 1992); self-defense training for loved ones (Guy et al., 1992); stayed with friends or family (Nicastro et al., 2000); training in management of assaultive behaviors (Guy et al., 1992); travel with companion (Fisher et al., 1999); increase perceived chances of outside intervention, e.g., fake arrival of others (Furby et al., 1992); increase actual chances of outside intervention, e.g., general appeal to anyone—yell "fire" or whistle; directed appeal—call police, summon nearest male (Furby et al., 1992)

MOVING INWARD (seeking self-improvement or insulation)

Accept Responsibility: (Stith et al., 1992)
Acceptance: (Wood & Conrad, 1983)
Cognitive Minimization: Can't imagine worse, think of worse experience (Meyer & Taylor, 1986)
Contemplation—Constructive: Active cognitive—try to anticipate how things turn out, go over it in your head, think about strategies (Harnish et al., 2000)
Contemplation—Destructive: Think of harming stalker, think of killing stalker (Blackburn, 1999)
Counter-disqualification: Attacking self (Wood & Conrad, 1983)
Denial: (Stith et al. 1992)

(Continued)

TABLE 11.1 *(Continued)*

MOVING INWARD (seeking self-improvement or insulation)

Distraction—Behavioral: Active—keep exceptionally busy, keep busy with work (Meyer & Taylor, 1986); avoidance—do things to take mind off situation, turn to work or other activities, daydream or fantasize (Harnish et al., 2000)

Distraction—Cognitive: Escape (Stith et al., 1992)

Drugs: Used alcohol or drugs (Levitt et al., 1996)

Ignoring/Immobility: Avoidance—ignoring harassment, doing nothing (Gruber, 1989); ignored legal action (Nicastro et al., 2000); ignored the behavior (Brewster, 2000; Cochran et al., 1997; Nicastro et al., 2000); ignored the problem (Levitt et al., 1996); ignored behavior or did nothing (U.S. Merit Systems Protection Board, 1988; Cochran et al., 1997); passive—ignoring it, walking away, pretending not to notice (Gruber & Bjorn, 1986)

Keep Documentation: Save and print harassing e-mails and messages (Miceli et al., 2001)

Manage Yourself: Control own thoughts/emotions/actions, assess the situation (Furby et al., 1992)

Neglect: Do not think about problem, decide it's not that bad a problem, ignore problem, act as though problem doesn't exist (Fritz, 1997)

Positive Reappraisal: Look for something good in what's happening, see things in a positive way, make light of situation (Harnish et al., 2000); suppression—put rape behind me, no reason to think about it (Meyer & Taylor, 1986)

Redefining the Situation: Viewing the situation as something other than harassment (Wood & Conrad, 1983)

Self Control: (Stith et al., 1992)

Spirituality: Religion—pray about or meditate on situation, trust in God (Harnish et al., 2000); spiritual belief/fantasy (Stith et al., 1992)

Stress Management: Stress reduction—think positive thoughts, techniques to reduce stress (Meyer & Taylor, 1986)

MOVING TOWARD/WITH (negotiating terms with other)

Capitulation: Went along with behavior (U.S. Merit Systems Protection Board, 1988)

Confrontation: Confront (Cochran et al., 1997; Fisher et al., 1999; Fremouw et al., 1997; Stith et al., 1992); threatened to tell others, reported behavior to an authority (Stockdale, 1998)

Deception/Manipulation: Hinting at sexual limitations, altering one's appearance, setting, or topic of conversation; giving false information (McCormack, 1979); unattractiveness—reduce/minimize assailant's propensity to rape—create bizarre/unattractive impression (Furby et al., 1992); use gender and age neutral names in Internet correspondence (Ogilvie, 2001)

Distraction: Told others to stop talking about it, told others to stop thinking about it, encouraged others to keep the experience a secret, distracted with other things (Ullman, 2000)

Face Protection/Negotiation: Defusion—pretense, masking, making do (Gruber, 1989); conventional multifunctional message—deflect harasser's threat or issue directive to stop or change behavior, while attempting to show consideration for harasser (Bingham & Burleson, 1989); rhetorical minimal message—redefine harasser's behavior as something other than harassment or redefine situation so harassment is seen as problematic, including denigration of harasser (Bingham & Burleson, 1989); rhetorical multifunctional message—redefine harassment situation, persuade harasser to retract threat or discontinue/change behavior, while deflecting negative identity implications for harasser (Bingham & Burleson, 1989); be nice—politely talk, tried to reason (Jason et al., 1984); face-protecting strategies—I'm not sure we're ready for this, we can do other things but not that, I can't unless you're committed to me (Afifi & Lee, 2000)

Face Protection/Humor: Deflect by joking or going along (Welsh, 1999); make a joke of the behavior (U.S. Merit Systems Protection Board, 1988); joking (Snow et al., 1991)

(Continued)

TABLE 11.1 *(Continued)*

MOVING TOWARD/WITH (negotiating terms with other)

Face Threat: Face-threatening strategies—I don't want to, it's getting late, "no", "stop it" (Afifi & Lee, 2000); defensive incivility (Snow et al., 1991)

Loyalty: Treat person with respect, take the person's perspective, maintain friendly relations with person, treat the person as you would want to be treated (Fritz, 1997)

Negotiation: Argued with stalker (Brewster, 2000); conventional minimal message—deflect harasser's threat and/or issue directive for harasser to stop and change behavior; may include reasons and threats or verbal aggression (Bingham & Burleson, 1989); conventional unifunctional message—deflect harasser's threat and/or issue directive for harasser to stop or change behavior; may refute counterarguments and provide reasons (Bingham & Burleson, 1989); excuses (Snow et al., 1991); expressive multifunctional message—express vague or confused thoughts and feelings toward harassment predicament with no negative affect (Bingham & Burleson, 1989); negotiation—direct request to stop, telling harasser to stop (Gruber, 1989); ask or tell person to stop (Malamut & Offermann, 2001); communicate face-to-face attention is unwanted (Blackburn, 1999); communicated via phone attention is unwanted (Blackburn, 1999); communicate via writing attention is unwanted (Blackburn, 1999); communicate don't want to see person (Jason et al., 1984); communicated attention unwanted via not returning calls (Blackburn, 1999); information—telling person sex was not desired (McCormack, 1979); logic—use rational but not moral arguments; moralizing—articulating rights of legitimacy; relationship conceptualizing—talking about the relationship (McCormack, 1979); polite refusal (Snow et al., 1991); requested person stop (Bjerregaard, 2000); asked/told person to stop (U.S. Merit Systems Protection Board, 1988); reasoning (Brewster, 2000); rhetorical unifunctional message—redefine harassment situation and persuade harasser to retract threat or discontinue/change behavior; may include consequences to noncompliance (Bingham & Burleson, 1989); self-evident justifications (Snow et al., 1991); talked to troublesome partner (Levitt et al., 1996); told suspect he/she was wrong (Nicastro et al., 2000); transcending the paradox by defining the situation as one of harassment (Wood & Conrad, 1983); reduce/minimize assailant's propensity to rape—avoid antagonizing assailant, don't miscommunicate intentions, appeal to assailant's sympathy or morals, reason with assailant (Furby et al., 1992); send message clearly stating that Internet messages are not appreciated and should be stopped (Miceli et al., 2001)

Nonverbal Display: Using facial expression, posture, physical distance, etc. (McCormack, 1979); studied seriousness—focusing attention on task; nonverbal cues of disinterest (Snow et al., 1991)

Reconciliation: Reconciled or "made up" with stalker (Fremouw et al., 1997); remain friends/were unclear in message (Jason et al., 1984)

Reward: Give gifts, provide services, flatter in exchange for compliance (McCormack, 1979)

Relationship Deescalation: Ended or tried to end relationship (Levitt et al., 1996)

Sympathy: Cried in front of perpetrator (Nicastro et al., 2000)

Voice: Confront person about problem, describe problem to person, tell person how you feel about the problem, etc. (Fritz, 1997)

MOVING AWAY (avoiding contact with other)

Availability Restriction: Absenteeism (Purcell et al., 2001); alter daily routines, schedule, lifestyle (Fremouw et al., 1997; Purcell et al., 2001); avoid (Fisher et al., 1999; Nicastro et al., 2000); avoid the person (Cochran et al., 1997; U.S. Merit Systems Protection Board, 1988); avoid going out of house, stay home (Kamphuis & Emmelkamp, 2001; Meyer & Taylor, 1986); avoid person (Levitt et al., 1996); withdrawal (Wood & Conrad, 1983); avoid working alone in office (Guy et al., 1992); avoid, curtail social outings (Blaauw et al. 2002; Pathé et al., 2000; Purcell et al., 2001); change careers, jobs (Bjerregaard, 2000; Blaauw et al. 2002; Meloy & Boyd, 2003; Pathé et al., 2000); change habit patterns, routine, travel routes

---

(Continued)

TABLE 11.1 *(Continued)*

MOVING AWAY (avoiding contact with other)

(Brewster, 2000; Kamphuis & Emmelkamp, 2001; Kohn, Flood, Chase, & McMahon, 2000; Meloy & Boyd, 2003; Pathé et al., 2000); go "underground" (Blaauw et al. 2002); flight (Snow et al., 1991); quit job or worked less; stop school (Blaauw et al. 2002; Kamphuis & Emmelkamp, 2001); establish distance or barrier between self and assailant, e.g., get out of house, run away (Furby et al., 1992)

Availability Restriction—Computer: ISP account blocking, computer firewall or filtering software protection (Miceli et al., 2001; Ogilvie, 2001)

Availability Restriction—Residence: Moved changed address, relocated (Bjerregaard, 2000; Blaauw et al. 2002; Brewster, 2000; Fisher et al., 1999; Kohn et al., 2000; Meloy & Boyd, 2003; Nicastro et al., 2000; Pathé et al., 2000; Purcell et al., 2001); moved to another city/changed addresses (Kamphuis & Emmelkamp, 2001)

Availability Restriction—Telephone: Caller ID/*69 (Brewster, 2000; Fisher et al., 1999; Nicastro et al., 2000); changed phone # (Bjerregaard, 2000; Brewster, 2000; Kamphuis & Emmelkamp, 2001; Meloy & Boyd, in press; Nicastro et al., 2000; Purcell et al., 2001); hang up when called (Fremouw et al., 1997); unlisted phone # (Blaauw et al. 2002; Guy et al., 1992); changed phone # or call-block (Brewster, 2000)

Exit: Change work routine, be transferred away, get person's work routine transferred away from you, leave company (Fritz, 1997)

Interactional Avoidance: Avoided the harasser—avoided contact (Cochran et al., 1997); do not acknowledge messages (Fisher et al., 1999); refusing to disclose personal data (Guy et al., 1992); withdraw—be reserved, shorten interaction, restrict topics, avoidance (Hess, 2002; Levitt et al., 1996)

Security—General: Protect self, e.g., changed phone number, moved (Jason et al., 1984); security measures (Blaauw et al. 2002; Fisher et al., 1999; Nicastro et al., 2000; Pathé et al., 2000); lights on, leaving (Brewster, 2000); locking doors/windows (Brewster, 2000); security system, installed (Bjerregaard, 2000)

Security—Personal: Precaution—lock car door, check door before opening, walk with keys ready (Meyer & Taylor, 1986); self-defense, class/training (Fisher et al., 1999; Guy et al., 1992; Nicastro et al., 2000)

Security—Residence: Home security (Kamphuis & Emmelkamp, 2001; Meloy & Boyd, 2003; Purcell et al., 2001)

Security—Work/Office: (Guy et al., 1992; Meloy & Boyd, 2003; Purcell et al., 2001)

Tie Signs: Displaying connection with others (Snow et al., 1991)

MOVING AGAINST (seeking/preparing to harm, threaten, intimidate, deter, or incapacitate other)

Advocacy Seeking: File formal complaint, report to immediate supervisor, report to law enforcement, report to office for handling complaints (Cochran et al., 1997; Malamut & Offermann, 2001); confrontation—organizational power structure—complaining through channels (Gruber, 1989)

Assault: Assaulted stalker (Blaauw et al. 2002); harmed stalker in self-defense (Blackburn, 1999); harmed stalker not in self-defense (Blackburn, 1999)

Coercion: Punishing or threatening to punish noncompliance (McCormack, 1979)

Confrontation—Aggressive: Ultimatums, strong or forceful language, physical defense (Gruber, 1989); assertive—attacking verbally, responding physically, taking or threatening to take the matter to someone in a position of authority (Gruber & Bjorn, 1986)

Counter-disqualification: Launching attacks at harasser (Wood & Conrad, 1983)

Incapacitation: Physically impede or incapacitate assailant, e.g., nonforceful means: give assailant drugs, get assailant drunk (Furby et al., 1992)

Legal Proceedings: Filed civil/criminal charges (Fisher et al., 1999); go to court (Bjerregaard, 2000); lawsuit (Blaauw et al. 2002); press charges (Nicastro et al., 2000)

Organization—Grievance: Filed grievance (Fisher et al., 1999)

(Continued)

TABLE 11.1 *(Continued)*

MOVING AGAINST (seeking/preparing to harm, threaten, intimidate, deter, or incapacitate other)

Physical Confrontation: Confronted physically (Nicastro et al., 2000); physically impede or incapacitate assailant, e.g., with physical force: weapon or physical struggle/fight (Furby et al., 1992)

Protective Order: (Bjerregaard, 2000; Blackburn, 1999; Fisher et al., 1999; Fremouw et al., 1997; Kohn et al., 2000; Nicastro et al., 2000); temporary restraining order (Meloy & Boyd, 2003)

Reporting—Organization: Reported behavior—lodged formal complaint (Cochran et al., 1997; Welsh, 1999); reported behavior to supervisor or other officials (U.S. Merit Systems Protection Board, 1988)

Reporting—Police: Contacted/called police (Bjerregaard, 2000; Blaauw et al. 2002; Fremouw et al., 1997; Kohn et al., 2000; Nicastro et al., 2000; Purcell et al., 2001)

Self-defense—Protection: Carried a whistle or other type of alarm (Fremouw et al., 1997)

Self-defense—Weapons: Repellent spray (Fremouw et al., 1997); bought gun (Bjerregaard, 2000; Kohn et al., 2000); weapon at home (Guy et al., 1992); weapon at the office (Guy et al., 1992); weapon, carried (Meloy & Boyd, 2003); weapon, obtained (Fisher et al., 1999)

Structural Constraint: Transfer, discipline, or give poor performance rating to harasser (U.S. Merit Systems Protection Board, 1988)

Third-Party Warning: Had someone warn the stalker (Fremouw et al., 1997)

Threat—Verbal: (Blackburn, 1999); threatened to call police (Nicastro et al., 2000); told stalker police made aware of attention (Budd & Mattinson, 2000); threatened to get stalker in trouble at work (Brewster, 2000); threatening to call police (Brewster, 2000); threaten to tell or told others (U.S. Merit Systems Protection Board, 1988); increase perceived chances of punishment, e.g., state you will press charges (Furby et al., 1992)

Threaten—Nonverbal: Increase perceived ability to cope with assailant, e.g., assume a karate stance, make it known you have a weapon (Furby et al., 1992)

Verbal Aggression: Cursed at suspect (Nicastro et al., 2000); hostile voice (Nicastro et al., 2000); angry letters to stalker (Blackburn, 1999); angry phone calls (Blackburn, 1999); yelled at stalker (Blackburn, 1999); yelled at suspect (Nicastro et al., 2000); expressive minimal message—react emotionally toward harasser—angry, hostile (Bingham & Burleson, 1989); expressive unifunctional message—criticize and condemn harasser, descriptions of complaint and justification for retaliation (Bingham & Burleson, 1989)

---

locus. A person's immobility may reflect an effort at denial, or an attempt to move within oneself. Immobility, however, is likely to function as an attempt to avoid the pursuit, cognitively or behaviorally. As such, a more active approach to moving away from someone entails all the various means of restricting the pursuer's access to oneself. *Meditation* represents a moving inward and moving toward. Efforts at positive reappraisal, forgiveness, and relationship redefinition would reflect this cluster of responses. *Social support* includes all those efforts to move toward and outward by eliciting the influence and input of others. Getting friends, family, or coworkers of the pursuer to redirect the pursuit, or seeking distraction or comfort through others represent such movement. *Intervention* efforts entail the pursuit of more forceful attempts to control, deter, or delimit the pursuer's actions through enlisting the assistance of others. This cluster includes the use of law enforcement, formal channels of regulation, and more aggressive actions such as having others threaten or harm the pursuer. Finally, *antipathy* describes internally directed actions that involve negative affect or cognition toward the pursuer, such as rumination and vengeful thinking. To our knowledge, no existing typology of coping responses has formulated such a taxonomic approach. It suggests blended types or clusters of responses that may reflect coping styles heretofore unanticipated. Despite extensive research on coping responses across these diverse literatures, relatively little research directly examines the efficacy of such responses. Seldom do such investigations proceed with a comprehensive taxonomy or sampling of coping responses. Therefore, this attempt at integrating these literatures should provide a platform from which such efforts can be pursued.

FUTURE DIRECTIONS FOR EXPLORING UNREQUITED LUST

Although scholarly knowledge about lust is accumulating (Regan & Berscheid, 1999), relatively few empirical claims regarding *unrequited* lust have been formally tested. Many of the claims about unrequited lust presented in this chapter are speculative. Conceptual refinements and empirical testing are needed to advance our understanding. In addition to the issues raised throughout this chapter, we offer some additional questions to guide future scholarship. First, because romantic love and lust are associated, it seems fruitful to investigate the connections between unrequited love and unrequited lust. Under what circumstances do they co-occur? What are their experiential similarities and differences? How and when do these phenomena influence one another? The narrative approach to gathering data employed by Baumeister et al. (1993) has yielded important insights about unrequited love. Such an approach could provide similar insights into unrequited lust.

Second, it would be helpful to explore how lovers, friends, lust objects, and researchers for that matter, discern the occurrence of unrequited lust. In what ways do lustful perons reveal their sexual desire to their objects? When do lustful persons endeavor to strategically reveal or conceal their lustful feelings? Aside from instances where a lustful person makes an overt verbal declaration, how is the lustful person's sexual desire inferred? What cues signal the mismatch between partners in their levels of lust? At what point does the perception of discrepancy in sexual desire rise to the level of nonreciprocation? We suspect that lustful persons and lust objects perceive, tolerate, and rationalize some degree of difference in sexual desire without coding it as "unrequited." Furthermore, the intriguing possibility that some individuals falsely infer that they are the object of another's lust merits consideration. What contextual and dispositional factors contribute to such misperceptions?

Finally, research should explore the various aspects of coping with the "discovery" of unrequited lust. In this chapter we proposed a taxonomy of coping responses for lust objects. The utility and comprehensiveness of this scheme requires empirical verification. Efforts should also be directed at identifying the coping mechanisms employed by lustful persons. What enables or motivates the lustful person to gradually quell desire for the lust object over time, displace the original lust object with a new one, or attempt to stimulate sexual desire in the nonreciprocating partner? Eventually coping research should demonstrate how lustful persons and lust objects successfully accomplish their emotional, self-presentational, and relational goals.

CONCLUSION

Lust. The very word evokes a sense of animal passion, of unconstrained impulse, and of palpable drive toward the fulfillment of some ancient compulsion. Stripped of such poetic license, lust is merely a sexual desire, one desire among many. Sexual desire itself has many manifestations other than mere sexual pleasure (Hill & Preston, 1996). However, we admit to a certain appreciation of poetic license. If humans really are more than mere reifications of biological impulse, poetry may be one of the only ways for us to peer deeply enough into the mirror of lust to appreciate its, and thus our own, complexity. In this chapter we have attempted to outline the many ways in which unrequited lust is almost always a problematic experience in human relationships.

Many related topics also could have been addressed in this outline (e.g., pedophilia, incest, sexual fantasy), but were left to other venues. Perhaps the most ironic oversight, however, is how problematic lust can be when given full reign, unconstrained by normative convention or the reciprocals from the object of desire. In closing then, we leave it to another observer of the human condition to proffer a final missive to those who would pursue lust fulfilled:

> The expense of spirit in a waste of shame
> Is lust in action; and till action, lust
> Is perjur'd, murderous, bloody, full of blame,
> Savage, extreme, rude, cruel, not to trust;
> Enjoy'd no sooner, but despised straight;
> Past reason hunted; and no sooner had,
> Past reason hated, as a swallow'd bait,
> On purpose laid to make the taker mad:
> Mad in pursuit and in possession so;
> Had, having, and in quest to have, extreme;
> A bliss in proof,–and prov'd, a very woe;
> Before, a joy propos'd; behind, a dream:
> Shakespeare (1991, p. 56), Sonnet CXXIX

REFERENCES

Afifi, W. A., & Burgoon, J. K. (1998). We never talk about that: A comparison of cross-sex friendships and dating relationships on uncertainty and topic avoidance. *Personal Relationships, 5,* 255–272.

Afifi, W. A., & Faulkner, S. L. (2000). On being "just friends": The frequency and impact of sexual activity in cross-sex friendships. *Journal of Social and Personal Relationships, 17,* 205–222.

Afifi, W. A., & Lee, J. W. (2000). Balancing instrumental and identity goals in relationships: The role of request directness and request persistence in the selection of sexual resistance strategies. *Communication Monographs, 67,* 284–305.

American Association of University Women. (1993). *Hostile hallways: The AAUW Survey on sexual harassment in America's schools.* Washington, DC: Author.

Anderson, K. J. (2001). Internet use among college students: An exploratory study. *Journal of American College Health, 50,* 21–26.

Aron, A., Aron, E. N., & Allen, J. (1998). Motivations for unreciprocated love. *Personality and Social Psychology Bulletin, 24,* 787–796.

Baumeister, R. F., Catanese, K. R., & Vohs, K. D. (2001). Is there a gender difference in strength of sex drive? Theoretical views, conceptual distinctions, and a review of relevant evidence. *Personality and Social Psychology Review, 5,* 242–273.

Baumeister, R. F., Wotman, S. R., & Stillwell, A. M. (1993). Unrequited love: On heartbreak, anger, guilt, scriptlessness, and humiliation. *Journal of Personality and Social Psychology, 64,* 377–394.

Baxter, L. A., & Bullis, C. (1985). Turning points in developing romantic relationships. *Human Communication Research, 12,* 469–493.

Baxter, L. A., & Wilmot, W. W. (1985). Taboo topics in close relationships. *Journal of Social and Personal Relationships, 2,* 253–269.

Belknap, J., & Erez, E. (1995). The victimization of women on college campuses: Courtship violence, date rape, and sexual harassment. In B. S. Fisher & J. J. Sloan (Eds.), *Campus crime: Legal, social, and policy perspectives* (pp. 156–178). Springfield, IL : Thomas.

Bell, R. A., & Daly, J. A. (1984). The affinity-seeking function of communication. *Communication Monographs, 51,* 91–115.

Berscheid, E., & Meyers, S. A. (1996). A social categorical approach to a question about love. *Personal Relationships, 3,* 19–43.

Bingham, S. G., & Burleson, B. R. (1989). Multiple effects of messages with multiple goals: Some perceived outcomes of responses to sexual harassment. *Human Communication Research, 16,* 184–216.

Bjerregaard, B. (2000). An empirical study of stalking victimization. *Violence and Victims, 15,* 389–406.

Blaauw, E., Winkel, F. W., Arensman, E., Sheridan, L., & Freeve, A. (2002). The toll of stalking: The relationship between features of stalking and psychopathology of victims. *Journal of Interpersonal Violence, 17,* 50–63.

Black, D. W., Belsare, G., & Schlosser, S. (1999). Clinical features, psychiatric comorbidity, and health-related quality of life in persons reporting compulsive computer use behavior. *Journal of Clinical Psychiatry, 60,* 839–844.

Blackburn, E. J. (1999). *"Forever yours": Rates of stalking victimization, risk factors and traumatic responses among college women*. Unpublished doctoral dissertation, University of Massachusetts, Boston.

Bleske, A. L., & Buss, D. M. (2000). Can men and women be just friends? *Personal Relationships, 7*, 131–151.

Bleske-Rechek, A. L., & Buss, D. M. (2001). Opposite-sex friendship: Sex differences and similarities in initiation, selection, and dissolution. *Personality and Social Psychology Bulletin, 27*, 1310–1323,

Blumstein, P., & Schwartz, P. (1983). *American couples*. New York: Pocket Books.

Brady, E. C., Chrisler, J. C., Hosdale, D. C., Osowiecki, D. M., & Veal, T. A. (1991). Date rape: Expectations, avoidance, strategies, and attitudes toward victims. *Journal of Social Psychology, 131*, 427–429.

Bratslavsky, E., Baumeister, R. F., & Sommer, K. L. (1998). To love or be loved in vain: The trials and tribulations of unrequited love. In B. H. Spitzberg & W. R. Cupach (Eds.), *The dark side of close relationships* (pp. 307–326). Mahwah, NJ: Lawrence Erlbaum Associates.

Brenner, V. (1997). Psychology of computer use: XLVII. Parameters of internet use, abuse and addiction: The first 90 days of the internet usage survey. *Psychological Reports, 80*, 879–882.

Brewster, M. P. (2000). Stalking by former intimates: Verbal threats and other predictors of physical violence. *Violence and Victims, 15*, 41–54.

Brown, M., & Auerback, A. (1981). Communication patterns in initiation of marital sex. *Medical Aspects of Human Sexuality, 15*, 105–117.

Budd, T., & Mattinson, J. (2000). *Stalking: Findings from the 1998 British crime survey* (Home Office Research, Research Findings No. 129). London: Research Development and Statistics Directorate.

Bureau of National Affairs. (1988). *Corporate affairs: Nepotism, office romance, and sexual harassment*. Washington, DC: Author.

Burgess, A. W., & Baker, T. (2002). Cyberstalking. In J. Boon & L. Sheridan (Eds.), *Stalking and psychosexual obsession: Psychological perspectives for prevention, policing and treatment* (pp. 201–220). West Sussex, England: Wiley.

Burkhart, B., & Fromuth, M.E. (1991). Individual psychological and social psychological understandings of sexual coercion. In E. Grauerholz & M. A. Koralewski (Eds.), *Sexual coercion: A sourcebook on its nature, causes, and prevention* (pp. 75–90). Lexington, MA: Lexington.

Byers, E. S. (1988). Effects of sexual arousal on men's and women's behavior in sexual disagreement situations. *Journal of Sex Research, 25*, 235–254.

Byers, E. S., & Heinlein, L. (1989). Predicting initiations and refusals of sexual activities in married and cohabiting heterosexual couples. *Journal of Sex Research, 26*, 210–231.

Byers, E. S., & Lewis, K. (1988). Dating couples' disagreements over the desired level of sexual intimacy. *Journal of Sex Research, 24*, 15–29.

Byers, E. S., Purdon, C., & Clark, D. A. (1998). Sexual intrusive thoughts of college men. *Journal of Sex Research, 35*, 359–369.

Cate, R. M., & Lloyd, S. A. (1992). *Courtship*. Thousand Oaks, CA: Sage.

Cerulo, K. A. (1997). Reframing sociological concepts for a brave new (virtual?) world. *Sociological Inquiry, 67*, 48–58.

Charney, D. A., & Russell, R. C. (1994). An overview of sexual harassment. *American Journal of Psychiatry, 151*, 10–17.

Clark, R. D., III. (1990). The impact of AIDS on gender differences in willingness to engage in casual sex. *Journal of Applied Social Psychology, 20*, 771–782.

Clark, R. E., & Labeff, E. E. (1986). Ending intimate relationships: Strategies of breaking off. *Sociological Spectrum, 6*, 245–267.

Cleek, M. G., & Pearson, T. A. (1985). Perceived causes of divorce: An analysis of interrelationships. *Journal of Marriage and the Family, 47*, 179–183.

Cochran, C. C., Frazier, P. A., & Olson, A. M. (1997). Predictors of responses to unwanted sexual attention. *Psychology of Women Quarterly, 21*, 207–226.

Cooper, A. (2000). Cybersex and sexual compulsivity: The dark side of the force. In A. Cooper (Ed.), *Cybersex: The dark side of the force* (pp. 1–3). Philadelphia, PA: Brunner–Routledge.

Cooper, A., Delmonico, D. L., & Burg, R. (2000). Cybersex users, abusers, and compulsives: New findings and implications. *Sexual Addiction & Compulsivity, 7*, 5–29.

Craig, M. E. (1990). Coercive sexuality in dating relationships: A situational model. *Clinical Psychology Review, 10*, 395–423.

Cupach, W. R., & Comstock, J. (1990). Satisfaction with sexual communication in marriage: Links to sexual satisfaction and dyadic adjustment. *Journal of Social and Personal Relationships, 7*, 179–186.

Cupach, W. R., & Metts, S. (1991). Sexuality and communication in close relationships. In K. McKinney & S. Sprecher (Eds.), *Sexuality in close relationships* (pp. 93–110). Hillsdale, NJ: Lawrence Erlbaum Associates.

Cupach, W. R., & Spitzberg, B. H. (1998). Obsessive relational intrusion and stalking. In B. H. Spitzberg & W. R. Cupach (Eds.), *The dark side of close relationships* (pp. 233–263). Mahwah, NJ: Lawrence Erlbaum Associates.

Cupach, W. R., Spitzberg, B. H., & Carson, C. L. (2000). Toward a theory of obsessive relational intrusion and stalking. In K. Dindia & S. Duck (Eds.), *Communication and personal relationships* (pp. 131–146). New York: Wiley.

Cyber-predators. (2002). *CQ Researcher, 12*(8), 169–192.

Davis, K. E., Ace, A., & Andra, A. (2000). Stalking perpetrators and psychological maltreatment of partners: Anger–jealousy, attachment insecurity, need for control, and break-up context. *Violence and Victims, 15,* 407–425.

DeLamater, J. D. (1981). The social control of sexuality. *Annual Review of Sociology, 7,* 263–290.

Dillard, J. P., & Witteman, H. (1985). Romantic relationships at work: Organizational and personal influences. *Human Communication Research, 12,* 99–116.

Dodd, E. H., Giuliano, T. A., Boutell, J. M., & Moran, B. E. (2002). Respected or rejected: Perceptions of women who confront sexist remarks. *Sex Roles, 45,* 567–577.

Drieschner, K., & Lange, A. (1999). A review of cognitive factors in the etiology of rape: Theories, empirical studies, and implications. *Clinical Psychology Review, 19,* 57–77.

Drigotas, S. M., & Rusbult, C. E. (1992). Should I stay or should I go?: A dependence model of breakups. *Journal of Personality and Social Psychology, 62,* 62–87.

Drigotas, S. M., Rusbult, C. E., & Verette, J. (1999). Level of commitment, mutuality of commitment, and couple well-being. *Personal Relationships, 6,* 389–409.

Dunn, J. L. (1999). What love has to do with it: The cultural construction of emotion and sorority women's responses to forcible interaction. *Social Problems, 46,* 440–459.

Dunn, J. L. (2002). *Courting disaster: Intimate stalking, culture, and criminal justice.* New York: Aldine, DeGruyter.

Egland, K. L., Spitzberg, B. H., & Zormeier, M. M. (1996). Flirtation and conversational competence in cross-sex platonic and romantic relationships. *Communication Reports, 9,* 105–117.

Eisaguirre, L. (1993). *Sexual harassment: A reference handbook.* Santa Barbara, CA: ABC-CLIO.

Ellis, L. (1989). *Theories of rape: Inquiries into the causes of sexual aggression.* New York: Hemisphere.

Emerson, R. E., Ferris, K. O., & Gardner, C. B. (1998). On being stalked. *Social Problems, 45,* 289–314.

Emmers-Sommer, T. M. (2002). Sexual coercion and resistance. In M. Allen, R. W. Preiss, B. M. Gayle, & N. A. Burrell (Eds.), *Interpersonal communication research: Advances through meta-analysis* (pp. 315–343). Mahwah, NJ: Lawrence Erlbaum Associates.

Felmlee, D. H. (1995). Fatal attractions: Affection and disaffection in intimate relationships. *Journal of Social and Personal Relationships, 12,* 295–311.

Felmlee, D. H. (1998). Fatal attraction. In B. H. Spitzberg & W. R. Cupach (Eds.), *The dark side of close relationships* (pp. 3–31). Mahwah, NJ: Lawrence Erlbaum Associates.

Finkelhor, D., Mitchell, K. J., & Wolak, J. (2000). *Online victimization: A report on the nation's youth.* Alexandria, VA: National Center for Missing and Exploited Children.

Fisher, B. S., Cullen, F. T., & Turner, M. G. (1999). *The extent and nature of the sexual victimization of college women: A national-level analysis.* Final Report submitted to the National Institute of Justice (NCJ 179977). Washington, DC: U.S. Department of Justice.

Fitzgerald, L. F. (1993). Sexual harassment: Violence against women in the workplace. *American Psychologist, 48,* 1070–1076.

Fitzgerald, L. F., Gelfand, M. J., & Drasgow, F. (1995). Measuring sexual harassment: Theoretical and psychometric advances. *Basic and Applied Social Psychology, 17,* 425–445.

Folkes, V. S. (1982). Communicating the reasons for social rejection. *Journal of Experimental Social Psychology, 18,* 235–252.

Fremouw, W. J., Westrup, D., & Pennypacker, J. (1997). Stalking on campus: The prevalence and strategies for coping with stalking. *Journal of Forensic Sciences, 42,* 664–667.

Fritz, J. M. H. (1997). Responses to unpleasant work relationships. *Communication Research Reports, 14,* 302–311.

Furby, L., Fischhoff, B., & Morgan, M. (1992). Preventing rape: How people perceive the options of defending oneself during an assault. In E. C. Viano (Eds.), *Critical issues in victimology: International perspectives* (pp. 174–189). New York: Springer.

Gelfand, M. J., Fitzgerald, L. F., & Drasgow, F. (1995). The structure of sexual harassment: A confirmatory analysis across cultures and settings. *Journal of Vocational Behavior, 47,* 164–177.

Gibson, W. (1984). *Neuromancer.* New York: Ace Books.

Gilbert, L. A., Walker, S. J., McKinney, S., & Snell, J. L. (1999). Challenging discourse themes reproducing gender in heterosexual dating: An analog study. *Sex Roles, 41,* 753–774.

Givens, D. B. (1983). *Love signals.* New York: Crown.

Goodson, P., McCormick, D., & Evans, A. (2001). Searching for sexually explicit materials on the Internet: An exploratory study of college students' behavior and attitudes. *Archives of Sexual Behavior, 30,* 101–118.

Griffiths, M. (1999). Internet addiction: Fact or fiction? *Psychologist, 12,* 246–250.

Griffiths, M. (2001). Sex on the internet: Observations and implications for internet sex addiction. *Journal of Sex Research, 38,* 333–342.

Gruber, J. E. (1989). How women handle sexual harassment: A literature review. *Sociology and Social Research, 74,* 3–7.

Gruber, J. E. (1990). Methodological problems and policy implications in sexual harassment research. *Population Research and Policy Review, 9,* 235–254.

Gruber, J. E., & Bjorn, L. (1986). Women's responses to sexual harassment: An analysis of sociocultural, organizational, and personal resource models. *Social Science Quarterly, 67,* 814–826.

Gutek, B. A. (1985). *Sex and the workplace.* San Francisco: Jossey-Bass.

Guy, J. D., Brown, C. K., & Poelstra, P. L. (1992). Safety concerns and protective measures used by psychotherapists. *Professional Psychology: Research and Practice, 23*, 421–423.

Hall, G. C. N. (1990). Prediction of sexual aggression. *Clinical Psychology Review, 10*, 229–245.

Harnish, J. D., Aseltine, R. H., Jr., & Gore, S. (2000). Resolution of stressful experiences as an indicator of coping effectiveness in young adults: An event history analysis. *Journal of Health and Social Behavior, 41*, 121–136.

Hatfield, E., & Rapson, R. L. (1987). Passionate love/sexual desire: Can the same paradigm explain both? *Archives of Sexual Behavior, 16*, 259–278.

Hatfield, E., Sprecher, S., Pillemer, J. T., Greenberger, D., & Wexler, P. (1988). Gender differences in what is desired in the sexual relationship. *Journal of Psychology and Human Sexuality, 1*, 39–52.

Heider, F. (1958). *The psychology of interpersonal relations.* Hillsdale, NJ: Lawrence Erlbaum Associates.

Hendrick, S. S., & Hendrick, C. (2002). Linking romantic love with sex: Development of the perceptions of love and sex scale. *Journal of Social and Personal Relationships, 19*, 361–378.

Herold, E. S., Mantle, D., & Zemitis, O. (1979). A study of sexual offenses against females. *Adolescence, 14*, 65–72.

Hess, J. A. (2002, July). *Measuring distance in personal relationships: The Relational Distance Index.* Paper presented at the International Association for Relationship Research Conference, Halifax, Nova Scotia, Canada.

Hicks, T. V., & Leitenberg, H. (2001). Sexual fantasies about one's partner versus someone else: Gender differences in incidence and frequency. *Journal of Sex Research, 38*, 43–50.

Hill, C. A., Blakemore, J. E. O., & Drumm, P. (1997). Mutual and unrequited love in adolescence and young adulthood. *Personal Relationships, 4*, 15–23.

Hill, C. A., & Preston, L. K. (1996). Individual differences in the experience of sexual motivation: Theory and measurement of dispositional sexual motives. *Journal of Sex Research, 33*, 27–45.

Hill, C. T., Rubin, Z., & Peplau, L. A. (1976). Breakups before marriage: The end of 103 affairs. *Journal of Social Issues, 32*, 147–168.

Hsu, B., Kling, A., Kessler, C., Knapke, K., Diefenbach, P., & Elias, J. E. (1994). Gender differences in sexual fantasy and behavior in a college population: A ten-year replication. *Journal of Sex & Marital Therapy, 20*, 103–118.

Hudson, W. W., Harrison, D. F., & Crosscup, P. C. (1981). Short-form scale to measure sexual discord in dyadic relationships. *Journal of Sex Research, 17*, 157–174.

Inose, H., & Pierce, J. R. (1984). *Information technology and civilization.* New York: Freeman.

Jason, L. A., Reichler, A., Easton, J., Neal, A., & Wilson, M. (1984). Female harassment after ending a relationship: A preliminary study. *Alternative Lifestyles, 6*, 259–269.

Kamphuis, J. H., & Emmelkamp, P. M. G. (2001). Traumatic distress among support-seeking female victims of stalking. *American Journal of Psychiatry, 158*, 795–798.

Kanin, E. J. (1984). Date rape: Unofficial criminals and victims. *Victimology: An International Journal, 9*, 95–108.

Kaplan, D. L., & Keys, C. B. (1997). Sex and relationship variables as predictors of sexual attraction in cross-sex platonic friendships between young heterosexual adults. *Journal of Social and Personal Relationships, 14*, 191–206.

Katz, G. (2001). Adolescents and young adults with developmental disabilities interface the internet: Six case reports of dangerous liaisons. *Mental Health Aspects of Developmental Disabilities, 4*(2), 77–84.

Katz, J. E. (1994). Empirical and theoretical dimensions of obscene phone calls to women in the United States. *Human Communication Research, 21*, 155–182.

Kedzie, C. R. (1997). A brave new world or a brave new world order? In S. Kiesler (Ed.), *Culture of the internet* (pp. 209–232). Mahwah, NJ: Lawrence Erlbaum Associates.

Keyton, J. (1996). Sexual harassment: A multidisciplinary synthesis and critique. In B. R. Burleson (Ed.), *Communication yearbook 19* (pp. 93–156). Thousand Oaks, CA: Sage.

Koeppel, L. B., Montagne-Miller, Y., O'Hair, D., & Cody, M. J. (1993). Friendly? Flirting? Wrong? In P. Kalbfleisch (Ed.), *Interpersonal communication: Communication in evolving relationships* (pp. 13–32). Hillsdale, NJ: Lawrence Erlbaum Associates.

Kohn, M., Flood, H., Chase, J., & McMahon, P. M. (2000). Prevalence and health consequences of stalking—Louisiana, 1998–1999. *Morbidity and Mortality Weekly Report, 49*(29), 653–655.

Koss, M. P., Dinero, T. E., Seibel, C. A., & Cox, S. L. (1988). Stranger and acquaintance rape: Are there differences in the victim's experience? *Psychology of Women Quarterly, 12*, 1–24.

Koss, M. P., & Harvey, M. R. (1991). *The rape victim: Clinical and community interventions* (2nd ed.). Newbury Park, CA: Sage.

Kraut, R., Patterson, M., Lundmark, V., Kiesler, S., Mukopadhyay, T., & Scherlis, W. (1998). Internet paradox: A social technology that reduces social involvement and psychological well-being? *American Psychologist, 53*, 1017–1031.

Laner, M. R., & Ventrone, N. A. (1998). Egalitarian dates/traditional dates. *Journal of Family Issues, 19*, 468–477.

Langhinrichsen-Rohling, J., Palarea, R. E., Cohen, J., & Rohling, M. L. (2000). Breaking up is hard to do: Unwanted pursuit behaviors following the dissolution of a romantic relationship. *Violence and Victims, 15*, 73–90.

Laumann, E. O., Gagnon, J. H., Michael, R. T., & Michaels, S. (1994). *The social organization of sexuality: Sexual practices in the United States*. Chicago: University of Chicago Press.

Leary, M. R. (2001). Toward a conceptualization of interpersonal rejection. In M. R. Leary (Ed.), *Interpersonal rejection* (pp. 3–20). New York: Oxford University Press.

Leary, M. R., Springer, C., Negel, L., Ansell, E., & Evans, K. (1998). The causes, phenomenology, and consequences of hurt feelings. *Journal of Personality and Social Psychology, 74*, 1225–1237.

Leitenberg, H., & Henning, K. (1995). Sexual fantasy. *Psychological Bulletin, 117*, 469–496.

Levitt, M. J., Silver, M. E., & Franco, N. (1996). Troublesome relationships: A part of human experience. *Journal of Social and Personal Relationships, 13*, 523–536.

Lloyd, S. A. (1991). The darkside of courtship: Violence and sexual exploitation. *Family Relations, 40*, 14–20.

Lobel, S. A., Quinn, R. E., St. Clair, L., & Warfield, A. (1994). Love without sex: The impact of psychological intimacy between men and women at work. *Organizational Dynamics, 23*, 5–16.

Lundberg-Love, P., & Geffner, R. (1989). Date rape: Prevalence, risk factors, and a proposed model. In M. A. Pirog-Good & J. E. Stets (Eds.), *Violence in dating relationships: Emerging social issues* (pp. 169–185). New York: Praeger.

MacKinnon, C. A. (1989). *Toward a feminist theory of the state*. Cambridge, MA: Harvard University Press.

Malamut, A. B., & Offermann, L. R. (2001). Coping with sexual harassment: Personal, environmental, and cognitive determinants. *Journal of Applied Psychology, 86*, 1152–1166.

Malamuth, N. M. (1996). The confluence model of sexual aggression: Feminist and evolutionary perspectives. In D. M. Buss & N. M. Malamuth (Eds.), *Sex, power, conflict: Evolutionary and feminist perspectives* (pp. 269–295). New York: Oxford University Press.

Markus, M. L. (1994). Finding a happy medium: Explaining the negative effects of electronic communication on social life at work. *ACM Transactions on Information Systems, 12*, 119–149.

McCabe, M. P., & Collins, J. K. (1984). Measurement of depth of desired and experienced sexual involvement at different stages of dating. *Journal of Sex Research, 20*, 377–390.

McCormick, N. B. (1979). Come-ons and put-offs: Unmarried students' strategies for having and avoiding sexual intercourse. *Psychology of Women Quarterly, 4*, 194–211.

McGrath, M. G., & Casey, E. (2002). Forensic psychiatry and the internet: Practical perspectives on sexual harassers in cyberspace. *The Journal of the American Academy of Psychiatry and the Law, 30*, 81–94.

McGuirl, K. E., & Wiederman, M. W. (2000). Characteristics of the ideal sex partner: Gender differences and perceptions of the preferences of the other gender. *Journal of Sex & Marital Therapy, 26*, 153–159.

McKenna, K. Y. A., Green, A. S., & Gleason, M. E. J. (2002). Relationship formation on the internet: What's the big attraction? *Journal of Social Issues, 58*, 9–31.

McKinney, K., & Maroules, N. (1991). Sexual harassment. In E. Grauerholz & M. A. Koralewski (Eds.), *Sexual coercion: A sourcebook on its nature, causes, and prevention* (pp. 29–44). Lexington, MA: Lexington.

McMaster, L. E., Connolly, J., Pepler, D., & Craig, W. M. (2002). Peer to peer sexual harassment in early adolescence: A developmental perspective. *Development and Psychopathology, 14*, 91–105.

Meloy, J. R., & Boyd, C. (2003). Female stalkers and their victims. *Journal of the American Academy of Psychiatry and the Law, 31*, 211–219.

Merkle, E. R., & Richardson, R. A. (2000). Digital dating and virtual relating: Conceptualizing computer mediated romantic relationships. *Family Relations, 49*, 187–192.

Messman, S. J., Canary, D. J., & Hause, K. S. (2000). Motives to remain platonic, equity, and the use of maintenance strategies in opposite-sex friendships. *Journal of Social and Personal Relationships, 17*, 67–94.

Metts, S., Cupach, W. R., & Bejlovec, R. A. (1989). "I love you too much to ever start liking you": Redefining romantic relationships. *Journal of Social and Personal Relationships, 6*, 259–274.

Metts, S., Cupach, W. R., & Imahori, T. T. (1992). Perceptions of sexual compliance-resisting messages in three types of cross-sex relationships. *Western Journal of Speech Communication, 56*, 1–17.

Metts, S., & Spitzberg, B. H. (1996). Sexual communication in interpersonal contexts: A script-based approach. In B. R. Burleson (Ed.), *Communication yearbook 19* (pp. 49–92). Thousand Oaks, CA: Sage.

Meyer, C. B., & Taylor, S. E. (1986). Adjustment to rape. *Journal of Personality and Social Psychology, 50*, 1226–1234.

Miceli, S. L., Santana, S. A., & Fisher, B. S. (2001). Cyberaggression: Safety and security issues for women worldwide. *Security Journal, 14*(2), 11–27.

Monsour, M. (1992). Meanings of intimacy in cross- and same-sex friendships. *Journal of Social and Personal Relationships, 9*, 277–295.

Monsour, M., Harris, B., Kurzweil, N., & Beard, C. (1994). Challenges confronting cross-sex friendships: "Much ado about nothing?" *Sex Roles, 31*, 55–77.

Monsour, M., Harvey, V., & Betty, S. (1997). A balance theory explanation of challenges confronting cross-sex friendships. *Sex Roles, 37*, 825–845.

Morris, W. (Ed.). (1979). *The American heritage dictionary of the English language*. Boston: Houghton Mifflin.

Morton, T. L., Alexander, J. F., & Altman, I. (1976). Communication and relationship definition. In G. R. Miller (Ed.), *Explorations in interpersonal communication* (pp. 105–125). Beverly Hills, CA: Sage.

Motley, M. T., & Reeder, H. M. (1995). Unwanted escalation of sexual intimacy: Male and female perceptions of connotations and relational consequences of resistance messages. *Communication Monographs, 62*, 355–382.

Muehlenhard, C. L., Danoff-Burg, S., & Powch, I. G. (1996). Is rape sex or violence? Conceptual issues and implications. In D. M. Buss & N. M. Malamuth (Eds.), *Sex, power, conflict: Evolutionary and feminist perspectives* (pp. 119–137). New York: Oxford University Press.

Muehlenhard, C. L., Harney, P. A., & Jones, J. M. (1992). From "victim-precipitated rape" to "date rape": How far have we come? *Annual Review of Sex Research* (Vol. 3, pp. 219–253). Mt. Vernon, IA: Society for the Scientific Study of Sex.

Murray, F. S. (1967). A preliminary investigation of anonymous nuisance telephone calls to females. *Psychological Record, 17*, 395–400.

Nardi, P. M., & Sherrod, D. (1994). Friendship in the lives of gay men and lesbians. *Journal of Social and Personal Relationships, 11*, 185–199.

Nicastro, A. M., Cousins, A. V., & Spitzberg, B. H. (2000). The tactical face of stalking. *Journal of Criminal Justice, 28*, 69–82.

Nice, M. L., & Katzev, R. (1998). Internet romances: The frequency and nature of romantic on-line relationships. *CyberPsychology & Behavior, 1*, 217–223.

Ogilvie, E. (2001). Cyberstalking. *Crime & Justice International, 17*(50), 9–10, 26–29.

Oliver, M. B., & Hyde, J. S. (1993). Gender differences in sexuality: A meta-analysis. *Psychological Bulletin, 114*, 29–51.

O'Meara, J. D. (1989). Cross-sex friendships: Four basic challenges to an ignored relationship. *Sex Roles, 21*, 525–543.

O'Sullivan, L. F., & Byers, E. S. (1993). Eroding stereotypes: College women's attempts to influence reluctant male sexual partners. *Journal of Sex Research, 30*, 270–282.

O'Sullivan, L. F., & Gaines, M. E. (1998). Decision-making in college students' heterosexual dating relationships: Ambivalence about engaging in sexual activity. *Journal of Social and Personal Relationships, 15*, 347–363.

Pam, A., Plutchik, R., & Conte, H. R. (1975). Love: A psychometric approach. *Psychological Reports, 37*, 83–88.

Parks, M. R., & Floyd, K. (1996). Making friends in cyberspace. *Journal of Communication, 46*, 80–97.

Parks, M. R., & Roberts, L. D. (1998). "Making MOOsic": The development of personal relationships on line and a comparison to their off-line counterparts. *Journal of Social and Personal Relationships, 15*, 517–537.

Paul, E. L., & Hayes, K. A. (2002). The casualties of "casual" sex: A qualitative exploration of the phenomenology of college students' hookups. *Journal of Social and Personal Relationships, 19*, 639–661.

Paul, E. L., McManus, B., & Hayes, A. (2000). "Hookups": Characteristics and correlates of college students' spontaneous and anonymous sexual experiences. *Journal of Sex Research, 37*, 76–88.

Pathé, M., Mullen, P. E., & Purcell, R. (2000). Same-gender stalking. *Journal of the American Academy of Psychiatry and the Law, 28*, 191–197.

Perlman, S. D., & Abramson, P. R. (1982). Sexual satisfaction among married and cohabiting individuals. *Journal of Consulting and Clinical Psychology, 50*, 458–460.

Pierce, C. A., & Aguinis, H. (2001). A framework for investigating the link between workplace romance and sexual harassment. *Group & Organization Management, 26*, 206–229.

Pool, I. d S. (1981). *The social impact of the telephone.* Cambridge, MA: MIT Press.

Pratarelli, M. C., Browne, B. L., & Johnson, K. (1999). The bits and bytes of computer/internet addiction: A factor analytic approach. *Behavior Research Methods, Instruments, & Computers, 31*, 305–314.

Purcell, R., Pathé, M., & Mullen, P. E. (2001). The prevalence and nature of stalking in the Australian community. *Australian and New Zealand Journal of Psychiatry, 36*, 114–120.

Quinn, K., Sanchez-Hucles, J., Coates, G., & Gillen, B. (1991). Men's compliance with a woman's resistance to unwanted sexual advances. *Journal of Offender Rehabilitation, 17*, 13–31.

Rawlins, W. K. (1982). Cross-sex friendship and the communicative management of sex-role expectations. *Communication Quarterly, 30*, 343–352.

Reeder, H. M. (2000). "I like you . . . as a friend": The role of attraction in cross-sex friendship. *Journal of Social and Personal Relationships, 17*, 329–348.

Regan, P. C. (1998). Of lust and love: Beliefs about the role of sexual desire in romantic relationships. *Personal Relationships, 5*, 139–157.

Regan, P. C., & Berscheid, E. (1995). Gender differences in beliefs about the causes of male and female sexual desire. *Personal Relationships, 2*, 345–358.

Regan, P. C., & Berscheid, E. (1999). *Lust: What we know about human sexual desire.* Thousand Oaks, CA: Sage.

Regan, P. C., & Dreyer, C. S. (1999). Lust? Love? Status? Young adults' motives for engaging in casual sex. *Journal of Psychology and Human Sexuality, 11*, 1–24.

Regan, P. C., Kocan, E. R., & Whitlock, T. (1998). Ain't love grand! A prototype analysis of romantic love. *Journal of Social and Personal Relationships, 15*, 411–420.

Ronfeldt, D. (1992). Cyberocracy is coming. *The Information Society, 8*, 243–296.

Roscoe, B., Strouse, J. S., & Goodwin, M. P. (1994). Sexual harassment: Early adolescent self-reports of experiences and acceptance. *Adolescence, 29*, 515–523.

Rose, S. M. (1985). Same- and cross-sex friendships and the psychology of homosociality. *Sex Roles, 12*, 63–74.

Rosenthal, D. A., & Smith, A. M. A. (1997). Adolescent sexual timetables. *Journal of Youth and Adolescence, 26*, 619–636.

Rotundo, M., Nguyen, D-H., & Sackett, P. R. (2001). A meta-analytic review of gender differences in perceptions of sexual harassment. *Journal of Applied Psychology, 86*, 914–922.

Rumbough, T. (2001). The development and maintenance of interpersonal relationships through computer-mediated communication. *Communication Research Reports, 18*, 223–229.

Samter, W., & Cupach, W. R. (1998). Friendly fire: Topical variations in conflict among same- and cross-sex friends. *Communication Studies, 49*, 121–138.

Sapadin, L. A. (1988). Friendship and gender: Perspectives of professional men and women. *Journal of Social and Personal Relationships, 5*, 387–403.

Savitz, L. (1986). Obscene phone calls. In T. F. Hartnagel & R. A. Silverman (Eds.), *Critique and explanation: Essays in honor of Gwynne Nettler* (pp. 149–158). New Brunswick, NJ: Transaction.

Schell, B. H., & Lanteigne, N. M. (2000). *Stalking, harassment, and murder in the workplace: Guidelines for protection and prevention.* Westport, CT: Quorum.

Schneider, C. S., & Kenny, D. A. (2000). Cross-sex friends who were once romantic partners: Are they platonic friends now? *Journal of Social and Personal Relationships, 17*, 451–466.

Schneider, J. P. (2000). Effects of cybersex addiction on the family: Results of a survey. *Sexual Addiction & Compulsivity, 7*, 31–58.

Schwartz, M. F., & Southern, S. (2000). Compulsive cybersex: The new tea room. *Sexual Addiction & Compulsivity, 7*, 124–144.

Sczesny, S., & Stahlberg, D. (2000). Sexual harassment over the telephone: Occupational risk at call centres. *Work & Stress, 14*, 121–136.

Shakespeare, W. (1991). *Complete sonnets* (Unabridged). New York: Dover Publications.

Sheffield, C. J. (1989). The invisible intruder: Women's experiences of obscene phone calls. *Gender and Society, 3*, 483–488.

Sidman, M. (1989). *Coercion and its fallout.* Boston, MA: Authors Cooperative.

Smith, M. D., & Morra, N. N. (1994). Obscene and threatening telephone calls to women: Data from a Canadian national survey. *Gender & Society, 8*, 584–596.

Snell, W. E., Jr., & Papini, D. R. (1989). The sexuality scale: An instrument to measure sexual-esteem, sexual-depression, and sexual-preoccupation. *Journal of Sex Research, 26*, 256–263.

Snow, D. A., Robinson, C., & McCall, P. L. (1991). "Cooling out" men in singles bars and nightclubs: Observations on the interpersonal survival strategies of women in public places. *Journal of Contemporary Ethnography, 19*, 423–449.

Snyder, D. K. (1979). Multidimensional assessment of marital satisfaction. *Journal of Marriage and the Family, 41*, 813–823.

Spitzberg, B. H. (1998). Sexual coercion in courtship relations. In B. H. Spitzberg & W. R. Cupach (Eds.), *The dark side of close relationships* (pp. 179–232). Mahwah, NJ: Lawrence Erlbaum Associates.

Spitzberg, B. H. (1999). An analysis of empirical estimates of sexual aggression victimization and perpetration. *Violence and Victims, 14*, 241–261.

Spitzberg, B. H. (2002). The tactical topography of stalking victimization and management. *Trauma, Violence, & Abuse, 3*, 261–288.

Spitzberg, B. H., & Cupach, W. R. (2001). Paradoxes of pursuit: Toward a relational model of stalking-related phenomena. In J. A. Davis (Ed.), *Stalking crimes and victim protection: Prevention, intervention, threat assessment, and case management* (pp. 97–136). Boca Raton, FL: CRC Press.

Spitzberg, B. H., & Cupach, W. R. (2002). The inappropriateness of relational intrusion. In R. Goodwin & D. Cramer (Eds.), *Inappropriate relationships: The unconventional, the disapproved, and the forbidden* (pp. 191–219). Mahwah, NJ: Lawrence Erlbaum Associates.

Spitzberg, B. H., & Hoobler, G. (2002). Cyberstalking and the technologies of interpersonal terrorism. *New Media & Society, 4*, 71–92.

Sprague, J., & Quadagno, D. (1989). Gender and sexual motivation: An exploration of two assumptions. *Journal of Psychology and Human Sexuality, 2*, 57–76.

Sprecher, S. (1989). Influences on choice of a partner and on sexual decision making in the relationship. In K. McKinney & S. Sprecher (Eds.), *Human sexuality: The societal and interpersonal context* (pp. 438–462). Norwood, NJ: Ablex.

Sprecher, S., Felmlee, D., Metts, S., Fehr, B., & Vanni, D. (1998). Factors associated with distress following the breakup of a close relationship. *Journal of Social and Personal Relationships, 15*, 791–809.

Sprecher, S., & Regan, P. C. (1998). Passionate and companionate love in courting and young married couples. *Sociological Inquiry, 68*, 163–185.

Sprecher, S., Schmeeckle, M., & Felmlee, D. (2002, August). *The principle of least interest: Consequences of inequality in emotional involvement for young adult romantic relationships.* Paper presented at the American Sociological Association Conference, Chicago, IL.

Stith, S. B., Jester, S. B., & Bird, G. W. (1992). A typology of college students who use violence in their dating relationships. *Journal of College Student Development, 33*, 411–421.

Stock, W. E. (1991). Feminist explanations: Male power, hostility, and sexual coercion. In E. Grauerholz & M. A. Koralewski (Eds.), *Sexual coercion: A sourcebook on its nature, causes, and prevention* (pp. 61–73). Lexington, MA: Lexington.

Stockdale, M. S. (1998). The direct and moderating influences of sexual harassment pervasiveness, coping strategies, and gender on work-related outcomes. *Psychology of Women Quarterly, 22*, 521–535.

Studd, M. V. (1996). Sexual harassment. In D. M. Buss & N. M. Malamuth (Eds.), *Sex, power, conflict: Evolutionary and feminist perspectives* (pp. 54–89). New York: Oxford University Press.

Surra, C. A., & Longstreth, M. (1990). Similarity of outcomes, interdependence, and conflict in dating relationships. *Journal of Personality and Social Psychology, 59*, 1–16.

Swain, S. O. (1992). Men's friendships with women. In P. Nardi (Ed.), *Men's friendships* (pp. 153–171). Newbury Park, CA: Sage.

Symons, D., & Ellis, B. (1989). Human male–female differences in sexual desire. In A. E. Rasa, C. Vogel, & E. Voland (Eds.), *The sociobiology of sexual and reproductive strategies* (pp. 131–146). New York: Chapman & Hall.

Tamres, L. K., Janicki, D., & Helgeson, V. S. (2002). Sex differences in coping behavior: A meta-analytic review and examination of relative coping. *Personality and Social Psychology Review, 6*, 2–30.

Tedeschi, J. T., & Felson, R. B. (1994). *Violence, aggression, and coercive actions*. Washington, DC: American Psychological Association.

Tennov, D. (1979). *Love and limerance*. New York: Stein and Day.

Thornhill, R., & Palmer, C. T. (2000). *A natural history of rape: Biological bases of sexual coercion*. Cambridge, MA: MIT Press.

Thornhill, R., & Thornhill, N. W. (1991). Coercive sexuality of men: Is there psychological adaptation to rape? In E. Grauerholz & M. A. Koralewski (Eds.), *Sexual coercion: A sourcebook on its nature, causes, and prevention* (pp. 91–108). Lexington, MA: Lexington.

Townsend, J. M., & Levy, G. D. (1990). Effects of potential partners' physical attractiveness and socioeconomic status on sexuality and partner selection. *Archives of Sexual Behavior, 19*, 149–164.

Ullman, S. E. (2000). Psychometric characteristics of the social reactions questionnaire. *Psychology of Women Quarterly, 24*, 257–271.

U. S. Merit Systems Protection Board. (1988). *Sexual harassment in the Federal Government: An update*. Washington, DC: U.S. Government Printing Office.

Vorauer, J. D., & Ratner, R. (1996). Who's going to make the first move? Pluralistic ignorance as an impediment to relationship formation. *Journal of Social and Personal Relationships, 13*, 483–506.

Vukovich, M. C. (1996). The prevalence of sexual harassment among female family practice residents in the United States. *Violence and Victims, 11*, 175–180.

Waldner-Haugrud, L. K., & Magruder, B. (1995). Male and female sexual victimization in dating relationships: Gender differences in coercion techniques and outcomes. *Violence and Victims, 10*, 203–215.

Waller, W. (1938). *The family: A dynamic interpretation*. New York: Gordon.

Warner, P. K. (1988). Aural assault: Obscene telephone calls. *Qualitative Sociology, 11*, 302–318.

Wästlund, E., Norlander, T., & Archer, T. (2001). Internet blues revisited: Replication and extension of an internet paradox study. *CyberPsychology & Behavior, 4*, 385–391.

Welsh, S. (1999). Gender and sexual harassment. In K. S. Cook & J. Hagan (Eds.), *Annual review of sociology* (Vol. 25, pp. 169–190). Palo Alto, CA: Annual Reviews.

Werking, K. J. (1997). *We're just good friends: Men and women in nonromantic relationships*. New York: Guilford.

Wheeler, J. G., George, W. H., & Dahl, B. J. (2002). Sexually aggressive college males: Empathy as a moderator in the "confluence model" of sexual aggression. *Personality and Individual Differences, 33*, 759–775.

Wiehe, V. R., & Richards, A. L. (1995). *Intimate betrayal: Understanding and responding to the trauma of acquaintance rape*. Thousand Oaks, CA: Sage.

Wiener, N. (1950). *The human use of human beings: Cybernetics and society*. Boston: Houghton Mifflin.

Williams, C. L., Giuffre, P. A., & Dellinger, K. (1999). Sexuality in the workplace: Organizational control, sexual harassment, and the pursuit of pleasure. In K. S. Cook & J. Hagan (Eds.), *Annual review of sociology* (Vol. 25, pp. 73–93). Palo Alto, CA: Annual Reviews.

Williams, F. (1991). *The new telecommunications: Infrastructure for the information age*. New York: Free Press.

Wilson, G. D. (1997). Gender differences in sexual fantasy: An evolutionary analysis. *Personality and Individual Differences, 22*, 27–31.

Wood, J. T., & Conrad, C. (1983). Paradox in the experience of professional women. *Western Journal of Speech Communication, 47*, 305–322.

Zweig, J. M., Barber, B. L., & Eccles, J. S. (1997). Sexual coercion and well-being in young adulthood: Comparisons by gender and college status. *Journal of Interpersonal Violence, 12*, 291–308.

12

Sexual Aggression in Romantic Relationships

F. Scott Christopher
Tiffani S. Kisler
Arizona State University

Although society often focuses on rapes by strangers, recent national survey findings reveal that relational partners account for 62% of the sexual assaults committed against women over the age of 18. Sexual assaults, attempted assaults, and less forceful means of aggression occur in the romantic relationships of adolescents, young adults, and married individuals, as well as among gays and lesbians. In this chapter, we examine sexual aggression and its correlates across all of these relationships. Initially, we review reports on the frequency of sexual aggression. Next, we explore the relational dynamics that play a role in this form of aggression. We then critically examine three levels of social support for sexual aggression—support that exists in the social networks of aggressors, support in the social organizations that aggressors belong to, and support that can be found in our culture. This is followed by an examination of individual characteristics that typify aggressors, and the negative outcomes that their victims often suffer. Finally, we evaluate the effectiveness of different prevention approaches and offer suggestions for future research.

INTRODUCTION

Sexual interactions between partners occur in many interpersonal relationships. Adolescents struggle with the question of how sexually intimate they should be as they begin to experience romantic attraction. Young adults engage in sexual dances in their developing relationships; sexual dances in which partners increase their synchronicity or fall out-of-step with one another. Married partners' knowledge of each others' likes and dislikes builds sexual patterns that most often result in a satisfied sexual life. Gays and lesbians seek out partners that help them to define and explore their sexuality.

Consensual interactions that increase sexual intimacy, or acceptance of a partner's wish to limit it, most often characterize the sexual lives of individuals who experience these relationships. However, this does not always describe individuals' sexual experiences. At times, those in relationships purposefully push to achieve their sexual desires in spite of their partners' silent resistance or vocal protestations. At other times, individuals choose to threaten or use force as a means to attain sexual goals.

We explore these forms of sexual aggression and their correlates in this chapter. We begin by examining how frequently sexual aggression occurs in different types of relationships. We then review the relational dynamics of sexual aggression. This is followed by an analysis of different forms of peer and social support for aggression. An examination of individual characteristics of sexual aggressors is next. Finally, we provide an overview of prevention efforts and their effectiveness.

Although we take an integrative approach by examining sexual aggression within the context of different romantic relationships, a caveat is in order. Research on sexual aggression in dating relationships began in the late 1960s (i.e., Kanin, 1967, 1969) but only drew the attention of a small number of researchers until the late 1980s when Koss' work on sexual aggression on college campuses (i.e., Koss, Gidycz, & Wisneiwskik, 1987) culminated in an ever-increasing number of scholars who examined this phenomenon. However, research interest into sexual aggression for other types of relationships has not kept pace. Far fewer investigators have examined sexual aggression in adolescent, gay, and lesbian relationships. Empirical inquiries into marital sexual aggression are even rarer; examination of sexual aggression among seniors does not exist. Our review is limited by these constraints.

THE FREQUENCY OF SEXUAL AGGRESSION IN RELATIONSHIPS

Conceptualizing Sexual Aggression

The term *sexual aggression*, as it is associated with close relationships, usually refers to interactions where one relationship member asserts his or her sexual wishes on an unwilling partner. It involves a number of influence tactics that, when used in concert, form an overall sexual aggression strategy (Christopher & Frandsen, 1990). Christopher (2001) argues that two over-arching forms of sexual aggression exist, sexual assault and sexual coercion. After examining the findings of a range of studies that categorized sexually aggressive men (Koss, Leonard, Beezley, & Oros, 1985), comparing the varied experiences of single women who were victimized (Koss & Oros, 1980), and factor analyzing items used to measure sexual influence tactics (Christopher & Frandsen, 1990), Christopher hypothesized that there are conceptual and empirical differences between sexual assault and sexual coercion. He asserts that sexual assault involves the use or threat of physical force. Christopher (2001) sees this form of aggression as easily identified and commonly viewed as a form of aggression. In comparison, sexual coercion is characterized by psychological, verbal, and sometimes persistent physical pressure in the absence of threats or use of force. Identifying experiences of sexual coercion is not as straightforward, and such experiences are not as commonly perceived as aggression.

Whereas Christopher (2001) formulated his conceptualization by using research involving single, young adults, recent work on sexual aggression in marriage supports his views. As part of a research project focused on married couples in therapy, Meyer, Vivian, and O'Leary (1998) created a measure of sexual aggression by factor analyzing items often found in inventories of sexual aggression that measured different aggressive tactics. Items that measured the use or threat of force composed one factor, whereas the second factor involved tactics that reflected the use of pressure.

Thus, Meyer et al.'s results suggest that Christopher's conceptualization of two forms of sexual aggression should be extended to include marital relationships.

Dating Relationships—Young Adult Women as Victims

Evidence exists of possible widespread sexual victimization against single women, especially against adolescents and young adults. In a landmark study using a national college probability sample, Koss, Gidyez, and Wisniewski (1987) found that more than half (53.7%) of the 3,000 college women they sampled suffered some form of sexual victimization by age 14. Of the victims, 27.5% experienced attempted rape or rape. More telling is that 59% of the rape victims reported that their dating partners raped them. Thus, single women are at greater risk for being a victim of sexual aggression from a date than they are from a stranger. Other researchers have also found similarly high rates of sexual aggression in dating relationships using campus-based convenience samples (e.g., Koss & Oros, 1982; Muehlenhard & Linton, 1987). Muehlenhard and Linton (1987), for instance, reported that 78% of college women in their sample endured some form of sexual aggression while dating, and Koss and Oros (1982) estimated that as many as 33% of college women may experience some form of sexual victimization from their dating partners. Although single campus studies have limited generalizability, the consistency between Koss et al.'s (1987) and others' findings establish that young adult, single women are often at risk for experiencing sexual aggression in their dating relationships.

The National Violence Against Women Survey (NVAWS) conducted by Tjaden and Thoennes (2000) provides the best estimate to date of the prevalence of sexual abuse among women. Their probability survey of 8,000 women revealed that 17.6% of the women were victims of rape or attempted rapes. Fully 62% of these violent acts occurred when the women were between the ages of 12 and 24 years. These findings further highlight the danger female adolescents and young adult women experience for becoming victims of sexual assault. This risk of victimization increased for those who were assaulted during these formative years. That is, victimization prior to age 18 doubled the probability that women in the NVAWS reported rape or rape attempts at a later age. Moreover, victimization past age 18 was most likely to occur at the hands of an intimate partner such as a current or former spouse, cohabitant, or a dating partner when compared to the likelihood of victimization by a family member or a stranger. Intimates accounted for 62% of sexual assaults for women older than 18 years. Moreover, women's chance of physical injury during a rape perpetrated by a current or past intimate partner was also higher when compared to incidents involving a stranger or nonintimate acquaintance.

Dating Relationships—Young Adult Men as Victims

Women are not the only victims of sexual aggression. Young adult, single males are also victimized; however, there is a paucity of research focused on this experience (Muehlenhard & Cook, 1988; Struckman-Johnson & Struckman-Johnson, 1994). Struckman-Johnson and Struckman-Johnson (1994) found that 24% of the single, college men in their sample reported incidents since age 16 in which they had experienced unwanted coercive sexual contact from a woman. In 22% of the incidents, sexual intercourse was involved, whereas 12% experienced unwanted sexual touching. Sexual contact was achieved by way of persuasion, intoxication, or threat of loss of love in 88% of these cases. Physical force, intimidation, and/or restraint were used in 12% of the incidents. More than 75% of the time this sexual aggression was initiated by an acquaintance or dating partner. Other reports vary by the form of aggressive tactic.

Waldner-Haugrud and Magruder (1995) found that among the single men in their sample, 28.6% were sexually coerced through partners' lies, 22.5% because of partner-induced guilt, and 56.9% because of intoxication. Muehlenhard and Cook (1988) also found that 22.7% of the men in their research engaged in unwanted sexual activity because of their dating partner's use of sexual coercion.

In addition to surveying women, the NVAWS also queried 8,000 men about their sexual victimization experiences. Based on these data, Tjaden and Thoennes (2000) report rates that are at odds with these small-sample studies. Only 3% of the men indicated that they were victims of rape or attempted rape, and their assailants were 5.5 times more likely to be male than female. Moreover, men were at greatest risk for this abuse when they were less than 12 years of age (48% of the cases reported) as compared to during adolescence (between the ages of 12 and 17—23% of the cases) or young adulthood (ages 18 to 25—17% of the cases). Intimate partners were also much less likely to perpetrate a rape among men (18% of the cases) when compared to nonintimate partners.

The findings of sexual victimization among men, however, need to be qualified when comparing rates for men to rates for women. Single women as a group experience more frequent sexual aggression (Christopher, Madura, & Weaver, 1998; Christopher, Owens, & Stecker, 1993a; Muehlenhard & Cook, 1988), and their aggression experiences characteristically involve more intimate sexual behaviors including oral–genital contact and intercourse (O'Sullivan, Byers, & Finkelman, 1998). In addition, women experience greater levels of distress as a result of being a victim of aggression, distress that generally has longer lasting and more serious consequences than those experienced by men (O'Sullivan et al., 1998; Struckman-Johnson, 1988; Tjaden & Theonnes, 2000).

Adolescents

Similar trends in rates of aggression have been found in adolescent samples (Davis, Peck & Storment, 1993; Patton & Mannison, 1995; Poitras & Lavoie, 1995; Small & Kerns, 1993). Poitras and Lavoie (1995) found 54.1% of girls and 13.1% of boys in 10th or 11th grade in heterosexual dating relationships were victims of sexual coercion. The aggressive tactics most commonly reported by victims involved verbal coercion where dating partners continually argued and placed pressure on their partners to obtain the desired behavior; sexual violence and use of physical force were reported with less frequency. Kissing, petting, or fondling were the most commonly identified unwanted sexual acts perpetrated against adolescents. Patton and Mannison (1995) found similarly high rates of female victimization; 53% of adolescent females in their sample reported an experience of aggression. Male victimization was also high with 45% of adolescent males reporting an experience. Small and Kerns (1993) examined the types of unwanted sexual contact reported by females in 7th, 9th, and 11th grades. Of the 21% of females who reported such experiences, 36% had been forced into intercourse; the remaining 64% underwent some type of unwanted touching or physical contact. Of the victims who experienced unwanted touching or physical contact, boyfriends were the perpetrators in 31% of the cases, friends in 22% of the cases, and first time dating partners in 18%. Small and Kerns (1993) found that by 11th grades, female adolescents were almost twice as likely as those in earlier grades to experience some form of sexual assault. Not all reports are as high as the overall rates found by Small and Kerns (1993). Davis, Peck, and Storment (1993) found lower rates for both male and female adolescents with 26% of girls and 11% of boys having experienced forced sexual contact. Even though there is divergence in reporting rates across studies, the rates nonetheless establish that sexual aggression is a surprisingly common dating experience during adolescence.

Marital Rape

Only a limited number of social scientists have investigated sexual aggression in marriage. This limited scrutiny may be the result of a commonly held view that forced sex inside of a marriage is antithetical because sex is an entitlement inherent in a marital contract. In fact, some states' laws have statutes supporting this view. We will explore this issue later in the chapter.

Two studies of marital sexual aggression stand out because of the quality of their design. Russell (1982) randomly surveyed women in the San Francisco area. In her sample, 1 in 7 married women, or 14%, reported that they were raped by their spouse. Of the women who were raped, 85% experienced complete penile–vaginal rape, 10% experienced attempted penile–vaginal rape, and 5% experienced forced or attempted oral, anal, or digital sexual contact. In each instance, the perpetrator was either their spouse or ex-spouse.

Finkelhor and Yllö's (1985) work constitutes the second study. They surveyed women who lived in the Boston area, whose children were between the ages of 6 and 14 and who lived with them. Moreover, they limited their study to victims of sexual assault; women who had engaged in sex because their spouse threatened or used physical force. Thus, their findings likely underrepresent the incidence of sexual aggression because incidents of sexual coercion probably co-occurred in these marriages but the researchers did not measure this. Fully 10% of the women in their study were raped by their spouse or a cohabitating partner, a figure strikingly similar to the 14% reported by Russell (1982). In more than one third of these instances (39%), the forced sex occurred 1 or 2 times; in 50% of the cases it occurred more than 20 times. Some women reported that aggression first happened early in their marriages. The likelihood of forced sex, however, increased dramatically as relationships deteriorated and ended. Ironically, a notable minority of the women, 28%, did not label their experience as rape.

Gay and Lesbian Relationships

Sexual coercion not only takes place within heterosexual relationships, it also occurs in gay and lesbian relationships. Unlike research showing differences in the rates of victimization for heterosexual men and women, gays and lesbians report similar levels of coercive experiences (Waldner-Haugrud & Gratch, 1997). Waldner-Haugrud and Gratch (1997), for example, found that 52% of their gay and lesbian sample experienced a sexually coercive incident at least once in their lifetime, and that severe forms of aggression were more common than the less severe forms. Fifty-five percent of gay men and 50% of lesbians experienced unwanted penetration, whereas 11% of gay men and 18% of lesbians experienced unwanted kissing. Not all reports involve such high and consistent victimization rates. Duncan (1990) found that approximately 31% of lesbian women and 12% of gay men in his sample were forced to have sex. These rates must be viewed with some caution as they involve small, convenience samples. Nonetheless, they indicate that sexual victimization at the hands of a relationship partner is not uniquely experienced by heterosexuals but also occurs among gays and lesbians.

Methodological Concerns

There are many difficulties in capturing accurate estimates of the frequency of sexual aggression in different populations. One of the overriding problems is the different ways that sexual aggression has been operationalized. The fact that this variable has been operationalized in a variety of ways across studies makes it difficult to get an accurate estimate of the prevalence of the problem. Although many researchers use Koss' Sexual Experience Survey (Koss et al., 1985), or variations thereof, it is not without limitations. Revisions in the wording of its items can result in differential reports in rates (Alksnis, Desmarais, Senn, & Hunter, 2000). Moreover, this instrument does not directly query respondents about whether they were raped.

Even though a national survey of violence provides a measure of the prevalence of rape and attempted rape (Tjaden & Thoennes, 2000), this still leaves unanswered the question of how many women and men experience sexual coercion instead of sexual assault. Nonetheless, it is important to recognize that this national data set demonstrates that rates of sexual coercion within close relationships are high. Because of the prevalence of sexual victimization within relationships, researchers have identified a number of relational correlates.

RELATIONAL DYNAMICS

The distribution of power and attempts to influence one's partner are qualities of any interpersonal relationship (Huston, 1983). Power distribution and choice of influence strategies in relationships are often tied to the gender of the partners (Falbo & Peplau, 1980). For instance, men more frequently choose direct influence strategies involving such tactics as assertion and open discussion, whereas women more frequently choose indirect strategies that include hinting, withdrawing, or attempting to manipulate a partner's emotions. Moreover, women who are involved in their relationship and in love oftentimes see themselves as possessing less power than their partners (Sprecher, 1985). Not surprisingly, sexually aggressive men are more attuned to the distribution of power in a relationship than are nonaggressive men (Lisak & Roth, 1988), suggesting they strategically choose when to engage in aggressive behavior, choices that allow them to retain power in their relationships.

Thus, relational power is an inherent quality of sexual aggression (Christopher, 2001; Finkelhor & Yllö, 1985). Sometimes its use is subtle. Muehlenhard and Linton (1987), for instance, revealed that single, sexually aggressive men were more apt to ask their dating partner out, to drive, and to pay for dating expenses than were their nonaggressive male peers. At other times, the use of power is more overt. Decisions to get a partner intoxicated, to lie, or to physically persist in light of resistance exemplify overt strategic choices characteristic of sexual coercion (Christopher & Frandsen, 1990). Perhaps the most overt display of power, however, comes when sexual aggression is paired with physical aggression as exemplified in marital rape.

Husbands who are sexually aggressive toward their spouse frequently couple physical and sexual aggression (Marshall & Holtzworth-Munroe, 2002; Russell, 1990; Tjaden & Theonnes, 2000). For instance, Marshall and Holtzworth-Munroe's (2002) investigation of married couples reveal that husbands' use of physical aggression was related to their use of threats and/or force to obtain sex from their wives. Finkelhor and Yllö (1985) developed a typology of marital rape that illustrates the different ways this occurs. In *forced-only* rapes, husbands were generally not physically abusive in other areas of the marriage and used only enough force to influence their wives to engage in sexual acts that the wives did not want to engage in. In contrast, wives who experienced *battering rapes* were in marriages where their spouse regularly beat them. Beatings often preceded or were a part of a rape for these women. The most sexually focused aggression, however, occurred in *obsessive rapes*. In these rapes, husbands forced their wife into humiliating and degrading sexual behaviors. These sometimes included sadistic acts such as being forced to engage in anal intercourse or to have multiple, concurrent coital partners. Tormenting and mistreating his wife resulted in increased sexual pleasure and gratification for the husband in these instances.

Husbands' use of physical aggression in marriages is associated with certain sexual interaction patterns. DeMaris' (1997) analysis of the National Survey of Families and Household reveals that couples engaged in sexual acts an average of 11 times a month in marriages where the husband was violent, but only 6.75 times a month in marriages where the husband was not violent. Additional analysis of a second data set by DeMaris and Swinford (1996) provide further insight into this interplay. Previous experiences of wives being forced to have sex by their husbands and continued threats of retaliation, predicted wives' fear of being hit if they argued or did something unwanted by their husbands. Thus, fear plays a role in relationships where physical and sexual aggression are paired.

Given that using power is an inherent part of sexual interaction for this form of aggression, some scholars have proposed that aggressive individuals attempt to control their partners in other areas of the relationship. Research supports this hypothesis. Stets and Pirog-Good's (1989) investigation of single men and women reveals that interpersonal control attempts predicted single men's use of mild and severe, and single women's use of severe sexual aggression. Christopher and McQuaid (1998) similarly find that aggressive men's nonsexual control attempts such as asserting that they set the rules of the relationship and keep their partner in line mediated the relationship between dyadic conflict and sexual aggression in dating relationships. The obvious conclusion from these findings is that acts of sexual aggression often co-occur with attempts to control a partner beyond the sexual realm of the relationship.

Power is not the only relationship dynamic involved in sexual aggression. Research focused on dating partnerships suggests that those who are sexually aggressive also have poor quality relationships. Single men and women who engage in sexually aggressive acts are often more ambivalent about continuing in their relationships and report higher levels of dyadic conflict than their nonaggressive peers (Christopher & McQuaid, 1998; Christopher, Owens, & Stecker, 1993a). Moreover, poor relational experiences, as evidenced by high levels of ambivalence and conflict, mediate the relationship between individual characteristics and sexual aggression for single men (Christopher, Owens, & Stecker, 1993b). Parallel findings exist in the marital rape literature. Finkelhor and Yllö (1985) describe the conflictual dynamics that characterize some marriages where wives engage in sex due to husbands' use of interpersonal coercion. In these instances, husbands get angry, deprive wives of money or goods, and otherwise utilize nonviolent threats in order to achieve sexual compliance in their spouses. In addition, these researchers report that the likelihood of sexual assault increases as marital relationships deteriorate. Thus, conflict punctuates these marriages.

Commitment also plays a role in sexual aggression (Christopher, 2001; Kanin, 1969, 1970). Believing that sexual liberties should accompany increased dyadic commitment can lead single men and women to more strongly pursue their sexual goals (Koss & Cleveland, 1997; Muehlenhard, Goggins, Jones, & Satterfield, 1991). Thus, it is not surprising that male and female sexual aggression more frequently occurs in the dating relationships of young adults with a monogamous as opposed to a casual commitment (Christopher, & McQuaid 1998; Christopher et al., 1993b). Adolescents, and especially female adolescents, are also at increased risk of being a victim of aggression when they are in an established dating relationship as compared to a relationship characterized by having only dated a few times (Patton & Mannison, 1995; Small & Kerns, 1993). Commitment plays a particularly salient role in sexually aggressive marriages. It is apparent that not only do some husbands see their marriage license as a license to rape (Finkelhor & Yllö, 1985; Russell, 1990), but that some young adults and adolescents believe that making a commitment to a relationship gives them license to achieve their sexual goals regardless of their partner's wishes.

Two additional, interrelated relational qualities are linked to sexual aggression—consensual sexual behaviors and communication difficulties. Kanin's (1969, 1970;

Kanin & Parcell, 1977) pioneering research showed that consensual sexual behaviors often preceded acts of single, male sexual aggression. In other words, these men's dating partners at times willingly engage in less intimate sexual behaviors such as kissing, having their breasts fondled, or even genital petting. However, their attempts to limit sexual intimacy to these behaviors can be unsuccessful when they are with the wrong dating partner. Engaging in consensual behaviors but then saying no to other behaviors may also send mix messages. Kanin speculated that the women in his study may not have understood that their dating partners perceived these less intimate sexual acts as communicating a willingness to engage in more intimate behaviors. More recent research provides additional insights into this dynamic. Sexually aggressive men often believe that dating partners lead them on, even when their partners do not intend this (Muehlenhard & Linton, 1987). Moreover, it may not matter if a woman says that she does not want to engage in a particular sexual behavior. Malamuth and Brown's (1994) work suggests that sexually aggressive men question the truthfulness of such assertions, even if the woman sends a clear and direct message of her wish to stop a sexual interaction.

It is important to note that acts of aggression are not limited to sexual behaviors that the couple has not experienced during their relationship. Contentions about sexual acts can focus on behaviors that the couple has previously engaged in, but on this particular occasion one partner is unwilling to do. This can occur in dating relationships either with the male partner or the female partner as the aggressor (Lloyd & Emery, 1999; O'Sullivan et al., 1998). Moreover, this also occurs in gay men's relationships (Hickson, Davies, Hunt, & Weatherburn, 1994). Nonetheless, there is an important caveat to these findings. Women's acts of sexual aggression are most likely to end with kissing or fondling, whereas men's acts are more apt to end in more intimate acts, including oral–genital contact and coitus (O'Sullivan et al., 1998; Tjaden & Theonnes, 2000; Waldner-Haugrud & Magruder, 1995). In addition, women's resistance during aggressive acts is stronger, and they experience more adverse reactions to sexually aggressive incidents compared to men.

The sexualized outlook aggressive men bring to their relationships may additionally influence relational interactions. In comparison to nonaggressive peers, single men who engage in sexual aggression have had more coital partners (Koss & Dinero, 1988; Koss et al., 1985), are more apt to have sex in uncommitted relationships (Lalumière, Chalmers, Quinsey, & Seto, 1996; Lalumière & Quinsey, 1996), and experience their first sexual encounter at a younger age (Koss & Dinero, 1988; Malamuth, Linz, Heavey, Barnes, & Acker, 1995). They actively search for new sexual encounters (Kanin, 1967) and are apt to experience more orgasms per week than nonaggressive peers (Kanin, 1983), while concurrently seeing their sexual life as unsatisfactory (Kanin, 1970, 1983).

Parallel findings can be found in the marital sexual aggression literature. Recall DeMaris' (1997) finding that couples reported high frequency of sex in marriages characterized by husbands' physical violence. Finkelhor and Yllö (1985) found that in certain, but not all marriages where marital rape occurred, there were divergent sexual desires between husbands and wives. Wives reported that their husbands would want sex up to four times a day, to engage in extreme sexual behaviors, and typically believed they were entitled to this level of sexuality.

Evidence additionally suggests that some sexually aggressive, single men, especially when compared to nonaggressive men, find sex paired with violence to be arousing. Koss and Dinero (1988) reported that aggressive, single men watch more violent pornography than nonaggressive men. Russell (1990) provides anecdotes of wives who were pressured to re-enact scenes from pornography witnessed by their husbands; scenes that included sadomasochism, bondage, having objects put inside their vaginas, and fellatio. Moreover, sexually aggressive men have self-reported greater sexual arousal when they listen to a guided imagery of a rape than nonaggressive men (Mosher & Anderson, 1986). Physical arousal to a rape story has additionally predicted engaging in sexually aggressive acts independent of other factors (Malamuth, 1986). Collectively, these findings portray sexually aggressive men as often examining their relationships through sexual filters and actively seeking new sexual adventures.

SOCIAL SUPPORT FOR SEXUAL AGGRESSION

Social support for sexual aggression exists on three levels. The first level reflects the immediate social network of aggressive men. Single, sexually aggressive men tend to be members of social groups who adhere to a strong masculine orientation. For instance, college women's reports of experiences with sexual assailants reflect disproportionately higher numbers of men who are members of fraternities and sports teams (Copenhaver & Grauerholz, 1991; Frinter & Rubinson, 1993). Additionally, fraternity members are more likely than independents to be sexually coercive (Lackie & de Man, 1997; Petty & Dawson, 1989; Tyler, Hoyt, & Whitbeck, 1998). These social organizations likely provide support for members' acts of sexual aggression by rewarding success in erotic achievements with increased social status.

The social support of peers can extend beyond support provided by formal organizations. A number of investigators report that single men's use of sexual coercion covaries with having friends who act similarly toward the female dating partners in their lives (Boeringer, Shehan, & Akers, 1991; DeKeseredy & Kelly, 1995; Garrett-Gooding & Senter, 1987). Moreover, such peers provide social reinforcement for behaving in a sexually aggressive manner, a form of reinforcement that is particularly salient to sexually aggressive men (Koss & Dinero, 1988; Petty & Dawson, 1989).

Peer group effects operate through a number of interpersonal mechanisms. DeKeseredy and Kelly (1995) demonstrate that forming a bond of friendship with similarly sexually aggressive peers predicts acts of sexual aggression. Moreover, peers help to give meaning to and provide positive support for sexually aggressive acts toward women according to their findings. Christopher and McQuaid (1998) also found that single men's discussion of relationship problems with their friends was indirectly related to their own sexual aggressiveness. It is possible that these discussions depicted women as sex objects (DeKeseredy & Kelly, 1995; Koss & Dinero, 1998) thereby degrading the female partners to lower status, a status that, from their perspective, allowed them to treat the women in an aggressive manner (DeKesserdy & Kelly, 1995; Kanin, 1970). Taken together, these findings suggest that aggressive peer groups help process relationship experiences in a manner that allows members to justify their behavior while reinforcing choices to exert overt sexual power (see Christopher, 2001 for an in-depth discussion).

Social support for sexual aggression concurrently exists on a broader cultural level. Consider that the first major scholarly work on marital rape published in 1982 by Diana Russell ignited a firestorm of controversy because Russell suggested that it was wrong for husbands to be legally exempt from raping their wives (Russell, 1990). The legal "exemption" for husbands originated in a proclamation by the Chief Justice of England in 1736.

> But the husband cannot be guilty of a rape committed by himself upon his lawful wife, for their mutual matrimonial consent and contract the wife hath given up herself in this kind unto the husband which she cannot retract. (Russell, 1990, p. 17)

Husband's legal exemption existed partially or completely in 47 states as of 1980 (Russell, 1990). Although complete exemptions are allowed in only four states today, the American Law Institute's Model Penal Code continues to recommend that spouses be exempt from sexual assault laws. Partial exemptions remain today in some states for cases where the wife is mentally incapacitated or disabled (Posner & Silbaugh, 1996).

Other forms of cultural support for sexual aggression are evident. Burt (1980, 1983) proposes that general societal support exists for men's sexual aggressiveness against women, especially when the men and women are in a romantic relationship. To measure this support, she developed a measure of rape myth acceptance. Research by Burt and others consistently reveals that single men are more accepting of rape myths than are single women (Lonsway & Fitzgerald, 1994), especially in the case where the men hold sex-role stereotyped beliefs (Muehlenhard, 1988).

Evidence of cultural support is additionally revealed in findings that show that individuals are not always quick to judge a sexually aggressive interaction as a rape. Researchers offered participants vignettes depicting sexual aggression that manipulate certain qualities of the characters in the story, and then asked participants whether a rape occurred (Schultz & DeSavage, 1975; Shotland & Goodstein, 1983). Young adults are quicker to conclude that a woman is raped if the woman forcefully resists, but they are slower to define an interaction as rape if she permits precoital sexual behaviors, partially disrobes, or offers little resistance. Moreover, participants are more apt to blame the female victim in the vignettes if she wears revealing clothing, allows precoital sexual interactions, has been drinking, or knows her partner (Kopper, 1996; Norris & Cubbins, 1992; Whatley, 1996). O'Neal (1998) extended this research by showing that individuals with a history of being sexually aggressive are even more apt to blame female victims than are those who are not sexually aggressive. Collectively, these findings demonstrate that young adults are not quick to conclude that an interaction involves sexual aggression and may even blame a victim for her experience. Peers and aggressors can use this lack of definitional clarity to justify their behavior. Furthermore, victimized women may be unwilling to share their experiences with others because they are unsure whether friends will blame them for the incident, a belief that likely contributes to victims' self-blame.

Similar beliefs can be found among adolescents even as young as 14 years of age (Goodchilds & Zellman, 1984). For instance, Davis, Peck, and Storment (1993) surveyed 9th to 12th graders and found that between one quarter and one third of the male students agreed that "It's OK for a boy to force a girl to have sex with him if..." (p. 222) the girl got the boy sexually excited, let the boy touch her above the waist, had dated the boy for a really long time, agreed to go home with him, wore revealing/sexy clothing, or had sex with the boy sometime before. Twenty-three percent of the boys agreed that force was acceptable if a girl got a boy sexually excited. Investigations using different attitude measures with a Canadian sample similarly found that adolescent boys, when compared to adolescent girls, were more accepting of parallel beliefs (Morrison, McLeod, Morrison, Anderson, & O'Connor, 1997). Underscoring these findings is the report by Zimmerman, Sprecher, Langer, and Holloway (1995) that 10th graders' ability to say no to a boy/girl friend who wanted to have sex when they did not want to was negatively related to peer influences. In other words, male and female adolescents saw themselves as less able to say "no" as peer influence increased. Thus, youths' attitudes supporting sexual aggression may indirectly contribute to its occurrence.

Lloyd and Emery's conceptualization of the gendered qualities inherent in dating roles represent the third level of social support for sexual aggression (Lloyd, 1991; Lloyd & Emery, 1999). These scholars posit that dating roles have three qualities that contribute to sexual aggression. They note that single men's dating role expectations include exerting control while on dates. A man typically asks the woman out, decides on the activity for the date, and eventually suggests a monogamous relationship if he wants one. In addition, men's role prescribes that they make the first sexual move and strive for increased sexual intimacy. Taken to a logical extreme, these role expectations will lead some men to conclude that they are in charge of their own and their partners' sexual wishes. Therefore, women's sexual wishes may be subjugated to the men's as men fulfill their dating role expectations.

The second quality of dating roles focuses on the role expectation that single women will become dependent on their dating relationship and, therefore, will strive to maintain the relationship even in times of distress. Women depend on men to advance the commitment level of the relationship while being the sexual gatekeepers. Moreover, if women are the caretakers of the relationship, it falls to them to engage in relationship repair strategies after acts of sexual aggression. This may also help explain why many women experience feelings of self-blame and fail to define their experiences as "rape" even when physical force was used against them (Koss et al., 1987; Lloyd & Emery, 1999).

Lloyd and Emery (1999) further point to the role of romance in dating relationships as the third relational role quality that contributes to sexual aggression. Romance in dating relationships is valued, often cultivated, and is positively sanctioned by partners, peers, and family. However, romance may lead partners in general, and women in particular, to overlook, excuse, or forgive sexual aggressiveness. It may additionally contribute to couples staying together even though sexual victimizing is a part of the relationship as couples provide excuses for the male partner's aggression (*He was drunk*), shift the blame for the incident to the female partner (*She should know better than to provoke him*), or downplay the seriousness of the incident (*It won't happen again*). In support of this conceptualization, Lloyd and Emery (1999) describe a number of women who, on telling their stories of sexual victimization in a relationship to these researchers, observed that if it were a friend relating a similar experience, they would tell the friend that she was a victim of rape and advise her to leave the relationship. However, these same women found it difficult to define their own experiences as rape even when their boyfriends used force to attain sex.

Other gendered qualities of dating roles may contribute to sexual aggression (Christopher, 2001). Single women's sexual and dating roles are inherently more restrictive than are men's roles. Woman are more likely to be judged sexually seductive and promiscuous than men in interpersonal interactions independent of their emotional closeness to a partner (Abbey, Cozzarelli, McLaughlin, & Harnish, 1987; Abbey & Melby, 1986). Other singles will judge a woman's sexual interest by her choice of clothing while not applying this same role expectation to men. Moreover, if a single woman is sexually interested in a man, she must be concerned about his reaction if she openly signals her interest (Muehlenhard & McCoy, 1991). Signaling sexual interest too early in a relationship can result in being labeled as "easy" or "loose"; labels that sexually aggressive men apply to the women they victimize (Kanin, 1970; 1983). Thus, a woman puts herself at risk if she shows sexual interest in a partner by her dress or her mannerisms, or may even be at risk because her date perceives her as sexually interested in him even though she is not.

SETTING AND USING INTOXICANTS

Privacy is a common prerequisite for engaging in sexual behavior in our society. Thus, it should not be surprising that most sexual aggression that takes place among singles is likely to occur in a place of privacy (i.e., Gwartney-Gibbs & Stockard, 1989). Although researchers have not always presented the same list of possible choices in their surveys, respondents most frequently report that their experiences of sexual aggression happened in a place that afforded privacy for the couple. Most often listed private places include houses or apartments (Miller & Marshall, 1987), parked cars (Muehlenhard & Linton, 1987), or fraternity houses (Copenhaver & Grauerholz, 1991).

Using intoxicants, usually in the form of alcohol but sometimes in the form of illegal drugs, is also a consistent predictor of sexual aggression across studies and in multivariate analyses. Some investigators demonstrate that men are more apt to be sexual aggressors when they have imbibed alcohol or taken drugs, whereas other investigators report that women are at increased risk of being victimized if they drink (Copenhaver & Grauerholz, 1991; Harrington & Leitenberg, 1994; Ward, Chapman, Cohn, White, & Williams, 1991). Still other investigators have found that drinking by either partner increases the risk of sexual aggression for young adults and adolescents (Harrington & Leitenberg, 1994; Koss & Dinero, 1989; Small & Kerns, 1991) as well as for gays and lesbians (Waldner-Haugrud & Gratch, 1997) and often plays a role in marital rape (Finkelhor & Yllö, 1985). Given that use of intoxicants consistently predicts sexual aggression across studies, it is not surprising that a recent meta-analysis shows that the relationship between alcohol use by singles and use of sexual aggression has a large average effect size, $d = .72$ (Christopher, Burch, & Kisler, 2001). Clearly, use of alcohol by either dyadic partner increases the risk of sexual aggression across all types of relationships and for different age groups.

What is not clear, however, is the processes involved in this association. One possible explanation is that sexual aggressors use alcohol to excuse their behavior. Certainly the qualitative reports of Lloyd and Emery (1999) reveal that some couples justify the male partner's behavior by citing the change in his behavior when he drinks as an important causal factor in the aggression. Nonetheless, other research shows that giving a partner alcohol is one of several influence tactics that form an overall sexually aggressive influence strategy (Christopher & Frandsen, 1990). In this instance, aggressors may hope that alcohol will lower the inhibitions and cloud the judgment of potential victims. These are not necessarily competing explanations and may operate simultaneously.

INDIVIDUAL CHARACTERISTICS

A great deal of scholarly effort has focused on identifying individual correlates of male sexual aggressors. These efforts have uncovered traits that covary with the use of aggression. A sizable number of researchers have examined the role of attitudes. Much of this research is based on Burt's (1980) foundational work. Recall that Burt speculated that members of society generally accept myths about rape. She demonstrated that belief in rape myths correlate with an acceptance of interpersonal violence, and a belief that men's and women's sexual relationships are inherently adversarial. Moreover, a comparison of convicted rapists with a community sample revealed that rapists were more apt to endorse rape myths and accept interpersonal violence (Burt, 1983).

Burt's assertions about the importance of examining the attitudes of sexual aggressors resonated with investigators who followed. Scholars have often included her measures in their studies with consistent results. Compared to single men who are not sexually aggressive, single, sexually aggressive men are more accepting of rape myths as well as of interpersonal violence (Byers & Eno, 1991; Malamuth, 1986; Muehlenhard & Linton, 1987), endorse the use of force (Garrett-Gooding & Senter, 1987; Rapaport & Burkhart, 1984), and identify force as a legitimate means of gaining sexual access (Koss & Dinero, 1988). Meta-analysis of such findings shows a strong, moderate relationship for comparisons between sexually aggressive and nonaggressive men (Christopher et al., 2001). In addition, belief in rape myths consistently predicts sexual aggressiveness in multivariate and structural equation models (Christopher et al., 1993b; Dean & Malamuth, 1997; Malamuth, Linz, Heavey, Barnes, & Acker, 1995; Malamuth,

Sockloski, Koss, & Tanaka, 1991). In reviewing these findings, Christopher (2001) hypothesized that these violent attitudes form an overarching attitudinal complex that is used to justify their own and their peer's acts of sexual aggression.

A parallel line of research examined sexual aggressors' gender attitudes. Several research teams found that single, sexually aggressive men, compared to nonaggressive male peers, possess more traditional attitudes about women's place in society (Koss et al., 1985; Muehlenhard & Falcon, 1990; Walker, Rowe, & Quinsey, 1993) and more strongly endorse masculinity (Dean & Malamuth, 1997; Sarwer, Kalichman, Johnson, Early, & Ali, 1993; Truman, Tokar, & Fischer, 1996). Meta-analyses of these studies reveal a small but consistent average effect size for both gender attitudes although averaged effect size for attitudes toward women ($d = .43$) is not quite as large as for masculinity ($d = .58$; Christopher et al., 2001).

Additionally scholars attempted to identify personality traits related to the use of sexual aggression. Positive associations exist for hostility toward women (Check, 1988; Christopher et al., 1993b; Kanin, 1970; Koss & Dinero, 1988; Malamuth et al., 1995), anger (Christopher et al., 1993b; Lisak & Roth, 1988; Mosher & Anderson, 1986), and dominance (Muehlenhard & Falcon, 1990). Collectively, meta-analysis suggests that these negative traits have a strong, moderate relationship to the use of sexual aggression (average $d = .58$; Christopher et al., 2001).

Hall and Hirschman (1991) proposed a conceptual framework for how these traits may operate. From their framework, most individuals' socialization results in internalized inhibitions against displays of aggression. Some individuals, however, experience emotions that weaken socialized inhibitions. Such *states of affective dyscontrol*, Hall and Hirschman's term, increase the likelihood of sexual aggression. There is research that supports their framework. Sexually aggressive, single men are more disinhibitted (Lisak & Roth, 1988), impulsive (Petty & Dawson, 1989), and apt to be thrill seekers (Lalumière & Quinsey, 1996) than are nonaggressive men, suggesting that they easily experience, and may seek out, emotively charged states. They additionally are less apt to understand social rules, feel responsible for their behavior, and to have prosocial values (Rapaport & Burkhart, 1984) thereby suggesting that their socialization had different outcomes from others. Furthermore, inhibitions may be weaker among these men because they have less empathy for their victims (Christopher et al., 1993b). Moreover, the role of anger and the hostility toward women are likely examples of the type of affective dyscontrol that can lead to sexual aggression.

MODELS OF MALE SEXUAL AGGRESSION

A number of scholars proposed conceptual models of male sexual aggression. These models vary in the assumptions inherent in the framework used. Some scholars use Evolutionary Psychology to frame their models. These perspectives look for adaptive explanations for the occurrence of sexual aggression. Thornhill and Thornhill's (1992) work is an example of this approach. Their view is built on certain assumptions about adaptive characteristics inherent in men's mating strategies. Specifically, men's mating strategies focus on procuring and retaining partners and on ensuring the paternity of any children that result from mating. These basic characteristics serve as a foundation for a set of hypotheses; hypotheses that they argue are supported by existing literature. They posit, for instance, that if men have a rape-specific adaptation, then a partner's consent should be unrelated to men's ability to achieve an erection, engage in coitus, and ejaculate. This reasoning can be extended to suggest that older men, and men of higher socioeconomic status, control more resources than younger men and men of lower socioeconomic status and thereby have greater opportunity to copulate with women. Thus, younger men and men with fewer resources are more apt to resort to coercing women to increase the chance of reproducing. Thornhill and Thornhill continue by speculating that men's concerns with punishment and the likelihood of detection are negatively associated with the probability of their use of coercion. This is based on the belief that as a species-specific adaptation, we are concerned with limiting the use of personal force. These two scholars also predict that men in established relationships are more apt to use sexual coercion if they detect or suspect a partner's infidelity. According to this framework, such coercion helps to ensure the certainty of paternity of any children that result from the pair-bond.

Malamuth (1998a, 1998b) also uses an evolutionary framework for his Confluence Model of sexual coercion. He posits that a confluence of three constellations of individual characteristics underlie coercive acts. First, coercive men possess a personality trait that causes them to assert their own interests at the expense of others. Second, an additional personality characteristic of these men is that they favor a short-term mating strategy—a choice that conflicts with female partners who typically choose a long-term strategy. Third, sexually aggressive men possess a constellation of emotions and attitudes that primes them to behave in coercive ways. Malamuth stresses that the interaction of these three influences drastically increases the probability that men will engage in sexually aggressive behavior.

Koss and Cleveland (1997) take an ecological approach. They begin with the assertion that men behave in reasonable ways when they are sexually aggressive because the societal context supports their behavior. More specifically, "permissive social ecologies" (p. 8) provide men with the opportunity to be aggressive while concurrently requiring women to accept being the victims of aggression. Included in these ecologies are the facts that society fails to clearly reject sexual aggression, thereby supporting rape-facilitating perceptions, that aggressive men often possess a collection of personality traits that predispose them to act in a coercive manner, and that such men find peer support for their actions. In addition, Koss and Cleveland (1997) cite the fact that women's experiences of sexual aggression are typically trivialized, and that women are often viewed as deserving victims, as additional components of a supportive ecology. In other words, these scholars underscore the role that social conditions play in supporting acts of sexual aggression.

Christopher (2001) uses Symbolic Interaction Theory to develop a model of sexual aggression in dating relationships. In this model, sexually aggressive men are conceptualized as possessing a constellation of supportive attitudes that contribute to the men's *self*-identity, an identity that is used to assign meaning to their own and their partner's actions and to justify their own aggression. Christopher speculates that the personality traits that are also part of the *self* of these men disinhibit socialization influences that normally block or control aggression. Peers are viewed as socializing agents who support sexually aggressive acts by providing positive meanings to these acts and by granting social status to those who engage in them. Moreover, when aggressive men make sexual role choices, they consider rewards they will likely receive from their peers, as well as how their peers will interpret their role-related behaviors. Christopher hypothesizes that increased relational commitment is often paired with sexual role expectations that have a theme of entitlement. Moreover, partners in these relationships may unintentionally support sexual aggressiveness in their relationship by recasting aggressive incidents in a favorable light and by putting themselves at increased risk by using alcohol.

VICTIM OUTCOMES

Several research teams have examined the adjustment of single women who have been sexually victimized in their dating relationships. Victimized women, when compared to nonvictimized peers, suffer higher levels of psychological trauma and distress

(Santello & Leitenberg, 1993; Shapiro & Schwartz, 1997; Zweig, Barber, & Eccles, 1997). They are also more apt to experience fear even in the safety of their own homes (Kelly & DeKeseredy, 1994). Their victimization may lead them to engage in more problem avoidance, social withdrawal, and self-criticism when faced with coping with their experiences, a problem solving style that suggests that these women disengage rather than actively face their trauma (Santello & Leitenberg, 1993).

Self-blame is frequently a strong part of their reaction. Emery and Lloyd's (1999) qualitative analysis of dating women's view of responsibility and blame highlights two themes in their reactions. First, victimized women typically offer excuses for their partner's aggressive behavior. They defuse his responsibility by offering excuses that center on his upbringing, his attitudes toward women and violence, his drinking, or the way he acts around friends. Second, they often take responsibility for their partner's behavior by believing that they put themselves at risk, that they should have been able to predict that their partner would behave aggressively, or that they should have been more assertive when saying no. Emery and Lloyd's findings may help explain why just over 70% of the women in Koss et al.'s (1987) survey did not believe they were victims of a crime even though their experience fit the legal definition of rape.

Victimization experiences for young, adolescent women can have a long temporal reach. Zweig, Crockett, Sayer, and Vicary's (1999) longitudinal study tracked young women from ninth grade to their early 20s. Women who experienced sexual coercion during adolescence, when compared to peers who did not, were more apt to evaluate the quality of their sexual experiences negatively. Women with adolescent experiences of sexual assault, however, endured more pervasive problems including greater depression, lower sexual-esteem, poorer body image, and poorer relationship quality.

Married women who are raped by their husbands report parallel outcomes. Finkelhor and Yllö (1985) found that these women described feelings of betrayal, anger, humiliation, and guilt. In addition, some incurred physical trauma to their genitals and rectum. Continued experiences were associated with greater long-term psychological effects (Russsell, 1990). Many of these women developed serious trust issues in their relationships, even after leaving their abusive husbands, and continued to feel fear even in nonsexual contexts (Finkelhor &Yllö, 1985). Not all women leave their sexually abusive marriages. Russell (1990) identified a number of reasons for this for the women in her study. Some lacked resources, support, and alternatives. Others blamed themselves and excused their husbands' behavior.

PREVENTION PROGRAMS

Interventionists developed prevention programs in an effort to reduce rates of sexual aggression. In effect, prevention intervention attempts to intercede in a problem area prior to the development of the problem. Efforts to intervene in sexual aggression have primarily focused on changing attitudes or behavior that, in turn, decrease the probability that sexually aggressive incidents will occur. For example, capitalizing on research findings, these programs often attempt to modify belief in rape myths and attitudes toward women or to increase victim empathy (Gidycz et al., 2001; Schewe & O'Donohue 1996; Yeater & O'Donohue, 1999). In addition, prevention intervention efforts targeted different populations. Some intervened with women, others with men, and still others used mixed-sex groups.

Interventions Focused on Women

Female interventions predominately focused on sexual assault education and self-defense strategies (Yeater & O'Donohue, 1999). Sexual assault educational approaches focus on enlightening women about their risk of and vulnerability to sexual assault. In an attempt to empower women, these programs target reducing risk-taking attitudes and behaviors.

Hanson and Gidycz's (1993) program exemplifies this approach. In their intervention, women watch a videotape that ends in a rape at a college party. Several risk factors are highlighted in the tape including alcohol use, problems in communication, and low assertiveness on the part of the female victim. A guided discussion among participants takes place that offers possible strategies for decreasing risks. The women in the program then view a second videotape that portrays potential responses to each risk in the original tape.

Breitenbecher and Scarce (2001) take a somewhat similar approach. Their program consists of a 90-minute session in which participants form groups of four to five women. The goal of the program is to change psychological barriers that keep single women from resisting sexual aggression that occurs while on a date. Groups are presented with a sexual vignette and asked to imagine themselves in the situation, to identify the emotions and cognitions they would experience, and to identify possible verbal and behavioral strategies they could use to reduce their risk. One larger group is formed from the smaller groups, and a guided discussion is used to reinforce strategies that emphasize direct, verbal communication as a prevention strategy.

Other programs focus on teaching women how to physically defend themselves if they are sexually assaulted. These programs typically train women how to respond to rape attempts by strangers rather than acquaintances or relationship partners. Yeater and O'Donohue (1999) criticize this approach. According to these scholars, the resistive techniques that are taught may not work with a relationship partner because the woman may already be in a physically compromising position when the assault begins. Moreover, they assert that rape attempts by strangers constitute a minority of instances of rape or attempted rape. Thus, these programs may apply to only a small number of sexually aggressive situations that women typically face.

To date, prevention programs aimed at single women have been largely unsuccessful (see Yeater & O'Donohue, 1999, for a review). There has been limited support for the assertion that changes in attitudes and knowledge by themselves result in women engaging in less risk-taking behavior and experiencing fewer instances of sexual victimization. Further, Yeater and O'Donohue (1999) identify common methodological problems shared by most prevention programs that target women. Many suffer from demand characteristics that may bias outcome measures. Samples often originate from low-risk populations, populations that may not respond the same as a high-risk population, thus confounding the external validity of the evaluations of the programs. In addition, few programs have an evaluation design that allows interventionists to conclude that the program resulted in a decrease in sexual assault rates. Moreover, programs do not always differentiate between participants who have never experienced sexual aggression from those who have been previously victimized. This may be a needed step in developing interventions as previously victimized women are at higher risk for experiencing repeat victimization (Breitenbecher & Scarce, 2001).

Interventions Focused on Men

Recognizing that sexual aggression is most frequently a male-centered phenomenon, some interventionists targeted young adult men. These programs are commonly designed to decrease men's belief in rape myths and increase their empathy for victims (Yeater & O'Donohue, 1999). Schewe and O'Donohue (1996) exemplify this approach. They implemented two short-term interventions that focused on changing beliefs that contribute to coercive sexual behavior and worked to increase victim empathy. The first intervention consisted of a 50-minute videotape in which the victims described their experiences. The goal was to encourage and increase victim empathy.

After the video, the men discussed possible consequences of rape. This was followed by an exercise in which participants were to gather as many arguments as possible to persuade a hypothetical man to not commit a rape. In the second intervention, men viewed a 50-minute videotape. The video underscored the importance of identifying and examining rape supportive cognitions. After the videotape, the group participated in a discussion of rape, followed by a second discussion involving the hypothetical man on the verge of attempting a rape.

Evaluations of the programs indicated that men in both treatments, when compared to no-treatment controls, made significant changes in the desired direction on measures of attraction to sexual aggression, rape myth acceptance, and acceptance of interpersonal violence. In addition, participants utilized more empathy-based and consequence-based arguments to convince the hypothetical man not to rape the woman.

Other interventions take similar approaches, although the design of their evaluations do not always allow for clear conclusions about their effectiveness (Yeater & O'Donohue, 1999). Berg (1993), for instance, conducted a 90-minute workshop utilizing audiotapes of sexual aggression victims designed to increase victim empathy and decrease belief in rape myths. Egidio and Robertson's (1981) 2-hour program included a lecture, a discussion, and two films on rape. Ring and Kilmartin (1992) also used a film, one that highlighted issues surrounding sex role socialization and intimacy. This was followed by experiential discussions that centered on the consequences of objectifying men and women's bodies and of repressing emotions.

Evaluations of these programs are not always well designed (Yeater & O'Donohue, 1999). Nonetheless, interventions focused on young adult men appear to have successfully intervened to bring about changes in attitudes that support sexual aggression. Moreover, some interventionists report that the posttest attitude changes achieved from their brief interventions continue to hold through a follow-up period. Still, there is a need to examine whether these changes are indicative of decreases in sexual aggression in the targeted groups.

Mixed-Gender Interventions

Some interventionists design programs for joint attendance by single men and women (but not necessarily couples). Similar to gender segregated interventions, these prevention efforts are often aimed at changing rape supportive attitudes, predominately rape myth acceptance and attitudes toward women (Gidycz et al., 2001; Yeater & O'Donohue, 1999). Programs generally consist of a 45-minute to 1-hour session. They commonly include a brief educational overview of sexual aggression and then diverge in the activities used to intervene. Frazier, Valtinson, and Candell (1994), for example, used an improvisational theater group in their program. Briskin and Gary (1986) emulated a quiz format to engender discussion about 24 rape myths. Ellis, O'Sullivan, and Sowards (1992) asked participants to imagine a close friend or relative disclosing that she was a sexual assault victim and then used discussion to highlight emergent themes.

These programs are generally successful at reducing belief in rape myths (Gidycz et al., 2001; Yeater & O'Donohue, 1999). However, these results must be viewed cautiously. Although there was commonly a reduction in rape myths, there was usually no reported reduction in perpetration or experience of sexual aggression. Iatrogenic effects, inadvertent and often unwanted effects that result from participation, are also of concern. Gidycz et al. (2001) found that men who had perpetrated prior to participating in their program were three times as likely to perpetrate in the follow-up period when compared to men who had not previously been sexually aggressive. Equally disturbing, Gidycz and colleagues (2001) found that while a majority of the participants rated their program as very successful, they did not think that the information applied to them. It appears that their intervention was unsuccessful at inducing a sense of vulnerability in participants. Other mixed-gender interventions failed to look at actual behavior change. In fact, Yeater and O'Donohue (1999) cite several methodological flaws with current programs including psychometrically poor dependent measures, small samples sizes, lack of power, and no indicant of actual change in sexually assaultive behavior.

Methodological and Programmatic Concerns

The overall limited effectiveness of prevention interventions has led researchers to list methodological problems in evaluation designs shared by many existing programs (Schewe & O'Donohue, 1996; Yeater & O'Donohue, 1999). Besides those already listed, the chief concern is that interventionists fail to measure short-and long-term behavior change in sexual aggression in men and in putting oneself at risk in women. Furthermore, Schewe and O'Donohue (1996) accuse many interventionists of taking a "shot gun" approach in their programs. They typically use a one time, 1- to 2-hour intervention format hoping this will effect a lasting change. Such simplistic approaches fail to recognize the complexity of forces that support sexual aggression, and it is unlikely that these brief interventions will effect long-term change in core attitudes.

Finally, Yeater and O'Donohue (1999) make some valuable suggestions to guide future programs. They recommend tailoring male and female programs to complement each other. In addition, they suggest focusing on comprehensive coverage of constructs that relate to behavior change, implementing skills for dealing with high-risk situations, measuring long-term impact, and assessing the generalizability of the skills taught. In addition, they note that developing strong programs with lasting effects is dependent on rigorous evaluations. It is necessary to have control groups and follow-up evaluation sessions in order to identify program components that maintain lasting effects.

CONCLUSIONS

This chapter provides one of the first overviews of sexual aggression that includes findings from studies focused on adolescents, young single adults, married individuals, gays, and lesbians. A few general conclusions can be drawn from this review. For example, although it is obvious that sexual aggression occurs across all of these relationships, more is known about what variables covary with this types of aggression in dating than in other types of relationships. Thus, one important direction for future research is to identify covariates that are universal across relationships from those that are more particular to specific types of romantic relationships. While attempting to accomplish this, researchers will have to ensure that they operationalize sexual aggression such that they measure both sexual coercion and sexual assault.

Moreover, the literature on sexual aggression has developed to the point where empirical investigations should be guided by theory. An array of theory-driven models and hypotheses have been advanced but not always tested. It is important to note, however, that some theories are narrower in focus than others. For instance, hypotheses and models informed by Evolutionary Psychology such as those offered by Thornhill and Thornhill (1992) as well as by Malamuth (1998a, 1998b) are tightly focused on mating strategies and do not always acknowledge results of other researchers whose work provides evidence that relational and social variables are associated with sexual aggression. While Christopher's (2001) use of Symbolic Interaction Theory allows him to hypothesize about the role of social and relational factors, his work is limited to premarital relationships and has not been applied to gay, lesbian, and married relationships characterized by sexual aggression. Thus, theoretical work is needed to explore the role of aggression that occurs in relationships other than dating relationships.

Nonetheless, we were also struck by the commonalities across findings that existed in the diversity of relationships represented by the corpus of this work. Foremost among these commonalities is that sexual aggression occurs across all types of close, romantic relationships. Given that it is a pervasive problem, it requires that intervention be guided by social policy that recognizes how complex and widespread a phenomenon sexual aggression actually is. Second, if prevention interventionists are going to succeed in reducing acts of sexual aggression, they must recognize and address the key role that relationship dynamics play in supporting acts of sexual aggression. Third, scholars must find ways to take their work to the public in a manner that engenders discussion about whether sexual coercion should continue to be tolerated and excused. Finally, although commonalities in findings exist across relationships, less is known about sexual aggression that occurs among adolescents, married, gays, and lesbians. Investigators will need to focus their attention on these populations if we are to gain a more thorough understanding of sexual aggression in relationships.

REFERENCES

Abbey, A., & Melby, C. (1986). The effects of nonverbal cues on gender differences in perceptions of sexual intent. *Sex Roles, 15*, 283–298.

Abbey, A., Cozzarelli, C., McLaughlin, K., & Harnish, R. J. (1987). The effects of clothing and dyad sex composition on perceptions of sexual intent: Do women and men evaluate these cues differently. *Journal of Applied Social Psychology, 17*, 108–126.

Alksnis, C., Desmarais, S., Senn, C., & Hunter, N. (2000). Methodological concerns regarding estimates of physical violence in sexual coercion: Overstatement or understatement? *Archives of Sexual Behavior, 29*, 323–334.

Berg, D. R. (1933). *The use of rape-specific empathy induction in rape education for college men: A theoretical and practical examination*. Unpublished master's thesis, University of Illinois, Urbana-Champaign, Illinois.

Boeringer, S. B., Shehan, C. L., & Akers, R. L. (1991). Social context and social learning in sexual coercion and aggression: Assessing the contribution of fraternity membership. *Family Relations, 40*, 58–64.

Breitenbecher, K. H., & Scarce, M. (2001). An evaluation of the effectiveness of a sexual assault education program focusing on psychological barriers to resistance. *Journal of Interpersonal Violence, 16*, 387–407.

Briskin, K. C., & Gary, J. M. (1986). Sexual assault programming for college students. *Journal of Counseling and Development, 65*, 207–208.

Burt, M. R. (1980). Cultural myths and supports for rape. *Journal of Personality and Social Psychology, 38*, 217–230.

Burt, M. R. (1983). Justifying personal violence: A comparison of rapists and the general public. *Victimology, 8*, 131–150.

Byers, E. S., & Eno, R. J. (1991). Predicting men's sexual coercion and aggression from attitudes, dating history, and sexual response. *Journal of Psychology and Human Sexuality, 4*, 55–70.

Check, J. V. P. (1988). Hostility toward women: Some theoretical considerations. In G. W. Russel (Ed.) *Violence in intimate relationships* (pp. 29–42). New York: PMA.

Christopher, F. S. (2001). *To dance the dance: A symbolic interactional exploration of premarital sexuality*. Mahwah, NJ: Lawrence Erlbaum Associates.

Christopher, F. S., & Frandsen, M. M. (1990). Strategies of influence in sex and dating. *Journal of Social and Personal Relationships, 7*, 89–107.

Christopher, F. S., Madura, M., & Weaver, L. (1998). Premarital sexual aggressors: A multivariate analysis of social, relational, and individual variables. *Journal of Marriage and the Family, 60*, 56–69.

Christopher, F. S., & McQuaid, S. (1998, June). *Dating relationships and men's sexual aggression: A test of a relationship-based model*. Paper presented at the biennial meeting of the International Society for the Study of Personal Relationships, Saratoga Springs, NY.

Christopher, F. S., Owens, L. A., & Stecker, H. L. (1993a). Exploring the dark side of courtship: A test model of male premarital sexual aggressiveness. *Journal of Marriage and the Family, 55*, 469–479.

Christopher, F. S., Owens, L. A., & Stecker, H. L. (1993b). An examination of single men and women's sexual aggressiveness in dating relationships. *Journal of Social and Personal Relationships, 10*, 511–527.

Christopher, F. S., Burch, S. C., & Kisler, T. S., (2001, November). *Men's use of sexual aggression in dating relationships: A meta-analysis.* Paper presented at the annual Society of Scientific Study of Sexuality Research, San Diego, C.A.

Copenhaver, S., & Grauerholz, E. (1991). Sexual victimization among sorority women: Exploring the link between sexual violence and institutional practices. *Sex Roles, 24,* 31–41.

Davis, T. C., Peck, G. Q., & Storment, J. M. (1993). Acquaintance rape and the high school student. *Journal of Adolescent Health, 14,* 220–223.

Dean, K. E., & Malamuth, N. M. (1997). Characteristics of men who aggress sexually and of men who imagine aggressing: Risk and moderating variables. *Journal of Personality and Social Psychology, 72,* 449–455.

DeKeseredy, W. S., & Kelly, K. (1995). Sexual abuse in Canadian university and college dating relationships: The contribution of male peer support. *Journal of Family Violence, 10,* 41–53.

DeMaris, A. (1997). Elevated sexual activity in violent marriages: Hypersexuality or sexual extortion? *The Journal of Sex Research, 34,* 361–373.

DeMaris, A., & Swinford, S. (1996). Female victims of spousal violence: Factors influencing their level of fearfulness. *Family Relations, 45,* 98–106.

Duncan, D. (1990). Prevalence of sexual assault victimization among heterosexual and gay/lesbian university students. *Psychological Reports, 66,* 65–66.

Egidio, R. K., & Robertson, D. E. (1981). Rape awareness for men. *Journal of College Student Development, 22,* 455–456.

Ellis, A. L., O'Sullivan, C. S., & Sowards, B. A. (1992). The impact of contemplated exposure to a survivor of rape on attitudes toward rape. *Journal of Applied Social Psychology, 22,* 889–895.

Emery, B., & Lloyd, S. (1999, November). *Survivors' perspectives on the long-term impact of sexual aggression.* Paper presented at the Annual Conference of the National Council on Family Relations.

Falbo, T., & Peplau, L. A. (1980). Power strategies in intimate relationships. *Journal of Personality and Social Psychology, 38,* 618–628.

Finkelhor, D., & Yllö, K. (1985). *License to rape: Sexual abuse of wives.* New York: Holt, Rinehart, & Winston.

Frazier, P., Valtinson, G., & Candell, S. (1994). Evaluation of a coeducational interactive rape prevention program. *Journal of Counseling and Development, 73,* 153–158.

Frinter, M. P., & Rubinson, L. (1993). Acquaintance rape: The influence of alcohol, fraternity membership, and sports team membership. *Journal of Sex Education and Therapy, 19,* 272–284.

Garrett-Gooding, J., & Senter, R. (1987). Attitudes and acts of sexual aggression on a university campus. *Sociological Inquiry, 57,* 348–371.

Gidycz, C. A., Layman, M. J., Rich, C. L., Crothers, M., Gylys, J., Matorin, A., & Jacobs, C. D. (2001). An evaluation of an acquaintance rape prevention program: Impact on attitudes, sexual aggression, and sexual victimization. *Journal of Interpersonal Violence, 16,* 1120–1138.

Goodchilds, J. D., & Zellman, G. L. (1984). Sexual signaling and sexual aggression in adolescent relationships. In N. M. Malamuth & E. Donnerstein (Eds.), *Pornography and Sexual Aggression,* (pp. 233–243). Orlando, FL: Academic Press.

Gwartney-Gibbs, P., & Stockard, J. (1989). Courtship aggression and mixed sex peer groups. In M. A. Pirog-Good and J. E. Stets (Eds.), *Violence in dating relationships: Emerging social issues* (pp. 185–204). New York: Praeger.

Hall, G. C. N., & Hirschman R. (1991). Toward a theory of sexual aggression: A quadripartite model. *Journal of Consulting and Clinical Psychology, 59,* 662–669.

Hanson, K. A., & Gidycz, C., A. (1993). Evaluation of a sexual assault prevention program. *Journal of Consulting and Clinical Psychology, 61,* 1046–1052.

Harrington, N. T., & Leitenberg, H. (1994). Relationship between alcohol consumption and victim behaviors immediately preceding sexual aggression by an acquaintance. *Violence and Victims, 9,* 315–324.

Hickson, F. C. I., Davies, P. M., Hunt, A. J., & Weatherburn, P. (1994). Gay men as victims of nonconsensual sex. *Archives of Sexual Behavior, 23,* 281–294.

Huston, T. L. (1983). Power. In H. Kelley, E. Berscheid, A. Christensen, J. Harvey, T. Huston, G. Levinber, E. McClintock, L. A. Peplau, & D. R. Peterson (Eds.), *Close Relationships* (pp. 169–219). New York: Freeman.

Kanin, E. J. (1967). An examination of sexual aggression as a response to sexual frustration. *Journal of Marriage and the Family, 29,* 428–433.

Kanin, E. J. (1969). Selected dyadic aspects of male sex aggression. *Journal of Sex Research, 5,* 12–28.

Kanin, E. J. (1970). Sex aggression by college men. *Medical Aspects of Human Sexuality, 4,* 28–40.

Kanin, E. J. (1983). Rape as a function of relative sexual frustration. *Psychological Reports, 52,* 133–134.

Kanin, E. J., & Parcell, S. R. (1977). Sexual aggression: A second look at the offended female. *Archives of Sexual Behavior, 6,* 67–76.

Kelly, K. D., & DeKeserdy, W. S. (1994). Women's fear of crime and abuse in college and university dating relationships. *Violence and Victims, 9,* 17–30.

Kopper, B. A. (1996). Gender, gender identity, rape myth acceptance, and time of initial resistance on the perception of acquaintance rape blame and avoidability. *Sex Roles, 34,* 81–93.

Koss, M. P., & Cleveland, H. H. (1997). Stepping on toes: Social roots of date rape lead to intractability and politicization. In M. D. Schwartz (Ed.), *Researching sexual violence against women: Methodological and personal perspectives* (pp. 4–21). Thousand Oaks, CA: Sage.

Koss, M. P., & Dinero, T. E. (1988). Predictors of sexual aggression among a national sample of male college students. In R. A. Prentky & V. L. Quinsey (Eds.), *Human sexual aggression: Current perspectives. Annals of the New York Academy of Sciences* (Vol. 528; pp. 133–146).

Koss, M. P., & Dinero, T. E. (1989). Discriminant analysis of risk factors for sexual victimization among a national sample of college women. *Journal of Consulting and Clinical Psychology, 57,* 242–250.

Koss, M. P., Gidycz, C. A., & Wisniewski, N. (1987). The scope of rape: Incidence and prevalence of sexual aggression and victimization in a national sample of higher education students. *Journal of Consulting and Clinical Psychology, 55,* 162–170.

Koss, M. P., Leonard, K. E., Beezley, D. A., & Oros, C. J. (1985). Nonstranger sexual aggression: A discriminant analysis of the psychological characteristics of undetected offenders. *Sex Roles, 12,* 981–992.

Koss, M. P., & Oros, C. J. (1980). *The "unacknowledged" rape victim.* Paper presented at the American Psychological Association meeting in Montreal, Canada.

Koss, M. P., & Oros, C. J. (1982). Sexual experiences survey: A research instrument investigating sexual aggression and victimization. *Journal of Consulting and Clinical Psychology, 50,* 455–457.

Lackie, L., & de Man, A. F. (1997). Correlates of sexual aggression among male university students. *Sex Roles, 37,* 451–457.

Lalumière, M. L., & Quinsey, V. L. (1996). Sexual deviance, antisociality, mating effort, and the use of sexually coercive behaviors. *Personality and Individual Differences, 21,* 34–48.

Lalumière, M. L., Chalmers, L. J., Quinsey, V. L., & Seto, M. C. (1996). A test of the mate deprivation hypothesis of sexual coercion. *Ethology and Sociobiology, 17,* 299–318.

Lisak, D., & Roth, S. (1988). Motivational factors in nonincarcerated sexually aggressive men. *Journal of Personality and Social Psychology, 55,* 795–802.

Lloyd, S. A. (1991). The darkside of courtship: Violence and sexual exploitation. *Family Relations, 40,* 14–20.

Lloyd, S. A., & Emery, B. C. (1999). *The darkside of dating: Physical and sexual violence.* Thousand Oaks, CA: Sage.

Lonsway, K. A., & Fitzgerald, L. F. (1994). Rape myths: In review. *Psychology of Women Quarterly, 18,* 133–164.

Malamuth, N. M. (1986). Predictors of naturalistic sexual aggression. *Journal of Personality and Social Psychology, 50,* 953–962.

Malamuth, N. M. (1998a). The confluence model as an organizing framework for research on sexually aggressive men: Risk moderators imagined aggression and pornography consumption. In R. Geen, & E. Donnerstein (Eds.), *Aggression: Theoretical and empirical reviews* (229–245). New York: Academic Press.

Malamuth, N. M. (1998b). An evolutionary-based model integrating research on the characteristics of sexually coercive men. In J. Adair, K. Dion, & D. Belanger (Eds.), *Advances in psychological science: Vol. 1. Personal social, and developmental aspects* (151–184). Hove UK: Psychology Press.

Malamuth, N. M., & Brown, L. M. (1994). Sexually aggressive men's perceptions of women's communications: Testing three explanations. *Journal of Personality and Social Psychology, 67,* 699–712.

Malamuth, N. M., Linz, D., Heavey, C. L., Barnes, G., & Acker, M. (1995). Using the confluence model of sexual aggression to predict men's conflict with women: A 10-year follow-up study. *Journal of Personality and Social Psychology, 69,* 353–369.

Malmuth, N. M., Sockloski, R. J., Koss, M. P., & Tanaka, J. S. (1991). Characteristics of aggressors against women: Testing a model using a national sample of college students. *Journal of Consulting and Clinical Psychology, 59,* 670–681.

Marshall, A., & Holtzworth-Munroe, A. (2002). Varying forms of husband sexual aggression: Predictors and subgroup differences. *Journal of Family Psychology, 16,* 286–296.

Meyer, S. L., Vivian, D., & O'Leary, D. K. (1998). Men's sexual aggression in marriage: Couples report. *Violence Against Women, 4,* 415–435.

Miller, B., & Marshall, J. C. (1987). Coercive sex on the university campus. *Journal of College Student Personnel, 47,* 38–47.

Morrison, T. G., McLeod, L. D., Morrison, M. A., Anderson, D., & O'Connor, W. E. (1997). Gender stereotyping, homonegativity and misconceptions about sexually coercive behavior among adolescents. *Youth and Society, 29,* 134.

Mosher, D. L., & Anderson, R. D. (1986). Macho personality, sexual aggression, and reactions to guided imagery of realistic rape. *Journal of Research in Personality, 20,* 77–94.

Muehlenhard, C. L. (1988). Misinterpreted dating behaviors and the risk of date rape. *Journal of Social and Clinical Psychology, 6,* 20–37.

Muehlenhard, C. L., & Cook, S. W. (1988). Men's self-reports of unwanted sexual activity. *Journal of Sex Research, 24,* 58–72.

Muehlenhard, C. L., & Falcon, P. L. (1990). Men's heterosocial skill and attitudes toward women as predictors of verbal sexual coercion and forceful rape. *Sex Roles, 23,* 241–259.

Muehlenhard, C. L., Goggins, M. F., Jones, J. M., & Satterfield, A. T. (1991). Sexual violence and coercion in close relationships. In K. McKinney and S. Sprecher (Eds.) *Sexuality in close relationships* (pp. 155–175). Hillsdale, NJ: Lawrence Erlbaum Associates.

Muehlenhard, C. L., & Linton, M. A. (1987). Date rape and sexual aggression in dating situations: Incidence and risk factors. *Journal of Counseling Psychology, 34,* 186–196.

Muehlenhard, C. L., & McCoy, M. (1991). Double standard/double bind: The sexual double standard and women's communication about sex. *Psychology of Women Quarterly, 15,* 447–461.

Norris, J., & Cubbins, L. A. (1992). Dating, drinking, and rape: Effects of victim's and assailant's alcohol consumption on judgments of their behavior and traits. *Psychology of Women Quarterly, 16*, 179–191.

O'Neal, K. (1998). *Attitudes about physical and sexual aggression in relationships.* Unpublished masters thesis, Arizona State University, Tempe, AZ.

O'Sullivan, L. F., Byers, E. S., & Finkelman, L. (1998). A comparison of male and female college students' experiences of sexual coercion. *Psychology of Women Quarterly, 22*, 177–195.

Patton, W., & Mannison, M. (1995). Sexual coercion in high school dating. *Sex Roles, 33*, 447–457.

Petty, G. M., & Dawson, B. (1989). Sexual aggression in normal men: Incidence, beliefs, and personality characteristics. *Personality and Individual Differences, 10*, 355–362.

Poitras, M., & Lavoie, F. (1995). A study of the prevalence of sexual coercion in adolescent heterosexual dating relationships in a Quebec sample. *Violence and Victims, 10*, 299–313.

Posner, R. A., & Silbaugh, K. B. (1996). *A guide to America's sex laws.* Chicago: The University of Chicago Press.

Rapaport, K., & Burkhart, B. R. (1984). Personality and attitudinal characteristics of sexually coercive college males. *Journal of Abnormal Psychology, 93*, 216–221.

Ring, T. E., & Kilmartin, C. (1992). Man to man about rape: A rape prevention program for men. *Journal of College Student Development, 33*, 82–84.

Russell, D. E. H. (1982). *Rape in marriage.* Bloomington, IN: Indiana University Press.

Russell, D. E. H. (1990). *Rape in marriage (Expanded and revised edition with new introduction).* Bloominton, IN: Indiana University Press.

Santello, M. D., & Leitenberg, H. (1993). Sexual aggression by an acquaintance: Methods of coping and later psychological adjustment. *Violence and Victims, 8*, 91–104.

Sarwer, D. B., Kalichman, S. C., Johnson, J. R., Early, J., & Ali, S. A. (1993). Sexual aggression and love styles: An exploratory study. *Archives of Sexual Behavior, 22*, 265–275.

Schewe, P. A., & O'Donohue, W. (1996). Rape prevention with high-risk males: Short term outcome of two interventions. *Archives of Sexual Behavior, 25*, 455–471.

Schultz, L. G., & DeSavage, J. (1975). Rape and rape attitudes on a college campus. In L. G. Schultz (Ed.), *Rape victimology* (pp. 77–90). Springfield: Thomas.

Shapiro, B. L., & Schwartz, J. C. (1997). Date rape: Its relationship to trauma symptoms and sexual self-esteem. *Journal of Interpersonal Violence, 12*, 407–419.

Shotland, R. L., & Goodstein, L. (1983). Just because she doesn't want to doesn't mean it's rape: An experimentally based causal model of the perception of rape in a dating situation. *Social Psychology Quarterly, 46*, 220–232.

Small, S. A., & Kerns, D. (1991, November). *Sexual coercion in adolescent relationships.* Paper presented at the annual meeting of the National Council on Family Relations, Denver, CO.

Small, S. A., & Kerns, D. (1993). Unwanted sexual activity among peers during early and middle adolescence: Incidence and risk factors. *Journal of Marriage and the Family, 55*, 941–952.

Sprecher, S. (1985). Sex differences in bases of power in dating relationships. *Sex Roles, 12*, 449–462.

Stets, J. E., & Pirog-Good, M. A. (1989). Sexual aggression and control in dating relationships. *Journal of Applied Social Psychology, 19*, 1392–1412.

Struckman-Johnson, C. (1988). Forced sex on dates: It happens to men, too. *Journal of Sex Research, 24*, 234–241.

Struckman-Johnson, C., & Struckman-Johnson, D. (1994). Men pressured and forced into sexual experience. *Archives of Sexual Behavior, 23*, 93–114.

Thornhill, R., & Thornhill, N. W. (1992). The evolutionary psychology of men's coercive sexuality. *Behavioral and Brain Science, 15*, 363–376.

Tjaden, P., & Thoennes, N. (2000). *Full report of the prevalence, incidence, and consequences of violence against women: Findings from the national violence against women survey* (NCJ 183781). Washington, DC: National Institute of Justice and the Centers for Disease Control and Prevention.

Truman, D. M., Tokar, D. M., & Fischer, A. R. (1996). Dimensions of masculinity: Relations to date rape supportive attitudes and sexual aggression dating situations. *Journal of Counseling & Development, 74*, 555–562.

Tyler, K. A., Hoyt, D. R., & Whitbeck L. B. (1998). Coercive sexual strategies. *Violence and Victims, 13*, 47–61.

Waldner-Haugrud, L. K., & Gratch, L. V. (1997). Sexual coercion in gay/lesbian relationships: Descriptives and gender differences. *Violence and Victims, 12*, 87–98.

Waldner-Haugrud, L. K., & Magruder, B. (1995). Male and female sexual victimization in dating relationships: Gender differences in coercion techniques and outcomes. *Violence and Victims, 10*, 203–215.

Walker, W. D., Rowe, R. C., & Quinsey, V. L. (1993). Authoritarianism and sexual aggression. *Journal of Personality and Social Psychology, 65*, 1036–1045.

Ward, S. K., Chapman, K., Cohn, E., White, S., & Williams, K. (1991). Acquaintance rape and the college social scene. *Family Relations, 40*, 65–71.

Whatley, M. A. (1996). Victim characteristics influencing attributes of responsibility to rape victims: A meta-analysis. *Aggression and Violent Behavior, 1*, 81–95.

Yeater, E. A., & O'Donohue, W. (1999). Sexual assault prevention programs: Current issues, future directions, and the potential efficacy of interventions with women. *Clinical Psychology Review, 19*, 739–771.

Zimmerman, R. S., Sprecher, S., Langer, L. M., & Holloway, C.D. (1995). Adolescents' perceived ability to
say "no" to unwanted sex. *Journal of Adolescent Research, 10*, 383–399.

Zweig, J. M., Barber, B. L., & Eccles, J. S. (1997). Sexual coercion and well-being in young adulthood:
Comparisons by gender and college status. *Journal of Interpersonal Violence, 12*, 291–308.

Zweig, J. M., Crockett, L. J., Sayer, A., Vicary, J. R. (1999). A longitudinal examination of the consequences
of sexual victimization for rural young adult women. *Journal of Sex Research, 36*, 396–409.

13

Sexual and Emotional Jealousy

Laura K. Guerrero
Arizona State University

Brian H. Spitzberg
San Diego State University

Stephen M. Yoshimura
University of Montana

In this chapter we review literature on both sexual and emotional jealousy. Jealousy is conceptualized as a cognitive, emotional, and behavioral response to a relationship threat. In the case of sexual jealousy, this threat emanates from knowing or suspecting that one's partner has had (or desires to have) sexual activity with a third party. In the case of emotional jealousy, an individual feels threatened by her or his partner's emotional involvement with and/or love for a third party. The experience and expression of jealousy is influenced by a number of factors, including culture, personality, and relational characteristics. Researchers taking an evolutionary perspective have also investigated and supported three hypotheses related to sex differences. First, men are more upset in response to sexual jealousy, whereas women are more upset in response to emotional jealousy. Second, men become especially jealous when a rival is high in status-related attributes such as dominance and wealth, whereas women become especially jealous when rivals are physically attractive. Third, men are more likely than women to express jealousy by engaging in behaviors such as displaying resources and competing physically with the rival, whereas women are more likely than men to enhance physical attractiveness. The evolutionary perspective on sex differences in jealousy has been challenged by those who support cognitive–interpretative and/or social structural frameworks for explaining sex differences in jealousy. Nonetheless, social evolutionary theory appears to provide a good theoretical starting point for studying jealousy. Synthesizing this work with research and theory related to individual, cultural, and relational factors would provide an even richer understanding of both sexual and emotional jealousy.

> *Like many married couples, one of the implicit rules of Kristen and Marc's relationship was that they would always be sexually faithful to one another. Recently, however, Kristen confessed to Marc that she had a one-night stand with someone 2 months earlier. Kristen explained that she had gone out drinking and dancing with some of her single friends one weekend while Marc was*

away on business. While at the nightclub with her friends, she met an attractive man who flattered her and made her feel exciting and beautiful. She told Marc that she had felt terribly guilty ever since and that she deeply regretted her actions. Kristen also assured Marc that the other man "meant nothing to her," that she had cut off all communication with him after their one night together, and that she would never be unfaithful again. As Marc listened to his wife, he felt as if his heart was beating so hard it would leave his chest. The thought of his wife with another man was almost too much to bear. Through all the emotion, he wondered if their marriage would ever be the same again.

INTRODUCTION

Although the vast majority of people in the United States (Christopher & Roosa, 1991; Hansen, 1985; Rathus, Nevid, & Fisher-Rathus, 1993; Thornton & Young-DeMarco, 2001; Treas & Giesen, 2000), indeed the world (Betzig, 1989), believe that marriages and serious dating relationships should be monogamous, research suggests that the scenario just described is not uncommon. Estimates of the percentage of spouses who engage in sexual infidelity vary considerably, suggesting that between 12 and 30% of marriages and cohabiting relationships (Laumann, Gagnon, Michael & Michaels, 1994; Patterson & Kim, 1991; Treas & Giesen, 2000; Wiederman, 1997), and around 40% of dating relationships (Wiederman & Hurd, 1999) report having at least one sexual affair during the course of their relationships. Emotional infidelity, which includes falling in love with or being emotionally attached to a third party, is also probably common in romantic relationships. Infidelity can cause irreparable harm to a relationship. Indeed, several studies have shown that sexual infidelity is often a factor predicting divorce (Betzig, 1989; Bradford, 1980; Cupach & Metts, 1986; Parker & Drummond-Reeves, 1993; Safron, 1979). Shackelford and Buss (1997b) put it well when they stated, "infidelity may have no rival in disrupting a marriage" (p. 793).

Both sexual and emotional infidelity are typically considered to be relational transgressions that lead to feelings of jealousy. Metts (1994) defined *relational transgressions* as violations of implicit or explicit relational rules (see also Jones, Moore, Schratter, & Negel, 2001). The prototypical type of relational transgression involves becoming sexually or emotionally involved with a third party. In fact, Metts (1994) reported that the top two relational transgressions listed by college students involved having extradyadic sex and wanting to or actually dating others. Similarly, Roscoe, Cavanaugh, and Kennedy (1988) found that dating or spending time with a rival, having extradyadic sex, and flirting or kissing someone else were the top three acts of betrayal reported by individuals in dating relationships. In most romantic relationships, infidelity is closely linked to jealousy. Indeed, Drigotas, Safstrom, and Gentilia (1999) conceptualized infidelity as consisting of two interrelated components—the belief that one's partner has violated a relational rule, and the fact that this relational violation typically leads to jealousy and rivalry.

Jealousy can have negative or positive effects on relationships. Jealousy is at the heart of many relationships' "first big fight" (Siegert & Stamp, 1994), and several researchers have demonstrated that jealousy associates negatively with relational satisfaction (Andersen, Eloy, Guerrero, & Spitzberg, 1995; Buunk & Bringle, 1987; Guerrero & Eloy, 1992; Salovey & Rodin, 1989). Yet, in some cases jealousy can be healthy rather than destructive. For example, after experiencing jealousy, people sometimes feel more passionate toward their partners, stop taking their partners for granted, and become more committed to their relationships (Pines, 1992). Jealousy is also adaptive in that it can help individuals ward off third-party threats and preserve the primary relationship (Buss, 1988).

In this chapter, we examine jealousy as a response to sexual and/or emotional infidelity within the context of romantic relationships. Because most of the research in this area has focused on heterosexual relationships, we adopt this focus throughout most of the chapter. However, new research on jealousy within homosexual relationships is included in various places within this chapter, and we are hopeful that this research trend will continue so that a clearer picture of the role that sexual orientation plays in the jealousy process will emerge. The chapter is organized into two main sections. First, we provide a general conceptualization of romantic jealousy, which includes differentiating jealousy from envy and rivalry, distinguishing sexual and emotional jealousy, and overviewing general factors that frame jealousy experience and expression. Second, we discuss evolutionary theory as an explanation for sex differences in the experience and expression of jealousy. This theory, which provides broad explanations for human behavior, has been used as a lens for investigating sexual and emotional jealousy more than any other theory. In this second section we also discuss the jealousy–violence link, summarize various ways that people respond to jealousy using communication, appraise the status of evolutionary theory as framework for explaining jealousy experience and expression, and suggest new theoretical avenues that might extend our knowledge regarding both sexual and emotional jealousy.

CONCEPTUALIZING JEALOUSY

Romantic jealousy is a cognitive, emotional, and behavioral response that occurs when the existence and/or quality of a person's primary relationship is perceived as being threatened by a third party (White & Mullen, 1989). Consistent with this definition, researchers commonly operationalize jealousy as a multidimensional construct. For example, Pfieffer and Wong's (1989) Multidimensional Jealousy Scale taps into the cognitive, emotional, and behavioral components of jealousy. Also consistent with this definition is the idea that jealousy always occurs within an actual or perceived triangle of relationships. This triangle includes a primary relationship (between the jealous person and the beloved), a secondary relationship (between the beloved and a rival), and a rival relationship (between the jealous person and the rival). This romantic triangle is one feature that makes jealousy unique and distinguishes it from related emotions such as envy and rivalry. Another feature is possession. Jealousy occurs when people are afraid they might lose something they value, such as an exclusive romantic relationship. Envy, by contrast, occurs when people want something that someone else has, and rivalry occurs when two or more people compete for something that neither of them has (Bryson, 1977; Guerrero & Andersen, 1998a; Parrott & Smith, 1993; Salovey & Rodin, 1986, 1989). The prototypical jealousy situation involves worrying that a rival will "steal" or "poach" a romantic partner away (Belske & Shackelford, 2001; Schmitt & Buss, 2001). Common examples of envy include wanting to have someone else's money, possessions, social position, or romantic relationship. Envy can also be experienced alongside jealousy, as when a jealous individual is envious of a rival's personal characteristics, such as physical attractiveness or wealth. Finally, common examples of rivalry include two people competing to secure a relationship with a desired romantic partner, and two or more people vying for a promotion at work (cf., Vecchio, 2000).

THE COGNITIVE APPRAISAL APPROACH

Cognitive appraisal theory has been used as a framework for explaining the complex set of thoughts, emotions, and behaviors that accompany the jealousy experience. This theoretical approach is predicated on the belief that emotions are the result of cognitive appraisals of stimuli within a given situation (Lazarus, 1991; Lazarus & Folkman, 1984; Lazarus & Lazarus, 1994). Accordingly, the situational and relational context provides a frame for helping people identify, interpret, and understand their emotions. White and Mullen (1989) applied Lazarus' cognitive appraisal approach to jealousy. In doing so, they argued that jealousy is experienced as a set of interrelated emotions, cognitions, and behaviors that occur in response to a relational threat (see also Guerrero & Andersen, 1998b). First, people experience a general state of heightened arousal due to the sudden perception of threat. Next, people make sense of the threat through primary and secondary appraisals. Primary appraisals focus on determining how real and serious the threat is. So Marc might ask himself questions such as "Was it really just a one-night stand?" and "Can I ever trust my wife again?" Primary appraisals also help people sort through and label their emotions. Jealousy tends to be associated with certain physiological sensations (i.e., heart, chest, breath; see Hupka, Zaleski, Otto, Reidl, & Tarabrina, 1996). Common jealousy-related emotions deriving from appraisals of these physiological reactions include feeling angry, fearful, sad, envious, and sexually aroused (Fitness & Fletcher, 1993; Guerrero & Yoshimura, 1999; Hupka, Otto, Tarabrina, & Reidl, 1993; Trost & Yoshimura, 1999; White & Mullen, 1989). As a result of primary appraisals, Marc might decide that he does not really fear losing his wife to a third party, but that he is angry at her and sad that the trust they had built over so many years has been shattered. In this case, Marc might feel that the quality of their relationship has been threatened more than its existence.

According to White and Mullen's application of cognitive appraisal theory, jealous individuals also make secondary appraisals that involve more specific evaluations of the jealousy situation, including possible causes and outcomes. There are four general types of secondary appraisals, which focus on (1) motives, (2) comparisons to the rival, (3) alternatives, and (4) potential loss. When appraising Kristen's motives, Marc might surmise that his wife's behavior was affected by her drinking, that she was bored and looking for excitement, and that her single friends may have been a bad influence on her. When comparing himself to the rival, Marc might question whether he is as attractive and successful as the man Kristen had sex with is. Marc might also think about his alternatives. If he cannot trust Kristen anymore, does he still want to be married to her? Perhaps he would be better off alone, or he would like to pursue other potentially attractive relational partners. Finally, Marc might assess the loss he would feel if his marriage ended or was permanently altered. He would likely weigh these feelings of loss against possible alternatives.

These types of secondary appraisals will then affect how Marc copes with the situation. Lazarus' work suggests that people often cope with emotions such as jealousy by trying to solve the problem and/or trying to alleviate negative affect (Lazarus & Folkman, 1984). Marc has a wide array of coping options at his disposal, including forgiving Kristen, seeking revenge by having an affair of his own, renegotiating relational rules regarding sexual exclusivity, acting indifferent, keeping closer tabs on Kristen, and terminating the relationship (Buss & Shackelford, 1997a; Guerrero & Andersen, 1998b; White & Mullen, 1989). These types of jealousy expressions are measured within Guerrero and colleague's Communicative Responses to Jealousy scale (Guerrero, Andersen, Jorgensen, Spitzberg, Eloy, 1995; Guerrero & Andersen, 1998b).

SEXUAL VERSUS EMOTIONAL JEALOUSY

Consistent with the notion that situational factors frame emotions, researchers have distinguished between two specific types of romantic jealousy—sexual jealousy and emotional jealousy (e.g., Buss, Larsen, Westen, & Semmelroth, 1992; Trost & Alberts, 1998). *Sexual jealousy* occurs when individuals know or suspect that their partners have had (or want to have) sexual activity with a third party. *Emotional jealousy*, on the other hand, occurs when individuals know or suspect that their partners are emotionally attached to and/or in love with a rival. Although people often experience sexual and emotional jealousy together, as is the case when a partner is having a long-term, emotionally involving affair, some situations produce more of one type of jealousy than the other. A one-night stand such as Kristen's is the prototypical situation that produces high levels of sexual jealousy with little or no emotional jealousy. By contrast, a situation where one's partner is especially close friends with a member of the opposite sex could produce high levels of emotional jealousy but little if any sexual jealousy. In addition, some evidence indicates that people vary in the extent to which one type of infidelity implies the other. For example, women may be more likely to presume that where there is sexual infidelity there is likely to be emotional infidelity, whereas men may be less likely to associate one with the other (DeSteno & Salovey, 1996; Glass & Wright, 1992; Harris & Christenfeld, 1996a, 1996b; cf. Buss, Larsen, & Westen, 1996; Cramer, Abraham, Johnson, & Manning-Ryan, 2001).

Different actions seem to trigger suspicion about sexual versus emotional infidelity. Shackelford and Buss (1997a) investigated cues to both sexual and emotional infidelity by having undergraduate students describe behaviors that would lead them to suspect that their partners were having sex with someone else and/or falling in love with someone else. Five types of behaviors were identified as leading primarily to suspicion of sexual infidelity: (1) *physical signs of disinterest in sexual exclusivity* (e.g., the partner smells like he or she had sex with someone else); (2) *revelations of sexual infidelity* (e.g., the partner confesses to having an affair); (3) changes in routine and sexual behavior (e.g., the partner starts trying new positions during sex); (4) *increased sexual interest and exaggerated displays of affection* (e.g., the partner talks about sex or says "I love you" more often than usual); and (5) *sexual disinterest/boredom* (e.g., the partner seems not to enjoy sex as much as she or he used to). From this list, it appears that changes in sexual attitudes and/or behaviors are a primary trigger of suspicion and could lead to sexual jealousy. People likely surmise that these changes in behavior are the direct result of having sexual contact with a third party. General increases in affection can also trigger sexual jealousy, particularly if one suspects that the partner is acting extra affectionate to cover up an affair, to alleviate guilty feelings, or to try to compensate for committing a relational transgression.

Seven behaviors were identified by Shackelford and Buss (1997a) as cues to emotional infidelity. Three of these behaviors indicate that relational closeness has decreased: (1) *relationship dissatisfaction and loss of love* (e.g., the partner says she or he would like to see other people); (2) *emotional disengagement* (e.g., the partner starts forgetting special dates and does not respond when you say "I love you"); and (3) *reluctance to spend time together* (e.g., the partner stops inviting you to family functions). The other four behaviors focus on changes in the partner's communication. First, people may suspect emotional infidelity when their partner uses *passive rejection and inconsiderate behavior* such as acting rude and being less loving and gentle when having sex. Second, *angry, critical, and argumentative communication* may trigger suspicions of emotional infidelity. For example, the partner might seem more critical and look for reasons to start an argument. Third, a *reluctance to talk about a certain person* may lead to suspicion that there is an emotional attachment between the partner and that person. Finally, *guilty and anxious communication*, such as acting nervous when coming home late or being unusually forgiving and apologetic, can trigger suspicion and emotional jealousy.

Finally, it is important to note that Shackelford and Buss (1997a) uncovered two behaviors that are equally indicative of sexual and emotional infidelity. The first of these, *apathetic communication*, occurs when the partner seems to be putting less effort into the relationship. Emotional disclosure, affection, and sex might all decrease, and the partner might stop trying to be cheerful and attractive. The second behavior that leads people to suspect both sexual and emotional infidelity is *increased contact with and reference to a third party.* Examples of this behavior include hearing your partner call you by a rival's name or seeing your partner wear something that belongs to a rival.

GENERAL FACTORS FRAMING JEALOUSY EXPERIENCE AND EXPRESSION

The various cues to sexual and emotional infidelity likely influence if and how people experience jealousy. A variety of other factors also influence the jealousy process, either by acting as causal agents or by framing the jealousy situation. Based on a review of theory and research on jealousy, Guerrero and Andersen (1998b) identified six general categories of antecedent factors that have the potential to influence all parts of the jealousy process: biology, culture, personality, relationship characteristics, the situation, and strategic moves.

Biology and Evolution

Perhaps the broadest explanation for jealousy comes from evolutionary theory. According to evolutionary perspectives, jealousy evolved as an adaptive mechanism that helped our ancestors retain their mates and maintain the pair bond (Buss et al., 1992; Kenrick & Trost, 1997). Pair bonding affords people with many adaptive benefits, including the provision of social, emotional, and financial support, increased paternal confidence for the male, and the shared resources that help couples successfully raise offspring (Daly & Wilson, 1983; Trost & Andersen, 1999). Thus, the disruption of the pair bond typically leads to jealousy because those benefits are threatened. Once infidelity has occurred, people can either attempt to repair the relationship, thereby retaining valued resources; or they can leave the relationship before making additional investments. However, a more adaptive strategy is to prevent infidelity from occurring in the first place. Indeed, jealousy may have evolved as a mechanism to trigger the use of mate retention behaviors that guard against infidelity (Buss, 1988; Buss & Shackelford, 1997a).

Evidence for the influence of evolutionary and biological factors on jealousy comes from three main sources. First, as we discuss later in this chapter, there is considerable evidence that many sex differences in jealousy experience and expression are consistent with evolutionary predictions (Buss, 1994). Second, jealousy is a universal experience found across cultures (Buss et al., 1999; Buunk & Hupka, 1987; Clanton & Smith, 1977; Hupka et al., 1985). Third, heightened arousal and other neurochemical processes accompany the jealousy experience, suggesting that reactions to relational threats became hardwired in human brains across the millennia (Ellis & Weinstein, 1986; Geary, DeSoto, Hoard, Sheldon, & Cooper, 2001; Hupka et al., 1996; Pines & Aronson, 1983; Trost & Andersen, 1999).

Culture

Culture also influences both jealousy experience and expression. In fact, Simpson and Kenrick (1997) pointed out that explanations based on culture and those based on genetic evolution work together to provide the best predictions for human behavior. They further argued that cultural differences might emerge for the evolutionary reason that people in groups have unique situations or geographic locations that would force them to adapt differently than other groups. Indeed, some studies suggest that cultural differences might exist at the foundation of the jealous experience, or the perception of threat. For example, individuals in the United States tend to consistently rate extramarital affairs as extremely negative events (Glenn & Weaver, 1979; Metts,

1994), whereas individuals from Sweden, Denmark, Belgium, and the Netherlands are less sensitive to such affairs (Buunk & Van Driel, 1989; Christensen, 1973). Another study suggests that Mexicans are more likely to identify distrust as a central issue in jealousy experience, whereas people from the United States and European countries are more likely to view sexual exclusivity as the central issue (Hupka et al., 1985). In Betzig's (1989) cross-cultural study, jealousy arose as a cause of divorce in North America and Insular Pacific cultures, but not in African, Circum-Mediterranean, East Eurasian, or South American cultures.

Evidence also suggests that people in different cultures and co-cultures (i.e., cultural groups found within a larger national culture) perceive jealous expressions as more or less acceptable. For example, in a comparison of two studies of jealousy and domestic assault in Britain and Spain, Delgado, Prieto, and Bond (1997) found that when jealousy was claimed as a motive for assault, Spanish respondents held the victim more responsible than British respondents, who attributed more responsibility to the assailant. In courtrooms in the United States, jealousy is used as an "excuse" to help husbands (more often than wives) avoid harsh punishments for violence enacted in the heat of emotion (Guerrero & Andersen, 1998a). Interestingly, Aune and Comstock (1997) found that Euro-American students tended to view their past jealousy expressions as socially appropriate, whereas Asian-American students were more likely to see their past jealousy expressions as inappropriate. Research also suggests that sexual jealousy is more prevalent and more acceptable in masculine, patriarchic cultures with rigid gender roles (Hofstede, 1980; Rathas, et al., 1993; Whitehurst, 1977) and in cultures where marriage and property ownership are important determinants of social status (Hupka & Ryan, 1990). Finally, although people from various cultures and co-cultures all tend to regulate jealousy expression through strategies such as downplaying the intensity of their feelings, members of some cultures appear to regulate jealousy expressions more than others. For example, Zammuner and Fischer (1995) found Dutch participants curb their expression of jealousy more than Italian participants.

Personality

In addition to evolutionary and cultural factors, personality factors influence how people interpret and cope with jealousy experiences and expression. Studies suggest that personality traits such as social anxiety, possessiveness, emotional dependency, and neuroticism have small to moderate positive associations with jealousy (Buunk, 1997; Guerrero & Spitzberg, 2002; White & Mullen, 1989; Xiaojun, 2002). The association between self-esteem and jealousy has also been examined, but findings have been inconsistent with relatively small effect sizes (Buunk, 1982a; Guerrero & Andersen, 1998b; Sheppard, Nelson, & Andreoli-Mathie, 1995; White & Mullen, 1989; cf. Peretti & Pudowsky, 1997). The strongest relationship appears to be a negative association between high self-esteem and anticipated jealousy, presumably because individuals with high self-esteem are confident that their relationships will not be seriously threatened by a third party (White & Mullen, 1989).

Jealousy experience and expression also vary based on people's attachment and love styles. People with secure attachment styles experience less jealousy than people with anxious or preoccupied styles (Guerrero, 1998; Hazan & Shaver, 1987; Knobloch, Solomon, & Cruz, 2001; Leak, Gardner, & Parsons, 1998; Sharpsteen & Kirkpatrick, 1997), most likely because anxious/preoccupied individuals have low levels of self-confidence and worry that their relational partners will abandon them. Jealous individuals who are insecure are also more likely to use indirect coping behaviors (such as surveillance or manipulation) rather than directly communicating with the partner about jealousy (Guerrero, 1998; McIntosh & Tangri, 1989; McIntosh & Tate, 1990). An individual's style of loving is also related to jealousy. White (1977) compared the jealousy experience of people possessing Lee's (1973) different love styles. Not surprisingly, individuals who identified with the mania (obsessive) and eros (passionate) love styles tended to experience relatively high levels of romantic jealousy. By contrast, individuals endorsing the ludic (game-playing) type of love reported relatively low levels of jealousy, probably because they desire low levels of relational commitment.

Relationship Characteristics

The type of relationship two people share is a critical factor framing how jealousy is experienced and expressed. In fact, Melamed (1991) found relationship status and length to moderate the influence that personality has on the experience of jealousy. Specifically, Melamed showed that correlations between jealousy and personality factors such as neuroticism and self-esteem were strongest among unmarried individuals who had only been together a short time. These correlations were weakest for married individuals.

Jealousy appears to be most likely when individuals feel love and attraction toward a partner, but the relationship is not yet fully committed. Couples who are seriously dating or cohabiting have been found to experience and express jealousy more often than couples in cross-sex friendships, casually dating relationships, and marriages (Aune & Comstock, 1991, 1997; Bringle & Boebinger, 1990; Guerrero, Eloy, Jorgensen, & Andersen, 1993; White, 1985). Similarly, Knox, Zusman, Mabon, and Shriver (1999) found that undergraduate students experienced more jealousy in newer romantic relationships (1 year or less) than in more established relationships (more than 1 year), and Aylor and Dainton (2001) found that married individuals experienced the least jealousy, whereas causal daters reported greater cognitive jealousy than serious daters. Knobloch et al. (2001) found a curvilinear relationship between relational intimacy and jealousy, suggesting that jealousy is particularly likely when relationships are characterized by moderate levels of intimacy. The public commitment associated with marriage may provide at least some buffer against jealousy by fostering relational security and limiting rivals. Those in casual dating relationships, on the other hand, may not be committed enough to worry about third-party involvements. In contrast, relational partners at moderate levels of intimacy may have more opportunities to interact with rivals than married individuals, while also being more emotionally involved than those in casual relationships. This combination of more rivals (as compared to married couples) and more emotional involvement (as compared to casual daters) may promote jealousy.

Relationship factors related to investment also affect jealousy. White (1981a, 1981b) found that jealousy is more likely when one person believes that she or he is putting more effort into the relationship than the partner. Similarly, Trost, Brown, and Morrison (1994) found that the amount of jealousy people reported increased as a function of how much they perceived they had invested into the relationship. Presumably, relational threats are heightened when people have put considerable time and effort into a relationship because these investments cannot be recovered if the relationship ends.

Trost et al. (1994) also found that sexual openness correlated positively with jealousy, probably because there is a higher chance that the partner will have a sexual affair in open relationships. The opposite pattern has been found in relationships where both partners value and endorse monogamy—in these relationships, people experience less jealousy because partners are more likely to be sexually faithful (Pines & Aronson, 1983). Importantly, however, if a sexual affair does occur, individuals in relationships that were previously defined as sexually exclusive rather than sexually open are likely to experience more intense distress because a valued rule was broken (Metts, 1994; White, 1981a, 1981b).

Situational Factors

If jealousy occurs because of a perceived threat to a relationship, it follows that attributional explanations (and all the associated biases) involved in the threat may affect the jealousy process. More specifically, whether a jealous person (and alternately, the person's partner) attributes a partner's behaviors as situational or dispositional may influence emotions, thoughts, expressions, and consequently, relational outcomes. For example, we know that people are likely to attribute others' behaviors to an internal cause even when their behavior may have identifiable situational explanations, but to attribute their own behavior to external causes (Ross, 1977; Taylor & Brown, 1988). In line with these assumptions, White and Mullen (1989) summarized research showing that the jealous person often perceives jealousy to be situational (e.g., "I was jealous because you were flirting with your ex-lover), whereas the partner often attributes jealousy to the jealous person (e.g., "You are so insecure about me talking to ex-lovers").

Situational justifications, excuses, and explanations are also used to try and explain jealousy-evoking behavior, including infidelity (Bringle & Buunk, 1991; Mongeau, Hale, & Alles, 1994; Mongeau & Schulz, 1997). For example, in the scenario at the beginning of this chapter, Kristen tells Marc that she was feeling lonely while he was out of town and was drinking at a nightclub with her single friends. *Situational justifications* involve trying to minimize the negative implications of the jealousy-evoking behavior. Common situational justifications for jealousy-evoking behavior include focusing on the degree of involvement (e.g., "it was only one night"), denying that a behavior was wrong (e.g., "I was only talking to him; I didn't mean to flirt"), or trying to downplay the importance of one's actions (e.g., "I only kissed her once"). *Situational excuses* involve trying to minimize responsibility for one's actions. To do so, people might focus on their inability to control their own behavior ("I was drunk") or they might shift the blame to someone else ("She tricked me into going up to her place"). Finally, *situational explanations* involve trying to accentuate the positive implications for the jealousy-evoking behavior. For example, a person might focus on positive relational outcomes (e.g., "Dating other people made me realize how much I love you") or positive motives for engaging in certain behaviors ("I talked with him for a long time because he was feeling rejected").

Some research suggests that individuals are more likely to use direct, relational communication when they attribute jealousy to the situation and/or the rival. McIntosh and Mathews (1992) found that individuals who tend to make situational rather than dispositional attributions of jealousy are more likely to engage in direct coping responses to jealousy, such as confronting their partners. Staske (1999) found that when romantic partners attribute jealousy to themselves or their partners, their expressions tend to be more focused on relationship concerns than when they attribute jealousy to rivals. For example, if Marc believes that Kristen was unfaithful because an attractive rival took advantage of her, he might perceive that the rival is to blame, Kristen is unlikely to cheat again, and there is little need to discuss relational issues. (Although he may, of course, still let Kristen know that he is upset.) On the other hand, if Marc believes that Kristen was to blame, he would more likely want to discuss relational issues, such as the state of their marriage and the renegotiation of relationship rules.

Strategic Moves

A special type of situation occurs when people intentionally induce jealousy. Between 70 to 80% of college students admit to attempting to induce jealousy in their relational partner (Brainerd, Hunter, Moore, & Thompson, 1996; Sheets, Fredendall, & Claypool, 1997). Many motives for jealousy induction have been suggested, including testing or assessing the state of the relationship, obtaining desired attention or rewards (such as more relational commitment), seeking revenge or punishment, bolstering self-esteem, and attempting to gain control (Brainerd et al., 1996; Buss, 2000; Fleis-chmann, Spitzberg, & Andersen, 2002; Sheets, Fredendall, & Claypool, 1997; White, 1980). Similarly, Baxter and Wilmot (1984) identified *triangle tests* as one type of strategy people use to help them assess the status of their relationships. Triangle tests include *fidelity checks*, such as seeing if a partner responds when an attractive person flirts with him or her, and *jealousy tests*, such as bringing up an old lover's name and gauging the current partner's reaction. These types of behaviors have also been cast as mate retention strategies that show one is appealing to others and therefore, is valuable as a mate (Buss, 1988; Buss & Shackelford, 1997a), and as vengeful communication (Yoshimura, 2002). Thus, although these tactics are sometimes effective in helping to retain mates, they can also backfire.

Jealousy can be induced using a variety of different strategies. Fleischmann et al. (2002) factor analyzed 22 induction tactics and found three general strategies that people use to induce jealousy in their partners—relational distancing, flirtation facades, and relational alternatives. Relational distancing tactics include keeping friends separate from one's partner and making plans with one's friends instead of the romantic partner. Flirtation facades include tactics such as sending flowers to oneself or leaving fake phone numbers for the partner to find. Finally, people can induce jealousy by suggesting relational alternatives, such as talking about past relationships or potential romantic partners. Structural equation modeling indicated that these three jealousy induction strategies mediated the relationship between jealousy induction goals (seeking revenge versus seeking rewards) and outcomes such as relational improvement and antisocial partner response. Surprisingly, all three jealousy induction strategies were positively related to perceived relational improvement for the person who reported engaging in the jealousy induction. Apparently, people who strategically employ jealousy induction perceive such activities to be relationally facilitative. Whether or not the partner who is the target of such jealousy induction perceives such facilitation has yet to be studied.

AN EVOLUTIONARY THEORY EXPLANATION FOR SEXUAL AND EMOTIONAL JEALOUSY

Although all of these factors undoubtedly influence jealousy experience and expression, most of the research that specifically focuses on sexual versus emotional jealousy has been guided by evolutionary theory. The evolutionary perspective on human behavior is a powerful approach that helps link human behavior to basic ideas about all biological life (Buss, 1995; Symons, 1979). Although the concept of evolution was discussed before Darwin (1859) assembled his work *On the Origin of Species*, Darwin made significant contributions that advanced new theory in both biological and psychological disciplines. One of his greatest contributions was to explain how species develop, change, and sometimes disappear through the process of natural selection. According to Darwin's theory, change occurs because (1) species' characteristics vary in type and quality, (2) offspring inherit their parents' physical characteristics, and (3) variation in characteristics leads to the differential reproductive success of descendents. Darwin surmised that as organisms reproduce, they pass on information that combines to form unique descendents. Over time and in different environments, some descendents will be more successful at surviving ("natural selection") and reproducing ("sexual selection") than will others. Of the characteristics that get reproduced, the most helpful will lead to survival and reproductive success, and thus, will be selected and carried on to future descendents. Conversely, those that are not helpful for either survival or proliferation will be eliminated.

Scholars later extended Darwin's work on evolution by advancing theories that centered on inclusive fitness (Hamilton, 1964; Williams, 1966). Based on biological discoveries surrounding human genes and genetic information, Hamilton argued that inheritance and selection could occur through *both* direct offspring reproduction and the reproductive success of genetic relatives. According to inclusive fitness theory, the success of all activities that promote genetic inheritance leads to the reproductive success of selected genes. From this perspective, for example, self-sacrifice makes reproductive sense if it leads to greater reproductive success of one's genetic relatives. Thus, the development of inclusive fitness theory contributed to an understanding of evolution at the genetic level rather than the individual level (i.e., the carrier of genes), which was a fundamental change in how biologists thought about the process of evolution (Buss, 1999; Simpson & Gangestad, 2001).

The connection between evolution and both emotion and behavior has been noted by modern scholars (e.g., Buss, 1994) as well as Darwin's original works. Based on his observations that emotions such as joy, fear, sadness, anger, surprise, and disgust were universally expressed among humans and other animals, Darwin (1871) argued that natural selection applied to behavior. Specifically, Darwin theorized that the abilities to send and receive emotional expressions were evolved mechanisms that came about because of their ability to help humans and other animals survive and reproduce. At the very least, he noted, "expression in itself, or the language of the emotions, as it has sometimes been called, is certainly of importance for the welfare of mankind" (Darwin, 1872, p. 366). Scholars have also used evolutionary theory to explain processes such as mate selection and retention (Bleske & Shackelford, 2001; Buss, 1984, 1988, 1989; Scheib, 2001; Schmitt, Shackelford, Duntley, Tooke, & Buss, 2001; Trost & Alberts, 1998). Thus, it is not surprising that modern scholars have used evolutionary theory to help explain jealousy experience and expression (Buss, 2000).

THE PARENTAL INVESTMENT MODEL

The parental investment model (Trivers, 1972), which extended Darwin's (1864, 1871) concept of sexual selection, provides a particularly suitable theoretical framework for studying both sexual and emotional jealousy. Sexual selection refers to the process whereby members of a species differentially select and compete for sexual access to potential mates (Darwin, 1871). According to Trivers (1972), sexual selection is driven by differential parental investments for men versus women. Moreover, men and women are differentially selective of mates based on the resources they have to lose if they make a poor mating choice.

Differential Parental Investment

According to the parental investment model, women throughout the ages have invested more biological and emotional resources into bearing and caring for their children. Biologically, women invest their bodies through 9 months of gestation and often through months of breastfeeding, which is a significantly higher biological investment than the quickly reproduced sex cells invested by men. Women are usually also the primary caretakers of their children from infancy through adulthood, with the amount of caretaking provided by fathers varying considerably. Thus, women make sizable investments to childrearing, both in terms of emotion and time. Because of their high level of parental investment, women should desire mates who provide them with good genetic material as well as the emotional and financial support necessary for successfully raising a child to adulthood. Consequently, women are predictably more selective when choosing potential mates than are men (Trivers, 1972). In fact, women are highly selective when choosing mates across a variety of situations, including dating, one-night stands, and marriage. By contrast, men are much less selective when selecting sexual partners for one-night stands, although they do become highly selective when forming long-term relationships (Clark & Hatfield, 1989; Kenrick, Sadalla, Groth, & Trost, 1990; Mathes, King, Miller, & Reed, 2002; cf. Scheib, 2001).

A different set of concerns guides men's mating behavior. Specifically, female internal gestation combined with a high degree of female selectivity leads to two important adaptive concerns for men: paternal confidence and intrasexual competition (Trivers, 1972). Men have adapted the concern over paternal confidence as a result of being unable to biologically carry offspring. Prior to the scientific advancements of genetic testing, generations of men could not be completely certain that the children whom they invested heavily in were biologically related to them. Thus, evolutionary theorists believe that men have evolved an attentiveness toward the sexual fidelity of mates (Buss, 1988, 2000; Daly & Wilson, 1988). Indeed, based on the few studies that have used blood samples or DNA testing, Baker and Bellis (1995) estimated that between 9% to 13% of children today have putative fathers who are not genetically related to them. As Buunk, Angleleitner, Oubaid, and Buss (1996) put it, paternal uncertainty "is not just a hypothetical possibility. It is a reality and probably has been throughout evolutionary history" (pp. 359–360). The second concern for men involves intrasexual competition. Although differential parental investment could lead both men and women into intrasexual competition, the high degree of female selectivity for potential partners situates men in more aggressive competition for access to the scarce resource of female reproduction (Trivers, 1972). By outlining the different reproductive concerns men and women have, the parental investment model has helped researchers predict and confirm differential enactment of such behavior as mate retention strategies (Buss, 1988; Buss & Shackelford, 1997a), rival derogation (Buss & Dedden, 1990), coercive control (Wilson, Jocic, & Daly, 2001), and violence (Daly & Wilson, 1988), all of which can be enacted in response to jealousy.

Mate Selection

Differential investment among members of the opposite sex also helps explain the unique dimensions on which men and women select mates. According to evolutionary theory, because men have limited access to potential mates due to both female selectiveness and intrasexual competition, men should be particularly concerned with finding a mate who is healthy and fertile and therefore likely to carry on his genes. This adaptive concern has been theorized to translate into a preference for sexually faithful and physically attractive partners, with features such as smooth skin and healthy bodies perceived as outward signs of fertility (Buss, 1994; Fink, Grammer, & Thornhill, 2001). By contrast, women should be more attentive to status and emotional faithfulness than men, because women desire a mate who can and will provide them with material and emotional support. Thus, women are more attentive than men to characteristics such as financial resources, dominance, ambitiousness, and emotional fidelity (Buss, 1995; Kenrick & Trost, 1997). Interestingly, however, some studies suggest that when a woman already has a long-term mate, extradyadic affairs might be sought in a manner similar to men's mate-selection strategies (see Gangestad & Simpson, 1990; Scheib, 2001).

Across studies, men do indeed report being more attentive to physical attractiveness than do women, and women tend to be more attentive to signs of status than do men (Li, Bailey, Kendrick, & Linsenmeier, 2002). For example, in a study of 9,474 individuals across 37 cultures, Buss and his colleagues (1990) found that men prefer attractiveness in mates more than do women, and women prefer income potential more than do men. Studies by Buss and Barnes (1986) and Kenrick et al. (1990) corroborated those results, showing that women were particularly attracted to status, whereas men emphasized physical attractiveness. Tooke and Camire (1991) uncovered further evidence suggesting that, when trying to attract romantic partners, men and women deliberately attempt to enhance these aspects of themselves; that is, women enhance physical attractiveness and men enhance signs of status. Men and women also seem attuned to the need to advertise these respective characteristics to the opposite sex; that is, men portray or signal status cues to attract women, and women portray attractiveness cues to attract men (e.g., Oda, 2001)

Although men are more attentive to physical appearance than women, both sexes prefer mates who appear outwardly healthy. As noted, when men are selecting mates, physical appearance is theorized to be a sign of fertility. Men prefer women who have hour-glass shaped figures with waist-to-hip ratios around .70, meaning that their waists are significantly smaller than their hips (Buss, 1989, 1994; Furnham, Lavancy, & McClelland, 2001; Singh & Young, 1995). Men have also reported a preference for large breasts; however, breast size appears less important than hip-to-waist ratio (Singh & Young, 1995). For women, physical fitness is important in that a potential mate must be strong and healthy enough to provide resources. Across various studies, women evaluate men as more physically fit and attractive when they are tall and moderately muscular, with broad shoulders and a waist-to-hip ratio of about 1.0, meaning that their hips and waists are close in size (Asthana, 2000; Buss, 1989, 1994). For both women and men, face and body symmetry, which are correlated to actual genetic fitness, have been found to be highly predictive of attractiveness (Grammer & Thornhill, 1994; Perrett et al., 1999; Rhodes, Proffitt, Grady, & Sumich, 1998).

APPLICATION OF THE PARENTAL INVESTMENT MODEL TO JEALOUSY

Research based on the parental investment model and general evolutionary theory leads to at least three predictions related to jealousy. First, men should experience more jealousy in response to sexual infidelity, whereas women should experience more jealousy in response to emotional infidelity. Second, men and women should differ in terms of the types of rival characteristics that exacerbate jealousy. Third, men and women should differ in the ways they respond to jealousy, with jealousy expression helping to alleviate adaptive concerns. The empirical research supporting each of these predictions is presented next.

Sex Differences in Sexual Versus Emotional Jealousy

Considerable research has focused on testing the evolutionary hypothesis that men react more strongly to sexual infidelity, whereas women react more strongly to emotional infidelity. With a few important exceptions (e.g., DeSteno & Salovey, 1996; Harris, 2002; Nannini & Meyers, 2000; Parker, 1997), this hypothesis has generally been supported (Buss et al., 1999; Cann, Mangum, & Wells, 2001; Cramer et al., 2001; White, 1981b; cf. Hupka & Bank, 1996). So in the scenario presented at the beginning of this chapter, it seems realistic to expect Marc to be particularly upset that Kristen had a sexual liaison with another man. If Kristen had been emotionally but not sexually involved with another man, one might guess that Marc would have been less upset. Additionally, according to evolutionary theory, it seems realistic that Kristen would try and explain away the threat by telling Marc that the affair "meant nothing to her" because in her mind emotional infidelity would be even worse than sexual infidelity.

In the first study to formally test sex differences in sexual versus emotional threats Buss et al. (1992) reasoned that men should experience more jealousy in response to sexual infidelity because sexual unfaithfulness reduces paternal confidence and increases the likelihood that a man will unknowingly invest valuable resources into a rival's offspring. By contrast, Buss et al. argued that women should experience more jealousy in response to emotional infidelity because they risk having their partner divert some of his resources to a rival. To test these hypotheses, Buss et al. conducted three studies. In the first study, respondents were asked to think of a committed romantic relationship and imagine that their partner had either (a) formed a deep emotional attachment to someone else or (b) enjoyed having passionate sexual intercourse with someone else. Respondents then circled which of these scenarios would be more distressing to them. Later in the questionnaire, respondents also chose one of the following scenarios as more upsetting: (a) imagining a partner trying different sexual positions with someone else, or (b) imagining a partner falling in love with someone else. Across both of these forced-choice options, men were more likely to choose the sexual scenario as more distressing, whereas women were more likely to choose the emotional scenario as more distressing.

In the second study, subjects' physiological responses were measured as they imagined that their partner was (a) having sexual intercourse with someone else or (b) falling in love with and forming an emotional attachment to someone else. For two of the three physiological measures (electrodermal activity and pulse rate), men showed significantly more arousal change in response to the sexual versus emotional scenario. Women displayed more change in electrodermal activity in response to the emotional as opposed to the sexual scenario.

Finally, the third study replicated results from the first study by having respondents choose whether having their partner fall in love with someone was more or less distressing than having their partner have sex with someone. The group of respondents in Study 3, which was limited to those who had been in exclusive sexual relationships, followed the same pattern as the group of respondents in Study 1—men tended to report being more distressed by sexual infidelity, whereas women tended to report being more distressed by emotional fidelity.

Researchers have supported this evolutionary hypothesis in different cultures. For example, Geary, Rumsey, Bow-Thomas, and Hoard (1995) examined patterns of jealousy in the United States and China. Across both samples, women were more distressed than men when imagining situations involving a partner's emotional infidelity, whereas men were more distressed than women when imagining situations involving sexual infidelity. People in the United States, however, reported more distress linked to sexual infidelity than their Chinese counterparts, regardless of sex. Similarly, Buunk, Angleitner, Oubaid, and Buss (1996) found that across samples from the United States, Germany, and the Netherlands men and women were more likely to report distress in reaction to sexual and emotional jealousy, respectively. This sex difference, however, was strongest in the United States. Wiederman and Kendall (1999) also found support for the evolutionary hypothesis regarding sex differences in a sample of Swedish college students. Another study conducted in New Zealand found support for a related difference in the way men and women experience relational threat (Mullen & Martin, 1994). As evolutionary theory would predict, jealous men were particularly concerned about losing the partner to a sexual rival, whereas jealous women were particularly concerned that the quality of their primary relationship would decline. Together, these findings suggest that differences in how men and women react to infidelity may be universal, but the strength of these reactions may vary based on culture.

Several scholars have challenged the evolutionary explanation by arguing that socialization and cognitive processes are more proximal predictors of differences in how women and men respond to sexual versus emotional jealousy. For example, DeSteno and Salovey (1996) cast "the choice between sexual infidelity and emotional infidelity" as a "false dichotomy for many individuals" (p. 371). They argued that men and women have different cultural beliefs regarding the covariation of sexual and emotional infidelity, with women more likely than men to believe that the opposite sex can enjoy sex outside an emotionally close relationship. Similarly, Harris and Christenfeld (1996a, 1996b) argued that men and women interpret evidence of infidelity differently. They argued that men are more bothered by sexual infidelity because they assume their wives and girlfriends would only have sex with someone they love. Women, they argued, are still bothered by sexual infidelity, but less so than men because they believe that their husbands and boyfriends can have extradyadic sex without necessarily being in love with the rival. Harris and Christenfeld's survey of undergraduate students confirmed their hypothesis that men and women do indeed interpret situations involving infidelity differently.

Other authors have challenged the work on evolutionary-based sex differences on methodological grounds. For example, Harris (2002) tested for differences between men and women in sexual versus emotional jealousy using both hypothetical and actual situations. She found that heterosexual men and women reported being more upset about sexual versus emotional infidelity, respectively, when using a forced choice method that involved hypothetical situations. However, when respondents recalled actual experiences of infidelity, both men and women focused more on their partner's emotional than sexual infidelity, regardless of sexual orientation. This finding led Harris to question the validity of using hypothetical scenarios to test the hypotheses regarding emotional versus sexual infidelity. Other researchers have challenged the validity of using forced choice as opposed to continuous measures when assessing emotional upset. DeSteno and Salovey (1996) stated that although the sex difference reported by Buss and his colleagues appears to be "readily replicable using the forced choice paradigm, we have been unable to replicate it using continuous measures" (p. 371). Similarly, in Parker's (1994, 1997) studies using continuous measures, both men and women responded more strongly to hypothetical situations involving sexual intimacy than those involving verbal intimacy. However, men were even more upset than women in response to sexual intimacy. Nannini and Meyers (2000) also found that sexual involvement, by itself or with emotional involvement, was more upsetting than emotional involvement alone. Undoubtedly, sexual infidelity is often perceived as an act of severe betrayal by both men and women, who, according to evolutionary theory, value the pair bond.

In response to these challenges, recent studies have tested the sexual versus emotional jealousy hypothesis by pitting evolutionary explanations against cognitive inference explanations, as well as by using different methodologies. For example, in addition to supporting this hypothesis using the traditional forced-choice method, Cramer et al. (2001) had respondents imagine a situation that involved both sexual and emotional infidelity. Respondents were then asked which part of the infidelity was most distressing to them. Consistent with the evolutionary hypothesis, men reported being more distressed by the sexual infidelity, whereas women reported being more distressed by the emotional infidelity. Cramer et al. argued that this finding ran counter to explanations involving differential interpretations of infidelity. Similarly, Wiederman and Kendall (1999) argued that they were able to rule out cognitive inference explanations by showing that attitudes regarding whether or not a person of the opposite sex could enjoy sex outside of an emotionally attached relationship were not related to the scenario (sexual versus emotional) that individuals chose as most distressing. In yet another study, Pietrzak, Laird, Stevens, and Thompson (2002) tested for sex differences in the same group of subjects using three different measures: the traditional forced-choice measure, continuous measures assessing the degree of emotional response to sexual versus emotional jealousy, and psychological measures assessing levels of arousal. In general, their findings supported the idea that men are more upset and aroused in response to sexual jealousy, whereas women are more upset and aroused in response to emotional jealousy.

The weight of the evidence so far suggests that men do indeed perceive sexual infidelity to be particularly threatening, whereas women perceive emotional infidelity to be the more salient threat. As further evidence for this distinction, Buunk (1984) found that for men, jealousy seems to be heightened when they believe that their girlfriends or wives engaged in an extrarelational affair because they have a need for sexual variety. For women, on the other hand, jealousy seems to be heightened when they believe that rivals are pressuring their boyfriends or husbands to form long-term relationship with them. However, it is important to note that when all of the above studies are considered together, it appears that situations involving both sexual and emotional infidelity are the most threatening of all, regardless of sex. Men may be more distressed than women when their partners have an emotionally meaningless one-night stand, whereas women may be more distressed than men when their partners have platonic but emotionally rich relationships with rivals. But an emotional and sexual attachment may be especially feared by both sexes. So Marc may have been somewhat relieved when Kristen assured him that she had no emotional involvement with the man with whom she slept.

Rival Characteristics Causing Increased Jealousy

Although research on sex differences in distress as a function of sexual versus emotional infidelity has been abundant, research on sex differences in the rival characteristics that lead to jealousy has been relatively sparse. According to evolutionary theory, people should experience heightened levels of jealous threat when rivals possess characteristics that are perceived as particularly attractive by the opposite sex, and/or that are lacking in themselves. Thus, women should be especially jealous when a rival is physically attractive, whereas men should be especially jealous when a rival possesses status-related characteristics, such as dominance and wealth.

Some support has been found for these predictions. For example, Dijkstra and Buunk (1998) presented respondents with scenarios where their partners were flirting with someone of the opposite sex. The scenarios were varied in terms of the physical attractiveness (high or low) of the rival, as shown in a photograph, and the degree of dominance (high or low) of the rival, as portrayed in a personality description. Consistent with evolutionary theory, women were more jealous when rivals were physically attractive, whereas men were more jealous when rivals were dominant. Buunk and Dijkstra (2001) obtained similar findings among a sample of gay men and women. Lesbians became more jealous than gay men in response to a scenario in which they were at risk of losing their relationship to a physically attractive rival. In contrast, gay men became more jealous than lesbians in response to a highly dominant rival. Interestingly, however, this sex difference may not be as functional for homosexual couples as heterosexual couples, in that lesbians may actually be attracted to status more than looks, whereas the opposite likely holds true for gay men. Relatedly, Bassett, Pearcey, and Dabbs (2001) compared the jealousy experiences of butch versus femme lesbians. Lesbians who classified themselves as butch were most jealous when rivals had resources such as wealth, whereas lesbians who classified themselves as femme were most jealous when rivals were physically attractive. Thus, jealousy was likely when rivals had traits valued by their partners in that one might expect femme lesbians to be more attracted to status and butch lesbians to be more attracted to looks, given their feminine and masculine orientations, respectively. At a broader level, these findings hint that human brains may have evolved so that being threatened by a rival's looks is part of a larger scheme of feminine traits, whereas being threatened by a rival's status is part of a large scheme of masculine traits. Alternatively, feminine individuals may be socially conditioned to pay attention to cues related to appearance when evaluating themselves and other women, whereas masculine individuals may be conditioned to pay more attention to status. Sometimes these feminine and masculine tendencies may operate even in situations where they are not very functional, as may be the case in gay relationships.

Other studies showed that the physical characteristics of rivals are evaluated in ways consistent with evolutionary theory. Dijkstra and Buunk (2001) found that women tended to experience heightened levels of jealousy when a rival had a low hip-to-waist-ratio, whereas men tended to experience heightened levels of jealousy when the rival had broad shoulders and small hips. When evaluating the threat that rivals posed, women were more likely to pay attention to the rival's waist, hips, and legs, whereas men were more likely to pay attention to the rival's shoulders, chest, and stomach. These findings suggest that men and women know what the opposite sex finds attractive, and they are especially jealous when a rival possesses those attractive attributes.

Research on derogating competitors also indirectly supports the idea that certain rival characteristics are more threatening than others. For instance, Buss and Dedden (1990) found that men and women were equally likely to derogate competitors in ways that were consistent with the parental investment model's predictions about differentially attractive characteristics. In addition, the derogatory messages most clearly consistent with the theory were also rated as the most effective. For example, women were more likely than men to remark on the poor physical appearance and sexual promiscuity of other women. Women also believed that derogating physical appearance was effective regardless of whether a man was seeking a short-term or long-term mate. Commenting on a competitor's sexual promiscuity, however, was only rated effective if the man was looking for a long-term mate. Men, on the other hand, were more likely than women to make derogatory comments about a rival's financial resources or physical strength and to try to defeat him in a physical or athletic competition.

Sex Differences in Jealousy Expression

In addition to derogating competitors, people have a wide variety of strategies at their disposal when responding to jealousy. Two of the most comprehensive typologies of jealousy-related behavior were developed by Buss (1988; Buss & Shackelford, 1997a), who examined mate retention tactics, and Guerrero and her colleagues (Guerrero et al., 1995; Guerrero & Andersen, 1998b), who examined communicative responses to jealousy (see Table 13.1). Several of the behaviors within these typologies have been found to differ according to sex in ways consistent with evolutionary theory.

In line with evolutionary predictions, jealous women report being more likely than jealous men to try and improve their physical appearance (Buss, 1988; Buss & Shackelford, 1997a; deWeerth & Kalma, 1993; Guerrero & Reiter, 1998; Mullen & Martin, 1994). This finding suggests that women are aware of the value that their partners place on physical attractiveness, and they strive to enhance attractiveness as a way to "win back" their partners. Enhancing physical appearance is also a relatively successful mate retention strategy for women, but not for men (Buss, 1988; Buss & Shackelford, 1997a).

Men, on the other hand, report responding to jealousy more than women by displaying financial resources and engaging in or trying to prevent intrasexual competition. So in the scenario with Marc and Kristen, Marc might respond to his sexual jealousy by buying expensive gifts for Kristen, restricting Kristen's access to rivals, and threatening the rival (Buss, 1988; Buss & Shackelford, 1997a; Guerrero & Reiter, 1998). Luci, Foss, and Galloway (1993) also found that men are more likely to think about taking aggressive action against rivals than are women, and some studies suggest that men are more likely than women to become sexually aggressive or promiscuous

TABLE 13.1

Jealousy-Related Behaviors

Buss' Mate Retention Tactics	Guerrero's Communicative Responses
Vigilance: Calling the partner at unexpected times to see who he or she was with; having friends check up on the partner.	*Surveillance:* Spying or checking up on the partner; pressing the redial button on the phone to see who the partner called last.
Mate Concealment: Refusing to introduce the partner to his or her same-sex friends; taking the partner away from gatherings where potential rivals are present.	*Restriction:* Restricting the partner's access to rivals at parties; keeping the partner close by when rivals are present.
Time Monopolization: Spending all of one's time with the partner so that meeting potential rivals was impossible; monopolizing the partner's time at social gatherings.	
Jealousy Induction: Flirting with another person in front of the partner; going out with others to make the partner jealous.	*Manipulation Attempts:* Flirting with others to make the partner jealous (counterjealousy inductions); trying to make the partner feel guilty; bringing up a rival's name to check for a reaction.
Emotional Manipulation: Crying when the partner said that he or she might go out with others; making the partner feel guilty for talking to others.	*Negative Affect Expression:* Crying in front of the partner; looking hurt; acting anxious when the partner is with a rival.
Commitment Manipulation: Asking the partner for marriage; getting the partner pregnant.	
Violence: Hitting rivals; starting fights with rivals; asking others to physically harm rivals; vandalizing the rival's property; slapping the rival.	*Violent Communication:* Roughly pulling the partner away from a rival; hitting or threatening to hit the partner.
	Violence Toward Objects: Throwing the partner's possessions out of the house; breaking dishes and/or slamming doors.
Punish Mate's Infidelity Threat: Expressing anger at partner for flirting with others; ignoring the partner; threatening to break up if the partner saw a rival again.	*Distributive Communication:* Arguing with the partner; being sarcastic; rude, and/or verbally aggressive.
	Active Distancing: Giving the partner the silent treatment; giving the partner cold or dirty looks; withdrawing affection and sexual favors.
	Relationship Threats: Threatening to end the relationship; to start dating other people; or to have a sexual affair of one's own.
Derogation of Competitors: Insulting rivals' appearances, strength, and/or intelligence; starting rumors about rivals; commenting on a rival's promiscuity.	*Derogating Competitors:* Expressing disbelief that anyone would be attracted to a rival; telling the partner the rival was a "ladies man" or "tease" who would hurt her or him.
Mate Derogation: Telling potential rivals negative information about the partner to deter them from approaching him or her; telling others that the partner might have a disease.	

TABLE 13.1

(*Continued*)

Buss's Mate Retention Tactics	Guerrero's Communicative Responses
Resource Display: Spending money on the partner; buying the partner expensive gifts; taking the partner out to a nice restaurant. *Appearance Enhancement:* Making one's face look nice; dressing more attractively and/or fashionably than usual. *Love and Care:* Saying "I love you;" going out of one's way to be kind; nice; and caring; becoming more affectionate than usual.	*Compensatory Restoration:* Sending flowers or gifts; saying "I love you" more than usual; trying to appear nicer or more physically attractive; being extra affectionate or complimentary.
Intrasexual Threats: Yelling and/or staring at perceived rivals; threatening rivals; warning rivals to "stay away" from the partner. *Verbal Possession Signals:* Telling potential rivals that the partner was "taken;" telling others about shared intimacy; introducing the partner as one's primary romantic partner. *Physical Possession Signals:* Kissing the partner in front of potential rivals; placing one's arm around the partner in front of others. *Possessive Ornamentation:* Wearing the partner's clothes; displaying pictures of the partner.	*Rival Contacts:* Threatening the rival; informing the rival that the partner is already in a relationship; telling the rival to stop seeing the partner. *Signs of Possession:* Putting an arm around the partner and saying "she's taken;" introducing the partner using terms such as "my girlfriend" or "my husband;" telling rivals they were (or plan to be) married; flashing a wedding ring.
Sexual Inducements: Giving in to the partner's sexual requests; acting sexy to distract the partner from rivals; performing sexual favors to prevent the partner from leaving the relationship.	No Similar Category
No Similar Category	*Integrative Communication:* Talking about jealous feelings with the partner; asking the partner probing questions; trying to reach an understanding or to renegotiate relationship rules; reassuring the partner that we can "work it out".
Submission and Debasement: Telling the partner that one would change for him or her; giving in to the partner's demands.	No Similar Category
No Similar Category	*Avoidance/Denial:* Denying jealous feelings; pretending to be unaffected by the situation; decreasing contact with the partner; avoiding jealousy-provoking situations.

Note. Similar categories of behaviors are listed side by side across the columns. Buss' make retention tactics compiled from Buss (1988) and Buss and Shackelford (1997b). Guerrero's communicative responses compiled from Guerrero et al. (1995) and Guerrero and Andersen (1998b).

with others as a jealousy response (Guerrero & Reiter, 1998; cf. deWeerth & Kalma, 1993). These last findings suggest that sex could be related to the threat of paternal uncertainty, in that evolutionary theory would predict that a man might be tempted to have sex outside of his primary relationship if he was worried about his partner's sexual faithfulness.

Men and women differ in other forms of jealous expression in ways that are not fully explainable by evolutionary theory. For example, across various studies jealous women more than jealous men have reported seeking support from others, trying to improve the relationship, demanding commitment from partners, expressing negative emotion, using integrative communication, and using verbal signals of possession (Amstutz, 1982; Buunk, 1981, 1982b; Buss & Shackelford, 1997a; Guerrero et al., 1993; Guerrero & Reiter, 1998; Parker, 1994; White, 1981b). These sex differences are consistent with White and Mullen's (1989) conclusion that jealous women are "more oriented toward solving relationship problems or directly expressing their emotions" (p. 129; see also Nadler & Dotan, 1992; cf. Buunk, 1982b; Francis, 1977). These results are partially explainable by evolutionary theory in that women are more oriented toward long-term mate retention and parental investment, and therefore, more oriented toward relational repair and maintenance. However, socialization may play a more direct role in explaining these sex differences. These findings also have practical relevance because research has shown that expressing negative jealous emotion while engaging in integrative communication is an especially effective way of coping with jealousy and enhancing relational satisfaction (Andersen et al., 1995; Guerrero & Andersen, 1998b). Other communicative responses to jealousy, including avoidance/denial, distributive communication, manipulation attempts, and violence, generally exacerbate the problem.

In addition to the behaviors related to resource display and mate guarding that were mentioned previously, jealous men report using submission and debasement (e.g., promising to do anything the partner wants) and getting drunk more than jealous women (Buss, 1988; Buss & Shackelford, 1997a; deWeerth & Kalma, 1993; Mathes, 1992; White & Mullen, 1989). These behaviors are not easily explained by evolutionary theory. In fact, Buss and Shackelford (1997a) admitted that they were at a loss to explain why men in both undergraduate and married samples reported using more submission and debasement than women. This finding is especially puzzling because dominant (yet prosocial) men are typically preferred to passive men (Scheib, 2001). Yet these findings are consistent with recent research on sex differences in communication during conflict and jealousy situations. Contrary to some early studies suggesting that males tend to be expressive in response to jealousy whereas females tend to be more communicatively avoidant (e.g., Buunk, 1982b; Francis, 1977), more recent research, typically employing more differentiated measures of jealousy response, indicates that females tend to be particularly expressive in response to jealousy and males tend to avoid and dissociate themselves (Aylor & Dainton, 2001; Nadler & Dotan, 1992). Males may also be more likely to use violence in response to jealousy (Smuts, 1996; Wilson et al., 2001). In relational contexts, females may have evolved more facility with modes of relational repair and negotiation because of the importance of long-term mate retention, whereas males may have developed greater comfort with submission, denial, and aggression, which would be efficient in short-term relationships. An alternative explanation for sex differences in submission and debasement is that jealous men might believe that it is important to show emotional faithfulness to their mates by being ingratiating. Tooke and Camire (1991) found that men often reported trying to appear exceptionally trustworthy and kind in their attempts to attract mates. Perhaps when they perceive the potential loss of their primary relationship, some men resort to tactics similar to those they initially engaged in to attract their partner.

Other jealous behaviors either consistently showed no sex difference or produced an inconsistent pattern across studies. With few exceptions, studies showed that strategies related to surveillance and vigilance seem to be enacted fairly equally by men and women, as are strategies related to nonverbal signs of possession, manipulation attempts, and increased displays of affection (Buss, 1988; Buss & Shackelford, 1997a; Guerrero & Reiter, 1998). Findings for avoidance/denial were inconsistent, with some studies showing that women use more of these strategies (deWeerth & Kalma, 1993; Guerrero et al., 1993), others showing men use more of these strategies (Mullen & Martin, 1994; Parker, 1994; White, 1981a, 1981b), and still others showing no differences (Guerrero & Reiter, 1998). Similarly, there is inconsistency across studies that examined verbal attacks, distributive communication, and relationship termination (or other relational threats) as responses to jealousy, with some authors reporting that women use these behaviors more, and others reporting that men use them more (Amstutz, 1982; deWeerth & Kalma, 1993; Guerrero et al., 1993; Mathes, 1992; Weghorst, 1980; White & Mullen, 1989). Future research should focus on personal, social, and situational factors that might mediate or moderate the association between gender and these jealous responses.

Violence and Jealousy

The most frequently studied behavioral response to jealousy is physical violence. The link between jealousy and aggression has long been presumed, as is evident in classic works such as Shakespeare's *Othello*. There are several reasons to expect this link to be real. First, clinical judgment and evaluation of violent patients often identified morbid jealousy as a proximate cause of violence (Mullen, 1996; Vaselle-Augenstein & Ehrlich, 1992). Second, jealousy is identified as a proximate cause of relational conflict, which in turn is associated with anger and aggression (Canary, Spitzberg, & Semic, 1998; Daly & Wilson, 1996; Siegert & Stamp, 1994; Spitzberg, 1997). This association between jealousy and conflict appears across both same- (Renzetti, 1988) and cross-sex romantic relationships (e.g., Daly & Wilson, 1996; Daly, Wilson, & Weghorst, 1982). Third, correlational data have fairly consistently revealed significant positive relationships between self-report measures of jealousy and measures of relational violence and aggression (Dutton, van Ginkel, & Landolt, 1996; Riggs, 1993; Simonelli & Ingram, 1998), although the effects are often moderated by sex. For example, Russell and Wells (2000) found that jealousy was a predictor of engaging in and receiving abuse for husbands but not for wives. Stets and Pirog-Good (1987) and Bookwala, Frieze, Smith, and Ryan (1992) found essentially the opposite. Specifically, Bookwala et al. found that jealousy was predictive of expressed violence for women (partial $r = .37$, $p < .05$) but not for men (partial $r = .04$, ns). Another moderator may be whether jealousy is operationalized as an attitude or a set of behaviors. Brainerd et al. (1996) found that approval of jealousy-inducing behaviors was unrelated to use of aggression ($r = .03$, ns), but use of jealousy-inducing behaviors was predictive of use of aggression ($r = .32$, $p < .001$). Fourth, jealousy has successfully discriminated between relationships and partners who are aggressive and/or violent and relationships and partners who are nonviolent (Barnett, Martinez, & Bluestein, 1995; Dutton et al., 1996; Holtzworth-Munroe, Stuart, & Hutchinson, 1997), although the effect sizes are sometimes relatively small (e.g., Follingstad, Bradley, Laughlin, & Burke, 1999; Ryan, 1995) or moderated by sex (Ryan, 1998). Related, it appears that violent males have less competent ways of responding to jealous situations than do nonviolent males (Holtzworth-Munroe & Anglin, 1991). Fifth, jealousy is often one of the most common post hoc attributions made by people reporting on the proximate causes of their relational violence. That is, when asked to attribute a cause of their relational violence, across a variety of studies jealousy is the most commonly selected cause (Cascardi & Vivian, 1995; Roscoe & Benaske, 1985; Roscoe & Callahan, 1985; Roscoe & Kelsey, 1986; Stamp & Sabourin, 1995; Sugarman & Hotaling, 1989). So common is this attribution that jealousy seems to be part of a cognitive schema of coercive control and aggression (Wilson et al., 2001), and therefore, aggression is often seen as a reasonably acceptable form of response to jealousy-provoking situations (Milardo, 1998).

Estimating the base rate of violence in the face of jealousy is difficult. On the one hand, it seems obvious that the overall "incidence of violent acts in those with jealousy is low" (Morenz & Lane, 1996, p. 90), and that jealousy plays an indirect role by facilitating or amplifying violent proclivities (Barnett et al., 1995). Violence is a relatively rare response to jealousy when compared to other types of responses, but among couples who report that violence has occurred in their relationships, jealousy is a leading cause for violent episodes. In Mullen and Martin's (1994) community sample, 15% of those surveyed "reported having been subjected to physical aggression as a result of a partner's jealousy," with no sex difference. Jealousy has been attributed as a "major" cause of wife battering (Buunk et al., 1996, p. 359). Morenz and Lane (1996) went further: "The most common form of murder-suicide in the United States, one-half to three-fourths, involves jealousy and is estimated to account for 1,000 to 1,500 deaths each year" (p. 89), typically involving precipitating events of partner rejection or imminent departure. Thus, although it is clear that jealousy does not usually result in violence, the evidence is convincing that when intimate violence occurs, it is often a currency of jealousy.

Why would this be? Evolutionary theory suggests that jealousy evolved as an adaptive complex of cognition, emotion, and behavior that facilitates mate retention. Jealousy leads to vigilance toward potential poachers of one's mate and arouses emotion that motivates mate-tending and guarding activities, including aggressive actions that prevent or limit sexual infidelity (Buss & Shackelford, 1997b; Daly, Wilson, & Weghorst, 1982). Such arousal and competitive motives lead then to potential escalation of intrasexual competition, which can take the form of violence (Buss & Shackelford, 1997b). Furthermore, jealousy necessarily implies a triangle of relationships, which means that there are obvious "targets" for one's emotional distress, although research shows that one's partner is far more likely to be the target of most of the controlling and aggressive tactics motivated by jealousy (Mathes & Verstraete, 1993; Paul, Foss & Galloway, 1993). Such a theoretical perspective is consistent with appraisal theories of jealousy and anger (see Canary et al., 1998; Guerrero & Andersen, 1998b), in which the evolved disposition to arousal from mate competition is interpreted in terms of attributions and threat potential. Such appraisals would then moderate the conditional behavioral responses, which would account for why jealousy sometimes leads to prosocial responses and sometimes leads to aggression.

It should be noted, however, that in one of the few studies to develop specific evolutionary predictions regarding jealousy and sex differences in aggression, deWeerth and Kalma (1993) found, contrary to expectations, that women were perceived as more likely to respond aggressively to discovering their partner's infidelity than men discovering their partner's infidelity. Similarly, Luci and Galloway (1994) found women were more likely than men to positively endorse the use of aggressive action (e.g., hitting, slapping, etc.) against unfaithful partners and rivals in situations involving sexual jealousy, and Luci, Foss, and Baenninger (1996) found women were more aggressive toward rivals than men. This sex-role reversal may reflect one of the instances in which contemporary cultural norms have interacted with evolutionary forces, or it may reflect that males restrain their violence if it threatens the very relationship that jealousy functions to protect. Thus, although evolutionary theory offers a plausible explanatory account for the link between jealousy and aggression, it also seems clear that more theoretical specification is needed to formulate testable empirical implications.

APPRAISING THE STATUS OF THE EVOLUTIONARY PERSPECTIVE ON JEALOUSY

For the past 2 decades evolutionary theory has provided the primary theoretical vehicle for describing and explaining differences in how women and men react to sexual versus emotional jealousy. In this section, we assess the contributions that the evolutionary perspective made in helping scholars to understand jealousy, and we suggest some complementary theoretical pathways that should be explored in the future. In doing so, we also provide some general assessments of the status of evolutionary theory as applied to social behavior.

In many ways, evolutionary theory has, to date, been a victim of its own success. Science proper has a natural ambivalence toward theories that seem excessively inclusive and indestructible (Popper, 1980). Although no scholar reasonably makes such claims of ubiquity and resilience, it is not uncommon to speak of an evolutionary paradigm, and to extend evolutionary accounts to rather esoteric domains in which social scientific theories had heretofore been reluctant to pursue. Evolutionary theory, by its very nature, threatens to dissolve the mind–body divide. In doing so, many scholars previously wedded to the cognitive or cultural paradigms find little solace in a theory so grounded in biology and biological history. Nevertheless, in recent years, evolutionary theory has itself evolved and adapted to the highly competitive ecological niche that is the marketplace of scientific rhetoric.

Here we evaluate the formal theoretical status of evolutionary theory as relevant to jealousy. Although there are numerous criteria on which to judge theory, the general standards of scope and power are particularly central (see Spitzberg, 2001). Here we focus on two interrelated qualities related to scope: (1) inclusiveness, which refers to the breadth of the theory, how much of a domain, or how many distinct domains, a theory claims; and (2) synthesis, which refers to the degree to which a theory absorbs other theories or resolves what otherwise appear to be contradictory claims of other theories. Power here refers to three criteria: (1) comparative competitiveness, which asks whether a theory has fared well in direct competition with alternative theoretical predictions or claims, (2) verification, which is the degree to which a theory's claims correspond to observed data, and (3) falsification, which refers to whether the theory makes predictions that are sufficiently risky to be (potentially) falsified through experiment and observation.

Evaluating Scope

Inclusiveness. Evolutionary theory is one of the broader theories in existence. In fact, it is one of the few theories that establishes a distinctly deep chronological frame of causality (Conway & Schaller, 2002) by addressing ultimate (i.e., phylogenetic), ontogenetic (developmental), and proximate (current environmental) causes of behavior (Simpson & Gangestad, 2001). The topical breadth of the theory is obvious from any reading of evolutionary texts. In addition to explaining sexual and emotional jealousy, various mid-level evolutionary theories have been used to explain mate preferences, sperm volume, sexual coercion, sexual fantasy, sequestering of women, incest taboos, morning sickness, fears and phobias, depression, aggression, competition, parental love, observational learning, child abuse, marital dissolution, color vision, conditional reasoning, judgment under uncertainty, aesthetics, self-deception, social illusions, maturational tempo, language acquisition, and so on (Ketelaar & Ellis, 2000,

p. 18; also see Simpson & Kenrick, 1997). Within the domain of jealousy, evolutionary theorists generated hypotheses related to various topics, including jealousy as a protective mechanism, sex differences in the experience and expression of jealousy, mate retention tactics, and rival characteristics that induce jealousy.

In addition, evolutionary theory applies to many different relationship types, including parent–child relationships, sibling relationships, friendships, romantic relationships, and relationships between strangers (Daly, Salmon, & Wilson, 1997; Simpson & Gangestad, 2001). Importantly, however, evolutionary predictions concerning jealousy have been applied most often to heterosexual romantic relationships. Given the theory's focus on reproduction and sexual jealousy, this emphasis makes sense. Nonetheless, evolutionary theory might also be fruitfully applied to issues such as competitiveness and jealousy in the workplace, sibling rivalry, and friendship jealousy. For example, Hill and Davis (2000) noted that

> the evolutionary perspective may help explain various forms of competitiveness in that people who are favored in domains such as the work place are more likely to be successful, attract mates, and ultimately, survive to procreate.

As we discuss later, researchers also examined sexual and emotional jealousy within homosexual relationships, with data producing inconsistent findings in relation to evolutionary theory.

Synthesis.   To date, evolutionary theory has not been extended in ways that clearly absorb many other theories. Indeed, one of the ongoing debates is the compatibility of cultural and cognitive theories with evolutionary theories. However, few (if any) evolutionary theorists claim that there is any incompatibility. The lack of incompatibility is claimed on at least two grounds. First, evolution clearly predates the existence of culture or cognition and, therefore, can be considered both progenitor and ongoing influence on culture and cognition. (e.g., Malamuth, 1996; Simpson & Gangestad, 2001). There are research programs pursuing existing theories from within an evolutionary perspective, including sex-role theory and sexual and relational coercion (Malamuth, 1996; Pratto, 1996), relational conflict, violence and jealousy (Daly & Wilson, 1988), and attachment theory and jealousy (Knobloch et al., 2001; Leak et al., 1998). Indeed, cognitive appraisal tendencies can be viewed as mental adaptations to survival challenges faced by ancestral peoples, which today may serve similar or novel functions. Cognitive appraisal models, therefore, reflect no intrinsic incompatibility with evolutionary theory (e.g., Guerrero & Andersen, 1998b; Nannini & Meyers, 2000; Pfeiffer & Wong, 1989; Staske, 1999). Given that both cognitive appraisal models and evolutionary theory were used to explain jealousy, a logical next step would be for researchers to merge these theories when making jealousy-related predictions.

Because jealousy is a complex combination of cognitions, emotions, and behaviors, it is not surprising that researchers studying jealousy in general (as opposed to sexual jealousy in particular) have begun to integrate theory to make predictions. For example, Guerrero (1998) noted the relevance of social exchange theory in explaining why insecurely attached individuals might be inclined to worry about the comparison level of alternatives in the form of partner loss to potential rivals, and Trost et al. (1994) used principles from both social exchange and evolutionary theories to make predictions related to jealousy. Guerrero and Afifi (1999) derived hypotheses about jealousy goals using theories related to uncertainty reduction, social exchange, and relational maintenance. Other researchers investigated jealousy and envy using social comparison theory (or the related concept of self-evaluation maintenance) as a theoretical lens (e.g., Hill & Davis, 2000; Rustemeyer & Wilbert, 2001; Salovey & Rodin, 1986) Given that responses to jealousy depend in part on who is perceived as blameworthy (e.g., self, partner, rival, or the "situation"), attribution theory seems to have substantial potential for contributing to a theory of jealousy that links affect and cognition with behavioral response. Thus, although theoretical integration thus far has not been very explicit or extensive when investigating sexual jealousy, the broader body of literature on jealousy suggests that there is substantial potential for such synthesis to occur. Progress toward understanding sexual and emotional jealousy is likely best served by merging principles from evolutionary theory with ideas from other theories that have successfully been used to study jealousy, including attachment theory, cognitive appraisal theory, social comparison theories, and social exchange theories. Indeed, a truly comprehensive theory of jealousy would include all of the factors reviewed earlier in this chapter—biology, culture, relationship characteristics, personality, situational factors, and strategic moves.

Evaluating Power

Competitiveness. To date, relatively few head-to-head competitions have been waged, and when they have, the tendency has been to locate the competition between different mid-range theories within the larger evolutionary parent theory, or to locate methodological nuances that might delimit the validity of evolutionary theory. Certainly, several theorists have begun the task of fleshing out predictions from evolutionary theory in contrast to competing theories (see, e.g., Ellis, 1989; Malamuth, 1996), but the empirical task of testing such networks of predictions is still in its infancy. Some of the research regarding whether males or females are more reactive to sexual versus emotional infidelity has been cast as a theoretical contrast rather than merely a methodological refinement (e.g., DeSteno & Salovey, 1996). In one of the few other attempts to pit an alternative theory's predictions regarding jealousy against evolutionary predictions, Rustemeyer and Wilbert (2001) found no support for a self-evaluation maintenance prediction and instead found results more in line with evolution. Other researchers pitted cognitive inference explanations for sex differences in jealousy against evolutionary explanations, with mixed results; some of these studies provide more support for a cognitive or social learning perspective on sex differences in jealousy (e.g., DeSteno & Salovey, 1996; Harris, 2002); others provide more support for an evolutionary perspective (Cramer et al., 2001; Wiederman & Kendall, 1999).

Eagly and Wood's (1999) comparison of evolutionary theory and social structural theory may have important implications for the study of jealousy. According to the social structural perspective, sex differences in mating behaviors are the result of differing social roles rather than evolution. Specifically, social structural theorists claim that men and women in contemporary societies learn to maximize rewards and efficiency by choosing mates who conform to cultural gender roles. In most modern societies, men still have more status and earning power than women, and labor is still divided along gender lines, with women spending more time doing domestic work and men spending more time earning wages. Thus, social structural theorists claim that women learn to value older men who have economic resources, whereas men learn to value women who can assume domestic duties related to the household and childcare. However, as cultural attitudes change toward gender equality, social structural theorists predict than these gender-linked preferences will weaken. To test this prediction, Eagly and Wood (1999) re-analyzed Buss et al.'s (1990) 37-culture data set, showing that sex differences in preferences for "good earning capacity," and "good housekeeper and cook" decreased as gender equality (as rated for each country) increased. Preferences for physical attractiveness, however, were generally not associated with gender equality.

The social structural perspective could also be applied to gender differences in sexual versus emotional jealousy. Many societies still endorse a double standard, whereby sexual experimentation is okay for men but not for women. Furthermore, in many societies females are taught to be sexual gatekeepers who refuse to have sex until a sufficient level of emotional intimacy has been achieved, whereas males are taught to be sexually assertive (Byers, 1996). These gender roles may in turn lead to sex differences in jealousy experience that are consistent with the evolutionary hypothesis that women are more upset over emotional infidelity whereas men are more upset over sexual infidelity. Of course, social structural and evolutionary explanations may work together to provide the best model of jealousy experience and expression.

Verification and Falsification. The distinction between verification and falsification is conceptually and practically subtle, warranting that these two criteria be discussed together. As Conway and Schaller (2002) pointed out, "Human beings— including scientists—are intuitive verificationists, not intuitive falsificationists. As humans, we do not care very much for what is not; we only really care for what is" (p. 155). Verification merely requires claims such as: if p, then q. When p is then observed, it is taken as evidence that theory p (technically, the theory from which p was deduced) is supported. Falsification tends to be a stricter requirement: if p, then *not* q, or if p, then r *and only r*. If q is observed, then the theory fails, or if anything other than r is observed, the theory fails. The value of falsification presupposes, however, that conditions can be established under which q or non-r could be observed *if* the theory is indeed false.

A good example of verification and falsification is in the scholarly debate surrounding sex differences in the experience of sexual and emotional jealousy. For some time the evidence that males were more jealous in response to sexual infidelity and females were more jealous in response to emotional infidelity was taken as verification of evolutionary principles related to mate retention and parental investment. But other theories could be, and were, shown to be capable of deriving such a prediction as well. If females are socialized to believe that sexual intimacy presupposes emotional intimacy, then scenarios describing sex would imply an emotional threat as well. Although research continues to seek various means of separating these dimensions of jealousy in an effort to more precisely verify this evolutionary claim, it remains to be determined what a falsifiable claim would be in regard to sexual versus emotional jealousy and sex differences. If a claim were deduced from evolutionary theory or one of its mid-range theories such as the parental investment model that females will only find emotional infidelity more jealousy-provoking than sexual infidelity under x, y, and z conditions, and no others, then the claim might be considered falsifiable.

Evolutionary theory also tends to make distributional predictions: if p, then there is a tendency to see q more than r. For example, if evolutionary principles are correct, males tend to engage in more short-term mating strategies than females, and females tend to engage in more long-term mating strategies than males. However, some scholars have begun investigating conditions under which females prefer short-term, or extra-pair, mating strategies (Scheib, 2001). Although females are predicted to generally prefer long-term mate retention, there may have been conditions through human evolution in which extra-pair mateships might have been adaptive for women. Specifically, the acquisition of good genes may be most valuable when women are already pair-bonded in a long-term relationship. In such situations, already having a partner to invest resources into the raising of offspring, the status aspects of a rival should be less salient than the rival's potential genetic contribution to offspring. Although there are also clear risks involved (e.g., being discovered by one's partner and thereby risking the survival of the relationship), it follows that women already in a pair-bonded relationship will be more influenced by physical attractiveness than status features of potential extra-pair mates (Scheib, 2001). Such an approach makes it unclear what constitutes a falsification of evolutionary theory by introducing a rationale by which observations contrary to the generally expected tendency are expected by the theory.

Similarly, it is unclear, to date, whether research on homosexual relationships provides points of falsification or points of refinement in relation to evolutionary predictions regarding jealousy. As a case in point, Sheets and Wolfe (2001) compared the reactions of homosexual and heterosexual individuals to situations involving emotional versus sexual infidelity. Heterosexual women, gay women, and gay men all reported experiencing greater distress in response to emotional infidelity. Only heterosexual men reported experiencing more distress in response to sexual infidelity. Sheets and Wolfe argued that this finding contradicts evolutionary hypotheses by showing that a stronger reaction to sexual infidelity (as compared to emotional infidelity) is not hard-wired into all men's brains, and that variables such as sexual orientation are more important than biological sex when determining reactions to jealousy. However, one could argue that these findings are consistent with evolutionary theory because heterosexual men are the only group for which paternal confidence would be an issue. Consistent with this idea, in at least two other studies (Bringle, 1995; Hawkins, 1990) homosexual men reported experiencing less sexual jealousy than heterosexual men.

Other studies using homosexual populations either call into question or suggest modification of some of the tenants of the evolutionary perspective on jealousy. This is not surprising given that many evolutionary hypotheses related to jealousy were derived from the parental investment model. In one study (Dijkstra et al., 2001), homosexual individuals showed a pattern of sex differences that was opposite to that of heterosexual individuals—gay men were more likely to choose emotional infidelity as more upsetting, whereas lesbians were more likely to choose sexual infidelity. Assuming that lesbians imagined their partners with another woman (as opposed to a man) this finding appears to run counter to evolutionary theory hypotheses even when issues of paternal certainty are considered. A cognitive inference explanation (DeSteno & Salovey, 1996; Harris & Christenfield, 1996a, 1996b) may explain such a finding, in that lesbians may assume that emotional attachment usually precedes sexual infidelity, whereas gay men may assume that sexual infidelity often occurs without emotional attachment. This explanation is consistent with research showing that gay men typically have more sexual partners and are less sexually faithful than lesbians or heterosexuals (Blumstein & Schwartz, 1983; Bringle, 1995). Findings seemingly contradictary to evolutionary theory were also found by Bassett et al. (2001), who compared the jealousy experiences of lesbians who classified themselves as butch versus femme. Counter to their prediction that butch lesbians would experience more sexual jealousy whereas femme lesbians would experience more emotional jealousy, there was no difference in sexual versus emotional jealousy. This nonfinding may be linked to the absence of paternal uncertainty and/or to issues related to intrasexual competition, with intrasexual competition being different for lesbians than for men who are trying to attract female mates. Clearly, these studies suggest that a simple "if p then q" equation does not always hold under condition x, with x representing the homosexual population. So if the Marc at the beginning of this chapter was involved with a Kristopher rather than a Kristen, we might expect his reaction (as well as Kristopher's explanation) to be somewhat different.

In summary, then, socioevolutionary theory has fared well by most criteria of evaluation. The theory is broad in scope, appears heuristic in producing specific and often novel predictions, and yet is sufficiently flexible in synthesizing existing and newly discovered empirical findings. The theory is most relevant to contexts in which mating and fitness are prominent potential concerns of the organism. As yet, however, it is still unclear (a) what the full scope of the theory is in relation to human behavior (i.e., what it should, and just as importantly, what it should not apply to), and (b) how it can be fruitfully integrated with nonevolutionary accounts (e.g., enculturation, personal experience, etc.). The same limitations could easily be lodged against most competing theories as well. Comparatively, therefore, socioevolutionary theory fares well relative to other social theories. The extent to which socioevolutionary theory has stimulated research and theoretical refinement in the arena of jealousy in particular illustrates the utility of the perspective.

CONCLUSION

Almost a century and a half ago, Darwin (1864) only dimly envisioned the transformational influence of his theory of evolution on the understanding of human behavior. At the very end of *The Origin*, he speculated:

> In the distant future I see open fields for far more important researches. Psychology will be based on a new foundation, that of the necessary acquirement of each mental power and capacity by gradation. Light will be thrown on the origin of man and his history. (Darwin, 1864, p. 424)

In the last few decades, evolution-inspired theories of human behavior have rapidly emerged. One of the most developed arenas of this theory has been in the area of understanding jealousy.

Jealousy is an evocative concept. "Jealousy is about infidelity, and infidelity has a moral dimension" (Mullen, 1991, p. 599). As a moral concept, jealousy tends to evoke negative evaluations, "where normality blends into pathology" (Hill & Davis, 2000, p. 507). However, evolutionary theorists view jealousy as a functional, normal, ambivalent product of our past. "Jealousy is an adaptive emotion, forged over millions of years, symbiotic with long-term love. It evolved as a primary defense against threats of infidelity and abandonment" (Buss, 2000, p. 56). "While jealousy is experienced by an individual, that experience is a function of his/her communication transactions" (Sprowl & White, 1989, p. 157). As such, jealousy is an inherently social and relational phenomenon. Evidence indicates that both infidelity and jealousy are relatively common relational experiences. As such, the management of jealousy is a challenge most individuals, and many if not most relationships, will face. It follows that one of the important tasks of social scientific theory and research is to find ways of making jealousy more a friend than an enemy in people's relations with others.

REFERENCES

Amstutz, D. (1982). *Androgyny and jealousy*. Unpublished doctoral dissertation, Northern Illinois University.

Andersen, P. A., Eloy, S. V., Guerrero, L. K., & Spitzberg, B. H. (1995). Romantic jealousy and relational satisfaction: A look at the impact of jealousy experience and expression. *Communication Reports, 8,* 77–85.

Aune, K. S., & Comstock, J. (1991). The experience and expression of jealousy: A comparison between friends and romantics. *Psychological Reports, 69,* 315–319.

Aune, K. S., & Comstock, J. (1997). Effect of relationship length on the experience, expression, and perceived appropriateness of jealousy. *The Journal of Social Psychology, 137,* 23–31.

Asthana, S. (2000). Female judgement of male attractiveness and desirability for relationships: Role of waist-to-hip ratio. *Psycho-Lingua, 30,* 60–64.

Aylor, B., & Dainton, M. (2001). Antecedents in romantic jealousy experience, expression, and goals. *Western Journal of Communication, 65,* 370–391.

Baker, R. R., & Bellis, M. A. (1995). *Sperm competition: Copulation, masterbation, and infidelity*. London: Chapman & Hall.

Barnett, O. W., Martinez, T. E., & Bluestein, B. W. (1995). Jealousy and romantic attachment in matrially violent and nonviolent men. *Journal of Interpersonal Violence, 10,* 473–486.

Bassett, J., Pearcey, S., & Dabbs, J.M., Jr. (2001). Jealousy and partner preference among butch and femme lesbians. *Psychology, Evolution and Gender 3*, 155–165.

Baxter, L. A., & Wilmot, W. W. (1984). Secret tests: Social strategies for acquiring information about the state of the relationship. *Human Communication Research, 11*, 171–201.

Bleske, A. L., & Shackelford, T. D. (2001). Poaching, promiscuity, and deceit: Combating mating rivalry in same-sex friendships. *Personal Relationships, 8*, 407–424.

Betzig, L. (1989). Causes of conjugal dissolution: A cross-cultural study. *Current Anthropology, 30*, 654–676.

Blumstein, P., & Schwartz, P. (1983). *American couples: Money, work, sex.* New York: Morrow.

Bookwala, J., Frieze, I. H., Smith, C., & Ryan, K. (1992). Predictors of dating violence: A multivariate analysis. *Violence and Victims, 7*, 297–311.

Bradford, L. (1980). The death of a dyad. In B. W. Morse & L. A. Phelps (Eds.), *Interpersonal communication: A relational perspective* (pp. 497–508). Minneapolis, MN: Burgess.

Brainerd, E. G., Jr., Hunter, P. A., Moore, D., & Thompson, T. R. (1996). Jealousy induction as a predictor of power and the use of other control methods in heterosexual relationships. *Psychological Reports, 79*, 1319–1325.

Bringle, R. G. (1995). Sexual jealousy in the relationships of homosexual and heterosexual men: 1980 and 1992. *Personal Relationships, 2*, 313–325.

Bringle, R. G., & Boebinger, K. L. G. (1990). Jealousy and the "third" person in the love triangle. *Journal of Social and Personal Relationships, 7*, 119–133.

Bringle, R. G., & Buunk, B. (1991). Extradyadic relationship and sexual jealousy. In M. McKinney & S. Sprecher (Eds.), *Sexuality in close relationships* (pp. 135–153). Hillsdale, NJ: Lawrence Erlbaum Associates.

Bryson, J. B. (1977, Month). *Situational determinants of the expression of jealousy.* Paper presented at the annual meeting of the American Psychological Association, San Francisco, CA.

Buss, D. M. (1984). *The evolution of desire: Strategies of human mating.* New York: Basic Books.

Buss, D. M. (1988). From vigilance to violence: Tactics of mate retention in American undergraduates. *Ethology and Sociobiology, 9*, 291–317.

Buss, D. M. (1989). Sex differences in human mate preferences: Evolutionary hypotheses tested in 37 cultures. *Behavioral and Brain Sciences, 12*, 1–49.

Buss, D. M. (1994). *The evolution of desire: Strategies of mate selection.* New York: Basic Books.

Buss, D. M. (1995). Evolutionary psychology: A new paradigm for psychological science. *Psychological Inquiry, 6*(1), 1–30.

Buss, D. M. (1999). *Evolutionary psychology: The new science of the mind.* Boston, MA: Allyn & Bacon.

Buss, D. M. (2000). *The dangerous passion: Why jealousy is as necessary as love and sex.* New York: Free Press.

Buss, D. M., Abbott, M., Angleitner, A., Asherian, A., & Biaggio, A. (1990). International preferences in selecting mates: A study of 37 cultures. *Journal of Cross-Cultural Psychology, 21*, 5–47.

Buss, D. M., & Barnes, M. (1986). Preferences in human mate selection. *Journal of Personality and Social Psychology, 50*, 559–570.

Buss, D. M., & Dedden, L. A. (1990). Derogation of competitors. *Journal of Personal and Social Relationships, 7*, 395–422.

Buss, D. M., Larsen, R. J., & Westen, D. (1996). Sex differences in jealousy: Not gone, not forgotten, and not easily explained by alternative hypotheses. *Psychological Science, 7*, 373–375.

Buss, D. M., Larsen, R., Westen, D., & Semmelroth, J. (1992). Sex differences in jealousy: Evolution, physiology, and psychology. *Psychological Science, 3*, 251–255.

Buss, D. M., & Shackelford, T. K. (1997a). From vigilance to violence: Mate retention tactics in married couples. *Journal of Personality and Social Psychology, 72*, 346–361.

Buss, D. M., & Shackelford, T. K. (1997b). Human aggression in evolutionary psychological perspective. *Clinical Psychology Review, 17*, 605–619.

Buss, D. M., Shackelford, T. K., Kirkpatrick, L. A., Choe, J. A., Lim, H. K., Hasegawa, M., Hasegawa, T., & Bennett, K. (1999). Jealousy and the nature of beliefs about infidelity: Tests of competing hypotheses about sex differences in the United States, Korea, and Japan. *Personal Relationships, 6*, 125–150.

Buunk, A. P., & van Driel, B. (1989). *Variant lifestyles and relationships.* Newbury Park, CA: Sage.

Buunk, B. (1981). Jealousy in sexually open marriages. *Alternative Lifestyles, 4*, 357–372.

Buunk, B. (1982a). Anticipated sexual jealousy: Its relationship to self-esteem, dependency, and reciprocity. *Personality and Social Psychology Bulletin, 8*, 310–316.

Buunk, B. (1982b). Strategies of jealousy: Styles of coping with extramarital involvement of the spouse. *Family Relations, 31*, 13–18.

Buunk, B. (1984). Jealousy as related to attributions for the partner's behavior. *Social Psychology Quarterly, 47*, 107–112.

Buunk, B. (1997). Personality, birth order, and attachment styles as related to various types of jealousy. *Personality and Individual Differences, 23*, 997–1006.

Buunk, B. P., Angleleitner, A., Oubaid, V., & Buss, D. M. (1996). Sex differences in jealousy in evolutionary and cultural perspective: Tests from the Netherlands, Germany and the United States. *Psychological Science, 7*, 359–363.

Buunk, B. P., & Bringle, R. G. (1987). Jealousy in love relationships. In D. Perlman & S. Duck (Eds.), *Intimate relationships: Development, dynamics, and deterioriation* (pp. 123–147). Beverly Hills, CA: Sage.

Buunk, B. P., & Dijkstra, P. (2001). Evidence from a homosexual sample for a sex-specific rival-oriented mechanism: Jealousy as a function of a rival's physical attractiveness and dominance. *Personal Relationships, 8,* 391–406.

Buunk, B. P., & Hupka, R. B. (1987). Cross-cultural differences in the elicitation of sexual jealousy. *Journal of Sex Research, 23,* 12–22.

Byers, E. S. (1996). How well does the traditional sexual script explain sexual coercion? Review of a program of research. *Journal of Psychology and Human Sexuality, 8,* 7–25.

Canary, D. J., Spitzberg, B. H., & Semic, B. A. (1998). The experience and expression of anger in interpersonal settings. In P. A. Andersen & L. K. Guerrero (Ed.), *The Handbook of Communication and Emotion* (pp. 189–213). San Diego, CA: Academic Press.

Cann, A., Mangum, J. L., & Wells, M. (2001). Distress in response to relationship infidelity: The roles of gender and attitudes about relationships. *Journal of Sex Research, 38,* 185–190.

Cascardi, M., & Vivian, D. (1995). Context for specific episodes of marital violence: Gender and severity of violence differences. *Journal of Family Violence, 10,* 265–293.

Christensen, H. T. (1973). Attitudes toward marital infidelity: A nine-culture sampling of university student opinion. *Journal of Comparative Family Studies, 4,* 197–214.

Christopher, F. S., & Roosa, M. W. (1991). Factors affecting sexual decisions in premarital relationships of adolescents and young adults. In K. McKinney & S. Sprecher (Eds.), *Sexuality in close relationships* (pp. 111–133). Hillsdale, NJ: Lawrence Erlbaum Associates.

Clanton, G., & Smith, L. G. (1977). *Jealousy.* Englewood Cliffs, NJ: Prentice-Hall.

Clark, R. D., & Hatfield, E. (1989). Gender differences in receptivity to sexual offers. *Journal of Psychology and Human Sexuality, 2,* 39–55.

Conway, L. G., III, & Schaller, M. (2002). On the verifiability of evolutionary psychological theories: An analysis of the psychology of scientific persuasion. *Personality and Social Psychology Review, 6,* 152–166.

Cramer, R. E., Abraham, W. T., Johnson, L. M., & Manning-Ryan, B. (2001–2002). Gender differences in subjective distress to emotional and sexual infidelity: Evolutionary or logical inference explanation? *Current Psychology, 20,* 327–336.

Cupach, W. R., & Metts, S. (1986). Accounts of relational dissolution: A comparison of marital and nonmarital relationships. *Communication Monographs, 53,* 311–334.

Daly, M., Salmon, C., & Wilson, M. (1997). Kinship: The conceptual hole in psychological studies of social cognition and close relationships. In J. A. Simpson and D. T. Kenrick (Eds.), *Evolutionary Social Psychology* (pp. 265–296). Mahwah, NJ: Lawrence Erlbaum Associates.

Daly, M., & Wilson, M. (1988). *Homicide.* Hawthorne, NY: Aldine, DeGruyter.

Daly, M., & Wilson, M. (1996). Evolutionary psychology and marital conflict. In D. M. Buss & N. M. Malamuth (Eds.), *Sex, power, conflict: Evolutionary and feminist perspectives* (pp. 9–28). New York: Oxford University Press.

Daly, M., Wilson, M. I., & Weghorst, S. J. (1982). Male sexual jealousy. *Ethology and Sociobiology, 3,* 11–27.

Darwin, C. (1859). *On the origin of species by means of natural selection, or the preservation of favoured races in the struggle for life.* New York: Appleton.

Darwin, C. (1871). *The descent of man and selection in relation to sex.* London: Murray.

Darwin, C. (1872). *The expression of the emotions in man and animals.* London: Murray.

Delgado, A. R., Prieto, G., & Bond, R. A. (1997). The cultural factor in lay perception of jealousy as a motive for wife battery. *Journal of Applied Social Psychology, 27*(20), 1824–1841.

DeSteno, D. A., & Salovey, P. (1996). Evolutionary origins of sex differences in jealousy: Questioning the fitness of the model. *Psychological Science, 7,* 367–372.

deWeerth, C., & Kalma, A. P. (1993). Female aggression as a response to sexual jealousy: A sex role reversal? *Aggression Behavior, 19,* 265–279.

Dijkstra, P., & Buunk, B. (1998). Jealousy as a function of rival characteristics: An evolutionary perspective. *Personality and Social Psychology Bulletin, 24,* 1158–1166.

Dijkstra, P., & Buunk, B. (2001). Sex differences in the jealousy-evoking nature of a rival's body build. *Evolution and Human Behavior, 22,* 335–341.

Drigotas, S. M., Safstrom, C. A., & Gentilia, T. (1999). An investment model prediction of dating infidelity. *Journal of Personality and Social Psychology, 77,* 509–524.

Dutton, D. G., van Ginkel, C., & Landolt, M. A. (1996). Jealousy, intimate abusiveness, and intrusiveness. *Journal of Family Violence, 11,* 411–423.

Eagly, A. H., & Wood, W. (1999). The origins of sex differences in human behavior: Evolved dispositions versus social roles. *American Psychologist, 54,* 408–423.

Ellis, C., & Weinstein, E. (1986). Jealousy and the social psychology of emotional experience. *Journal of Social and Personal Relationships, 3,* 337–357.

Ellis, L. (1989). *Theories of rape: Inquiries into the causes of sexual aggression.* New York: Hemisphere.

Fink, B., Grammer, K., & Thornhill, R. (2001). Human (Homo sapiens) facial attractiveness in relation to skin texture and color. *Journal of Comparative Psychology, 115,* 92–99.

Fitness, J., & Fletcher, G. J. O. (1993). Love, hate, anger and jealousy in close relationships: A prototype and cognitive appraisal analysis. *Journal of Personality and Social Psychology, 65,* 942–958.

Fleischmann, A. A., Spitzberg, B. H., & Andersen, P. A. (2002). *Tickling the monster: Jealousy induction in relationships.* Unpublished manuscript, available from B. H. Spitzberg, San Diego State University.

Follingstad, D. R., Bradley, R. G., Laughlin, J. E., & Burke, L. (1999). Risk factors and correlates of dating violence: The relevance of examining frequency and severity levels in a college sample. *Violence and Victims, 14*, 365–380.

Francis, J. L. (1977). Toward the management of heterosexual jealousy. *Journal of Marriage and Counseling, 3*, 61–69.

Furnham, A., Lavancy, M., & McClelland, A. (2001). Waist to hip ratio and facial attractiveness: A pilot study. *Personality and Individual Differences, 30*, 491–502.

Gangestad, S. W., & Simpson, J. A. (1990). Toward an evolutionary history of female sociosexual variation. *Journal of Personality, 58*, 69–96.

Geary, D. C., DeSoto, M. C., Hoard, M. K., Sheldon, M. S., & Cooper, M. L. (2001). Estrogens and relationship jealousy. *Human Nature, 12*, 299–320.

Geary, D. C., Rumsey, M., Bow-Thomas, C. C., & Hoard, M. K. (1995). Sexual jealousy as a facultative trait: Evidence from the pattern of sex differences in adults from China and the United States. *Ethology and Sociobiology, 16*, 355–383.

Glass, S. P., & Wright, T. L. (1992). Justifications for extramarital relationships: The association between attitudes, behaviors, and gender. *The Journal of Sex Research, 29*, 361–387.

Glenn, N. D., & Weaver, C. N. (1979). Attitudes toward premarital, extramarital, and homosexual relations in the U.S. in the 1970's. *Journal of Sex Research, 15*, 108–118.

Guerrero, L. K. (1998). Attachment-style differences in the experience and expression of romantic jealousy. *Personal Relationships, 5*, 273–291.

Guerrero, L. K., & Afifi, W. A. (1999). Toward a goal-oriented approach for understanding communicative responses to jealousy. *Western Journal of Communication, 63*, 216–248.

Guerrero, L. K., & Andersen, P. A. (1998a). The dark side of jealousy and envy: Desire, delusion, desperation, and destructive communication. In B. H. S. and W. R. Cupach (Eds.), *The dark side of close relationships* (pp. 33–70). Mahwah, NJ: Lawrence Erlbaum Associates.

Guerrero, L. K., & Andersen, P. A. (1998b). Jealousy experience and expression in romantic relationships. In P. A. Andersen & L. K. Guerrero (Eds.), *Handbook of communication and emotion: Research, theory, applications, and contexts* (pp. 155–188). San Diego, CA: Academic Press.

Guerrero, L. K., Andersen, P. A., Jorgensen, P. F., Spitzberg, B. H., & Eloy, S. V. (1995). Coping with the green-eyed monster: Conceptualizing and measuring communicative responses to romantic jealousy. *Western Journal of Communication, 59*, 270–304.

Guerrero, L. K., & Eloy, S. V. (1992). Relational satisfaction and jealousy across marital types. *Communication Reports, 5*, 23–31.

Guerrero, L. K., Eloy, S. V., Jorgensen, P. F., & Andersen, P. A. (1993). Hers or his? Sex differences in the communication of jealousy in close relationships. In P. Kalbfleisch (Ed.), *Interpersonal communication: evolving interpersonal relationships* (pp. 109–131). Hillsdale, NJ: Lawrence Erlbaum Associates.

Guerrero, L. K., & Reiter, R. L. (1998). Expressing emotion: Sex differences in social skills and communicative responses to anger, sadness, and jealousy. In D. J. Canary & K. Dindia (Eds.), *Sex differences and similarities in communication* (pp. 321–350). Mahwah, NJ: Lawrence Erlbaum Associates.

Guerrero, L. K., & Spitzberg, B. H (2002, February). *The dark side of love: Possessiveness and distrust as predictors of communicative responses to jealousy.* Paper presented at the annual meeting of the Western States Communication Association, Long Beach, CA.

Guerrero, L. K., & Yoshimura, S. M. (1999, May). *General threat and specific emotions as predictors of communicative responses to jealousy.* Paper presented at the International Communication Association, San Francisco, CA.

Grammer, K., & Thornhill, R. (1994). Human (homo sapiens) facial attractiveness and sexual selection: The role of symmetry and averageness. *Journal of Comparative Psychology, 108*, 233–242.

Hamilton, W. D. (1964). The genetical evolution of social behavior (I and II). *Journal of Theoretical Biology, 7*(1–16), 17–52.

Hansen, G. (1985). Dating jealousy among college students. *Sex Roles, 12*, 713–721.

Harris, C. R. (2002). Sexual and romantic jealousy in heterosexual and homosexual adults. *Psychological Science, 13*, 7–12.

Harris, C. R., & Christenfeld, N. (1996a). Gender, jealousy, and reason. *Psychological Science, 7*, 364–366.

Harris, C. R., & Christenfeld, N. (1996b). Jealousy and relational responses to infidelity across gender and culture. *Psychological Science, 7*, 378–379.

Hawkins, R. O. (1990). The relationship between culture, personality, and sexual jealousy in men in heterosexual and homosexual relationships. *Journal of Homosexuality, 19*, 67–84.

Hazan, C., & Shaver, P. (1987). Conceptualizing romantic love as an attachment process. *Journal of Personality and Social Psychology, 52*, 511–524.

Hill, R., & Davis, P. (2000). "Platonic jealousy": A conceptualization and review of the literature on non-romantic pathological jealousy. *British Journal of Medical Psychology, 73*, 505–517.

Hofstede, G. (1980). *Culture's consequences: International differences in work-related values.* Beverly Hills, CA: Sage.

Holtzworth-Munroe, A., & Anglin, K. (1991). The competency of responses given by maritally violent versus nonviolent men to problematic marital situations. *Violence and Victims, 6*, 257–269.

Holtzworth-Munroe, A., Stuart, G. L., & Hutchinson, G. (1997). Violent versus nonviolent husbands: Differences in attachment patterns, dependency, and jealousy. *Journal of Family Psychology, 11,* 314–331.

Hupka, R. B., & Bank, A. L. (1996). Sex differences in jealousy: Evolution or social construction? *Cross-Cultural Research, 30,* 24–59.

Hupka, R. B., Otto, J., Tarabrina, N. V., & Reidl, L. (1993). Cross-cultural comparisons of nouns associated with jealousy and the related emotions of envy, anger and fear. *Cross-Cultural Research, 27,* 181–211.

Hupka, R. B., Buunk, B., Falus, G., Fulgosi, A., Ortega, E., Swain, R., & Tarabrina, N. V. (1985). Romantic jealousy and romantic envy: A seven nation study. *Journal of Cross-Cultural Psychology, 16,* 423–446.

Hupka, R. B., & Ryan, J. M. (1990). The cultural contribution to jealousy: Cross-cultural aggression in sexual jealousy situations. *Behavior Science Research, 24,* 51–71.

Hupka, R. B., Zaleski, Z., Otto, J., Reidl, L., & Tarabrina, N. V. (1996). Anger, envy, fear, and jealousy as felt in the body: A five-nation study. *Cross-Cultural Research, 30,* 243–264.

Jones, W. H., & Burdette, M. P. (1994). Betrayal in relationships. In A. L. Weber & J. H. Harvey (Eds.), *Perspectives on close relationships* (pp. 243–262). Needham Heights, MA: Allyn & Bacon.

Jones, W. H., Moore, D. S., Schratter, A., & Negel, L. A. (2001). Interpersonal transgressions and betrayals. In R. M. Kowalski (Eds.), *Behaving badly: Aversive behaviors in interpersonal relationships* (pp. 233–256). Washington, DC: American Psychological Association.

Kenrick, D. T., Sadalla, E. K., Groth, G., & Trost, M. R. (1990). Evolution, traits, and the stages of human courtship: Qualifying the parental investment model. *Journal of Personality, 58,* 97–116.

Kenrick, D. T., & Trost, M. R. (1997). Evolutionary approaches to relationships. In S. Duck (Ed.), *Handbook of personal relationships* (2nd ed., pp. 151–177). Chichester, England: Wiley.

Ketelaar, T., & Ellis, B. J. (2000). Are evolutionary explanations unfalsifiable? Evolutionary psychology and the Lakatosian philosophy of science. *Psychological Inquiry, 11,* 1–21.

Knobloch, L. K., Solomon, D. H., & Cruz, M. G. (2001). The role of relationship development and attachment in the experience of romantic jealousy. *Personal Relationships, 8,* 205–224.

Knox, D., Zusman, M. E., Mabon, L., & Shriver, L. (1999). Jealousy in college student relationships. *College Student Journal, 33,* 328–329.

Laumann, E. O., Gagnon, J. H., Michael, R. T., & Michaels, S. (1994). *The social organization of sexuality: Sexual practices in the United States.* Chicago: University of Chicago Press.

Lazarus, R. S. (1991). *Emotion and adaptation.* New York: Oxford University Press.

Lazarus, R. S., & Folkman, S. (1984). *Stress, appraisal, and coping.* New York: Springer.

Lazarus, R. S., & Lazarus, B. N. (1994). *Passion and reason: Making sense of our emotions.* New York: Oxford University Press.

Leak, G. K., Gardner, L. E., & Parsons, C. J. (1998). Jealousy and romantic attachment: A replication and extension. *Representative Research in Social Psychology, 22,* 21–27.

Lee, J. A. (1973). *The colors of love: An exploration of the ways of loving.* Don Mills, Ontario: New Press.

Li, N. P., Bailey, J. M., Kenrick, D. T., & Linsenmeier, J. A. W. (2002). The necessities and luxuries of mate preferences: Testing the tradeoffs. *Journal of Personality and Social Psychology, 82,* 947–955.

Luci, P., Foss, M. A., & Galloway, J. (1993). Sexual jealousy in young women and men: Aggressive responsiveness to partner and rival. *Aggressive Behavior, 19,* 401–420.

Luci, P., Foss, M. A., & Baenninger, M. (1996). Double standards for sexual jealousy: Manipulative morality or a reflection of evolved sex differences? *Human Nature, 7,* 291–321.

Luci, P., & Galloway, J. (1994). Sexual jealousy: Gender differences in response to partner and rival. *Aggressive Behavior, 20,* 203–211.

Malamuth, N. M. (1996). The confluence model of sexual aggression: Feminist and evolutionary perspectives. In D. M. Buss & N. M. Malamuth (Eds.), *Sex, power, conflict: Evolutionary and feminist perspectives* (pp. 269–295). New York: Oxford University Press.

Mathes, E. W. (1992). *Jealousy: The psychological data.* Lanham, MD: University Press of America.

Mathes, E. W., King, C. A., Miller, J. K., & Reed, R. M. (2002). An evolutionary perspective on the interaction of age and sex differences in short-term sexual strategies. *Psychological Reports, 90,* 949–956.

Mathes, E. W., & Verstraete, C. (1993). Jealous aggression: Who is the target, the beloved or the rival? *Psychological Reports, 72,* 1071–1074.

McIntosh, E. G., & Mathews, C. O. (1992). Use of direct coping resources in dealing with jealousy. *Psychological Reports, 70,* 1037–1038.

McIntosh, E. G., & Tangri, S. S. (1989). Relationship between jealous feelings and behaviors. *Perceptual and Motor Skills, 69,* 765–766.

McIntosh, E. G., & Tate, D. T. (1990). Correlates of jealous behaviors. *Psychological Reports, 66,* 601–602.

Melamed, T. (1991). Individual differences in romantic jealousy: The moderating effect of relationship characteristics. *European Journal of Social Psychology, 21,* 455–461.

Metts, S. (1994). Relational transgressions. In W. R. Cupach and B. H. Spitzberg (Eds.), *The dark side of interpersonal communication* (pp. 217–239). Hillsdale, NJ: Lawrence Erlbaum Associates.

Milardo, R. M. (1998). Gender asymmetry in common couple violence. *Personal Relationships, 5,* 423–438.

Mongeau, P. A., Hale, J. L., & Alles, M. (1994). An experimental investigation of accounts and attributions following sexual infidelity. *Communication Monographs, 61,* 301–312.

Mongeau, P. A., & Schulz, B. E. (1997). What he doesn't know won't hurt him (or me): Verbal responses and attributions following sexual infidelity. *Communication Reports, 10,* 143–152.

Morenz, B., & Lane, R. L. (1996). Morbid jealousy and criminal report. In L. B. Schlesinger (Ed.), *Explorations in criminal psychopathology: Clinical syndromes with forensic implications* (pp. 78–97). Springfield, IL: Thomas.

Mullen, P. E. (1991). Jealousy: The pathology of passion. *British Journal of Psychiatry, 158,* 593–601.

Mullen, P. E. (1996). Jealousy and the emergence of violent and intimidating behaviours. *Criminal Behaviour and Mental Health, 6,* 199–205.

Mullen, P. E., & Martin, J. L. (1994). Jealousy: A community study. *British Journal of Psychiarty, 164,* 35–43.

Nadler, A., & Dotan, I. (1992). Commitment and rival attractiveness: Their effects on male and female reactions to jealousy-arousing situations. *Sex Roles, 26,* 293–310.

Nannini, D. K., & Meyers, L. S. (2000). Jealousy in sexual and emotional infidelity: An alternative to the evolutionary explanation. *The Journal of Sex Research, 37,* 117–122.

Oda, R. (2001). Sexually dimorphic mate preference in Japan. *Human Nature, 12,* 191–206.

Parker, B. L., & Drummond-Reeves, S. J. (1993). The death of a dyad: Relational autopsy, analysis, and aftermath. *Journal of Divorce and Remarriage, 21,* 95–119.

Parker, R. G. (1994, November). *An examination of the influence of situational determinants upon strategies for coping with romantic jealousy.* Paper presented at the annual meeting of the Speech Communication Association, New Orleans, LA.

Parker, R. G. (1997). The influence of sexual infidelity, verbal intimacy, and gender upon primary appraisal processes in romantic jealousy. *Women's Studies in Communication, 20,* 1–25.

Parrott, W. G., & Smith, R. H. (1993). Distinguishing the experiences of envy and jealousy. *Journal of Personality and Social Psychology, 64,* 906–920.

Patterson, J., & Kim, P. (1991). *The day America told the truth.* New York: Prentice-Hall.

Paul, L., Foss, M. A., & Galloway, J. (1993). Sexual jealousy in young women and men: Aggressive responsiveness to partner and rival. *Aggressive Behavior, 19,* 401–420.

Peretti, P. O., & Pudowski, B. C. (1997). Influence of jealousy on male and female college daters. *Social Behavior and Personality, 25,* 155–160.

Perrett, D. I., Burt, D. M., Penton-Voak, I. S., Lee, K. J., Rowland, D. A., & Edwards, R. (1999). Symmetry and human facial attractiveness. *Evolution and Human Behavior, 20,* 295–307.

Pfeiffer, S. M., & Wong, P. T. P. (1989). Multidimensional jealousy. *Journal of Social and Personal Relationships, 6,* 181–196.

Pietrzak, R. H., Laird, J. D., Stevens, D. A., & Thompson, N. S. (2002). Sex differences in human jealousy: A coordinated study of forced-choice, continuous rating scale, and physiological responses of the same subjects. *Evolution and Human Behavior, 23,* 83–94.

Pines, A. (1992). *Romantic jealousy: Understanding and conquering the shadow of love.* New York: St. Martin's Press.

Pines, A., & Aronson, E. (1983). Antecedents, correlates, and consequences, of sexual jealousy. *Journal of Personality, 51,* 108–136.

Popper, K. (1980). Science: Conjectures and refutations. In E. D. Klemke, R. Hollinger, & A. D. Kline (Eds.), *Introductory readings in the philosophy of science* (pp. 19–34). Buffalo, NY: Prometheus.

Pratto, F. (1996). Sexual politics: The gender gap in the bedroom, the cupboard, and the cabinet. In D. M. Buss & N. M. Malamuth (Eds.), *Sex, power, conflict: Evolutionary and feminist perspectives* (pp. 179–230). New York: Oxford University Press.

Rathus, S. A., Nevid, J. S., & Fisher-Rathus, L. (1993). *Human sexuality in a world of diversity.* Boston: Allyn & Bacon.

Renzetti, C. M. (1988). Violence in lesbian relationships: A preliminary analysis of causal factors. *Journal of Interpersonal Violence, 3,* 381–399.

Rhodes, G., Proffitt, F., Grady, J. M., & Sumich, A. (1998). Facial symmetry and the perception of beauty. *Psychonomic Bulletin and Review, 5,* 659–669.

Riggs, D. S. (1993). Relationship problems and dating aggression: A potential treatment target. *Journal of Interpersonal Violence, 8,* 18–35.

Roscoe, B., & Benaske, N. (1985). Courtship violence experienced by abused wives: Similarities in patterns of abuse. *Family Relations, 34,* 419–424.

Roscoe, B., & Callahan, J. E. (1985). Adolescents' self-report of violence in families and dating relations. *Adolescence, 20,* 545–553.

Roscoe, B., Cavanaugh, L. E., & Kennedy, D. R. (1988). Dating infidelity: Behaviors, reasons, and consequences. *Adolescence, 89,* 36–43.

Roscoe, B., & Kelsey, T. (1986). Dating violence among high school students. *Psychology: A Quarterly Journal of Human Behavior, 23,* 53–59.

Ross, L. (1977). The intuitive psychologist and his shortcomings. In L. Berkowitz (Ed.), *Advances in Experimental Social Psychology* (Vol. 10, pp. 173–220). New York: Academic Press.

Russell, R. J. H., & Wells, P. A. (2000). Predicting marital violence from the Marriage and Relationship Questionnaire: Using LISREL to solve an incomplete data problem. *Personality and Individual Differences, 29,* 429–440.

Rustemeyer, R., & Wilbert, C. (2001). Jealousy within the perspective of self-evaluation maintenance theory. *Psychological Reports, 88,* 799–804.

Ryan, K. M. (1995). Do courtship-violent men have characteristics associated with a "battering personality"? *Journal of Family Violence, 10,* 99–120.

Ryan, K. M. (1998). The relationship between courtship violence and sexual aggression in college students. *Journal of Family Violence, 13*, 377–394.

Safron, C. (1979). Troubles that pull couples apart: A Redbook report. *Redbook, 83*, 138–141.

Salovey, P., & Rodin, J. (1986). Differentiation of social-comparison jealousy and romantic jealousy. *Journal of Personality and Social Psychology, 50*, 1100–1112.

Salovey, P., & Rodin, J. (1989). Envy and jealousy in close relationships. In C. Hendrick (Ed.), *Close relationships* (pp. 221–246). Newbury Park, CA: Sage.

Scheib, J. E. (2001). Context-specific mate choice criteria: Women's trade-offs in the contexts of long-term and extra-pair mateships. *Personal Relationships, 8*, 371–390.

Schmitt, D. P., & Buss, D. M. (2001). Human mate poaching: Tactics and temptations for infiltrating existing mateships. *Journal of Personality and Social Psychology, 80*, 894–917.

Schmitt, D. P., Shackelford, T. K., Duntley, J., Tooke, W., & Buss, D. M. (2001). The desire for sexual variety as a key to understanding basic human mating strategies. *Personal Relationships, 8*, 425–456.

Shackelford, T. K., & Buss, D. M. (1997a) Cues to infidelity. *Personality and Social Psychology Bulletin, 23*, 1034–1045.

Shackelford, T. K., & Buss, D. M. (1997b). Anticipation of marital dissolution as a consequence of spousal infidelity. *Journal of Social and Personal Relationships, 14*, 793–808.

Sharpsteen, D. J., & Kirkpatrick, L. A. (1997). Romantic jealousy and adult romantic attachment. *Journal of Personality and Social Psychology, 72*, 627–640.

Sheets, V. L., & Wolfe, M. D. (2001). Sexual jealousy in heterosexuals, lesbians, and gays. *Sex Roles, 44*, 255–276.

Sheets, V. L., Fredendall, L. L., & Claypool, H. M. (1997). Jealousy evocation, partner reassurance, and relationship stability: An exploration of the potential benefits of jealousy. *Evolution and Human Behavior, 18*, 387–402.

Sheppard, V. J., Nelson, E. S., & Andreoli-Mathie, V. (1995). Dating relationships and infidelity: Attitudes and behaviors. *Journal of Sex and Marital Therapy, 21*, 202–212.

Siegert, J. R., & Stamp, G. H. (1994). "Our first big fight" as a milestone in the development of close relationships. *Communication Monographs, 61*, 349–351.

Simonelli, C. J., & Ingram, K. M. (1998). Psychological distress among men experiencing physical and emotional abuse in heterosexual dating relationships. *Journal of Interpersonal Violence, 13*, 667–681.

Simpson, J. A., & Kenrick, D. T. (Eds.). (1997). *Evolutionary social psychology*. Mahwah, NJ: Lawrence Erlbaum Associates.

Simpson, J. A., & Gangestad, S. W. (2001). Evolution and relationships: A call for integration. *Personal Relationships, 8*, 341–356.

Singh, D., & Young, R. K. (1995). Body weight, waist-to-hip ratio, breasts, and hips: Role in judgments of female attractiveness and desirability for relationships. *Ethology and Sociobiology, 16*, 483–507.

Smuts, B. (1996). Male aggression against women: An evolutionary perspective. In D. M. Buss & N. M. Malamuth (Eds.), *Sex, power, conflict: Evolutionary and feminist perspectives* (pp. 231–368). New York: Oxford University Press.

Spitzberg, B. H. (1997). Intimate violence. In W. R. Cupach & D. J. Canary (Eds.), *Competence in interpersonal conflict* (pp. 174–201). New York: McGraw-Hill.

Spitzberg, B. H. (2001). The status of attribution theory *qua* theory in personal relationships. In V. Manusov & J. H. Harvey (Eds.), *Attribution, communication behavior, and close relationships* (pp. 353–371). Cambridge, England: Cambridge University Press.

Sprowl, S. P., & White, C. L. (1989). Gender differences in the social construction of romantic jealousy: An exploratory study. In C. M. Lont & S. A. Friedley (Eds.), *Beyond boundaries: Sex and gender diversity in communication* (pp. 157–173). Fairfax, VA: George Mason University.

Staske, S. A. (1999). Creating relational ties in talk: The collaborative construction of relational jealousy. *Symbolic Interaction, 22*, 213–246.

Stets, J. E., & PirogGood, M. A. (1987). Violence in dating relationships. *Social Psychology Quarterly, 50*, 237–246.

Sugarman, D. B., & Hotaling, G. T. (1989). Dating violence: Prevalence, context, and risk markers. In M. A. Pirog-Good & J. E. Stets (Eds.), *Violence in dating relationships: Emerging social issues* (pp. 3–32). New York: Praeger.

Symons, D. (1979). *The evolution of human sexuality*. New York: Oxford University Press.

Taylor, S. E., & Brown, J. D. (1988). Illusion and well-being: A social psychological perspective on mental health. *Psychological Bulletin, 103*, 193–210.

Thornton, A., & Young-DeMarco, L. (2001). Four decades of trends in attitudes toward family issues in the United States: The 1960s through the 1990s. *Journal of Marriage and Family, 63*, 1009–1037.

Tooke, W., & Camire, L. (1991). Patterns of deception in intersexual and intrasexual mating strategies. *Ethology and Sociobiology, 12*, 345–364.

Treas, J., & Giesen, D. (2000). Sexual infidelity among married and cohabiting Americans. *Journal of Marriage and the Family, 62*, 48–60.

Trivers, R. L. (1972). Parental investment and sexual selection. In B. Campbell (Ed.), *Sexual selection and the descent of man: 1871–1971* (pp. 136–179). Chicago, IL: Aldine.

Trost, M. R., & Alberts, J. K. (1998). An evolutionary view on understanding sex effects in communicating attraction. In D. J. Canary and K. Dindia (Eds.), *Sex differences and similarities in communication* (pp. 233–255). Mahwah, NJ: Lawrence Erlbaum Associates.

Trost, M. R., & Andersen, P. A. (1999, May). *Interpersonal communication as an adaptive function: The selection of human communication abilities through evolutionary processes.* Paper presented at the annual meeting of the International Communication Association, San Francisco, CA.

Trost, M. R., Brown, S., & Morrison, M. (1994, November). *Jealousy as an adaptive communication strategy.* Paper presented at the annual meeting of the Speech Communication Assocation, New Orleans, LA.

Trost, M. R., & Yoshimura, S. M. (1999, February). *The emotion profiles for expressing jealousy.* Paper presented at the annual meeting of the Western States Communication Association, Vancouver, British Columbia, Canada.

Vaselle-Augenstein, R., & Ehrlich, A. (1992). Male batterers: Evidence for psychopathology. In E. C. Viano (Ed.), *Intimate violence: Interdisciplinary perspectives* (pp. 139–154). Washington, DC: Hemisphere.

Vecchio, R. P. (2000). Negative emotion in the workplace: Employee jealousy and envy. *International Journal of Stress Management, 7,* 161–179.

Weghorst, S. J. (1980, June). *Behavioral correlates of self-reported jealousy in a field experiment.* Paper presented at a meeting of the Animal Behavior Society, Ft. Collins, CO.

White, G. L. (1977). *Jealousy and attitudes toward love.* Unpublished manuscript.

White, G. L. (1980). Inducing jealousy: A power perspective. *Personality and Social Psychology Bulletin, 6,* 222–227.

White, G. L. (1981a). A model of romantic jealousy. *Motivation and Emotion, 5,* 295–310.

White, G. L. (1981b). Jealousy and partner's perceived motives for attraction to a rival. *Social Psychology Quarterly, 44,* 24–30.

White, G. L. (1985). *Gender, power, and romantic jealousy.* Unpublished manuscript.

White, G. L., & Mullen, P. E. (1989). *Jealousy: Theory, research, and clinical strategies.* New York: Guilford.

Whitehurst, R. N. (1977). Jealousy and American values. In G. Clanton & L. G. Smith (Eds.), *Jealousy* (pp. 136–239). Englewood Cliffs, NJ: Prentice-Hall.

Wiederman, M. W. (1997). Extramarital sex: Prevalence and correlates in a national survey. *Journal of Sex Research, 34,* 167–174.

Wiederman, M. W., & Hurd, C. (1999). Extradyadic involvement during dating. *Journal of Social and Personal Relationships, 16,* 265–274.

Wiederman, M. W., & Kendall, E. (1999). Evolution, sex, and jealousy: Investigation with a sample from Sweden. *Evolution and Human Behavior, 20,* 121–128.

Williams, G. C. (1966). *Adaptation and natural selection.* Princeton, NJ: Princeton University Press

Wilson, M., Jocic, V., & Daly, M. (2001). Extracting implicit theories about the risk of coercive control in romantic relationships. *Personal Relationships, 8,* 457–477.

Xiaojun, W. (2002). Relationship between jealousy and personality. *Acta Psychologica Sinica, 34,* 175–182.

Yoshimura, S. M. (2002). *An evolutionary approach to communicating vengeance in romantic relationships.* Unpublished doctoral dissertation, Arizona State University.

Zammuner, V. L., & Fischer, A. H. (1995). The social regulation of emotions in jealousy situations: A comparison between Italy and the Netherlands. *Journal of Cross Cultural Psychology, 26,* 189–208.

IV

Sexuality in Special Types of Couples and Contexts

14

Sexuality in the Relationships of Lesbians and Gay Men

Letitia Anne Peplau
Adam Fingerhut
Kristin P. Beals
University of California, Los Angeles

This chapter presents research on sexuality in the intimate relationships of lesbians and gay men. It begins with a brief historical perspective on gay and lesbian couples and a consideration of the climate of sexual prejudice faced by contemporary lesbians and gay men. Separate sections review scientific research on sexual frequency, sexual satisfaction, gender-based sexual roles, and sexual exclusivity, first for gay male couples and then for lesbian couples. Attention is also given to the impact of HIV on gay couples and to a controversy about reports of low sexual frequency in lesbian couples. As relevant, comparisons among gay, lesbian, and heterosexual couples are provided. Directions for future research are noted throughout. A concluding section summarizes key findings, highlights limitations in existing research, and calls attention to topics about sexuality in gay and lesbian relationships that merit further investigation.

INTRODUCTION

This chapter investigates sexuality in the committed relationships of lesbians and gay men, a topic that has received relatively little attention. Relationship researchers have typically focused on such nonsexual aspects of gay and lesbian couples as love, commitment, power and the division of labor, perhaps in reaction to public stereotypes of homosexuals as hypersexual. Sex researchers have studied specific forms of gay and lesbian sexual activity and, more recently, the sexual transmission of HIV, but have largely ignored the relationship context. In contrast, this chapter focuses explicitly on sexuality in lesbian and gay couples.

An important starting point is to recognize that most lesbians and gay men want to have a committed, intimate relationship. In a recent national survey (Kaiser Foundation, 2001), 74% of lesbians and gay men said that if they could legally marry someone of the same sex, they would like to do so some day. Most (68%) lesbians and gay men rated "legally-sanctioned gay and lesbian marriages" as very important to them. We do not know the exact percentages of lesbians and gay men who are currently in committed relationships. In an early study conducted in San Francisco, a majority of respondents were currently in a "relatively stable relationship": 51% of White gay men, 58% of Black gay men, 72% of White lesbians, and 70% of Black lesbians (Bell & Weinberg, 1978). In a recent large-scale survey of lesbians, 65% reported currently being in a same-sex primary relationship (Morris, Waldo, & Rothblum, 2001). In contrast, a recent survey of more than 2,600 Black lesbians and gay men found that only 41% of women and 20% of men reported being "in a committed relationship" (Battle, Cohen, Warren, Fergerson, & Audam, 2002). The reasons for differences among existing studies in the percentages of lesbians and gay men who report being in a committed relationships are unknown, but may reflect differences in characteristics of the samples (e.g., age, ethnicity, length of relationship), the specific questions asked, or the historical time period.

Information about the percentage of gay and lesbian adults who live together with a same-sex partner has recently become available from the 2000 U.S. Census and other national surveys (e.g., Black, Gates, Sanders, & Taylor, 2000; Human Rights Campaign, 2001; Kaiser Foundation, 2001). The best estimate is that about 25 to 30% of gay men and lesbians live with a same-sex partner. Statistics on cohabitation do not include lesbians and gay men in committed relationships who maintain separate residences. Taken together, research indicates that personal relationships constitute a context for sexual expression for many lesbians and gay men.

This chapter reviews the available research on sexuality in same-sex relationships. We begin by briefly considering historical trends in same-sex relationships and the contemporary social climate of sexual prejudice and discrimination that today's gay and lesbian couples confront. Then we review empirical studies, first for gay men and then for lesbian women. In a concluding section, we consider useful directions for future research.

THE SOCIAL CONTEXT

A Historical Perspective on Gay and Lesbian Couples

Same-sex romantic and erotic attractions have been widely documented throughout history and across differing cultures (e.g., Duberman, Vicinus, & Chauncey, 1989). Social historians have provided fascinating chronicles of the varied forms of same-sex love and sexuality that existed in 18th and 19th century America (e.g., Faderman, 1981; Katz, 2001). Noticeably absent from historical accounts, however, is the "homosexual couple" as we know it today—an intimate partnership between two self-identified gay or lesbian partners. Two historical changes were prerequisites for modern gay and lesbian couples: the decline of marriage as a cornerstone of adult life and the emergence of the homosexual as a distinct type of person.

In most times and places, heterosexual marriage was an essential component of adult status in the community with few exceptions (e.g., nuns and priests). Same-sex relations, therefore, occurred either prior to or in conjunction with marriage. As Murray (2000) recently documented, same-sex relations tended to take one of three forms: age-structured, gender-based, or egalitarian. Many cultures have had age-structured forms of same-sex sexuality. In Melanesia, for example, male youths engaged in socially scripted sexual relations with older males. This same-sex sexual behavior was normative, considered essential for masculine development, and had no implications for the youths' social identity. Once boys matured into men, they were expected to marry a woman (Herdt, 1981). Other cultures have used gender categories to structure same-sex relations. In Latin America, the "passive" (feminine) male participating in anal sex is considered homosexual. The "active" (masculine) male is not viewed as distinctive or atypical (Carrier, 1995). Murray called the third form of homosexuality "egalitarian" because it occurs among peers who are relatively equal in status. Kendall (1999, p. 169) described a pattern in southern Africa in which "long-term loving, intimate, and erotic relationships between women were normative." The women in these relationships were typically married but also had a special same-sex friendship that was publicly acknowledged and honored. Their social identity was that of a married woman, not of "lesbian."

The growth of industrial capitalism and "labor for wages allowed more and more men, and some women, to detach themselves from a family-based economy and strike out on their own" (D'Emilio & Freedman, 1988, p. 227). In 19th century America, for example, it became possible for employed women or those with independent means to form long-term same-sex partnerships known in New England as "Boston marriages" (Faderman, 1981). Close same-sex relationships were particularly common among academic women, as seen in the lifelong relationship of Jeannette Mark and Mary Woolley, who met in 1895 at Wellesley College. Woolley eventually became president of Mt. Holyoke College. At that time, women in romantic same-sex relationships expressed their passionate love for each other openly. "Ah, how I love you, " President Grover Cleveland's sister, Rose, wrote to her friend Evangeline in 1890. "All my whole being leans out to you. . . . I dare not think of your arms" (cited in Goode, 1999, p. 33). Given prevailing beliefs about women's sexuality, these romantic relationships were not viewed as sexual or socially deviant. "It is probable that many romantic friends, while totally open in expressing and demonstrating emotional and spiritual love, repressed any sexual inclinations . . . since . . . women were taught from childhood that only men or bad women were sexually aggressive" (Faderman, 1981, p. 80).

A second historical change was the emergence, in the years before World War I, of the homosexual person as a new personal identity based on the individual's erotic and romantic attractions (Katz, 1995). At the close of the 19th century, early sexologists, psychoanalysts, and physicians began to distinguish between heterosexuals and "sexual inverts" as types of people. At the same time, "some individuals began to interpret their [own] desires as a characteristic that distinguished them from the majority, . . . elaborated an underground sexual subculture, . . . [and created] a social milieu that nurtured their emergent sense of identity" (D'Emilio & Freedman, 1988, p. 227). Migration to urban centers, experiences serving in the military, and many other events contributed to the development of a shared sense of group identity based on sexual orientation—a "gay consciousness." Over time, gay and lesbian communities have grown larger and developed distinctive businesses, organizations, social services, and activities. During the 20th century, men and women who identified as gay and lesbian forged intimate relationships as alternatives to heterosexual marriage. Gradually, gay and lesbian couples have became a more visible part of American society.

Sexual Prejudice and Discrimination

Although public attitudes toward homosexuality are changing, the sexual relationships of lesbians and gay men in the United States continue to develop within a social climate of sexual prejudice (Herek, 2000). Representative national surveys conducted during the past 30 years show that Americans' attitudes about homosexuality have become more tolerant (see review by Loftus, 2001). Currently, a strong majority of Americans (often 75% or more) approves of laws to protect the civil rights of lesbians and gay men in such areas as employment and housing. Further, 76% of Americans "completely agree" with the statement,"Society should not put any restrictions on sex between consenting adults in the privacy of their own home" (Kaiser Foundation, 2001). However, public attitudes about the morality of same-sex sexuality are much more negative. The General Social Survey, a biannual national probability sample of U.S. adults, asked respondents, "What about sexual relations between two adults of the same sex—do you think it is always wrong, almost always wrong, wrong only sometimes, or not wrong at all?" In 1998, 56% of respondents chose "always wrong" and only 31% chose "not wrong at all" (Loftus, 2001). In other recent national surveys (reviewed by Loftus, 2001), about half of Americans agreed that "homosexual behavior is morally wrong" and indicated that "allowing gays and lesbians to legally marry would undermine the traditional American family."

The lives of lesbians and gay men are colored by these negative social attitudes (Meyer & Dean, 1998). In a telephone survey of 405 gay, lesbian, and bisexual adults from 15 major U.S. cities, 74% of respondents reported that they had experienced some form of prejudice or discrimination because of their sexual orientation, and 32% had been the target of violence against themselves or their property (Kaiser Foundation, 2001). For some gay men and lesbians, simply being seen together as a couple can lead to insults or physical violence. The brutal beating of actor Trev Broudy, 33, is one example (Musbach, 2002). Shortly after midnight one evening in 2002, Trev embraced and said goodbye to a male friend on a quiet street in West Hollywood, California. Moments later, three men who had witnessed the embrace jumped out of their car, armed with a baseball bat and metal pipe, and savagely attacked Trev, sending him to the critical care unit of a local hospital. Fortunately, most lesbians and gay men are not attacked. Yet they are vulnerable to such dangers. This may be why most lesbians (73%) in one study (Loulan, 1987) reported that they do not hold hands with a partner in public. A climate of fear must surely affect the intimate relationships of lesbians and gay men, although research on this important topic is currently lacking.

STUDYING SEXUALITY IN GAY AND LESBIAN RELATIONSHIPS

Before reviewing research findings about sexuality in the relationships of lesbians and gay men, a few words are in order about the available databases. Many studies that examined gay and lesbian sexuality focused on specific sexual behaviors rather than on relationships (e.g., Laumann, Gagnon, Michael, & Michaels, 1994). Current conclusions about sexuality in the committed relationships of lesbians and gay men are based on a few major investigations. These are supplemented by smaller and more focused studies. None of the studies is representative, and most samples are disproportionately young, White, urban, and relatively well educated. Further, most studies were published 10 or 20 years ago. The key studies used in this review are described (in alphabetical order by first author):

- Bell and Weinberg (1978) studied both gay men (575 Whites and 111 Blacks) and lesbians (229 Whites and 64 Blacks). Participants were recruited from bars, personal contacts, gay organizations, gay baths, and advertisements in the San Francisco Bay area. This project included a smaller subset of men and women in couple relationships.
- Blumstein and Schwartz (1983) studied both partners from 957 gay male, 772 lesbian, 653 heterosexual cohabiting, and 3,656 married couples recruited in diverse ways including newspaper and media stories in Seattle, San Francisco, New York, and elsewhere. This project is known as the "American Couples Study."
- Bryant and Demian (1994) studied 706 lesbians and 560 gay men in couple relationships. Participants were recruited nationwide by advertisements in the gay press and also through gay churches and organizations.

- Harry (1984) collected questionnaire responses from 1,556 gay men about their relationship experiences. Men were recruited through gay organizations, publications, and community locations in Chicago. (Note: In his 1984 book, Harry also reported secondary analyses of data collected by Bell and Weinberg, 1978.)
- Jay and Young (1979) reported survey responses from 250 lesbians and 419 gay men. Among this sample, 80% of the lesbians and 49% of the gay men were part of a couple.
- Kurdek (1991) studied both partners in 77 gay male, 58 lesbian, 36 heterosexual cohabiting, and 49 married couples. Participants were recruited by ads and personal contacts, largely from the Midwest.
- Lever (1995) studied 2,525 lesbian women who responded to a survey published in the *Advocate*, a national gay and lesbian publication. Among this sample, 68% of women were in a primary relationship.
- McWhirter and Mattison (1984) studied 156 gay male couples from the San Diego area who were recruited through friendship networks and personal contacts.
- Peplau, Cochran, Rook, and Padesky (1978) studied 127 lesbians recruited in Los Angeles. In this sample, 61% of women were in an ongoing romantic/sexual relationship with a woman.

In the following sections, we review and discuss research on sexuality in the relationships of gay men and lesbians. Our review is presented separately for men and then for women. There are two main reasons for this approach. First, researchers have asked somewhat different research questions about sexuality in gay and lesbian couples. Second, there is growing evidence that human sexuality takes somewhat different forms in men and women (Peplau, 2003). Analyses that consider men and women together run the risk of taking men's experiences as the norm and missing important aspects of women's sexuality (Peplau & Garnets, 2000). After presenting findings for gay men and lesbians, we discuss comparisons among gay, lesbian, and heterosexual couples.

SEXUALITY IN THE RELATIONSHIPS OF GAY MEN

Our knowledge of sexuality in gay men's relationships is necessarily limited to the topics that researchers have investigated. In this section, we review studies of sexual frequency, sexual satisfaction, gender-based sexual roles, sexual exclusivity, and the impact of HIV on gay men's relationships.

Sexual Frequency

Researchers studying the sexuality of gay couples have often charted the frequency of sexual contact between male partners. (For a comprehensive list of references on gay male relationships from 1958–1992, see Deenen, Gijs, and van Naerssen, 1994a.) In an early study, Jay and Young (1979) asked participants how often they had sex with their current "lover." There was considerable variation in sexual frequency: 2% of men reported having sex more than once per day, 9% once per day, 38% several times per week, 40% once or twice per week, and 11% less than once per week. The median frequency was once or twice a week.

In a more recent study, Deenen, Gijs, and van Naerssen (1994b) also reported variability in couples' sexual frequency. They used ads in newspapers and gay publications to recruit 320 Dutch men currently in a gay relationship. Participants ranged in age from 20 to 77, and relationship length varied from 10 months to 37 years. In their sample, 2% of the couples had sex 6 or more times per week, 25% three to five times per week, 43% one to two times per week, and 17% one to three times per month. The remaining 13% of couples had sex with one another less than one to three times per month. Again, the modal couple in this sample had sex once or twice a week. Diverse sexual frequency also characterized a sample of 325 Black gay men studied by Peplau, Cochran, and Mays (1997). Asked how often they had sex with their current partner during the past month, 50% of men said one to three times a week, 10% had sex more often, and 41% had sex less often. Because none of these samples is representative of gay men in the population, findings do not provide general base rates for sexual activity among gay male couples. However, they do demonstrate that sexual frequency differs considerably from one couple to another.

Data consistently demonstrate that, on average, the longer a gay male couple is together, the less frequently they engage in sexual activity with each other. Blumstein and Schwartz (1983) found a steady decline in frequency associated with relationship length. Of the couples who had been together 2 years or less, 67% had sex three or more times per week. This contrasted with 32% of the couples who had been together between 2 to 10 years, and only 11% of the couples together more than 10 years. In this sample, increased age also had a significant independent association with lower sexual frequency, although the effect of age was smaller than the effect for duration of the relationship. Two other studies (Bryant & Demian, 1994; McWhirter & Mattison, 1984) reported a similar temporal pattern: the most sexually active gay couples were those who had been together 1 year or less.

Sexual Satisfaction and Its Correlates

Another topic receiving much attention in research about sexuality in gay male couples is sexual satisfaction and its correlates. McWhirter and Mattison (1984) found that the vast majority of gay couples in their sample were sexually satisfied. Asked to "rate the current quality" of their sexual relationship with their partner, 83% of men said they were "satisfied" and an additional 7% reported being "very satisfied." In a study of younger gay men in relationships (median length of 15 months), the mean rating of sexual satisfaction was 5.8 on a 7-point scale (Peplau & Cochran, 1981). A study of Black gay men also found high ratings of sexual satisfaction, with a mean score of 5.5 on a 7-point scale (Peplau et al., 1997).

It will come as no surprise that sexual satisfaction and sexual frequency are correlated. Data from the American Couples sample clearly demonstrate this pattern: 85% of gay men who had sex three or more times per week were sexually satisfied, as compared with 69% for men having sex between one and three times per week, 45% for men having sex between once a week and once a month, and 26% for those having sex less than once per month. The correlation between sexual frequency and sexual satisfaction for gay men was $r = .50$ (controlling for age and duration of relationship). Similarly, Deenen et al. (1994b) also found a significant association between sexual frequency and satisfaction ($B = .57$). Of course, these associations tell us nothing about the direction of causality. It seems likely that frequent sex can improve general feelings of sexual satisfaction and also that sexual enjoyment can increase the frequency of sexual encounters.

Sexual satisfaction is also associated with global measures of relationship satisfaction among gay men. Deenen et al. (1994b) showed that sexual satisfaction and relationship satisfaction were significantly correlated ($r = .35, p < .001$). Similarly, Bryant and Demian (1994) reported that a high level of "quality of sexual interaction" was significantly correlated with relationship quality ($r = .26, p < .001$). In one of the few studies of Black gay men (Peplau et al., 1997), overall relationship satisfaction was also significantly correlated with sexual satisfaction ($r = .44, p < .001$) and with sexual frequency ($r = .19, p < .001$). A study of young, White gay men

(Peplau & Cochran, 1981) also found an association between sexual satisfaction and the importance men placed on "dyadic attachment," a measure assessing the importance of shared activities, sexual exclusivity, and knowing the relationship will endure into the future. Higher scores on dyadic attachment were correlated with greater sexual satisfaction ($r = .25$, $p < .05$).

One of the most detailed analyses of sexuality in couples was conducted by Kurdek (1991). In addition to assessing sexual satisfaction, he also assessed three other attitudinal components of sexuality. These were the importance of fidelity, the importance of trying new sexual techniques and activities, and beliefs about sexual perfection (e.g., "I get upset if I think I have not completely satisfied my partner sexually"). For gay couples, sexual satisfaction was positively correlated with global relationship satisfaction ($r = .44$, controlling for the effects of income and length of relationship). In contrast, attitudes about sexual fidelity and new sexual techniques were unrelated to gay men's global relationship satisfaction. Finally, beliefs about personal sexual perfection were negatively correlated with global relationship satisfaction. Kurdek (1991) viewed these beliefs as dysfunctional because they establish exaggerated or unrealistic standards for sexual performance.

Gender Roles and Sexual Activity

Given the power that gender roles often have in defining the behavior of men and women in heterosexual relationships, the lay public sometimes wonders how two men in a relationship pattern their interactions. Some people assume that one man adopts the "feminine," passive role, and the other partner adopts the "masculine," dominant role. Do contemporary gay male couples actually adopt these "butch" and "femme" roles? At the outset, it is important to acknowledge that most gay couples, like a growing number of heterosexual couples, are in dual-worker relationships where both partners share financial responsibilities. When gay partners live together, they typically share in homemaking activities as well (e.g., Kurdek, 1993).

Jay and Young (1979) asked gay men, "How often do you 'role-play' (butch/femme, masculine/feminine, husband/wife, dominant/submissive) in your relationships?" The most common response was "never" (47%), followed by "very infrequently" (23%). Only 2% of men "always" adopted such roles. When asked more specifically about their sexual interactions, only 24% of the gay men stated that they frequently adopted gendered roles; most men did not. Similarly, McWhirter and Mattison (1984, p. 276) noted that the men in their study "do not assume male and female roles in their sex with each other."

Evidence concerning gender roles also comes from investigations of the specific sexual activities of gay male partners, most often concerning anal sex. By analogy to heterosexual couples, is one gay partner typically the "insertor" (husband) and the other the "insertee" (wife)? Further, do these roles indicate a partner's degree of masculinity within the relationship? In a secondary analysis of data collected by Bell and Weinberg (1978), Harry (1984) found no association between a man's role in anal sex and other measures of masculinity/femininity including performing traditionally gender-typed household chores (e.g., cooking or home repairs) and interviewer ratings of the man's degree of "masculinity versus effeminacy." In the American Couples Study, gay men who took the insertor role in anal sex with their primary partner were generally less emotionally expressive and more rational in problem solving, traits that are traditionally defined as masculine. However, gay men who took the insertor role were also more likely to back down during an argument, a behavior demonstrating subordinate status. Thus, it is not clear that specific sexual acts are necessarily indicative of general patterns of masculinity or dominance in a gay male relationship. Blumstein and Schwartz (1983) concluded that "for both partners, anal intercourse is associated with being masculine: in couples where both partners are forceful, out-going, and aggressive, there is more anal sex" (p. 244). Similarly, Harry (1984, p. 43) concluded that "valuing masculinity in the self is quite strongly related to valuing masculinity in erotic partners."

There are problems with efforts to associate specific sexual acts with masculinity or dominance. One problem is that some gay men never engage in anal sex with their partner, preferring other sexual techniques. A second issue is the versatility with which gay men often approach their sexual interactions. Bell and Weinberg (1978) reported that many gay men took both the insertor and insertee roles in sex. Of the gay men in their sample, 80% performed the insertive role in anal sex in the previous year, and 69% received anal sex in the previous year. McWhirter and Mattison (1984) also found that among couples engaging in anal sex, the majority did not adopt strict roles as to who would be the insertor and insertee. Additionally, Lever (1994) found that of those men who said they liked being "on top" during anal intercourse, 72% also liked being on bottom. So, although some men may have distinct preferences for the sexual activities they most enjoy, many gay men are versatile in the sexual roles they assume.

A final issue in regard to gender roles and sexuality concerns which partner typ-ically initiates sexual interaction. In heterosexual couples, both partners sometimes initiate sex, but it is more often the male partner who takes the lead (Impett & Peplau, 2003). The American Couples Study asked participants which partner more frequently initiates sex (i.e., lets "the [partner] know one would like to have sex"). Only 12% of wives said that they usually initiate sex compared to 51% of husbands who said they usually initiate sex. In contrast, 31% of gay men indicated that they initiate sex more than their partner, 32% that the partner initiates sex more often, and 37% that both partners initiate sex equally often. These results are not surprising given that gay couples lack guidelines about which partner should be the sexual leader.

In summary, sexual interactions among modern gay couples do not typically fit into neat and dichotomous categories of "masculine" and "feminine" behavior or roles. This is consistent with much research indicating that the associations between specific sexual activities and masculinity/femininity are variable across relationships, cultural contexts, and historical periods (Murray, 2000). Two gaps in current knowl-edge suggest useful directions for future research. First, studies of those gay men who do prefer gendered roles in their sexual relationships would be informative. Second, because the norms and values of gay subcultures evolve and change over time, it would be useful to know how successive age cohorts of gay men incorporate themes of masculinity and femininity into their erotic relationships, and how this issue differs across diverse contemporary gay subcultures.

Sexual Exclusivity and Sexual Openness

A distinctive feature of contemporary gay men's relationships is the tendency to form sexually open (nonmonogamous) relationships. This may reflect the fact that regardless of sexual orientation, men tend to have more permissive attitudes toward casual or uncommitted sex than do women, and the size of this male–female difference in attitudes is relatively large (e.g., Bailey, Gaulin, Agyei, & Gladue, 1994; Kurdek, 1991). In this section we assess sexual exclusivity in gay male couples, consider how gay male couples negotiate nonmonogamy, and examine how sexual openness affects relationship satisfaction.

How Common is Nonmonogamy? Sexual exclusivity is by no means the norm among contemporary gay couples. In understanding patterns of monogamy versus sexual openness, it is useful to distinguish between partners' agreements about sexual openness and their actual behavior. Unfortunately, not all researchers systematically measured both agreements and behavior. A recent study surveyed 115 gay men who obtained a "civil union" under a new Vermont law that affords gays the legal benefits of marriage (Campbell, 2002). Among this highly committed group of gay men who had been in their relationships for an average of 12 years, 83% of men characterized their relationship as sexually exclusive. Most men acted entirely in accord with this arrangement; 61% of the sample reported being sexually exclusive in their behavior since their current relationship began. In contrast, other studies find lower rates of sexual exclusivity (see early review by Harry, 1984). For example, in Harry and DeVall's (1978) sample of gay men in committed relationships, only 32% of partners agreed to be "faithful" and fewer, only 25% of the men studied, were sexually "faithful" in their behavior during the past year. A third of couples agreed to have a sexually nonexclusive relationship, and the remaining 35% disagreed about sexual exclusivity. In all, 75% of the men had sex with someone other than their partner during the past year. Bryant and Demian (1994) reported that 63% of gay men considered their relationship to be sexually exclusive, although a third of these men broke their monogamy agreement at least once. In a sample of African American gay men, 65% reported that they had extradyadic sex since their current relationship began (Peplau et al., 1997).

Another consistent finding is that the longer a gay male couple stays together, the more likely the partners are to have sex outside the primary relationship (Harry, 1984; Harry & DeVall, 1978). In the American Couples Study sample, 66% of the male couples who had been in a relationship 2 years or less had engaged in extradyadic sex, whereas 94% of the couples who had been together 10 years or more had done so. McWhirter and Mattison (1984) found that 73% of their male couples began their relationship with an understanding, sometimes explicit, sometimes implicit, that the relationship would be sexually exclusive. Yet, 100% of those couples who had been together 5 years or longer had engaged in extradyadic sexual relations. Thus, it appears that even those gay men who start a relationship with intentions of being monogamous either change their intentions or fail to live up to this standard.

In understanding patterns of monogamy versus sexual openness, it is important to recognize that extradyadic sex comes in a variety of forms. Some couples have an explicit and consensual agreement to be open to outside sexual affairs. It is clear to both partners that extradyadic sex is acceptable. Other couples agree to be sexually monogamous. For these couples, a partner who has sex outside the relationship is "cheating." For still other couples, rules about monogamy are not explicitly discussed and any agreement is implicit. Unfortunately, much of the research on sexual exclusivity has failed to distinguish among these various types of couples or to account for discrepancies between agreements and actual behavior. Future research should examine these issues in greater detail and consider their possible consequences for the well-being of the couple.

Negotiating Sexual Openness.   Because extradyadic sex is common among gay couples, partners often make agreements concerning the nature of their sexual relationship. Although some couples' agreements are unstated, it is often the case that gay male partners discuss their beliefs about sexual exclusivity and openness. Once a decision is made as to whether a couple will be exclusive or not, a whole host of "rules" must often be negotiated.

Although clinical psychologists and counselors working with gay couples once viewed extradyadic affairs as evidence of instability, gay affirmative therapists today often help gay couples to work through the negotiations of an open relationship (LaSala, 2001; McWhirter & Mattison, 1984). In her book on creating and maintaining gay relationships, Tessina (1989) devoted an entire chapter to the negotiation of "fidelity contracts." Such a contract may or may not include provisions allowing for extradyadic sex. According to Tessina, violating the rules of the contract is the "enemy," not extradyadic sex itself.

A study of open gay relationships in the United Kingdom (Hickson, Davies, Hunt, Weatherburn, McManus, & Coxon, 1992) investigated sexual contracts. Among the 252 men who had a "regular partner," 56% had a nonmonogamous relationship. Most men (73%) in a sexually open relationship had a set of rules to define the boundaries of nonmonogamy. These regulations concerned honesty, politeness, emotional attachment to other partners, threesomes, and safer sex. What worked for one couple did not necessarily work for others. For example, some couples agreed that they would talk openly about all extradyadic affairs; other couples agreed to stay silent. Some couples agreed that anal sex with other partners was permitted; others viewed it as acceptable as long as a condom is used; still others outlawed it altogether. What mattered was not the rule itself, but rather that both partners accepted and adhered to their self-generated rules. Interestingly, many of the men in the study who were part of a supposed closed relationship also had rules regarding sexual infidelity that constituted a sort of just-in-case clause. These men viewed their monogamy contracts as flexible, a finding in line with previous evidence (e.g., McWhirter & Mattison, 1984) that many men who begin a sexually exclusive relationship shift to a pattern of sexual openness over time.

Sexual Exclusivity and Satisfaction.   Does sexual exclusivity affect relationship satisfaction and stability in gay male couples? Blasband and Peplau (1985) found no significant differences between gay men in exclusive and nonexclusive relationships on measures of love or liking for the partner, closeness, satisfaction, commitment, or relationship longevity. From these results, Blasband and Peplau concluded that "both open and closed relationships can be experienced as very positive and rewarding" (p. 409). Kurdek (1991, 1988) found similar results: Attitudes about fidelity were not associated with reports of global relationship satisfaction, and behavioral patterns of sexual exclusivity versus nonexclusivity were not associated with sexual satisfaction or relationship quality.

Research suggests that for gay men, agreement about exclusivity versus openness is more important to relationship satisfaction than any specific type of behavior. Harry (1984) reported that men were equally satisfied in relationships with an agreement to be exclusive or to be nonexclusive. In a study of couples of mixed HIV status, Wagner, Remien, and Carballo-Dieguez (2000) compared couples who agreed either to be monogamous or to have a consensually open relationship with couples in which extradyadic affairs were secret or only partially known to the partner. When both partners adhered to an explicit agreement about sex, scores on measures of sexual satisfaction, relationship satisfaction, affectional expression, and dyadic consensus were higher. These findings may indicate that agreement promotes satisfaction, but it is equally plausible that unhappy men are less willing to negotiate an agreement with their partner and so conceal their extradyadic affairs.

Gay Male Couples and the AIDS Crisis

All gay men in the United States have been affected by the epidemic of AIDS and concerns about the sexual transmission of HIV infection. In response to the AIDS crisis, striking changes were reported in the sexual practices of gay men, most notably increases in condom use and declines in rates of unprotected anal intercourse (see review by Paul, Hays, & Coates, 1995). Research focusing specifically on HIV in the context of committed gay relationships is limited and has centered on two issues: how the AIDS epidemic has affected sexual behavior in gay male couples and how couples manage their sexual relations when one partner is HIV positive.

The AIDS Crisis and Risky Sex in Gay Male Couples.   Has the sexual behavior of gay couples changed from the pre-AIDS era to the present? Unfortunately, no definitive data-based answer to this question is available. Rutter and Schwartz (1996) suggested that from the 1970s to the 1990s gay men's attitudes shifted toward greater endorsement of monogamy but their actual sexual behavior did not undergo a corresponding change. After reviewing available evidence, Nardi (1997, p. 77) concluded that "there is little evidence supporting the claims of increases in coupling and settling down into domesticity" as a response to AIDS. Rather, Nardi suggested, what may have changed is the way gay men talk about relationships, giving greater emphasis to committed relationships and talking less about their casual sexual encounters. Nardi reviewed the few studies indicating that rates of reporting monogamy may have increased in the 1980s, but expressed skepticism about whether these self-reports accurately depict actual behavior. Currently, reliable empirical evidence on changes in sexual exclusivity among gay male couples is lacking.

Another question is whether partners in intimate gay relationships in the era of AIDS are practicing safer sex with each other, for instance by using condoms, avoiding the exchange of bodily fluids, or getting tested regularly for HIV. Although research on this point is inadequate, it appears that many gay couples do not consistently follow safer-sex guidelines. Gay men may be more likely to protect themselves when having sex with casual partners than with a long-term partner. For example, in a study conducted in Switzerland, gay men in a steady relationship reported using a condom for anal sex an average of 57% of the time with their primary partner compared to 89% of the time with casual partners (Moreau-Gruet, Jeannin, Dubois-Arber, & Spencer, 2001).

A study of 46 gay male couples from southern California (Appleby, Miller, & Rothspan, 1999) investigated men's reasons for not following safer-sex guidelines. Many couples assumed they were not at risk, either because both partners had tested negative for HIV or because they had discussed their sexual histories. However, this assumption of safety may be false because of continued extradyadic sexual contacts and the time lag between contracting HIV and actually testing positive. Another common reason for not using condoms with a steady partner was the view that condoms reduce pleasure. Men also cited relationship maintenance reasons. Some gay men viewed unprotected sex as a way to demonstrate love, trust, and commitment to a partner. Men also worried that using a condom might signal a lack of trust, especially if a partner asked to switch from unprotected sex to protected sex. More than half the respondents (53%) said that such a request would elicit suspicion of an affair. In order to avoid raising concerns about infidelity and trust, some gay men may find it easier to engage in risky sex with their partner.

In summary, there is reason to believe that many gay men in couple relationships do not consistently practice safer sex, at least in part because of feelings of safety and trust. This may not be a wise strategy, however. The risk associated with unprotected sex with a steady partner was illustrated in a recent study of gay men in the Netherlands (Davidovich, de Wit, Albrecht, Geskus, Stroebe, & Coutinho, 2001). In this longitudinal project, more than 75% of younger men (under age 30) who contracted HIV between 1984 to 1993 got it from a casual sex partner. In contrast, 67% of younger men who contracted HIV between 1994 and 2000 were infected by a steady partner. According to the researchers (p. 1307), "it appears that young gay men have adopted, over time, safer sex practices with casual partners but to a lesser extent with steady partners." The researchers urged health professionals to pay increased attention to the sexual behaviors of younger gay men in couple relationships.

When a Partner is HIV Positive.   When one partner in a couple is HIV positive and the other is not, the couple is said to be serodiscordant (or discordant, for short).

The safest course of action for these couples is to use condoms and/or avoid high-risk behaviors such as engaging in anal sex or exchanging fluids during oral sex. Little is currently known about how discordant couples manage sexual risks. Although some of these couples are following safer-sex guidelines, others are not. In a study of 786 Swiss men with a steady partner (Moreau-Gruet et al., 2001), many discordant couples practiced safer sex. For example, 29% of discordant couples refrained from anal sex compared to 14% of HIV-negative couples. Among those who did have anal sex with their partner, 85% of discordant couples reported consistent condom use compared to only 35% of HIV-negative couples. In contrast, a study of 75 discordant gay couples from New York City found that 76% of couples reported engaging in anal sex in the past year and only half of these couples reported always using condoms (Wagner, Remien, & Carballo-Dieguez, 1998).

Research also demonstrates that many partners in HIV discordant couples participate in extradyadic sex. In a study of 63 HIV discordant couples, Wagner et al. (2000) found that extradyadic sex was frequent. In half the couples, both partners had at least one sexual affair during the past year. In 18 other couples, one partner had an affair. The likelihood of having an affair was only slightly greater among HIV-negative men than among men who had tested positive for HIV.

Although informative, these preliminary findings about the impact of HIV on gay men's relationships provide few clues about the psychological and interpersonal impact of HIV. Based on interviews with a small sample of HIV-positive men, Powell-Cope (1995) described problems that discordant couples face in trying to protect the HIV-negative partner and to maintain or regain a sense of intimacy. Some couples she interviewed "mourned" the loss of the spontaneous sexual expression they enjoyed before HIV became a concern. Some couples tried to deemphasize the importance of sexual activity in their lives together, focusing instead on other ways to express intimacy and caring. Research is needed to understand the emotional impact of HIV/AIDS, the negotiations that occur between discordant partners about the nature and meaning of their sexual interactions, and the impact of HIV on sexual and relationship quality.

SEXUALITY IN THE RELATIONSHIPS OF LESBIAN WOMEN

This section reviews empirical findings about sexuality in the relationships of lesbian women, focusing on sexual frequency, the controversy surrounding the meaning of "sex" for lesbians, sexual satisfaction and its correlates, gender roles and sexuality, and sexual exclusivity in lesbian relationships. As relevant, comparisons with gay male and heterosexual couples will also be provided.

Sexual Frequency

Several studies assessed the frequency of sexual behavior among lesbian women in a current relationship (e.g., Blumstein & Schwartz, 1983; Bryant & Demian, 1994; Califa, 1979; Lever, 1995, Loulan, 1987). In an early study, Jay and Young (1979) asked lesbians how often they "have sex" in their relationship. There was considerable variation in sexual frequency in this sample. One percent of women reported having sex more than once a day, 4% once a day, and the majority, 57%, had sex several times a week. Twenty-five percent of women had sex once a week and 8% less often. For 5% of women, sex was not currently a part of their relationship. Another study asked lesbians how often they "engaged in sexual activity that included genital stimulation" with their current partner during the past month (Peplau, Cochran, Rook, & Padesky, 1978). One third of women had sex once a week, and 37% had sex more often. About

21% of women had sex once or twice during the month, and 8% had not had sex during the past month. A national study of 398 Black lesbian women in committed relationships also asked about sexual frequency during the past month (Peplau et al., 1997). In this sample, 11% of women indicated having sex more than three times a week, 47% indicated one to three times per week, and 41% of women reported having sex less than once a week. These data are useful in illustrating the variability in sexual frequency among lesbian couples, but cannot be seen as general base rates because all studies use nonrepresentative samples.

Sexual frequency declines over time in lesbian relationships (e.g., Loulan, 1987, Peplau et al., 1978). Data from the American Couples Study are illustrative. Among women who had been together 2 years or less, 76% had sex one to three times a week or more. Among couples together for 2 to 10 years, the comparable figure was 37% and for couples together more than 10 years, only 27% had sex one to three times a week or more. Both the partners' age and the duration of the relationship contributed to this pattern, but relationship length was a stronger factor than age for lesbians. Lever's (1995) survey also found that sexual frequency was negatively associated with the length of time that a lesbian couple had been together. In the first year of a relationship, a third of couples had sex three or more times a week, in the second year this declined to 20%, and after the second year it was 10%.

Comparative research investigated reports of sexual frequency among lesbian, gay male, and heterosexual couples. Three patterns were found. First, across all types of couples, there is a general decline in sexual frequency as relationships continue over time (e.g., Blumstein & Schwartz, 1983; Christopher & Sprecher, 2000). Second, in the early stages of a relationship, gay male couples have sex more often than other couples. Perhaps the best evidence on this point comes from the American Couples Study. Among couples who had been together 2 years or less, 67% of gay men reported having sex with each other three or more times per week. This compared with 45% of the married couples, and 33% of the lesbian couples. This pattern of differences between gay male versus other couples occurred primarily among short-term relationships and not among couples who had been together for 10 years or longer. After a decade of togetherness, only 11% of the gay couples had sex three or more times per week as compared with 18% of heterosexual married couples, and 1% of lesbians.

A third pattern is that lesbian couples report having sex less often than either heterosexual or gay male couples. The American Couples study compared sexual frequency among lesbian, gay male, and heterosexual couples who had been together less than 2 years, 2 to 10 years, or more than 10 years. At each stage, lesbians reported having sex less often. More recently, Lever compared responses from lesbians who participated in the *Advocate* survey to national data on heterosexuals. She concluded that "after only two years together, lesbians have sex less frequently than married heterosexual couples do after ten years" (1995, p. 25).

The Controversy Over Lesbian Sexuality

The empirical finding that lesbian couples have sex less frequently than other couples and that sexual frequency declines rapidly in lesbian relationships is sometimes referred to as "lesbian bed death." Iasenza (2002, p. 112) noted that lesbian bed death "has become not only the subject of jokes by lesbian comics but a syndrome that a fair number of lesbian psychotherapy clients and their therapists believe actually exists."

The interpretation of this pattern is currently controversial (see review by Fassinger & Morrow, 1995). A frequent suggestion has been that gender socialization leads women to repress and ignore sexual feelings, and that the impact of this socialization is magnified in a relationship with two female partners (e.g., Nichols, 1987). Another view has been that women have difficulty being sexually assertive or taking the lead in initiating sexual activities with a partner, leading to low levels of sexual activity. Blumstein and Schwartz (1983, p. 214) suggested that "lesbians are not comfortable in the role of sexual aggressor and it is a major reason why they have sex less often than other kinds of couples." A third possibility is based on the presumption that men are generally more interested in sex than women. In this view, both lesbian and heterosexual women may experience low sexual desire because of work pressures, the demands of raising children, health issues, and so on. In heterosexual couples, the male partner's greater level of desire and willingness to take the initiative in sex encourages the woman to engage in sexual activity. This does not occur in lesbian couples. Efforts to test these possibilities systematically would be useful.

A more fundamental challenge is presented by those who suggest that conventional definitions of "sex" are the problem (e.g., McCormick, 1994). In Western cultural traditions, sex is what you do with your genitals, real sex means heterosexual intercourse, and penile penetration is the gold standard of human sexuality. Some sexual acts are labeled "foreplay," suggesting that they don't count as real sex. Recently, researchers asked a large sample of college students if they would say they had "had sex" if they had engaged in each of several activities (Sanders & Reinisch, 1999). Less than half the college students responded that they would say they "had sex" if they engaged only in oral–genital contact. In contrast, 99.5% considered penile intercourse to be "having sex." Critics argue that using a male norm of penile penetration as the standard for sex creates problems for understanding women's sexuality, particularly for women who are intimate with other women.

One concern is methodological. Is the wording of sex surveys equally appropriate to lesbian, gay, and heterosexual respondents? In a recent health survey for teens, the Vermont Department of Health asked respondents whether they had had "intercourse with males only, females only, both males and females, or neither" (cited in Rothblum, 2000). Just how would a lesbian teen answer this question? What does it mean for two girls to have "intercourse?" Surveys about sexuality in adult lesbian relationships may inadvertently suffer from similar problems. We do not know how lesbian respondents interpreted the question posed by Blumstein and Schwartz (1983), "About how often in the past year did you and your partner have sexual relations?" In a more recent study, Lever (1995) tried to clarify terminology by explaining, "When we say 'have sex with' we mean a situation in which at least one person's genitals were stimulated." Research is needed to assess the impact of different ways of asking questions about women's sexual experiences.

Another question goes beyond methods to ask how researchers can more fruitfully conceptualize women's sexuality. A study that allowed lesbian participants to define "sexual activity" as they wanted suggests that a broader conceptualization might be useful (Loulan, 1987). In this sample, over 90% of lesbians included hugging, cuddling, and kissing as sexual activities. More than 80% listed holding body to body as well as touching and kissing breasts. Similarly, in the *Advocate* survey (Lever, 1995), many women were enthusiastic about nongenital activities. On a 5-point scale from "I love it" to "I don't like it and won't do it," 91% of lesbians said they "love" hugging, caressing, and cuddling; 82% love French kissing; and 74% love just holding hands. Reflecting on this issue, Rothblum (1994, p. 634) asked whether lesbians "can reclaim erotic, nongenital experiences as real sex?" Future research should examine more closely what lesbian women consider "sex" and then, using women's own definitions, determine the frequency of sexual behavior over the course of lesbian relationships.

A further issue concerns whether low sexual frequency should be considered a problem, as suggested in the term "lesbian bed death." Fassinger and Morrow (1995, p. 200) challenged this view: "Is lack of sexual desire or genital activity a 'problem' in a loving and romantic woman-to-woman relationship? From whose point of view? ... Who determines what is sexually normative for lesbians?" Indeed, both historical analyses of 19th century American women (e.g., Faderman, 1981) and contemporary accounts of lesbians highlight the existence of passionate and enduring relationships between women that do not involve genital sexuality. Rothblum and Brehony (1993) have reclaimed the 19th century term "Boston marriage" to describe romantic but asexual relationships between lesbians today. Such relationships call into question the assumption that an absence of genital sex is necessarily a sign of a dysfunctional relationship.

Sexual Satisfaction and Its Correlates

In an early study of lesbians (Peplau et al., 1978), most women reported being highly satisfied with the sexual aspects of their current relationship (mean of 5.9 on 7-point scale of overall sexual satisfaction). Nearly three fourths of the women found sex extremely satisfying, and only 4% reported that sex was not at all satisfying. In another study, Eldridge and Gilbert (1990) found mean sexual satisfaction scores of 5.4 on a 7-point scale. In a sample of Black lesbians in committed relationships, the mean sexual satisfaction score was 5.7 on a 7-point scale (Peplau et al., 1997). In short, many lesbians describe sex in their current relationship as very rewarding.

Comparative studies find much similarity between the sexual satisfaction of lesbian, gay, and heterosexual couples. In the American Couples Study, 68% of lesbians, 63% of gay men, 68% of wives, and 67% of husbands were classified as satisfied with their sex life (Blumstein & Schwartz, 1983). In another comparative study, Kurdek (1991) found no differences in sexual satisfaction scores among lesbian, gay, and heterosexual couples.

Greater sexual satisfaction is associated with greater sexual frequency. For example in the American Couples Study, 95% of lesbians who had sex three times a week or more were satisfied with their sex life. The percentage of participants satisfied with their sex life dropped significantly with declines in frequency. Only 37% of lesbians who had sex less than once a month were satisfied with their sex life. The correlation between sexual frequency and sexual satisfaction was .48 (controlling for age and length of relationship). A similar correlation between sexual frequency and sexual satisfaction ($r = .46$, $p < .001$) was reported by Peplau et al. (1978).

Research suggests other possible correlates of sexual satisfaction that deserve further study. In the American Couples Study, sexual satisfaction was greater for lesbians in couples where partners were relatively equal in initiating sex and in refusing to have sex (Blumstein & Schwartz, 1983). For example, 83% of lesbians reporting equality of refusal were sexually satisfied compared to 58% of couples reporting unequal refusal. Another study found an association between sexual satisfaction and the importance women gave to a measure of "dyadic attachment," comprised of questions about shared activities, sexual fidelity, and knowing that the relationship would endure into the future (Peplau et al., 1978). Women who scored high on dyadic attachment reported greater sexual satisfaction ($r = .20$, $p < .05$).

Another factor that may contribute to sexual satisfaction in lesbian couples concerns orgasm. Comparative studies suggest that lesbians have orgasms more often during sexual interactions than do heterosexual women. Kinsey, Pomeroy, Martin, and Gebhard (1953) compared heterosexual women who had been married for 5 years with lesbians who had been sexually active for 5 years. Among these women, 17% of the heterosexuals compared to only 7% of the lesbians never had an orgasm. Only 40% of the heterosexual women had orgasm easily (i.e., 90–100% of the time they had sex) compared to 68% of the lesbians. These findings may, as Kinsey suggested, reflect differences in the knowledge and sexual techniques of women's partners. But differences in the emotional quality of sexual experiences may be equally important. Four other studies also reported high rates of orgasm among lesbians in relationships (e.g., Jay & Young, 1979; Lever, 1995; Loulan, 1987; Peplau et al., 1978). There appears to be a paradox in lesbian relationships. On the one hand, lesbian relationships may increase the likelihood of orgasm. On the other hand, many lesbians emphasize their enjoyment of nongenital kissing and cuddling, activities that are not necessarily associated with orgasm. A better understanding of these issues is needed.

An important question is whether sexuality is related to the overall well-being of a relationship. Kurdek (1991) found that sexual satisfaction was positively correlated with relationship satisfaction among lesbians ($r = .59$, $p < .01$), as well as among gay male and heterosexual couples. For lesbians (but not for gay men), greater discrepancies in partners' reports of sexual satisfaction were negatively correlated with global relationship satisfaction ($r = -.43$, $p < .01$). In a study that included both partners of 275 lesbian couples, Eldridge and Gilbert (1990) also found that scores on a multi-item measure of "sexual intimacy" were significantly correlated with relationship satisfaction ($r = .39$, $p < .001$). In the Peplau et al. (1997) study of African American lesbians, overall relationship satisfaction was correlated with both sexual satisfaction ($r = .46$, $p < .001$) and sexual frequency ($r = .35$, $p < .001$).

In summary, for both lesbians and gay men, sexual satisfaction is linked to overall relationship satisfaction. Future research might examine the strength of this association once other predictors of relationship quality such as emotional intimacy and conflict are taken into account (cf. Eldridge & Gilbert, 1990; Kurdek, 1994).

Gender Roles and Sexual Activity

Research conducted from the 1970s to the present has generally refuted the idea that in lesbian couples, one partner adopts a "butch" or masculine role and the other a "femme" or feminine role. Most lesbians are in dual-worker relationships and, when partners live together, they typically share both homemaking and financial responsibilities (Kurdek, 1993). The study by Jay and Young (1979) asked lesbians, "How often do you 'role-play' (butch/femme, masculine/feminine, husband/wife, dominant/submissive) in your relationship?" Only 10% of women said that they did this somewhat or very frequently. When asked specifically about sexuality, 17% of women said they did this somewhat or very frequently. Most women said they never engaged in butch–femme behavior, either sexually or in other aspects of their relationship. This, of course, contrasts markedly with heterosexual couples in which male and female partners often enact gendered social and sexual roles.

In a survey by Loulan (1990), most lesbians were familiar with butch–femme roles and were able to rate themselves and their partner on a butch–femme continuum. At the same time, most women said that these roles were not important in their relationships, and no association was found between these labels and women's sexual behavior (e.g., initiating sex, specific sexual behaviors). The *Advocate* study (Lever, 1995) asked women to rate themselves and their partner on a 7-point scale from "very femme/feminine" to "very butch/masculine." Most women rated themselves and their partner in the middle of the scale. About one fourth of the women described themselves as being in a butch/femme pairing, 17% characterized themselves and their partner as femme–femme and 8% as butch–butch. Lever (1995, p. 28) found "very little evidence that images of masculinity or femininity relate to who takes the role of the sexual aggressor within relationships." In general, research conducted during the past 30 years suggests that consistent butch–femme roles are largely absent from lesbian relationships, and that self-perceptions of masculinity and femininity are not closely tied to sexual behavior.

At the same time, it is useful to understand historical changes in the enactment and meaning of butch/femme roles among American lesbians (Faderman, 1991). In the 1950s, gender-based roles were an important part of some urban lesbian subcultures

(Davis & Kennedy, 1989). Women had to adopt either a butch or femme role to gain social acceptance. Intimate relationships were deemed appropriate only between a butch and a femme partner. In the 1970s, lesbian feminists tended to reject such roles as imitations of patriarchal, heterosexual patterns that limited women's potential. Instead, images of lesbian androgyny (e.g., jeans, T-shirts, comfortable shoes, no makeup) were encouraged. In the 1980s, a newer version of butch–femme roles reemerged in some middle and upper-class urban lesbian communities, in part as a reaction to the lesbian "clones" of the 1970s. "Many young women who claimed butch or femme identities in the 1980s saw themselves as taboo–smashers and iconoclasts" (Faderman, 1991, pp. 263–264). From their perspective, neo butch and femme styles were seen as transcending traditional definitions of masculinity and femininity and as claiming the full range of human traits and behaviors as appropriate for women. Still others argued that butch–femme roles were a way to enhance eroticism through the attraction of personal differences in appearance and behavior. According to Nichols (1987, p. 115), butch–femme advocates "are acknowledging that physical appearance is important to sexuality, that at least sometimes, opposites attract, and that these opposites may be, to an extent, modeled after gender roles, affirming that it is all right to have different tastes and preferences, that we do not all need to act or look alike."

In short, the butch–femme distinction is a familiar theme to most contemporary lesbians. Women from different age cohorts are likely to perceive issues surrounding butch and femme styles rather differently. Our knowledge of how this theme affects lesbian relationships today is relatively limited. In-depth studies of specific age cohorts and subcultural groups would be especially valuable.

Sexual Exclusivity and Sexual Openness

Among contemporary lesbian couples, sexual exclusivity appears to be the norm (Blumstein & Schwartz, 1983; Peplau et al., 1978). In the survey by Bryant and Demian (1994), 91% of lesbians said their current relationship was sexually exclusive and 90% said they had never broken their agreement about being monogamous. In the *Advocate* survey (Lever, 1995), roughly 80% of lesbians said that their current relationship was monogamous and many of the rest said they were trying to be sexually exclusive. In a recent study of 160 lesbians from Vermont who obtained "civil union" status for their relationships (Campbell, 2002), 92% of women reported that their relationship (mean length of 9 years) was sexually exclusive both in principle and in practice. Only 4% indicated that they had had sex with another person since their relationship began.

Most research on lesbian sexuality has studied White women. In an investigation of 398 Black lesbians in relationships (mean length of just over 2 years), more variation was found in sexual exclusivity (Peplau et al., 1997). More than half of the women (54%) said they had not had sex with someone else since their current relationship began, but a significant minority (46%) had had extradyadic sex, usually with only one person. Similarly, most lesbians (57%) said that they and their partner had an agreement that did not permit sex with others, but again, a sizeable minority did not have an exclusivity agreement.

Comparative studies suggest that there are several important differences between patterns of sexual exclusivity for gay male couples versus lesbian and heterosexual couples. Data from the American Couples Study are illustrative. First, there are differences in attitudes about monogamy. In the American Couples Study, 71% of lesbians, 84% of wives, and 75% of husbands indicated that it was important to be monogamous, but only 36% of gay men held this view. Second, there were major differences in actual behavior. Only a minority of lesbians (28%), wives (21%), and husbands (26%) reported having engaged in extradyadic sex, compared to 82% of gay men. Third, among those individuals who had engaged in extradyadic sex, gay men reported having a greater number of outside partners. Specifically, 43% of gay men who had extradyadic sex reported 20 or more other sex partners, compared to only 7% of husbands, 3% of wives, and 1% of lesbians. Fourth, among those who had extradyadic sex, only 7% of gay men reported having a single outside sex partner, compared to 29% of husbands, 43% of wives, and 53% of lesbians. Fifth, because some instances of extradyadic sex may occur early in a relationship and then not be repeated, Blumstein and Schwartz (1983) also asked about recent experiences of outside sex. Regardless of the length of their relationship, gay men were substantially more likely than other groups to report having extradyadic sex during the past year. Finally, Kurdek (1991) reported that sexual fidelity was positively related to relationship satisfaction for lesbian and heterosexual couples, but not for gay male couples.

CONCLUDING COMMENTS

Several general patterns emerge from this review of empirical studies. For both lesbians and gay men, sex is typically satisfying. There is a reciprocal association between sexual satisfaction and relationship satisfaction; each can enhance or detract from the other. Sexual satisfaction is linked to sexual frequency. In long-term couples, the frequency of sex decreases over time. This trend is most pronounced among lesbian couples, who are sometimes characterized as experiencing "lesbian bed death." The interpretation of low sexual frequency among long-term lesbian couples is controversial and has led some researchers to question conventional ways of conceptualizing and measuring women's sexuality.

Few contemporary lesbians and gay men characterize their sexual interactions as involving consistent gendered, butch (masculine) versus femme (feminine), roles. Many lesbians and gay men show flexibility and variety in their sexual activities. Nor is there a consistent link between performing traditionally masculine versus feminine activities in a relationship (e.g., cooking or doing home repairs) and sexual interactions. Nonetheless, issues of masculinity and femininity continue to be a topic of discussion between partners in intimate lesbian and gay relationships and also in the media and other aspects of lesbian and gay communities. The meaning of concepts such as butch and femme has changed over time and varies by social class.

One of the major differences between lesbian and gay male couples concerns sexual exclusivity versus openness in relationships. Simply put, monogamy is the norm for most lesbian relationships, and sexual openness is the norm for most gay male relationships. For gay men, sexual openness does not necessarily diminish the quality of a primary relationship, particularly when partners adhere to mutually acceptable agreements about extradyadic sex. The AIDS epidemic has raised concerns for all sexually active gay men. Research does not yet provide clear answers about how gay couples are responding to this challenge and the extent to which sexual exclusivity may have increased. Some evidence suggests that gay men may engage in risky sexual practices with their intimate partners as a way to demonstrate love and trust.

The scientific database concerning sexuality in lesbian and gay relationships continues to be woefully limited. Available studies are biased toward younger, urban, White lesbians and gay men. Convenience samples are the norm, and may underrepresent couples who are not open about their sexual orientation (Christopher & Sprecher, 2000). Further, as Tolman and Diamond (2001, p. 50) observed, researchers have often adopted "an improverished approach to adult sexuality that tabulates acts, instead of eliciting their meanings and contexts." Perhaps most troubling, virtually no new research on sexuality in gay and lesbian couples has been conducted during the past 10 years.

Many important topics about sexuality in relationships merit further attention. Two topics are illustrative. First, we know very little about sexuality among older gay and lesbian couples. In a study of 41 older lesbians, Cole and Rothblum (1991) found that menopause appeared to have relatively little effect on women's sexuality. The researchers suggested that menopause may have less impact on lesbians than on heterosexual women because "lesbian women are not as intercourse or penetration focused as heterosexual women and therefore the physiological changes of menopause might not be so disruptive" (p. 192). Second, research on sexual coercion in same-sex couples would be valuable. In heterosexual dating and married couples, sexual coercion is typically initiated by the male partner and is often interpreted by researchers as related to male aggressiveness and beliefs about male privilege. Evidence that forced sexual activities also occur in gay and lesbian relationships (e.g., Merrill & Wolfe, 2000; Waldner-Haugrud & Gratch, 1997) raises important questions about the nature and origins of sexual abuse in intimate relationships. (See Christopher and Kisler, chapter 12, this volume.)

New studies would benefit substantially from more sophisticated methodologies. The use of more representative samples, such as the recent national survey conducted for the Kaiser Foundation (2001), is helpful. So, too, are studies of specific populations with known characteristics, such as lesbians and gay men seeking government recognition for their relationships through civil unions (e.g., Campbell, 2002). Many studies relied on fairly basic descriptive analyses, rather than testing theory-based models or using multivariate approaches to consider the effects of several factors simultaneously. Further, research has emphasized general trends and has not focused attention on exceptions. It would be valuable to know more about nontypical groups, such as gay men in sexually exclusive relationships or lesbians who incorporate butch–femme themes into their sexual lives. Given the ongoing changes in gay and lesbian subcultures, ethnographic studies of sexual relationships among specific communities would be informative. Finally, the importance of culture in shaping aspects of gay and lesbian relationships and sexuality highlights the value of studies of lesbians and gay men from ethnic minority communities, as well as studies of how acculturation influences the sexuality of gay men and lesbians who emigrate from one country to another. Studies will be especially valuable that go beyond merely comparing ethnic groups and instead attempt to link relationship experiences to specific cultural norms, values, and attitudes.

REFERENCES

Appleby, P. R., Miller, C., & Rothspan, S. (1999). The paradox of trust for male couples: When risk is part of loving. *Personal Relationships, 6,* 81–93.

Bailey, J. M., Gaulin, S., Agyei, Y., & Gladue, B. A. (1994). Effects of gender and sexual orientation on evolutionarily relevant aspects of human mating psychology. *Journal of Personality and Social Psychology, 66,* 1081–1093.

Battle, J., Cohen, C. J., Warren, D., Fergerson, G., & Audam, S. (2002). *Say it loud, I'm Black and I'm proud: Black Pride Survey 2000.* New York: The Policy Institute of the National Gay and Lesbian Task Force. Retrieved December 1, 2002 from www.ngltf.org

Bell, A. P., & Weinberg, M. S. (1978). *Homosexualities: A study of diversity among men and women.* New York: Simon & Schuster.

Black, D., Gates, G., Sanders, S., & Taylor, L. (2000). Demographics of the gay and lesbian population in the United States. *Demography, 37,* 139–154.

Blasband, D., & Peplau, L. A. (1985). Sexual exclusivity versus openness in gay male couples. *Archives of Sexual Behavior, 14,* 395–412.

Blumstein, P., & Schwartz, P. (1983). *American couples: Money, work, sex.* New York: Morrow.

Bryant, A. S., & Demian (1994). Relationship characteristics of American gay and lesbian couples: Findings from a national survey. *Journal of Gay and Lesbian Social Services, 1,* 101–117.

Califa, P. (1979). Lesbian sexuality. *Journal of Homosexuality, 4*(3), 255–266.

Campbell, S. M. (2002, July 6). *Gay marriage: A descriptive study of civil unions in Vermont.* Poster presented at the International Conference on Personal Relationships, Halifax, Nova Scotia, Canada.

Carrier, J. M. (1995). *De los otros: Mexican male homosexual encounters.* New York: Columbia University Press.

Christopher, F. S., & Sprecher, S. (2000). Sexuality in dating, marriage and other relationships: A decade review. *Journal of Marriage and the Family, 62,* 999–1017.

Cole, E., & Rothblum, E. D. (1991). Lesbian sex at menopause: As good as ever or better than ever. In B. Sang, J. Warshow, & A. J. Smith (Eds.), *Lesbians at midlife* (pp. 184–193). San Francisco: Spinsters Book Co.

Davidovich, U., de Wit, J., Albrecht, N., Geskus, R., Stroebe W., & Coutinho, R. (2001). Increase in the share of steady partners as a source of HIV infection: A 17-year study of seroconversion among gay men. *AIDS, 15,* 1303–1308.

Davis, M., & Kennedy, E. L. (1989). Oral history and the study of sexuality in the lesbian community: Buffalo, New York, 1940–1960. In M. B. Duberman, M. Vicinus, & G. Chauncey (Eds.), *Hidden from history: Reclaiming the gay and lesbian past* (pp. 426–440). New York: New American Library.

D'Emilio, J., & Freedman, E. B. (1988). *Intimate matters: A history of sexuality in America.* New York: Harper & Row.

Deenen, A. A., Gijs, L., & van Naerssen, L. X. (1994a). Thirty-five years of research into gay relationships. *Journal of Psychology & Human Sexuality, 7,* 19–39.

Deenen, A. A., Gijs, L., & van Naerssen, L. X. (1994b). Intimacy and sexuality in gay male couples. *Archives of Sexual Behavior, 23,* 421–431.

Duberman, M. B., Vicinus, M., & Chauncey, G. (Eds.). (1989). *Hidden from history: Reclaiming the gay and lesbian past.* New York: New American Library.

Eldridge N. S., & Gilbert, L. A. (1990). Correlates of relationship satisfaction in lesbian couples. *Psychology of Women Quarterly, 14,* 43–62.

Faderman, L. (1981). *Surpassing the love of men.* New York: Morrow.

Faderman, L. (1991). *Odd girls and twilight lovers: A history of lesbian life in twentieth-century America.* New York: Columbia University Press.

Fassinger, R. E., & Morrow, S. L. (1995). Overcome: Repositioning lesbian sexualities. In L. Diamant & R. D. McAnulty (Eds.), *The psychology of sexual orientation, behavior, and identity: A handbook* (pp. 197–219). London: Greenwood.

Goode, E. E. (1999). Intimate friendships. In L. Gross & J. D. Woods (Eds.), *The Columbia reader on lesbians and gay men in media, society, and politics* (pp. 33–36). New York: Columbia University Press.

Harry, J. (1984). *Gay couples.* New York: Praeger.

Harry, J., & DeVall, W.B. (1978). *The social organization of gay males.* New York: Praeger.

Herdt, G. H. (1981). *Guardians of the flute.* New York: Macmillan.

Herek, G. M. (2000). The psychology of sexual prejudice. *Current Directions in Psychological Science, 9,* 19–22.

Hickson, F. C. I., Davies, P. M., Hunt, A. J., Weatherburn, P., McManus, T. J, & Coxon, A. P. M. (1992). Maintenance of open gay relationships: Some strategies for protection against HIV. *AIDS Care, 4,* 409–419.

Human Rights Campaign (2001, August 22). *Gay and lesbian families in the United States.* Washington, DC: Author.

Iasenza, S. (2002). Beyond "lesbian bed death": The passion and play in lesbian relationships. *Journal of Lesbian Studies, 6(1),* 111–120.

Impett, E. A., & Peplau, L. A. (2003). Sexual compliance: Gender, motivational, and relationship perspectives. *Journal of Sex Research, 40,* 87–100.

Jay, K., & Young, A. (1979). *Out of the closets: Voices of gay liberation.* New York: BJ Publishing Group.

Kaiser Foundation (2001, November). *Inside-out: A report on the experiences of lesbians, gays and bisexuals in America and the public's view on issues and policies related to sexual orientation.* Menlo Park, CA: Author.

Katz, J. N. (1995). *The invention of heterosexuality.* New York: Dutton.

Katz, J. N. (2001). *Love stories: Sex between men before homosexuality.* Chicago: University of Chicago Press.

Kendall, (1999). Women in Lesotho and the (Western) construction of homophobia. In E. Blackwood & S. E. Wieringa (Eds.), *Female desires: Same-sex relations and transgender practices across cultures* (pp. 157–180). New York: Columbia University Press.

Kinsey, A. C., Pomeroy, W. B., Martin, C. E., & Gebhard, P. H. (1953). *Sexual behavior in the human female.* Philadelphia: Saunders.

Kurdek, L. A. (1988). Relationship quality of gay and lesbian cohabiting couples. *Journal of Homosexuality, 15(3/4),* 93–118.

Kurdek, L. A. (1991). Sexuality in homosexual and heterosexual couples. In K. McKinney & S. Sprecher (Eds.), *Sexuality in close relationships* (pp. 177–191) Hillsdale, NJ: Lawrence Erlbaum Associates.

Kurdek, L. A. (1993). The allocation of household labor in homosexual and heterosexual cohabiting couples. *Journal of Social Issues, 49(3),* 127–139.

Kurdek, L. A. (1994). Areas of conflict for gay, lesbian, and heterosexual couples: What couples argue about influences relationship satisfaction. *Journal of Marriage and the Family, 56,* 923–934.

LaSala, M. C. (2001). Monogamous or not: Understanding and counseling gay male couples. *Families in Society, 82,* 605–611.

Laumann, E. O., Gagnon, J. H., Michael, R. T., & Michaels, S. (1994). *The social organization of sexuality.* Chicago: University of Chicago Press.

Lever, J. (1994, August 23). The 1994 Advocate survey of sexuality and relationships: The men. *Advocate*, 18–24.

Lever, J. (1995, August 22). The 1995 Advocate survey of sexuality and relationships: The women. *Advocate*, 22–30.

Loftus, J. (2001). America's liberalization in attitudes toward homosexuality, 1973 to 1998. *American Sociological Review, 66*, 762–782.

Loulan, J. (1987). *Lesbian passion: Loving ourselves and each other*. San Francisco: Spinsters/Lute.

Loulan, J. (1990). *The lesbian erotic dance: Butch, femme, androgyny and other rhythms*. San Francisco: Spinsters.

McCormick, N. B. (1994). *Sexual salvation*. Westport, CT: Praeger.

McWhirter, D. P., & Mattison, A. M. (1984). *The male couple: How relationships develop*. Englewood Cliffs, NJ: Prentice-Hall.

Merrill, G. S., & Wolfe, V. A. (2000). Battered gay men. *Journal of Homosexuality, 39*(2), 1–29.

Meyer, I. H., & Dean, L. (1998). Internalized homophobia, intimacy, and sexual behavior among gay and bisexual men. In G. M. Herek (Ed.), *Stigma and sexual orientation* (pp. 160–186). Thousand Oaks, CA: Sage.

Moreau-Gruet, F., Jeannin, A., Dubois-Arber, F., & Spencer, B. (2001). Management of the risk of HIV infection in male homosexual couples. *AIDS, 15*, 1025–1035.

Morris, J. F., Waldo, C. R., & Rothblum, E. D. (2001). A model of predictors and outcomes of outness among lesbian and bisexual women. *American Journal of Orthopsychiatry, 71*, 61–71.

Murray, S. O. (2000). *Homosexualities*. Chicago: University of Chicago Press.

Musbach, T. (2002, September 5). Gay actor beaten, hate crime suspected. Retrieved November 4, 2002, from http://www.Planetout.com/news/article.html?2002/09/05/1

Nardi, P. M. (1997). Friends, lovers, and families: The impact of AIDS on gay and lesbian relationships. In M. P. Levine, P. M. Nardi, & J. H. Gagnon (Eds.), *In changing times* (pp. 55–82). Chicago: University of Chicago Press.

Nichols, M. (1987). Lesbian sexuality: Issues and developing theory. In Boston Lesbian Psychologies Collective (Ed.), *Lesbian psychologies* (pp. 97–125). Chicago: University of Illinois Press.

Paul, J. P., Hays, R. B., & Coates, T. J. (1995). In A. R. D'Augelli & C. J. Patterson (Eds.) *Lesbian, gay, and bisexual identities over the lifespan* (pp. 345–397). New York: Oxford University Press.

Peplau, L. A. (2003). Human sexuality: How do men and women differ? *Current Directions in Psychological Science, 12*(2), 37–40.

Peplau, L. A., & Cochran, S. D. (1981). Value orientations in the intimate relationships of gay men. *Journal of Homosexuality, 6*(3), 1–19.

Peplau, L. A., Cochran, S. D., & Mays, V. M. (1997). A national survey of the intimate relationships of African American lesbians and gay men. In B. Greene (Ed.), *Ethnic and cultural diversity among lesbians and gay men* (pp. 11–138). Thousand Oaks, CA: Sage.

Peplau, L. A., Cochran, S., Rook, K., & Padesky, C. (1978). Loving women: Attachment and autonomy in lesbian relationships. *Journal of Social Issues, 34*(3), 7–27.

Peplau, L. A., & Garnets, L. D. (2000). (Eds.). Women's sexualities: New perspectives on sexual orientation and gender. *Journal of Social Issues, 56*(2), whole number.

Powell-Cope, G. M. (1995). The experiences of gay couples affected by HIV infection. *Qualitative Health Research, 5*, 36–52.

Rothblum, E. D. (1994). Transforming lesbian sexuality. *Psychology of Women Quarterly, 18*, 627–641.

Rothblum, E. D. (2000). Sexual orientation and sex in women's lives: Conceptual and methodological issues. *Journal of Social Issues, 56*(2), 193–204.

Rothblum, E. D., & Brehony, K. A. (Eds.). (1993). *Boston marriages: Romantic but asexual relationships among contemporary lesbians*. Amherst: University of Massachusetts Press.

Rutter, V., & Schwartz, P. (1996). Same-sex couples: Courtship, commitment, context. In A. E. Auhagen, & M. von Salisch (Eds.), *The diversity of human relationships* (pp. 197–223). New York: Cambridge University Press.

Sanders, S. A., & Reinisch, J. M. (1999). Would you say you "had sex" if...? *Journal of the American Medical Association, 281*(3), 275–277.

Tessina, T. (1989). *Gay relationships for men and women: How to find them, how to improve them, how to make them last*. Los Angeles, CA: Tarcher.

Tolman, D. L., & Diamond, L. M. (2001). Desegregating sexuality research: Cultural and biological perspectives on gender and desire. *Annual Review of Sex Research, 12*, 33–74.

Wagner, G. J., Remien, R. H., & Carballo-Dieguez, A. (1998). Extramarital sex: Is there an increased risk for HIV transmission? A study of male couples of mixed HIV status. *AIDS Education and Prevention, 3*, 245–256.

Wagner, G. J., Remien, R. H., & Carballo-Dieguez, A. (2000). Prevalence of extra-dyadic sex in male couples of mixed HIV status and its relationship to psychological distress and relationship quality. *Journal of Homosexuality, 39*, 31–46.

Waldner-Haugrud, L., & Gratch, L. (1997). Sexual coercion in gay/lesbian relationships: Descriptive and gender differences. *Violence and Victims, 12*, 87–96.

15

Exploring Marital Sexuality: Peeking Inside the Bedroom and Discovering What We Don't Know—But Should!

F. Scott Christopher
Tiffani S. Kisler
Arizona State University

Even though marriage represents the only relationship where society positively sanctions most forms of sexual expression, relationship scientists have paid surprisingly little attention to marital sexuality. In an attempt to spur new empirical interest, we offer foundational and prospective views on this area of study in this chapter. We begin by proposing that Symbolic Interaction Theory represents a viable framework for reviewing past work and informing future research. We review major lines of existing research that have focused on variations in coital frequency and sexual satisfaction, and on the dynamics of extramarital liaisons. Next, frequent sexual dysfunctions are examined as one way of illuminating the potential sexual role expectations of married couples. Finally, we explore promising new areas of research by integrating theory with new empirical findings on the covariation between marital sexuality and the demands of multiple roles, such as parental and work, within marriage.

> *If a couple puts a marble into a jar every time they have sex for the first year of their marriage, and then they take a marble out every time they have sex after their first anniversary, the jar will never be empty.*

This old saw describes one ignoble view of sex in marriage.[1] Although a humorist may delight in such an assessment, relationship scholars prefer theoretical and empirically driven approaches. Unfortunately, if scholars were to use the corpus of

---

[1] We use the term "marriage" to refer to heterosexual couples who have experienced a civil or religious wedding ceremony.

371

empirical-based knowledge about marital sexuality to paint a picture of marital sexuality for the public, it would not be a very detailed or richly colored picture. A few lines may coalesce into a vague, somewhat recognizable shape. However, the picture would lack form and would not be very satisfying. This is an unfortunate state of affairs as a greater number of sexual acts occur in marriage than in any other relational state. Moreover, marriage represents the only relationship where sexual intercourse is fully sanctioned by society.

In this chapter, we address this shortcoming by initially offering Symbolic Interaction Theory as a guiding framework for examining marital sexuality. We follow this with a review of the major lines of existing research in the area. Next, we examine sexual problems married couples frequently present when they seek therapy. We do this in an attempt to identify common sexual role expectations that individuals bring to their marriages. Finally, we suggest possible areas of research that warrant investigation by integrating theory with promising new empirical findings.

A THEORETICAL FRAMEWORK

Science progresses best when guided by theory. Symbolic Interactionism provides one framework investigators can use to pose research questions when investigating marital sexuality. In brief, this theory focuses on the symbolic qualities and meanings that emerge from dyadic interactions (see Christopher, 2001 and Longmore, 1998 for more in-depth descriptions). Meaning evolves from each individual's *Self* where one's symbolic environment is created. Meanings are aggregated into roles that emerge from interactions with one's dyadic partner. Roles include a position that defines the role and behavioral expectations for oneself and for one's partner. Roles are hierarchically arranged within the *Self* according to their saliency or importance for one's identity (Stryker & Statham, 1985). Roles that are pivotal to defining one's *Self* are more salient than roles of lesser importance, and, therefore, they are more apt to influence role-related choices and behavior. Roles can include demands placed on the individual and these can produce conflict. Intra-individual role conflict occurs when individuals experience conflicting demands within themselves from two or more competing roles they are trying to simultaneously enact. Dyadic or inter-individual role conflict occurs when partners do not agree about the role expectations they hold for each other and for themselves. In the sections that follow, we highlight ways that Symbolic Interactionism can be used to guide research.

EXISTING RESEARCH

Scholarly interest in marital sexuality has existed since the 1930s (Terman, 1938). However, the focus of this interest has generally been limited to a small number of variables. Changes in coital frequency represent one popular focus, whereas links between marital and sexual satisfaction represent a second. Other scholars investigated extramarital sexuality either by investigating attitudes or behavior (see Willetts, Sprecher, & Beck, chapter 3, this volume, for additional insight into these areas of investigation).

Identifying changes in coital frequency has been a primary area of interest for scholars of marital sexuality. Terman (1938) was one of the first to systematically document that frequency of marital coitus decreases across time. His finding was replicated in a range of studies although age and time in marriage potentially confound one another in many of these investigations (Ard, 1977; Blumstein & Schwartz, 1983; Jasso, 1985; Kinsey, Pomeroy, & Martin, 1948; Laumann, Gagnon, Michael, & Michaels, 1994; Marsiglio & Donnelly, 1991; Smith, 1994). Scholarly interest in this variable continued into the 1990s (Christopher & Sprecher, 2000; Edwards & Booth, 1994) with similar findings, although this research suggests the most dramatic drop in frequency may occur in the first few years of marriage (Call, Sprecher, & Schwartz, 1995; Greenblat, 1983) followed by a more gradual decline.

A number of empiricists have looked for links between coital frequency and marital satisfaction or happiness. Investigating the link between these two variables also has a long history. Terman (1938) was again one of the first to test for this relationship. He found that these two variables were only weakly related. Others similarly revealed that coital frequency and marital satisfaction are linked, although the bivariate association reported in these investigations is stronger than what Terman originally found (Ard, 1977; Call et al., 1995; Laumann et al., 1994; Smith, 1994). Contemporary studies often include measures of coital frequency and just as often find that even though frequency decreases with time, married individuals are by-and-large satisfied with their sexual interactions (Blumstein & Schwartz, 1983; Greeley, 1991; Laumann et al., 1994). Thus, coital frequency by itself may not be the best indicator of how satisfied spouses are with their relationship.

Marital satisfaction and sexual satisfaction are interrelated (see Sprecher & Cate, chapter 10, this volume). Early analyses of Burgess and Cottrell's 1930s sample showed a notable relationship between these variables (Dentler & Pineo, 1960). Later studies, including those conducted in the 1990s, consistently support this association across a range of samples (Blumstein & Schwartz, 1983; Cupach & Comstock, 1990; Edwards & Booth, 1994; Greeley, 1991; Haavio-Mannila & Kontula, 1997; Henderson-King & Veroff, 1994; Kurdek, 1991; Lawrance & Byers, 1992, 1995; Oggins, Leber, & Veroff, 1993). The direction of this relationship is not completely clear. Most scholars propose that sexual satisfaction is a predictor of marital satisfaction. However, Lawrance and Byers hypothesized that the opposite is true. Hendersen-King and Veroff (1994) further posit that the relationship is actually reciprocal, possibly a more accurate depiction of the true dynamics of marriage.

As noted, investigating extramarital sexuality (Parkinson, 1991), either by examining attitudes about extramarital liaisons (Bukstel, Roeder, Kilmann, Laughlin, & Sotile, 1978; Singh, Walton, & Williams, 1976) or by asking about actual instances of engaging in sex with someone other than one's spouse (Athanasiou & Shaver, 1969; Bercheid, Walster, & Bohrnstedt, 1973; Edwards & Booth, 1976; Glass & Wright, 1977; Hunt, 1974; Laumann, et al., 1994; Travis & Sadd, 1977), represents a popular topic of research for scholars of marital sexuality. A consistent finding across studies is that a large majority of our society does not accept married individuals having sex outside of their marriage (Laumann, et al., 1994; Singh et al., 1976; Smith, 1994; see also Willetts, Sprecher, & Beck, chapter 3, this volume). Behavior and attitudes, however, do not always match. Estimates of how many married individuals actually engage in extramarital sex have varied across time and methodologies (Parkinson, 1991). Whereas early research set the rate at 40% for married men (Athanasiou & Shaver, 1969) and between 36% and 30% for married women (Athanasiou & Shaver, 1969; Levin, 1975). Laumann et al.'s (1994) more current research with the National Health and Social Life Survey (NHSLS) suggests that 25% of married men and 15% of married women experience sex with a nonspousal partner at least once in their marriage. These numbers become even lower when respondents are asked about the previous year of their marriage (about 4% for both men and women). Other national probability studies of this time period generally confirm Laumann et al.'s findings (Billy, Tanfer, Grady, & Klepinger, 1993; Forste & Tanfer, 1996; Greeley, 1991; Smith, 1994; Wiederman, 1997). Thus, although extramarital sexual contact occurs, it is not as frequent as many may believe.

A few insights into marital sexuality can be garnered from these investigations. Assuming good health, it is apparent that couples gradually decrease their frequency of coitus the longer they are together (Christopher & Sprecher, 2000; Edwards & Booth,

1994). Coital frequency, in turn, can be an indicator of marital happiness and satisfaction (Edwards & Booth, 1994) as well as sexual satisfaction (Greeley, 1991; Laumann et al., 1994), but it is not always a good one. The reasons for this association must be inferred as scholars have not developed and tested explanatory models. Moreover, even with the decrease in frequency, married couples for the most part remain fairly satisfied with their sexual relationships (Laumann et al., 1994), and this satisfaction with their sex life contributes to couples' marital satisfaction. Nonetheless, not all married individuals are satisfied, and decreased sexual satisfaction, with a concurrent drop in marital satisfaction, likely contributes to individuals engaging in extramarital affairs (Bringle & Buunk, 1991). The actual frequency of married individuals engaging in extramarital coitus at any given time, however, is relatively low.

Given the general lack of breadth in variables used by investigators in this area, alternative approaches are needed to illuminate the relational dynamics of marital sexuality. One approach is to examine sexual difficulties that frequently arise in marriage. Scrutinizing these can provide insight into what married couples expect in their sexual interactions.

SEXUAL DIFFICULTIES AND MARITAL SEXUAL ROLE EXPECTATIONS

Symbolic Interaction Theory suggests that married couples negotiate their sexual roles in their relationships. Yet, no empirical or theoretical investigation to date has identified commonly held role expectations that these couples have for their sex life. Baxter (1986) offers one approach for shedding light on this area. She proposed that understandings about role expectations for relationships could be gained by examining violations of relational rules. Applying her logic, identifying typical sexual problems that are presented in marital therapy can provide insights into expectations about sexual roles in marriage. Frequent sexual problems that couples present in therapy include performance problems (premature ejaculation, erectile dysfunction, female orgasmic disorder), dissatisfaction with frequency of sexual relations, dissatisfaction with the type and duration of sexual encounters, infidelity, and infertility (Winceze & Carey, 2001; see also Aubin & Heiman, chapter 20, this volume, for additional information on sexual dysfunction).

Performance Problems

Many sexual dysfunctions interfere with a couple's ability to have successful sexual interactions. These dysfunctions vary by gender. The *Diagnostic and Statistical Manual of Mental Disorders*, (DSM IV; American Psychiatric Association, 1994) identifies low sexual desire, arousal problems, and sexual pain as the most common sexual dysfunctions for women. The most common sexual dysfunctions for men are premature ejaculation, erectile dysfunction, and low sexual desire. Although sexual dysfunctions are somewhat more frequent among those who are divorced, widowed, or dating, married individuals experience dysfunction as well (Laumann, Paik, & Rosen, 1999) and often seek counseling to alleviate the problems (Winceze & Carey, 2001). Other factors besides marital status plays a role in sexual dysfunctions. Laumann et al. (1999), for instance, found that women report higher rates of sexual dysfunction than men do by a ratio of 43% men unaffected to 31% of women unaffected. Men and women also vary as to what contributes to their dysfunctions. Complications with health are more likely to affect all facets of men's sexual performance, whereas for women, health problems generally only relate to a woman experiencing symptoms of sexual pain. This traditional belief about women's dysfunction, however, has recently been challenged

(Tiefer, 2001). Feelings relating to social status and quality of life also impact sexual functioning. Social status variables such as age and deteriorating social economic status, unlike health factors, have a stronger impact on women's sexual functioning than on men's (Laumann et al, 1999). For women, social status variables affect all areas of their sexual functioning whereas it is mainly related to erectile dysfunction in men.

This group of common presenting problems provides insights into possible violations of sexual role expectations that married couples experience. Two problems, erectile dysfunction and painful intercourse, likely demonstrate that *married couples expect sexual intercourse to occur*. Moreover, seeking therapy for low sexual desire potentially reflects a common expectation that *sexual interactions will occur with some degree of regularity*. Attempts to alleviate problems of painful coitus and orgasmic dysfunction concomitantly demonstrate an expectation that *sex should be pleasurable*. Finally, opting for treatment for premature ejaculation suggests that couples have role expectations about *how long a couple should spend in their sexual interactions once interactions are initiated*.

Dissatisfaction with Frequency of Sexual Relations

As we showed in this review, sexual frequency has long been of interest to those who study marital sexual interaction. It is also possible that many married partners base their judgments about the quality of their sexual relationship on the frequency of their interactions and perceive it as a problem when this frequency changes. These problems can be exacerbated when partners have differing expectations for how frequently they should experience intercourse, and such differences can lead couples to seek therapy (Winceze & Carey, 2001). These differences again reflect role expectations that *sexual interactions should occur with some degree of regularity*. Moreover, expectations of frequency will likely differ across couples, and this is a topic worthy of future investigations. Furthermore, sexual role expectations of regular coital interaction additionally suggest that sex serves a functional purpose in the marital relationship, as couples are dissatisfied when it is missing or too infrequent. This points to the need to understand marital sexual roles within the broader context of the marital relationship.

Dissatisfaction with Type and Duration of Sexual Encounters

Some couples seek therapy because their sex life has become routine. This may result in a decrease in pleasure and/or satisfaction. Routinization of sex can also potentially result in sexual interactions of shorter duration. Alternatively, conflicting role demands, such as those experienced because of parenting and employment roles, may leave less time or energy to spend adequate time meeting one's partner's sexual needs. These presenting problems are additional indicants that married couples expect that their *sexual role enactments will be mutually pleasurable*. However, some married individuals may further expect their *partners to be open to new sexual explorations and to be flexible in attending to their sexual wishes*. Not having these sexual role expectations met may lead some couples to seek therapy.

Infidelity

Couples often enter therapy due to issues of infidelity. Glass and Wright (1997) suggest that as couples enter into a marital relationship, they expect monogamy from their partner and failure to remain monogamous is a direct violation of the marital agreement. Men and women sometimes differ in what triggers distress with a violation of monogamy (Buss, 1999; Cann, Mangum, & Wells, 2001). For women, violations of monogamy focus more on issues of emotional intimacy, whereas men more typically focus on issues of physical intimacy. Problems with monogamy are further complicated by the rise in the popularity and the use of the Internet for sexual reasons (Cooper, Scherer, Boies, & Gordon, 1999; Young, Griffin, Cooper, O'Mara, & Buchanan, 2000). Visiting pornographic sites or seeking sexually oriented chat room relationships may not be viewed by the involved spouse as cheating because it takes place via a computer. However, one's partner may take a different view and such actions can damage the relationship.

Glass and Wright (1997) report that individuals experiencing infidelity from a spouse vary greatly in the way they respond to the violation of their marital agreement. In fact, these researchers assert that the strength of the reaction is related to an individual's belief regarding monogamy and commitment within a marriage. Those who have an easier time coping with issues of infidelity hold the assumption that infidelity is likely to occur within marital relationships; thus, acts of infidelity fit their role expectations. Justifications for infidelity are hypothesized to differ between men and women. Glass and Wright (1997) suggest that women take more of a relational focus such as falling in love as a justification, whereas men are more individually focused such as citing the excitement of a sexual conquest. Furthermore, Glass and Wright (1985) propose that women relate sex with love, whereas men focus mainly on the sexual acts.

Such presenting problems imply that *couples typically expect their spouses to be monogamous in their sexual relationships*. This is not surprising given general social disapproval for extramarital sexual encounters (Smith, 1994). However, it also suggests that what constitutes a violation of the role expectation of monogamy varies in as yet undiscovered ways. For instance, if a spouse visits pornography sites on the Internet, does this constitute a violation of monogamy? If the same spouse visits chat rooms, does this cross the line? If the spouse phones an individual after meeting this person in a chat room and engages in phone sex or develops a friendship, is this outside of the negotiated boundaries established in the marriage? Not all couples may have discussed these possibilities, and these are topics worthy of future research.

Infertility

A surprising 15% of American married couples will experience fertility problems and will eventually seek professional help in conceiving (Meyers, Diamond, Kezur, Scharf, Weinshel, & Rai, 1995). The genesis of such difficulties with conceiving is approximately equally distributed between reproductive issues with the woman, the man, and the two of them as a couple. Diagnosis entails privacy violations for the couple as professionals examine their sexual interactions in minute detail. Furthermore, treatment can result in regimented sexual interaction and doubts about their *Self*-definitions as women, men, or as sexual beings (Pepe & Byrne, 1991; Porter & Christopher, 1984). Infertility problems highlight the fact that one sexual role that many married couples experience is sex as an avenue for having children. Meanings attached to sex may radically change as the couple attempts to have a child and realizes the limited opportunities that exist for conception. Investigations into the sexuality of infertile couples could provide insights into their sexual role expectations. Obviously, *many couples expect conception* as a role outcome. However, the fact that fertility problems can lead individuals to question their femininity or masculinity suggests that marital sexuality may be interrelated to one's gender role for many married people. Again, this points to potential role expectations that many couples have for their sexual roles.

PROMISING NEW DIRECTIONS FOR RESEARCH

There are a number of reasons why it is important to explore new areas of research for marital sexuality. First, although it has been popular to examine coital frequency, it has not proven to be an overly heuristic variable (Christopher & Sprecher, 2000; Parkinson, 1991). By now, the decrease in frequency across marital duration and/or age is well documented. The ability to predict coital frequency, even with a host of available variables and using a national data set, however, has been somewhat elusive as demonstrated by examining the size of squared multiple correlations (i.e., Call et al., 1995). Perhaps the fact that this variable has not provided many clues about marital sexuality beyond its association with time in the marriage and marital satisfaction is understandable. What specifically can be inferred from measuring coital frequency? Many investigators used this as a barometer of the health of the sexual relationship if not the marriage itself. By-and-large, findings across studies show that couples who have more frequent sex are happier or more satisfied than those having less frequent sex (Birchler & Webb, 1977; Edwards & Booth, 1976, 1994; Greeley, 1991; Henderson-King & Veroff, 1994; Hunt, 1974). Even this consistent finding leaves unanswered the question of what measuring coital frequency actually reflects. Imagine that relationship scholars measured love solely by asking married couples how frequently they explicitly professed their love to their spouse. This may not accurately reflect the level of love spouses' experience. Similarly, asking about coital frequency may not be a critical or sensitive item for investigations of marital sexuality.

A second reason exists for exploring new areas of research for marital sexuality. There is emerging evidence that women's cognitive representations of their sexual *Self* are structured differently than are men's. This evidence originates in work by Cryanowski and Andersen (1998) who investigated sexual self-schemas. According to these researchers, sexual self-schemas are "cognitive generalizations about sexual aspects of oneself that are derived from past experience, are manifest in current experience, are influential in the processing of sexually relevant social information, and guide sexual behavior" (Andersen, Cryanowski, & Espindle, 1999, p. 646). These scholars conceptualize sexual self-views as regulating cognitive processes and sexual behaviors. According to their research, women's and men's sexual schemas have three components. Women's component of romance–passion parallel's men's component of passion–loving. Both of these components facilitate linking sexual behaviors with romantic feelings toward one's partner. Similarly, men's component of open minded–liberal acts in a similar manner to women's open–direct self-views in that both facilitate sexual activity. Differences emerge in the third components. For men, this component reflects power–aggression, for women it reflects their embarrassment with their sexuality. Thus, men's sexual self-views potentially include a power and or aggression quality whereas women's potentially include a theme of anxiousness. These gender differences in how men and women see themselves sexually have the potential to impact how they relate to one another in relationships (Cyranowski & Andersen, 1998; Andersen et al., 1999). For instance, if men hold a sexual self view strongly influenced by a sense of power and aggression, it can lead to sexually aggressive acts in a dating relationship or marriage (see Christopher & Kisler, Chapter 12, this volume for a review). Women whose sexual self-perception is filled with embarrassment and anxiety are at risk for experiencing sexual dysfunction (see Aubin & Heiman, Chapter 20, this volume, for an in-depth discussion of sexual dysfunction).

A third reason for exploring new research areas originates in advances in understanding sexual arousal. For years, researchers have capitalized on the fact that most couples follow a progression of sexual behaviors that begins with kissing, advances to fondling, and culminates in intercourse by creating scales that measure these steps. Although this typical progression of sexual interaction increases men's arousal at each step, this is not true of women (Geer & Broussard, 1990). Instead, women find some intermediate steps of the progression as arousing as sexual intercourse and are not as aroused by other steps. The body of research on sexual arousal also illuminated additional interesting differences between men and women (Everaerd, Laan, Both, & Van Der Velde, 2000; Everaerd, Laan, & Spiering, 2000). Scholars in this area differentiate between subjective arousal, or arousal that is recognized and reported by the individual, and objective arousal, or arousal that is measured by physiological instruments. Whereas subjective and objective arousal generally co-occur in men, this is not the case for women. Women's reports of subjective sexual arousal appear to be contingent on the meaning they put on the social and relational context in which they find themselves at the time. In other words, most women are more apt to subjectively report being aroused while also being physically aroused when their sexual interactions are experienced in a relational context. Given that this context is marriage for most women, it is even more important that marital sexuality is more fully and critically examined. Collectively, the arousal literature suggests a strong need to investigate men's and women's experiences of marital sexuality individually and dyadically.

Finally, although most couples are satisfied with their sexual interactions, all are not (Laumann, Paik, & Rosen, 1999). As we established, significant numbers of individuals and couples seek therapy and counseling for sexual problems every year. Therapists who attempt to guide these couples are more apt to achieve therapeutic goals if they have a better understanding of what constitutes "normal" sexual interactions in marriage. One need only look to the pervasive influence of Masters and Johnson's (1966) model of human sexual response on intervention to recognize the potential effect of a broader research agenda for marital sexuality.

The Demands of Multiple Roles Within Marriage

One research question worthy of exploration is how do married individuals and couples resolve role conflict when it includes their sexual roles? Married couples in our society often face multiple demands on their time as a couple. Two roles in particular may potentially create role conflict with their sexual roles, parenting roles and work roles. In fact, Parkinson (1991), in her review of 6 decades of research of marital sexuality, concluded that the birth of children and employment demands represented two factors that are likely to have a notable impact on marital sexuality.

Parental Role and Marital Sexuality.   A limited number of researchers examined the effect children have on marital sexuality. Having children is negatively related to coital frequency (Blumstein & Schwartz, 1983; Greenblat, 1983; Jasso, 1985) as well as couples' preferred frequency of intercourse (Doddridge, Schumm, & Bergen, 1987). In some instances, having young children contributes to limits in some married couples' sexual life. Donnelly's (1993) analysis of a national data set showed that married individuals with preschool children are at increased risk for being in a "sexually inactive marriage" as defined by not having had sex in the previous month. Ironically, her analysis further revealed that the more children couples had, the more frequent was their sexual activity.

Children may also affect married individuals' evaluations of their sex life. Henderson-King and Veroff (1994) found that children's effects vary by ethnic group. For instance, when children were present in the family, the Black wives and husbands in the study negatively evaluated their sexual interaction; the same relationship did not hold for the White wives and husbands. Having children in the household was also negatively related to Black husbands' rating of joyful sex, but positively related to White husbands' ratings of the same variable. These ethnic differences may have emerged because the Black families in this study were more apt to include children not fathered by the wife's husband. The possible resulting family tensions in these stepfamilies may have led to increases in sexual upset and less sexual joy for these spouses. In addition, the seeming depressive impact of children on coital frequency and sexual evaluation was likely linked to the multitude of role demands associated with being a parent. However, some of the decrease may also reflect social attitudes. Friedman, Weinberg, and Pines' (1998) Israeli sample comprised of university students and professionals saw the roles of sexuality and motherhood as exclusive of one another. Thus, women may experience role conflict when they attempt to simultaneously define themselves as "sexy" and "motherly" if they accept the social attitude that these roles are incompatible.

The equivocal nature of the findings suggests that for some couples, having children is associated with decreases in marital sexual interaction. However, the dynamics of this have not been investigated and represent a potentially productive area of research. There are a number of plausible explanations for this decrease that could be tested. The transition to parenthood results in multiple role changes, especially for women (Demo & Cox, 2000). Couples often become more child-oriented and gender-traditional in their household roles (Cowan & Cowan, 1992). Thus, couples may have fewer opportunities for sex given the time demands of the parenting role and the decreases in privacy. Couples may have to create times for sex as opposed to relying on spontaneous interactions. Moreover, it is unclear whether the shift to more traditional gender-stereotyped roles affects the sexual relationship. If wives or husbands resent this shift, such negative feelings could mediate their sexual attraction for their spouse. Additionally, couples may find that children decrease the available resources in the family. These might include tangible resources such as family finances and space but may also include limits on time and spousal attention. This could, in turn, result in dyadic role conflict that would have the potential of spilling over into their sexual role. However, not all of the findings reviewed showed negative effects; positive effects were also evident. Other couples may find the addition of children increases their investment in family life, and they may also find parental roles rewarding. This might positively influence their feelings of sexual attraction toward one another. Moreover, wives' positive evaluations of their husbands in their father role could trigger wives' subjective sexual arousal as the relational context becomes conducive for this.

Other questions arise from changes that result from pregnancy and adding children to the family. Do women's body images during and after pregnancy impact their sexual role? Do husbands and wives consider the parental role demands of their spouse when making decisions about approaching them for intercourse? In other words, do spouses consider how tired their husband or wife may be, or whether they need additional sleep time to face the demands of the next day, before initiating a sexual interaction? Finally, what is the temporal reach of the sexual role negotiations that take place during the transition to parenthood? Do the sexual roles negotiated at this important transition in the relationship have a lasting impact on the sexual interaction of the couple? Investigating these questions highlights the heuristic possibilities for research in this area (Haugen, Schmutzer, & Wenzel, Chapter 17, this volume, addresses some of these questions).

Work Roles and Marital Sexuality.   One of the challenges of marital life is how to juggle the often conflicting demands placed on couples by their work and family roles. Pressure from work, for instance, can negatively influence married individuals' coital frequency (Jasso, 1985). Demands from the job can also result in couples working different shifts, and this in turn can be associated with sexual dissatisfaction and problems (White & Keith, 1990). In other instances, time spent at work may exceed the normal 40-hour week. On first consideration this would seem to be a challenge for marital couples, however, Shibley-Hyde, DeLamater, and Durik (2001) examined the NHSLS data and found that those who worked more than 40 hours a week were no more likely to experience sexual problems or lower sexual satisfaction than were those who worked the normal 40-hour week.

It might not be the number of hours worked that is important, rather it might be one's work role experience that influences one's marital sexuality. Shibley-Hyde et al. (2001) revealed work-related differences in a second study. Using a community sample, they looked at the ability of family and work variables to predict an array of sexual outcomes. Their findings revealed that aspects of the spouses' work role were associated with married couples' sexual life (Shibley-Hyde et al., 2001). Husbands' ratings of the quality of their work role, for example, were negatively associated with couples' frequency of intercourse. Moreover, an interaction between husbands' and wives' work-role quality showed that husbands' sexual attraction to their spouse was highest when the husbands' work quality was high, but the wives' was concurrently low. In addition, wives' sexual satisfaction was highest when their spousal-role salience[2] was high but their work-role salience was low. These findings suggest that a high-quality work experience for husbands may decrease intercourse frequency but concurrently increase feelings of sexual attraction toward their wives. At the same time, wives' sexual satisfaction appears to be greatest when her identity is tied more to her family role than to her work role.

Shibley-Hyde and her colleagues (2001) demonstrate the importance of expanding research beyond simply looking at coital frequency. Their research highlights the viability of examining such variables as sexual attractiveness of one's spouse and sexual satisfaction. Moreover, the strong predictive value of identity salience in their findings underscores the value of using Symbolic Interaction Theory in guiding research in marital sexuality.

There are additional work-related areas that warrant research. For instance, evidence exists that work complexity[3] has a positive impact on family life (see Perry-Jenkins, Repetti, & Crouter, 2000, for a review). It is possible that work complexity may also positively influence work role saliency, which Shibley-Hyde et al. (2001) has shown influences marital sexuality. Chronic job stress also affects the marital environment by increasing role conflict and contributing to feelings of being overloaded (Perry-Jenkins et al., 2000). It would not be surprising if this type of stress additionally negatively influenced spouses' sexual interaction. Similar to the literature on parenting, not all of the findings for work point to negative effects on marital sexuality. Thus, high investments in one's employment with satisfactory outcomes potentially could positively influence marrieds' sexual lives, especially in the case of husbands. In addition, wives with high spousal-role salience may be more apt to perceive their arousal in sexual interactions with their husbands. This in turn could contribute to their sexual and marital satisfaction. Each of these plausible explanations shows the rich potential for researching ties between worklife and marital sexuality.

Sexuality and Marital Interaction

Marital interactional researchers provided descriptions of different styles of marital interaction, some more functional than others. For instance, Gottman (1993) describes four marital interaction styles that were functional for the couples in his study. *Complementary couples* are respectful of each other, divide power within the relationship into different domains, and have moderate levels of intimacy. *Conflict-minimizing couples*

---

[2] Role saliency reflects the relative importance a role plays in defining one's *Self*.
[3] Work complexity refers to the level of self-direction, control, and planning individuals have in their employment.

adhere to more traditional gender roles within their marriages, emphasize family and religious values, and avoid expressing strong emotions such as anger. *Best friends couples* are characterized by equitable power arrangements, an emphasis on sharing, and being strongly committed to their marriage. *Emotionally expressive couples* are volatile and strongly express a full range of emotions, whether it is anger or joy.

McCarthy (1999) speculated on the sexual strengths and vulnerabilities of each of these styles. He posits that many of the qualities of complementary couples would promote sexual desire. These include experiencing intimacy within the relationship, reinforcing each other's competencies, and spending time validating the worth of one's spouse. McCarthy continues that this type of couple may be at risk for sex becoming routinized and being assigned a lower priority in the couple's lives as they negotiate the role demands of marital life. Conflict minimizing couples, from McCarthy's perspective, would minimize sexual conflicts, follow traditional arrangements of having the husband initiate and dominate the couple's sexual life, and would also be at risk for falling into a routine sexual pattern that may eventually marginalize the importance of sex.

McCarthy (1999) postulates that the remaining two marital styles are less stable than the previous two. Sex for best friend couples energizes and reinforces their marriage according to McCarthy. It plays a key role in their relationship and experiences of intimacy. Nonetheless, their marital role expectations may be so high that it is difficult for the couple to live up to them; thus, they may become disappointed and disillusioned. Because high levels of emotionality characterize emotionally expressive couples, McCarthy speculates that their sex is likely to be passionate, vibrant, and fun. Sex is apt to be spontaneous and playful for these couples. However, if sex becomes routine, or if a sexual dysfunction cannot be resolved quickly, McCarthy believes that these individuals may turn to affairs for their sexual excitement or may dissolve their marriages to look for more exciting alternatives.

Although McCarthy's hypothesized interactions between marital interaction styles and sexual roles do not presently have empirical support, his work points to the importance of considering the dynamics of marriage when investigating marital sexuality. Other work provides further evidence that considering marital dynamics when investigating marital sexuality is an important and potentially fruitful avenue of investigation. For instance, Shibley-Hyde et al.'s (2001) study of the impact of work on marital sexuality was also unique in that they measured the saliency of the spousal role. This proved to be a key variable. After controlling for education and income, higher spousal salience was positively related to wives sexual satisfaction and how attractive they found their husbands, as well as husbands' sexual attraction to their wives. Interaction effects showed that spousal feelings of sexual attraction for both husbands and wives were at their highest when spousal salience was high for both. Thus, spouses' definition of *Self* in the marital role is related to their sexual relationship.

Prior research also suggests that the quality and quantity of sex positively covaries with the love one has for a spouse (Aron & Henkemeyer, 1995; Grote & Frieze, 1998; Sprecher & Regan, 1998), that the type of love changes across time, and that such changes are related to sexual satisfaction (Grote & Frieze, 1998). Other research points to the importance of investigating communication. How couples communicate about sexuality, and whether they are satisfied with their communication, plays a role in overall marital satisfaction (Byers & Demmons, 1999; Cupach & Comstock, 1990). Moreover, sexual communication is related to how sexually rewarding and costly married individuals rate their sexual interactions (Lawrance & Byers, 1995). Yet, it is not entirely clear how well couples communicate in the sexual realm as much sexual communication is nonverbal (Cupach & Metts, 1991). Couples may lack a language that allows them to negotiate satisfactory sexual roles in their marriage.

Nonetheless, current findings related to marital dynamics underscore the importance of placing marital sexual interaction within the context of the larger relationship in future investigations.

CONCLUSIONS

Twenty years ago, Greenblat (1983) in writing about marital sexuality stated that "this form of sex—the only widely accepted, fully socially legitimate form of sex—remains more the topic of jokes than of serious social scientific investigations" (p. 289). Although advancements have been made since Greenblat's statement, they are not as numerous nor as rich as advancements made in other areas of sexuality over the past 2 decades. As our title states, this chapter allowed us to "peek inside the bedroom and discover what we don't know—but should." We reviewed existing research, examined possible expectations married individuals may have about their sexual roles, and explored possible new directions for future research. The stage is set for future research—to know more about what occurs in the marital bedroom. Such research can be theoretically grounded, as we demonstrated by the use of Symbolic Interactionism in this chapter. It can move beyond the traditional variables of coital frequency and satisfaction to include new variables such as sexual-role saliency and expectations, as well as physical arousal, spousal attraction, and sexual *Self*-views. In addition, it can investigate how marital sexuality is woven into the normal fabric of marital and family life. Theoretically grounded research that uses an array of sexual measures and explores the interrelationship of sexuality to other relational phenomenon will allow us to paint a much more complete picture of marital sexuality in the future.

REFERENCES

American Psychiatric Association (1994). *Diagnostic and statistical manual of mental disorders*, (4th ed.). Washington, DC: Author.

Andersen, B. L., Cyranowski, J. M., & Espindle, D. (1999). Men's Sexual Self-schema. *Journal of Personality and Social Psychology, 76*, 645–661.

Ard, B. M. (1977). Sex in lasting marriages: A longitudinal study. *Journal of Sex Research, 13*, 274–285.

Aron, A., & Henkemeyer, L. (1995). Marital satisfaction and passionate love. *Journal of Social and Personal Relationships, 12*, 139–146.

Athanasiou, R., & Shaver, P. (1969). A questionnaire on sex. *Psychology Today, 3*, 64–69.

Baxter, L. A. (1986). Gender differences in the heterosexual relationship rules embedded in break-up accounts. *Journal of Social and Personal Relationships, 3*, 289–306.

Berscheid, E., Walster, E., & Bohrnstedet, G. (1973). The body image report. *Psychology Today, 7*, 119–131.

Billy, J. O. G., Tanfer, K., Grady, W. R., & Klepinger, D. H. (1993). The sexual behavior of men in the United States. *Family Planning Perspectives, 25*, 52–60.

Birchler, G. R., & Webb, L. J. (1977). Discriminating interaction behavior in happy and unhappy marriages. *Journal of Consulting and Clinical Psychology, 45*, 494–495.

Blumstein, P., & Schwartz, P. (1983). *American couples*. New York: Morrow.

Bringle, R. G., & Buunk, B. P. (1991). Extradyadic relationships and sexual jealousy. In K. McKinney & S. Sprecher (Eds.), *Sexuality in close relationships* (pp. 135–153). Hillsdale, NJ: Lawrence Erlbaum Associates.

Bukstel, L. H., Roeder, G. D., Kilmann, P. R., Laughlin, J., & Sotile, W. M. (1978). Projected extramarital involvement in unmarried college students. *Journal of Marriage and the Family, 40*, 337–340.

Buss, D. M. (1999). *Evolutionary psychology*. Boston: Allyn & Bacon.

Byers, E. S., & Demmons, S. (1999). Sexual satisfaction and sexual self-disclosure within dating relationships. *The Journal of Sex Research, 36* (2), 180–189.

Call, V., Sprecher, S., & Schwartz, P. (1995). The incidence and frequency of marital sex in a national sample. *Journal of Marriage and the Family, 57*, 639–650.

Cann, A., Mangum, J. L., & Wells, M. (2001). Distress in response to relationship infidelity: The roles of gender and attitudes about relationships. *Journal of Sex Research, 38*, 185–190.

Christopher, F. S. (2001). *To dance the dance: A symbolic interactional exploration of premarital sexuality*. Mahwah, NJ: Lawrence Erlbaum Associates.

Christopher, F. S., & Sprecher, S. (2000). Sexuality in marriage, dating, and other relationships: A decade review. *Journal of Marriage and the Family, 62,* 999–1017.

Cooper, A., Scherer, C. R., Boies, S. C., & Gordon, B. L. (1999). Sexuality on the Internet: From sexual exploration to pathological expression. *Professional-Psychology: Research and Practice, 30,* 154–164.

Cowan, C. P., & Cowan, P. (1992). *When partners become parents: The big life change for couples.* New York: Basic Books.

Cupach, W. R., & Comstock, J. (1990). Satisfaction with sexual communication in marriage. Links to sexual satisfaction and dyadic adjustment. *Journal of Social and Personal Relationships, 7,* 179–186.

Cupach, W. R., & Metts, S. (1991). Sexuality and communication in close relationships. In K. McKinney and S. Sprecher's (Eds.), *Sexuality in close relationships* (pp. 93–110). Hillsdale, NJ: Lawrence Erlbaum Associates.

Cyranowski, J. M., & Anderson, B. L. (1998). Schemas, sexuality, and romantic attachment. *Journal of Personality and Social Psychology, 74,* 1364–1379.

Demo, D., & Cox, M. (2000). Families with young children: A review of research in the 1990s. *Journal of Marriage and the Family, 62,* 876–895.

Dentler, R. A., & Pineo, P. (1960). Marital adjustment and personal growth of husbands: A panel analysis. *Marriage and the Family, 22,* 45–48.

Doddridge, R., Schumm, W. R., & Bergen, M. B. (1987). Factors related to decline in preferred frequency of sexual intercourse among young couples. *Psychological Reports, 60,* 391–395.

Donnelly, D. A. (1993). Sexually inactive marriages. *The Journal of Sex Research, 30,* 171–179.

Edwards, J. N., & Booth, A. (1976). Sexual behavior in and out of marriage: An assessment of correlates. *Journal of Marriage and the Family, 38,* 73–83.

Edwards, J. N., & Booth, A. (1994). Sexuality, marriage, and well-being: The middle years. In A. S. Rossi (Ed.), *Sexuality across the life course* (pp. 233–259). Chicago: The University of Chicago Press.

Everaerd, W., Laan E. T., Both, S., & Van Der Velde, J. (2000). Female sexuality. In L. T. Szuchman and F. Muscarella (Eds.), *Psychological perspectives on human sexuality* (pp. 101–146). New York: Wiley.

Everaerd, W., Laan E. T., & Spiering, M. (2000). Male sexuality. In L. T. Szuchman and F. Muscarella (Eds.), *Psychological perspectives on human sexuality* (pp. 60–100). New York: Wiley.

Forste, R. T., & Tanfer, K. (1996). Sexual exclusivity among dating, cohabitating, and married women. *Journal of Marriage and the Family, 58,* 33–47.

Friedman, A., Weinberg, H., & Pines, A. M. (1998). Sexuality and motherhood: Mutually exclusive in perception of women. *Sex Roles, 38,* 781–800.

Geer, J. H., & Broussard, D. B. (1990). Scaling heterosexual behavior and arousal: Consistency and sex differences. *Journal of Personality and Social Psychology, 58,* 664–671.

Glass, S. P., & Wright, T. L. (1977). The relationship of extramarital sex, length of marriage, and sex differences on marital satisfaction and romanticism: Athanasiou's data reanalyzed. *Journal of Marriage and the Family, 39,* 691–703.

Glass, S. P., & Wright, T. L. (1985). Sex differences in type of extramarital involvement and marital dissatisfaction. *Sex Roles, 12,* 1101–1119.

Glass, S. P., & Wright, T. L. (1997). Reconstructing marriages after the trauma of infidelity. In W. K. Halford and J. Markman (Eds.), *Clinical handbook of marriage and couple interventions* (pp. 471–507). New York: Wiley.

Gottman, J. (1993). The roles of conflict engagement, escalation, and avoidance in marital interaction: A longitudinal view of five types of couples. *Journal of Consulting and Clinical Psychology, 61,* 6–15.

Greeley, A. M. (1991). *Faithful attraction: Discovering intimacy, love, and fidelity in American marriage.* New York: Doherty.

Greenblat, C. S. (1983). The salience of sexuality in the early years of marriage. *Journal of Marriage and the Family, 45,* 289–299.

Grote, N. K., & Frieze, I. H. (1998). "Remembrance of things past": Perceptions of marital love from its beginnings to the present. *Journal of Social and Personal Relationships, 15,* 91–109.

Haavio-Mannila, E., & Kontula, O. (1997). Correlates of increased sexual satisfaction. *Archives of Sexual Behavior, 26,* 399–419.

Henderson-King, D. H., & Veroff, J. (1994). Sexual satisfaction and marital well-being in the first years of marriages. *Journal of Social and Personal Relationships, 11,* 509–534.

Hunt, M. (1974). *Sexual behavior in the 1970s.* Chicago: Playboy Press.

Jasso, G. (1985). Marital coital frequency and the effects of spouses' ages and marital duration, birth and marriage cohorts, and period influences. *American Sociological Review, 50,* 224–241.

Kinsey, A. C., Pomeroy, W. B., & Martin, C. E. (1948). *Sexual behavior in the human male.* Philadelphia: Saunders.

Kurdek, L. A. (1991). Sexuality in homosexual and heterosexual couples. In K. McKinney & S. Sprecher. *Sexuality in close relationships.* Hillsdale, NJ: Lawrence Erlbaum, pp. 177–191.

Laumann, E. O., Gagnon, J. H., Michael, R. T., & Michaels, S. (1994). *The social organization of sexuality: Sexual practices in the United States.* Chicago: The University of Chicago Press.

Laumann, E. O., Paik, A., & Rosen, R. C. (1999). Sexual dysfunction in the United States: Prevalence and predictors. *Journal of the American Medical Association, 281,* 537–544.

Lawrance, K., & Byers, E. S. (1992). Development of the interpersonal exchange model of sexual satisfaction in long-term relationships. *The Canadian Journal of Human Sexuality, 1*, 123–128.

Lawrance, K., & Byers, E. S. (1995). Sexual satisfaction in long-term heterosexual relationships: The interpersonal exchange model of sexual satisfaction. *Personal Relationships, 2*, 267–285.

Levin, R. J. (1975, October). The *Redbook* report on premarital and extramarital sex. *Redbook, 145*, 38–40.

Longmore, M. A. (1998). Symbolic interactionism and the study of sexuality. *Journal of Sex Research, 35*, 44–57.

Marsiglio, W., & Donnelly, D. (1991). Sexual intercourse in later life: A national study of married persons. *Journal of Gerontology, 46*, 338–344.

Masters, W. H., & Johnson, V. E. (1966). *Human sexual response*. Boston: Little, Brown.

McCarthy, B. W. (1999). Marital style and its effects on sexual desire and functioning. *Journal of Family Psychotherapy, 10*, 1–12.

Meyers, M., Diamond, R., Kezur, D., Scharf, C., Weinshel, M., & Rai, D. (1995). An infertility primer for family therapists: Medical, social, and psychological dimensions. *Family Process, 34*, 219–229.

Oggins, J., Leber, D., & Veroff, J. (1993). Race and gender differences in black and white newlyweds' perceptions of sexual and marital relationships. *The Journal of Sex Research, 30*, 152–160.

Parkinson, A. B. (1991). Marital and extramarital sexuality. In S. J. Bahr (Ed.), *Family research: A sixty-year review, 1930–1990* (pp. 65–96). New York: Lexington/Macmillian.

Pepe, M. V., & Byrne, J. T. (1991). Women's perception of immediate and long-term effects of failed infertility treatment on marital and sexual satisfaction. *Family Relations, 40*, 303–309.

Perry-Jenkins, M., Repetti, R. L., & Crouter, A. (2000). Work and family in the 1990s. *Journal of Marriage and the Family, 62*, 981–998.

Porter, N. L., & Christopher, F. S. (1984). Infertility: Towards an awareness of a need among family life practitioners. *Family Relations, 33*, 309–315.

Shibley-Hyde, J., DeLamater, J. D., & Durik, A. M. (2001). Sexuality and the dual-earner couple, part II: Beyond the baby years. *Journal of Sex Research, 38*, 10–23.

Singh, B. K., Walton, B. L., & Williams, J. S. (1976). Extramarital sexual permissiveness: Conditions and contingencies. *Journal of Marriage and the Family, 38*, 701–712.

Smith, T. W. (1994). *The demography of sexual behavior*. Menlo Park, CA: Kaiser Family Foundation.

Sprecher, S., & Regan, P. C. (1998). Passionate and companionate love in courting and young married couples. *Sociological Inquiry, 68*, 163–185.

Stryker, S., & Statham, A. (1985). Symbolic interaction and role theory. In G. Lindzey & E. Aronson (Eds.), *Handbook of social psychology* (pp. 311–377). New York: Random House.

Terman, L. M. (1938). *Psychological factors in marital happiness*. New York: McGraw-Hill.

Tiefer, L. (2001). A new view of women's sexual problems: Why new? Why now? *Journal of Sex Research, 38*, 89–96.

Travis, C., & Sadd, S. (1977). *The Redbook report on female sexuality*. New York: Delacorte.

White, L., & Keith, B. (1990). The effect of shift work on the quality and stability of marital relations. *Journal of Marriage and the Family, 52*, 453–462.

Wiederman, M. W. (1997). Extramarital sex: Prevalence and correlates in a national survey. *The Journal of Sex Research, 34*, 167–174.

Winceze, J. P., & Carey, M. P. (2001). *Sexual dysfunction: A guide for assessment and treatment* (2nd ed.). New York: Guilford.

Young, K. S., Griffin, S. E., Cooper, A., O'Mara, J., & Buchanan, J. (2000). Online infidelity: A new dimension in couple relationships with implications for evaluation and treatment. *Sexual Addiction and Compulsivity, 7*, 59–74.

16

Family Foundations of Sexuality

Terri D. Fisher
The Ohio State University at Mansfield

This chapter explores the role of the family in sexual development during the childhood and adolescent years. There is little evidence for the influence of early childhood family interactions on subsequent sexual behavior or attitudes. Family communication about sex, even with adolescents, is a relatively low-frequency behavior, with uncertain outcome. Parental attitudes regarding adolescent sexuality seem to be conveyed to offspring and are related to teen sexual activity. The closeness of the parent–adolescent relationship is also an important predictor of adolescent sexual behavior. Mixed findings regarding the effect of parental monitoring or control may well be due to a curvilinear relationship between the degree of such parental supervision and adolescent sexual activity. The greater likelihood of sexual activity among teens living in a single-parent household is in part due to lack of supervision, but may be due to greater family instability as well. Older siblings also appear to be significant influences on adolescent sexuality.

INTRODUCTION

Families and sexuality are inextricably linked. Without sexual intercourse, there would be no babies and thus no families, at least if one's definition of a family includes a child or two. Yet, the family is the last place that many would think of when contemplating sex in a relational context. Nonetheless, it is likely that there is much sexual learning that occurs within the family, regardless of whether or not the parents make a conscious effort to teach the children about sexuality. Sex, being part of life, is also part of family life, even though normally only the adult partners in the family actually experience sex with one another. Indeed, the majority of teens are still living with parents when they begin to engage in sexual behaviors.

Although there has been much theoretical speculation regarding childhood sexual socialization, particularly from a psychoanalytic perspective, this chapter will only address the actual empirical research that has been done in this area. There are not yet many research-based conclusions that can be drawn about the relationship between various types of family sexual socialization and their subsequent impact on sexual *relationships*. The bulk of research in this area has primarily examined different family variables and their connection to adolescent sexual behavior. The focus has been on adolescent sexuality as a public health issue, concerning questions of age at sexual debut, number of sexual partners, contraceptive use, and pregnancy. This concentration on the problems related to adolescent sexuality means that there is little, if any, research that has been concerned with sexual adjustment or pleasure. Of course, the emphasis on the problematic aspects of teen sexuality reflects the realities of funding. No agency is likely to pour big money into a study of adolescent sexual pleasure. Researchers conducting federally funded research in particular need to frame their research questions in ways that are politically astute, which means focusing on prevention issues.

The research on sexuality and family variables has been plagued by many methodological difficulties, resulting in inconsistent findings in a number of areas. In addition, until recently, many of the studies in this area consisted of limited samples and a correlational approach with data collected at only one point in time, limiting an understanding of the multitude of biological, social, and psychological factors that likely impact on adolescent sexuality. Nonetheless, there seems to have been a tendency on the part of researchers to infer causality even when the data are strictly correlational, thus impeding the development of models that acknowledge the multifactoral influences on the development of sexuality (a refreshing exception is Christopher's recent [2001] application of Symbolic Interactional Theory to adolescent sexuality). This area of research, has, for the most part, remained remarkably atheoretical, lacking much in the way of a unifying theory that would result in studies that move beyond a descriptive or exploratory approach.

This chapter explores the major areas in which research on the family foundations of sexuality has been conducted, beginning with sexual learning in early childhood and family sexual discussions. In addition, the areas of parental values, family closeness, parental monitoring or control, parental marital status, and siblings is examined. The relationship between each of these variables and subsequent adolescent sexual behavior is also discussed.

EARLY SEXUAL LEARNING

Although subject to much speculation, there is little empirical research regarding the impact of the family on early sexual development (with the exception of incest experiences, a topic that falls outside the purview of this chapter). Okami (1995) reviewed the empirical evidence for the claim that in children, exposure to parental nudity, exposure to parental sexuality, and sleeping with the parents constitute subtle sexual abuse that will result in negative repercussions. He found very little evidence to support such a claim. The strongest study of those reviewed by Okami was one by Lewis and Janda (1988) in which the researchers surveyed college students about childhood exposure to nudity within the family. In males, memories of such exposure in early childhood was related to less current discomfort with physical contact and affection. In females, this early exposure to family nudity was related to greater frequency of sexual activity. For both sexes, memories of family nudity that occurred between the ages of 6 and 10 were related to a greater tendency to engage in casual sexual relationships. It is possible, however, that family nudity is a proxy variable for permissive sexual attitudes or a greater willingness on the part of parents to be open regarding sexuality. Those parents who are more comfortable with nudity are likely to also be more comfortable acknowledging the pleasurable aspects of sexual behavior.

Okami, Olmstead, Abramson, and Pendleton (1998) reported the results of a longitudinal study of children from conventional or nonconventional families, differentiated primarily by marital status of the parents, with those in the nonconventional group consisting of intentionally single mothers, couples in group-living situations, and cohabiting couples. Okami et al. were interested in whether early childhood exposure to parental nudity or actually observing the parents having sex (the "primal scene") impacted the subsequent sexual behavior of the children. For boys, exposure to parental sexuality reduced their likelihood of having contracted an STD or getting someone pregnant, although these events were somewhat more likely in girls exposed to parental sexual activity. Exposure to parental nudity was related to a lesser likelihood of having sexual intercourse during adolescence, but more positive sexual experiences among those who were sexually active. In males, family nudity was negatively related to substance use, petty theft, and shoplifting. In general, there was little evidence of any harm whatsoever from exposure to parental nudity or sexual behavior. Okami, Weisner, and Olmstead (2002) also used this same sample of families to examine the practice of cosleeping, that is, parents and children sharing a bed. Once again, no evidence of harm was found. In fact, at age 6, there was a small, positive relationship between bed sharing and cognitive competence in the child.

It has often been asserted that parents provide children with education about sexuality regardless of whether it is done explicitly, by the absence of dialogue regarding sexual behavior, or by means of parents' reactions to sex play on the part of the child, to nudity, to masturbation, and to all of the other sex-related situations that can occur in family life. There is little research, however, that has attempted to validate this declaration. Fox and Inazu (1980) speculated that indirect sources of family influence on sexual behavior (for example, the general sexual climate in the household, attitudes toward nudity and physical affection, etc.) are likely stronger than direct communication: "At the same time, however, and somewhat ironically, the focus on direct communication is of interest precisely because of its limitations. Because of its relative weakness, it provides the most conservative and restrictive test for parental influence on children's sexual behavior" (p. 26). It might also be that the focus on direct communication is due to the fact that it is easier to measure than is nonverbal communication. Mosher (1998) provided some convincing examples of how the reactions of parents to various situations could impact the affective responses of children to sexual pleasure and release, but his work is at this point mostly theoretical.

Recently, Joffe and Franca-Koh (2001) examined the issue of nonverbal family sexual communication by means of a retrospective study of British young adults between the ages of 21 and 35. The participants were asked to report their pre- and postpubertal memories of various ways that affection was shown by their parents to one another, of the ways that nudity was handled in the home, and of their awareness of parental sexuality and mother's menstruation. These elements were considered by the researchers to constitute nonverbal sexual communication. Joffe and Franca-Koh found that general nonverbal sexual communication was significantly and negatively correlated with the age of first intercourse, such that those who grew up in a household with more nonverbal sexual communication reported a younger age of onset of sexual activity. This significant correlation appears to be due primarily to the *handling of nudity* factor, which measured the extent of nudity and degree of bathroom privacy that occurred in the home both before and after puberty. The authors suggest that "witnessing nonverbal openness in the home, particularly nudity, is linked to a sense of comfort with one's sexuality and therefore with an earlier entry into this activity" (p. 26). As mentioned previously, however, it is also possible that this variable is indicative of more permissive attitudes toward sexuality on the part of the parents. Thus, parents' sexual attitudes might be influencing the approach to sexuality of the adolescents more than family nudity per se.

In the Joffe and Franca-Koh study, general nonverbal sexual communication was not related to number of sexual partners, although the *expression of affection* factor was, such that those who grew up in a household with more affection exhibited between the parents reported a smaller number of lifetime sexual partners. Nonverbal sexual communication was not linked to contraceptive use nor was it related to the overall sex guilt score, although it was related to a few of the individual items in that those who reported greater nonverbal sexual communication were less likely to answer the items in a way that indicated sex guilt.

Our knowledge in this area is likely to remain sparse, for childhood sexuality is perhaps the most taboo of all possible research areas. Many of the standard problems and limitations of sex research are magnified when it comes to the study of children and sexuality. Consequently, almost all of the research on the family foundations of sexuality has been done with adolescents, including very late adolescents who are college students. Indeed, researchers have tended to be rather flexible in their use of the term "adolescents." Studies claiming adolescent participants have sometimes used subjects as young as 10 or as old as 25. Consistent findings are not likely to be found when some studies include preteens and others involve young adults. The research that has been done with adolescents on family foundations of sexuality has focused primarily on the process of learning about sex and the family correlates of adolescent sexual behavior. There is no research of which I am aware in which a relationship between early family socialization and the way in which the individual later incorporates sexuality into relationships was examined.

PARENT–CHILD COMMUNICATION ABOUT SEXUALITY

Parents are often spectacularly unaware of the sexual activity of their teenage offspring. Jaccard, Dittus, and Gordon (1998) found that 47% of mothers whose children had already engaged in sexual intercourse were unaware of this and believed that their children were virgins. The closer the mother–child relationship, the more likely mothers were to underestimate the sexual activity of their children. This tendency was unrelated to employment status of mothers or to family size. Similarly, Blum (2002) reported that 49% of teens who reported that they were nonvirgins had mothers who believed that their offspring had not yet experienced sexual intercourse.

Perhaps because they tend to underestimate the sexual precocity of their children, parents are not usually the primary source of information about sexuality for adolescents. Teens are much more likely to learn about sex from their friends than from their parents (Ansuini, Fiddler-Woite, & Woite, 1996; Nicholas & Tredoux, 1996) and to talk about sex with their friends rather than their parents (Pistella & Bonati, 1998). In many households, there is little or no communication about sexuality between parents and their offspring (Darling & Hicks, 1983; Fisher, 1986a, 1988; King & Lorusso, 1997). Incredibly, even in a sample of families of sons between the ages of 12 and 25 with hemophilia and HIV, nearly half of the parents reported that they *never* discussed sexuality or safer sex with their sons (Parsons et al., 1998). Rosenthal, Senserrick, and Feldman (2001) found that most parents are perceived as problematic, inactive, or ineffective communicators about sexuality. When communication does occur, it is much more likely to involve the child's mother than the father (Barone & Wiederman, 1997; Downie & Coates, 1999; Fisher, 1987; Hutchinson & Cooney, 1998; Nicholas & Tredoux, 1996; Nolin & Petersen, 1992; Raffaelli, Bogenschneider, & Flood, 1998; Rosenthal & Feldman, 1999). This is true regardless of whether the child is a son or a daughter. Fox and Inazu (1980) succinctly described this situation by suggesting that within the realm of family sex education "fathers were most notable for their lack of participation"(p. 9).

Daughters are more likely to be communicated with about various aspects of reproduction than are sons (Blum, 2002; DiIorio, Kelley, & Hockenberry-Eaton, 1999; Downie & Coates, 1999; Fisher, 1988; Lefkowitz, Kahlbaugh, & Sigman, 1996; Leland & Barth, 1993; Nolin & Petersen, 1992; Raffaelli et al., 1998; Rosenthal & Feldman, 1999), although not regarding the exploration of their sexuality (Downie & Coates, 1999). This common finding of greater communication with daughters, however, could be, at least in part, a function of the way that sexual communication has typically been measured. Many instruments designed to quantify sexual communication include the topic of menstruation, an issue much more likely to affect a girl than a boy. On the other hand, mothers tend to talk more in general with their daughters than with their sons (DiIorio et al., 1999; Leaper, Anderson, & Sanders, 1998). Perhaps reflecting the greater frequency of discussion, daughters tend to be more favorable in their evaluation of their mothers as sex educators than are sons, and mothers are evaluated more favorably than fathers by both daughters and sons (Feldman & Rosenthal, 2000; Rosenthal et al., 2001).

All of these findings must be tempered with the realization that parents and their offspring often don't agree as to whether or not communication about sex has actually occurred. Parents consistently report more frequent and extensive discussions about sexuality than do adolescents (Jaccard et al., 1998; King & Lorusso, 1997). By means of focus groups, Kahn (1994) determined that parents and their offspring have different criteria for determining whether an exchange constituted a *conversation*. In addition, she found that if discussion of a particular topic occurred more often or in greater depth with someone other than the parents, the adolescents tended to discount the conversation with the parents. Similarly, King and Lorusso (1997) report that among the 59% of college students in their study who indicated that they had never had a meaningful discussion with either of their parents about sex, 60% had parents who believed that there had been such discussions. Jaccard et al. (1998) found only a correlation of .13 between mothers' and teens' reports of sexual communication.

This lack of agreement as to amount of discussion about sexuality should come as no surprise to those familiar with the work of Larson and Richards (1994), who found that adolescents and their parents live in "divergent realities," often not even agreeing as to whether or not they are in the same room as the other. Rosenthal, Feldman, and Edwards (1998) suggested that the lack of consensus regarding family sexual communication may be due to the limited perspective on the part of adolescents regarding what actually constitutes a conversation about sex. That is, parents, being more experienced with sexual activity, might take a broader view than their children about what conversational topics might be considered related to sex. Raffaelli et al. (1999) suggested that the apparent disagreement regarding reports of family sexual discussion may be due to methodological inconsistencies such as asking about sexual discussions that might have occurred at any time during the adolescent's life, assessing parent–child communication by means of a single item, obtaining information from only one member of the parent–child dyad, and neglecting the role of fathers in family sexual communication.

Predictors and Characteristics of Family Sexual Discussions

Several studies examined the characteristics of parents who are more likely to talk to their children about sexuality. Fisher (1990) found that mothers who talked to their college students about sexuality were more likely to be open regarding general family communication and were more likely to have had a mother who had discussed sex with them. Fathers who discussed aspects of sexuality with their children were also more likely to be open in general family communication, were more likely to have had a father who had discussed sexuality with them, and reported more years of formal education. Raffaelli et al. (1998) studied characteristics of parents who talked to their 8th- to 12th- grade children about sexuality and found that being female, having higher general communication levels, having a greater parental belief that other teens were engaging in sexual activity, having greater parental concerns about adolescent sexual activity, and mothers' having greater feelings of competence in sexual communication were all predictors of higher levels of sexual communication.

In their study of the reservations of African American mothers about sexual discussions with their teens, Jaccard, Dittus, and Gordon (2000) found that the two most prevalent reasons for hesitation about discussing sex with adolescents were concerns about embarrassing the teen and worry that the teen might ask a question to which they do not know the answer (a legitimate concern, based on the 1996 findings of Hockenberry-Eaton, Richman, DiIorio, Rivero, and Maibach that many parents were unable to define basic reproductive and sexual terms). The strongest predictors of communication level were "the concern that the discussion would be embarrassing, the concern that the teen would not take her seriously, the concern that the teen would think she was prying, and the concern that the teen might ask her something she does not know" (p. 204), with each of these factors related to lower levels of sexual communication.

Lefkowitz, Kahlbaugh, and Sigman (1996) observed the conversations of mothers and their early adolescent offspring in an attempt to understand the dynamics of parent–child sexual discussions. Compared to other types of conversations, talks pertaining to sex tended to have less turn taking by the participants, fewer words, and more domination by the mothers. Mother–daughter dyads spoke more overall than did mother–son dyads, because of less discussion with their sons on the part of mothers. Mothers spoke twice as often as their children during discussions about sexuality. Lefkowitz et al. discovered that the emotional relationship between parents and their offspring was unrelated to the nature of the conversational exchange during talks about sex.

By means of a 2-year longitudinal study, Kahlbaugh, Lefkowitz, Valdez, and Sigman (1997) analyzed the affective nature of mother–adolescent communication about sexuality during the early and middle adolescent years. They found that mothers tended to be more didactic and dominant when discussing dating and sexuality than when discussing conflicts or everyday topics, and this tendency increased over the 2-year period. Kahlbaugh et al. suggested that this was due to the perceived importance of the topic on the part of the mothers.

Yowell (1997) analyzed audiotaped conversations between early adolescent girls and their mothers about appropriate social and physical behavior between a hypothetical middle school couple. The conversations took place in the home and lasted between 25 and 60 minutes. She also interviewed mothers and daughters regarding the nature of their interactions and communication. Based on these conversations, Yowell classified the mother's communication style into one of three categories. Mothers with the *power–assertive* communicative style were rather dogmatic and tended to have daughters who were passively engaged during sexual discussions. Mothers with a *conflicted* communicative style tended to feel ambivalence about sexual discussions and their daughters were likely to be avoidant during conversations about sex. Mothers who used a *collaborative* communicative style were open and tolerant during the discussions, and their daughters tended to be actively engaged during sexual talks. These three conversational styles were unrelated to the degree of pubertal development of the daughter.

Rosenthal et al. (1998) administered semistructured interviews to mothers of 16-year-old sons and daughters regarding the style, content, and frequency of the conversations about sexuality held with their children. Qualitative analyses revealed five basic communication styles on the part of the mother. *Avoidant communicators* tended not to discuss sex-related issues at all. *Reactive communicators* reported only a few sexual discussions with their adolescent children, with these talks tending to be triggered by some relevant situation or pressing issue, such as a child's romantic involvement. *Opportunistic communicators* had infrequent sexual discussions with their children, but were more willing to discuss sexuality than those mothers in the reactive category. The opportunistic mothers tended to use events such as a television show or the life situation of a friend or family member to serve as the catalyst for a sexual discussion. Those mothers who reported *child-initiated communication* waited for the adolescent child to ask questions or start a conversation. Mothers in the *mutually interactive communication* category reported mutual, open, and intimate discussions with their teenage children that were initiated at various times either by the parent or by the child.

O'Sullivan, Meyer-Bahlburg, and Watkins (2001) held focus groups for urban African American and Latino mothers and their daughters between the ages of 6 and 13, in an attempt to gain greater knowledge of the content of family sexual communication. They found that mothers typically conveyed three major messages: the hazards of sex, the responsibility of the girl to prevent sexual interaction, and the need for the girl to disclose any sexual or romantic interactions with boys to the mother. There was no mention of pleasure or of positive aspects of sexuality, and mothers were perceived by daughters to greatly exaggerate the risks of sexual intercourse. The daughters tended to reassure the mothers of their intentions to avoid engaging in sexual activity, but their pledges were often insincere and the girls tended to avoid disclosing sexual or romantic information to the mother (in many cases, neglecting to tell the mother when menarche occurred). O'Sullivan et al. concluded that given the relatively "antagonistic" roles that girls and their mothers play, that perhaps the girls should seek sexual information from other sources.

A more positive solution was proposed by Lefkowitz, Sigman, and Au (2000), who provided some mothers of early adolescents with two training sessions designed to help them learn how to competently discuss sexuality and AIDS. The mothers in the intervention group became more comfortable and effective in their sexual discussions with their children, both during an assessment period as well as later. There was some evidence that the intervention resulted in increased knowledge by daughters about AIDS.

Parents are particularly unlikely to talk about sexual risk factors such as STDs and HIV/AIDS, and they are not likely to explain how to take steps to minimize the risks of sexuality, although African American parents have been found to be more likely to do so than White parents (Hutchinson & Cooney, 1998). Baumeister, Flores, and Marin (1995) found in their study of Latina adolescents' perceptions of sexual information provided by parents that of five possible topics (menstruation, sexual intercourse, STDs, body parts related to sex, and birth control), parents were least likely to discuss birth control with their daughters.

Rosenthal and Feldman (1999) examined the factor structure of various sex-related topics discussed by parents and found four distinct domains. *Development and society concerns* include topics related to physical development and bodily changes as well as topics that are societal issues such as pregnancy, abortion, and homosexuality. *Sexual safety* topics consist of issues like STDs and contraception. The *experiencing sex* category consists of topics such as dating, sexual desire and satisfaction, and different types of sexual practices. Finally, *solitary sexual activity* includes discussion of masturbation and wet dreams. The 16-year-old students in the sample believed communication from parents regarding the areas of *experiencing sex* and *solitary sexual activity* to be relatively unimportant as a topic of discussion with their parents. They were more willing to accept communication regarding *sexual safety*, but Rosenthal and Feldman concluded that "parents are not preferred sources of information or influence when it comes to dealing with sexuality" (p. 848). Wood, Senn, Desmarais, Park, and Verberg (2002) examined early and middle adolescents' evaluation of sources of information about dating. They found that friends and sex education teachers were rated as more important sources of this information than were parents or the media, although adults (parents and teachers) were perceived to be more accurate sources of information.

The Relationship of Parent–Child Sexual Communication With Adolescent Sexual Behavior

Jaccard and Dittus (1991) suggested that parents can influence the sexual behavior of their teenage children by serving as role models, influencing their social and emotional development, instilling appropriate values, and serving as sources of information. Of these four possible routes of influence, the last seems to be the easiest to accomplish and prescribe. Therefore, it is encouraging to believe that parent–child discussions about sex will result in more responsible sexual behavior (waiting longer to engage in sexual intercourse, having few sexual partners, utilizing contraception, etc.). In fact, for quite some time, the conventional wisdom, backed by selected research findings, has been that parent–child communication about sexuality is a fine preventative measure for avoiding some of the pitfalls of adolescent sexuality, despite the fact that there have always been those who feared that teaching children about sexuality would cause them to immediately become sexually active. Indeed, parents are typically told that they should discuss various aspects of sexuality with their children, regardless of the discomfort such a discussion might entail (Simanski, 1998). It remains unclear, however, whether or not there is any relationship between family sexual communication and adolescent sexual behavior because the results of the research in this area have been remarkably inconsistent.

Although some researchers have found the commonly touted relationship between sexual communication and a lower likelihood of "irresponsible sexual behavior" (Darling & Hicks, 1982; Davis & Friel, 2001; DiIorio et al., 1999; Forste & Heaton, 1988; Holtzman & Rubinson, 1995; Hutchinson & Cooney, 1998; Jaccard & Dittus, 1991; Jaccard, Dittus, & Gordon, 1996; Kotchick, Dorsey, Miller, & Forehand, 1999; Leland & Barth, 1993; R. A. Lewis, 1973; Mueller & Powers, 1990; Murry, 1996; Pick & Palos, 1995), other researchers have failed to find such a relationship (Barone & Weiderman, 1997; Casper, 1990; Cvetkovich & Grote, 1983; Fisher, 1987; Handelsman, Cabral, & Weisfield, 1987; Kastner, 1984; Newcomer & Udry, 1984; Wright, Peterson, & Barnes, 1990) and still others have found an inverse relationship (Darling & Hicks, 1982; Davis & Friel, 2001; Fox & Inazu, 1980; Inazu & Fox, 1980; Widmer, 1997). Some researchers have found mixed results, with the relationship varying as a function of the sex of the adolescent or the sex of the parent, although not in any consistent way (DeLamater & MacCorquodale, 1979; Fisher, 1988; Moore, Peterson, & Furstenberg, 1986; Newcomer & Udry, 1985; Somers & Paulson, 2000; Spanier, 1976; Treboux & Busch-Rossnagel, 1990). If there is an actual impact of family sexual communication on adolescent sexual behavior, not only is it not clear whether such communication would serve to deter or to encourage adolescent sexual activity, the size of such an effect is also unknown. One could argue that an "effect" that remains so elusive must not be particularly strong in the first place, although it is possible that the different findings are due to the varied samples, age groups, and methodologies that have been used. Indeed, the area of parent–child communication about sexuality is fraught with methodological difficulties (for excellent reviews of some of the issues, see Miller, 1998; Warren, 1995).

Messages and Topics.   One likely reason for the inconsistent findings is the multitude of ways in which family sexual communication has been measured (Fisher, 1993). Only a few studies have taken a close look at the messages that were conveyed by parents during sexual communication. Darling and Hicks (1982) found that messages about sex conveyed by parents to their adolescent offspring fall into three major categories: *sex as dangerous*, *sex as dirty*, and *sex as positive*. In a subsequent study, Darling and Hicks (1983) categorized these parental messages into five areas: a sexual double standard exists, sex is bad, sex should be delayed, save sex for marriage, and love is a prerequisite for sex (pp. 235–236). Ward and Wyatt (1994), in a retrospective study of the purported effects of childhood sexual messages on adolescent sexual behavior, found that White women who recalled receiving negative verbal messages from childhood tended to engage in riskier sexual behavior during the teen years than those who received more positive or instructional messages during childhood. Ward and Wyatt also asked about nonverbal sexual communication, defined as parents communicating information about sex by means of their behavior (e.g., a display of physical affection). Those participants who recalled an absence of such nonverbal messages, especially during adolescence, tended to report riskier adolescent sexual behavior. There were no such associations for the sample of African American women. Ward and Wyatt suggest that researchers should not measure general family sexual communication but instead should more closely examine the type or tone of the communication.

Murray (1994) suggested that the "effect" of parent–child sexual discussions may be related to the topics covered. In her sample of randomly selected, African American adolescent females, having had a discussion with parents about how pregnancy occurs was related to sexual abstinence, but discussing topics such as menstruation, sexually transmitted diseases, and contraception was not. Thus, it could be that the attempt to develop a good global scale of family sexual communication might be misguided. A recent study (Romo, Lefkowitz, Sigman, & Au, 2002) yielded similar findings. In a study of Latino mothers and their 12- to 15-year-old offspring, Romo et al. found, based on a structural equation model, that although extensive discussion of maternal sexual beliefs and values was related to less likelihood of the adolescent engaging in sexual activity 1 year later, maternal comments about their adolescent children's dating and sexuality experiences were related to a *greater* likelihood of sexual activity 1 year later. Therefore, the content of the sexual discussions seems to make a big difference with regard to the impact of those discussions. Disclosure regarding teenage sexual and dating experiences on the part of the mothers was related to adolescent reports of greater openness in their relationship with mother and more conservative attitudes toward premarital sex 1 year later. Therefore, Romo et al. suggest that self-disclosure appears to be a useful sexual communication strategy on the part of mothers.

Parental Attitudes.   Generally, parents' attitudes toward premarital sex have not been taken into account when examining the relationship between family sexual communication and adolescent sexual behavior (Jaccard & Dittus, 1991), with a few exceptions. Moore et al. (1986) found that family sexual discussions were related to lower levels of sexual activity only among girls from families in which the parents had traditional attitudes, and Fisher (1989) found that only the sexual behavior of female college students with parents who had permissive sexual attitudes was correlated with the amount of family sexual discussion such that more communication about sexuality was related to a greater likelihood that the daughter had experienced sexual intercourse. More recently, Dittus and Jaccard (2000) found that the adolescent children of mothers who were opposed to adolescent sexual intercourse were less likely to engage in sexual activity or to become pregnant. Jaccard et al. (2000), commenting on the same data set, asserted that

> To the extent that there is a causal link between these variables, then it would be prudent for parents who are strongly opposed to premarital sex to convey this disapproval to their teen. It is interesting to consider the notion that whether the teen accurately perceives the position of the mother is not the primary issue for discouraging sexual intercourse in young teens. Rather, it is the teen's perception of the mother's position, independent of the accuracy of the perception, that is predictive. (p. 259)

Similarly, Blum (2002) reported that adolescents tend to underestimate the degree of disapproval of teenage sexual behavior felt by their mothers. Mother's disapproval of such behavior only had a deterrent effect on sexual initiation when the adolescent accurately perceived the mother's attitudes. Interestingly, younger adolescents (but not older ones) were much more likely to accurately perceive their mother's disapproval of their having sex when they had close relationships with their mothers.

It seems obvious in retrospect that any impact of sexual communication from the parents must be moderated by the viewpoint of the parents toward sexuality in general and premarital sex in particular. Nonetheless, very little is known with certainty about this relationship, much less about how the content of family sexual discussions might differ as a function of parental values. It is likely that discussing sex with a very conservative parent might have far different implications than would a sexual discussion with a more permissive parent. It is clear that parental attitudes must be included as a moderating variable in future research.

Other Considerations.   Another factor that seems to account for inconsistent findings is the age of the adolescent. A study by Treboux and Busch-Rossnagel (1995) indicated that for high school and college-age female adolescents, the impact of sexual discussions with their mothers and of the adolescent's perception of the mother's sexual attitudes was strongest among 9th and 10th graders, with those teenage girls who reported discussing a greater number of sexual topics with their mothers holding more conservative sexual attitudes. Older adolescents are less satisfied with and more negative about sexual discussions with their mothers (Lefkowitz, Romo, Corona, Au, & Sigman, 2000).

K. B. Rodgers (1999) examined sexual risk taking as a function of family communication by assessing the number of sexual partners in the past year, the consistency of contraceptive use, and contraceptive effectiveness in high school students who voluntarily engaged in sexual intercourse. She found no direct connection between family sexual communication and sexual risk taking. There was, however, an interaction between parental support and communication for male participants. Males with parents who were not supportive but who did discuss sexual issues were the most likely to be engaging in high-risk sexual behavior. Rodgers suggested that this could be due to the poor parent–child relationship interfering with the quality of sexual communication, apparently resulting in sexual discussions that are less effective than no discussions at all.

Whitaker, Miller, May, and Levin (1999) found that sexual discussions with mothers were related to a greater likelihood of sexually active teenagers using condoms and discussing sexual risk with their partners, but only if the mothers were effective communicators during the conversations about sex, as indicated by their children's ratings of the mothers' comfort, skill, and openness during such discussions. This is an intriguing finding, because previous researchers have not considered the skill and comfort levels of parents when examining the possible impact of family sexual communication. Another factor examined by this group of researchers (K. S. Miller, Levin, Whitaker, & Xu, 1998) is the timing of sexual discussions. If a mother discussed condoms prior to her adolescent child engaging in sexual intercourse, it was much more likely that the adolescent would use condoms at first intercourse, at most recent intercourse, and in general. This variable of timing of sexual discussions is another very important factor that previous researchers have not considered.

Whitaker and Miller (2000) suggested that the impact of parent–child communication regarding sexuality may be indirect, operating by means of a diminished impact of peer influence. In their study of African American and Hispanic adolescents between the ages of 14 and 16, they found that peer norms about sex were more strongly related to adolescent sexual behavior when parents did not discuss with their children the issue of when to start having sex. Similarly, peer norms regarding condoms were more strongly related to adolescent condom use when parents did not discuss condoms with their children. Teens whose parents had discussed these issues with them were more likely to believe that parents (as opposed to peers) were the best source of information about sex. Whitaker and Miller suggested that family sexual discussions function not only to provide information but also to reinforce the values of the parents and protect the adolescents from peer pressure.

Conclusions. It seems that there is no clear relationship between parent–child communication about sexuality and subsequent adolescent sexual activity. Whether or not family sexual discussions serve as a deterrent to risky sexual behavior apparently depends on the age of the child when the communication takes place, what topics are discussed, the comfort level of the parents, and the values of the parent. It seems without basis to advise all parents to discuss aspects of sexuality with their children if the only goal of such discussion is to discourage teens from engaging in sexual behavior. It is likely, however, that family discussions about sex might yield benefits yet to be determined.

Relationship of Parent–Child Sexual Communication With Adolescent Sexual Knowledge and Attitudes

As mentioned previously, parents are very rarely the primary source of information about sexuality. Given that, it is perhaps not surprising that factual information from parents is unlikely to have much impact on the sexual knowledge database of teens. Most studies indicate that there is no apparent relationship between the amount or type of family sexual communication and the accuracy of adolescents' sexual knowledge (Bennett & Dickinson, 1980; Fisher, 1986b, 1988; Hansson, Jones, & Chernovetz, 1979; Sigelman, Derenowski, Mullaney, & Siders, 1993; Warren & St. Pierre, 1973), although Somers and Paulson (2000) recently found a connection between degree of parent–child sexual communication and sexual knowledge in high school students, and the Sigelman et al. (1993) study found a significant relationship between parents' knowledge of myths about the transmission of AIDS and the knowledge of their children about these myths when parents reported higher levels of communication about sex. Despite these two exceptions, the bulk of the research indicates that whatever effect family discussions about sexuality might have, it is not likely to result in increased knowledge on the part of the children.

Parents and teens who report high levels of communication about sexuality with one another do tend to have sexual attitudes that are very highly correlated with each other, relative to families that report lower levels of sexual communication (Fisher, 1986a, 1987, 1988). Although this relationship appears to have been examined by very few researchers, the results are consistent across several different samples. These results suggest that parent–child communication about sexuality could be an effective means for parents to convey values to their children. In fact, Treboux and Busch-Rossnagel (1995) determined that the effects of sexual discussion with mothers and of adolescents' perception of parental approval of sexual behavior operate indirectly on female adolescent sexual behavior by way of the sexual attitudes of the adolescent.

This intergenerational transmission of values was recently explored by B. C. Miller, Norton, Fan, and Christopherson (1998) who reported the results of their excellent short-term longitudinal study in which structural equation modeling was used to examine both direct and indirect effects of family and biological variables on aspects of adolescent sexual behavior measured at three different points in time. They found that the quality of parent–child sexual communication did not directly affect adolescent sexual behavior, but it did affect the teens' sexual values (with high quality communication being related to a greater likelihood of adolescents valuing sexual abstinence). In turn, adolescent sexual values were related to adolescent sexual behavior, with abstinence values having a strong negative direct effect on intention to have sex in the next year and a moderate negative direct effect on actual sexual activity. This finding is all the more remarkable given the fairly restricted range of values, in light of the fact that 85% of the participating families were Mormon. A study by Taris, Semin, and Bok (1998) resulted in the finding that adolescents from families in which the parent–child interactions were of high quality were more likely to share the sexual values of their mothers than were teens from families with a poor family climate. The results of these newer studies, combined with those of the earlier Fisher studies, give strong indication that values transmission could indeed be an important mechanism by which families can influence their adolescent offspring.

PARENTAL VALUES

There is not a lot of research examining the effect of parents' sexual values on the sexual behavior of their children, but the results have been consistent. Small and Luster (1994) found that having parents with permissive values regarding teenage sexual behavior was strongly associated with greater sexual experience in both male and female adolescents. Hovell et al. (1994) also found mothers' permissive attitudes about adolescent sexuality were positively related and mothers' belief that one should wait until marriage to have intercourse was negatively related to adolescent sexual intercourse. Dittus, Jaccard, and Gordon (1997) found that fathers' as well as mothers' sexual attitudes were predictors of the sexual behavior of inner city African American teens. A study by Taris and Semin (1997b) indicated that in families with a high quality of interaction, differences in sexual attitudes between parents and adolescents resulted in significantly less disagreement than in families with poor quality interaction. K. S. Miller, Forehand, and Kotchick (1999) found a clear relationship between mothers having more conservative sexual attitudes and their adolescent offspring reporting less frequent intercourse and fewer sexual partners. Dittus and Jaccard (2000) examined a subsample of the Longitudinal Study of Adolescent Health, the largest study of adolescent health ever conducted, consisting of a nationally representative sample of students in the 7th through 11th grades. They found that the adolescents' perception of disapproving maternal attitudes toward adolescent sexual behavior at time one of testing was predictive of less likelihood of having engaged in sexual intercourse or having become pregnant 1 year later. Davis and Friel (2001) also demonstrated that mothers who disapprove of adolescent sex are more likely to have teenage children who tend to postpone sexual involvement. Meschke, Barthlomae, and Zentall (2002) suggested that the impact of parental values on the sexual behavior of adolescents may be moderated by the quality of the relationship between parent and adolescent, in that the parents' values may have more of an impact on the adolescent if the parents are warm and supportive.

Of course, any apparent relationship between the sexual behavior or attitudes of parents and those of their children after controlling for all relevant demographic variables could be due to social learning factors or to common genetic factors. Most researchers in this area have ignored the possibility that there are individual differences with regard to basic level of sex drive as well as sociosexuality (Simpson & Gangestad, 1991; Simpson, Wilson, & Winterheld, chapter 4, this volume) that may well be genetically based. It is entirely possible that permissive parents have permissive children, not because of the social transmission of their ideas, but because they share a biologically based tendency toward such. This seems likely, especially in light of the finding by Jaccard et al. (1998) that adolescents are often unaware of the sexual attitudes of their parents, with a correlation of only .28 between mothers' reports of their disapproving attitudes regarding teenage sexual activity and the adolescents' perceptions of their mothers' attitudes. An earlier study (1996) by these same authors yielded a correlation of .22 between adolescents' perceptions of their mothers' attitudes toward premarital sex and their mothers' actual attitudes.

FAMILY CLOSENESS

One area of consensus in the research literature is that parent–child closeness and/or the quality of their nonsexual communication is fairly consistently linked to lower levels of sexual activity (Dittus & Jaccard, 2000; Fisher, 1987; Fleuridas, Creevy, & Vela, 1997; Inazu & Fox, 1980; Jaccard, Dittus, & Gordon, 1996; Karofsky, Zeng, & Kosorok, 2000; Metzler, Noell, Biglan, Ary, & Smolkowski, 1994; B. C. Miller, 1998; B. C. Miller et al., 1997 [found in females only]; Newcomer & Udry, 1987; St. Lawrence, Brasfield, Jefferson, Allyene, & Shirley, 1994) and a greater likelihood of the use of birth control (Dittus & Jaccard, 2000; Jaccard et al., 1996). There are, however, some interesting exceptions to this pattern of findings. A recent two-wave panel study by Taris and Semin (1997a) indicated that a close parent–child relationship is related to *earlier* onset of sexual activity 1 year later. McLaughlin, Chen, Greenberger, and Biermeier (1997) found that White females (but not males or Asian-American females) reported more autonomy from parents in decision making if they had more sexual partners but more conflict with parents if they reported no sexual partners. K. B. Rodgers (1999) did not find a significant impact of family supportiveness on high-risk sexual behavior in high school students; nor did Upchurch, Aneshensel, Sucoff, and Levy-Storms (1999), who reported that parental socioemotional support did not have an effect on adolescent sexual behavior independent of other family variables.

Whitbeck, Conger, and Kao (1993) suggested that the small inconsistency in research findings in this area might be due to the likelihood that the effects are largely indirect. They found that adolescent girls lacking supportive parental relationships are more likely to develop emotionally intimate relationships with their peers as a means of compensation, which affects both their sexual attitudes and their susceptibility to peer influence, and concluded that "the quality of the parent–child relationship creates the emotional context that contributes to the relative strength of peer group influences" (p. 274). Whitbeck, Yoder, Hoyt, and Conger (1999) found that poor family relationships were more predictive of age at first sexual intercourse than were positive family relationships. The warmth and supportiveness of the mother was not related to early sexual intercourse, although mother rejection certainly was. These family variables, however, were not nearly as predictive of adolescent sexual behavior as were certain nonfamily variables, (grade level, deviant peers, permissive sexual attitudes, steady dating, and alcohol use).

Using data from the National Longitudinal Study of Adolescent Health, Davis and Friel (2001) found that when girls perceived positive relationships with their mothers they seemed to postpone engaging in sexual intercourse. This relationship was not found for boys. A close mother–child relationship reported by the adolescents was unrelated to number of sexual partners for adolescents of either sex. However, when the mothers evaluated the relationship positively, there was a clear delay in age of onset of sexual intercourse for both sons and daughters, and a reduction in the number of sexual partners reported by daughters. The amount of interaction between mother and adolescent (as reported by the adolescents) was unrelated to number of sexual partners for both sexes and to age of sexual debut for boys. Unexpectedly, however, those girls who reported spending more time with their mothers reported a slightly *earlier* age at first intercourse.

Whitbeck, Hoyt, Miller, and Kao (1992) determined that the closeness of the family affected adolescent sexual behavior indirectly through depressed affect, which in females was associated with an increased likelihood of sexual activity during adolescence. Whitbeck et al. suggested that these girls might have tried to compensate for the distant relationship with their parents by developing more intimate relationships outside the family as a means of experiencing warmth and support. For males, lack of closeness in family relationships resulted in an increased likelihood of alcohol use, which was, in turn, closely associated with a greater likelihood of adolescent sexual activity.

Lynch (2001) attempted to apply two important developmental theories to the first wave of data from the National Longitudinal Study of Adolescent Health. Bronfenbrenner's Ecological Systems Theory (1992) stresses the interconnections between the individual and various aspects of the environment (family, institutions, cultures). In his Problem Behavior Theory, Jessor (1992) suggested that various adolescent problem behaviors such as drug use, delinquency, and risky sexual activity are all related to one another. Lynch found moderate support for both of these models. Interestingly, the family interaction/bonding variables had their strongest impact on adolescent sexual activity indirectly, by means of a negative impact on substance use, which was a powerful predictor of sexual activity, particularly for younger adolescents.

In Blum's (2002) summary of findings from the National Longitudinal Study of Adolescent Health, he reported that mothers who were satisfied with their relationship with their daughters had daughters who were less likely to indicate that they had engaged in sexual intercourse. This relationship was not found for sons, however. When adolescents of either sex reported a close relationship with their mothers (conceptualized as connectedness), they were significantly less likely to have made the transition to engaging in sexual intercourse, except among the 10th- and 11th-grade girls (the oldest in the sample).

Multivariate Studies of Family Closeness

Very few studies have examined this warmth/closeness/good general communication variable simultaneously with family sexual communication, so it is not yet clear how these variables interrelate. Fisher (1987) found that general family communication was unrelated to family sexual communication using a bivariate correlational analysis; but in a subsequent study with a similar sample (Fisher, 1990), which utilized a multiple regression analysis involving many variables, there was indeed a significant correlation. Luster and Small (1994) found clear-cut relationships between lack of family closeness, low levels of parental supervision, and lack of discussion about contraception (for females) and high risk adolescent sexual behavior (defined as having had more than one sexual partner and rarely if ever using contraception). Revealingly, however, for many variables there were no significant differences between sexual abstainers and those adolescents who engaged in responsible sexual behavior (defined as having had only one sexual partner and consistently using contraception). More recently, K. S. Miller et al. (1999) examined the role of numerous family variables as predictors of sexual behavior in African American and Hispanic high school students who participated in the study with their mothers. After controlling for demographic variables and structural family variables (which were not significant predictors), the major predictors of reduced and responsible adolescent sexual behavior were higher levels of parental monitoring, better general communication, and more conservative maternal sexual attitudes.

Somers and Paulson (2000) explored the association of family closeness and parental sexual communication in high school students and found these variables in combination were unrelated to adolescent sexual experience. Parental communication about sexuality was more closely related to extent of adolescent sexual behavior than was family closeness, but in a positive direction such that those teens who reported higher levels of sexual communication also reported *higher* levels of sexual behavior. The authors believe that this likely reflects an increase in sexual discussions occurring as the result of sexual activity on the part of the adolescents, but because all of the data were collected at one point in time (and only from the adolescents), it is impossible to verify this hypothesis. Somers and Paulson also acknowledge that their findings could be due to the uncontrolled variable of age of the adolescent (which is a very strong predictor of experiencing sexual intercourse). Whitaker and Miller (2000) added parental monitoring and parental closeness measures to their original analysis and determined that the indirect effect of parent–child communication on the impact of peer norms was independent of these two variables.

Although closeness to parents appears to be one of the strongest family-related correlates of delayed sexual activity (Miller, Benson, & Galbraith, 2001), it is not obvious whether it is a direct or an indirect effect. If it is a direct effect, it could be that the closeness of the parent–child relationship serves as a motivation for the teen to resist sexual activities. On the other hand, it is possible that the family closeness eliminates the need for the adolescent to seek warmth and understanding outside the family, which could lead to premature sexual encounters. Certainly, to the degree that adolescent sexual intercourse may be viewed as an act of rebellion, one would expect it to be less likely when family ties are strong.

PARENTAL MONITORING OR CONTROL

The amount of monitoring or control to which an adolescent is subjected is the one family variable examined in this chapter that is most amenable to change, and yet relatively few researchers have attempted to examine the impact of supervision on adolescent sexual behavior. Based on the research that has been done, there still seems to be no consensus regarding the relationship between monitoring or control on the part of the parents and sexual behavior on the part of the adolescent. Nonetheless, the situation has improved somewhat since 1981, when Fox lamented:

> It would appear that, although teenagers complain often and loudly about parental restrictions and rules, although the family is generally expected to continue to safeguard and protect its children by monitoring their behavior, and although parents appear to worry endlessly about how, in fact, to do this, there is little research on this family function. (Fox, 1981, pp. 108–109)

The earliest study to directly examine this question was that of Jessor and Jessor (1975) who found that their (nonspecified) measure of parental control over adolescent behavior significantly distinguished between virgins and nonvirgins for both males and females in high school as well as for male college students, such that the adolescents who had not yet experienced sexual intercourse had parents who exerted greater control. A follow-up to this study in 1983 indicated that regardless of the age at which the transition to nonvirgin status was made, parental controls were significantly more lax for those making the transition. A strength of this later study is that it was prospective, allowing conclusions to be drawn as to the direction of the relationship.

Since the Jessor and Jessor studies, a number of other researchers found support for a relationship between degree of monitoring or strictness by the parents and a lower probability of having engaged in sexual intercourse on the part of adolescents (Hogan & Kitagawa, 1985; Hovell et al, 1994; Metzler et al., 1994; K. S. Miller, et al., 1999; Moore et al., 1986; K. B. Rodgers, 1999; Small & Luster, 1994; Upchurch et al., 1999). Other studies, however, failed to provide support for the relationship (Biglan et al., 1990;

Cvetkovich & Grote, 1983; Inazu & Fox, 1980; Jaccard & Dittus, 1991; Newcomer & Udry, 1984). In fact, Upchurch et al. (1999) analyzed data from a longitudinal study of adolescents between the ages of 12 and 17 and found that both male and female adolescents who reported that their parents exerted high levels of control were more likely to begin having sexual intercourse at an early age. It is important, however, to keep in mind that this measure of control was reported only by the adolescent and could have reflected the degree of alienation from the parent that the adolescent felt.

A study by B. C. Miller, McCoy, Olson, and Wallace (1986) helps to clarify the seemingly contradictory results of these studies. These researchers found a curvilinear relationship between the adolescent's perception of parental strictness and dating rules and whether or not the adolescent had engaged in sexual intercourse. Adolescents were most likely to have had intercourse if they reported that their parents were "not strict" or had no rules governing their dating. The lowest rates of intercourse were among those teens who reported that their parents were halfway between "moderate" and "strict" (4 on a scale of 1 to 5) or who indicated that the number of dating rules that they had been given by their parents was somewhere between "moderate" and "many." Adolescents reporting "very strict" parents or "many rules" were significantly more likely than this moderately strict group to have had sexual intercourse, although this relationship was only significant when the male and female data were combined. Evidence for this curvilinear relationship between dating rules and sexual intercourse was present based on parents' reports as well. The possibility of a nonlinear relationship has not typically been examined by researchers in this area, but might well help to explain the inconsistent findings. This study by Miller et al., although quite convincing, begs for replication with a different population, although Kurdek and Fine (1994) demonstrated a curvilinear relationship between general adolescent adjustment and family control.

Whitbeck et al. (1999) found that higher levels of monitoring on the part of the mother were related to a lesser likelihood of adolescent sexual intercourse only among younger adolescents. After ninth grade, monitoring was actually positively related to sexual behavior. Whitbeck et al. concluded that there is diminishing parental influence on sexual behavior as adolescents grow older. Unfortunately, their sample was limited to students in Grades 8 through 10, and it is impossible to know whether that trend would continue through the high school years or whether parental influence has a curvilinear effect, with greater impact in early and in late adolescence. Lynch (2001) also reported a significant decline in the impact of family variables on sexual behavior in the high school years relative to the junior high years.

K. B. Rodgers (1999), in her study of high school students who had engaged in sexual intercourse, found that both males and females who were monitored by their parents were less likely to engage in high-risk sexual behavior. Contrary to the author's hypothesis, the effectiveness of monitoring was not enhanced by parental supportiveness. Rodgers suggested that perhaps monitoring, in and of itself, conveys concern and care to the teen. This study also examined the impact of psychological control on the part of the parents by means of guilt. This tactic seemed to increase the likelihood of high-risk sexual behavior among the female adolescents, with the father's psychological control having more of an impact than the mother's. Rodgers speculated that high levels of control through guilt could prevent daughters from developing the maturity and internalized morality that would facilitate responsible sexuality.

Longmore Manning, and Giordano (2001) recently looked at the possibility that preadolescent parenting strategies could be essential in determining the timing of adolescent dating and sexual experience, arguing that "parental behavior prior to the onset of adolescence provides a basic foundation for young people who later must make behavioral choices outside of parental purview" (p. 332). They used data from the two waves of the National Survey of Families and Households that included information obtained from interviews with parents regarding the degree of supportive parenting, monitoring, and coercive control provided and adolescents' reports of their sexual and dating behavior 4 years later. They found that for both males and females, timing of first date was not influenced by parental strategies, and early monitoring (as determined by restrictions on child's behavior and amount of time spent without supervision) was the only significant parenting predictor of timing of first sexual intercourse, with those parents who reported greater monitoring of their children prior to the teenage years being more likely to have adolescents who delay sexual intercourse.

In this area, the samples and analyses have generally been of good quality, although many of the measures lack demonstrated reliability and validity. Teenagers may not be the best judges of the relative strictness of their own parents, although their perceptions are likely what matters most. Although the majority of studies yielded at least one significant relationship between the level of supervision or parental monitoring received by adolescents and the occurrence of sexual activity, generally the relationship appears to be relatively small and not a straightforward one.

PARENTAL MARITAL STATUS

There are numerous studies that have indicated that adolescents are more likely to engage in intercourse if they are living in any family structure other than residing with both original parents (Meschke, Zweig, Barber, & Eccles, 2000 [found in females only]; B. C. Miller & Bingham, 1989 [solely females in sample]; Murray, 1994; Murray, 1996; Stern, Northman, & Van Slyck, 1984; Upchurch et al., 1999; Whitbeck & Simons, 1994), although in the Miller and Bingham study, when age, race, social class, and religion were controlled, the impact of parental marital status was largely reduced. Upchurch et al. (1999) found that adolescent males and females living in a reconstituted family were at particular risk of an early sexual debut. They attributed this to the stress of adjusting to a new family structure.

Newcomer and Udry (1987) suggested that the reason for the greater rate of sexual activity among teenagers living in single-parent households is because of the lower degree of general parental control present in such households. There is ample evidence that single parents use parenting strategies that are related to higher rates of adolescent deviant behavior (Demo, 1992; McLanahan & Booth, 1989). Obviously, in a single-parent family, there is only one parent to take on the job of keeping track of the adolescent. Dornbusch et al. (1985) demonstrated that single-parent households headed by mothers were characterized by an absence of joint decision making processes, which was associated with delinquency even when controlling for parental education and socioeconomic status. The presence of any other adult in the household was related to higher levels of parental control and lower levels of various types of delinquency, especially for males. The nature of the parent–child relationship is likely different in a single-parent household as well, although Upchurch et al. (1999) found no support for the notion that extent of parent–adolescent interaction varied by family structure.

In her study of lower-class and lower-middle-class White girls attending a recreation center, Hetherington (1972) found that those girls who had experienced father absence because of divorce were more flirtatious and interested in boys than were girls whose fathers had died. Hetherington did not directly measure sexual behavior, and it is uncertain if these findings regarding the differences between daughters of widows and daughters of divorced women would still hold true today. Nonetheless, this study remains an intriguing suggestion of the impact that father absence could have on female sexuality and suggests that there could be more going on than a simple lack of monitoring.

Capaldi, Crosby, and Stoolmiller (1996) found in their sample of adolescent males who lived in higher crime areas that parental marital status did not predict the adolescent transition to having sexual intercourse. Rather, it was the total number of family transitions that was related to the boys' sexual behavior. A divorce is considered a family transition, as is a marriage. They suggested (as have others) that this could be due to the parents serving as models of sexual behavior, with the sexual elements of a new relationship being more apparent to an adolescent than the sexual aspects of a long-standing marriage. This same impact of parental marital changes on adolescent sexual behavior was found by B. C. Miller et al. (1997) for boys in their nationally representative sample. For the girls, however, it was mother's marital status that was a better predictor, with girls in a single-parent home being more likely to engage in intercourse. Miller et al. suggested that this could indicate a socialization effect for females, with sexual attitudes mediating the effect of mothers' marital status on females. This hypothesis was based on the findings of Whitbeck and Simons (1994) that mothers' dating behaviors were a direct influence on the sexual behavior of sons, but an indirect influence on daughters by means of mothers' sexual attitudes. Kotchick et al. (1999) found a positive relationship between maternal sexual risk-taking behavior (multiple sexual partners, inconsistent condom use) and adolescent sexual risk-taking behavior in a sample of Black and Hispanic families headed by single mothers. However, when they included variables pertaining to the quality of family sexual communication and mothers' attitudes regarding adolescent sexuality, this relationship was no longer significant. Rather, open and receptive sexual communication between mother and adolescent was negatively related to adolescent sexual risk taking.

In an intriguing test of competing hypotheses regarding the impact of parental marital status on adolescent sexual behavior, Wu and Thomson (2001) found that for White adolescent females, the number of changes in the family situation was significantly related to an earlier age at first intercourse, supporting the idea that it is instability in the family that leads to a greater likelihood of the adolescent engaging in sexual intercourse. For African American adolescent females, however, living in a single-parent household or in a family with a stepfather was linked to an earlier age at first intercourse, which lends support to the view that earlier intercourse in such households is due to lack of parental control (because stepfathers tend to be less effective at monitoring behavior than biological or adoptive fathers). Interestingly, there was no relationship between age at first intercourse and being born to an unmarried mother or extended time spent in a single-parent household or the extended absence of a biological father for teens of either race. The authors found little support for the hypothesis that being raised by a single parent provides a role model for sex outside of marriage (a socialization hypothesis).

Recently, Davis and Friel (2001) found that when the nature of the mother–child relationship and parental involvement as well as maternal sexual attitudes were controlled in a multivariate model, family structure was unrelated to timing of adolescent sexual debut except for girls in single-parent families. Family structure was not at all related to number of sexual partners reported by adolescents. Instead, the relationship between mother and adolescent as well as the mother's attitudes about adolescent sexuality and the level of her discussions of sex was related to the onset of sexual intercourse in teens. The authors believe that earlier findings of a relationship between parental marital status and adolescent sexual activity were probably due to the previously discussed moderating variable of parental control or monitoring.

Although parental marital status appears to be an important predictor of adolescent sexual behavior, there is much work to be done to fully understand the dynamics behind this relationship. Apparently the effect of living in a single-parent household may differ as a function of race, parenting style, and perhaps other variables that have not yet been examined. In addition, there appears to be no research on the impact of parents who are in the process of ending their relationship on the sexual behavior of their teenage children. Such a study could provide important insights regarding the role of the family in adolescent sexual decision making.

SIBLINGS

Older siblings not only serve as an important source of sexual information (Ansuini et al., 1996), they may also influence sexual behavior in their younger brothers and sisters, with their own sexual behaviors being significant predictors of the sexual behavior of younger siblings (Haurin & Mott, 1990; Pick & Palos, 1995; J. L. Rodgers & Rowe, 1990). J. L. Rodgers and Rowe (1988) demonstrated that younger siblings are more likely to experience sexual intercourse at an earlier age than older siblings, even when time period and age is controlled. In a subsequent study designed to test various possible explanations of this finding, J. L. Rodgers, Rowe, and Harris (1992) found no support for explanations based on a tendency on the part of younger siblings to report or remember an earlier age of first intercourse (a telescoping effect) or on older sibling modeling of sexual behavior. There was some evidence for the notion that older siblings provide their younger siblings with sexual opportunities and settings, and stronger support for the possibility that younger siblings are more physically mature at a particular age than were their older siblings. Although Rodgers et al. did not test for differential treatment on the part of parents, they suggested that this sibling effect could also be a function of increased parental permissiveness and decreased monitoring of younger siblings. The results of a study by Widmer (1997) suggest that older brothers are particularly influential regarding the age at which their younger siblings first experience intercourse. Older brothers who had not yet experienced intercourse were very likely to have younger siblings who were also virgins, but older brothers who had engaged in intercourse tended to have siblings who were nonvirgins. This relationship was especially strong for younger brothers, although the effect was present for younger sisters as well. No such correlation in behavior was found for older sisters and their siblings.

It also was found that the younger sisters of young women who become pregnant during their adolescence are significantly more likely to become pregnant themselves (East, 1996; East, Felice, & Morgan, 1993; Powers, 2001). East et al. (1993) found that having many sexually active sisters was significantly correlated to permissive sexual attitudes, but when this variable was combined with various sister- and girlfriend-related variables in a regression analysis, other variables became more important. In particular, if the presence of an older sister who had a baby in adolescence was considered, the number of sexually active sisters was no longer a significant predictor for girls' sexual attitudes or behavior. East (1996) reported that compared to other younger sisters, those girls with an older sister who had given birth during the teen years were significantly more accepting of nonmarital adolescent childbearing, gave younger ages as the appropriate time for various life transitions, had lower expectations for education and career, and more likely to have engaged in certain problem behaviors. These findings were not due to differences in various socioeconomic and demographic indicators. East suggested that

> having an adolescent childbearing sister as a role model may increase younger sisters' vulnerability for early parenthood by enhancing their acceptance of nonmarital adolescent childbearing, by altering their perceptions of the timing of typical normative transitions, by inculcating pessimistic future expectations, and by causing an increase in problem behaviors. (p. 279)

CONCLUSIONS

Although the impact of early family-based sexual learning and family sexual discussions on adolescent sexual behavior, knowledge, and attitudes is still unclear, there is now greater understanding of the dynamics of parent–child sexual communication and the variables that must be controlled in research on the topic. It does seem apparent that there is a strong connection between the sexual attitudes of parents and those of their adolescent children, although the reasons for this similarity remain unknown. Despite the few exceptions, parent–child closeness appears to be strongly related to many desirable sex-related behaviors on the part of adolescents such as older age at first intercourse, fewer sexual partners, and greater likelihood of contraceptive use. Although the optimal amount of parental monitoring may not yet be known, it seems likely that too little monitoring is related to an earlier onset of sexual behavior on the part of teens. The marital status of parents also seems to be connected to adolescent sexuality, although it cannot be conclusively stated exactly how or why. Finally, enough is known about the influential role of siblings on sexual behavior of their younger brothers and sisters to be tantalizing, but there is still much more to learn in this area.

Some have questioned the degree of influence that parents can ever have on the behavior of their children (Harris, 1995). The results of studies in most of areas of possible family influence on sexuality provide little support to refute that view. It could be, however, that the behaviors that are most influenced by the family have not yet been studied. Certainly, we know next to nothing about the family's role in the development of sexual adjustment and pleasure, erotophilia, one's view of the role of sex in a relationship, etc., nor has there been research looking at the impact of the family on sexual behavior beyond the adolescent years. It could also be that the biologically and socially based components of the adolescent sex drive simply overwhelm parental influences in many cases.

Weinstein and Thornton (1989) argued that there would only be a simple relationship between parental variables and adolescent sexual behavior to the degree that parents have a "homogeneously restrictive" set of values. They further indicated that there has been a trend toward more diverse sexual values on the part of parents, leading to more complex interactions between parental attitudes and adolescent sexual behavior, perhaps accounting for the fact that earlier studies were more likely to indicate a straightforward relationship between family relationships and the sexual behavior and values of adolescent offspring. It is certainly true that researchers cannot assume that all parents are opposed to their own teenagers engaging in sexual behaviors, nor can it be assumed that the influence and example of all parents would be a responsible, positive one.

Regardless of the outcomes, research on the family influences on adolescent sexuality has come a long way since early attempts to study the impact of family sexual communication as typified by a study by A. G. Miller (1974) misleadingly entitled, "The Relationship Between Family Interaction and Sexual Behavior in Adolescence," in which the family interactions of nine young, unmarried mothers were compared to those of seven Girl Scouts. The studies done in the past decade were much improved over those done in the past, with larger and more representative samples, more complex analyses, and often a longitudinal approach. Nonetheless, there is still much that is unknown or unclear regarding the family foundations of sexuality.

Because it is influenced by a combination of biological, social, and cultural factors, adolescent sexuality is a moving target to try to study. Future researchers of family foundations of sexual behavior would do well to take into account the age and developmental status of the adolescent participants, the characteristics and values of their parents, and the timing of the particular family interactions being studied. More uniform methodology and attempts at replication of previous findings would enhance consistency in findings. In addition, it is time to begin to study sexuality within a relational context rather than as a completely isolated activity (see McKinney & Sprecher, 1991). It might be that an important feature of learning about sex within the family is its impact on the child's view of the proper role of sexuality within relationships. Finally, theory-based and programmatic research is needed to truly advance our knowledge of how the family can lay a foundation for future sexual development.

REFERENCES

Ansuini, C. G., Fiddler-Woite, J., & Woite, R. S. (1996). The source, accuracy, and impact of initial sexuality information on lifetime wellness. *Adolescence, 31,* 283–289.

Barone, N. M., & Wiederman, M. W. (1997). Young women's sexuality as a function of perceptions of maternal sexual communication during childhood. *Journal of Sex Education and Therapy, 22,* 33–38.

Baumeister, L. M., Flores, E., & Marin, B. V. (1995). Sex information given to Latino adolescents by parents. *Health Education Research, 10,* 233–239.

Bennett, S. M., & Dickinson, W. B. (1980). Student–parent rapport and parent involvement in sex, birth control, and venereal disease education. *The Journal of Sex Research, 16,* 114–130.

Biglan, A., Metzler, C. W., Wirt, R., Ary, D., Noell, J., Ochs, L., French, C., & Hood, D. (1990). Social and behavioral factors associated with high-risk sexual behavior among adolescents. *Journal of Behavioral Medicine, 13,* 245–261.

Blum, R. W. (2002). Mothers' influence on teen sex: Connections that promote postponing sexual intercourse. University of Minnesota, Center for Adolescent Health and Development.

Bronfenbrenner, Y. (1992). Ecological systems theory. In R. Vasta (Ed.), *Six theories of child development* (pp. 187–250). London: Jessica Kingsley.

Capaldi, D. M., Crosby, L., & Stoolmiller, M. (1996). Predicting the timing of first sexual intercourse for at-risk adolescent males. *Child Development, 67,* 344–359.

Casper, L. M. (1990). Does family interaction prevent adolescent pregnancy? *Family Planning Perspectives, 22,* 109–114.

Christopher, F. S. (2001). *To dance the dance: A symbolic interactional exploration of premarital sexuality.* Mahwah, NJ: Lawrence Erlbaum Associates.

Cvetkovich, G., & Grote, B. (1983). Adolescent development and teenage fertility. In D. Byrne & W. A. Fisher (Eds.), *Adolescents, sex and contraception* (pp. 109–123). Hillsdale, NJ: Lawrence Erlbaum Associates.

Darling, C. A., & Hicks, M. W. (1982). Parental influence on adolescent sexuality: Implications for parents as educators. *Journal of Youth and Adolescence, 11,* 231–245.

Darling, C. A., & Hicks, M. W. (1983). Recycling parental sexual messages. *Journal of Sex and Marital Therapy, 9,* 233–243.

Davis, E. C., & Friel, L. V. (2001). Adolescent sexuality: Disentangling the effects of family structure and family context. *Journal of Marriage and Family, 63,* 669–681.

DeLamater, J., & MacCorquodale, P. (1979). *Premarital sexuality: Attitudes, relationships, behavior.* Madison: University of Wisconsin Press.

Demo, D. H. (1992). parent–child relations: Assessing recent changes. *Journal of Marriage and the Family, 54,* 104–117.

DiIorio, C., Kelley, M., & Hockenberry-Eaton, M. (1999). Communication about sexual issues: Mothers, fathers, and friends. *Journal of Adolescent Health, 24,* 181–189.

Dittus, P. J., & Jaccard, J. (2000). Adolescents' perceptions of maternal disapproval of sex: Relationship to sexual outcomes. *Journal of Adolescent Health, 26,* 268–278.

Dittus, P. J., Jaccard, J., & Gordon, V. V. (1997). The impact of African American fathers on adolescent sexual behavior. *Journal of Youth and Adolescence, 26,* 445–465.

Dornbusch, S. M., Carlsmith, J. M., Bushwall, S. J., Ritter, P. L., Leiderman, H., Hastorf, A. H., & Gross, R. T. (1985). Single parents, extended households, and the control of adolescents. *Child Development, 56,* 326–341.

Downie, J., & Coates, R. (1999). The impact of gender on parent–child sexuality communication: Has anything changed? *Sexual and Marital Therapy, 14,* 109–121.

East, P. L. (1996). The younger sisters of childbearing adolescents: Their attitudes, expectations, and behaviors. *Child Development, 67,* 267–282.

East, P. L., Felice, M. E., & Morgan, M. C. (1993). Sisters' and girlfriends' sexual and childbearing behavior: Effects on early adolescent girls' sexual outcomes. *Journal of Marriage and the Family, 55,* 953–963.

Feldman, S. S., & Rosenthal, D. A. (2000). The effect of communication characteristics on family members' perceptions of parents as sex educators. *Journal of Research on Adolescence, 10,* 119–150.

Fisher, T. D. (1986a). An exploratory study of communication about sex and the sexual attitudes of early, middle and late adolescents and their parents. *Journal of Genetic Psychology, 147*, 543–557.

Fisher, T. D. (1986b). Parent–child communication and young adolescents' sexual knowledge and attitudes. *Adolescence, 21*, 517–527.

Fisher, T. D. (1987). Family communication and the sexual behavior and attitudes of college students. *Journal of Youth and Adolescence, 16*, 481–495.

Fisher, T. D. (1988). The relationship between parent–child communication about sexuality and college students' sexual behavior and attitudes as a function of parental proximity. *The Journal of Sex Research, 24*, 305–311.

Fisher, T. D. (1989). An extension of the findings of Moore, Peterson, and Furstenberg (1986) regarding family sexual communication and adolescent sexual behavior. *Journal of Marriage and the Family, 51*, 637–639.

Fisher, T. D. (1990). Characteristics of mothers and fathers who talk to their adolescent children about sexuality. *Journal of Psychology and Human Sexuality, 3*, 53–70.

Fisher, T. D. (1993). A comparison of various measures of family sexual communication: Psychometric properties, validity, and behavioral correlates. *The Journal of Sex Research, 30*, 229–238.

Fleuridas, C., Creevy, K., & Vela, E. (1997). Sexual risk-taking in college students and functional families of origin. *Families, Systems & Health, 15*, 185–202.

Forste, R. T., & Heaton, T. B. (1988). Initiation of sexual activity among female adolescents. *Youth and Society, 19*, 250–268.

Fox, G. L. (1981). The family's role in adolescent sexual behavior. In T. Ooms (Ed.), *Teenage pregnancy in a family context* (pp. 73–129). Philadelphia: Temple University Press.

Fox, G. L., & Inazu, J. K. (1980). Patterns and outcomes of mother–daughter communication about sexuality. *Journal of Social Issues, 36*, 7–29.

Handelsman, C. D., Cabral, R. J., & Weisfeld, G. E. (1987). Sources of information and adolescent sexual knowledge and behavior. *Journal of Adolescent Research, 2*, 455–463.

Hansson, R. D., Jones, W. H., & Chernovetz, M. E. (1979). Contraceptive knowledge: Antecedents and implications. *Family Coordinator, 28*, 29–34.

Harris, J. R. (1995). Where is the child's environment? A group socialization theory of development. *Psychological Review, 102*, 458–489.

Haurin, R. J., & Mott, F. (1990). Adolescent sexual activity in the family context: The impact of older siblings. *Demography, 27*, 537–557.

Hetherington, E. M. (1972). Effects of father absence on personality development in adolescent daughters. *Developmental Psychology, 7*, 313–326.

Hockenberry-Eaton, M., Richman, M. J., DiIorio, C., Rivero, T., & Maibach, E. (1996). Mother and adolescent knowledge of sexual development: The effects of gender, age, and sexual experience. *Adolescence, 31*, 35–47.

Hogan, D. P., & Kitagawa, E. M. (1985). The impact of social status, family structure and neighborhood on the fertility of Black adolescents. *American Journal of Sociology, 90*, 825–855.

Holtzman, D., & Rubinson, R. (1995). Parent and peer communication effects on AIDS-related behavior among U.S. high school students. *Family Planning Perspectives, 27*, 235–240, 268.

Hovell, M., Sipan, C., Blumberg, W., Atkins, C., Hofstetter, C. R., & Kreitner, S. (1994). Family influences on Latino and Anglo adolescents' sexual behavior. *Journal of Marriage and the Family, 56*, 973–986.

Hutchinson, M. K., & Cooney, T. M. (1998). Patterns of parent–teen sexual risk communication: Implications for intervention. *Family Relations, 47*, 185–194.

Inazu, J. K., & Fox, G. L. (1980). Maternal influence on the sexual behavior of teenage daughters. *Journal of Family Issues, 1*, 81–102.

Jaccard, J., & Dittus, P. (1991). *Parent–teen communication: Toward the prevention of unintended pregnancies.* New York: Springer-Verlag.

Jaccard, J., Dittus, P. J., & Gordon, V. V. (1996). Maternal correlates of adolescent sexual and contraceptive behavior. *Family Planning Perspectives, 28*, 159–185.

Jaccard, J., Dittus, P. J., & Gordon, V. V. (1998). Parent–adolescent congruency in reports of adolescent sexual behavior and in communications about sexual behavior. *Child Development, 69*, 247–261.

Jaccard, J., Dittus, P. J., & Gordon, V. V. (2000). Parent–teen communication about premarital sex: Factors associated with the extent of communication. *Journal of Adolescent Research 15*, 187–208.

Jessor, R. (1992). Risk behavior in adolescence: A psychosocial framework of understanding and action. *Developmental Review, 12*, 374–390.

Jessor, S. L., & Jessor, R. (1975). Transition from virginity to nonvirginity among youth: A social-psychological study over time. *Developmental Psychology, 11*, 473–484.

Joffe, H., & Franca-Koh, A. C. (2001). Parental non-verbal sexual communication: Its relationship to sexual behaviour and sexual guilt. *Journal of Health Psychology, 6*, 17–30.

Kahlbaugh, P., Lefkowitz, E. S., Valdez, P., & Sigman, M. (1997). The affective nature of mother–adolescent communication concerning sexuality and conflict. *Journal of Research on Adolescence, 7*, 221–239.

Kahn, J. R. (1994). Speaking across cultures within your own family. In J. M. Irvine (Ed.), *Sexual cultures and the construction of adolescent identities* (pp. 285–309). Philadelphia: Temple University Press.

Karofsky, P. S., Zeng, L., & Kosorok, M. R. (2000). Relationship between adolescent–parental communication and initiation of first intercourse by adolescents. *Journal of Adolescent Health, 28*, 41–45.

Kastner, L. S. (1984). Ecological factors predicting adolescent contraceptive use: Implications for intervention. *Journal of Adolescent Health Care, 5*, 79–86.

King, B. M., & Lorusso, J. (1997). Discussions in the home about sex: Different recollections by parents and children. *Journal of Sex and Marital Therapy, 23*, 52–60.

Kotchick, B. A., Dorsey, S., Miller, K. S, & Forehand, R. (1999). Adolescent sexual risk-taking behavior in single-parent ethnic minority families. *Journal of Family Psychology, 13*, 93–102.

Kurdek, L. A., & Fine, M. A. (1994). Family acceptance and family control as predictors of adjustment in young adolescents: Linear, curvilinear, or interactive effects? *Child Development, 65*, 1137–1146.

Larson, R., & Richards, M. H. (1994). *Divergent realities: The emotional lives of mothers, fathers, and adolescents.* New York: Basic Books.

Leaper, C., Anderson, K. J., & Sanders, P. (1998). Moderators of gender effects on parents' talk to their children: A meta-analysis. *Developmental Psychology, 34*, 3–27.

Lefkowitz, E. S., Kahlbaugh, P. E., & Sigman, M. D. (1996). Turn-taking in mother–adolescent conversations about sexuality and conflict. *Journal of Youth and Adolescence, 25*, 307–321.

Lefkowitz, E. S., Romo, L. F., Corona, R., Au, T. K., & Sigman, M. (2000). How Latino American and European American adolescents discuss conflicts, sexuality, and AIDS with their mothers. *Developmental Psychology, 36*, 315–325.

Lefkowitz, E. S., Sigman, M., & Au, T. K. (2000). Helping mothers discuss sexuality and AIDS with adolescents. *Child Development, 71*, 1383–1394.

Leland, N., & Barth, R. (1993). Characteristics of adolescents who have attempted to avoid HIV and who have communicated with parents about sex. *Journal of Adolescent Research, 8*, 58–76.

Lewis, R. A. (1973). Parents and peers: Socialization agents in the coital behavior of young adults. *The Journal of Sex Research, 9*, 156–170.

Lewis, R. J., & Janda, L. H. (1988). The relationship between adult sexual adjustment and childhood experiences regarding exposure to nudity, sleeping in the parental bed and parental attitudes toward sexuality. *Archives of Sexual Behavior, 17*, 349–362.

Longmore, M. A., Manning, W. D., & Giordano, P. C. (2001). Preadolescent parenting strategies and teens' dating and sexual initiation: A longitudinal analysis. *Journal of Marriage and Family, 63*, 322–335.

Luster, T., & Small, S. A. (1994). Factors associated with sexual risk-taking behaviors among adolescents. *Journal of Marriage and the Family, 56*, 622–632.

Lynch, C. O. (2001). Risk and protective factors associated with adolescent sexual activity. *Adolescent and Family Health, 2*, 99–107.

McKinney, K., & Sprecher, S. (1991). Introduction. In K. McKinney & S. Sprecher (Eds.), *Sexuality in close relationships* (pp. 1–8). Hillsdale, NJ: Lawrence Erlbaum Associates.

McLanahan, S., & Booth, K. (1989). Mother-only families: Problems, prospects, and politics. *Journal of Marriage and the Family, 31*, 557–580.

McLaughlin, C. S., Chen, C., Greenberger, E., & Biermeier, C. (1997). Family, peer, and individual correlates of sexual experience among Caucasian and Asian American late adolescents. *Journal of Research on Adolescence, 7*, 33–53.

Meschke, L. L., Bartholomae, S., & Zentall, S. R. (2000). Adolescent sexuality and parent–adolescent processes: Promoting healthy choices. *Family Relations, 39*, 143–154.

Meschke, L. L., Zweig, J. M., Barber, B. L., & Eccles, J. S. (2000). Demographic, biological, psychological, and social predictors of the timing of first intercourse. *Journal of Research on Adolescence, 10*, 315–338.

Metzler, C. W., Noell, J., Biglan, A., Ary, D., & Smolkowski, K. (1994). The social context for risky sexual behavior among adolescents. *Journal of Behavioral Medicine, 17*, 419–438.

Miller, A. G. (1974). The relationship between family interaction and sexual behavior in adolescence. *Journal of Community Psychology, 2*, 285–288.

Miller, B. C. (1998). *Families matter: A research synthesis of family influences on adolescent pregnancy.* Washington, DC: National Campaign to Prevent Teen Pregnancy.

Miller, B. C., Benson, B., & Galbraith, K. A. (2001). Family relationships and adolescent pregnancy risk: A research synthesis. *Developmental Review, 21*, 1–38.

Miller, B. C., & Bingham, C. R. (1989). Family configuration in relation to the sexual behavior of female adolescents. *Journal of Marriage and the Family, 51*, 499–506.

Miller, B. C., McCoy, J. K., Olson, T. D., & Wallace, C. M. (1986). Parental discipline and control attempts in relation to adolescent sexual attitudes and behavior. *Journal of Marriage and the Family, 48*, 503–512.

Miller, B. C., Norton, M. C., Curtis, T., Hill, E. J., Schvaneveldt, P., & Young, M. H. (1997). The timing of sexual intercourse among adolescents: Family, peer, and other antecedents. *Youth and Society, 29*, 54–83.

Miller, B. C., Norton, M. C., Fan, X., & Christopherson, C. R. (1998). Pubertal development, parental communication, and sexual values in relation to adolescent sexual behaviors. *Journal of Early Adolescence, 18*, 27–52.

Miller, K. S., Forehand, R., & Kotchick, B. A. (1999). Adolescent sexual behavior in two ethnic minority samples: The role of family variables. *Journal of Marriage and the Family, 61*, 85–98.

Miller, K. S., Levin, M. L., Whitaker, D. J., & Xu, X. (1998). Patterns of condom use among adolescents: The impact of mother–adolescent communication. *American Journal of Public Health, 88*, 1542–1544.

Moore, K. A., Peterson, J. L., & Furstenburg, F. F. (1986). Parental attitudes and the occurrence of early sexual activity. *Journal of Marriage and the Family, 48*, 777–782.

Mosher, D. L. (1998). Guilt and sexuality in adolescents. In J. Bybee (Ed.), *Guilt and children*. San Diego, CA: Academic Press.

Mueller, K. E., & Powers, W. G. (1990). Parent–child sexual discussion: Perceived communicator style and subsequent behavior. *Adolescence, 25,* 469–482.

Murry, V. M. (1994). Black adolescent females: A comparison of early versus late coital initiators. *Family Relations, 43,* 342–348.

Murry, V. M. (1996). An ecological analysis of coital timing among middle-class African American adolescent females. *Journal of Adolescent Research, 11,* 261–279.

Newcomer, S. F., & Udry, J. R. (1984). Mothers' influence on the sexual behavior of their teenage children. *Journal of Marriage and the Family, 46,* 477–485.

Newcomer, S. F., & Udry, J. R. (1985). Parent–child communication and adolescent sexual behavior. *Family Planning Perspectives, 17,* 169–174.

Newcomer, S. F., & Udry, J. R. (1987). Parental marital status effects on adolescent sexual behavior. *Journal of Marriage and the Family, 49,* 235–240.

Nicholas, L., & Tredoux, C. (1996). Early, late and non-participants in sexual intercourse: A profile of black South African first-year university students. *International Journal for the Advancement of Counseling, 19,* 111–117.

Nolin, M., & Petersen, K. (1992). Gender differences in parent–child communication about sexuality: An exploratory study. *Journal of Adolescent Research, 7,* 59–79.

Okami, P. (1995). Childhood exposure to parental nudity, parent–child co-sleeping, and "primal scenes": A review of clinical opinion and empirical evidence. *The Journal of Sex Research, 32,* 51–64.

Okami, P., Olmstead, R., Abramson, P. R., & Pendleton, L. (1998). Early childhood exposure to parental nudity and scenes of parental sexuality ("primal scenes"): An 18-year longitudinal study of outcome. *Archives of Sexual Behavior, 27,* 361–384.

Okami, P., Weisner, T., & Olmstead, R. (2002). Outcome correlates of parent–child bedsharing: An eighteen-year longitudinal study. *Developmental and Behavioral Pediatrics, 23,* 244–253.

O'Sullivan, L. F., Meyer-Bahlburg, H. F. L., & Watkins, B. X. (2001). Mother–daughter communication about sex among urban African-American and Latino families. *Journal of Adolescent Research, 16,* 269–292.

Parsons, J. T., Butler, R., Kocik, S., Norman, L., Nuss, R., & the Adolescent Hemophilia Behavioral Intervention Evaluation Projects (HBIEP) Study Group. (1998). The role of the family system in HIV risk reduction: Youths with hemophilia and HIV infection and their parents. *Journal of Pediatric Psychology, 23,* 57–65.

Pick, S., & Palos, P. A. (1995). Impact of the family on the sex lives of adolescents. *Adolescence, 30,* 667–675.

Pistella, C. L. Y., & Bonati, F. A. (1998). Communication about sexual behavior among adolescent women, their family, and peers. *Families in Society: The Journal of Contemporary Human Services, 79,* 206–211.

Porter, C. P., Oakley, D., Ronis, D. L., & Neal, R. W. (1996). Pathways of influence on fifth and eighth graders' reports about having had sexual intercourse. *Research in Nursing and Health, 19,* 193–204.

Powers, D. A., (2001). Unobserved family effects on the risk of a first premarital birth. *Social Science Research, 30,* 1–24.

Raffaelli, M., Bogenschneider, K., & Flood, M. F. (1998). Parent–teen communication about sexual topics. *Journal of Family Issues, 19,* 315–333.

Raffaelli, M., Smart, L. A., Van Horn, S. C., Hohbein, A. D., Kline, J. E., & Chan, W. L. (1999). Do mothers and teens disagree about sexual communication? A methodological reappraisal. *Journal of Youth and Adolescence, 28,* 395–402.

Rodgers, J. L., & Rowe, D. C. (1988). Influence of siblings on adolescent sexual behavior. *Developmental Psychology 24,* 722–728.

Rodgers, J. L., & Rowe, D. C. (1990). Adolescent sexual activity and mildly deviant behavior: Sibling and friendship effects. *Journal of Family Issues, 11,* 274–293.

Rodgers, J. L., Rowe, D. C., & Harris, D. G. (1992). Sibling differences in adolescent sexual behavior: Inferring process models from family composition patterns. *Journal of Marriage and the Family, 54,* 142–152.

Rodgers, K. B. (1999). Parenting processes related to sexual risk-taking behaviors of adolescent males and females. *Journal of Marriage and the Family, 61,* 99–109.

Romo, L. F., Lefkowitz, E. S., Sigman, M., & Au, T. K. (2002). A longitudinal study of maternal messages about dating and sexuality and their influence on Latino adolescents. *Journal of Adolescent Health, 31,* 59–69.

Rosenthal, D. A., & Feldman, S. S. (1999). The importance of importance: Adolescents' perceptions of parental communication about sexuality. *Journal of Adolescent 22,* 835–851.

Rosenthal, D. A., Feldman, S. S., & Edwards, D. (1998). Mum's the word: Mothers' perspectives on communication about sexuality with adolescents. *Journal of Adolescence, 21,* 727–743.

Rosenthal, D., Senserrick, T., & Feldman, S. (2001). A typology approach to describing parents as communicators about sexuality. *Archives of Sexual Behavior, 30,* 463–482.

Sigelman, C. K., Derenowski, H. A., Mullaney, H. A., & Siders, A. T. (1993). Parents' contributions to knowledge and attitudes regarding AIDS. *Journal of Pediatric Psychology, 18,* 221–235.

Simanski, J. W. (1998). The birds and the bees: An analysis of advice given to parents through the popular press. *Adolescence, 33,* 33–45.

Simpson, J. A., & Gangestad, S. W. (1991). Individual differences in sociosexuality: Evidence for convergent and discriminant validity. *Journal of Personality and Social Psychology, 60,* 870–883.

Small, S. A., & Luster, T. (1994). Adolescent sexual activity: An ecological, risk-factor approach. *Journal of Marriage and the Family, 56,* 181–192.

Somers, C. L., & Paulson, S. E. (2000). Students' perceptions of parent–adolescent closeness and communication about sexuality: Relationships with sexual knowledge, attitudes, and behavior. *Journal of Adolescence, 23,* 629–644.

Spanier, G. B. (1976). Formal and informal sex education as determinants of premarital sexual behavior. *Archives of Sexual Behavior, 5,* 39–67.

Stern, M., Northman, J. E., & Van Slyck, M. R. (1984). Father absence and adolescent "problem behaviors": Alcohol consumption, drug use and sexual activity. *Adolescence, 19,* 301–312.

St. Lawrence, J. S., Brasfield, T. L., Jefferson, K. W., Allyene, E., & Shirley, A. (1994). Social support as a factor in African-American adolescents' sexual risk behavior. *Journal of Adolescent Research, 9,* 292–310.

Taris, T. W., & Semin, G. R. (1997a). Parent–child interaction during adolescence, and the adolescent's sexual experience: Control, closeness, and conflict. *Journal of Youth and Adolescence, 26,* 373–398.

Taris, T. W., & Semin, G. R. (1997b). Quality of mother–child interaction, differences in sexual attitudes, and intergenerational disagreement on sexuality. *Early Child Development and Care, 136,* 65–78.

Taris, T. W., Semin, G. R., & Bok, I. A. (1998). The effect of quality of family interaction and intergenerational transmission of values on sexual permissiveness. *Journal of Genetic Psychology, 159,* 237–250.

Treboux, D., & Busch-Rossnagel, N. A. (1990). Social network influences on adolescent sexual attitudes and behaviors. *Journal of Adolescent Research, 5,* 175–189.

Treboux, D., & Busch-Rossnagel, N. A. (1995). Age differences in parent and peer influences on female sexual behavior. *Journal of Research on Adolescence, 5,* 469-487.

Upchurch, D. M., Aneshensel, C. S., Sucoff, C. A., & Levy-Storms, L. (1999). Neighborhood and family contexts of adolescent sexual activity. *Journal of Marriage and the Family, 61,* 920–933.

Ward, L. M., & Wyatt, G. E. (1994). The effects of childhood sexual messages on African-American and White women's adolescent sexual behavior. *Psychology of Women Quarterly, 18,* 183–201.

Warren, C. (1995). Parent–child communication about sex. In T. J. Socha and G. H. Stamp (Eds.), *Parents, children and communication: Frontiers of theory and research* (pp. 173–201). Mahwah, NJ: Lawrence Erlbaum Associates.

Warren, C. L., & St. Pierre, R. (1973). Sources and accuracy of college students' sex knowledge. *Journal of School Health, 43,* 588–590.

Weinstein, M., & Thornton, A. (1989). Mother–child relations and adolescent sexual attitudes and behavior. *Demography, 26,* 563–577.

Whitaker, D. J., & Miller, K. S. (2000). Parent–adolescent discussions about sex and condoms: Impact on peer influences of sexual risk behavior. *Journal of Adolescent Research, 15,* 251–273.

Whitaker, D. J., Miller, K. S., May, D. C., & Levin, M. L. (1999). Teenage partners' communication about sexual risk and condom use: The importance of parent–teenager discussions. *Family Planning Perspectives, 31,* 117–121.

Whitbeck, L. B., Conger, R. D., & Kao, M.-Y. (1993). The influence of parental support, depressed affect, and peers on the sexual behaviors of adolescent girls. *Journal of Family Issues, 14,* 261–278.

Whitbeck, L., Hoyt, D., Miller, M., & Kao, M. (1992). Parental support, depressed affect, and sexual experiences among adolescents. *Youth and Society, 24,* 166–167.

Whitbeck, L. B., & Simons, R. L. (1994). The effects of divorced mothers' dating behaviors and sexual attitudes on the sexual attitudes and behaviors of their adolescent children. *Journal of Marriage and the Family, 56,* 615–622.

Whitbeck, L. B., Yoder, K. A., Hoyt, D. R., & Conger, R. D. (1999). Early adolescent sexual activity: A developmental study. *Journal of Marriage and the Family, 61,* 934–946.

Widmer, E. D. (1997). Influence of older siblings on initiation of sexual intercourse. *Journal of Marriage and the Family, 59,* 928–938.

Wood, E., Senn, C. Y., Desmarais, S., Park, L., & Verberg, N. (2002). Sources of information about dating and their perceived influence on adolescents. *Journal of Adolescent Research, 17,* 401–417.

Wright, D. W., Peterson, L. R., & Barnes, H. L. (1990). The relations of parental employment and contextual variables with sexual permissiveness and gender role attitudes of rural early adolescents. *Journal of Early Adolescence, 10,* 382–398.

Wu, L. L., & Thomson, E. (2001). Race differences in family experience and early sexual initiation: Dynamic models of family structure and family change. *Journal of Marriage and Family, 63,* 682–696.

Yowell, C. M. (1997). Risks of communication: Early adolescent girls' conversations with mothers and friends about sexuality. *Journal of Early Adolescence, 17,* 172–196.

17

Sexuality and the Partner Relationship During Pregnancy and the Postpartum Period

Erin N. Haugen
Peter A. Schmutzer
Amy Wenzel
University of North Dakota

Although much work has examined the manner in which pregnancy and childbirth disrupt aspects of sexual functioning (i.e., frequency of intercourse), little work has considered how this disruption affects the quality of the partner relationship during the transition to parenthood. In this chapter, research investigating sexual functioning during pregnancy and the postpartum period is reviewed. It is evident that sexual functioning during pregnancy and the postpartum period changes as compared to sexual functioning prior to conception. Patterns of sexual activity are variable, but the frequency of sexual activity generally declines throughout pregnancy and slowly begins to increase around the second month postpartum (cf. von Sydow, 1999). Other variables such as sexual interest and arousal appear to follow a similar pattern, although there is a subset of individuals who experience increased interest during this time period. There are a wide variety of factors that affect sexual functioning during pregnancy and the postpartum period, such as breastfeeding status, parity, age, and subjective experiences of pain. However, a number of methodological limitations temper the conclusions that can be drawn from this literature, and research in this area to date has been largely atheoretical. Future researchers are encouraged to consider changes in sexual functioning in light of changes in the quality of the partner relationship and identify the factors that might enhance this relationship at a time when sexual activity is occurring at a relatively low level.

INTRODUCTION

The transition to parenthood represents a time characterized by some of the most dramatic life changes and adjustments. Despite the fact that considerable research evaluated the manner in which sexual functioning changes during pregnancy and the postpartum period, little work placed these changes in a family systems context or examined how these changes affect various aspects of the partner relationship. Although people sometimes attribute fluctuations in the sexual relationship to hormonal changes, it is more common for research investigating sexual functioning during pregnancy and the postpartum period to find that physical (e.g., pain) and psychosocial (e.g., fear of harming the baby or becoming pregnant again) factors explain significant variance in sexual functioning throughout this period. The disruption of sexual functioning certainly can be disturbing for some couples, but it is heartening that most couples who have recently given birth do not meet diagnostic criteria for a sexual disorder (Bitzer & Alder, 2000). On the other hand, of women who seek therapy for sexual difficulties, many indicate that the onset of their sexual problems occurred following the birth of a child (Flowers & Flowers, 1985). Thus, it is important to understand the normative changes in sexual functioning that occur during pregnancy and the postpartum period in order to provide education to childbearing couples as well as to identify factors that might put couples at risk for relational difficulties during this stressful time.

This chapter reviews literature pertaining to sexual functioning during pregnancy and the postpartum period. Specifically, this review discusses the manner in which sexual activity, sexual interest, sexual desire, and other sexual variables change throughout the transition to parenthood. In addition, sexual difficulties (e.g., dyspareunia) that are prominent during this time are discussed. Furthermore, the literature pertaining to the effects of breastfeeding on postpartum sexuality is evaluated, as breastfeeding is a behavior that is unique to the postpartum period. Moreover, nonsexual factors that pertain to the partner relationship, such as relationship satisfaction, are addressed in the context of the transition to parenthood. Finally, methodological limitations of this body of literature are discussed, as well as directions for future research.

SEXUAL ACTIVITY

In this section, changes during the transition to parenthood regarding sexual intercourse and other nonintercourse sexual behaviors, such as breast stimulation and oral–genital behaviors, are considered. Sexual activity is defined as particular sexual behaviors in which individuals or couples engage during intimate times that involve genital contact, even if intercourse does not occur. Results from several studies suggest that sexual activity changes during pregnancy and the postpartum period. For example, in a study that utilized data from the National Survey of Families and Households, Call, Sprecher, and Schwartz (1995) found that pregnancy had a negative effect on sexual activity. However, this effect was moderated by the composition of the household; the presence of children younger than four years old was associated with a decrease in level of sexual activity, whereas the presence of children older than 5 was associated with an increase in level of sexual activity.

Overall, a general pattern of sexual activity emerged from this literature. Many researchers report that the frequency of sexual activity declines during pregnancy, reaches a point near zero during the immediate postpartum period, and slowly begins to increase thereafter (Barclay, McDonald, & O'Loughlin, 1994; Georgakopoulos, Dodos, & Mechleris, 1984; Lumley, 1978; von Sydow, Ullmeyer, & Happ, 2001). Several variables account for the reduction of sexual activity throughout pregnancy, including somatic symptoms (e.g., nausea, fatigue), increased physical size, physical pain, and fear of harming the fetus (von Sydow, 1999). In addition, De Judicibus and McCabe (2002) found that at 12 weeks postpartum, depressive symptomatology, fatigue, dyspareunia, and breastfeeding were the variables that were most likely to interfere with sexual functioning.

Factors that influence sexual activity in pregnancy may vary as a function of gender. For example, Miller and Friedman (1989) identified that, for men, greater emotional satisfaction and the degree to which they viewed their partners as attractive were positively related to the amount of sexual activity in which they engaged with their partners. In contrast, emotional satisfaction did not predict frequency of sexual activity in women; rather, women who felt unattractive, experienced conflict over their new role as a parent, and reported physical discomfort due to pregnancy engaged in sexual activity less frequently than women who denied such difficulties. After childbirth, females report that variables such as pain (at the episiotomy site) and fear of pregnancy contribute to decreased frequency of sexual activity as compared to pre-pregnancy levels (Lumley, 1978).

In addition, several researchers report that some women who are pregnant or in the postpartum period initiate sexual activity less often than they did prior to con- ception. In a questionnaire study of self-reported sexual functioning obtained from 52 pregnant women, women reported that they generally initiated sexual activity with their partners less often in the third trimester than they did before their pregnan- cies (Reamy, White, Daniell, & Le Vine, 1982). Similarly, results from a cross-sectional study of 141 pregnant women suggested that approximately 51% of women in the sample reported a decrease in their own initiation of sexual activity as compared to before pregnancy (Bartellas, Crane, Daley, Bennett, & Hutchens, 2000). Because the term "sexual activity" encompasses a number of sexual behaviors, it is important to clearly understand the specific type of activity being measured in order to accurately evaluate empirical findings. We divided research examining specific types of sexual activity in pregnant and postpartum couples into two categories: coital activity and noncoital activity.

Coital Activity

In general, research indicates that one of three patterns characterizes the frequency of coital activity during pregnancy. Each of these patterns was uncovered by research using a number of different methodological approaches, such as cross-sectional anal- ysis, longitudinal analysis, and analysis of retrospective reports. First, some studies demonstrate that the frequency of coital activity declines linearly as pregnancy pro- gresses. For example, Solberg, Butler, and Wagner (1973) obtained data to support this contention by interviewing 260 women immediately after childbirth for retrospective reports of their sexual behavior in pregnancy. In addition, Elliott and Watson (1985) interviewed 128 women eight times from weeks 13 to 39 of pregnancy, and their re- sults confirmed that the frequency of coital activity declines gradually throughout pregnancy. Similarly, results from a cross-sectional study of 141 pregnant women suggested that 96%, 89%, and 67% engaged in vaginal intercourse during the first, second, and third trimesters, respectively. Moreover, 71% of this sample reported that the frequency of coital activity was lower than their pre-pregnancy rates (Bartellas et al., 2000).

In contrast, other research suggests a different pattern of sexual activity, such that coital frequency is similar during the first and second trimesters but decreases dra- matically during the third trimester. For example, in a sample of 119 primiparous women interviewed at weeks 12, 24, and 36 of pregnancy, approximately 52% to 55% of women engaged in coitus one to three times per week during the first and sec- ond trimesters of pregnancy, respectively. However, this declined to approximately 33% of women in the third trimester. Moreover, an additional 36% of women denied engaging in coital activity at all during the final trimester of pregnancy, which is considerably higher than the 10% and 7% of women who denied intercourse during trimesters one and two, respectively (Kumar, Brant, & Robson, 1981; Robson, Brant, & Kumar, 1981). Similarly, in a cross-sectional study of 216 women who completed questionnaires pertaining to sexual functioning during each trimester of pregnancy, 37% and 25% of women engaged in coital activity two times each week during the first and second trimesters, respectively. In the third trimester, 20% of women continued to engage in coitus two times each week. In addition, 37% stopped engaging in coital activity, which is considerably higher than the 9% and 4% who did not engage in coital activity during the first and second trimesters, respectively (Tolor & DiGrazia, 1976). Moreover, in a prospective study of 52 women who completed questionnaires during the first, second, third, and late third trimesters of pregnancy, approximately 40% and 35% of women engaged in coital activity four to eight times within a two-week interval during the first and second trimesters, respectively. At the third and late third trimesters, the subset of women who continued to engage in coitus reportedly did so only one to three times within a two-week interval (Reamy et al., 1982). Finally, in their sample of 219 women who completed questionnaires two to four days after childbirth regarding sexual functioning during each trimester of pregnancy, Hart, Cohen, Gingold, and Homburg (1991) found that 59% and 48% of women engaged in coital activity during trimesters one and two, whereas the rate declined to 31% of women in the third trimester.

A third pattern of coital activity emerged from a smaller number of studies, such that compared to the first trimester, coital activity increases slightly in the second trimester before dropping dramatically in the third trimester. For example, El Tomi, Al Bustan, and Abokhadour (1993) indicated that among 160 pregnant Kuwaiti women, 20% endorsed a decrease in coital frequency during the first trimester as compared to pre-pregnancy levels. In the second trimester, these women generally reported a slight increase, although rates were still below pre-pregnancy levels of coital activity. Interestingly, an additional 20% of women who did not report decreased sexual intercourse in the first trimester reported an increase in coital frequency during the second trimester. In general, although there are some women who report an increase in coital activity during the second trimester, as evidenced by the findings just described, researchers typically report that sexual functioning is still below pre-pregnancy levels (e.g., Falicov, 1973). However, regardless of the differences between studies documenting the frequency of coital activity in the first and second trimesters, it has been demonstrated uniformly that the most dramatic shift in rates of sexual intercourse occurs in the third trimester.

Researchers identified several factors that explain the decrease in coital activity during pregnancy. Oftentimes, couples are forced to alter the positions used for coitus due to physical discomfort, such as breast tenderness (Barclay et al., 1994). Hart et al. (1991) found that as pregnancy progressed, the male superior position was used less often, and at term, 82% of the couples still engaging in sexual activity used the side-by-side position (cf. Reamy et al., 1982; Solberg et al., 1973). In addition, some women are advised by their physicians to abstain from intercourse during late pregnancy because of factors such as increased risk for obstetric complications or early delivery (Calhoun, Selby, & King, 1981). Other researchers found that coital activity varies as a function of age. For example, in a questionnaire study of 205 women expecting their first child, Pepe and colleagues (1988) found that the decline in sexual activity during pregnancy was more evident in older women. Specifically, during pregnancy, no women in this study between 15 and 20 years of age refused intercourse, approximately 25% of women ages 21 to 35 did so, and approximately 80% of women 36 to 40 years of age did so.

After childbirth, coital activity continues to be practiced at a lower level than it was practiced prior to conception. In her metacontent analysis, von Sydow (1999) estimated that most women resume sexual intercourse at approximately six to eight weeks postpartum. Other researchers found that sexual activity resumes at approximately five to seven weeks postpartum (e.g., Glazener, 1997), with 19% of women resuming sexual activity within the first month postpartum (Byrd, Hyde, DeLamater, & Plant, 1998; Hyde, DeLamater, Plant, & Byrd, 1996). However, there is wide variability both within samples as well as across studies. For example, Adinma (1996) found that some women reported resuming sexual activity as early as 3 days after childbirth, whereas others reported abstinence until the 84th week postpartum. Overall, 49% of Adinma's sample reported that they resumed sexual intercourse between the 6th and 11th week postpartum. On average, women reported resumption of sexual intercourse at 16.5 weeks postpartum, a value much higher than that estimated by von Sydow (1999). However, it is likely that this value is elevated due to a significant proportion of outliers who did not resume intercourse until the 36th week postpartum or beyond.

One important point to consider is that some research suggests that the decision to resume sexual intercourse in the postpartum period is strongly influenced by a desire to satisfy the needs of one's partner. For example, Barrett and colleagues (1999) found that 80% of women in their sample resumed sex by the 7th month postpartum. Of these women, 28% indicated that their partners initiated resumption of sexual intercourse. Although this is not a substantial number, there appears to be a subset of women who may prefer an even longer time before resuming coital activity. It is possible that they engage in intercourse out of obligation to their partner, perhaps out of a sense of guilt or even pressure. Despite the fact that some women may experience emotional conflict regarding when to resume sexual activity, there is evidence to suggest that early resumption of sexual activity does not affect healing of the perineum in an adverse manner (Richardson, Lyon, Graham, & Williams, 1976).

In general, the frequency of coital activity appears to increase throughout the first year postpartum, with the most substantial increase occurring in the first few postpartum months. For example, Elliott and Watson (1985) found that sexual behavior decreases gradually throughout pregnancy, increases sharply during first three months postpartum, and continues to rise through the remaining nine months postpartum. In an impressive study in which women and men were recruited for participation in the Wisconsin Maternity Leave and Health project (i.e., not specifically for sex research), 570 women and 550 men were interviewed during pregnancy and the first year postpartum (Byrd et al., 1998; Hyde et al., 1996). Results indicated that 17%, 89%, and 92% of women reported having intercourse at 1 month, 4 months, and 12 months, respectively. The mean frequency in which women engaged in sexual intercourse in the past month was 0.42, 5.27, and 5.12 at these respective time intervals. However, not all studies report such optimistic findings about sexual functioning in the postpartum period. In a longitudinal study conducted across the first year postpartum, one group of researchers reported that approximately 60%, 66%, and 59% of women engaged in coitus at 12, 26, and 52 weeks postpartum, and over half of the women in this sample reported reduced frequency of coitus throughout the first year postpartum compared to the month before conception (Kumar et al., 1981; Robson et al., 1981).

Several factors account for the variability among reports of the time at which couples indicate that they resume sexual intercourse after childbirth. For example, Hyde et al. (1996) reported that women who had a cesarean section (27%) were more likely to resume coital activity at one month postpartum than were women who had a vaginal delivery (18%). This finding is surprising, given that the recovery from a cesarean section commonly takes longer than recovery from a vaginal delivery (Bailey, 1989). Age of the mother may also influence the time at which couples resume intercourse after the birth of a child. In a sample of 160 Kuwaiti women who were interviewed every four weeks from the twelfth week of pregnancy to the 6th month postpartum, women who were 30 to 34 years of age generally surpassed their pre-pregnancy levels of coital activity, whereas women 20 to 29 years of age reported levels below those estimated before conception. However, the authors provided no explanation for these findings (Al Bustan, El Tomi, Faiwalla, & Manav, 1995). There is also evidence to suggest that couples who give birth to their first child resume coital activity more slowly than couples with more than one child (Fischman, Rankin, Soeken, & Lenz, 1984). In addition, women commonly cite family planning as a reason for delaying the resumption of coital activity. In fact, Adinma (1996) reported that the most common reason given by women who resumed sexual intercourse later than average (i.e., after 16.5 weeks postpartum) was family planning, such that 41% of these women indicated that this was the primary factor in their decision. Finally, Bitzer and Alder (2000) indicated that some women are advised by their physicians to refrain from sexual activity for at least four weeks following delivery.

It is difficult to draw definitive conclusions from this literature, as each study reviewed assessed coital activity at different time intervals and used different dependent measures (e.g., dichotomous assessments of coital activity, frequency of coital activity). Moreover, nearly all studies relied on self-report inventories designed by the investigator rather than standardized measures of sexual functioning. Nevertheless, there are a few patterns that can be observed across studies. First, research documented three patterns that characterize coital activity during pregnancy, all of which suggest a substantial decrease in frequency of coital activity during the third trimester of pregnancy. Second, coital activity gradually increases throughout the first year postpartum, although there is wide variability in the time at which couples resume sexual activity, and many women report that the frequency of coital activity during this time is still below pre-pregnancy levels. Because most researchers do not follow their samples beyond the first year postpartum, it is difficult to pinpoint the time at which coital activity returns to pre-pregnancy levels, or if it ever does. Third, it appears that age is a variable that moderates the frequency of coital activity during both pregnancy and the postpartum period. Interestingly, older childbearing women report a lower frequency of coital activity during pregnancy, but their levels of coital activity during the postpartum period approximate pre-pregnancy levels to a greater degree that the postpartum coital activity of younger women. However, it is possible that older women generally engage in coital activity less often (see Christopher & Kisler, chapter 15, this volume), so perhaps the difference in the frequency between postpartum coital activity and the frequency of coital activity at other times in their lives is not as dramatic as it is for younger women.

Noncoital Activity

Many studies examining sexual functioning in pregnancy and the postpartum period equate coital activity with sexuality and fail to include measures of noncoital activity. However, noncoital activity clearly is an important aspect of the sexual lives of these couples and in many cases is preferable to coital activity. For example, Kenny (1973) investigated pregnant women's attitudes about alternatives to sexual intercourse, and 82% indicated that they favored petting to mutual climax. Tolor and DiGrazia (1976) recruited women in their first, second, and third trimesters of pregnancy and women who were six weeks postpartum and found that women in their sample generally preferred to engage in noncoital activity more than coital activity. Although vaginal stimulation was the most preferred sexual activity during the first trimester, clitoral and breast stimulation were the most preferred sexual activities during all other time periods. In contrast, in their sample of 30 couples who completed questionnaires and interviews in the third trimester of pregnancy and at seven months postpartum, von Sydow et al. (2001) found that similar to intercourse, the frequency of breast stimulation decreased in pregnancy and the postpartum period. Hyde et al. (1996) found that during the second trimester, 92% of women engaged in petting, which decreased to 65% at one month postpartum but increased to 91% and 94% at four and twelve months postpartum, respectively. Miller and Friedman (1989) indicated that 83% of their pregnant couples reported engaging in noncoital genital activity at least one time per week, but only 48% of these couples had sexual intercourse at least one time per week. The relative frequency of noncoital activity compared to coital activity may depend on the particular assessment interval, as Alder and Bancroft (1983) indicated that genital contact that did not lead to intercourse was more frequent than intercourse in the first three weeks following childbirth but that around eight weeks postpartum, intercourse became the most frequent type of genital contact. In addition, couples may engage in noncoital activities before resuming intercourse following the birth of their child. For example, Ryding (1984) found in a sample of 50 postpartum women that 40% engaged in noncoital activities with their partners before the first act of intercourse.

In addition to noncoital genital activity, some researchers evaluated the frequency of nongenital activity, such as the desire to be held. For example, in a prospective study, White, Reamy, and Southward (1983) asked 52 pregnant military wives to rate their desire to be held in addition to sexual activity during the three trimesters of pregnancy. Results indicated that women reported a moderate desire to be held throughout pregnancy, which was similar to their desire before pregnancy. In addition, there was no relation between the desire to be held and the frequency of sexual intercourse, as the women who reported the greatest desire to be held did not necessarily report the highest frequency of sexual intercourse. Moreover, Tolor and DiGrazia (1976) found that when women did not desire to engage in intercourse, the most frequent alternative was a desire to be held. Results reported by Miller and Friedman (1989) suggest that nongenital affectionate activity is quite common in pregnant couples, as 94% of their sample report that they engage in this activity more than once a week during pregnancy. Similarly, von Sydow et al. (2001) found that French kissing was practiced more often than any genital activity during the third trimester of pregnancy and at seven months postpartum, although this is likely similar to what is found in the general population.

Although few studies have evaluated masturbation during pregnancy and the postpartum period, it appears that the frequency of this activity for women follows a somewhat similar pattern as the frequency of sexual intercourse. Solberg et al. (1973) reported that approximately 40 to 50% of women in their sample masturbated during pregnancy. In addition, in their sample of 219 Israeli women who completed questionnaires during pregnancy, Hart et al. (1991) reported that female masturbation was unchanged in the first and second trimesters of pregnancy (15%), whereas there was a slight decrease in the third trimester (9%). In Hyde et al.'s (1996) study of 570 childbearing women and their partners, approximately 23% of women reportedly masturbated in the second trimester of pregnancy and also at 4 and 12 months postpartum. However, at one month postpartum, this declined to 13% of women in their sample. Regardless of the time interval, the frequency of masturbation for women in this sample was quite low—an average of less than once per month. In contrast, male masturbation remained relatively constant throughout pregnancy and after childbirth, with some reports indicating that approximately 44% of men masturbated during the second trimester of pregnancy through the first year postpartum (Byrd et al., 1998; Hyde et al., 1996). Moreover, at 12 months postpartum, men masturbated approximately 2.4 times per month (Hyde et al., 1996), whereas von Sydow et al. (2001) found that men in their sample masturbated approximately four times per month during pregnancy and the postpartum period. Interestingly, this rate of male masturbation is considerably higher than what Laumann, Gagnon, Michael,

and Michaels (1994) found in their study of 3,432 individuals in the general population, suggesting that male partners of pregnant and postpartum women find sexual
outlets outside of the partner relationship. Thirty couples that were pregnant with
their first child were interviewed by von Sydow et al. (2001) in the third trimester
and again at seven months postpartum. Similar to the findings reported by Hyde and
her colleagues, rates of male masturbation remained constant throughout pregnancy
and after childbirth, and rates of female masturbation were steady during pregnancy,
ceased following childbirth, and resumed at approximately three months postpartum.
Unlike the Hyde et al. (1996) study, however, women reported that they masturbated
approximately three times a month.

Few studies obtained data regarding oral sex practices during pregnancy and the
postpartum period. Solberg et al. (1973) found that of the 99 pregnant women in their
sample, 32% performed fellatio, 17% received cunnilingus, and 50% used both types
of oral sex equally or simultaneously. Hart et al. (1991) reported a decrease in the
frequency of oral sex throughout pregnancy, especially during the third trimester.
That is, 35% of women engaged in oral sex before the third trimester, whereas 18%
of women engaged in oral sex thereafter. However, the authors reported only the
dichotomous variable of whether or not participants engaged in oral sex activity and
did not report the frequency of these behaviors. Moreover, there was no differentiation
between acts of fellatio and cunnilingus, such that the authors did not indicate whether
this was a cumulative frequency of fellatio and cunnilingus or whether it was only
one of those activities. Similarly, in their sample of pregnant couples, Barclay et al.
(1994) found that 76% reported that they engaged in oral sex, but the authors did not
indicate during which trimester(s) couples engaged in these practices and whether
the frequency declined throughout pregnancy.

In a more comprehensive examination of oral sex practices in pregnancy and the
postpartum period, Hyde et al. (1996) and Byrd et al. (1998) found that approximately 45% of their couples engaged in fellatio from the second trimester of pregnancy
through the completion of the first year postpartum, except during the first month
postpartum, when fellatio decreased to approximately 33%. In addition, cunnilingus
was practiced by 45% of the couples at 4 and 12 months postpartum and by 30%
and 8% during the second trimester and the first month postpartum, respectively.
Similarly, von Sydow et al. (2001) found that for individuals who engaged in oral
sex, fellatio was practiced slightly more often than cunnilingus during both late pregnancy and seven months postpartum. These patterns of results conflict to some degree
with the results from Laumann et al.'s (1994) analysis of sexual activities practiced
by individuals representative of the general population, as these researchers collected
data suggesting that men endorse giving oral sex as often as they received it. Rates of
cunnilingus may be particularly decreased during the postpartum period, as Barrett
et al. (1999) found it was the only sexual activity that was practiced less frequently in
the postpartum period than in pregnancy.

In sum, it appears that noncoital activity is an important facet of sexual activity for
pregnant and postpartum couples, particularly during periods in which the woman
may be experiencing discomfort that disrupts sexual intercourse. However, like coital
activity, noncoital activity is practiced at lower rates in the third trimester of pregnancy
and in the first few weeks postpartum compared to early pregnancy and later in
the postpartum period. In addition, affectionate nongenital activity appears to be
practiced by nearly all expectant parents and is desired even by individuals who have
ceased engaging in coital or genital activity. We suspect that this sort of activity may
be important in preserving the closeness of couples as they transition to parenthood,
especially in instances in which other factors (e.g., discomfort, time, sleep deprivation)
prevent couples from engaging in other types of sexual activity.

SEXUAL INTEREST AND DESIRE

Some researchers include measures of sexual interest and desire in their investigation of sexual functioning during pregnancy and the postpartum period. Often these results parallel those found regarding sexual activity. In fact, Solberg et al. (1973) indicated that female sexual interest during pregnancy was consistently associated with frequency of sexual activity, as individuals who reported decreased sexual interest generally endorsed lower rates of coital activity than others who reported no change or increased sexual desire. Moreover, von Sydow (1999) estimated that female sexual interest varies in a similar manner as frequency of sexual activity, such that it is unchanged or declines somewhat in the first trimester and decreases markedly during the third trimester.

Female sexual interest appears to decline throughout pregnancy but generally remains at least at a moderate level until the third trimester. For example, Tolor and DiGrazia (1976) indicated that women in their sample reported "moderate" to "considerable" sexual interest during each trimester of pregnancy. In a sample of 160 pregnant Kuwaiti women who were interviewed in 4-month intervals, El-Tomi et al. (1993) found that 10%, 20%, and 8% of women reported increased sexual desire compared to pre-pregnancy levels during the first, second, and third trimesters, respectively. On the other hand, Elliott and Watson (1985) reported that 35% of women endorsed a sharp decrease in sexual interest during pregnancy, and an additional 24% of women reported a gradual decrease. Robson et al. (1981) found that 55% of their 119 female participants indicated that their sexual desire decreased in early pregnancy. Some researchers identify the second trimester as being particularly variable with regard to sexual desire. For example, 73% of Kenny's (1973) sample reported the same level of sexual desire as during the first trimester, whereas 24% reported increased sexual desire compared to the first trimester (see Falicov, 1973 for similar results with a small sample). In contrast to these findings, other researchers report a decrease in sexual desire during the second trimester, and in one sample the decrease in sexual desire was associated with dyspareunia, or the experience of pain during sexual intercourse (Hart et al., 1991; Reamy & White, 1985).

Not surprisingly, the most substantial changes in sexual interest and desire occur at or around the third trimester (e.g., De Judicibus & McCabe, 2002). Masters and Johnson (1966) found that approximately 20% of pregnant women reported that their partners lost sexual interest in them beginning in the late second trimester to the early third trimester. Hart et al. (1991) indicated that 57% of their sample reported low sexual desire in the third trimester of pregnancy. In a sample of 50 postpartum women who were interviewed in the immediate postpartum period regarding sexual functioning during pregnancy and after childbirth, Ryding (1984) found that significantly more women reported decreased sexual desire in the third trimester as compared to the first two trimesters of pregnancy. In contrast, Barclay et al. (1994) indicated that as pregnancy progressed, 91% of their couples desired to make love more often or believed that their partners would like to make love more often. However, these results must be interpreted with caution, as they are based on a sample size of 12 couples, and the authors did not provide a distinction between the two types of sexual desire.

Several factors may influence female sexual interest during pregnancy. For example, many researchers suggest that changing physical attractiveness (e.g., abdominal growth, breast changes) of pregnant women disrupts female sexual desire (Alteneder & Hartzell, 1997; Bitzer & Alder, 2000; Solberg et al., 1973; White & Reamy, 1982). In addition, women often attribute the slight decline in sexual interest during the first trimester to physical symptoms (e.g., nausea, fatigue) and the decline in sexual interest throughout pregnancy to increased emotional lability, sexual fears (e.g., harming the fetus), and somatic changes (Bitzer & Alder, 2000). Also, age may be predictive of sexual desire during pregnancy. For example, Pepe et al. (1988) found in their sample of 205 postpartum women questioned about their sexual behavior in pregnancy that 64% of 25 women who were 15 to 20 years old reported decreased desire, whereas all 40 women who were 36 to 40 years old indicated decreased sexual desire. However, not all variables that seem logically related to decreases in sexual desire have been confirmed empirically, as De Judicibus and McCabe (2002) indicated that fatigue, depressive symptomatology, relationship satisfaction, work-role conflict, and mother-role conflict failed to predict sexual desire during pregnancy.

Although male sexual desire does not decrease as dramatically as female sexual desire, one report indicated a decline of sexual desire for sexual activity in a subset of men. In a study of 112 couples that were interviewed retrospectively regarding their sexual behavior during pregnancy, approximately 40% of women indicated a decrease in desire throughout the first two trimesters of pregnancy, whereas 9% and 17% of men reported a similar decline in the first and second trimesters, respectively. During the third trimester, a substantial proportion of women reported decreased interest in sexual activity (75%), and over half of their partners reported a similar decline (64%). The authors attributed the decline in male sexual desire to fear of hurting the child during sexual intercourse and to the growing abdomen of their pregnant female partners (Bogren, 1991). However, these reports were retrospective, which may be subject to a number of sources of reporting bias (see Wiederman, chapter 2, this volume).

After childbirth, female sexual interest generally remains low until the third to fourth month postpartum (von Sydow, 1999). For example, Kumer et al. (1981) reported that women at 12 weeks postpartum who reported decreased sexual desire were more likely to have coitus less than one time per week than women who reported a greater level of desire. De Judicibus and McCabe (2002) found that compared to pre-pregnancy levels of sexual desire, women reported lower levels of sexual desire at 12 weeks postpartum, and Fischman et al. (1984) documented that decreased sexual desire extends throughout the first year postpartum in at least half of postpartum women. Glazener (1997) indicated that over 20% of her sample reported a complete lack of sexual desire throughout months 2 to 18 postpartum. On the other hand, Hyde et al. (1996) reported that at one year following the birth of their children, 56% of the women in their sample never experienced decreased desire. In addition, the rate at which sexual desire increases after childbirth varies. Elliott and Watson (1985) found that during the first year postpartum, 31% of their sample reported a sharp increase in sexual desire, and 29% endorsed random fluctuation. Robson et al. (1981) indicated that at three months postpartum, 57% of women in their sample reported decreased sexual desire as compared to pre-pregnancy levels, although 25% of the women in their sample stated that they enjoyed sexual intercourse more than before pregnancy. Furthermore, there is a sharp contrast between the levels of sexual desire reported by women and men in the postpartum period, as Fischman et al. (1984) indicated that over 60% of men reported an unchanged desire for sex, whereas only 37% of the women reported the same.

Several factors may account for the decrease in sexual desire reported by women after childbirth. In a sample of 33 postpartum women, Kenny (1973) surprisingly found that 43% of women with more than one child felt as if childbirth increased their sexual desire, whereas only 8% first-time mothers indicated the same. However, it is unclear whether women in this sample were using pregnancy or the period of time prior to conception as a reference point. De Judicibus and McCabe (2002) found that at 12 weeks postpartum, female sexual desire was predicted by relationship satisfaction and fatigue. At six months postpartum, the absence of depressive symptomatology, relationship satisfaction, and acceptance of the mother role predicted higher levels of female sexual desire.

In sum, female sexual interest declines during pregnancy, especially in the third trimester, and remains decreased throughout the beginning of the postpartum period. However, a minority of women experience an increase in sexual desire, particularly in the second trimester of pregnancy. In the postpartum period, sexual interest appears to increase around the 3rd or 4th month following childbirth, although there is also a subset of women who report decreased levels of sexual desire throughout the first year postpartum and into the second year. The metacontent analysis by von Sydow (1999) suggests that, on average, women resume coital activity before they experience an increase in sexual desire, although researchers in this area have yet to identify whether this affects the quality of the partner relationship. In addition, there is evidence for significant gender differences in sexual desire throughout the time associated with childbirth, such that men generally desire sexual activity more than women. Although this gender difference is similar to what is found in the general population (cf. Laumann et al., 1994), such a discrepancy has the potential to decrease satisfaction with the partner relationship. Thus, it is important for health professionals to educate couples about this difference in desire so that they formulate realistic expectations for sexual activity during this time.

OTHER SEXUAL VARIABLES

Orgasm

Changes associated with childbirth affect orgasmic functioning in a similar manner as the sexual variables considered thus far, such that orgasmic capability is impaired during pregnancy and the postpartum period in at least a subset of women. For example, in a sample of 140 pregnant women, 51% reported no change in their frequency of orgasm during sexual intercourse, whereas 34% reported a decreased ability to achieve orgasm (Bartellas et al., 2000). Some researchers report a linear decline in the frequency of orgasms throughout pregnancy (e.g., Hart et al., 1991; Reamy et al., 1982). In their cross-sectional study of women in each trimester of pregnancy and at six weeks postpartum, Tolor and DiGrazia (1976) found that the frequency of orgasm declined from the first two trimesters to the last trimester. Another group of researchers found in their sample of 119 primiparous women that 60% experienced orgasm more than half of the time in which they engaged in sexual intercourse during the first and second trimesters. By the third trimester, only 42% of the women who continued to engage in coital activity experienced orgasm more than half the time (Kumar et al., 1981; Robson et al., 1981). Moreover, Solberg et al. (1973) found that women generally reported that the strength and intensity of orgasms diminished during pregnancy.

Interestingly, some women may achieve orgasm more easily during pregnancy than at other times in their life. Fogel and Lauver (1990) noted that some women may experience their first orgasm during pregnancy. Barclay et al. (1994) reported that during the first trimester, 52% their sample indicated that the frequency of orgasm was the same as before pregnancy and that 24% of their sample reported an increase in the frequency of orgasm. Masters and Johnson (1966) indicated that of 101 women assessed during the second trimester, 82 reported an increased ability to achieve orgasm, often beyond pre-pregnancy levels. They determined that sexual responsiveness during pregnancy is more closely related to parity and social status than to the somatic concerns of pregnancy.

The ability to reach orgasm during pregnancy does not appear to depend on the particular method of sexual stimulation during pregnancy. For example, Solberg et al. (1973) found no relation between position used and orgasmic frequency of women in their sample. In addition, the orgasmic frequency with masturbation and hand stimulation by one's partner did not change throughout pregnancy. However, during the last month of pregnancy, more women indicated that they "rarely or never" achieved orgasm through oral–genital stimulation (58%) as compared to before pregnancy (16%). Reamy et al. (1982) found that women did not indicate any preference for the method to achieve orgasm during pregnancy. However, during the second trimester, coitus was the most frequent method of sexual activity, whereas in the first and early third trimesters, coitus and manual and oral stimulation were used equally.

In contrast, postpartum women generally report greater difficulty in achieving orgasm as compared to pre-pregnancy levels, particularly during the first three months after childbirth. Factors such as fatigue, the inability to relax, and dyspareunia reportedly interfere with this process (Falicov, 1973; Reamy & White, 1985). In addition, some evidence suggests a relation between low levels of sexual desire and difficulty achieving orgasm (Kumar et al., 1981; Solberg et al., 1973). However, there appears to be a gradual return to pre-pregnancy levels of orgasm throughout the first year postpartum. In a sample of 30 couples who completed questionnaires at 7 months postpartum men reported that they reached orgasm more frequently than females during intercourse. However, females reported that they reached orgasm more frequently when they engaged in coital activity and clitoral stimulation simultaneously than when they engaged in coital activity alone (von Sydow, 2002). In their questionnaire-based study of 98 women who were seven weeks postpartum, Barrett et al. (1999) found that difficulty reaching orgasm increased significantly within the first three months postpartum, followed by a gradual return to pre-pregnancy levels. In contrast, other researchers find that women reach their pre-pregnancy levels of orgasm fairly quickly after childbirth. For example, Tolor and DiGrazia (1976) reported that women in their sample generally reached their pre-pregnancy orgasmic ability at six weeks postpartum.

This change in sexual responsiveness may be upsetting to postpartum couples and interfere with their sexual satisfaction. For example, Elliott and Watson (1985) found in their sample of 128 women and 87 men that at six months postpartum, 48% of women were "somewhat bothered" by their own change in sexual responsiveness, which was similar to their dissatisfaction at 12 months postpartum (47%). In contrast, only 20% of men were bothered by their own change at six months postpartum, which declined to 12% at one year after the birth of their children. On the other hand, several men reported dissatisfaction with their partners' change in sexual responsiveness. Specifically, 43% and 39% of men were bothered by their wives' change at 6 and 12 months postpartum, respectively. There is also evidence to suggest that male partners do not accurately estimate the frequency of orgasm in their female partners during postpartum coital activity. For example, von Sydow (2002) found that men believed their partners reached orgasm during intercourse more frequently than females reported. In contrast, women accurately estimated the frequency of orgasm in males during intercourse.

In sum, the ability to achieve orgasm during pregnancy and the postpartum period follows a similar pattern to the other sexual variables reviewed thus far. Many of the factors that affect frequency of coital activity and sexual desire (e.g., pain) also interfere with the frequency with which new mothers reach orgasm during sexual activity. Research by Elliot and Watson (1985) suggests that lack of sexual responsiveness has the potential to create problems in the partner relationship. Thus, it is important for expectant couples to be educated about the normal variability in sexual responsiveness associated with childbirth so that a temporary inability to achieve orgasm is not interpreted as being indicative of underlying distress in the partner relationship.

Sexual Satisfaction

Most research suggests that women experience less satisfaction with the sexual relationship as pregnancy progresses and that it takes some time following childbirth to achieve pre-pregnancy levels of sexual satisfaction. For example, Elliott and Watson (1985) found that 40% of women in their sample reported a sharp decrease in satisfaction with sex during pregnancy. Research generally demonstrates that women who receive little or no pleasure from sexual activity before pregnancy are more likely to either stop engaging in sexual activity in the first trimester of pregnancy or continue to derive little pleasure from sexual activity than do women who enjoy sexual activity before becoming pregnant (Kumar et al., 1981). Moreover, Robson et al. (1981) reported that sexual enjoyment and frequency of coitus are correlated at every assessment interval throughout pregnancy and the postpartum period. Linking orgasmic frequency with sexual satisfaction, Reamy et al. (1982) indicated that orgasmic women in their sample who were either pleased or indifferent about their pregnancies reported greater satisfaction with their sexual lives during the middle of pregnancy than did nonorgasmic women who were unhappy about their pregnancies. Moreover, orgasmic women tended to report greater levels of sexual satisfaction than did nonorgasmic women.

Similar to other variables of sexual functioning, some studies documented a linear decline in sexual satisfaction during pregnancy (e.g., Kumar et al., 1981; Reamy et al., 1982), whereas other researchers reported a more variable pattern of sexual satisfaction. For example, Falicov (1973) found that second trimester sexual satisfaction was greater than first trimester satisfaction, although it was still below pre-pregnancy levels of sexual satisfaction (cf. Kumar et al., 1981; Tolor & DiGrazia, 1976). In their sample of 128 women who were interviewed in 4-week intervals from the 13th week of pregnancy through the first year postpartum, Elliott and Watson (1985) indicated that a majority of women having sex in early pregnancy reported no change in sexual enjoyment. Specifically, of the 99 women who reported engaging in sexual activity, 71% indicated a similar sexual enjoyment as compared to before pregnancy, whereas an additional 6% found it more enjoyable than before pregnancy. In contrast, Bogren (1991) found that during the first trimester, 35% of women and 22% of men experienced decreased sexual satisfaction as compared to pre-pregnancy levels. As would be expected, these numbers increased to 55% and 76% of men and women, respectively, who experienced diminished sexual satisfaction in the third trimester. Other researchers also documented substantial declines in sexual satisfaction during the third trimester of pregnancy (De Judicibus & McCabe, 2002; Kumar et al., 1981; Robson et al., 1981; Tolor & DiGrazia, 1976). Moreover, there is evidence to suggest that compared to younger women, women older than 25 years of age experience particularly decreased sexual satisfaction during the third trimester and that men older than 25 years old experience this during the final two trimesters of pregnancy (Bogren, 1991).

Interestingly, some research shows that a majority of women report satisfaction with sexual activity during the first few months of the postpartum period. For example, one group of researchers reported that of the women engaging in sexual intercourse at 12 weeks postpartum, over two thirds reported satisfaction with their level of sexual activity, which increased to 80% at one year postpartum. However, 40% of these women found coitus less enjoyable than before pregnancy (Kumar et al., 1981; Robson et al., 1981). Elliott and Watson (1985) indicated that 32% of women in their sample reported a sharp increase in satisfaction with sexual activity soon after childbirth and that 52% of women who were three months postpartum were "definitely" satisfied with their sex lives. In addition, De Judicibus and McCabe (2002) indicated that although women reported lower levels of sexual satisfaction than before pregnancy, they reported greater sexual satisfaction at 12 weeks postpartum as compared to the third trimester of pregnancy. von Sydow (2002) collected other data suggesting that both members of the couple generally find sexual activity to be moderately to highly pleasant and exciting, although men are more satisfied with these activities than are women.

In sum, sexual satisfaction appears to decline throughout pregnancy, but unlike other sexual variables reviewed in this chapter, relatively high levels of satisfaction are achieved fairly early in the postpartum period. However, it is often unclear from these studies whether levels of satisfaction have a similar meaning as reports of pre-pregnancy levels of satisfaction or whether women report satisfaction because infrequent sexual activity matches their current level of sexual desire. Moreover, very few studies assessed men's level of sexual satisfaction following childbirth. It will be important for future research to track men's and women's levels of sexual satisfaction across pregnancy and the postpartum period, as differing levels might exacerbate difficulties in the partner relationship that occur as both individuals adjust to their new roles as parents.

SEXUAL DIFFICULTIES

As mentioned throughout the chapter thus far, there are several factors that affect the degree to which couples engage in sexual activity during pregnancy and the postpartum period. Many of these factors not only account for variability in couples' sexual activity, but they also serve to make couples vulnerable to more serious sexual difficulties. During pregnancy, factors such as fears related to the baby (e.g., harming the fetus, miscarriage), somatic symptoms (e.g., tiredness, nausea), increasing abdominal size, and pain during sexual activity (e.g., painful penetration) exert a strong influence on the frequency and type of sexual activity in which couples engage (Falicov, 1973). In addition, some couples may actually report phobic anxiety pertaining to sexual intercourse (e.g., Hames, 1980). Physical problems are common in the postpartum period, with some reports indicating that only 13% of women claim no problems (Glazener, Abdalla, Stroud, Naji, Templeton, & Russell, 1995). For example, Barrett et al. (1999) indicated that 80% of women experienced at least one sexual problem such as painful intercourse, tiredness, decreased vaginal lubrication, lack of vaginal muscle tone, or difficulty reaching orgasm during the first three months postpartum, which decreased to two thirds of women at six months postpartum. In the following section are more extensive discussions of two variables that have been examined the most with regard to sexual difficulties—physical pain and sexual fears.

Physical Pain

Several women report that they experience pain during sexual activity. For example, Bartellas et al. (2000) found that 40% of 133 women indicated that breast discomfort occurred frequently in early pregnancy. Dyspareunia is a relatively common problem reported by pregnant women, and its presence typically increases throughout the course of pregnancy. For example, Reamy and White (1985) found that during the first trimester, 18% of women indicated that they experienced some pain associated with coitus, which increased to 32% of women during the late third trimester. In addition, they found that women expecting their first child reported painful sex more often than women who already had children. In late pregnancy, women over 27 years of age more frequently reported painful intercourse than did younger women.

Dyspareunia is also relatively common after childbirth, but it tends to decrease as the postpartum period progresses. However, there is evidence to suggest that women who experience dyspareunia before pregnancy have a four-fold chance of experiencing it at six months postpartum (Barrett et al., 2000). In a sample of 328 women interviewed during the first five to seven weeks postpartum, of those women who resumed sexual activity, approximately 40% experienced dyspareunia during the first act of coitus (Grudzinskas & Atkinson, 1984). In one sample, factors such as giving birth with an intact perineum or not receiving an episitotomy were associated with decreased coital pain (Kline et al., 1994). In addition, painful intercourse may be associated with the type of delivery. For example, Ryding (1984) found that 10% of women experienced dyspareunia after a normal vaginal delivery, 22% after an episi-totomy or perenial rupture, and 40% after a cesarean section. Parity of the pregnant or postpartum women may also be an influential factor in the degree to which couples experience sexual difficulties, as Kline and colleagues (1994) found that women expecting their first child experienced more perenial pain and sexual problems than women who already had a child. Moreover, it has been demonstrated that physical discomfort is associated significantly with lack of sexual satisfaction and a longer period of sexual abstinence after childbirth (Fischman et al., 1984), although not all researchers confirm these associations (e.g., Al Bustan et al., 1995). An additional problem that may be present after childbirth is vaginal bleeding. In one sample of 42 couples who completed questionnaires following the birth of their first child, 38% of the couples felt that vaginal bleeding inhibited their sexual activity. In addition, approximately 24% of males indicated that breast changes inhibited their sexual activity because of tenderness and leakage (Hames, 1980).

Fortunately, the presence of physical pain typically abates over time. Glazener (1997) found that 42% of women in this sample reported perineal pain following discharge from the hospital, which declined to 22% at eight weeks postpartum and to 10% at 12 to 18 months postpartum. In another study, it was found that approximately 40% of women having sex experienced soreness or pain during coitus at 12 weeks postpartum. These rates declined to 18% at six months postpartum and to 8% at one year postpartum (Kumar et al., 1981; Robson et al., 1981). In a cross-sectional study assessing women at 4 and 12 months postpartum, approximately 62% of women who were 4 months postpartum indicated physical discomfort with sex, compared to 16% of women who were 12 months postpartum.

Sexual Fears

During pregnancy, men and women commonly express fear of harming the fetus during coital activity. For example, some researchers found a negative correlation between frequency of sexual intercourse in the first trimester and expression of fears by the mother that sexual intercourse would damage or harm the fetus (Kumar et al., 1981; Robson et al., 1981). In addition, Falicov (1973) found that fear of harming the fetus or provoking miscarriage interfered with desire to engage in sexual intercourse for over half of the women in this sample, although these fears declined throughout pregnancy. Moreover, Reamy and White (1985) indicated that during the first and second trimesters, fear and anxiety regarding the pregnancy correlated positively with dyspareunia.

Research found that approximately half of pregnant women express this concern. Masters and Johnson (1966) interviewed 43 pregnant women in their first trimester and found that 26 of these women expressed concerns regarding harm to the fetus, many of whom did not communicate these fears to their partners. In addition, Lumley (1978) found that 40% of couples in this sample reported a transient fear of harming the fetus during pregnancy. Moreover, Bartellas et al. (2000) indicated that 49% of their sample experienced fear of harming the fetus at some point during pregnancy, and 55% of the sample believed that their partner shared this fear. Although women reported stable levels of this fear throughout pregnancy, they believed that their partners became more fearful of harming the fetus as pregnancy progressed. Bogren (1991) also found that fear of harming the fetus was a prominent concern for women throughout the entire pregnancy, which led to decreased sexual desire during the same time interval. However, Bogren (1991) indicated that similar fears in men were related to a decrease in sexual desire only in the third trimester. There is also some evidence to suggest that women who are fearful during pregnancy express a desire to engage in noncoital activity more than women who do not express similar anxiety. Specifically, White et al. (1983) indicated that women who were fearful indicated a greater desire to be held than women who did not report such fears.

Although these fears are distressing to many pregnant couples, it appears that unless women are experiencing a high-risk pregnancy, sexual activity during pregnancy is not harmful. Pugh and Fernandez (1953) indicated that although lack of coital activity is commonly attributed to the complications of late pregnancy and delivery, sexual intercourse and these complications are unrelated. In addition, Perkins (1979) failed to find an association between sexual activity (with or without orgasm) and premature rupture of membranes or low birth weight infants. However, pregnant couples should be aware that fatal air embolism may occur during pregnancy as a result of inflation of air into the vagina during oral sex (Eckert, Katchis, & Dotson, 1991; Fyke, Kazmier, & Harms, 1985). Some pregnant couples also express concerns regarding engaging in sexual intercourse and the onset of premature labor, though empirical research has failed to establish any association (e.g., Perkins, 1979; Rayburn & Wilson, 1980). At times women are advised by their medical doctors to abstain from sexual activity in certain circumstances, such as instances in which they experience pelvic pain, bleeding, or premature rupture of the membrane (Bitzer & Alder, 2000).

During the postpartum period, a prominent concern for couples is fear of harming the woman during sexual activity. For example, despite high levels of sexual desire, 37% of women in one sample delayed intercourse due to fear of soreness (Falicov, 1973). Bailey (1989) found that couples reported fear of resuming sexual intercourse if the woman experienced an episiotomy or laceration, which was mainly because these women feared that they would split open. Moreover, Hames (1980) reported that 55% of women reported that the most significant factor inhibiting resumption of sexual intercourse was the feeling of pain, whereas 64% of men reported that they feared sexual intercourse would harm their wives. Concerns of another pregnancy are also prevalent within the first few months after childbirth, such that couples report initiating contraceptive use less than one week before sexual intercourse is resumed (Glazener, 1997). Approximately 42% to 90% of women report using contraception during sexual intercourse within the first three months postpartum (Alder & Bancroft, 1988; Glazener, 1997).

In sum, it appears that sexual difficulties are prominent throughout the transition to parenthood. One of the most distressing difficulties is dyspareunia, which tends to become more problematic as pregnancy progresses but decreases throughout the first year postpartum. Several factors, such as type of delivery, parity, and vaginal bleeding may influence the degree to which pregnant and postpartum women experience sexual pain, which in turn, disrupts sexual activity. In addition, although a substantial number of pregnant women and their partners report fear of harming the fetus during sexual activity, it appears that sexual activity may be harmful to the fetus only in high-risk pregnancies. During the postpartum period, fears of harming the women during sexual activity or becoming pregnant again are also present, but they decrease with time.

BREASTFEEDING

Breastfeeding is an important variable to consider with regard to sexual functioning, as many women believe that breastfeeding inhibits sexual desire, although it often is a source of sexual arousal in and of itself. In many Western cultures, the female breast serves two functions, both of which serve as a means to help propagate our species and to ensure its survival (Llewellyn-Jones, 1978). The primary function of the mother's breast is to provide her infant with nutrition necessary for that infant's survival. The second function, more common in Western societies than in other parts of the world (Dettwyler, 1995), is erotic in nature (Llewellyn-Jones, 1978). The female breast stimulates sexual arousal in both men and women, which may function as a precursor to sexual intercourse. For some women, the sexual arousal resulting from suckling and fondling of the breast commonly experienced during sexual encounters and foreplay with a partner is also experienced as they breastfeed their infants. For a few women, that experience may provide even more pleasure than coital activity (Llewellyn-Jones, 1978). Jessup and Powers (1987) also pointed out the duality of the female breast as a means to nourish one's child as well as the important role it holds in foreplay, serving as a mechanism of sexual arousal for both women and men. Although some women reported that their breasts were not included in foreplay during lactation, other women found that their larger breasts were more sensitive during lactation and that they became a more central part of sexual activity than before birth (Jessup & Powers, 1987).

Newton (1992) explained the connection between breastfeeding and sexual pleasure by identifying several psychophysiological similarities between lactation and sexual intercourse. During both suckling and sexual arousal, women experience uterine contractions, nipple erection, breast stroking and nipple stimulation, and similar vascular changes in the skin (Newton, 1992). However, human sexuality is variable, and Dettwyler (1995) stated, "Sometimes breastfeeding is pleasurable and sometimes it is painful. Most of the time, for most women, it is simply neutral" (p. 263).

Aspects of the sexual relationship of a couple in which the mother is breastfeeding may be affected, although results found in the literature are often conflicting (Alteneder & Hartzell, 1997; Romito, 1988). Alder and Bancroft (1983) found differing rates of frequency of sexual intercourse six weeks after the birth of a child when comparing breastfeeders and nonbreastfeeders, with breastfeeders reporting a lower frequency of sexual intercourse than their nonbreastfeeding counterparts. Hyde et al. (1996) reported that nonbreastfeeding women were more likely to resume sexual intercourse at one month postpartum than breastfeeders by a rate of almost two to one. Additionally, breastfeeding mothers resumed sexual intercourse with their partners more slowly than bottle feeders if their babies required continued feeding during the night (Alder & Bancroft, 1983).

Alder and Bancroft (1988) confirmed and expanded on their earlier findings, reporting that at three months postdelivery, not only had breastfeeders resumed normal sexual activity levels later than artificial feeders, but they also reported more pain during sexual intercourse and a notable reduction in sexual interest and enjoyment compared to pre-pregnancy levels. However, these differences were diminished markedly at six months following childbirth. Fatigue caused by sleep disturbance is thought to be a contributing factor to the lower frequency of sexual intercourse as well as to the increase in duration of time following birth that couples resume sexual intercourse. Alder (1989) reported that breastfed babies were more likely to wake during the night than nonbreastfed babies, which provides some support for the idea that fatigue in breastfeeding women may be connected to a lack of sexual desire. Thus, fatigue due to lack of sleep may confound the apparent negative relation between breastfeeding and sexual desire.

Romito (1988) suggested that other factors involved with breastfeeding may also play important roles in the nature of the sexual activities of couples. For instance, breastfeeding mothers shared fewer activities with their partners, which may contribute to a lack of closeness between the partners. In addition, breastfeeding women reported greater disappointment in the degree to which their partners participated in baby care than did bottle-feeding mothers, although prior to birth, both groups of women had expected the same levels of cooperation from their partners. Jessup and Powers (1987) hypothesized that mothers provide their babies with high levels of tactile stimulation in the course of their daily activities, such as bathing and breast-feeding, during which they also receive tactile stimulation in return. Consequently, it is possible that the breastfeeding mother might "feel 'touched out' by the end of the day. The result might be that she requires less caressing from her husband, which he might perceive as a rejection of his attempts for closeness" (Jessup & Powers, 1987, p. 45). Although the aforementioned factors often result in less closeness and sexual intimacy between couples in which the woman breastfeeds her infant, Romito (1988) suggested that if partners make conscious efforts to participate more in the care of their children, the loss of closeness between the couple can be avoided, and the level of closeness may even increase. Jessup and Powers (1987) stated that the period of time during which a breastfeeding mother might feel "touched out" is a passing phase in the lactation period and that an explanation of this phenomenon to the couple may help minimize resulting strains in the relationship.

Although the literature reviewed suggests that breastfeeding has a detrimental effect on sexual functioning and intimacy, other studies examining postpartum sexual adjustment have resulted in somewhat different conclusions. For example, Masters and Johnson (1966) found that although half of the women in their sample reported decreased levels of sexual activity at three months postpartum, breastfeeding mothers composed the group with the highest levels of sexual interest and activity. Falicov (1973) reported similar findings in a study that examined women at two and seven months postpartum, with breastfeeders reporting not only higher levels of sexual desire, but also an increased capacity for arousal and orgasm. Kenny (1973) studied 33 breastfeeding women and concluded that breastfeeding had little impact on their sexual activity and that breastfeeding women reported somewhat less desire in the first few months postpartum, although their desire increased with time.

The physical changes that occur in women following childbirth in relation to breast-feeding may also result in adjustments, both positive and negative, in the sexual activities of a couple. Hames (1980) conducted a study examining the sexual needs and interests of postpartum couples that asked both the wives and husbands about the effect of postpartum breast changes on their normal sexual activities. Sixty-four percent of the females in Hames' (1980) study reported no changes in their normal sexual activity as a result of breast changes following delivery. A lesser percentage of females, 24%, reported that breast tenderness and milk leakage were the main factors that inhibited their normal sexual activities, and 12% of the females reported that breast changes (e.g., larger breast size) increased and enhanced their normal sexual activities following birth. Of the men in this sample, 60% reported no changes in normal sexual activity because of postdelivery breast changes, 21% reported that breast leakage inhibited normal sexual activity, and 19% reported that the increased size of their wives breasts enhanced their normal sexual activities (Hames, 1980). It is important to note that when asked, "what factors, if any, prevented [you] from resuming sexual intercourse following the delivery of the baby" (Hames, 1980, p. 314), the most significant factor reported by men was a fear of hurting their wives. No issues pertaining to breastfeeding, breast change, or milk leakage were reported.

Just as changes in sexual activity are reported with the onset of breastfeeding, changes in sexual activity on cessation of breastfeeding also occur. Forster, Abraham, Taylor, and Llewellyn-Jones (1994) studied lactating women as they weaned their babies from breastfeeding and found that women who stop breastfeeding their first child experience an increase in sexual activity and frequency of sexual intercourse within three to four weeks following cessation of breastfeeding. These results must be interpreted cautiously, however, as the body of literature examining sexuality and the cessation of breastfeeding is extremely limited at this time.

The available research literature on sexual adjustment during breastfeeding in the postpartum period leaves one with no clear conclusions. Some studies showed evidence of a decline in sexual activity and a longer duration before commencing sexual intercourse in couples in which the mother breastfeeds, and other studies reported that there is no difference in sexual activity or functioning between breastfeeders and nonbreastfeeders. The best course of action for health professionals may be to educate parents and potential parents about the variation of responses that couples may have in terms of sexual functioning and satisfaction as a result of breastfeeding.

TRANSITION TO PARENTHOOD

The impact of childbirth on the quality of a couple's relationship can be dramatic. The transition from childless couple to parenthood brings with it a number of changes to a couple's social relationships, daily activities and responsibilities, and work and social systems (Alder, 1989; Moss, Bolland, Foxman, & Owen, 1986). Everything from couples' relationships with their own parents, their role in their extended families, and their partner relationships may be affected. An examination of several early studies of marital satisfaction of new parents brings to light somewhat disheartening findings (Moss et al., 1986). Alder (1989) reported that beginning when couples first become parents, they experience a decline in martial satisfaction that continues through the childbearing years. Cowan and colleagues (1985) conducted a longitudinal study comparing parents and childless couples and concluded that "couples who became parents were more likely to report increased conflict and disagreement in their marriages and were less likely to view themselves as 'lovers' in their relationship" (p. 478). From a series of three interviews with 400 primiparous couples beginning during the 5th month of pregnancy and ending at five months postpartum, Meyerowitz and Feldman (1966) found increased complaints of sexual incompatibility, thoughts of being unable to express feelings to their spouse, feelings of not sharing leisure time, and an inability to discuss the husband's work during the postpartum period. Marital satisfaction may only begin to increase, in fact, when the children leave home (Alder, 1989; see Christopher & Kisler, chapter 15, this volume, for more discussion).

Wallace and Gotlib (1990) conducted a study to examine the stability of marital adjustment following birth. They found that both husbands and wives peak in their global ratings of marital adjustment at one month following childbirth and show a significant decrease at six months postpartum, illustrating that couples do not simply return to their pre-pregnancy levels of marital adjustment at six months postpartum. For women, the single best predictor of marital adjustment following childbirth was the level of marital adjustment reported while they were pregnant (Wallace & Gotlib, 1990). One noteworthy finding of the Wallace and Gotlib study was that characteristics of the infant did not explain additional variability in postpartum marital adjustment.

Other studies have come to different conclusions, finding that only a small number of new parents showed signs of serious crisis and that many found that parenthood enhanced their relationships in terms of happiness and satisfaction (Moss et al., 1986). In a study conducted by Meyerowitz and Feldman (1966), primiparous couples with more differentiated marriages were more likely to report an increase in marital satisfaction following birth as compared to those with more companion-like marriages. Additionally, participants in the study strongly agreed that having a baby improved their relationship. It should be noted, however, that compared with findings at five weeks after delivery, at five months postpartum, 20% fewer couples reported that things in their relationship were going well, indicating a downward trend in marital satisfaction as time progressed in the postpartum period.

Several factors may account for the variability in manner in which childbearing affects the partner relationship. For example, a commonly observed finding is that the decline in marital satisfaction following childbirth is often more pronounced for women than for men (Belsky, Spanier, & Rovine, 1983). In addition, couples tended to spend more time on "instrumental tasks and less time on emotional aspects of their functioning" (Belsky et al. 1983, p. 570) following childbirth. Thus, it follows that couples who retain a high level of relationship satisfaction are those that take time to facilitate emotional connectedness. As indicated in the aforementioned Meyerowitz and Feldman (1966) study, the degree to which couples are differentiated or companionlike appears to play a role in the manner in which parenthood affects ratings of satisfaction in the marriage relationship.

The transition to parenthood appears to be a challenge for many couples, particularly for those couples whose relationships are already distressed. In addition to increased demands on time, individuals must struggle with a new way of defining their role in their family as well as the degree to which they can contribute to their varying roles in society. Stress resulting from guilt or being upset with the quality of one's sexual relationship can only exacerbate difficulties in the transition to parenthood. Although it is almost certain that the nature of couples' sexual relationships will change with parenthood, because sexual satisfaction is closely associated with relationship satisfaction, it is important for new parents to continue to attend to this aspect of their lives.

METHODOLOGICAL CAVEATS

Although it is evident from this review that a great deal of research has been conducted on sexual functioning during pregnancy and the postpartum period, several questions remain unanswered. First, there is very little focus on the manner in which the transition to parenthood affects male sexuality. In fact, approximately one third of studies examining sexuality in pregnancy and the postpartum period include data reported from the male partner (von Sydow, 1999). Although men certainly would not be experiencing the physical discomfort during sexual activity that is reported by women during this time period, it is likely that environmental factors (e.g., getting up with the infant in the middle of the night) and psychological factors (e.g., anxiety about harming the partner) would affect the male sexual activity cycle. Second, there are no known studies that examine aspects of the sexual relationship following childbirth in lesbian couples. Third, to determine whether changes in the sexual and partner relationship differ from changes that couples experience during other stressful life events, researchers need to include comparison groups of couples who are not in the transition to parenthood (Hobbs, Bramwell, & May, 1999). It is important to identify the percent of variance in changes in sexual activity that are attributed generally to stressful life events as well as the unique percentage of variance that is attributed to childbirth.

It is difficult to determine causality with the data available in the literature. Many investigations are entirely retrospective, and even in prospective studies that follow longitudinal samples beginning in pregnancy, pre-pregnancy levels of sexual functioning are obtained from retrospective reports. Moreover, prospective data beyond the third month postpartum is lacking (von Sydow, 1999), which is problematic if one hopes to identify the point at which sexual functioning goes back to pre-pregnancy levels or assumes a new level of normalcy. In addition, because the human sexual activity cycle is highly variable, more data points are needed, particularly during pregnancy, to obtain a clearer picture of the patterns of sexual functioning throughout the transition to parenthood. For example, some women indicate that the beginning of the third trimester is similar to the second trimester of pregnancy and that problems related to sexual intercourse began during the latter six weeks of the third trimester (Kenny, 1973). Thus, separating the third trimester into two different assessment intervals, similar to the methodology used in Reamy and White (1985), would provide more data points and a clearer picture of the pattern of sexual functioning during pregnancy.

The measurement of sexual variables also makes it difficult to compare results across studies and to draw meaningful conclusions about the nature of sexual functioning in pregnancy and the postpartum period. For example, rather than using standardized measures to assess aspects of sexuality, researchers commonly develop their own measures, resulting in studies that evaluate sexual functioning through instruments that vary in quality and interpretability. In addition, some investigators evaluate coital activity as the primary measure of sexual functioning (e.g., Grudzinskas & Atkinson, 1984; Tolor & DiGrazia, 1976) rather than examining other variables such as sexual enjoyment, arousal, and satisfaction (e.g., Robson et al., 1981). Other researchers equate sexual activity with sexual interest rather than evaluating sexual interest directly (e.g., Barclay et al., 1994). Although an increasing number of researchers include measures other than coital activity to assess sexuality, there is no consensus regarding how to define variables such as sexual interest, enjoyment, and satisfaction. Moreover, few studies collect data pertaining to noncoital activity. When these variables are assessed, they are often evaluated for the presence or absence of the behavior rather than measured based on frequencies, continuums, and time periods in which these behaviors occur.

FUTURE RESEARCH

One of the most serious limitations of this body of literature is that the research conducted to date has not been guided by any theoretical framework, and there is no comprehensive model of sexual functioning during pregnancy and the postpartum period. It is important for future researchers to utilize theoretical models from the mainstream close relationships literature (see DeLameter & Hyde, chapter 1, this volume) to conceptualize couples' relational and sexual adjustment during this time period. For example, it is likely that individuals of childbearing age have well defined scripts for the amount of sexual activity in which they engage with their partners. The presence of one or more small children will likely disrupt each individual's sexual script, and the couple will find themselves in a position in which they must redefine their expectations for intimacy. Moreover, according to evolutionary theory, the period following childbirth might be a time of substantial differences in expectations between men and women with regard to preferred levels of sexual activity and investment in the relationship. It is possible that postpartum women will be especially sensitive to the degree to which they perceive their partners as providing for them and their offspring. On the one hand, men might respond to this expectation with enthusiasm in order to ensure that their children are healthy and will pass on their genes. Alternatively, because the level of sexual activity typically is quite low in the third trimester of pregnancy and the first few months postpartum, men might be more likely than at other times during the course of the relationship to pursue extramarital affairs. Thus, the time period focused on in this chapter presents an unique opportunity to provide empirical validation for aspects of evolutionary theory, particularly aspects that pertain to issues other than mate selection.

Based on the observations made in the previous section, we advise researchers to attend to a number of methodological issues in future studies. The literature is saturated with studies examining the percentage of women engaging in coital activity at various intervals during pregnancy and the postpartum period. To contribute unique knowledge to this line of study, we suggest that researchers investigate the frequency in which pregnant and postpartum couples engage in a number of types of sexual activity, ranging from nongenital activity (e.g., kissing, holding) to noncoital genital activity (e.g., fellatio, cunnilingus). In addition to data describing sexual activity, it will be important for future researchers to measure sexual desire, sexual arousal, sexual responsiveness (i.e., orgasm), and sexual satisfaction. Consistent with the recommendations put forth by von Sydow (1999), we also identify a number of design choices that would make significant methodological contributions to this area. These strategies include (a) assessing both partners' reports of sexual functioning, (b) including a comparison group of nonchildbearing couples, (c) using established instruments with sound psychometric properties to facilitate comparison across studies, and (d) obtaining the most accurate estimates of pre-pregnancy sexual functioning as possible.

Moreover, the impact of altered sexual functioning in pregnancy and the postpartum period on the partner relationship has yet to be addressed in a systematic or comprehensive manner. Research reviewed in this chapter suggests that, on average, women resume coital activity without an accompanying increase in desire and that male partners' level of sexual desire usually is higher than female partners' level of sexual desire. The short- and long-term relational effects of these discrepancies are unclear. We suggest that researchers measure aspects of the quality of the relationship during the transition to parenthood, including consensus, coherence, satisfaction, and intimacy. In addition, it is unclear whether levels of sexual activity *ever* reach pre-pregnancy levels after the birth of a child. Thus, it is clear that future research must follow couples beyond the first year postpartum. In fact, we suggest that a much needed longitudinal study would involve the recruitment of couples *before* they become pregnant to measure prospectively pre-pregnancy levels of sexual functioning and the tracking of these couples throughout pregnancy, the first year postpartum, and at least one year thereafter in order to achieve a broader longitudinal view of the manner in which childbirth affects sexual functioning and the partner relationship.

Finally, we suggest that future research should examine the variables that might moderate the relation between breastfeeding and sexual functioning, as it is difficult to draw conclusions from existing studies that investigate this issue. It is possible, for example, that women experiencing postpartum depression have more difficulty tolerating the physical effects of breastfeeding than do nondepressed women, which would make them particularly prone to experiencing dysfunction in other aspects of their lives such as the sexual relationship. Another possibility is that decreased sexual functioning due to breastfeeding occurs because of expectations—if women foresee that they will experience sexual difficulties (as is commonly reported anecdotally by expectant mothers), then they might experience them because of a self-fulfilling prophesy. Research in other areas of sexuality (e.g., alcohol use and sexual functioning) has demonstrated that expectations play a large role in sexual arousal (see Wenzel, Jackson, & Brendle, chapter 22, this volume).

CONCLUSIONS

Although results vary across studies, all types of coital and noncoital activities decline throughout pregnancy and begin to increase again 6 to 12 weeks following childbirth. Other variables, such as sexual interest and arousal, appear to coincide with the general pattern of sexual activity. New parents may approach sexual activity with apprehension because of physical pain or fears of causing damage, although these anxieties dissipate over time. However, it is unclear when, if ever, sexual activity goes back to what couples experienced before pregnancy. It is quite possible that couples achieve a new sense of normalcy in their sexual relationship. On the other hand, it is important to recognize that although there is disruption in sexual activity, it is distressing only for a subset of couples (De Judicibus & McCabe, 2002). Few women report a complete loss of desire and abandonment of sexual activity.

It is also important to acknowledge that, although sexuality throughout the transition to parenthood appears to be disrupted as compared to pre-pregnancy sexuality, it does not mean that there is a problem with sexual functioning per se. As Hobbs et al. (1999) noted, there has been little work done to examine whether couples regard decreased sexual activity to be problematic in the close relationship, and if they do, why they regard it as being problematic. Rather, couples are entering a new realm in which many aspects of their lives are being redefined, including their relationship with their partner. At times, sexual activity brings couples together in the face of stress, sleep deprivation, and multiple demands; at other times, it may be a source of frustration. The research reviewed in this chapter suggests that it is important for expectant parents to be educated about changes in sexual functioning that may accompany childbirth and to formulate realistic expectations about how their new child will impact their sex life. Above all, we suggest that couples approach these changes with open communication, empathy, and sensitivity, all of which will ease any discomfort associated with these changes and will serve to enhance the partner relationship.

REFERENCES

Adinma, J. I. B. (1996). Sexual activity during pregnancy and after pregnancy. *Advances in Contraception, 12*, 53–61.
Al Bustan, M. A., El Tomi, N. F., Faiwalla, M. F., & Manav, V. (1995). Maternal sexuality during pregnancy and after childbirth in Muslim Kuwaiti women. *Archives of Sexual Behavior, 24*, 207–215.
Alder, E. (1989). Sexual behaviors in pregnancy, after childbirth and during breastfeeding. *Balliere's Clinical Obstetrics and Gynaecology, 3*, 805–821.
Alder, E., & Bancroft, J. (1983). Sexual behaviour of lactating women: A preliminary communication. *Journal of Reproductive and Infant Psychology, 1*, 47–52.
Alder, E., & Bancroft, J. (1988). The relationship between breast feeding persistence, sexuality and mood in postpartum women. *Psychological Medicine, 18*, 389–396.
Alteneder, R. R., & Hartzell, D. (1997). Addressing couples' sexuality concerns during the childbearing period: Use of the PLISSIT model. *Journal of Obstetric, Gynecologic, and Neonatal Nursing, 26*, 651–658.
Bailey, V. R. (1989). Sexuality—before and after birth. *Midwives Chronicle, 102*, 24–26.
Barclay, L. M., McDonald, P., & O'Loughlin, J. A. (1994). Sexuality and pregnancy: An interview study. *The Australian and New Zealand Journal of Obstetrics and Gynaecology, 34*, 1–7.
Barrett, G., Pendry, E., Peacock, J., Victor, C., Thakar, T., & Manyonda, I. (1999). Women's sexuality after childbirth: A pilot study. *Archives of Sexual Behavior, 28*, 179–191.
Bartellas, E., Crane, J. M. G., Daley, M., Bennett, K. A., & Hutchens, D. (2000). Sexuality and sexual activity in pregnancy. *British Journal of Obstetrics and Gynaecology, 107*, 964–968.
Barrett, G., Pendry, E., Peacock, J., Victor, C., Thakar, R., & Manyonda, I. (2000). Women's sexual health after childbirth. *BJOG, 107*, 186–195.
Belsky, J., Spanier, G. B., & Rovine, M. (1983). Stability and change in marriage across the transition to parenthood. *Journal of Marriage and the Family, 45*, 567–577.
Bitzer, J., & Alder, J. (2000). Sexuality during pregnancy and the postpartum period. *Journal of Sex Education and Therapy, 25*, 49–58.
Bogren, L. Y. (1991). Changes in sexuality in women and men during pregnancy. *Archives of Sexual Behavior, 20*, 35–45.
Byrd, J. E., Hyde, J. S., DeLamater, J. D., & Plant, E. A. (1998). Sexuality during pregnancy and the year postpartum. *The Journal of Family Practice, 47*, 305–308.
Calhoun, L. G., Selby, J. W., & King, H. E. (1981). The influence of pregnancy on sexuality: A review of the current evidence. *The Journal of Sex Research, 17*, 139–151.
Call, V., Sprecher, S., & Schwartz, P. (1995). The incidence and frequency of marital sex in a national sample. *Journal of Marriage and the Family, 57*, 639–652.
Cowan, C., Cowan, P., Heming, G., Garrett, E., Coysh, W., Curtis-Boles, H., & Boles, A. (1985). Transition to parenthood: His, hers, and theirs. *Journal of Family Issues, 6*, 461–481.

De Judicibus, M. A., & McCabe, M. P. (2002). Psychological factors and the sexuality of pregnant and postpartum women. *The Journal of Sex Research, 39*, 94–103.

Dettwyler, K. A. (1995). Sexuality and breastfeeding. *Journal of Human Lactation, 11*, 263–264.

Eckert, W. G., Katchis, S., & Dotson, P. (1991). The unusual accidental death of a pregnant woman by sexual foreplay. *The American Journal of Forensic Medicine and Pathology, 12*, 247–249.

Elliott, S. A., & Watson, J. P. (1985). Sex during pregnancy and the first postnatal year. *Journal of Psychosomatic Research, 29*, 541–548.

El Tomi, N. F., Al Bustan, M., & Abokhadour, N. (1993). Maternal sexuality during pregnancy and after childbirth in Kuwait. *International Quarterly of Community Health Education, 13*, 163–173.

Falicov, C. J. (1973). Sexual adjustment during first pregnancy and postpartum. *American Journal of Obstetrics and Gynecology*, 991–1000.

Fischman, S. H., Rankin, E. A., Soeken, K. L., & Lenz, E. R. (1984). Changes in sexual relationships in postpartum couples. *JOGNN, 15*, 58–63.

Flowers, J. S., & Flowers, C. E. (1985). Psychosexual and psychosomatic gynecology. In D. H. Nichols & J. R. Evrard (Eds.), *Ambulatory gynecology* (pp. 117–139). New York: Harper & Row.

Fogel, C. I., & Lauver, D. (1990). *Sexual health promotion*. Philadelphia: Saunders.

Forster, C., Abraham, S., Taylor, A., & Llewellyn-Jones, D. (1994). Psychological and sexual changes after the cessation of breastfeeding. *Obstetrics and Gynecology, 84*, 872–876.

Fyke, F. E., Kazmier, F. J., & Harms, R. W. (1985). Venous air embolism: Life-threatening complication of orogenital sex during pregnancy. *The American Journal of Medicine, 78*, 333–336.

Georgakopoulos, P. A., Dodos, D., & Mechleris, D. (1984). Sexuality in pregnancy and premature labor. *British Journal of Obstetrics and Gynaecology, 91*, 891–893.

Glazener, C. M. A. (1997). Sexual function after childbirth: Women's experiences, persistent morbidity and lack of professional recognition. *British Journal of Obstetrics and Gynaecology, 104*, 330–335.

Glazener, C. M. A., Abdalla, M., Stroud, P., Naji, S., Templeton, A., & Russell, I. T. (1995). Postnatal maternal morbidity: Extent, causes, prevention, and treatment. *British Journal of Obstetrics and Gynaecology, 102*, 282–287.

Grudzinskas, J. G., & Atkinson, L. (1984). Sexual function during the puerperium. *Archives of Sexual Behavior, 13*, 85–91.

Hames, C. T. (1980). Sexual needs and interests of postpartum couples. *JOGN Nursing, 9*, 313–315.

Hart, J., Cohen, E., Gingold, A., & Homburg, R. (1991). Sexual behavior in pregnancy: A study of 219 women. *Journal of Sex Education and Therapy, 17*, 86–90.

Hobbs, K., Bramwell, R., & May, K. (1999). Sexuality, sexual behaviour, and pregnancy. *Sexual and Marital Therapy, 14*, 371–383.

Hyde, J. E., DeLamater, J. D., Plant, E. A., & Byrd, J. M. (1996). Sexuality during pregnancy and the year postpartum. *The Journal of Sex Research, 33*, 143–151.

Jessup, D. J., & Powers, D. C. (1987). Lactation and its effects on sexuality. *Journal of Pediatric and Perinatal Nutrition, 1*, 43–49.

Kenny, J. A. (1973). Sexuality of pregnant and breastfeeding women. *Archives of Sexual Behavior, 2*, 215–229.

Kline, M. C., Gauthier, R. J., Robbins, J. M., Kaczorowski, J., Jorgensen, S. H., Franco, E. D., Johnson, B., Waghorn, K., Gelfand, M. M., Guralnick, M. S., Luskey, G. W., & Joshi, A. K. (1994). Relationship of episitotomy to perinatal trauma and morbidity, sexual dysfunction, and pelvic floor relaxation. *American Journal of Obstetrics and Gynecology, 171*, 591–598.

Kumar, R., Brant, H. A., & Robson, K. M. (1981). Childbearing and maternal sexuality: A prospective survey of 119 primiparae. *Journal of Psychosomatic Research, 25*, 373–383.

Laumann, E. O., Gagnon, J. H., Michael, R. T., & Michaels, S. (1994). *The social organization of sexuality: Sexual practices in the United States*. Chicago: The University of Chicago Press.

Llewellyn-Jones, J. D. (1978). Breast feeding and sexuality. *Australian Nurses Journal, 8*, 22–24.

Lumley, J. (1978). Sexual feelings in pregnancy and after childbirth. *Australian and New Zealand Journal of Obstetrics and Gynaecology, 18*, 114–117.

Masters, W., & Johnson, V. (1966). *Human sexual response*. Boston: Little, Brown.

Meyerowitz, J. H., & Feldman, H. (1966). Transition to parenthood. *Psychiatric Research Report, 20*, 78–84.

Miller, W. E., & Friedman, S. (1989). Male and female sexuality during pregnancy: Behavior and attitudes. *Journal of Psychology & Human Sexuality, 1*, 17–37.

Moss, P., Bolland, G., Foxman, R., & Owen, C. (1986). Marital relations during the transition to parenthood. *Journal of Reproductive and Infant Psychology, 4*, 57–67.

Newton, N. (1992). Interrelationships between sexual responsiveness, birth, and breast feeding. *Pre- and Peri-Natal Psychology Journal, 6*, 317–336.

Pepe, F., Panella, M., Pepe, P., Paneleea, P., Amaru, A., Cantarella, M., Russo, G., & Privitera, C. D. (1988). Sexual behaviour in relation to age: A study of 205 puerperal women. *Clinical Experiments in Obstetrics and Gynaecology, 15*, 24–30.

Perkins, R. P. (1979). Sexual behavior and response in relation to complications of pregnancy. *American Journal of Obstetrics and Gynecology, 134*, 498–505.

Pugh, W. E., & Fernandez, F. L. (1953). Coitus in late pregnancy. *Obstetrics and Gynecology, 2*, 636.

Rayburn, W. F., & Wilson, E. A. (1980). Coital activity and premature delivery. *American Journal of Obstetrics and Gynecology, 15*, 972–974.

Reamy, K. J., & White, S. E. (1985). Dyspareunia in pregnancy. *Journal of Psychosomatic Obstetrics and Gynaecology, 4,* 263–270.

Reamy, K., White, S. E., Daniell, W. C., & Le Vine, E. S. (1982). Sexuality and pregnancy: A prospective study. *The Journal of Reproductive Medicine, 27,* 321–327.

Richardson, A. C., Lyon, J. B., Graham, E. E., & Williams, N. L. (1976). Decreasing postpartum sexual abstinence time. *American Journal of Obstetrics & Gynecology, 126,* 416–417.

Robson, K. M., Brant, H. A., & Kumar, R. (1981). Maternal sexuality during first pregnancy and after childbirth. *British Journal of Obstetrics and Gynaecology, 88,* 882–889.

Romito, P. (1988). Mothers' experience of breastfeeding. *Journal of Reproductive and Infant Psychology, 6,* 88–99.

Ryding, E. L. (1984). Sexuality during and after pregnancy. *Acta Obstetrica et Gynecologica Scandinavica, 63,* 679–682.

Solberg, D. A., Butler, J., & Wagner, N. N. (1973). Sexual behavior in pregnancy. *New England Journal of Medicine, 288,* 1098–1103.

Tolor, A., & DiGrazia, M. D. (1976). Sexual attitudes and behavior patterns during and following pregnancy. *Archives of Sexual Behavior, 5,* 539–551.

von Sydow, K. (1999). Sexuality during pregnancy and after childbirth: A metacontent analysis of 59 studies. *Journal of Psychosomatic Research, 47,* 27–49.

von Sydow, K. (2002). Sexual enjoyment and orgasm postpartum: Sex differences and perceptual accuracy concerning partners' sexual experience. *Journal of Psychosomatic Obstetrics and Gynecology, 23,* 147–155.

von Sydow, K., Ullmeyer, M., & Happ, N. (2001). Sexual activity during pregnancy and after childbirth: Results from the Sexual Preferences Questionnaire. *Journal of Psychosomatics Obstetrics & Gynecology, 22,* 29–40.

Wallace, P. M., & Gotlib, I. H. (1990). Marital adjustment during the transition to parenthood: Stability and predictors of change. *Journal of Marriage and the Family, 52,* 21–29.

White, S. E., Reamy, K., & Southward, G. M. (1983). Nurturant needs of pregnancy: Sexual, psychological, and demographic correlates. *Journal of Psychosomatic Obstetrics and Gynaecology, 2–4,* 243–249.

White, S. E., & Reamy, K. (1982) Sexuality and pregnancy: A review. *Archives of Sexual Behavior, 11,* 429–444.

18

Sexuality in Midlife and Later Life Couples

Elisabeth O. Burgess
Georgia State University

As the American population continues to age, concerns about sexuality in midlife and later life couples will become more and more important. Diverse life course experiences shape opportunities for sexual partnership, sexual attitudes, and sexual behavior in later life. Therefore, this chapter explores the ways that aging influences sexual behavior. Research suggests that the incidence and frequency of sexual activity are lower among older cohorts than younger ones. These changes are due to physiological changes with aging and changes in the opportunity to engage in sexual activities. Finally, this chapter concludes with a discussion of problems with current research on sexuality and aging.

> *When I get older, losing my hair,*
> *Many years from now.*
> *Will you still be sending me a Valentine,*
> *Birthday greetings, bottle of wine...*
> *Will you still need me,*
> *Will you still feed me,*
> *When I'm sixty-four.*
>
> > *(The Beatles, "When I'm sixty-four")*

This Beatles song, a whimsical examination of love, romance, and aging, addresses the desire for an intimate partner with aging.[1] The generation that came of age listening to the music of the Beatles and questioning the social and sexual norms of their parents and grandparents now approaches "sixty-four." Are Baby Boomers shattering traditional notions of sexuality and aging? Are they growing old with long-term

---

The author would like to acknowledge Dawn M. Baunach, Mindy Stombler, and editors of this Handbook for their editorial advice and additional suggestions on earlier drafts of this manuscript. In addition, Jennifer Osborne and Cristina Gheorghui provided assistance with library and administrative work.

[1] A note on language. The term "aging" is used to refer to the process of growing older, which includes midlife adults as well as older adults.

partners? Does the aging result in an inevitable decline in sexual activity, satisfaction, and well-being? This chapter explores our current understanding of sexuality and aging by (1) identifying the demographic profile of older adults; (2) addressing current patterns of sexuality among midlife and older adults; (3) exploring changes in sexuality with aging; and (4) making suggestions for future research.

TWENTY-FIRST CENTURY CONTEXT

Contemporary midlife and older adults are aging in a very different climate than their parents and grandparents. Tremendous shifts in the age distribution of the population have coincided with dramatic changes in attitudes about sexuality. As a result, middle age and older adults are redefining the images of sexuality and aging.

The demographic changes in the age distribution of the U.S. population have been dramatic. Since 1900, the percentage of Americans over the age of 64 has more than tripled (4.1% in 1900 to 12.4% in 2000). A hundred years ago, life expectancy at birth was about 56 years of age. In contrast, a child born in 2000 can anticipate living 76.9 years. The Baby Boom generation, now in their 40s and 50s, can expect to be part of the largest generation of elders in American history. By 2020 approximately 20% of the population will be over 65 (U.S. Census, 2000).

Longer lives and greater numbers of older adults have already begun to shift our concept of the life course. No longer do adults spend the majority of their lives bearing and rearing children. Instead, the life course now includes the new stages of "empty nest" and "retirement." Late life can now be broken down into three categories—young–old, middle–old, and old–old—not measured by merely chronological, but also by social and physical well-being (Neugarten & Neugarten, 1996). These demographic shifts have altered our definitions of the middle and old age. Traditional geriatric attitudes and behavior no longer apply to the healthier and more active midlifers and seniors.

An additional consideration for understanding contemporary patterns of aging is gender. Men and women experience aging differently in several ways. For example, in the United States, women live approximately 7 years longer than men. These additional years of life increase the probability that women, particularly heterosexual women, will face later life without a partner. In addition, heterosexual men still partner with younger women and are more likely to remarry after divorce. As a result, at age 55 men are more likely to be married (75%) than are women (66%). This gap becomes even wider among the older age groups. By age 75, 70% of men remain married, as compared to 34% of women (U.S. Census, 2000).

Furthermore, aging does not occur in a vacuum. Peer experience and historical events influence the acceptability of different sexual activities and lifestyle choices. Contemporary middle age and older adults have experienced profound social change as a result of the postwar economic boom and the social movements of civil rights, women's liberation, sexual revolution, and gay and lesbian liberation. The impact of these movements depends largely on exposure. During the peak of these social changes, midlife Baby Boomers were impressionable youth and young adults, experimenting with new social and sexual practices. In contrast, current cohorts of older adults came of age during periods that were more conservative with regard to sexual attitudes and practices. In a study of adults ages 18 to 59, Laumann, Gagnon, Michael, and Michaels (1994) found that older adults were more likely to express traditional or conservative values about sexuality. Jacoby (1999) reported that women and men ages 45 to 59 were more likely to approve of a variety of sexual activities, including sex between unmarried partners, oral sex, and masturbation, than older age groups. In this study, age differences in sexual attitudes were more disparate for women and men. Overall these findings suggest that historical changes in attitudes about sexuality continue and that younger cohorts will practice a wider variety of sexual behavior as they age.

Moreover, experiences of aging are very diverse; in addition to age and gender, social class, race, health status, and sexual orientation also shape patterns of aging. Because of poor working and living conditions and inadequate health care, working class and poor adults experience more health problems and a greater number of functional disabilities over the life course and at younger ages than those from middle and upper class (George, 1996). Poor health in middle and later life negatively impacts sexual behavior and satisfaction for both men and women. Current cohorts of racial and ethnic minority elders face discrimination and prejudice that often limits access to education, jobs, health care, and housing (George, 1996; Williams & Wilson, 2001). In addition to lowering health status, persistent levels of inequality places strains on the marital and family life of many African American elders; as a result they experience lower rates of marriage when compared to Whites (Staples, 1988; Treas, 1995). Older immigrants frequently were raised in cultures with different sets of values about family and sexuality (Treas, 1995). Gays and lesbians also face a lifetime of discrimination, which can result in low levels of social support from family. Additionally, older cohorts of gays and lesbians may be less likely to have long-term partners because of historical patterns of social stigma, which discouraged them from living openly as homosexuals and limited partnership opportunity (Fullmer, Shenk, & Eastand, 1999: Kimmel, 1993).

Finally, despite recent demographic changes and the heterogeneity of older adult life styles, ageism still has a strong influence on our attitudes about aging. Young, middle age, and older adults are often ill informed about normative patterns of aging and often rely on stereotypes in order to understand sexuality and older adults (Hillman & Stricker, 1994; Levy, 1994; Walker & Ephross, 1999). Older cohorts may even lack the vocabulary to discuss sexuality (David, 2002). Access to older adult populations may be inhibited by ageist gatekeepers, such as health care administrators and adult children, who are trying to protect older adults (Starr & Wiener, 1981). Exacerbating this problem is the lack of nationally representative research on sexuality in later life. Any research on sexuality is difficult to fund, but, when funding sources are limited, the older adults are often the first eliminated from the sample (Laumann et al., 1994). In the case of the National Health and Social Life Survey (NHSLS), when federal funding vanished, Laumann and his colleagues were faced with the difficult decision of how to reduce the proposed sample size of this national sex survey from 20,000 respondents to fewer than 4,000. In order to maintain a nationally representative sample, they reduced the age range of the sample to ages 18 to 59 (Laumann et al., 1994).[2] Although this survey does not contain older adults, it does provide some useful age group comparisons.

PATTERNS OF SEXUAL BEHAVIOR IN MIDLIFE AND LATER ADULTHOOD

Sex is good. Engaging in sexuality helps to preserve psychological and physical well-being and may, in turn, reduce various physical and mental health problems associated with age (Bortz & Wallace, 1999; Edwards & Booth, 1994; Trudel, Turgeon, & Piche,

---

[2] Laumann et al. (1994) limited the sample in several other ways including eliminating the non-English speaking adults and those living in group homes or institutional settings such as college dormitories or nursing homes.

2000). However, sexuality and aging has been a neglected area of research, and what is known about this topic is skewed by a variety of methodological flaws (see the following). Despite this, research indicates that aged individuals remain sexual beings. In this section, I explore the incidence and frequency of sexual activity, the connections among health, well-being, and sexual satisfaction, and sexual activity and satisfaction among gay, lesbian, and bisexual elders.

Incidence and Frequency of Sexual Activity by Age

The first large samples of middle age and older adults for sexuality research were published in the early 1980s. The Starr-Wiener Report (Starr & Wiener, 1981) surveyed 800 adults ages 60 and older. Starr and Weiner's questionnaire consisted of 50 open-ended questions designed to address a broad range of issues including sexual behavior, sexual fantasies, sexual satisfaction, change in sexuality over time, and attitudes regarding sexual norms. Starr and Wiener sampled groups of seniors around the country. After giving a lecture on "Love, Intimacy, and Sex in the Later Years" at senior centers, the researchers asked the audience to contribute to the understanding of sex and aging by filling out a survey and returning it in the self-addressed, stamped envelope. The resulting 14% response rate included 800 adults from across the country, 35% were male, 65% were female, and 47.8% of respondents were married. The respondents wrote enthusiastically about their interest in sex and sexuality. In addition to sexual frequency and satisfaction, Starr and Weiner asked respondents about the length of sex acts (20% reported 30 minutes or more) and communication about sexual desires (50% talked to their partners about "what you like in sex"). This research confirmed that older adults maintained an interest in sexuality and sexual practices.

Brecher (1984) in collaboration with the Consumer's Union, publisher of *Consumer Reports*, surveyed 4,246 midlife and older adults (ages 50–93). After placing a notice in *Consumer Reports*, Brecher received over 10,000 requests for the survey. This extensive survey contained over 200 items addressing issues of friendship, love, and sex, as well as demographic and health information. Many sections asked for retrospective and current accounts of attitudes and behavior. Although many respondents reported a decline in sexual intercourse with age, particularly among the oldest respondents, they engaged in a variety of other sexual behaviors. Because approximately 75% of this sample was married, Brecher explored numerous connections between marital happiness and sexual activity. Seventy-five percent of wives and 87% of husbands felt that "the sexual side of your marriage" was moderately or very important. In addition, Brecher included statistics on the differences in sexual attitudes and behaviors for happy and unhappy marriages and reported on attitudes about extramarital sexuality and open marriages. For example, both husband and wives who were having intercourse with their spouse were more likely to be happily married than those in inactive marriages, and older adults who were comfortable discussing sexual issues with their spouse were more likely to be happily married than those less comfortable discussing sex. Additionally, Brecher found that men reported extramarital affairs since age 50 three times more frequently than women.

Although these studies provided documentation that older adults were sexually engaged, they did not provide analysis of factors linked to sexual activity. These studies confirmed that sexual interest continued into later life, but the qualitative results provided more description than explanation. The lack of representative data meant that it was not possible to generalize from these findings to the general population of older adults.

More recent cross-sectional research suggests considerable variability in sexual activity among middle age and older adults. This research sought to confirm findings from earlier studies that linked declines in sexual activity to age (Edwards & Booth,

1976; Kinsey, Pomperoy, & Martin, 1948; Kinsey, Pomperoy, Martin & Gebhard, 1953; Udry, Deven, & Coleman, 1982). Midlife and older adults who are married or cohabiting are the most likely to be sexually active and have greater frequency of sexual activities than do singles of the same age. Using data from 807 older (60+) married respondents from the National Survey of Families and Households (NSFH), Marsiglio and Donnelly (1991) examined sexual frequency through analysis of the question, "About how often did you and your husband/wife have sex during the past month?" More than 50% of married persons in this study reported having sex at least once a month (Marsiglio & Donnelly, 1991). But there was a considerable difference in the sexual activity of those ages 60 to 65 (more than 60% once a month) and those over 65 (less than 45% once a month). In addition, Marsiglio and Donnelly examined the predictors of sexual frequency among the 423 sexually active respondents, finding that age and marital duration were both negatively related to sexual frequency.

Other studies found similar differences in age groups. Matthias, Lubben, Atchison, and Schweitzer (1997) explored sexual activity and satisfaction among a group of 1,217 older adults participating in a Los Angeles area health promotion trial. Respondents, who were interviewed by telephone, were English-speaking elders, age 70 or over, and not suffering from any dementia or terminal illness. Matthias et al. (1997) found that about one third of this sample "had sexual relationships" in the last month. Because partnership status is negatively related to age, particularly for women, gender is central to the understanding of sexual activity in later life (Jacoby, 1999; Laumann et al., 1994; Matthias et al., 1997). Married women were 24 times more likely to report sexual activity than single women. In contrast, marital status was not a significant factor for the incidence of male sexual activity. Reporting on data from the AARP/Modern Maturity Sexuality Study, Jacoby (1999) illustrated that about half of the 45- to 59-year-old group have sex once a week, but less than 30% of adults over 74 have sex that frequently.

Not only are older adults continuing to have sex, but they are also engaging in a wide array of noncoital behaviors (Brecher, 1984; Johnson, 1998; Starr & Weiner, 1981). For example, Bretschneider and McCoy (1988) found that the majority of adults (80 years and older) in their sample often engaged in mutual caressing. This survey of 202 White men and women from Northern California found that older adults reported continuity between past and present levels of sexual behavior of every type except for coitus. This suggests that even among the oldest–old, sexual interest earlier in life may predict attitudes and some behaviors in later life.

Patterns of sexual frequency in midlife and later life can also be understood by exploring cross-sectional data that contains young and middle-age adults. Laumann et al. (1994) found considerable gender differences in rates of sexual activity among mid–life cohorts. Sexual activity rates for men declined moderately for respondents from the late 40s through the 50s. For women, rates of sexual activity decreased steadily from the early 30s to the early 50s and then fell more dramatically in the late 50s. When they supplemented their data with material from the General Social Survey, Laumman et al. (1994) found that by age 74 more than 70% of the women were sexually inactive compared to only 35% of men in that age group.

Some research suggests that biological age is not the sole cause of declines in sexual activity. The longer a couple is together, the more familiar they become with one another and, therefore, the novelty of sexual activity may begin to wane. Thus, duration of relationship may be negatively related to sexual frequency. In one of the most extensive studies of couples to date, Blumstein and Schwartz (1983) surveyed approximately 6,000 couples (married, cohabiting, gay, and lesbian) and conducted in-depth interviews and follow-up surveys of 300 couples. They found that whereas sexual frequency declined with relationship duration and age, there were some differences by type of couple. For married couples the influence of duration of relationship and age were about equal. In contrast, the sexual frequency of heterosexual cohabiting couples was significantly impacted by duration and not by age. For the sexual frequency of gay and lesbian couples, both duration and age were influential but duration had a stronger impact.

Furthermore, Call, Sprecher, and Schwartz (1995) examined the incidence and frequency of marital sex across age groups using data from the 1988 National Survey of Families and Households. Examining 6,785 married respondents and 679 cohabitors, Call et al. (1995) modeled the incidence and frequency of sex. Highest rates of sex (at least once a month) occurred in younger age groups. Incidence of sex dropped substantially after age 65 and even more dramatically after age 75. The frequency of marital sex was approximately 12 times a month for couples ages 19 to 24, 5 times a month for those ages 50 to 54 and 2 times a month for those ages 65 to 69. Taking other time-related variables into account, duration of marriage was not a significant predictor of sexual frequency. In contrast, age retains the strongest negative impact on the frequency of marital sex. This suggests that except for a brief period at the beginning of the marriage, sexual frequency is better predicted by age than by duration.

Most longitudinal research indicates that sexual frequency may decline with age. Edwards and Booth (1994) examined the relationship between well-being and sexuality in midlife married persons. They examined three wave panels of interview data collected from 1980 through 1988 in order to examine issues of stability and change in marriages. Dissatisfaction with and loss of interest in marital sex increased over time, while psychological well-being and marital quality decreased. Younger cohorts of midlife adults employed a broader range of sexual techniques and more frequent sex than older cohorts. Women were more dissatisfied with marital sex than men. Men from older cohorts were more dissatisfied than men from younger cohorts. Finally, although sexual activity tended to decline with age and marital duration, after the first years of marriage, the decline was gradual and modest. Another longitudinal study that examined changes in marital sex was Udry (1980). Examining data from three waves of a 4-year panel study on the frequency of intercourse in young marriages, Udry (1980) found that length of marriages "subsumes the effect of all other variables" (p. 324). Because his was a young sample, issues of age are less likely to confound those of duration. As such, this research provides strong support for the finding that the fastest rate of decline in sexual frequency is in the early years of marriage.

Health, Well-Being, and Sexual Satisfaction

Health and relationship quality have significant impacts on probability of engaging in sexual activity. Some research indicates that respondents' physical health (or fitness) positively relates to sexual activity (Bortz & Wallace, 1999; Johnson, 1998; McKinlay & Feldman, 1994). Marsiglio and Donnelly (1991) found spouse's health related to the likelihood of having sex in the past month, but health was not related to sexual frequency. In a representative study of 1,709 men from Massachusetts, ages 40 to 70, McKinlay and Feldman (1994) found that men in good health reported more involvement in sexual activity and higher levels of satisfaction. In their longitudinal panel study, Edwards and Booth (1994) established that dissatisfaction with and loss of interest in marital sex increased over time, while psychological well-being and marital quality decreased. Although well-being influences sexuality, Edwards and Booth argued that the relationship may be reciprocal. Focus groups with 14 Canadian women suggested that it is the male partner's health, in particular sexual health (erectile functioning) that dictates coital frequency (Loehr, Verma, & Seguin, 1997).

In contrast to patterns of sexual activity, there is less change in the enjoyment of and satisfaction with sexuality in old age. In a survey of 657 women ages 50 to 89, Johnson (1998) found that one third of women reported higher levels of sexual interest and sexual satisfaction than in the past. Moreover, sexually active women experienced higher levels of sexual interest and sexual satisfaction. Matthias et al. (1997) determined that sexual activity and mental health were predictors of increased sexual satisfaction for both men and women. Interestingly, sexual activity is not a requirement of sexual satisfaction (Marsiglio & Donnelly, 1991; Matthias et al., 1997). Matthais et al. (1997) found that more than 50% of older adults who were not sexually active in the past month were satisfied or very satisfied with their levels of sexual activity. These reports of sexual satisfaction among sexually inactive older adults implied that some older adults are content with low sexual activities.

Patterns of Sexual Behavior for Gay, Lesbian, and Bisexual Older Adults

Patterns of sexual activity and satisfaction for gay and lesbian adults are not well understood. Much of the research on older gays and lesbians focuses on identity issues and the stigma of homosexuality (Duberman, 1997; Friend, 1991; Gershick, 1998; Gray & Dressel, 1985; Lee, 1991; Quam & Whitford, 1992). Although these topics are essential for understanding life-span adjustment and discrimination, they fail to address changes in sexual behavior and satisfaction with aging. Berger (1996) was one of the first researchers to examine sexual behavior in gay males in a large sample. His research, originally conducted in 1978 to 1979, included surveys of 112 gay men who were age 40 or older and 10 in-depth interviews with a subsample of these men. Similar to heterosexual men, gay men have a continued interest in sexual activity. The rates of gay male sex are higher than that found in heterosexual samples. Berger (1996) reported 61% of his sample engaged in sex once a week or more. Not surprisingly, almost 50% of men reported being satisfied with sex. Moreover, sexual satisfaction was positively related to life satisfaction. In a sample of Chicago gay men, Pope and Schulz (1990) found that sexual activity decreased in older age groups. Although 81% of men ages 40 to 49 had sex at least once a week, only 43% of men over 60 had sex once a week. In contrast, Deenen, Gijs, and van Naerssen (1994) found that among Dutch partnered gay men rates of sexual frequency were lower for men in longer relationships than for those in shorter relationships.

Studies of older lesbians are less likely to ask explicit questions about sexuality as compared to those on gay men, but they are more likely to emphasize relationship dynamics. In a snowball sample of 110 midlife lesbians from around the United States, Sang (1993) found that 26% of the women were celibate. But, the majority of midlife lesbians in this sample felt that their sex lives were more exciting now than in the past. Kehoe (1988) collected surveys from a snowball sample of 100 lesbians over age 60. More than 50% of the older lesbians in this national sample had not had sexual relations with another woman in the last year. In contrast to gay men, 43% of whom had had sex in the past week (Pope & Schultz, 1990), only 18% of lesbians had had sex in the last week (Kehoe, 1988). As with heterosexual women (Marsiglio & Donnelly, 1991; Matthias et al., 1997), levels of sexual satisfaction for older lesbians are not perfectly correlated with levels of sexual activity. Although only 21% of lesbians reported being sexually active about once a month or more often, 33% of lesbians reported being somewhat or very satisfied with their sex lives over the past year (Kehoe, 1988). Moreover, Kehoe (1988) reported that sex was not the primary reason for relationships among partnered lesbians. Instead, gender is a key factor in understanding sexuality for both homosexual and heterosexual older adults. Regardless of sexual orientation, women are more likely than men to report not having had sex in the past year and to lack opportunities to find sexual partners.

There is very little research on older bisexual or transgender adults. Weinberg, Williams, and Pryor (2001) report on research from a longitudinal panel study of 56 San Francisco bisexuals who where interviewed from 1983 through 1996. These 23 men, 28 women, and 5 transgender individuals were ages 35 to 67 in 1996. They found decreases in sexual involvement with age primarily due to life course factors such as workplace responsibilities and childrearing. Of additional interest, respondents' contact with the bisexual subculture tended to decrease with age, as did the salience of the bisexual identity.

In sum, most middle age and older adults continue their interest in sexual activities, but experience some decline in activity with age.

CHANGES IN SEXUALITY WITH AGING

Changing Bodies, Changing Minds

Human lives are constantly in flux. The passage of time marks shifts in biology, life stages, experience, and emotional well-being. Sex and sexuality are no exception. These changes may be the result of physiological changes, environmental variation, or an interaction of the two. In the world with Viagra and Botox, American culture discourages physical evidence of aging. Pop a pill, get a shot, have a surgery, and stay young. These temporary fixes may mask the outward appearance of aging, but human bodies and minds inevitably change with the passage of the years. Although many of these changes are intrinsic to the aging process, they are also sensitive to disease, health status, and psychological well-being (Bortz & Wallace, 1999; Keil, Sutherland, Knapp, Waid, & Gazes, 1992; Kingsberg, 2000; Whitbourne, 1990). As such, the depth and degree of physiological change is variable. In addition, the physiological change differs dramatically for men and women.

Changes in the Male Body.   The male body ages as a result of hormonal changes, loss of muscle tone, and other normal physiological shifts. Whereas some researchers refer to these changes as "male menopause," Metz and Miner (1995; 1998) argued that there is no definitive evidence of a discrete transition. The process is gradual and begins as early as the 30s. In midlife, men begin to experience a decrease in orgasmic functioning. The result is shorter orgasms, fewer orgasmic contractions, and less seminal fluid (Masters & Johnson, 1966). Later in life, men experience additional change; including reduction in the viscosity and volume of seminal fluid, decrease in force of ejaculate, less rigidity in erections, and more difficulty maintaining and regaining erections (Laumann, Paik, & Rosen, 2001; Theinhaus, Conter, & Bosmann, 1986; Weg, 1983). These changes can be exacerbated by poor health, alcohol abuse, or prescription drug use (McKinlay & Feldman, 1994; Metz & Miner, 1998; Schiavi, 1994; 1999).

The Massachusetts Male Aging Study (MMAS) collected detailed information about the physical and mental health and sexual activity of 1,709 men, ages 40 to 70 (McKinlay & Feldman, 1994). Unlike many studies that rely exclusively on self-reported health, the MMAS researchers collected medical and health data, including height, weight, and blood sample. Although good health was related to involvement and satisfaction with sex, having undergone prostate surgery was the only physical health issue associated with sexual difficulties. In fact, mental health was an important factor for understanding male sexual difficulties. Higher levels of anger and depression were significant predictors of sexual difficulties. McKinlay and Feldman (1994) found that aging had a negative impact on erectile function, including frequency of erections, awakening with erections, and trouble attaining and maintaining erections. In addition, men in older age groups experienced more trouble ejaculating and were more likely to report pain with intercourse. Although these findings are based on cross-sectional data, retrospective questions included in the survey suggest that these patterns are age related.

The physical changes to a man's body influence his perception of himself and his sexual functioning. The dominant sociocultural models of sexuality emphasize the male phallus (Teifer, 1995). Men who focus their sexual pleasure on penile functioning and quick coital experiences will be deeply disappointed by the changes in the performance. On the other hand, the changes in male functioning give men a chance to slow down, experience the more sensual pleasures, and experiment with a variety of sexual practices. For heterosexual men, the slower process of erection may put them more in synch with their female partners (Marsiglio & Greer, 1991).

Changes in the Female Body. For women, menopause determines many of the physiological changes, which can begin as early as age 35. The reduction of estrogen, progesterone, and androgen levels results in the thinning of the vaginal walls, decreased vaginal lubrication, diminished fullness of labia, and a shrinking and loss of elasticity of the vaginal barrel (Deeks & McCabe, 2001; Mansfield, Koch & Voda, 2000; Weg, 1983). As with men, orgasmic response remains but contractions may be fewer and weaker and there is less general body involvement (Masters & Johnson, 1966).

Although contemporary midlife women are more knowledgeable about menopause than earlier generations of women, there is a tendency in both the scientific literature and popular culture to equate all negative health and sexual experiences to menopause. Cole and Rothblum (1990) argued that the language of menopause with its emphasis on symptoms tends to pathologize this experience. Mansfield et al. (2000) found that the midlife women in their sample attributed negative sexual functioning or decrease in sexual frequency to menopause. In contrast, positive sexual experiences or maintenance of frequency were attributed to lifestyle or environmental factors. Deeks and McCabe (2001) surveyed 304 Australian partnered women (ages 35 to 65) about menopause and sexual functioning. The responses were divided into three groups representing menopausal status (premenopausal, perimenopausal, or postmenopausal) and regression analysis was used to determine the predictive value of this status on sexual functioning. Deeks and McCabe (2001) found that menopausal status was the best predictor of sexual dysfunction such that postmenopausal women were most likely to report experiencing sexual dysfunction. On the other hand, age was a better predictor of sexual satisfaction and frequency. Older women were less likely to be sexually satisfied and had lower frequency of sexual intercourse.

Using data from the National Health and Social Life Survey (NHSLS), Laumann et al. (2001) examined the prevalence of sexual problems among adults who have been sexually active in the past 12 months. With the exception of trouble lubricating, older women, ages 50 to 59, were less likely to experience sexual problems than women in the youngest age cohort. In contrast to older men, who experienced more difficulty with sexual problems as they age, women's sexual anxiety reduced with age. Regardless of age, unmarried adults experienced higher levels of sexual dysfunction.

Finally, ageist societal beliefs about beauty and youth may constrain older women's body image and self-esteem (Hurd, 2000). The majority of the 22 women (ages 61 to 92) in this qualitative study had negative feelings about their bodies. By focusing on the maintenance of physical health, older women were able to counter negative cultural perspectives about older women's bodies (Hurd, 2000). However, anxiety about weight and beauty plague women throughout the life course. Older women, regardless of sexual orientation, are perceived as asexual or sexually unappealing (Fullmer et al., 1999). Discomfort with one's body may cause women to avoid sexual activity with a partner. Also, it may discourage older women from seeking out partners when they are widowed or divorced. These findings suggest that additional factors interact with menopause.

Influence of Physiological Change on Couples. Physiological aging can have a variety of impacts on midlife and aging couples. Older couples who are ill-informed about normative patterns of aging may feel embarrassment or stress when they face sexual problems. Stereotypes about aging bodies serve to further erode sexual self-esteem. Moreover, there is no guarantee that a couple will experience these changes at the same time. In fact, research suggests that men experience more difficulty with physiological changes with age than do women (Edwards & Booth, 1994; Laumann et al., 2001). This sexual asynchrony can lead to miscommunication, cessation of sexual activity, or even the end of a relationship (Leiblum, 1990). Despite these negative implications, many older couples reported considerable rewards from late life sexuality. Sexual encounters became less goal-oriented, and the focus was more on intimacy (Brecher, 1984; Starr & Weiner, 1981). Several of the older gay men in Kimmel's (1993) sample felt the increased levels of intimacy with aging more than made up for decreases in sexual frequency. Lesbian couples emphasize the importance of relationships and intimacy across all age groups (Blumstein & Schwartz, 1983). In sum, aging couples need new sexual scripts to address the impact of physiological changes on sexual pleasure (Levy, 1994).

Opportunity Structure

Although sexuality is certainly a physical act requiring the cooperation of both the body and mind, sociocultural factors profoundly structure the sexual experiences of middle and later life couples. Changes such as increased levels of privacy and decreased fear of pregnancy may result in rediscovered pleasures for many couples.

In midlife, a women's fertility begins to decrease, and with menopause it ceases. Because modern heterosexual couples seek to limit the number of children, a major emphasis of sexuality in early adulthood involves issues of scheduling or preventing pregnancies (Brecher, 1984). The attention to contraception and birth control can be costly, both financially and emotionally. For sexually active younger couples, the fear of unwanted pregnancy can limit sexual freedom and spontaneity. Midlife and later life couples frequently speak of the relief of no longer fearing pregnancy (Brecher, 1984; Starr & Wiener, 1981).

Another important event that occurs in midlife is the launching of children. Depending on number of children and age at conception, couples may begin to experience "empty-nests" in their 40s. Whereas some couples may experience angst at such a dramatic shift in the parenting and family roles, many are pleased with the freedom (Huyck, 2001). The privacy provided by living without children can add spark to even the most conservative sex life. No longer do couples need to worry about closed doors or loud noises (Brecher, 1984).

The later years do not always bring peace and quiet to older couples. A variety of life events can create stress and lack of privacy for older couples, which can decrease opportunity for sexual activity. Carolan and Allen (1999) found that midlife demands such as busy children, extended family, and workplace commitments limited the time available for spouses. The passage of time does not always bring relief. It is not unusual for adult children to remain in the parents' home well into their 20s as they gain the education and experience to move out on their own. Additionally, divorced children and grandchildren may find solace in the family homestead. On the other hand, intimacy may provide a welcome distraction for the day-to-day struggles. Harper and Schaalje (1999) argued that perceived intimacy mediated the negative impact of daily stressor on marital quality. For African American couples in Carolan and Allen's study, religious practices and spiritual beliefs also buffered every day stressors in midlife.

Shared lives can be very exciting sexually when given the freedom to act on pleasures. Many older adults reported that this is the best time of their life sexually

(Brecher, 1984; Starr & Weiner, 1981). Relationships of long duration build trust and intimacy. Physiological changes slow down the lovemaking process, making it more sensual and often more pleasurable. Retirement brings additional flexibility in timing of sexual rendezvous. For some older adults, age brings increased self-acceptance and less need to seek the social or family approval for sexual partners or practices. For instance, Berger (1996) found that older gay men tend to be less anxious about their homosexuality than young men. Fifty percent of midlife lesbians felt that their sex lives were better because they were now able to be more open, had increased levels of communication, and had decreased pressure to experience orgasm (Sang, 1993).

Environmental factors may also influence sexuality in later life in negative ways. For example, physical and social changes with age may bring conflict to a partnership. Changes in marital status, such as divorce or death of a spouse, can thrust an inexperienced, mature adult back into the sexual marketplace. Furthermore, physical or cognitive impairment of a spouse may alter the relationship and bring the additional burden of caregiving into the home.

Whereas some couples crave the opportunity to reconnect in midlife, other couples may not see eye-to-eye. During early adulthood and childrearing, individual attention can easily drift from intimate relations to the stresses of work and children. As such, sexual frequency decreases most dramatically in the first year or two of marriage (Call et al., 1995; Udry, 1980). A segment of these couples may drift into periods of celibacy. Although significant numbers of adults are not sexually active (Laumann et al., 1994), sex researchers rarely examine whether this celibacy is by choice. Although lack of a partner may be the most common reason for celibacy, married men and women may also experience stages of sexual inactivity. If one partner is dissatisfied with a lack of sexual activity, he or she is experiencing involuntary celibacy—desire for sexual activity but absence of a willing partner (Donnelly, Burgess, Anderson, Davis, & Dillard, 2001). Not only do involuntary celibates' partners stop engaging in sex with them, they often withdraw all forms of sexual affection. As a result, involuntary celibates often face periods of depression and feelings of frustration. For the majority of partnered involuntary celibates, sexual activity declines gradually (Donnelly, Burgess, & Anderson, 2001). Despite the lack of sexual activity, the majority of respondents reported loving their partners and being happy in the relationship in areas other than sex.

Reentry into the sexual marketplace can be frightening for a mature adult still recovering from divorce or the death of a partner. Dating norms, issues of sexual health, and safety have changed significantly over the past few decades (Levy, 1994; Starr & Weiner, 1981). Moreover, heterosexual women face a lack of available male partners. Single women in Starr and Weiner's (1981) research were often frustrated and angry by the lack of available men. Brecher (1984) reported that 40% of unmarried sexually active women were engaging in affairs with married men. Twenty-nine percent of unmarried women chose sexual partners who were 10 or more years older or younger than they were (Brecher, 1984). In contrast, Starr and Weiner (1981) found that most unmarried women channeled their energy elsewhere either toward nonsexual activities such as exercise or gardening or through fantasy and self-stimulation. This difference may be a function of the nonrepresentative samples. Sexually active adults may be more likely to volunteer to participate in sex research such as the Consumer Union study (Brecher, 1984).

Those who do find new partners have a different array of issues to address in late life. No longer do they have the shared life history with this partner (Starr & Weiner, 1981). However, new relationships bring spark and often a willingness to explore new things (Starr & Weiner, 1981). In a study of 10 African American couples, Carolan and Allen (1999) found that increased levels of confidence and maturity in midlife enhanced their relationships.

Dating in later life emphasizes companionship. Talbott's (1998) study of 64 older widows (age 60 or older) found that most were interested in men, but few were concerned about remarriage. Widows who have been married multiple times and those whose marriage was of short duration were the most likely to consider remarriage when dating. Most of the older men and women in Bulcroft and O'Connor's (1986) study of 35 single adults, age 60 and older, from the Twin City area of Minnesota felt that dating was a way to fight off loneliness. Although most of these dating singles were sexually active, friendship was a higher priority in a date. Using data from the NSFH, Bulcroft and Bulcroft (1991) examined dating patterns of 1,421 previously married singles, ages 55 and older. Males were more likely to date at all ages and more likely to be interested in partnership. Older respondents had lower rates of dating and less interest in remarriage or cohabitation. Surprisingly, dating did not appear to have much effect on happiness or levels of depression.

Older couples may still love each other dearly, but now health problems may become the focus of the relationship. Caring for a sick partner can put considerable strain on traditional patterns of intimacy. Many caregiving spouses compensate for decline in coital activities by increasing sensual activities such as caressing and masturbation (Bretschneider & McCoy, 1988; Pitzele, 1995). The stress of caregiving may be particularly difficult if the health problem is dementia. Wright (1990) found that the quality of sex and affection often declined for couples when one partner was suffering from Alzheimer's disease, but this did not necessarily lead to marital distress. In contrast, when the afflicted spouse exhibited heightened sexuality as a manifestation of the illness, this behavior placed an additional strain on the marriage. Furthermore, when caregiving responsibilities continue for long periods of time, the burden might drain the caregiving spouse's physical and emotional health and, thus, lower levels of sexual involvement (Wright, 1998). One option for burdened caregivers is assisted living or nursing facilities. Although these institutions provide additional support and care, the trade off is lack of privacy and lack of opportunity for intimacy (Mulligan & Palguta, 1991; White, 1982; Wright, 1998).

In sum, a variety of opportunities structure the experiences of sexuality with aging. These physical and social factors can facilitate or constrict the incidence and frequency of sexual activities. Factors such as lower levels of fertility, children leaving home, and increased levels of privacy create more chances for sexual fulfillment in the lives of older adults. In comparison, issues such as intergenerational households, caregiving responsibilities, and widowhood or divorce may impede the prospect of being sexually active.

PROBLEMS WITH EXTANT RESEARCH

Alfred Kinsey was the first sex researcher to attempt to explore the sexual behaviors of older adults. But in *Sexual Behavior in the Human Male* (1948) and *Sexual Behavior in the Human Female* (1953), Kinsey and his collaborators devote the majority of their attention to subjects from 16 to 55 years of age. When they focused on adults over 60, the emphasis was on decline in sexual frequency (Starr & Weiner, 1983). Contemporary sex researchers who study midlife and older adults also continue to produce findings based on flawed assumptions or methods. This research is largely atheoretical, emphasizes androcentric models of sexuality, and is replete with sampling problems. Each of these issues is discussed in the next section.

Theory

Many different theoretical perspectives have been applied to the study of sexuality, including structural functionalism, exchange, social construction, feminism, poststructuralism, and evolutionary theory; yet, most of the research on aging fails to specify and elicit theoretical perspectives (see DeLamater & Hyde, chapter 1, this volume). Two key areas that contribute to this lack of theoretical specificity are the prominence of descriptive research and the disciplinary focus. Much of the research in this area is merely descriptive, focusing on demographic trends and basic statistics. Who is having sex? How often are they having it? How satisfied are they with sexual frequency? As a result we know that older men report having more sex than older women (Bortz & Wallace, 1999; Jacoby, 1999); older adults who are sexually active have sex a few times a month (Marsiglio & Donnelly, 1991; Starr & Weiner, 1981); and most seniors are satisfied with their sexual activity (Johnson, 1998; Matthias et al., 1997). There are many ways that one can interpret such data. Call et al. (1995) used the theoretically informed concept of "habituation" to explain the significance of length of partnership on sexual frequency. This perspective informs their research questions, methodology, and discussion of the findings. Without a well thought out theoretical perspective it is difficult to analyze findings.

In addition, much of the research on older sexuality is medical or therapeutic in nature. Although there is nothing wrong with this perspective, this research focuses on individual pathologies and ignores larger social and environmental factors of sexuality and aging. The emphasis is on curing "problems" rather than on understanding or explaining large-scale patterns of behavior. Well-researched areas of sexuality should strive to address both micro-level and macro-level factors influencing attitudes and behaviors.

Androcentric Model of Sex

Conventional definitions of sexual behavior emphasize a limited model of sexuality. This emphasis is on heterosexual coitus within a consenting relationship. The majority of the research discussed in this chapter measures the incidence or frequency of "having sex" or "sexual intercourse" (cf. Call et al., 1995; Marsiglio & Donnelly, 1991; Matthias et al.,1997). This androcentric model emphasizes male pleasure and orgasm (Teifer, 1995). As such, this perspective effectively silences the voices of women. While coitus is an essential part of procreative sex, it is only one avenue by which to reach sexual pleasure. The focus on this limiting perspective leads to gaps in our understanding of sexuality and aging.

Recent research suggests that adults under the age of 60 engage in a wide array of sexual practices (Laumann et al., 1994). Middle age and older adults, who are no longer interested in conceiving children, may feel even less restricted to coital activities. Whereas some researchers, such as Brecher (1984) and Starr and Weiner (1981), have asked questions about noncoital activities, their findings are descriptive, based on nonrepresentative samples. Neither research was based on a theoretical perspective. Instead, in the spirit of Kinsey's research, both were attempts to demonstrate the numerous and varied sexual attitudes and behaviors of older adults.

By examining noncoital activities across age groups, researchers can address whether diversity in sexual activity represents a continuity of behavior or whether it shifts with age, length of relationship, health status, or cohort differences. In addition to ignoring the variety of sexual liaisons of heterosexual couples, the androcentric model fails to address the sexual behaviors of gays and lesbians, who do not engage in coitus at any age. Furthermore, although research on sexual patterns of young adults consistently asks about nonmarital partners, research on older adults assumes that sexuality occurs only within marriage.

In her book on peer marriage, Schwartz (1994) introduced an alternative to traditional androcentric models of sexuality. Schwartz argued that passion in an equitable relationship can be sexy. Whereas "traditional sexuality is more about chase and capture," peer passion emphasizes the thrill of shared passions (p. 85). Peer relationships provide more opportunity for either party to initiate sex and the freedom to explore eroticism in a safe environment. By reinventing sexual acts and attitudes at all ages, couples may feel less discomfort or anxiety about changes in physical functioning with age.

Sampling Problems

The final problem with extant research on midlife and older adults regards sampling. Our understanding of the sexual behavior of this population is based on limited samples. Although it is not necessary for all research to adhere to the strict standards of quantitative sampling methods, the dearth of random, nationally representative, longitudinal, or dyadic research on this population is inexcusable. An additional problem arises from the overuse of convenient samples and clinical populations.

Very few studies of sexuality and aging use data from nationally representative random surveys. If researchers want to do comparative research or address issues of generalizability, it is necessary to have samples that are representative. Without such data, much research is merely descriptive. Some research addressing age group differences has used the National Survey of Families and Households (Call et al., 1995; Marsiglio & Donnelly, 1991) and the National Health and Social Life Survey (Laumann et al., 1994; Laumann et al., 2001). Both of these studies provide large samples that allow for the inclusion of multiple variables and sophisticated statistical analysis. Despite these benefits, neither of these studies provides sufficient data to address diverse issues of aging. One benefit of the NSFH sample is that it includes older adult respondents. This allows for analysis of age groups into the 70s (Call et al., 1995). Unfortunately, this survey was not designed as a sexuality survey; thus, the measures of sexual behavior are limited to issues of "frequency." The NHSLS has the opposite problem. Because it was designed as a sexuality survey it address a wide range of issues regarding sexual behavior, but the sample is limited to adults below the age of 60. As Laumann et al. (1994) discusses, lack of federal funding for sexuality research frequently limits the parameters of quality samples. An additional benefit of cross-sectional samples is the ability to make useful comparisons across cultures. This will allow researchers to explore how patterns of sexual behavior in midlife and beyond are similar and different across cultures.

A second problem with sexuality research is the reliance on cross-sectional data to make assumptions about change over time. Although cross-sectional data can provide useful information about differences between various age groups, it cannot address issues of development or tease out cohort and age effects. This is particularly important for research on couples where the additional issue of length of relationship can confound measures of change over time. George and Weiler (1981) argue that cross-sectional research overestimates rates of decline in sexual activity at the aggregate level, suggesting that stability may be a dominant component in patterns of sexual activity. But, as they point out, focus on aggregate data may also have flaws such as masking patterns of individual change over time. Several longitudinal panel studies have explored issues of sexuality for married midlife adults (Edwards & Booth , 1994), for midlife bisexual adults (Weinberg et al., 2001), and for sexual frequency in young married adults (Udry, 1980).

Some research attempts to address flaws in cross-sectional data by having participants remember sexual patterns from earlier. For instance, Deeks and McCabe (2001) asked respondents to report the frequency of sexual intercourse 1 year ago. Starr and Weiner (1981) asked respondents, "How does sex feel now compared with when you were younger? (Better, Same, Worse)." McKinlay and Feldman (1994) asked men age

60 and older, "Compared to when you were in your 40s, do you feel sexually aroused? (More now than then, about the same now as then, less now than then.)" This leads to a retrospective bias, the over- or underestimation of past behaviors due to the fallibility of memory.

Finally, very little of this research addresses couples. Many sexual activities require the presence of two or more persons. Reports of sexual frequency or satisfaction based on a sole respondent are only addressing one part of the story. Gathering data from both partners has many benefits. First, it allows researchers to compare results and to learn the different perspectives within the relationship. Blumstein and Schwartz (1983) were able to do this in their extensive study, *American Couples*. Second, accessing spouse's data is an effective way of addressing the problem of missing data. Call et al. (1995) found that older adults were significantly less likely to respond to the sexuality question on the NSFH when compared to younger respondents. By substituting spouse data for missing data, these researchers were able to increase the reliability of their findings (Call et al., 1995). Finally, for some issues of sexuality, gender may play a significant role in reporting. Double standards about sexual behavior for men and women may influence responses to sexuality research. For example, it is more socially desirable for men to have numerous sexual partners than it is for women (Brown & Sinclair, 1999). Adults in older cohorts may even be more likely to rely on these negative gender stereotypes than younger cohorts.

Finally, sexuality research on older populations has focused too often on middle class, White heterosexual respondents. Although there has been an increase in research on older homosexual populations (Berger, 1996; Kehoe, 1988), there is less research on other populations. In addition to examining these populations in cross-sectional research, there is a need for more in-depth studies of sexuality among older African Americans, Latinos, immigrants, and working-and lower-class heterosexual and homosexual adults. Because the older adult population is becoming more diverse, there is an increased need to understand the patterns of behavior among these special populations.

FUTURE DIRECTIONS AND CONCLUSIONS

As the bulge of the Baby Boom generation moves from midlife to old age, our understanding of sexuality in late life will shift considerably. The size and power of this generation has manipulated American social experiences for almost 5 decades. In order to understand the future impact of the Boomers, contemporary researchers need to gain a better grasp on issues of sexuality and aging in the present. Despite the strength of the Baby Boom cohort to create change, it is important to realize that this is not a homogeneous cohort. In fact, it is the most diverse American generation to reach midlife. Leading edge Boomers have different experiences from their younger peers. High rates of marital dissolution and increased acceptance of gay and lesbian unions in this generation have altered cultural understandings of relationships.

Although the depth and breadth of research on sexuality and aging continue to improve, researchers must strive to fill in the gaps in our knowledge of sexuality and aging. More application of theory, broader definitions of sexuality and sex, and improved research methods could all contribute to future research. By reaching across disciplines, sexuality scholars and gerontologists can explore common theoretical perspectives and build on research of other fields. This interdisciplinary perspective would challenge traditional models of sexuality and aging by incorporating a wide ranging understanding of the topic.

Furthermore, researchers must reach beyond the narrow scope of existing research on sexuality and aging. Future research must include a wider array of respondents.

This can be done through oversampling of neglected populations or through in-depth examination of a particular group. The sexual practices and values of racial and ethnic minorities and people from diverse socioeconomic backgrounds are all but ignored in extant research on sexuality and aging (Thienhaus et al., 1986). Race, ethnicity, and socioeconomic status impact life course changes at all stages of life. African Americans have lower rates of marriage than Whites. New immigrants may come from cultures with different social and sexual values. Working class and poor adults experience higher rates of disability and have different patterns of mental and physical health. Each of these factors—marital status, values, and health—can influence sexual frequency and satisfaction in midlife or later, but few have explored the interaction with race and class. With increases in life expectancy across all social groups, middle age and older adults are becoming more diverse, and it is essential that sexuality research reflect these changes.

In addition, interdisciplinary research teams should move beyond cross-sectional studies, which confound issues of age, cohort, and historical period. Findings based on age-group differences are tricky to interpret without comparison data (Deacon, Minichiello, & Plummer, 1995). Future research must incorporate prospective longitudinal designs. In order to adequately address change over time, research should include three or more time points. Ideal research would include cohort-sequential designs in order to address issues of aging and cohort patterns.

In conclusion, the majority of relationships continue to be sexually vital through midlife and aging. The topic of sexuality and aging poses an unique challenge to researchers because it requires an understanding of multiple disciplines. The sexual life course of relationships is influenced by physiological, psychological, and environmental factors; each of which contributes to the overall well-being of the couple.

REFERENCES

Berger, R. M. (1996). *Gay and gray: The older homosexual man* (2nd ed.). New York: Haworth.

Blumstein, P., & Schwartz, P. (1983). *American couples*. New York: Morrow.

Bortz, W. M., & Wallace, D. H. (1999). Physical fitness, aging, and sexuality. *Western Journal of Medicine, 170*, 167–169.

Brecher, E. L. (1984). *Sex and aging: A Consumers' Union report*. Boston: Little, Brown.

Bretschneider, J., & McCoy, N. (1988). Sexual interest and behavior in the health of 80–102 year-olds. *Archives of Sexual Behavior, 17*, 109–129.

Brown, N. R., & Sinclair, R. C. (1999). Estimating number of lifetime sexual partners: Men and women doing it differently. *The Journal of Sex Research, 36*, 292–297.

Bulcroft, R. A., & Bulcroft, K. A. (1991). The nature and functioning of dating in later life. *Research on Aging, 13*, 244–260.

Bulcroft, K., & O'Connor, M. (1986). The importance of dating relationships on quality of life for older persons. *Family Relations, 35*, 397–401.

Call, V., Sprecher, S., & Schwartz, P. (1995). The incidence and frequency of marital sex in a national sample. *Journal of Marriage and the Family, 57*, 639–652.

Carolan, M. T., & Allen, K. R. (1999). Commitments and constraints for African American couples in midlife. *Journal of Family Issues, 20*, 3–24.

Cole, E., & Rothblum, E. (1990). Commentary on "Sexuality and the midlife woman." *Psychology of Women Quarterly, 14*, 509–512.

David, P. (2002). Sex in the nineties: Exploring sexuality and intimacy in older Jewish women. *Journal of Social Work in Long Term Care, 1*, 47–55.

Deacon, S., Minichiello, V., & Plummer, D. (1995). Sexuality and older people: Revisiting the assumptions. *Educational Gerontology, 21*, 497–513.

Deeks, A. A., & McCabe, M. P. (2001). Sexual function and the menopausal woman: The importance of age and partner's sexual functioning. *Journal of Sex Research, 38*, 219–225.

Deenen, A. A., Gijs, L., & van Naerssen, A. X. (1994). Intimacy and sexuality in gay male couples. *Archives of Sexual Behavior, 23*, 421–431.

Donnelly, D., Burgess, E., Anderson, S., Davis, R., & Dillard, J. (2001). Involuntary celibacy: A life course analysis. *Journal of Sex Research, 38*, 159–179.

Donnelly, D., Burgess, E., & Anderson, S. (2001—). *When you're married, you kinda expect a little sex: Marital involuntary celibacy.* Paper presented at the meeting of the Southern Sociological Society, Atlanta, GA.

Duberman, M. (Ed.). (1997). *A queer world: The center for lesbian and gay studies reader.* New York: New York University Press.

Edwards, J. N., & Booth, A. (1976). Sexual behavior in and out of marriage: An assessment of correlates. *Journal of Marriage and the Family, 38*, 73–81.

Edwards, J. N., & Booth, A. (1994). Sexuality, marriage, and well-being: The middle years. In A. S. Rossi (Ed.), *Sexuality across the life course* (pp. 233–259). Chicago: University of Chicago Press.

Fullmer, E. M., Shenk, D., & Eastland, L. J. (1999). Negotiating identity: A feminist analysis of the social invisibility of older lesbians. *Journal of Women and Aging, 11*, 131–148.

Friend, R. A. (1990). Older lesbian and gay people: A theory of successful aging. *Journal of Homosexuality, 20*, 99–118.

George, L. K. (1996). Social factors and illness. In R. H. Binstock & L. K. George (Eds.), *Handbook of aging and the social sciences* (4th ed., pp. 229–252). New York: Academic Press.

George, L. K., & Weiler, S. J. (1981). Sexuality in middle and late life. *Archives of General Psychiatry, 38*, 919–923.

Gershick, Z. Z. (Ed.). (1998). *Gay old girls.* New York: Alyson Books.

Gray, H., & Dressel, P. (1985). Alternative interpretations of aging among gay males. *The Gerontologist, 25*, 83–87.

Harper, J. M., & Schaalje, B. G. (2000). Daily hassles, intimacy, and marital quality in later life. *American Journal of Family Therapy, 28*, 1–18.

Hillman, J. L., & Stricker, G. (1994). A linkage of knowledge and attitudes toward elderly sexuality: Not necessarily a uniform relationship. *The Gerontologist, 34*, 256–260.

Hurd, L. C. (2000). Older women's body image and embodied experience: An explanation. *Journal of Women and Aging, 12*, 77–97.

Huyck, M. H. (2001). Romantic relationships in later life. *Generations, 25*, 9–18.

Jacoby, S. (1999). Great sex: What's age got to do with it? *Modern Maturity, 42*, 41–45.

Johnson, B. K. (1998). A correlational framework for understanding sexuality in women age 50 and older. *Health Care for Women International, 19*, 553–565.

Kehoe, M. (1988). Lesbians over 60 speak for themselves. *Journal of Homosexuality, 16*, 1–111.

Keil, J. E., Sutherland, S. E., Knapp, R. G., Waid, L. R., & Gazes, P. C. (1992). Self-reported sexual functioning in elderly Blacks and Whites: The Charleston Heart Study experience. *Journal of Aging and Health, 4*, 112–125.

Kimmel, D. C. (1993). Adult development and aging: A gay perspective. In L. D. Garnets & D. C. Kimmel (Eds.), *Psychological perspectives on lesbian and gay male experiences* (pp. 517–534). New York: Columbia University Press.

Kingsberg, S. A. (2000). The psychological impact of aging in sexuality and relationships. *Journal of Women's Health and Gender-Based Medicine, 9*, S33–S38.

Kinsey, A. C., Pomperoy, B., & Martin, E. (1948). *Sexual behavior in the human male.* Philadelphia: Saunders.

Kinsey, A. C., Pomperoy, B., Martin, E., & Gebhard, P. H. (1953). *Sexual behavior in the human female.* Philadelphia: Saunders.

Laumann, E. O., Gagnon, J. H., Michael, R. T, & Michaels, S. (1994). *The social organization of sexuality: Sexual practices in the United States.* Chicago: University of Chicago Press.

Laumann, E. O., Paik, A., & Rosen, R. C. (2001). Sexual dysfunction in the United States: Prevalence and predictors. In E. O. Laumann & R. T. Michael (Eds.), *Sex, love, and health in America: Private choices and public policies* (pp. 352–376) Chicago: University of Chicago Press.

Lee, J. A. (Ed.). (1991). *Gay midlife and maturity.* New York: Haworth.

Leiblum, S. R. (1990). Sexuality and the midlife woman. *Psychology of Women Quarterly, 14*, 495–508.

Levy, J. A. (1994). Sex and sexuality in later life stages. In A. S. Rossi (Ed.), *Sexuality across the life course* (pp. 287–309). Chicago: University of Chicago Press.

Loehr, J., Verma, S., & Seguin, R. (1997). Issues of sexuality in older women. *Journal of Women's Health, 6*, 451–457.

Mansfield, P. K., Koch, P. B., & Voda, A. M. (2000). Midlife women's attributions for their sexual response changes. *Health Care for Women International, 21*, 543–559.

Marsiglio, W., & Donnelly, D. (1991). Sexual relations in later life: A national study of married persons. *Journal of Gerontology: Social Sciences, 46*, S338–344.

Marsiglio , W., & Greer, R. A. (1994). A gender analysis of older men's sexuality: Social, psychological, and biological dimensions. In E. Thompson (Ed.), *Older men's lives* (pp. 122–139). Thousand Oaks, CA: Sage.

Masters, W. H., & Johnson, V. E. (1966). *Human sexual response.* Boston: Little, Brown.

Matthias, R. E., Lubben, J. E., Atchison, K. A., and Schweitzer, S. O. (1997). Sexual activity and satisfaction among very old adults: Results from a community-dwelling Medicare population survey. *The Gerontologist, 37*, 6–14.

McKinlay, J. B., & Feldman, H. A. (1994). Age-related variation in sexual activity and interest in normal men: Results from the Massachusetts male aging study. In A. S. Rossi (Ed.), *Sexuality across the life course* (pp. 261–285). Chicago: University of Chicago Press.

Metz, M. E., & Miner, M. H. (1995). Male "menopause," aging, and sexual function: A review. *Sexuality and Disability, 13,* 287–307.

Metz, M. E., & Miner, M. H. (1998). Psychosexual and psychosocial aspects of male aging and sexual health. *The Canadian Journal of Human Sexuality, 7,* 245–259.

Mulligan, T., & Palguta, R. F. (1991). Sexual interest, activity, and satisfaction among male nursing home residents. *Archives of Sexual Behavior, 20,* 199–204.

Neugarten, B. L., & Neugarten, D. A. (1996). The changing meanings of age. In D. A. Neugarten (Ed.), *The meanings of age: Selected papers of Bernice L. Neugarten* (pp. 72–77). Chicago: Chicago University Press.

Pitzele, S. K. (1995). Chronic illness, disability, and sexuality in people older than fifty. *Sexuality and Disability, 13,* 309–325.

Pope, M., & Schulz, P. (1990). Sexual attitudes and behavior in midlife and aging homosexual males. *Journal of Homosexuality, 20,* 169–177.

Quam, J. K., & Whitford, G. S. (1992). Adaptation and age-related expectations of older gay and lesbian adults. *The Gerontologist, 32,* 367–374.

Sang, B. E. (1993). Existential issues of midlife lesbians. In L. D. Garnets & D. C. Kimmel (Eds.), *Psychological perspectives on lesbian and gay male experiences* (pp. 500–516). New York: Columbia University Press.

Schiavi, R. C. (1994). The effect of chronic disease and medication on sexual functioning. In A. S. Rossi (Ed.), *Sexuality across the life course* (pp. 313–339). Chicago: University of Chicago Press.

Schiavi, R. C. (1999). *Aging and male sexuality.* New York: Cambridge University Press.

Schwartz, P. (1994). *Love between equals: How peer marriage really works.* New York: The Free Press.

Staples, R. (1988). An overview of race and marital status. In H. P. McAdoo (Ed.), *Black families* (pp.187–190). Newbury Park, CA: Sage.

Starr, B. D., & Weiner, M. B. (1981). *The Starr–Weiner report on sex and sexuality in the mature years.* Briarcliff Manor, NY: Stein & Day.

Talbott, M. M. (1998). Older widows' attitudes towards men and remarriage. *Journal of Aging Studies, 12,* 429–441.

Teifer, L. (1995). *Sex is not a natural act and other essays.* Boulder, CO: Westview.

Theinhaus, O. J., Conter, E. A., & Bosmann, H. B. (1986). Sexuality and aging. *Aging and Society, 6,* 39–54.

Treas, J. 1995. Older Americans in the 1990s and beyond. *Population Bulletin, 50,* 2–43.

Trudel, G., Turgeon, L., & Piche, L. (2000). Marital and sexual aspects of old age. *Sexual and Relationship Therapy, 15,* 381–406.

Udry, J. R. (1980). Changes in frequency of marital intercourse from panel data. *Archives of Sexual Behavior, 9,* 319–325.

Walker, B. L., & Ephross, P. H. (1999). Knowledge and attitudes toward sexuality of a group of elderly. *Journal of Gerontological Social Work, 31,* 85–107.

Weinberg, M. S., Williams, C. J., & Pryor, D. W. (2001). Bisexuals at midlife: Commitment, salience, and identity. *Journal of contemporary ethnography, 30,* 108–208.

Weg, R. B. (1983). The physiological perspective. In R. B. Weg (Ed.), *Sexuality in the later years: Roles and behavior* (pp. 39–80). New York: Academic Press.

Whitbourne, S. K. (1990). Sexuality in the aging male. *Generations, 14,* 28–31.

White, C. B. (1982). Sexual interest, attitudes, knowledge, and sexual history in relation to sexual behavior in the institutionalized aged. *Archives of Sexual Behavior, 11,* 11–21.

Williams, D. R., & Wilson, C. M. (2001). Race, ethnicity, and aging. In R. H. Binstock & L. K. George (Eds.), *Handbook of aging and the social sciences,* (5th ed., pp. 160–178). New York: Academic Press.

Wright, L. K. (1991). The impact of Alzheimer's disease on the marital relationship. *The Gerontologist, 31,* 224–237.

Wright, L. K. (1998). Affection and sexuality in the presence of Alzheimer's disease: A longitudingal study. *Sexuality & disability, 16,* 167–179.

19

Sex in "His" Versus "Her" Relationships

Kathleen D. Vohs
University of British Columbia

Kathleen R. Catanese
Case Western Reserve University

Roy F. Baumeister
Florida State University

This chapter discusses several new theories about gender, sexuality, and intimate relationships. First, evidence pertaining to whether men and women differ in the strength of sexual motivation (i.e., sex drive) is reviewed. Across 12 diverse areas of sexuality, we found conclusively that men have a stronger sex drive than women, a difference that has implications for the timing, course, and function of sex within close relationships. We next detail a theory called Erotic Plasticity, which describes differences in the flexibility and malleability of men's and women's sex drive. We provide evidence in support of the idea that women's sexual preferences, desires, and overall sex drive is more responsive to sociocultural, personal, and situational influences relative to men's sex drive. Last, we discuss a provocative new theory called Sex Exchange Theory that depicts sexual negotiations between men and women as driven by social exchange principles. In this analysis, the "resource" of sex resides within a woman, who must receive equitable resources from a man (e.g., emotional support, respect, material goods, relationship stability) in exchange for sexual encounters with her. Using the frameworks presented in this chapter, a variety of findings from the literatures of sexuality, gender, and close relationships can be interpreted.

The aim of this chapter is to review three theories of sexuality in the context of gender. We begin with a question that is fundamental to comprehending gender differences in sexuality in other domains, which is: Do men and women differ in the strength of sex drive? A review of the literature led us to conclude that they reliably do, with men generally desiring sex much more frequently and intensely than women. Next, we detail a theory of erotic plasticity, which describes gender differences in the degree to which a person's sex drive is open to influence from social, situational, and cultural factors. Last, we discuss a new theory, called the Sex Exchange Theory, that describes the dynamic relationships among gender, strength of sex drive, sexual activity, and social benefits within a couple. A discussion of these theories will be used to reflect and explain gender differences, including differences that implicate mainly the individual and those affecting the dyad.

SEX DRIVE

This section presents a summary of a literature review pertaining to whether men and women differ in strength of sex drive (Baumeister, Catanese, & Vohs, 2001). Evidence gathered from 12 distinct areas of sexuality (e.g., masturbation, sexual fantasies and thoughts, desired number of sex partners) consistently and conclusively show that men have a stronger sex drive than women.

The issue of whether men and women differ in sex drive is an important one on multiple levels (see Baumeister et al., 2001). Ideally, average sex drive would be equal in men and women, such that small individual variations would be the only hindrance to sexual harmony; and most heterosexual couples could easily match each other in sexual desire, thereby producing a lasting harmony. However, if men and women do differ in sex drive, sexual and relational harmony may be difficult to achieve. Relational conflicts about sex drive may be especially problematic if differences in sex drive are unrecognized as being related to gender and, as a result, each member of the couple attributes such differences to the relationship or to the other person. Thus, an unacknowledged pattern of gender differences in sex drive may create unnecessary problems within relationships.

Gender differences in sex drive are also important at the individual level, especially in terms of an individual's self-perceptions. If a woman sees herself as having a weaker sex drive than her male partner but believes that, on average, women's sex drive is equivalent to men's, then she may see herself as inadequate. This perception could then create more problems for the woman, personally and in terms of her relationships. Conversely, if a man believes that his sex drive should be equal to his female partner's but finds that he desires sex more than she does, he may believe that he would be better with a woman with higher sex drive or that he is hypersexual or abnormal.

Last, society may benefit from understanding whether there are gender differences in sex drive. If society assumes that women want sex as much as men do, this assumption may guide and shape expectations for sexuality and successful relationships. For instance, society might expect that problems resulting from low sex drive are unusual and rare in females, rather than relatively common (as they actually are). These types of erroneous assumptions may very well create unrealistic expectations within relationships.

Recognition of gender differences in sex drive may result in a change in societal standards and treatment approaches for both men and women. Accordingly, pharmaceutical companies may not put their monies into research to find ways to increase or enhance female sex drive. On the legal front, imagine a rape trial in which the jurors all believe that women who dress in a provocative manner were wanting to get sex as a result. This belief could change their judgments about the culpability of the defendant.

Is the answer already well known? Prior to our literature search (as described in Baumeister et al., 2001), we reviewed several textbooks on sexuality and found that the question of gender differences in sex drive remained open or unresolved. These textbooks either avoided the issue of gender difference in sex drive or tentatively implied that there is no difference. For instance, Crooks and Baur (1999) claimed that the idea of stronger male sex drive is wrong: "A long-standing assumption in many Western societies is the mistaken belief that women are inherently less sexually inclined than men" (p. 68). Allgeier and Allgeier (2000) recognized and acknowledged the existence of a widespread belief that men have stronger desires for sex, but they did not comment on whether the stereotype was supported or unsupported by research. Hyde and DeLamater (1997) wrote a section entitled, "Greater Sex Drive in Women?" but did not consider the idea that men have a stronger sex drive. Hyde and DeLamater's review concluded that evidence favors the view that sex drive does not differ between genders. Thus, although there are numerous implications for personal and relational well-being, sex researchers and theorists had not yet provided a definitive answer as to whether there is a gender difference in sex drive.

Evidence for Differences in Sexual Motivation

We started hunting for published evidence in research databases to assess what was known about whether men and women differ on strength of sex drive. In doing so, we distinguished between sex drive and sexual enjoyment and focused exclusively on the former. We defined sex drive as sexual motivation, such as craving for sexual activity and sexual pleasure. Conceptually, sex drive encompasses both frequency and intensity of sexual desires.

Our approach in investigating this question was to think about two hypothetical persons of the same sex (two men or two women) and assuming that one of them had a stronger sex drive than the other. What would be the likely consequences of having a stronger sex drive? In other words, in what ways would these two people differ because of their varying sex drive? We made a list of expected areas of difference and then searched the literature for evidence that compared men against women on each of these.

We reviewed two sex journals, *The Journal of Sex Research* and *Archives of Sexual Behavior*, the former from 1965 to late 2000 and the latter beginning in1990 to late 2000. These journals were chosen for more thorough review based on their outstanding reputations for peer-reviewed empirical (quantitative and qualitative) research and theoretical advances in sexuality research. PSYCHINFO and MEDLINE databases were also consulted for articles referring to specific operationalizations (e.g., number of sex partners), and also sexual motivation or libido. Our search yielded empirical evidence that was classified into 12 different categories: sexual thoughts, fantasies, and spontaneous arousal; desired frequency of sex; desired number of sex partners; masturbation; willingness to forego sex; emergence of sexual desire; seeking versus avoiding and initiating versus refusing; liking for various sexual practices; sacrificing resources to get sex; favorable attitudes toward sex; prevalence of low sexual desire; and self-rated sex drive.

In our review, we saw a strong pattern of findings indicating that men have a stronger sex drive than women. In terms of our categories, we found that, relative to women, men think about sex more frequently (e.g., Eysenck, 1971;Laumann, Gagnon, Michael, & Michaels, 1994); more often experience sexual arousal (e.g., Knoth, Boyd, & Singer, 1988); have a greater number of fantasies, which occur more often and are more varied (e.g., Leitenberg & Henning, 1995); desire sex more frequently (e.g., Klusmann, 2002; McCabe, 1987); desire to have more sexual partners (e.g., Buss & Schmidt, 1993); masturbate more often (e.g, Oliver & Hyde, 1993); want sex sooner within a relationship (e.g., Sprecher, Barbee, & Schwartz, 1995); are less willing to live without sexual activity (e.g., Kinsey, Pomeroy, Martin, & Gebhard, 1953; Leiblum & Rosen, 1988); engage in more initiation of sex (e.g., O'Sullivan & Byers, 1992); expend more resources (e.g., time, money) to get sex (see Elias, Bullough, Elias, & Brewer, 1998); take more risks and make more sacrifices for sex (e.g., Blumstein & Schwartz, 1983); desire and enjoy more varied sexual practices (e.g., Laumann et al., 1994); possess more favorable and more liberal, permissive attitudes toward sexual activities (e.g., Laumann et al., 1994); self-report a stronger sex drive (e.g. Mercer & Kohn, 1979), and are less satisfied with their sex lives within their close relationships (Sprecher, 2002). Men are less likely to complain of low sex drive in themselves and more likely to complain about low sex drive in their partners.

In fact, no measure in any study showed women to have a stronger drive than men. Although some measures or some studies reported no differences between the sexes, even these were rare. On the whole, men showed stronger and more robust sexual motivation than did women. Despite the fact that, biologically, women can have more orgasms (which is not to necessarily say that they experience more sexual pleasure, but rather can achieve orgasm more frequently; however, men achieve orgasm more consistently, see Kinsey et al., 1953), they desire sex and sexual gratification less than men do. This conclusion is not a value judgment, nor is it a statement of how all women and all men behave. This conclusion is based on gender differences across many men and women and does not apply to an individual man or woman. Indeed, there is much variability within the sexes, and this is important to consider when speaking of individuals. However, on the whole, men have a stronger sex drive than do women.

Several areas of the sexuality literature are notable when reviewing gender differences in sex drive. One of the most telling is in the area of masturbation, which is highly sensitive to differences in sex drive because there are fewer constraints associated with it than with other sexual activities. Masturbation is less affected by societal pressures and the need for a partner, and there is some suggestion that, in the past, society has directed more efforts toward stopping boys and men, rather than girls and women, from masturbating. (Of course, this may be partly a function of the fact that boys and men are more likely to masturbate than girls and women.) In support of the idea that there are societal inhibitors about masturbation, research on people who do not masturbate indicates that men are more inhibited than women by guilt or interpersonal concerns (Arafat & Cotton, 1974). Despite these possible obstacles to male masturbation, a meta-analytic review found that gender differences in masturbation is quite large and reliable, with men much more likely than women to engage in it (Oliver & Hyde, 1993). Furthermore, women who do not masturbate generally cite lack of desire as the primary reason (Arafat & Cotton, 1974).

Masturbation is commonly thought of as a "solo" activity—private, independent, and performed in the absence of a willing sexual partner. This is a misconception. Both men and women masturbate privately even when they are a part of a dyadic sexual relationship and having regular sexual activity. However, men who have a regular sex partner masturbate more consistently and more often than do women who have a regular sex partner. Klusmann (2002) found that 84% of men in relationships masturbated at least once a month. In contrast, only 60% of women masturbated at least once a month while in a sexually active relationship. For men, this rate did not decrease over the course of the relationship, whereas for women masturbation rates decreased by 6%. In fact, almost 50% of men reported masturbation at an even greater rate than once a month—indeed almost 50% of men in relationships reported that they masturbate more than once a week. Only 16% of the women in relationships surveyed masturbated more than once a week (Klusmann, 2002).

These data confirm that both men and women masturbate even in the context of a sexually active relationship, but that men masturbate much more than women. Because men (in general) do not have as much sex as they desire, it is possible that they supplement their total sexual output with masturbation. They may also masturbate for more practical reasons, such as when their partners are absent or unwilling to have sex. Notably, both of these possibilities follow from the idea that men have a stronger sex drive than women.

It is easy to imagine how conflict might develop when masturbation takes place within a relationship. Women who have a weaker sex drive and masturbate less might have a difficult time understanding why their partner continues to masturbate despite his involvement in a sexually active relationship. This misunderstanding could potentially lead to conflict within the relationship, especially if a woman takes it to indicate some inadequacy in her sexual skill or abilities. She may believe that her partner does not love her as much anymore, that she is sexually inadequate, or that he prefers self-pleasuring more than sex with her. This situation could place a strain on the relationship, a strain that may be compounded by a societal expectation that men and women are identical in strength of sex drive. Considering these possibilities makes it easy to see how a gender difference in strength of sex drive (combined with the belief that there is no such difference) has serious implications for harmony within close relationships.

Desired frequency of sexual intercourse is another highly relevant index of sex drive. Given that this measure involves internal wishes and desire for sexual activity, as opposed to actual sex partners or amounts of sex, it is more sensitive to sexual motivation because the presence of a willing partner is not a requirement. On this measure, there are a plethora of studies showing that men desire more sexual activity than do women. In the beginning stages of a heterosexual relationship, for example, women want to wait longer than men before having sex with their new partner, and this difference is reliable regardless of whether waiting is assessed using calendar time, number of dates, or time since acquaintance (Buss & Schmitt, 1993; Cohen & Shotland, 1996; Sprecher et al., 1995). Furthermore, at all stages of a heterosexual relationship, men want sex more often than women. Indeed, McCabe (1987) found that, across all levels of relationship longevity, women reported that they were getting as much sexual intercourse as they wanted, whereas men consistently reported wanting more sexual intercourse than what they were getting.

In a recent study of German university students in heterosexual relationships, Klusmann (2002) found that men were more likely to complain that they were not getting sex often enough, and this effect occurred more as the relationship progressed. Early in the relationship, men and women were strikingly similar in desire for sex and tenderness (although men wanted sex slightly more and women wanted tenderness slightly more). Over time, however, men desired about the same amount of sex, but their desire for tenderness decreased. In contrast, women's desire for sex dropped, yet they wanted more tenderness (Klusmann, 2002). In other words, as relationships develop and evolve, men may be getting less sex than they want, and women may be getting less tenderness than they want. This mismatch could quickly lead to misunderstandings or problems within the couple.

A look at the sex patterns of same-gender couples is revealing of sex drive because it removes the possibility of one confound in the heterosexual relationship literature—the fact that the woman may not want to have sex with her male partner for fear of pregnancy—and because sex within same-gender couples is free from the influence of the opposite-gender partner and thus reflects the average sexual activity within each gender separately (see also Peplau, Fingerhut, & Beals, chapter 14, this volume).

Despite these possible equalizers, gay male couples have more sex than lesbian couples (Blumstein & Schwartz, 1983; Iasenza, 2000). In one study, almost half (47%) of White homosexual men reported having sex more than once a week, whereas that amount of sex was being had by only a third (32%) of White homosexual women (Bell & Weinberg, 1978). After being together for awhile, some lesbian couples appear to stop having sex altogether—a phenomenon referred to as "lesbian bed death" (see Iasenza, 2000)—whereas this decline is significantly less likely to occur among gay male couples. Prior to the prevalence of HIV and AIDS in the United States in the 1970s and 1980s, homosexual men were known to have had hundreds of sex partners, some even reporting that they would have half a dozen sex partners in a single night (e.g., Shilts, 1987). This level of promiscuity was not usually seen among lesbians. Hence, across all levels of relationship status and when examining sexual orientation, men desire more sex than do women.

Other, more troubling, sexual improprieties may be partially attributable to gender differences in sex drive. For instance, males are more likely than females to use coercive means and physical force to obtain sex (Anderson & Struckman-Johnson, 1998). Previous research has indicated that men are also more likely than women to have extramarital affairs and other extradyadic sexual activity, with one recent large-scale study showing overwhelming confirmation of this finding (e.g., Laumann et al., 1994). Gay men are more likely than lesbians to have extradyadic sexual relationships (Blumstein & Schwartz, 1983). Although gender differences in sex drive do not excuse or rationalize possible immoral or illegal activities, inequities in sexual motivation may help explain how these patterns emerge.

One common consequence of the gender difference in sex drive involves relationship dissolution. The impact of gender differences in sex drive on close relationships depends on the importance of sex for each member of the relationship. If men desire sex more often than women, then they may place greater importance on their sexual satisfaction than women do on their sexual satisfaction. If men are not getting as much sex as they desire, it follows that they may be dissatisfied with their sex lives, a feeling that may spill over to affect satisfaction with their relationships.

Although some studies have reported no gender differences in sex life satisfaction (Klusmann, 2002), other research has demonstrated that satisfaction with one's sex life in the context of a sexual relationship is more important for men than for women. A longitudinal study of romantic couples (Sprecher, 2002) found that sexual satisfaction decreases over time for men and women, but this effect is stronger for men. In addition, relative to women, sexual satisfaction is more strongly and more consistently associated with relationship quality over time for men.

Greater importance of sexual satisfaction for men in relationships is exemplified in data on determinants of relationship dissolution. Overall sexual satisfaction and overall relationship satisfaction have differing effects on relationship stability, effects that are qualified by gender. One recent study demonstrated that relationship dissatisfaction predicted relationship dissolution for women, but not for men. Conversely, sexual dissatisfaction predicted relationship dissolution for men, but not for women. These data suggest that couples are more likely to breakup when men are not happy with their sex life and when women are not happy with the overall relationship (Sprecher, 2002).

Given that the evidence clearly points to a gender difference in sex drive, the next question is why these strong and consistent differences occur. As is perhaps to be expected, explanations for why men and women differ in sex drive focus on both nature and culture. In reviewing the evidence on the role of biology (Baumeister et al., 2001), we conclude that testosterone is the main candidate, given that it occurs at much different levels among men and women (with adult men having 7–8 times as much testosterone as adult women; see Dabbs, 2000) and has been shown to affect sexual responses. In particular, testosterone is related to sexual initiation, whereas estrogen appears to be related to sexual receptivity (e.g., Shifren et al., 2000; Singh, Vidaurri, Zambarano, & Dabbs, 1999). Some medical and biobehavioral studies that manipulate testosterone levels report significant influences on sex drive, although there were some mixed or null results. Recent studies have also focused on increasing testosterone in men as they age to counteract several effects, including declining sex drive (Gooren, 1998).

We examined data from very different countries with very different cultural teachings and beliefs about sex (e.g., the Netherlands, India, Colombia), and they also support the idea that men have a stronger sex drive than women. Sociologists and anthropologists also concluded that different cultures demonstrate similar gender differences in sexual motivation (see Baumeister et al., 2001, for a more detailed review). In sum, we believe that biology may be a more important determinant than culture in producing differences in sex drive.

In closing, there is a strong and reliable gender difference in sex drive, with men having and desiring more varied and frequent sexual activity relative to women. We reiterate that there is as much variability within the genders as there is between, but that it is also important to fully grasp the reliability and robustness of gender differences in sex drive. This gender difference in sex drive has important implications for the satisfaction and happiness of individuals in relationships and for the success of the relationship in the long term. If a couple disagrees about how much sex to have, the odds are that the man will be the one wanting more and this may lead to serious problems, misunderstandings, and disagreement over time.

EROTIC PLASTICITY

There have been two overarching views of sexual motivation that have dominated sexuality research in the past and fueled the debate between nature and nurture (see DeLamater & Hyde, 1998). The social constructionist view of sexuality maintains that culture, social influence, and learning determine the script of sexual attitudes and behaviors for both men and women (see Staples, 1973). On the other side of the debate are the evolutionary theorists who rely on the belief that rather than being shaped by culture and society, sexuality is shaped mainly by genetics, innate desires, and an evolutionary plan (Buss & Schmidt, 1993; Trivers, 1972). In this section, we suggest an interesting interplay between these two perspectives: namely, that women's sexual experiences are more guided by social construction, the situation, and relational context; whereas men's sexual experiences are more dependent on evolutionary forces and innate drives than on interpersonal context.

The basic idea is that women's sexuality seems to be more socially flexible and malleable. Men's sexuality is more consistent over time and situation and more resistant to social and cultural influences. *Erotic plasticity* refers to the degree to which sexuality is shaped by social, cultural, and situational variables. In other words, erotic plasticity refers to the way in which people's sexual desires, the degree to which they feel these desires, and the way in which they express these desires vary depending on sociocultural factors and contextual differences. If sexuality is resistant to these variables, it exhibits low erotic plasticity. If sexuality changes at differing levels of large overarching factors such as education and religion or as more immediate factors such as situational context vary, then it exhibits high erotic plasticity.

The theory of female erotic plasticity (Baumeister, 2000) proposes that the female sex drive exhibits greater variability and flexibility in response to social, cultural, and situational factors than the male sex drive. In contrast, male sexuality is less responsive to these factors and driven more by biological determinants and evolutionary forces. So although men and women are dependent on both nature and culture in shaping their sexual lives, women are *more* dependent on culture, and men are *more* dependent on nature.

This section examines the three predictions that the theory of female erotic plasticity permits as well as the evidence for these three tenants of the theory proposed by Baumeister (2000). We look at changes in intra-individual sexuality over time, the effect of social and cultural variables on sexuality, and the consistency between sexual attitudes and behaviors for both men and women as individuals and within relationships. After examining the evidence for female erotic plasticity, we explore possible reasons for why female erotic plasticity might exist. Finally, we look at some general implications of the theory.

Evidence for Female Erotic Plasticity

The theory of erotic plasticity makes three specific predictions about women's sexuality. First, it predicts that individual women's sexuality should change more over time than men's sexuality. If women's sexuality is more malleable, this flexibility should manifest itself in greater changes over time. Second, erotic plasticity predicts that social and cultural factors should have greater effects on women's sexuality than on men's sexuality. Social and cultural factors such as education, socioeconomic status, and religion are strong influences on most people's lives. If women's sexuality is more easily influenced and changeable to begin with, social and cultural factors should affect women's sexuality more strongly than they should affect men's. Third, women will show a greater gap between their attitudes and their behaviors on sexual dimensions compared to men. Plasticity means that situational factors have greater scope for influence. We now present evidence that is consistent with the theory of erotic plasticity for the specific hypotheses.

Do Aspects of Women's Sexuality Change More Over Time Than Do Men's?

The idea that women's sexuality is less consistent over time than men's is not a new one. Indeed, both the Kinsey Reports (Kinsey, Pomeroy, & Martin, 1948; Kinsey et al., 1953) and Masters and Johnson's (1966) research on human sexual response noted that women's sexual activity went through far greater fluctuations over time. Men, on the other hand, were generally consistent and stable in their sexual activities and desires over time. Other studies also find that the frequency of women's sexual activities such as masturbation rise and fall more over time than do men's. Whereas men's masturbation remains consistent over time, as women age, their rate of masturbation actually increases (Adams & Turner, 1985). Women's individual attitudes about sexuality also change more over time than do men's, such that they tend to represent the cultural *Zeitgeist* of that period (Harrison, Bennett, Globetti, & Alsikafi, 1974).

There is also a gender difference in stability of sexual orientation over time. Lesbian women are far more likely to have had heterosexual relations than gay men (Bell & Weinberg, 1978; Kinsey et al., 1948, 1953; Laumann et al., 1994; Rosario et al., 1996; Savin-Williams, 1990; Schfer, 1976; Whisman, 1996). Lesbians often have heterosexual relationships throughout their lives (Rust, 1992), and heterosexual women also initiate lesbian affairs (Dixon, 1984). Such patterns are far less common among gay or heterosexual men. Finally, lesbians are also less likely to view their own homosexuality as unchanging, exclusive, and irreversible than gay men (see Golden, 1987). Thus, the weight of the evidence provides support for the prediction that women's sexuality changes more over time than does men's.

The greater malleability of women's sexuality compared to the consistency and stability of men's sexuality over time has strong implications for close relationships. Individual changes in women most certainly will affect their partners, whether her partners are male or female. Any personal change has the ability to affect the person with whom one shares a close, sexual relationship. For instance, if women are more likely to change their sexual behaviors and preferences over time, it is possible that these changes will serve to match or mismatch their partner's sexual preferences. A higher degree of match between partners' sexuality is likely to increase the harmony within a relationship, whereas a higher degree of mismatch may create discord within the relationship.

Not only does the theory of erotic plasticity have consequences within relationships, but it also has consequences for sex patterns (especially in women) across relationships, with different sex partners. Women's sexual behaviors may not stay constant from partner to partner. Instead, her behaviors may shift depending on her needs and desires as influenced by her current male partner. These shifts may be most evident at the onset of relationships, when sexual intimacy and passion is high for both partners (Baumeister & Bratslavsky, 1999) and both partners desire a high degree of sexual activity (Klusmann, 2002). As time goes on, however, women's sexual desire may weaken, and once again men and women may find themselves in situations of quite dissimilar sexual desires and preferences.

The greater malleability of women also implies that attempts at persuasion to try new sexual behaviors may be more successfully directed at women than men. Men may be more likely to stay with sexual partners who agree to engage in the particular sexual practices they find most appealing. Given that men's sexual preferences and activities are more consistent and stable over time, if he hasn't already been interested in a particular activity in the past, he may not elect to try it as a result of his female partner's request.

Do Social and Cultural Factors Affect Women's Sexuality More Than Men's Sexuality?

Social and cultural factors have great influence on most people's lives. If we compare people on their reactions to cultural movements or on social factors such as education and religion, we will see that these factors play a very important role in shaping the individual. Erotic plasticity predicts that these factors also play a very important role for sexuality. Specifically, if women's sexuality is more malleable and adaptable, these social and cultural factors should have an even greater impact on shaping women's sexuality compared to men's. Indeed, women's sexuality does seem to be more heavily shaped by social and cultural factors including the sexual revolution, education, religion, politics, and peer group.

The sexual revolution clearly had a greater impact on women's sexuality than on men's. Following the sexual revolution, there were far greater decreases for women than for men in the number of virgins on college campus (Sherwin & Corbett, 1985) and the age of various first sexual experiences (Schmidt & Sigusch, 1972). Women's attitudes about sex also changed more than men's attitudes during the mid- to late-20th century (Croake & James, 1973).

Religion and education also have a greater impact on women's sexuality than on men's. Although both men and women who are highly educated share liberal attitudes toward sex, it is only among women that different levels of education correspond to different behaviors and desires about sex. Compared to less educated women, highly educated women are more likely to report having anal sex, giving and receiving oral sex, and finding more types of sexual activities appealing (Laumann et al., 1994). They are also more likely to report being lesbian or bisexual than less educated women (Laumann et al., 1994). The researchers did not find similar differences between men of different education levels. Comparing nonreligious people to religious fundamentalists, we see the opposite pattern. More religious women are less likely to report engaging in oral sex, homosexuality, and contraception than less religious women. There is less of a gap between religious and nonreligious men on these activities (Laumann et al., 1994).

The convergence of conclusions from religion and education is methodologically powerful because this research addresses two major institutional forces, which would be presumed to have different directions of influence on sex drive. And they do, but only for women. Among women, more education leads to more sexual permissiveness, whereas more religion leads to less sexual permissiveness, The fact that women are more affected by both factors, and thus in both directions, helps to rule out ceiling effect explanations (such that there was already such a high baseline that no other movement upward was possible) and other possibilities. Instead, it appears that female sexuality is more receptive than male sexuality to sociocultural forces.

The idea that women's sexuality is more responsive to social and cultural factors has both positive and negative predictions for close relationships. Surely the sexual revolution both harmed and improved relationships. Anecdotal experiences of the impact of this period include a heightened awareness and enjoyment of sex for women. This aspect of the sexual revolution probably had a positive effect on many relationships for men and women. Conversely, it may have also ruined marriages in which women's newfound sexual interest and experience found its way outside the primary relationship.

The effect of social and cultural factors like education, politics, religion, or cultural climate on women's sexuality also makes for costs and benefits to relationships. Moving from one country to another, for example, means a shift in cultural and social environments. Women may be more successful at acculturating to these new sexual norms than are men. This possibility could well influence the health of the relationship as it seeks to survive a new environment.

Do Women Show Lower Attitude–Behavior Consistency on Sexual Dimensions Than Men?

Attitudes are not always that good at predicting people's behaviors. There are many factors that can account for discrepancies between one's attitude about a certain topic and how one acts when actually confronted with the behavior. In a perfect world, there might be no interferences. But in reality, contextual factors and external demands can often drive a wedge between how we think we should act and what we actually do. The theory of erotic plasticity predicts that sexuality will change based on situational factors and external pressures. If women show greater erotic plasticity than men, they should show more susceptibility to these situational factors and external pressures. This will be reflected in a greater discrepancy between their attitudes about sexuality and the ways in which they actually behave when given the opportunity.

Sure enough, women show greater discrepancies than men do between their attitudes and behaviors on such sexual issues as infidelity, condom use, and homosexual activity (see Baumeister, 2000). When considering less serious forms of infidelity, such as kissing or holding hands, the correlation between attitudes and actual behaviors is considerably weaker for women in dating relationships compared to their male counterparts (Hansen, 1987). Women also show less consistency between their attitudes toward using condoms and their behavior in actually using them as compared to men. Women are more committed to using condoms than men are, but both men and women fail to use condoms at the same rate (Herold & Mewhinney, 1993). Men's intentions to use condoms and the actual rate at which they use them is more closely aligned. Women don't actually live up to their lofty intentions to have safe sex.

Finally, although women find homosexuality more desirable than men do, they are less likely to have actually indulged in their desires (Laumann et al., 1994). Thus, there is a greater inconsistency between women's attitudes and behaviors concerning homosexuality than between men's attitudes and behaviors. These discrepancies between attitude and behavior support the theory of female erotic plasticity. It is possible that the larger attitude–behavior gap for women is because women's sexual behaviors are more influenced by those things such as situational context, social pressures, and the immediate demands of the situation that often interfere with attitudes and intentions. Men, on the other hand, may be less swayed by these factors, and so men are more able to stick to their original attitude even when the situation changes.

The fact that there is weaker attitude–behavior consistency in women may have some of the most serious consequences on close relationships because it involves whether people follow through with their sexual attitudes, intentions, and verbal commitments. This is especially important in relationships when both actions and intentions invariably affect one's partner. Sexual relationships involve a great deal of negotiation—when, where, and in what ways to have sexual relations. Decisions between men and women who are having sex must also be made with regard to issues like birth control and reproductive health. This tenant of erotic plasticity predicts that women will be more likely to compromise their initial attitudes and beliefs surrounding these types of issues in relationships.

Men and Erotic Plasticity

If social and cultural factors have more influence on women, are men more influenced by genetic factors? Genetics do, in fact, account for more variance for men, as compared to women, in the age at which they first start having sex (Dunne et al., 1977). In addition, although the results are not yet fully conclusive, evidence is beginning to point toward a greater role of genetic factors in producing male homosexuality than in female homosexuality (see Bailey & Pillard, 1995). One recent study supports this by showing that homosexuality in men, but not women, is significantly determined by number of older brothers. The greater the number of older brothers, the more likely the man is to be gay. The author believes that this is because the mother's body "remembers" and builds up a genetic response to having carried male fetuses, who are genetically different form her own female constitution. This research supports the idea that men's sexuality may be more genetically and biologically determined than women's (Bogaert, 2003).

One exception to the general pattern of greater female erotic plasticity relates to male childhood experiences. Evidence suggests that although relatively stable over time, men's sexuality seems to be responsive to external forces during a critical developmental stage in early childhood. During this time, boys may be especially susceptible to outside forces that will shape their sexual development. For example, more males than females exhibit unusual sexual practices, or paraphilias. Paraphilias seem to have their basis in childhood experiences (Money, 1990; Reinisch, 1990). These paraphilias do not change much over time: men do not whimsically adopt or exchange them, and they are very difficult to extinguish even when a man seeks therapy to help him. Another example of ways in which males are more affected by childhood sexual experiences relates to sexual dysfunction. There is a stronger link between prepubescent sexual experience and sexual dysfunction for males than for females (Laumann, Paik, & Rosen, 1999). This critical childhood period in which outside factors may shape male sexuality is also exhibited in homosexuality. The one external factor that seems to play a role in shaping male homosexuality is proximity to an urban area. Growing up in an urban versus rural area predicts homosexuality more so for men than for women, even after controlling for migration patterns (Laumann et al., 1994).

Finally, recent experimental research concerning the mating preferences of goats and sheep points to a critical socialization period in childhood among males (Kendrick, Hinton, Atkins, Haupt, & Skinner, 1998) but not females. The researchers created a situation in which newborn sheep were reared by goats and newborn goats were reared by sheep. They were later returned to their own species when they were old enough to mate. When the females were returned to their species, they were able to mate with goats or sheep, irrespective of being reared with the opposite species. This fits the pattern of female erotic plasticity in which female sexuality is adaptive and flexible. The researchers were surprised to find very peculiar mating patterns among the males, however. The males were not adaptive or flexible in their mating patterns. But surprisingly, they would only mate with the species that they had been reared with and not their own. Because the males would not mate with their own species, these findings contradict a purely biological explanation—indeed, mating with the other species cannot produce offspring. Instead, the males showed a pattern of "sexual imprinting" (Kendrick et al., 1998) in which the species by which they were reared (yet not the biological descendents of) determined their mating preferences. Females did not show the pattern of sexual imprinting and instead were able to adapt their mating preferences to both the species by which they were reared and their biologically appropriate partners.

Explanations for Female Erotic Plasticity

The idea of differential erotic plasticity for men and women naturally evokes the question of possible mechanisms that may be responsible for these effects. We review three such explanations, focusing on differential power (physical and otherwise), the nature of sexual scripts for men and women, and differences in the strength of sexual motivation.

Differential Power Theory.   The differential power theory (see Baumeister, 2000) asserts that one possible explanation for female erotic plasticity revolves around the issue of strength and power. The physically weaker sex may generally have to adapt to the strength of the stronger sex. The demand on women to be flexible in response to male sexual desire may have shaped female sexuality to be more flexible and adaptable. Men have traditionally possessed more strength and power, not only physically, but politically, economically, and socially. The differential power theory predicts that a woman should be more flexible in the political, economic, and social spheres because men have traditionally held the most power in these areas. There is preliminary evidence suggesting that women are not more flexible overall than men (Christiansen, 1977; Eley, Lichtenstein, & Stevenson, 1999), and these findings do not lend much support to the differential power theory.

The Changeability of Women.   A second plausible explanation for female erotic plasticity concerns the change inherent in the female sexual script. This explanation rests on the assumption that change is built into the female sexual role. Because the costs of pregnancy are far greater for women then men, women are more sexually selective than men. Women begin with the attitude against having sex, and then must change their minds from no to yes when they settle on an acceptable sexual partner. Men, on the other hand, are less conservative about their sexual choices and more willing to have sex with a woman sooner (see Cohen & Shotland, 1996; Oliver & Hyde, 1993). The change of mind from no to yes is the critical choice point that women must make in sexual decision making. This attitude shift from saying no to sex to saying yes to sex could potentially provide the basis for erotic plasticity. It is an inherently flexible movement and would shape malleability in other sexual domains.

Research on sexual fantasies give us a glimpse into the plausibility of this explanation. One of the most common and most arousing sexual fantasies for women involves the initial resisting and eventual enjoyment of sex (Cowan & Dunn, 1994). Both men and women found it exciting and arousing for a woman to change her mind and eventually enjoy sex. Although there is no solid evidence to refute or support this explanation, we do know that women's change from a negative response to a sexual offer to a positive one is appealing for both men and women. It is possibly built into the sexual script and could set the stage for the development of erotic plasticity.

Strength of Sex Drive.   Finally, strength of sex drive may dictate its relative plasticity. If a sex drive is particularly strong, it would be more difficult to alter, direct, or suppress. A weaker sex drive would be more pliable and flexible. If women exhibit more erotic plasticity, it is possible that this plasticity is the result of a weaker sex drive. As we saw earlier, women do exhibit a milder sex drive than men (see Baumeister et al., 2001). This milder sex drive may explain why women show more flexibility to situation, social, and cultural demands on their sexuality.

One possible means of testing this explanation would be to examine the effect of strength of sex drive on erotic plasticity within gender. If within gender, people with weaker sex drives show more erotic plasticity regardless of sex, this would lend support to the strength of sex drive explanation. Another approach would be to see if plasticity is reversed with motivations that are stronger among women than men. Many experts regard the desire to have and care for children to be stronger in women than in men. Does this result in greater "parental plasticity" among men? Several signs suggest that the answer is yes, although a more systematic review of the literature is needed. The mother–child bond seems to remain fairly stable across cultural and historical boundaries, whereas the father role changes quite a bit, and indeed even in American society the past half century has seen greater changes in fathers than in mothers. Although preliminary, this finding suggests that weaker motivations produce greater plasticity—and that the main cause of female erotic plasticity may be found in the differential strength of sex drive.

Erotic Plasticity: A Summary

This section examined the theory of female erotic plasticity. We saw that compared to men, women's sexuality responds more flexibly to social, cultural, and situational factors. Women's sexuality show more intra-individual sexual variability over time, is more responsive to social and cultural factors, and exhibits a wider gap between attitude and behavior. We proposed three possible explanations for these findings. At this point in time, there is not enough evidence to either support or refute any of these three explanations, although what evidence is available favors the view that the female sex drive has higher plasticity because it is milder.

Female erotic plasticity has implications for society as a whole as well as the individual and his or her relationships. For society in general, popular culture would find it more effective and productive to aim its sexual agenda at women than at men. Given women's greater adaptability and flexibility to cultural factors, society would find it easier to control, redirect, or shape women's sexuality. Female erotic plasticity also has implications for clinical practice. If women's sexuality is more flexible than men's, sex therapists would find it easier to work with and treat female sexual problems than male problems. The implications are also far reaching for the individual and his or her relationships. Women may find themselves more willing and able to compromise in sexual situations, and men may find themselves more resilient to adapting to changing situations and external pressures. Finally, in the search for sexual self-knowledge, women may find it a murkier, more ambiguous terrain, whereas men find it more consistent and more reliable.

SEX EXCHANGE THEORY

Social exchange theory is an approach that seeks to explain human interactions by analyzing the costs and benefits for each participant. In essence, it treats all interactions as quasi-economic deals in which people give each other social rewards such as attention, pleasure, information, or affection. Sex exchange theory (Baumeister &

Vohs, in press) is an extension of that approach to sex, specifically to heterosexual interactions.

The core idea of sex exchange theory is that sex is a female resource that is given and received within the context of a romantic relationship (Baumeister & Vohs, in press). More precisely, sex is something that the woman gives to the man. Therefore, he must normally give her something else in exchange: commitment, affection, money, material possessions, or attention. This view flies in the face of popular ideals that depict sex as a mutual pleasuring between equal partners, but perhaps that popular ideal was something men used to trick women into giving sex without getting anything in return. In any case, we think that sex exchange theory fits many of the facts about men, women, and sexual relations.

The notion of sex as a female resource follows directly from the gender difference in sex drive, given that the woman is in an advantageous bargaining position insofar as she desires sex less than the man. He must persuade her and perhaps sweeten the deal by offering her an added inducement. That is why he will buy her dinner rather than the reverse. This inequity creates an atmosphere ripe for exchange, and there is a variety of exchange-related consequences that may result from these conditions. In this section, we detail evidence in support for three consequences that follow from the theory.

Central to the theory, an imbalance of sexual motivations means that the least-interested party (the woman) can decide to supply sex when it appears that there will be benefits to doing so (see Waller & Hill, 1951). The benefits that the woman may demand before allowing sex to occur vary widely but likely contenders are access to monetary compensation or material gifts, securing love or commitment, or obtaining attention and status. In reality, anything that the woman desires could be a part of the exchange process. A second consequence of a sexual marketplace is that supply-and-demand laws would apply. Specifically, the more demand for the product (in this case, the more that a man wants sex with a particular woman), the more the supplier (i.e., the woman) can require before making the exchange. Third, in sex exchange theory, the local community is a very important setting within which to consider the supply-and-demand curves. Each local community constitutes a sexual marketplace, in which supply, demand, and other factors establish a "going rate"—in the sense of a standard, normative price—of how much the man should appropriately give in order to obtain sex.

There are several ancillary points to be noted with regard to the theory. Sex exchange theory does not state that the process occurs explicitly, but it can be explicit at times. One obvious example of when the exchange process is made explicit is in the case of prostitution. However, within most couples, we believe that sex exchange operates at a nonconscious level, with neither person in the couple consciously specifying or deciding to run the sexual relationship in this manner. Rather, we believe that men and women act according to what "feels right" for them in the relationship and what "feels right" is best predicted by the man giving social benefits to the woman for sex.

Another aspect of the theory is that it is not isomorphic with either a feminist approach to sex nor an evolutionary approach to sex, but rather it is compatible with the two perspectives. Feminists' view men as historically wanting to suppress women as a way to gain power over them. The current theory is consistent with such an approach because it explains, at least in terms of sexual activity, why men would want more power over women: when men have more power than women, men can get away with getting sex in return for fewer or less costly benefits.

Along evolutionary lines, the current theory is consistent with the idea that males of many species have had to find ways to persuade females to mate with them. Indeed, male bonobos that want to mate have been known to entice females with food (de Waal, 1995). Evolutionary theory has also depicted men as desiring attractive women over unattractive women, and this too agrees with sex exchange theory. In the current theory, the exchange rate is higher when gaining access to sex with a beautiful woman compared to gaining access to sex with a less attractive woman.

Evidence in Support of Sex Exchange Theory

With regard to the first prediction of the theory, that sex is a female resource and that men exchange social benefits for it, there are several lines of evidence in support. First, men view sexual gratification as a benefit that they receive from women in relationships. Women believe that relationships benefit them in a more psychological way through increased self-confidence (Sedikides, Oliver, & Campbell, 1994). A more explicit, though extreme, form of the sex exchange relationship is prostitution. With regard to the question of whether sex is a male or female resource, it is highly telling that there are far greater numbers of male clients of prostitutes who are willing to pay money for (most often) sex with a woman. A recent large investigation of clients of prostitution found "not ... a single instance of a woman reporting that she had purchased sex from a man" (Atchison, Fraser, & Lowman, 1998, p. 198).

In the context of romantic sexual relationships, evidence shows that men desire sex more than women do and earlier in the relationship. In a consensual sexual relationship, then, when the man wants sex before (and more) than the woman, she is the one to decide when the couple has sex. Research supports this view that women act as the sexual "gatekeepers"—there is only a slight correlation between when men wanted to have sex within a specific relationship and when sex actually commenced; whereas the correlation between preferred and actual time until sex was almost perfectly matched for women (Cohen & Shotland , 1996). Thus, when the man wants to have sex, he must wait. When the woman wants to have sex, however, the couple has sex. Because the man wants to have sex but must wait for the woman, he is likely to try to boost his chances by providing benefits to the woman.

Last, the data on sexual infidelities supports the sex exchange idea in that men are more likely than women to place greater importance on the faithfulness of their partners rather than on their own. In contrast, women value their own faithfulness with just as much importance as that of their partners (Regan & Sprecher, 1995). This finding fits nicely with the exchange theory of sex because it illustrates the implicit meaning attached to fidelity as the protection of an exchanged benefit within the relationship. Men appear to place greater value on the sexual benefits that they receive from their partner.

Another study on fidelity also revealed (perhaps surprisingly) that both men and women would feel more distressed by their partner having sex with a man than with a woman (Wiederman & LaMar, 1998). This finding supports sex exchange theory by highlighting that when men have sex with someone in another relationship, he robs the primary relationship to a greater extent than does a female interloper.

With regard to the idea that supply-and-demand processes underlie sex exchange, we found evidence that there is a belief among girls and women that they must receive at least the words of love before engaging in sex. One study (Wilson, 1978) found that girls who engaged in sex with a boy who had not stated his love (whether it was sincerely felt or not) would gain a reputation for being sexually promiscuous. Notably, the bad name such girls would acquire was given by other girls, not boys, which dovetails nicely with the idea that women are the ones to push for higher benefits (i.e., words of love) before giving sex as a method of boosting supply-and-demand rates.

We also found that after the exchange of benefits are made, men can demand sex from their female relationship partners to a greater extent than can women. In particular, in many cultures, the institution of marriage constitutes grounds for men to demand sex of their wives (Betzig, 1989). A cross-cultural analysis of divorce found that in over 90 cultures (approximately half of those studied), acts of adultery and/or refusal of sex on the part of women are cause for the man to be granted a divorce. In only two cultures, however, were women allowed a divorce in the case of a man's sexual infidelity. If we assume that marriage is a social benefit for most women and that, once married, this benefit has been given, then these findings fit the idea that the woman's role is to supply sex to the man.

The notion of a local marketplace is also central to sex exchange theory. We examined changes in sexual norms that correspond to changes in the relative numbers of sexually mature males and females (sometimes known as operational sex ratio, especially in the animal literature). A review of sex ratios in different societies reveals that the balance of men to women in an area has a sizable impact on the sexual norms in that area (Guttentag & Secord, 1983). This investigation found that when women are scarce, frequency of sex drops and length of time before having sex rises. Presumably this pattern occurs because (in the parlance of the current theory) women can give less sex overall and demand more benefits for it. The opposite was also found to hold: when there are more women than men, sex is more prevalent and sexual norms are much looser (i.e., more extradyadic sex, more premarital sex). Under these conditions, women may have to compete with each other to a greater extent to attract an acceptable man and therefore may have to give away sex at a lower rate.

The significance of local marketplaces on sex exchange can be seen in the African country of Rwanda. The 1994 genocide decimated and imprisoned men and resulted in a practice among the remaining women called "husband-sharing" (*kwinjira*). Women not only compete with other women to attract a man, but they must also share the few men that exist in the community. Because of the increased sharing of sexual partners, husband-sharing has resulted in alarming rates of HIV/AIDS transmission in the region. Health officials liken husband-sharing to something like male prostitution. Rwandan women share husbands in an effort to fulfill their sexual needs and to replace the children that they lost in the genocide (Gough, 2000). Women are giving away sex in order to secure the benefits that they receive from this action—children and all that they represent for women in an impoverished and male-deprived country. Thus, the Rwandan case illustrates that scarcity plays an important role in determining the patterns of give-and-take in a local community.

Sex Exchange: A Summary

This last section detailed sex exchange theory (Baumeister & Vohs, in press), which describes the exchange of benefits between two people with unequal sexual motivations. In particular, sex exchange theory predicts that men (or the person in the relationship most interested in getting sex) will offer social benefits such as commitment, attention, love, or material goods to women (or the person less interested in sex) in an attempt to get sex. This theory is perhaps most applicable to the commencement of sex within a relationship, but there is evidence (e.g., Betzig, 1989) that some degree of exchange may be required even in long-term couples for the relationship not to dissolve. We look forward to research testing specific tenets of this theory, especially those that diverge from existing (e.g., feminist or evolutionary) views of gender and sex, for more direct evidence of sex exchange.

GENDER AND SEXUAL PATTERNS: DIFFERENCES AND SIMILARITIES

We began with the idea that there are both similarities and differences in how men and women approach sex and that these differences had implications for the individual, his or her intimate relationships, and society. Although the similarities were not highlighted as much as the differences, men and women are both motivated to have sex, albeit men more than women. Thus, gender differences in sex drive reflect differences in degree, not in the basic drive to have sexual activity. Plasticity theory points to gender differences in the relative importance of nature, biology, and innate drives (for men) versus social factors, intrapersonal states, and culture (for women). Of course, the sexual responses of both men and women are influenced by nature and culture. The idea of plasticity theory, however, goes further than merely restating this truism to specifying the degree to which men and women are influenced differentially by nature or culture. Last, although the analysis of sex through the lens of sex exchange theory does make a more qualitative statement about the nature of the sexual relationship by gender, it is not necessarily tied to gender. Rather, this is a theory of supply-and-demand and of least and most interested parties. Thus, to the extent that one person—of either gender—is more desiring of sex from another, sex exchange patterns are likely to emerge.

DIRECTIONS FOR FUTURE RESEARCH

Future research on gender differences in sex drive, erotic plasticity, and sex exchange should focus on theoretical development and empirical testing while also emphasizing dyadic, as well as individualistic, effects. An overarching theory of sexuality that incorporates the interaction of sex drive, erotic plasticity, and sex exchange remains an important outstanding quest. Differences in sex drive may be a common starting point for tests of both erotic plasticity and sex exchange. Strength of sex drive could be used to assess for degree of plasticity, and it may also serve as a gauge by which to measure the relative importance or benefits of sex (as in sex exchange theory). Likewise, social, cultural, and environmental factors may play the dual role of adjusting female sexual behavior while also creating a marketplace that determines sex exchange.

A study of the effect of modernization on adolescent sexual behavior among people in sub-Saharan Africa may shed light on the way in which these theories interact with one another. Over a 5-year period, age of first intercourse was significantly reduced by greater access to education, media, and urban living for adolescent girls, but not boys. Sexual behavior in boys was less consistently affected by these factors, with data from some countries showing that modernization was related to early sexual activity in boys, whereas it was related to later sexual activity in others (Gupta & Majy, 2003). The authors speculated that modernization provided girls and women with greater lifestyle choices, which thereby reduced girls' reliance on males for resources in exchange for sexual favors. However, not all girls took advantage of modernization; for them, the need to have sex in order to get resources from men may have actually increased, which may have contributed to the cases in which boys' sexual activity occurred at an earlier age.

These results are intriguing because they highlight the interaction between plasticity and sex exchange. Sex exchange is based on the local market and the local environment. When the environment shifts (in this case, in the form of modernization), so too does sexuality for women, but not for men. Thus, women's sexuality is malleable over time based on changes in the environment, and the conditions of exchange vary according to these environmental changes as well as their corresponding changes in female sexuality.

Experimental methods should also be developed to determine the relative contribution of each theory for explaining aspects of the others theories. Laboratory research can also be conducted to further clarify the predictions of individual theories. For example, methods could be developed to test the underlying explanations presented for erotic plasticity. We proposed (Baumeister et al., 2001) that erotic plasticity is enabled by women's weaker sex drive. Future research should test the effect of strength of sex drive on measures of erotic plasticity within gender. Laboratory tests should be designed to test for mediators and moderators for these gender differences.

Finally, future research on these theories should do more to incorporate the dynamics of a couple into each of the three theories about sexuality presented in this chapter. This is especially important for theories of gender differences in strength of sex drive as well as erotic plasticity. The theory of gender differences in strength of sex drive mainly emphasizes individual differences between men and women. Future research on this theory should seek to understand how changes in the sex drive of one member of a partnership affects the other member. This research should look for effects at both the level of the couple and the level of the individual. Erotic plasticity emphasizes the impact of broader constructs such as social and cultural factors and age. Research on this theory should shed light on how these larger social and cultural factors specifically impact the dyad as well as the individual.

In sum, we hope that researchers will approach the question of gender differences in sexuality with the goal of investigating not only *how* men and women differ but also *why*. With this as the goal, we will be much closer to gaining a clearer understanding of sexuality on a more basic level, as well as it what it means for "him" and "her."

REFERENCES

Adams, C. G., & Turner, B. F. (1985). Reported change in sexuality from young adulthood to old age. *Journal of Sex Research, 21,* 126–141.

Allgeier, E. R., and Allgeier. A. R. (2000). *Sexual interactions* (5th ed.). Boston: Houghton Mifflin.

Anderson, P. B., & Struckman-Johnson, C. (Eds.) (1998). *Sexually aggressive women: Current perspectives and controversies.* New York: Guilford.

Arafat, I. S., & Cotton, W. L. (1974). Masturbation practices of males and females. *Journal of Sex Research, 10,* 293–307.

Atchison, C., Fraser, L., & Lowman, J. (1998). Men who buy sex: Preliminary findings of an exploratory study. In J. Elias, V. Bullough, V. Elias, & G. Brewer (Eds.), *Prostitution* (pp. 172–203). Amherst, NY: Prometheus.

Bailey, J. M., & Pillard, R. C. (1995). Genetics of human sexual orientation. *Annual Review of Sex Research, 6,* 126–150.

Baumeister, R. F. (2000). Gender differences in erotic plasticity: The female sex drive as socially flexible and responsive. *Psychological Bulletin, 126,* 347–374.

Baumeister, R. F., & Bratslavsky, E. (1999). Passion, intimacy, and time: Passionate love as a function of change in intimacy. *Personality and Social Psychology Review, 3,* 210–221.

Baumeister, R. F., Catanese, K. R., & Vohs, K. D. (2001). Is there a gender difference in strength of sex drive? Theoretical views, conceptual distinctions, and a review of relevant evidence. *Personality and Social Psychology Review, 5*(3), 242–273.

Baumeister, R. F., & Vohs, K. D. (in press). Sexual economics: Sex as female resource social exchange in heterosexual interactions. *Personality and Social Psychology Review.*

Bell, A. P., & Weinberg, M. S. (1978). *Homosexualities: A study of diversity among men and women.* New York: Simon & Schuster.

Betzig, L. (1989). Causes of conjugal dissolution: A cross-cultural study. *Current Anthropology, 30,* 654–676.

Blumstein, P. W., & Schwartz, P. (1983). *American Couples.* New York: Simon & Schuster.

Bogaert, A. F. (2003). Number of older brothers and social orientation: New tests and the attraction/behavior distinction in two national probability samples. *Journal of Personality and Social Psychology, 84,* 644–652.

Buss, D. M., & Schmitt, D. P. (1993). Sexual strategies theory: An evolutionary perspective on human mating. *Psychological Review, 100,* 204–232.

Christiansen, K. O. (1977). A preliminary study of criminality among twins. In S. Mednick & K. Christiansen (Eds.), *Biosocial bases of criminal behavior* (pp. 89–108). New York: Gardner.

Cohen, L. L., & Shotland, R. L. (1996). Timing of first sexual intercourse in a relationship: Expectations, experiences, and perceptions of others. *Journal of Sex Research, 33,* 291–299.

Cowan, G., & Dunn, K. F. (1994). What themes in pornography lead to perceptions of the degradation of women? *Journal of Sex Research, 31,* 11–21.

Croake, J. W., & James, B. (1973). A four year comparison of premarital sexual attitudes. *Journal of Sex Research, 9,* 91–96.

Crooks, R., & Baur, K. (1999). *Our sexuality*. Pacific Grove, CA: Brooks/Cole.

Dabbs, J. M. (2000). *Heroes, rogues, and lovers: Testosterone and behavior*. New York: McGraw-Hill.

DeLamater, J. D., & Hyde, J. S. (1998). Essentialism vs. social constructionism in the study of human sexuality. *Journal of Sex Research, 35*, 10–18.

de Waal, F. B. M. (1995). Sex as an alternative to aggression in the bonobo. In P. R. Abramson & S. D. Pinkerton (Eds.), *Sexual nature, sexual culture* (pp. 37–56). Chicago: The University of Chicago Press.

Dixon, J. K. (1984). The commencement of bisexual activity in swinging married women over age thirty. *Journal of Sex Research, 20*, 71–90.

Dunne, M. P., Martin, N. G., Statham, D. J., Slutske, W. S., Dinwiddie, S. H., Bucholz, K. K., Madden, P. A. F., & Heath, A. C. (1997). Genetic and environmental contributions to variance in age at first sexual intercourse. *Psychological Science, 8*, 211–216.

Eley, T. C., Lichtenstein, P., & Stevenson, J. (1999). Sex differences in the etiology of aggressive and nonaggressive antisocial behavior: Results from two twin studies. *Child Development, 70*, 155–168.

Elias, J. E., Bullough, V. L., Elias, V., & Brewer, G. (1998). *Prostitution: On whores, hustlers, and johns*. New York: Prometheus.

Eysenck, H. J. (1971). Masculinity–femininity, personality and sexual attitudes. *Journal of Sex Research, 7*, 83–88.

Golden, C. (1987). Diversity and variability in women's sexual identities. In the Boston Lesbian Psychologies Collective (Eds.), *Lesbian psychologies: Explorations and challenges* (pp. 19–34). Urbana, IL: University of Illinois Press.

Gooren, L. J. (1998). Endocrine aspects of aging in the male. Molecular and Cellular Endocrinology, *145*, 153–159.

Gough, D. (2000, February 13). Rwanda AIDS risk increases: "Husband sharing" causes concern. *The Cleveland Plain Dealer*, p. A9.

Gupta, N., & Majy, M. (2003). Sexual initiation among adolescent girls and boys: Trends and differentials in sub-Saharan Africa. *Archives of Sexual Behavior, 32*, 41–53.

Guttentag, M., & Secord, P. F. (1983). *Too many women? The sex ratio question*. Beverly Hills, CA: Sage.

Hansen, G. L. (1987). Extradyadic relations during courtship. *Journal of Sex Research, 23*, 382–390.

Harrison, D. A., Bennett, W. H., Globetti, G., & Alsikafi, M. (1974). Premarital sexual standards of rural youth. *Journal of Sex Research, 10*, 266–277.

Herold, E. S., & Mewhinney, D. M. K. (1993). Gender differences in casual sex and AIDS prevention: A survey of dating bars. *Journal of Sex Research, 30*, 36–42.

Hyde, J. S., & DeLamater, J. (1997). *Understanding human sexuality* (6th ed.). Boston, MA: McGraw-Hill.

Iasenza, S. (2000). Lesbian sexuality post-Stonewall to post-modernism: Putting the "lesbian bed death" concept to bed. *Journal of Sex Education and Therapy, 25*, 59–69.

Kendrick, K. M., Hinton, M. R., Atkins, K., Haupt, M. A., & Skinner, J. D. (1998). Mothers determine sexual preferences. *Nature, 395*, 229–230.

Kinsey, A. C., Pomeroy, W. B., Martin, C. E., & Gebhard, P. H. (1953). *Sexual behavior in the human female*. Philadelphia: Saunders.

Kinsey, A. C., Pomeroy, W. B., & Martin, C. E. (1948). *Sexual behavior in the human male*. Philadelphia: Saunders.

Klusmann, D. (2002). Sexual motivation and the duration of partnership. *Archives of Sexual Behavior, 31*, 275–287.

Knoth, R., Boyd, K., & Singer, B. (1988). Empirical tests of sexual selection theory: Predictions of sex differences in onset, intensity, and time course of sexual arousal. *Journal of Sex Research, 24*, 73–89.

Laumann, E. O., Gagnon, J. H., Michael, R. T., & Michaels, S. (1994). *The social organization of sexuality: Sexual practices in the United States*. Chicago: University of Chicago Press.

Laumann, E. O., Paik, A., & Rosen, R. C. (1999). Sexual dysfunction in the United States: Prevalence and predictors. *Journal of the American Medical Association, 281*, 537–544.

Leiblum, S. R., & Rosen, R. C. (1988). Changing perspectives on sexual desire. In S. Leiblum & R. Rosen (Eds.), *Sexual desire disorders* (pp. 1–20). New York: Guilford.

Leitenberg, H., & Henning, K. (1995). Sexual fantasy. *Psychological Bulletin, 117*, 469–496.

Masters, W. H., & Johnson, V. E. (1966). *Human sexual response*. Boston: Little, Brown.

McCabe, M. P. (1987). Desired and experienced levels of premarital affection and sexual intercourse during dating. *Journal of Sex Research, 23*, 23–33.

Mercer, G. W., & Kohn, P. M. (1979). Gender difference in the integration of conservatism, sex urge, and sexual behaviors among college students. *Journal of Sex Research, 15*, 129–142.

Money, J. (1990). *Vandalized lovemaps*. Buffalo, NY: Prometheus.

Oliver, M. B., & Hyde, J. S. (1993). Gender differences in sexuality: A meta-analysis. *Psychological Bulletin, 114*, 29–51.

O'Sullivan, L., & Byers, E. S. (1992). College students' incorporation of initiator and restrictor roles in sexual dating interactions. *Journal of Sex Research, 29*, 435–446.

Reinisch, J. M. (1990). *The Kinsey Institute new report on sex*. New York: St. Martin's.

Regan, P. C., & Sprecher, S. (1995). Gender differences in the value of contributions to intimate relationships: Egalitarian relationships are not always perceived to be equitable. *Sex Roles, 33*, 221–238.

Rosario, M., Meyer-Bahlburg, H. F. L., Hunter, J., Exner, T. M., Gwadz, M., & Keller, A. M. (1996). The psychosexual development of urban lesbian, gay, and bisexual youths. *Journal of Sex Research, 33*, 113–126.

Rust, P. (1992). The politics of sexual identity: Sexual attraction and behavior among lesbian and bisexual women. *Social Problems, 39*, 366–386.

Savin-Williams, R. C. (1990). *Gay and lesbian youth: Expressions of identity.* New York: Hemisphere.

Schfer, S. (1976). Sexual and social problems of lesbians. *Journal of Sex Research, 12*, 50–69.

Schmidt, G., & Sigusch, V. (1972). Changes in sexual behavior among young males and females between 1960–1970. *Archives of Sexual Behavior, 2*, 27–45.

Sherwin, R., & Corbett, S. (1985). Campus sexual norms and dating relationships: A trend analysis. *Journal of Sex Research, 21*, 258–274.

Sedikides, C., Oliver, M. B., & Campbell, W. K. (1994). Perceived benefits and costs of romantic relationships for women and men: Implications for exchange theory. *Personal Relationships, 1*, 5–21.

Shifren, J. L., Braunstein, G. D., Simon, J. A., Casson, P. R., Buster, J. E., Redmond, G. P., Burki, R. E., Ginsburg, E. S., Rosen, R. C., Leiblum, S. R., Jones, K. P., Daugherty, C. A., Caramelli, K. E., & Mazer, N. A. (2000). Transdermal testosterone treatment in women with impaired sexual function after oophorectomy. *New England Journal of Medicine, 343*, 682–688.

Singh, D., Vidaurri, M., Zambarano, R. J., & Dabbs, J. M. (1999). Lesbian erotic role identification: Behavioral, morphological, and hormonal correlates. *Journal of Personality and Social Psychology, 76*, 1035–1049.

Shilts, R. (1987). *And the band played on: Politics, people, and the AIDS epidemic.* New York: Viking/Penguin.

Sprecher, S. (2002). Sexual satisfaction in premarital relationships: Associations with satisfaction, love, commitment, and stability. *Journal of Sex Research, 39*, 190–196.

Sprecher, S., Barbee, A., & Schwartz, P. (1995). "Was it good for you, too?": Gender differences in first sexual experiences. *Journal of Sex Research, 32*, 3–15.

Staples, R. (1973). Male–female sexual variations: Functions of biology or culture. *Journal of Sex Research, 9*, 11–20.

Waller, W., & Hill, R. (1951). *The family: A dynamic interpretation.* New York: Dryden. (Original work published in 1938)

Whisman, V. (1996). *Queer by choice.* New York: Routledge.

Wiederman, M. W., & LaMar, L. (1998). "Not with him you don't!": Gender and emotional reaction to sexual infidelity during courtship. *Journal of Sex Research, 35*, 288–297.

Wilson, D. (1978). Sexual codes and conduct: A study of teenage girls. In C. Smart & B. Smart (Eds.), *Women, sexuality, and social control.* London: Routledge and Kegan Paul.

V

Applications and Clinical Aspects

20

Sexual Dysfunction From a Relationship Perspective

Sylvie Aubin
Julia R. Heiman
University of Washington, Seattle

Fundamental to the study of sexuality and its problems is the analysis of two individuals interacting in a very specific context. Sexual dysfunctions are primarily studied from a clinical management perspective. Currently, the assessment and treatment of individuals with sexual dysfunctions are based on a normative five-phase sexual response model of sexual functioning. Problems in sexual functioning are categorized using the phases and defined by physiological and/or psychological symptoms serving as criteria for clinical diagnosis. Relationship components are conceptualized as consequences and listed among the other symptom criteria to meet diagnosis. One shortcoming of the functional, symptom criteria model includes the emphasis on individual versus relationship symptoms and as a result, the paucity of research and theoretical models to explain sexual dysfunctions from the perspective of the couple. Assessment of sexual problems within the couple requires knowledge in the area of human sexual interactions. One must thus be familiar with the process of assessing sexual dysfunctions from an integrative approach, with the various diagnostic tools and methods, and with sexual relationship patterns. We offer a three-dimensional system comprised of interacting personal or relationship variables influencing the onset and course of sexual dysfunctions. Variables may predispose, precipitate, or maintain sexual problems and are best understood from a developmental perspective, emphasizing the importance of situating the onset and impact of sexual problems within partners' histories as individuals and as a couple. Among the influential relationship variables, the dimension of disparity between partners is a systemic construct that is central to most theoretical explanations of sexual dysfunctions and a relevant clinical management issue. Couples with sexual problems may thus present with significant differences between partners as to their recognition and tolerance of sexual symptoms as well as their cognitive, emotional, and/or sexual relationships. Sexual dysfunctions may, but do not always, significantly impact couples' quality of life. Consequences are generally observed on both sexual and nonsexual interactions and are associated with diminished frequency and quality of partner-related sexual activities and often limited couple closeness. Couple closeness, defined in part as nonsexual intimacy is characterized by diminished frequency and quality of affectionate, loving behaviors and by decreased communication and/or mutual supportive listening abilities. Fortunately, partners' coping skills and resources serve as important mediating variables in limiting the consequences of sexual dysfunctions on couple and sexual relationships. The effectiveness of partners' reactive coping skills may positively alter the course of their sexual difficulties and contribute to the survival of both couple and sexual relationships.

INTRODUCTION

The analysis of sexual problems within the relationship context is based on the underlying assumption that although sexual difficulties may be identified in one partner, the history of personal and couple interactions significantly influences the nature of sexual difficulties. More specifically, relationship patterns such as how partners perceive and manage their sexual problems are key components in the understanding of the onset and course of sexual dysfunctions within the couple.

Over the course of their relationship, couples typically report a variety of transient sexual difficulties. Sexual complaints may include problems in partners' sexual response (e.g., sexual desire, arousal, orgasm) or problems in partners' degree of sexual pleasure and satisfaction with the frequency and/or quality of sexual encounters. Sexual complaints often relate to problems in sexual functioning and may lead to, depending on the severity and impact of the problem on the individual and/or the relationship, to sexual dysfunctions.

A limited number of authors in the field focused on the relationship determinants and offered relationship-based theoretical models to explain sexual dysfunctions. Available models integrate a variety of constructs from psychodynamic, object-relation theories; cognitive, behavioral, or social learning theories; or systemic, interactional theories. For example, sexual problems may be explained by differences between partners in their sexual scripts, roles, or beliefs (e.g., Beck, 1988; Gagnon, Rosen, & Leiblum, 1982; Rosen, & Leiblum, 1988); by problems in their interaction patterns, exchanges, or emotional and intimacy needs (e.g., Byers, 1999; McCarthy, 1998(b); Schnarch, 1991; Verhulst & Heiman, 1979, 1988); or by difficulties in their sexual attraction, skills, or sexual cues (e.g., Hurlbert, Apt, Hurlbert, & Pierce, 2000; Kaplan, 1995; Pridal & LoPiccolo, 2000).

This chapter discusses the diagnostic assessment of sexual dysfunctions in couples from a clinical perspective (e.g., the clinical management of couples with sexual dysfunctions). Reflecting the limitations of research in this area and the available theoretical models, formulations and observations are heavily based on clinical reports and practical experience, with references to empirical research where available. Our focus here is more on heterosexual couples, though many issues we raise apply to same-sexed couples as well. Research specific to sexual dysfunctions in same-sex couples is needed, and we refer the reader to chapter 12 of this volume or to chapters in Leiblum & Rosen's books (2000) for more in-depth discussions of *same-sex* sexuality issues.

This chapter is divided into three main sections: (1) the diagnostic assessment and clinical issues specific to determining sexual dysfunctions within the relationship, (2) a description of the multifaceted nature and symptoms of sexual dysfunctions and the influential variables impacting the onset and course of sexual dysfunctions, and (3) a clinical case discussion illustrating the complexities of assessing sexual dysfunctions within the relationship.

DIAGNOSTIC ASSESSMENT OF SEXUAL DYSFUNCTIONS WITHIN THE COUPLE

Historical Trends in the Study and Clinical Management of Sexual Dysfunctions

Despite researchers' admonitions for considering sexual dysfunctions from a relationship perspective, it is surprising that studies focusing on sexual dysfunctions within the couple are relatively rare compared to studies of sexual dysfunctions from the perspective of the individual. Historically, researchers in this field gained scientific attention by first describing and measuring the human sexual response in laboratory setting (Masters & Johnson, 1966) and then by offering effective treatment methods beginning with Masters and Johnson's book on sexual dysfunctions (1970). To a lesser extent, research was also shaped by the integration of sexual dysfunctions into the American Psychiatric Association's (APA) Diagnostic and Statistical Manual of Mental Disorders, now in its fourth and revised edition (DSM-IV-TR; APA, 2000). Sexual difficulties became framed under a psychiatric or medical model. This model conceptualizes sexual dyfunctions as diseases and defines sexual problems into a list of symptoms, serving as criteria for diagnosis. In addition, the description of sexual symptoms focuses on aspects of functioning (e.g., erection, lack of orgasm) and is individual based not couple based.

This categorization impacted the clinical management and study of sexual dysfunctions. For example, studies have tended to prioritize areas of individual functioning that have been affected as opposed to looking at the affected relationship areas. Even though Masters and Johnson's early work clearly involved the couple, the diagnostic emphasis remained on the etiology of individual symptoms (Bretschneider & McCoy, 1988; Masters & Johnson, 1970).

Currently, there is a rapidly expanding emphasis on individual and physiological treatments for sexual dysfunctions. This highly medicalized model has been strengthened by the clinical and commercial success of sildenafil citrate (Viagra™) for erectile disorder, with other medications for this condition currently in development (Laumann, Paik, & Rosen, 1999; Leiblum & Rosen, 2000). Despite the medical, individual-based approach to sexual dysfunctions, a number of clinicians and researchers now stress the importance of an integrative and/or couple-based approach for managing sexual problems. The integrative approach includes a variety of assessment modalities, such as couple and individual clinical interviews, questionnaires, and/or physiological measures (Heiman, 2001, 2002; Leiblum & Rosen, 2000; Pridal & LoPiccolo, 2000; Schnarch, 1991; Wincze & Carey, 2001). Treatment approaches are typically designed to target relationship determinants of sexual dysfunctions, such as sexual issues, nonsexual intimacy issues, emotional or cognitive regulation, and communication skills of both partners (Hawton & Catalan, 1986; Heiman, 2000; Heiman & Meston, 1997a; Johnson & Greenberg, 1985; MacPhee, Johnson, & Van Der Veer, 1995; McCarthy & McCarthy, 1984; Pridal & LoPiccolo, 2000; Schnarch, 1997; Spence, 1997; Trudel, Marchand, Ravart, Aubin, Turgeon, & Fortier, 2001). In addition, support for couple treatment of sexual dysfunctions can be found from research results showing favorable treatment prognosis, specifically for hypoactive sexual desire in women (Basson., 2000; McCarthy & McCarthy, 1984; Trudel, 2000).

Given the important medical breakthroughs in the treatment of erectile disorder (Laumann et al., 1999; Leiblum & Rosen, 2000), sex researchers and couples alike are faced with the challenge of integrating medical interventions into their work and lives and of keeping in mind the centrality of sexual dysfunctions as occurring within a relationship context (Hawton & Catalan, 1986).

Classification of Sexual Dysfunctions and Their Symptoms Criteria

Establishing a sexual dysfunction diagnosis implies knowledge about normal sexual functioning. Masters and Johnson's (1966) research rationale was to provide a four-phase model of human sexual response to serve as a basis for defining normal male and female sexual functioning and as a comparative framework for diagnosing sexual problems. Later modified by Kaplan (1974, 1979) to include sexual desire as the first phase, the five-phase sexual response model (i.e., sexual desire, excitation, plateau, orgasm, resolution) is used by the American Psychiatric Association's (APA) Diagnostic and Statistical Manual (APA, 2000), the World Health Organization's (WHO) International Classification of Diseases (ICD-10; WHO, 1992) and the International Consensus Development Conference Panel (Basson et al., 2000)to categorize male and female sexual dysfunctions. We will use the DSM-IV-TR with some modifications from the Consensus Panel because it is a widely used system for clinical research in the United States (Heiman, 2001; Tiefer, Hall, & Tarvis, 2002).

Current diagnosis of sexual dysfunctions found in both classification systems include sexual desire disorders (i.e., hypoactive sexual desire and sexual aversion), sexual arousal disorders (i.e., female sexual arousal and male erectile disorder), and orgasmic disorders (i.e., female and male orgasmic disorders and premature ejaculation). Also included are sexual pain-related disorders, predominantly diagnosed in women, such as dyspareunia, vaginismus, and noncoital sexual pain disorder. For sexual dysfunctions that present with a specific etiology or that do not meet the criteria for a particular type of sexual dysfunction, the DSM-IV-TR (APA, 2000) categorizes them as due to a general medical condition, as substance induced, or as not otherwise specified. We outlined the sexual dysfunctions and their diagnostic criteria in Table 20.1 for the Consensus Panel (WHO, 2000) and in Table 20.2 for the DSM-IV-TR (APA, 2000).

Modest modifications to the DSM-IV-TR (APA, 2000) with respect to female sexual dysfunctions, have been set forth by the Consensus Panel (Basson et al., 2000). This classification system broadens diagnosis by including as sexual symptoms other nongenital or intercourse determinants and/or interactions such as noncoital sexual pain disorders and allows for an estimate of etiological factors to be psychological or physiological or both, rather than splitting off the biological/medical factors as the DSM-IV-TR does. Despite the Consensus Panel's recommendations, authors evaluate that the proposed reinforced the "status quo" of categorization approach to female sexual dysfunctions and does not address the crucial issue of how appropriate it is to label a sexual problem into a "dysfunction" (Bancroft, Loftus, & Long, 2003). Other criticisms of the response cycle model, such as how restrictive the range of diagnostic categories are, led researchers to propose subcategories of sexual dysfunctions (Basson, 2000, 2001a; Basson et al., 2000; Heiman, 2002) and include other types of sexually related problems such as sexual dissatisfaction (Basson et al., 2000; Byers, 2001; Hendry et al., 1999; Lue et al., 1999).

Assessment of sexual problems is based on a list of symptoms serving as diagnostic criteria that present with considerable overlap in subjective and physiological components (e.g., listed symptoms in one type of sexual dysfunction can also be found in another; Basson et al., 2000; Heiman & Meston, 1997b; Segraves & Segraves, 1991). In addition, there are similarities within the diagnostic systems in their proposed list of sexual problems and in their definition. We will precede our discussion of the various sexual dysfunctions with some highlights of diagnostic areas that are common to both systems—More specifically, their use of diagnostic modifiers and/or identifiers and their use of personal and/or interpersonal distress as symptoms criteria.

Each diagnosis requires establishing modifiers. Modifiers allow for greater specificity in diagnostic assessment by determining whether sexual dysfunctions are *lifelong* or *acquired* and *generalized* or *situational* and by specifying the etiologic origin

TABLE 20.1

Female Sexual Dysfunctions Defined by International Consensus Development Conference on Female Sexual Dysfunction

Sexual Dysfunction	Diagnostic Criteria
Sexual desire disorders A. Hypoactive sexual desire disorder	Hypoactive sexual desire disorder is the persistent or recurrent deficiency (or absence) of sexual fantasies/thoughts, and/or desire for, or receptivity to, sexual activity, which causes personsl distress.
B. Sexual aversion disorder	Sexual aversion disorder is the persistent or recurrent phobic aversion to and avoidance of sexual contact with a sexual partner, which causes personal distress.
Sexual arousal disorder	Sexual arousal disorder is the persistent or recurrent inability to attain or maintain sufficient sexual excitement, causing personal distress. It may be expressed as a lack of subjective excitement or a lack of genital (lubrication/swelling) or other somatic responses.
Orgasmic disorder	Orgasmic disorder is the persistent or recurrent difficulty, delay in, or absence of attaining orgams following sufficient stimulation and arousal, which causes personal distress.
Sexual pain disorders A. Dyspareunia	Dyspareunia is recurrent or persistent genital pain associated with sexual intercourse.
B. Vaginismus	Vaginismus is recurrent or persistent involuntary spasm of the musculature of the outer third of the vagina that interferes with vaginal penetration, which causes personal distress.
C. Noncoital sexual pain disorder	Recurrent or persistent genital pain induced by noncoital sexual stimulation.

Note. Goldstein, Graziottin, Heiman, Johanness, Laan, Levin, & McKenna, (1999). Female sexual dysfunction. In Jardin, Wagner, Khoury, Giuliano, Padma-Nathan, & Rosen, (Eds.), *Erectile dysfunction*. Plymouth England: Plymbridge Dist. (p. 531).

(APA, 2000; Basson et al., 2000). Etiological specifiers include psychological causes, medical/organic causes, a combination of both, or unknown causes. The DSM-IV-TR specifies to verify for the presence of concomitant Axis I disorders (e.g., depression, anxiety, substance use) and/or general medical conditions that might explain the sexual dysfunction. Co-morbid mental or medical causes to sexual problems can thus be classified separately and defined as "sexual dysfunction due to a general medical condition" or as "substance induced sexual dysfunction." In sum, both systems utilize the same diagnostic specifiers but in comparison to the Consensus Panel, the DSM-IV-TR categorizes sexual dysfunctions that are caused exclusively by mental or medical conditions under different diagnostic entities and/or codes.

In order to be diagnosed with a sexual dysfunction, the sexual problem must cause personal and/or relationship distress. The inclusion of "personal distress" for the Consensus Panel or "marked distress and/or interpersonal difficulty" for the DSM-IV-TR emphasizes the role of psychological or emotional variables related to the impact of the sexual problem on the individual and/or on the relationship. These criteria present the diagnostic challenge of defining distress from the individual's versus the evaluator's standpoint, accounting for partners' differential awareness and threshold for recognizing distress (Heiman, 2000). Fugl-Meyer and Sjogren Fugl-Meyer's (1999) study is one of the few to clearly differentiate between the presence of sexual

TABLE 20.2

Sexual Dysfunctions Defined by the DSM-IV-TR

Sexual Dysfunction	Diagnostic Criteria
Sexual desire disorders 302.71 Hypoactive sexual desire disorder	A. Persistently or recurrently deficient (or absent) sexual fantasies and desire for sexual activity. The judgment of deficiency or absence is made by the clinician, taking into account factors that affect sexual functioning, such as age and the context of the person's life. B. The disturbance causes marked distress or interpersonal difficulty. C. The sexual dysfunction is not better accounted for by another Axis I disorder (except another sexual dysfunction) and is not due exclusively to the direct physiological effects of a substance (e.g., a drug abuse, a medication) or a general medical condition.
302.79 Sexual aversion disorder	A. Persistent or recurrent extreme aversion to, and avoidance of, all (or almost all) genital sexual contact with a sexual partner. B. The disturbance causes marked distress or interpersonal difficulty. C. The sexual dysfunction is not better accounted for by another Axis I disorder (except another sexual dysfunction).
Sexual arousal disorders 302.72 Female sexual arousal disorder	A. Persistent or recurrent inability to attain, or to maintain until completion of the sexual activity, an adequate lubrication/swelling response of sexual excitement. B. The disturbance causes marked distress or interpersonal difficulty. C. The sexual dysfunction is not better accounted for by another Axis I disorder (except another sexual dysfunction) and is not due exclusively to the direct physiological effects of a substance (e.g., a drug abuse, a medication) or a general medical condition.
302.72 Male erectile disorder	A. Persistent or recurrent inability to attain, or to maintain until completion of the sexual activity, an adequate erection. B. The disturbance causes marked distress or interpersonal difficulty. C. The sexual dysfunction is not better accounted for by another Axis I disorder (except another sexual dysfunction) and is not due exclusively to the direct physiological effects of a substance (e.g., a drug abuse, a medication) or a general medical condition.

Orgasmic disorders
302.73 Female orgasmic disorder

A. Persistent or recurrent delay in, or absence of, orgasm following a normal sexual excitement phase. Women exhibit wide variability in the type or intensity of stimulation that triggers orgasm. The diagnosis of female orgasmic disorder should be based on the clinician's judgment that the woman's orgasmic capacity is less than would be reasonable for her age, sexual experience, and the adequacy of sexual stimulation she receives.

B. The disturbance causes marked distress or interpersonal difficulty.

C. The sexual dysfunction is not better accounted for by another Axis I disorder (except another sexual dysfunction) and is not due exclusively to the direct physiological effects of a substance (e.g., a drug abuse, a medication) or a general medical condition.

302.74 Male orgasmic disorder

A. Persistent or recurrent delay in, or absence of, orgasm following a normal sexual excitement phase during sexual activity that the clinician, taking into account the person's age, judges to be adequate in focus, intensity, and duration.

B. The disturbance causes marked distress or interpersonal difficulty.

C. The sexual dysfunction is not better accounted for by another Axis I disorder (except another sexual dysfunction) and is not due exclusively to the direct physiological effects of a substance (e.g., a drug abuse, a medication) or a general medical condition.

302.75 Premature ejaculation

A. Persistent or recurrent ejaculation with minimal sexual stimulation before, on, or shortly after penetration and before the person wishes it. The clinician must take into account factors that affect duration of the excitement phase, such as age, novelty of the sexual partner or situation, and recent frequency of sexual activity.

B. The disturbance causes marked distress or interpersonal difficulty.

C. The premature ejaculation is not due exclusively to the direct effects of a substance (e.g., withdrawal from opiates).

(Continued)

483

TABLE 20.2

(Continued)

Sexual Dysfunction	Diagnostic Criteria
Sexual pain disorders 302.76 Dyspareunia (not due to a general medical condition)	A. Recurrent or persistent genital pain associated with sexual intercourse in either a male or a female. B. The disturbance causes marked distress or interpersonal difficulty. C. The disturbance is not caused exclusively by vaginismus or lack of lubrication, is not better accounted for by another Axis I disorder (except another sexual dysfunction) and is not due exclusively to the direct physiological effects of a substance (e.g., a drug abuse, a medication) or a general medical condition.
306.51 Vaginismus (not due to a general medical condition)	A. Recurrent or persistent involuntary spasm of the musculature of the outer third of the vagina that interferes with sexual intercourse. B. The disturbance causes marked distress or interpersonal difficulty. C. The disturbance is not better accounted for by another Axis I disorder (e.g., somatization disorder) and is not due exclusively to the direct physiological effects of a general medical condition.
Sexual dysfunction due to a general medical condition	A. Clinically significant sexual dysfunction that results in marked distress or interpersonal difficulty predominates in the clinical picture B. There is evidence from the history, physical examination, or laboratory findings that the sexual dysfunction is fully explained by the direct physiological effects of a general medical condition. C. The disturbance is not better accounted for by another mental disorder (e.g., major depressive disorder).
625.8 Female hypoactive sexual desire disorder due to… 608.89 Male hypoactive sexual desire disorder due to… 607.84 Male erectile disorder due to… 625.0 Female dyspareunia due to… 608.89 Male dyspareunia due to… 625.8 Other female sexual dysfunction due to… 608.89 Other male sexual dysfunction due to…	

Substance-induced sexual dysfunction

291.8 Alcohol; 292.89 Amphetamine (or Amphetamine-Like Substance); 292.89 Cocaine; 292.89 Opioid; 292.89 Sedative, Hypnotic, or Anxiolytic; 292.89 Other (or Unknown Substance)

A. Clinically significant sexual dysfunction that results in marked distress or interpersonal difficulty predominates in the clinical picture

B. There is evidence from the history, physical examination, or laboratory findings that the sexual dysfunction is fully explained by substance use as manifested by either (1) or (2):

   (1) the symptoms in Criterion A developed during, or within a month of, substance intoxication

   (2) medication use is etiologically related to the disturbance

C. The disturbance is not better accounted for by a sexual dysfunction that is not substance induced. Evidence that the symptoms are better accounted for by a sexual dysfunction that is not substance induced might include the following: the symptoms precede the onset of the substance use or dependence (or medication use); the symptoms persist for a substantial period of time (e.g., about a month) after the cessation of intoxication, or are substantially in excess of what would be expected given the type or amount of the substance used or the duration of use; or there is other evidence that suggests the existence of an independent nonsubstance induced sexual dysfunction (e.g., a history of recurrent nonsubstance-related episodes).

302.70 Sexual dysfunction not otherwise specified

This category includes sexual dysfunctions that do not meet criteria for any specific sexual dysfunction. Examples include:

1. No (or substantially diminished) subjective erotic feelings despite otherwise normal arousal and orgasm

2. Situations in which the clinician has concluded that a sexual dysfunction is present but is unable to determine whether it is primary, due to a general medical condition, or substance induced.

Note. American Psychiatric Association. (2000). *Diagnostic and statistical manual of mental disorders* (Text revision). Washington, DC: Author.

dysfunctions and partners' perception of sexual problems as problematic or distressful. Interestingly, the authors found important gender differences in the concordance rates between the presence and the recognition of sexual dysfunctions as problematic. For example, 69% of men reporting erectile dysfunction perceived it as a problem, whereas only 45% of women reporting orgasmic disorder perceived it as a problem. A recent review of four other studies assessing the prevalence of sexual problems in women concluded that only a third to a half of women identified as having a sexual problem considered themselves as having a sexual problem or marked distress about their sexuality (Bancroft et al, 2003)

Sexual Desire Disorders

Sexual desire disorders include hypoactive sexual desire and sexual aversion. Associated affective, cognitive, and behavioral symptoms include low sexual desire, fantasies, sexual thoughts, pleasure, and sexual receptivity (APA, 2000; Aubin, Trudel, Ravart, Marchand, & Heiman, 2001; Basson, 2001b; Basson et al., 2000; Heiman, 2001; Heiman, Epps, & Ellis, 1995; Kaplan, 1995; Levine, 1988; Nutter & Condron, 1983; Rosen & Leiblum, 1995; Trudel et al., 2001). Affected individuals rarely initiate and/or tend to avoid sexual activities with the partner (Renshaw, 2001; Trudel, 2000; Trudel, Aubin, & Matte, 1995). Sexual aversion, a rare sexual disorder for which we have no available prevalence rates, presents as key diagnostic symptoms of anxiety and phobic states toward sexual activities, often leading to avoidance of partner genital sexual contact (Heiman, 2002; Kaplan, 1995; Rosen & Leiblum, 1989).

Hypoactive sexual desire is regarded by most authors as more prevalent in females than in males (33.4% versus 15.8% for men; Heiman, 2002; Simons & Carey, 2001) and as the most challenging sexual dysfunction to treat (Heiman & Meston, 1997a; Leiblum & Rosen, 2000; Trudel, 1991). Hypoactive sexual desire etiology is for both genders multidimensional (e.g., associated with a variety of psychological and/or medical factors), highly case specific, and for most cases of female hypoactive sexual desire, related to the quality of couple relationships (Heiman, 2001; McCarthy, 1984; Trudel, et al., 2001). Relationship components that are associated with hypoactive sexual desire include an excessively low or high degree of cohesiveness in nonsexual intimate activities (e.g., couple closeness); poor couple adaptation to life transitions, e.g., first child (Apt & Hurlbert, 1992; Heiman, 2002); history of sexual trauma (Heiman, 2001; Heiman & Meston, 1997b; Trudel, Ravart, & Matte, 1993; Walker et al., 1999); and co-existing arousal, orgasm, or pain disorders (Aubin et al., 2001; Barbach, 1976; Rosen & Leiblum, 1989). Hypoactive sexual desire diagnosis within the couple can be further complicated by partner disparities in sexual desire or by hypoactive sexual desire symptoms posing as causes or effects of other relationship issues. Thus, it is useful to determine whether a desire problem is in fact only a disparity in desire between partners and to identify whether desire is primary or secondary to other sexual dysfunctions such as orgasmic and/or pain problems.

Sexual Arousal Disorders

Arousal disorders, female sexual arousal disorder and erectile dysfunction, refer to a decreased or lack of genital response, with prevalence estimates ranging from 14% to 52% in women (it usually concerns the symptom of lubrication rather than arousal) and from 10% to 53% in men (Heiman, 2002; Kuriansky, Sharpe, & O'Connor, 1982; Simons & Carey, 2001). In women, the main symptoms are lack of vaginal lubrication or swelling with a subjective awareness of insufficient sexual excitement or arousal (Basson, 2001b; Basson et al., 2000; APA, 2000; Heiman, 2002). For men, lack of penile response serves as the principal criterion for diagnosis (APA, 2000; Basson et al.,

2000). Compared to other sexual dysfunctions, arousal disorders along with sexual pain problems have recently become highly researched areas, probably because of the interest in genital vasocongestive agents such as sildenafil citrate (Heiman & Meston, 1997a; Leiblum & Rosen, 2000; Trudel, 2000).

Affective and relationship components of arousal dysfunctions, though often not the main focus of research, include problems with sexual desire, subjective excitement, pleasure, and enjoyment along with avoidance of sexual activities with the partner. Important cognitive and emotional factors are associated with performance anxiety, more specifically an expectation to attain or maintain a desired state of arousal (Althof, 1992; Beck & Barlow, 1986; Beck, Barlow, & Sakheim, 1983; Heiman, 2002; LoPiccolo, 1992; Rosen, Leiblum, & Spector, 1994; Rowland & Heiman, 1991). From our experience, both partners typically report feeling anxious, tense, or nervous before and during sexual activity followed by frustration and sadness from experiencing another disappointing sexual encounter.

Orgasmic Disorders

Orgasm disorders are also common. Laumann et al. (1999) estimate that 24.1% of women reported orgasm problems in the last year compared to 8.3% of men, whereas 28.5% of men reported having orgasm too early (Simons & Carey, 2001). Characteristic symptoms range from rapid orgasm to absent orgasm. The criteria for both the DSM-IV-TR and the Consensus Panel specify that orgasm problems occur despite sufficient sexual stimulation or a normal sexual excitement phase. The DSM-IV-TR further specifies to consider women's variability in the type or intensity of stimulation for triggering orgasm and for men, the variability in the type of context for reaching orgasm. Orgasmic disorders can thus be diagnosed as situational or specific to a particular type of sexual stimulation (e.g., intercourse, manual, oral stimulation) or specific to a particular context (e.g., partner versus individual sexual activities). Generalized orgasmic disorders are characterized by the inability to reach orgasm from any type of sexual stimulation or context.

Studies consistently show that women's source of orgasmic stimulation is primarily clitoral and that inability to reach orgasm for both sexes is more common in couple than in solitary types of activities such as masturbation (Heiman, 2000; Heiman & LoPiccolo, 1988; Kaplan, 1989). In addition, orgasm problems are often linked to performance anxiety and include distinctive relationship components. For example, in women with partner-related orgasmic disorder, there is a "partner spectator effect," defined as a women's perception of her partner as a spectator to her sexual performance, resulting in anxiety and inability to reach orgasm. Our clinical observations of couples diagnosed with situational, partner-related orgasmic disorder have shown that couples are usually aware of the partner's ability to reach orgasm through solitary masturbation. This information may cause additional pressure and feelings of sexual inadequacy and frustration for both partners. Couples often report being caught in a sexual performance ritual where they find themselves heavily focused on the objective of reaching orgasm for the diagnosed individual.

Sexual Pain Disorders

Sexual pain disorders (e.g., dyspareunia) frequently present with medical conditions acting as causal, precipitating, or maintaining factors (Heiman, 2002; Leiblum & Segraves, 2000; Schover, 2000). Pain during sexual activity is estimated to affect 14.4% of women and 3% of men, with vaginismus affecting less than 5% of women (Heiman, 2002; Heiman & Meston, 1997b; Wincze & Carey, 2001). For both sexes, assessment of symptoms includes a detailed description of the subject's experience of pain during both coital activities and noncoital sexual stimulation and is labeled as dyspareunia. Assessment for diagnostic specification includes pain sensation (e.g., dull, sharp), intensity (e.g., mild to moderate), and precise location (e.g., superficial at intromission or deep during thrusting). In addition, all sexual pain disorders require careful physical examination by a provider knowledgeable in the area of genital and pelvic pain.

Studies have identified that female dyspareunia often coexists with other sexual dysfunctions or medical conditions. They range from female sexual arousal disorder, to medical conditions such as vulvar vestibulitis syndrome (Bergeron, 1999; Bergeron, Binik, Khalife, & Padigas, 1997; Maurice, 1999), vaginal dryness from menopausal states, hormonal treatments, or postsurgical atrophy (Heiman & Meston, 1997b; McCoy, 2001; Schover, 2000). Male sexual pain, although not as well documented, commonly refers to pain during erection, ejaculation, or penetration. Predisposing and/or co-existing medical conditions range from anatomical deformation of the penis (e.g., angulation, priapism) such as in Peyronie's disease, to post-prostatectomy complications (Lue et al., 1999; Schover, 2000).

Vaginismus is described as the involuntary contractions of the muscle located at the outer third of the vagina, creating a barrier to penile entry. Some authors do not see vaginismus as a distinct diagnostic syndrome because it overlaps or coexists with dyspareunia (Reissing, Binik, & Khalife, 1999). It is usually diagnosed in younger women, may be found during the initial gynological exam, and often generalizes to any type of genital intromission. Significant affective and relationship components are pain-related fears and anxieties about sexual contact and pregnancy that negatively impact the couple's repertoire of sexual activities (Leiblum, 2000; Trudel, 2000).

In order to address the dimension of clinical subjectivity necessitated by diagnosis (e.g., the evaluator's clinical judgment and/or opinion), it is helpful to use a multi-modal approach to couple assessment. In addition to diagnostic interviewing, it is clinically relevant to include empirically valid and reliable questionnaires (Daker-White, 2002). Questionnaires may evaluate partners' overall sexual functioning (e.g., Derogatis Sexual Functioning Inventory by Derogatis & Melisaratos, 1979) or be more specific to female sexual functioning (e.g., Female Sexual Function Index by Rosen et al., 2000, Brief Index of Sexual Functioning for Women by Taylor, Rosen, & Leiblum, 1994, Sexual Function Questionnaire by Quirk et al., 2002) or male sexual functioning (e.g., International Index of Erectile Function by Rosen, Riley et al., 1997, Brief Sexual Function Questionnaire for Men by Reynolds et al., 1988) and/or to couple adaptation (e.g., Dyadic Adjustment Scale by Spanier, 1976, Personal Assessment of Intimacy in Relationships by Schaefer & Olson, 1980). Interestingly, most questionnaires assessing male or female sexual functioning include relatively few items specific to the relationship dimension and/or include the partner when they were compared to the total number of items. For example, the International Index of Erectile Function includes 1 question out of 15 about the individual's sexual satisfaction with his partner (Rosen et al., 1997).

In addition to diagnostic interviewing and questionnaires, assessment of sexual dysfunctions may include objective, physiological measures. Assessment methods now utilize techniques that allow for better diagnostic precision of concurrent physical conditions and also provide verification of sexual responses linked to sexual symptoms. For example, these may include for men penile arteriography, dynamic infusion pharmacocavernosometry, or nocturnal tumescence and rigidity assessment (Hendry et al., 1999). For women, aside from the genital pain disorders, which require specialized exam and diagnostic workups, a variety of technologies are currently being tested that may include duplex doppler, ultrasonography, and pelvic imaging. Even though these methods need further testing, they may help to clarify differences in women's perception of objective (e.g., physical) versus subjective (e.g., psychological self-report) aspects of their sexual responses as well as help detect physiological or sensory disorders (Heiman, 1998, Heiman et al., 2001; Laan, Everaerd, Van der velde, & Geer, 1995; Maravilla et al., 2001; Meston & Frohlich, 2000).

Models of Sexual Dysfunctions Within the Couple

Assessment of sexual problems from a relationship perspective requires that the clinician not only possesses knowledge about sexual symptoms and their determinants but, most important, understands how interpersonal relationships are implicated in the development and maintenance of sexual dysfunctions. In our experience, theoretical models that integrate sociocultural, cognitive, and systemic constructs helped to further our comprehension of the mechanism of influence of interpersonal relationships on sexual problems. This section includes an overview of these models and provides a conceptual framework for discussing the clinical implications and issues of diagnosing sexual dysfunctions within the couple, the topic of the next section.

Early in the diagnostic process, the clinician is faced with the dilemma of distinguishing sexual dysfunctions from disparities in sexual desire, response, and behavior between partners (Leiblum & Rosen, 2000). Reported distress and areas of dissatisfaction often relate to the expected frequency of sexual activities and to the content of the sexual scenario. We define sexual scenario as the actual or expected repertoire of sexual activities that typically take place during a sexual encounter with the partner. Partners have mental representations or cognitive–emotional schemas of what constitutes good and poor sexual scenarios and of how each of them should respond sexually (Heiman, 2001; Heiman & Meston, 1997a; Spence, 1997; Trudel, 2000; Trudel et al., 2001). In addition, partners not only differ in their desired frequency of sexual encounters but in their preferred sexual scenarios, contexts, and exchanges (Crowe & Ridley, 1987; Laumann, Gagnon, Michael, & Michaels, 1994; Zilbergeld & Ellison, 1980). Desire discrepancy by itself is not considered a dysfunction but if not addressed by couples, may lead to sexual dysfunctions.

The onset and maintenance of hypoactive sexual desire (Heiman, 2001; Verhulst & Heiman, 1988) or orgasmic disorders (Heiman, 2000) can be understood using a systemic model of explanation. Sexual interactions between partners are organized into three interdependent levels or subsystems consisting of symbolic, affect-regulated, or sensate interactions. Briefly, symbolic level interactions refer to the "interactional fit" (Verhulst & Heiman, 1988, p. 249) between partners as to how congruent they are in their exchanges, ideas, cognitive scripts, or views of the world. Affect-regulated interactions concern the coordination and regulation of affective states, comprised of four types of interactions; namely, attachment (e.g., intimacy, affection, and the affective bond), exploratory (e.g., sensory contact and familiarity), ranking-order (e.g., partners' social position—submission, domination, and control) and territorial (e.g., ownership rights and space). Sensate exchanges refer to sensory, neurophysiological motor responses that are related to partners' differential sexual response pace such as sexual desire, arousal, or orgasm attainment. Problems in any of the three subsystems may create sexual polarization and emotional distancing between partners, which is an important relationship-based symptom for most sexual dysfunctions. We provide further examples of interactions throughout the next sections and refer to reader to the works of Verhulst & Heiman (1979, 1988) for more details on this model.

Discrepancies between partners concerning their sexual interactions may also be examined using a social scripting approach. Based on sociocultural theory (e.g., the production of behavior within social life), this model places a particular emphasis on cognitive and interpersonal dimensions of sexual interactions using the construct of sexual scripts (Gagnon, Rosen, & Leiblum, 1982; Simon & Gagnon, 1986). Essentially, scripts consist of cognitive maps (e.g., define sexual situations, name the actors, direct the behaviors) and establish rules of sexual conduct (e.g., appropriateness of sexual behaviors as in what context and with whom). Sexual scripts are either performative (e.g., current) or ideal (e.g., wished for). Performative scripts may be analyzed in terms of four key attributes: complexity, rigidity, conventionality, and satisfaction (Gagnon, Rosen, & Leiblum, 1982). Problems with sexual scripts may precede, maintain, or develop as a consequence of sexual dysfunctions. For example, in couples with erectile disorder, performative scripts are typically restricted, repetitive, inflexible, and unsatisfying for both partners (Rosen, Leiblum, & Spector, 1994). In addition, scripts difficulties often relate to significant discrepancies between and/or within partners' scripts (Aubin et al., 2001; Rosen & Leiblum, 1988). Between-script discrepancies are defined as a lack of congruence (e.g., differences are too great or narrow) between partners as to their performative and/or ideal scripts, whereas within-script discrepancies refer to a lack of congruence in a partner's self-performative versus ideal scripts. In couples with hypoactive sexual desire, significant script discrepancies between partners are known to negatively affect the experience of sexual desire and initiation (Aubin et al., 2001; Rosen & Leiblum, 1988).

Theoretical formulations of the social scripting approach thus help to conceptualize the couple as a micro-culture, promoting not only individual but also couple norms of sexual conduct (Feldman, Goldstein, Hatzichristou, Krane, & McKinlay, 1994; Gagnon, Rosen, & Leiblum, 1982; Rosen & Leiblum, 1988; Verhulst & Heiman, 1988). Partners are immersed in the process of social comparison by having access to two referential models. First, the dominant culture and sexual role models displayed in educational programs, family, social interactions, or the media and second, the sexual partner.

The partner's sexual expectations and ideal scripts about how the other should respond sexually significantly shape the patterns of sexuality and may be implicated in the course of some sexual dysfunctions. Pressure to meet the partner's expectations often merges with sexual self-expectations. Based on Bowen's Family Theory (Bowen, 1978), Schnarch referred to this phenomenon as a lack of individuation or as a reflected sense of self and postulates that it is a product of emotional fusion between partners (Schnarch, 1991, 2000). He also presented this notion as a potential explanation for couples with hypoactive sexual desire (Schnarch, 1991, 2000). Schnarch postulates that hypoactive sexual desire is not a symptom of other relationship problems but a process of the relationship, reflecting a partner's adaptation or functioning. He argues that hypoactive sexual desire originates from unresolved personal differentiation or self-validation between partners. This systemic position is characterized by partners' low tolerance of sexual anxiety or discomfort, personal attribution or self-blame for the partner's sexual problem, feelings of disappointment or anger, and by partners' tendency to define sexual adequacy in terms of one's ability to please the other. The emotional and interpersonal consequences of this position serve specific individual needs of self-validation or self-protection from rejection or disappointment for both partners. For example, the low-desire partner may express his/her need to self-validate by controlling the frequency of sexual activities or his/her need to protect one's self from the partner's disappointment by avoiding or not initiating sexual activities. The high-desire partner may express his/her low differentiation by first blaming himself or herself for the partner's low sexual desire and express his or her need of self-protection by later blaming the partner or the partner's relationship history.

Clinical Issues in Determining Diagnosis From a Relationship Perspective

As proposed by the theoretical models, determining diagnosis for sexual dysfunctions within the couple is a challenging task because of the presence of significant disparities between partners. We will thus end this section with further discussions on partner disparities because it constitutes an unique aspect and important part of evaluating sexual problems within the couple.

A couple's sexual dysfunction can arise from or be influenced by the nature of inter-actional exchanges and/or social scripts (Gagnon et al., 1982; Rosen & Leiblum, 1988), by sexual myths and/or stereotypes (Barbach, 1976; Beck, 1988; Zilbergeld, 1992), by differences in couple sexual norms or by differences in cognitive schemas and/or attribution styles (Anderson & Cyranowski, 1995; Anderson, Cyranowski, & Espin-dle, in press; Beck & Barlow, 1986; Heiman, 2001; Money, 1986). Differences between the sexes in couple sexual ideals and interactions are in turn influenced by norms of sexual conduct that have traditionally been ascribed to each gender. Recently, assess-ment of sexual dysfunctions within the couple has paid greater attention to differences between partners in the subjective and behavioral aspects of sexual desire. Researchers distinguished sexual receptivity from pro-activity, a category now proposed for sex-ual desire for women (i.e., to accommodate for more than one category of normal, though frequently gender-typed, sexual desire and response). In addition, differences between the sexes in sexual desire and pro-activity can still be observed (Lawrence, Taylor, & Byers 1996; McCoy, 2001; Walker et al., 1999). Compared to women, men still display a greater number of initiations for couple sexual activities and higher fre-quencies of sexual desire, thoughts, and fantasies (Byers, & Heinlein, 1989; Laumann et al., 1994; Laumann et al., 1999; Leitenberg & Henning, 1995; Trudel, 2000). Whether they experience similar levels of responsive desire is unknown.

The nature of cognitive and emotional interference (i.e., what partners are thinking and feeling during their sexual encounters) is another area where one can identify differential profiles of responses between partners presenting with specific types of sexual dysfunctions. Sexual concerns and expectations reported by women with hy-poactive sexual desire are referred to as *response-based concerns* such as being able to elicit sexual desire and experience arousal during the sexual encounter (Rosen et al., 1997; Trudel, 2000). In comparison, men with erectile disorder often report *performance-based concerns* or anxieties such as erectile functioning and the ability to elicit pleasure and orgasm for the partner (Beck & Barlow, 1986; Trudel, 2000). These concerns may develop into negative perceptions of the self or into catastrophic or fatalistic thinking patterns that often serve, over time, to worsen sexual symptoms. Improvements of sexual symptoms are thus related to the constructive management of these thinking patterns and are focused on the experience of desire and pleasure either for the self or for the partner.

The meaning, priority, and primary purpose of sex are other areas of divergence that affect couples and influence the course of sexual dysfunctions. Differences in the priority of sex can be a function of many factors including (a) regularity in one's attempts at sexual exposure, (b) physical and psychological sexual readiness, (c) part-ners' needs to relieve sexual tension, (d) synchronization between partners' sexual rhythms or pace in sensate exchanges, and (f) the connection between sex and non-sexual relationships (Masters & Johnson, 1970; McCoy, 2001; Verhulst & Heiman, 1979, 1988). Partners thus differ in their attempts at maintaining active sexual connections either cognitively through fantasies or behaviorally through sexual activities that may occur or not with the partner (e.g., solitary masturbation versus partner-related sexual activities). Some authors have suggested that compared to women, men are more active at maintaining sexual connections. They propose that it could be due in part to men's regular attempts at exposure to sexuality combined with greater sexual desire, readiness, and need to alleviate sexual tension (Basson, 2000a; Heiman, 2001; Laumann et al., 1994).

Another area of difference between partners relates to differential timing in their need for intimacy and emotional connection or closeness. Nonsexual intimacy, behaviorally defined as loving behaviors or emotionally defined as feeling close to the partner, have been reported by women as important motivators for engaging in sex with the partner and as rewarding aspects of sexual relationships (Byers, 1999). For men, nonsexual intimacy and closeness can be achieved through sexuality where sexual interactions serve as the primary form of expressing and receiving love. Finally, other differences between partners are implicated in the course of sexual dysfunctions and relate to divergent sexual attraction, initiation rituals, and what partners find sexually arousing or satisfying (e.g., the types of sexual caresses and activities such as oral, anal, or coital positions) (Kaplan, 1995).

In summary, the diagnostic assessment of male and female sexual dysfunctions is currently based on a categorization approach and commonly uses as diagnostic reference tools the DSM-IV-TR with recent recommendations by the International Consensus Development Conference Panel, the latter being specific to female sexual dysfunctions. Following the works of Masters and Johnson and of Kaplan, each classification system lists sexual dysfunctions in accordance with a five-phase sexual response model (as well as genital pain disorders) and defines sexual problems into psychological and physiological symptoms serving as criteria for diagnosis. Clinically relevant diagnostic components relate to the use of diagnostic modifiers and the inclusion of psychological distress as a symptom criteria. Modifiers allow for the specification of onset, context of occurrence, and etiology; whereas the affective consequence of sexual dysfunctions, defined as personal and/or interpersonal distress, accounts for the individual's recognition of a problem and a negative effect on himself or herself and/or on the relationship. In addition, it is important to note that when assessing sexual dysfunctions within the couple, problem and distress recognition are criteria that have shown significant gender differences.

Mainly to address the various shortcomings of the categorization model, authors now stress the use of a multimodal approach to assessment, integrating psychological and physiological measures, and they emphasize the importance of relationship determinants in the onset and course of sexual dysfunctions. Of the various relationship determinants, the dimension of disparities between partners not only poses as a significant contributor to sexual symptoms but also as a central component for explaining the onset and maintenance of certain sexual dysfunctions or other sexual problems. Systemic-based models to explain sexual dysfunctions thus focus on the analysis of partner disparities in areas such as sexual desire, activity, priority, meaning of sex, and timing for intimacy. Whether problematic or not, differences between partners are important clinical issues and may present as challenges to diagnosing sexual dysfunctions from a relationship perspective.

INFLUENTIAL VARIABLES ON SEXUAL DYSFUNCTIONS WITHIN THE COUPLE

Couples diagnosed with sexual dysfunctions generally report having the problem for a number of years. For example, in a recent study of couples with hypoactive sexual desire in women, desire problems were reported by women for an average of 6 years (Trudel et al., 2001). Problems with sexual functioning may continue for a number of reasons, and we will discuss three reasons. First, there are differences between partners in problem recognition and tolerance. Second, predisposing and/or precipitating factors identified as relationship stressors may influence the course of sexual dysfunctions. Third, partners' coping style, particularly avoidance versus actively coping, may be involved in the persistence of sexual difficulties. The first two will be the focus of this section and the third will be covered in the last section.

Recognition and Tolerance of Sexual Symptoms

Partners differ in their individual timing and awareness of their sexual problems. Perceptual awareness of sexual difficulties relates to partners' abilities to be introspective about their experience of both sexual and couple distress. How partners interpret distress relates to the concept of differential levels of tolerance for discomfort, more specifically related to the consequences of the problem on the self, the partner, and the relationship. Various authors suggest that women are more aware of and less willing to tolerate relationship distress that may or not stem from sexual dysfunction (Birchler & Webb, 1975; Edwards, 1981; Fugl-Meyer & Sjogren Fugl-Meyer, 1999; Heiman & Meston, 1997b). For example, sexual desire in women is more readily disrupted by relationship factors, and relationship conflicts are thought to be the single most common cause of hypoactive sexual desire in women (Rosen & Leiblum, 1995; Trudel, 2000; Trudel et al., 2001). Study results from Bancroft et al. (in press) also support the link between sexual and relationship distress in women. When examining the predictors of distress about sexuality among women, Bancroft and colleagues found that sexual distress strongly related to women's subjective response during sexual activity with the partner. Subjective response was defined into a composite measure of feeling pleasure, feeling emotionally close, not feeling indifferent, or having unpleasant feelings. Authors concluded that womens' emotional well-being, report of positive and/or negative feelings, and emotional closeness to the partner during the sexual encounter were identified as strong determinants of distress about the relationship and of sexual distress.

Other studies found that sexual dysfunctions do not necessarily lead to relationship distress or to unsatisfying sexual and/or couple relationships. A notable proportion of satisfied or happily married couples with sexual problems report being sexually satisfied despite their sexual dysfunctions (Frank, Anderson, & Rubenstein, 1978; Heiman & Meston, 1997b; Heiman, 2000). Partners' tolerance is thus heavily influenced by relationship distress and sexual satisfaction. Our clinical observations corroborate with research results indicating that low couple and sexual satisfaction are associated with lower tolerance of sexual dysfunctions.

A partner's decision to address his or her sexual problem is also influenced by explicit or implicit survival threats to the relationship and by witnessing distress in the other partner. For example, young couples eager to start a family but unable to complete coitus due to vaginismus, erectile disorder, or delayed or absent ejaculation may jeopardize their plans to have children and potentially endanger the relationship (Heiman & Meston, 1997a). In addition, the level of distress displayed by the partner often motivates partners to address the problem. For example, men with premature ejaculation often refer to the women's discontent as their main reason for wanting to resolve the problem. For lifelong and generalized hypoactive sexual desire, couples are faced with a problem that shows little progress over time even though partners were aware of the problem when they originally got involved. The painful decision of whether to stay in a relationship with infrequent sexual encounters and few pleasurable, sexually satisfying activities is contemplated by both partners (LoPiccolo, 1992; Rosen & Leiblum, 1995; Trudel, 2000).

The assessment of couples' history with sexual dysfunctions generally aims at determining whether symptoms are lifelong or present from the very beginning of the relationship. Sexual symptoms also may be acquired or follow a clearly identifiable event occurring at a specific point later in the relationship. The onset of sexual dysfunctions can be sudden or gradual. For instance, when asked about when the problem started, partners mention the arrival of children as not only an important couple transition but also a period linked to decreases in nonsexual and sexual intimacy (Apt & Hurlbert, 1992; Heiman & Grafton-Becker, 1989; Heiman & Meston, 1997).

Not surprisingly, sexual and couple relationship problems existing prior to the arrival of children typically are exacerbated because of increased demands and stress on couples. Lifelong sexual dysfunctions often correlate with individual-based predisposing factors and may persist throughout the relationship history, whereas acquired sexual dysfunctions stem from relationship-based factors and may resolve at some point in the relationship. The specific nature of these factors and their potential influence on sexual symptoms are discussed next.

Predisposing and/or Precipitating Factors to Sexual Dysfunctions

Sexual dysfunctions diagnosis includes a history of variables influencing the onset and course of sexual symptoms throughout the couple's history. Hawton's psychosocial model is of clinical utility for the classification of causal variables into three factors—the predisposing, precipitating, and maintaining factors (Hawton & Catalan, 1986). According to Hawton, assessment of sexual problems aims at identifying the multidimensional determinants, defined as psychological, social/relational, or medical factors that either predispose, precipitate, or maintain sexual symptoms.

Based on Hawton's model of assessing influential factors from an historical perspective (e.g., factors related to onset are usually assessed first), we describe the predisposing and precipitating factors in this section and discuss maintaining factors throughout the last two sections of the chapter. We integrate maintaining factors into the last sections of the chapter because these sections focus on presenting the course of sexual dysfunctions across the couple's developmental lifespan and integrating partners' coping strategies. We consider coping strategies as similar to maintaining factors because of their influence on maintaining sexual symptoms and for their occurrence within the context of the couple's various developmental phases.

Predisposing factors to sexual dysfunctions usually exist prior to and/or at the outset of the current relationship and are considered important variables in diagnosing individuals with primary and generalized sexual dysfunctions (e.g., the sexual problem is lifelong and manifests itself across all types of sexual activities). Research shows that compared to other types of sexual dysfunctions, primary and generalized sexual problems are more treatment resistant (Heiman, 2002; Kaplan, 1995; Leiblum & Rosen, 2000; McCarthy, 1997; Wincze & Carey, 2001). Predisposing psychosocial factors may include early traumatic sexual experiences, disturbed family patterns, and repeated exposure to negative sexual education messages or experiences. For instance, studies consistently report that sexually victimized individuals are at higher risk of developing sexual dysfunctions that are carried from one relationship to another or through multiple relationships (Heiman, 2001; Heiman & Meston, 1997a; Laumann et al., 1999; Maurice, 1999; Trudel, 1991). Negative, faulty educational or parental messages, although rarely independent causes, also correlate with increased vulnerability to sexual dysfunctions. For example, development of sexual identity, body image, first coital encounter, and sexual trauma are crucial components of women's history that can predispose to sexual dysfunctions (Heiman, 2000; Heiman, Gladue, Roberts, & LoPiccolo, 1986; Heiman & Meston, 1997a). In addition, women taught to believe that the main purpose of sex is to satisfy men's sexual needs and that sexual assertiveness and attainment of orgasm are mainly the men's sexual responsibilities are more susceptible to developing desire or orgasm problems (Barbach, 1976; Cotten-Huston & Wheeler, 1983; Ellis, 1977).

Congenital physical conditions may also predispose to sexual dysfunctions. They range from basic neuroendocrine functions to anatomical formation of the genital area to biologically induced syndromes, such as juvenile-onset diabetes. Conditions can either be reversible, medically controlled, or irreversible (Kaplan, 1983). For instance, a woman with a small vaginal structure can be predisposed to both female dyspareunia and female sexual arousal disorder. Men with erectile disorder caused by congenital Peyronie's disease can be predisposed to male dyspareunia because of the pain felt during penetration and/or ejaculation (Lue et al., 1999).

Precipitating factors consist of events in couples' distant past that have an effect on the functioning of the present relationship. Precipitating events are best understood as stressful events that produce a destabilizing effect on partners, forcing them into script or role changes, which in turn negatively impact sexual and couple relationships. Precipitating events are often associated with acquired or secondary sexual dysfunctions. Sexual dysfunctions may thus be precipitated by a specific event and are secondary to periods of "normal" adequate sexual functioning. For some couples, personal or relational events may trigger or precipitate sexual symptoms that, although mild in the beginning of the relationship, progressively evolve into sexual dysfunction. The distinction between lifelong versus acquired sexual dysfunctions may thus be difficult to establish due to the presence of mild sexual symptoms early in the relationship history and the absence of a period of "normal" sexual functioning.

Other precipitating factors of sexual dysfunctions include normative developmental events serving as distinct biological markers (e.g., specific age-related periods along the individual lifespan) that may or may not be accompanied by acute illness or medical procedures (Havighurst, 1981; Levinson, Darrow, Klein, Levinson, & McKee, 1978). Useful as diagnostic reference points with their associated clinical features, each biological marker encompasses a range of physical and psychosocial changes that may have significant effects on sexual functioning.

Biological markers associated with reproduction that impact sexuality include the onset of menses and ongoing menstrual cycles, the first ejaculation (Dennerstein et al., 1994; Sanders, Warner, & Backstrom, 1983), and the pregnancy period with prenatal and postnatal changes, lactation, and postpartum states. Research has shown important biological changes for women that are related to pregnancy, especially the trimestrial phase (Apt & Hurlbert, 1992), continued lactation (Alder & Bancroft, 1988), and menapause (Heiman & Meston, 1997b; McCoy, 2001). All have been found to affect not only womens' overall quality of life but also their experience of sexuality. For example, during pregnancy, the presence of physical symptoms such as interrupted sleep, lower energy levels, fatigue, and discomfort may act as important stressors and diminish sexual desire and the frequency of sexual activities (see Haugen, Schmutzer, & Wenzel, chapter 17, this volume, for further discussion on the issues related to the effects of pregnancy and postpartum sexuality on the relationship). Finally, the transition to menopause, with symptoms such as hot flashes, vaginal dryness, and atrophy, may negatively affect sexual desire and arousal states (Bancroft, Graham, & McCoy, 2001; Heiman, 1998; Heiman & Meston, 1997b; Leiblum & Sachs, 2002; McCoy & Davidson, 1985). Currently, researchers are critically exploring replacing levels of hormones for both genders.

Sexual problems associated with transitional periods are characterized for the majority of women by decreased sexual desire, arousal, orgasm capacity, and frequency of sexual activities, which may be diagnosed as sexual dysfunctions (Bancroft et al., in press; Heiman & Meston, 1997b; Leiblum & Sachs, 2002; Meyers, et al., 1990). For instance, female dyspareunia is commonly diagnosed as a result of vaginal atrophy because of estrogen deficiencies or the postsurgery effects of either hysterectomy or oophorectomy (Carlson, Miller, & Fowler, 1994; Darling & McKay Smith, 1993; Heiman & Meston, 1997b; McCarthy, 1999; Sherwin & Gelfand, 1987).

For men, changes in sexual functioning associated with age may be accompanied by a progressive decline in sexual desire, arousal, and/or genital response (Bancroft et al., in press). For example, men over the age of 50 may experience age-related diminished sexual desire, penile rigidity, or ability to sustain the erection at some point during the sexual encounter. In response to these changes, 34.8% of men between 40 to

70 years old may develop erectile disorder (Heiman, 2002; Heiman & Meston, 1997b; Leiblum & Segraves, 2000; Martin, 1981; Wincze & Carey, 2001). For other men, decreased production of testosterone with age may be associated with decreased sexual desire and for a small percentage of men be clinically diagnosed as hypogonadism, a condition influencing the development of hypoactive sexual desire and/or erectile disorder (Maurice, 1999; Schiavi, Schreiner-Engel, Mandeli, Schanzer, & Cohen, 1990). We will further illustrate in the next section how partners' attempts to cope with sexual midlife changes not only influence sexual symptoms but also affect the survival of the relationship.

Parallel to biological, lifespan, and other health-related changes acting as precipitants of sexual dysfunctions, psychosocial maturation characterized by identity formation, career choice, and role changes have also been identified as correlates of the aging process. Our clinical observations show that choice of a sexual partner and commitment to a relationship are developmental challenges that can either activate sexual dysfunctions or be threatened by the presence of sexual dysfunctions. For instance, a young man developing premature ejaculation within the context of a new relationship may experience considerable anxiety over the fear of rejection and, as a consequence, hinder his chances of being in a long-term relationship. If the relationship ends without him having a chance to improve his ejaculatory control, performance anxiety and fear of another relationship loss will be carried into the next relationship. Sexual experimentation, a new relationship, and how partners cope with premature ejaculation can either maintain, exacerbate, or alleviate the problem.

Finally, the presence of sudden, unexpected events may be important turning points in the history of a couple's relationship. For instance, partners with a school-age child diagnosed with attention deficit and hyperactivity disorder may report stressful periods both at home and at work. Partners' often notice that during these periods, almost all of their energy and time are devoted to the disruptive child, leaving limited time for each other.

The severity and medical management of certain health events are also known for having direct negative effects on sexual functioning or for precipitating sexual dysfunctions. For example, the diagnosis of major depression and treatment with medication are associated with important sexual side effects such as diminished sexual desire and, with Selective Serotonine Reuntake Inhibitors, increased latency or inability to obtain orgasm (Heiman, 2002; Heiman & Meston, 1997a; Maurice, 1999; Trudel, 2000). Other common events known to precipitate sexual dysfunctions (Schover, 2000) include unexpected pregnancy, job loss, sudden change in partners' physical health (e.g., cardiovascular disease, cancer) or psychological health (e.g., stress-related anxiety, burn-out, or depression).

Developmental Phases Specific to the Couple

Along with partners' individual developmental events or adult life phases, couples also follow a predictable path of development comprised of events serving as markers of change and adaptation (Havighurst, 1981; Levinson et al., 1978). Developmental phases specific to the couple are also known to affect sexual relationships and the course of sexual symptoms. For descriptive purposes, we can divide the time sequence into three phases: the honeymoon phase, the working/responsible phase, and the retirement phase.

The Honeymoon Phase.   Of the three phases, the honeymoon phase is often remembered by couples as a peak period in their sexual functioning and in their degree of couple closeness. Compared to the other relationship phases, the portrait of couples during the honeymoon phase usually includes high frequencies of sexual initiations and activities, a more elaborate sexual scenario due to the experimentation of various types of sexual activities and regular attempts at establishing nonsexual intimacy. Despite the emotional stress of establishing new, exciting but uncertain couple and sexual relationships, the honeymoon phase may be considered as one of the couple's rare periods of "dyadic synchrony" or of high couple cohesiveness. Partners focus on and engage in mutual efforts at building the foundations of the relationship (e.g., fantasizing about the self in relation to the partner, observing, questioning, interpreting interactions, expressing, initiating, or being receptive to ways of increasing intimacy). Once secure, partners' focus shifts to external conditions of the relationship (e.g., building the nest, discussing children, meeting financial responsibilities).

The course of sexual dysfunctions is influenced by adaptation to each phase and is to be understood within the context of past and upcoming future events. For example, it is clinically relevant to assess female hypoactive sexual desire within the context of the duration of the relationship because hypoactive sexual desire symptoms may manifest differently during the couple's various developmental phases. Hypoactive sexual desire symptoms during the honeymoon phase may be mild in severity when compared to more severe symptoms found during the working/responsible couple phase. Research results show that the transition from the honeymoon into the working/responsible phase is often characterized by increased responsibilities that coincide with reduced couple time and reduced frequency of sexual activities, which may in turn precipitate hypoactive sexual desire disorder (Basson, 2000; Heiman & Meston, 1997a). Considering the high degree of couple cohesiveness and, for some couples the absence of sexual problems, partners often refer to the honeymoon phase as an ideal period of their sexual functioning that they wish they could return to (e.g., I wish my partner could initiate sex as she/he did when we started being sexual. I know it was a special time, but if she was able to do it then, why can't she do it again?).

Despite their sexual difficulties, couples with sexual dysfunctions often present with a high degree of couple cohesiveness in their desire to form a relationship. However, couples with sexual dysfunctions differ from couples without sexual problems in their experience of positive versus negative emotions, in their level of cognitive interference with sexual feelings, and in their attempts at building intimacy that can be manifest from the very beginning of the relationship (Beck & Barlow, 1986; Beck, Barlow & Sakheim, 1983; Rowland & Heiman, 1991). For example, on starting a new relationship, a man with erectile disorder may experience a strong desire to build a relationship but, at the same time, report intense fears of performance failure. He may experience attraction and excitement at the same time as having disturbing thoughts such as "I probably won't be able to have or keep my erection and satisfy her." She, in turn, may be affected by his fears but, more important, may witness his hesitant or inconsistent attempts at building intimacy and may question his intentions and commitment to the relationship. For these couples, the honeymoon phase may not be a positive, early phase of their relationship because of sexual symptoms that threaten the survival of the relationship.

For couples experiencing an idealized honeymoon phase, the positive components of this period can serve to temporarily buffer the severity of sexual dysfunctions and, for some couples, completely mask sexual symptoms that preceded the relationship. For example, during the honeymoon phase of the relationship, women with acquired hypoactive sexual desire present with less severe sexual symptoms by reporting more frequent, spontaneous sexual desire versus receptive sexual desire (i.e., internally versus externally motivated sexual desire) and show greater initiation of sexual activities with the partner. At later stages of the relationship, changes in the nature of sexual desire may occur and are characterized by more frequent receptive versus spontaneous sexual desire with sexual activities most often occurring in response to the partner's sexual initiation. Moreover, as the relationship ages, other hypoactive sexual desire symptoms may worsen and can range from a lack of either spontaneous or receptive sexual desire to an absence of sexual initiations and/or frequent refusal of the partner's sexual initiations. Thus, as previously noted, the criteria for female hypoactive sexual desire should reflect relationship maturation and transformations in the nature of sexual desire. Adding the dimension of changes in sexual desire within the context of long-term relationships improves diagnostic specificity for women with hypoactive sexual desire (Basson, 2001b; Heiman, 2001).

In addition to changes in hypoactive sexual desire symptoms as the couple evolves, partners' desire for intimacy is influenced by the presence of stressful, negative relationship-based events (e.g., conflicts over unresolved problems, territorial or ranking order conflict, repeated disappointing sexual experiences). Unresolved conflicts and ongoing negative sexual encounters are often associated with physical and/or emotional distancing between partners that may be followed by a postconflict reconciliation period where partners try to reconnect.

The presence of sexual difficulties in the honeymoon and early phase of the relationship may trigger a variety of emotional, cognitive, and behavioral reactions from both partners that serve as coping attempts. Despite the generally positive effects of a new relationship on partners' desire for intimacy, sexual difficulties can be felt by partners as an unpleasant intruder. Cognitively, partners begin to form causal interpretations such as questioning the history of the problem with previous sexual partners and wondering if they are sexually inadequate or if they are not attractive sexually.

Sexual problems may also be seen by young couples as obstacles that are part of the normal adjustment process of adapting to many relationship aspects such as learning to cope with each other's personal problems, lifestyle preferences, opinions, and choices. Sexual adjustments may thus be attributed to the novelty of the relationship and its challenges (e.g., performance anxiety, fears of rejection). For both partners, sexual symptoms may be tolerated in the hope that problems will be worked through as the couple moves into a secure, trusting relationship. They may also deal with their insecurity by seeking greater sexual or nonsexual intimacy such as showing mutual support, engaging in positive, loving behaviors, exploring their sexuality verbally or nonverbally, and/or trying to adapt their sexual encounters to the sexual problem.

Adjustment to sexual dysfunctions early in the relationship is often characterized by mixed outcomes. Important mediating variables on the adjustment process often relate to the history of the sexual problem and to partners' cognitive–emotional management of symptoms. For example, our clinical observations indicate that adjustment is more likely to be difficult when sexual symptoms persist over multiple relationships and/or show little progress. In addition, the way partners interpret and react to sexual symptoms correlates with adjustment. As will be discussed in the last section of the chapter, coping strategies such as retreating and isolating from the partner to deal with feelings of shame, frustration, or sadness not only results in poor long-term adjustment to sexual symptoms but also compromises the survival of the relationship.

The Working/Responsible Phase.   As the relationship evolves from the honeymoon phase into the working/responsible phase, partners typically face responsibilities and practical demands that negatively affect the attention and time spent on each other, including their sexual relationship. For instance, partners may be actively involved in securing their relationship, defined as making important financial and/or career investments (e.g., buying a house, establishing a career path), deciding about having children, and engaging in other goal-oriented commitment decisions. These events can be significant event markers on the couple's sexuality (Apt et al., 1992; Heiman & Meston, 1997a; Leiblum & Sachs, 2002; Spence, 1997). For example, adaptation to these transitional events impacts couples' frequency and quality of sexual interactions, sometimes causing sexual dysfunctions or compromising their mutual efforts at resolving the sexual problem.

Career choice and establishment are often identified as important psychosocial lifespan events in the lives of men and women (Havighurst, 1981; Levinson et al., 1978). Adaptation to the role of the working individual with increasing demands and responsibilities impacts couple and sexual relationships and can activate sexual dysfunctions. For example, the cumulative effect of fulfilling many roles at once is a well-known precipitating factor for hypoactive sexual desire in women (Trudel et al, 2001). The chronic demands of the dual roles of career and parenting can interfere with womens' connection with their individual sexual desire and/or their connection to their role as a sexual partner. In addition, how partners define and set personal expectations and attempt to fulfill career and parenting roles are important moderating variables in understanding the impact of these transitional periods on sexuality. Dealing with the partner's distress and responding to the partner's sexual expectations often serve as additional pressures, evolving into relationship tension and diminishing desire for sexual intimacy. In some cases of hypoactive sexual desire in women, territorial conflicts such as how space and time are structured can result in chronic emotional and physical distancing between partners and is mentioned by both partners as the most distressing consequence (or cause) of hypoactive sexual desire disorder.

The Retirement Phase.   In the couple's mature years, sexuality and sexual dysfunctions are experienced in the context of characteristic midlife and late-life developmental events. These events may include a midlife sexual crisis, an intense period where one's sexuality along with other life areas are reexamined; the presence of challenging mental or physical health conditions; or simply facing the reality of aging and mortality. As previously mentioned, normative sexual changes linked to age include a gradual diminution of sexual response speed and intensity (e.g., slower arousal), increased time to reach orgasm, and less intense orgasms.

Empirical reports from important epidemiological research such as the Laumann and colleagues study (1994) show that couples do maintain some level of active sexual life into their later years (Bretschneider & McCoy, 1988; Leiblum & Segraves, 2000; Martin, 1981; Schiavi et al., 1990). Aside from these reports, we still have limited knowledge about the state of ongoing sexual dysfunctions in older couples, the state of persisting sexual symptoms, and their effects on couple and sexual relationships. In addition, some individuals may remain sexually functional but no longer engage in sex because of a lack of interest, which may not be diagnosed as a sexual dysfunction (e.g., if individuals are not reporting distress or do not regard it as a problem).

The retirement phase is often associated with the children leaving home. For some couples, this period symbolizes a positive reunification, a time to focus again on the internal aspects of their relationship (e.g., quality of communication, couple closeness, and desire for intimacy) and work on those aspects in need of attention, including sexuality. At this stage of couple life, the prospect of growing old in a peaceful and mutually supportive relationship can serve as an important motivator for couples to accept or resolve their problems. For other couples, the departure of the children elicits feelings of anxiety, sadness, or frustration at having to deal with long-lasting, unresolved couple and sexual relationship problems. For these couples, the thought of spending the latter part of life with the partner activates the decision to end their troubled relationship.

Although we proposed that most aging couples (i.e., age of relationship) go through a predictable sequence of developmental phases, each phase follows partners' development as aging individuals (i.e., age of partners). Some phases are more representative of the lives of younger versus older partners because of events partners of varying age typically face. We defined events as relationship stressors because of their negative influence on the onset and course of sexual symptoms. Relationship stressors are associated with significant shifts in relationship patterns such as taking partners' attention and energy away from their couple and sexual relationships.

For example, the working/responsible phase typically concerns younger partners, includes a number of adaptation changes, and is characterized by partners' high involvement in childbirth and care, dual careers, and for some, caring of immediate parents and/or relatives. The burden of these events may be mediated by partners' mutual sharing of responsibilities that may in turn lead to a differential impact on the couple. For example, Schwartz (1994) proposes that compared to traditional marriages, peer marriages are based on equality and are characterized by partners' mutual sharing of childrearing, chores, and decision making. Peer marriages thus result in intense companionship, a collaborative working alliance, and a breakdown of gender-specific task allocation. It would be interesting to study the incidence and management of sexual dysfunctions in peer versus traditional marriages and to specifically compare the outcome of sexual symptom resolution. We speculate that equal sharing may be associated with a better outcome because of the increased likelihood that a collaborative alliance in major relationship areas may generalize to the sharing of responsibility for sexual symptoms. This, in turn, may limit the severity and consequences of sexual problems for peer couples.

The retirement phase concerns older partners. For the most part, influential events on couple and sexual relationships relate to mental and/or physical health changes and to significant modifications in the support system such as the loss of loved ones, relatives, or friends. Other events that may compromise the quality of couple and sexual relationships include the ongoing support and care of grown-up children and/or grandchildren. In addition to these loads, older partners are at increased risk of facing illness. This may result in important shifts in the nature of relationship interactions such the negative impact of the patient–caregiver role on their couple and sexual lives.

COPING WITH THE CONSEQUENCES OF SEXUAL DYSFUNCTIONS

Despite widespread media coverage of Viagra™ for treating erectile disorder and public health messages from the office of the Surgeon General (2001)stating that "sexuality is a fundamental part of human life" (p. ii), couples rarely discuss sexual matters. For some couples, sexual issues are linked to personal taboos and/or give rise to mutual feelings of uneasiness or shame; whereas for others, sexuality is associated with feelings of guilt, frustration, or helplessness.

Timing of the impact of sexual symptoms on couples is not only influenced by specific events in the couple's developmental phases but also by partners' coping style or mutual attempts at alleviating the problem. Despite an absence of empirical research specific to partners' strategies for coping with sexual dysfunctions, we will present, in this last section, our clinical observations of couples' reactive coping that may serve to maintain sexual dysfunctions .

In men and women, coping with sexual problems is often a function of their usual coping styles for other relationship difficulties. Couples, however, report that sexual problems are especially challenging because of their potential and unpredictable consequences. The process of coping with sexual dysfunctions may thus consist of covert (i.e., internal) or overt (i.e., external) strategies that may involve the self and/or the partner. Covert coping attempts include recognition, contemplation of solutions, and formation of behavioral intentions. Overt coping includes the actual application of solutions with and without the partner. Assessment of each partner's history of overt coping often shows that each of them attempted a variety of strategies such as research-ing the sexual problem (e.g., self-help books, visiting web sites, talking to significant others), altering the sexual scenario (e.g., trying or avoiding various sexual activities), experimenting with sexual aids (e.g., sexual toys, over-the-counter or other nonpre-scribed substances) or seeking professional help (e.g., medication, individual and/or couple sex therapy).

Partners typically exhibit different rates of readiness to engage in the coping pro-cess. The more active partner may feel frustrated at the slow progress, whereas the passive, slower-paced partner may feel pressured and frustrated at lagging behind and/or being pushed into overt coping. In addition, each partner may feel controlled by the other's coping style. For instance, it is not uncommon for the partner with sex-ual symptoms to overutilize behavioral intentions such as intending to address the sexual problem or contemplating solutions such as trying specific treatment methods for the problem (e.g., medication). Overutilization of covert strategies may either stag-nate or worsen sexual symptoms and reduce the partner's credibility about his/her willingness to address the problem.

Over the course of the couple relationship, long-term coping with sexual dysfunc-tions typically includes periods of active versus passive coping. Active periods of coping occur in response to worsening of sexual symptoms and include overt coping strategies such as partners' trial of various solutions that may lead to temporary relief of the problem. Passive periods of coping are characterized by covert strategies and by tolerance of sexual symptoms.

Whether sexual symptoms are short- or long-term in duration, the process of ac-tive coping commonly starts with partners' recognition of the sexual dysfunction (i.e., recognizing that there is a sexual problem) that may be influenced by the couple's tran-sition to a specific phase of their relationship. For example, the end of the honeymoon phase often results in a much clearer perception of sexual difficulties, combined with unsettled feelings of disappointment and frustration at persisting sexual symptoms. As a result, some couples try to actively cope and limit the consequences of sexual dysfunctions on their relationship, whereas other couples adopt a passive coping style characterized by partners' decisions, from implicit understandings between them, to stay in the relationship in spite of problematic sexuality.

We indicated earlier that partners' reactive patterns and history of coping attempts can either maintain sexual problems or influence the frequency of sexual activities with the partner. Our clinical observations also indicate that partners' coping attempts to deal with the problem may result in the survival of the couple relationship as opposed to the survival of the sexual relationship. There is an important distinction between the survival of the couple and the maintenance of couple sexual activities. Dysfunctional sexuality does not necessarily lead to couple dissolution and for a significant propor-tion of couples, sexual symptoms are endured over a number of years (Trudel et al., 2001). Long-term adaptation to sexual dysfunctions and gradual cessation of coping attempts are likely consequences of emotional fatigue from repeated disappointing results, difficulty maintaining coping attempts, or gradual acceptance of the problem. For these couples, adaptation to sexual dysfunctions may result in a relationship with no sexual activities (McCabe, 1997; McCarthy, 1997).

Sexual consequences of sexual dysfunctions generally include significant modi-fications in the frequency of sexual activities, the quality of sexual encounters, and the degree of sexual cohesion between partners. Couples with sexual dysfunctions typically report a diminished frequency of sexual activities and describe a ritualized, unsatisfying sexual interaction pattern comprised of a predictable sequence of sexual events culminating, if possible, in orgasm (Heiman, 2000, Leiblum & Segraves, 2000; Spence, 1997; Trudel et al., 2001). Altering the sexual interaction pattern, such as ex-perimenting with different genital, oral, or coital positions, is usually the couple's first coping attempt to deal with the sexual problem. For example, a couple with erectile disorder may try to solve the problem by experimenting with various types of sexual activities, excluding penetration activities, or finding alternative ways to experience arousal and orgasm.

Assessment of couples' coping with long-term sexual dysfunctions often shows a pattern of limited sexual interactions. For example, couples describe a restricted range of sexual contexts with identified times and performance of specific sexual activities in an attempt to create optimal conditions for sexual encounters to occur. In addition, partners' ineffective coping reactions, such as the abrupt interruption of the sexual encounter or emotional outbursts because of unattained sexual responses, reinforce partners' personal responsibility for their sexual failures. Our clinical work corroborates research results showing the effects of sexual dysfunctions on each partner's subjective experience of his or her sexual encounters and on partner's degree of sexual cohesiveness. For example, couples with hypoactive sexual desire show reduced levels of perceptual congruence in their actual versus desired frequency of sexual activities, in their actual versus expected sexual pleasure for the self and/or the partner, and in their degree of sexual satisfaction (Aubin et al., 2001; Basson et al., 2000; Kaplan, 1983; Trudel, 2000; Trudel, Fortin, & Matte, 1997).

For couples in which the male partner has erectile disorder, it is not uncommon to find clinically important disparities between partners as to how they rate the importance of penile penetration to their sexual enjoyment. The male partner typically reports penile penetration as very or extremely important to his enjoyment of sexual encounters. For his partner, penile penetration is often considered less central to her sexual enjoyment, and sexual pleasure instead derives from other types of sexual activities and/or the conditions surrounding sexual activities such as increased intimacy and closeness (Basson, 2000, 2001b; McCabe, 1997; McCarthy, 1998b; Spence, 1997). Partners' differences in their rating of penile penetration to their enjoyment also apply to couples without erectile difficulties. Our clinical observations, however, indicate that couples with erectile disorder present with greater disparities in their ratings when compared to ratings of couples without erectile disorder. Greater disparities in ratings for sexually dysfunctional couples may be in part explained by partners' different cognitive focus during their sexual encounters. For example, the male partner often reports on his increased attention to his penile performance, whereas the woman reports on her increased attention to other aspects of the sexual encounter.

Partners with sexual dysfunctions generally agree that negative emotional, cognitive, and behavioral sexual consequences from repeated disappointing sexual encounters determine how they perceive their current and future sexual encounters (Ellis, 1977; Gagnon et al., 1982; Trudel, 1991). For example, when thinking about having a sexual encounter with his partner, a man with premature ejaculation is emotionally and cognitively reminded of his own and/or his partner's anxiety and frustration. He also anticipates having problems in feeling pleasure and arousal but most important, predicts that he again will reach orgasm prematurely (Kaplan, 1989).

Similar cognitive–emotional consequences of sexual dysfunctions have also been observed in women. Rosen and Leiblum (1989) suggested that the emotional consequences of hypoactive sexual desire correspond more to "response" anxiety than to "performance" anxiety. When asked to engage in a sexual encounter, a woman with hypoactive sexual desire may refuse her partner's sexual initiation based on her anticipation that she will not be able to respond with desire, pleasure, or arousal during the sexual encounter. Interestingly, some women with hypoactive sexual desire do report being able to reach orgasm with limited sexual desire, a situation analogous to the male ejaculation with limited sexual desire or pleasure.

From a dyadic perspective, it is interesting to highlight differences between partners regarding what they specifically recall or find most distressing about their sexual experiences. Men with sexual dysfunctions often retain vivid images associated with failed sexual encounters, such as the timing of their ejaculation or loss of their erection. For partners of men with erectile disorder, images of the men's frustration, anger, or unhappiness as well as the men's questioning of their own attractiveness are mentioned as primary sources of distress. Men with erectile disorder report being very disappointed and frustrated at not being able to perform or feeling inadequate and diminished in their "manhood" and at not being able to satisfy their partner. Although the women recognize their own feelings of disappointment and anger, they also tend to stress how they feel sad and helpless at witnessing the partner's negative reactions and how limited an impact their attempts to help had.

Patterns of different cognitive–emotional responses between partners are also seen in couples with female sexual dysfunctions. Some women diagnosed with secondary hypoactive sexual desire (e.g., loss of sexual desire secondary to a period of normal sexual desire) report feeling very troubled by not knowing why they lost their sexual desire, distressed by refusing their partner's sexual advances, and frustrated by their partners' persisting faulty causal attributions of their refusals (Trudel et al., 2001). Partners of women with hypoactive sexual desire may experience significant distress from questioning their own sexual skills as a causal explanation for the women's lack of sexual desire. Cognitively, the men will look for inadequacies in their sexual abilities and conclude that if their partner does not desire them sexually, it must be because they have not succeeded in fulfilling them sexually. Although this may be true of some couples, the majority of women with hypoactive sexual desire do not consider their partners' sexual skills as a causal factor for their lack of sexual desire and assuming so builds resentment and frustration in both partners.

Even though sexual symptoms most clearly impact couples' sexual relationships, our clinical observations indicate that it is when symptoms permeate the areas of communication and nonsexual intimacy that women, as compared to men, exhibit lower tolerance for the sexual problem and decide to engage in the process of coping. We clinically noted that couples' communication is influenced by partners' negative cognitive–emotional states such as sadness, anger, or frustration that are linked to their sexual problems. Research specifically shows that couples with sexual dysfunctions present with diminished frequency of communication about the sexual problem and a negative impact of sexual dysfunctions on partners' disclosing and listening skills (Ackerman & Carey, 1995; Spence, 1997; Snyder & Berg, 1983; Trudel et al., 2001; Zimmer, 1989).

The gradual buildup of emotional hurts over negative sexual experiences may severely affect the couple's communication by leading to a higher incidence of overt criticisms or reproaches and/or ceasing of any active listening (Baucom & Epstein, 1990; Beck, 1988; McCabe, 1997; Trudel, Boulos, & Matte, 1993; Trudel et al., 1997). In our clinical experience, partners often describe circular discussions where they are left with the overwhelming feelings of not being understood and of helplessness and hopelessness about their future as a sexual couple. For other couples, sexual problems are mentioned in the context of emotional turmoil, resulting in truncated communication and defensive listening about how each partner experiences the problem.

The influence of sexual dysfunctions on communication is mediated by couples' coping and/or communication responses. We borrow from other authors' characterization of couples' coping and/or communication responses as either passive/avoidant versus overt/emotionally expressive (Gottman & Levenson, 1992; Jacobson & Folette, 1985; McCarthy, 1999; Wright, 1985). The passive/avoidant coping response is usually defined as the internalization of emotions and/or avoidance of verbal communication or interaction with the partner about negative emotional states. States of anger or sadness may be passively expressed by engaging in a retreat or isolation from the partner.

The overt/emotionally expressive coping response generally refers to the expression of emotions and/or attempts to engage in verbal communication or interaction with the partner. Negative emotional states are usually expressed by reaching out verbally to the partner.

Partners may exhibit different coping and/or communication responses to cope with sexual problems. For example, one partner may use passive/avoidant coping, such as lack of verbal communication or physical contact, and the other partner may use overt/emotional coping, such as disclosure of sexual discontent and confrontation. To a certain extent, partners learn to adjust and accept their differences in coping. We noted, however, that ongoing problems in partners' management of their different coping styles are associated with maintenance of sexual symptoms and reduced levels of couple intimacy.

Dysfunctional sexuality, just like functional sexuality, is thus identified by the majority of couples as an important source of conflict because of differences or misunderstandings in coping and/or communication responses. Maintenance of sexual symptoms is often associated with ongoing feelings of frustration or sadness. For example, these feelings may be expressed through sexual indifference, refusals, or avoidance by one partner and through sexual criticisms or confrontation by the other, reducing partners' desire for intimacy (Baucom & Epstein, 1990; Beck, 1988; Renshaw, 2001; Schnarch, 1991; Verhulst & Heiman, 1988).

As discussed next, couples' frequency and quality of nonsexual intimacy can be dramatically affected by sexual dysfunctions. Research results show that partners' attempts at building nonsexual intimacy are sometimes scarce and often overtaken by avoidance strategies that are generalized from sexual to nonsexual intimacy situations (Bancroft, Graham, & McCord, 2001; McCabe, 1997; McCarthy, 1999; Purnine & Carey, 1997; Spence, 1997; Trudel, 2000). Nonsexual intimacy is behaviorally defined as the couples' repertoire of verbal, nonverbal, and behavioral attempts to convey a message of love and appreciation for the other. Nonsexual intimacy also refers to the frequency and quality of time partners spend together as a couple. Both nonsexual and sexual intimacy, because of their strong ties with love and trust, represent significant areas of distress for most couples with sexual dysfunctions. Specific consequences of sexual problems to the couple are characterized by the progressive avoidance of sexual encounters with the partner as well as avoidance of affectionate physical contact and, as a result, the reduced expression of positive, loving feelings toward the other (McCabe, 1997; Pridal & LoPiccolo, 2000).

For couples with sexual dysfunctions, we clinically observed that the frequency of time spent with the partner in relaxed, pleasurable activities is relatively low if compared to the honeymoon phase or prior to the onset of sexual problems. It is, however, not clear how sexual dysfunctions relate to each partner's greater involvement in other nonrelationship tasks such as career advancement and childrearing during the couple's working/provider phase. Working outside of the home or raising children implies time demands that decrease the opportunities for individual pursuits as well as joint leisure activities (i.e., not task or project driven). It is often difficult to identify whether these conditions cause sexual dysfunctions or whether sexual dysfunctions maintain these conditions. Comparing couples before versus after the onset of sexual dysfunctions or couples with versus without sexual dysfunctions on the frequency and quality of couple time would be promising avenues.

The distinction between sexual and nonsexual intimacy can be ambiguous. Partners' confusion occurs when physical, nonsexual behaviors such as nongenital caressing or other affectionate physical gestures are misinterpreted as sexual initiations (LoPiccolo, 1977). In addition, it is typically more difficult for men than women to be intimate without the hope of a sexual result, particularly when sexual encounters become less frequent or irregular (McCabe, 1997).

For some couples with sexual dysfunctions, the avoidance of physical intimacy may be due to performance fears or a buildup of negative feelings toward the partner (Heiman, 2001; McCabe, 1997; McCarthy, 1984; Renshaw, 2001). Revisiting unpleasant cognitive–emotional consequences of sexual dysfunctions for the self or for the partner (e.g., to experience one's own or the other's feelings of sadness or frustration) negatively affects partners' decisions to engage in any form of intimacy. Lack of clarification of one's intentions, miscommunication of needs for closeness, and the absence of negotiation about a nonsexual outcome often interfere with nonsexual and/or sexual intimacy. For some couples, physical proximity becomes intolerable, and they agree to a sexual moratorium that may include separate sleeping arrangements.

This type of emotional and/or physical distancing places a serious strain on both partners. Spouses often report feeling frustrated or sad at the lack of physical contact and emotional intimacy, at not feeling close to each other, or at not being able to express or receive positive loving affection with the partner (Pridal & LoPiccolo, 2000). We borrow from the systemic concept of a vicious cycle of not having sex because of lack of couple closeness or of not having couple closeness because of lack of sexuality for understanding partners' resistance to intimacy (Verhulst & Heiman 1979; Wright, 1985). For example, a woman with a partner with premature ejaculation may complain of her inability to express positive loving feelings because of her fear of evoking a sexual response in her partner and reminding him of his sexual dysfunction. He, in turn, may complain of feeling sexually inadequate, undesired, or unloved because of her lack of affectionate behaviors and/or sexual initiation.

We conclude this section with a discussion of couples who engage in sexual activities that may or not include sexual experimentation outside the relationship. Some partners cope with sexual dysfunctions by resorting to personal ritualized sexual scenarios or to extramarital relationships. Because of their secretive, hidden nature, out-of-relationship strategies destabilize essential components of the couple system, such as partners' mutual honesty, trust, and sense of security (Ackerman & Carey, 1995; Leitenberg & Henning, 1995). With disclosure, there is often an effort to manage feelings of betrayal and anger as well as to try to rebuild mutual feelings of love and trust. This recovery process may impair the desire for intimacy and may delay addressing a sexual dysfunction. For example, the longer duration extramarital affair requires a more complex recovery process for both partners and carries a greater risk of worsening sexual symptoms.

Although it seems tempting to conclude that some partners engage in separate sexual lives because of their enduring sexual problems (Pittman, 1989), this argument certainly is not true of all couples with sexual dysfunctions. A closer examination of partners' personal sexual history may sometimes lead one to question whether these coping strategies are used specifically to deal with sexual symptoms or if they are more reflective of a personal coping style for dealing with a variety of problems, including sexual dysfunctions. For instance, an individual with a sexual dysfunction or with a diagnosed partner may justify a history of extramarital relationships as a coping strategy, using it as an excuse for his or her inability to deal with extramarital relationship urges or other commitment issues.

In summary, assessment of the history, etiological nature, and consequences of sexual symptoms on the couple relationship is characterized by a complex set of interacting personal and/or relationship variables. Despite meeting the predetermined symptom criteria for a sexual dysfunction, diagnosed couples present with an unique clinical portrait of how sexual symptoms emerged and developed. Thus, important variations may be observed from one couple to another in the duration of symptoms that may in part be due to differences between partners in symptom recognition and tolerance. Partners typically differ in their perception of distress and the extent of the problem on the viability and overall quality of their relationship.

As a result, these disparities delay addressing the sexual problem and contribute to increases in the severity of symptoms over time.

The etiological nature of sexual symptoms is not only multidimensional but also specific to each couple's relationship history. Based on Hawton's model, we organized influencing variables into predisposing, precipitating, or maintaining factors. Factors stem from the individual and/or from the relationship and may consist of psychosocial and/or physiological events. Influential events serve as markers for the onset of sexual symptoms and are also known for their impact on the course of sexual symptoms. Expanding on Hawton's model, we presented influential factors from the perspective of the developing couple and highlighted their occurrence along three phases of couple development. The lifespan perspective helps to identify the multifactorial influences on sexual symptoms and to conceptualize symptoms as intrinsically tied to the historical context and events of the aging couple. Identified as similar to maintaining variables, partners' coping skills and resources were last discussed and recognized for their significant mediating effects of limiting the consequences of sexual dysfunctions on couple and sexual relationships. Disparities between partners in coping styles and/or effectiveness of strategies contribute to the severity of sexual symptoms and influence the consequences of symptoms on communication and on nonsexual and sexual intimacy. Prolonged use of avoidance, defensive listening, or negative confrontation to deal with sexual symptoms significantly diminishes partners' degree of closeness, which in turn leads to diminished nonsexual and sexual intimacy.

CASE DISCUSSION

The following couple case example was chosen because it reflects today's clinical challenges of assessing sexual dysfunctions from a relationship perspective. It serves to illustrate the complex interaction of physiological and psychological determinants related to the onset and course of sexual symptoms. In addition, the case discussion describes how differences in partners' coping responses can maintain erectile disorder and negatively impact on sexual and couple relationships. We will present a systemic assessment of sexual dysfunctions including our analysis of influential variables and partners' coping responses. The names and certain personal information have been altered to protect the identity of the consulting couple.

Roger and Louise

Roger, 58, had retired as a police officer 3 years earlier, and Louise, 51, was a nurse-practitioner employed in a nursing home. They had been married for 13 years and had no children. Roger had a married 23 year-old daughter from a previous marriage. Roger's urologist referred them to therapy after his physical exams and test results showed no physiological etiology for his erectile disorder.

A multimodal approach was used to diagnose the erectile disorder and evaluate other relationship variables. Three assessment modalities were chosen and consisted of (a) semistructured couple and individual interviews (e.g., one for each partner), (b) self-report questionnaires, and (c) release of Roger's medical report and tests results. The semistructured interviews provided information on the nature of the erectile disorder in terms of its onset, course, and influential variables as well as partner's personal, sexual, and relationship history and the current sexual quality of life for the couple.

Self-report questionnaires allowed to gather information about the erectile disorder (e.g., International Index of Erectile Function by Rosen et al., 1997), partners' sexual functioning (e.g., Brief Sexual Function Questionnaire for Men by Reynolds et al., 1988; Female Sexual Function Index by Rosen et al., 2000), couple adjustment (e.g., Dyadic Adjustment Scale by Spanier, 1976), and partners' psychological adjustment (e.g., Brief Symptom Inventory by Derogatis & Melisaratos, 1983).

A summary analysis of results of the International Index of Erectile Function questionnaire (Rosen et al., 1997) served to confirm a secondary and situational type of erectile disorder, with symptoms of moderate intensity and with no medical etiology. The latter specifier was also corroborated by negative medical test results. Although not meeting the diagnostic criteria or reaching test score significance for hypoactive sexual desire disorder on the other male and female sexual functioning questionnaires (Reynolds et al., 1988; Rosen et al., 2000), problems with diminished sexual desire and with partners' cognitive–emotional responses were noted. Results showed that both partners reported frequent avoidance of couple sexual activities, diminished sexual pleasure, and low sexual satisfaction with the frequency and quality of sexual activities. Significant results to the Dyadic Adjustment Scale questionnaire (Spanier, 1976) were obtained and indicated difficulties in partners' overall level of marital adjustment and more specifically in their involvement of mutual couple activities and satisfaction with the frequency of affectionate expression and overall sexual life. No significant results were obtained for partners' psychological adjustment either measured by the global indices of distress or by the primary symptom dimensions of the Brief Symptom Inventory questionnaire (Derogatis & Melisaratos, 1983).

Information gathered from the semistructured interviews revealed that during his sexual history, Roger reported having erectile disorder for about 2 years with onset after he had surgery for chronic obstructive sinusitus. He suffered postsurgery complications, including infection, for about 6 months and mostly recalled feeling fatigued, helpless, and depressed because of his limited energy and activity level. Louise recalled this period as difficult because of her "double caring shifts" at work and at home. She also mentioned feeling fatigued, but she was mostly puzzled and frustrated by the slow recovery process from a procedure she knew had a short recovery time.

Two years after the surgery, both described that their lack of sexual intimacy and the erectile disorder had reached a point, when Louise confronted Roger about their intimacy and sexuality problems, that could no longer be explained by the surgery. She also disclosed her doubts about the future of their relationship. The next week, Roger came home with a Viagra™ prescription, only to witness Louise's greater anger and frustration. It was shortly after this incident that, at Roger's suggestion, they entered couple sex therapy.

Analysis of the influential variables and consequences of the erectile disorder on Roger and Louise's couple and sexual relationships indicated that the erectile disorder was closely tied to the physical and emotional consequences of Roger's surgery. Although direct physical etiology for the erectile disorder had been ruled out, postsurgery fatigue and discomfort contributed to it. In addition, important mediating variables that served to maintain the erectile disorder were Roger's and Louise's different coping styles, characterized by Roger's lack of assertiveness and passive/avoidant style and Louise's emotionally reactive and active/confrontational style.

Attending to Roger's physical needs shifted the couple into a caregiver–patient role that, although acceptable for awhile, progressively steered them away from their relationship and sexual feelings. Difficulties in managing this transitional period were present early on. Both expected a smooth recovery but within a few weeks, exhibited different reactions to postsurgery symptoms, adding relationship complications to the physical ones.

Roger felt anxious and helpless about his surgery outcome. He felt guilty about Louise's extra workload and various dissatisfactions. At the same time, he felt increasingly frustrated at Louise for not understanding and for pressuring him into a recovery process that he felt he had little control over. He dealt with these feelings mostly by internalizing them and by retreating, not wanting to cause further distress. He also kept his decreased sexual desire and erections to himself, thinking it was probably due to the surgery and would improve with time. Thus Roger decided that he would wait to engage in sexual activity until he felt better and had his sexual stamina back. In the meantime, if Louise made a sexual initiation, he would decline.

According to Louise, she was aware that postsurgery complications were relatively rare for Roger's type of surgery. He was expected to resume normal life within a few weeks of the surgery. She reported feeling very concerned about Roger's complications, but she also felt surprised and a little frustrated. She willingly stepped into the caregiver role, thinking that it would only be for a short time. She thus felt increasingly anxious at the lack of progress and the complications. She felt stressed about fulfilling multiple roles, at work and at home, recognizing the burden of being the only one managing the household chores. She also felt irritated by Roger's depressive mood and apathy. She described him as being mostly passive, referring to his inability to reach out to her and express his inner feelings and to his lack of appreciative feedback for all her work. She also felt disappointed about his sexual withdrawal and rare attempts at physical contact or affection.

After making a few subtle attempts at intimacy, she detected Roger's passive resistance from his lack of responding to her or for not engaging in further intimacy. She decided, without telling Roger, that she would not pressure him and would wait for him to let her know when he felt ready for sex. Louise began to suspect something else other than the surgery might be causing his sexual apathy. She felt sad because she remembered thinking that even though they probably would not be able to have sexual intercourse, she hoped that they could still engage in some other form of intimacy such as petting.

Louise's usual way of dealing with her feelings was to let her partner know about her concerns, questions, or dissatisfactions. For example, she mentioned having expressed to Roger how concerned and disappointed she felt about the surgery complications and how stressful it was for her to fulfill her multiple roles. She also emphasized how upset she felt about their limited discussions and at the way he was passively coping with his postsurgery symptoms. She mentioned attempting to communicate her intimacy frustrations by pointing out to Roger how unappreciated she felt because of his lack of positive, caring comments or demonstrations of affection.

Roger recognized that Louise told him very frequently how she felt. However, he specified that he was easily overwhelmed by Louise's emotional reactions. During their discussions, he tried to be supportive by listening to her and by not interrupting, even though he did not agree with her about his lack of appreciation. He tried to express his disagreement by pointing out his efforts at being a good listener and by referring to his appreciation of her help and involvement during his postsurgery recovery. Louise's typical response was to revert back to her dissatisfactions and his lack of understanding about his behaviors causing her distress. Their discussions would often escalate emotionally until Roger ended the conversation by leaving the room or paying attention to other matters. He justified his retreat by stating that the more Louise attempted to prompt him into further discussion or action, the more they would become angry. He believed that the best way to handle anger was to stop the conversation because it might lead to more hurtful words or actions.

As time went by, Roger and Louise felt increasingly frustrated and saddened, not only from their circular discussions and compromised intimacy, but also from Roger's ongoing erectile disorder. Roger was very distressed about his sexual problem. He felt ashamed and inadequate and wondered why he still had erection problems long after his surgery. He also noticed that his sexual stamina was still missing, as evidenced by continuing erection difficulties and by not feeling very sexual, referring to his decreased sexual desire. Roger mentioned having several fears about his sexual problems. He was particularly afraid of learning that there were no physical causes to his sexual problems, but that instead there was a psychological basis to his erectile disorder. He also feared Louise's negative reactions, such as blaming herself or him for being an inadequate sexual partner. He felt unable to deal with these fears and address his sexual problems. Instead, he continued to wish that his sexual problems would get better with time and that he would try to make efforts at having more regular sexual encounters when he had erections hard enough to allow for penetration.

As a result, Roger and Louise's sexual encounters occurred sporadically (once a month), initiated most often by Roger and significantly altered in quality. Both described that sex happened only in the morning and on days where Louise had not worked an overnight shift. On waking with a morning erection, Roger would wake Louise, and both would quickly engage in penetration in order not to lose the erection. After a few thrusts, Roger would typically lose his erection and the encounter would be interrupted. Repeated episodes of this sexual scenario resulted in their complete avoidance of intimacy either by not discussing or engaging in it. In addition, both referred to the buildup of emotional hurt as getting in the way of being affectionate and acknowledged how it presented them from getting closer. Other variables in Roger and Louise's history of couple and sexual relationships predisposed and/or maintained the erectile disorder. Assessment of their sexuality prior to the surgery indicated important disparities in their sexual desire, sexual initiations, attainment of orgasm, and expectations of sexuality. Sexual encounters were almost always instigated by Louise and occurred about three times a week. Their usual sexual scenario included a short period of mutual caressing and a significant proportion of time spent on penile penetration until Louise reached orgasm followed by Roger's orgasm.

Louise explained that sexuality was an important expression of love and commitment and that it was the only time where she felt truly connected with Roger. Moreover, she viewed penetration as a special experience of total couple fusion, allowing her to feel sexually excited and able to achieve orgasm. For Louise, sex was an important part of couple life that should happen naturally unless there is a medical problem. She further admitted feeling uncomfortable with using "artificial" sexual aids such as sexual toys or medication such as Viagra™, perceiving them as intruders in the bedroom.

Roger strongly believed that a man should be committed to his spouse and able to satisfy her, not only sexually but also in other relationship areas. He felt his sexual needs therefore should be met through sexuality within the couple, adding that he derived most of his sexual pleasure from Louise's sexual arousal and attainment of orgasm. He had noticed, however, that prior to the surgery, he started to have trouble keeping his erections long enough for Louise to achieve orgasm, sometimes causing them to interrupt their sexual encounter. Both attributed these problems to Roger's adaptation to the stress of retirement and hoped that "maybe next time, it wouldn't happen."

Although Roger agreed with Louise that sex is an important way of expressing love and feeling connected to her, he recalled feeling just as close to her in other contexts, such as when they had dinner out or played golf. He also admitted having always felt uneasy about Louise's high sexual desire, frequency of sexual initiations, and intensity during their sexual encounters. He sometimes wished for more playful, leisurely sex that could include some extra help when he experienced erectile problems.

Other contributing variables to Roger's and Louise's sexual difficulties concern personal and couple lifespan events. There were normative sexual changes with age, such as Roger's decreased ability to sustain his erection and his loss of penile rigidity. For Louise, menopausal vaginal dryness became a problem, although that was satisfactorily improved by hormone replacement therapy. Roger's sexual changes, however, were left unaddressed, as they had not yet been able to reach a mutually satisfactory solution. Developmentally, Roger and Louise were moving toward the retirement phase of their lives, with accompanying mixed emotions of positive antic- ipations of future projects and increased time spent together, along with uncertainty about their changing roles.

In summary, our clinical impressions were that Roger's surgery and postsurgery recovery period posed as turning points in Roger and Louise's history and were associated with important changes in their couple and sexual relationships. These couple lifespan events served to activate erectile difficulties into a diagnosis of erectile disorder and to escalate ongoing dysfunctional relationship issues. Other variables were identified as predisposing variables to the erectile disorder. They related to significant disparities between Roger and Louise in specific areas of their couple and sexual relationships. These disparities were first observed in their sensate exchanges (e.g., Louise's greater sexual desire, arousal, and specific pace for orgasm) and second, in their perception and rigid beliefs about sexuality within the couple (e.g., the greater importance of sex and penetration for Louise, the connections of sex to love and intimacy, and the nature of sex as a natural act without sexual aids).

In addition, Roger's and Louise's divergent cognitive–emotional style of coping, analogous to ranking-order subsystem interactions (e.g., Roger's lack of assertiveness and passive coping style versus Louise's emotionally reactive and overt coping style) posed as significant maintaining variables on the erectile disorder, and repercussions were observed on the majority of their couple and sexual relationships. Their com- munication was characterized by inefficient problem-solving strategies to deal with Roger's age-related changes. By not verifying personal attributions for the erectile dis- order and by miscommunicating each other's desire for intimacy, they locked them- selves into a vicious communication cycle of attack–retreat. Their nonsexual intimacy was characterized by the progressive avoidance of nonsexual, affectionate behaviors mainly because of the emotional hurts and/or cognitive–emotional connections with their sexuality. Their sexuality was characterized by sporadic sexual encounters, a limited sexual scenario, and by the interruption of sexual encounters when Roger lost his erection.

CONCLUSION

The nature and consequences of sexual dysfunctions have been studied primarily from a clinical perspective; namely, how to assess and treat sexual problems. The indicated approach for the assessment of sexual dysfunctions within the couple is integrative and/or multimodal and includes a collection of methods, both subjective and ob- jective. Subjective measures are collected through clinical interviews and self-report questionnaires, whereas objective measures are mainly obtained from laboratory- induced sexual arousal measurements of genital and other nongenital responses. De- spite efforts to provide operational and reliable guidelines for assessing sexual dys- functions, the field currently lacks research aimed at the empirical testing of methods and instruments, especially from the relationship perspective. We need to improve the definition of sexual dysfunctions and to identify the clinically relevant couple and sexual features as influential factors on sexual dysfunctions. For example, we agree with Bancroft et al.'s (2001) recommendations to question the appropriateness of la- beling women's sexual problems as sexual dysfunctions. As mentioned earlier, sexual difficulties may be indicative of an adaptive coping response to mental health or rela- tionship problems or to other life events (Bancroft et al., in press; Laumann et al., 1999). Further studies are needed to distinguish sexual dysfunctions from sexual problems resulting from life circumstances and to delineate individual from relationship-based variables affecting women's sexual response.

We also suggest to look more closely at the validity and diagnostic efficiency of the integrative, multimodal approach by isolating the effectiveness of methodologies, by varying the format of application, by comparing both partners' responses, and by using quantitative and qualitative measures of couple and sexual relationships.

Because the management of sexual dysfunctions is being influenced by the medical approach to diagnose and treat individuals versus couples (Tiefer, 1986), there is a pressing need to clarify how the couple influences the onset and course of sexual dysfunctions as well as to develop a treatment response. Specifically, studies are needed to document the role of disparities between partners and on partners' cognitive–emotional responses as coping strategies to deal with sexual symptoms. As suggested by most systemic or other relationship-based theories, sexual dysfunctions may be explained by significant differences between partners in the way they perceive and manage their couple and/or sexual interactions. Empirical studies are needed to delineate the exact nature and extent of partners' differential sexual preferences and expectations as well as differences in their needs for love and intimacy that may place them at risk of developing sexual dysfunctions. In addition, considering the negative impact of sexual dysfunctions on couple closeness and intimacy, we need to know more about partners' long-term coping with sexual dysfunctions. For example, what methods and strategies partners use over time, how symptoms are cognitively processed (e.g., perceived and interpreted), and aside from avoidance, what other nonconstructive relationship strategies are associated with maintenance of sexual symptoms.

Data would be helpful to describe the longevity of sexual dysfunctions, their trajectory across the couple's lifespan, their effects on couple and sexual relationships from the couple's younger to older years, and the end points and outcomes of sexual symptoms using different age cohorts of couples (Basson, 2001b). In particular, we could learn from a study of couples with and without sexual dysfunctions, with different types of sexual problems, and the empirical documentation of clinically observed gender differences in the experience of sexuality and sexual dysfunctions.

From a diagnostic standpoint, it is important to expand on the clinical dimensions of relationship distress and satisfaction as diagnostic criteria for both female and male sexual dysfunctions (Basson, 2001a; Basson et al., 2000; Byers, 2001; Fugl-Meyer & Sjogren Fugl-Meyer, 1999; Heiman & Grafton-Becker, 1989). We suggest specifying the sources of sexual distress, such as distinguishing relationship from personal distress and identifying factors in partners' differential cognitive–emotional coping styles. In addition, treating couple versus individual sexual satisfaction as separate entities would improve our understanding of the relative contribution of each set of variables to sexual dysfunctions.

Despite our efforts to profile a basic clinical portrait of couples with sexual dysfunctions, we recognize that we have only outlined some of the relationship issues. Many other clinical observations, systemic or theoretical formulations, and/or interactions specific to sexually functional couples (e.g., same sex, elderly, various ethnicities) and those with different etiologies of sexual dysfunctions (e.g., physical disability) are not described. We tried throughout this chapter to sensitize the reader to the lack of studies, leaving doubts as to the generalizability of our clinical findings and hypotheses. We look forward to more research in this area, particularly across ethnicities and cultures.

ACKNOWLEDGMENT

The authors would like to acknowledge the Ford Foundation for supporting Dr. Sylvie Aubin with a 2-year postdoctoral fellowship as part of the Sexuality Research Fellowship Program of the Social Sciences Research Council, facilitating the preparation and writing of this chapter.

REFERENCES

Ackerman, M. D., & Carey, M. P. (1995). Psychology's role in the assessment of erectile dysfunction: Historical precedents, current knowledge, and methods. *Journal of Consulting and Clinical Psychology, 63*(6), 862–876.

Althof, S. E. (1992). Psychogenic impotence: Treatment of men and couples. In S. R. Leiblum, R. C. Rosen (Eds.), *Principles and practice of sex therapy: Update for the 1990's* (pp. 237–265). New York: Guilford.

Althof, S. E. (1995). Pharmacological treatment of rapid ejaculation. *Psychiatric Clinics of North America, 18,* 85–94.

American Psychiatric Association. (2000). *Diagnostic and statistical manual of mental disorders* (Text revision). Washington, DC: Author.

Anderson, B. L. (1983). Primary orgasmic dysfunction: Diagnostic considerations and review of treatment. *Psychological Bulletin,93,* 105–136.

Anderson, B. L., & Cyranowski, J. M. (1995). Women's sexual self-schema. *Journal of Personality and Social Psychology, 67,* 1079–1100.

Anderson, B. L., Cyranowski, J. M., & Espindle, D. (in press). Men's sexual self-schema. *Journal of Personality and Social Psychology.*

Alder, E., & Bancroft, J. (1988). The relationship between breast feeding persistence, sexuality and mood in post-partum women. *Psychological Medicine, 18,* 389–396.

Apt, C. V., & Hurlbert, D. F. (1992). Motherhood and female sexuality beyond one year postpartum: A study of military wives. *Journal of Sex Education and Therapy, 18,* 104–114.

Arentewicz, G., & Schmidt, G. (1983). *The treatment of sexual disorders.* New York: Basic Books.

Aubin, S., Trudel, G., Ravart, M., Marchand., A., & Heiman, J. R. (2001, June). *Changes in perceptual congruence hypoactive sexual desire symptoms in couples: Selected analysis from a cognitive-behavioral treatment program.* Poster presented at the 27th Annual Meeting of the International Academy of Sex Research, Montreal, Quebec, Canada.

Aubin, S., Trudel, G., Ravart, M., Marchand., A., & Heiman, J. R. (2002, June). *Defining hypoactive sexual desire in women using clinical outcome data related to symptoms criteria and subject self-report.* Poster presented at the 28th Annual Meeting of the International Academy of Sex Research, Hamburg, Germany.

Bancroft, J., Graham, C. A., & McCord, C. (2001). Conceptualizing women's sexual problems. *Journal of Sex and Marital Therapy, 27,* 95–103.

Bancroft, J., Loftus, J., & Long, J. S. (2003). Distress about sex: A national survey of women in heterosexual relationships. *Archives of Sexual Behavior, 32*(3), 209–211.

Barbach, L. (1982). *For each other: Sharing sexual intimacy.* New York: Anchor.

Barbach, L. (1976). *For yourself: The fulfillment of female sexuality.* New York: Anchor.

Basson, R. (2000). The female sexual response: A different model. *Journal of Sex & Marital Therapy, 26,* 51–65.

Basson, R. (2001a). Commentary: Are the complexities of women's sexual function reflected in the new consensus definitions of dysfunctions? *Journal of Sex & Marital Therapy, 27,* 105–112.

Basson, R. (2001b). Human sex response cycles. *Journal of Sex & Marital Therapy, 27,* 33–43.

Basson, R., Berman, J., Burnett, A., Derogatis, L., Ferguson, D., Fourcroy, J., Goldsein, I., Graziottin, A., Heiman, J. H., Lann, E., Leiblum, S., Padma-Nathan, H., Rosen, R., Segraves, K., Segraves, T., Shabsigh, R., Sipski, M., Wagner, G., & Whipple, B. (2000). Report of the International Consensus Development Conference on Female Sexual Dysfunction: Definitions and classifications. *Journal of Urology, 163,* 888–893.

Baucom, D. H., & Epstein, N. (1990). *Cognitive-behavioral marital therapy.* New York: Brunner/Mazel.

Beck, A. T. (1988). *Love is never enough.* New York: Harper & Row.

Beck, J., & Barlow, D. H. (1986). Effects of anxiety and attentional focus on sexual responding—I. Psysiological patterns and erectile dysfunction. *Behavior Research and Therapy, 24,* 9–17.

Beck, J., Barlow, D. H., & Sakheim, D. K. (1983). The effects of attentional focus and partner arousal on sexual responding in functional and dysfunctional men. *Behavior Research and Therapy, 21,* 1–8.

Bergeron, S. (1999, June). *A randomized comparison of vestibulectomy, biofeedback, and cognitive-behavioral therapy in the treatment of vulvar vestibulitis.* Paper presented at the 25th Annual Meeting of the International Academy of Sex Research, Stony Brook, New York.

Bergeron, S., Binik, Y. M., Khalife, S., & Padigas, K. (1997). Vulvar vestibulitis syndrome: A critical review. *Clinical Journal of Pain, 13,* 27–42.

Birchler, G. R., & Webb, L. (1975). A social learning formulate of discriminating interaction behaviors in happy and unhappy marriages. *Journal of Consulting and Clinical Psychology, 45,* 494–495.

Bowen, M. (1978). *Family therapy in clinical practice.* New York: Aronson.

Bretschneider, J. G., & McCoy, N. L. (1988). Sexual interest in healthy 80- to 103-year-olds. *Archives of Sexual Behavior, 17*(4), 109–129.

Byers, E. S. (1999). The interpersonal exchange model of sexual satisfaction: Implications for sex therapy with couples. *Canadian Journal of Counseling, 33*(2), 95–111.

Byers, E. S. (2001). Evidence for the importance of relationship satisfaction for women's sexual functioning. *Women and Therapy, 24*(1/2), 23–26.

Byers, E. S., & Heinlein, L. (1989). Predicting initiations and refusals of sexual activities in married and cohabiting heterosexual couples. *The Journal of Sex Research, 26*(2), 210–231.

Carlson, K. J., Miller, B. A., & Fowler, F. J. (1994). The Maine Women's Health Study I. Outcomes of hysterectomy. *Obstetrics and Gynecology, 83*, 556–565.

Cotten-Huston, A. L., & Wheeler, K. A. (1983). Preorgasmic group treatment: Assertiveness, marital adjustment and sexual function in women. *Journal of Sex and Marital Therapy, 9*, 296–302.

Crowe, M., & Ridley, J. (1987). The negotiation timetable: A new approach to marital conflicts involving male demands and female reluctance for sex. *Sexual and Marital Therapy, 1*, 157–173.

Cyranowski, J. M., & Anderson, B. L. (1998). Schemas, sexuality, and romantic attachment. *Journal of Personality and Social Psychology, 74*, 1079–1100.

Daker-White, G. (2002). Reliable and valid self-report outcome measures in sexual (dys)function: A systematic review. *Archives of Sexual Behavior, 31*(2), 197–209.

Darling, C. A., & McKay Smith, Y. M. (1993). Understanding hysterectomies: Sexual satisfaction and quality of life. *Journal of Sex Research, 30*, 324–335.

Dennerstein, L., Gotts, G., & Brown, J. B., et al. (1994). The relationship between the menstrual cycle and female sexual interest in women with PMS complaints and volunteers. *Psychoneuroendocrinology, 19*, 293–304.

Derogatis, L. R., & Melisaratos, N. (1979). The DSFI: A multidimensional measure of sexual functioning. *Journal of Sex and Marital Therapy, 5*, 244–281.

Derogatis, L. R., & Melisaratos, N. (1983). The brief symptom inventory: An introductory report. *Psychological Medicine, 13*, 595–605.

Edwards, J. (1981). Viewpoints, how prevalent is lack of sexual desire in marriage? *Medical Aspects of Human Sexuality, 15*(9), 73–83

Eidelson, R. J., & Epstein, N. (1982). Cognition and relationship maladjustment: Development of a measure of dysfunctional relationship beliefs. *Journal of Consulting and Clinical Psychology, 50*, 715–720.

Ellis, A. (1977). The rational-emotive approach to sex therapy. Dans A. Ellis et R. Grieger (Eds.), *Handbook of rational-emotive therapy* (pp. xxx). New York: Springer.

Feldman, H. A., Goldstein, I., Hatzichristou, D. G., Krane, R. J., & McKinlay, J. B. (1994). Impotence and its medical and psychosocial correlates: Results of the Massachusetts Male Aging Study. *Journal of Urology, 151*, 54–61.

Fish, L. S., Fish, R. C., & Sprenkle, D. H. (1984). Treating inhibiting sexual desire: A marital therapy approach. *American Journal Family Therapy, 12*(3), 3–12.

Fisher, S. (1973). *The female orgasm.* New York: Basic Books.

Frank, E., Anderson, C., & Rubenstein, D. (1978). Frequency of sexual dysfunction in normal couples. *New England Journal of Medicine, 299*, 111–115.

Friedman, J. M., & Hogan, D. R. (1985). Sexual dysfunction: Low sexual desire. In D. H. Barlow (Ed.), *Clinical handbook of psychological disorders* (pp. ?). New York: Guilford.

Fugl-Meyer, A. R., & Sjogren Fugl-Meyer, K. (1999). Sexual disabilities, problems, and satisfaction in 18–74 year old Swedes. *Scandinavian Journal of Sexology, 3*, 79–105.

Gagnon, J. H., Rosen, R. C., & Leiblum, S. R. (1982). Cognitive and social aspects of sexual dysfunction: Sexual scripts in sex therapy. *Journal of Sex and Marital Therapy, 8*, 44–56.

Goldstein, I., Graziottin, A., Heiman, J. R., Johannes, C., Laan, E., Levin, R. L., & McKenna, K. E. (1999). Female sexual dysfunction. In A. Jardin, G. Wagner, S. Khoury, F. Giuliano, H. Padma-Nathan, & R. Rosen, (Eds.), *Erectile dysfunction* (pp. 509–556). Plymouths, England: Plymbridge Dist.

Goldstein, I., Lue, T. F., Padma-Nathan, H., Rosen, R. C., Stern, W. D., & Wicker, P. A. (1998). Oral sildenafil in the treatment of erectile dysfunction. *New England Journal of Medicine, 338*, 1397–1404.

Gottman, J. H., & Levenson, R. W. (1992). Marital processes predictive of later dissolution: Behavior, physiology, and health. *Journal of Personality and Social Psychology, 63*(2), 221–233.

Havighurst, R. J. (1981). Personality and patterns of aging. In L. D. Steinberg (Ed.), *The life cycle* (pp. 341–348). New York: Columbia University Press.

Hawton, K., Catalan, J., & Fagg, J. (1991). Low sexual desire: Sex therapy results and prognostic factors. *Behaviour Research and Therapy, 29*, 217–224.

Hawton, K., & Catalan, J. (1986). Prognostic factors in sex therapy. *Behaviour Research and Therapy, 24*, 377–385.

Heiman, J. R. (1998). Psychophysiological models of female sexual response. *International Journal of Impotence Research, 10*(2), s94–s97.

Heiman, J. R. (2000). Orgasmic disorders in women. In S. R. Leiblum, R. C. Rosen (Eds.), *Principles and practice of sex therapy* (3rd ed., pp. 118–153). New York: Guilford.

Heiman, J. R. (2001). Sexual desire in human relationships. In W. Evaraerd, E. Laan, & S. Both (Eds.), *Sexual appetite, desire and motivation: Energetics of the sexual system* (pp. 117–134). Amsterdam: The Royal Netherlands Academy of Arts and Sciences.

Heiman, J. R. (2002). Sexual dysfunction: Overview of prevalence, etiological factors, and treatments. *The Journal of Sex Research, 39*(1), 73–78.

Heiman, J. R., Epps, P. H., & Ellis, B. (1995). Treating sexual desire disorders in couples . In N. S. Jacobson & A. S. Gurman (Eds.), *Clinical handbook of couple therapy* (pp. 471–495). New York: Guilford.

Heiman, J. R., Gladue, B. A., Roberts, C. W., & LoPiccolo, J. (1986). Historical and current factors discriminating sexually functional from sexually dysfunctional married couples. *Journal of Marital and Family Therapy, 12*(2), 163–174.

Heiman, J. R., & Grafton-Becker, V. (1989). Orgasmic disorders in women. In S. R. Leiblum, R. C. Rosen (Eds.), *Principles and practice of sex therapy: Update for the 1990's* (pp. 51–88). New York: Guilford.

Heiman, J. R., & LoPiccolo, J. (1983). Clinical outcome of sex therapy: Effects of daily versus weekly treatment. *Archives of General Psychiatry, 40,* 443–449.

Heiman, J. R., & LoPiccolo , J. (1988). *Becoming orgasmic. A sexual growth program for women* (Rev. ed.). New York: Prentice-Hall.

Heiman, J. R., Maravilla, K. R., Hackbert, L., Delinganis, A. V., Heard, A., Garland, P., Carter, W., Weisskoff, R. M., & Peterson, B. (2001, June). *Vaginal photoplethysmography and pelvic imaging: A comparison of measures.* Paper presented at the 27th Annual Meeting of the International Academy of Sex Research, Montreal, Quebec, Canada.

Heiman, J. R., & Meston, C. (1997a). Empirically validated treatment for sexual dysfunction. *Annual Review of Sex Research, 8,* 148–194.

Heiman, J. R., & Meston, C. (1997b). Evaluating sexual dysfunction in women. *Clinical Obstetrics and Gynecology, 40*(3), 616–629.

Hendry, W. F., Althof, S. E., Bensonm G. S., Haensel, S. M., Hull, E. M., Kihars, K., & Opsomer, R. J. (1999). Male orgasmic and ejaculatory disorders. In A. Jardin, G. Wagner, S. Khoury, F. Giuliano, H. Padma-Nathan, & R. Rosen (Eds.), *Erectile dysfunction* (pp. 477–506). Plymouth, England: Plymbridge.

Hurlbert, D. F., Apt, C. V., Hurlbert, M. K., & Pierce, A. P. (2000). Sexual compatibility and the sexual desire–motivation relation in females with hypoactive sexual desire disorder. *Behavior Modification, 24*(3), 325–347.

Jacobson, N. S., & Folette, W. C. (1985). Clinical significance of improvement resulting from two behavioral marital therapy components. *Behavior Therapy, 16,* 249–262.

Johnson, S. M., & Greenberg, L. S. (1985). Emotionally focused couples therapy: An outcome study. *Journal of Marital and Family Therapy, 11*(3), 313–317.

Kaplan, H. S. (1974). *The new sex therapy.* New York: Brunner/Mazel.

Kaplan, H. S. (1977). Hypoactive sexual desire. *Journal of Sex and Marital Therapy, 3*(1), 3–9.

Kaplan, H. S. (1979). *Disorders of sexual desire.* New York: Brunner/Mazel.

Kaplan, H. S. (1983). *The evaluation of sexual disorders: Psychological and medical aspects.* New York: Brunner/Mazel.

Kaplan, H. S. (1989). *Premature ejaculation. Overcoming premature ejaculation.* New York: Brunner/Mazel.

Kaplan, H. S. (1995). *The sexual desire disorders : Dysfunctional regulation of sexual motivation.* New York: Brunner/Mazel.

Kinsey, A. C., Pomeroy, W. B., & Martin, C. E. (1948). *Sexual behavior in the human male.* Philadelphia: Saunders.

Kinsey, A. C., Pomeroy, W. B., Martin, C. E., & Gebhard, P. (1953). *Sexual behavior in the human female.* Philadelphia: Saunders.

Kuriansky, J. B., Sharpe, L., & O'Connor, D. (1982). The treatment of anorgasmia: Long-term effectiveness of a short-term behavioral group therapy. *Journal of Sex and Marital Therapy, 8,* 29–43.

Laan, E., Everaerd, W., Van der velde, J., & Geer, J. H. (1995). Determinants of subjective experience of sexual arousal in women: Feedback from genital arousal and erotic stimulus content. *Psychophysiology, 5b*,(32), 444–451.

Laumann, E. O., Gagnon, J. H., Michael, R. T., & Michaels, S. (1994). *The social organization of sexuality: Sexual practices in the United States.* Chicago: University of Chicago Press.

Laumann, E. O., Paik, A., & Rosen, R. C. (1999). Sexual dysfunction in the United States: Prevalence and predictors. *Journal of the American Medical Association, 281,* 537–544.

Lawrence, K. A., Taylor, D., & Byers, E. S. (1996). Differences in men's and women's global, sexual, and ideal—sexual expressiveness and instrumentality. *Sex Roles, 34*(5/6), 337–357.

Leiblum, S. R. (2000). Vaginismus: A most perplexing problem. In S. R. Leiblum & R. C. Rosen (Eds.), *Principles and practice of sex therapy* (3rd ed., pp. 181–202). New York: Guilford.

Leiblum, S., Bachman. G., & Kemmann, E, et al., (1983). Vaginal atrophy in the post-menopausal women: The importance of sexual activity and hormones. *Journal of the American Medical Association, 249,* 2195–2198.

Leiblum, S. R., & Rosen, R. C. (2000). Introduction: Sex therapy in the age of Viagra. In S. R. Leiblum & R. C. Rosen (Eds.), *Principles and practice of sex therapy* (3rd ed., pp. 1–13). New York: Guilford.

Leiblum, S. R., & Sachs, J. (2002). *Getting the sex that you want. A women's guide to becoming proud, passionate, and pleased in bed.* New York: Crown.

Leiblum, S. R., & Segraves, R. T. (2000). Sex therapy with aging adults. In S. R. Leiblum & R. C. Rosen (Eds.), *Principles and practice of sex therapy* (3rd ed., pp. 423–448). New York: Guilford.

Leitenberg, H., & Henning, K. (1995). Sexual fantasy. *Psychological Bulletin, 117,* 469–496.

Levine, S. B. (1988). Intrapsychic and individual aspects of sexual desire. In S. R. Leiblum & R. C. Rosen (Eds.), *Sexual desire disorders* (pp. 21–44). New York: Guilford.

Levinson, D. J., Darrow, C. N., Klein, E. B., Levinson, M. H., & McKee, B. (1978). *The seasons of a man's life.* New York: Knopf.

LoPiccolo, J. (1977). Direct treatment of sexual dysfunction in the couple. In J. Money & H. Musaph (Eds.), *Handbook of sexology* (pp. ?). New York: Elsevier/North-Holland.

LoPiccolo, J. (1992). Post-modern sex therapy for erectile failures. In R. C. Rosen, & S. R. Leiblum (Eds.), *Erectile disorders: Assessment and treatment* (pp. ?). New York: Guilford.

LoPiccolo, J., & Friedman, J. M. (1988). Broad-spectrum treatment of low sexual desire: Integration of Cognitive, Behavioral and Systemic Therapy. In S. R. Leiblum & R. C. Rosen (Eds.), *Sexual desire disorders.* (pp. 107–144). New York: Guilford.

Lue, T. F., Gelbard, M. K., Gueglio, G. G., Jordan, G. H., Levive, L. A., Moreland, R., Pryor, J., Ralph, D., & Yachia, D. (1999). Peyronie's Disease. In A. Jardin, G. Wagner, S. Khoury, F. Giuliano, H. Padma-Nathan, & R. Rosen (Eds.), *Erectile dysfunction* (pp. 437–475). Plymouth, England: Plymbridge.

MacPhee, D. C., Johnson, S. M., & Van Der Veer, M. C. (1995). Low sexual desire in women: The effects of marital therapy. *Journal of Sex & Marital Therapy, 21*(3), 159–182.

Maravilla, K. R., Garland, P., Cao, Y., Heiman, J. R., Weisskoff, R., Carter, W., & Peterson, B. (2001, June). *Imaging the female sexual arousal response in the MR magnet: An attractive approach to the subject.* Paper presented at the 27th Annual Meeting of the International Academy of Sex Research. Montreal, Quebec, Canada.

Martin, C. E. (1981). Factors affecting sexual functioning in 60–79-year-old married males. *Archives of Sexual Behavior, 10*(5), 399–420.

Masters, W. H., & Johnson, V. (1966). *Human sexual response.* Boston: Little, Brown.

Masters, W. H., & Johnson, V. (1970). *Human sexual inadequacy.* Boston: Little, Brown.

Masters, W. H., Johnson, V., & Kolodny, R. C. (1988). *Masters and Johnson on sex and human loving.* Boston: Little, Brown.

Maurice, W. L. (1999). *Sexual medicine in primary care.* St. Louis, MO: Mosby.

McCabe, M. P. (1997). Intimacy and quality of life among sexually dysfunctional men and women. *Journal of Sex & Marital Therapy, 23*(4), 276–290.

McCarthy, B. W. (1984). Strategies and techniques for the treatment of inhibited sexual desire. *Journal of Sex and Marital Therapy, 10*(2), 97–104.

McCarthy, B. W. (1997). Strategies and techniques for revitalizing a nonsexual marriage. *Journal of Sex and Marital Therapy, 23*(3), 231–240.

McCarthy, B. W. (1998a). *Couple sexual awareness.* New York: Carroll and Graf.

McCarthy, B. W. (1998b). Integrating Viagra into cognitive–behavioral couples' sex therapy. *Journal of Sex Education and Therapy, 23*(4), 302–308.

McCarthy, B. W. (1999). Marital style and its effects on sexual desire and functioning. *Journal of Family Psychotherapy, 19*(3), 1–12.

McCarthy, B. W., & McCarthy, E. (1984). *Sexual awareness: Enhancing sexual pleasure.* New York: Carrol & Graf.

McCoy, N. L. (2001). Female sexuality during aging. *Functional Neurobiology of Aging, 54,* 769–779.

McCoy, N. L., & Davidson, J. M. (1985). A longitudinal study of the effects of menopause on sexuality. *Maturitas, 7,* 203–210.

Meston, C. M., & Frohlich, P. F. (2000). The neurobiology of sexual function. *Archives of General Psychiatry, 57,* 1012–1030.

Meyers, L. S., Dixen, J., Morrisette, D., & et al. (1990). Effects of estrogen, androgen, and progestin on psychophysiology and behavior in post-menopausal women. *Journals of Clin Endocrinol. Metab., 70,* 1124–1131.

Money, J. (1986). *Lovemaps: Clinical concepts of sexual erotic healthy and pathology, paraphilias, and gender transposition in childhood, adolescence and maturity.* New York: Irvington.

Nutter, D. E., & Condron, M. K. (1983). Sexual fantasy and activity patterns of females with inhibited sexual desire versus normal controls. *Journal of Sex and Marital Therapy, 9,* 276–282.

Office of the Surgeon General. (2001). *The surgeon general's call to action to promote sexual health and responsible sexual behavior.* Washington, DC: U.S. Government Printing Office.

Pittman, F. (1989). *Private lies. Infidelity and the betrayal of intimacy.* New York: Norton.

Pridal, C. G., & LoPiccolo, J. (2000). Multielement treatment of desire disorders: Integration of cognitive, behavioral, and systemic therapy. In S. R. Leiblum, R. C. Rosen (Eds.), *Principles and practice of sex therapy* (3rd ed., pp. 57–81). New York: Guilford.

Purnine, D. M., & Carey, M. P. (1997). Interpersonal communication and sexual adjustment: The roles of understanding and agreement. *Journal of Consulting and Clinical Psychology, 65*(6), 1017–1025.

Quirk, F. H., Heiman, J. R., Rosen, R. C., Laan, E., Smith, M. D., & Boolell, M. (2002). Development of a sexual function questionnaire for clinical trials of female sexual dysfunction. *Journal of Women's Health & Gender-Based Medicine, 11*(3), 277–289.

Reissing, E., Binik, Y. M., & Khalifè, S. (1999). Does vaginismus exist?: A critical review of the literature. *Journal of Nervous and Mental Disease, 187,* 261–274.

Renshaw, D. C. (2001). Women coping with a partner's sexual avoidance. *Family Journal, 9*(1), 11–16.

Reynolds, C. F., Frank, E., Thase, M. E., Houck, J., Jennings, R., Howell, J. R., Liliefend, S. O., & Kupfer, D. J. (1988). Assessment of sexual function in depressed, impotent, and healthy men: Factor analysis of a brief sexual function questionnaire for men. *Psychiatry Research, 24,* 231–250.

Rosen, R., Brown, C., Heiman, J., Leiblum, S., Meston, C., Shabsigh, R., Ferguson, D., & D'Agostino, R. (2000). The Female Sexual Function Index (FSFI): A multidimensional self-report instrument for the assessment of female sexual function. *Journal of Sex and Marital Therapy, 26,* 191–208.

Rosen, R. C., Lane, R. M., & Menza, M. (1999). Effects of SSRIs on sexual function: A critical review. *Journal of Clinical Psychopharmacology, 19*, 67–85.

Rosen, R. C., & Leiblum, S. R. (1988). A sexual scripting approach to problems of desire. In S. R. Leiblum, R. C. Rosen (Eds.), *Sexual desire disorders* (pp. 168–191). New York: Guilford.

Rosen, R. C., & Leiblum, S. R. (1989). Assessment and treatment of desire disorders. In S. R. Leiblum & R. C. Rosen (Eds.), *Principles and practice of sex therapy, update for the 1990's* (pp. 19–47). New York: Guilford.

Rosen, R. C., & Leiblum, S. R. (1995). *Case studies in sex therapy.* New York: Guilford.

Rosen, R. C., & Leiblum, S. R. (1995). Hypoactive sexual desire. *The Psychiatric Clinics of North America, 18*(1), 107–121.

Rosen, R. C., Leiblum, S. R., & Spector, I. P. (1994). Psychologically based treatment for male erectile disorder: A cognitive–interpersonal model. *Journal of Sex and Marital Therapy, 20*(2), 67–85.

Rosen, R. C., Riley, A., Wagner, G., Osterloch, I. H., Kirkpatrick, J., & Mishra, A. (1997). The International Index for Erectile Function (IIEF): A multidimensional scale for assessment of erectile dysfuncton. *Urology, 49*, 822–830.

Rowland, D. L., & Heiman, J. R. (1991). Self-reported and genital arousal changes in sexually dysfunctional men following a sex therapy program. *Journal of Psychosomatic Research, 35*(4/5), 609–619.

Sanders, D., Warner, P., & Backstrom, T. (1983). Mood, sexuality, hormones and the menstrual cycle. I. Changes in mood and physical state: Description of subjects and method. *Psychosomatic Medicine, 45*, 487–501.

Schaefer, M. T., & Olson, D. H. (1980). Personal assessment of intimacy in relationships: Assessing intimacy: The pair inventory. *Journal of Marital and Family Therapy, 7*, 47–60.

Schiavi, R. C., Schreiner-Engel, P., Mandeli, J., Schanzer, H., & Cohen, E. (1990). Healthy aging and male sexual function. *American Journal of Psychiatry, 147*, 35–46.

Schiavi, R. C., & Segraves, R. J. (1995). The biology of sexual function. *Psychiatric Clinics of North America, 18*, 7–23.

Segraves, K. B., & Segraves, R. T. (1991). Hypoactive sexual desire disorders: Prevalence and comorbidity in 906 subjects. *Journal of Sex and Marital Therapy, 7*, 55–58.

Schnarch, D. (1991). *Constructing the sexual crucible.* New York: Norton.

Schnarch, D. (1997). *Passionate marriage.* New York: Norton.

Schnarch, D. (2000). Desire problems: A systemic perspective. In S. R. Leiblum & R. C. Rosen (Eds.), *Principles and practice of sex therapy* (3rd ed., pp. 17–56). New York: Guilford.

Schover, L. R. (2000). Sexual problems in chronic illness. In S. R. Leiblum & R. C. Rosen (Eds.), *Principles and practice of sex therapy* (3rd ed., pp.). New York: Guilford.

Schwartz, P. (1994). *Love between equals. How peer marriage works.* New York: The Free Press.

Schwartz, M. F., & Masters, W. H. (1988). Inhibited sexual desire: The Masters and Johnson Institute treatment model. In S. R. Leiblum & R. C. Rosen (Eds.), *Sexual desire disorders* (pp. 229–242). New York: Guilford.

Sherwin, B. B., & Gelfand, M. M. (1987). The role of androgen in the maintenance of sexual functioning in oopherectomized women. *Psychosomatic Medicine, 49*, 397–409.

Simons, J. S., & Carey, M. P. (2001). Prevalence of sexual dysfunctions: Results from a decade of research. *Archives of Sexual Behavior, 30*, 177–217.

Simon, W., & Gagnon, J. H. (1986). Sexual scripts: Permanence and change. *Archives of Sexual Behavior, 15* (2), 97–120.

Snyder, D. K., & Berg, P. (1983). Determinants of sexual dissatisfaction in sexually distressed couples. *Archives of Sexual Behavior, 12*, 237–246.

Spanier, G. B. (1976). Dyadic Adjustment Scale: Measuring dyadic adjustment: New scales for assessing the quality of marriage and similar dyads. *Journal of Marriage and the Family, 38*, 15–28.

Spence, S. H. (1997). Sex and relationships. In W. K. Halford & H. J. Markham, (Eds.). *Clinical handbook of marriage and couples interventions* (pp. 73–105). New York: Wiley.

Taylor, F., Rosen, R. C., & Leiblum, S. R. (1994). Self-report assessment of female sexual functioning: Psychometric evaluation of the brief index of sexual functioning for women. *Archives of Sexual Behavior, 23*, 627–643.

Tiefer, L. (1986). In pursuit of the perfect penis: The medicalization of male sexuality. *American Behavioral Scientist, 29*, 579–599.

Tiefer, L., Hall, M., & Tarvis, C. (2002). Beyond dysfunction: A new view of women's sexual problems. *The Journal of Sex and Marital Therapy, 28*(s), 225–232.

Trudel, G. (1991). A review of psychological factors in low sexual desire. *Sexual and Marital Therapy, 6*(3), 261–272.

Trudel, G. (2000). *Les dysfonctions sexuelles. Évaluation et traitement par des méthodes psychologique, interpersonnelle et biologique.* Québec, Canada: Presses de l'Université du Québec.
" Sexual Dysfunctions. Quatation and Treatment using Psychological, interpersonal and Biological Methods."

Trudel, G., Aubin, S., & Matte, B. (1995). Sexual behaviors and pleasure in couples with hypoactive sexual desire. *Journal of Sex Education and Therapy, 21*, 210–216.

Trudel, G., Boulos, M. A., & Matte, B. (1993). Dyadic adjustment in couples with hypoactive sexual desire. *Journal of Sex Education and Therapy, 19*(1), 31–36.

Trudel, G., Fortin, C., & Matte, B. (1997). Sexual interaction and communication in couples with hypoactive sexual desire. *Scandinavian Journal of Behavior Therapy, 26,* 49–53.

Trudel, G., Marchand, A., Ravart, M., Aubin, S., Turgeon, L., & Fortier, P. (2001). The effect of a cognitive–behavioral group treatment program on hypoactive sexual desire in women. *Sexual and Relationship Therapy, 16,* 145–164.

Trudel, G., Ravart, M., & Matte, B. (1993). The use of the multiaxial diagnostic system for sexual dysfunctions in the assessment of hypoactive sexual desire. *Journal of Sex and Marital Therapy, 19*(2), 123–130.

Verhulst, J., & Heiman, J. R. (1979). An interactional approach to sexual dysfunction. *American Journal of Family Therapy, 7,* 19–36.

Verhulst, J., & Heiman, J. R. (1988). A systems perspective on sexual desire. In S. R. Leiblum & R. C. Rosen (Eds.), *Sexual desire disorders* (pp. 243–267). New York: Guilford.

Walker, E. A., Gelfand, A., Katon, M. J., Doss, M. P., Von Korff, M., Bernstein, D., & Russo, J. (1999). Adult health status of women HMO members with histories of childhood abuse and neglect. *American Journal of Medicine, 107,* 332–339.

Wenninger, K., & Heiman, J. R. (1998). Relating body image to psychological and sexual function in child abuse survivors. *Journal of Traumatic Stress, 11,* 543–562.

Wincze, J. P., & Carey, M. P. (2001). *Sexual dysfunction. A guide for assessment and treatment.* New York: Guilford.

World Health Organization. (1992). *ICD-10. International classification of diseases and related problems.* Geneva, Switzerland: Author.

Wright, J. (1985). *Survival startegies for couples. A self-help book.* Buffalo, NY: Prometheus Books.

Zilbergeld, B. (1992). *The new male sexuality.* New York: Bantam Books.

Zilbergeld, B., & Ellison, C. R. (1980). Desire discrepancies and arousal problems in sex therapy. In S. R. Leiblum & L. A. Pervin (Eds.), *Principles and practice of sex therapy* (pp. 65–106). New York: Guilford.

Zimmer, D. (1989). Interaction patterns and communication skills in sexually distressed, maritally distressed, and normal couples: Two experimental studies. *Journal of Sex and Marital Therapy, 9*(4), 251–265.

Zimmer, D., Borchardt, E., & Fischle, C. (1983). Sexual fantasies of sexually distressed and nondistressed men and women: An empirical comparison. *Journal of Sex and Marital Therapy, 9*(1), 38–50.

21

Safer Sex and Sexually Transmitted Infections From a Relationship Perspective

Seth M. Noar
Rick S. Zimmerman
Katherine A. Atwood
University of Kentucky

Although being in a close relationship has many social and emotional benefits, there is growing evidence that close relationships may be risky in terms of sexually transmitted infections (STIs) including HIV. Specifically, there is significant evidence that adolescents and young adults are inadvertently putting themselves at risk within the context of their close relationships. Data supporting this hypothesis are reviewed within three areas of research: early initiation of first sexual intercourse, condom use and partner risk assessment, and actual STI incidence. Although there are considerable complexities with regard to the association between close (and casual) relationships and STI risk, we conclude from the literature reviewed that, for adolescents and young adults, close relationships are often risky with regard to STIs. Implications of this review are discussed, and a number of future lines of research are offered.

INTRODUCTION

This chapter discusses how close relationships and relationship characteristics are related to sexually transmitted infection (STI) risk for heterosexual adolescents and young adults in the United States.[1] We begin by first discussing the epidemiology

---

[1] In this chapter we chose to focus on heterosexual adolescents and young adults in the United States. We recognize that similar work with other populations in the United States (e.g., gay and bisexual adolescents and young adults), as well as with populations outside the United States is very important. A full treatment of the issues discussed here, as applied to these other populations, is beyond the scope of the current chapter.

of STIs including HIV/AIDS, patterns of condom use in adolescent and young adult populations, and general issues with regard to the current state of the literature on relationship characteristics and safer sexual behavior. We then further set the context of the chapter by briefly discussing the development of close relationships and sexuality in adolescents and young adults. Next, we move into the substantive literature of this review. First, protective aspects of being in a close relationship are explored and discussed. Then, the risk-related aspects of being in a close relationship are examined within three areas: early sexual initiation, condom use and partner risk assessment, and incidence of STI infection. Finally, the chapter concludes with implications of these findings and suggested directions for future research. Throughout the chapter, literature is reviewed, and in some cases new, unpublished findings from our research program are presented to help answer questions that have yet to be answered fully by the existing literature.

EPIDEMIOLOGY

Sexually transmitted infections have been, and continue to be, a significant problem in the United States. In fact, it is estimated that more than 65 million people are currently living with an *incurable* STI, and further that approximately 15 million people become infected with an STI each year (Cates, 1999; Centers for Disease Control and Prevention [CDC], 2000a). This STI epidemic has been called a *hidden epidemic*, as many of these infections go unrecognized and untreated for long periods of time (CDC, 2000a). These figures do not include HIV/AIDS, which has had its greatest effect on men who have sex with men (MSM) and injecting drug use populations, and for which evidence suggests has been increasingly affecting heterosexual populations over the last several years (CDC, 1999; Karon, Fleming, Steketee, & De Cock, 2001). In fact, the CDC documented 807,075 cumulative cases of AIDS at the end of the year 2001 (CDC, 2001). In women, heterosexual contact accounted for 41% of these cases, injecting drugs accounted for 39%, and other risks accounted for 20% of cases. In men, MSM accounted for 55% of these cases, injecting drugs accounted for 22%, engaging in both these activities accounted for 8%, heterosexual contact accounted for 5%, and other risks accounted for 10% of cases.

Both adolescents (ages 10–19) and young adults (ages 20–24) are at higher risk for contracting STIs including HIV when compared to their older adult counterparts (CDC, 2000a; Karon et al., 2001). It is estimated that adolescents account for one quarter of new STIs each year (CDC, 2000a), and adolescents and young adults combined account for a majority of new infections each year (CDC, 2000b). These proportions of STIs in younger populations have been attributed to a number of factors (CDC, 2000c), including (a) their likelihood of having multiple sexual partnerships, rather than single, long-term partnerships, (b) their likelihood of engaging in unprotected intercourse, (c) their likelihood of, in some cases, selecting partners at higher risk, (d) for some STIs, such as Chlamydia, an increased physiological susceptibility for young women, and (e) the multiple barriers to quality STI services for this age group, ranging from issues of access to comfort and confidentiality concerns. In addition, it should be noted that other STIs themselves are risk factors for the contraction of HIV due to biological and behavioral factors (see CDC, 1998; Pinkerton & Layde, 2002), indicating that these epidemics are also related to one another.

CONDOM USE

Using condoms consistently, defined as *every time* one has sexual intercourse, is the most effective way for sexually active individuals to protect themselves from STIs including HIV. Data from several studies, however, suggest that consistent condom use among adolescents and young adults tends to be the exception, not the rule (Cates, 1990; Seidman & Rieder, 1994). Across several studies that examined consistent condom use in adolescents, all reported that less than 50% of individuals used condoms consistently (Cates, 1990). In a large survey of undergraduate college students, 88% were found to be sexually active, but only 18% of these students reported consistently using condoms (Seidman & Rieder, 1994). Further, in a nationally representative study, only 7% of sexually active heterosexuals ages 18 to 29 used condoms consistently (Leigh, Temple, & Trocki, 1993). Finally, Choi and Catania (1996) reported, from two national surveys, that 16% and 24% of at-risk heterosexuals in this same age group (18–29) used condoms consistently.

Condom use at one intercourse occasion such as last intercourse yields higher percentages of condom use as compared to percentages of consistent condom use, as one might expect. That is, as the data indicate, fewer individuals use condoms consistently than use condoms occasionally or not at all. Across several studies, Cates (1990) reported that between 38% and 66% of adolescents used a condom at last intercourse. Ku, Sonenstein and Pleck (1994) reported from the 1990–1991 National Survey of Adolescent Males that only 53% of sexually active males ages 17 to 22 years old used a condom at first intercourse with a new partner. They also found that condom use at first intercourse *decreased* with age. Condom use at first intercourse with a new partner for 17 to 18 year olds was 59%, whereas for 21 to 22 year olds it was 46% (Ku et al., 1994). These data, in sum, clearly indicate that both adolescents and young adults tend to use condoms *inconsistently*, putting themselves at risk for STIs including HIV.

RELATIONSHIP CHARACTERISTICS AND THE HIV PREVENTION LITERATURE

The data on both STIs and condom use in adolescents and young adults has led many to emphasize the importance of comprehensive prevention efforts targeted at heterosexually active youth (e.g., Rotherum-Borus, O'Keefe, Kracker, & Foo, 2000). However, prevention efforts can only be as effective as the research that supports such efforts. The HIV prevention literature is vast, and researchers have learned much about both what motivates and discourages safer sexual behaviors in young men and women. However, the majority of literature that focuses on condom use, STIs, and risk factors for STIs such as early initiation of sexual activity has focused on predictors of the behaviors of interest, without always considering the context in which sexual behavior takes place. Studies of predictors of early initiation of sexual activity (e.g., DiIorio et al., 2002; Thorton, 1990), condom use (e.g., Sheeran, Abraham & Orbell, 1999) and STIs (e.g., Coker et al., 1994; Rosenberg, Gurvey, Adler, Dunlop, & Ellen, 1999) have shed light on the correlates and predictors of these behaviors and outcomes. However, such studies have not always taken into account important relational and contextual influences on sexual behavior.

Specifically, what has been studied less often is the impact of relationship characteristics on STI and HIV risk behavior. This is the case for many reasons. First, theories of health behavior (e.g., Ajzen & Fishbein, 1980; Ajzen & Madden, 1986; Bandura, 1986; Becker, 1974; Prochaska, DiClemente, & Norcross, 1992) as well as theories proposed specifically for HIV-related behavior (Catania, Kegeles, & Coates, 1990; Fisher & Fisher, 1992) do not explicitly posit relationship characteristics as important to STI risk behavior. Second, from a methodological point of view, relationships are sometimes difficult to conceptualize and measure. Human sexuality researchers, relationship researchers, and HIV prevention researchers have not often fused their research programs together to find the best ways to understand HIV-related risk from a relationship perspective (e.g., Kelly & Kalichman, 1995). Finally, for a variety of reasons, it is unlikely that the association between relationship characteristics and condom use is a simple, linear association (e.g., Kordoutis, Loumakou, & Sarafidou, 2000; Ku et al., 1994). This makes associations between relationship characteristics and safer sexual behavior more difficult to find, as sexual relationships are quite dynamic in nature and may demand new methodologies and prospective designs to tease apart and uncover effects.

The key exception to relationship characteristics not being a focus in the HIV prevention literature is the main (also described as primary or steady)/casual partner distinction (e.g., Comer & Nemeroff, 2000; Misovich, Fisher & Fisher, 1997). Researchers have made distinctions between sexual partners who are main partners as compared to those who are more casual in nature. Differences found between these types of partners will be discussed. Further, it is encouraging that increasing numbers of researchers are stressing the importance of contextual factors such as relationship characteristics and their association with STI risk (e.g., Amaro, 1995; Canin, Dolcini, & Adler, 1999; Katz, Fortenberry, Zimet, Blythe, & Orr, 2000; Kelly & Kalichman, 1995; Ku et al., 1994; Logan, Cole, & Leukefeld, 2002; Mays & Cochran, 1988; Misovich et al., 1997; Noar, Morokoff, & Redding, 2001; Sheeran et al., 1999). This includes characteristics such as length and type of relationship (Canin et al., 1999; Katz et al., 2000; Ku et al., 1994; Misovich et al., 1997), gender and power dynamics within relationships (e.g., Amaro, 1995; Logan et al., 2002; Mays & Cochran, 1988; Noar & Morokoff, 2002), and partner support of condom use (e.g., Noar et al., 2001, Sheeran et al., 1999). Thus, a literature on this topic has begun to emerge.

DEVELOPMENT OF CLOSE RELATIONSHIPS AND SEXUALITY

There are a number of reasons that adolescents and young adults may choose to be in close relationships. These include companionship and commitment (Cate, Levin, & Richmond, 2002; Shulman & Kipnis, 2001; Sternberg, 1986; Zimmer-Gembeck, Siebenbruner, & Collins, 2001), support and security (Duemmler & Kobak, 2001; Shulman & Kipnis, 2001; Zimmer-Gembeck et al., 2001), closeness, intimacy and love (Adams, Laursen, & Wilder, 2001; Cate et al., 2002; Sternberg, 1986; Taradash, Connolly, Pepler, Craig, & Costa, 2001; Zimmer-Gembeck et al., 2001), as well as desires for romance, passion, and expression of sexuality (Shulman & Seiffge-Krenke, 2001; Sternberg, 1986). The ultimate goal of entering into a close relationship for many may be the hope of finding a lifelong relationship partner. Being in a close relationship is also related to a number of positive emotional, social, and health outcomes (e.g., Furman, Brown, & Feiring, 1999; Zimmer-Gembeck et al., 2001).

Close relationships in adolescence and young adulthood can be described as having unique characteristics as compared to those of older adults. As this is the period in individuals' lives when they tend to date many partners, such relationships tend to be briefer than adult relationships and in some cases may include multiple partnerships at the same time, sometimes described as *concurrent* partnerships (CDC, 2000c). Thorton (1990) conducted seminal work on courtship and adolescent sexuality, which he examines through a developmental perspective. He posits that in Western societies, adolescent peer groups tend to be demarcated along gender lines. As adolescents mature, the formulation of opposite sex friendships and relationships become gradually more important and become an integral part of the maturation process (Thorton, 1990). This eradicating of barriers between the genders and the development of relationships is often incremental. As young people begin to date, the duration and frequency of time they spend together tends to increase, as does their emotional, romantic, and subsequent sexual involvement (Porter, Oakley, Guthrie, & Killion, 1999; Thorton, 1990). Thorton (1990) and other researchers suggest that as young couples become emotionally committed to one another and experience increasing levels of sexual involvement, their expectations about what is considered permissible within the relationship also expand to meet this new and exciting terrain of sexual intimacy (Peplau, Rubin, & Hill, 1977; Thorton, 1990). As they reach one threshold of sexual involvement, their level of self-efficacy grows, preparing them for a next level of intensive sexual involvement (Thorton, 1990).

This research, conducted on White youth in Detroit, also suggests that dating at an earlier age leads to a greater probability of being in a steady relationship at an earlier age, which in turn leads to a greater frequency of sexual activity in one's teen years (Thorton, 1990). Though, Thorton (1990) suggests that there is tremendous variation with regard to these processes and the speed at which adolescents and young adults move through this trajectory, depending on such factors as race/ethnicity, family composition, social values, interpersonal skills, pubertal development, peer norms, religious affiliation, and neighborhood characteristics (see also Fisher, chapter 16, this volume). Other researchers have posited similar developmental theories related to adolescent romantic relationships (e.g., Shulman & Seiffge-Krenke, 2001), although some have pointed out substantial differences related to factors such as race (Smith & Udry, 1985). Scholars in the field have also made the point that the study of adolescent romantic relationships is still somewhat in its infancy, and that further conceptual and empirical work is warranted (Brown, Feiring, & Furman, 1999).

PROTECTIVE ASPECTS OF CLOSE RELATIONSHIPS

When we examine close relationships, it quickly becomes obvious that they have the potential to offer protective aspects with regard to STI risk. If two partners are truly mutually monogamous and infection-free and are not engaging in any other behaviors that would put them at risk for HIV (e.g., injection drug use), then they are clearly not at risk for STIs and can engage in fulfilling sexual encounters without condoms and without worry of infection. In addition, individuals in close relationships may be better situated to come to know a partner's disease status as compared to individuals in casual relationships or encounters (Wolitski & Branson, 2002), as communication about these issues is likely to be better (e.g., Bowen & Michal-Johnson, 1989). However, as we discuss later, though *perceptions* are that communication about STI status is better in close relationships, the reality may be that it is *not* much better at getting at a partner's true STI status. Further, some emerging data suggest that condom use (and non-use) is more habitual in main or close relationships as compared to those that are more casual (de Visser & Smith, 2001; de Wit, Stroebe, de Vroome, Sandfort, & Van Griensven, 2000). Thus, *if* those in a relationship choose to use condoms, it may be easier for them to maintain consistent condom use, as opposed to having to renegotiate condom use each time with a casual partner. In addition, some emerging literature suggests that alcohol plays more of a risk-related role in casual sexual encounters as compared to close relationships (Cooper & Orcutt, 2000; Corbin & Fromme, 2002). Finally, Warszawski and Meyer (2002) found that individuals were likely to tell their close partner if they found out they had an STI, but were very unlikely to tell any casual partners. If this unpleasant situation were to arise, close partners would be at a great advantage of finding out about the STI, and could take appropriate action to protect themselves. If the close partner had already become infected with the STI, this would allow the individual to get treatment for the STI sooner than if one found out on their own. Further, because many STIs do not have observable symptoms and can cause permanent damage if undetected for long periods of time, it would be a great advantage to find out sooner rather than later if one had an STI (CDC, 2000a, 2000c).

RISK-RELATED ASPECTS OF CLOSE RELATIONSHIPS

Despite these protective aspects of relationships, there is growing evidence that individuals in close relationships may be at increased risk for STIs and that certain characteristics of close relationships may contribute to that risk. In the following sections, the risk-related impact of being in a close relationship is reviewed within three areas: early sexual initiation, condom use and partner risk assessment, and STI incidence.

Close Relationships and Early Sexual Initiation

Initiation of sexual intercourse is one of the key developmental thresholds separating adolescence from young adulthood, and the crossing of this threshold occurs at relatively young ages in the United States. According to the 1997 National Youth Risk Behavior Survey, 38% of 9th graders reported ever having sex (Kann & Kinchen, 1998). In some instances first intercourse occurs even earlier than this, with 7% of adolescents reporting that they engaged in intercourse before the age of 13. Males are more likely to engage in sexual intercourse before the age of 13 than females (15% versus 7%) and Blacks more than Hispanics or Whites (22% versus 8% and 4%, respectively). By the 12th grade, 61% of high school students report having had sexual intercourse (Kann & Kinchen, 1998).

Studies found that young sexual initiators (14 years of age or younger) have a greater number of sexual partners and engage in a higher frequency of unprotected sexual intercourse during the high school years when compared to those who initiate sexual intercourse at a later age (Coker et al., 1994). Young initiators also experience a greater likelihood of unintended pregnancy (Brooks-Gunn & Furstenberg, 1989; Coker et al., 1994; Greenberg, Magder, & Aral, 1992; Hayes, 1987), HIV, and other STI's (Coker et al., 1994; Greenberg et al., 1992).

Because data demonstrated that the age of one's first intercourse experience is so important, a large literature has sought to understand the predictors of first intercourse. This has included the developmental (Thorton, 1990), biological (Crockett, Bingham, Chopak, & Vicary, 1996; Udry & Billy, 1987), familial (Hogan & Kitagawa, 1985; Miller, McCoy, Olson, & Wallace, 1986), psychological (DiIorio et al., 2002; Meschke, Zweig, Barber, & Eccles, 2000), and socioeconomical (Heaton & Jacobson, 1994; Meschke et al., 2000) factors that come into play when intercourse is initiated. However, the one component that is frequently overlooked is the *relationship* between the initiate and his or her partner, even though this may be very important (Manning, Longmore, & Giordano, 2000). Studies find that adolescents who are in a relationship at an early age are likely to have more permissive attitudes about sexual intercourse (Miller et al., 1986; Thorton, 1990). Further "being in a relationship" or "dating someone" may afford the opportunity to see this person alone and in turn have sexual intercourse with him or her (Dorius, Heaton, & Steffen, 1993; Porter et al., 1999).

In addition, a small number of studies examined the impact of dating or being in a relationship on initiation of sexual intercourse and found that adolescents who are *dating* at an early age are more likely to engage in *first sexual intercourse* at a younger age (Dorius et al., 1993; Miller et al., 1986; Thorton, 1990). Thorton's (1990) study of 916 White 18 year olds in Detroit, discussed earlier in this chapter, examined both *first date* and *first steady relationship* and their associations with initiation of sexual intercourse. In regard to first date, 50% of males who began dating at age 13 or younger experienced first intercourse by age 15 or younger, as compared to 10% of those who began dating at age 16. Among females, 30% of those who began dating by age 13 or younger reported having sexual intercourse by age 15, compared to *none* of the females who started dating at age 16. In addition, those who first dated at an earlier age had a higher number of sexual partners as compared to those who began dating at a later age. This difference is presumably because those who begin dating earlier have more opportunity and time for the formulation of sexual partnerships as compared to those who start later. In regard to first steady relationship, those whose first steady relationship was at an early age were more likely to experience first sexual intercourse at a younger age, as compared to those whose first steady relationship occurred at a later age (Thorton, 1990).

Thorton (1990) suggests that there is a gradual trajectory over time of noncoital behaviors leading to first sexual intercourse in White adolescents. However, several studies have reported that African American adolescents initiate sex at an earlier age (Hayes, 1987; Kann & Kinchen, 1998; Smith & Udry, 1985), and that this trajectory is significantly more abbreviated (Smith & Udry, 1985). In an urban longitudinal study of 1,368 youth ages 12 to 15, no predictable progression of precoital activity was found among African American youth (Smith & Udry, 1985). African American males and females were more likely to report that they had intercourse as compared to other "petting behaviors," with intercourse directly following "necking." In contrast, Whites experienced a longer "preparatory" period before intercourse including kissing, necking, light petting, heavy petting, and then intercourse (Smith & Udry, 1985). Thus, these data suggest that there may be less of an association between relationship status and early sexual initiation in African American adolescents as compared to Whites (e.g., Dorious et al., 1993), though there is clearly a need for more research in this area.

Condom Use and Initiation of Sexual Intercourse.   Though data suggest that in some cases those in relationships are more likely to initiate sexual activity, literature also suggests that those in relationships at first intercourse are more likely to use contraception. That is, when researchers compare first intercourse experiences of those in a relationship to those whose first intercourse experience occurred with a casual partner, relationship status is associated with contraceptive use. In Manning and colleagues' analysis of 1,593 female initiates in the National Survey of Family Growth, those who were in a relationship at first intercourse were more likely to use contraception when compared to those whose first intercourse occurred with a casual partner (Manning et al., 2000). In fact, 52% of those who "just met" their first sexual partner used *no method* of birth control compared to 24% of those "going steady" (Manning et al., 2000). They and others (Ford, Sohn, & Lepkowski, 2002) hypothesize that adolescents in close relationships may have some shared understanding that the relationship may become sexual and therefore may be more apt to communicate the need for contraception to their sex partner (Manning et al., 2000). Further, if condom use does occur at first intercourse, it has been found to be associated with subsequent condom use (Miller & Levin, 1998; St. Lawrence & Scott, 1996). Although being in a relationship may result in early age at first intercourse, there appears to be the opportunity for discussions about sexual decision making and contraception within the relationship before intercourse occurs. Interventions targeting young adolescent couples provide a unique opportunity to instill health protective behaviors before more high-risk behaviors are firmly entrenched and considered normative to them (e.g., El-Bassel et al., 2001).

New Findings.   Our research group recently collected data from 2,965 rural teens participating in an HIV and pregnancy prevention intervention in their 9th-grade health classes (Zimmerman, Hansen, Cupp, & Brumley-Shelton, 2003). Data reported

TABLE 21.1

Relationship at First Sexual Intercourse and Associated Outcomes

Relationship Status at First Intercourse	Contraceptive Use at First Intercourse		Lifetime Prevalence	Most Recent Sexual Experience (with a different partner)		
	Condom N = 706	Hormonal Methods N = 706	Treated for STI N = 685	Alcohol Use N = 418	Marijuana Use N = 416	Condom Used N = 415
Just met	32%	4%	11%	41%	44%	56%
Casual relationship	36%	5%	7%	26%	27%	61%
Serious relationship	41%	9%	3%	17%	16%	80%

Note. All comparisons (in the columns) are statistically significant, $p < .05$.

here are from the baseline and follow-up (4 to 6 months later) surveys. A majority (54%) were male, most were either age 14 (41%) or 15 (45%), and 96% were White. Of these students, 854 (29%) reported ever having sexual intercourse: 21% of these had first done so by age 12, another 27% started at age 13, 38% at age 14, and the remainder at older ages. A small minority of students (8% overall, 11% of males, 5% of females) had their first sexual experience with someone they had just met. The remainder was nearly evenly divided between casual friends (casual acquaintances, friends, or casual dating partners) with 46% in this category (54% of males and 37% of females) and serious dating partners with 48% in this category (33% of males and 56% of females).

Among these sexually active students ($N = 854$), we found strong associations between relationship status with first sexual partner and condom and other contraceptive use, lifetime STI prevalence, and later risky sexual behavior (see Table 21.1). The closer the relationship, the greater the likelihood of both condom use and hormonal birth control use during the first sexual experience. Also, the closer the relationship at the first sexual intercourse experience, the *less negative* later consequences and *less risky* later sexual behavior was likely to be. Those who had their first sexual intercourse experience with someone they just met were more than four times more likely to have been treated for an STI than those who were in a serious relationship the first time they had sex. In addition, at the most recent sexual experience with a subsequent partner, alcohol and marijuana use were significantly greater and condom use was less likely for individuals in more casual partnerships during their first sexual experience (Zimmerman et al., 2003).

To help determine whether relationship at this first sexual experience was merely a correlate of other risk-promoting characteristics or itself implicated as a predictor of subsequent behavior, we conducted a logistic regression in which we controlled for personality characteristics (sensation-seeking and impulsivity) and gender. Even after controlling for these variables, adolescents whose first sexual experience was with someone they had just met were significantly less likely to have used a condom and more likely to have used alcohol or marijuana when they most recently had sex. This suggests that the relationship with first sexual partner may establish a pattern of risky sexual behavior that continues through later sexual encounters.

In sum, the associations among close relationships, first sexual intercourse, and safer sex are quite complex and the first sexual experience is a very important event in the lives of adolescents. In addition, as is obvious in the next section, the dynamics that exist in and around these very early sexual relationships and experiences (e.g., condom use more likely with a close partner at first intercourse) are quite different than later sexual experiences of adolescents and young adults.

Close Relationships, Condom Use, and Partner Risk Assessment

Main/Casual Distinction.   As already noted, the most common distinction made with regard to relationships in the HIV prevention literature is the main/casual distinction (Comer & Nemeroff, 2000; Misovich et al., 1997). Main or steady partners are typically defined as close partners that one sees regularly, whereas casual partners may involve one-time sexual encounters or any additional sexual partners an individual has besides his or her main partner. Using this distinction, a robust finding has emerged in the literature: Individuals are *less* likely to use condoms with main partners as compared to casual partners. And, this has been reported not only in heterosexual adolescents and young adults, but also in other populations including gay men, injection drug users, commercial sex workers, and heterosexual adults (see Misovich et al., 1997, for a review). It appears that individuals, correctly or incorrectly, view their close, main partner relationships as less risky than casual sexual relationships.

However, this quite consistent finding is at odds with studies of adolescents at first intercourse reviewed in the previous section of this chapter. As already noted, condoms are more likely to be used at a first intercourse occasion if the partners are in a relationship, as compared to those who have casual sex the first time. It appears that in these early sexual relationships, being close with someone is protective and may lead to condom use. However, it also appears that with regard to relationships that are subsequent to one's first sexual intercourse experience, that this phenomenon essentially reverses itself. That is, main partners are subsequently viewed as less risky or not risky at all as compared to casual partners. In addition, it is likely that older adolescents with main partners are more likely to be using hormonal birth control, and by extension, further increasing the perception that condoms are not needed. This has resulted in the rather consistent finding in many studies of sexually active adolescents and young adults that individuals use condoms less often with main than with casual partners (Misovich et al., 1997).

In addition, this finding has broad implications for individuals' STI risk and thus for prevention efforts. That is, if individuals' perceptions about the safety of their main, close relationship are incorrect (e.g., their partner has an STI), then by not using condoms they are putting themselves at considerable risk. In fact, researchers have suggested that individuals are inadvertently putting themselves at risk for STIs and HIV within the context of their close relationships (Baker, Morrison, Gillmore, & Schock, 1995; Katz et al., 2000; Kelly & Kalichman, 1995; Mays & Cochran, 1988; Metts & Fitzpatrick, 1992; Misovich et al., 1997; Noar, 2001; O'Leary, 2000). These findings have led researchers to encourage increased condom use in main relationships, unless individuals know for certain that their partner is not infected with STIs or at risk for becoming infected (Civic, 2000; Misovich et al., 1997; O'Leary, 2000).

Condom Use Over Time in Close Relationships.   Other data extend this main/casual finding within close relationships. Ku et al. (1994) has proposed the *sawtooth hypothesis* that posits that within a close relationship, condom use will vary over time, with the direction of condom use decreasing and creating a sawtooth pattern. Using data from the National Survey of Adolescent Males (NSAM), Ku et al. (1994) demonstrated that condom use tends to be highest at the beginning of a relationship and decreases over the course of a relationship. Specifically, 53% of young men used condoms at initial intercourse with their close partner, whereas only 44% used condoms with that same partner at their most recent intercourse occasion. In addition, use of other contraceptive methods followed the reverse path. Namely, only 29% of young men's partners used birth control (other than condoms) at initial intercourse with their close partner, whereas 48% used birth control with that same partner at their most recent intercourse occasion. Other researchers have also found a negative association between time in a relationship and condom use, indicating that as relationships progress, condom use diminishes (Civic, 2000; Fortenberry, Tu, Harezlak, Katz, & Orr, 2002; Saul et al., 2000). These data support the notion of the *contraceptive switch,* which is the idea that partners start off using condoms and then as the relationship progresses, move to a hormonal contraceptive method such as birth control pills (Civic, 2000; Hammer, Fisher, Fitzgerald, & Fisher, 1996; Ku et al., 1994; Maticka-Tyndale, 1992). The obvious implication here is that as the relationship continues and gets close, individuals are less likely to see the other as an STI risk, and they opt for a more convenient (but not protective in terms of STIs) contraceptive method such as birth control pills.

When Do New Relationships Become Close Ones?   Fortenberry et al. (2002) examined the question of when a new relationship becomes a main or steady relationship, in the sense that condoms are no longer perceived to be needed. Using adolescents and young adults (mean age 17.6 years, range 13–22) and gathering data over time, they found that condom use tended to stop in most relationships at about 3 weeks from the beginning of sexual initiation within that relationship. This suggests that within quite a short amount of time, adolescents and young adults go from viewing one another as *casual* partners who they may need to protect themselves from to *main* or *close* partners who they perceive to be safe. The sawtooth pattern proposed by Ku et al. (1994) was observed in Fortenberry and colleagues' (2002) data in *new* partnerships, whereas established main partnerships demonstrated virtually no change in condom use over time. At 3 weeks time, both groups (new and established partnerships) were using condoms approximately 40% of the time, whereas new partnerships had previously been using condoms 66% of the time. Researchers have shown that condom use (and nonuse) are quite habitual in nature (Trafimow, 2000; Yzer, Siero, & Buunk, 2001), and more specifically that condom *nonuse* in close relationships may be more driven by habit as compared to casual relationships in which various situational characteristics (e.g., using alcohol, acting impulsively "in the moment") may be more important (Corbin & Fromme, 2002; de Visser & Smith, 2001; de Wit et al., 2000; Lynam, Zimmerman, & Monteith, 2003; Zimmerman, Lynam, & Monteith, 2003).

Unsafe Sex Within the Context of a Casual Relationship.   These data beg the question: What are the processes that lead individuals to perceive a partner (casual or main) to be safe in terms of STIs? It is clear that condom use and sexual *behavior* with main versus casual partners are quite different, suggesting that *perceptions* of these partner types are different as well. It is also clear that new or casual partners can become main partners relatively quickly in the eyes of adolescents and young adults. The decision to abandon condom use in some cases comes only after a very short amount of time has passed, when partners may not know one another's actual risk status. Thus, it is important here to examine both the literature that looks at the process of partner risk assessment in new or casual partners, as well as those processes that affect risk assessment in more established, main partner relationships. In addition, a reasonable proportion of adolescents and young adults have multiple sexual partners; for example, having both a main and casual partner (35%; Leigh et al., 1993). In these cases individuals may be engaging in both types of partner risk assessment concurrently.

First, we note that some adolescents and young adults use partner selection instead of condom use to avoid STIs (Civic, 2000; Keller, 1993; Maticka-Tyndale, 1991, 1992; Williams et al., 1992). In fact, Maticka-Tynadale (1992) found that the major rule used by young adult college students to avoid HIV was selection of what they perceived to be uninfected partners. This is despite data that suggest that using condoms consistently is the best way to protect against disease, even as compared to other strategies such as reducing number of sexual partners (Pinkerton & Abramson, 1993; Reiss & Leik, 1989). Even more intriguing is that the literature has demonstrated that individuals use superficial partner characteristics when assessing the STI risk of a potential sexual partner. Adolescents and young adults, when confronted with new partners, appear to equate superficial characteristics such as greater attractiveness of the partner and the appearance of health (Clark, Miller, Harrison, Kay, & Moore, 1996; Sheer & Cline, 1994), similarities to self (Malloy, Fisher, Albright, Misovich, & Fisher, 1997), general knowledge and liking of the person (Misovich, Fisher, & Fisher, 1996; Misovich et al., 1997; Williams et al., 1992), familiarity with the person (Swann, Silvera, & Proske, 1995), and "just knowing" a partner is safe (Civic, 2000; Keller, 1993) with lower STI risk. What these characteristics have in common, of course, is that there is no evidence that *any* of them are related to a partner's actual STI or HIV risk status. In addition, the belief that one can tell an uninfected partner from an infected partner has been found to be related to decreased condom use and lack of other HIV preventive intentions and behaviors in adolescents and young adult college students (Clark et al., 1996; Misovich et al., 1996). These data together indicate that some adolescents and young adults engage in unprotected intercourse with new or casual partners after engaging in a superficial risk assessment process that apparently satisfies them, but in reality does not in any way directly address the STI risk of their sexual partner.

One study found that individuals knew very little about the STI risk of partners at first intercourse, and additionally that individuals had made few attempts to find out any such information (Ingham, Woodcock, & Stenner, 1991). Perhaps worse than using superficial characteristics to try and assess a partner's risk status is the fact that some individuals do not engage in any risk assessment at all (Bowen & Michal-Johnson, 1989; Ingham et al., 1991; Keller, 1993; Overby & Kegeles, 1994). What researchers do not always take into account is that sex is by no means a reasoned and rational behavior, but rather involves intense emotions and sexual desire that may jeopardize both one's motivation and ability to stop and think about safe sex (Canin et al., 1999; Civic, 2000; Donohew et al., 2000; Kelly & Kalichman, 1995). Particularly in casual situations, but also in monogamous relationships, lust may take over and sex may occur without the use of protection. In fact, sex "just happening" has been given as a reason for not using condoms (Civic, 2000; Keller, 1993), and research supports the perception that for some, condoms "ruin the moment" and decrease pleasure (Sacco, Levine, Reed, & Thompson, 1991; Sacco, Rickman, Thompson, Levine, & Reed, 1993). Contrary to a rational, thoughtful process that some enter into with regard to partner risk assessment, others do not appear to engage in risk assessment at all. This may be particularly true of individuals with impulsive decision-making styles (Donohew et al., 2000), in casual sexual encounters where arousal and spontaneity may cloud one's judgment (Canin et al., 1999), and in situations where alcohol or illicit substances are involved (Cooper & Orcutt, 2000; Corbin & Fromme, 2002; Leigh & Stall, 1993; Lowry et al., 1994).

Further, another study found evidence of what the authors called the "ultimate irony" with regard to casual relationships (Bowen & Michal-Johnson, 1989, p. 15). In a sample of 243 college students, these researchers found that talk about HIV risk between casual partners was perceived to be too serious a topic relative to the seriousness of the sexual encounter. Thus, because the relationship (or lack thereof) was not perceived to be at all serious, it did not warrant talking about a serious topic such as HIV status and risk. As a result, some may have engaged in unprotected sex with a partner of unknown risk status (Bowen & Michal-Johnson, 1989).

Additionally, studies document the fact that some individuals will lie or minimize their past risky behaviors in order to persuade a partner to have sex (Cochran & Mays, 1990; Mays & Cochran, 1993; Stebleton & Rothenberger, 1993). In a study of 422 sexually active college students, Cochran and Mays (1990) found that a reasonable proportion of individuals (34% of men and 10% of women) told a lie to get a partner to have sex, and that significant proportions of individuals would lie in order to have sex again in the future. In addition, of those who had multiple sexual partners (32% of men and 23% of women), the majority reported that their main partner did not know about the additional partner(s). Further, men were significantly more likely to have lied, to be willing to lie in the future, and to have had multiple sexual partners. What is particularly interesting is that both men and women reported being lied to (Cochran & Mays, 1990), and both report knowing that partners will often minimize their risk histories in order to obtain sex (Mays & Cochran, 1993). Despite this knowledge, some men and women use sex partner questioning to gather information about a partner's risk history (Civic, 2000; Mays & Cochran, 1993). Swann et al. (1995) reported that individuals thought they could tell a difference between someone who was lying about their risk history compared to someone who was not. As it turns out, individuals could not, in fact, detect when a partner was lying about their HIV status (Swann et al., 1995). Unfortunately, in some cases, questioning a sex partner about their sexual history may serve in a manner that actually *enhances* sexual risk, rather than diminishing it (Civic, 2000; Cline, Freeman, & Johnson, 1990; Cline, Johnson, & Freeman, 1992; Mays & Cochran, 1993). That is, it appears that in some cases individuals ask potential partners questions about their risk histories, get answers that satisfy them, and then go on to have unprotected sex. In fact, Civic (2000) found that the number one reason that college students did not use condoms was that they claimed to know their partner's sexual history, despite the fact that they had not necessarily seen any hard evidence (e.g., STI test results). Though individuals sometimes obtain information that satisfies them in terms of safety, this is by no means a definitive indication that the partner is not infected with an STI.

However, the other side of this coin should be recognized and at some level applauded. Unlike the superficial and idiosyncratic decision rules used by many to attempt to assess partner risk, questioning a partner about his or her sexual history *is* a strategy that is at least relevant to STI risk. And, several studies indicate that a fair number of individuals use strategies such as questioning a sexual partner to try and assess a partner's actual STI risk (Clark et al., 1996; Cline et al., 1990; Cline et al., 1992; Keller, 1993; Mays & Cochran, 1993; Quina, Harlow, Morokoff, Burkholder, & Deiter, 2000; Rickert, Sanghvi, & Wiemann, 2002). As already noted, what is unclear is how effective such partner questioning might be in leading to behaviors that are truly safe in nature. Whereas some researchers appear to remain skeptical about the utility of partner questioning (Cline et al., 1990; Cline et al., 1992; Cochran & Mays, 1990; Misovich et al., 1997), the potential for successful partner questioning to reduce sexual risk has not been well studied (Wolitski & Branson, 2002). In fact, Quina et al. (2000) found in a community sample of women that those women who questioned their partners regarding sexual history were *more* likely to engage in safer sexual behaviors. Clearly, more research in this area is needed to assess if and how questioning a sexual partner can be used as a risk reduction strategy. Further, though researchers suggest that condom use is the best protective strategy, avoiding sex with high-risk partners should also be a high priority, as condoms are not 100% protective in all cases (e.g., Hearst & Hulley, 1988). Certain forms of sex partner questioning, if successful in nature, could at the very least promote dialogue between partners and perhaps lead to a decision to avoid sexual contact with a person who may be infected with an STI.

Unsafe Sex Within the Context of a Close Relationship. Within the context of a close relationship, there are several factors that may reduce the perceived STI risk and increase the chance of individuals having unprotected sex. Many of these factors are interrelated, and include trust, commitment, and investment (Civic, 2000; Cline et al., 1990; Hammer et al., 1996; Katz et al., 2000; Lock, Ferguson, & Wise, 1998;

Maticka-Tyndale, 1992; Misovich et al., 1997; Overby & Kegeles, 1994; Saul et al., 2000; Williams et al., 1992; Wingood & DiClemente, 1998), relational concerns taking precedence over health concerns (Bowen & Michal-Johnson, 1989; Cline et al., 1990; Hammer et al., 1996), and the idea that being in a monogamous relationship *in and of itself* makes one safe (Catania, Stone, Binson, & Dolcini, 1995; Civic, 2000; Comer & Nemeroff, 2000; Hammer et al., 1996; Keller, 1993; Misovich et al., 1997; Overby & Kegeles, 1994).

Trust itself is very powerful in relationships, and many activities couples engage in may facilitate the building of trust. However, in the sexual context it appears that couples feel that trust translates into automatic safety from STIs (Hammer et al., 1996; Lock et al., 1998; Overby & Kegeles, 1994; Williams et al., 1992). In some cases, adolescents engage in unsafe sexual practices with their main partner to demonstrate trust (Lock et al., 1998). It is also clear that condom use within the context of a close relationship can represent mistrust and arouse suspicions of cheating (Choi, Rickman, & Catania, 1994; Oncale & King, 2001; Overby & Kegeles, 1994; Wingood & DiClemente, 1998), especially if one were to make a suggestion to use condoms when they were not being used previously (Hammer et al., 1996; O'Donnell, Doval, Vornfett, & DeJong, 1994). Simply *talking about* STI risk is viewed as a violation of trust in some cases (Bowen & Michal-Johnson, 1989; Cline et al., 1990). In addition, the *contraceptive switch* that some couples make when they transition from condoms to hormonal birth control is seen as a very intimate and trust-building step in both adolescent and young adult relationships (Hammer et al., 1996; Maticka-Tyndale, 1992). Further, some studies found an association between trust and commitment-related beliefs and condom use. For instance, the belief that asking a partner to use condoms means you are implying they are unfaithful (Overby & Kegeles, 1994; Wingood & DiClemente, 1998), as well as the belief that losing a partner may mean losing additional friends and family (Saul et al., 2000) have both been found to be related to lower rates of condom use. In addition, higher relationship quality has been found to be related to lower rates of condom use in adolescent and young adult relationships (Katz et al., 2000). In sum, because of its many connotations, trust is clearly a major impediment to safer sexual behaviors such as condom use within close relationships.

Along with building trust, couples also seek to keep their relationships intact and moving forward in a positive manner. However, in some cases relational concerns can, in the sexual context, take precedence over health concerns such as STI risk (Bowen & Michal-Johnson, 1989; Cline et al., 1990; Hammer et al., 1996). Because relationships are perceived as fragile by young men and women (Hammer et al., 1996), there may be missed opportunities to talk about and assess risk. Bowen and Michal-Johnson (1989), in their sample of 243 college students, found that 40% of the sample wanted to talk about AIDS in their relationship but did *not* do so. Concern for the potential negative impact that the conversation might have on the relationship was a major reason for not doing so. Cline et al. (1990) found in a college sample that talk about AIDS clearly took a backseat position to other relationship concerns. In addition, when couples did talk about AIDS, it tended to be a very general conversation rather than specifics about how to reduce risk within the context of their relationship (Cline et al., 1990).

Perhaps the most perplexing finding is the misconception that being in a monogamous relationship, in and of itself, makes one safe. Comer and Nemeroff (2000) conducted a very interesting study in which individuals were given various scenarios to respond to with a range of safer or risky sexual decisions. The three scenarios were sex with a casual partner, sex with a main partner who was emotionally safe (but no risk information given), and sex with a main partner with risk information given (e.g., information about person's past sexual relationships, their actual negative HIV status, etc.). As expected, they found that individuals rated the casual condition as more risky than the other two conditions. However, what was particularly noteworthy was that they did *not* find a difference with regard to individuals' perceived risk or intention to use condoms in response to the two *main* partner scenarios. This study clearly makes the point that individuals in relationships blur emotional with physical safety (cf. Comer & Nemeroff, 2000) and assume that because one is in a close, monogamous relationship that one is automatically safe. Indeed, because the *emotionally safe* main partner scenario was described as a close, intimate relationship, participants *assumed* that it was a low STI risk scenario. They did not view this scenario as risky even though they had no sexual risk information about the partner, as compared to the other main partner condition where they had sexual risk information and knew the partner was safe.

Similarly, Overby and Kegeles (1994), in their study of minority female adolescents, found that young women perceived themselves at low risk for HIV despite high-risk practices, with much of the explanation for this being that they were in a monogamous relationship. The researchers concluded that "These findings suggest both a lack of recognition of the cumulative importance of their own and others past relationships and behaviors" (Overby & Kegeles, 1994, p. 225). Adolescents and young adults appear to enter monogamous relationships and within a short amount of time decide that their partner is safe from STIs and HIV, despite no direct evidence of this. Further, in addition to the fact that one partner may be infected with an STI when the individuals enter the relationship, Cochran and Mays' (1990) data on college students in which a significant minority had multiple sexual partners and the majority (68% of men and 59% of women) reported that their main partner was unaware of their multiple sexual partners is certainly relevant here. Studies also found significant proportions of adolescents who were in main partner relationships to have additional sexual partners as well (45%; Rosenberg et al., 1999). In addition, one study that surveyed both individuals and their main partners found that individuals underestimated the previous risk behavior of their main sexual partners. In fact, more than one third of the sample thought their main partner had not engaged in a series of risk behaviors such as injection drug use or ever having had sex with a man (for men only), when they actually had (Ellen, Vittinghoff, Bolan, Boyer, & Padian, 1998). If one partner is faithful and has unprotected sex with the other partner who has multiple sexual partners or other risk characteristics, than this first partner is clearly taking a risk, while likely thinking they are safe within their "monogamous" relationship.

In addition, Keller (1993) found that the number one reason cited by college students for not using condoms was that they were in a relationship. These data are clear: adolescents and young adults believe, by virtue of being in a close relationship, that they are invulnerable to STIs including HIV. Despite data regarding lying and cheating behaviors (Cochran & Mays, 1990), and the fact that they report knowing that many individuals minimize their risk histories (Mays & Cochran, 1993), these young men and women seem to think that monogamy simply implies safety. In this age group this finding has important implications because adolescents and young adults are often *serially monogamous,* entering into short-term relationship after relationship (CDC, 2000c; Corbin & Fromme, 2002; Misovich et al., 1997; Rosenberg et al., 1999). This finding has serious consequences for individuals in this age group, as those who pursue a path of serial monogamy may never see *any* partner as a risk if they employ this rule.

New Findings. Our research group recently collected data from 18 to 25-year-old young adults in college and from the community using a random digit dialing procedure and corroborated Comer and Nemeroff's (2000) findings while examining this phenomenon from a different angle (Noar, Zimmerman, & Palmgreen, 2003). In our sample of 606 young adults (58% female) collected from two cities in Kentucky and Tennessee, we asked individuals to rate the likelihood that a person in a certain scenario would contract an STI. First, individuals were asked how likely it was that a person would get an STI if they *always* used condoms with their partner (partner type not specified). Eighteen percent thought this was somewhat or very likely. This perhaps reflects the fact that condoms may not be 100% effective against *every* STI, and the efficacy of condoms certainly decreases when they are not used correctly. However, 34% thought it was somewhat or very likely that an individual would get an STI by having unprotected sex with a *main/steady partner*, as compared to 82% who thought it was somewhat or very likely with a *casual partner*. Thus, these data reveal that young adults see main partners as significantly safer than casual partners. Further, these data suggest that young adults view either consistent condom use or unsafe sex with a main partner as protective from STIs. Clearly, consistent condom use with a partner is a much safer behavior than unsafe sex with a main partner of unknown STI status.

Because of the many misconceptions discussed related to the difference between partners' perceived and actual STI risk status, numerous researchers have suggested that the Surgeon General's advice in the 1980s to *know your partner* as an HIV prevention strategy should be abandoned or at the very least modified (Cline et al., 1990; Hammer et al., 1996; Ingham et al., 1991; Misovich et al., 1996, 1997; Williams et al., 1992). Certainly, adolescents and young adults would benefit from a more in-depth explanation of what, if anything, the *know your partner* advice might achieve in terms of sexual risk reduction. Knowing superficial characteristics about one's partner most likely does not offer protection against STIs. However, if partners are able to communicate and as a result, get tested and know one another to be disease free, or consistently use condoms as a result of communicating, then certainly *knowing your partner* at this level is quite beneficial.

Sexual Assertiveness, Negotiation, and Communication.   The case has been made that safer sexual behavior is different from other health behaviors in a number of ways, most notably that it is a dyadic behavior involving two people that occurs in a relationship context (Amaro, 1995; Kelly & Kalichman, 1995; Ku et al., 1994; Logan et al., 2002; Mays & Cochran, 1988; Metts & Fitzpatrick, 1992; Noar, Morokoff, & Harlow, 2002a; Noar et al., 2001). Other health behaviors such as exercise, smoking cessation, and eating a healthy diet are more individualistic and do not occur in a dyadic, relationship context. This has led researchers to study patterns of communication and sexual assertiveness between partners. A sizeable literature finds that individuals who are communicative and sexually assertive specifically with regard to safer sexual behavior and condom use are more likely to engage in safer sexual behaviors including condom use (Grimley, Prochaska, & Prochaska, 1993, 1997; Harlow, Quina, Morokoff, Rose, & Grimley, 1993; Morokoff et al., 1997; Noar, 2003; Noar et al., 2001, Noar, Morokoff, & Redding, 2002b; Redding et al., 2002; Sheeran et al., 1999; Zamboni, Crawford, & Williams, 2000). Sexual communication and assertiveness have been found to be positively related to condom use (Grimley et al., 1993; Harlow et al., 1993; Noar, 2003; Noar, Morokoff, & Harlow, in press; Noar et al., 2001, 2002a, 2002b; Redding et al., 2002; Sheeran et al., 1999; Zamboni et al., 2000) and negatively related to unprotected intercourse (Harlow et al., 1993; Noar et al., 2002b). Thus, condom-specific communication and assertiveness appear to operate as protective factors related to risky and safer sexual behaviors in young men and women. These communicative behaviors can take place within the context of main or casual sexual relationships. Little research has examined these behaviors separately in casual as compared to main partner relationships, however, in order to understand differences in how communication might be carried out in the various relationship contexts. Grimley et al. (1993) examined sexual assertiveness for condom use in a heterosexually active sample of college men and women ($N = 248$) in both main and casual partners. They found that higher levels of sexual assertiveness were associated with more consistent condom use with both main and casual partners. More research that considers communication and assertiveness in different relationship contexts is warranted.

Research has more extensively examined the role of gender in the communication process, and demonstrated that women tend to take a more active role in this communication process, with men taking a more passive role (Carter, McNair, Corbin, & Williams, 1999; Debro, Campbell, & Peplau, 1994; Lock et al., 1998; Noar et al., 2002a). This may be in part because males are the ones who actually wear condoms, leaving women in a position where they more often need to make a request that condoms be used. It may also be that traditional gender role dynamics and pregnancy concerns put the contraceptive responsibility on the female, leaving women in a position where they may more often take the initiative to communicate about safer sex as compared to men (Amaro, 1995; Noar & Morokoff, 2002; Quina, Harlow, Morokoff, & Saxon, 1997; Troth & Peterson, 2000). As the risk status of casual and main partners is often unknown, it remains a high priority to encourage both young men and women to be assertive about safer sexual behaviors with their partners until it is clear that the relationship is monogamous *and* that partners have been tested and are free of STIs including HIV. Encouraging sexual assertiveness means instilling several skills in young men and women, including the ability to insist on condom use with a partner, the ability to insist on condom use with a resistant partner, and the ability to refuse unprotected sex if a partner refuses to use a condom (Noar et al., 2002b). As we continue to learn about the dynamics of communication in both close and casual relationships, we become better able to design interventions that promote healthy communication between partners that results in sexual behaviors that do not put individuals at risk for STIs.

Close Relationships and STI Incidence

As mentioned earlier, the consequences of STIs in young people are significant. For instance, human papillomavirus (HPV) infection in adolescents has been associated with increased risk of cervical neoplasia (American Academy of Pediatrics, 1994). Hepatitis B and C have been associated with cirrhosis and carcinoma, and untreated chlamydia in young women can lead to pelvic inflammatory disease and sterility (American Academy of Pediatrics, 1994).

Because of these substantial health risks, numerous studies have attempted to identify correlates of STI diagnosis in an effort to stem the tide of transmission. Such studies have identified early age at first intercourse (Coker et al., 1994), previous STIs (Crosby, Leichliter, & Brackbill, 2000), multiple, concurrent, or high-risk sexual partners (Morris & Kretzschmar, 1997; Mosure et al., 1997; Rosenberg et al., 1999; Stergachis et al., 1993), inconsistent use of condoms (Cates, 1990; CDC, 2001; Steiner, Cates, & Lee, 1999), and substance use (Ellen, Langer, Zimmerman, Cabral, & Fichtner, 1996) as predictors of STI infection.

The critical component that is frequently overlooked in studies of STIs is the role of the relationship in STI transmission (Rosenberg et al., 1999). Whereas studies of safer sex already reviewed examined the association between relationship type and condom use, such studies rarely include biologic markers of infection. Including biologic markers would mean actually testing individuals for STIs, and there are several reasons for the absence of biologic markers in such studies. First, outside of STI clinics, it is very challenging to recruit minors or young adults for STI testing. Although there are now less invasive urine-based tests for chlamydia and gonorrhea, and tests under development for trichomoniasis (Blake, 2001), their use is not widespread. Second, although adolescent research on relationship characteristics and STIs is needed, it has been debated whether parental consent is required for testing programs that involve research. Obtaining parental consent poses significant challenges and raises questions about sampling bias. Finally, although STI outcomes are important, there is considerable complexity in trying to make the case that a certain STI was transmitted within a specific relationship. Whereas biologic measures can assess the presence of infection, researchers are less able to detect whether the infection is a new (incident) infection or the recurrence of a previous infection (Fishbein & Pequegnat, 2000). This blurring of the distinction between incidence and prevalence adds to the complexity of linking STI infection to specific partners when it is unclear when the infection occurred. To assess the association between relationship type and the biologic STI outcome, one would need to conduct longitudinal studies of populations who are infection free at the start of the study. One would then need to test both the individual and their past and current sexual partners repeatedly throughout the study, in order to make determinations regarding from whom an STI was transmitted.

In addition, long-standing sociologic research methods such as social network analysis are needed to better understand the spread of infection within sexual networks, including the timing, duration, and extent of overlap in multiple partnerships and the shared sexual behaviors between the individual and his or her sexual network (Laumann, Gagnon, Michael, & Michaels, 1994; Morris & Kretzschmar, 1997; Potterat et al., 1999). The few studies that have assessed the extent of overlap in multiple partnerships and their association with an STI diagnosis have examined relationship *concurrency*, defined as having sex with a main partner and other sex partners during the same time interval. In studies of adolescents (Rosenberg et al., 1999) and adults (Potterat et al., 1999), researchers have found that the greater the number of concurrent sexual partners, the greater the odds of STI. The data suggest that having a larger number of concurrent sexual partners increases the number of people to whom the individual is connected to at a given time, thereby increasing the possibility of exposure to infection. What is alarming is that the data suggest that relationship concurrency among adolescents is not uncommon. In Rosenberg and colleagues' (1999) study of 283 adolescents in an STI clinic, one third were not completely monogamous with their main partner. In an analysis of the Adolescent Health Survey of 13 to 17 year olds, 56% reported having two or more sexual partners, and of those, more than half reported being involved in these partnerships during the same period of time (Ford et al., 2002). Other researchers have found significant evidence of concurrency of sexual partnerships in adolescents and young adults (Garnett et al., 1996; Oliver & Hyde, 1993).

What makes these concurrent partnerships so key to disease transmission is that individuals tend to be involved with sex partners who engage in similar levels of sexual activity (Garnett et al., 1996). This suggests that one's concurrent partners also have concurrent partners, expanding the sexual network to which an individual is connected (Rosenberg et al., 1999). As mentioned previously in this chapter, individuals may be more likely to use condoms with casual partners to protect themselves from infection from the "outside," but less likely to introduce condoms into established relationships (e.g., Friedman et al., 2001; Misovich et al., 1997). Thus, for main partners to remain uninfected, both partners in a couple need to be vigilant about using condoms during any other sexual encounter. This logic, of course, presumes that both partners in a close relationship view the relationship in the same way. Should a sexual partner define more than one relationship as "close," and thereby engage in unprotected sexual intercourse with multiple partners, then clearly those partners are at increased risk of contracting an STI.

New Findings.   In conjunction with the CDC, we conducted 30 to 40 minute interviews with 3,000 STI clients in six major cities over a 2-year period in 1990 and 1991

(Ellen et al., 1996; Langer, Zimmerman, & Cabral, 1994). For over half of the sample, results of laboratory tests for STIs were linked to the interview data. This gave us the unique opportunity to assess the association among relationship status, use of condoms with main and other partners, and current STIs. For our analyses here we selected participants under age 30 who did not identify as gay, had had sex in the past 3 months, and were tested for STIs ($N = 880$). Results indicated that those who had intercourse (in the last 3 months) with someone they considered to be a main sexual partner had a slightly lower prevalence of STIs (82%) as compared to those who had intercourse only with individuals they did not consider to be main sexual partners (90%), though this difference was not statistically significant. Length of time in the main sexual partnership was unrelated to STI prevalence. However, among those with a main partner, those with zero to two additional partners were less likely to receive an STI diagnosis (82%) than those with three or more additional partners (90%). Surprisingly, there were no significant differences in STI prevalence among those with zero, one, or two other partners in addition to a main partner. These associations were most clear and consistent for gonorrhea and nongonococcal urethritis, which were also the most prevalent STIs in this sample. In addition, we found that men who never used condoms with their main partners exhibited the clearest pattern. Among these men, 84% of those with no additional partners had an STI as compared to 96% of those with five or more additional partners, with those in between these groups exhibiting a fairly linear pattern. Overall, these results suggest that being in a main relationship may be protective in some instances, although the combination of engaging in unprotected sex in a main relationship and having multiple additional partners may be especially risky with regard to STIs.

IMPLICATIONS AND DIRECTIONS FOR FUTURE RESEARCH

There are several areas that future research should explore. First, a better understanding of close relationships and relationship factors is key to understanding both the STI and HIV epidemics. These infections do not occur in a vacuum, nor do they always occur in casual relationships. Rather, sexual behavior often takes place in the context of close relationships, and as we have seen, this often puts individuals at risk as their guard tends to be down. New research should include ways to better assess types of relationships, moving beyond the main/casual distinction, for instance, to finer gradations of relationships in terms of intimacy, quality, and other important factors. Further research is needed that more precisely measures the quality, level of intimacy, duration, and frequency of contact with *first* sexual partners as well, as the literature has demonstrated the enormous influence that first sexual experiences have on later behaviors.

In addition, many questions remain with regard to *first* sexual experiences. Do such experiences set one on a more positive or negative trajectory in terms of risky sexual experiences later in life, depending on the context (type of relationship, age of individual) in which they occur? The data here suggest that this may be the case. In addition, what is the "ideal" age of first sexual intercourse? Whereas early initiation of sexual intercourse is correlated with risky outcomes as compared to later initiation, the mechanisms through which this risk occurs are unclear. Is it merely that starting one's sexual experiences at an earlier age affords more time for negative experiences, or is there a more complex explanation with regard to early initiators? In particular, to what extent do individual differences (e.g., personality variables such as impulsivity or sensation-seeking) and demographic factors (e.g., gender, race, social class) interact with these early sexual experiences to affect later sexual risk taking? Finally, there appears to be a bit of a conundrum in that those in relationships initiate earlier, which appears to be associated with negative outcomes; whereas those who initiate early who are in close relationships tend to use condoms in those instances, which is positive. The complexity of initiation and its relation to later positive and negative consequences deserves more research attention. Evidence presented here suggests that interventions to reduce sexual risk should be designed both to delay initiation of sexual activity and to discourage sexual activity within casual partnerships.

In addition, it remains very important to continue to understand the process by which individuals assess their sexual partners' risk. The data we presented that demonstrate that individuals see main partners as much *less* of an STI risk than casual partners beg for more research to understand the process of why this is the case. It is important that such work is done in high-risk populations such as at-risk heterosexual women, commercial sex workers, and men who have sex with men (e.g., Gold & Skinner, 1996; Gold, Skinner, & Hinchy, 1999; Offir, Fisher, Williams, & Fisher, 1993), as most studies on this topic have been conducted using college students (who are at lower risk than these other populations). It also remains important to examine the potential effectiveness of sex partner questioning and partner selection strategies on STI risk behavior. Though some strategies may be problematic in nature, some may hold promise in terms of reducing sexual risk taking. Researchers note that there has been little research on the effectiveness of such strategies (Canin et al., 1999; Wolitski & Branson, 2002). Thus, all we can say at this point is that individuals use various strategies, but we have little information about which strategies may be effective versus ineffective.

Related to this, we cannot realistically expect individuals to use condoms consistently throughout their entire life. Thus, we need to better educate adolescents and young adults when, and under what circumstances, discontinuing condom use is advisable. It is currently a reality that many couples discontinue condom use at a relatively early point in a serious relationship and as a result, may be putting themselves at risk. Couples need to know that they are safe from STIs before discontinuing condom use, and changing the risk perceptions and risky behaviors within relationships will likely involve education as well as communication skill building. As discussed, research on communication and assertiveness about condom use has largely ignored relationship status and partner type. Future work should examine differences in communication patterns between close and casual partners. Common sense tells us that different partner types will talk differently with one another about condom use, though this is an open, empirical question.

In addition, research on how condoms can become a symbol of safety and caring in relationships, rather than mistrust, is important (Choi et al., 1994; Hammer et al., 1996; Sherman & Latkin, 2001). Noar et al. (2002a) found that some individuals, especially women, used a strategy that entailed telling their partner how much they cared about them in order to get the partner to use a condom. In this same vein, it would seem critical to examine how condoms can come to represent more of a symbol of caring for a partner's health, rather than the perceptions of mistrust and other negative connotations currently associated with condoms.

Further, it is critical that we have better data related to actual STIs and relationship type. Though such studies may be difficult to undertake, they nonetheless should be conducted. The better we can document the association between types of relationships and STIs, the better able we will be to address the risky relationship contexts. In fact, interventions that focus on couples and include relationship factors as a focus may be more effective than individually focused interventions (Canin et al., 1999; El-Bassel et al., 2001; Katz et al., 2000; Misovich et al., 1997). Few such interventions have been developed or evaluated, and this remains a high priority as well. Such interventions would have the opportunity to address the multiple barriers to condom use that occur within relationships.

Finally, as social psychological theory drives much of the work in HIV prevention, such theory should be expanded to include contextual influences such as relationship factors (Canin et al. 1999; Noar et al., 2001; Sheeran et al., 1999). How one might go about expanding such theoretical frameworks is a question to be carefully considered. For instance, the Theory of Planned Behavior (TPB; Ajzen & Madden, 1986) proposes that an individual's attitudes, subjective norms, and perceived behavioral control with regard to a behavior explain health-related behaviors such as condom use. Sheeran and colleagues (Sheeran et al., 1999; Sheeran & Taylor, 1999) proposed additions to this theory such as considering a sexual *partner's* normative beliefs about condom use. In addition, they suggest that a partner's attitude about condom use is important as well, and provide empirical evidence from meta-analyses in support of these variables (Sheeran et al., 1999; Sheeran & Taylor, 1999). Further, Bryan, Fisher, and Fisher (2002) suggest that a construct they call *preparatory behaviors* be added to the TPB. They conceptualize these behaviors, which are thought to directly precede actual condom use, as buying condoms, carrying condoms, and communicating about condom use with a partner. Empirical evidence for this addition to the TPB has also been provided (Bryan et al., 2002; Sheeran et al., 1999). These suggested additions to theory reflect the dyadic and relationship-oriented nature of sexual encounters and the desire to extend theory to better understand safer sexual behavior. Further, other theories have either added or proposed similar additions in attempts to better take into account relationship factors that are associated with condom use (e.g., Grimley et al., 1993, 1997; Noar et al., 2001, 2002b). Our research group's current work in model development proposes using Fishbein's Integrated Behavior Change Model (Fishbein, 2000), and incorporating situational and environmental variables such as relationship status and alcohol and other substance use to understand sexual behavior and condom use (Zimmerman, Cupp, Atwood, Feist-Price, & Donohew, 2003; Zimmerman, Noar, Feist-Price, Anderman, & Cupp, 2003).

In addition, theories from human sexuality and the study of relationships, such as social exchange theories (Sprecher, 1998) and sexual scripts (Edgar & Fitzpatrick, 1993; Gagnon, 1990), may be useful in further informing the expansion of current theoretical frameworks or perhaps leading to the creation of new frameworks. Most current theories of safer sexual behavior (such as the TPB) do not take into account various dynamics related to sex, such as gender and power-related dynamics. Sexual scripts (Gagnon, 1990) are a framework for understanding the sexual behavior of, for instance, heterosexual couples. Such scripts describe the typical or "traditional" manner in which sex occurs, including who initiates sex as well as other dynamics within a sexual situation. Where safer sexual behaviors such as condom use fit into the sexual script is an issue that remains largely unexplored (Noar, 2002). For instance, who initiates condom use, how does it happen, and what are the sometimes nonverbal communications and negotiations that take place around condom use? Further, do these vary according to type of sexual partner, the sexual situation, or other situational variants? And, what are the roles of emotion, passion, lust, and sexual arousal in relation to safer sexual behavior? These are issues that have been touched on by some literature but that have not been systematically studied or integrated into an explanatory safer sexual framework or theory. An understanding of exactly how condom use fits into sexual scripts, described in a frame-by-frame type of model, would be quite useful both in terms of understanding safer sexual behavior and in creating new interventions. Said another way, if we know where the "weak link" is in the metaphorical chain (e.g., sexual script) that leads to condom use, we may be better able to intervene and strengthen such a link. This is a much larger step than adding a small number of new variables to an existing theory, such as has been suggested with the TPB. However, such research might result in a better understanding of safer sexual behavior through a broader understanding of situational influences and dynamics that take place in sexual situations.

ACKNOWLEDGMENT

The authors wish to thank T. K. Logan and Sharon Lock for helpful comments made on an earlier version of this chapter and Megan Dyer for her assistance in locating and retrieving references.

REFERENCES

Adams, R. E., Laursen B., & Wilder, D. (2001). Characteristics of closeness in adolescent romantic relationships. *Journal of Adolescence, 24,* 353–363.

Ajzen, I., & Fishbein, M. (1980). *Understanding attitudes and predicting behavior.* Englewood Cliffs, NJ: Prentice-Hall.

Ajzen, I., & Madden, T. J. (1986). Prediction of goal-directed behavior: Attitudes, intentions, and perceived behavioral control. *Journal of Experimental Social Psychology, 22,* 453–474.

Amaro, H. (1995). Love, sex, and power: Considering women's realities in HIV prevention. *American Psychologist, 50*(6), 437–447.

American Academy of Pediatrics, Committee on Adolescence. (1994). Sexually transmitted diseases. *Pediatrics, 94*(4), 568–573.

Baker, S. A., Morrison, D. M, Gillmore, M. R., & Schock, M. D. (1995). Sexual behaviors, substance use, and condom use in a sexually transmitted disease clinic sample. *The Journal of Sex Research, 32*(1), 37–44.

Bandura, A. (1986). *Social foundations of thought and action: A social cognitive theory.* Englewood Cliffs, NJ: Prentice-Hall.

Becker, M. H. (1974). The health belief model and personal health behavior. *Health Education Monographs, 2*(4), entire issue.

Blake, D. R. (2001). The future is here: Noninvasive diagnosis of STDs in teens. *Contemporary OB/GYN, 46*(3), 103–110.

Bowen, S. P., & Michal-Johnson, P. (1989). The crisis of communicating in relationships: Confronting the threat of AIDS. *AIDS & Public Policy Journal, 4*(1), 10–19.

Brooks-Gunn J., & Furstenberg, F. E. (1989). Adolescent sexual behavior. *American Psychologist, 44,* 249–257.

Brown, B. B., Feiring, C., & Furman, W. (1999). Missing the love boat: Why researchers have shied away from adolescent romance. In W. Furman, B. B. Bradford, & C. Feiring (Eds.), *The development of romantic relationships in adolescence* (pp. 1–16). Cambridge, UK: Cambridge University Press.

Bryan, A., Fisher, J. D., & Fisher, W. A. (2002). Tests of the mediational role of preparatory safer sexual behavior in the context of the theory of planned behavior. *Health Psychology, 21*(1), 71–80.

Canin, L., Dolcini, M. M., & Adler, N. E. (1999). Barriers to and facilitators of HIV–STD behavior change: Intrapersonal and relationship-based factors. *Review of General Psychology, 3*(4), 338–371.

Carter, J. A., McNair, L. D., Corbin, W. R., & Williams, M. (1999). Gender differences related to heterosexual condom use: The influence of negotiation styles. *Journal of Sex & Marital Therapy, 25,* 217–225.

Catania, J. A., Kegeles, S. M., & Coates, T. J. (1990). Towards an understanding of risk behavior: An AIDS risk reduction model (ARRM). *Health Education Quarterly, 17*(1), 53–72.

Catania, J. A., Stone, V., Binson, D., & Dolcini, M. M. (1995). Changes in condom use among heterosexuals in wave 3 of the Amen Survey. *The Journal of Sex Research, 32*(3), 193–200.

Cate, R. M., Levin, L. A., & Richmond, L. S. (2002). Premarital relationship stability: A review of recent research. *Journal of Social and Personal Relationships, 19*(2), 261–284.

Cates, W. (1990). The epidemiology and control of sexually transmitted diseases in adolescents. *Adolescent Medicine: State of the Art Reviews, 1*(3), 409–427.

Cates, W. (1999). Estimates of the incidence and prevalence of sexually transmitted diseases in the United States. *Sexually Transmitted Diseases, 26*(Suppl. 4), S2–S7.

Centers for Disease Control and Prevention. (1998). HIV prevention through early detection and treatment of other sexually transmitted diseases—United States. Recommendations of the advisory committee for HIV and STD prevention. *Morbidity and Mortality Weekly Report, 47,* 1–24.

Centers for Disease Control and Prevention. (2001) HIV/AIDS Surveillance-General Epidemiology. L178 slide series through 2001. Retrieved August 24, 2002 from http://www.cdc.gov/hiv/graphics/images/l178/l178–8.htm

Centers for Disease Control and Prevention. (2000a). *Tracking the hidden epidemics: Trends in STDs in the United States.* Atlanta, GA: Department of Health and Human Services, Division of STD Prevention.

Centers for Disease Control and Prevention. (2000b). *STD 2000 surveillance slides.* Retrieved August 24, 2002 from http://www.cdc.gov/std/2000Slides.htm

Centers for Disease Control and Prevention. (2000c). *Sexually transmitted disease surveillance, 1999.* Atlanta, GA: Department of Health and Human Services, Division of STD Prevention.

Centers for Disease Control and Prevention. (2001). *HIV/AIDS surveillance report, 13*(2). Atlanta, GA: Department of Health and Human Services.

Choi, K. H., & Catania, J. A. (1996). Changes in multiple sexual partnerships, HIV testing, and condom use among U.S. heterosexuals 18 to 49 years of age, 1990 and 1992. *American Journal of Public Health, 86*(4), 554–556.

Choi, K. H., Rickman, R., & Catania, J. A. (1994). What heterosexual adults believe about condoms [Letter to the editor]. *The New England Journal of Medicine, 331*(6), 406–407.

Civic, D. (2000). College students' reasons for nonuse of condoms within dating relationships. *Journal of Sex & Marital Therapy, 26*, 95–105.

Clark, L. F., Miller, K. S., Harrison, J. S., Kay, K. L., & Moore, J. (1996). The role of attraction in partner assessments and heterosexual risk for HIV. In S. Oskamp & S. C. Thompson (Eds.), *Understanding and preventing HIV risk behavior: Safer sex and drug use* (pp. 80–99). Thousand Oaks, CA: Sage.

Cline, R. J. W., Freeman, K. E., & Johnson, S. J. (1990). Talk among sexual partners about AIDS: Factors differentiating those who talk from those who do not. *Communication Research, 17*(6), 792–808.

Cline, R. J. W., Johnson, S. J., & Freeman, K. E. (1992). Talk among sexual partners about AIDS: Interpersonal communication for risk reduction or risk enhancement? *Health Communication, 4*(1), 39–56.

Cochran, S. D., & Mays, V. M. (1990). Sex, lies, and HIV [Letter to the editor]. *The New England Journal of Medicine, 322*(11), 774–775.

Coker, A. L., Richter, D. L., Valois, R. F., McKeown, R. E., Garrison, C. Z., & Vincent, M. L. (1994). Correlates and consequences of early initiation of sexual intercours. *Journal of School Health, 64*(9), 372–378.

Comer, L. K., & Nemeroff, C. J. (2000). Blurring emotional safety with physical safety in AIDS and STD risk estimations: The casual/regular partner distinction. *Journal of Applied Social Psychology, 30*(12), 2467–2490.

Cooper, M. L., & Orcutt, H. K. (2000). Alcohol use, condom use and partner type among heterosexual adolescents and young adults. *Journal of Studies on Alcohol, 61*, 413–419.

Corbin, W. R., & Fromme, K. (2002). Alcohol use and serial monogamy as risks for sexually transmitted diseases in young adults. *Health Psychology, 21*(3), 229–236.

Crockett, L. J., Bingham, R., Chopak, J. S., & Vicary, J. R. (1996). Timing of first sexual intercourse: The role of social control, social learning and problem behavior. *Journal of Youth and Adolescence, 25*(1), 89–111.

Crosby, R., Leichliter J. S., & Brackbill R. (2000). Longitudinal prediction of sexually transmitted diseases among adolescents: Results from a national survey. *American Journal of Preventive Medicine, 18*(4), 312–317.

Debro, S. C., Campbell, S. M., & Peplau, L. A. (1994). Influencing a partner to use a condom: A college student perspective. *Psychology of Women Quarterly, 18*, 165–182.

de Visser, R., & Smith, A. (2001). Relationship between sexual partners influences rates and correlates of condom use. *AIDS Education and Prevention, 13*(5), 413–427.

de Wit, J. B. F., Stroebe, W., de Vroome, E. M. M., Sandfort, T. G. M., & Van Griensven, G. J. P. (2000). Understanding AIDS preventive behavior with casual and primary partners in homosexual men: The theory of planned behavior and the information–motivation–behavioral–skills model. *Psychology and Health, 15*, 325–340.

DiIorio, C., Resnicow, K., Thomas, S., Wang, D. T., Dudley, W. N., Van Marter, D. F., & Lipana, J. (2002). Keepin' it R.E.A.L!: Program description and results of baseline assessment. *Health Education and Behavior, 29*(1), 104–123.

Donohew, L., Zimmerman, R. S., Cupp, P. S., Novak, S., Colon, S., & Abell, R. (2000). Sensation seeking, impulsive decision-making, and risky sex: Implications for risk-taking and design of interventions. *Personality and Individual Differences, 28*, 1079–1091.

Dorius, G. L., Heaton, T. B., & Steffen, P. (1993). Adolescent life events and their association with the onset of sexual intercourse. *Youth & Society, 25*(1), 21–24.

Duemmler, S. L., & Kobak, R. (2001). The development of commitment and attachment in dating relationships: Attachment security as relationship construct. *Journal of Adolescence, 24*, 401–415.

Edgar, T., & Fitzpatrick, M. A. (1993). Expectations for sexual interaction: A cognitive test of the sequencing of sexual communication behaviors. *Health Communication, 5*(4), 239–261.

El-Bassel, N., Witte, S. S., Gilbert, L., Sormanti, M., Moreno, C., Pereira, L., Elam, E., & Steinglass, P. (2001). HIV prevention for intimate couples: A relationship-based model. *Families, Systems, & Health, 19*(4), 379–395.

Ellen, J. M., Langer, L. M., Zimmerman, R. S., Cabral, R. J., & Fichtner, R. (1996). The link between the use of crack cocaine and the sexually transmitted diseases of a clinic population: A comparison of adolescents with adults. *Sexually Transmitted Diseases, 23*(6), 511–516.

Ellen, J. M., Vittinghoff, E., Bolan, G., Boyer, C. B., & Padian, N. S. (1998). Individuals' perceptions about their sex partners' risk behavior. *The Journal of Sex Research, 35*(4), 328–332.

Fishbein, M. (2000). The role of theory in HIV prevention. *AIDS Care, 12*(3), 273–278.

Fishbein, M., & Pequegnat, W. (2000). Evaluating AIDS prevention interventions using behavioral and biological outcome measures. *Sexually Transmitted Diseases, 27*(2), 101–110.

Fisher, J. D., & Fisher, W. A. (1992). Changing AIDS-risk behavior. *Psychological Bulletin, 111*(3), 455–474.

Ford, K., Sohn, W., & Lepkowski, J. (2002). American adolescents: Sexual mixing patterns, bridge partners, and concurrency. *Sexually Transmitted Diseases, 29*, 13–19.

Fortenberry, J. D., Tu, W., Harezlak, J., Katz, B. P., & Orr, D. P. (2002). Condom use as a function of time in new and established adolescent sexual relationships. *American Journal of Public Health, 92*(2), 211–213.

Friedman, S. R., Flom, P. L., Kottiri, B. J., Neaigus, A., Sandvol, M., Curtis, R., Des Jarlais, D. C., & Zenilman, J. M. (2001). Consistent condom use in the heterosexual relationships of young adults who live in a high-HIV-risk neighbourhood and do not use "hard drugs." *AIDS Care, 13*(3), 285–296.

Furman, W., Brown, B. B., & Feiring, C. (Eds.). (1999). *The development of romantic relationships in adolescence.* Cambridge, UK: Cambridge University Press.

Gagnon, J. H. (1990). The explicit and implicit use of the scripting perspective in sex research. *Annual Review of Sex Research, 1*, 1–43.

Garnett, G. P., Hughes, J. P., Anderson, R. M., Stoner, B. P., Aral, S. O., Whittington, W. L., Handsfield, H. H., & Holmes, K. K. (1996). Sexual mixing patterns of patients attending sexually transmitted disease clinics. *Sexually Transmitted Diseases, 23*, 248–257.

Gold, R. S., & Skinner, M. J. (1996). Judging a book by its cover: Gay men's use of perceptible characteristics to infer antibody status. *International Journal of STD & AIDS, 7*, 39–43.

Gold, R. S., Skinner, M. J., & Hinchy, J. (1999). Gay men's stereotypes about who is HIV infected: A further study. *International Journal of STD & AIDS, 10*, 600–605.

Greenberg, J., Magder, L., & Aral, S. (1992). Age of first coitus. A marker for risky sexual behavior in women. *Sexually Transmitted Diseases, 19*, 331–334.

Grimley, D. M., Prochaska, G. E., & Prochaska, J. O. (1993). Condom use assertiveness and the stages of change with main and other partners. *Journal of Applied Biobehavioral Research, 1*(2), 152–173.

Grimley, D. M., Prochaska, G. E., & Prochaska, J. O. (1997). Condom use adoption and continuation: A transtheoretical approach. *Health Education Research, 12*(1), 61–75.

Hammer, J. C., Fisher, J. D., Fitzgerald, P., & Fisher, W. A. (1996). When two heads aren't better than one: AIDS risk behavior in college-age couples. *Journal of Applied Social Psychology, 26*(5), 375–397.

Harlow, L. L., Quina, K., Morokoff, P. J., Rose, J. S., & Grimley, D. M. (1993). HIV risk in women: A multifaceted model. *Journal of Applied Biobehavioral Research, 1*(1), 3–38.

Hayes, C. D. (1987). *Risking the future: Adolescent sexuality, pregnancy, and childbearing.* Washington, DC: National Academy Press.

Hearst, N., & Hulley, S. B. (1988). Preventing the heterosexual spread of AIDS: Are we giving our patients the best advice? *Journal of the American Medical Association, 259*(16), 2428–2432.

Heaton, T. B., & Jacobson, C. K. (1994). Race differences in changing family demographics in the 1980s. *Journal of Family Issues, 15*, 290–308.

Hogan, D. P., & Kitagawa, E. M. (1985). The impact of social status, family structure and neighborhood on the fertility of Black adolescents *American Journal of Sociology, 90*, 825–855.

Ingham, R., Woodcock, A., & Stenner, K. (1991). Getting to know you . . . Young people's knowledge of their partners at first intercourse. *Journal of Community & Applied Social Psychology, 1*, 117–132.

Kann, L., & Kinchen S. A. (1998). Youth risk behavior surveillance—United States, 1997. *MMWR CDC Surveillance Summary, 47*(SS-03), 1–89.

Karon, J. M., Fleming, P. L., Steketee, R. W., & De Cock, K. M. (2001). HIV in the United States at the turn of the century: An epidemic in transition. *American Journal of Public Health, 91*, 1060–1068.

Katz, B. P., Fortenberry, J. D., Zimet, G. D., Blythe, M. J., & Orr, D. P. (2000). Partner-specific relationship characteristics and condom use among young people with sexually transmitted diseases. *The Journal of Sex Research, 37*(1), 69–75.

Keller, M. L. (1993). Why don't young adults protect themselves against sexual transmission of HIV? Possible answers to a complex question. *AIDS Education and Prevention, 5*(3), 220–233.

Kelly, J. A., & Kalichman, S. C. (1995). Increased attention to human sexuality can improve HIV–AIDS prevention efforts: Key research issues and directions. *Journal of Consulting and Clinical Psychology, 63*(6), 907–918.

Kordoutis, P. S., Loumakou, M., & Sarafidou, J. O. (2000). Heterosexual relationship characteristics, condom use and safe sex practises. *AIDS Care, 12*(6), 767–782.

Ku, L., Sonenstein, F. L., & Pleck, J. H. (1994). The dynamics of young men's condom use during and across relationships. *Family Planning Perspectives, 26*, 246–251.

Laumann, E. O., Gagnon, J. H., Michael, R. T., & Michaels, S. (1994).*The social organization of sexuality: Sexual practices in the United States.* Chicago, IL: University of Chicago Press.

Langer, L. M., Zimmerman, R. S., & Cabral, R. J. (1994). Perceived versus actual condom skills among clients at sexually transmitted disease clinics. *Public Health Reports, 109*, 683–687.

Leigh, B. C., & Stall, R. (1993). Substance use and risky sexual behavior for exposure to HIV: Issues in methodology, interpretation, and prevention. *American Psychologist, 48*(10), 1035–1045.

Leigh, B. C., Temple, M. T., & Trocki, K. F. (1993). The sexual behavior of U.S. adults: Results from a national survey. *American Journal of Public Health, 83*(10), 1400–1408.

Lock, S. E., Ferguson, S. L., & Wise, C. (1998). Communication of sexual risk behavior among late adolescents. *Western Journal of Nursing Research, 20*(3), 273–294.

Logan, T., Cole, J., & Leukefeld, C. (2002). Women, sex, and HIV: Social and contextual factors, meta-analysis of published interventions, and implications for practice and research. *Psychological Bulletin, 128*(6), 851–885.

Lowry, R., Holtzman, D., Truman, B. I., Kann, L., Collins, J. L., & Kolbe, L. J. (1994). Substance use and HIV-related sexual behaviors among U.S. high school students: Are they related? *American Journal of Public Health, 84*(7), 1116–1120.

Lynam., D., Zimmerman, R. S., & Monteith, M. (2003). *Thinking about condom use and impulsivity: Results from an experimental study.* Manuscript in preparation.

Malloy, T. E., Fisher, W. A., Albright, L., Misovich, S. J., & Fisher, J. D. (1997). Interpersonal perception of the AIDS risk potential of persons of the opposite sex. *Health Psychology, 16*(5), 480–486.

Manning, W. D., Longmore, M. A., & Giordano, P. C. (2000). The relationship context of contraceptive use at first intercourse. *Family Planning Perspectives, 32*(3), 104–110.

Maticka-Tyndale, E. (1991). Sexual scripts and AIDS prevention: Variations in adherence to safer-sex guidelines by heterosexual adults. *The Journal of Sex Research, 28*(1), 45–66.

Maticka-Tyndale, E. (1992). Social construction of HIV transmission and prevention among heterosexual young adults. *Social Problems, 39*(3), 238–252.

Mays, V. M., & Cochran, S. D. (1988). Issues in the perception of AIDS risk and risk reduction activities by Black and Hispanic/Latina women. *American Psychologist, 43*(11), 949–957.

Mays, V. M., & Cochran, S. D. (1993). Ethnic and gender differences in beliefs about sex partner questioning to reduce HIV risk. *Journal of Adolescent Research, 8*(1), 77–88.

Meschke, L. L., Zweig, J. M., Barber, B. L., & Eccles, J. S. (2000). Demographic, biologic, psychological, and social predictors of timing of first intercourse *Journal of Research on Adolescence, 10*(3), 315–339.

Metts, S., & Fitzpatrick, M. A. (1992). Thinking about safer sex: The risky business of "know your partner" advice. In T. Edgar, M. A. Fitzpatrick, & V. S. Freimuth (Eds.), *AIDS: A communication perspective* (pp. 1–19). Hillsdale, NJ: Lawrence Erlbaum Associates.

Millstein, S. G., Igra, V., Gans, J. (1996). Delivery of STD/HIV preventive services to adolescents by primary care physicians. *Journal of Adolescent Health, 24,* 131–142.

Miller, K. S., & Levin, M. L. (1998). Patterns of condom use among adolescents: The impact of mother–adolescent communication. *American Journal of Public Health, 88*(10), 1543–1545.

Miller, B. C., McCoy, J. K., Olson T. D., & Wallace, T. M. (1986). Parental discipline and control attempts in relation to adolescent sexual attitudes and behavior. *Journal of Marriage and Family, 48*(3), 503–512.

Misovich, S. J., Fisher, J. D., & Fisher, W. A. (1996). The perceived AIDS-preventive utility of knowing one's partner well: A public health dictum and individuals' risky sexual behaviour. *The Canadian Journal of Human Sexuality, 5*(2), 83–90.

Misovich, S. J., Fisher, J. D., & Fisher, W. A. (1997). Close relationships and elevated HIV risk behavior: Evidence and possible underlying psychological processes. *Review of General Psychology, 1*(1), 72–107.

Morokoff, P. J., Quina, K., Harlow, L. L., Whitmire, L., Grimley, D. M., Gibson, P. R., & Burkholder, G. J. (1997). Sexual assertiveness scale (SAS) for women: Development and validation. *Journal of Personality and Social Psychology, 73*(4), 790–804.

Morris, M., & Kretzschmar M. (1997). Concurrent partnerships and the spread of HIV. *AIDS, 11*(5), 641–648.

Mosure, D. J., Berman, S., Fine, D., Delisle, S., Cates, W., & Boring, J. R. (1997). Genital Chlamydia infections in sexually active female adolescents: Do we really need to screen everyone? *Journal of Adolescent Health, 20,* 6–13.

Noar, S. M. (2001). Sexual negotiation and the influence of gender and power in heterosexually active men and women. *Dissertation Abstracts International, 62*(09), 4277B.

Noar, S. M. (2002). Eyes wide shut or open? What we are learning about men, masculinity, and safer sex. *Society for the Psychological Study of Men and Masculinity Bulletin, 7*(3), 7–9.

Noar, S. M. (2003). The role of structural equation modeling in scale development. *Structural Equation Modeling: A Multidisciplinary Journal, 10*(4), 622–647.

Noar, S. M., & Morokoff, P. J. (2002). The relationship between masculinity ideology, condom attitudes, and condom use stage of change: A structural equation modeling approach. *International Journal of Men's Health, 1,* 43–58.

Noar, S. M., Morokoff, P. J., & Harlow, L. L. (2002a). Condom negotiation in heterosexually active men and women: Development and validation of a condom influence strategy questionnaire. *Psychology and Health, 17*(6), 711–735.

Noar, S. M., Morokoff, P. J., & Harlow, L. L. (in press). *Condom influence strategies in an ethnically diverse community sample of men and women.* Journal of Applied Social Psychology.

Noar, S. M., Morokoff, P. J., & Redding, C. A. (2001). An examination of transtheoretical predictors of condom use in late adolescent heterosexual men. *Journal of Applied Biobehavioral Research, 6*(1), 1–26.

Noar, S. M., Morokoff, P. J., & Redding, C. A. (2002b). Sexual assertiveness in heterosexually active men: A test of three samples. *AIDS Education and Prevention, 14*(4), 330–342.

Noar, S. M., Zimmerman, R. S., & Palmgreen, P. (2003). *The influence of relationship type on young adults' STD, HIV and pregnancy-related risk perceptions.* Manuscript in preparation.

O'Donnell, L., Doval, A. S., Vornfett, R., & DeJong, W. (1994). Reducing AIDS and other STDs among inner-city Hispanics: The use of qualitative research in the development of video-based patent education. *AIDS Education and Prevention, 6*(2), 140–153.

Offir, J. T., Fisher, J. D., Williams, S. S., & Fisher. W. A. (1993). Reasons for inconsistent AIDS-preventive behaviors among gay men. *The Journal of Sex Research, 30*(1), 62–69.

O'Leary, A. (2000). Women at risk for HIV from a primary partner: Balancing risk and intimacy. *Annual Review of Sex Research, 11,* 191–234.

Oliver, M. B., & Hyde, J. S. (1993). Gender differences in sexuality: A meta-analysis. *Psychological Bulletin, 114,* 20–51.

Oncale, R. M., & King, B. M. (2001). Comparison of men's and women's attempts to dissuade sexual partners from the couple using condoms. *Archives of Sexual Behavior, 30*(4), 379–391.

Overby, K. J., & Kegeles, S. M. (1994). The impact of AIDS on an urban population of high-risk female minority adolescents: Implications for intervention. *Journal of Adolescent Health, 15*, 216–227.

Peplau, L. A., Rubin, Z., & Hill, C. T. (1977). Sexual intimacy in dating relationships. *Journal of Social Issues, 3*, 86–109.

Pinkerton, S. D., & Abramson, P. R. (1993). Evaluating the risks: A Bernoulli process model of HIV infection and risk reduction. *Evaluation Review, 17*(5), 504–528.

Pinkerton, S. D., & Layde, P. M. (2002). Using sexually transmitted disease incidence as a surrogate marker for HIV incidence in prevention trials: A modeling study. *Sexually Transmitted Diseases, 29*(5), 298–307.

Porter, C. P., Oakley D. J., Guthrie, B. J., & Killion, C. (1999). Early adolescents' sexual behaviors. *Issues in Comprehensive Pediatric Nursing, 22*, 129–142.

Potterat, J. J., Zimmerman-Rogers, H., Muth, S. Q., Rothenberg, R. B., Green, D. L., Taylor, J. E., Bonney, M. S., & White, H. A. (1999). Chlamydia transmission: Concurrency, reproduction number, and the epidemic trajectory. *American Journal of Epidemiology, 150*, 1331–1339.

Prochaska, J. O., DiClemente, C. C., & Norcross, J. C. (1992). In search of how people change: Applications to addictive behaviors. *American Psychologist, 47*(9), 1102–1114.

Quina, K., Harlow, L. L., Morokoff, P. J., Burkholder, G., & Deiter, P. J. (2000). Sexual communication in relationships: When words speak louder than actions. *Sex Roles, 42*(7/8), 523–549.

Quina, K., Harlow, L. L., Morokoff, P. J., & Saxon, S. E. (1997). Interpersonal power and women's HIV risk. In N. Goldstein and J. L. Manlowe (Eds.), *The gender politics of HIV/AIDS: Perspectives on the pandemic in the United States* (pp. 188–206). New York: New York University Press.

Redding, C. A., Morokoff, P. J., Noar, S. M., Meier, K. S., Rossi, J. S., Koblin, B., Brown-Peterside, P., Mayer, K., Harlow, L., White, S., & Gazabon, S. (2002, April). Evaluating transtheoretical model-based predictors of condom use in at-risk men and women. In P. J. Morokoff (Chair), *Theory-based approaches to HIV prevention*. Symposium conducted at the Twenty-Third Annual Scientific Sessions of the Society of Behavioral Medicine, Washington, DC.

Reiss, I. L., & Leik, R. K. (1989). Evaluating strategies to avoid AIDS: Number of partners vs. use of condoms. *The Journal of Sex Research, 26*(4), 411–433.

Rickert, V. I., Sanghvi, R., & Wiemann, C. M. (2002). Is lack of sexual assertiveness among adolescent and young adult women a cause for concern? *Perspectives on Sexual and Reproductive Health, 34*(4), 178–183.

Rosenberg, M. D., Gurvey, J. E., Adler, N., Dunlop, M. B. V., & Ellen, J. M. (1999). Concurrent sex partners and risk for sexually transmitted diseases among adolescents. *Sexually Transmitted Diseases, 26*(4), 208–212.

Rotherum-Borus, M. J., O'Keefe, Z., Kracker, R., & Foo, H. (2000). Prevention of HIV among adolescents. *Prevention Science, 1*, 15–30.

Sacco, W. P., Levine, B., Reed, D., & Thompson, K. (1991). Attitudes about condom use as an AIDS-relevant behavior: Their factor structure and relation to condom use. *Psychological Assessment: A Journal of Consulting and Clinical Psychology, 3*(2), 265–272.

Sacco, W. P., Rickman, R. L., Thompson, K., Levine, B., & Reed, D. L. (1993). Gender differences in AIDS-relevant condom attitudes and condom use. *AIDS Education and Prevention, 5*(4), 311–326.

Saul, J., Norris, F. H., Bartholow, K. K., Dixon, D., Peters, M., & Moore, J. (2000). Heterosexual risk for HIV among Puerto Rican women: Does power influence self-protective behavior? *AIDS and Behavior, 4*(4), 361–371.

Seidman, S. N., & Rieder, R. O. (1994). A review of sexual behavior in the United States. *American Journal of Psychiatry, 151*, 330–341.

Sheer, V. C., & Cline, R. J. (1994). The development and validation of a model explaining sexual behavior among college students: Implications for AIDS communication campaigns. *Human Communication Research, 21*(2), 280–304.

Sheeran, P., Abraham, C., & Orbell, S. (1999). Psychosocial correlates of heterosexual condom use: A meta-analysis. *Psychological Bulletin, 125*(1), 90–132.

Sheeran, P., & Taylor, S. (1999). Predicting intentions to use condoms: A meta-analysis and comparison of the theories of reasoned action and planned behavior. *Journal of Applied Social Psychology, 29*(8), 1624–1675.

Sherman, S. G., & Latkin, C. A. (2001). Intimate relationship characteristics associated with condom use among drug users and their sexual partners: A multilevel analysis. *Drug and Alcohol Dependence, 64*, 97–104.

Shulman, S., & Kipnis, O. (2001). Adolescent romantic relationships: A look from the future. *Journal of Adolescence, 24*, 337–351.

Shulman, S., & Seiffge-Krenke, I. (2001). Adolescent romance: Between experience and relationships. *Journal of Adolescence, 24*, 417–428.

Smith, E. A., & Udry, J. R. (1985). Coital and non-coital sexual behaviors of White and Black adolescents. *American Journal of Public Health, 75*(10), 1200–1203.

Sprecher, S. (1998). Social exchange theories and sexuality. *The Journal of Sex Research, 35*(1), 32–43.

St. Lawrence, J. S., & Scott, C. P. (1996). Examination of the relationship between African American adolescents' condom use at sexual onset and later sexual behavior: Implications for condom distribution programs. *AIDS Education and Prevention, 8*, 258–266.

Stebleton, M. J., & Rothenberger, J. H. (1993). Truth or consequences: Dishonesty in dating and HIV/AIDS-related issues in a college-age population. *Journal of American College Health, 42*, 51–54.

Steiner, M. J., Cates, W., & Lee, W. (1999). The real problem with male condoms is nonuse. *Sexually Transmitted Diseases, 26*(8), 459–462.

Stergachis, A., Scholes, D., Heidrich, F. E., Sherer, D. W., Holmes, K. K., & Stamm, W. E. (1993). Selective screening for Chlamydia Trachomatis infection in a primary care population of women. *American Journal of Epidemiology, 138*(3), 143–153.

Sternberg, R. J. (1986). A triangular theory of love. *Psychological Review, 93*(2), 119–135.

Swann, W. B., Silvera, D. H., & Proske, C. U. (1995). On "knowing your partner": Dangerous illusions in the age of AIDS? *Personal Relationships, 2*, 173–186.

Taradash, A., Connolly, J., Pepler, D., Craig, W., & Costa, M. (2001). The interpersonal context of romantic autonomy in adolescence. *Journal of Adolescence, 24*, 365–377.

Thorton, A. (1990). The courtship process and adolescent sexuality. *Journal of Family Issues, 11*(3), 239–275.

Trafimow, D. (2000). Habit as both a direct cause of intention to use a condom and as a moderator of the attitude-intention and subjective norm-intention relations. *Psychology and Health, 15*, 383–393.

Troth, A., & Peterson, C. C. (2000). Factors predicting safe-sex talk and condom use in early sexual relationships. *Health Communication, 12*(2), 195–218.

Udry, J. R., & Billy, J. O. (1987). Initiation of coitus in early adolescence. *American Sociological Review, 52*, 841–855.

Warszawski, J., & Meyer, L. (2002). Sex difference in partner notification: Results from three population based surveys in France. *Sexually Transmitted Infections, 78*, 45–49.

Williams, S. S., Kimble, D. L., Covell, N. H., Weiss, L. H., Newton, K. J., Fisher, J. D., & Fisher, W. A. (1992). College students use implicit personality theory instead of safer sex. *Journal of Applied Social Psychology, 22*(12), 921–933.

Wingood, G. M., & DiClemente, R. J. (1998). Partner influences and gender-related factors associated with noncondom use among adult African American women. *American Journal of Community Psychology, 26*(1), 29–51.

Wolitski, R. J., & Branson, B. M. (2002). "Gray area behaviors" and partner selection strategies: Working toward a comprehensive approach to reducing the sexual transmission of HIV. In A. O'Leary (Ed.), *Beyond condoms: Alternative approaches to HIV prevention* (pp. 173–198). New York: Kluwer Academic/Plenum.

Yzer, M. C., Siero, F. W., & Buunk, B. P. (2001). Bringing up condom use and using condoms with new sexual partners: Intentional or habitual? *Psychology and Health, 16*, 409–421.

Zamboni, B. D., Crawford, I., & Williams, P. G. (2000). Examining communication and assertiveness as predictors of condom use: Implications for HIV prevention. *AIDS Education and Prevention, 12*(6), 492–504.

Zimmer-Gembeck, M. J., Siebenbruner, J., & Collins, W. A. (2001). Diverse aspects of dating: Associations with psychosocial functioning from early to middle adolescence. *Journal of Adolescence, 24*, 313–336.

Zimmerman, R. S., Cupp, P. K., Atwood, K., Feist-Price, S., & Donohew, R. L. (2003). *A new model of initiation of sexual activity in adolescents.* Manuscript in preparation.

Zimmerman, R. S., Hansen, G., Cupp, P. K., & Brumley-Shelton, A. (2003). *The impact of rural teens' first sexual encounters on later sexual behavior.* Manuscript in preparation.

Zimmerman, R. S., Lynam, D., & Monteith, M. (2003). *Understanding sexual decision-making: Validation of a new paradigm.* Manuscript in preparation.

Zimmerman, R. S., Noar, S. M., Feist-Price, S., Anderman, E., & Cupp, P. K. (2003). *A comprehensive model of health behavior change: Application to adolescent Candom use.* Manuscript in preparation.

22

Psychopathology, Sexuality, and the Partner Relationship

Amy Wenzel

Lydia C. Jackson

Jennifer R. Brendle
University of North Dakota

Although the past decade has witnessed an increase in the number of studies examining the effects of psychopathology on close, romantic relationships, little work has investigated the interplay between psychopathology, close relationships, and sexual functioning. In this chapter information about relationship and sexual functioning is integrated for several types of psychopathology, including depression, mania, borderline personality disorder, anxiety disorders, eating disorders, and alcoholism. In general, there appears to be a bidirectional association between psychopathology and the quality of close relationships, such that symptoms of psychopathology impair functioning in relationships, and problems in relationships exacerbate symptoms of psychopathology. Depressed and anxious individuals appear to suffer from pervasive sexual dysfunction, as many of these individuals report difficulties with desire, arousal, and orgasm. In contrast, other types of psychopathology are characterized by a more complex pattern of sexual functioning, such that individuals with some disorders engage in normative levels of sexual activities but report a lack of enjoyment or particular types of dysfunction. This review clearly suggests that the quality of romantic and sexual relationships in individuals with psychopathology is impaired; however, continued research must be conducted to identify the causal relations among these variables.

INTRODUCTION

Psychopathology is a term that refers to disturbed behavior, emotions, and/or cognitions, which is classified according to guidelines put forth in the *Diagnostic and Statistical Manual of Mental Disorders* (DSM-IV; American Psychiatric Association [APA], 1994). Although most types of psychopathology are associated with deleterious interpersonal consequences, only recently have researchers begun to consider the manner in which psychopathology affects the partner relationship, with little literature focusing particularly on intimacy and sexual functioning. The lack of investigation in this area is surprising, as decreased sexual desire is one sign of some types of psychopathology, particularly depression (Garvey, 1985). Clinical psychologists who are trained in identifying and conceptualizing psychopathology should be taught to recognize sexual disturbance, as the DSM-IV includes nine types of primary sexual dysfunction and eight paraphilias under the broad heading of "Sexual and Gender Identity Disorders" (APA, 1994). Unfortunately, our impression is that oftentimes these clinical syndromes are omitted from or only considered in a cursory manner in psychopathology courses, and sexual disturbance is only infrequently the subject matter of articles in mainstream clinical psychology journals.

Despite the fact that individuals receiving mental health treatment often have substantial concerns about their sexual functioning and satisfaction, existing literature suggests that clinicians rarely inquire directly about sexuality, and patients rarely spontaneously volunteer this information (cf. Ashton, Hamer, & Rosen, 1997). Although there could be several reasons for this (e.g., discomfort with subject matter), there is some evidence that clinicians feel there is not enough literature on the topic that is specific enough to be useful in treatment planning (Pinderhughes, Grace, & Reyna, 1972). The present chapter reviews existing literature that characterizes the manner in which psychopathology is associated with sexual dysfunction, particularly in individuals who are involved in close, romantic relationships. Although this review likely will leave the reader with more questions than answers, it provides a framework to assimilate results from existing studies, makes apparent issues that will be important for future research to address, and highlights important treatment considerations.

PSYCHOPATHOLOGY IN INDIVIDUALS WITH SEXUAL DYSFUNCTION

There are two approaches that have been used to study the relation between psychopathology and sexuality—examining the prevalence of psychopathology in individuals with sexual dysfunction and examining the prevalence of sexual dysfunction in individuals with psychopathology. The former approach has been adopted in two studies. First, Derogatis, Meyer, and King (1981) examined diagnoses and symptoms of psychopathology in 325 individuals (199 men, 126 women) who sought treatment from a sexual behavior clinic for a sexual disorder. Psychiatric diagnoses were assigned to 34% of men with premature ejaculation, 37% of men with impotence, 50% of women with inhibited orgasm, and 88% of women with vaginismus or dyspareunia. On a common self-report measure of psychiatric symptoms, both men and women scored at or higher than the 87th percentile on a global symptom index, indicating that they endorsed symptoms at a rate much higher than individuals in the general population. However, the specific types of symptoms most frequently endorsed varied as a function of gender: men most often reported symptoms of anxiety and depression, whereas women most often reported symptoms of depression and interpersonal sensitivity. In all, this study systematically demonstrated that symptoms of psychopathology are elevated above average in individuals presenting for treatment with sexual concerns.

Although Derogatis et al. (1981) demonstrated an association between sexual disturbance and psychopathology, conclusions about etiology could not be drawn because only current concerns pertaining to these two areas were assessed. In contrast, Schreiner-Engel and Schiavi (1986) examined the prevalence of lifetime psychopathology in 46 individuals who were diagnosed with inhibited sexual desire but did not meet diagnostic criteria for any current psychopathology and 36 matched controls.

Results indicated that 73% of male patients and 71% of female patients had a history of affective disorders (i.e., major depression, intermittent depression) as compared to 32% and 29% of control men and women, respectively. In 88% of the male patients and all of the female patients with a history of affective disorder, the sexual disturbance developed concurrently with or after the initial depressive episode. The authors concluded that sexual and affective disorders might share a common etiology.

These studies indicate that psychopathology is common in individuals who seek treatment for sexual disturbance. Moreover, even if individuals seeking treatment for sexual disturbance are free of psychopathology, there is a strong likelihood that they have experienced psychopathology in the past, making them vulnerable to future emotional distress. It is possible that the sexual side effects of psychopathology last far longer than other symptoms of psychopathology. Nevertheless, it is unclear whether results from these studies can generalize to individuals with sexual disturbance who do not seek treatment. For example, it is possible that emotional distress associated with psychopathology exacerbates concern and attention toward sexual dysfunction, which would in turn prompt these individuals to seek treatment. Individuals with no history of psychopathology, then, might develop adaptive skills to cope with their sexual dysfunction and, therefore, would be less likely to seek treatment. If such a scenario were to be true, rates of co-occurring sexual dysfunction and psychopathology would vary widely as a function of the setting in which the sample is identified and recruited. Thus, it will be important for epidemiological researchers to examine sexual disturbance and symptoms of psychopathology in a large community sample.

One caveat pertaining to the usefulness of these studies to the topic at hand is that aspects of the partner relationship were not assessed. Schreiner-Engel and Schiavi (1986) noted that their patients' inhibited sexual desire was a source of distress in their relationship, but this conclusion was drawn from anecdotal reports rather than through systematic assessment. At present, the extent to which psychopathology and sexual dysfunction each contribute unique variance to explain partner relational disturbance remains uncertain.

SEXUAL DYSFUNCTION IN INDIVIDUALS WITH PSYCHOPATHOLOGY

A greater number of studies examined various types of sexual dysfunction in individuals with particular types of psychopathology. The general strategy of these studies was to identify a sample of individuals with one particular type of psychopathology and to examine different aspects of sexuality, either by interview or self-report. Physiological data are rarely collected, although a few studies examined sexual responsivity in alcoholic individuals in order to investigate the manner in which alcohol intake affects sexual functioning (e.g., Wilson, Lawson, & Abrams, 1978) as well as to examine biological changes associated with chronic alcohol use (e.g., Tan, Johnson, Lambie, Vijaysenan, & Whiteside, 1984). Literatures pertaining to emotional disorders (i.e., depression, mania, borderline personality disorder, anxiety disorders), eating disorders, and alcoholism are reviewed.

Emotional Disorders

Depression. It has long been accepted that depressed individuals have difficulty in their interpersonal functioning (e.g., Coyne, 1976). Researchers found that the lack of an intimate, trusting relationship with a romantic partner is an important factor in susceptibility to depression (Brown & Harris, 1978) and that family functioning is more disturbed in depressed patients than in patients with other types of psychopathology (Miller & Kobakoff, 1986). The past decade witnessed the development of several lines of research focused particularly on the effects of depression on the partner or marital relationship. In general, there appears to be a bidirectional association between depression and relationship distress (cf. McLeod & Eckberg, 1993; O'Mahen, Beach, & Banawan, 2001). Specifically, empirical research demonstrated that depression predicts marital dissatisfaction even when prior levels of marital dissatisfaction are controlled (e.g., Beach, Martin, Blum, & Roman, 1993), and other studies have shown that marital dissatisfaction at one assessment predicts depression at a second assessment (e.g., Fincham, Beach, Harold, & Osbourne, 1997). Moreover, depression in one individual is related to distress experienced by the partner. For instance, McLeod and Eckberg (1993) reported that partners of depressed individuals are less satisfied with their marriages than nondepressed individuals, that they regard their depressed spouses as demanding, and that they often avoid interacting with them. This cyclical pattern of relationship conflict and the depression leads to divorce in many cases. In their sample of recently divorced psychiatric patients, Briscoe et al. (1973) reported that 40% of the women and 34% of the men had major depressive disorder. In 40% of these cases, the depressive disorder appeared to contribute to the divorce, rather than result from it (Briscoe & Smith, 1973).

Not surprisingly, depressed individuals often complain of sexual dysfunction in addition to problems in their partner relationship. According to Garvey (1985), at least 50% of depressed patients complain of decreased libido. Several reasons may account for the decline in sexual functioning associated with depression. One possibility is that the quality of a depressed individual's sexual relationship covaries with the degree of distress that characterizes his or her partner relationship, as research documented the strong association between relationship satisfaction and sexual satisfaction (see Sprecher & Cate, chapter 10, this volume). Second, general symptoms of depression, such as rumination, loss of interest or pleasure, or social isolation, may impair sexual functioning in the same manner as they affect many areas of an individual's life (cf. Clayton, 2001; Garvey, 1985). Third, depression may exert effects on a particular phase of sexual functioning, such as desire, arousal, or orgasm, because of biological effects, particularly those that occur in the hypothalamic–pituitary axis (Clayton, 2001). A related complication is that antidepressant medications often cause adverse sexual side effects (to be reviewed in a separate section). To date, little empirical research has examined the nature of sexual functioning in depression, and none has done so with the intent of investigating the extent to which each of these factors uniquely disrupts sexual functioning in depressed individuals.

In an attempt to examine the association between depression and a number of relationship variables including sexuality, Zieba, Dudek, and Jawor (1997) administered self-report inventories of relationship and sexual functioning to depressed individuals (19 males, 17 females) 2 years after discharge from a psychiatric hospital. They divided the patients into two groups: those with persistent depressive symptoms and those with mild or remitted depressive symptoms. Compared with the remitted patients, persistently depressed patients reported a poorer overall relationship quality, a lesser involvement in the household, a diminished sense of security and acceptance by the partner, and an inability to express feelings. Persistently depressed patients tended to withdraw from conflict situations and think more often about divorce as a coping strategy. Interestingly, male patients regarded the impact of depression on their marital functioning more negatively and were less satisfied in their marriages than female patients. Regardless of whether or not these patients were currently depressed, many individuals in both groups reported sexual problems—30% of the sample had ceased sexual activity altogether, and another 43% had "sporadic, unsatisfactory contact." Thus, although distress in the partner relationship improved as depressive symptoms improved, remitted depressive individuals continued to experience sexual disturbance.

In a more comprehensive examination of sexual functioning in depression, Kennedy, Dickens, Eisfeld, and Bagby (1999) recruited depressed outpatients (55 males, 79 females) who had not been treated with antidepressant medication and administered a self-report inventory assessing change in sexual functioning in the past month. Forty-one percent of the male patients and 50% of the female patients reported a decrease in sexual drive. Approximately 30 to 40% of both men and women endorsed difficulties with other behaviors associated with sexual desire, such as interest in sexually explicit material, fantasizing about sex, and masturbation. Arousal was problematic for many men in their sample: 34% indicated that they had "less vigorous erections," and 46% indicated an inability to sustain an erection. Women also endorsed arousal difficulties, as 50% indicated decreased sexual arousal, and 40% reported difficulty obtaining vaginal lubrication. Orgasm generally was less of a problem for the sample, although a substantial minority of men endorsed problems with either premature ejaculation (12%) or delayed ejaculation (22%), and 15% of women endorsed "difficulty having orgasm." Contrary to expectation, there was no correlation between the severity of depression and the extent of sexual dysfunction. In all, results from this study suggest that depression has a substantial effect on all stages of the sexual response cycle in both men and women, though particularly so on sexual desire and arousal.

Other studies have focused on the effects of depression on sexual functioning in men only. For example, Howell et al. (1987) instructed medication-free depressed men and age-matched controls to complete self-report inventories of sexual functioning and behavioral logs of sexual activity. Results from self-report inventories suggested that depressed men perceived less pleasure from sexual experience and had a more negative body image than nondepressed men. Although depressed and nondepressed men logged a similar number of sexually active days, depressed men indicated less sexual interest and satisfaction. In a follow-up study by this same group of researchers (Nofzinger et al., 1993), it was found that men who remitted from depression expressed more sexual satisfaction than men whose depression did not remit. In fact, improvements on an interview measure of depression correlated significantly with increased percentages of sexually active days, increased sex drive, and decreased complaints about sexual function. Interestingly, depressed men had more abnormalities in nocturnal penile tumescence ratings than nondepressed individuals that did not change as depression remitted, confirming results from Zieba et al. (1997) that some aspects of sexual dysfunction may persist beyond the depressive episode.

In contrast to the studies described above that used clinical samples of depressed patients, McVey (1997) examined sexual functioning in women presenting for treatment for hypoactive sexual desire. Based on Beck Depression Inventory scores, he divided his sample into three groups: nondepressed ($n = 43$), mildly depressed ($n = 42$), and depressed ($n = 46$). Although there were no differences between groups in self-reported sexual desire intensity, depressed women reported less sexual excitability than nondepressed women, and both depressed and mildly depressed women reported less sexual assertiveness and fantasy than nondepressed women. Women in McVey's sample completed 12 sessions of orgasm consistency training. Although over half of the women in all three groups dropped out of treatment, depressed women were significantly more likely to discontinue participation in the intervention. Analyses of treatment completers indicated that all three groups made equal gains in treatment, particularly in sexual desire intensity and in approaching behavior. Thus, results from this study suggest that depression may be an obstacle to address in keeping women in treatment but that treatment is effective for individuals who are able to complete an entire program.

In all, the few studies that have been conducted in this area confirm subjective complaints of decreased libido associated with depression. In addition, research indicates that arousal and orgasm also are disrupted in at least a subset of depressed individuals (Kennedy et al., 1999). Even when depressive symptoms remit, individuals may experience continued sexual disturbance (Nofzinger et al., 1993; Zieba et al., 1997), which confirms the data obtained by Schreiner-Engel and Schiavi (1986) with their sample of individuals with inhibited sexual desire who were free of current psychopathology. Because symptoms of depression, relationship distress, and sexual dysfunction frequently covary, the direction of causality among these variables is unknown. It is possible that each of these factors might exert causal influence on the other two in particular situations depending on the unique circumstances of each couple. It will be important for future empirical research to examine the unique variance contributed by relationship distress, general symptoms of depression, and side effects from pharmacological treatment on sexual functioning and satisfaction. Moreover, it is important for clinicians to educate depressed patients and their partners about the nature of possible sexual dysfunction associated with depression in order to limit the extent to which partners misinterpret disinterest in sex to problems in the relationship.

Mania.   The presence of a manic episode is a key ingredient in the diagnosis of bipolar disorder, a type of psychopathology characterized by alternating periods of heightened mood and activity and depression. One DSM-IV criterion (APA, 1994) used to determine the presence or absence of a manic episode is increased goal-directed activity, which includes excessive participation in sexual activities and increased sexual drive, fantasies, and behavior. This criterion suggests that mania may alter some aspects of an individual's sexual functioning, and if it is the direction of indiscriminant sexual activity, then there might be adverse consequences on the partner relationship. Results from one study confirmed the importance of studying the nature of intimate relationships in individuals with bipolar disorder, as 57% of bipolar patients in the sample experienced "broken marriages" (Brodie & Leff, 1971). Despite the fact that promiscuity and/or sexual experimentation are often observed in individuals experiencing a manic episode, little research has examined sexual behavior in individuals who are diagnosed with bipolar disorder.

In an empirical study to examine an aspect of sexual functioning in manic individuals, Jamison, Gerner, Hammen, and Padesky (1980) asked 35 bipolar patients to note differences in the intensity in their sexual relationships (among other characteristics) during periods of mania as compared to periods of normal functioning. Approximately 60% of the patients indicated that sexual intensity increased either "somewhat" or "very much" during mania, although these rates were lower than rates of changes they observed in at least some other areas of functioning, such as productivity and alertness. Female patients, but not male patients, rated increases in sexual intensity as the most enjoyable change experienced. Jamison et al. noted that these kinds of changes are extremely rewarding and may deter individuals from seeking out the necessary treatment.

The little research that exists suggests that many individuals diagnosed with bipolar disorder experience distress in their relationships and that a substantial percentage of bipolar individuals perceive that manic episodes are associated with a positive change in the manner in which they experience sexual activity. However, no known studies have investigated the manner in which mania affects stages of the sexual response cycle, such as desire, arousal, or orgasm. Moreover, the reasons for dysfunction associated with the partner relationships of bipolar individuals are unclear. Although indiscriminant sexual activity during mania certainly could be one explanation for the termination of relationships, it is likely that relationship distress also occurs in the context of the overall level of stress that the course of the disorder creates for care-takers and/or family members. Thus, there is a substantial need for future research to investigate systematically several aspects of relationship and sexual functioning in bipolar individuals, both in the context of a manic episode as well as in the context of subsequent depression.

Borderline Personality Disorder.   A personality disorder is an "enduring pattern of inner experience and behavior that deviates markedly from the expectation of the individual's culture, is pervasive and inflexible, has an onset in adolescence or early adulthood, is stable over time, and leads to distress and impairment" (APA, p. 629). Clinicians have long observed that certain personality characteristics are associated with distinct expressions of sexual behavior (e.g., Abraham & Beumont, 1981; Kuriansky, 1988). The greatest amount of empirical work has focused on borderline personality disorder (BPD), as this pathology has been linked strongly with a history of sexual abuse and is associated with significant disturbance in interpersonal functioning (Linehan, 1993). It is included here in the section on emotional disorders because it frequently co-occurs with depression (Gunderson & Phillips, 1991), and it is characterized by extreme emotion dysregulation that results in marked reactivity of mood (APA, 1994; Linehan, 1993).

One of the key diagnostic characteristics of BPD is the presence of unstable, intense interpersonal relationships. Based on this diagnostic criterion, it is logical to predict that the close, romantic relationships of individuals with BPD would be characterized by a great deal of dysfunction. Daley, Burge, and Hammen (2000) confirmed that borderline symptoms predicted romantic chronic stress, relationship conflict, partner satisfaction, abuse, and unwanted pregnancy in late adolescent girls. However, these outcomes were better accounted for by a cumulative index of features associated with several personality disorders rather than by borderline characteristics alone. This finding suggests the need to conduct careful empirical investigations of relationship functioning in individuals with a variety of personality disorders. On the other hand, these results must be interpreted with caution, as the sample comprised participants representing the spectrum of borderline symptoms, with very few exhibiting symptoms at a clinically significant level. Moreover, because their sample consisted of girls recruited when they were approximately 18 years old, it is possible that borderline symptoms would indeed exert negative effects on relationship functioning later in adulthood.

In an attempt to characterize the manner in which BPD affects aspects of sexuality, Hurlbert, Apt, and White (1992) examined sexual functioning in 32 women with BPD and 32 women without BPD who were enrolled in a marital enrichment program. Women with BPD scored higher than non-BPD women on inventories assessing sexual assertiveness, erotophilia, sexual esteem, sexual preoccupation, sexual depression, and sexual dissatisfaction. In addition, a higher percentage of women with BPD responded positively to single items assessing the likelihood of having an affair, history of abuse, presence of a sexual problem in the partner, current sexual boredom, homosexual attraction, and sexual problems in the current relationship. Although these responses seem to indicate that women with BPD are generally characterized by a heightened sex drive, a high percentage of these women indicated that they do not usually experience orgasm during sexual activities with their partners.

The authors interpreted these findings to suggest that the BPD group's high scores on the sexual assertiveness and sexual esteem scales reflect hypersexuality or promiscuity and that their high scores on the erotophilia and preoccupation scales suggest the use of sex to achieve a variety of psychological ends, such as intimacy. It is certainly the case that individuals with BPD experience chronic feelings of emptiness and make frantic attempts to avoid abandonment and to feel close to others. Because a high percentage of women with BPD indicated that they were experiencing problems in their current sexual relationship and that they would consider having an affair, the authors' explanation is viable. On the other hand, the diagnosis of BPD is associated with a host of negative stereotypes, and it is possible that high scores on the sexual assertiveness, erotophilia, sexual esteem scales could be interpreted positively to reflect adaptive aspects of the sexual functioning of individuals with this personality disorder. Therapists working with these patients should explore the manner in which these characteristics can be channeled in a healthy direction to enhance their close, romantic relationships.

Anxiety Disorders. According to Barlow (2002), many early accounts of sexual dysfunction promoted the assumption that anxiety causes disturbance, either through performance fears (e.g., Masters & Johnson, 1970) or through the physiological inhibition of arousal (e.g., Kaplan, 1974). Some research indeed confirmed that anxiety inhibits sexual arousal (e.g., Beggs, Calhoun, & Wolchik, 1987). However, other studies found evidence indicating that anxiety either has no effect on sexual arousal or even enhances it (e.g., Barlow, Sakheim, & Beck, 1983; Elliot & O'Donohue, 1997; Palace & Gorzalka, 1990), although these findings have been obtained using samples of sexually functional individuals rather than samples of sexually dysfunctional individuals. In general, empirical studies designed to examine the relation between anxiety and arousal in both sexually functional and dysfunctional individuals suggest a complex interplay of physiological, emotional, and cognitive factors that together determine the extent to which sexual arousal is reactive to anxiety or fear (see Barlow, 2002, for a comprehensive review).

In sexually functional individuals, emotions may "transfer," such that the experience of one emotion (e.g., anxiety) in turn makes a second one (e.g., sexual arousal) more intense (Zillman, 1983). However, several factors relating to the experience of anxiety may inhibit this transfer of emotions in sexually dysfunctional individuals. For example, sexually dysfunctional individuals are distracted by performance demands, as these demands elicit negative self-evaluative thoughts that center on the adequacy of their physiological responding, quality of their performance, and possible embarrassment or humiliation (e.g., Barlow, 1986). In addition, there is evidence that sexually functional individuals report positive affect in sexual contexts but that sexually dysfunctional individuals report negative affect. Barlow (2002) speculated that negative affect facilitates the avoidance of sexual cues, both of which reinforce negative beliefs about performance. Sexually dysfunctional individuals also perceive themselves as having less control over their sexual responding than functional individuals. Thus, in dysfunctional individuals, anxiety disrupts sexual functioning through the elicitation of negative affect, which in turn narrows their attention on performance concerns. Almost as if it were a self-fulfilling prophesy, performance subsequently suffers, and the dysfunctional individual avoids future sexual encounters because beliefs of his or her sexual inadequacy (Barlow, 2002).

Although Barlow's (2002) cognitive–affective model of sexual dysfunction clearly outlines the mechanism by which anxiety affects sexual performance, few investigations have examined sexual functioning in groups of individuals identified as anxious, and no known investigations have attempted to validate this model with individuals who experience anxiety at a clinically significant level. The anxiety disorder that one would logically expect to be associated with sexual disturbance is social anxiety disorder, a syndrome in which individuals report pervasive fears of embarrassment or scrutiny by others. Results from early studies suggest that heterosocial anxiety (i.e., social anxiety in interacting with members of the opposite gender) disrupts behavior when meeting an opposite sex person for the first time, such that heterosocially anxious individuals have difficulty initiating conversation or making eye contact (e.g., Curran, Little, & Gilbert, 1978; Twentyman & McFall, 1975). Recent research demonstrated that the close, romantic relationships of socially anxious individuals are characterized by a lack of intimacy (Wenzel, 2002), impaired communication skills (Wenzel, Graff-Dolezal, Macho, & Brendle, 2003), conflict avoidance, and interpersonal dependency (Davila & Beck, 2002). In an attempt to examine several aspects of sexuality in socially anxious individuals, Leary and Dobbins (1983) found that heterosocially anxious participants reported less sexual experience, less frequent sexual activity, fewer sexual partners, more apprehension about sex, and a higher incidence of sexual dysfunctions than participants low in heterosocial anxiety. Interestingly, high- and low-anxious participants did not differ on their knowledge or attitudes regarding sex.

The greatest number of studies examining sexuality and anxiety disorders focus on individuals with obsessive compulsive disorder, as it is logical that obsessions about morality or contamination might interfere with aspects of sexual functioning. In a self-report study utilizing samples of outpatients with obsessive compulsive disorder and outpatients with generalized anxiety disorder, obsessive compulsive patients reported greater levels of nonsensuality, sexual avoidance, and anorgasmia (Aksaray, Yelken, Kaptanoglu, Oflu, & Ozaltin, 2001). Moreover, Van Minnen and Kampman (2002) found that obsessive compulsive patients had more sexual dysfunctions and were less satisfied with their sexual relationship than patients with panic disorder, although both patient groups reported lower sexual desire and fewer sexual contacts than nonanxious individuals. In contrast, other researchers reported that obsessive compulsive disorder is not characterized by sexual impairment (Freund & Steketee, 1989; Staebler, Pollard, & Merkel, 1993). Thus, the literature on this disorder has yielded mixed findings, although it should be noted that there has not been careful documentation of the particular kinds of obsessions and compulsions exhibited by patients, preventing speculation as to whether obsessive compulsive content (e.g., morality, contamination) mediates the relation between obsessive compulsive symptoms and sexual disturbance.

Fewer studies examined sexual functioning in individuals with other types of anxiety disorders. In one questionnaire study (Ware et al., 1996), patients with generalized anxiety disorder, panic disorder, and social anxiety disorder were more likely to report sexual dysfunction than nonanxious individuals. However, specific areas of sexual disturbance varied as a function of diagnostic group. Specifically, patients with panic disorder rated sex as less important than nonanxious individuals, whereas patients with social anxiety disorder reported less likelihood of enjoying sexual contacts with their partners than nonanxious individuals. In contrast, there were no specific differences between patients with generalized anxiety disorder and nonanxious individuals. The authors of this study suggested that patients with generalized anxiety disorder, panic disorder, and social anxiety disorder are high at risk for experiencing difficulties in sexual functioning but that patients with panic disorder and social anxiety disorder may be at a significantly higher level of risk than generalized anxiety patients. On the other hand, Katz and Jardine (1999) reported a positive association between chronic worry (a key feature of generalized anxiety disorder) and sexual aversion and a negative association between chronic worry and sexual desire.

There are far too few existing studies to draw definitive conclusions about the manner in which clinically significant expressions of anxiety affect sexual functioning. However, it appears that social anxiety interferes with developing meaningful partner relationships, and if these relationships are formed, it affects intimacy, communication, and problem solving. Individuals with other anxiety disorders (e.g., generalized anxiety disorder, obsessive compulsive disorder) report low sexual desire, decreased enjoyment, infrequent orgasm, and decreased sexual activity. According to Barlow's (2002) model, it is possible that sexual dysfunction in anxiety disorders is related to heightened levels of negative affect and negative self-statements about performance. However, it is unclear whether these disturbances are specific to a particular type of pathology or, more generally, to the life interference and distress associated with having any type of anxiety disorder.

A number of directions are evident for future research examining the manner in which anxiety disorders disturb sexual functioning. The relation between anxiety and sexual disturbance has the most developed theoretical framework of any areas of psychopathology in this chapter. It would be useful to test Barlow's (2002) model of anxious apprehension and sexual dysfunction with patients representing each specific type of anxiety disorder to identify the particular flavor of negative affect and self-statements that are elicited during sexual activity. Such information would have direct bearing on the process of addressing sexual dysfunction in the context of cognitive behavioral therapy. For example, it is possible that the general distracting effects of worry disrupt sexual performance in patients with generalized anxiety disorder much in the same way as general distraction disrupts performance in sexually functional individuals (cf. Abrahamson, Barlow, Sakheim, Beck, & Athanasiou, 1985). In contrast, the negative self-statements associated with performance concerns account for the largest percentage of variance in explaining sexual dysfunction in social anxiety disorder. If this were the case, two very different treatment strategies would be in order. Additionally, it is important to link the manner in which sexual disturbance in anxiety disorders relates to more general relationship functioning. Anxiety disorders researchers are becoming increasingly concerned with the interpersonal consequences of this type of psychopathology (e.g., Chambless et al., 2002; Davila & Beck, 2002; Emmelkamp & Gerlsma, 1994; Wenzel, 2002), although there is no existing information about the interplay between anxiety, sexual functioning, and the quality of close relationships.

Psychotropic Medication.   According to Narrow, Regier, Rae, Manderscheid, and Locke (1993), psychotropic medication is the most common treatment for depression in the United States. Moreover, many clinicians also consider psychotropic medication a first-line treatment for anxiety disorders (Craske & Barlow, 2001). At least part of the action of these medications is to increase levels of serotonin and GABA, neurotransmitters that inhibit sexual arousal (Milner, Tandon, Tomori, & Florence, 1999). Thus, it is not surprising that individuals with psychopathology who are treated with psychotropic medication for depression or anxiety disorders experience sexual disturbance. As a result, many patients fail to comply with their treatment regimen (Segraves, 1992). According to Montejo-Gonalez et al. (1997), between one third and one half of patients taking psychotropic medication seriously consider discontinuing it because of resulting sexual dysfunction.

The greatest amount of research on the sexual side effects of psychotropic medications centers on antidepressant medications, which, despite their name, are commonly prescribed for *both* depression and anxiety disorders. In their review of the sexual side effects of antidepressants, Margolese and Assalian (1996) concluded that these medications have been associated with decreased libido, increased impotence, painful erection, spontaneous erection, priapism, lack of vaginal lubrication, delayed orgasm, painful orgasm, anorgasmia, spontaneous ejaculation, retarded ejaculation, and ejaculation without orgasm. That is, there is evidence to suggest that antidepressant medications exert adverse effects on nearly every aspect of sexual functioning. In addition, available literature indicates that specific classes of antidepressants, such as the tricyclic and tetracyclic antidepressants (e.g., imipramine [Trofranil]), monoamine oxidase inhibitors (MAOIs; e.g., phenelzine [Nardil]), selective serotonin reuptake inhibitors (SSRIs; e.g., fluoxetine [Prozac]), and atypical antidepressants (e.g., venlafaxine [Effexor]), have been associated with some disturbance in each major phase of the sexual response cycle—sexual desire, excitement, and orgasm (Margolese & Assalian,

1996). Moreover, sexual dysfunction persists for at least 6 months in approximately 94% of patients taking antidepressants who report sexual side effects, and many of these patients perceive the dysfunction to increase in severity the longer they are medicated (Montejo-Gonzalez et al., 1997).

Specific rates of sexual disturbance vary dramatically among studies; in fact, in their review of the literature published since the 1970s, Montejo-Gonzalez et al. (1997) reported that documented rates of sexual dysfunction in patients taking antidepressant medication range from 1 to 96%. However, it is generally estimated that *at least* 25 to 30% of patients taking antidepressant medications experience adverse sexual side effects (Ashton et al., 1997; Fava & Rankin, 2002; Segraves, 1998). Although a long list of specific dysfunctions has been documented (as previously listed), the *most* commonly reported sexual side effects associated with these medications include decreased sexual desire, delayed ejaculation, or anorgasmia (Fava & Rankin, 2002; Milner et al., 1999). These difficulties were documented even in healthy volunteers who take these medications for a short period of time (Balon, 1998; Montejo-Gonzalez et al., 1997). One commonly prescribed medication that seems to be an exception to this rule is the atypical antidepressant buproprion (Wellbutrin), as less than 5% of individuals taking this medication report impotence or decreased libido (Margolese & Assalian, 1996). More than 80% of patients who discontinue SSRIs and switch to buproprion because of sexual side effects report at least partial resolution of their sexual difficulties (Walker et al., 1993). According to Margolese & Assalian (1996), other medications associated with fewer sexual side effects that are increasingly being prescribed are nefazodone (Serzone) and mirtazapine (Remeron).

Although many studies have reported rates of sexual dysfunction associated with particular types of antidepressant medications, few investigations have been comparative in nature. Because studies vary dramatically in methodological variables such as inclusion and exclusion criteria of participants, presence or absence of comorbid psychopathology, duration of time on medication, and dosage of medication, it is difficult to draw meaningful conclusions across studies. Thus, results from studies examining effects of at least two medications in the same design are particularly useful in identifying the medications that are most likely to minimize aversive side effects.

Few studies have been conducted to compare sexual side effects in older classes of antidepressants, such as the tricyclic antidepressants and the MAOIs. However, in a well-designed exception, Harrison et al. (1985, 1986) found that 21% and 27% of men and women, respectively, taking imipramine (i.e., a tricyclic antidepressant) and 30% and 36% of men and women, respectively, taking phenelzine (i.e., an MAOI) reported orgasmic difficulty. In contrast, nearly all recently conducted comparative studies focused on differences between specific SSRIs, as this class of antidepressants now is by far the most commonly prescribed in the United States. For example, in a retrospective chart review, Shen and Hsu (1995) identified that approximately 30% of patients taking fluoxetine (Prozac), 20% of patients taking paroxetine (Paxil), and 36% of patients taking sertraline (Zoloft) reported side effects, differences that were not statistically significant. In a prospective, multisite study involving direct interviews with patients, Montejo-Gonzalez et al. (1997) reported no significant differences among four types of SSRIs, although the absolute rates of sexual dysfunction were higher than those previously listed (65% of patients taking paroxetine, 59% of patients taking fluvoxamine [Luvox], 56% of patients taking sertraline, 54% of patients taking fluoxetine), and paroxetine was associated with more disturbance specifically in the area of orgasm than the other medications. Modell, Katholi, Modell, and DePalma (1997) sent a questionnaire assessing the presence of various side effects to outpatients taking fluoxetine, sertraline, paroxetine, or the atypical antidepressant, buproprion (Wellbutrin). Approximately 73% of the individuals taking any of the three SSRIs (i.e., fluoxetine, sertraline, paroxetine) reported adverse sexual side effects, in contrast to only 14% of the individuals taking buproprion. In fact, 77% of the individuals taking buproprion endorsed at least one area of improved sexual functioning. In all, comparative studies generally find no differences in the sexual side effects associated with medications *within* a particular class, but there are clear differences *between* classes of antidepressants.

According to Fava and Rankin (2002), sexual side effects of antidepressant treatment generally decrease over time, so physicians often wait several weeks to determine whether a dosage change or an adjunct intervention is necessary. Decreasing the dosage of medication often addresses the problem, although care must be taken so that the dose does not go below a therapeutic level. An alternative strategy is to prescribe an adjunct medication to specifically address the sexual side effects (Aizenberg, Noar, Zemishlany, & Weizman, 1999). Adjunct medications either might be one of the antidepressants that are associated with relatively low rates of sexual dysfunction, such as buproprion, or other pharmacological agents, such as yohimbine or sildenafil (Viagra). Rothschild (1995) described a "drug holiday" protocol, in which patients are instructed to discontinue taking medications after the Thursday morning dose and resume at their previous dosage at noon on Sunday. It is suggested that they engage in sexual activities during this hiatus and observe whether aspects of their sexual functioning improve. Results from his trial suggest that drug holidays effectively reduced the sexual side effects of sertraline and paroxetine, but not fluoxetine, while not appreciably increasing depressive symptoms. Rothschild noted that medications with a relatively short half-life, such as sertraline and paroxetine, might be ideal for drug holidays to manage sexual side effects.

Much less has been written about the effects of other classes of psychotropic medication on sexual functioning. However, sexual dysfunction has been documented in several benzodiazepines, or anti-anxiety medications (e.g., diazepam [Valium]) and lithium (Balon, 1998; Blay, Ferrez, & Calil, 1982; Milner et al., 1999). Benzodiazepines facilitate GABA transmission, which inhibits sexual arousal in a similar manner as does serotonin. Thus, use of these medications has been shown to exacerbate disturbance in sexually dysfunctional individuals, and some of its more general side effects (e.g., drowsiness) indirectly decrease sexual interest and arousal (Milner et al., 1999). Lithium is a mood stabilizer that often is prescribed to individuals with bipolar disorder. Because hypersexuality is a common symptom of this disorder, patients being treated with lithium often mistake a return to a relatively normal sex drive as being indicative of sexual dysfunction. Moreover, it may be associated with a decrease in sexual drive or activity because of secondary effects such as weight gain and decreased activity level (Milner et al., 1999).

In all, the use of psychotropic medication puts individuals with depression or anxiety disorders at risk for experiencing sexual disturbance above and beyond dysfunction that occurs because of their psychopathology. Emotional disorders create stress in any romantic relationship, and although psychotropic medication may improve many of the symptoms that an individual experiences, their use may place further strain on the partner relationship by prolonging sexual dysfunction. It is important for clinicians to assess the quality of the partner relationship when deciding on the preferred modality of treatment for emotional disorders. It is well established that couple's therapy reduces depressive symptoms in women to the same degree as well-established individual psychotherapies (e.g., O'Leary & Beach, 1990). Perhaps couple's therapy should be regarded as the first-line treatment for depressed women who report substantial distress in their partner relationship. Even if clinicians prescribe or refer for psychotropic medication, another use of couple's therapy would be to promote understanding and tolerance between partners with regard to adverse sexual side effects and to encourage alternative ways of expressing intimacy within the relationship during the course of pharmacological treatment. At minimum, clinicians should educate patients and their partners about the normalcy of sexual side effects associated with psychotropic medications.

Eating Disorders

A hallmark feature of eating disorders, particularly anorexia nervosa and bulimia nervosa, is a preoccupation with body weight and size (APA, 1994). Anorexic individuals maintain the irrational belief that parts of their body are overweight despite the fact that others view them as extraordinarily thin or even emaciated. Because body image is perceived as central to well-being in both anorexic and bulimic individuals, it is logical to predict that sexual functioning would correlate negatively with the degree to which these individuals have body image concerns. Indeed, much empirical research has confirmed that women with histories of eating disorders report decreased sexual desire and a decreased frequency of sexual acts when they perceive their body weight as being too high (e.g., Abraham, 1998; Abraham et al., 1985; Jagstaidt, Golay, & Pasini, 1996).

A pervasive theme in the literature is that anorexic and bulimic individuals differ with regard to their sexual behavior. Anorexic individuals, or individuals who restrict their food intake, are often regarded by clinicians as sexually inhibited and uninterested, whereas bulimic individuals, or individuals who engage in purging behavior, are often seen as promiscuous and more likely to engage in sexual experimentation (cf. Coovert, Kinder, & Thompson, 1989). Thus, a number of studies examining sexuality in eating disorders have been designed to compare the two groups with each other rather than to a control group of individuals without eating disorders, making it difficult to draw conclusions about the extent to which their sexual functioning is abnormal compared to individuals in the general population. There are two purposes of the following review: (a) to consider the manner in which symptoms relating to each eating disorder are associated with impaired sexual functioning compared to individuals without eating disorders, and (b) to compare sexual disturbance in anorexia with sexual disturbance in bulimia. To accomplish these aims, we first review studies examining only one eating disorder, paying particular attention to those studies employing non-eating disorder control groups, and we subsequently examine results from studies comparing both types of eating disorders in the same design.

Anorexia Nervosa. Surprisingly few studies examined samples of individuals with anorexia without comparing them to bulimia, presumably because most researchers who conduct research in this area break down their results as a function of anorexia subtype (restricting versus purging; see comparison below). In an uncontrolled study, Morgan, Lacey, and Reid (1999) demonstrated that the frequency of sexual fantasy increased as anorexic inpatients approached their target body weight, although these rates were still below normative values. On the other hand, Kaufer and Katz (1983) found no difference in the sexual content in Rorschach responses between anorexic and nonanorexic individuals.

In the most comprehensive comparison of anorexic and nonanorexic individuals, Raboch and Faltus (1991) found that anorexic women were more likely to report difficulties with anorgasmia and low sexual desire. In all, 53% of their anorexia sample endorsed a "primary disturbance of sex life," and another 27% of this sample indicated that their sex life had deteriorated after the onset of their disorder. Raboch and Faltus noted that the patients who scored lowest on their self-report inventory of sexual functioning tended to be those who had irregular menstrual cycles. In addition, they observed that sexual dysfunction was most pronounced in anorexics who had disturbed partner relationships. Although direction of causality between relational and sexual disturbance could not be determined from this study's design, it suggests that individuals with anorexia who experience disturbance in one domain are likely to experience difficulty in the other.

Bulimia Nervosa.   A greater number of studies examined aspects of sexuality in samples of bulimic individuals than in samples of anorexic individuals, and results from these studies highlight both similarities and differences in the sexual functioning of bulimic and nonbulimic individuals. For example, bulimic individuals were shown to demonstrate adequate dating competence (Katzman & Wolchik, 1984), and they are similar to nonbulimic individuals on many variables pertaining to their sexual and relationship history (e.g., age at first significant relationship, age at first intercourse, number of sexual partners, length of longest relationship; Abraham et al., 1985). However, controlled studies also suggest that these individuals are characterized by a number of sexual disturbances. Specifically, bulimic individuals report less sexual enjoyment than nonbulimic individuals, which they attribute to their overdependence on their partner and desire to be thinner (Allerdissen, Florin, & Rost, 1981). They also are more likely than nonbulimic individuals to endorse symptoms of sexual disorders, including anorgasmia, vaginismus, dyspareunia, low sexual desire, intercourse experienced from a spectator perspective, and use of alcohol as a disinhibitor (Jagstaidt et al., 1996). Interestingly, Abraham et al. (1985) found that bulimic individuals were more likely to achieve orgasm through masturbation than nonbulimic individuals (94% vs. 47%), but that they were less likely to achieve orgasm through intercourse (37% vs. 71%). However, it is important to note that bulimic and nonbulimic individuals are similar in some other domains of sexual functioning, including arousal, sexual fantasy, frequency of intercourse per month, masturbation with orgasm, and homosexual experiences (Jagstaidt et al., 1996).

There is some evidence that immediately after treatment, bulimic individuals engage in less sexual activity than they had when their symptoms were active (Pyle, Mitchell, & Eckert, 1981). However, trends toward decreased frequency of sexual behavior seem to normalize after some time, as Abraham (1998) found that former bulimic patients report having fairly normative sexual relationships 10 to 15 years after treatment. Although these former patients were engaging in sexual activities at a level consistent with that reported by the general population, 86% of the sample admitted that they sometimes withdrew from their partners because of concerns about body weight (Abraham, 1998). In addition, this follow-up study demonstrated that marital difficulties were associated with having active eating disorder symptoms, and 45% of the sample believed that relationship difficulties exacerbated the course of their eating disorder. Thus, at least as measured by patients' perceptions, eating disorder symptomatology and relationship disturbance are closely related, and rates of sexual dysfunction are highest in periods of time when eating disorder symptoms reach a clinically significant level.

Comparison of Restrictors and Purgers.   Contrary to clinical lore, the empirical literature varies with regard to whether bulimics and "purging" anorexics have more sexual experience than "restricting" anorexics. Restricting anorexics are significantly emaciated individuals who achieve this by restricting their food intake, whereas purging anorexics are significantly emaciated individuals who achieve this by compensatory behavior (e.g., vomiting, laxatives). Some studies comparing the two groups report that a higher percentage of purgers had at least one previous steady boyfriend, had sexual intercourse, had engaged in oral sex, and/or had taken oral contraceptives than restrictors or dieters (Abraham & Beumont, 1981; Beumont, Abraham, & Simson, 1981; Beumont, George, & Smart, 1976; Dykens & Gerrard, 1986; Garfinkel, Moldofsky, & Garner, 1980). Several psychological variables have been posited to explain these differences, such as guilt about sex (Freeman, Thomas, Solyom, & Koopman,

1985) and negative attitudes toward sex (Leon, Lucas, Colligan, Ferdinand, & Kamp, 1985), both of which are more frequently endorsed in restricting anorexics than in purging anorexics. On the other hand, other studies found no difference between the two groups in their sexual experience (e.g., Casper, Eckert, Halmi, Goldberg, & Davis, 1980). In fact, Rothschild, Fagan, Woodall, and Andersen (1991) reported that restrictors and purgers had equally low scores on a global index of sexual functioning, which fell below the first percentile when compared to scores obtained in the general population. Fifty percent of the eating disorder patients in this sample rated their present sexual relationship as "poor," suggesting that both groups of patients were equally dysfunctional.

Despite the fact that evidence exists to support the notion that bulimic individuals are more sexually experienced than anorexic individuals, results from some studies suggest that they report less pleasure associated with sexual behavior. For example, Casper et al. (1980) indicated that their purging patients reported less interest in sex and less posttreatment sexual experience than their restricting patients. Garfinkel (1981) examined chart data of anorexic inpatients classified as bulimic or restricting and found that bulimic patients indeed had more extensive sexual histories than anorexic patients, but that they were more likely to report a lack of sexual enjoyment. Morgan, Wiederman, and Pryor (1995) noted that bulimic individuals may use sex for instrumental purposes, such as to gain control or acceptance rather than to satisfy sexual desires. Thus, motivation for secondary gain might account for differences in rates of sexual activity between restricting and purging eating disorder patients.

The majority of existing research examined sexual functioning in eating disorder patients at the time they are receiving treatment. In contrast, Morgan et al. (1995) examined sexual functioning in former anorexic and bulimic patients approximately 2 years after they had presented for treatment at their Eating Disorders Treatment Clinic. Results must be interpreted with caution because significantly fewer former anorexics returned the questionnaire than former bulimics; nevertheless, this study provides important information about the long-term functioning of individuals with these eating disorders. On recovery from their eating disorder, both groups of former patients reported that they had intercourse less frequently (i.e., approximately once per week) and desired it less frequently (i.e., approximately twice a week) than the rates typically reported in the general population (cf. Schover, Friedman, Weiler, Heiman, & LoPiccolo, 1980). Most of these individuals either did not masturbate or did so less than once a month, rates that again are much less that what are observed in the general population. Approximately 78% of the former patients reported that they experience negative emotions during sex as compared to approximately 35% of the general population, and approximately 39% of the sample indicated that they had significant "sex relationship problems." The only difference between diagnostic groups in current sexual functioning was in their perception of their competence as a sexual partner, as anorexics scored lower than bulimics in this domain.

Eating Disorders: Conclusions.   A number of conclusions can be drawn from this review. First, it is clear that eating disorders are associated with impairments in close relationships and in sexual adjustment. However, sexual functioning is not uniformally abnormal, as individuals, particularly those with bulimia, are similar to noneating disordered individuals on variables such as frequency of past and present intercourse and masturbation. Although individuals who are treated successfully for eating disorders tend to resume fairly normal sexual functioning, body image concerns continue to impair sexual desire at times in which individuals feel that their weight is higher than is desired. Finally, although there is some evidence to the contrary, it appears that bulimic women are more sexually experienced than anorexic women who lose weight predominantly by restricting, which may be due to psychological variables associated with bulimia such as sex guilt or motivation to achieve secondary gain. It will be important to understand the manner in which these mediating psychological variables develop and facilitate these two very different styles of weight management. For example, some research suggests that restrictors are characterized by a rigid, overly controlled personality style, whereas purgers are characterized by a histrionic, overly-indulgent personality style, and that these characterological features (rather than eating disorder symptoms) determine the type of sexual behavior that is expressed (Abraham & Beumont, 1981).

Although many of the studies described examined relationship satisfaction or quality in a global manner, few elicited the specific manner in which eating disorder symptomatology, sexual dysfunction, and relationship functioning exert reciprocal influences. Based on her clinical experience, Zerbe (1996) speculated that eating disorder patients use eating as a coping strategy rather than developing the skills to obtain social support from their close relationships in times of stress. That is, individuals with eating disorders may not have the necessary skills to develop healthy romantic relationships. From this standpoint, it would be important to incorporate into treatment psychoeducation to normalize patients' knowledge of healthy relationships and social skills in order to help them achieve that goal. In addition, Simpson and Ramberg (1992) described eating disorder cases in which sexual avoidance played a functional role in the relationship, as the partners of these patients expressed some of their own discomfort with and aversion toward sex. These case descriptions highlight the need to conduct a functional analysis of eating disorder patients' sexual disturbance, as it may be secondary to a more central relationship problem.

As has been demonstrated to this point in the chapter, it will be important for future research in this area to make methodological improvements to draw conclusions that are meaningful and generalizable. For example, almost no research in this area focuses on symptomatology and sexuality in male eating disorder patients (but see Herzog, Norman, Gordon, & Pepose, 1984, for an exception). It is acknowledged that the prevalence of eating disorders in males is significantly lower than in females (APA, 1994), but at this point, we know virtually nothing about the partner relationships and sexual adjustment of males with anorexia and bulimia. Second, nearly every study reviewed herein used samples of individuals who were hospitalized as inpatients or being treated as outpatients. Thus, the extent to which the findings are generalizable to individuals in the community with eating disorders who are not currently seeking treatment is questionable. Finally, because relational and sexual disturbances are central to eating disorder pathology, it will be important for future research to uncover the manner in which dysfunction in these areas predicts severity of symptoms, probability of relapse, and long-term psychosocial adjustment.

Alcoholism

Although alcoholism researchers have long recognized the importance of close relationships in affecting the course of the disease (e.g., Jensen, 1979), only recently have researchers begun to examine empirically the association between alcohol use and aspects of the partner relationship (see Dolan & Nathan, 2002 for a review). Consistent with the intuitive notion that relationships of alcoholic individuals are distressed, Whalley (1978) reported that alcoholic men were more likely to be separated from their spouses than nonalcoholic men, and Schuckit (1972) described a similar observation for alcoholic women. In addition, wives often point to drinking as the cause of their marital and family difficulties and develop drinking problems after the dissolution of their marriage (Roberts & Leonard, 1997). On the other hand, there is also evidence that similar levels of alcohol use by both partners, even if it is heavy use, often contributes to a stable relationship culture and high levels of harmony. In addition, longitudinal data suggest that wives' drinking frequency is negatively related to husbands' subsequent alcohol dependence symptoms, suggesting that a wife who drinks on a regular basis reduces her husband's vulnerability to alcohol dependence (Roberts & Leonard, 1997). Thus, alcohol abuse often is the cause and consequence of relationship distress, but if both partners adjust their drinking to a level comfortable to both parties, then it may be less problematic than one might expect (Dolan & Nathan, 2002).

Very little research examined the interplay between alcohol use, relationship functioning, and sexuality, although a variable often assessed in research examining sexual functioning in alcoholic individuals is the degree to which alcohol facilitates comfort with intimate behavior. In general, there are two lines of inquiry that address the manner in which alcohol use affects sexual functioning. In some studies, participants are given (or think they are being given) alcohol, and indices of sexual arousal are obtained in a laboratory setting (e.g., Wilson & Lawson, 1976a, 1976b). Effects of alcohol intake on sexual arousal were examined in this manner in samples of non-alcoholic college-age students (e.g., Wilson & Lawson, 1976a) as well as adults who abused alcohol for several years (e.g., Wilson, Lawson, & Abrams, 1978). In contrast, other researchers recruit individuals representing a wide range of drinking habits (e.g., Klassen & Wilsnack, 1986) or individuals diagnosed with an alcohol use disorder (e.g., Beckman, 1979) and gather data on their sexual history, attitudes, interest, and performance, usually through a self-report or interview format. Each of these areas of research will be discussed next.

Effects of Alcohol Intake on Arousal.   Alcohol intake alters sexual functioning through both physiological and psychological mechanisms, and similar patterns have been demonstrated in college student samples and clinical samples of individuals with alcoholism (Lang & Frank, 1990). For men, there is a mildly enhancing effect of alcohol on sexual responsivity at low blood alcohol content (BAC) levels, but there is a subsequent decrease in sexual responsivity when BAC increases above 0.05 (Wilson & Lawson, 1976b). In contrast, women experience reduced vaginal blood flow even at BAC levels below 0.05 (Crowe & George, 1989). Although men's self-reports of arousal parallel this physiological effect, women subjectively report that their arousal increases as alcohol dose increases (e.g., Wilson & Lawson, 1976a). Crowe and George (1989) speculated that women might be less able than men to detect changes in physiological arousal. Moreover, there is some evidence that low doses of alcohol enhance overall arousal, and it is possible that women mistake this activation for sexual arousal (Lang & Frank, 1990). Lindman (1992) also suggested that women are more likely to associate guilty feelings with sex, and it is possible that they experience arousal associated with alcohol because their self-evaluation is impaired.

Although arousal appears to diminish with increasingly higher doses of alcohol, both men and women are more likely to engage in sexual activity while intoxicated than while sober. Crowe and George (1989) attribute this paradox to disinhibition, which can be explained by both pharmacological and psychological mechanisms. Specifically, increasing doses of alcohol results in cognitive impairment, which may cause individuals to make decisions to engage in sexual acts that they would not normally do when they are sober. In addition, people often have the expectation that alcohol use gives "permission" to engage in socially unacceptable behaviors. Thus, even if people intuitively know that alcohol interferes with arousal, these secondary effects of alcohol increase the level of sexual activity. Because both alcohol ingestion and sexual activity are highly reinforcing, it is not surprising that people develop alcohol use problems, particularly after perceiving success with social and intimate interactions that occur while intoxicated.

Alcohol Use and Sexual Dysfunction in Community Samples.   Few studies examined self-reported sexual dysfunction in community samples of individuals who are not alcoholics, but work by Wilsnack and Wilsnack represents an unique exception (cf. Wilsnack, Wilsnack, & Klassen, 1984). In their national survey, they identified groups of light drinking or abstaining individuals, moderate-to-heavy drinking individuals (i.e., four or more drinks per week), former problem drinkers, and abstaining individuals who were formerly heavy drinkers approximately 1 year prior. Klassen and Wilsnack (1986) reported that the majority of women drinkers perceived that drinking reduced sexual inhibitions and helped them to feel closer to and more open with others, although they were more likely to perceive themselves as targets of sexual advances rather than being more sexually assertive. Women who abstained from drinking in the previous 12 months were more sexually traditional than moderate-to-heavy drinkers (e.g., lowest rates of premarital intercourse). Klassen and Wilsnack attributed this difference to one of two factors—either that alcohol served as a sexual disinhibitor, or that both drinking and sexual behavior are regulated by a more general moral value system. Moderate drinkers scored lower than both light and heavy drinkers on measures of sexual dysfunction, suggesting that these women might have achieved an optimal level of moderation or balance in several areas of their lives. In a report on the analysis of the second wave of their longitudinal data, they indicated that sexual dysfunction found in their first assessment was the strongest predictor of continued drinking at the time of their second assessment (Wilsnack, Plaud, Wilsnack, & Klassen, 1997). These data suggest that sexual dysfunction might be a risk factor for later alcohol use.

Sexual Dysfunction in Alcoholics.   Chronic alcohol abuse has detrimental effects on sexual functioning in men and women, as evidenced by both physiological and self-report data. Crowe and George (1989) reviewed evidence suggesting that chronic alcohol use decreases testosterone production and increases femininzation (e.g., testicular atrophy, impotence) in men (cf. Powell, 1984; Schiavi, 1990; Tan et al., 1984). During sleep, alcoholic men have diminished tumescent latency and a decreased number of maximum penile tumescent episodes as compared to nonalcoholic men (Schiavi, 1990). Schiavi also indicated that chronic alcohol intake affects peripheral neurological processes that underlie erectile dysfunction, such that the myelin and axon degeneration that occurs could affect sexual functioning by decreasing tactile sensitivity or by producing unpleasant sensations in response to genital stimulation. However, an encouraging observation is that many impotent alcoholics had been abstinent for a shorter period of time than former alcoholics exhibiting normal sexual functioning, which suggests that some of these physiological effects may be reversible (Tan et al., 1984; but see Lemere & Smith, 1973 for conflicting findings). Far less is known about the physiological changes associated with chronic alcohol use in women, although Crowe and George (1989) reviewed data from animal studies suggesting that chronic alcohol use causes ovarian weight reduction and disrupts the estrous cycle in females.

There are several documented types of sexual dysfunction associated with alcoholism in men, including lack of sexual desire, impotence, difficulty maintaining erection, and premature ejaculation (Jensen, 1979; Powell, 1984; see Schiavi, 1990, for a comprehensive review). Data from Whalley's (1978) study suggests that of these difficulties, erectile dysfunction is the most pronounced, although Wilsnack et al. (1997) reported that ejaculation and orgasm dysfunction were the most significant difficulties in their community sample of male heavy drinkers. Alcoholic women report dissatisfaction with their sexuality (Beckman, 1979) and low levels of interest, arousal, pleasure, lubrication, and orgasm (Covington & Kohen, 1984). In fact, in Covington and Kohen's (1984) sample of 35 newly recovering alcoholic women, 85% reported some sort of sexual dysfunction. According to Crowe and George (1989), 50% of male and female alcoholics report that drinking relieves sexual problems, but 25% of alcoholic women and 60% of alcoholic men are considered sexually dysfunctional. In addition, alcoholic women report high levels of psychological variables relating to sexual dysfunction, including a fear of intimacy, performance anxiety, and guilt about sexuality (Heiser & Hartmann, 1987).

Although female alcoholics often are associated with the stereotype of promiscuity, empirical data yielded mixed findings to support this characterization. For example, alcoholic women in Beckman's (1979) study indicated that they were more likely than normal controls, psychiatric controls, and alcoholic men to engage in sexual activity while drinking. Over half of these women (55%) indicated that they were more likely to have intercourse with people they would not if they had not been drinking, and 41% reported that they would engage in sexual acts while drinking that they otherwise would not. Jensen (1984) found that alcoholic women were more likely to have been diagnosed with a sexually transmitted disease than nonalcoholic women. In contrast, results from two studies (Covington & Kohen, 1984; Heiser & Hartmann, 1987) failed to find results supporting increased rates of sexual activity while drinking, but results from the former study indicated that newly recovering alcoholic women in their samples endorsed a greater variety of sexual experiences than nonalcoholic women. Based on clinical experience, Schuckit (1972) concluded that very few alcoholic women are promiscuous, but instead that most are depressed, in dysfunctional marriages, and are sexually naïve. Evidence also is mixed with regard to whether men exhibit promiscuity in the context of heavy drinking (Whalley, 1978; Wilsnack et al., 1997).

Confirming the implications of Wilsnack and colleagues' longitudinal data, many researchers uncovered evidence in female alcoholics suggesting that sexual dysfunction indeed is a predisposing factor for heavy drinking. For example, Apter-Marsh (1984) found that 20% of her sample of recovered alcoholic women reported dyspareunia before they started drinking heavily. Although these women engaged in more frequent sexual activity during the time in which they were drinking the most, it was also during this time that the had the lowest percentage of orgasms during intercourse. Covington and Kohen (1984) reported that 79% of 35 newly recovering female alcoholics endorsed some sort of dysfunction prior to heavy drinking. Other researchers indicate that alcoholic women have low sexual self-esteem (cf. Lindman, 1992). For example, Heiser and Hartmann (1987) reported that alcoholic women are more likely than nonalcoholic women to believe their partner is not physically attractive to them, that they might not be sexually responsive, and that something is wrong with them.

Unfounded sexual attitudes also were linked with chronic alcohol use. Jensen (1979) indicated that alcoholic men who falsely believe that alcohol enhances arousal were more likely to report sexual dysfunction than alcoholic men who did not hold this belief. Moreover, Apter-Marsh (1984) indicated that 80% of her sample of recovering female alcoholics believed that alcohol improved their sexual functioning when they were drinking (see Covington & Kohen, 1984, for similar results), although nearly all the women abandoned that belief in sobriety. Similarly, Beckman (1979) found that female alcoholics were more likely than normal controls and psychiatric controls to endorse desiring and enjoying intercourse more while drinking than while sober. Heiser and Hartmann (1987) indicated that alcoholic women are more likely than nonalcoholic women to believe that alcohol induces sexual relaxation, sexual enhancement, assertiveness, and even sexual satisfaction.

Taken together, the data reviewed in these three sections suggest that some alcoholic individuals, particularly women, might begin drinking heavily to increase closeness with others, to relieve anxiety associated with social interaction and intimacy, and/or to overcome possible sexual dysfunction (cf. Covington & Surrey, 1997). Many of these individuals are characterized by low self-esteem and are critical of themselves, so the attention they receive from others while drinking is a welcomed change and likely contributes to the cycle of addiction. Despite the fact that sexual performance clearly decreases under the influence of alcohol, cognitive impairment and the positive affective experience associated with intimate encounters while drinking reinforce the perception that alcohol increases sexual functioning. Not surprisingly, periods of sobriety bring about many doubts with regard to interpersonal and sexual competence.

Sexual Functioning in Sobriety.   The time of sobriety presents many challenges to aspects of an alcoholic individual's sexuality. Recovering alcoholic women report fears that their bodies are permanently impaired or have "shut down" after drinking, and they also experience guilt, shame, and anger about their sexual behavior while drinking (Apter-Marsh, 1984). Covington and Kohen (1984) indicated that approximately three fourth of newly recovered alcoholic women endorsed some sort of sexual dysfunction. However, many of these women reported dysfunction prior to the onset of heavy drinking, making it unclear whether the transition to sobriety exacerbates dysfunction or represents a regression to pre-drinking levels of sexual functioning. Some evidence suggests that the course of sexual dysfunction during sobriety varies as a function of gender, as men may experience years of sexual dysfunction following the discontinuation of heavy drinking, whereas dysfunction in women gradually improves through the first 6 to 12 months of sobriety (Apter-Marsh, 1984).

One common aspect of alcoholism treatment is Antabuse, a pharmacological agent that induces vomiting if alcohol is ingested. Results from several studies suggest that recovering alcoholic men believe there is a direct association between Antabuse and the onset of sexual disturbance. For example, half of the dysfunctional men in Jensen's (1984) sample attributed their sexual problems to Antabuse. Moreover, Powell (1984) observed that delayed ejaculation was particularly salient in individuals treated with Antabuse. He suggested that sexual problems associated with chronic alcohol use should be normalized and that patients should be "given permission" not to engage in sexual acts until they are ready to do so. Schiavi (1990) cautioned that Antabuse could be a confounding factor that accounts for much of the observed sexual dysfunction in male alcoholics. Thus, it is important to consider the number of individuals who are taking Antabuse when interpreting data pertaining to sexual functioning in recovering alcoholics. There is little discourse on the effects of Antabuse on sexual functioning in female alcoholics, as treatment with Antabuse typically is reserved for only the most severe alcoholics, most of whom are men (Nancy Vogeltanz-Holm, personal communication, October 2002).

Alcoholism: Conclusions.   Sexual dysfunction is both a cause and a consequence of heavy drinking. Alcohol intake clearly inhibits sexual arousal, and chronic alcohol use is associated with detrimental physiological effects on reproductive organs in both men and women. Newly recovering alcoholics report dysfunction in all major stages of the human sexual response cycle—desire, arousal, and orgasm. Moreover, alcoholic individuals sometimes make poor sexual decisions while under the influence, such as engaging in sexual activity with people whom they would not have if they were sober. Particularly in alcoholic women, these decisions are associated with emotional distress, low self-esteem, and fear that they will not be sexually functional unless they are using alcohol. Sexual dysfunction continues as alcoholic individuals adjust to sobriety, and restoration to normative levels of sexual functioning often takes several months or even years.

As so far discussed, most types of psychopathology have been unequivocally associated with impaired relationship and sexual functioning. In contrast, in some instances, heavy drinking by both partners creates a relationship culture characterized by stability, engagement in a shared activity, and mutual understanding (cf. Dolan & Nathan, 2002). However, the maintenance of such a culture surely is a "slippery slope," as there is no guarantee that the health-related, emotional, and interpersonal consequences of chronic alcohol use will follow a similar course in both members of the couple. As these consequences lead to increased or decreased alcohol consumption in one partner, the culture will be disrupted, potentially leading to violated expectations and increased relationship conflict. Moreover, in couples in which only one partner is a heavy drinker, the time of sobriety is not necessarily one of increased harmony. As Jensen (1984) noted, many alcoholics struggle to regain their role in familial relationships after they have stopped drinking, and partners are often ambivalent and wonder whether the gains they made in treatment will last.

Several methodological points are of note for continued research into the nature of sexual and relationship functioning in individuals who abuse alcohol. Schiavi (1990) emphasized the importance of using a multifactorial conceptualization of alcoholism that integrates psychosocial and biological variables to understand its effects on human sexuality. To date, most research examining the effects of alcohol use on sexuality have been based on self-report data, such as interviews and questionnaires, which are subject to reporting bias due to social desirability and distorted memory (see Wiederman, chapter 2, this volume). Recommendations for future research include conducting more detailed physiological assessments of sexual response and gathering collateral data to provide the partner's perspective of the couple's sexual functioning. In addition, nearly all studies examining the effects of alcohol use disorders on sexuality rely on participants who recently have started or finished treatment programs. Because these participants are not actively drinking, it is unclear whether data collected during this time apply to functioning during the period in which they were drinking heavily. In addition, their physical and psychological stasis also has been radically altered, making it questionable as to whether their functioning is representative of *any* time in their lives. Although a longitudinal study of a nationally representative sample would address this issue, Klassen and Wilsnack (1986) questioned whether their sample of heavy drinkers was at all similar to individuals who have been diagnosed with alcohol use disorders. Ideally, it would be useful to gather data on sexual functioning from alcoholic individuals before they start treatment, while they are in treatment, and after they have adjusted to sobriety.

IMPLICATIONS FOR TREATMENT

It is evident from this review that sexual dysfunction is a major correlate of psychopathology. Thus, clinicians should assume that at least a subset of individuals in their caseload are experiencing sexual difficulties. Although most patients with psychopathology do not spontaneously report sexual disturbance, over half endorse difficulty if specifically asked by their clinician (Montejo-Gonzalez et al., 1997). By routinely asking about sexual functioning, clinicians are able to (a) accurately monitor sexual dysfunction, (b) model that it is acceptable to talk about sexual concerns, and (c) provide a message that sexual difficulties are common in individuals who are being treated for psychopathology. When clinicians learn that patients are experiencing sexual disturbance associated with their psychopathology, they may choose from a number of interventions, including psychoeducation, couple or sex therapy (see McCarthy, Bodnar, & Handal, chapter 23, this volume), or a pharmacological adjunct to enhance sexual functioning.

Educating patients about sexual dysfunction associated with psychopathology and pharmacological treatment of psychopathology is imperative, as it will allow for patients to make informed decisions about the modality of treatment that is in their best interest. Moreover, it is recommended here that patients' partners attend at least one appointment with the patient so that they learn about the interplay between psychopathology, relationship quality, and sexual functioning. Not only will such an interaction help to modify partners' expectations for relationship and sexual functioning during the course of treatment, but it also has the potential to promote an environment of acceptance and understanding rather than conflict and disillusionment. If successful, this might facilitate symptom remission above and beyond that associated with the treatment that patients are receiving.

CONCLUSION

A general conclusion that can be drawn from this review is that all types of psychopathology are associated with distress in the close relationship and at least some sort sexual dysfunction. It appears that the association between psychopathology and relationship distress is bidirectional, such that symptoms of psychopathology impair functioning in relationships, and problems in relationships exacerbate symptoms of psychopathology. This association has been demonstrated empirically by depression researchers (see O'Mahen et al., 2001), but it also can be inferred from the review of the other types of psychopathology. For example, individuals with eating disorders are often so preoccupied with their body shape and image that they experience a great deal of discomfort in their sexual relationship. Conversely, many individuals who had recovered from eating disorder pathology indicated that problems in their relationship were associated with relapse (Morgan et al., 1995). In addition, individuals diagnosed with alcohol use disorders often report high rates of relationship conflict (e.g., Whalley, 1978), but it was also documented that some individuals begin drinking heavily after the dissolution of a romantic relationship (Roberts & Leonard, 1997). It will be important for future researchers to document empirically this bidirectional association in individuals with types of psychopathology other than depression.

Patterns of sexual dysfunction, however, vary as a function of particular type of psychopathology. Some types of psychopathology, such as depression and anxiety disorders, are characterized by pervasive sexual dysfunction, such that a significant percentage of individuals with these disorders endorse disturbance in sexual desire, arousal, and orgasm. Although research examining long-term sexual functioning in individuals with anxiety disorders has not been conducted, available evidence suggests that sexual dysfunction persists in depressed individuals well after their symptoms have remitted. In contrast, individuals with bulimia and borderline personality disorder (BPD) present with a more complex pattern of dysfunction. Although the frequency of their sexual activity is at a rate that is average or higher than average compared to the frequency of healthy individuals, they often deny enjoyment in these activities and endorse orgasmic dysfunction. Interestingly, the researchers who arrived at these observations in both of these literatures suggest that individuals with these pathologies engage in sexual activity for secondary gain (Hurlbert et al., 1992; Morgan et al., 1995). These findings raise the possibility that a primarily biological mechanism underlies the generalized dysfunction observed in depression and anxiety but that a primarily psychological mechanism underlies the pattern of sexual functioning in bulimia and BPD.

Mania, in contrast, is associated with increased sexual activity, and there are no known reports of sexual dysfunction in the context of a manic episode. However, it is unclear whether increased sexual activity is an expression of more general increases in goal-directed activity or whether biological changes that occur during a manic episode facilitate increases in sex drive. Many alcoholic individuals also report increased sexual activity in periods of heavy drinking. However, there is evidence that sexual dysfunction predates heavy drinking in many alcoholic individuals (Apter-Marsh, 1984), and prolonged alcohol use has the potential to result in severe physiological changes that cause sexual dysfunction (Crowe & George, 1989). This pattern of results highlights that fact that frequency of sexual activity is not necessarily an accurate marker of functionality in sexual relationships.

It is evident from this literature review that studies examining the association between psychopathology and relational dysfunction are not conducted from a relational perspective and are largely atheoretical. At this point, much work needs to be done to examine how different types of psychopathology affect the partner relationship, especially when the individual with psychopathology has some sort of sexual dysfunction. It is likely that sexual dysfunction associated with psychopathology violates the partner's sexual script, which establishes one's expectations for the amount and type of typical sexual activity. Moreover, it is logical that the partner would feel that he or she is contributing much more to the relationship than the individual with psychopathology, which violates basic principles of exchange theory (see Byers & Wang, chapter 9, this volume). It will be important for future researchers to assess the degree to which psychopathology affects *partners'* perceptions of the quality of the romantic and sexual relationship, not only to understand this issue in a broader theoretical context, but also to identify additional acceptance and change techniques that could be integrated into a couple's intervention.

Despite the important observation over 25 years ago that depression adversely affects interpersonal functioning (Coyne, 1976), programs of research examining the interpersonal sequelae of psychopathology are just beginning to develop. To date, most of this research has investigated the effects of psychopathology on relationship satisfaction (e.g., Wenzel, 2002), stress and conflict (e.g., Davila & Beck, 2002), and communication (e.g., Chambless et al., 2002). It is imperative for future researchers to begin to consider the manner in which psychopathology affects sexual functioning, as the quality of the sexual relationship and the quality of the partner relationship are closely associated (Sprecher & Cate, chapter 10, this volume). Although a number of studies were reviewed in this chapter, most used small samples, convenience samples of individuals who were participating in larger studies, or individuals who were assessed during the course of treatment. All of these factors limit what can be said about sexual functioning in individuals with psychopathology who are representative of the general population. We encourage future researchers to integrate literatures from clinical psychology, psychiatry, communication, and human sexuality disciplines to develop a comprehensive framework for conceptualizing sexual dysfunction and relationship distress in individuals with psychopathology.

REFERENCES

Abraham, S. (1998). Sexuality and reproduction in bulimia nervosa patients over 10 years. *Journal of Psychosomatic Research, 44,* 491–502.

Abraham, S. F., Bendit, N., Mason, C., Mitchell, H., O'Connor, N., Ward, J., Young, S., & Llewellyn-Jones, D. (1985). The psychosexual histories of young women with bulimia. *Australian and New Zealand Journal of Psychiatry, 19,* 72–76.

Abraham, S., & Beumont, P. J. V. (1981). Varieties of psychosexual experience in patients with anorexia nervosa. *International Journal of Eating Disorders, 1,* 10–20.

Abrahamson, D. J., Barlow, D. H., Sakheim, D. K., Beck, J. G., & Athanasiou, R. (1985). Effects of distraction on sexual responding in functional and dysfunctional men. *Behavior Therapy, 16,* 503–515.

Aiznberg, D., Noar, S., Zemishlany, Z., & Weizman, A. (1999). The serotonin antagonist mainserin for treatment of serotonin reuptake inhibitor-induced sexual dysfunction in women: An open label study. *Clinical Neuropharmacology, 22,* 347–350.

Aksaray, G., Yelken, B., Kaptanoglu, C., Oflu, S., & Ozaltin, M. (2001). Sexuality in women with Obsessive Compulsive Disorder. *Journal of Sex & Marital Therapy, 27,* 273–277.

Allerdissen, R., Florin, I., & Rost, W. (1981). Psychological characteristics of women with bulimia nervosa (bulimerexia). *Behavior Analysis and Modification, 4,* 313–317.

American Psychiatric Association (1994). *Diagnostic and statistical manual of mental disorders, (4th ed.)* Washington, DC: Author.

Apter-Marsh, M. (1984). The sexual behavior of alcoholic women while drinking and during sobriety. *Alcoholism Treatment Quarterly, 1,* 35–48.

Ashton, A. K., Hamer, R., & Rosen, R. C. (1997). Serotonin reuptake inhibitor-induced sexual dysfunction and its treatment: A large-scale retrospective study of 596 psychiatric outpatients. *Journal of Sex and Marital Therapy, 23,* 165–175.

Balon, R. (1998). The effects of antidepressants on human sexuality: Diagnosis and Management Update 1998. *Primary Psychiatry, 5,* 35–44.

Barlow, D. H. (1986). Causes of sexual dysfunction: The role of anxiety and cognitive interference. *Journal of Consulting and Clinical Psychology, 54,* 140–148.

Barlow, D. H. (2002). *Anxiety and its disorders (2nd ed.).* New York: Guilford.

Barlow, D. H., Sakheim, D. K., & Beck, J. G. (1983). Anxiety increases sexual arousal. *Journal of Abnormal Psychology, 92,* 49–54.

Beach, S. R. H., Martin, J. K., Blum, T. C., & Roman, P. M. (1993). Subclinical depression and role fulfillment in domestic settings: Spurious relationships, imagined problems, or real effects? *Journal of Psychopathology and Behavioral Assessment, 15,* 113–128.

Beckman, L. J. (1979). Reported effects of alcohol on the sexual feelings and behavior of women alcoholics and nonalcoholics. *Journal of Studies on Alcohol, 40,* 272–282.

Beumont, P. J. V., Abraham, S. F., & Simson, K. G. (1981). The psychosexual histories of adolescent girls and young women with anorexia nervosa. *Psychological Medicine, 11,* 131–140.

Beumont, P. J. V., George, G. C. W., & Smart, D. E. (1976). "Dieters" and "vomiters and purgers" in anorexia nervosa. *Psychological Medicine, 6,* 617–622.

Beggs, V. E., Calhoun, K. S., & Wolchik, S. A. (1987). Sexual anxiety and female sexual arousal: A comparison of arousal during sexual anxiety stimuli and sexual pleasure stimuli. *Archives of Sexual Behavior, 16,* 311–319.

Blay, S. L., Ferrez, M. P. T., & Calil, M. H. (1982). Lithium-induced male sexual impairment: Two case reports. *Journal of Clinical Psychiatry, 43,* 497–498.

Briscoe, C. W., & Smith, J. B. (1973). Depression and marital turmoil. *Archives of General Psychiatry, 29,* 811–817.

Briscoe, C. W., Smith, J. B., Robins, E., Marten, S., & Gaskin, F. (1973). Divorce and psychiatric disease. *Archives of General Psychiatry, 29,* 119–125.

Brodie, H., & Leff, M. (1971). Bipolar depression: A comparative study of patient characteristics. *American Journal of Psychiatry, 127,* 1086–1090.

Brown, G. W., & Harris, T. O. (1978). *Social origins of depression: A study of psychiatric disorder in women.* London: Tavistock.

Casper, R. C., Eckert, E. D., Halmi, K. A., Goldberg, S. C., & Davis, J. M. (1980). Bulimia: Its incidence and clinical importance in patients with anorexia nervosa. *Archives of General Psychiatry, 37,* 1030–1035.

Chambless, D. L., Fauerbach, J. A., Floyd, F. J., Wilson, K. A., Remen, A. L., & Renneberg, B. (2002). Marital interaction of agoraphobia women: A controlled, behavioral observation study. *Journal of Abnormal Psychology, 111,* 502–512.

Clayton, A. H. (2001). Recognition and assessment of sexual dysfunction associated with depression. *Journal of Clinical Psychiatry, 62,* 5–9.

Coovert, D. L., Kinder, B. N., & Thompson, J. K. (1989). The psychosexual aspects of anorexia nervosa and bulimia nervosa: A review of literature. *Clinical Psychology Review, 9,* 169–180.

Covington, S. S., & Kohen, J. (1984). Women, alcohol, and sexuality. *Advances in Alcohol and Substance Abuse, 4,* 41–56.

Covington, S. S., & Surrey, J. L. (1997). The relation model of women's psychological development: Implications for substance abuse. In R. W. Wilsnack & S. C. Wilsnack (Eds.), *Gender and alcohol: Individual and social perspectives* (pp. 335–351). New Brunswick, NJ: Rutgers Center of Alcohol Studies.

Coyne, J. C. (1976). Depression and the response of others. *Journal of Abnormal Psychology, 85,* 186–193.

Craske, M. G., & Barlow, D. H. (2001). Panic disorder and agoraphobia. In D. H. Barlow (Ed), *Clinical handbook of psychological disorders: A step-by-step treatment manual* (3rd ed.; pp. 1–59). New York: Guilford.

Crowe, L. C., & George, W. H. (1989). Alcohol and human sexuality: Review and integration. *Psychological Bulletin, 105,* 374–386.

Curran, J. P., Little, L. M., & Gilbert, F. S. (1978). Reactivity of males of differing heterosexual social anxiety to female approach and nonapproach cue conditions. *Behavior Theapy, 9,* 961.

Daley, S. E., Burge, D., & Hammen, C. (2000). Borderline personality disorder symptoms as predictors of four-year romantic relationship dysfunction in young women: Addressing issues of specificity. *Journal of Abnormal Psychology, 109,* 451–460.

Davila, J., & Beck, J. G. (2002). Is social anxiety associated with impairment in close relationships? A preliminary investigation. *Behavior Therapy, 33,* 427–446.

Derogatis, L. R., Meyer, J. K., & King, K. M. (1981). Psychopathology in individuals with sexual dysfunction. *American Journal of Psychiatry, 138,* 757–763.

Dolan, S. L., & Nathan, P. E. (2002). When one marital partner is an alcoholic. In J. H. Harvey & A. Wenzel (Eds.), *A clinician's guide to maintaining and enhancing close relationships* (pp. 215–229). Mahwah, NJ: Lawrence Erlbaum Associates.

Dykens, E. M., & Gerrard, M. (1986). Psychological profiles or purging bulimics, repeat dieters, and controls. *Journal of Consulting and Clinical Psychology, 54,* 283–288.

Elliot, A. N., & O'Donohue, W. T. (1997). The effects of anxiety and distraction on sexual arousal in a nonclinical sample of heterosexual women. *Archives of Sexual Behavior, 26,* 607–624.

Emmelkamp, P. M. G., & Gerlsma, C. (1994). Marital functioning and the anxiety disorders. *Behavior Therapy, 25,* 407–429.

Fava, M., & Rankin, R. (2002). Sexual functioning and SSRIs. *Journal of Clinical Psychiatry, 63 (suppl. 5),* 13–16.

Fincham, F. D., Beach, S. R. H., Harold, G. T., & Osbourne, L. N. (1997). Marital satisfaction and depression: Longitudinal relationships for husbands and wives. *Psychological Science, 3,* 351–357.

Freeman, R. J., Thomas, C. D., Solyom, L., & Koopman, R. F. (1985). Clinical and personality correlates of body size overestimation in anorexia nervosa and bulimia nervosa. *International Journal of Eating Disorders, 4,* 439–456.

Freund, B., & Steketee, G. (1989). Sexual history: Attitudes and functioning of Obsessive–Compulsive Patients. *Journal of Sex & Marital Therapy, 15,* 31–41.

Garfinkel, P. E. (1981). Some recent observations on the pathogenesis of anorexia nervosa. *Canadian Journal of Psychiatry, 26,* 218–223.

Garfinkel, P. E., Moldofksy, H., & Garner, D. M. (1980). The heterogeneity of anorexia nervosa: Bulimia as a distinct subgroup. *Archives of General Psychiatry, 37,* 1036–1040.

Garvey, M. J. (1985). Decreased libido in depression. *Medical Aspects of Human Sexuality, 19,* 30–34.

Gunderson, J. G., & Phillips, K. A. (1991). A current view of the interface between borderline personality disorder and depression. *American Journal of Psychiatry, 148,* 967–975.

Harrison, W. M., Rabkin, J. G., Erhardt, A. A., et al. (1986). Effects of antidepressant medication on sexual function: A controlled study. *Journal of Clinical Psychopharmacology, 6,* 144–149.

Harrison, W. M., Stewart, J., Erhardt, A. A., et al. (1985). A controlled study of the effects of antidepressants on sexual function. *Psychopharmacology Bulletin, 21,* 85–88.

Heiser, K., & Hartmann, U. (1987). Disorders of sexual desire in a sample of women alcoholics. *Drug and Alcohol Dependence, 19,* 145–157.

Herzog, D. B., Norman, D. K., Gordon, C., & Pepose, M. (1984). Sexual conflict and eating disorders in 27 males. *American Journal of Psychiatry, 141,* 989–990.

Howell, J. R., Reynolds, C. F., Thase, M. E., Frank, E., Jennings, J. R., Houck, P. R., Berman, S., Jacobs, E., & Kupfer, D. J. (1987). Assessment of sexual function, interest, and activity in depressed men. *Journal of Affective Disorders, 13,* 61–66.

Hurlbert, D. F., Apt, C., & White, L. C. (1992). An empirical examination into the sexuality of women with borderline personality disorders. *Journal of Sex and Marital Therapy, 18,* 231–242.

Jagstaidt, V., Golay, A., & Pasini, W. (1996). Sexuality and bulimia. *New Trends in Experimental and Clinical Psychiatry, 12,* 9–15.

Jamison, K. R., Gerner, R. H., Hammen, C., & Padesky, C. (1980). Clouds and silver lining: Positive experiences associated with primary affective disorders. *American Journal of Psychiatry, 137,* 198–202.

Jensen, S. B. (1979). Sexual customs and dysfunction in alcoholics. *British Journal of Sexual Medicine, 10,* 29–31.

Jensen, S. B. (1984). Sexual function and dysfunction in younger married alcoholics: A comparative study. *Acta Psychiatrica Scandinavica, 69,* 543–549.

Kaplan, H. S. (1974). *The new sex therapy.* New York: Brunner/Mazel.

Katzman, M. A., & Wolchik, S. A. (1984). Bulimia and binge eating in college women: A comparison of personality and behavioral characteristics. *Journal of Consulting and Clinical Psychology, 52,* 423–428.

Kaufer, J. F., & Katz, J. L. (1983). Rorschach responses in anorectic and nonanorectic women. *International Journal of Eating Disorders, 3,* 65–74.

Katz, R. C., Jardine, D. (1999). The relationship between worry, sexual aversion, and low sexual desire. *Journal of Sex & Marital Therapy, 25,* 293–296.

Kennedy, S. H., Dickens, S. E., Eisfeld, B. S., & Bagby, R. M. (1999). Sexual dysfunction before antidepressant therapy in major depression. *Journal of Affective Disorders, 56,* 201–208.

Klassen, A. C., & Wilsnack, S. C. (1986). Sexual experience and drinking among women in a U.S. national survey. *Archives of Sexual Behavior, 15,* 363–392.

Kuriansky, J. B. (1988). Personality style and sexuality. In R. A. Brown & J. R. Field (Eds.), *Treatment of sexual problems in individual and couples therapy* (pp. 23–47). Costa Mesa, CA: PMA.

Lang, A. R., & Frank, D. I. (1990). Drinking and sexual functioning—Acute doses of alcohol and sexual response. *Clinical Practice in Sexuality, 5,* 10–18.

Leary, M. R., & Dobbins, S. E. (1983). Social anxiety, sexual behavior, and contraceptive use. *Journal of Personality and Social Psychology, 45,* 1347–1354.

Lemere, F., & Smith, J. W. (1973). Alcohol–induced sexual impotence. *American Journal of Psychiatry, 130,* 212–213.

Leon, G. R., Lucas, A. R., Colligan, R. C., Ferdinand, R. J., & Kamp, J. (1985). Sexual, body-image, and personality attributes in anorexia nervosa. *Journal of Abnormal Child Psychology, 13,* 245–258.

Lindman, R. (1992). Alcohol and female disinhibition. In K. Bjorkqvist & P. Niemola (Eds.), *Of mice and women: Aspects of female aggression* (pp. 241–250). San Diego, CA: Academic Press.

Linehan, M. M. (1993). *Cognitive–behavioral treatment of borderline personality disorder.* New York: Guilford.

Margolese, H. C., & Assalian, P. (1996). Sexual side effects of antidepressants: A review. *Journal of Sex and Marital Therapy, 22,* 209–217.

Masters, W. H., & Johnson, V. E. (1970). *Human sexual inadequacy.* Boston: Little, Brown.

McLeod, J. D., & Eckberg, D. A. (1993). Concordance for depressive disorders and marital quality. *Journal of Marriage and the Family, 55,* 733–746.

McVey, T. B. (1997). Depression among women with hypoactive sexual desire: Orgasm consistency training and effect on treatment outcome. *Canadian Journal of Human Sexuality, 6,* 211–220.

Miller, I. W., & Kobakoff, G. I. (1986). Family functioning in psychiatric patients. *Comprehensive Psychiatry, 25,* 438–452.

Milner, K., Tandon, R., Tomori, O., & Florence, T. (1999). Psychotropic medication and sexual dysfunction. In P. F. Buckley (Ed.), *Sexuality and serious mental illness* (pp. 173–195). Amsterdam: Harwood.

Modell, J. G., Katholi, C. R., Modell, J. D., & DePalma, R. L. (1997). Comparative sexual side effects of buproprion, fluoxetine, paroxetine, and sertraline. *Clinical Pharmacology and Therapy, 61,* 476–487.

Montejo-Gonzalez, A. L., Liorca, G., Izquierdo, J. A., Ledesma, A., Bousono, M., Calcedo, A., Carrasco, J. L., Ciudad, J., Daniel, J., de la Gandara, J., Derecho, J., Franco, M., Gomz, M. J., Macias, J. A., Martin, T., Perez, V., Sanchez, J. M., Sanchez, S., & Vicens, E. (1997). SSRI-induced sexual dysfunction: Fluoxetine, paroxetine, setraline, and fluvoxamine in a prospective, multicenter, and descriptive clinical study of 344 patients. *Journal of Sex and Marital Therapy, 23,* 176–194.

Morgan, C. D., Wiederman, M. W., & Pryor, T. L. (1995). Sexual functioning and attitudes of eating disordered women: A follow-up study. *Journal of Sex and Marital Therapy, 21,* 67–77.

Morgan, J. F., Lacey, J. H., & Reid, F. (1999). Anorexia nervosa: Changes in sexuality during weight restoration. *Psychosomatic Medicine, 61,* 541–545.

Narrow, W. E., Regier, D. A., Rae, D. S., Manderscheid, R. W., & Locke, B. Z. (1993). Use of services by persons with Mental and addictive disorders: Findings from the National Institute of Mental Health Epidemiological Catchment Area Program. *Archives of General Psychiatry, 50,* 95–107.

Nofzinger, E. A., Thase, M. E., Reynolds, C. F., Frank, E., Jennings, J. R., Garamoni, G. L., Fasiczka, A. L., & Kupfer, D. J. (1993). Sexual function in depressed men: Assessment by self-report, behavioral, and nocturnal penile tumescence measures before and after treatment and after treatment with CBT. *Archives of General Psychiatry, 50,* 24–30.

O'Mahen, H. A., Beach, S. R. H., & Banawan, S. F. (2001). Depression in marriage. In J. H. Harvey & A. Wenzel (Eds.), *Close romantic relationships: Maintenance and enhancement* (pp. 299–319). Mahwah, NJ: Lawrence Erlbaum Associates.

O'Leary, K. D., & Beach, S. R. H. (1990). Marital therapy: A viable treatment for depression and marital discord. *American Journal of Psychiatry, 147,* 183–186.

Palace, E. M., & Gorzalka, B. B. (1990). The enhancing effects of anxiety on arousal in sexually dysfunctional and functional women. *Journal of Abnormal Psychology, 99,* 403–411.

Pinderhughes, C. A., Grace, E. B., & Reyna, L. J. (1972). Psychiatric disorders and sexual functioning. *American Journal of Psychiatry, 125,* 1276–1283.

Powell, D. J. (1984). Treatment of impotence in male alcoholics. *Alcoholism Treatment Quarterly, 1,* 65–83.

Pyle, R. L., Mitchell, J. E., & Eckert, E. D. (1981). Bulimia: A report of 34 cases. *Journal of Clinical Psychiatry, 42,* 60–64.

Raboch, J., & Faltus, F. (1991). Sexuality of women with anorexia nervosa. *Acta Psychiatrica Scandinavica, 84,* 9–11.

Roberts, L. J., & Leonard, K. E. (1997). Gender differences and similarities in the alcohol and marriage relationship. In R. W. Wilsnack & S. C. Wilsnack (Eds.), *Gender and alcohol: Individual and social perspectives* (pp. 289–311). New Brunswick, NJ: Rutgers Center of Alcohol Studies.

Rothschild, A. J. (1995). Selective serotonin reuptake inhibitor-induced sexual dysfunction: Efficacy of a drug holiday. *American Journal of Psychiatry, 152,* 1514–1516.

Rothschild, B. S., Fagan, P. J., Woodall, C., & Andersen, A. E. (1991). Sexual functioning of female eating-disordered patients. *International Journal of Eating Disorders, 10,* 389–394.

Schiavi, R. C. (1990). Chronic alcoholism and male sexual dysfunction. *Journal of Sex and Marital Therapy, 16,* 23–33.

Schover, L. R., Friedman, J., Weiler, S., Heiman, J., & LoPiccolo, J. (1980). *A multi-axial descriptive system for the sexual dysfunctions: Categories and manual.* Stony Brook, NY: State University of New York at Stony Brook.

Schreiner-Engel, P., & Schiavi, R. (1986). Lifetime psychopathology in individuals with low sexual desire. *The Journal of Nervous and Mental Disease, 174,* 646–651.

Schuckit, M. A. (1972). Sexual disturbance in the woman alcoholic. *Medical Aspects of Human Sexuality, 6,* 44–65.

Segraves, R. T. (1992). Overview of sexual dysfunction complicating the treatment of depression. *Journal of Clinical Psychiatry Monograph, 10,* 4–10.

Segraves, R. T. (1998). Antidepressant-induced sexual dysfunction. *Journal of Clinical Psychiatry, 59,* 48–54.

Shen, W. W., & Hsu, J. H. (1995). Female sexual side effects associated with selective serotonin reuptake inhibitors: A descriptive clinical study of 33 patients. *International Journal of Psychiatry in Medicine, 25,* 239–248.

Simpson, W. S., & Ramberg, J. A. (1992). Sexual dysfunction in married female inpatients with anorexia and bulimia nervosa. *Journal of Sex and Marital Therapy, 18,* 44–54.

Staebler, C. R., Pollard, C. A., & Merkel, W. T. (1993). Sexual history and quality of current relationships in patients with Obsessive Compulsive Disorder: A comparison with two other psychiatric samples. *Journal of Sex & Marital Therapy, 19,* 147–153.

Tan, E. T. H., Johnson, R. H., Lambie, D. G., Vijaysenan, M. E., & Whiteside, E. A. (1984). Erectile impotence in chronic alcoholics. *Alcoholism: Clinical and Experimental Research, 8,* 297–301.

Twentyman, C. T., & McFall, R. M. (1975). Behavioral training of social skills in shy males. *Journal of Consulting and Clinical Psychology, 43,* 384–395.

Van Minnen, A., & Kampman, M. (2000). The interaction between anxiety and sexual dysfunction: A controlled study of sexual functioning in women with anxiety disorders. *Sexual Relationship Therapy, 15,* 47–57.

Walker, P. W., Cole, J. O., Gardner, E. A., Hughes, A. R., Johnston, J. A., Batey, S. R., & Lineberry, C. G. (1993). Improvement in fluoxetine-associated sexual dysfunction in patients switched to buproprion. *Journal of Clinical Psychiatry, 54,* 459–465.

Ware, M. R., Emmanuel, N. P., Johnson, M. R., Brawman-Mintzer, O., Knapp, R., Crawford-Harrison, M., & Lydiard, R. B. (1996). Self-reported sexual dysfunctions in anxiety disorder patients. *Psychopharmacology Bulletin, 32,* 530.

Wenzel, A. (2002). Characteristics of close relationships in individuals with social phobia: A preliminary comparison with nonanxious individuals. In J. H. Harvey & A. Wenzel (Eds.), *A clinician's guide to maintaining and enhancing close relationships* (pp. 199–213). Mahwah, NJ: Lawrence Erlbaum Associates.

Wenzel, A., Graff-Dolezal, J, Macho, M., & Brendle, J. R. (2003). *Relationship communication skills and social skills in socially anxious and nonanxious individuals in the context of romantic relationships.* Manuscript submitted for publication.

Whalley, L. J. (1978). Sexual adjustment of male alcoholics. *Acta Psychiatrica Scandinavica, 58,* 281–298.

Wilsnack, R. W., Wilsnack, S. C., & Klassen, A. D. (1984). Women's drinking and drinking problems: Patterns from a 1981 survey. *American Journal of Public Health, 74,* 1231–1238.

Wilsnack, S. C., Plaud, J. J., Wilsnack, R. W., & Klassen, A. D. (1997). Sexuality. gender, and alcohol use. In R. W. Wilsnack & S. C. Wilsnack (Eds.), *Gender and alcohol: Individual and social perspectives* (pp. 250–288). New Brunswick, NJ: Rutgers Center of Alcohol Studies.

Wilson, G. T., & Lawson, D. M. (1976a). Effects of alcohol on sexual arousal in women. *Journal of Abnormal Psychology, 85,* 489–497.

Wilson, G., & Lawson, D. (1976b). Expectancies, alcohol, and sexual arousal in male social drinkers. *Journal of Abnormal Psychology, 85,* 587–594.

Wilson, G. T., Lawson, D. M., & Abrams, D. B. (1978). Effects of alcohol on sexual arousal in male alcoholics. *Journal of Abnormal Psychology, 87,* 609–616.

Zerbe, K. J. (1996). The emerging sexual self of the patient with an eating disorder: Implications for treatment. In M. F. Schwartz & L. Cohn (Eds.) *Sexual abuse and eating disorders* (pp. 134–154). Philadelphia: Brunner/Mazel.

Zieba, A., Dudek, D., & Jawor, M. (1997). Marital functioning in patients with major depression. *Sexual and Marital Therapy, 12,* 313–320.

Zillman, D. (1983). Transfer of excitation in emotional behavior. In J. T. Cacioppo & R. E. Petty (Eds.), *Social psychophysiology: A sourcebook.* New York: Guilford.

23

Integrating Sex Therapy and Couple Therapy

Barry W. McCarthy
L. Elizabeth Bodnar
Mitsouko Handal
American University

This chapter provides an overview of current approaches to understanding and changing sexual dysfunction. There are a wide range of approaches, but we will primarily focus on the cognitive–behavioral couple sex therapy model (McCarthy, 2002a). Although there is a plethora of theoretical and clinical writing about the role of sexual satisfaction and sexual dysfunction in relationships, there is a dearth of empirical data. This chapter will explore hypotheses about the origin of sexual problems, types of sexual dysfunction, clinical assessment protocols, intervention strategies and techniques, sequelae of sexual problems in couple relationships, and the importance of a relapse prevention program so that sexuality can play an enhancing role in the couple relationship.

Traditionally, couple therapy has underplayed the importance of sexuality and sexual dysfunction. The term "couple therapy" is more inclusive than the customary term "marital therapy," which originally focused on legally married heterosexual couples. Couple therapy can include gay and lesbian couples, cohabiting couples, and unmarried couples. Couple therapy can involve a range of issues including family conflicts, communication difficulties, parenting difficulties, financial conflicts, division of household tasks, as well as intimacy and sexuality. Dysfunctional sex has traditionally been viewed as a symptom of a more basic relationship issue with the assumption that if the relational problem was understood and changed, the sexual problems would automatically be cured. If the sexual dysfunction did not resolve on its own, then clinicians assumed that sensate focus exercises would resolve the sexual problem.

The original sex therapy model by Masters and Johnson (1970) emphasized sexuality as a couple issue, the use of sensate focus exercises (taking turns giving and receiving touch from nongenital touch to genital touch), with a focus on resolving arousal and orgasm dysfunctions. Kaplan (1974) introduced a sex therapy model focused on desire, arousal, and orgasm, which serves as the basis for the DSM-IV-TR diagnostic criteria for sexual dysfunction. Kaplan's system was based on a psychiatric/psychodynamic model, which tried to integrate psychological, relational, and behavioral approaches. Weeks and Giambriatta (2002) advocated an integration of medical and couple approaches to understanding and changing sexual dysfunction. The major text in the sex therapy field, Leiblum and Rosen (2000), focuses on recently developed medical interventions while emphasizing the crucial role of psychological and systematic approaches. However, the medicalization of sexual dysfunction conceptualization and treatment has become a major controversy in the sex therapy field.

Tiefer (2001) uses a feminist analysis to challenge the medical model, especially for female sexuality. The introduction of Viagra (Goldstein et al., 1998) has had a dramatic impact on changing both the professional's and lay public's understanding of sexual dysfunction, particularly erectile dysfunction. Viagra is the first user-friendly medical intervention for sexual dysfunction, but it has been misused and overused as a stand-alone intervention, without addressing psychological or systemic factors (McCarthy, 1999a). If medical interventions are to be employed successfully in the treatment of male and female sexual dysfunction, a comprehensive assessment and intervention model is necessary (Bancroft, Graham, & McCord, 2001). McCarthy (2002a) argued that medical interventions have to be integrated into the couple style of sexual intimacy, pleasure, and eroticism. Medical interventions can be a valuable adjunctive resource, but at essence sexuality is an interpersonal process. Approaching the treatment of sexual dysfunction in a comprehensive manner necessitates the integration of couple therapy, sex therapy, and in some cases medical interventions.

COUPLE THERAPY AND SEX THERAPY

Couple therapy and sex therapy are different, yet complementary, modalities. The field of marital therapy has changed both in numbers and status over the past 20 years, whereas sex therapy has stagnated and decreased. Among the reasons for this are a proliferation of marital therapy training programs, licensure for marriage therapists, insurance reimbursement for marriage therapy, cultural shift to encourage marriage, and increased professional prestige. In contrast, there are few recognized sex therapy training programs, no licensure or insurance reimbursement for sex therapy, the medicalization of sexual problems and treatment, and the negative public and professional perceptions generated by the recovered memories of child sexual abuse and value-oriented sexual controversies. Although sex therapy is not widely utilized in marriage counseling, sexuality plays an important role in marriage. A clinical adage is that when sexuality functions well in a relationship it serves a small but integral role, contributing 15 to 20% to marital vitality and satisfaction. The major functions of sexuality are as a shared pleasure, a means to deepen and reinforce intimacy, and a tension reducer to deal with the stresses of life and marriage (McCarthy, 2003). However, when sexuality is dysfunctional, conflictual, or nonexistent, it plays an inordinately powerful role, draining the relationship of vitality and threatening its viability. Paradoxically, bad sex plays a more influential negative role than the enhancing role of good sex. The traditional couple approach of treating sexual issues as symptoms of individual or couple pathology, or even worse treating them with benign neglect, is not theoretically acceptable or empirically supported.

Sex therapy is best understood as a subspecialty. To be a successful sex therapist the clinician needs skills in the assessment and treatment of individuals, couples, and sexual function and dysfunction. Ideally, sex therapy would be well-integrated with couple therapy (McCarthy, 2001a). However, many couple therapists would rather not work directly with sexual issues, preferring instead to make a referral to a sex therapist.

Reasons for this include lack of knowledge, lack of interest, feelings of incompetence, as well as the possibility of raising personal and value issues for the clinician.

CORE SKILLS OF SEX THERAPY

To better understand how sex therapy could be integrated into couple therapy, it is useful to explore the intricacies of sex therapy. Sex therapy is described by traditional couple therapists as limited, behavioral, and even mechanistic (Scharff & Bagnini, 2002). In reality, high quality sex therapy is a challenging subspecialty. It requires the therapist to be comfortable and skilled at assessment, individual therapy, couple therapy, and sexual function and dysfunction. The clinician has to be aware of each individual, the couple relationship, and the role of marital sexuality.

The four core skills in cognitive–behavioral sex therapy are (a) taking a comprehensive sexual history in a nonjudgmental manner; (b) designing and implementing a sex therapy program specific to each dysfunction and couple; (c) assigning, processing, and individualizing sexual exercises; and (d) designing and implementing a relapse prevention program.

The change model in cognitive–behavioral sex therapy is based on personal responsibility for sexuality and working as an intimate team. The client who blames the spouse or blames himself/herself subverts the change process. The client who is narcissistic, dependent, or isolated can defeat the goals of therapy. The optimal approach is to be honest with oneself and each other about conditions for good sex, as well as anxieties and inhibitions that block sexual response. Sharing these anxieties and inhibitions and challenging them via the personal responsibility/intimate team model is crucial to the therapeutic process. Ideally, the partners' view each other as sexual friends, with each partner's arousal facilitating the other's (the "give to get" pleasuring guideline).

The Sexual History

Couple therapists are used to taking extensive family histories and examining patterns of individual, couple, and family communication and norms. An example is extended family genograms, which carefully examine patterns of marriage, divorce, children, and close relationships (McGoldrick, Gerson, & Shellenberger, 1999). However, couple therapists often ignore sexual history questions or give only cursory attention to sexual problems and dysfunctions (Gurman, 2002).

The comprehensive individual sexual history is the main assessment technique in sex therapy. Sexual histories are conducted individually so the person is able to give an uncensored report of his or her sexual strengths and weaknesses, both before the marriage and during the marriage. The recommendation in traditional couple therapy is not to see the individual alone because the clinician will be triangulated by secrets (Glass & Wright, 1997). Although dealing with secrets is a complex clinical issue, a greater danger is not knowing about crucial factors that may impact the change process. For example, if the clinician did not know that the man had a paraphilia arousal pattern or that the woman was involved in a comparison affair, the therapy would be subverted because central factors were not addressed.

To truly understand the role of sexuality, it is essential to understand sexuality in context and its meaning for the individual and couple. If the history is conducted with the partner present, the clinician is less likely to obtain a true picture because at least 75% of individuals admit to sensitive or secret material (McCarthy, 2002b). Shameful secrets about the past have a powerful effect on the individual's sexual self-esteem and can subvert couple sexuality (Lipman, MacMillan, & Boyle, 2001). Disclosing, processing, and dealing with past sexual experiences frees the person and relationship. The couple feedback session (to be discussed in detail in the next section) is a therapeutic setting to deal with the harmful effects of past sexual secrets.

The typical partner response to learning of a spouse's past sexual secret is to be empathic and supportive. The partner is usually more accepting and less judgmental about the problem than the person with the secret. Past sexual secrets include guilt over masturbation, an unwanted pregnancy or sexually transmitted disease, abusive or traumatic childhood or adolescent experiences, sexual experimentation with someone of the same sex, or being sexually humiliated or rejected. The person's sense of these as "shameful secrets" that were not processed at the time or subsequently, give these experiences excessive power over adult sexuality. The spouse, especially the wife, is willing and eager to be a "partner in healing" (Maltz, 2001), which includes accepting and processing the past negative sexual experiences, feeling deserving of sexuality as a positive part of the person's life and relationship, and developing a comfortable and functional sexual relationship.

Present sensitive or secret material is more emotionally complex, more difficult to share, and is potentially more destabilizing for the person and the relationship. Present secrets might involve a male variant arousal pattern (pornography, cybersex, fetishism), an extramarital affair, a preference for masturbation to couple sex, homosexual relationships, or a lack of physical attraction or love. Obviously, these secrets can impair sex therapy and in some cases result in a sham therapy contract, that is, not addressing the core psychological and sexual issues which cause or maintain the problem behaviors. This is a strong argument for conducting individual history-taking. These sensitive, yet central, factors would not be disclosed during a couple session.

The clinician needs to respectfully and carefully explore the function and meaning of the present secret. For example, the man who is involved in a compartmentalized or high opportunity/low involvement affair that he is willing to give up is in a very different position than the man who is thinking of leaving the marriage for a comparison affair that has evolved in seriousness and intensity over the past 6 months. Another example is the woman who feels alienated from the spouse and has no motivation to engage in intimate sex, instead preferring to use fellatio to "service" him. This contrasts with the woman who enjoys sex and does fellatio as a way to avoid painful intercourse. These examples illustrate the crucial importance of not only identifying sexual secrets and sensitive material, but also understanding their causes, dimensions, and meanings in order for the clinician to formulate an intervention plan.

The Couple Feedback Session

The couple feedback session is the core intervention in cognitive–behavioral sex therapy. The clinician takes the material he or she has gathered from the initial couple session, each individual history, and phone consultations with previous therapists (individual or couple), as well as physicians they have consulted. The feedback session has a threefold focus: (a) to establish a new understanding of the sexual problem with positive expectations of change as the couple functions as an intimate team; (b) to propose a therapeutic plan that focuses on specific individual, couple, and sexual changes, as well as potential traps to monitor; and (c) to assign a sexual homework exercise and encourage the couple to process and clarify material from the feedback session. Ideally, the couple leaves the feedback session with a clear understanding of the individual responsibility–intimate team model of change, motivation to address the sexual problem, and willingness to process the feedback and clarify (with each other and the therapist) personal and couple vulnerabilities. Couples who have shared previously sensitive and secret material feel increased awareness and freedom to discuss past and present sexual experiences. They are energized and optimistic, but realize this will be a complex change process, not a miracle cure.

The Sex Therapy Process and Exercises

A core strategy in cognitive–behavioral sex therapy is to use semistructured sexual exercises to facilitate changing attitudes, behaviors, and emotions. Some sex therapy models do not use sexual exercises (Schnarch, 1991). Instead they focus on the function and meaning of sexuality indirectly through the individuation process. However, the majority of sex therapy models utilize sexual exercises as a critical element in the change process. A vital skill for the therapist is to describe, process, design, refine, and individualize sexual exercises. The exercises provide a continuous assessment to identify anxieties, inhibitions, and lack of skills. They help the couple build sexual comfort and skill. This assessment–feedback–intervention process, which depends on both the exercises and doing a fine grain assessment of attitudes, behaviors, and feelings during the therapy session, is central to sex therapy. The clinician does not simply ask whether the behavior occurred and whether it was successful, but explores comfort, skill, attitudes, and feelings.

Although some couples proceed easily through the sex therapy process in 10 to 15 sessions, many do not (Heiman & Meston, 1999). Couples who benefit the most from sex therapy are dealing with an acute problem, have a solid relationship, are motivated and not ambivalent, have a female dysfunction, the problem is anxiety and/or lack of sexual skill, and the dysfunction is primary (lifelong). Conversely, the more difficult couples to treat are conflictual, have a secondary dysfunction (acquired), a male dysfunction (especially inhibited desire), a chronic and severe dysfunction, a pattern of avoiding touch, and a strict pass–fail approach to intercourse (McCarthy & McCarthy, 2003). Individual personality factors and the couple relationship can strongly impact therapy process and outcome.

Taking responsibility for sexuality means that it is not the partner's responsibility to "give" the other person desire, arousal, or orgasm. Each person is responsible for her or his desire, arousal, and orgasm. The role of the partner is to be active and involved, especially to be responsive to requests and nonverbal guidance, as well as open to the partner's pleasure and eroticism. Schnarch (1991) has emphasized the role of individuation and self-validation (as opposed to validation from the partner) as a crucial factor in healthy sexuality. Lobitz and Lobitz (1996) extended this concept to a view of intimate sexuality, which integrates personal responsibility and genuine intimacy as the model for satisfying sexuality.

Sexuality is primarily an interpersonal process. The couple functions as an intimate team in terms of developing a couple sexual style where they share pleasure, eroticism, arousal, intercourse, and orgasm. The intimate team process challenges the blame–counterblame interaction that poisons sexual desire. The conceptualization of sex as a team sport and approaching the sexual problem as the common enemy is highly motivating. In the intimate team process, one partner does not turn against or blame the other partner, the couple wins or loses as a team.

The exercises are more comprehensive than the Masters and Johnson (1970) sensate focus exercises. Each set of exercises is divided into four component exercises that gradually build sexual comfort and skill. The format begins with the giver–pleasurer sequence, which transitions to intimate, interactive pleasuring. Exercises include nongenital pleasuring, genital pleasuring, self-exploration/masturbation, nondemand pleasuring, bridges to sexual desire, eroticism and arousal, intercourse as a pleasuring experience, special turn-ons, sexuality and aging, enhancing your sexual relationship, you as a sexual person, becoming a sexual couple, increasing female arousal, female orgasm, learning ejaculatory control, arousal and erections, and overcoming ejaculatory inhibition (McCarthy & McCarthy, 2002).

Sexual exercises are a primary medium in the change process. Reading and discussing concepts and exercises changes attitudes, doing exercises changes behavioral comfort and skill, and processing exercises and integrating new experiences into sexual self-esteem changes emotional response.

There is not "one right way to be sexual." Each couple must develop their unique sexual style. Exercises can serve a diagnostic function (to identify anxieties and inhibitions), a change function (to build comfort and skill), and an integrative function (to develop a functional, enduring sexual relationship). Does the couple enjoy a variety of ways or places to be sexual or do they prefer predictable Saturday night sex under the covers? Do they enjoy sexual connection three times a week or once every 2 weeks? Do they value a variety of pleasuring scenarios and techniques or do they prefer one or two pleasuring techniques? Do they enjoy erotic sex to orgasm or is orgasm limited to intercourse? Do they prefer taking turns or mutual stimulation? Do they enjoy multiple stimulation or single stimulation? Is touching and sexuality used to heal from an argument or do they need to feel emotionally close before having sex? Is sexuality an important, integrated part of their relationship or a small, compartmentalized part? Is sex primarily for pleasure, intimacy, tension-reduction, or conception? Is sex a way to feel more intimate and connected or a way to maintain emotional distance? Talking about, doing, processing, and individualizing exercises help the couple accept and utilize the multiple meanings and dimensions of sexuality.

Some couples say they never feel as open and intimate as during pleasuring or afterplay, other couples say they never feel as lonely or alienated as they do in bed. For example, the man who has a fetish arousal pattern has to shut out the woman in order to be aroused. Another example is the wife who has loving feelings toward the husband, but experiences sexual aversion.

Desire and satisfaction are the core components of sexuality. Although arousal and orgasm are important and integral, they are not as important as desire and satisfaction.

When sexuality functions well, it is a positive and central component of the marriage. However, when sexuality is dysfunctional, nonexistent, affected by an extramarital affair, or stressed by a fertility problem (unwanted pregnancy or infertility), sexuality plays an inordinately powerful role, draining the marriage of intimacy and good feelings. Sexual problems are a major cause of divorce in the first 3 years of marriage.

SEX THERAPY STRATEGIES AND TECHNIQUES FOR EACH DYSFUNCTION

Cognitive–behavioral sex therapy is a semistructured, focused intervention that includes a four-session assessment phase. Therapy sessions usually involve 10 to 25 couple meetings and a relapse prevention program of 1 to 2 sessions with follow-up meetings every 6 months for 2 years (McCarthy, 2002a). In addition to this general sex therapy model, there are specific strategies and exercises for each dysfunction. The most frequent female sexual dysfunctions (by frequency) are: (a) secondary inhibited sexual desire; (b) primary inhibited sexual desire; (c) secondary nonorgasmic response during partner sex; (d) dyspareunia (painful intercourse); (e) primary nonorgasmic response during partner sex; (f) female arousal dysfunction; (g) primary nonorgasmic response; and (h) vaginismus. The most common male sexual dysfunctions (by frequency) are: (a) premature ejaculation—usually primary; (b) erectile dysfunction—almost always secondary; (c) inhibited sexual desire—almost always secondary; and (d) ejaculatory inhibition—primary in younger males, secondary in older males.

Primary (lifelong) dysfunction means there has always been a problem (i.e., primary nonorgasmic response means the woman has never been orgasmic by any means). Secondary (acquired) dysfunction means the person has been functional, but now experiences a problem (i.e., secondary erectile dysfunction means the man has a history of erections and successful intercourse but now has an erectile dysfunction). Many couples experience more than one dysfunction. For example, the man with erectile dysfunction develops secondary inhibited sexual desire. In dealing with complex cases, the clinician utilizes the assessment/intervention process to sequence interventions in an optimal manner. If a woman's secondary arousal dysfunction and secondary inhibited desire occur in the context of primary dyspareunia, interventions and exercises focus on building comfort and reducing pain. Once pain-free sex is reestablished, it is likely that arousal and desire will easily return. On the other hand, when inhibited sexual desire is a primary problem, it becomes the focus of interventions and exercises, instead of arousal or orgasm.

Strategies and Techniques for Female Sexual Dysfunction

Although treatments for each female dysfunction comprise distinct interventions and exercises, there are three guiding strategies. First, traditional female sexuality has emphasized intimacy and pleasuring, but deemphasized eroticism. Sex therapy interventions integrate intimacy, pleasuring, and eroticism. Perhaps the reason that women find sex therapy easier and more inviting than men is that the permission-giving and integrative strategies are compatible with the meaning and content of female sexuality (Heiman, 2000). In other words, erotic scenarios and techniques are not a stand-alone performance goal, but fit into the intimate pleasuring context. Basson (2001) elaborates on the concept of responsive female desire and the desire/arousal feedback loop. Rather than female sexual desire being a spontaneous physical urge, it is often a result of perceiving an opportunity to be sexual and awareness of the potential benefits to her and the relationship (emotional closeness, building acceptance, physical closeness). She allows herself to be less passive and move from sexual compliance to seeking sexual contact and erotic situations. Women's sexual desire is often responsive rather than a spontaneous sexual event.

The second guiding strategy is the woman is encouraged to develop her "sexual voice" so that she can request the type and sequence of touching and erotic scenarios that promote her sexual receptivity and responsivity. So much of female sexuality is in reaction to the male's sexual initiatives. "Foreplay" is to get the woman ready for intercourse, it is the man who decides when to transition to intercourse. Female sexuality is more variable and complex than male sexuality. This does not mean better or worse, just different. Women appreciate the concept of "nondemanding pleasuring" rather than "foreplay." Pleasuring recognizes the importance of touching for its own sake, inside and outside the bedroom, nongenital and genital touch, and that not all touching leads to intercourse. The woman's "sexual voice" means that her sensual and erotic feelings and needs are as important as the man's. She can proceed at her pace rather than the sexual scenario being driven by the man's erection and needs. Especially important is the recognition that sensuality is the underpinning of sexual response. Pleasuring involves mutual give and take, not his "working on her." She can decide when and how to transition from pleasuring to eroticism and when to transition to intercourse. Also, she decides whether she wants to give or receive multiple stimulation during intercourse.

The third guiding strategy involves female orgasm and sexual satisfaction. The male model is sex equals intercourse and that orgasm is the only measure of satisfaction. Female orgasmic response is more flexible and variable than male orgasmic response. In a given sexual experience she might be singly orgasmic, nonorgasmic, or multiorgasmic and could occur during the pleasuring phase, during intercourse, or through afterplay. Only one in four women follow the male pattern of having one orgasm during intercourse through thrusting alone. Many women find it easier to be orgasmic with erotic stimulation—manual, oral, or rubbing. Some women are never orgasmic during intercourse but are regularly orgasmic with erotic stimulation. This is a normal sexual response pattern, not a sexual dysfunction. The majority of women who are orgasmic during intercourse use multiple stimulation. Multiple stimulation during intercourse can include clitoral stimulation by either partner, breast or anal stimulation, fantasizing or talking, kissing, stimulating the partner, feeling aroused by his arousal, and varying intercourse positions—particularly those that allow more body contact and her control of movement.

Inhibited desire is by far the major female sexual dysfunction (Basson, 2000). There are two strategies for dealing with inhibited sexual desire. First, the clinician establishes the woman's emotional and sexual conditions for sexual receptivity and responsivity. Second, the clinician encourages the woman to build bridges to sexual desire. Traditionally, female sexual desire was contingent on romantic love, sense of attractiveness, a strong and positive relationship, and the man being a great lover. The sex therapy concept is that the woman has a noncontingent right to sexual pleasure and desire. Women who are overweight, in a stressful relationship, are nonorgasmic, or have a history of sexual trauma have a right to sexual pleasure and desire. Conditions for good sex include freedom from fear of pregnancy or sexually transmitted diseases and intimate coercion or threats of negative consequences, as well as feelings of personal validation, acceptance, and freedom to be both intimate and erotic.

Bridges to sexual desire (McCarthy, 1995) include ways of thinking about and anticipating a sexual encounter, which are personally inviting. The essence of sexual desire is a positive anticipation and a feeling she deserves sexual pleasure. Exercises to enhance desire include increasing comfort, enhancing attraction, building trust, and creating erotic scenarios and techniques. The theme of the exercises is to develop ways of thinking about, experiencing, and feeling sexual that are good for the woman and the relationship. Cognitively and behaviorally, the woman becomes aware of the situations and scenarios in which she desires to initiate a sexual encounter and/or in which she would be responsive to a sexual initiation. Rather than "one right way" to feel desire, the therapist helps the woman and couple develop her, his, and their bridges to sexual desire. The challenge to the clinician is to individualize a treatment plan that utilizes information from individual dynamics, the relationship, their situation and values, and feedback and processing exercises. Individual psychological factors that most inhibit sexual desire are anger, depression, and a history of unprocessed or poorly processed negative sexual incidents. Relational factors include an emotionally distant relationship, ambivalence about the spouse or marriage, a history of intimate coercion, and disappointment or resentment toward the spouse or marriage. Situational and value factors include lack of time or privacy for sexuality, distractions from children or extended family, devaluation of marital sex, or settling for a marginal marriage with mediocre sex.

Breaking the cycle of inhibited sexual desire might require androgen supplements and creating erotic scenarios for one woman, while for another couple it requires emotionally focused therapy to reduce anger and increase bonding. Typically both emotional and sexual factors need to be addressed. Again, the theme is that high-quality sex therapy is comprehensive.

Arousal problems require different strategies and exercises. A central element in understanding female arousal is the congruence of subjective and objective arousal. Feeling "turned on" proceeds or occurs simultaneously with objective arousal (i.e., lubrication and readiness for intercourse). Arousal exercises give the woman permission to experiment with pleasuring and erotic scenarios, so that she can learn to identify and appreciate her arousal pattern(s). Does she prefer single or multiple stimulation, does she like taking turns or is mutual stimulation more arousing, is it better to start with oral–genital or breast stimulation, does she want to control the transition and sequencing of eroticism or leave it to him, how do they decide to transition to intercourse?

Some women feel subjectively aroused, but are poor lubricators. Other women are easily lubricated, even though they do not feel subjective arousal. The most common intervention for lubrication problems is to use an external lubricant, often K-Y Jelly. Women tend to be comfortable with K-Y Jelly due to familiarization during gynecological exams. Other women prefer a sensuous lotion, providing it is water-based and hypoallergenic, such as abalone oil, aloe vera, or a fruit flavored lotion. The newest medical intervention is Viagra, which is not yet approved for female arousal dysfunction. Other techniques to increase arousal include external turn-ons such as mirrors, dancing, music, X- or R-rated videos, or being sexual outdoors. The most common psychological turn-ons are using fantasies, anticipating an erotic date, feeling emotionally close and intimate, and being turned on by a partner's arousal.

Pain issues, whether dyspareunia or vaginismus, can be particularly complex. These problems require working cooperatively with a gynecologist to ensure appropriate diagnosis, as well as to prevent a major physical factor, such as an untreated sexually transmitted disease, tear in the vaginal wall, or infected Bartholin gland, from being overlooked.

Binik, Pukall, Reissing, & Khalife (2001) argued that dyspareunia and vaginismus are best understood as pain disorders. Therefore, the treatment team should consist of a physician with a subspecialty in sexual pain, a physical therapist with a subspecialty in pelvic musculature, and a sex therapist. This is in sharp contrast to the traditional marriage therapist who interprets the sexual pain as a symptom of relationship distress or a power struggle. This again highlights the importance of a comprehensive assessment and a treatment plan that uses interventions and exercises as a feedback loop.

The traditional focus in sex therapy for female dysfunction was orgasm. The assumption was that if the woman could learn to be orgasmic, then everything else would fall into place. The mistaken belief was that orgasm equals satisfaction. Although orgasm is a natural, integral component of female sexuality, it is not the ultimate measure of function or satisfaction. Three excellent self-help books on female sexuality (Foley, Kope, & Sugrue, 2002; Ellison, 2001; Leiblum & Sachs, 2002) emphasized that orgasm needs to be understood in the context of the woman's desire, arousal, and satisfaction pattern. There is not one right orgasm style. The woman develops an arousal–orgasm pattern(s) with which she is comfortable and that fits her preferences and needs. New performance myths about orgasm include that multiple orgasms are better, "G" spot orgasm is the ultimate, the importance of having an orgasm during intercourse, the importance of orgasm each time sex occurs, or whatever the new performance fad might be. The healthy way to understand female orgasm is as a normal extension of the pleasure–eroticism–arousal process. Orgasm is experienced as a satisfying aspect of the woman's and couple's sexual style. Exercises for arousal and orgasm help the woman and couple explore and confront inhibitions that interfere with the erotic flow. Important assessment/interventions include the woman using self-stimulation to orgasm with the partner holding her, focusing on multiple stimulation with erotic nonintercourse sex, letting go and using "orgasm triggers," transitioning to intercourse at high levels of arousal, using multiple stimulation during intercourse, and using vibrator stimulation before, during, or after intercourse. This is not to force orgasm, but to reduce the barriers to orgasm and increase eroticism and arousal. She allows the sensations and feelings to flow to orgasm. Orgasm is an important part of the pleasure–eroticism–arousal process, not a pass–fail test separate from it.

Strategies for Male Sexual Dysfunction

Many of the same strategies and techniques in sex therapy for female dysfunction are relevant for male sexual dysfunction. Others are gender specific or dysfunction specific. The major strategy is for the man to adopt a variable, flexible, pleasure-oriented approach to sexuality. The sexual socialization of young men emphasizes sex as easy, predictable, performance oriented, and, most critically, autonomous. In other words, the male needs nothing from the partner in order to experience desire, arousal, and orgasm. This double standard learning about sexual performance might serve the young man well, but is detrimental for the middle years and older men, especially for marital sexuality (McCarthy, 2001b). With the advent of Viagra in 1998, men hoped that they could return to easy, predictable, autonomous erections. Viagra is the first user-friendly medical intervention to improve erectile functioning and can be a valuable resource if integrated into the couple lovemaking style. However, Viagra is not a magic cure. Much of the dropout rate from Viagra treatment is due to unrealistic expectations of returning the man to the sexual performance of his 20s. In contrast, sex therapy seeks to reinforce an intimate, interactive, pleasure-oriented approach to sexuality, with Viagra as an additional resource (Althof, 2000).

Although each male sexual dysfunction has specific interventions and exercises, the core strategy is for the man to alter attitudes toward pleasure and mutuality, which enables him to see the woman as an intimate ally in developing a comfortable, functional couple sexual style.

For premature ejaculation, Metz and McCarthy (2003) emphasize the importance of a comprehensive approach to assessing the nine types of premature ejaculation (four biological/physical, four psychological/relational, and a mixed type involving other sexual dysfunctions) and utilizing a treatment package to address all the issues so that the man will not relapse. Previously, premature ejaculation was viewed as a simple problem with a standard intervention of increasing awareness of the point of ejaculatory inevitability and then employing the stop–start technique (which involves stopping penile stimulation and waiting 15 to 60 seconds until the urge to ejaculate has dissipated), first with manual stimulation and then during intercourse. Although this is all that is needed for a significant number of men, it is not enough for two large groups. The first group is comprised of males who have a biological predisposition to premature ejaculation (their neurological system is "hard-wired" for rapid sexual response). These males often benefit from medication (either antidepressant or anti-anxiety) as an adjunct in learning ejaculatory control. The second, and even larger group, experience relationship distress, which is either a cause of or a reaction to premature ejaculation. These men need to focus on rebuilding intimacy and psychosexual skills.

The couple working together as an intimate team is particularly important in successfully implementing an ejaculatory control program. The woman plays an active, involved role in ejaculatory stimulation. Like other aspects of sexuality, this change process has a fundamental interpersonal component, which focuses the couple on increasing empathy, closeness, and cooperation.

The man needs to establish positive, realistic goals for ejaculatory control, not a super-macho, perfectionistic criterion of 30 minutes of intercourse. In fact, lovemaking sessions vary between 15 to 45 minutes of which 2 to 7 minutes involves intercourse. Few couples engage in intercourse that lasts for more than 10 minutes in spite of what males claim or the media hypes. A simple, but crucial, component of ejaculatory control is to have a regular rhythm of sexual contact, whether that is twice a week or once every 10 days. The most difficult situation for ejaculatory control is the man-on-top position, using short, rapid thrusts. The couple learns to become more comfortable with alternate intercourse positions, slower thrusting, and circular thrusting.

As noted in the female sexual dysfunction section, the goal is not to have the woman perform like the man, that is, a single orgasm during intercourse. The goal of ejaculatory control is to allow intercourse to be pleasurable for the couple with the man experiencing some choice over when he ejaculates. The sexual experience need not end because the man has ejaculated. Afterplay is an integral, though often ignored, component of sexuality. Afterplay can enhance sexual satisfaction, especially for women. Afterplay can include additional erotic stimulation for the woman to orgasm, but more typically involves emotional and physical sharing. Afterplay can be a genuine coming together that adds to the context and meaning of intimate sexuality.

Treatment of erectile dysfunction was revolutionized by the introduction of Viagra in 1998 (Goldstein et al., 1998). However, contrary to the advertising hype, the efficacy of Viagra alone is mixed at best and the dropout rate is high. For Viagra to be effective for couples, it needs to be integrated into their lovemaking style. The unrealistic expectation that Viagra alone will completely solve a couple's sexual problem, sets the male up for further sexual dysfunction. Viagra can be a valuable resource in that it works to increase vasocongestion and reduce performance fears, but it needs to be integrated into the couple's intimacy, pleasuring, and eroticism style (Rosen, 2000).

Males with erectile dysfunction often develop inhibited sexual desire because sex has become a source of embarrassment and failure rather than pleasure and satisfaction. Too much of the man's self-esteem is placed on his penis with the unrealistic performance demand that it respond no matter what is affecting him physically, psychologically, or relationally. To regain erectile comfort and confidence, both the man and his partner need to change behaviors, attitudes, and emotional responses.

Returning to 100% predictable, nonself-conscious sex after a sensitizing experience of erectile difficulty is not a realistic expectation. The quality of the sexual relationship can improve if the man views the partner as his intimate ally, is open to pleasurable and erotic stimulation, and is open to her help in initiating the transition from eroticism to intercourse and her guidance of intromission. Men try to rush intromission by initiating intercourse as soon as they become erect because they fear losing the erection. The sex therapy strategy is just the opposite. Arousal and erection is a natural result of relaxing, being open to giving and receiving pleasurable touch, being receptive to her erotic stimulation, enjoying the erotic flow, letting her guide intromission at high levels of arousal, and enjoying multiple stimulation during intercourse.

A very important guideline is to accept that whether once every ten times, once a month, or once a year, the man will not have an erection sufficient for intercourse (McCarthy, 2001c). Rather than being a source of panic or a feeling of failure, the couple can be open to two backup scenarios: transitioning into a nondemand sensual experience or using erotic, nonintercourse sex to reach high arousal and orgasm for one or both partners. The man and couple accept that sexuality is about giving and receiving pleasure, not about a pass–fail intercourse performance.

Inhibited sexual desire for males is almost always a secondary dysfunction. The exception may be a secret sexual agenda, such as a paraphiliac arousal pattern, a homosexual orientation, or a preference for masturbation with pornography over couple sex. There are two major causes of secondary inhibited sexual desire. The first is embarrassment and frustration because of sexual dysfunction, particularly erectile dysfunction. The second is a result of aging (Butler & Lewis, 2002). Whether the couple stops being sexual at 40, 50, 60, 70, or 80, it is almost always the man's decision, conveyed nonverbally and indirectly. If sex cannot be easy and predictable, he may be unwilling to adopt a flexible, variable couple style of sex. For these men, feeling in control and the traditional double standard is more important than sharing pleasure with the spouse.

Revitalizing sexual desire is an excellent example of the personal responsibility– intimate team model of change. The man has to confront and change his self-defeating assumptions and feelings about sexuality. The woman can support these changes, but cannot make them for him. Together they build a new sexual style where both partners value intimacy, pleasuring, and eroticism. As with exercises for female sexual dysfunction, they build his, her, and couple bridges to sexual desire. Of special importance is his valuing pleasurable and erotic expression, not just intercourse. He learns to accept that there is normal variation in sexual experiences, including that 5 to 15% of sexual encounters will be mediocre, unsatisfying, or dysfunctional (Frank, Anderson, & Rubinstein, 1978). By accepting these concepts, he reinforces the cycle of positive anticipation, pleasure-oriented sexuality, and a regular rhythm of sexual contact. He can avoid the cycle of anticipatory anxiety, tense or failed sex, and avoidance.

Ejaculatory inhibition is the least discussed male sexual dysfunction. Yet, it very much interferes with both his and their sexual satisfaction. In the most severe form, it means total inability to ejaculate. More commonly, the man can ejaculate with masturbation and often with partner manual or oral stimulation, but not during intercourse. Usually, these couples do not seek therapy until they want to become pregnant (Perelman, 2001).

A common pattern with aging (affecting as many as 15% of men over 50 years of age) is intermittent ejaculatory inhibition (Butler & Lewis, 2002). This means the man wants to reach orgasm, but is unable to do so. The primary strategy is to encourage the couple to work together to enhance erotic stimulation, specifically multiple stimulation during intercourse. The man often is reluctant to ask the partner for additional stimulation, feeling that a "real man" can do it alone. With the aging of the man and the aging of the relationship, there is an increased need for intimate, interactive stimulation. The "give to get" pleasuring guideline becomes even more important with aging. The man who values intimacy, pleasuring, and eroticism, as well as embraces a variable, flexible couple sexual style, ensures healthy sexual functioning with aging.

Young males with a primary problem of ejaculatory inhibition need a different set of strategies and exercises. Sometimes, the cause is an idiosyncratic masturbation pattern, which is not transferable to couple sex. Examples include the man who reaches orgasm rubbing a flaccid penis against bed sheets or using two-finger light touch to ejaculate. A more common pattern is the man who becomes quickly erect at low levels of subjective arousal and immediately initiates intercourse. A helpful strategy in this case is to request pleasurable and erotic stimulation and not transition to intercourse until his subjective arousal is a "7" on a 10-point scale (0 is neutral, 5 is initial erection, 10 is orgasm). Exercises focus on multiple erotic stimulation and identifying "orgasm triggers" to utilize during couple sex. The emphasis is on intimate, interactive sexuality, where the woman's involvement and eroticism are central.

DEVELOPING A COUPLE SEXUAL STYLE

An excellent example of integrating marital and sex therapy is the process of helping the couple agree on a sexual style that is congruent with their marital style. Gottman (1999) identified four couple styles that can promote marital satisfaction and stability. By order of frequency, these styles are: complementary, conflict minimizing, best friend, and emotionally expressive. One size does not fit all. Each person has preferences for autonomy versus coupleness, degree of emotional intimacy, the way to deal with differences and conflicts, and the role and meaning of sexuality (McCarthy, 1999b).

Complementary Couple

The complementary couple style allows each person to maintain autonomy while enjoying a solid, intimate couple bond. Each person's worth and contributions are acknowledged and validated. Each person has his or her domains of influence. When there are conflicts, it is usually decided on the basis of whose domain it is. The couple establishes a level of emotional intimacy that allows a genuine connection. They are open to problem solving and have confidence in their ability to deal with conflict without building resentment. They maintain individuality while simultaneously sharing interests and fun. The traps for this marital style include taking each other for granted, growing apart, resenting tasks and not feeling validated, and believing that the relationship is no longer equitable.

Sexuality is an important component of the complementary couple style. The essence of the marital bond is a respectful, trusting friendship with sexuality energizing the bond and creating special feelings. This style of couple may take sexuality for granted, thus allowing sexuality to atrophy. They may feel estranged or resentful and consequently withhold sex. Finally, they may get overly involved in other activities resulting in a lack of time and/or energy for sex.

Conflict Minimizing Couple

The conflict minimizing couple style is the most traditional and most stable. It is also the least emotionally intimate style. Traditional gender roles are reinforced with the man and woman having clear domains with little overlap or need for negotiation. The couple emphasizes children, extended family, and religion. Differences are expected, but conflicts are routinely avoided, especially emotional conflicts. This is the calmest and most predictable style of marriage.

The trap of this couple style is that they do not address problems in the acute stage, so that by the time the couple addresses the problem, it has become chronic or severe. They lack conflict resolution skills. Gender roles are rigid, and they do not expect to be positively influenced by each other. Resentment toward the partner and relationship can build and then explode in unexpected and disturbing ways. The couple can grow so far apart that there is a lack of genuine connection, resulting in a devitalized marriage.

The role of sexuality is often underplayed among conflict minimizing couples. Sexuality is viewed as the man's domain and the woman is not expected to value erotic sex. Sex is primarily for procreation. These couples find it easier to accept sexual dysfunction and avoid sexual conflict. However, if there is an unexpected problem, such as infertility or an unwanted pregnancy, the couple may feel overwhelmed and destabilized. Furthermore, the lack of a vital sexual relationship can cause the couple to feel cheated and disappointed in the spouse and marriage. These couples may miss out on an intimate relationship and the pleasures of sexuality.

Best Friend Couple

Best friend relationships are our cultural ideal. The partner is viewed as the "soul mate." This style can be the most emotionally intimate. When these marriages work well they are close, vital, and highly satisfying. However, this style of marriage is not a good fit for the majority of couples. This style lacks a balance between autonomy and intimacy. Expectations of the spouse and marriage tend to be too high, resulting in disappointment, primarily for the female. Rather than falling into the best friend style, both people need to carefully assess whether this style meets each individual's needs and the marriage's needs. If both people want a best friend marriage, they need to devote the time and energy to maintain a vital marital bond.

Sexually, the best friend couple style can be very satisfying because of the sense of equity and valuation of intimacy. The best friend couple tends to put creativity and eroticism into their sexual life. However, there is a danger that high levels of closeness will overwhelm the eroticism and desire components of the relationship. If there is a dysfunction or problem, the spouse is less likely to confront the issue because of sympathy for the partner. Although it is healthy to be empathetic, supportive, and sexually encouraging, it is problematic to be sympathetic, tentative, and avoidant (this can lead to self-consciousness and is felt as anti-erotic). If there is an extramarital affair, feelings of hurt and betrayal are more likely to dominate and paralyze the best friend couple. It then becomes more difficult to rebuild trust and sexual desire. These couples rarely recover from an affair without marital therapy (Spring, 1996).

Emotionally Expressive Couple

The emotionally expressive couple is the most vibrant, but also the most unstable. In terms of intimacy, the relationship is like an accordion; sometimes very close and other times angry and distant. When both people prefer the emotionally expressive style and maintain psychological boundaries during conflict, the couple can have a satisfying relationship. These couples experience a strong connection and realize their emotions, both positive and negative, are genuine.

The trap of this couple style is the frequency of fighting and the volatile nature of the relationship. It is one thing to say to a partner, "I am angry with you" or even "You disgust me" but is very destructive to say, "I wish I had never married; you are a bad person" or "If I get the chance, I am going to destroy your relationship with our children." The latter statements violate a psychological boundary and breaks the bond of respect and trust. "Hitting below the belt" in a heated argument to intentionally cause harm takes conflict to an extreme and destructive level.

Sexually, emotionally expressive couples have a vital, erotic connection, which can help bridge the gap of alienation in bad times. In good times, sexuality makes the relationship especially exciting. The sense of being alive and open to spontaneity and eroticism is a special characteristic of this marital style. On the other extreme, the impulsiveness and explosiveness can result in an extramarital affair or an attack–counterattack confrontation after a disappointing sexual encounter. These relationships can have too much drama and not enough trust and intimacy. Paradoxically, although emotionally expressive couples have more explosive emotional and sexual incidents, they are also more resilient in recovering from these incidents. For example, emotionally expressive couples are more likely to recover from an affair than conflict minimizing couples and best friend couples because they focus on present emotions and emotional rebuilding.

There is not one right marital style for all couples. The couple can choose a primary marital style and then modify and individualize it based on their values, preferences, and situation. Some couples begin with one marital style and then transition to a different one. The most common pattern is to change from a best friend couple to a complementary couple. It is important to tailor sex therapy to the individual couple style, thus effectively integrating couple and sex therapy.

PRIMARY PREVENTION AND SECONDARY INTERVENTION OF SEXUAL PROBLEMS

A core understanding of the relationship between couple therapy and sexual dysfunction (and the need for sex therapy) is to accept the positive, yet limited, role of sexuality in a relationship. People should not begin a relationship or marriage because of sex nor should they stay in the relationship or marriage for sex. That imbues sex with a power it does not deserve. The essence of the relational bond is respect and trust. At base, a relationship is a respectful, trusting commitment to share your lives. Emotional and sexual intimacy cannot compensate for lack of respect or trust.

Sexual dysfunction, extramarital affairs, and conflict over fertility are major stresses on the marital bond, draining the relationship of vitality and possibly leading to dissolution. Ideally, the way to deal with sexual problems is prevention. The romantic love and passionate sex at the beginning of the relationship are special and give the couple the motivation to take the emotional risk to become seriously involved. However, romantic love and passionate sex by their very nature are fragile and ephemeral, seldom lasting even a year. Even for those couples where it continues until marriage, it seldom lasts a year into the marriage.

A crucial task in primary prevention of sexual dysfunction is to transition to a couple sexual style that is centered on mature intimacy and sharing pleasure rather than romantic love and passionate sex (McCarthy, 2003). A long-term relationship has a solid base when both partners value intimacy, pleasuring, and eroticism, as well as think of each other as intimate sexual friends. Couples who value sex as shared pleasure, a means to reinforce and deepen intimacy, and a tension reducer are able to enjoy the multiple functions of sex in their lives and relationship. Perhaps most important for couple vitality is recognition of the multitude of pathways to connection—affection, sensuality, playfulness, eroticism, and intercourse. Touching is valued for itself, not as "foreplay" for intercourse. A hug can be as valuable as an orgasm.

Another strategy for primary prevention of sexual dysfunction is to maintain positive and realistic expectations: 40 to 50% of sexual experiences involve equal desire, arousal, and orgasm; 20 to 25% are very good for one spouse and good for the other; 20 to 25% are good for one partner and the other partner "goes along for the ride"; and 5 to 15% are mediocre, dissatisfying, or dysfunctional (Frank, Anderson, & Rubinstein, 1978). Couples who are able to laugh about or at least shrug off mediocre or negative sexual experiences have a resilient sexual relationship. Encouraging these kinds of relational sexuality serves a primary prevention function among couples.

When there is a sexual problem, conflict, or dysfunction, secondary intervention becomes crucial. Secondary intervention means dealing with the sexual issue in the acute phase before it becomes chronic or severe. If a sexual problem has not spontaneously remitted within 6 months, it is unlikely to do so. The first 6 months is the best time to seek therapy or at least a professional assessment of the problem. Optimally the assessment is conducted with the couple rather than just with the individual experiencing the dysfunction or conflict. Couples usually seek the counsel of a marital therapist before consulting a sex therapist. Thus, marital therapists are likely to see couples in the acute stage of sexual dysfunction.

Dealing with a problem in the acute stage is easier than dealing with a chronic problem because couples tend to show higher levels of motivation. There is hope for change and layers of resentment and blame have not been firmly built. The couple is more open to new understandings and willing to try new change strategies. Expectations and energy are very different when it is the first therapy experience rather than the fourth attempt to resolve the problem. It is easier to address a problem after 6 months than 6 years, when avoidance has grown strong. Permission-giving, providing information, and suggesting strategies and techniques are often enough to help motivated couples resolve the sexual dysfunction. If this does not help, the couple can be referred to sex therapy.

Emotional intimacy and sexual intimacy are different, yet complementary dimensions of a healthy relationship. Emotional intimacy involves making self-disclosures, sharing emotions, feeling close, and feeling your partner is your ally. Sexual intimacy is a way to share pleasure, deepen connection, and reduce tension. Sexuality generates special energy and feelings. It allows the sharing of one's self and one's body in a very special way. Conflictual, dysfunctional, or nonexistent sexuality drains the relationship of intimacy and ultimately may threaten the viability of the relationship. This is especially true in the first 3 years of marriage. Contrary to the popular myth that affairs occur out of boredom after years of marriage, the most common time to have an affair is in the first 3 years of marriage. In addition, an unplanned or unwanted pregnancy can destabilize a marriage. Also contrary to popular belief, the most common time to experience sexual dysfunction, particularly inhibited sexual desire, is in the first 3 years of marriage. The rate of nonsexual marriages (being sexual less than 10 times in a year) is higher among couples married for 2 years than 20 years (McCarthy & McCarthy, 2003). Interestingly, increased emotional intimacy resulting from marital therapy has been found to decrease sexual desire and functioning. The marital intervention inadvertently reduces desire and eroticism (Markman, Floyd, Stanley, & Storaaslir, 1983). Both marriage and sex therapists must be careful to reinforce sexuality as a positive and integrated element in the marital bond. Marital therapists need to ensure they do not perpetuate sexual myths or double standard approaches to sexuality by not addressing the issues.

THE PLISSIT MODEL: COUPLE THERAPY AND SEX THERAPY

A helpful conceptual model for the link between couple and sex therapy is the four-stage PLISSIT model of intervention (Annon, 1974). The PLISSIT model provides a format for couple therapists to choose what types and levels of sexual interventions to integrate into their therapeutic repertoire. The four stages of PLISSIT are (1) permission-giving; (2) limited information; (3) specific suggestions; and (4) intensive sex therapy.

The majority of couples seeking therapy do not want to focus on sexuality issues. The majority of couple therapists are not interested in being trained for or conducting sex therapy. The PLISSIT model advocates that all mental health and counseling personnel be comfortable providing clients with positive sexuality information in a respectful, empathic, and permission-giving manner. Some couple therapists will choose to give specific suggestions for dealing with an acute sexual dysfunction or conflict. Some couples therapists will do sex therapy, whereas others will refer the couple to a sex therapist.

The permission-giving component of the PLISSIT model encourages the couple to view sexuality as a positive, integral part of their relationship and to value the many functions and dimensions of sexuality within the relationship. The person's right to express himself or herself free from fear of an unwanted pregnancy, sexually transmitted disease, or sexual coercion is affirmed. Couple sexuality is viewed as mutual, voluntary, pleasure-oriented, and energizing.

The limited information component includes normalizing occasional mediocre or failed sexual experiences; the importance of sexual comfort; utilizing a variety of pleasuring and erotic scenarios; integrating intimacy, pleasuring, and eroticism; being aware of normal sexual changes with aging; and being aware of physical health behaviors and medications that may interfere with sexual functioning. The clinician helps the couple confront common sexual myths such as all loving couples have a sexually functional relationship, so sexual problems are always a sign of a relationship problem; intimacy is the essence of sexuality; you can never have too much intimacy; angry, alienated couples cannot have a good sexual relationship; incest only occurs in severely pathological or alcoholic families; child sexual abuse and sexual trauma always need to be dealt with before issues of couple sexuality; extramarital affairs are always a sign of marital dissatisfaction; extramarital affairs only occur after many years of marriage; infertility affects self-esteem, not the sexual relationship; marital sex is less frequent and satisfying than sex among nonmarried couples; marriage therapy is the intervention of choice, sex therapy is a last resort; medical treatments for sexual dysfunction make sex therapy irrelevant; traditional couple communication techniques are necessary for improved sexual functioning; conflict, stress, and anger are counter indications for utilizing sexual exercises; unless intimacy is strong, use of pleasuring exercises and erotic scenarios have minimal impact; the more specific the sexual problem, the less effective is sex therapy; desire problems are better treated by individual or marital therapy; sexual compulsion/addiction problems are best treated by an inpatient 12-step program; married couples have similar levels of sexual development; and people choose partners of similar pathology.

These myths point out how important it is for marital therapists to be aware of the multicausal, multidimensional aspects of sexual function and dysfunction. Especially important is to realize that although there is a positive relationship between marital satisfaction and sexual satisfaction for most couples (Sprecher, 1998), it is a myth that increasing sexual frequency will resolve marital problems or that just because sex is functional, that sexuality is satisfying.

A growing number of couple therapists are comfortable utilizing specific suggestions and sexual interventions. Examples may include use of nondemand pleasuring exercises with a temporary prohibition on intercourse (the most common suggestion), using stop–start technique to improve ejaculatory control, using self-exploration/masturbation exercises (with or without a vibrator) for primary nonorgasmic dysfunction, using wax and wane exercises to regain erectile comfort and confidence, identifying erotic scenarios to build bridges to sexual desire, and assigning self-help books for information and attitude changes. Sexuality is a valued component of a relationship. Sexuality is not treated with benign neglect by the therapist or the couple.

THE ROLE OF THE SEX THERAPIST AS A TRAINER, CONSULTANT, AND SUPERVISOR

An efficacious and efficient role for the sex therapist is that of trainer, consultant, and supervisor (McCarthy, 2001a). Not every clinician can or should practice sex therapy. Yet all couple therapists should be sexual permission-givers and provide accurate sexual information. Workshops and consultations can cover a range of fairly common sexual issues to increase couple therapists' knowledge, comfort, and skill in dealing with sexual issues. Issues could include sexual dysfunction; contraception; infertility; sterilization; affairs; STDs and HIV/AIDS; sexual effects of medical illness or medications; revitalization of a nonsexual relationship; sexuality for single, divorced, or widowed people; marital style and sexual functioning; use of Viagra, hormone replacement, testosterone, and other medical interventions; sex after 60; levels of intimacy and sexual desire; and relapse prevention strategies and techniques. This allows couple therapists to become more comfortable and skilled in utilizing specific sexual suggestions. Furthermore, this can provide the clinician with an assessment–intervention format to decide when a case should be referred for sex therapy.

Another way to increase the clinician's comfort and skill level is the clinical and case-based supervision process, whether individual or group. Supervision can provide couple therapists a place to explore and develop competence in sex therapy. Just as important, the supervision process provides a milieu to explore how sexual issues affect the clinician in terms of comfort and personal values. The couple therapist can become comfortable assigning, monitoring, and individualizing sexual exercises.

Sexuality has a number of symbolic and emotional meanings that need to be explored. However, the couple therapist cannot use this as a rationale to avoid dealing directly with sexual attitudes, behaviors, and feelings. Although understanding personal and relational meanings and context are very important, the clinician is cautioned not to divert from sexuality issues. Therapists must be aware that addressing sexual issues may be perceived as intrusive, voyeuristic, or inappropriate. Boundary and ethical issues need to be carefully considered, but not used as a rationale to avoid or ignore dealing directly with sexual dysfunction or conflict.

Supervision can also address variant or deviant male erotic patterns. The needs of the individual or couple in addressing these problems is paramount and should override a therapist's own political or value beliefs. Assessing and changing variant sexual behavior is a subspecialty therapeutic skill. The clinician must recognize that some clients and/or problems are better to refer than to treat himself or herself.

Not all clinicians should treat all couples or all problems. A good example is the treatment of gay couples. Some clinicians have little interest in gay issues, are uncomfortable with gay couples, or have religious or moral beliefs that are anti-gay. The appropriate intervention would be to make a referral to a gay-friendly therapist.

SEX THERAPY AS A SUBSPECIALTY OF COUPLE THERAPY

Couple therapy and sex therapy are different, but complementary. The sex therapist cannot conduct high quality, comprehensive sex therapy without being comfortable and competent in dealing with general relationship issues.

The issue is not couple therapy versus sex therapy; it is "both–and" not "either–or." The traditional idea that sexual problems will clear up when relationship problems are resolved has little empirical support. This is particularly true for sexual problems that involve lack of knowledge, comfort, or skill, as well as primary sexual dysfunction and chronic sexual dysfunction (especially inhibited desire). In these cases, a specific sexual intervention is required (LoPiccolo & Friedman, 1988).

When the marital therapist drops the sexual focus to explore relationship or individual dynamics, he or she inadvertently reinforces sexual self-consciousness and avoidance. The more avoidance, the higher the anxiety. Avoidance fosters self-consciousness that interferes with erotic flow. Anticipatory anxiety, distraction, performance anxiety, and self-consciousness subvert the sexual response cycle. The sex therapist recognizes and processes a therapeutic impasse, but uses an integrative approach of redesigning and individualizing sexual exercises, continuing to explore the relationship between subjective and objective arousal, as well as understanding individual and relationship issues.

The marital therapy field has grown, whereas the sex therapy field has stagnated and even declined. However, this does not mean the need for competent, caring professional help for sexual problems has lessened. The extraordinary growth in sexuality self-help materials, books, and Internet resources has not translated into a lower rate of sexual problems and dysfunction. In many instances, the information has created new performance myths and set unrealistic, intimidating expectations. There has been a dramatic increase in prescriptions written by physicians (chiefly internists and family practitioners) for Viagra and, to a lesser degree, testosterone (Tiefer, 2000). Although medical interventions can be a valuable resource as part of a comprehensive treatment program, medication alone is seldom a "magic cure" for sexual dysfunction. Human sexuality is primarily an interpersonal process, not a medical phenomenon. Psychological, relational, and sexual skill factors play a crucial role, especially with the aging of the person and the aging of the relationship. The medical intervention has to be coordinated with couple therapy and integrated into the couple intimacy, pleasuring, eroticism styles.

Sex therapy interventions focus on implementing a biopsychosocial model. The therapist helps each individual make specific requests and determine what they are comfortable implementing and what does not fit for them. For example, a common intervention with Viagra is for the woman to initiate the transition to intercourse and guide intromission. However, there are women who are not comfortable with putting the penis inside of them and men who are not comfortable in giving up control. In these cases, the usual suggestion would be countertherapeutic, raising self-consciousness rather than facilitating arousal and intercourse. The clinician is comfortable helping the couple process sexual techniques and feelings. The focus is to increase sexual awareness and comfort, not to make sex self-conscious and clinical.

SUMMARY

Couple therapy and sex therapy are different, but complementary therapeutic modalities. Ideally the same therapist would be comfortable and competent in integrating both approaches in a single therapy contract.

The PLISSIT model provides a four-dimensional format to examine levels of intervention. The majority of couple therapists can become comfortable with the permission-giving and informational aspects of sexual counseling. An increasing number are gaining comfort and confidence with specific sexual suggestions. However, when confronting a complex sexual dysfunction, a chronic and severe sexual problem, or a secret or sensitive sexual conflict, the clinician needs to change to a sexually focused intervention or make a referral to a subspecialist—a sex therapist. The unique skills of the sex therapist include taking a detailed individual sexual history, formulating a feedback and treatment plan, assigning and processing sexual exercises, confronting and changing attitudes, behaviors, and emotions that interfere with sexuality, and designing relapse prevention program.

In the future, there will be much more empirical research to study the complex process of sexual function and dysfunction. Among a variety of couples, including gay and lesbian couples, nonmarried couples, and couples of different ages, socioeconomic status, and cultural background the need for empirical research and outcome data is clear.

In understanding the functions and meanings of sexuality for the individual and couple, the therapist has to be specific and explicit so the couple can honestly explore and change their intimate sexual relationship. The therapist has to understand the context and meaning of sexuality and its role in the relationship. To understand the relationship between couple therapy and sexual problems and dysfunction, it is imperative to accept the positive, yet limited role healthy sexuality has in marriage. It is equally important to understand the large negative impact sexual problems and dysfunction can have. That is why sexual problems and dysfunction have to be confronted directly, whether by the couple therapist who is comfortable with and trained to deal with sexual issues or by a sex therapist. Sex issues and dysfunction cannot be treated with benign neglect or hope of improvement if the relationship improves. Sexuality is an integral component in a relationship and needs to be directly addressed to resolve conflicts and dysfunction. Sexuality should not be allowed to control or subvert the relationship. Healthy sexuality needs to play a 15 to 20% function of energizing and making special the marital bond.

REFERENCES

Althof, S. (2000). Erectile dysfunction. In S. Leiblum & R. Rosen, *Principles and practices of sex therapy* (3rd ed., pp. 242–275). New York: Guilford.

Annon, J. (1974). *The behavioral treatment of sexual problems*, Honolulu, HI: Enabling Systems.

Bancroft, J., Graham, C., & McCord, C. (2001). Conceptualizing women's sexual problems. *Journal of Sex and Marital Therapy, 27,* 95–104.

Basson, R. (2000). The female sexual response. *Journal of Sex and Marital Therapy, 26,* 51–65.

Basson, R. (2001). Using a different model for female sexual response to address women's problematic low sexual desire. *Journal of Sex and Marital Therapy, 27,* 395–404.

Binik, Y., Pukall, C., Reissing, E., & Khalife, S. (2001). The sexual pain disorders. *Journal of Sex and Marital Therapy, 27,* 113–116.

Butler, R., & Lewis, M. (2002). *The new sex and love after sixty.* New York: Ballantine.

Ellison, C. (2001). *Women's sexualities.* Oakland, CA: New Harbinger.

Foley, S., Kope, S., & Sugrue, D. (2002). *Sex matters for women,* New York: Guilford.

Frank, E., Anderson, C., & Rubinstein, R. (1978). Frequency of sexual dysfunction in normal couples. *New England Journal of Medicine, 299,* 111–115.

Glass, S., & Wright, T. (1997). Reconstructing marriages after the trauma of infidelity. In W. Halford & H. Markman (Eds.), *Clinical handbook of marriage and couples interventions* (pp. 471–507). New York: Wiley.

Goldstein, I., Lue, T., Padma-Nathan, H., Rosen, R., Steers, W., & Wicker, P. (1998). Oral Sildenafil in the treatment of erectile dysfunction. *New England Journal of Medicine, 338,* 1397–1404.

Gottman, J. (1999). *The seven principles for making marriage work.* New York: Crown.

Gurman, A. (2002). Brief integrative marital therapy. In A. Gurman & N. Jacobson (Eds.), *Clinical handbook of couple therapy* (3rd ed., pp. 180–220). New York: Guilford.

Heiman, J. (2000). Orgasmic disorders in women. In S. Leiblum & R. Rosen (Eds.), *Principles and practice of sex therapy* (3rd ed., pp. 118–152). New York: Guilford.

Heiman, J., & Meston, C. (1999). Empirically validated treatment for sexual dysfunction. *Annual Review of Sex Research, 6,* 148–197.

Kaplan, H. (1974). *The new sex therapy.* New York: Brunner/Mazel.

Leiblum, S., & Rosen, R. (Eds.). (2000). *Principles and practice of sex therapy* (3rd ed.). New York: Guilford.

Leiblum, S., & Sachs, T. (2002). *Getting the sex you want.* New York: Crown.

Lipman, F., MacMillan, H., & Boyle, M. (2001). Childhood abuse and psychiatric disorders among single and married mothers. *American Journal of Psychiatry, 158,* 73–77.

Lobitz, W., & Lobitz, G. (1996). Resolving the sexual intimacy paradox. *Journal of Sex and Marital Therapy, 22,* 71–84.

LoPiccolo, J., & Friedman, J. (1988). Broad spectrum treatment of low sexual desire. In S. Leiblum & R. Rosen (Eds.), *Sexual desire disorders* (pp. 107–144). New York: Guilford.

Maltz, W. (2001). *The sexual healing journey.* New York: Harper Collins.

Markman, H., Floyd, F., Stanley, S., & Storaaslir, (1983). Prevention of marital distress. *Journal of Consulting and Clinical Psychology, 56,* 210–217.

Masters, W., & Johnson, V. (1970). *Human sexual inadequacy.* Boston: Little, Brown.

McCarthy, B. (1995). Bridges to sexual desire. *Journal of Sex Education and Therapy, 21,* 132–141.

McCarthy, B. (1999a). Integrating Viagra into cognitive–behavioral sex therapy. *Journal of Sex Education and Therapy, 23,* 302–308.

McCarthy, B. (1999b). Marital style and its effects on sexual desire and functioning. *Journal of Family Psychotherapy, 10*(3), 1–12.

McCarthy, B. (2001a). Integrating sex therapy, strategies, and techniques into marital therapy. *Journal of Family Psychotherapy, 12*(3), 45–53.

McCarthy, B. (2001b). Male sexuality after fifty. *Journal of Family Psychotherapy, 12*(1), 29–37.

McCarthy, B. (2001c). Relapse prevention strategies and techniques with erectile dysfunction. *Journal of Sex and Marital Therapy, 24,* 1–8.

McCarthy, B. (2002a). Sexuality, sexual dysfunction, and couple therapy. In A. Gurman & N. Jacobson (Eds.), *Clinical handbook of couple therapy* (3rd ed., pp. 629–652). New York: Guilford.

McCarthy, B. (2002b). Sexual secrets, trauma, and dysfunction. *Journal of Sex and Marital Therapy, 28,* 353–359.

McCarthy, B. (2003). Marital sex as it ought to be. *Journal of Family Psychotherapy, 14*(2), 1–12.

McCarthy, B., & McCarthy, E. (2002). *Sexual awareness: Couple sexuality for the twenty-first century.* New York: Carroll and Graf.

McCarthy, B., & McCarthy, E. (2003). *Rekindling desire: A step by step program to help low-sex and no-sex marriage.* New York: Brunner/Routledge.

McGoldrick, M., Gerson, R., & Shellenberger, S. (1999). *Genograms: Assessment and Intervention.* New York: Norton.

Metz, M., & McCarthy, B. (2003). *Coping with premature ejaculation.* Oakland, CA: New Harbinger.

Perelman, M. (2001). Integrating Sildenafil in sex therapy. *Journal of Sex Education and Therapy, 26,* 13–21.

Rosen, R. (2000). Medical and psychological interventions for erectile dysfunction. In S. Leiblum & R. Rosen (Eds.), *Principles and practice of sex therapy* (3rd ed., pp. 276–304). New York: Guilford.

Scharff, J., & Bagnini, C. (2002). Object relations couple therapy. In A. Gurman & N. Jacobson (Eds.), *Clinical handbook of couple therapy* (3rd ed., pp. 59–85). New York: Guilford.

Schnarch, D. (1991). *Constructing the sexual crucible*. New York: Norton.

Sprecher, S. (1998). Social exchange theories and sexuality. *The Journal of Sex Research, 35*, 32–43.

Spring, J. (1996). *After the affair*. New York: HarperCollins.

Tiefer, L. (2000). Sexology and the pharmaceutical industry. *Journal of Sex Research, 37*, 273–283.

Tiefer, L. (2001). A new view of women and sexual problems. *Journal of Sex Research, 38*, 89–96.

Weeks, G., & Giambriatta, N. (2002). *Hypoactive sexual desire*. New York: Norton.

VI

Commentaries

What We Know About Sexuality in Intimate Relationships

Pepper Schwartz
Department of Sociology University of Washington

This book presents a very broad, detailed, and current review of research on sexuality in intimate relationships. I have been given the happy, but daunting, task to think about a meta-level analysis of what might be thought of as the accumulated weight of these fine papers.

I am sure that every reader could, after reading this book, come to different conclusions—all defensible, and in a way, all correct. So, my own view, presented here, acknowledges its partiality and particularity. Nonetheless, I hope to look at a few themes that emerge to me and pose some observations and, perhaps, some questions that are intriguing enough to inspire some further research by scholars or students drawn to this area of research.

I find five areas of focus that combine to give us a bird's eye view. The first is what I would call *theoretical or large-scale empirical observations* about sexuality or sexual acts as practiced in love and intimate relationships. The second is *an overview of who does what to whom how often—and why*. The third is looking at *sexuality over the lifecycle*. The fourth examines *clinical aspects of sexual function and dysfunction in relationships*, and the fifth focuses on *darker, sadder aspects of sexuality*. Of course, some of these overlap—and I use these distinctions just to make it easier to catalogue all the elements of sexuality discussed in this book. All five ultimately add up to the "sexual landscape" of intimate relationships.

THEORETICAL AND EMPIRICAL OVERVIEWS

One of the major advances in studying sexuality has been to locate the major variables of diagnostic interest. Chief among them, of course, is gender. In DeLamater and Hyde's chapter on the conceptual and theoretical issues in close relationships, gender interacts with dyadic (rather than individualist) models to help us understand what social factors construct sexuality as we know it. This chapter is important, essential really, because it lays out behavioral science's claim as the mother science of sexuality. Few authors, and certainly not these, discount or minimize the biological aspects of sexuality, but here the introduction to sexuality is one that is a product of the social rather than the physical world. Gender has been utilized for the last 30 or 40 years as an important analytic tool for the study of sexuality, but the interactive aspects of gender (subtle and apparent) linked with the interactive issues of intimate relationships has, oddly enough, not been so obviously necessary to many researchers. For example, Kinsey's work—still, perhaps, the most influential work ever done on sexuality in the Western world, treats men and women as individuals and only couples their sexuality when counting sexual frequency or other sexual acts that obviously involve a partner. The idea that sexuality is changed by interaction—and changed by the circumstances of interaction—never fully penetrated his early work or the flurry of research that came afterward.

Of course we know now that much of what was presented as couple research was through the prism of male researcher's visions of sexuality and didn't really frame questions from both a male and female perspective. (For example, the whole idea of mating sexual frequency to sexual satisfaction as the main way of assessing sexual satisfaction could hardly have been the first way women would have independently constructed measurement; yet for years no one questioned it as the major way to assess sexual success.)

The new way of using couple data has more of a symbolic interactionist frame and therefore is a significant change in the way we study sexuality. It is not just male and female perspective that is studied, nor differences in male and female preferences or attitudes, but rather that *any* couple constitutes a separate sexual reality from any individual, and thus gender is just one complication of couplehood rather than a complete explanation of what accounts for differences, problems, or needs. This gets even more interesting when couplehood and gender are differentiated further by whether there is gender redundancy or distinction (i.e., heterosexual couples being distinct by gender) or whether homosexual couples act differently (or similarly) according to whether or not same-sex couples have a different culture and prioritization of needs than heterosexual couples.

As DeLamater and Hyde show, and as demonstrated in other chapters, part of the reconfiguration of sexuality studies is this addition of other major frames and variables. Unfortunately, as I review most of the chapters, the inclusion of variables such as race, ethnicity, or religiosity is still ghettoized—meaning that the authors must cite studies that look at Black, Hispanic, or Asian couples in small, separate studies rather than as part of a comparable sample so that explanations of similarity or differences can be adequately made. The exceptions to this are the large national studies such as the National Health and Social Life Survey study and others—but the deficit in these studies and comparisons is that comparisons are made, but the authors of these quantatative studies rarely make interpretations that help us understand the social forces that create these differences.

The scholars throughout this book tend to call for an integrative model—a model that takes in the classic social science dimensions to be considered, that recognizes that emotions and personality differences need to be taken into account, and that uses biological information both to help frame the question and explain behaviors. Still, this call for integration remains rather plaintive. There are very few studies that actually include teams from very different disciplines.

Probably the most controversial, and more often than not the outlier in the call for integration of theories and behavioral models, is sociobiological theory and interpretation of data through that lens. After a period of feminists (and biologists') fervent criticism, socio-biologists have settled down mostly to having disputes with each other. Although there is a certain nod to the theory by including it in overviews of sexual theories, there are few writers (except in some textbooks) that include reproductive strategies as part of the explanations for sexual conduct—unless that person is primarily a sociobiologist, psychobiologist, or some other derivative science. Although sociobiology scares many behavioral scientists by positing that the most important relations between the sexes have one pithy ultimate explanation (reproductive fitness), it seems to me that, like Freudian theory, there are some fascinating insights to be gained by understanding how the genders must have developed different mating strategies given the different physical roles they play in reproduction, and that to use that insight doesn't mean one has to buy all the data that true believers feel flows from that proposition.

Thus, like some of the other theories and variables mentioned here, this point of view stays marginalized, so that even while recognizing it, text writers and scholars from other disciplines tend to ignore its heuristic propositions and interesting empirical work.

This also appears to be true about Attachment Theory. Attachment Theory seems to be utilized primarily by scholars who use it as their only theoretical frame. In this case, I understand why it may be so ghettoized. Although Attachment Theory can be easily used to study child behavior and is useful for understanding clinical approaches to children's behavioral difficulties, it becomes somewhat more difficult to apply to adult behavior because the proximal clinical approach is unavailable. The theory may be able to explain *why* someone is having problems in adulthood establishing intimacy, trust, or sexual vulnerability and acceptance with a partner, but it remains essentially descriptive of early childhood rather than usefully prescriptive about what to do about present circumstances. Feeny and Noller do an admirable job teaching us how different kinds of attachment predict adult heterosexual and homosexual sexual patterns—but it is not clear how this interacts with more recent socialization, behavioral experience, and change over the life cycle. Perhaps attachment might be more attractive to a sociologist like myself or clinicians if there was a literature on how attachment styles might be changed in later life for a more positive, growth producing, intimate relationship style.

The theories most utilized in the chapters in this book are a combination of symbolic interaction, script and role theories (the production of couple issues and perceptions), and economic theories (e.g., exchange theory) or, in a less fancy way, the approach of studying why people do things based on what they get out of it or perceive they are getting out of it. This vision of sexuality (predicting behavior based on costs and benefits to each partner) is very disturbing to the romantic imagery westerners would like to nurture (students particularly object to it), but in fact, I think most people do use an economic model—even if they don't conceptualize it that way. The chapter by Byers and Wang shows the complexity—and the utility—of understanding how sexuality works in exchange relationships. As they indicate, it is hard to discover how the exchange works because nonsexual accounts (lack of influence with your partner, not doing the dishes, smarting from a criticism) may be in the equation of sexual negotiation. They also show how this frame, unlike many others, understands that the couple is not in some dyadic vacuum but rather exists in a larger world of possible—and impossible—rewards and costs. Men and women, being "economic" creatures, rationally assess their chances and costs in a real world formula and make their choices according to what they think their realistic options are. (They may be terribly wrong of course, but they are making their assessments to the best of their abilities. This explains so much about why observers are sometimes flummoxed trying to understand other people's relationships! "Good deals," etc. vary extraordinarily from person to person.)

As you can see, I am drawn to this model for the study of sexuality in general, and there are a number of sexual frames that I would recommend to the reader. I cannot spend the time I might want to here, but I will mention that an extremely useful comment in the chapter by Byers and Wang refers to the static nature of how exchange theory is usually used and how inappropriate that is for long-term relationships. Sexuality, unless it is a commercial exchange, is not a "spot market" (an economic term for a one time exchange) but rather, keeps an account that builds toward lifetime equity but does not, cannot, expect equal exchange on every moment of sexual conduct. (Not only would this be difficult—it would be boring!) What needs to be done is to see how exchange expectations change from the beginning of relationships throughout the life cycle and how they differ in happy versus unhappy relationships or sexually satisfying relationships versus unsatisfactory sexual relationships. Byers and Wang's comment on extending this perspective to all kinds of relationships is totally on point.

What frame does bring in interactivity (building a relationship and relationship skills through social interaction, exchange, and perhaps a developmental model of couple sexuality)? A new frame that has exciting possibilities for understanding both individual (and gendered) scripts and relationship outcomes is helped by using the perspective of *sociosexuality*. Sociosexuality—a term not used, oddly enough, among sociologists but which incorporates sociological, psychological, and biological perspectives—is, I think, a real step forward in helping us to understand the predictors of individual and life course profiles of sexuality in relationships. Simpson, Wilson, and Winterheld date the earliest invocation of the concept from Kinsey's work—but it has been transformed into a more applied concept since then. The theory takes the larger variable of cultural impact on individual and collective scripts (directives for action and attitudes) and divides the world into people who for various reasons have greater and lesser openness to interacting with, and accumulating, romantic and sexual partners. One of the questions that floats through many of the chapters in this book is that of sexual commitment and loyalty or, translated into practical terms, of monogamy or nonmonogamy. Using the frame of restricted (more monogamous) and unrestricted (potentially less monogamous), the analyst escapes using gender as a surrogate for this tendency and can use an entirely new—and more accurate—frame to understand how people act in sexual relationships. In fact, I like this concept a lot because it shows that sometimes gender is *not* the most useful comparative frame and that by using gender, we often invent a dichotomized vision of sexuality that is more often a continuum. Also, by using gender, we obscure what a more accurate comparative frame may be. This is especially true in areas where our knee-jerk reaction is that there is a male/female division rather than a division on class, or personality, or culture.

GENDER, ACTS, AND ACTORS

Gender is now the main way we look at behaviors and acts—and there are certainly differences in perspectives, preferences, and in experience depending on whether one is a man or a woman. Vohs, Catanese, and Baumeister take on some of the hard and heavily debated questions that, depending on your point of view, speak either to the convergence of gender—or to the unalterable and essential differences. The authors avoid fence sitting (a safer place to be in these debates) and after reviewing a variety of data, indicate that there is no doubt that men have a stronger sex drive than women, a finding that has obvious implications for the timing, meaning, and practice of sex within relationships. Softening this finding, however, is their second, almost universally agreed on research finding that, indeed, women's sexuality is more flexible and culturally malleable than men's. Thus, given cultural permission, freedom, and technological protection from unwanted pregnancies or disease, women's sexuality can be quite different under permissive and protective conditions than under restrictive ones.

If both findings are accepted, it does put into question the importance of the first question—especially as there is likely to be many women and men with similar sex drives even if there are more men at the high end of the scale and more women at the low end. Furthermore, there is danger in men or women comparing themselves to large-scale differences when their individual case may be an outlier. Although the authors defend the need to know who has the greater sex drive by saying that knowing women have a lesser sex drive will help ameliorate problems between men and women over sexual differences in desire, I think they are wrong. For example, they say, among other things, that

> if a woman sees herself as having a weaker sex drive than her male partner but believes that, on average, women's sex drive is equivalent to men's, then she may see herself as inadequate. This perception could then create more problems for the woman, personally and in terms of her relationships. Conversely, if a man believes that his sex drive should be equal to his female partner's but finds that he desires sex more than she does, he may believe that he would be better with a woman with higher sex drive or that he is hypersexual or abnormal. (Vohs, Catanese, & Baumeister, chapter 19, this volume)

This approach is a little scary. First of all, it sets up a definition that tells women that if they have little desire, it is just normal. After all, they are women and naturally would desire less sex than men. This stops the woman from looking at other reasons why she might have less desire; for example, that she is with the wrong partner, or that she is depressed, or that he is a clumsy lover. Indeed, what would be wrong in saying that "on average" women's sexual drive is equivalent to men's? Indeed, new data on young men and women show significant increases in numbers of partners and amount of recreational sex. Also, there are data that in older couples, women's sexual interest outstrips men's—precisely because variety is not as important to most women as it seems to be to most men, and thus, interest is less extinguished over time. In addition, it seems specious to say that men would think they were oversexed because their female partner had less desire; the overall view, scientifically correct or not, is that women do desire less sex—few men would think they were hypersexed to demand sex more often. This is one of those examples where the larger conclusion should not be brought down to the individual level. Differences that exist in large populations almost never predict an individual profile. If low sex drive exists in many females, it should be recognized in those females and not assumed to be true of all females. Care should also be taken to include cultural change. For example, my own work, *American Couples*: Money, Work, and Sex (Blumstein & Schwartz, 1983) is often cited to show low sexual desire in lesbians compared to gay men. True enough. But it is also true that since those data were gathered, young lesbians have had a cultural movement that included a more positive, proactive, and intense approach to sexuality. I believe the lesbian couple profiles look a good deal different today than they did in the late 1970s and early 1980s when the *American Couples* study was researched and written up. Vohs, Catanese, and Baumeister in all fairness, do acknowledge that this plasticity in women does show up in changes in women's sexual patterns over time.

Another main discriminator used in sexuality research besides gender is *sexual orientation*. The past 20 years produced a flowering of scholarship on gay men and lesbians and Peplau, Fingerhut, and Beals give us a good overview of some of the best. What is interesting here are some of the holes in the literature; most interesting to me is how little there is, relatively speaking, on same-sex dating and courtship. Necessarily, articles on gay couples include a historical contextualization: specifically, sexuality before and after AIDs. As often happens when doing comparisons between heterosexual and same-sex couples, one group illuminates the other. In this case, it brings to mind the fact that the same kind of contextualizations (e.g., sexuality studied during the period of time when herpes was discovered, sexuality during high unemployment periods versus good economies, or sexuality during wartime versus peace, etc.) are almost never used to explain why certain effects might be observed in a given study done at a specific time but not replicated under other conditions. Mostly, however, looking at gay and lesbian couples makes the observer more aware than ever of the continuity of gender rather than the differences between same-sex and opposite-sex couples. This is especially true when looking at values and behaviors associated with extradyadic sex. Gay men stand alone here in their commitment to a certain amount of sexual openness, whereas lesbians and heterosexual wives are much more conservative. Husbands are less liberal about extradyadic sex than are gay men but are certainly less likely to be monogamous than are wives.

These differences don't really reveal the extent of difference between the *culture* of nonmonogamy available to gay men and the nonmonogamy that happens in heterosexual relationships. Nonmonogamy is a fascinating aspect of sexual behavior precisely because of its front stage and back stage differences (values versus actual behavior) and because of the differences in how it is perceived in gay versus straight life. Moreover, in overview studies on sexual behavior, non monogamy is always discussed at length because it indicates that there is a second reality to sexuality in intimate relationships: a common need to go outside of them and create sexual thrills or supplementary intimacy (or an escape strategy from the main relationship). In the chapter on sexuality in an exchange perspective, extradyadic sex is analyzed in a cost and benefit framework, obviously different depending on a given individual's sociosexuality. Enumerated costs include fear of exposure or guilt at trespassing previous vows. Other frameworks in exchange theory include thinking of extramarital sex as a compensatory factor for relationships that are perceived as inequitable. Socio-biologists explain differences in male and female behavior by looking at gendered differences in reproductive fitness; sociologists explain it by the norms and enforcement for those norms that reinforce men's greater power and control in intimate relations.

Why extramarital sex happens is, however, not as startling as the fact that it does happen, and sometimes contrary to the person's religiosity or values, or in spite of the destructive outcomes, if it is discovered. This is an arena of study that has to admit the obvious: Humans are more often than not irrationally appetitive animals. Sometimes we want what we want when we want it—values and consequences be damned—or at least, delayed. Extradyadic sex shows us that love is not the same as sexual desire, love is not only not necessary for sexual desire, but sexual desire lives in its own wild state—sometimes acculturated and tamed, but sometimes just plain willful.

This is a good idea to keep in mind when we look at all the chapters on sexual behavior. In the chapter by Willetts and Sprecher, a careful review of data from large random sample data sets (and few large nonrandom ones), we get a good sense of the structured nature of most sexual conduct. Sexuality differs in an orderly way by age, duration of relationship, and by how and when sexuality occurs in relationships. Once one reads these statistics several important political questions come to mind. Chief among them for me is how can we be a nation where adolescents are sexually active (premarital sex occurs for 85% of men and 80% of women and the majority of Americans practice of premarital sex) and yet still preach a doctrine of abstinence and refuse prime time commercial space for contraceptives? The degree of hypocrisy, not to mention ill preparedness, that we expose adolescents to is breathtaking.

Material in other chapters shows a decline of sexual education even as premarital sex and exposure to sexual materials becomes ubiquitous. Some of this is explained by the strength of conservative groups affecting national social policy, but even the promise of money and votes to politicians furthering a conservative sexual agenda doesn't entirely explain the inconsistency between public law and policy and private behavior. There is something in the general public's discomfort with sexuality (no matter what they are doing in their own lives) that allows discontinuity of behavior, values, and law in American society. This is particularly clear on American values of premarital sex for adolescents where a majority disapprove of sex before marriage, but a significant percentage of those who disapprove will have themselves had premarital sex during their adolescent years. Perhaps this discontinuity comes from the fact that we know that many, maybe most, boys and girls have highly compromised, disappointing, and risky first sexual experiences. Still, it is curious that we choose to rectify the situation by believing that we can enforce abstinence (even though that has not happened since the second sexual revolution in the late 60s and 70s) rather than providing more informed and better sexual and emotional conditions for first sexual experiences.

The danger of our position becomes maddeningly clear when we read the chapter, "Safer Sex and Sexually Transmitted Infections From a Relationship Perspective" by Noar, Zimmerman, and Atwood. Epidemics of sexually transmitted diseases have been dangerous to people throughout time but modern mobility, the increasingly younger age of sexual participants, and the greater number of partners have made sexually transmitted disease of far greater concern in the last 30 years than in previous periods of history. Close relationships have shown to be a protection against sexually transmitted disease (particularly against AIDs) because in most, but not all, populations they are associated with more use of condoms, more monogamy, and fewer number of partners. Younger people, however, are less likely to be in committed relationships, and the use of condoms, when used at all, decreases after the first 3 weeks. Accordingly, the data show that the youngest sexually active people are at higher risk for sexually transmitted diseases as well as for the HIV virus. Condom use tends to decrease over time. However, the response to this risk has been, from my perspective, irrationally moralistic. Concentrating on exhortations to morality are no substitute for sexual health information, provision of condoms and other barrier method contraceptives, and teaching social skills so that partners can talk to each other about sex and sexual safety. Given what we know about the ineffectiveness of abstinence based programs (for example, the 2001 Bearman study published in the American Sociological Review, a meta analysis that concluded that such programs could delay first intercourse but did not stop sex before marriage and made it more likely that unprotected intercourse would occur when intercourse eventually took place), it seems hard to understand why there is no realistic public health response to the sexually provocative and active society adolescents inhabit.

Of course, even if better sexual education programs were put in place, there is still the issue of irrational desire—desire that wants satisfaction in the short run, even with almost certain dire health costs in the future. This is why some social scientists and medical researchers believe that the answer lies in inoculation rather than in individual responsibility. Sad as that perspective may be, why should it surprise us? Why should we be so moralistic about it? We, as a nation, simply cannot reconcile ourselves to the fact that we *will* be sexual, we have been sexual throughout history, and only intense supervision, terminal diseases, and stigmatization could possibly bring back sexual sobriety—and only temporarily until medical salvation and new ways to escape the consequences establish themselves.

THE SEXUAL LIFE CYCLE

The easiest, and most awesome, organization of sexual information is to follow its development and change over the life cycle. Of course that life cycle starts with infants. In this book, we have chapters that look at family systems and how they affect the way we look at our bodies and develop our sexual interests, first as children and later as adults. Parents are interested in two main questions. First, how does my conduct affect my child's sexual values and behaviors? For example, what happens if my child walks in on me and my partner having sex? If I am a single mom, how will it affect my child if I have a partner stay overnight? What is the impact of walking around nude in front of a 5 year old? Second, parents want to know what they should say to their children about sex and sexuality.

The review of the literature in the chapter, "Family Foundations of Sexuality," is contradictory about the impact of parental nudity, but in general points to correlations already associated with permissive sexual attitudes, which include a more liberal approach to timing and quantity of sexual behaviors. There was no evidence of pathology. More information, and less contradictory information lies in the area of parental communication about sexuality to children and adolescents. In sum: children want more information, parents do less educating than they think they do, and children are under educated about sexual information and sexual conduct. What is striking is how little almost half of all parents know about their children's sexual lives! Discomfort about the topic creates an ostrich-like head-in-the-sand approach in all too many households. Thus, the overall picture of the child and adolescent part of the sexual life cycle is one of parallel, hidden worlds between most children and their parents—leaving children to pick up rumor and experience unguided by parental wisdom and emotional support.

There is some continuation of a disconnect between families and adolescents as adolescents get older, into young adulthood and learn about first loves, lusts, and other essential elements of courtship and sexual attraction. In chapter 5, Regan brings us back to the strong emotional and physiological arousal in attraction—and its potential for violence as well as love. Quoting Shakespeare, she reminds us of the woeful limits of scientific analysis! The intensity, longing, worship, and despair in love poems reminds us why love and lust have been considered pathological in many (maybe most) societies throughout history. This volatile state of passionate lust is distinguished from love, as discussed in chapter 7 by Hendrick and Hendrick, who discuss the problems of categorizing lust—the issue being whether lust is a connection to love and not just an end in itself. Love, of course is not available to everyone, but the connection and commitment to one person seems an almost general desire of Western civilization and correlates with sexual satisfaction as well.

The ambition to find a one-person commitment lays the structure for most of the passage of the sexual life cycle. The early literature on attraction, detailed by Regan, points out the importance of defining "sex appeal." Sociobiologists would have us believe it can be reduced to a ratio of waist to hips measurements and facial symmetry. However, these are not data based on real life choices, nor do they take into account the reconfiguration of attraction based on cultural status markers (e.g., money or strength). To amend her quote from Shakespeare, my suspicion is that instead of placing "desire not truly in our hearts, but in our eyes," it would be more correct to say that desire is more truly in our social categories and childhood aspirations and learned tastes. Shakespeare may be more eloquent than me—but I can account for a good many odd looking people getting hooked up—and he can't!

Perhaps one place to look at how this all comes together is in the analysis of first sexual involvements in romantic relationships. Metts coins a concept that I have also used and find valuable: the idea that there are *turning points*—in this case, a passion turning point—where love and sexual attraction combine to create a first sexual experience that has interpersonal meaning. Metts comes up with 13 steps or turning points that increase intimacy, sexuality, and commitment. The order of these steps is consequential for relationship development.

We have seen some actual consequences of the way people categorize when each behavior is appropriate and what constitutes a sexual turning point. Metts brings up the issue that a minority of people will label oral sex as "sex" and so its meaning in a relationship may be catalogued by many people as a lower level of intimacy. The ambiguity of the meaning of oral sex was, of course, utilized by President Clinton and sparked a national debate of "what is sex?" If a nation and a sexually experienced man can use the "steps of sexuality" idiosyncratically, how likely is it that two people can correlate the same meaning to an act or a sequence of intimacy in a relationship?

It is challenging to try and interpret sexual behavior through the life cycle when language not only changes by culture, but within culture , depending on a person's location in the life cycle. The life cycle is a perfect example of how courtship, sexual satisfaction, or sexual function are affected by age (and perhaps also affect aging). Oddly enough, many researchers assume that age and phase of relationship will covary and therefore dating and youth are often presumed to be synchronized. In fact, given the divorce rate, delay of age of marriage, etc., dating happens at any point of the life cycle. Sometimes ignoring this fact creates an awkward lack of fit once the frame of older daters is included in the consideration of sexuality and dating. For example, the "love at first sight" phenomenon might be similar for dating couples of all ages—but it might not. Sex on the second date might be *de rigueur* among 20 year olds, but more complex in its implications for 50 year olds.

This is, explicitly recognized by the organization of this book as the sexual life cycle is part of the book's format. Still, it is easy to forget that dating happens in midlife as well as in the teen or young adult years simply because the preponderance of research is on young people. Likewise, the chapter on exploring marital sexuality often envisions the couples in a vacuum rather than sorted by age or sexual experience or number of previous spouses. Still, the chapter is a good corrective to our haphazard analysis of marital sexuality.

The sexual life cycle is profoundly interesting when seen through a sequence of chapters in this book. In chapter 15, by Christopher and Kisler, the authors draw our attention to how simplistically marital sexuality is usually treated in the literature. As the authors mention, sexual "success" in marriage is most easily measured by coital frequency, and often, that is the whole approach to the matter. Intuitively we know that sexual frequency is a meager and often misleading measure; nonetheless, it pops up in almost every article on sexual satisfaction. In the same way, extramarital sexuality is often taken to be the result of sexual dissatisfaction—another misleading correlation because we know that extramarital sexuality can be the result of a number of motivations or even of happenstance.

Many of the examinations of marital sexuality have tried to overcome this rather sterile conceptualization by looking at sexual dysfunction in the couple, and Christopher and Kisler, in chapter 12, cover that literature as well. Still, we know that there must be something in between sexual frequency and nonmarital or dysfunctional sex that describes couple's ordinary experience of marital sexuality! Surely the nuances of intimacy, of exploration, of fantasy, or attempts at transformation deserve a place in our understanding of couples in bed (or on the dining room table, for that matter). Perhaps what we need more of are in-depth, daily sexual biographies, with qualitative interviews about the ebb and flow of sexual intimacy, degrees of satisfaction (boredom or excited anticipation and growth) and turning points or stasis—but not much of this exists outside of novels.

Still, we do take a stab at understanding the hidden life of couples by looking at specific frames in the life cycle. Christopher and Kisler in chapter 15 and Haugen, Schmutzer, and Wenzel in chapter 17 look at a known pressure points for couples' sexual lives—the 9 months of pregnancy (also for some with fertility problems, the period before a desired pregnancy spent trying to get pregnant), the postpartum period of 1 or more years, and indeed, all the years of childrearing that continue throughout the youth of a couple's life. The record is pretty clear here: All of this takes its toll on the couple's commitment and satisfaction. It occurred to me as I read this familiar and depressing review of the facts that a productive study might be one that compared couples whose sexual lives did not suffer during these periods (or who had relatively little negative impact) with those who had the more ordinary sparse and attenuated sex life that usually occurs with pregnancy, postpartum, and childrearing. Both sets of authors set up a number of possible hypotheses for why these conditions exist—but I long for the nitty-gritty details of what is happening intrapsychically and interpersonally. I would also like to have a competition between variables rather than a long list of what might explain the downward slope of most couples' sex lives in this period. Is it the lack of spontaneity? Or is the lack of spontaneity because of anger over inequitable conditions, lower discretionary cash, etc.? In other words, how much of what is happening is due to the impact of children, to secondary consequences of having children, or to previous values about children, sexuality, marriage, or all three of those? In addition, Christopher and Kisler, Haugen, Schmutzer, and Wenzel explore some interesting hypotheses about how the world of work affects couple's sexuality, and I have no doubt that future research will show that how couples feel about work and how they cope with it, affects their postchildren sexual life immensely.

What is important to remember is a point Haugen et al. make right up front: *That after child birth, sexual patterns are changed.* Couples, in general, do not go back to the pattern established before pregnancy. What has changed is the couple's view of each other and the way sexuality proceeds from this moment forward. How much, getting practical here, could be ameliorated if there was peer parenting, better accommodation of the work place to parenthood, and more postpartum education on sexuality and happiness in the relationship? After reading Haugen et al. I kept musing over how little practical sexual counseling we give new parents and how little continuing counseling couples get about how important it is to keep the physical connection that they once so prized as a central part of their relationship.

This takes us to at least one central issue about female sexuality: why is it that so many women have less desire after having children? Is there a physiological change for some women that has nothing to do with psychological or sociological issues? If so, what are its descriptors and what can be done to help women who are flummoxed and worried about their own lack of erotic energy? Certainly I have interviewed women who have lost their ability to be easily aroused and do not want to give up that ability.

On the other hand, one also sees women who are totally immersed in motherhood and see their husbands/partners as an annoying interruption of baby love. A number of other examples come to mind. Although the authors quote Hyde et al. as showing that the majority of women do reclaim their sexual desire, the fact is a very large number of women have a much less intense sexual appetite once children are on the scene. Interesting clues are presented, for example, in the work that shows some women experience a decline in the ease and intensity of orgasm, suggesting either emotional or physiological changes. I would think that the former might be more implicated only because most women get back to prepregnancy orgasmic levels, but that is only a guess and there may be some pregnancy or birth sequella (for example, different consequences of Cesarean surgery or other kinds of surgery where nerves are cut) that are purely physiological in origin.

This work is important and, I think, not well enough represented in popular parent and women's magazines read by pregnant women and new mothers and fathers. The decrease in desire, satisfaction, and orgasm are ordinary, not extraordinary, events. But surely, how these changes affect a couple must depend on what the couple thinks these changes mean and how much they attribute to change in the relationship versus biological causes.

Many of these decreases happen in middle-age and older couples of course—but most people seem to accept aging as the explanation without looking further. This is unfortunate because older men and women are so ready to buy the idea that aging inevitably causes attenuated sex lives that this belief turns into a "self fulfilling prophesy." That is, by believing something will happen, one makes sure it does! As Burgess mentions in chapter 18, this belief in the decline of sexual frequency and sexual pleasure starting in middle age can have dire consequences for a couple. Because people stay active and live fuller lives longer, the loss of a familiar sexual life is not only needless, it is also a spur to divorce for unsuspecting partners who believe they can just put sex in a dead file. Now that better living through chemistry has become part of the culture, it is clear that older partners who are not ready to become chaste after 50 will create new pressures and expectations for their sexual relationships. Although some study has been done on men who use Viagra and other new drugs created to enhance erectile function, it is clear we don't know much about how the potential resurrection of potency and frequency is affecting older (and some younger) couples. Certainly the issue of female desire will get additional scrutiny in middle age. Menopause or relationship issues coterminous with menopause has a correlation with less sexual interest in a number of women. With the advent of a number of pharmaceutical companies investing in drugs that will increase sexual desire in women, it remains to be seen if women will embrace these drugs in the same astounding fashion that men all over the globe have. Will older women without live-in partners use these drugs and will they increase interest in dating or re-pairing in older women? The sociology of sexuality in older men and women is being reinvented as I write, and it bears observation and study by researchers (who, of course, have a vested interest in the outcomes).

Finally, these same life cycle variables are chronicled in the chapter on lesbian and homosexual couples. Unlike the stereotypes of the past, I think it is generally well accepted that, like other men and women, gay men and lesbians generally aim to be partnered at some time in their lives. Their ambition is to have a lifetime partner even if the achievement of that goal is harder for them because they have no legal standing in most states as a couple and there is the likelihood of a lack of support for the couple's welfare in their families of origin. Still, couplehood is the norm after a period of coming out and self definition that has its analogues, but is not a complete match in the history of heterosexuals whose definition of their sexuality has an easier route.

Studies of same-sex couples are generally more sophisticated than studies of heterosexuals because it is obvious that the social context has to be taken into account. For example, the sexual history of each couple is dependent on a variety of social factors (living in repressive Virginia versus accepting Vermont, for example) and in order to understand some couple dynamics, it is clear that the clinician or researcher would have to understand the impact of social factors that would ordinarily affect any couple's adjustment but are more likely to be an issue in gay versus heterosexual couples. (An example of an ordinary issue that might be more potent for same-sex couples would be not only the acceptance of families of origin and "in laws" but what kind of day-to-day support—or aggravation—they might provide.) Furthermore, definitions of what the relationship "is" have to be more conscious—for example, the couple has to state to each other whether or not they are living together or "married" in a way that heterosexuals bypass by having legal status available to them. Although heterosexuals may have sexual issues that impede their sexual adjustment, most do not have to decide just how heterosexual they are; lesbians, on the other hand, may often have to self-assess—and then convince a partner—of their loyalty to a lesbian partnership. Finally, the literature clearly shows that cultural values about homosexuality, however liberal, still do not automatically convey approval and support to most young people who are developing a gay identity. Thus, the literature on the life cycle of young gay couples is often concerned with just how solid and happy a young gay or lesbian person is with their sexual orientation and how this affects their relationship and their sexual satisfaction and practice.

The data on same-sex relationships used to be weighted toward studying the individual coming out process, but now there is a lot of research on the inside of couples' lives. Long overdue, same-sex couples can now have a more realistic picture of what life together might be like and what sexual issues may present themselves because excellent scholars have been covering more than a few topics superficially. No one topic is over stressed—the only exception to that rule being years of research on extra-relationship sex, which has remained an area of concentrated research because of gay men's lesser allegiance to monogamy (which is culturally anomalous) and of course because of all the AIDs research on the topic. As Peplau et al. point out, research has been hampered because of lack of funding for random samples, but I believe that many of the nonrandom samples have been useful studies, and the attributions of any given set of findings to a larger population have been cautiously presented (in most, though not all, cases).

Looking over the review of the sexuality of same-sex couples, it struck me how much more similar gay and lesbian couples' sexuality is to heterosexual couples than single gay sexuality is to single heterosexual sexual patterns. There are continuities with heterosexual couples in the satisfactions and wear and tear of daily intimate relationships. It is also true that gay and lesbian couples have a wide variety of intragroup differences in sexual practices and values.

Still, the most enduring and intriguing difference between gay men and just about everyone else is their ability to be committed and still, as many conservative observers might see it, "unfaithful." (indeed, many gay men may also code it as such, because extradyadic sex happens in many gay relationships that have intentions of being monogamus). The reality of sexual openness does create some very interesting material for researchers (and perhaps for heterosexuals or lesbians who have cravings for a bit more sexual freedom within their relationship) in offering opportunities to study how sexual openness is negotiated, how some sex is judged to be dangerous or a trespass, whereas other kinds are allowed; how couples handle jealousy; and which kinds of sexual liaisons destabilize a relationship and which kinds can be integrated into a long-term commitment without ill effect.

Mentioned in passing by Peplau et al. but worthy of a bit more reflection here, is how gay couple life has shaped the helping and therapeutic professions. Instead of therapists helping gay men find their way back to some cultural norm, many therapists have situated themselves in the subculture and helped unhappy partners consider an adaptation to a new norm of sexual openness. This is an interesting issue for on the one hand, it shows how social change and relationship theories can change and modify previous professional opinion, it also brings up the issue of whether or not this "gay affirmative" counseling is really in the client's best interests (because openness is good for the relationship and for the individual) or is simply an accommodation to a social fact that is not in the best interests of the couple. More and better research (some of which is helpfully presented in the Peplau et al. chapter) on the real sequella of open marriages (gay or heterosexual) would help inform this potential professional conundrum.

The chapter on gay and lesbian couples, similar as it is with the concern of all couples in most respects is different in one very important area—the impact of AIDs. Although heterosexuality has been affected by AIDs (see the excellent review of the literature in chapter 21 on safer sex), it is painfully true that no group has been affected as much as gay men. The linkage between sex and death, the high stakes that trust presents, the need for honesty between partners, and the anger and resentment that gay men must feel toward their unfair and special exposure to this disease has had to have its impact on the interior life of couples (especially for HIV positive individuals and their partners). This has been covered most poignantly in plays and movies and is covered in a less emotional way in this volume. But over and above the facts, figures, and correlations, the AIDs plague is a sad reality behind and between the lines of scientific discussion as one considers the special problems of gay love in the 20th and 21st centuries.

Contemplating the nightmarish presence of AIDs, horrific even with present drugs that control progress of the disease for many men and women, makes the chapters on general issues of sexual dysfunction less heartbreaking, even as we consider their serious impact on relationships. The truth is that sex isn't easy—and that like any other behavior, people may be more or less talented at it, more or less enthusiastic to do it, and more or less well matched to a partner. Add that to the cultural malaise American society has exhibited historically and contemporaneously on this subject, and it is obvious that many couples have difficult and even disastrous sexual issues.

The good news from the chapters in this volume is how sophisticated sex therapy has become and how much broader the research on the subject has grown. Masters and Johnson's model of human sexual response, revolutionary and helpful as their work has been, is no longer a hegemonic model. Many brilliant practitioners and researchers now offer highly specialized alternative approaches, ones that suit people of different values, experiences, ages, and sexual orientations. Gender differences and contextual issues (such as inequity in marriage) that have been ignored historically, are now taken into account and allow for relationship adjustment to be a part of the improvement of the couple's sexual life. McCarthy, Bodnar, & Handal's overview of the field shows how the focus of therapy has, happily, broadened from a body parts approach to this larger contextual frame. This has been matched, however, by far more information about how the body works (or doesn't). So there is a much greater ability to parcel out biological, psychological, and relational variables that complicate sexual, personal, and couple satisfaction. McCarthy et al.'s list of ways to help couples address psychological and sociological beliefs about sexuality that may impede personal satisfaction or undermine couple reconciliation is particularly instructive.

Both McCarthy et al. and Aubin and Heiman spend time on the newest key phrase in clinical approaches to sexuality: inhibited sexual desire. McCarthy et al. believe that "inhibited sexual desire for males is almost always a secondary dysfunction" caused by erectile dysfunction or concomitant physiological problems of aging (chapter 23, this volume). (Exceptions are having a different sexual orientation than the relationship you are in or some paraphiliac or unique arousal pattern that will not or cannot be accommodated by a partner.) This takes the reader into the new world of sexuality and chemistry—the marriage of the clinical professions to the new classes of performance wonder drugs, the first of which has been named Viagra. If you want to know what an impact it has had, consider this: One study found that, along with Coca Cola, it was the most well-known brand name in the world!

Of course, Viagra has also changed sexual therapy. Aubin and Heiman take us deeper into this world explaining that sex therapy has changed to accommodate the ability to help men (also to assess to what extent drugs, hormones, etc. might also help women) with inhibited desire or orgasmic difficulty. Stepping carefully among different diagnostic tools that label who is and who is not sexually dysfunctional (in order not to pathologize nonorgasmic women or women with low sexual interest), it is still hard for the sensitive clinician to see rare or absent orgasm or rare or absent desire as merely one point on a sexual continuum (as feminist sex researcher and social critic, Leonore Tieffer, suggests we might).

The world of sexual therapy has entered an era of more medicalized terminology, and female sexuality has been firmly enclosed within it. Terms like HSD (hypoactive sexual desire) and FSAD (female sexual arousal disorder) are now part of a therapeutic tool kit—part of well-meaning therapists' clinical response to women's (or their partners') complaints of lack of desire or lack of adequate arousal (self-defined) during sex. The good news is that women and their partners do not have to suffer in silence about fears of sexual inadequacy or feel hopeless about gaining back (or learning) sexual response. *The bad news is that a baseline of normalcy seems to have been created out of thin air.* No real baseline of sexual functioning exists—only a vision of what sex can be like for some people (easy arousal, frequent desire, etc.) and therefore, so the thinking goes, what ought to be available to all people. Women and men who do not fit the profile of the sexually "normal" (for all that we know may actually be the sexually talented) are put in a pathological diagnostic category. However, as I see it, this may be grossly unfair. It may be that, for example, there is just a certain number of people who cannot run fast or for long periods of time, but nonetheless are not labeled as pathologically deficient in running. Still, we have decided that sexual interest and orgasm are a right for everyone. In a society where sex is accepted as a given and glorified in cinematic scenes of high passion, it is impossible to think that people would happily exclude themselves from that vision of sexuality. Responsible clinicians, like Aubin and Heiman, are trying very hard not to push a single version of sexual competence on anyone, but offer help to those who experience "personal distress"; but there is always the problem that begins when one person's distress is caused by their partner's demands for their treatment because the partner is unwilling to settle for, what is for them, an inadequate sex life. Trying to reconcile different sexual appetites and enjoyment in a relationship is a daunting task for therapists. Somewhat easier are transient (though persistent and difficult) problems caused by sexual trauma in the past, or issues that are relationship specific which may be solved by resolution of the psychiatric damage from the event or events or changing or ending the relationship. Aubin and Heiman also alert us to the life cycle issues that change and often create sexual issues such as the physiological and psychological concomitants of aging.

The trickiest problem is to find out how much of any given dysfunction is an artifact of the relationship itself. Aubin and Heiman indicate that hypoactive sexual desire is the most challenging sexual dysfunction to treat and is associated with very high or very low couple closeness, poor adaptation to major turning points in a couple's life (for example, having a child, having a past sexual trauma, differences in desire, or other relationship issues). Those other relationships issues might be extraordinarily embedded in the couple's history or as superficial (but torturous) as individual weight gain or inequitable conditions leading to resentment and a cycle of attacks and counterattacks that freeze the emotional temperature of the partners. Couples may come in for a sexual issue that has morphed into a relationship crisis, or conversely, go to a therapist for a relationship deficiency that can be traced to or complicated by sexual complaints. Here, analysis is more of an art than a science (just as all good science has a bit of art in it). Patients' conscious and unconscious use of sex makes it necessary for the therapist to dig a bit deeper to find out if lack of sexual desire is being used as a self-punishment, a punishment for a partner, an aversive response because of past sexual experiences or imagery, or an inhibition due to low lying anger or depression. The authors mention how scripts of expectation, of roles or norms, or self-expectation can complicate sexual arousal or behavior. Figuring out how each person's script interacts with their stage in the life cycle (and the challenges of that part of their life) makes the analyst's job an ever-changing challenge.

But all of this seems more intuitive, more accessible to logic than the last part of this book: sexual pathology. These chapters remind me of the combustibility of thwarted, twisted, or compulsive sexual desire. I would, for example, catalogue depression as a condition that thwarts desire. Wenzel, Jackson, and Brendle as well as several other authors, remind us how common and destructive depression is. Nothing vibrant survives under the dark cloud of depression. Although social scientists can never describe depression as accurately as some novelists who have described their own depression or others (e.g., William Styron), nonetheless, the list of concomitant sexual dysfunctions that accompany depression should alert both partners and therapists to how diagnostic low sexual desire might be in signaling a partner's depression. Also in this category, the ill effects of alcoholism on short- and long-term sexual functioning—a fact that should, but doesn't, deter young men from drinking excessively—is also well described. Alas, even though the effects of alcohol can cause relative or full impotence, many men still become victims of its use.

Alcohol becomes an interesting variable throughout our discussions of sexuality—particularly when it comes to twisted and compulsive desire. Cupach and Spitzberg's very interesting chapter on unrequited lust shows how a lack of mutual desire is not always deterrent enough to stop willful sexual desire. Passion has been described as a drug—both psychologically and physiologically. As such, it transports an individual out of a rational approach and substitutes one of euphoria, intense need, grandiosity, willfulness, or even anger and aggressiveness. Passion and a culture that venerates and excuses acts made in the name of love (for example, John Hinkley who shot President Reagan so that he could "impress Jodi Foster") revs up the sexual motor and sets the stage for antisocial acts. These can vary from speaking unwanted sentiments to the sorts of aggressive acts detailed in chapter 12 by Christopher and Kisler. At a minimal level, agitation can occur between committed partners who have different sexual appetites; at the bizarre level, one stranger can be demanding sex from another.

Unrequited lust ends up on the police blotter when date rape, or just plain old rape, occurs. It is hard to believe that not so long ago, a large percentage of the public believed that rape was rare and usually invented (for example, the awful phrase used in a well-known court case about how rape was unlikely because it was like trying to thread a moving needle). After half a century of political agitation, the woman's movement has changed the nation's sensibilities about rape, changed the court system, and, through aligned research, awakened the sexological community to rape and sexual aggression as a major social issue in relationships. Christopher and Kisler, in reviewing the literature on various kinds of sexual victimization (attempted rape, date rape, marital rape, and stranger rape) sensitizes us to the fact that sex is often the setting for playing out the need for control, gender stereotypes, prejudices, and even inchoate rage. The full picture of a society that breeds sexual aggression becomes apparent—through social institutions that denigrate women and/or provide a context for drunken, impersonal sex (e.g., some fraternities), to the idea that a husband has a right to have sex with his wife no matter what she personally desires, to the idea that sexual display (e.g., mini skirts or plunging necklines) are meant to unfairly inflame male desire and therefore are a "come on" that gives a woman "what she is asking for" (even if she insists, when sexually confronted, that she is not interested or available). An insidious belief is that if sexual play begins, there is a point of "no return" that entitles the man to proceed, no matter what. The authors rightly point out that rape may always be with us, but it will certainly be with us if these cultural beliefs are not mitigated.

Most of us can feel superior reading about such willful and dangerous sexuality—unless we read the chapter on sexual and emotional jealousy, by Guerrero, Spitzberg, and Yoshimura. Who among us has not felt the "green-eyed monster" of rejection, loss, or possessiveness fill us with anger, revenge, or despair. We are, after all, talking about our deepest need—for love and commitment—and when it is thwarted, we may succumb to twisted emotions and loss of rationality. Not only the loss of a loved or desired person is involved. As the authors show, rage often results because our own identity, our own worthiness is on the line. We are diminished, vanquished, by a superior rival—or an inferior one—who "proves" to us that we were not ever really appreciated. In other words, whatever the attributes of our rival—we are flattened by their existence. Whether it is men's greater propensity to sexual jealousy or women's greater likelihood of emotional jealousy, the anger and sorrow men and women feel is experienced by most human beings sometime during their lifetime.

These are some of the important, layered, and nuanced aspects of sexuality in relationships. Although the editors have put together an amazing breadth of articles on the subject, what one is struck by is that many more chapters, with many more subject areas, could be added. Sex is a part of everything human we do—every emotion, attachment, and intrapsychic act. Sexual issues in a relationship inform us as much about each individual as they do about the relationship, and as much about the culture as they do about ourselves. Then again, romantic and sexual interaction has its own reality, over and above cultural or individual beliefs, values, needs, or desires.

And that is what makes studying sexuality in close relationships so complex and enlightening. Its pleasure and pitfalls help us analyze our emotional lives, just as our emotional lives help us understand the pliant and diurnal nature of our sexuality. This book gives us a look at so much of what we want to know and have to know. It points to the many questions we must answer to help give adequate answers to the issues that bedevil us. To read about sexuality in close relationships is to understand how much we don't understand, as well as to celebrate our increasing knowledge about a subject so much at the heart of our deepest connections.

25

Sexuality in Close Relationships: Concluding Commentary

Daniel Perlman
University of British Columbia
Susan Campbell
Middlebury College

This chapter provides a commentary on the contents of the *Handbook of Sexuality in Close Relationships*. These reflections focus on (a) three emphases of the volume (defining sex, relational aspects of sexuality, problematic aspects of relationships); (b) the book's treatment of culture and selected demographic type variables (gender, race, sexual orientation); (c) the major theoretical approaches prominent in the volume (attachment, evolutionary, social exchange, and symbolic interaction); (d) five topics that might have received more attention (meta-analysis, international perspectives, the funding context of sex research, disciplinary perspectives other than psychology, and public policy implications of the current knowledge base); and finally (e) future directions in terms of sampling, methods, theory, and developmental perspectives. We conclude that this volume amply testifies to the value of considering relational aspects of sexuality.

On December 1, 1994, then U.S. Surgeon General Joycelyn Elders said: "In regard to masturbation, I think that that is something that is a part of human sexuality, and it is a part of something that perhaps should be taught." Two weeks later, after a public furor over this remark, President Clinton requested Elders' resignation. Although U.S. society may have become more sexually permissive in the second half of the 20th century, in the mid-1990s it still was not ready for government officials to publicly advocate solitary forms of sexual stimulation. Instead, the American public primarily sanctions sex in couple relationships. Whereas many sex researchers undoubtedly privately applauded Elders' remark, studies going back to Kinsey (Kinsey, Pomeroy, & Martin, 1948, p. 512) demonstrate that the most common form of sexual expression is in relationships. Thus, the focus of this *Handbook* on sexuality in relationships is justified.

Factors associated with our sexuality include aspects of the individual, properties of the dyad, and larger social influences. In commenting on the sexual dysfunction area,

Aubin and Heiman depict there having been an "individual-based approach to sexual dysfunction" (chapter 20, this volume). Our perception is that the study of sexuality more generally has traditionally been in the domains of those concerned either with the individual or with larger social forces. In 1961, Lester Kirkendall published a volume on *Premarital Intercourse and Interpersonal Relations* but it wasn't until the 1990s that anthologies dealing with dyadic aspects began appearing (e.g., McKinney & Sprecher, 1991b). The present volume expands that tradition and represents a milestone in its development.

Our goal in this chapter is to reflect on the contents of the volume. En route, our belief in the value of studying sexuality from the perspective of intimate relationships will be evident. We start with three contemporary emphases we see manifest in this volume: the question of what is sex, the relational approach, and the inclusion of problematic aspects of sexuality in relationships. In the middle segments of the chapter we reflect on the volume in terms of its treatment of selected demographic type variables (gender, race, sexual orientation) and its treatment of theory. From there we identify a few topics of interest to us that get less attention, and finally end with future directions for the field. Our reflections complement Schwartz's companion commentary, dealing with some of the same issues as she covers (theory, gender, and the dark side of sex) but differing in others (e.g., our concern with omissions vs. Schwartz's well-taken observations on the life span). Our chapter also looks back, building on the wisdom of the book as a whole, on some of the issues DeLamater and Hyde raise in their first chapter. Thus, to some extent our observations are designed as a bookend that brings the volume full circle back to its starting point.

NEW EMPHASES MANIFEST IN THIS VOLUME

What is Sex?

Sex researchers have traditionally focused on sexual behaviors such as sexual touching and intercourse, especially penile–vaginal intercourse. In their first chapter, DeLamater and Hyde criticize this formulation as being too narrow. Throughout the volume, contributors return frequently to definitional issues. In discussing sex in conjunction with the transition to parenthood, Haugen, Schmutzer, and Wenzel distinguish between coital and noncoital sex. Wiederman notes that in survey research respondents attribute different meanings to the question of "have you had sex?" Some members of the public think oral–genital contact such as Bill Clinton had with Monica Lewinski constitutes sex; others do not! In this same vein, Peplau, Fingerhut, and Beals wonder whether the wording of sex surveys is equally appropriate to lesbians, gays, and heterosexual respondents. McCarthy, Bodnar, and Handal discuss male versus female sexuality, whereas Burgess sees traditional definitions of sex as male centric, especially as applied to middle and old age sexuality.

It is fair to conclude that the thrust of the contributors' views (e.g., Hendrick & Hendrick) is toward broader, more complex definitions of sexuality. From the laypersons' perspective, sex takes different forms and has different meanings. Clearly researchers need to be able to ask laypersons about their sexuality. In doing so, cross-cultural techniques such as differential item functioning may help in giving assurances that indexes have similar meanings across different populations (Holland & Wainer, 1993; van de Vijver & Poortinga, 1997). DeLamater and Hyde give specific definitions such as that of sexual health offered by the sexual health model. For us, another profitable avenue that might be explored is going beyond lay concepts to constructs defined from a theoretical perspective. Although this may incur some decrement in social scientists' ability to converse with the public and policy makers, it may contribute to the advancement of the scientific enterprise.

Sexuality in Close Relationships

At the core of this volume is the issue of sexuality in close relationships. Sprecher and McKinney (1993) outlined how sex is an interpersonal act involving disclosure, intimacy, love, interdependence, affection, relationship maintenance, and the like. Writing in this tradition, Sprecher and Cate see sexuality as a component of relationship phenomena. For many people in North American society, although certainly not all, emotional closeness is a condition that legitimates sexual intimacy (cf. Hendrick & Hendrick, chapter 7, this volume: "Today, falling in love . . . is a sufficient condition for having sex"). So love and relationships go together.

Underlying the dyadic study of sexuality are at least two premises. First, dyads are different than the sum of their parts. Put differently, a person's sexual activities depend not only on their own attributes but also those of their partner. So, a hypothetical male, John, will have a different sexual relationship if he partners with Mary rather than Jane or Jake. Second, there are phenomena and processes such as interpersonal power and influence that only occur at the dyadic level.

Although several contributors call for taking further steps in the relational study of sexuality (e.g., the editors in their Introduction; Willetts, Sprecher, & Beck; Simpson, Wilson, & Winterheld; Regan; Metts; Feeney & Noller; Fisher; Aubin & Heiman; Noar, Zimmerman, & Atwood), impressive strides forward have been made. The relational study of sexuality points to a number of ways of looking at the intertwining of these phenomena. We examine their intersection in two ways: first by commenting more abstractly on the interconnections among different types of variables and second in terms of the nature of some of the substantive questions that have been asked.

Interconnections Among Five Types of Variables. In general, researchers can examine independent, dependent, control, mediating, and moderating variables. Experimental researchers establish conditions so they can infer that a manipulated, independent variable caused a change in the dependent variable. In the current volume, this type of causal thinking about independent and dependent variables is manifest in Feeney and Noller's assertion that attachment "security promotes healthy long-term sexual relationships." Apropos of control variables, Metts is concerned with how attachment styles influence the growth of relationships after partners have engaged in their first sexual involvement. She wanted to be sure this influence was independent of such factors as the age of respondents or their history of previous sexual partners. So in her regression analysis she entered age and history first as control variables, finding that even after doing this, attachment played a role. Illustrative of mediational questions, Feeney and Noller tested a model that attachment security fosters positive attitudes toward communication that in turn promotes safer sex. In this work, positive attitudes are a mediator. Peplau, Fingerhut, and Beals report that for lesbians the discrepancy in partners' satisfaction with their sexual relationship is negatively associated with overall relational satisfaction. This association isn't found among gay males. Thus in this case, type of relationship (lesbian vs. gay) moderates or alters the correlation between factors (satisfaction discrepancy and global satisfaction).

Relationship factors can enter sex research as any one of these five types of variables. Most research on sexuality is correlational in nature. The most frequently reported type of finding in this volume is simply an association between variables, sometimes after holding constant various control variables, especially demographic type control variables. Determining cause and effect from these associations is difficult (e.g., is sexual satisfaction an independent variable that causes changes in marital satisfaction as a dependent variable or vice versa; Sprecher & Cate, chapter 10, this volume). Nonetheless researchers often have predictor and outcome variables and sometimes, as did Feeney and Noller, evoke causal thinking. The search for mediating and moderating factors or how variables cluster together to form types is less common. Although it is not necessarily true, it is easy to see relationship states (satisfaction) as predictor or outcome variables and relationship processes (conflict, communication) as mediating variables.

Interests and Questions Asked.   One can also see across this collection of chapters different interests and ways questions about relationships have been asked. A classic descriptive question of concern to sex researchers is the number of relationships in which people have engaged in various sexual activities. In the era of HIV/AIDS, that question has assumed new meaning because having more partners is a prime risk factor for sexually transmitted diseases (Michael, 1997). Relationship researchers are finding, however, that even being in stable, intimate relationships can leave partners vulnerable to disease transmission (Noar, Zimmerman, & Atwood, chapter 21, this volume).

A second recurrent question in this collection is how aspects of relationships and sex change over time. For instance, Metts looks at how partners' communication about love and commitment influences feelings of regret and/or relationship escalation at the time of first sex and affects later relationship quality. Feeney and Noller track how lesbians' relationships with their mothers change during the transition in which they announce their sexual orientation. Haugen, Schmutzer, and Wenzel examine what happens during pregnancy. Burgess integrates information on sex in relationships as adults age. Some of these questions are linked to lifespan development but these phenomena can be kept intellectually and sometimes empirically separate (see Burgess, chapter 18, this volume).

Another noteworthy feature is the number of categories of relationships that have been considered. Most obvious, there are the relationships in which sexual behavior occurs: dating, romantic, cohabiting, married, new versus old, lesbian, gay, extramarital, and relationships at different points in the lifecycle. Complementing this list, Cupach and Spitzberg consider lust in friendships, cyber (or technologically mediated) relationships, and the relations between coworkers. Presumably there are sexual behaviors that are unique to or more pronounced in specific relationships (e.g., gay men's nonmonogamous bonds; lesbians' higher rates of orgasm; Peplau, Fingerhut, & Beals) or relationships among variables that differ between relational contexts (as our earlier discussion of moderators illuminated). Yet as the replication of other findings illustrates, some phenomena cut across relationship types (e.g., "comparative studies find much similarity between the sexual satisfaction of lesbian, gay, and heterosexual couples" Peplau, Fingerhut, & Beals, chapter 14, this volume). So it is crucial to look for both differences and similarities among relationships of different types.

Beyond the focal sexual dyad itself, other relationships warrant consideration. Past relationships can influence present ones as was shown by Noar, Zimmerman, and Atwood's finding that adolescents whose first coital experience occurred in an established (as opposed to a casual) relationship were more likely to use contraceptives in their subsequent sexual liaisons. In the case of jealousy (Guerrero, Spitzberg, & Yoshimura), there is a person threatening the sexual dyad. In extrarelational affairs (Willetts, Sprecher, & Beck; Byers & Wang), there are two sexual dyads interweaving with one another. Fisher highlights how family members, including parents and siblings, influence children's sexuality. The extent to which youth are peer, as opposed to family, oriented is also associated with their sexual behavior. As studies such as these illustrate, networks of relationships influence dyads.

Pros and Cons of a Relational Approach.   As Weiderman notes, studying partners is "messy" because their data violate the usual statistical assumption of independence among respondents. Yet there are payoffs. Not only can researchers look at how wives' behavior correlates with wives' outcomes, but they can also examine cross-partner effects—how wives' behavior influences their spouses' outcomes. Furthermore, as already indicated, some phenomena such as relational roles only become apparent in dyads. For example, in this volume there is a concern with different parties (e.g., perpetrators and victims) in sexual aggression (Christopher & Kisler, in chapter 12), unrequited lust (Cupach & Spitzberg), and jealousy (Guerrero, Spitzberg, & Yoshimura). In a similar vein, there is the sexual initiator and the person who responds (Byers & Wang), his and her sexuality (Vohs, Catanese, & Baumeister), as well as the insertor and the insertee in gay sex (Peplau, Fingerhut, & Beals).

To sum up the emphasis on relationships, this volume illuminates the number of ways relationships and sexuality intersect with one another. Focusing on relationships adds questions to the study of sexuality and vice versa. Relational aspects of sexuality are linked to health and other important outcomes (see Noar, Zimmerman, & Atwood; Burgess). Other levels of analysis are important, but certainly this volume amply testifies to the value of considering relational aspects of sexuality. Doing so provides fertile ground for social scientists seeking to predict and understand either or both.

The Dark Side of Sexuality in Relationships

A third emphasis of this volume, as Schwartz also notes, is the dark side of relational sexuality. Marriage and family texts have mentioned sexual problems for some time. But our perception is that this topic was covered briefly. For instance, the 1981 edition of Kephart's successful text, *The Family, Society, and the Individual*, had three pages on sexual adjustment and maladjustment. He identified four complaints (e.g., premature ejaculation), saying there was "no need to go into detail" (Kephart, 1981, p. 365) and cited research that marital sex was "improving" as indexed by higher rates of coitus and orgasm.

In this volume, paralleling a similar trend in the study of close relationships (Perlman, 2000), the problematic side of sexuality is a prominent component. There is a subsection of the book on "The Dark Side of Sex" (see chapters on lust, aggression, and jealousy by Cupach & Spitzberg; Christopher & Kisler [chapter 12], and Guerrero, Spitzberg, & Yoshimura). Later in the volume there is a chapter on sexual dysfunction (Aubin & Heiman). Several other chapters at least touch on bleak aspects of sex in discussing the costs of sex (Byers & Wang), sexually transmitted diseases (Noar, Zimmerman, & Atwood), sexual conflicts (Sprecher & Cate), male–female tensions in sexual desire (Vohs, Catanese, & Baumeister), sexual declines with the arrival of children and with aging (Haugen, Schmutzer, & Wenzel; Burgess), and sexual problems associated with psychopathologies (Wenzel, Jackson, & Brendle). Christopher and Kisler (chapter 15) creatively use sexual problems as a way of identifying marital role expectations.

A few statistics illustrate the prevalence of sexual problems in contemporary relationships. Christopher and Kisler (chapter 12) cite one study in which 53% of adolescent females and 45% of males reported having experienced sexual aggression. Estimates of the prevalence of sexual arousal disorders (e.g., lack of vaginal lubrication or penile response) vary considerably but range as high as 52% in women and 53% in men (Aubin & Heiman). Over the past year, 24% of women report having had orgasm problems and 29% of men report premature ejaculation (Aubin & Heiman).

One might perceive the sky is falling. Yet, one of the paradoxes of the dark elements of relationships and sexuality is the high level of satisfaction people report in both domains. As Sprecher and Cate (chapter 10, this volume) point out, "research indicates that most individuals involved in a committed relationship are sexually satisfied. For example, Laumann, Gagnon, Michael, and Michaels (1994), with NHSLS data, found that 88% of the married respondents reported being either extremely or very physically pleased."

There are probably multiple factors that can help to explain this paradox. First, many respondents may have a positivity bias in their satisfaction ratings. Matlin and Stang (1978) detected a Pollyanna principle in language, memory, and thought. Second, even though there are costs to sexual relationships, Byers and Wang find that the rewards are more common. Third, some of the problems that people experience may be fairly isolated events that occurred in the past or outside their primary sexual liaison. They may be referring to satisfaction in relationships that are working in the present.

Even if on balance people are predominantly satisfied with their sexual relationships, we nonetheless believe the problematic aspects of sex warrant careful scrutiny. As McCarthy, Bodnar, and Handal argue,

> when sexuality is dysfunctional, conflictual (including differences in desired frequency), or nonexistent, it plays an inordinately powerful role, draining the relationship of vitality and threatening its viability. Paradoxically, bad sex plays a more influential negative role than the enhancing role of good sex. (chapter 23, this volume)

Furthermore, once people develop a sexual dysfunction; their own or their partners' expectations and thoughts may help to sustain it (see Aubin & Heiman). On the other hand, whatever the mechanisms, we are pleased that some problems apparently do not weigh heavily in people's overall judgments of their sexual lives and that therapists have well-developed techniques for helping clients overcome sexual dysfunctions (McCarthy, Bodnar, & Handal).

GENDER AND SEXUALITY

Gender Differences

Whereas we have been discussing newer directions manifest in the volume, we want to turn next to one of *the* classic topics for sex researchers and other social scientists: the role of gender. Canary and Dindia's (1998) consideration of gender differences in communication helps put this discussion in a broader context. They divided researchers concerned with gender into two camps: those with what they call "alpha biases" and those with "beta biases." Those with an alpha bias observe that gender differences are pervasive, and they accentuate the differences between men and women. Those with a beta bias note that the magnitude of any differences is small and may be due to other factors than gender per se. For them, men's and women's interactions are to a greater degree and in more ways similar than they are dissimilar.

Turning more specifically to the present volume, DeLamater and Hyde ask, "Are there gender differences in sexuality in close relationships?" (chapter 1, this volume). The authors of this handbook seem to answer this question with a resounding, "Yes . . . sometimes." There are perhaps more proponents of gender differences among sexuality researchers than in many other research domains, and this may be due to the relatively large size of some gender differences in sexuality, especially when compared to other types of gender differences (e.g., in cognitive abilities, Hyde & Linn, 1988). The summary of gender differences reported in the chapters in this volume is consistent with other recent summaries of gender differences in sexuality (e.g., Peplau, 2003).

Sexual Desire.   One area of focus for sexuality researchers interested in gender differences has been sexual desire. Several chapters in this volume feature research showing greater sexual desire and interest among men than among women. Vohs and colleagues focus on sexual motivation, as measured by the "frequency and intensity of sexual desires" (Vohs et al., chapter 19, this volume). They cite several types of evidence, the most direct being that men generally report wanting sex more often than do women. Haugen and colleagues echo this finding in their chapter on sexuality during pregnancy: They cite fluctuations in female sexual desire across the trimesters of pregnancy and note that "there is evidence for significant gender differences in sexual desire throughout the time associated with childbirth, such that men generally desire sexual activity more than women." Vohs et al. also refer to frequency of masturbation, sexual aggression, and extradyadic sex as being higher among males than among females. Willetts, Sprecher, and Beck cite evidence that males, both in adolescence and as adults, have more sexual partners than do females, and are more likely to engage in sex outside their primary relationship.

The Importance of Sexual Versus Relational Factors.   Another area in which researchers point to evidence of gender differences in sexuality is the relative importance of sexual versus relational variables to the meaning and functioning of the relationship. In general, women seem to place greater emphasis on relational characteristics than do men, whereas sexual factors play a more important role for men than for women. One example comes from research on sociosexuality, described by Simpson and colleagues. Women are more likely than men to report that they require emotional closeness in a relationship before having sex, and are less approving of "casual sex" than are men (Simpson & Gangestad, 1991). Simpson and Gangestad (1991) refer to this cluster of attitudes as sociosexual orientation, with women falling on the more "restricted" end of the continuum, and men being more "unrestricted."

Another example of this general pattern involves research on sexual and emotional jealousy. Guerrero, Spitzberg, and Yoshimura, for example, describe research suggesting that men are more upset by a partner's sexual infidelity, whereas women are more upset by a partner's emotional infidelity; thus, women are more likely to focus on the relational, rather than the sexual, betrayal. They also cite evidence of gender differences in expressions of jealousy suggesting that jealous women (more than jealous men) may respond to sexual unfaithfulness by "trying to improve the relationship [and] demanding commitment from the partner" (chapter 13, this volume).

Other references to the differential importance of relational and sexual factors for women and men can be found in other chapters and elsewhere in the literature. In their chapter on marital sexuality, Christopher and Kisler note that an examination of sexuality in the marital context is particularly important for women, as "women's reports of subjective sexual arousal appear to be contingent on the meaning they put on the social and relational context in which they find themselves" (chapter 15, this volume). In another chapter, Metts describes research investigating the effects of a couple's first sexual involvement on relationship quality. Interestingly, she found no differences between men and women in relationship satisfaction and commitment, and no differences in the degree of regret or sense of relationship escalation experienced after a first sexual encounter. However, she found that regret after the first sexual involvement was a negative predictor of relationship satisfaction *only for men*, whereas a sense of relationship escalation after sex was a positive predictor of satisfaction *only for women*. Thus, the determining factor for men involved the interpretation of the sexual event, whereas for women it involved the implications of sex for the meaning of the relationship. This is consistent with the findings from a recent paper by Sprecher (2002), who examined the importance of sexual satisfaction for relationship functioning. She found that, although sexual satisfaction was associated with relational satisfaction, love, and commitment for both women and men, the associations were stronger for men. Moreover, sexual satisfaction (but not relationship satisfaction) predicted the likelihood of a relationship breaking up over time for men, but not for women; whereas relationship satisfaction (but not sexual satisfaction) predicted breaking up for women.

Sexual Coercion and Aggression.   Another area of difference between men and women is in experiences related to sexual coercion and aggression. In chapter 12, Christopher and Kisler review research and theory related to sexual aggression in romantic relationships and found that although the incidence of aggression varies widely depending on the samples and definitions of aggression used, women are much more frequently the victims of sexual aggression, and aggressive acts against women are more sexually "intimate" than those against men. In the context of experiencing jealousy in a romantic relationship, men are more likely than women to respond by threatening the rival or by becoming sexually aggressive with the partner (Guerrero, Spitzberg, & Yoshimura).

Caveats About Gender Differences

Research identifying gender differences inevitably raises questions about the ways in which men and women are similar, as well as about the size and importance of those differences. It is, in some respects, difficult to evaluate the degree to which men and women are similar in their relational sexuality. As Wiederman (chapter 2, this volume) noted, "The overriding goal of researchers appears to be generating results that attain statistical significance," referring, of course, to significant *differences*. The statistical challenge of attempting to retain the null hypothesis aside, there is a sense in which the most interesting questions regarding gender are presumed to be about simple differences. But it is possible to analyze data and consider their meaning in ways that allow both differences *and* similarities to emerge. For example, Hendrick and Hendrick describe several gender differences that appear in their own work on attitudes regarding love and sexuality: Women are more likely to be friendship-oriented and less likely to take a game-playing approach to love than are men. They also note, however, that despite some consistent differences, a pattern of similarity can be observed by exploring correlations among love and sexuality variables; in their studies, the correlations for men are rarely different from those for women. They conclude that "any discussion of gender and sexuality in intimate relationships must embrace both gender differences and gender similarities" (chapter 7, this volume).

Even when differences exist, we should not presume that all differences are created equal. Wiederman emphasizes (as have others) the importance of reporting measures of effect size, but few researchers have done so. For example, Vohs and colleagues cite studies that pertain to gender differences in sexual motivation and conclude that "there is a strong and reliable gender difference in sex drive" (Vohs, Catanese, & Baumeister, chapter 19, this volume), but it is unclear from this conclusion, and presumably from the studies cited, whether this difference is a sizable one. In one exception to this general avoidance of effect sizes, Simpson and colleagues acknowledge that men are, on average, less restricted in their sociosexuality than are women, but point out that "the variability in responses that exists *within* each gender greatly exceeds that which exists *between* men and women" (Simpson, Wilson, & Winterheld, chapter 4, this volume). They cite studies showing that knowing a person's gender accounts for only 9% of the variance in desired number of sexual partners and 25% of the variance in interest in casual sex. Much explanatory power can be gained, then, by looking beyond the male/female dichotomy.

There are other avenues of research on sexuality in relationships in which questions of difference are only implicitly addressed because of our presumptions about women and men. An illustrative example comes from research on sexual aggression. Because women are more commonly the victims of sexual violence than are men, few studies have asked questions about the frequency of male victims of this type of aggression. In chapter 12, Christopher and Kisler note, however, that recent work has begun to explore the experiences of male victims of sexual violence. Some of these studies show surprising numbers of adult males (nearly one fourth in one study) who have "experienced unwanted coercive sexual contact from a woman" (Christopher & Kisler, chapter 12, this volume). One recent paper examined the experience of sexual coercion among female prisoners and found that approximately half of the incidents of sexual coercion (ranging from sexual groping to rape) occurred at the hands of a female perpetrator (Struckman-Johnson & Struckman-Johnson, 2002). Presumptions about gender differences may therefore lead researchers to fail to ask questions that point to important exceptions to those differences.

ETHNICITY, RACE, AND CULTURE

DeLamater and Hyde point out that "in contrast to the attention given to gender, research on sexuality in close relationships has seldom focused on race or ethnicity" (chapter 1, this volume). This observation is generally reflected in the chapters in this volume. A few chapters (e.g., Fisher; Hendrick & Hendrick; Metts; Willetts, Sprecher, & Beck) refer to the occasional study employing a non-White sample, but otherwise, little reference is made to research that explicitly considers the role of race and ethnicity. This despite the observation by DeLamater and Hyde that there is evidence from large-scale surveys such as the NHSLS (Laumann, Gagnon, Michael, & Michaels, 1994) suggesting that ethnicity is associated with significant differences in sexual behaviors.

There is slightly more attention paid to the role of culture. In addition to the chapters that cite an occasional study employing non-Western samples (e.g., Vohs, Catanese, & Baumeister; Willetts, Sprecher, & Beck), a few authors specifically devote a section of their chapters to a consideration of cross-cultural research. Guerrero and colleagues, for example, consider the influence of culture on the feeling and expression of jealousy, citing data from a number of different studies, representing a wide variety of cultures. Similarly, Simpson, Wilson, and Winterheld cite an ambitious study conducted by Schmitt and colleagues (2003) testing various predictions about sociosexuality in more than 50 different countries. This research revealed a number of cross-cultural similarities (e.g., women are, on average, more restricted than men), and several differences, as well. For example, "gender differences in sociosexuality tend to be larger in environments that pose more daunting barriers to reproduction (e.g., in harsh or pathogen-prevalent environments), and smaller in cultures that have greater political and economic gender equality" (Simpson, Wilson, & Winterheld, chapter 4, this volume).

These exceptions regarding race, ethnicity, and culture aside, the majority of chapters in this volume do not address any of these issues. These chapters focus, at least implicitly, on their respective topics in a North American context. Although this may partly reflect the geographical location of the authors (only Feeney and Noller live outside of the United States or Canada), an important reason seems to be the scarcity of published research using ethnically diverse or non-American samples. Numerous authors (e.g., Aubin & Heiman; Burgess; Sprecher & Cate) make this point, and call for researchers to broaden their samples. Peplau and colleagues go a step further, pointing out that "studies will be especially valuable that go beyond merely comparing ethnic groups and instead attempt to link relationship experiences to specific cultural norms, values and attitudes" (Peplau, Fingerhut, & Beals, chapter 14, this volume). We agree, and would add that, as with issues related to gender, questions of ethnic group and cultural similarity are as informative and interesting as questions of difference. The relative absence of data addressing these issues leaves researchers unable to draw meaningful conclusions about the generalizability of both research and theory related to sexuality in relationships.

SAME-GENDER RELATIONSHIPS

Based on the research summarized in the chapters in this volume, it would seem that there is much work to be done to provide a full account of the nature of same-gender sexual relationships. Relationships researchers focused little attention on same-gender couples, and research specifically examining sexuality in these relationships is particularly rare. This lack of relevant data leads some authors to explicitly focus their chapters on sexuality in heterosexual relationships (e.g., Byers & Wang's chapter on social exchange theory, Aubin & Heiman's chapter on sexual dysfunction in relationships). Even when a topic has been studied extensively among gay populations, authors may still choose to explicitly omit discussion of gay and/or lesbian samples from the discussion (e.g., Noar, Zimmerman, & Atwood's chapter on safer sex).

Some contributors to this volume describe a relatively small number of relevant studies in a separate section of their chapter, noting the ways in which same-gender couples are similar to or different from heterosexual couples (e.g., Burgess). Feeney and Noller cite several studies of attachment and relationship functioning using gay and/or lesbian samples. They conclude that the distribution of attachment styles and the role of attachment in relationship functioning is similar in heterosexual and homosexual individuals. On the other hand, they conclude that although research using heterosexual samples confirms the centrality of the parent–child relationship in the formation of attachment style, research on gay men suggests that "attachment security may be influenced more strongly by peer relationships than by early parenting" (Feeney & Noller, chapter 8, this volume). Moreover, these authors highlight the influence of attachment on an experience exclusive to gay and lesbian individuals— "coming out." Two studies suggested that for gay men and lesbians, attachment style may be significantly associated with the timing, extent, and effects of disclosure regarding their sexual orientation.

Such conclusions are difficult to draw with confidence, however, when there are no more than a handful of relevant studies. For example, in chapter 12 on sexual aggression in relationships, Christopher and Kisler must make do with only two studies reporting sexual coercion rates among gay and lesbian couples (conducted with relatively small, nonrandom samples).[1] The most common reference to same-gender relationships among the chapters in this volume is the lament by authors that more work is needed to extend the findings they discussed to gay and lesbian populations (e.g., DeLamater & Hyde; Metts; Byers & Wang; Sprecher & Cate; Christopher & Kisler; Burgess).

Peplau, Fingerhut, and Beals, whose chapter focuses exclusively on this topic, provide the most extensive treatment of sexuality in same-gender relationships in this volume. These authors, too, note that "the scientific database concerning sexuality in lesbian and gay relationships continues to be woefully limited" (Peplau, Fingerhut, & Beals, chapter 14, this volume). Nonetheless, on the basis of available research evidence, they draw several important conclusions: Most individuals in gay and lesbian relationships report high levels of sexual satisfaction, and satisfaction with sex is significantly associated with other relationship variables (e.g., commitment and satisfaction). Some gender differences observed in heterosexual couples are reflected in differences between gay and lesbian couples; namely, that gay men report more frequent sexual interactions, both within and outside their current relationships, than do lesbian women. Despite this, the sexual relationships of gay men and lesbian

---

[1] Bartholomew, Landolt, and Oram's 1999 unpublished paper reports sexual aggression among a representative sample of gay Canadian males.

women tend not to be explicitly gendered (i.e., involving the adoption of explicitly butch/femme roles).

THEORETICAL FRAMEWORKS FOR
UNDERSTANDING SEXUALITY

In the first chapter of this volume, DeLamater and Hyde identify conceptual issues for sex researchers and then discuss five theoretical positions. In trying to reflect on the volume as a whole, it is worthwhile to return to the theme of theories. Three fundamental tasks of science are description, the empirical examination of the relationships among variables (sometimes called prediction), and explanation. In science, the desire to explain the relationships among variables leads to the development of theories. As commonly defined, theories involve a set of constructs and the postulated interrelationships among them. Theories typically rest on assumptions about how to view phenomena. Because they provide frameworks for understanding and explaining relationships among phenomena, they can provide a basis for analyzing new situations and for predicting empirical relationships. Scholars such as Kurt Lewin (1951) believe that theories have practical value in that they can be used to change behavior and solve everyday problems.

How important are theories in sex research? Matters of description are arguably more central in this field than in many other domains. Laypersons as well as social scientists have wanted to know when do youths first engage in sex, how often do people have sex, in what practices do they engage, how satisfied are people with their sexual activities, etc. In an analysis of articles published in the *Journal of Sex Research* and the *Archives for Sexual Behavior* during the period from 1971 to 1990, Ruppel (1994) found that three fourths were primarily data reports. Weis (1998c) argued that "relatively little sexuality research is oriented to testing theoretical hypotheses" (p. 1). Sprecher and Cate (see also Fisher) echo this sentiment saying, "Our impression is that much research on sexuality and close relationships has no theoretical underpinnings" (Sprecher & Cate, chapter 10, this volume). Certainly there are authors in this volume who explicitly note that their main goal is description (e.g., Willetts, Sprecher, & Beck) and many others whose treatment of issues is largely at the level of description or identification of the correlations among variables (e.g., Burgess). Nonetheless, we believe sexual science is making strides forward in accessing or developing well-formulated, useful theoretical perspectives.

The Theoretical Perspectives Used

Classic Theories. DeLamater and Hyde focus on five theoretical positions: evolutionary psychology, social exchange, sexual scripts, symbolic interaction, and role theory. One of the landmark publications regarding theoretical approaches to sexuality was the 1998 special issue of the *Journal of Sex Research* entitled, "The Use of Theory in Research and Scholarship on Sexuality" (Weis, 1998b). In the introduction to that set of articles, Weis (1998c) discusses 25 classic works of sexual theory (e.g., Freud, Reiss, Triviers, Gagnon & Simon, Byrne). In his conclusion, Weis (1998a) identifies and evaluates 39 theoretical perspectives that have been or could be used in research on sexuality. The core of the collection is the presentation of what Weis, as editor, considered the five leading contemporary perspectives on sexuality: evolutionary (i.e., Buss's sexual strategies approach), social exchange, symbolic interactionism, social learning, and systems.

Comparing DeLamater and Hyde with Weis, they agree in identifying three theories as major: evolutionary psychology, social exchange, and symbolic interaction. In the current volume, each of these perspectives is prominent. For example, Simpson, Wilson, Winterheld draw heavily on the evolutionary tradition in their analysis of sociosexuality as do Guerrero, Spitzberg, and Yoshimura in their analysis of jealousy. Byers and Wang take an exchange approach (see also Vohs, Catanese, & Baumeister), whereas Christopher and Kisler (chapter 15) explore marital sexuality from a symbolic interactionist stance.

Of the seven theories featured by DeLamater, Hyde, and Weis, the following four receive less attention in this volume: role theory, script theory, social learning theory, and the systems perspective. Although the notion of roles, especially gender roles, can be found in a few chapters of the present work (e.g., Peplau, Fingerhut, & Beals; Christopher & Kisler, chapter 15), we do not see as much influence of role theory as does Schwartz in her companion commentary. Perhaps this is because we have as a criterion of influence explicit testing of role theories ideas rather than more causal use of the role notion as an ad hoc explanatory concept. For us it is noteworthy that Biddle, who is recognized as the leading advocate of role theory, is not cited elsewhere in the book after DeLamater and Hyde's chapter. Systems approaches do not enjoy much prominence either (see Aubin & Heiman for brief consideration). Social learning and script theory get somewhat more attention. For instance, Byers and Wang incorporate the social learning perspective as a component of their presentation of an integrative social exchange model. Metts as well as Sprecher and Cate discuss script theory as it applies to topics of concern to them.

In Weis' (1998a) evaluation of theories of sexuality, he rated the systems approach low in both conceptual clarity and testability. Although it may seem useful to practitioners, with these attributes it is not surprising that it is less influential in research investigations. Social learning models were prominent in the study of relationships in the 1970s, but they are having less influence in that domain during the 1990s (Perlman & Duck, 2003). A similar trend seems apparent in the area of sexuality. Among the 39 theories considered by Weis, role theory was among the few for which he did not identify any recent references. So role theory, too, seems to be declining in standing.

New Theoretical Approaches to Sexuality.   This volume advances two approaches relatively new to the sexuality domain: attachment theory (Feeney & Noller) and a theory of erotic plasticity (Vohs, Catanese, & Baumeister). The attachment perspective shares some of its intellectual roots with evolutionary as well as psychodynamic perspectives. In its current form, it traces back especially to John Bowlby and has become a very influential viewpoint in the close relationships literature (Perlman & Duck, 2003). It is a theory concerned with both normative phenomena (e.g., separation) and individual differences. It is the individual differences aspect of attachment theory, namely attachment dimensions or styles, which is having the greatest impact on sexuality research.

Vohs, Catanese, and Baumeister's theory of erotic plasticity can be synthesized into three propositions and a preferred explanation: compared to men, women show greater variability over time in their sexuality, they are more influenced by social and cultural factors, and finally, their attitudes and behavior are more likely to be discrepant. In this volume, Peplau, Fingerhut, and Beals' treatment of sexuality in lesbians and gay men is largely a synthesis of empirical findings. Elsewhere, however, Peplau and her associates provided an explanation for women's sexual orientation. Like Vohs, Catanese, and Baumeister, Peplau (see Peplau & Garnets, 2000) believes that different factors may be needed to explain men and women's sexual orientation. Peplau sees women's sexuality as changeable over time and situations (see Peplau, 2003). So, the line of thinking advanced by Vohs, Catanese, and Baumeister is proving useful not only for explaining gender differences but also for explaining intragender variability in specific domains.

Comparisons Among Theories

Substantive Comparisons.   DeLamater and Hyde do a nice job of comparing theories on five criteria that stem from their discussion of conceptual issues. In editing a collection of articles on theories in the *Journal of Sex Research*, Weis (1998c) asked contributors to address a series of 11 topics. Other than being concerned with the dyad or individual as the unit of analysis, Weis mostly identified additional dimensions along which these theoretical viewpoints can be compared. For instance, some of his questions are:

- What are the theory's discipline origins and affiliations?
- What are each theory's assumptions?
- What are the theory's major concepts?
- What aspects of sexuality does the theory address?

In their comparison of close relationships theories, Perlman and Fehr (1986) add even more comparison points such as to what extent do various theories see behavior as a function of personal attributes or dynamics (e.g., motives, cognitions) operating within the person versus properties between actors or even circumstances/factors external to the dyad? Do theories focus on contemporary forces affecting behavior or are they more concerned with historical, childhood factors?

To illustrate some of these comparisons, consider the evolutionary versus the social exchange approach. The evolutionary approach traces its intellectual history back to Darwin. Evolutionary theorists (e.g., Buss, 1998) assume that human nature has evolved via natural selection, with men and women facing different adaptive problems in some domains of their lives, and therefore in those domains, they have come to differ from one another. Both sexes, however, have an inherent tendency to perpetuate their genes. Buss and his associates use such key concepts as sexual desire, intrasexual competition, long- and short-term mating strategies, and mate retention tactics. This theory has been used to analyze mate selection, restricted versus unrestricted sexual orientation (see Simpson, Wilson, & Winterheld), sexual satisfaction (Sprecher & Cate), jealousy (see Guerrero, Spitzberg, & Yoshimura), infidelity, and conflict, among other topics (see Guerrero, Spitzberg, and Yoshimura's discussion of the theory's broad scope). Evolutionary theorists believe that the species has adapted to its environmental context, but those adaptations become encoded in the individual's genes. Thus, human behavior is rooted in the species' history rather than being heavily influenced by contemporary forces.

The social exchange approach has it intellectual antecedents in several disciplines including economics, sociology, and psychology (Sprecher, 1998). In the mid-20th century, such scholars as Blau, Homans, and Thibaut and Kelley formulated classic exchange viewpoints. Slightly later Hatfield and her associates developed the equity line of this theoretical family. Social exchange theorists generally assume that social behavior is a series of exchanges in which individuals try to minimize their costs while maximizing their rewards. As articulated by Byers and Wang, the main social exchange concepts are rewards, costs, equity (and equality), comparison level, and comparison level for alternatives. They apply their model to four topics: sexual partner selection, sexual frequency, sexual satisfaction (cf. Sprecher & Cate, chapter 10, this volume), and extradyadic sexual relationships. In seeing social behavior as a series of exchanges, this viewpoint focuses attention at the dyadic level. Concepts such as the individual's comparison level consider the individual's history of interactions, but individuals are constantly calculating the equity of their relationships and assessing their comparison level for alternatives. So this perspective places more emphasis on contemporary influences on behavior.

Of the five theories (evolutionary, exchange, symbolic interactionism, attachment, and erotic plasticity), four are what might be considered "imported theories" in the sense that they were largely developed to explain other phenomena and then applied to issues of sexuality. Erotic plasticity is unique in having been developed to address a sexual issue. With the exception of symbolic interactionism with its roots in sociology, most of these theories have a significant portion of their origins in psychology. Two of the theories (attachment and especially evolutionary) also have part of their intellectual heritage in biology. Three of the five theories (evolutionary, social exchange, and attachment) are dominant perspectives in the study of close relationships (Perlman & Duck, 2003). One might speculate that the intertwining of theoretical concepts in this volume and the close relationships area is due to this volume's focusing on interpersonal aspects of sexuality. This does not, however, seem to be altogether the case. A similar degree of overlap can be seen in the *Journal of Sex Research's* special issue on theory that did not limit its attention to interpersonal aspects of sexuality.

Evaluative Comparisons.   In this volume, Guerreo, Spitzburg, and Yoshimura evaluate evolutionary theory using five criteria. They conclude that "socioevolutionary theory has fared well by most of the criteria" (chapter 13, this volume). Weis (1998a) applies a broader set of eight criteria to the evaluation of 25 different theories: conceptual clarity, internal consistency, testability, parsimony, recognition of human pluralism and context, research generated, empirical support, and applicability to human sexuality. He gives somewhat higher marks to the social exchange camp than to evolutionary theories, rating social exchange higher on conceptual clarity, internal consistency, testability, and parsimony. He rates symbolic interactionism and evolutionary psychology as roughly the same, although he praises symbolic interactionism for greater recognition of human pluralism but sees evolutionary psychology as having higher conceptual clarity. By most criteria commonly used, what might be considered the four senior theories featured in this volume (attachment, evolutionary psychology, social exchange, and symbolic interaction) can be judged successful. As articulated and developed by outstanding scholars whose impact has cut across disciplinary boundaries, they have become dominant viewpoints in the study of sexuality. Each of these theories has generated a considerable body of research, and each has helped give understanding to diverse aspects of sexuality.

Are these theories the ultimate conceptual frameworks for the study of sexuality? We suspect not. As we noted previously, social learning and role theories once garnered more attention than they are receiving now. Prototypically we see theories as being introduced, gaining adherents, generating research, being challenged, being defended, and eventually giving way to substantially revised or new formulations. Over time, ideas get refined, take new directions, and are combined in novel ways. For instance, in chapter 19, this volume, Vohs, Catanese, and Baumeister identify their views as part of the social exchange tradition yet they are embarking on what might be considered a new branch of this work. Nonetheless, we see the contribution of attachment, evolutionary psychology, social exchange, and symbolic interaction as very substantial—they have been of enduring value over many decades. Although the current versions of these viewpoints probably won't be as prominent 30, 50, or 100 years from now, they likely will influence thinking for many years to come and have earned their place in the history of human sexuality and in broader fields as well.

OMISSIONS AND LESS EXTENSIVELY COVERED AREAS

This is a big volume that admirably covers many topics. It does so in considerable detail. We appreciate that it isn't realistic for editors to include everything. Books would get too big, expensive, and unwieldy. Nonetheless, we feel there are areas to which others might profitably want to give more attention. We will comment on our choice of five such topics: meta-analysis, international perspectives, the funding context in which research is undertaken, disciplinary perspectives other than psychology, and public policy implications of the current knowledge base. Others undoubtedly might identify additional topics (e.g., contraception and abortion).

Meta-analysis

Meta-analyses are studies that statistically combine findings from several existing studies. Oliver and Hyde's (1993) analysis of gender differences in sexual attitudes and behavior is a well-known example. A few authors in this collection mention meta-analyses (see DeLamater & Hyde; Noar, Zimmerman, & Atwood; Schwartz) but even brief citations are rare. As the study of sexuality in close relationships matures and accumulates many studies involving common variables, we see the value of giving more attention to meta-analysis. It allows researchers to see overall trends across several studies that may not be statistically significant in every article individually. Consistent findings strengthen one's confidence in the outcome. One can also check for the homogeneity of effects to see if they hold across the whole pool of studies or whether other factors can be found that moderate (or qualify) findings. Meta-analysis can also assess the likelihood of the so-called "file draw problem." This is the concern that editorial biases favoring significant results may lead to isolated statistically significant but unreliable findings getting published when in fact there are many other nonsignificant studies that have remained in researchers' file draws. Apropos of our discussion of gender differences, another advantage of meta-analysis is that it can be used to obtain indicators of effect sizes.

The United States Viewpoint

Earlier we underscored the relative lack of attention to culture. In part, as we noted, this is because a great deal of research on sexuality in close relationships has been done in North America. But we do not think this fully explains the level of attention devoted to culture. For example, at the same time that Laumann, Gagnon, Michael, and Michaels did their frequently cited U.S. study, at least two other major European Union national surveys were conducted, one in France (Bozon & Leridon, 1996), the other in Britain (Wellings, Field, Johnson, & Wadworth, 1994). Certainly these studies have findings that could help put the U.S. findings in a broader context (see Michael et al., 1998). The British findings are mentioned in passing in this volume (Willetts, Sprecher, & Beck), but the English language report of the massive French survey is not even mentioned.

It is not only that most authors examine their respective topics in a North American context. They also unconsciously do it with a North American point of view. In terms of its sexual mores, the United States is undoubtedly unique in some ways. For example Willetts, Sprecher, and Beck cite evidence that U.S. respondents held more negative attitudes toward extramarital sex than did respondents from any other country in a 23-nation survey. In the interpersonal realm, North America is considered an individualistic as opposed to a collectivist society (Markus & Kitayama, 1991). Presumably these sorts of differences color and influence the types of questions and interpretations authors have regarding sexuality. Where, for example, in this collection do we see examination of the sexual adjustment of newlyweds in arranged marriages or the shame to extended family members of extramarital affairs that might be of concern to people living in more collectivist cultures? Or what about the sexual aspects of the growing European LAT ("Living Apart Together") relational form (see de Jong Gierveld & Peeters, 2003) that involves intimate partners choosing to maintain separate residents?

Funding

Doing research requires resources. Even if one takes what we consider to be an unrealistic classic view of science itself as value free, public granting agencies and private foundations dictate the allocation of funds to various research priorities. Older readers will recall the infamous golden fleece awards that Senator Proxmire gave for what he considered to be useless expenditures of public moneys. He bestowed one of these on Hatfield and Berscheid's love research (Shaffer, 1977). In a March 1975 press release, Proxmire wrote: "I believe that 200 million other Americans [besides Proxmire himself] want to leave some things in life a mystery . . . So National Science Foundation—get out of the love racket. Leave that to Elizabeth Barrett Browning and Irving Berlin" (as quoted in Shaffer, 1977, p. 816).

One might hope that at times when governments were unwilling to support sex research, private foundations would fill the breach. But that has not always been the case. In the 1950s, threats to the tax-exempt status of the Rockefeller Foundation by right-wing members of congress frightened nearly all major foundations from supporting sex studies (Michael et al., 1998).

Scattered across the present volume are hints of how funding, or lack of funding, has shaped research knowledge. Fisher quips, "No agency is likely to pour big money into a study of adolescent sexual pleasure" (Fisher, chapter 16, this volume). Willetts, Sprecher, and Beck as well as Burgess noted how funding problems restricted Laumann, Gagnon, Michael, and Michaels (1994) from conducting the full scope of their project. The proposal for conducting the first steps of their national survey, which was highly evaluated and approved by the scientific review panel, was denied money after Senator Helms opposed funding of surveys of human sexual behavior (Laumann, Gagnon, & Michael, 1994). Ultimately they received private support, but in the process, the adequate sampling of special subgroups such as homosexuals was compromised and sampling of adults over 59 got dropped completely.

For Laumann's group, there was a silver lining in the funding difficulties they faced. They observe, "Ironically, our failure to secure government funding freed us to abandon the overly compromised, narrowly targeted survey instrument in favor of the much more comprehensive approach" (Laumann, Gagnon, Michael, & Michaels, 1994, p. 41). The breadth and depth of their study differentiates it from the aforementioned English and French surveys and may partially explain why it receives more attention.

Shaffer (1977) contends that the attack on Hatfield and Berscheid's research was part of a general anti-intellectualism. In the 1990s, sex research continued in the United States but was sheltered under calls for proposals that invited work on the "proximate determinants of fertility" rather than explicitly calling for sex studies (Laumann, Gagnon, & Michael, 1994). In recent years, U.S. support of sex research has been significantly focused on HIV/AIDs and public health issues.

At the time of this writing, conservative political views have considerable influence in U.S. government decisions. Conservatives frequently approach sex from a moral and religious vantage point. Many hold that sex research is an undesirable envision of privacy. Cornerstones of their philosophy include pro-traditional family attitudes; anti-gay opinions; and opposition to premarital sex, abortion, and divorce. Despite evidence on the lack of parent–child communication regarding sex (Fisher), many conservatives oppose sex education, feeling it should be left to the family. If their children are exposed to sex education in the schools, many conservatives favor a "Just say no," abstinence-type approach (see Schwartz for an assessment of the outcome of these programs). Advocates of such values undoubtedly place a lower general priority on sex research, would prefer studies of sex within marital relationships than in other forms of sexual unions, see less purpose to studies of contraceptive behavior among teens, and the like.

Our point here, however, is not specifically how the values of conservatives are shaping research on sexuality. Other groups trying to influence public policy—whether liberal democrats, feminists, Marxians, drug company lobbyists, or even the American Psychological Association—have their agendas, too. Generally we see the direction of science as influenced in part by political and ideological forces. Sex research, perhaps more so than many areas of research, is impacted. Our bottom line is that a more systematic mapping out of how political and ideological factors are shaping sex research is warranted.

Disciplines Represented

The disciplinary mix of scholars represented in this book includes sociologists, family scientists, and communications experts. Historians, philosophers, and Shakespeare get cited. The vast majority of the work reported in this volume was, however, conducted by psychologists. More broadly, the kinds of questions asked and the theoretical perspectives applied to answering those questions are for the most part psychological. The emphasis on individual, and to a lesser extent, dyadic behaviors and assessments is reflected in chapters on sexual and relationship satisfaction, love, lust, jealousy, and attachment. We see this emphasis as a reflection of a broader cultural and historical trend in our understanding of sexuality and relationships. Heterosexual marriage and the meaning and structure of the family have shifted enormously over the last century. The links of marriage and the family with economic and religious structures have weakened over time (Jones, Tepperman, & Wilson, 1995), and the notion of marriage as an institution conferring rights and obligations to spouses and their families is less prominent. Our notions of sexuality as being most appropriate in the context of marriage and for the purposes of procreation have become more permissive as well (Hyde & DeLamater, 2000). With these shifts, more emphasis has been placed on marriage and all other forms of intimate relationships as a means of achieving self-fulfillment, in which partners define their relationships as successful to the extent that they are personally and mutually satisfying (Jones et al., 1995). In this context, questions of a psychological nature take on greater importance, and the relative impact of broader societal structures is less obvious, although no doubt still consequential.

What is missing as a result of the emphasis on a psychological perspective on sexuality in relationships? Sociological approaches (e.g., script theory) do receive some treatment in these chapters (e.g., Sprecher & Cate), but usually as one of a variety of theoretical approaches that one might consider. The research summarized typically ignores variables such as class, education, and race and does not address the ways in which institutions such as religion, medicine, and the law play a role in the construction of meaning around sexuality and relationships.

Also missing from this volume is the inclusion of work utilizing a physiological approach to the study of sexuality. Although evolutionary theory (mentioned in several chapters) does refer to biological processes, including the genetic transmission of behavioral predispositions, these processes are not explicitly examined in research tied to the theory. There are, however, clearly opportunities for researchers to expand the study of sexuality in close relationships to include questions related to biological processes and mechanisms. For example, Metts reviews work related to the "passion turning point" in a relationship, the experience of the initial sexual experience. One might ask whether this experience and the psychological variables associated with it (e.g., attachment) are associated with hormonal (e.g., testosterone) or neurochemical (e.g., phenylethylamine) shifts. In addition, we would agree with DeLamater and Hyde that neural plasticity opens a variety of avenues for sexuality research, and that theorists and researchers should work to integrate biological influences into their understanding of sexuality in relationships.

Public Policy

A final omission we see in this volume is a lack of attention to the wealth of public policy implications that might be derived from the volume's rich body of knowledge. We believe that the psychological and U.S.-centric biases we have been discussing plus the nature of sexuality in the United States may contribute to this. First, whereas some psychologists have policy interests, it is much more common for them to think in terms of the psychopathology and therapy issues that the editors feature in the applied section of the volume or preventive programs such as those to avoid sexual abuse (Christopher & Kisler, chapter 12). Second, as Michael et al. (1998) note, Americans are not strong in their resolve to develop effective public health policies pertaining to sex. With their emphasis on individualism and less government involvement, we suspect it is less common for U.S. citizens than for those in northern European social democracies to think along those lines. Finally, Michael et al. (1998) argue that the U.S. public's lack of resolve regarding policy is influenced by their sex attitudes and behavior: "the greater diversity of sexual behavior and the greater degree of absolute opinion about improper sexual behavior make it much more difficult to mount an effective public health effort in the United States" (p. 753). In other words, the United States is a comparatively diverse society, with significant segments of the population being both sexually restrictive and sexually permissive. This makes it difficult to design public health campaigns that fit everybody. Furthermore, holding absolute opinions against issues such as nonmarital sex, abortion, and homosexuality, significant segments of U.S. society do not want public money directed to those behaviors.

FUTURE DIRECTIONS

Many of the authors in this volume consider limitations of the work on their topic and make suggestions for the directions of future research. Some of their suggestions deal with substantive aspects of their area. But, more generic issues run across many of their remarks. Four recurrent themes stand out: the need for better sampling, the value of strong methods including longitudinal research, the desire for more theory-based research, and the need to consider developmental issues.

Sampling

Roughly half of the authors in this collection refer to the need for better sampling. Some call for large, representative samples (Willetts, Sprecher, & Beck; Peplau, Fingerhut, & Beals; Wenzel, Jackson, & Brendle). Others want to see phenomena of interest to them studied in specific types of relationships (e.g., Simpson, Wilson, & Winterheld's and Regan's concern with long-term relationships; Burgess) or a more diverse set of relationships including "understudied" segments of the population (Metts; Byers & Wang; Sprecher & Cate; Christopher & Kisler, chapter 12; Peplau, Fingerhut, & Beals; Noar, Zimmerman, & Atwood). In domains such as the transition to parenthood, comparison groups not undergoing the transition are valuable (Haugen, Schmutzer, & Wenzel).

Dating back to appraisals of the Kinsey studies, sampling issues—including the problem of volunteer bias or what Weiderman calls nonresponse error—have been a longstanding concern to sex researchers. Yet, sampling challenges are always worth repeating, especially for sexuality as a field in which curiosity about what is "normal" or typical for the population as a whole runs high. We share in seeing the advantages of studying diverse groups so that we have an adequate picture of the sexuality of subsegments of society. Large, representative samples allow more accurate generalizations to the population as a whole and thereby facilitate development of public policy implications (see Willetts, Sprecher, & Beck). Sampling not only influences the ability to make population estimates, but it can also influence the association found between variables (Weiderman). It is little wonder that sex researchers place a premium on representative samples.

Methodology

Along with better sampling, authors in this collection believe the future of research on sexuality in close relationships will be enhanced by improved methodology.

- One common methodological wish is for longitudinal studies (Willetts, Sprecher, & Beck; Regan; Feeney & Noller; Sprecher & Cate; Burgess). In terms of studying life transitions, it is valuable to employ prospective designs that start collecting data before the event and that follow people for sufficiently long periods after the transition (Haugen, Schmutzer, & Wenzel). Longitudinal studies permit researchers to examine change over time and the influence of early events on later ones.
- Contributors point to further development in the area of measurement (Willetts, Sprecher, & Beck; cf. Haugen, Schmutzer, & Wenzel). Ideal properties here include precision (Willetts, Sprecher, & Beck), reliability (Regan), validity (Regan), multiple-item scales (Feeney & Noller), and moving beyond self-report to include physiological assessment (Wenzel, Jackson, & Brendle).
- Metts as well as Sprecher and Cate see a role for diary or experience sampling methods, in part as a way of alleviating memory biases.
- Haugen, Schmutzer, and Wenzel believe researchers should get both partners' reports (cf. Metts). In identifying new emphases of this volume, we already discussed advantages of dyadic data. In this section on future directions for research we note that Simpson, Wilson, and Winterheld as well as Regan would like researchers to consider questions on how the matching of partners on sexual restrictiveness and sexual desire influence relationships (cf. Haugen, Schmutzer, & Wenzel; Aubin & Heiman). Collecting dyad data allows addressing this type of question.
- Peplau, Fingerhut, and Beals note the dearth of multivariate studies involving gays and lesbians. Although multivariate statistical techniques are well developed, areas remain where it would still be valuable to discriminate how much different variables contribute to overall patterns (Byers & Wang, Regan).
- Sprecher and Cate would like diverse, sophisticated methodologies (cf. Peplau, Fingerhut, & Beals). Although this volume rests most heavily on quantitative, correlational approaches, a few contributors think qualitative techniques (e.g., narrative data) could help enrich our understanding (Cupach & Spitzberg). Complementing this advice, Sprecher and Cate as well as Peplau, Fingerhut, and Beals think gains might be made from studying deviant cases (outliers and exceptions). Vohs, Catanese, and Baumeister identify issues that could be examined experimentally.

Theory

Another recurrent theme revolves around the use of theory in sex research. In general, there is a desire for the empirical work in the field to be more grounded in theory (Willetts, Sprecher, & Beck; Sprecher & Cate; Christopher & Kisler, chapters 12 and 15; Fisher; Burgess). Haugen, Schmutzer, and Wenzel advocate that the empirical grounding be with theories of close relationships. Some authors call for broader, more integrative theorizing (DeLamater & Hyde; Vohs, Catanese, & Baumeister) as well as testing all aspects of existing theories (Byers & Wang). Noar, Zimmerman, and Atwood want contextual influences (e.g., relationship factors) added to the social psychological theories that frequently guide research on HIV prevention. Others want new theoretical formulations, perhaps grounded in existing empirical findings. This harkens back to Reiss's (1967) approach in the 1960s. Regan champions more carefully examination of extant theories themselves.

Complementing the call for theoretically grounded endeavors, some contributors exhort future researchers to go beyond finding differences to explaining why they occur (Willetts, Sprecher, & Beck; Vohs, Catanese, & Baumeister). In light of the value of theories in providing explanations (as well as the other functions they serve), we endorse this call for greater use of theory.

Developmental Issues

Related to the desire for more longitudinal studies, some authors promote additional attention to developmental issues. These can be divided into those pertaining to the lifespan and those pertaining to the development course of relationships. In the first chapter, DeLamater and Hyde advocate both. Apropos of a lifespan approach, they note that "Each stage of development—childhood, adolescence, adulthood, and later life—is associated with biological development and changes, distinctive social influences, and developmental and coping tasks" (Detamater & Hyde, chapter 1, this volume). Others echo this prompt for further illumination of developmental stages (e.g., Feeney and Noller with regard to attachment and Fisher with regard to the family foundations of sexual behavior). Many of the chapters in this volume are at least loosely associated with specific developmental periods. Byers and Wang give voice to the need for studying relationships developmentally. They ask questions such as: Is the social exchange perspective equally applicable at different relationship stages? Do the importance of various social exchange components vary at different relationship stages? How do changes in equity impact on sexual relationships? DeLamater and Hyde note that some scholars reject developmental theories. Certainly, one can debate about stages and the like, but it is our impression that the relationship area has generally found it profitable to use at least a rudimentary notion that relationships grow, sustain themselves, and decline.

Future Directions—Echo or Truly New?

Regan observed that over a decade ago McKinney and Sprecher (1991b) encouraged contributors to an earlier volume to speculate on beneficial directions for the field. They, too, dealt with issues like diary methods and longitudinal designs. Has anything changed in prescriptions for the future? We think so. Although sampling, methods, and theory are classic ingredients of any research domain, in the area of sexuality there have been clear advances since the McKinney and Sprecher book. There have been new, large-scale national surveys; there has been some shifting of dominant theoretical perspectives; knowledge about sexuality in close relationships has advanced considerably; we know a good deal more about how to handle dyadic data; and the like. So the suggestions about sampling, methods, and theory are offered from a different starting point. Furthermore, in this volume there are a number of suggestions about the directions in which specific areas of research should proceed. They offer a wealth of ideas for future work.

SUMMARY AND CONCLUSIONS

The goal of this chapter has been to provide a commentary on the contents of the *Handbook of Sexuality in Close Relationships*. In the first section of the chapter on novel emphases of the volume, we claimed that contemporary researchers are broadening the definition of sexuality, studying sex from a relational perspective, and giving more attention to the problematic, dark aspects of sexuality.

In the next section of the chapter, we concluded that the authors in this handbook answer the question "Are there gender differences in sexuality in close relationships?" with a resounding, "Yes . . . . sometimes." We illustrated areas with gender differences (e.g., sexual desire, responsiveness to sexual vs. relational factors, aggression) and noted caveats to the gender difference literature (e.g., statistical significance doesn't indicate the magnitude or practical importance of the difference). From gender we went to ethnicity, race, culture, and sexual orientation. Research on these topics is valued yet could still profitably be further developed.

Next we discussed theories, noting the prominence of four perspectives in this volume: attachment, evolutionary psychology, social exchange, and symbolic interaction. We discussed the functions of theories, and we compared and evaluated them. Although there is a considerable body of purely descriptive research on sexuality, we judged the four senior theories featured in this volume to be highly successful in terms of classic evaluative criteria.

As we moved toward the end of the chapter, we identified five topics we would like to see get more attention: meta-analysis, international perspectives, the funding context in which research is undertaken, disciplinary perspectives other than psychology, and public policy implications of the current knowledge base. In reflecting on international perspectives and funding, we implicitly acknowledged the importance we attribute to the way problems are framed. Finally, we ended with a synopsis of the contributors' recommendations for future research. These include advances in four domains: sampling, methods, theory, and developmental issues.

This volume has examined sexuality in close relationships. For the relationship area, the last 2 decades have been a period of exciting growth. As Berscheid and Reis (1998) state:

> The sheer volume of recent research on interpersonal relationships within social psychology and allied disciplines reflects the fact that relationship science in the latter half of the 1990s resembles a boomtown during the gold rush days of the American West. Relationship science is young, sprawling, dynamic, [and] enthusiastic. (p. 253)

We are encouraged by this activity. In a period of such vitality, it is not surprising that relationship scholars were interested in addressing such logically related topics as sexuality. And for sex researchers, welcoming and elaborating an interpersonal perspective appears to have made equal sense.

We believe that many of the challenges and trends that have occurred in the study of close relationships (Perlman & Duck, 2003) can also be seen in the current volume that weds sexuality and relationships. For instance, there is considerable overlap in the prominent theories, both areas are concerned with such topics as the types of relationships, both face many similar methodological concerns, both have become concerned with problematic phenomena, and the like.

Compared with McKinney and Sprecher's 1991 anthology, the current volume abundantly bears witness to the progress that has been made combining the study of sexuality and close relationships. At the beginning of the earlier book, the editors noted researchers had begun studying sexuality in close relationships but hoped their publication would "help generate additional research ideas on the topic" (McKinney

& Sprecher, 1991a, p. 4). The current volume undoubtedly has at least four to five times as many words as its predecessor. The number of chapters has gone from 9 to 25 with a corresponding increase in the range of topics covered. The literature on which the current volume is based is more extensive—there is simply more of it, more questions have been addressed, and questions have been addressed more deeply. Today we have a more sophisticated and nuanced understanding. Whereas the earlier volume was a tasty sampler, a prelude, the current volume deserves its title as a Handbook.

Providing a commentary on the chapters of this book has been a pleasure for us. We agree with the assumption of the volume that it is profitable to approach sexuality and close relationships together. One can have either without the other, but their intersection is a crucial aspect of many people's lives. As the contents of this volume abundantly testify, studying them together enriches the study of each.

REFERENCES

Bartholomew, K., Landolt, M. A., & Oram, D. (1999, August). *Abuse in male same-sex relationships: Prevalence, incidence, and injury.* Paper presented at the 1999 Annual Convention of the American Psychological Association, Boston, MA.

Berscheid, E., & Reis, H. (1998). Attraction and close relationships. In D. T. Gilbert, S. T. Fiske, & G. Lindzey (Eds.), *The handbook of social psychology* (4th ed., pp. 193–281). New York: McGraw-Hill.

Bozon, M., & Leridon, H. (Eds.). (1996). *Sexuality and the social sciences: A French survey on sexual behavior* (G. Rogers, Trans.). Brookfield, VT: Dartmouth Publishing Co.

Buss, D. M. (1998). Sexual strategies theory: Historical origins and current status. *Journal of Sex Research, 35,* 19–31.

Canary, D. J., & Dindia, K. (Eds.). (1998). Prologue: Recurring issues in sex differences and similarities in communication. In D. J. Canary & K. Dindia (Eds.), *Sex differences and similarities in communication: Critical essays and empirical investigations of sex and gender in interaction* (pp. 1–17). Mahwah, NJ: Lawrence Erlbaum Associates.

de Jong Gierveld, J., & Peeters, A. (2003). The interweaving of repartnered older adults' lives with their children and siblings. *Ageing and Society, 23,* 187–205.

Holland, P. W., & Wainer, H. (Eds.). (1993). *Differential item functioning.* Hillsdale, NJ: Lawrence Erlbaum Associates.

Hyde, J. S., & DeLamater, J. D. (2000). *Understanding human sexuality.* New York: McGraw-Hill.

Hyde, J. S., & Linn, M. C. (1988). Gender differences in verbal ability: A meta-analysis. *Psychological Bulletin, 104,* 53–69.

Jones, C. L., Tepperman, L., & Wilson, S. J. (1995). *The futures of the family.* Englewood Cliffs, NJ: Prentice-Hall.

Kinsey, A. C., Pomeroy, W. B., & Martin, C. E. (1948). *Sexual behavior in the human male.* Philadelphia: Saunders.

Kephart, W. M. (1981). *The family, society, and the individual* (5th ed.). Boston: Houghton Mifflin.

Kirkendall, L. A. (1961). *Premarital intercourse and interpersonal relations.* New York: Julian Press.

Laumann, E. O., Gagnon, J. H., & Michael, R. T. (1994). A political history of the National Sex Survey of Adults. *Family Planning Perspectives, 26*(1), 34–38.

Laumann, E. W., Gagnon, J. H., Michael, R. T., & Michaels, S. (1994). *The social organization of sexuality: Sexual practices in the United States.* Chicago: University of Chicago Press.

Lewin, K. (1951). Problems of research in social psychology. In D. Cartwright (Ed.), *Field theory in social science: Selected theoretical papers* (pp. 155–169). New York: Harper & Brothers.

Markus, H. R., & Kitayama, S. (1991). Culture and the self: Implications for cognition, emotion, and motivation. *Psychological Review, 98,* 224–253.

Matlin, M. W., & Stang, D. J. (1978). *The Pollyanna principle: Selectivity in language, memory, and thought.* Cambridge, MA: Schenkman.

McKinney, K., & Sprecher, S. (Ed.). (1991a). Introduction. In K. McKinney & S. Sprecher (Eds.), *Sexuality in close relationships* (pp. 1–8). Hillsdale, NJ: Lawrence Erlbaum Associates.

McKinney, K., & Sprecher, S. (Ed.). (1991b). *Sexuality in close relationships.* Hillsdale, NJ: Lawrence Erlbaum Associates.

Michael, R. T. (1997). The National Health and Social Life Survey: Public health findings and their implications. In S. L. Isaacs & J. R. Knickman (Eds.), *To improve health and health care: 1997. The Robert Wood Johnson Foundation anthology* (pp. 232–250). San Francisco : Jossey-Bass. Retrieved June 22, 2003, from http://www.rwjf.org/publications/publicationsPdfs/library/oldhealth/chap11.htm

Michael, R. T., Wadsworth, J., Feinleib, J., Johnson, A. M., Laumann, E. O., & Wellings, K. (1998). Private sexual behavior, public opinion, and public health policy related to sexually transmitted diseases: A U.S.–British comparison. *American Journal of Public Health, 88,* 749–754.

Oliver, M. B., & Hyde, J. S. (1993). Gender differences in sexuality: A meta-analysis. *Psychological Bulletin, 114,* 29–51.

Peplau, L. A. (2003). Human sexuality: How do men and women differ? *Current Directions in Psychological Science, 12,* 37–40.

Peplau, L. A., & Garnets, L. D. (2000). A new paradigm for understanding women's sexuality and sexual orientation. *Journal of Social Issues, 56,* 329–350.

Perlman, D. (2000). El lado oscuro de las relaciones [The dark side of relationships]. *Revista de Psicologia Social y Personalidad, 17,* 95–121.

Perlman, D., & Duck, S. (2003). The seven seas of the study of personal relationships: From "The Thousand Islands" to interconnected waterways. In A. Vangelisti & D. Perlman (Eds.), *Cambridge handbook of personal relationships.* Manuscript in preparation.

Perlman, D., & Fehr, B. (1986). Theories of attraction: The analysis of interpersonal attraction. In V. J. Derlega & B. A. Winstead (Eds.), *Friendship and social interaction* (pp. 9–40). New York: Springer-Verlag.

Reiss, I. L. (1967). *The social context of premarital sexual permissiveness.* New York: Holt, Rinehart & Winston.

Ruppel, H. J., Jr. (1994). *Publication trends in the sexological literature: A comparison of two contemporary journals.* Unpublished doctoral dissertation, Institute for the Advanced Study of Human Sexuality, San Francisco, CA.

Schmitt, D. P., Alcalay, L., Allik, J., Ault, L., Austers, I., Bennett, K. L., et al. (2003). Universal sex differences in the desire for sexual variety: Tests from 52 nations, 6 continents, and 13 islands. *Journal of Personality and Social Psychology, 85,* 85–104.

Shaffer, L. S. (1977). The golden fleece: Anti-intellectualism and social science. *American Psychologist, 32,* 814–823.

Simpson, J. A., & Gangestad, S. W. (1991). Individual differences in sociosexuality: Evidence for convergent and discriminant validity. *Journal of Personality and Social Psychology, 60,* 870–883.

Sprecher, S. (1998). Social exchange theories and sexuality. *Journal of Sex Research, 35,* 32–43.

Sprecher, S. (2002). Sexual satisfaction in premarital relationships: Associations with satisfaction, love, commitment and stability. *Journal of Sex Research, 39,* 190–196.

Sprecher, S., & McKinney, K. (1993). *Sexuality.* Newbury Park, CA: Sage.

Struckman-Johnson, C., & Struckman-Johnson, D. (2002). Sexual coercion reported by women in three Midwestern prisons. *Journal of Sex Research, 39,* 228–240.

van de Vijver, F. J., & Poortinga, Y. H. (1997). Towards an integrated analysis of bias in cross-cultural assessment. *European Journal of Psychological Assessment, 13,* 29–37.

Weis, D. L. (1998a). Conclusion: The state of sexual theory. *Journal of Sex Research, 35,* 100–114.

Weis, D. L. (1998b). The use of theory in research and scholarship on sexuality [Special issue]. *Journal of Sex Research, 35*(1).

Weis, D. L. (1998c). The use of theory in sexuality research. *Journal of Sex Research, 35,* 1–9.

Wellings, K., Field, J., Johnson, A., & Wadworth, J. (1994). *Sexual behavior in Britain: The national survey of sexual attitudes and lifestyles.* New York: Penguin.

Author Index

H

Subject Index

Note: Page numbers in *italic* refer to figures; those in **boldface** refer to tables. Page numbers followed by "n" refer to footnotes.